Presents:

ESSENTIAL
X-MEN
VOL. 4

Collecting UncannyX-Men #162-79 & Annual #6

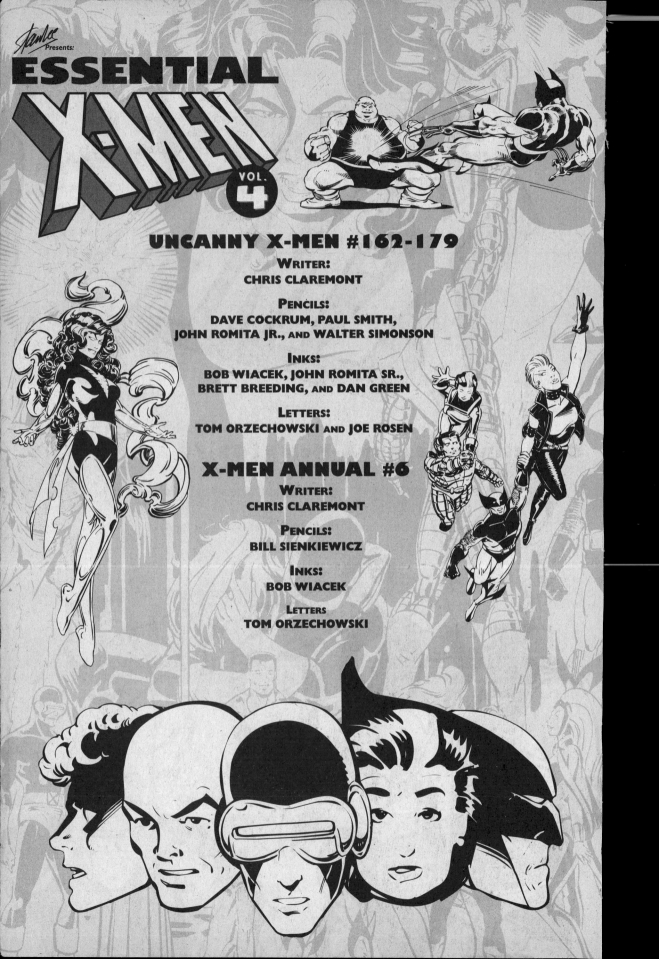

Stan Lee Presents:

ESSENTIAL X-MEN VOL. 4

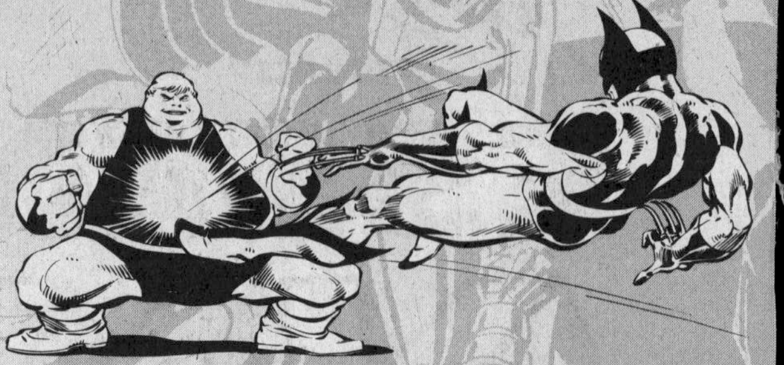

UNCANNY X-MEN #162-179

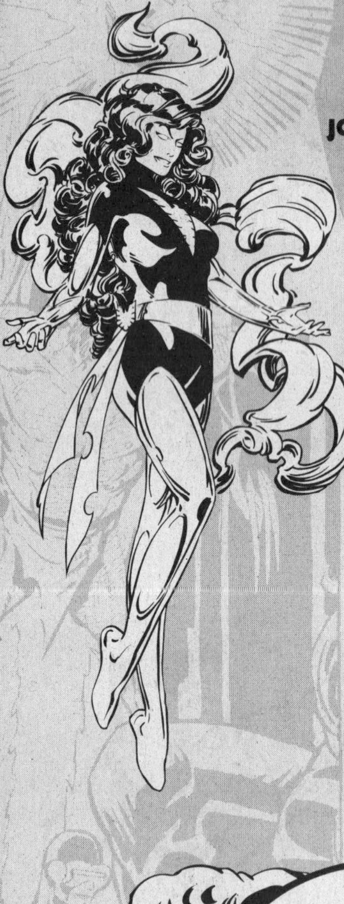

WRITER:
CHRIS CLAREMONT

PENCILS:
DAVE COCKRUM, PAUL SMITH,
JOHN ROMITA JR., AND WALTER SIMONSON

INKS:
BOB WIACEK, JOHN ROMITA SR.,
BRETT BREEDING, AND DAN GREEN

LETTERS:
TOM ORZECHOWSKI AND JOE ROSEN

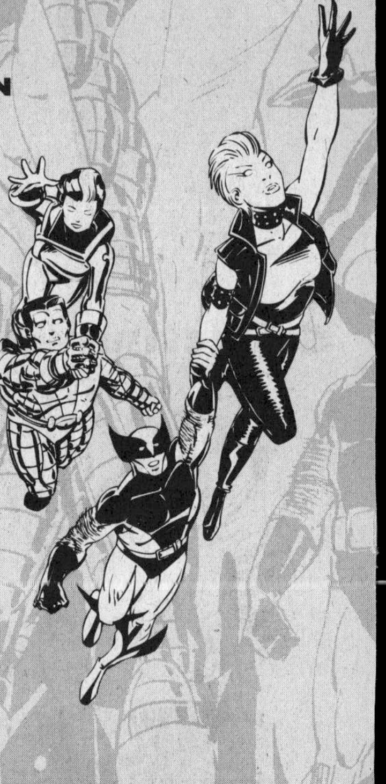

X-MEN ANNUAL #6

WRITER:
CHRIS CLAREMONT

PENCILS:
BILL SIENKIEWICZ

INKS:
BOB WIACEK

LETTERS
TOM ORZECHOWSKI

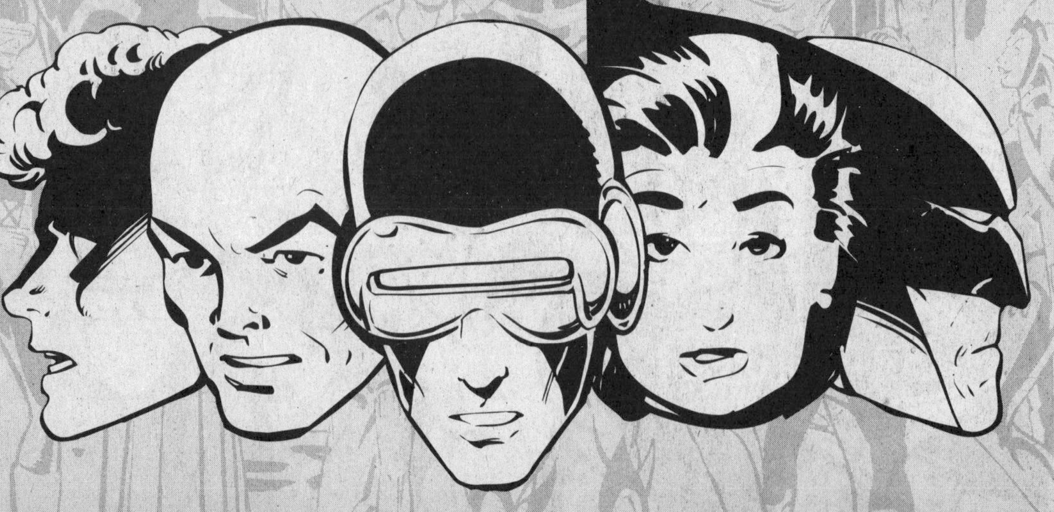

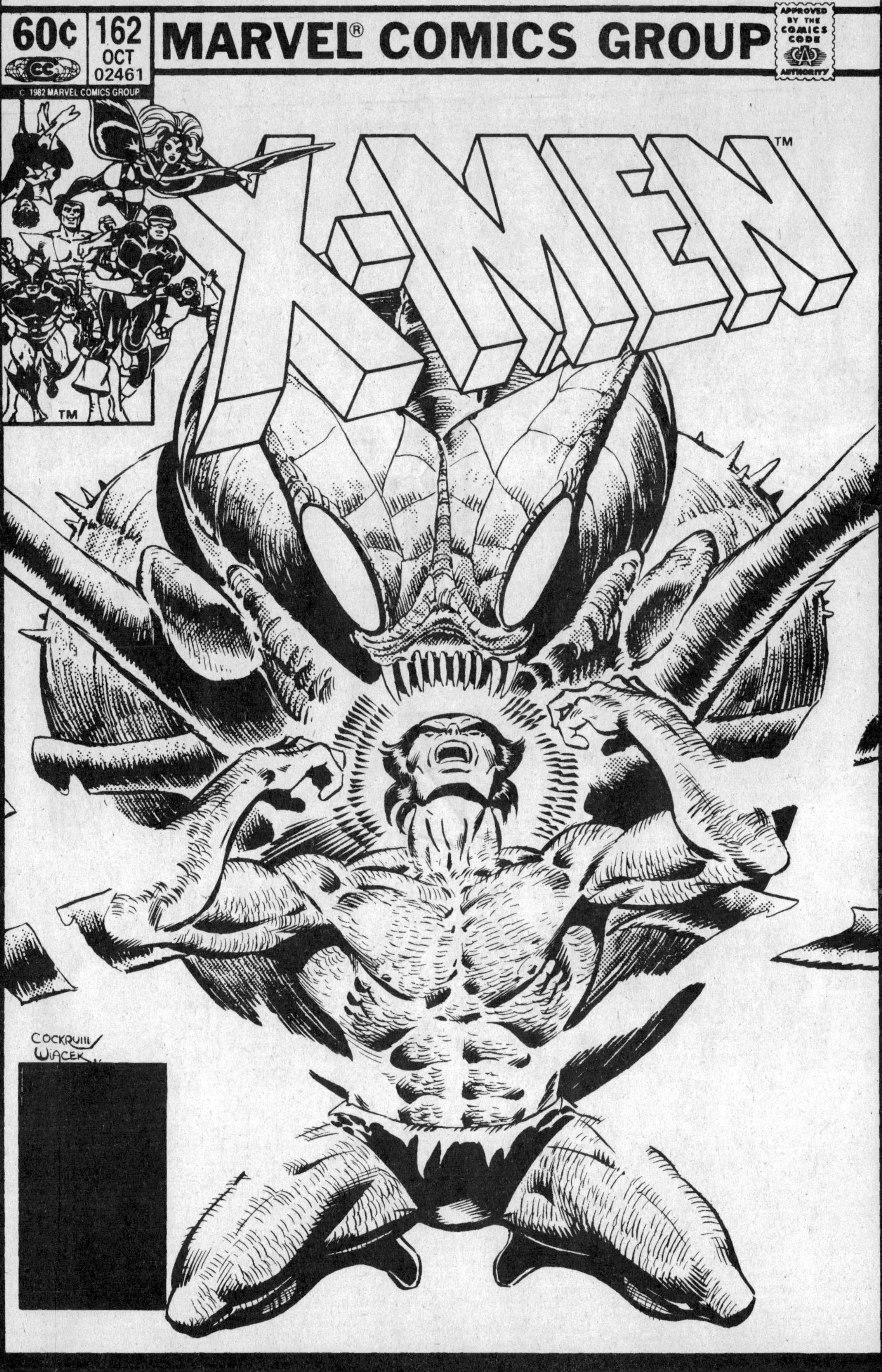
60¢
162
OCT
02461
MARVEL® COMICS GROUP
APPROVED BY THE COMICS CODE AUTHORITY
© 1982 MARVEL COMICS GROUP
X-MEN™
COCKRUM/
WIACEK

REPRINT CREDITS:

COVER ART
PAUL SMITH

COVER COLORS
CHRIS DICKEY

COVER DESIGN
COMICRAFT'S JG ROSHELL

INTERIOR DESIGN
MIKHAIL BORTNIK

ASSISTANT EDITOR
MATTY RYAN

COLLECTIONS EDITOR
BEN ABERNATHY

MANUFACTURING MANAGER
BERNADETTE THOMAS

DIRECTOR – EDITORIAL OPERATIONS
BOB GREENBERGER

EDITOR IN CHIEF
JOE QUESADA

PRESIDENT
BILL JEMAS

SPECIAL THANKS:
Elizabeth Maya, Tom Brevoort, Doreen Mulryan, and the generosity of Ralph Macchio

ESSENTIAL X-MEN® VOL. 4 Contains material originally published in magazine form as UNCANNY X-MEN Vol. 1 #'s 162-179. and X-MEN ANNUAL # 6. Published by MARVEL COMICS, Bill Jemas, President; Frank Fochetta, Senior Vice President, Publishing; Joe Quesada, Editor-in-Chief; Stan Lee, Chairman Emeritus. OFFICE OF PUBLICATION: 387 PARK AVENUE SOUTH, NEW YORK, N.Y. 10016. Copyright © 1982, 1983, 1984 and 2001 Marvel Characters, Inc. All rights reserved. X-MEN (including all prominent characters featured in this issue and the distinctive likenesses thereof) is a registered trademark of MARVEL CHARACTERS, INC. No part of this book may be printed or reproduced in any manner without the written permission of the publisher. Printed in the U.S.A. First Printing, May, 2001. ISBN # 0-7851-0775-4. GST. #R127032852. MARVEL COMICS is a division of MARVEL ENTERPRISES, INC. Peter Cuneo, Chief Executive Officer; Avi Arad, Chief Creative Officer.

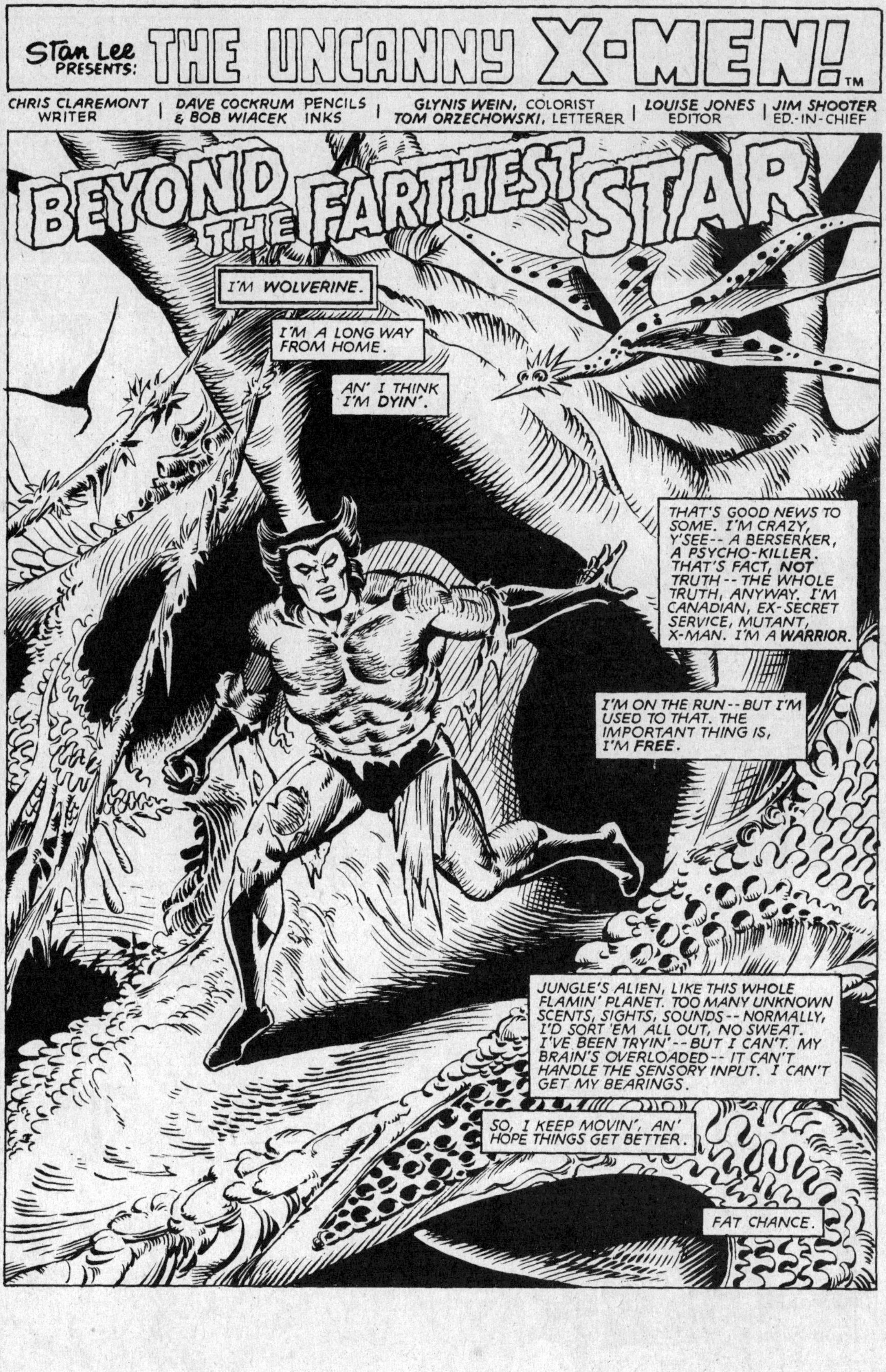
Stan Lee PRESENTS: THE UNCANNY X-MEN!™
CHRIS CLAREMONT WRITER | DAVE COCKRUM PENCILS & BOB WIACEK INKS | GLYNIS WEIN, COLORIST TOM ORZECHOWSKI, LETTERER | LOUISE JONES EDITOR | JIM SHOOTER ED.-IN-CHIEF
BEYOND THE FARTHEST STAR
I'M WOLVERINE.
I'M A LONG WAY FROM HOME.
AN' I THINK I'M DYIN'.
THAT'S GOOD NEWS TO SOME. I'M CRAZY, Y'SEE-- A BERSERKER, A PSYCHO-KILLER. THAT'S FACT, NOT TRUTH -- THE WHOLE TRUTH, ANYWAY. I'M CANADIAN, EX-SECRET SERVICE, MUTANT, X-MAN. I'M A WARRIOR.
I'M ON THE RUN -- BUT I'M USED TO THAT. THE IMPORTANT THING IS, I'M FREE.
JUNGLE'S ALIEN, LIKE THIS WHOLE FLAMIN' PLANET. TOO MANY UNKNOWN SCENTS, SIGHTS, SOUNDS -- NORMALLY, I'D SORT 'EM ALL OUT, NO SWEAT. I'VE BEEN TRYIN' -- BUT I CAN'T. MY BRAIN'S OVERLOADED -- IT CAN'T HANDLE THE SENSORY INPUT. I CAN'T GET MY BEARINGS.
SO, I KEEP MOVIN', AN' HOPE THINGS GET BETTER.
FAT CHANCE.

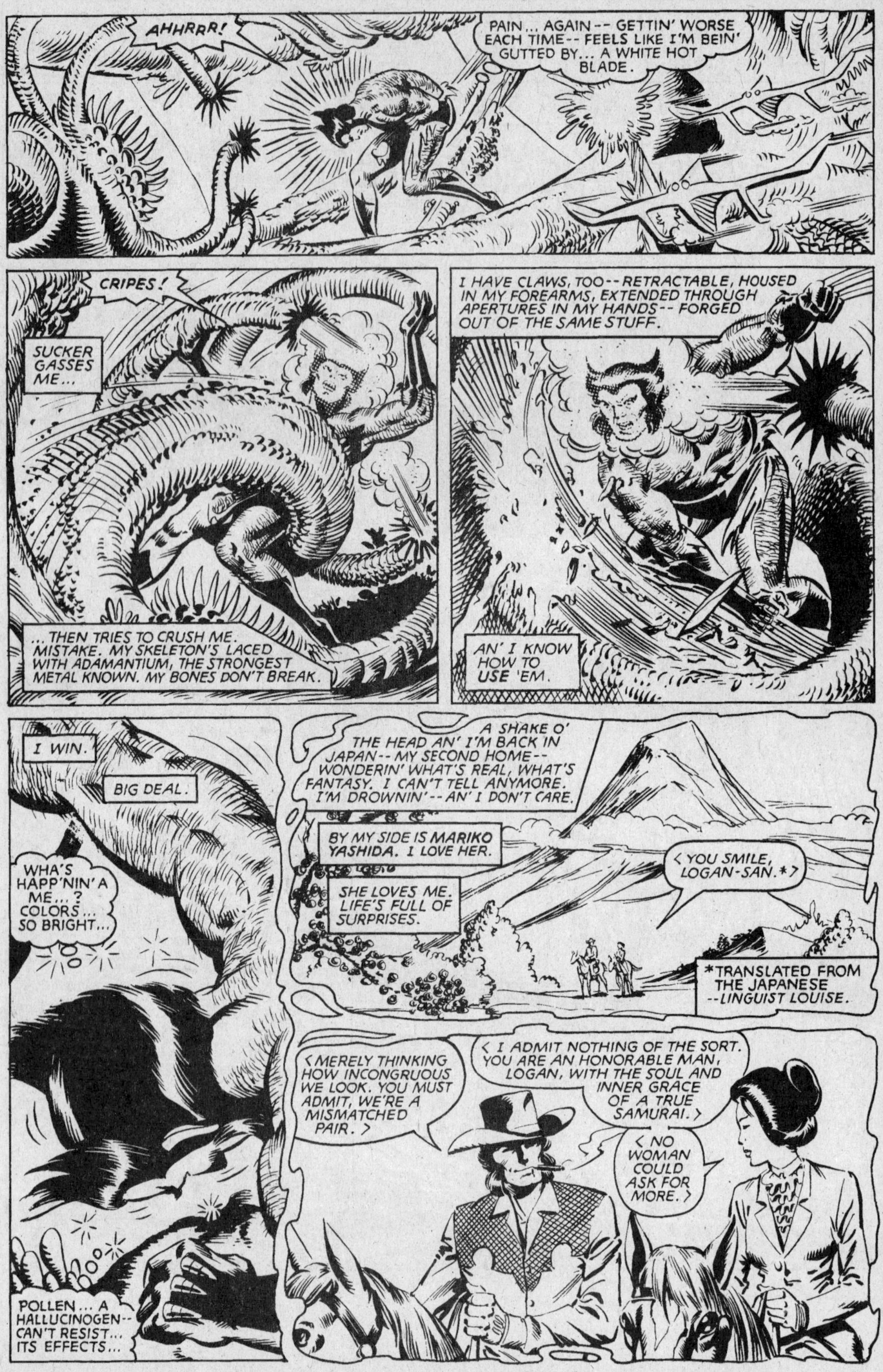
AHHRRR!
PAIN... AGAIN-- GETTIN' WORSE EACH TIME-- FEELS LIKE I'M BEIN' GUTTED BY... A WHITE HOT BLADE.
CRIPES!
SUCKER GASSES ME...
...THEN TRIES TO CRUSH ME. MISTAKE. MY SKELETON'S LACED WITH ADAMANTIUM, THE STRONGEST METAL KNOWN. MY BONES DON'T BREAK.
I HAVE CLAWS, TOO-- RETRACTABLE, HOUSED IN MY FOREARMS, EXTENDED THROUGH APERTURES IN MY HANDS-- FORGED OUT OF THE SAME STUFF.
AN' I KNOW HOW TO USE 'EM.
I WIN.
BIG DEAL.
WHA'S HAPP'NIN' A ME...? COLORS... SO BRIGHT...
POLLEN... A HALLUCINOGEN-- CAN'T RESIST... ITS EFFECTS...
A SHAKE O' THE HEAD AN' I'M BACK IN JAPAN-- MY SECOND HOME-- WONDERIN' WHAT'S REAL, WHAT'S FANTASY. I CAN'T TELL ANYMORE. I'M DROWNIN'-- AN' I DON'T CARE.
BY MY SIDE IS MARIKO YASHIDA. I LOVE HER.
SHE LOVES ME. LIFE'S FULL OF SURPRISES.
<YOU SMILE, LOGAN-SAN.*>
*TRANSLATED FROM THE JAPANESE --LINGUIST LOUISE.
<MERELY THINKING HOW INCONGRUOUS WE LOOK. YOU MUST ADMIT, WE'RE A MISMATCHED PAIR.>
<I ADMIT NOTHING OF THE SORT. YOU ARE AN HONORABLE MAN, LOGAN, WITH THE SOUL AND INNER GRACE OF A TRUE SAMURAI.>
<NO WOMAN COULD ASK FOR MORE.>

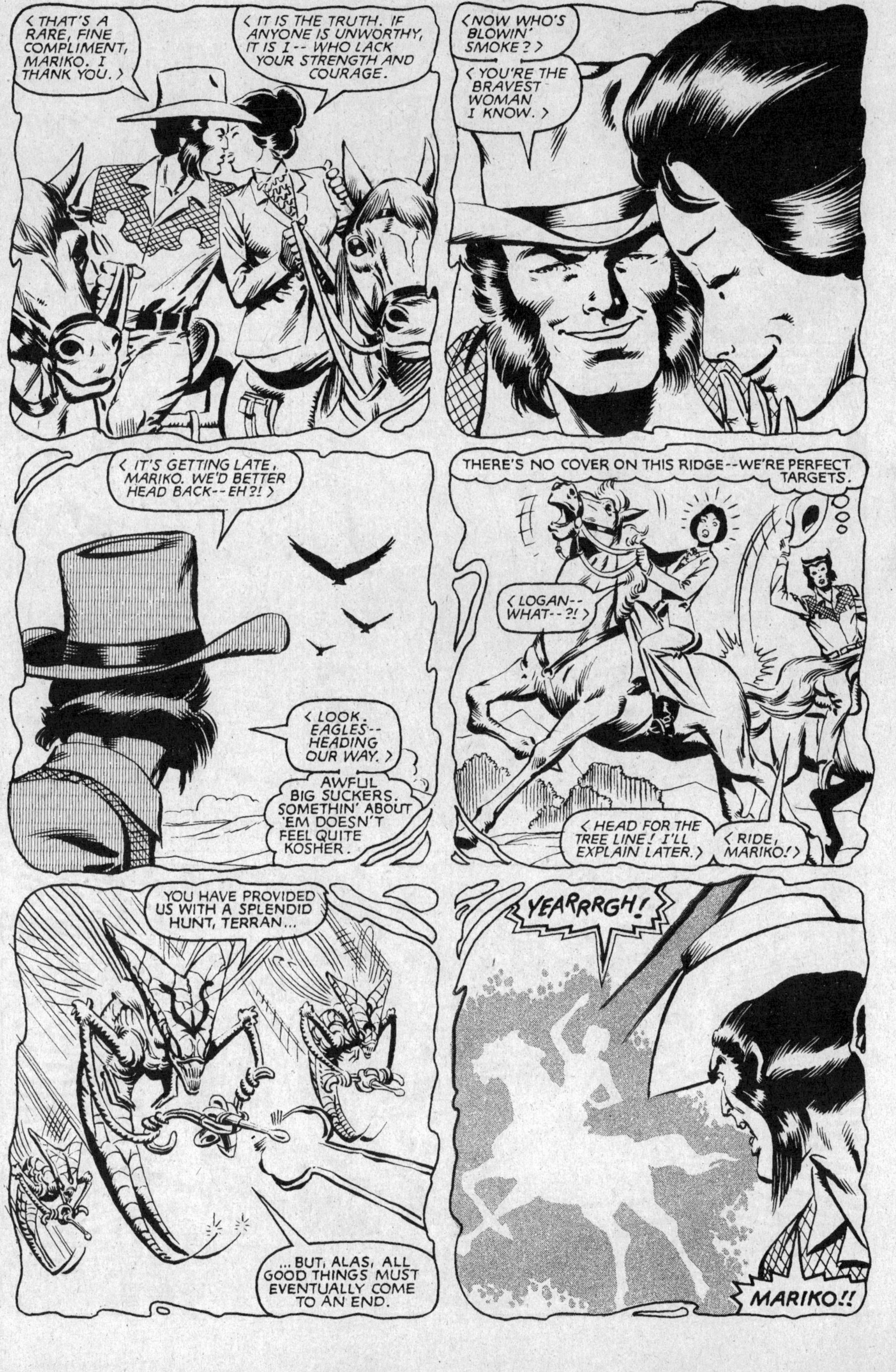
< THAT'S A RARE, FINE COMPLIMENT, MARIKO. I THANK YOU. >
< IT IS THE TRUTH. IF ANYONE IS UNWORTHY, IT IS I -- WHO LACK YOUR STRENGTH AND COURAGE. >
< NOW WHO'S BLOWIN' SMOKE? >
< YOU'RE THE BRAVEST WOMAN I KNOW. >
< IT'S GETTING LATE, MARIKO. WE'D BETTER HEAD BACK-- EH?! >
< LOOK. EAGLES-- HEADING OUR WAY. >
AWFUL BIG SUCKERS. SOMETHIN' ABOUT 'EM DOESN'T FEEL QUITE KOSHER.
THERE'S NO COVER ON THIS RIDGE--WE'RE PERFECT TARGETS.
< LOGAN-- WHAT--?! >
< HEAD FOR THE TREE LINE! I'LL EXPLAIN LATER. >
< RIDE, MARIKO! >
YOU HAVE PROVIDED US WITH A SPLENDID HUNT, TERRAN...
... BUT, ALAS, ALL GOOD THINGS MUST EVENTUALLY COME TO AN END.
YEARRRGH!
MARIKO!!

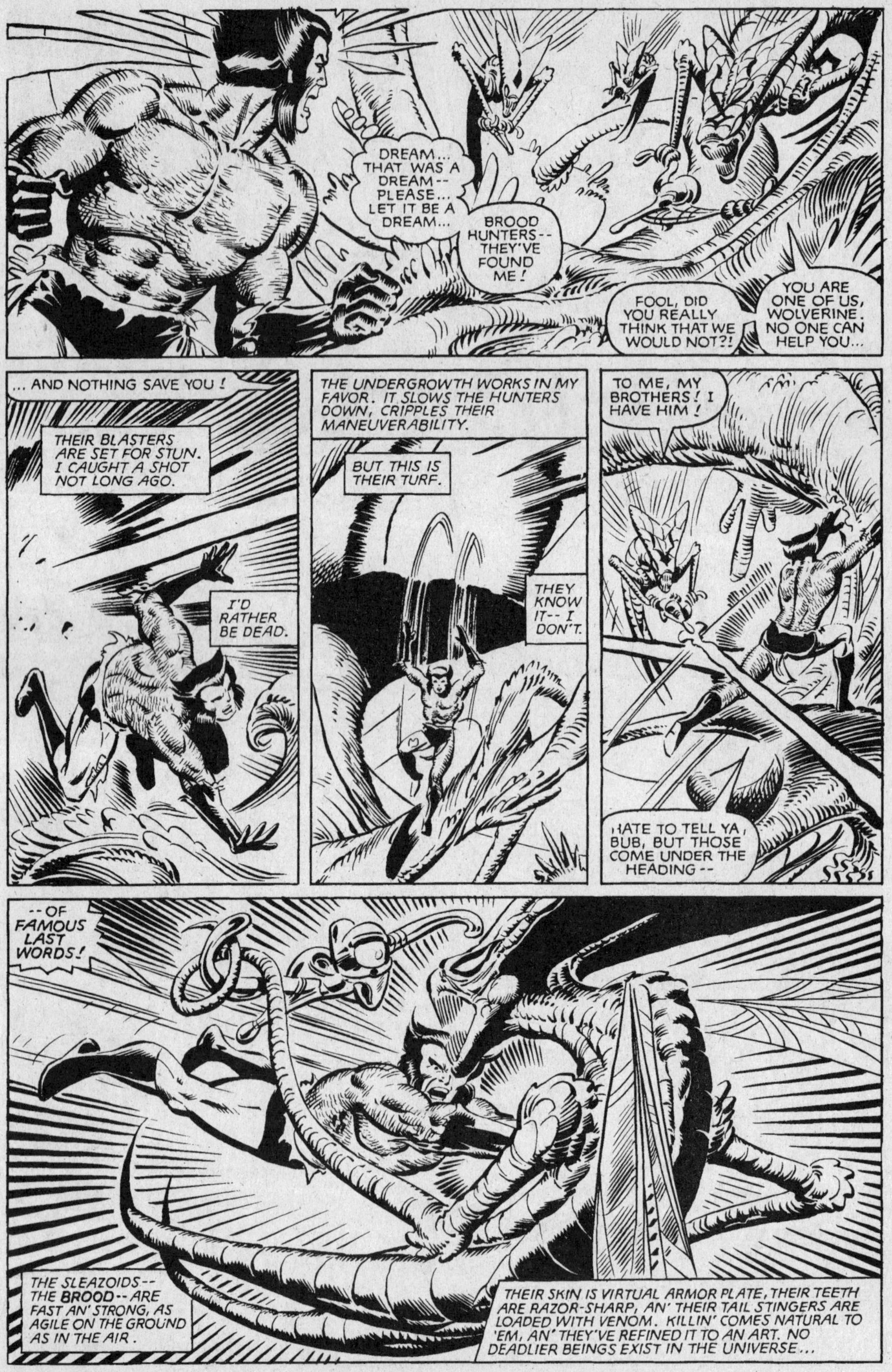
DREAM... THAT WAS A DREAM-- PLEASE... LET IT BE A DREAM...
BROOD HUNTERS-- THEY'VE FOUND ME!
FOOL, DID YOU REALLY THINK THAT WE WOULD NOT?!
YOU ARE ONE OF US, WOLVERINE. NO ONE CAN HELP YOU...
... AND NOTHING SAVE YOU!
THEIR BLASTERS ARE SET FOR STUN. I CAUGHT A SHOT NOT LONG AGO.
I'D RATHER BE DEAD.
THE UNDERGROWTH WORKS IN MY FAVOR. IT SLOWS THE HUNTERS DOWN, CRIPPLES THEIR MANEUVERABILITY.
BUT THIS IS THEIR TURF.
THEY KNOW IT-- I DON'T.
TO ME, MY BROTHERS! I HAVE HIM!
HATE TO TELL YA, BUB, BUT THOSE COME UNDER THE HEADING --
-- OF FAMOUS LAST WORDS!
THE SLEAZOIDS-- THE BROOD-- ARE FAST AN' STRONG, AS AGILE ON THE GROUND AS IN THE AIR.
THEIR SKIN IS VIRTUAL ARMOR PLATE, THEIR TEETH ARE RAZOR-SHARP, AN' THEIR TAIL STINGERS ARE LOADED WITH VENOM. KILLIN' COMES NATURAL TO 'EM, AN' THEY'VE REFINED IT TO AN ART. NO DEADLIER BEINGS EXIST IN THE UNIVERSE...

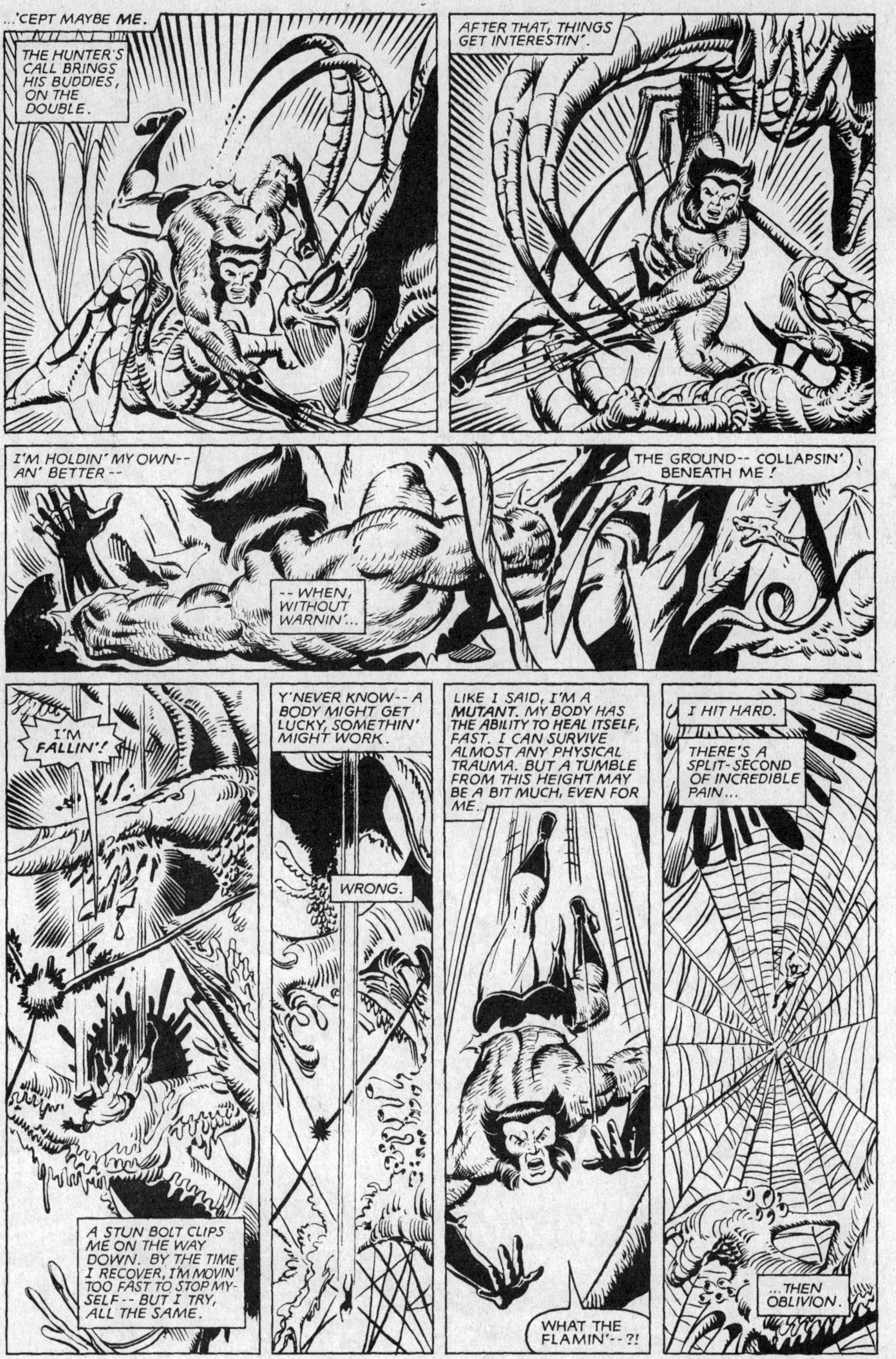
...'CEPT MAYBE ME.
THE HUNTER'S CALL BRINGS HIS BUDDIES, ON THE DOUBLE.
AFTER THAT, THINGS GET INTERESTIN'.
I'M HOLDIN' MY OWN-- AN' BETTER --
-- WHEN, WITHOUT WARNIN'...
THE GROUND-- COLLAPSIN' BENEATH ME!
I'M FALLIN'!
A STUN BOLT CLIPS ME ON THE WAY DOWN. BY THE TIME I RECOVER, I'M MOVIN' TOO FAST TO STOP MY-SELF -- BUT I TRY, ALL THE SAME.
Y'NEVER KNOW-- A BODY MIGHT GET LUCKY, SOMETHIN' MIGHT WORK.
WRONG.
LIKE I SAID, I'M A MUTANT. MY BODY HAS THE ABILITY TO HEAL ITSELF, FAST. I CAN SURVIVE ALMOST ANY PHYSICAL TRAUMA. BUT A TUMBLE FROM THIS HEIGHT MAY BE A BIT MUCH, EVEN FOR ME.
WHAT THE FLAMIN'--?!
I HIT HARD.
THERE'S A SPLIT-SECOND OF INCREDIBLE PAIN...
...THEN OBLIVION.

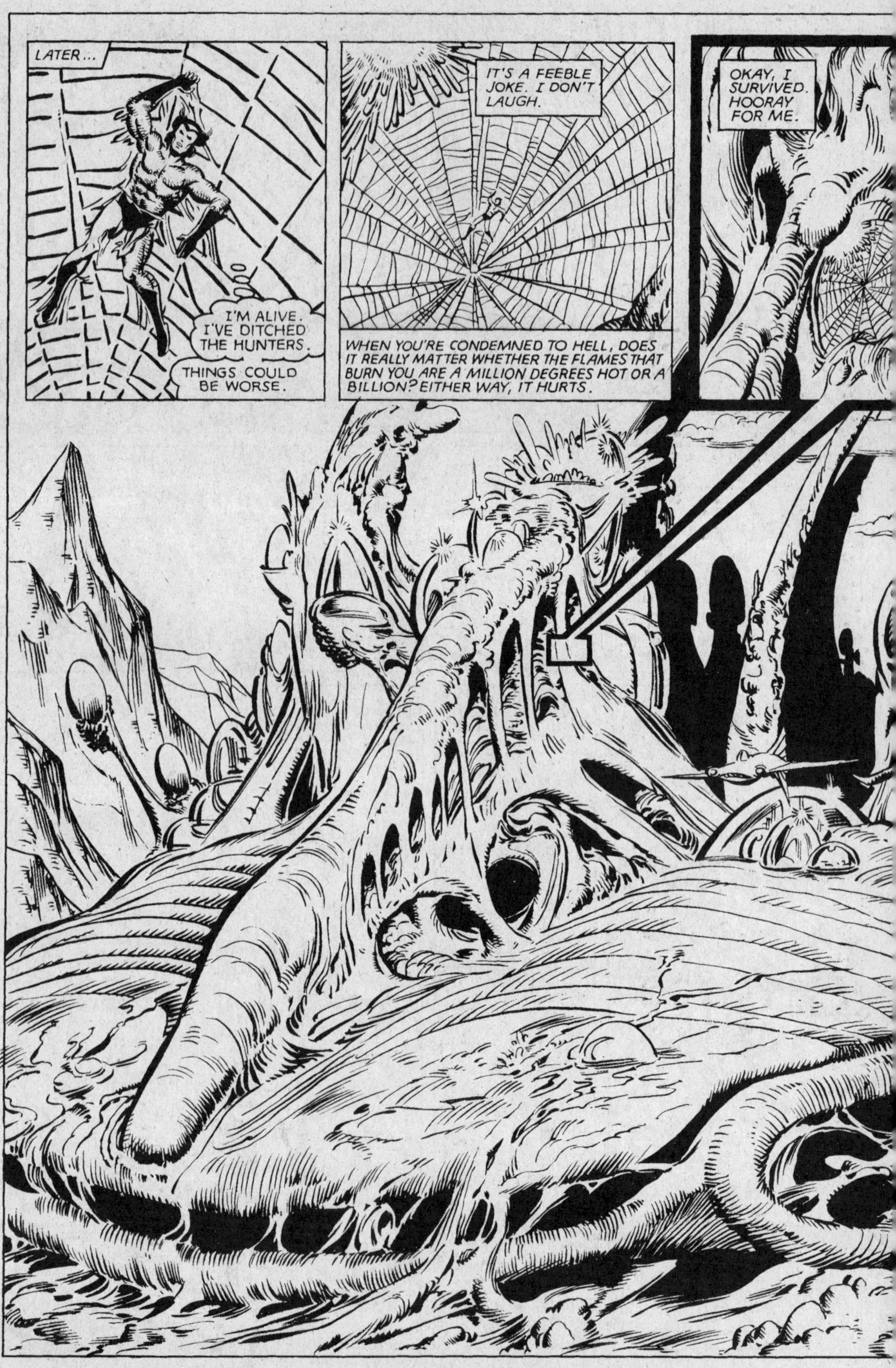
LATER...
I'M ALIVE. I'VE DITCHED THE HUNTERS.
THINGS COULD BE WORSE.
IT'S A FEEBLE JOKE. I DON'T LAUGH.
WHEN YOU'RE CONDEMNED TO HELL, DOES IT REALLY MATTER WHETHER THE FLAMES THAT BURN YOU ARE A MILLION DEGREES HOT OR A BILLION? EITHER WAY, IT HURTS.
OKAY, I SURVIVED. HOORAY FOR ME.

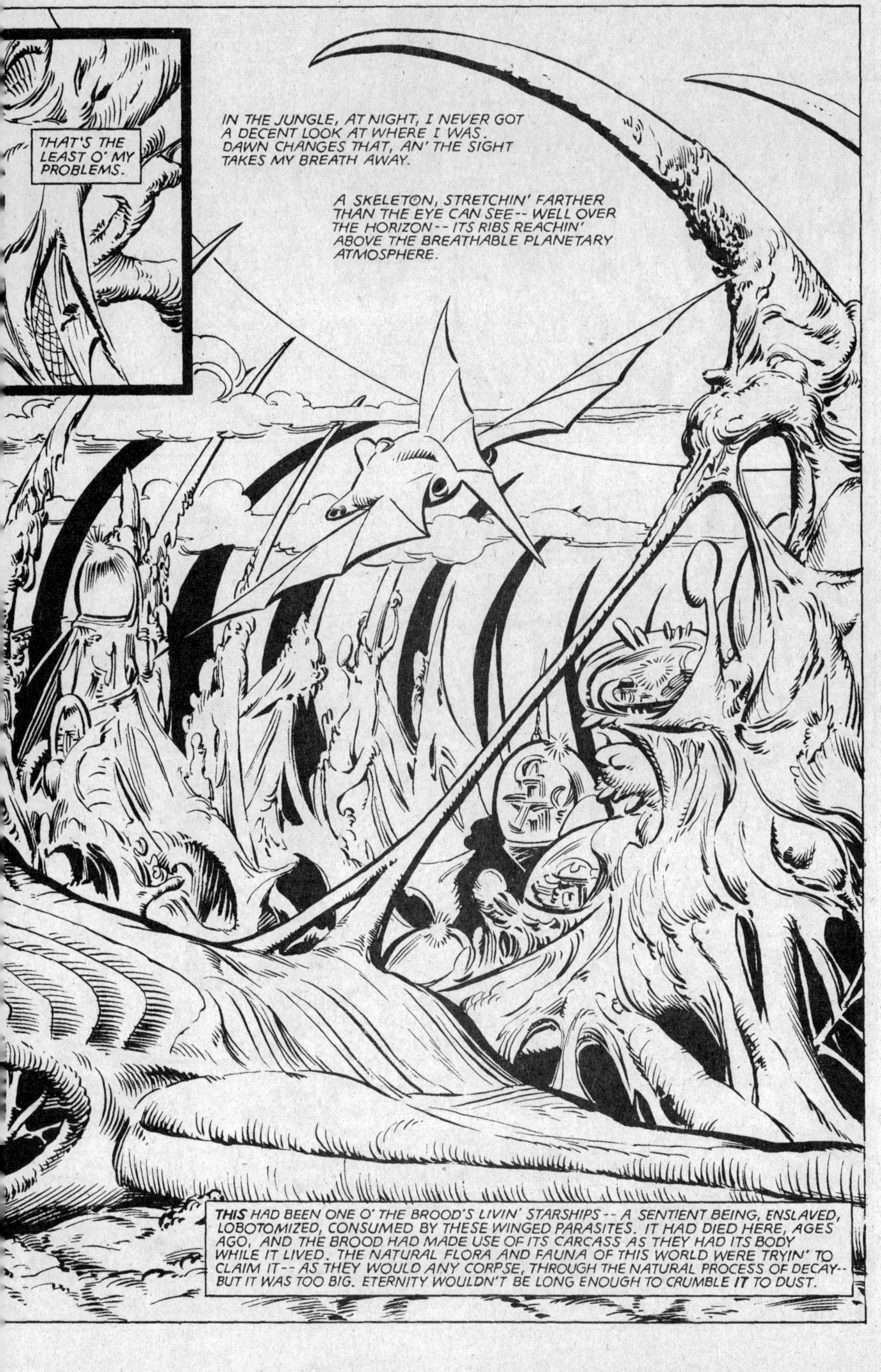

THAT'S THE LEAST O' MY PROBLEMS.
IN THE JUNGLE, AT NIGHT, I NEVER GOT A DECENT LOOK AT WHERE I WAS. DAWN CHANGES THAT, AN' THE SIGHT TAKES MY BREATH AWAY.
A SKELETON, STRETCHIN' FARTHER THAN THE EYE CAN SEE-- WELL OVER THE HORIZON-- ITS RIBS REACHIN' ABOVE THE BREATHABLE PLANETARY ATMOSPHERE.
THIS HAD BEEN ONE O' THE BROOD'S LIVIN' STARSHIPS -- A SENTIENT BEING, ENSLAVED, LOBOTOMIZED, CONSUMED BY THESE WINGED PARASITES. IT HAD DIED HERE, AGES AGO, AND THE BROOD HAD MADE USE OF ITS CARCASS AS THEY HAD ITS BODY WHILE IT LIVED. THE NATURAL FLORA AND FAUNA OF THIS WORLD WERE TRYIN' TO CLAIM IT -- AS THEY WOULD ANY CORPSE, THROUGH THE NATURAL PROCESS OF DECAY-- BUT IT WAS TOO BIG. ETERNITY WOULDN'T BE LONG ENOUGH TO CRUMBLE IT TO DUST.

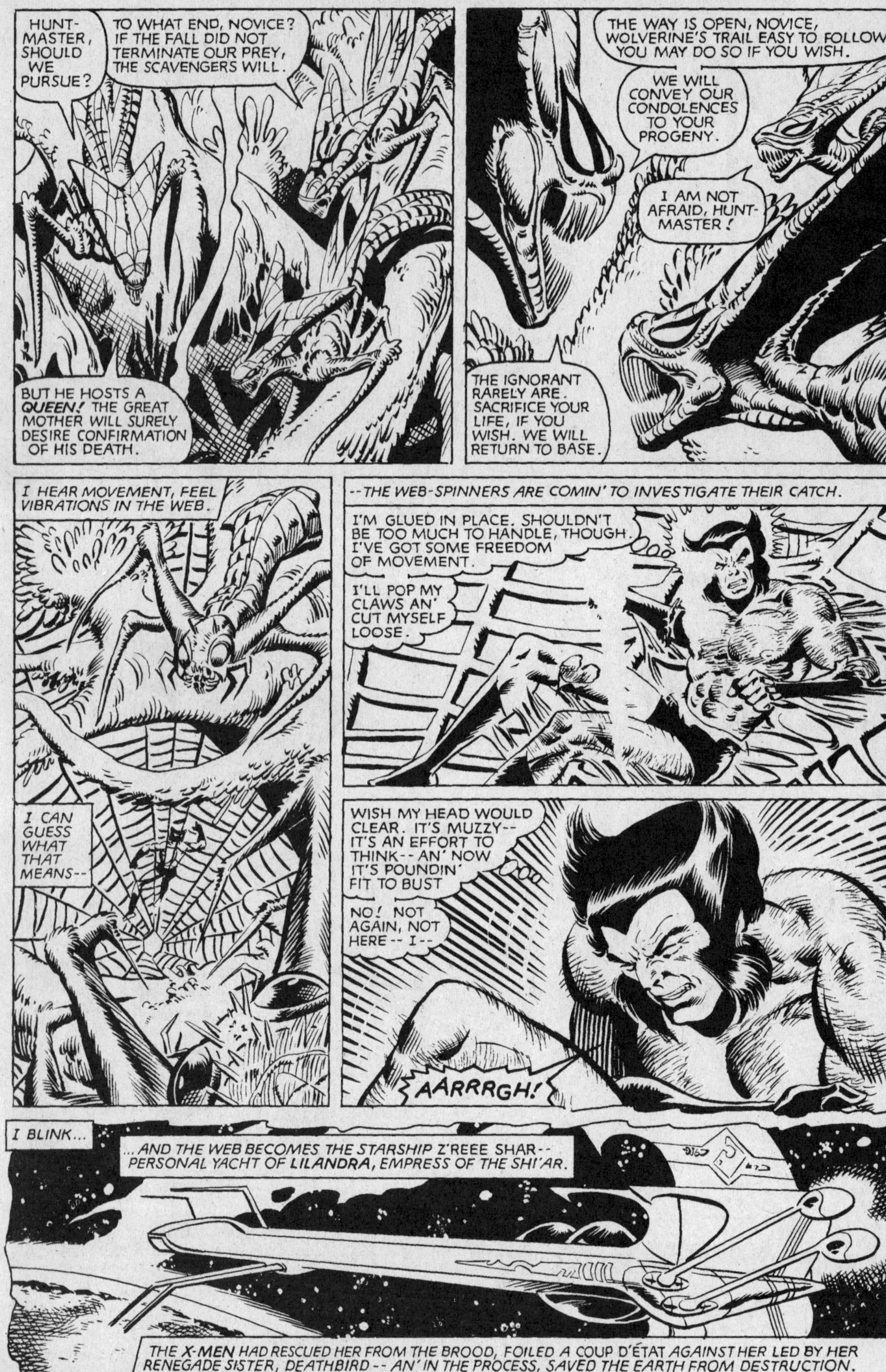
HUNT-MASTER, SHOULD WE PURSUE?
TO WHAT END, NOVICE? IF THE FALL DID NOT TERMINATE OUR PREY, THE SCAVENGERS WILL.
BUT HE HOSTS A QUEEN! THE GREAT MOTHER WILL SURELY DESIRE CONFIRMATION OF HIS DEATH.
THE WAY IS OPEN, NOVICE, WOLVERINE'S TRAIL EASY TO FOLLOW. YOU MAY DO SO IF YOU WISH.
WE WILL CONVEY OUR CONDOLENCES TO YOUR PROGENY.
I AM NOT AFRAID, HUNT-MASTER!
THE IGNORANT RARELY ARE. SACRIFICE YOUR LIFE, IF YOU WISH. WE WILL RETURN TO BASE.
I HEAR MOVEMENT, FEEL VIBRATIONS IN THE WEB.
I CAN GUESS WHAT THAT MEANS--
--THE WEB-SPINNERS ARE COMIN' TO INVESTIGATE THEIR CATCH.
I'M GLUED IN PLACE. SHOULDN'T BE TOO MUCH TO HANDLE, THOUGH. I'VE GOT SOME FREEDOM OF MOVEMENT.
I'LL POP MY CLAWS AN' CUT MYSELF LOOSE.
WISH MY HEAD WOULD CLEAR. IT'S MUZZY-- IT'S AN EFFORT TO THINK-- AN' NOW IT'S POUNDIN' FIT TO BUST
NO! NOT AGAIN, NOT HERE -- I--
AARRRGH!
I BLINK...
...AND THE WEB BECOMES THE STARSHIP Z'REEE SHAR-- PERSONAL YACHT OF LILANDRA, EMPRESS OF THE SHI'AR.
THE X-MEN HAD RESCUED HER FROM THE BROOD, FOILED A COUP D'ÉTAT AGAINST HER LED BY HER RENEGADE SISTER, DEATHBIRD -- AN' IN THE PROCESS, SAVED THE EARTH FROM DESTRUCTION.

TO SHOW HER APPRECIATION, LIL INVITED US ABOARD HER YACHT FOR A BANQUET -- PART CELEBRATION, PART FAREWELL. SHE WAS RETURNIN' HOME AN' WANTED TO THANK US --

--ME, CAROL DANVERS, CYCLOPS, STORM, COLOSSUS, NIGHTCRAWLER, AN' KITTY PRYDE.

COLOSSUS WASN'T REALLY IN THE MOOD FOR A PARTY, ON ACCOUNT OF HIS SISTER, ILLYANA.

PETEY, WHAT'S DONE IS DONE. MOPIN' WON'T CHANGE ANYTHING -- IT CERTAINLY WON'T MAKE ILLYANA A CHILD AGAIN.*

I KNOW, WOLVERINE, BUT IT IS A HARD REALITY TO FACE.

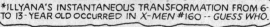

*ILLYANA'S INSTANTANEOUS TRANSFORMATION FROM 6- TO 13-YEAR OLD OCCURRED IN X-MEN #160 -- GUESS WHO.

MUCH ABOUT OUR BATTLE WITH THE DEMON-LORD BELASCO IS DIFFICULT TO COPE WITH -- NOT THE LEAST OF WHICH WAS MY CONFRONTATION WITH MY OLDER SELF.

THAT STORM WAS A SORCERESS. SHE SAID HALF MY HERITAGE WAS BOUND TO THE ARTS ARCANE. BUT HOW?! I AM A MUTANT, NOT A MAGICIAN.

COULD I TRULY POSSESS SUCH TALENTS?

SUDDENLY...

BEHOLD, FOOLS! LILANDRA, MAJESTRIX SHI'AR, IS NO MORE! LONG LIVE THE NEW EMPRESS! ME!

DEATH-BIRD!

A TRAP. WE TRIED TO REACT...

...BUT A STASIS BOMB ENDED THE FIGHT AS SOON AS IT HAD BEGUN.*

*SEE LAST ISH--L.

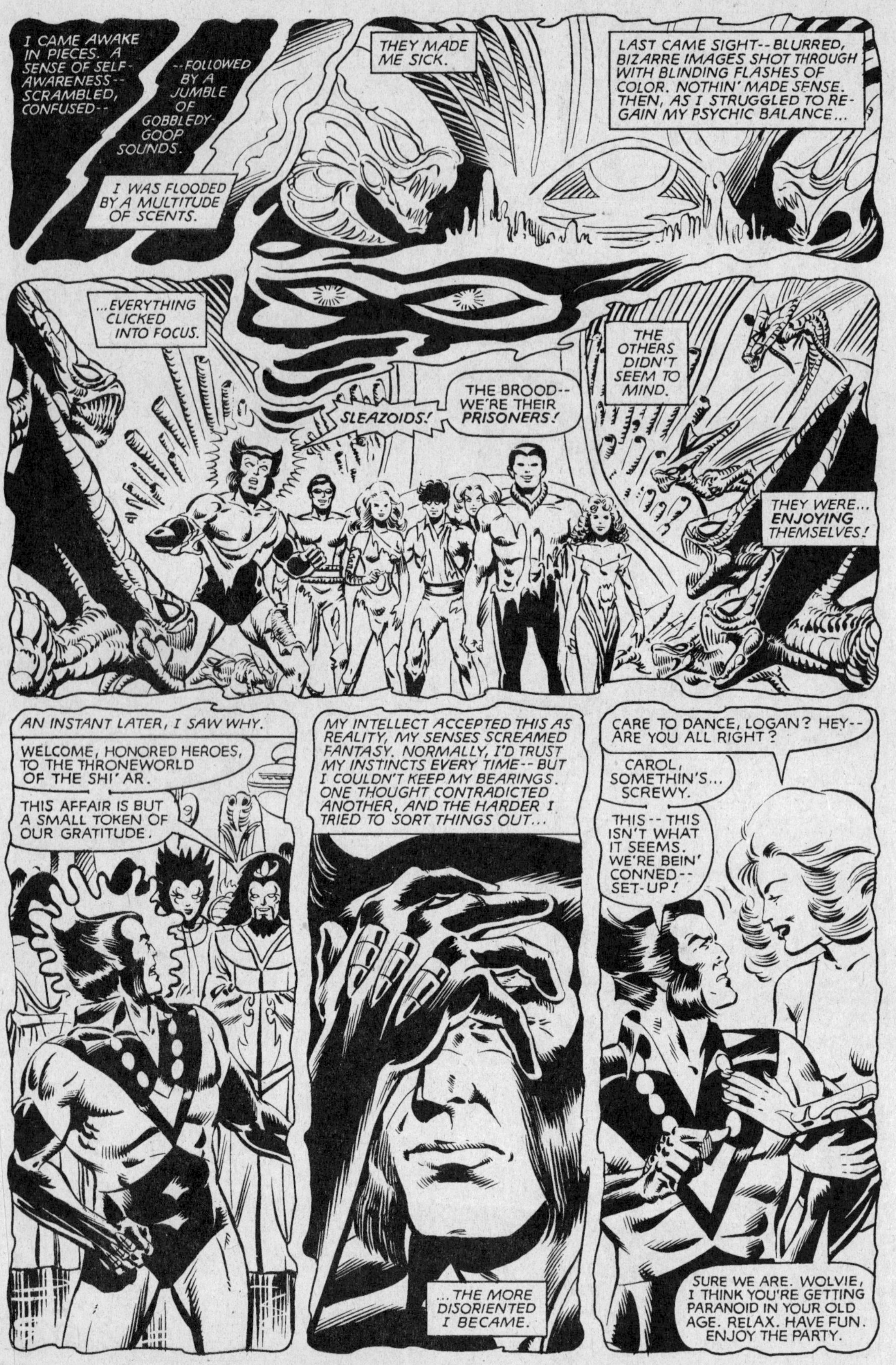
I CAME AWAKE IN PIECES. A SENSE OF SELF-AWARENESS--SCRAMBLED, CONFUSED--
--FOLLOWED BY A JUMBLE OF GOBBLEDY-GOOP SOUNDS.
I WAS FLOODED BY A MULTITUDE OF SCENTS.
THEY MADE ME SICK.
LAST CAME SIGHT--BLURRED, BIZARRE IMAGES SHOT THROUGH WITH BLINDING FLASHES OF COLOR. NOTHIN' MADE SENSE. THEN, AS I STRUGGLED TO REGAIN MY PSYCHIC BALANCE...
...EVERYTHING CLICKED INTO FOCUS.
SLEAZOIDS!
THE BROOD--WE'RE THEIR PRISONERS!
THE OTHERS DIDN'T SEEM TO MIND.
THEY WERE... ENJOYING THEMSELVES!
AN INSTANT LATER, I SAW WHY.
WELCOME, HONORED HEROES, TO THE THRONEWORLD OF THE SHI'AR.
THIS AFFAIR IS BUT A SMALL TOKEN OF OUR GRATITUDE.
MY INTELLECT ACCEPTED THIS AS REALITY, MY SENSES SCREAMED FANTASY. NORMALLY, I'D TRUST MY INSTINCTS EVERY TIME--BUT I COULDN'T KEEP MY BEARINGS. ONE THOUGHT CONTRADICTED ANOTHER, AND THE HARDER I TRIED TO SORT THINGS OUT...
...THE MORE DISORIENTED I BECAME.
CARE TO DANCE, LOGAN? HEY--ARE YOU ALL RIGHT?
CAROL, SOMETHIN'S... SCREWY.
THIS--THIS ISN'T WHAT IT SEEMS. WE'RE BEIN' CONNED--SET-UP!
SURE WE ARE. WOLVIE, I THINK YOU'RE GETTING PARANOID IN YOUR OLD AGE. RELAX. HAVE FUN. ENJOY THE PARTY.

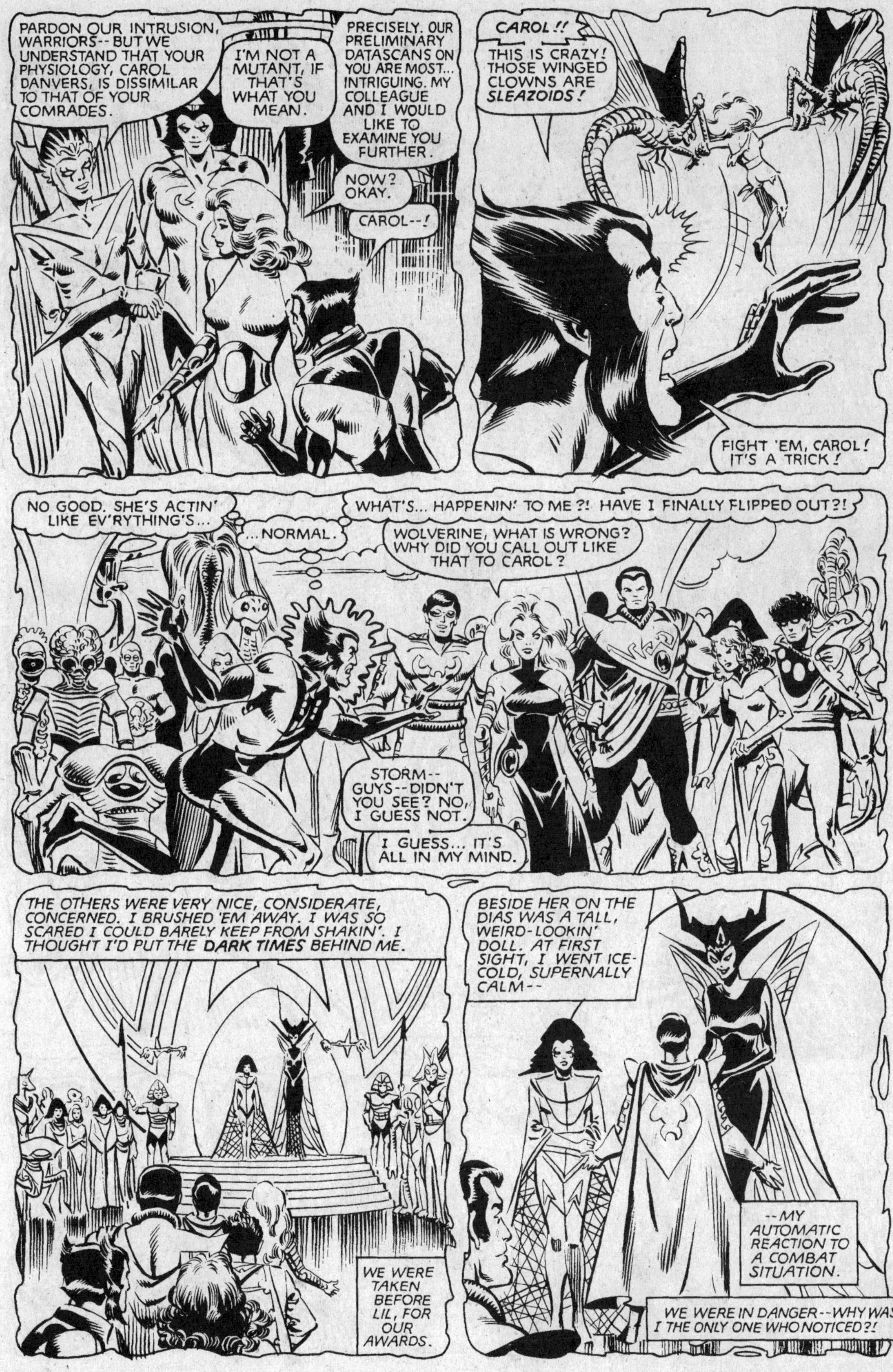
PARDON OUR INTRUSION, WARRIORS-- BUT WE UNDERSTAND THAT YOUR PHYSIOLOGY, CAROL DANVERS, IS DISSIMILAR TO THAT OF YOUR COMRADES.
I'M NOT A MUTANT, IF THAT'S WHAT YOU MEAN.
PRECISELY. OUR PRELIMINARY DATASCANS ON YOU ARE MOST... INTRIGUING. MY COLLEAGUE AND I WOULD LIKE TO EXAMINE YOU FURTHER.
NOW? OKAY.
CAROL--!
CAROL!!
THIS IS CRAZY! THOSE WINGED CLOWNS ARE SLEAZOIDS!
FIGHT 'EM, CAROL! IT'S A TRICK!
NO GOOD. SHE'S ACTIN' LIKE EV'RYTHING'S...
...NORMAL.
WHAT'S... HAPPENIN' TO ME?! HAVE I FINALLY FLIPPED OUT?!
WOLVERINE, WHAT IS WRONG? WHY DID YOU CALL OUT LIKE THAT TO CAROL?
STORM-- GUYS--DIDN'T YOU SEE? NO, I GUESS NOT.
I GUESS... IT'S ALL IN MY MIND.
THE OTHERS WERE VERY NICE, CONSIDERATE, CONCERNED. I BRUSHED 'EM AWAY. I WAS SO SCARED I COULD BARELY KEEP FROM SHAKIN'. I THOUGHT I'D PUT THE DARK TIMES BEHIND ME.
WE WERE TAKEN BEFORE LIL, FOR OUR AWARDS.
BESIDE HER ON THE DIAS WAS A TALL, WEIRD-LOOKIN' DOLL. AT FIRST SIGHT, I WENT ICE-COLD, SUPERNALLY CALM--
--MY AUTOMATIC REACTION TO A COMBAT SITUATION.
WE WERE IN DANGER--WHY WAS I THE ONLY ONE WHO NOTICED?!

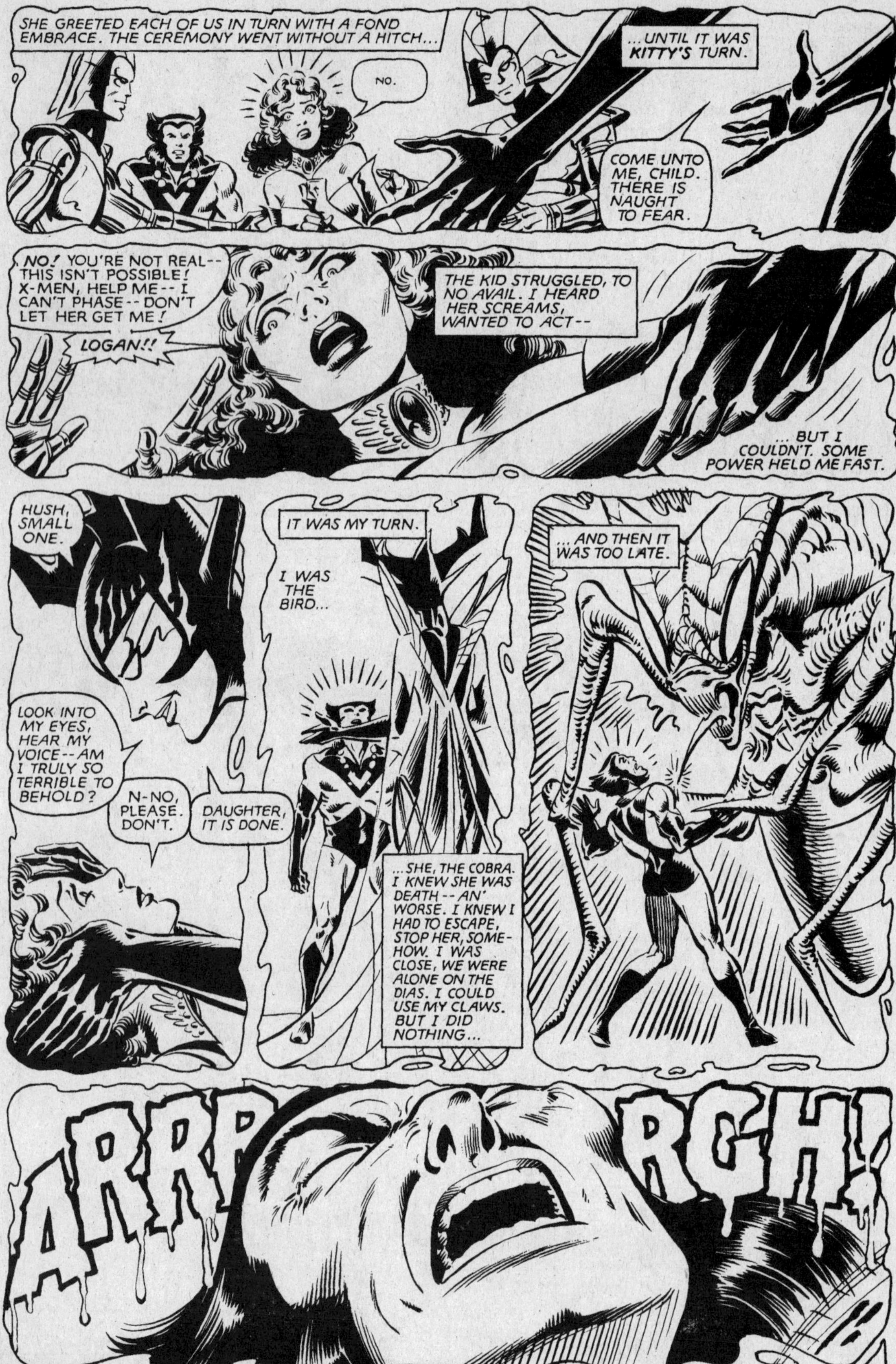
SHE GREETED EACH OF US IN TURN WITH A FOND EMBRACE. THE CEREMONY WENT WITHOUT A HITCH...
NO.
...UNTIL IT WAS KITTY'S TURN.
COME UNTO ME, CHILD. THERE IS NAUGHT TO FEAR.
NO! YOU'RE NOT REAL-- THIS ISN'T POSSIBLE! X-MEN, HELP ME-- I CAN'T PHASE-- DON'T LET HER GET ME!
LOGAN!!
THE KID STRUGGLED, TO NO AVAIL. I HEARD HER SCREAMS, WANTED TO ACT--
...BUT I COULDN'T. SOME POWER HELD ME FAST.
HUSH, SMALL ONE.
LOOK INTO MY EYES, HEAR MY VOICE--AM I TRULY SO TERRIBLE TO BEHOLD?
N-NO, PLEASE. DON'T.
DAUGHTER, IT IS DONE.
IT WAS MY TURN.
I WAS THE BIRD...
...SHE, THE COBRA. I KNEW SHE WAS DEATH--AN' WORSE. I KNEW I HAD TO ESCAPE, STOP HER, SOMEHOW. I WAS CLOSE, WE WERE ALONE ON THE DIAS. I COULD USE MY CLAWS. BUT I DID NOTHING...
...AND THEN IT WAS TOO LATE.
ARRRGH!

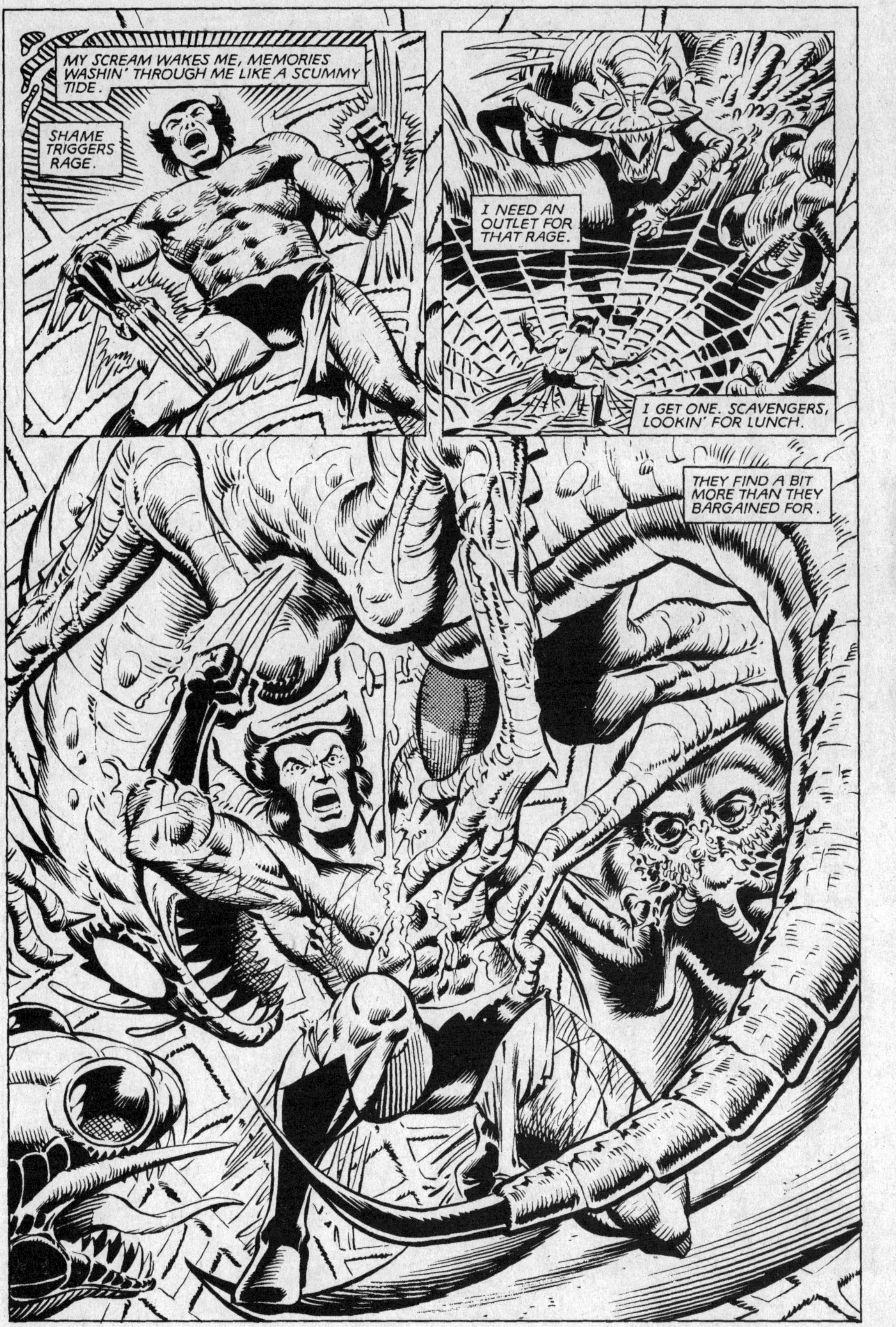
MY SCREAM WAKES ME, MEMORIES WASHIN' THROUGH ME LIKE A SCUMMY TIDE.
SHAME TRIGGERS RAGE.
I NEED AN OUTLET FOR THAT RAGE.
I GET ONE. SCAVENGERS, LOOKIN' FOR LUNCH.
THEY FIND A BIT MORE THAN THEY BARGAINED FOR.

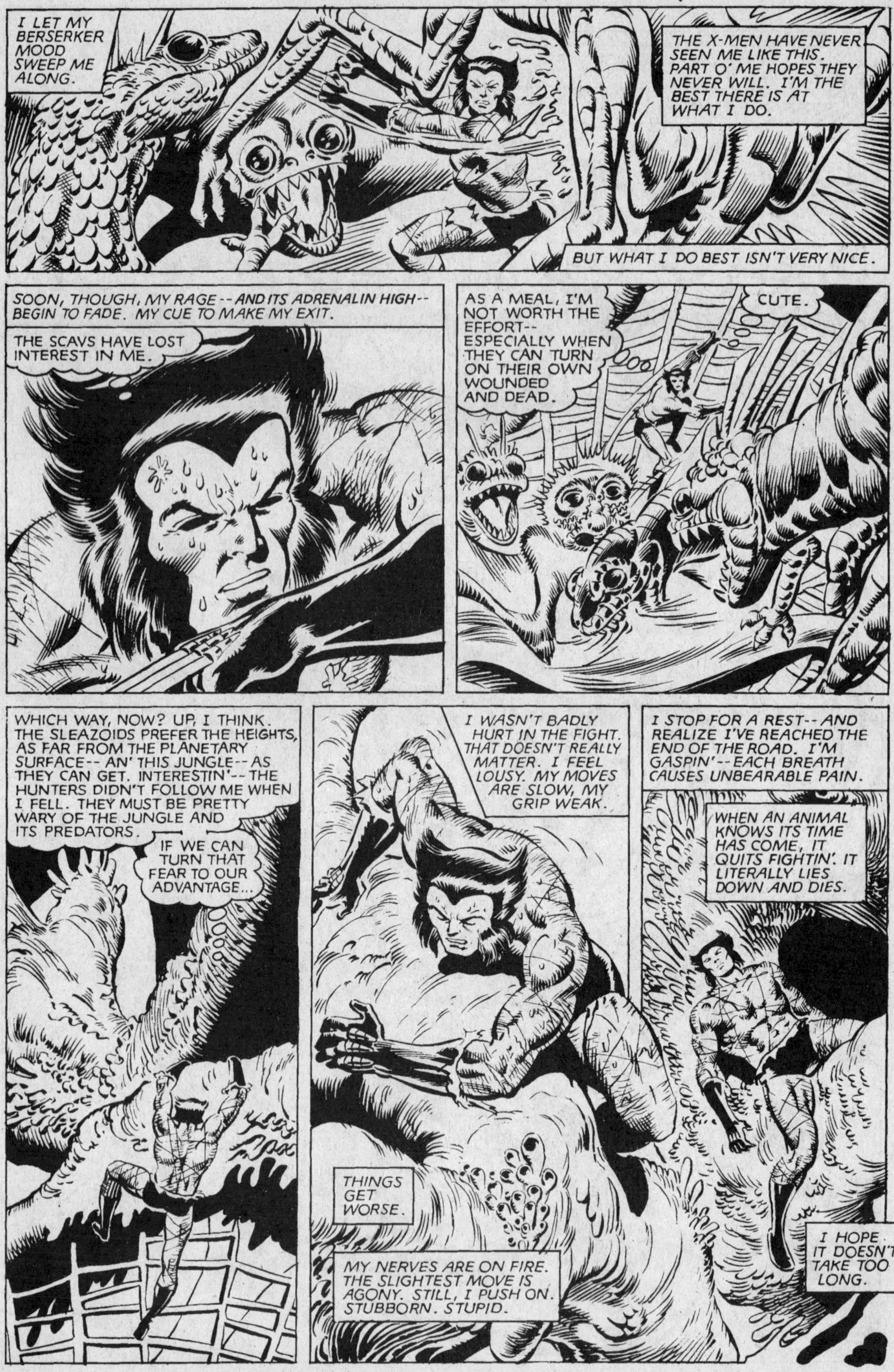
I LET MY BERSERKER MOOD SWEEP ME ALONG.
THE X-MEN HAVE NEVER SEEN ME LIKE THIS. PART O' ME HOPES THEY NEVER WILL. I'M THE BEST THERE IS AT WHAT I DO.
BUT WHAT I DO BEST ISN'T VERY NICE.
SOON, THOUGH, MY RAGE -- AND ITS ADRENALIN HIGH -- BEGIN TO FADE. MY CUE TO MAKE MY EXIT.
THE SCAVS HAVE LOST INTEREST IN ME.
AS A MEAL, I'M NOT WORTH THE EFFORT -- ESPECIALLY WHEN THEY CAN TURN ON THEIR OWN WOUNDED AND DEAD.
CUTE.
WHICH WAY, NOW? UP, I THINK. THE SLEAZOIDS PREFER THE HEIGHTS, AS FAR FROM THE PLANETARY SURFACE -- AN' THIS JUNGLE -- AS THEY CAN GET. INTERESTIN' -- THE HUNTERS DIDN'T FOLLOW ME WHEN I FELL. THEY MUST BE PRETTY WARY OF THE JUNGLE AND ITS PREDATORS.
IF WE CAN TURN THAT FEAR TO OUR ADVANTAGE...
I WASN'T BADLY HURT IN THE FIGHT. THAT DOESN'T REALLY MATTER. I FEEL LOUSY. MY MOVES ARE SLOW, MY GRIP WEAK.
THINGS GET WORSE.
MY NERVES ARE ON FIRE. THE SLIGHTEST MOVE IS AGONY. STILL, I PUSH ON. STUBBORN. STUPID.
I STOP FOR A REST -- AND REALIZE I'VE REACHED THE END OF THE ROAD. I'M GASPIN' -- EACH BREATH CAUSES UNBEARABLE PAIN.
WHEN AN ANIMAL KNOWS ITS TIME HAS COME, IT QUITS FIGHTIN'. IT LITERALLY LIES DOWN AND DIES.
I HOPE IT DOESN'T TAKE TOO LONG.

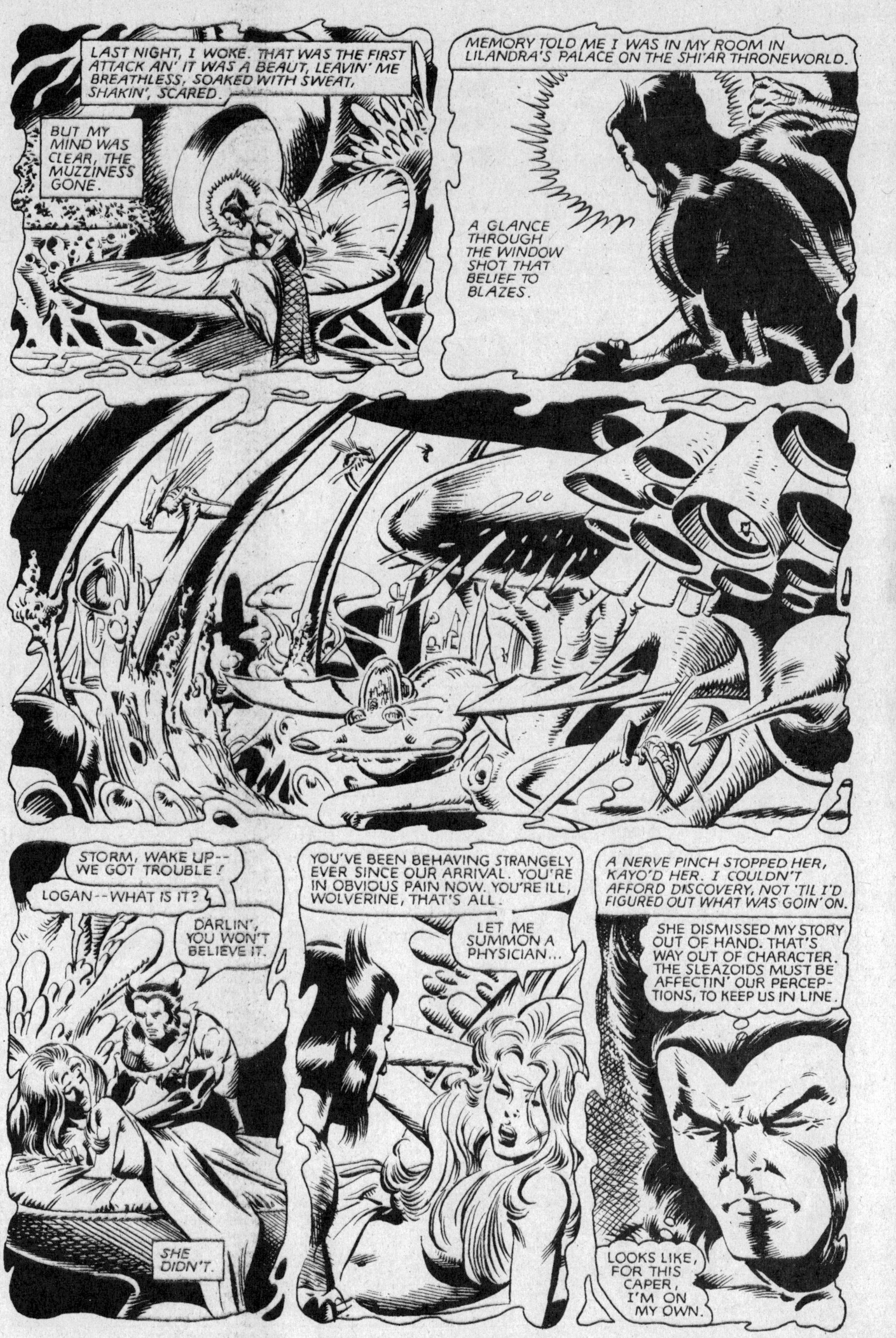
LAST NIGHT, I WOKE. THAT WAS THE FIRST ATTACK AN' IT WAS A BEAUT, LEAVIN' ME BREATHLESS, SOAKED WITH SWEAT, SHAKIN', SCARED.
BUT MY MIND WAS CLEAR, THE MUZZINESS GONE.
MEMORY TOLD ME I WAS IN MY ROOM IN LILANDRA'S PALACE ON THE SHI'AR THRONEWORLD.
A GLANCE THROUGH THE WINDOW SHOT THAT BELIEF TO BLAZES.
STORM, WAKE UP-- WE GOT TROUBLE!
LOGAN--WHAT IS IT?
DARLIN', YOU WON'T BELIEVE IT.
SHE DIDN'T.
YOU'VE BEEN BEHAVING STRANGELY EVER SINCE OUR ARRIVAL. YOU'RE IN OBVIOUS PAIN NOW. YOU'RE ILL, WOLVERINE, THAT'S ALL.
LET ME SUMMON A PHYSICIAN...
A NERVE PINCH STOPPED HER, KAYO'D HER. I COULDN'T AFFORD DISCOVERY, NOT 'TIL I'D FIGURED OUT WHAT WAS GOIN' ON.
SHE DISMISSED MY STORY OUT OF HAND. THAT'S WAY OUT OF CHARACTER. THE SLEAZOIDS MUST BE AFFECTIN' OUR PERCEPTIONS, TO KEEP US IN LINE.
LOOKS LIKE, FOR THIS CAPER, I'M ON MY OWN.

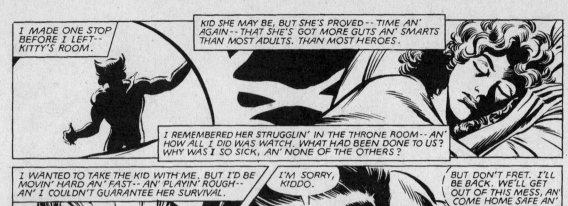

I MADE ONE STOP BEFORE I LEFT-- KITTY'S ROOM.

KID SHE MAY BE, BUT SHE'S PROVED-- TIME AN' AGAIN-- THAT SHE'S GOT MORE GUTS AN' SMARTS THAN MOST ADULTS. THAN MOST HEROES.

I REMEMBERED HER STRUGGLIN' IN THE THRONE ROOM-- AN' HOW ALL I DID WAS WATCH. WHAT HAD BEEN DONE TO US? WHY WAS I SO SICK, AN' NONE OF THE OTHERS?

I WANTED TO TAKE THE KID WITH ME. BUT I'D BE MOVIN' HARD AN' FAST-- AN' PLAYIN' ROUGH-- AN' I COULDN'T GUARANTEE HER SURVIVAL.

I'M SORRY, KIDDO.

BUT DON'T FRET. I'LL BE BACK. WE'LL GET OUT OF THIS MESS, AN' COME HOME SAFE AN' SOUND, YOU GOT MY WORD.

FOR NOW, SHE WAS BETTER OFF WHERE SHE WAS.

THE PROMISE SOUNDED HOLLOW.

SUDDENLY, AN IMAGE FLASHED THROUGH MY MIND-- KITTY CRADLED IN MY ARMS, MY RIGHT HAND LYIN' BELOW HER BREASTBONE, THE STACCATTO CLICK OF CLAWS EXTENDING, RETRACTING, THE LIGHT FADIN' FROM HER EYES...

WHAT HAD BEEN DONE TO US, TO MAKE ME THINK SUCH THINGS?!

ELSEWHERE IN THE PALACE, I FOUND THE ANSWER.

A CADRE OF SLEAZOIDS HAD GATHERED FOR A CEREMONY. THE OBJECT OF THEIR ATTENTION WAS AN OLD FOE OF THE X-MEN, A RENEGADE MEMBER OF LILANDRA'S IMPERIAL GUARD: FANG.

I GRINNED. SERVED THE SUCKER RIGHT IF THE BROOD-- FOR WHOM HE'D WORKED TO OVERTHROW LIL-- WERE GONNA REWARD HIS TREACHERY WITH TORTURE OR EXECUTION.

HE WAS PLEADIN'. THEY WERE LAUGHIN'. SURPRISINGLY, I UNDERSTOOD THEIR LANGUAGE.

FANG'S BODY BEGAN TO SMOKE. HE SHRIEKED. I STOPPED GRINNIN'.

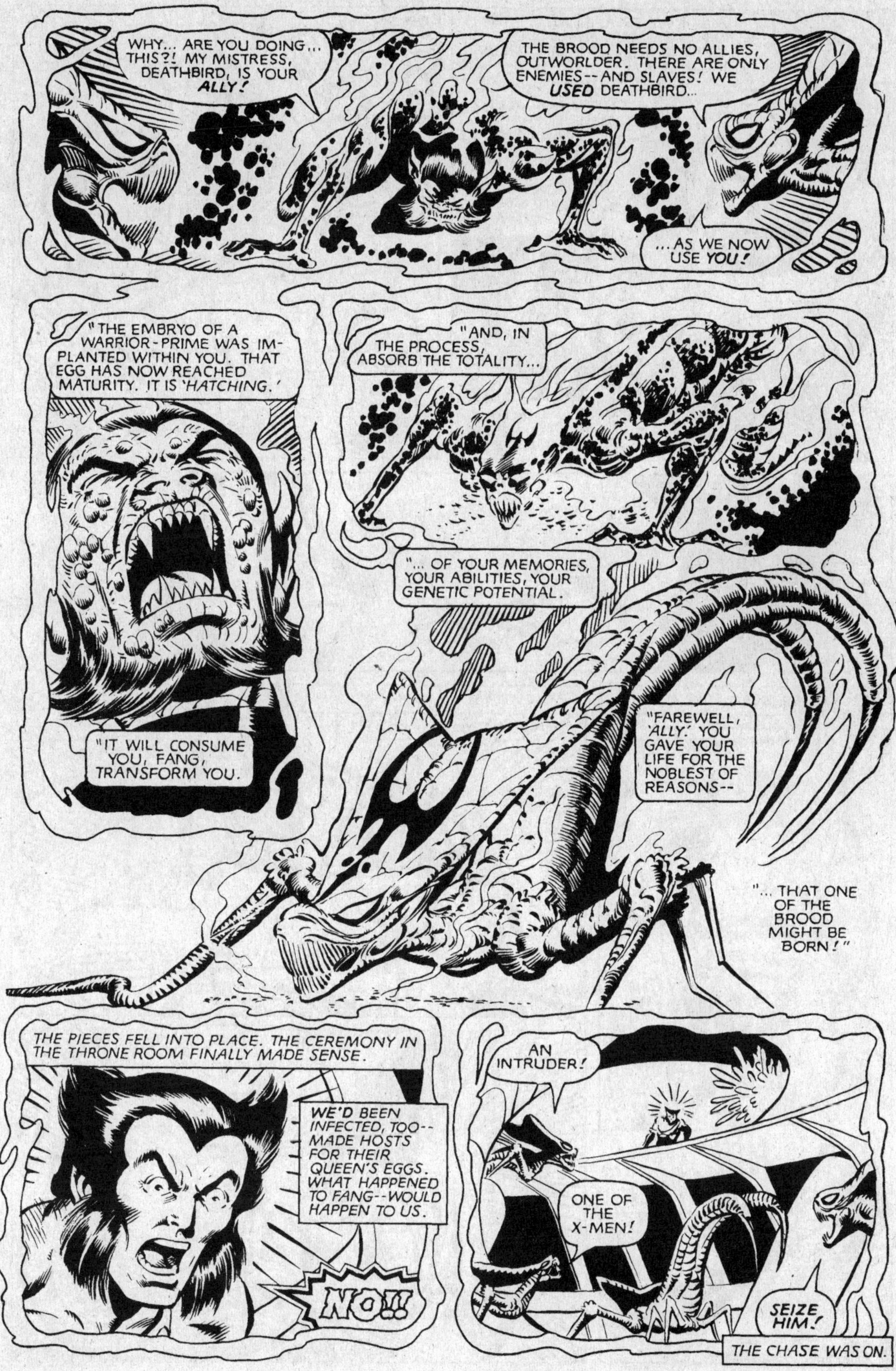

WHY... ARE YOU DOING... THIS?! MY MISTRESS, DEATHBIRD, IS YOUR ALLY!
THE BROOD NEEDS NO ALLIES, OUTWORLDER. THERE ARE ONLY ENEMIES--AND SLAVES! WE USED DEATHBIRD...
...AS WE NOW USE YOU!
"THE EMBRYO OF A WARRIOR-PRIME WAS IMPLANTED WITHIN YOU. THAT EGG HAS NOW REACHED MATURITY. IT IS 'HATCHING.'
"IT WILL CONSUME YOU, FANG, TRANSFORM YOU.
"AND, IN THE PROCESS, ABSORB THE TOTALITY...
"... OF YOUR MEMORIES, YOUR ABILITIES, YOUR GENETIC POTENTIAL.
"FAREWELL, 'ALLY.' YOU GAVE YOUR LIFE FOR THE NOBLEST OF REASONS--
"... THAT ONE OF THE BROOD MIGHT BE BORN!"
THE PIECES FELL INTO PLACE. THE CEREMONY IN THE THRONE ROOM FINALLY MADE SENSE.
WE'D BEEN INFECTED, TOO--MADE HOSTS FOR THEIR QUEEN'S EGGS. WHAT HAPPENED TO FANG--WOULD HAPPEN TO US.
NO!!
AN INTRUDER!
ONE OF THE X-MEN!
SEIZE HIM!
THE CHASE WAS ON.

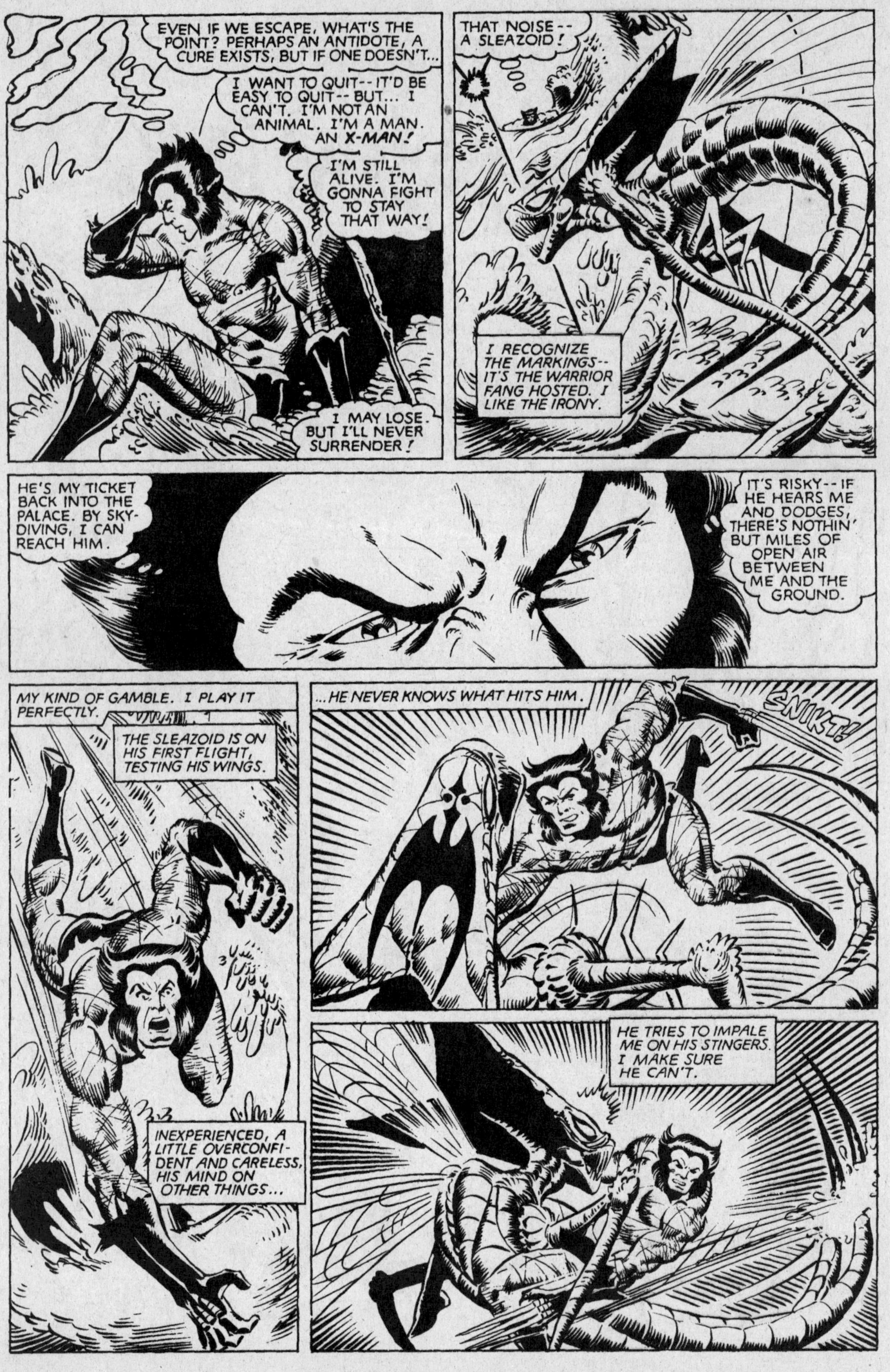

EVEN IF WE ESCAPE, WHAT'S THE POINT? PERHAPS AN ANTIDOTE, A CURE EXISTS, BUT IF ONE DOESN'T...
I WANT TO QUIT-- IT'D BE EASY TO QUIT-- BUT... I CAN'T. I'M NOT AN ANIMAL. I'M A MAN. AN X-MAN!
I'M STILL ALIVE. I'M GONNA FIGHT TO STAY THAT WAY!
I MAY LOSE. BUT I'LL NEVER SURRENDER!
THAT NOISE-- A SLEAZOID!
I RECOGNIZE THE MARKINGS-- IT'S THE WARRIOR FANG HOSTED. I LIKE THE IRONY.
HE'S MY TICKET BACK INTO THE PALACE. BY SKY-DIVING, I CAN REACH HIM.
IT'S RISKY-- IF HE HEARS ME AND DODGES, THERE'S NOTHIN' BUT MILES OF OPEN AIR BETWEEN ME AND THE GROUND.
MY KIND OF GAMBLE. I PLAY IT PERFECTLY.
THE SLEAZOID IS ON HIS FIRST FLIGHT, TESTING HIS WINGS.
INEXPERIENCED, A LITTLE OVERCONFI-DENT AND CARELESS, HIS MIND ON OTHER THINGS...
...HE NEVER KNOWS WHAT HITS HIM.
SNIKT!
HE TRIES TO IMPALE ME ON HIS STINGERS. I MAKE SURE HE CAN'T.

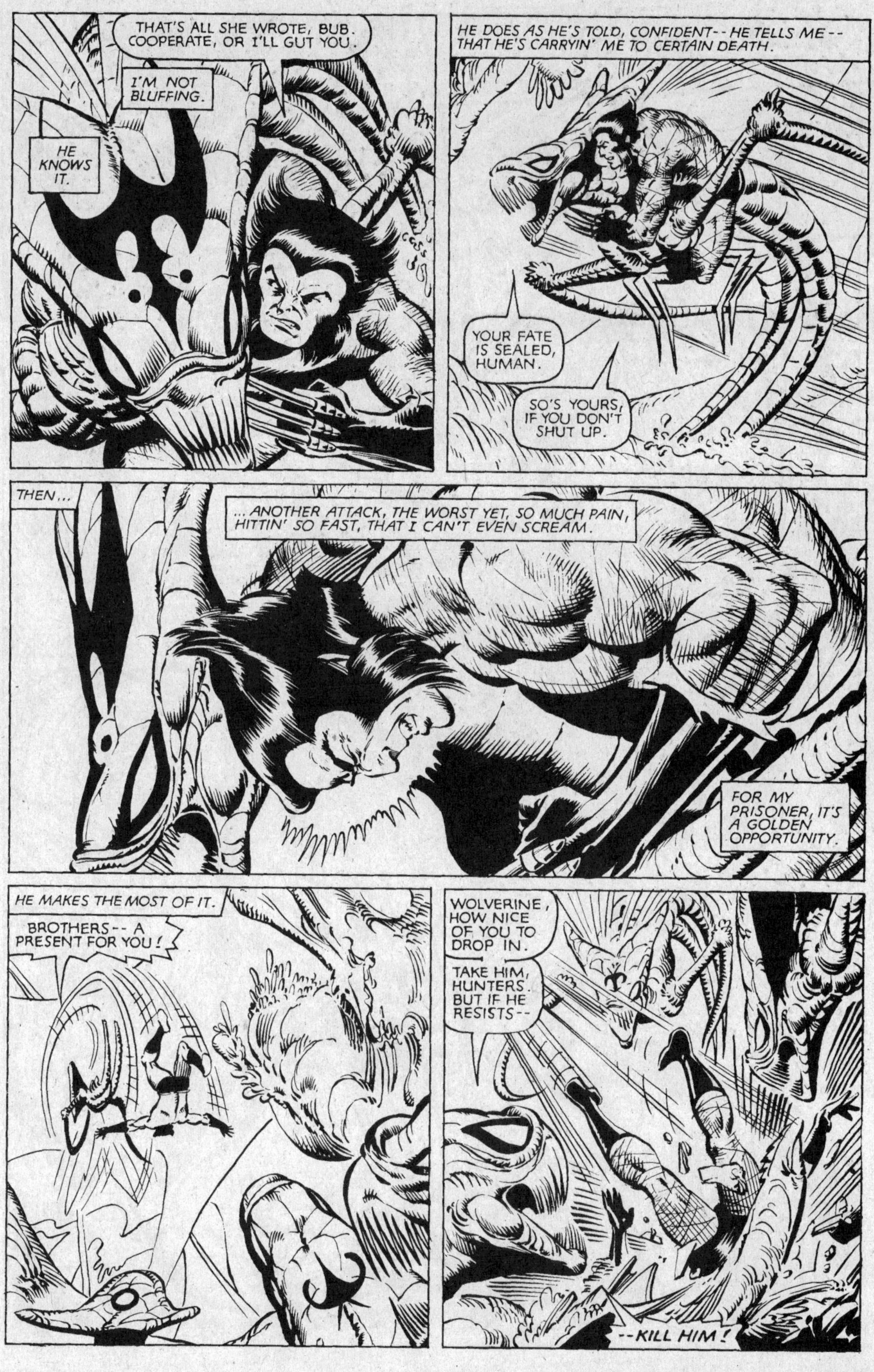
THAT'S ALL SHE WROTE, BUB. COOPERATE, OR I'LL GUT YOU.
I'M NOT BLUFFING.
HE KNOWS IT.
HE DOES AS HE'S TOLD, CONFIDENT-- HE TELLS ME-- THAT HE'S CARRYIN' ME TO CERTAIN DEATH.
YOUR FATE IS SEALED, HUMAN.
SO'S YOURS, IF YOU DON'T SHUT UP.
THEN...
...ANOTHER ATTACK, THE WORST YET, SO MUCH PAIN, HITTIN' SO FAST, THAT I CAN'T EVEN SCREAM.
FOR MY PRISONER, IT'S A GOLDEN OPPORTUNITY.
HE MAKES THE MOST OF IT.
BROTHERS-- A PRESENT FOR YOU!
WOLVERINE, HOW NICE OF YOU TO DROP IN.
TAKE HIM, HUNTERS. BUT IF HE RESISTS--
--KILL HIM!

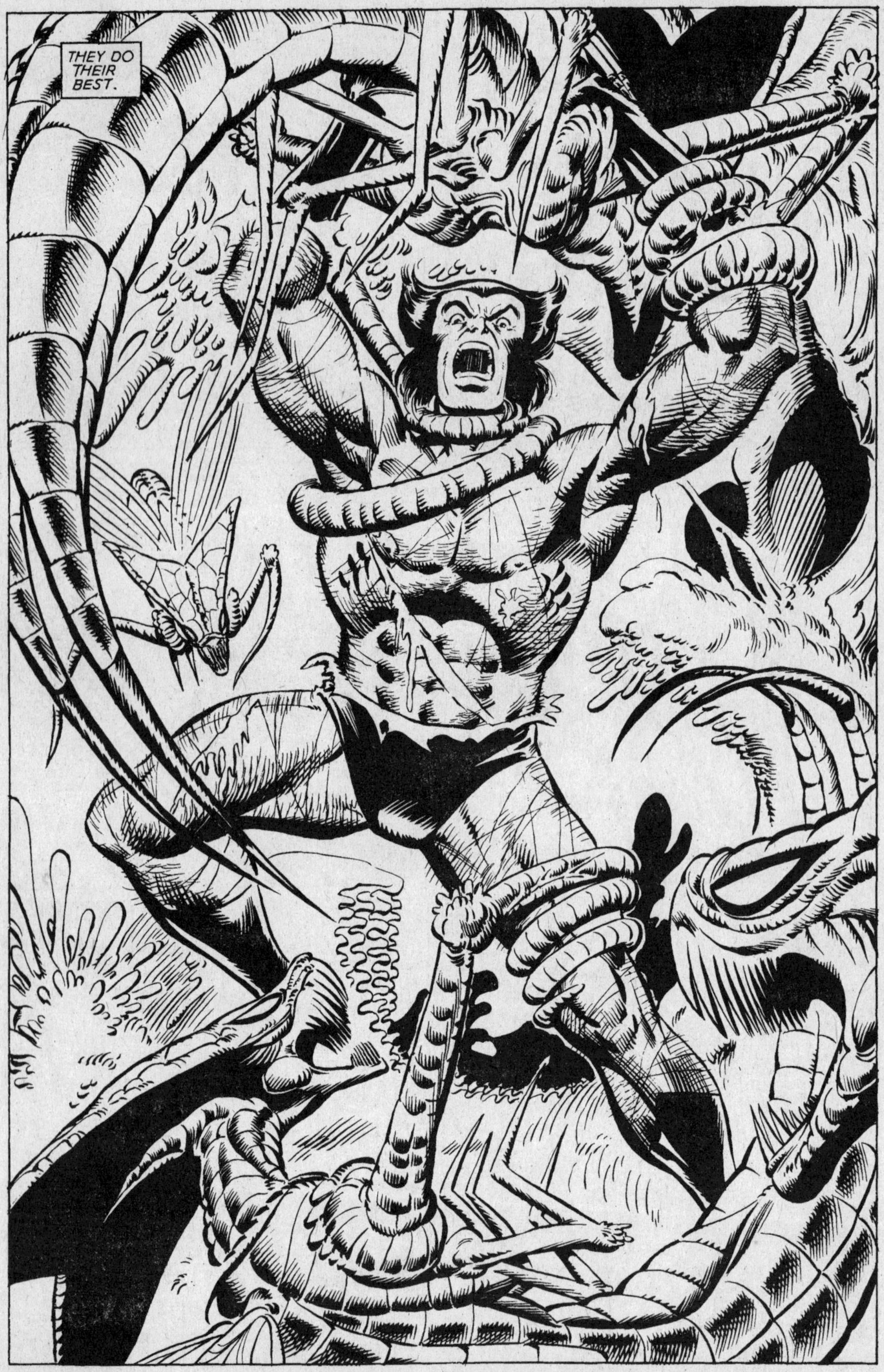
THEY DO THEIR BEST.

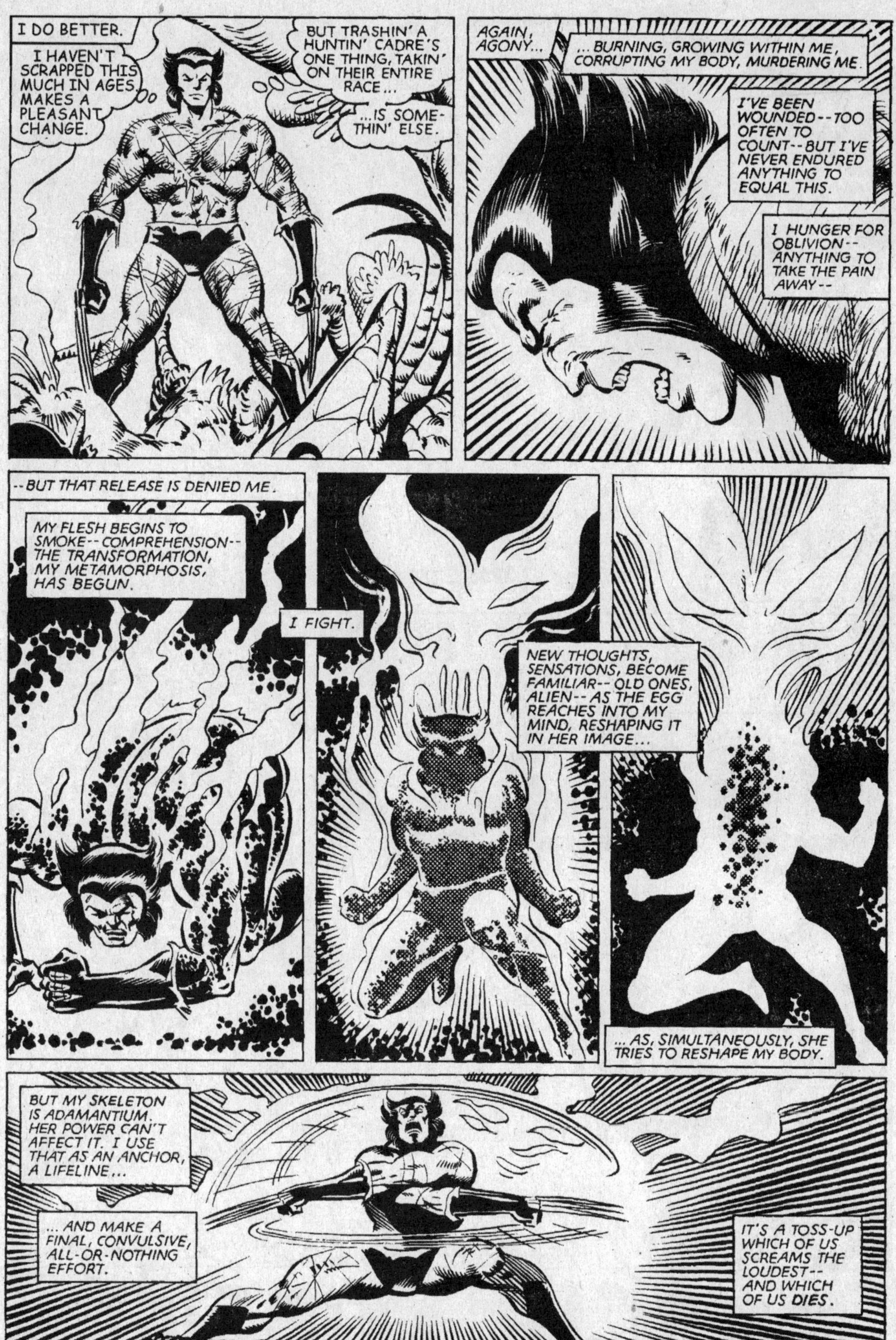
I DO BETTER.
I HAVEN'T SCRAPPED THIS MUCH IN AGES. MAKES A PLEASANT CHANGE.
BUT TRASHIN' A HUNTIN' CADRE'S ONE THING, TAKIN' ON THEIR ENTIRE RACE...
...IS SOMETHIN' ELSE.
AGAIN, AGONY...
...BURNING, GROWING WITHIN ME, CORRUPTING MY BODY, MURDERING ME.
I'VE BEEN WOUNDED--TOO OFTEN TO COUNT--BUT I'VE NEVER ENDURED ANYTHING TO EQUAL THIS.
I HUNGER FOR OBLIVION--ANYTHING TO TAKE THE PAIN AWAY--
--BUT THAT RELEASE IS DENIED ME.
MY FLESH BEGINS TO SMOKE--COMPREHENSION--THE TRANSFORMATION, MY METAMORPHOSIS, HAS BEGUN.
I FIGHT.
NEW THOUGHTS, SENSATIONS, BECOME FAMILIAR--OLD ONES, ALIEN--AS THE EGG REACHES INTO MY MIND, RESHAPING IT IN HER IMAGE...
...AS, SIMULTANEOUSLY, SHE TRIES TO RESHAPE MY BODY.
BUT MY SKELETON IS ADAMANTIUM. HER POWER CAN'T AFFECT IT. I USE THAT AS AN ANCHOR, A LIFELINE...
...AND MAKE A FINAL, CONVULSIVE, ALL-OR-NOTHING EFFORT.
IT'S A TOSS-UP WHICH OF US SCREAMS THE LOUDEST--AND WHICH OF US DIES.

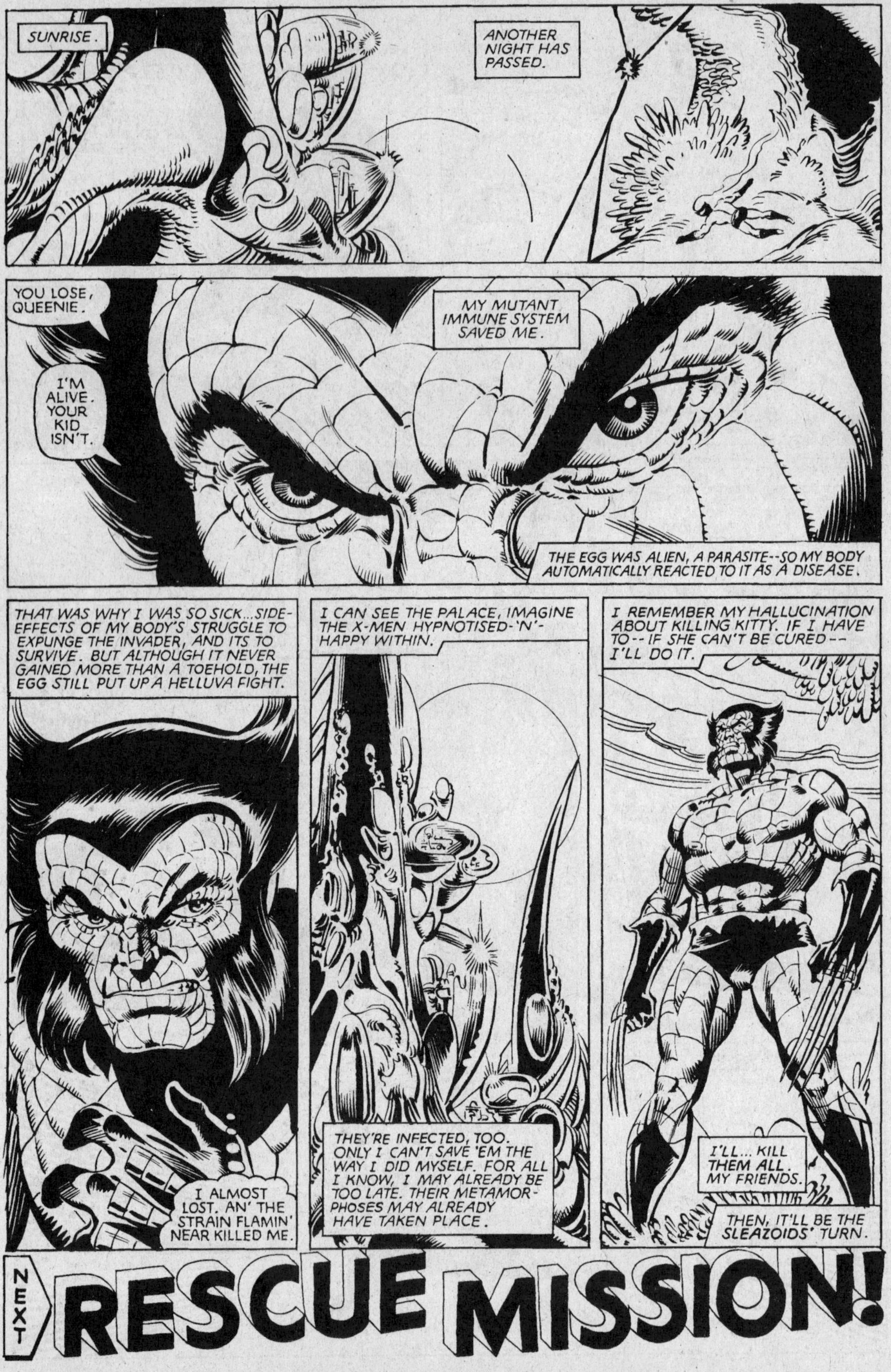

SUNRISE.
ANOTHER NIGHT HAS PASSED.
YOU LOSE, QUEENIE.
I'M ALIVE. YOUR KID ISN'T.
MY MUTANT IMMUNE SYSTEM SAVED ME.
THE EGG WAS ALIEN, A PARASITE--SO MY BODY AUTOMATICALLY REACTED TO IT AS A DISEASE.
THAT WAS WHY I WAS SO SICK...SIDE-EFFECTS OF MY BODY'S STRUGGLE TO EXPUNGE THE INVADER, AND ITS TO SURVIVE. BUT ALTHOUGH IT NEVER GAINED MORE THAN A TOEHOLD, THE EGG STILL PUT UP A HELLUVA FIGHT.
I ALMOST LOST. AN' THE STRAIN FLAMIN' NEAR KILLED ME.
I CAN SEE THE PALACE, IMAGINE THE X-MEN HYPNOTISED-'N'-HAPPY WITHIN.
THEY'RE INFECTED, TOO. ONLY I CAN'T SAVE 'EM THE WAY I DID MYSELF. FOR ALL I KNOW, I MAY ALREADY BE TOO LATE. THEIR METAMOR-PHOSES MAY ALREADY HAVE TAKEN PLACE.
I REMEMBER MY HALLUCINATION ABOUT KILLING KITTY. IF I HAVE TO -- IF SHE CAN'T BE CURED -- I'LL DO IT.
I'LL... KILL THEM ALL. MY FRIENDS.
THEN, IT'LL BE THE SLEAZOIDS' TURN.
NEXT
RESCUE MISSION!

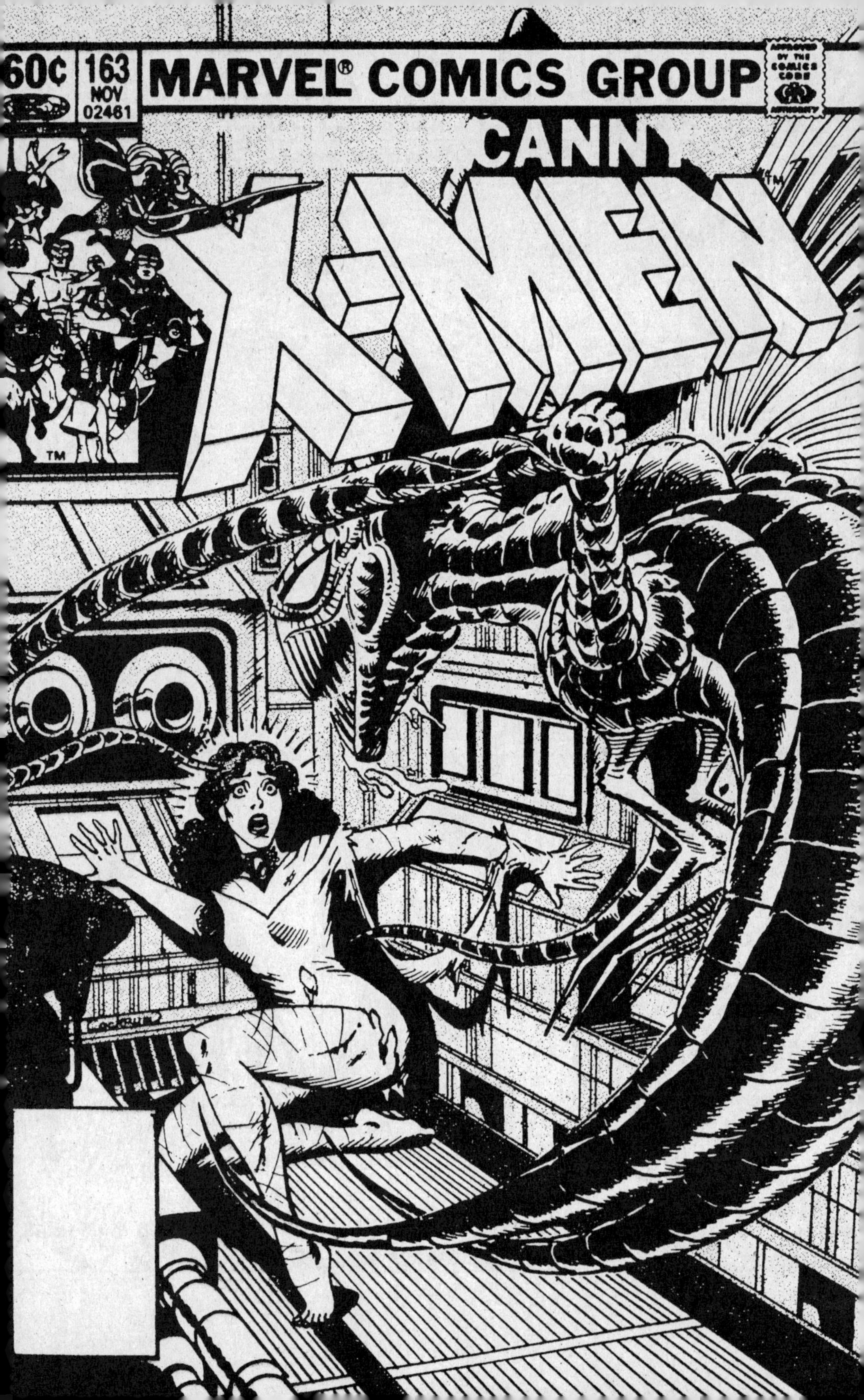
60¢
163
NOV
02461
MARVEL® COMICS GROUP
CANN
X-MEN
TM

RESCUE MISSION

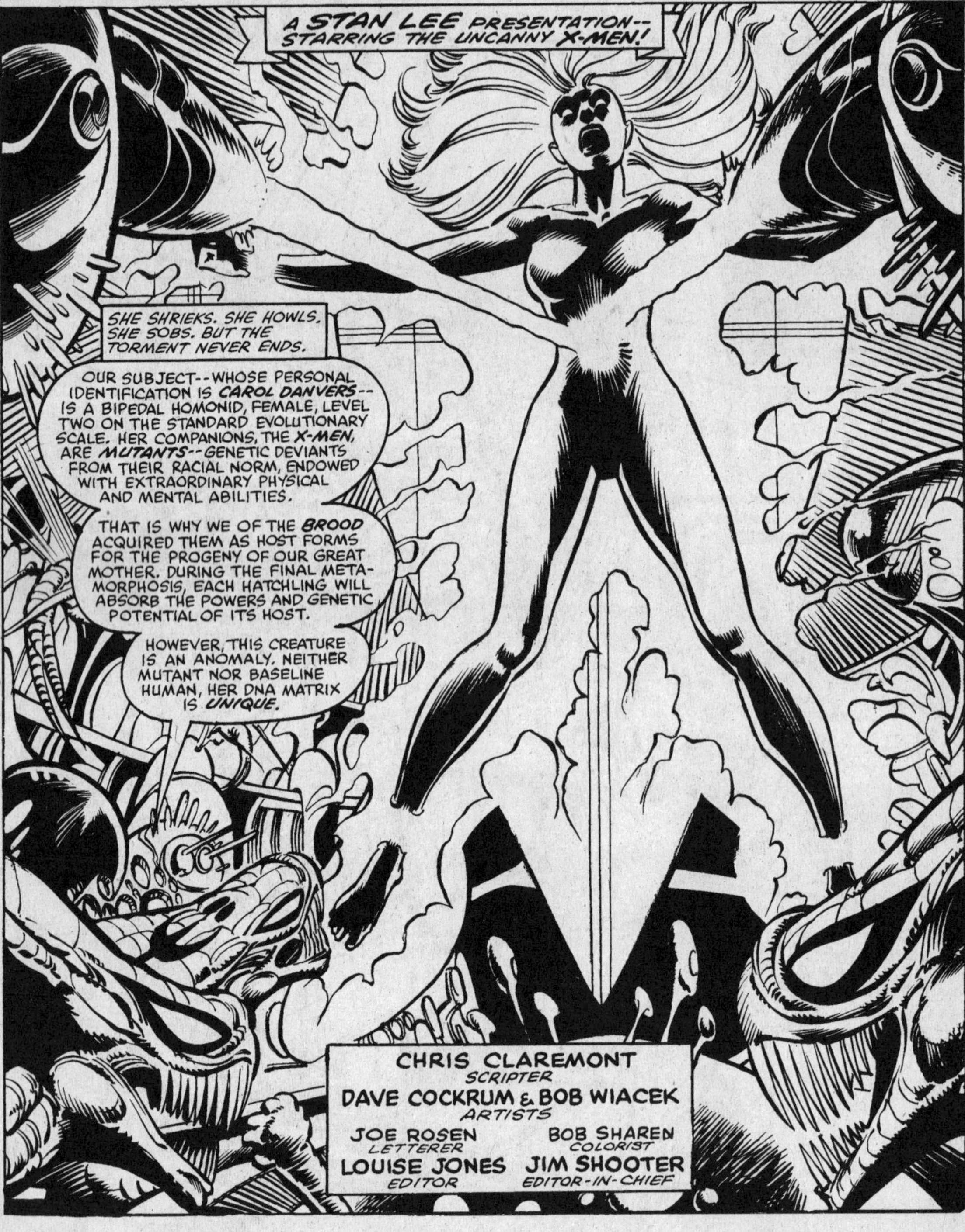
A STAN LEE PRESENTATION-- STARRING THE UNCANNY X-MEN!
SHE SHRIEKS. SHE HOWLS. SHE SOBS. BUT THE TORMENT NEVER ENDS.
OUR SUBJECT--WHOSE PERSONAL IDENTIFICATION IS CAROL DANVERS--IS A BIPEDAL HOMONID, FEMALE, LEVEL TWO ON THE STANDARD EVOLUTIONARY SCALE. HER COMPANIONS, THE X-MEN, ARE MUTANTS--GENETIC DEVIANTS FROM THEIR RACIAL NORM, ENDOWED WITH EXTRAORDINARY PHYSICAL AND MENTAL ABILITIES.
THAT IS WHY WE OF THE BROOD ACQUIRED THEM AS HOST FORMS FOR THE PROGENY OF OUR GREAT MOTHER. DURING THE FINAL METAMORPHOSIS, EACH HATCHLING WILL ABSORB THE POWERS AND GENETIC POTENTIAL OF ITS HOST.
HOWEVER, THIS CREATURE IS AN ANOMALY. NEITHER MUTANT NOR BASELINE HUMAN, HER DNA MATRIX IS UNIQUE.
CHRIS CLAREMONT SCRIPTER
DAVE COCKRUM & BOB WIACEK ARTISTS
JOE ROSEN LETTERER
BOB SHAREN COLORIST
LOUISE JONES EDITOR
JIM SHOOTER EDITOR-IN-CHIEF

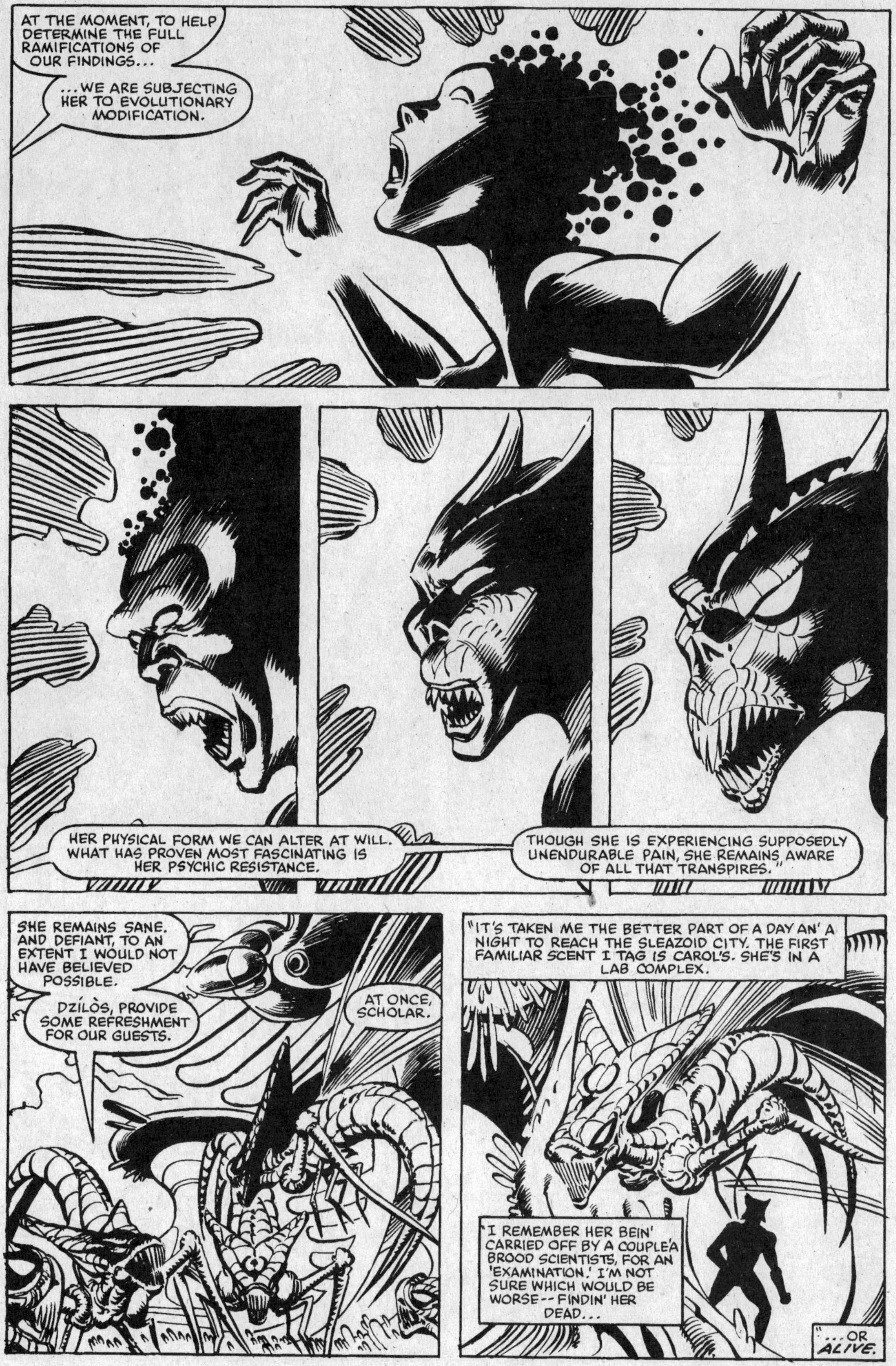
AT THE MOMENT, TO HELP DETERMINE THE FULL RAMIFICATIONS OF OUR FINDINGS...
...WE ARE SUBJECTING HER TO EVOLUTIONARY MODIFICATION.
HER PHYSICAL FORM WE CAN ALTER AT WILL. WHAT HAS PROVEN MOST FASCINATING IS HER PSYCHIC RESISTANCE.
THOUGH SHE IS EXPERIENCING SUPPOSEDLY UNENDURABLE PAIN, SHE REMAINS AWARE OF ALL THAT TRANSPIRES."
SHE REMAINS SANE. AND DEFIANT, TO AN EXTENT I WOULD NOT HAVE BELIEVED POSSIBLE.
DZÍLÒS, PROVIDE SOME REFRESHMENT FOR OUR GUESTS.
AT ONCE, SCHOLAR.
"IT'S TAKEN ME THE BETTER PART OF A DAY AN' A NIGHT TO REACH THE SLEAZOID CITY. THE FIRST FAMILIAR SCENT I TAG IS CAROL'S. SHE'S IN A LAB COMPLEX.
"I REMEMBER HER BEIN' CARRIED OFF BY A COUPLE'A BROOD SCIENTISTS, FOR AN 'EXAMINATION.' I'M NOT SURE WHICH WOULD BE WORSE-- FINDIN' HER DEAD...
"...OR ALIVE.

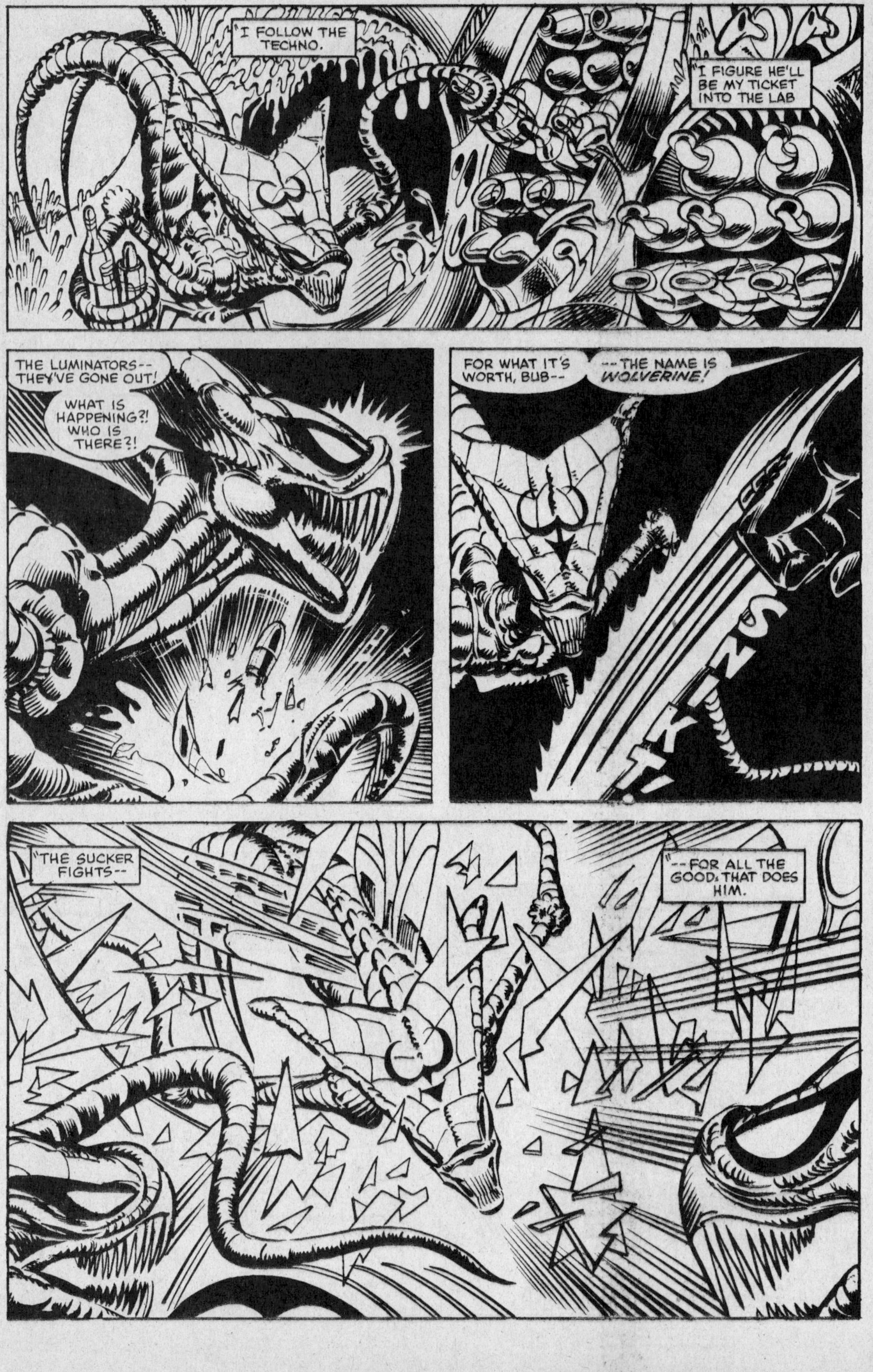
"I FOLLOW THE TECHNO.
"I FIGURE HE'LL BE MY TICKET INTO THE LAB
THE LUMINATORS-- THEY'VE GONE OUT!
WHAT IS HAPPENING?! WHO IS THERE?!
FOR WHAT IT'S WORTH, BUB--
--THE NAME IS WOLVERINE!
SNIKT!
"THE SUCKER FIGHTS--
"--FOR ALL THE GOOD THAT DOES HIM.

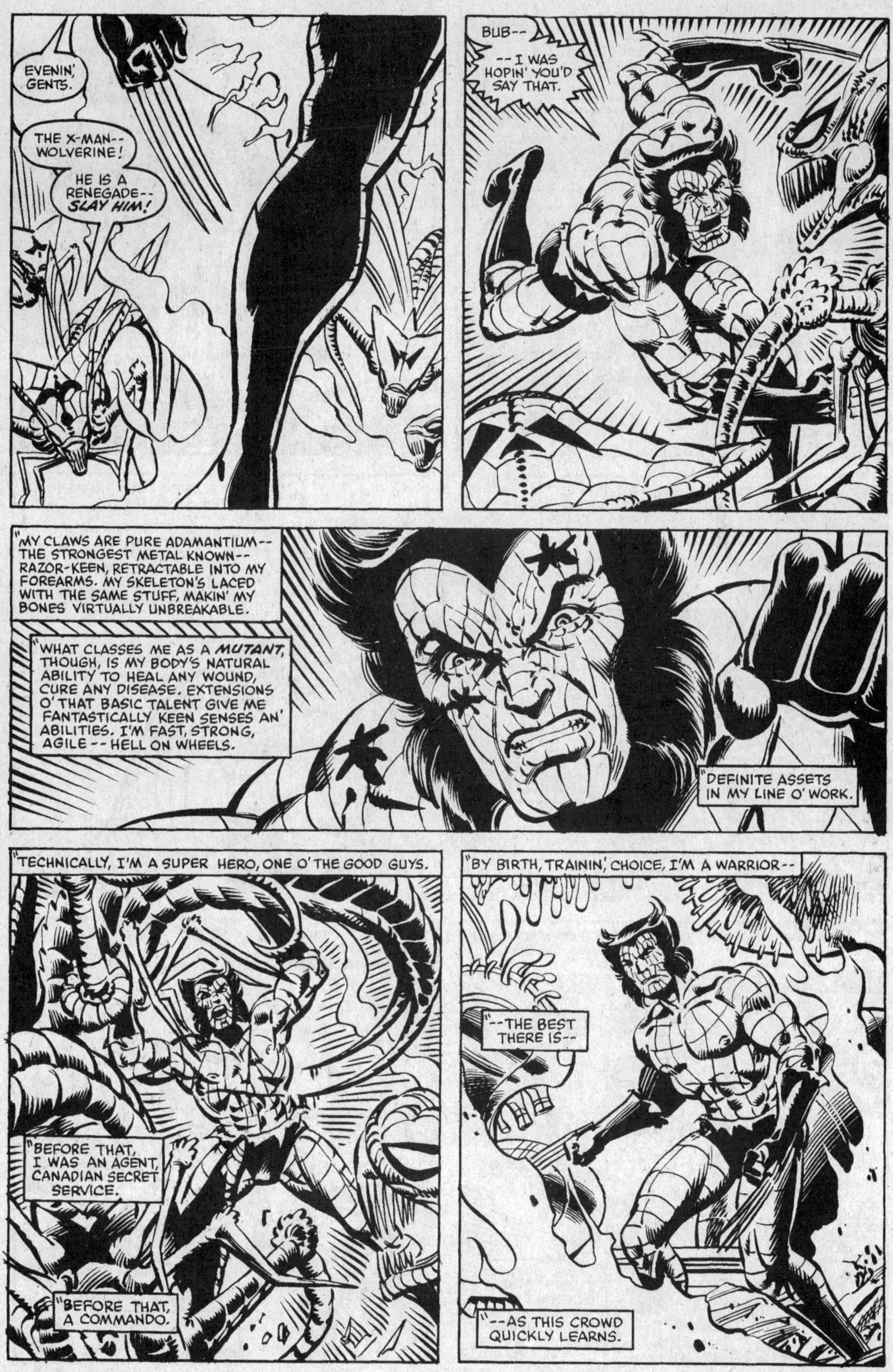
EVENIN', GENTS.
THE X-MAN--WOLVERINE!
HE IS A RENEGADE--SLAY HIM!
BUB--
--I WAS HOPIN' YOU'D SAY THAT.
"MY CLAWS ARE PURE ADAMANTIUM--THE STRONGEST METAL KNOWN--RAZOR-KEEN, RETRACTABLE INTO MY FOREARMS. MY SKELETON'S LACED WITH THE SAME STUFF, MAKIN' MY BONES VIRTUALLY UNBREAKABLE.
"WHAT CLASSES ME AS A MUTANT, THOUGH, IS MY BODY'S NATURAL ABILITY TO HEAL ANY WOUND, CURE ANY DISEASE. EXTENSIONS O' THAT BASIC TALENT GIVE ME FANTASTICALLY KEEN SENSES AN' ABILITIES. I'M FAST, STRONG, AGILE--HELL ON WHEELS.
"DEFINITE ASSETS IN MY LINE O' WORK.
"TECHNICALLY, I'M A SUPER HERO, ONE O' THE GOOD GUYS.
"BEFORE THAT, I WAS AN AGENT, CANADIAN SECRET SERVICE.
"BEFORE THAT, A COMMANDO.
"BY BIRTH, TRAININ', CHOICE, I'M A WARRIOR--
"--THE BEST THERE IS--
"--AS THIS CROWD QUICKLY LEARNS.

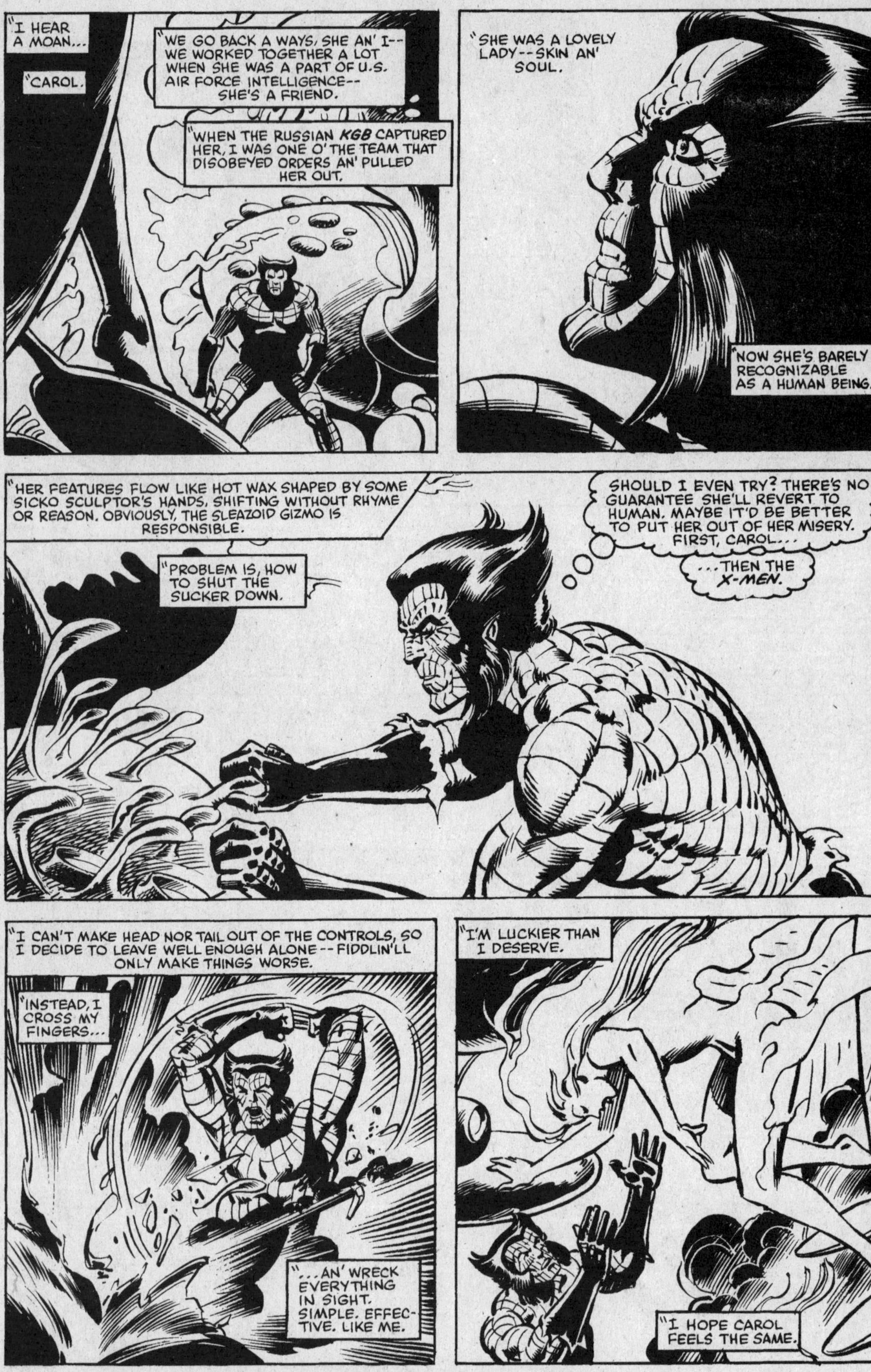
"I HEAR A MOAN...
"CAROL.
"WE GO BACK A WAYS, SHE AN' I-- WE WORKED TOGETHER A LOT WHEN SHE WAS A PART OF U.S. AIR FORCE INTELLIGENCE-- SHE'S A FRIEND.
"WHEN THE RUSSIAN KGB CAPTURED HER, I WAS ONE O' THE TEAM THAT DISOBEYED ORDERS AN' PULLED HER OUT.
"SHE WAS A LOVELY LADY--SKIN AN' SOUL.
"NOW SHE'S BARELY RECOGNIZABLE AS A HUMAN BEING.
"HER FEATURES FLOW LIKE HOT WAX SHAPED BY SOME SICKO SCULPTOR'S HANDS, SHIFTING WITHOUT RHYME OR REASON. OBVIOUSLY, THE SLEAZOID GIZMO IS RESPONSIBLE.
"PROBLEM IS, HOW TO SHUT THE SUCKER DOWN.
SHOULD I EVEN TRY? THERE'S NO GUARANTEE SHE'LL REVERT TO HUMAN. MAYBE IT'D BE BETTER TO PUT HER OUT OF HER MISERY. FIRST, CAROL...
...THEN THE X-MEN.
"I CAN'T MAKE HEAD NOR TAIL OUT OF THE CONTROLS, SO I DECIDE TO LEAVE WELL ENOUGH ALONE--FIDDLIN'LL ONLY MAKE THINGS WORSE.
"INSTEAD, I CROSS MY FINGERS...
"...AN' WRECK EVERYTHING IN SIGHT. SIMPLE. EFFECTIVE. LIKE ME.
"I'M LUCKIER THAN I DESERVE.
"I HOPE CAROL FEELS THE SAME.

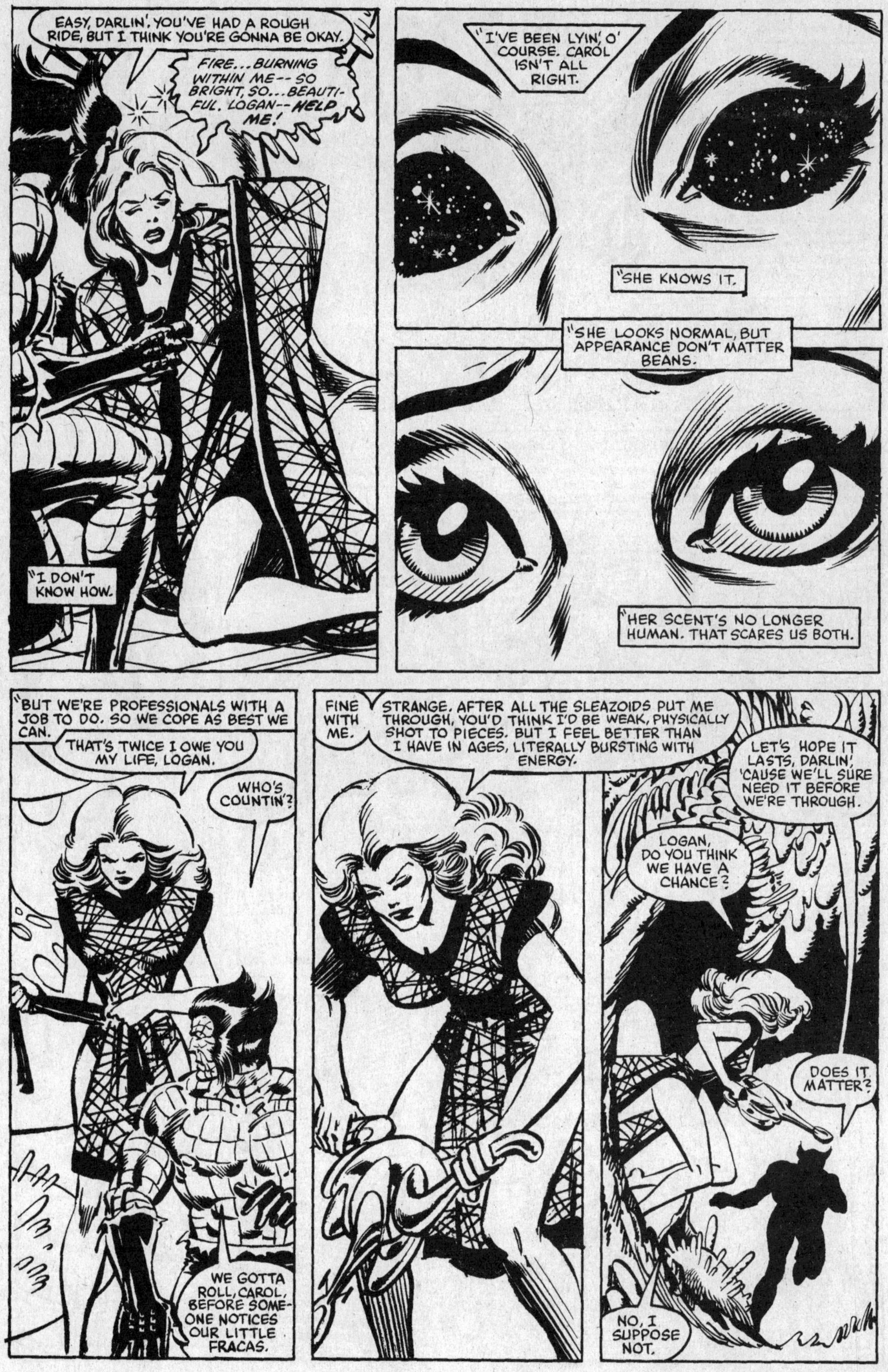
EASY, DARLIN'. YOU'VE HAD A ROUGH RIDE, BUT I THINK YOU'RE GONNA BE OKAY.
FIRE... BURNING WITHIN ME-- SO BRIGHT, SO... BEAUTI-FUL. LOGAN-- HELP ME!
"I DON'T KNOW HOW.
"I'VE BEEN LYIN', O' COURSE. CAROL ISN'T ALL RIGHT.
"SHE KNOWS IT.
"SHE LOOKS NORMAL, BUT APPEARANCE DON'T MATTER BEANS.
"HER SCENT'S NO LONGER HUMAN. THAT SCARES US BOTH.
"BUT WE'RE PROFESSIONALS WITH A JOB TO DO. SO WE COPE AS BEST WE CAN.
THAT'S TWICE I OWE YOU MY LIFE, LOGAN.
WHO'S COUNTIN'?
WE GOTTA ROLL, CAROL, BEFORE SOME-ONE NOTICES OUR LITTLE FRACAS.
FINE WITH ME.
STRANGE. AFTER ALL THE SLEAZOIDS PUT ME THROUGH, YOU'D THINK I'D BE WEAK, PHYSICALLY SHOT TO PIECES. BUT I FEEL BETTER THAN I HAVE IN AGES, LITERALLY BURSTING WITH ENERGY.
LET'S HOPE IT LASTS, DARLIN', 'CAUSE WE'LL SURE NEED IT BEFORE WE'RE THROUGH.
LOGAN, DO YOU THINK WE HAVE A CHANCE?
DOES IT MATTER?
NO, I SUPPOSE NOT.

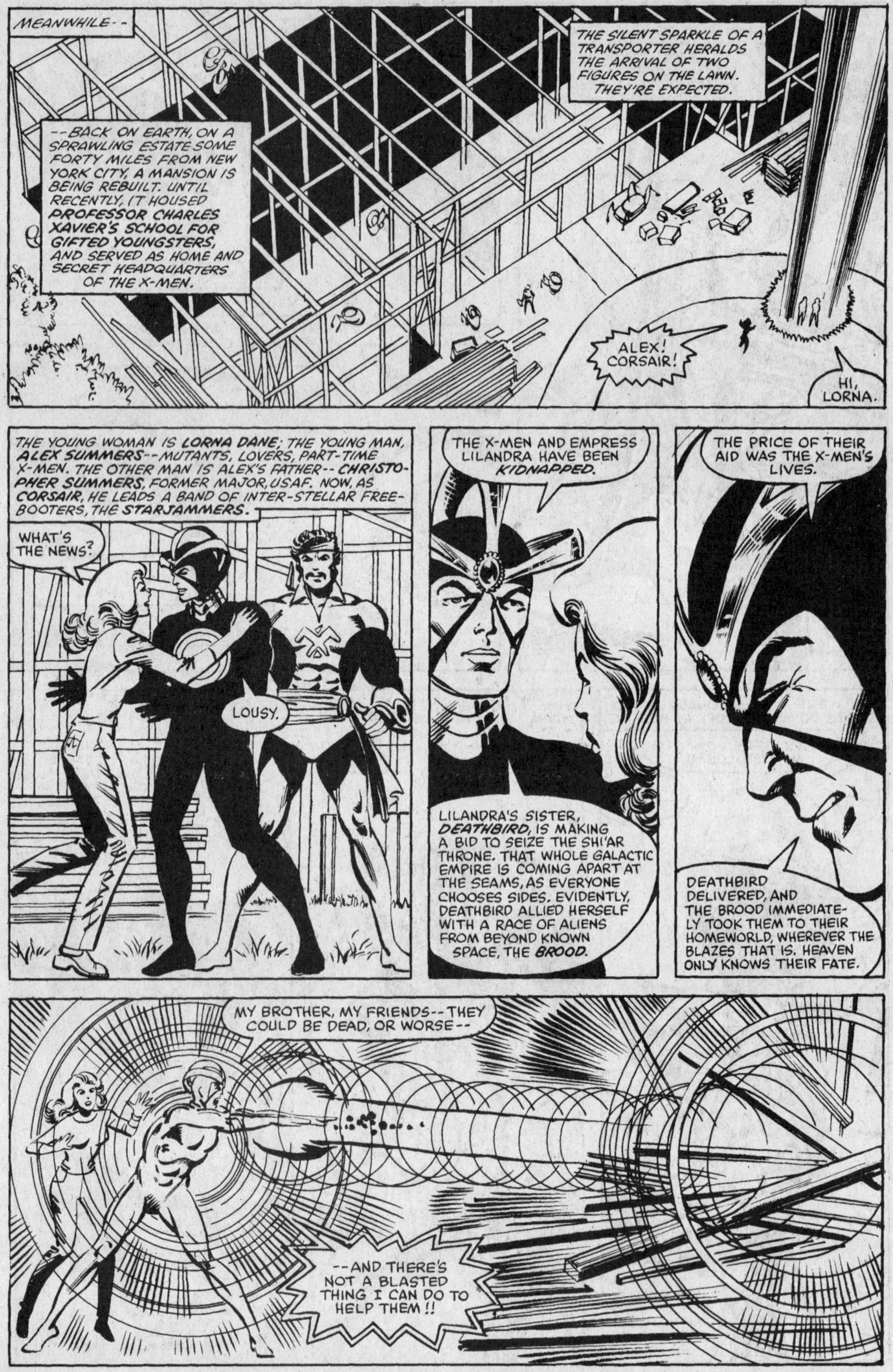
MEANWHILE--
--BACK ON EARTH, ON A SPRAWLING ESTATE SOME FORTY MILES FROM NEW YORK CITY, A MANSION IS BEING REBUILT. UNTIL RECENTLY, IT HOUSED PROFESSOR CHARLES XAVIER'S SCHOOL FOR GIFTED YOUNGSTERS, AND SERVED AS HOME AND SECRET HEADQUARTERS OF THE X-MEN.
THE SILENT SPARKLE OF A TRANSPORTER HERALDS THE ARRIVAL OF TWO FIGURES ON THE LAWN. THEY'RE EXPECTED.
ALEX! CORSAIR!
HI, LORNA.
THE YOUNG WOMAN IS LORNA DANE; THE YOUNG MAN, ALEX SUMMERS--MUTANTS, LOVERS, PART-TIME X-MEN. THE OTHER MAN IS ALEX'S FATHER--CHRISTOPHER SUMMERS, FORMER MAJOR, USAF. NOW, AS CORSAIR, HE LEADS A BAND OF INTER-STELLAR FREE-BOOTERS, THE STARJAMMERS.
WHAT'S THE NEWS?
LOUSY.
THE X-MEN AND EMPRESS LILANDRA HAVE BEEN KIDNAPPED.
LILANDRA'S SISTER, DEATHBIRD, IS MAKING A BID TO SEIZE THE SHI'AR THRONE. THAT WHOLE GALACTIC EMPIRE IS COMING APART AT THE SEAMS, AS EVERYONE CHOOSES SIDES. EVIDENTLY, DEATHBIRD ALLIED HERSELF WITH A RACE OF ALIENS FROM BEYOND KNOWN SPACE, THE BROOD.
THE PRICE OF THEIR AID WAS THE X-MEN'S LIVES.
DEATHBIRD DELIVERED, AND THE BROOD IMMEDIATELY TOOK THEM TO THEIR HOMEWORLD, WHEREVER THE BLAZES THAT IS. HEAVEN ONLY KNOWS THEIR FATE.
MY BROTHER, MY FRIENDS--THEY COULD BE DEAD, OR WORSE--
--AND THERE'S NOT A BLASTED THING I CAN DO TO HELP THEM!!

Panel 1:
AN ENERGY BOLT-- ARE WE UNDER ATTACK?!

CORSAIR REACTS AUTOMATICALLY, WITH THE SPEED OF THOUGHT, USING THE PHASING JEWELS ON HIS GLOVES TO SUMMON HIS HAND WEAPONS. IN A SPLIT-SECOND, HE'S READY FOR ACTION.

Panel 2:
SORRY, DAD. MY FAULT. FALSE ALARM.

I UNDERSTAND, SON. WE ALL NEED TO BLOW OFF SOME STEAM.

Panel 3:
YOU SEEM T' BE A MITE NERVOUS, MAJOR.

BETTER NERVOUS THAN DEAD, DR. MACTAGGERT.

GOOD POINT. MIGHT I ASK YUIR PLANS?

MY SON HAS BEEN KIDNAPPED. I INTEND TO RESCUE HIM. OR AVENGE HIM.

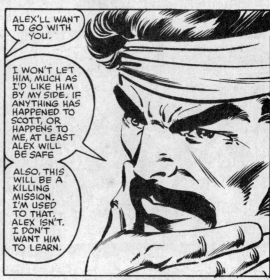

Panel 4:
ALEX'LL WANT TO GO WITH YOU.

I WON'T LET HIM, MUCH AS I'D LIKE HIM BY MY SIDE. IF ANYTHING HAS HAPPENED TO SCOTT, OR HAPPENS TO ME, AT LEAST ALEX WILL BE SAFE.

ALSO, THIS WILL BE A KILLING MISSION. I'M USED TO THAT. ALEX ISN'T. I DON'T WANT HIM TO LEARN.

Panel 5:
WE'LL BE WARPING OUT OF ORBIT AS SOON AS I BEAM UP. I WANTED TO SAY GOOD-BYE TO YOU AND PROFESSOR XAVIER.

CHARLES ISN'T HERE. HE'S TAKING THIS VERY HARD, CHRIS--NOT SO MUCH THAT THE X-MEN ARE IN DANGER, BUT THAT, FOR ALL HIS POWER, HE WAS AND IS UNABLE TO DO ANYTHING ABOUT IT.

HE'S A STRONG MAN, MOIRA. HE'LL RECOVER.

Panel 6:
HE'S LOST THE WOMAN HE LOVES AND HIS BELOVED X-MEN, HIS FAMILY. HE'S ALONE, CHRIS. AYE, HE'S STRONG, BUT EVEN THE STRONGEST BACK HAS ITS BREAKING POINT.

I FEAR, FOR CHARLEY, THIS MAY BE IT.

FAREWELL, CORSAIR. GOOD LUCK.

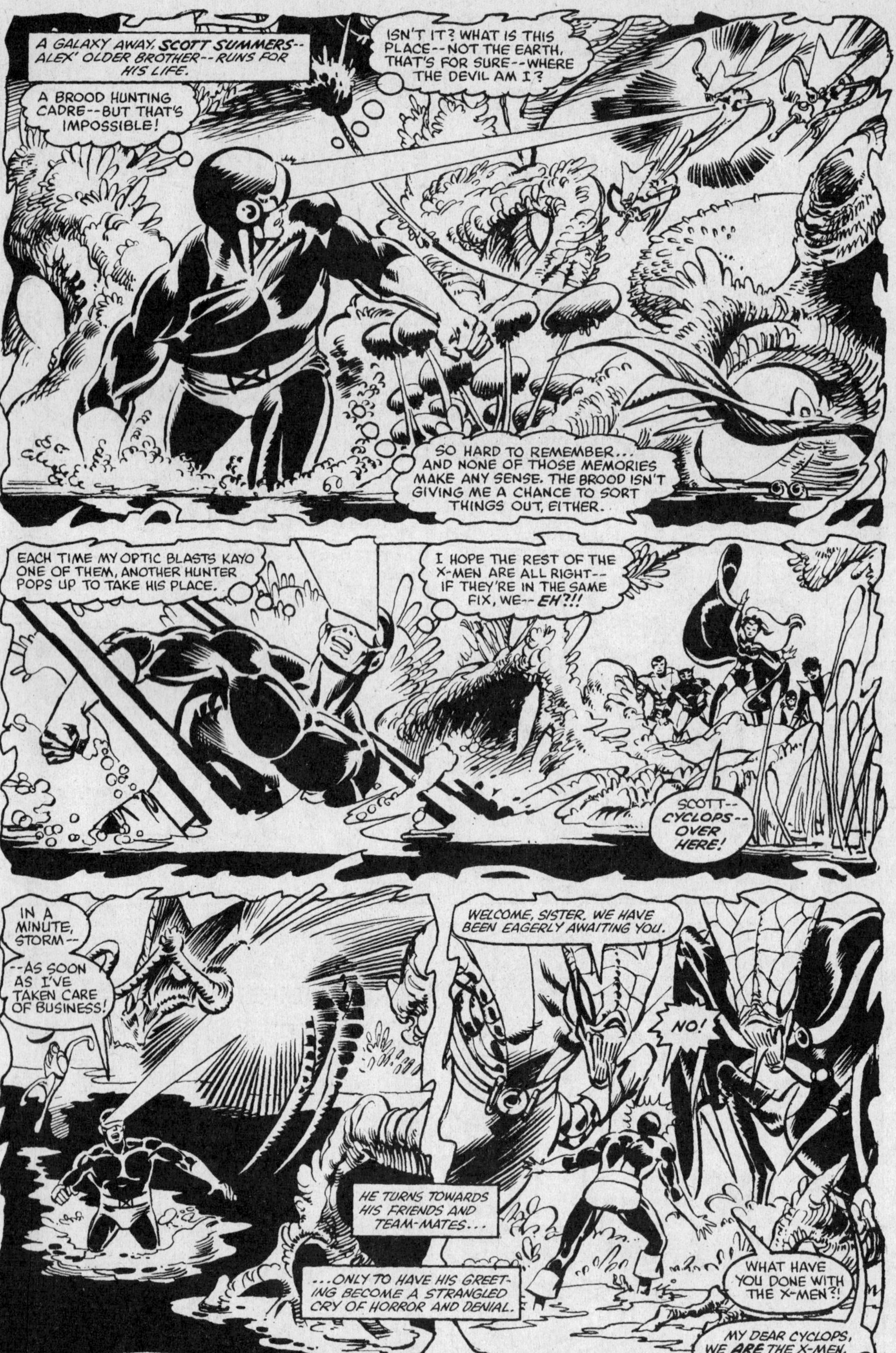
A GALAXY AWAY, SCOTT SUMMERS-- ALEX' OLDER BROTHER--RUNS FOR HIS LIFE.
A BROOD HUNTING CADRE--BUT THAT'S IMPOSSIBLE!
ISN'T IT? WHAT IS THIS PLACE--NOT THE EARTH, THAT'S FOR SURE--WHERE THE DEVIL AM I?
SO HARD TO REMEMBER... AND NONE OF THOSE MEMORIES MAKE ANY SENSE. THE BROOD ISN'T GIVING ME A CHANCE TO SORT THINGS OUT, EITHER.
EACH TIME MY OPTIC BLASTS KAYO ONE OF THEM, ANOTHER HUNTER POPS UP TO TAKE HIS PLACE.
I HOPE THE REST OF THE X-MEN ARE ALL RIGHT-- IF THEY'RE IN THE SAME FIX, WE-- EH?!!
SCOTT-- CYCLOPS-- OVER HERE!
IN A MINUTE, STORM--
--AS SOON AS I'VE TAKEN CARE OF BUSINESS!
WELCOME, SISTER. WE HAVE BEEN EAGERLY AWAITING YOU.
NO!
HE TURNS TOWARDS HIS FRIENDS AND TEAM-MATES...
...ONLY TO HAVE HIS GREETING BECOME A STRANGLED CRY OF HORROR AND DENIAL.
WHAT HAVE YOU DONE WITH THE X-MEN?!
MY DEAR CYCLOPS, WE ARE THE X-MEN.

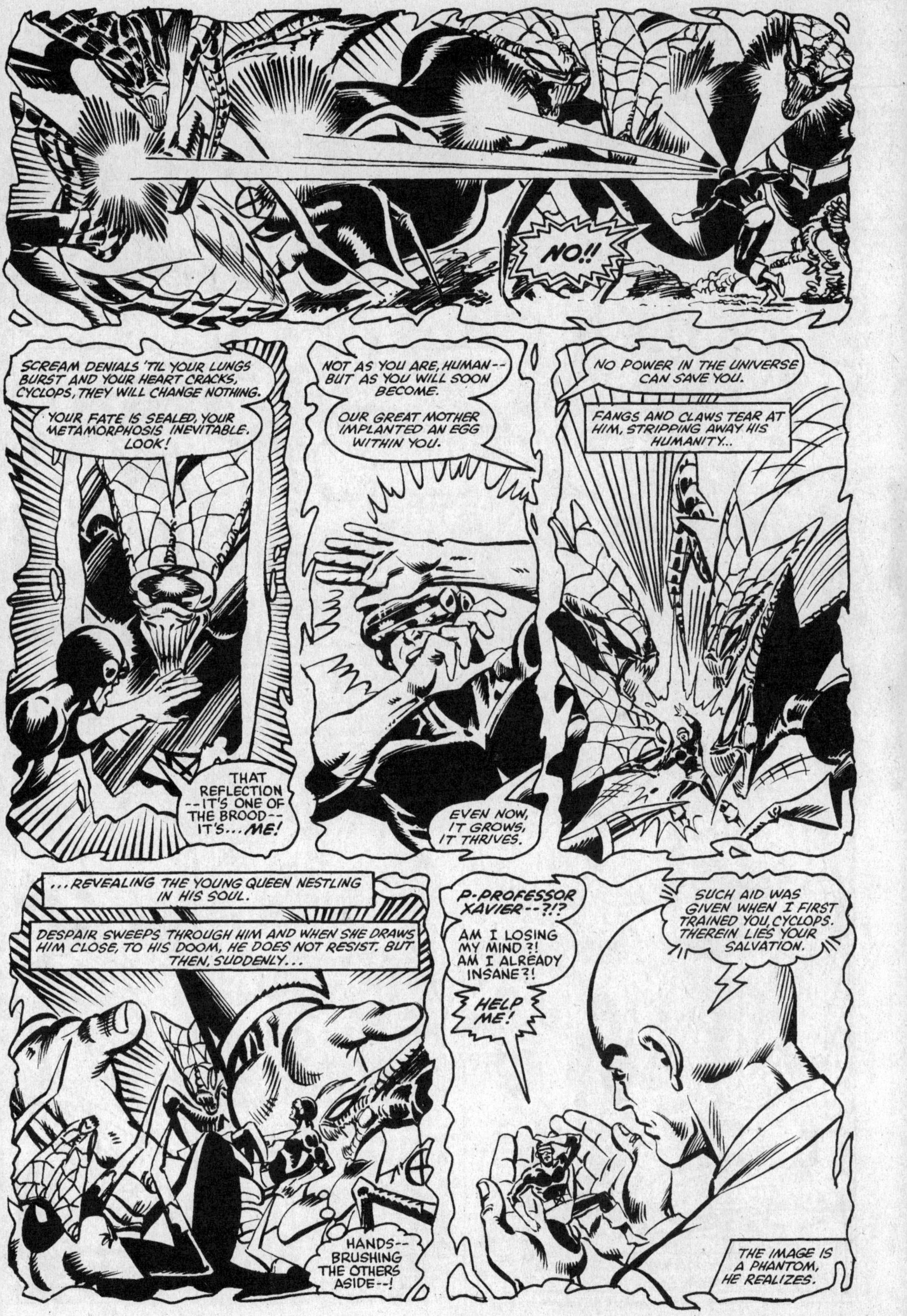
NO!!
SCREAM DENIALS 'TIL YOUR LUNGS BURST AND YOUR HEART CRACKS, CYCLOPS, THEY WILL CHANGE NOTHING.
YOUR FATE IS SEALED, YOUR METAMORPHOSIS INEVITABLE. LOOK!
THAT REFLECTION --IT'S ONE OF THE BROOD-- IT'S... ME!
NOT AS YOU ARE, HUMAN-- BUT AS YOU WILL SOON BECOME.
OUR GREAT MOTHER IMPLANTED AN EGG WITHIN YOU.
EVEN NOW, IT GROWS, IT THRIVES.
NO POWER IN THE UNIVERSE CAN SAVE YOU.
FANGS AND CLAWS TEAR AT HIM, STRIPPING AWAY HIS HUMANITY...
...REVEALING THE YOUNG QUEEN NESTLING IN HIS SOUL.
DESPAIR SWEEPS THROUGH HIM AND WHEN SHE DRAWS HIM CLOSE, TO HIS DOOM, HE DOES NOT RESIST. BUT THEN, SUDDENLY...
HANDS-- BRUSHING THE OTHERS ASIDE--!
P-PROFESSOR XAVIER--?!?
AM I LOSING MY MIND?! AM I ALREADY INSANE?!
HELP ME!
SUCH AID WAS GIVEN WHEN I FIRST TRAINED YOU, CYCLOPS. THEREIN LIES YOUR SALVATION.
THE IMAGE IS A PHANTOM, HE REALIZES.

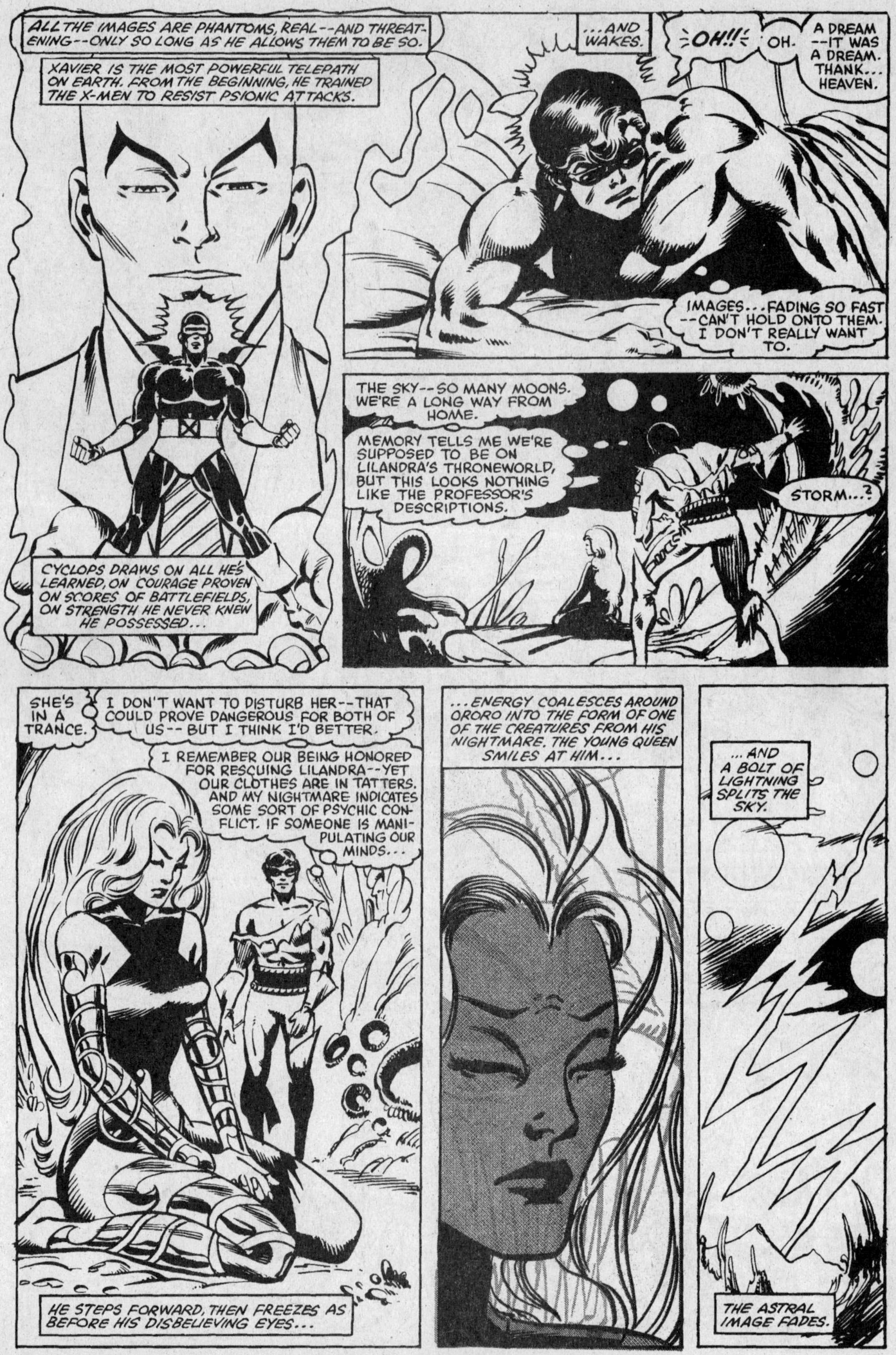

ALL THE IMAGES ARE PHANTOMS, REAL--AND THREATENING--ONLY SO LONG AS HE ALLOWS THEM TO BE SO.
XAVIER IS THE MOST POWERFUL TELEPATH ON EARTH. FROM THE BEGINNING, HE TRAINED THE X-MEN TO RESIST PSIONIC ATTACKS.
CYCLOPS DRAWS ON ALL HE'S LEARNED, ON COURAGE PROVEN ON SCORES OF BATTLEFIELDS, ON STRENGTH HE NEVER KNEW HE POSSESSED...
...AND WAKES.
OH!!
OH.
A DREAM --IT WAS A DREAM. THANK... HEAVEN.
IMAGES... FADING SO FAST --CAN'T HOLD ONTO THEM. I DON'T REALLY WANT TO.
THE SKY--SO MANY MOONS. WE'RE A LONG WAY FROM HOME.
MEMORY TELLS ME WE'RE SUPPOSED TO BE ON LILANDRA'S THRONEWORLD, BUT THIS LOOKS NOTHING LIKE THE PROFESSOR'S DESCRIPTIONS.
STORM...?
SHE'S IN A TRANCE.
I DON'T WANT TO DISTURB HER--THAT COULD PROVE DANGEROUS FOR BOTH OF US-- BUT I THINK I'D BETTER.
I REMEMBER OUR BEING HONORED FOR RESCUING LILANDRA--YET OUR CLOTHES ARE IN TATTERS. AND MY NIGHTMARE INDICATES SOME SORT OF PSYCHIC CONFLICT. IF SOMEONE IS MANIPULATING OUR MINDS...
HE STEPS FORWARD, THEN FREEZES AS BEFORE HIS DISBELIEVING EYES...
...ENERGY COALESCES AROUND ORORO INTO THE FORM OF ONE OF THE CREATURES FROM HIS NIGHTMARE. THE YOUNG QUEEN SMILES AT HIM...
...AND A BOLT OF LIGHTNING SPLITS THE SKY.
THE ASTRAL IMAGE FADES.

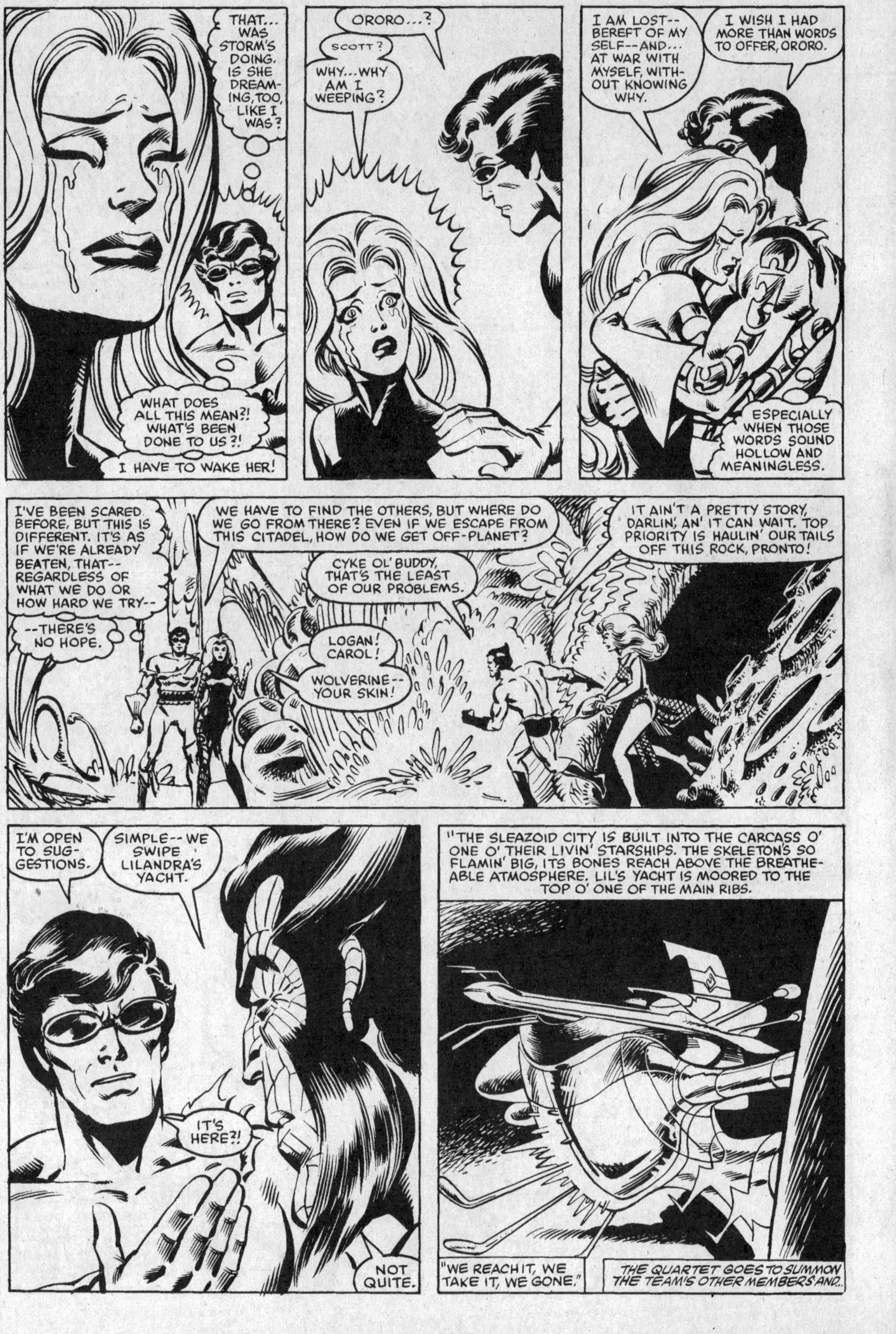

THAT... WAS STORM'S DOING. IS SHE DREAMING, TOO, LIKE I WAS?
WHAT DOES ALL THIS MEAN?! WHAT'S BEEN DONE TO US?!
I HAVE TO WAKE HER!
ORORO...?
SCOTT?
WHY...WHY AM I WEEPING?
I AM LOST-- BEREFT OF MY SELF--AND... AT WAR WITH MYSELF, WITHOUT KNOWING WHY.
I WISH I HAD MORE THAN WORDS TO OFFER, ORORO.
ESPECIALLY WHEN THOSE WORDS SOUND HOLLOW AND MEANINGLESS.
I'VE BEEN SCARED BEFORE, BUT THIS IS DIFFERENT. IT'S AS IF WE'RE ALREADY BEATEN, THAT--REGARDLESS OF WHAT WE DO OR HOW HARD WE TRY--
--THERE'S NO HOPE.
WE HAVE TO FIND THE OTHERS, BUT WHERE DO WE GO FROM THERE? EVEN IF WE ESCAPE FROM THIS CITADEL, HOW DO WE GET OFF-PLANET?
CYKE OL' BUDDY, THAT'S THE LEAST OF OUR PROBLEMS.
LOGAN! CAROL!
WOLVERINE-- YOUR SKIN!
IT AIN'T A PRETTY STORY, DARLIN', AN' IT CAN WAIT. TOP PRIORITY IS HAULIN' OUR TAILS OFF THIS ROCK, PRONTO!
I'M OPEN TO SUGGESTIONS.
SIMPLE-- WE SWIPE LILANDRA'S YACHT.
IT'S HERE?!
NOT QUITE.
"THE SLEAZOID CITY IS BUILT INTO THE CARCASS O' ONE O' THEIR LIVIN' STARSHIPS. THE SKELETON'S SO FLAMIN' BIG, ITS BONES REACH ABOVE THE BREATHEABLE ATMOSPHERE. LIL'S YACHT IS MOORED TO THE TOP O' ONE OF THE MAIN RIBS.
"WE REACH IT, WE TAKE IT, WE GONE."
THE QUARTET GOES TO SUMMON THE TEAM'S OTHER MEMBERS AND...

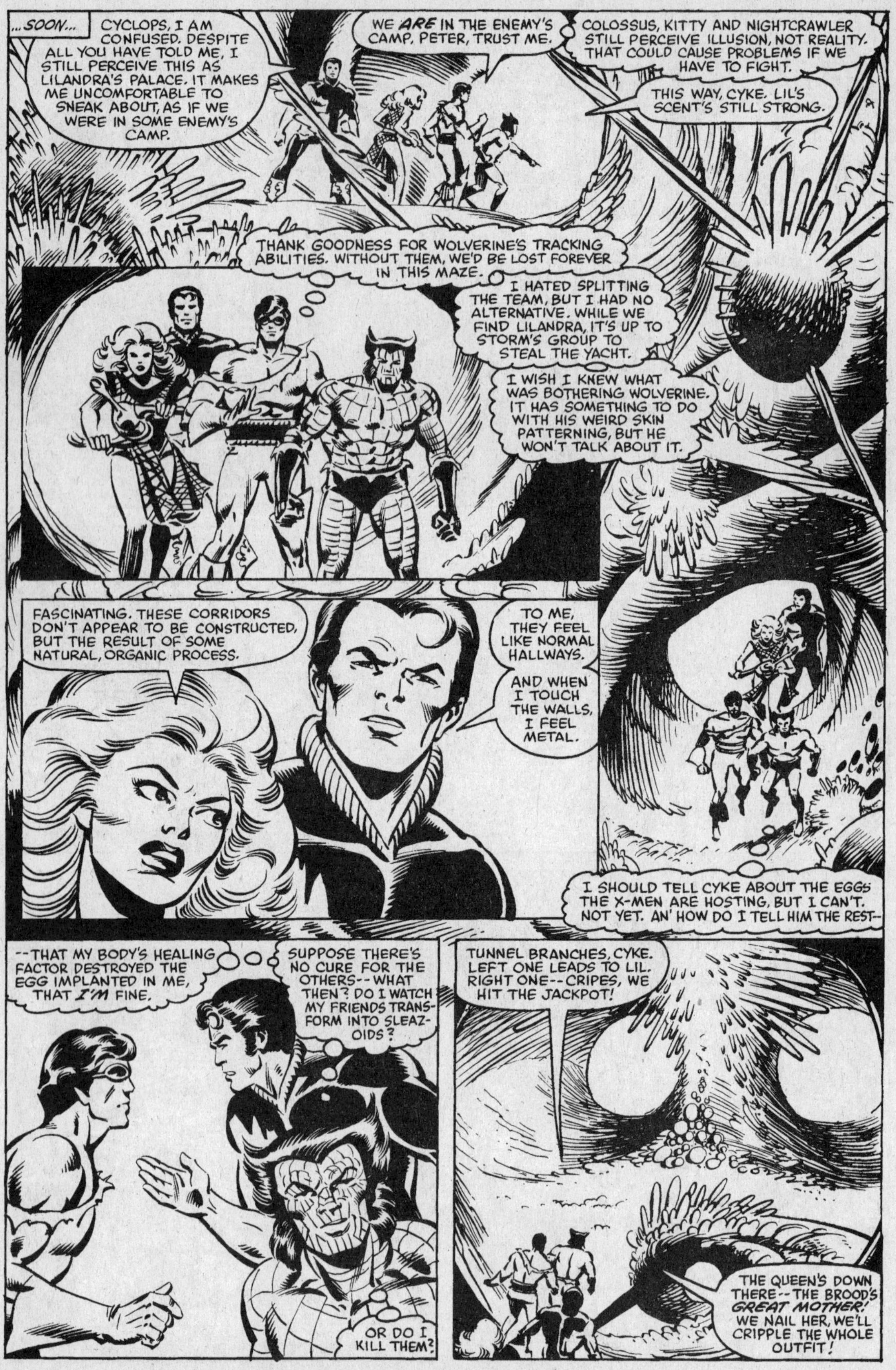
...SOON...
CYCLOPS, I AM CONFUSED. DESPITE ALL YOU HAVE TOLD ME, I STILL PERCEIVE THIS AS LILANDRA'S PALACE. IT MAKES ME UNCOMFORTABLE TO SNEAK ABOUT, AS IF WE WERE IN SOME ENEMY'S CAMP.
WE ARE IN THE ENEMY'S CAMP, PETER, TRUST ME.
COLOSSUS, KITTY AND NIGHTCRAWLER STILL PERCEIVE ILLUSION, NOT REALITY. THAT COULD CAUSE PROBLEMS IF WE HAVE TO FIGHT.
THIS WAY, CYKE. LIL'S SCENT'S STILL STRONG.
THANK GOODNESS FOR WOLVERINE'S TRACKING ABILITIES. WITHOUT THEM, WE'D BE LOST FOREVER IN THIS MAZE.
I HATED SPLITTING THE TEAM, BUT I HAD NO ALTERNATIVE. WHILE WE FIND LILANDRA, IT'S UP TO STORM'S GROUP TO STEAL THE YACHT.
I WISH I KNEW WHAT WAS BOTHERING WOLVERINE. IT HAS SOMETHING TO DO WITH HIS WEIRD SKIN PATTERNING, BUT HE WON'T TALK ABOUT IT.
FASCINATING. THESE CORRIDORS DON'T APPEAR TO BE CONSTRUCTED, BUT THE RESULT OF SOME NATURAL, ORGANIC PROCESS.
TO ME, THEY FEEL LIKE NORMAL HALLWAYS.
AND WHEN I TOUCH THE WALLS, I FEEL METAL.
I SHOULD TELL CYKE ABOUT THE EGGS THE X-MEN ARE HOSTING, BUT I CAN'T. NOT YET. AN' HOW DO I TELL HIM THE REST--
--THAT MY BODY'S HEALING FACTOR DESTROYED THE EGG IMPLANTED IN ME, THAT I'M FINE.
SUPPOSE THERE'S NO CURE FOR THE OTHERS--WHAT THEN? DO I WATCH MY FRIENDS TRANSFORM INTO SLEAZOIDS?
OR DO I KILL THEM?
TUNNEL BRANCHES, CYKE. LEFT ONE LEADS TO LIL. RIGHT ONE--CRIPES, WE HIT THE JACKPOT!
THE QUEEN'S DOWN THERE--THE BROOD'S GREAT MOTHER! WE NAIL HER, WE'LL CRIPPLE THE WHOLE OUTFIT!

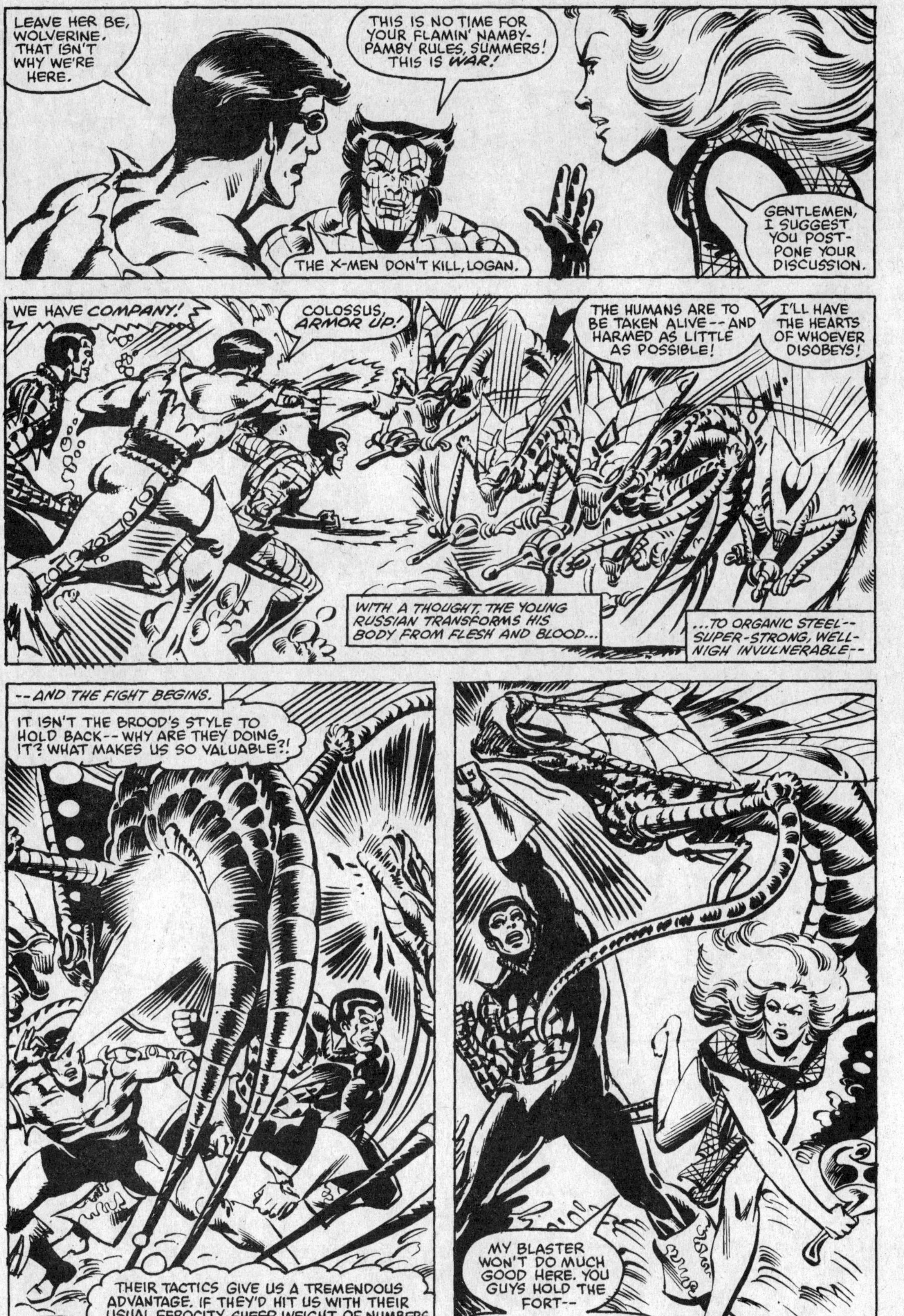

LEAVE HER BE, WOLVERINE. THAT ISN'T WHY WE'RE HERE.
THIS IS NO TIME FOR YOUR FLAMIN' NAMBY-PAMBY RULES, SUMMERS! THIS IS WAR!
THE X-MEN DON'T KILL, LOGAN.
GENTLEMEN, I SUGGEST YOU POSTPONE YOUR DISCUSSION.
WE HAVE COMPANY!
COLOSSUS, ARMOR UP!
THE HUMANS ARE TO BE TAKEN ALIVE--AND HARMED AS LITTLE AS POSSIBLE!
I'LL HAVE THE HEARTS OF WHOEVER DISOBEYS!
WITH A THOUGHT, THE YOUNG RUSSIAN TRANSFORMS HIS BODY FROM FLESH AND BLOOD...
...TO ORGANIC STEEL--SUPER-STRONG, WELL-NIGH INVULNERABLE--
--AND THE FIGHT BEGINS.
IT ISN'T THE BROOD'S STYLE TO HOLD BACK--WHY ARE THEY DOING IT? WHAT MAKES US SO VALUABLE?!
THEIR TACTICS GIVE US A TREMENDOUS ADVANTAGE. IF THEY'D HIT US WITH THEIR USUAL FEROCITY, SHEER WEIGHT OF NUMBERS WOULD HAVE OVERWHELMED US.
MY BLASTER WON'T DO MUCH GOOD HERE. YOU GUYS HOLD THE FORT--
--I'LL SPRING LILANDRA!

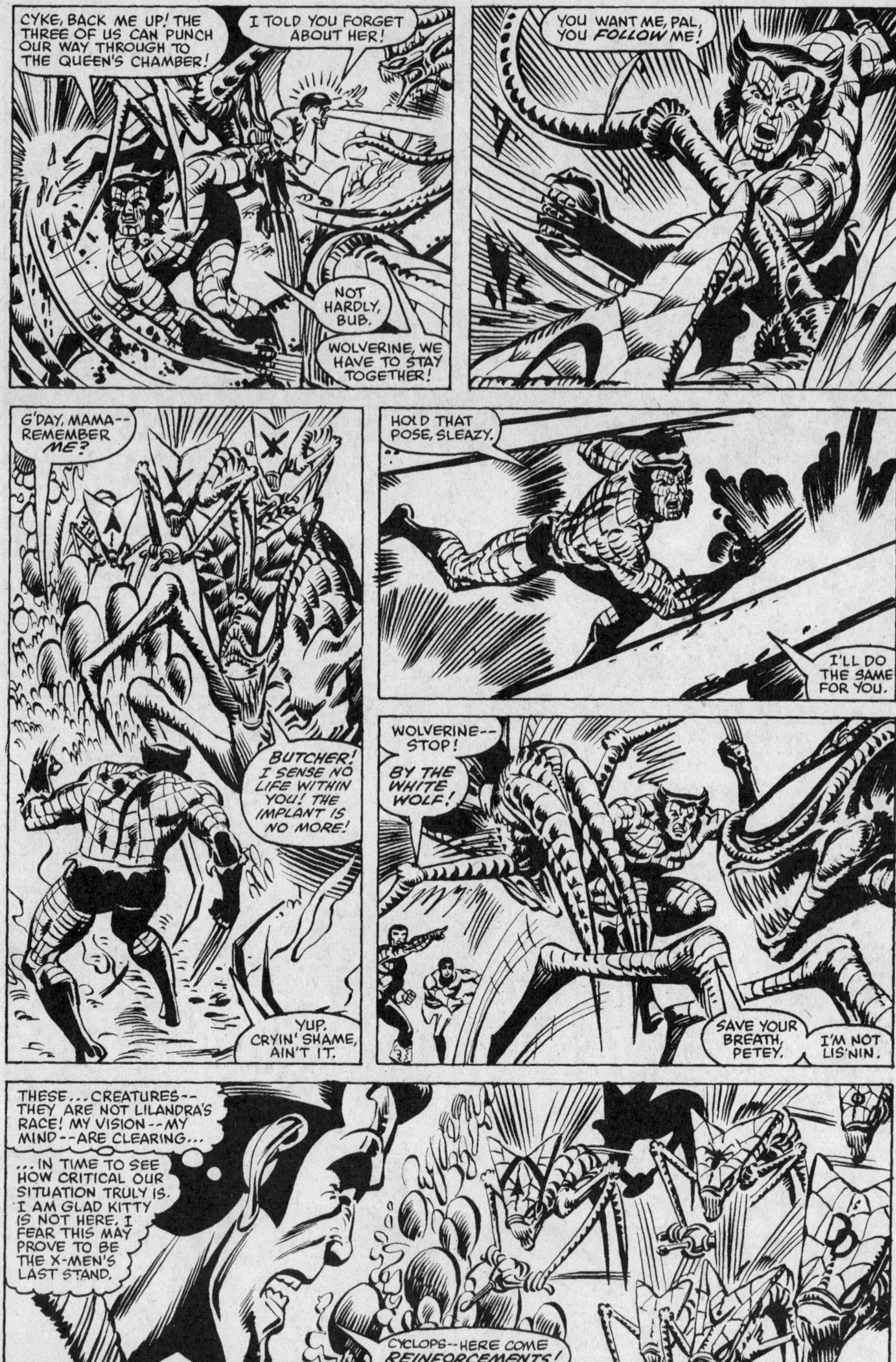
CYKE, BACK ME UP! THE THREE OF US CAN PUNCH OUR WAY THROUGH TO THE QUEEN'S CHAMBER!
I TOLD YOU FORGET ABOUT HER!
NOT HARDLY, BUB.
WOLVERINE, WE HAVE TO STAY TOGETHER!
YOU WANT ME, PAL, YOU FOLLOW ME!
G'DAY, MAMA-- REMEMBER ME?
BUTCHER! I SENSE NO LIFE WITHIN YOU! THE IMPLANT IS NO MORE!
YUP. CRYIN' SHAME, AIN'T IT.
HOLD THAT POSE, SLEAZY.
I'LL DO THE SAME FOR YOU.
WOLVERINE-- STOP!
BY THE WHITE WOLF!
SAVE YOUR BREATH, PETEY.
I'M NOT LIS'NIN.
THESE... CREATURES-- THEY ARE NOT LILANDRA'S RACE! MY VISION--MY MIND--ARE CLEARING...
...IN TIME TO SEE HOW CRITICAL OUR SITUATION TRULY IS. I AM GLAD KITTY IS NOT HERE. I FEAR THIS MAY PROVE TO BE THE X-MEN'S LAST STAND.
CYCLOPS--HERE COME REINFORCEMENTS!

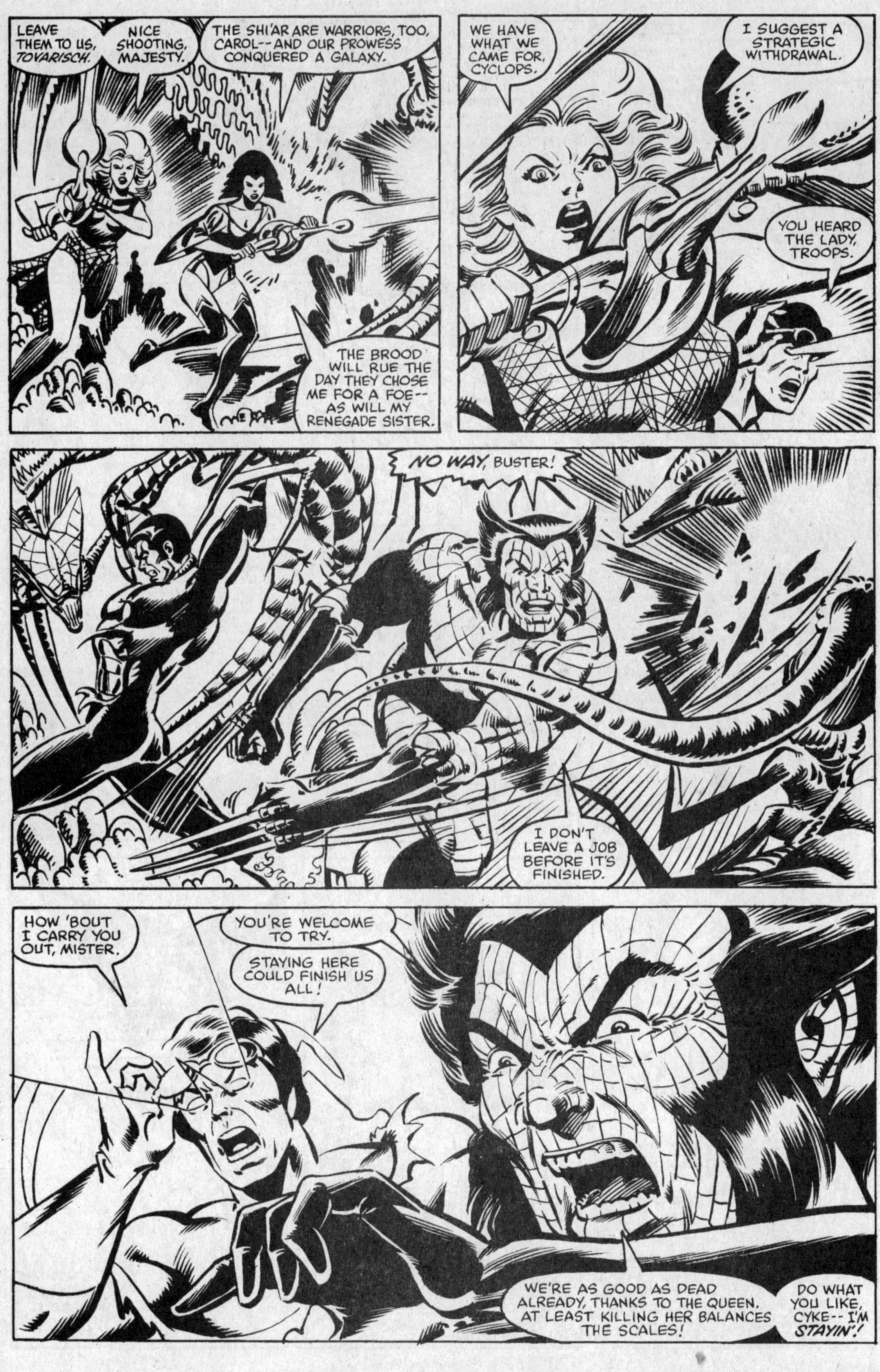

LEAVE THEM TO US, *TOVARISCH.*
NICE SHOOTING, MAJESTY.
THE SHI'AR ARE WARRIORS, TOO, CAROL--AND OUR PROWESS CONQUERED A GALAXY.
THE BROOD WILL RUE THE DAY THEY CHOSE ME FOR A FOE--AS WILL MY RENEGADE SISTER.
WE HAVE WHAT WE CAME FOR, CYCLOPS.
I SUGGEST A STRATEGIC WITHDRAWAL.
YOU HEARD THE LADY, TROOPS.
NO WAY, BUSTER!
I DON'T LEAVE A JOB BEFORE IT'S FINISHED.
HOW 'BOUT I CARRY YOU OUT, MISTER.
YOU'RE WELCOME TO TRY.
STAYING HERE COULD FINISH US ALL!
WE'RE AS GOOD AS DEAD ALREADY, THANKS TO THE QUEEN. AT LEAST KILLING HER BALANCES THE SCALES!
DO WHAT YOU LIKE, CYKE-- I'M *STAYIN'!*

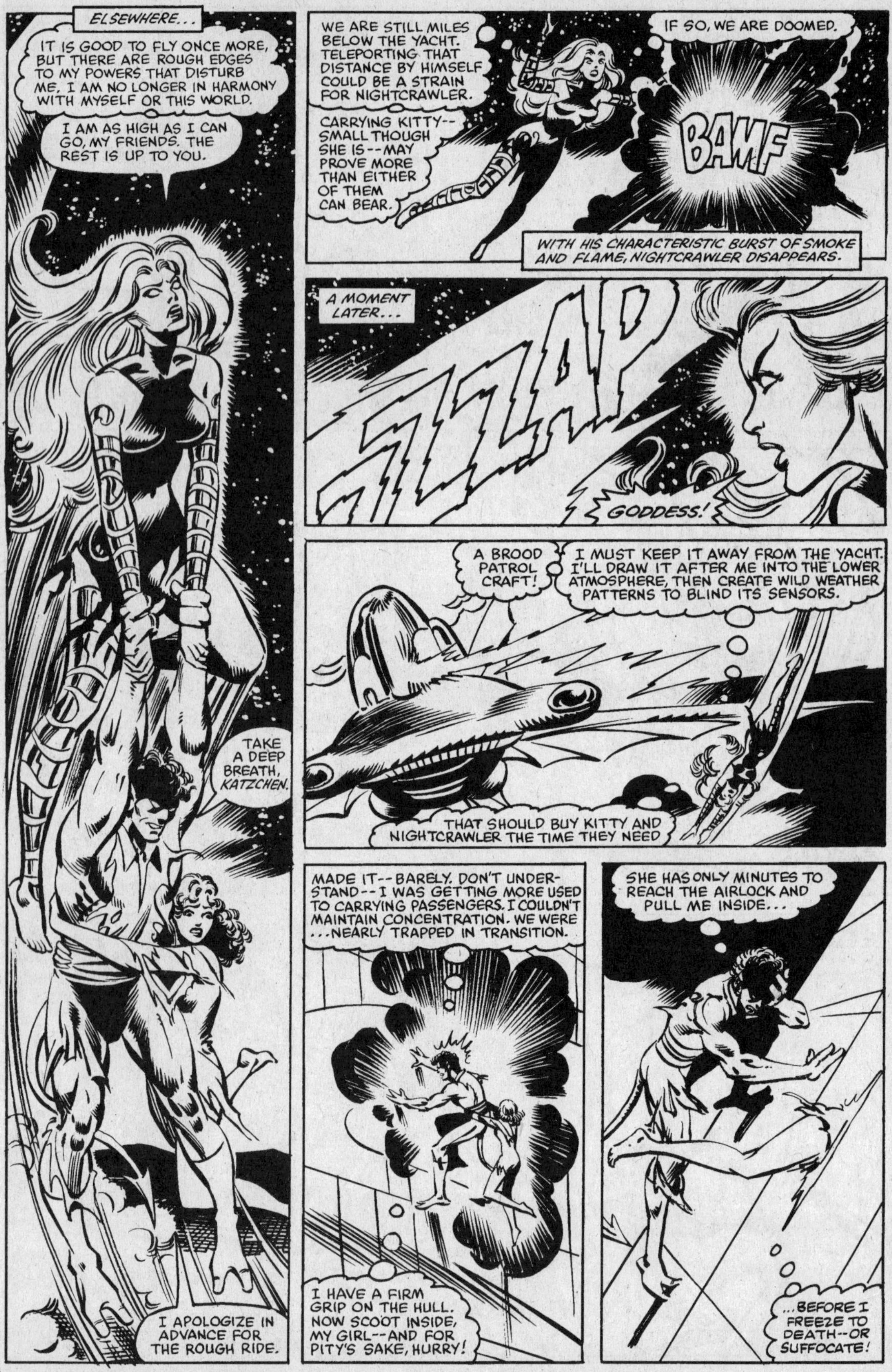
ELSEWHERE...
IT IS GOOD TO FLY ONCE MORE, BUT THERE ARE ROUGH EDGES TO MY POWERS THAT DISTURB ME. I AM NO LONGER IN HARMONY WITH MYSELF OR THIS WORLD.
I AM AS HIGH AS I CAN GO, MY FRIENDS. THE REST IS UP TO YOU.
TAKE A DEEP BREATH, KATZCHEN.
I APOLOGIZE IN ADVANCE FOR THE ROUGH RIDE.
WE ARE STILL MILES BELOW THE YACHT. TELEPORTING THAT DISTANCE BY HIMSELF COULD BE A STRAIN FOR NIGHTCRAWLER.
CARRYING KITTY-- SMALL THOUGH SHE IS--MAY PROVE MORE THAN EITHER OF THEM CAN BEAR.
IF SO, WE ARE DOOMED.
BAMF
WITH HIS CHARACTERISTIC BURST OF SMOKE AND FLAME, NIGHTCRAWLER DISAPPEARS.
A MOMENT LATER...
SZZAP
GODDESS!
A BROOD PATROL CRAFT!
I MUST KEEP IT AWAY FROM THE YACHT. I'LL DRAW IT AFTER ME INTO THE LOWER ATMOSPHERE, THEN CREATE WILD WEATHER PATTERNS TO BLIND ITS SENSORS.
THAT SHOULD BUY KITTY AND NIGHTCRAWLER THE TIME THEY NEED
MADE IT--BARELY. DON'T UNDERSTAND--I WAS GETTING MORE USED TO CARRYING PASSENGERS. I COULDN'T MAINTAIN CONCENTRATION. WE WERE ...NEARLY TRAPPED IN TRANSITION.
I HAVE A FIRM GRIP ON THE HULL. NOW SCOOT INSIDE, MY GIRL--AND FOR PITY'S SAKE, HURRY!
SHE HAS ONLY MINUTES TO REACH THE AIRLOCK AND PULL ME INSIDE...
...BEFORE I FREEZE TO DEATH--OR SUFFOCATE!

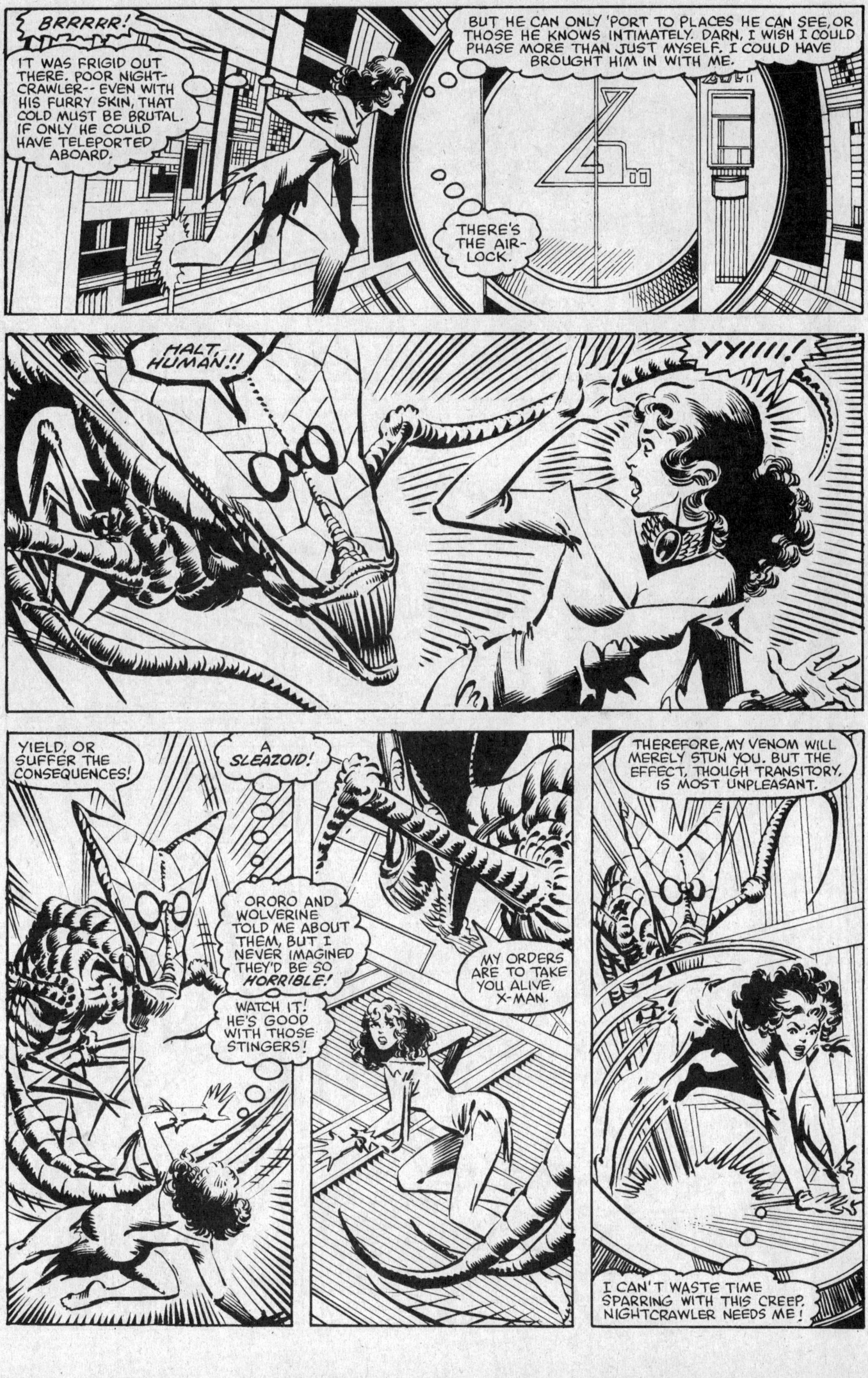
BRRRRR!
IT WAS FRIGID OUT THERE. POOR NIGHT-CRAWLER-- EVEN WITH HIS FURRY SKIN, THAT COLD MUST BE BRUTAL. IF ONLY HE COULD HAVE TELEPORTED ABOARD.
BUT HE CAN ONLY 'PORT TO PLACES HE CAN SEE, OR THOSE HE KNOWS INTIMATELY. DARN, I WISH I COULD PHASE MORE THAN JUST MYSELF. I COULD HAVE BROUGHT HIM IN WITH ME.
THERE'S THE AIR-LOCK.
HALT, HUMAN!!
YYIIII!
YIELD, OR SUFFER THE CONSEQUENCES!
A SLEAZOID!
ORORO AND WOLVERINE TOLD ME ABOUT THEM, BUT I NEVER IMAGINED THEY'D BE SO HORRIBLE!
WATCH IT! HE'S GOOD WITH THOSE STINGERS!
MY ORDERS ARE TO TAKE YOU ALIVE, X-MAN.
THEREFORE, MY VENOM WILL MERELY STUN YOU. BUT THE EFFECT, THOUGH TRANSITORY, IS MOST UNPLEASANT.
I CAN'T WASTE TIME SPARRING WITH THIS CREEP. NIGHTCRAWLER NEEDS ME!

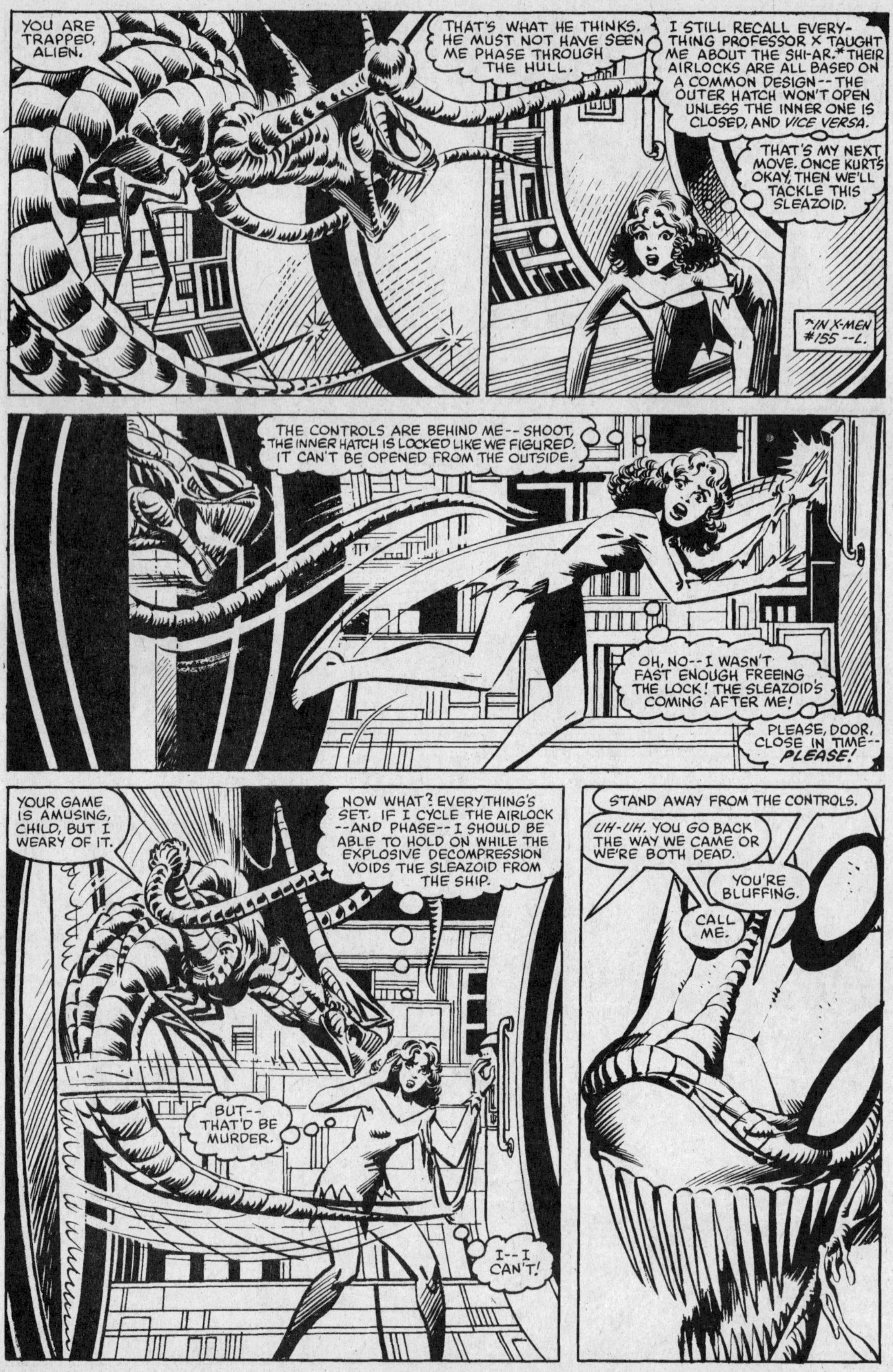

YOU ARE TRAPPED, ALIEN.
THAT'S WHAT HE THINKS. HE MUST NOT HAVE SEEN ME PHASE THROUGH THE HULL.
I STILL RECALL EVERYTHING PROFESSOR X TAUGHT ME ABOUT THE SHI-AR.* THEIR AIRLOCKS ARE ALL BASED ON A COMMON DESIGN -- THE OUTER HATCH WON'T OPEN UNLESS THE INNER ONE IS CLOSED, AND VICE VERSA.
THAT'S MY NEXT MOVE. ONCE KURT'S OKAY, THEN WE'LL TACKLE THIS SLEAZOID.
*IN X-MEN #155 --L.
THE CONTROLS ARE BEHIND ME -- SHOOT, THE INNER HATCH IS LOCKED LIKE WE FIGURED. IT CAN'T BE OPENED FROM THE OUTSIDE.
OH, NO -- I WASN'T FAST ENOUGH FREEING THE LOCK! THE SLEAZOID'S COMING AFTER ME!
PLEASE, DOOR, CLOSE IN TIME -- PLEASE!
YOUR GAME IS AMUSING, CHILD, BUT I WEARY OF IT.
NOW WHAT? EVERYTHING'S SET. IF I CYCLE THE AIRLOCK -- AND PHASE -- I SHOULD BE ABLE TO HOLD ON WHILE THE EXPLOSIVE DECOMPRESSION VOIDS THE SLEAZOID FROM THE SHIP.
BUT -- THAT'D BE MURDER.
I -- I CAN'T!
STAND AWAY FROM THE CONTROLS.
UH-UH. YOU GO BACK THE WAY WE CAME OR WE'RE BOTH DEAD.
YOU'RE BLUFFING.
CALL ME.

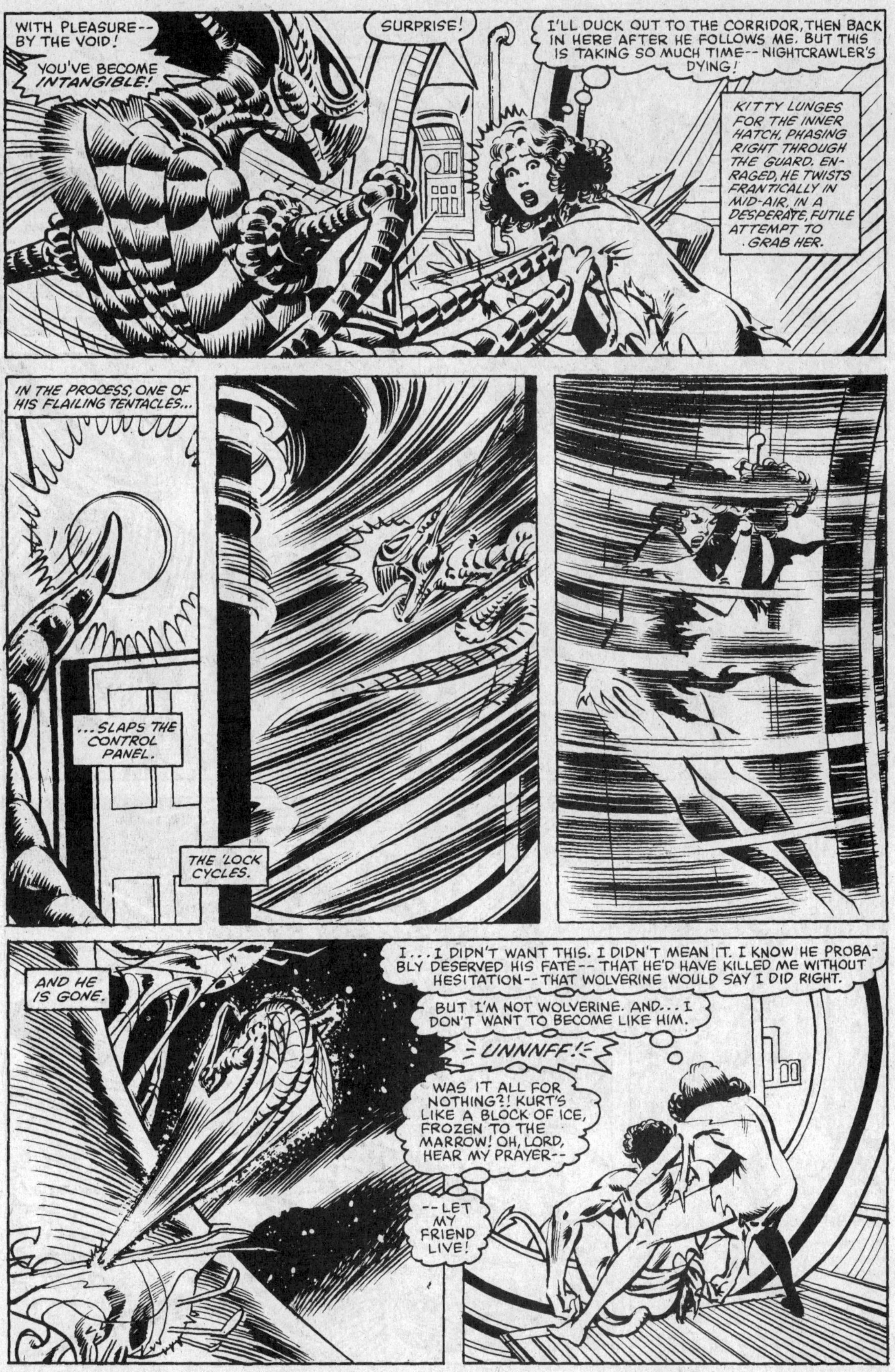
WITH PLEASURE-- BY THE VOID!
YOU'VE BECOME *INTANGIBLE!*
SURPRISE!
I'LL DUCK OUT TO THE CORRIDOR, THEN BACK IN HERE AFTER HE FOLLOWS ME. BUT THIS IS TAKING SO MUCH TIME-- NIGHTCRAWLER'S DYING!
KITTY LUNGES FOR THE INNER HATCH, PHASING RIGHT THROUGH THE GUARD. ENRAGED, HE TWISTS FRANTICALLY IN MID-AIR, IN A DESPERATE, FUTILE ATTEMPT TO GRAB HER.
IN THE PROCESS, ONE OF HIS FLAILING TENTACLES...
...SLAPS THE CONTROL PANEL.
THE 'LOCK CYCLES.
AND HE IS GONE.
I... I DIDN'T WANT THIS. I DIDN'T MEAN IT. I KNOW HE PROBABLY DESERVED HIS FATE-- THAT HE'D HAVE KILLED ME WITHOUT HESITATION-- THAT WOLVERINE WOULD SAY I DID RIGHT.
BUT I'M NOT WOLVERINE. AND... I DON'T WANT TO BECOME LIKE HIM.
UNNNFF!
WAS IT ALL FOR NOTHING?! KURT'S LIKE A BLOCK OF ICE, FROZEN TO THE MARROW! OH, LORD, HEAR MY PRAYER--
--LET MY FRIEND LIVE!

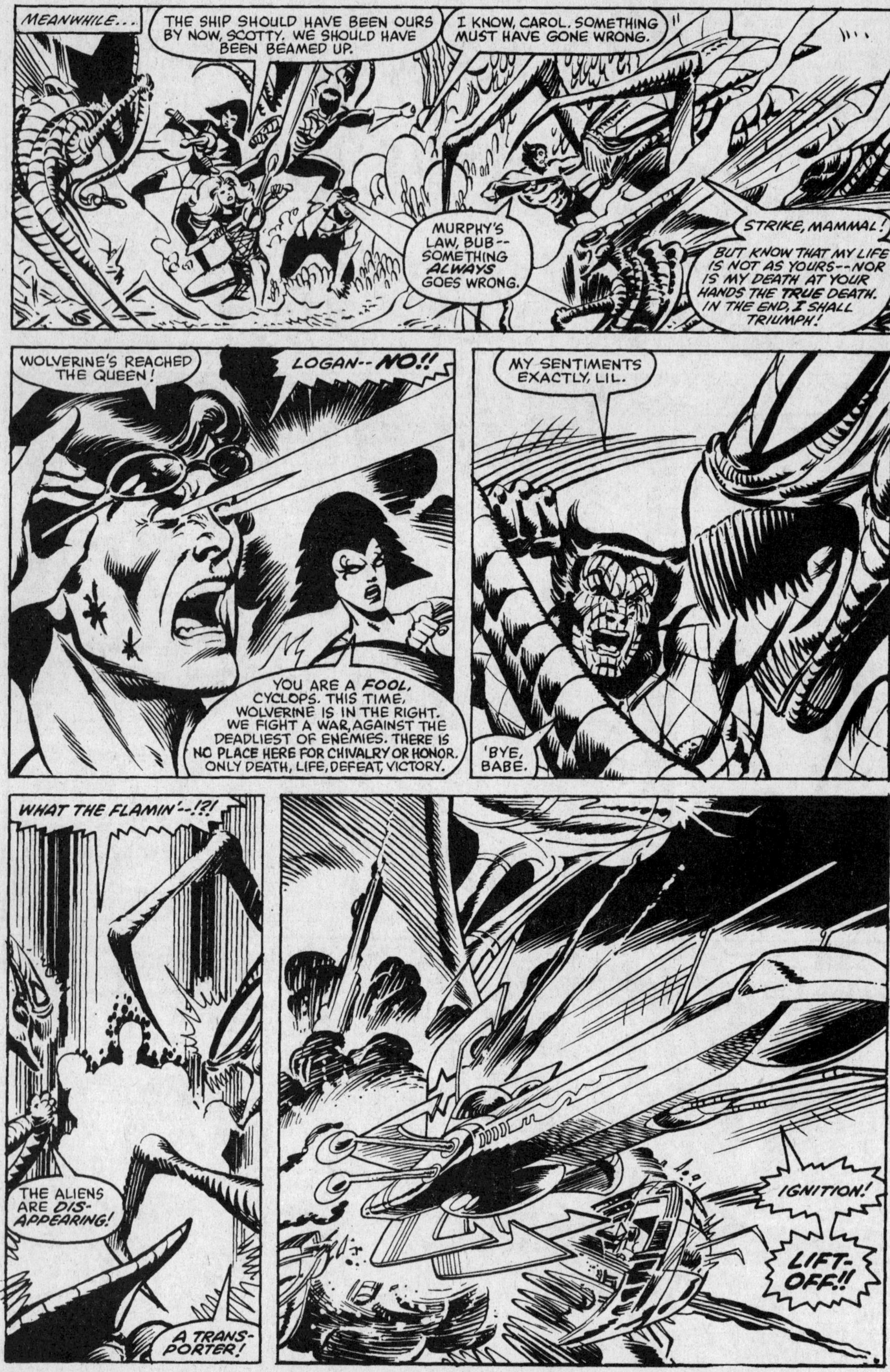
MEANWHILE...
THE SHIP SHOULD HAVE BEEN OURS BY NOW, SCOTTY. WE SHOULD HAVE BEEN BEAMED UP.
I KNOW, CAROL. SOMETHING MUST HAVE GONE WRONG.
MURPHY'S LAW, BUB-- SOMETHING ALWAYS GOES WRONG.
STRIKE, MAMMAL!
BUT KNOW THAT MY LIFE IS NOT AS YOURS--NOR IS MY DEATH AT YOUR HANDS THE TRUE DEATH. IN THE END, I SHALL TRIUMPH!
WOLVERINE'S REACHED THE QUEEN!
LOGAN--NO!!
YOU ARE A FOOL, CYCLOPS. THIS TIME, WOLVERINE IS IN THE RIGHT. WE FIGHT A WAR, AGAINST THE DEADLIEST OF ENEMIES. THERE IS NO PLACE HERE FOR CHIVALRY OR HONOR. ONLY DEATH, LIFE, DEFEAT, VICTORY.
MY SENTIMENTS EXACTLY, LIL.
'BYE, BABE.
WHAT THE FLAMIN'--!?!
THE ALIENS ARE DIS-APPEARING!
A TRANS-PORTER!
IGNITION!
LIFT-OFF!!

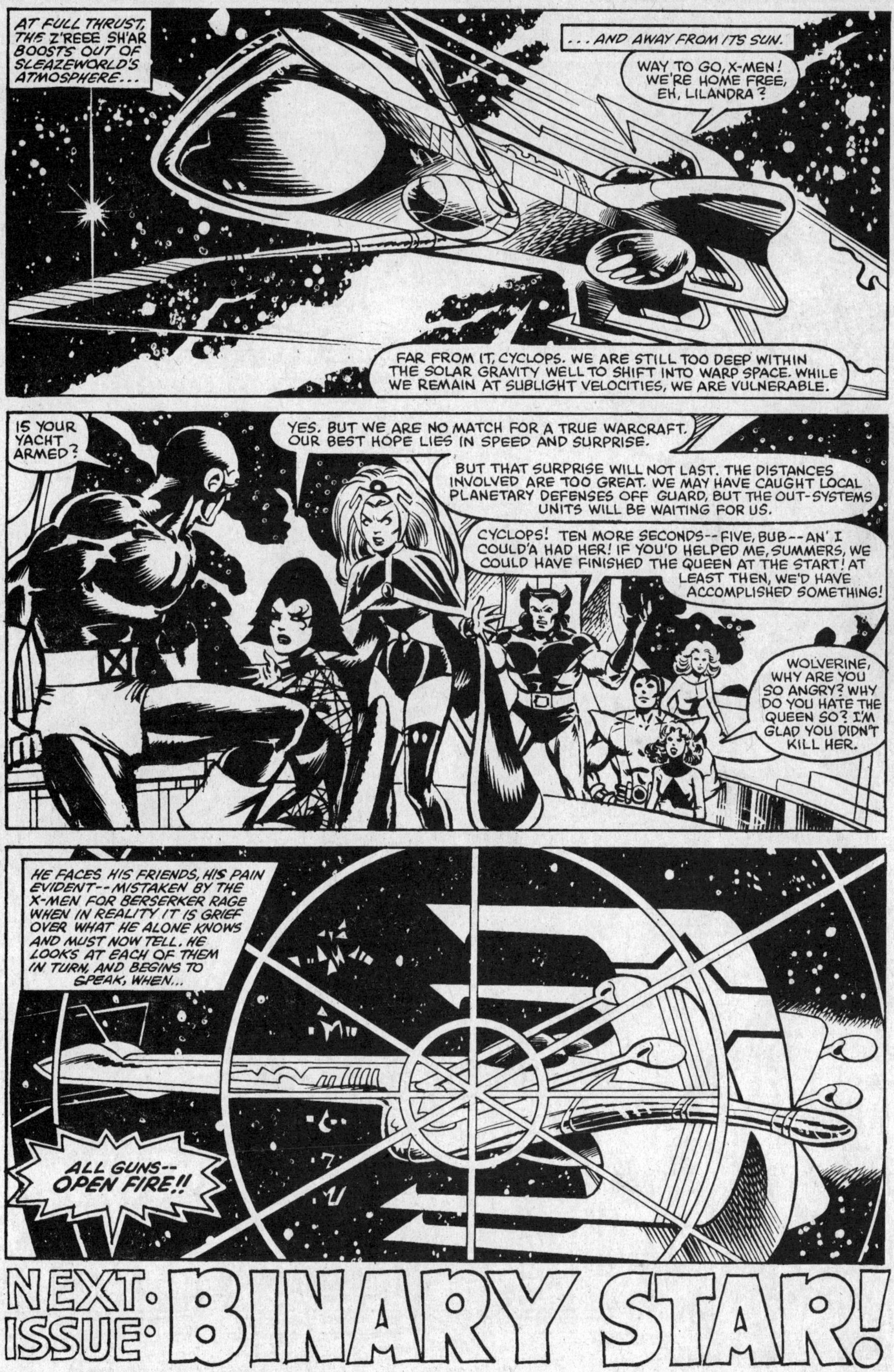
AT FULL THRUST, THE Z'REEE SH'AR BOOSTS OUT OF SLEAZEWORLD'S ATMOSPHERE...
...AND AWAY FROM ITS SUN.
WAY TO GO, X-MEN! WE'RE HOME FREE, EH, LILANDRA?
FAR FROM IT, CYCLOPS. WE ARE STILL TOO DEEP WITHIN THE SOLAR GRAVITY WELL TO SHIFT INTO WARP SPACE. WHILE WE REMAIN AT SUBLIGHT VELOCITIES, WE ARE VULNERABLE.
IS YOUR YACHT ARMED?
YES. BUT WE ARE NO MATCH FOR A TRUE WARCRAFT. OUR BEST HOPE LIES IN SPEED AND SURPRISE.
BUT THAT SURPRISE WILL NOT LAST. THE DISTANCES INVOLVED ARE TOO GREAT. WE MAY HAVE CAUGHT LOCAL PLANETARY DEFENSES OFF GUARD, BUT THE OUT-SYSTEMS UNITS WILL BE WAITING FOR US.
CYCLOPS! TEN MORE SECONDS--FIVE, BUB--AN' I COULD'A HAD HER! IF YOU'D HELPED ME, SUMMERS, WE COULD HAVE FINISHED THE QUEEN AT THE START! AT LEAST THEN, WE'D HAVE ACCOMPLISHED SOMETHING!
WOLVERINE, WHY ARE YOU SO ANGRY? WHY DO YOU HATE THE QUEEN SO? I'M GLAD YOU DIDN'T KILL HER.
HE FACES HIS FRIENDS, HIS PAIN EVIDENT--MISTAKEN BY THE X-MEN FOR BERSERKER RAGE WHEN IN REALITY IT IS GRIEF OVER WHAT HE ALONE KNOWS AND MUST NOW TELL. HE LOOKS AT EACH OF THEM IN TURN, AND BEGINS TO SPEAK, WHEN...
ALL GUNS-- OPEN FIRE!!

NEXT• ISSUE• BINARY STAR!

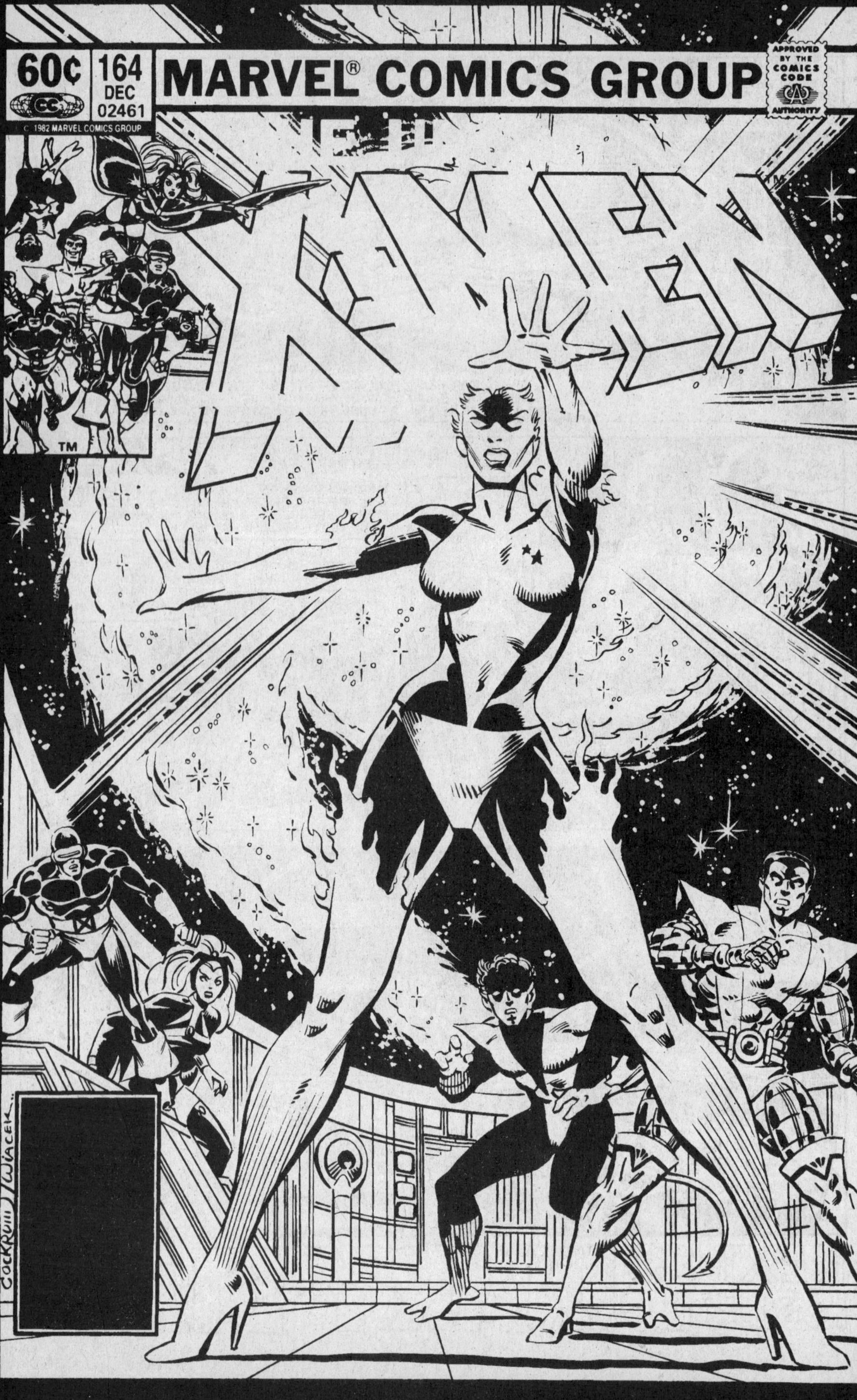
60¢
164
DEC
02461
MARVEL® COMICS GROUP
APPROVED BY THE COMICS CODE AUTHORITY
© 1982 MARVEL COMICS GROUP
TM
COCKRUM / WIACEK

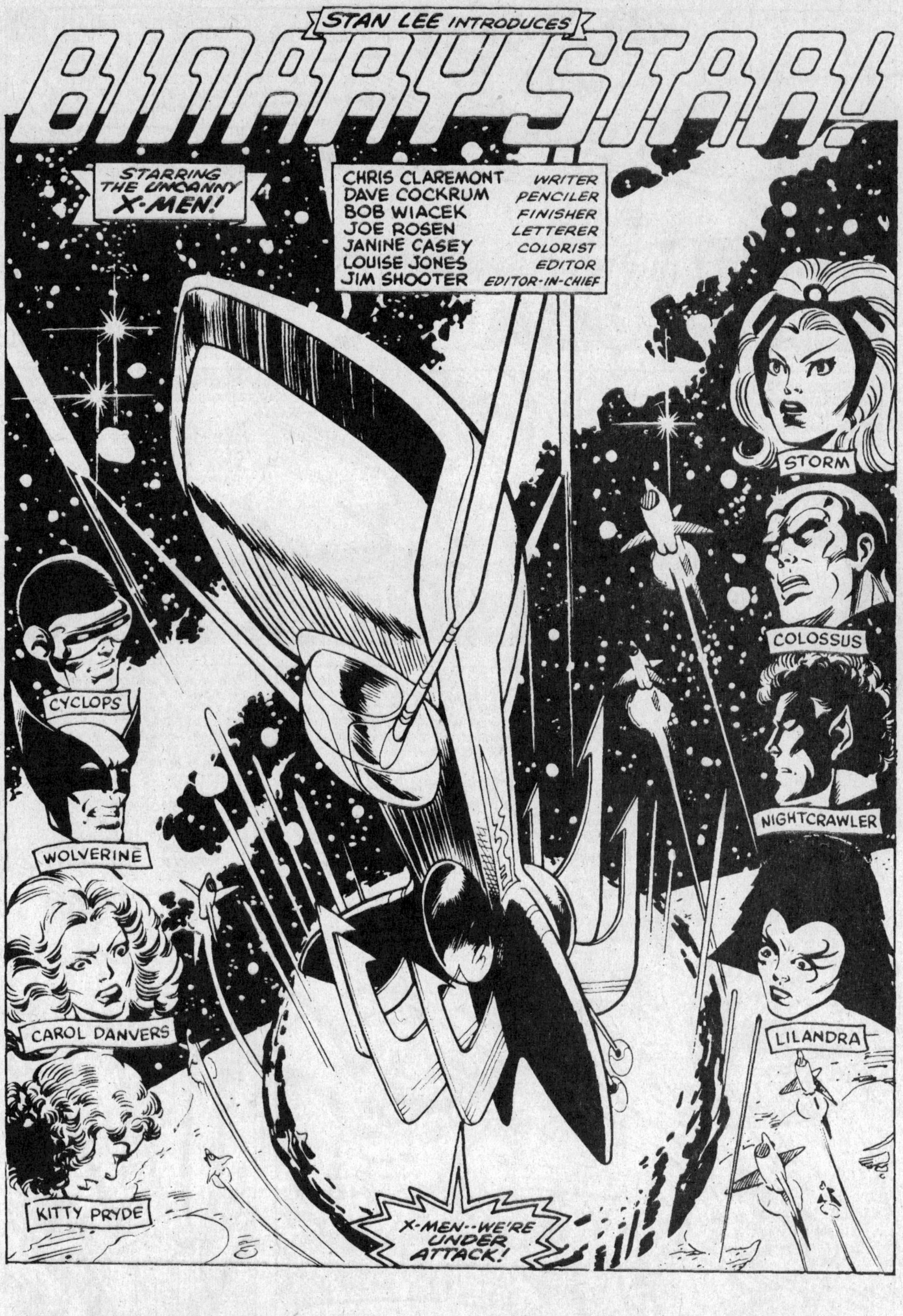

STAN LEE INTRODUCES
BINARY STAR!
STARRING THE UNCANNY X-MEN!
CHRIS CLAREMONT WRITER
DAVE COCKRUM PENCILER
BOB WIACEK FINISHER
JOE ROSEN LETTERER
JANINE CASEY COLORIST
LOUISE JONES EDITOR
JIM SHOOTER EDITOR-IN-CHIEF
STORM
COLOSSUS
NIGHTCRAWLER
LILANDRA
CYCLOPS
WOLVERINE
CAROL DANVERS
KITTY PRYDE
X-MEN--WE'RE UNDER ATTACK!

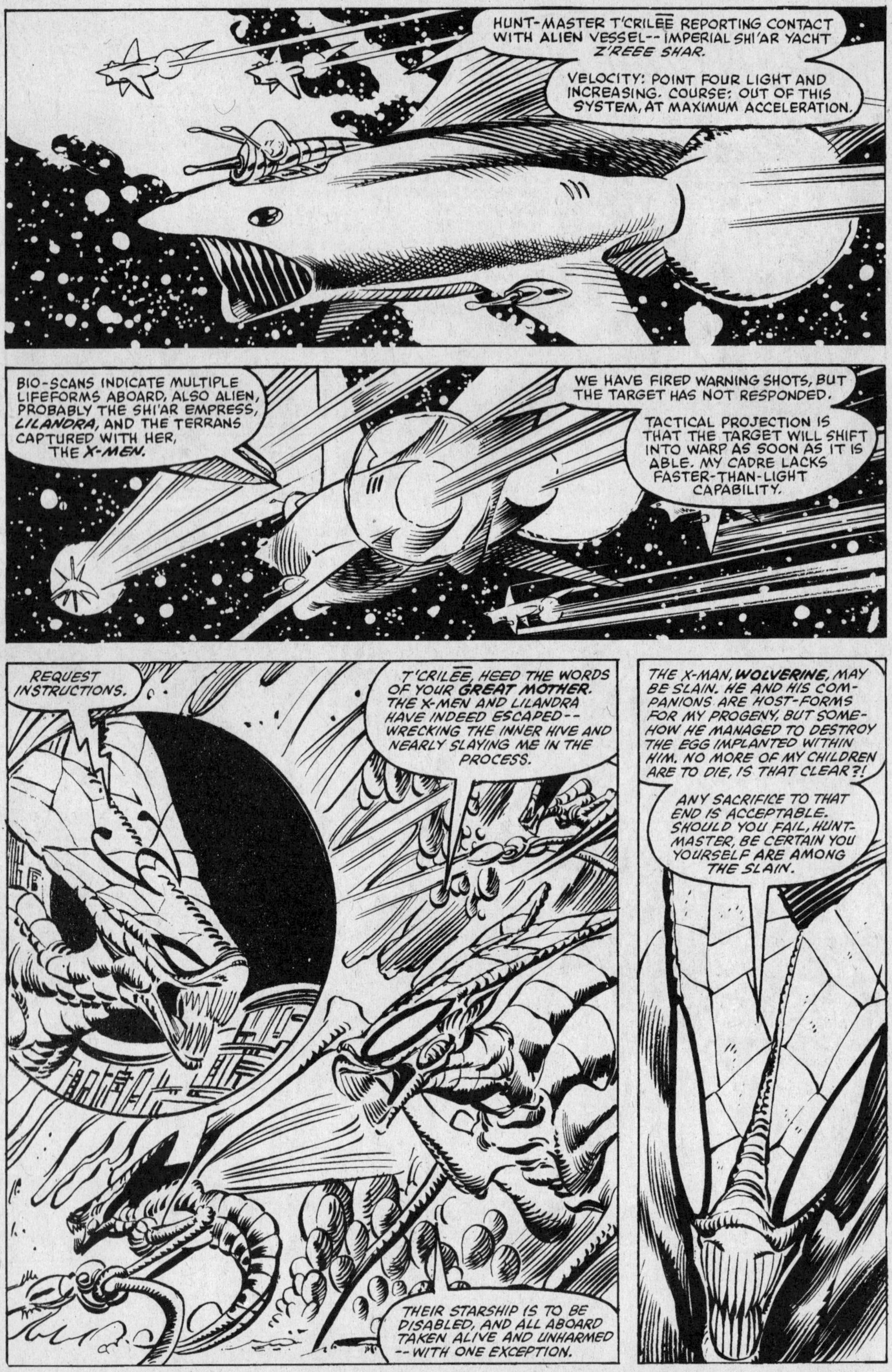

HUNT-MASTER T'CRILĒĒ REPORTING CONTACT WITH ALIEN VESSEL-- IMPERIAL SHI'AR YACHT Z'REEE SHAR.
VELOCITY: POINT FOUR LIGHT AND INCREASING. COURSE: OUT OF THIS SYSTEM, AT MAXIMUM ACCELERATION.
BIO-SCANS INDICATE MULTIPLE LIFEFORMS ABOARD, ALSO ALIEN, PROBABLY THE SHI'AR EMPRESS, LILANDRA, AND THE TERRANS CAPTURED WITH HER, THE X-MEN.
WE HAVE FIRED WARNING SHOTS, BUT THE TARGET HAS NOT RESPONDED.
TACTICAL PROJECTION IS THAT THE TARGET WILL SHIFT INTO WARP AS SOON AS IT IS ABLE. MY CADRE LACKS FASTER-THAN-LIGHT CAPABILITY.
REQUEST INSTRUCTIONS.
T'CRILĒĒ, HEED THE WORDS OF YOUR GREAT MOTHER. THE X-MEN AND LILANDRA HAVE INDEED ESCAPED-- WRECKING THE INNER HIVE AND NEARLY SLAYING ME IN THE PROCESS.
THEIR STARSHIP IS TO BE DISABLED, AND ALL ABOARD TAKEN ALIVE AND UNHARMED --WITH ONE EXCEPTION.
THE X-MAN, WOLVERINE, MAY BE SLAIN. HE AND HIS COMPANIONS ARE HOST-FORMS FOR MY PROGENY, BUT SOMEHOW HE MANAGED TO DESTROY THE EGG IMPLANTED WITHIN HIM. NO MORE OF MY CHILDREN ARE TO DIE, IS THAT CLEAR?!
ANY SACRIFICE TO THAT END IS ACCEPTABLE. SHOULD YOU FAIL, HUNT-MASTER, BE CERTAIN YOU YOURSELF ARE AMONG THE SLAIN.

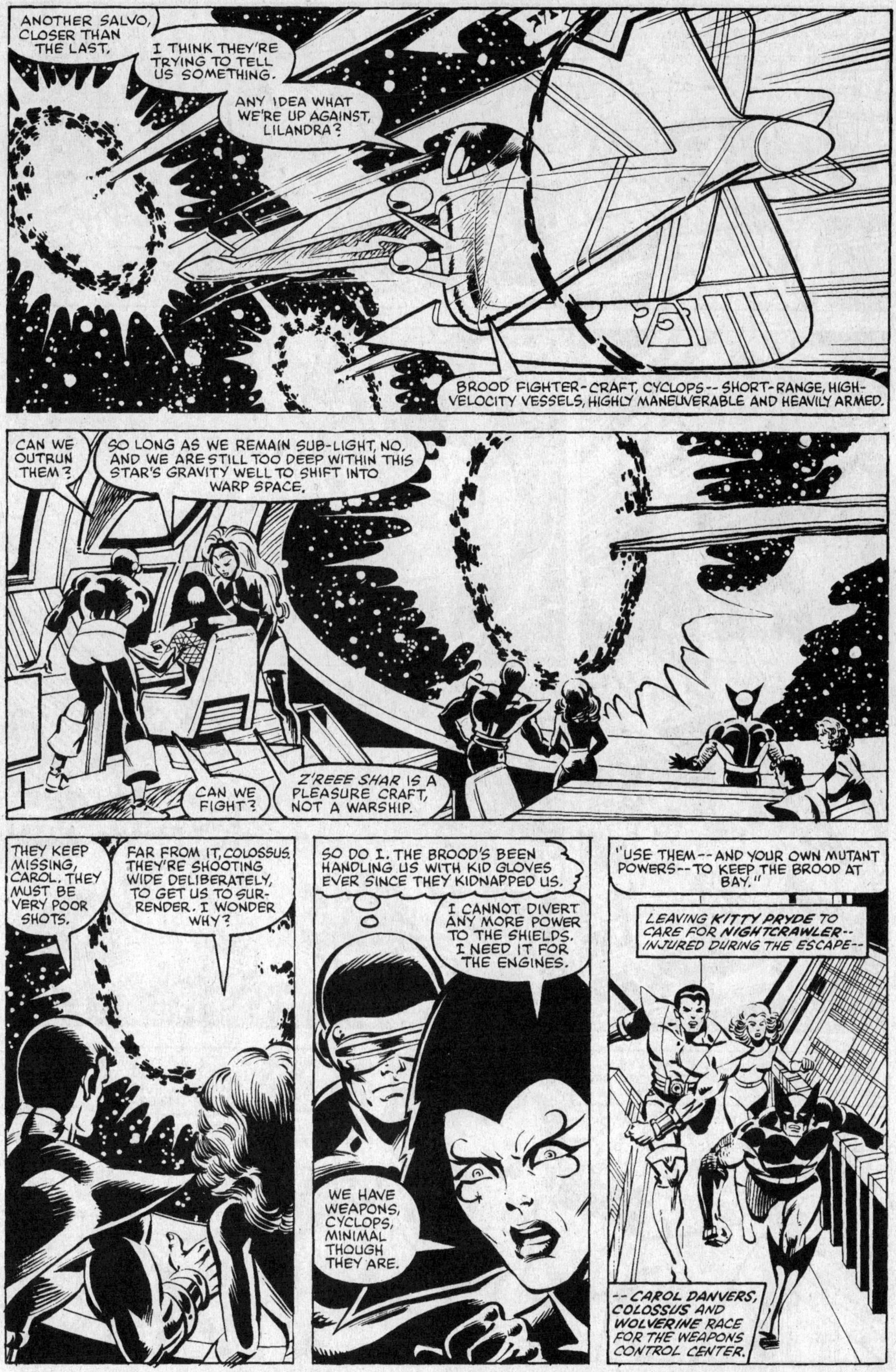

ANOTHER SALVO, CLOSER THAN THE LAST.
I THINK THEY'RE TRYING TO TELL US SOMETHING.
ANY IDEA WHAT WE'RE UP AGAINST, LILANDRA?
BROOD FIGHTER-CRAFT, CYCLOPS -- SHORT-RANGE, HIGH-VELOCITY VESSELS, HIGHLY MANEUVERABLE AND HEAVILY ARMED.
CAN WE OUTRUN THEM?
SO LONG AS WE REMAIN SUB-LIGHT, NO. AND WE ARE STILL TOO DEEP WITHIN THIS STAR'S GRAVITY WELL TO SHIFT INTO WARP SPACE.
CAN WE FIGHT?
Z'REEE SHAR IS A PLEASURE CRAFT, NOT A WARSHIP.
THEY KEEP MISSING, CAROL. THEY MUST BE VERY POOR SHOTS.
FAR FROM IT, COLOSSUS. THEY'RE SHOOTING WIDE DELIBERATELY, TO GET US TO SURRENDER. I WONDER WHY?
SO DO I. THE BROOD'S BEEN HANDLING US WITH KID GLOVES EVER SINCE THEY KIDNAPPED US.
I CANNOT DIVERT ANY MORE POWER TO THE SHIELDS. I NEED IT FOR THE ENGINES.
WE HAVE WEAPONS, CYCLOPS, MINIMAL THOUGH THEY ARE.
"USE THEM -- AND YOUR OWN MUTANT POWERS -- TO KEEP THE BROOD AT BAY."
LEAVING KITTY PRYDE TO CARE FOR NIGHTCRAWLER -- INJURED DURING THE ESCAPE --
-- CAROL DANVERS, COLOSSUS AND WOLVERINE RACE FOR THE WEAPONS CONTROL CENTER.

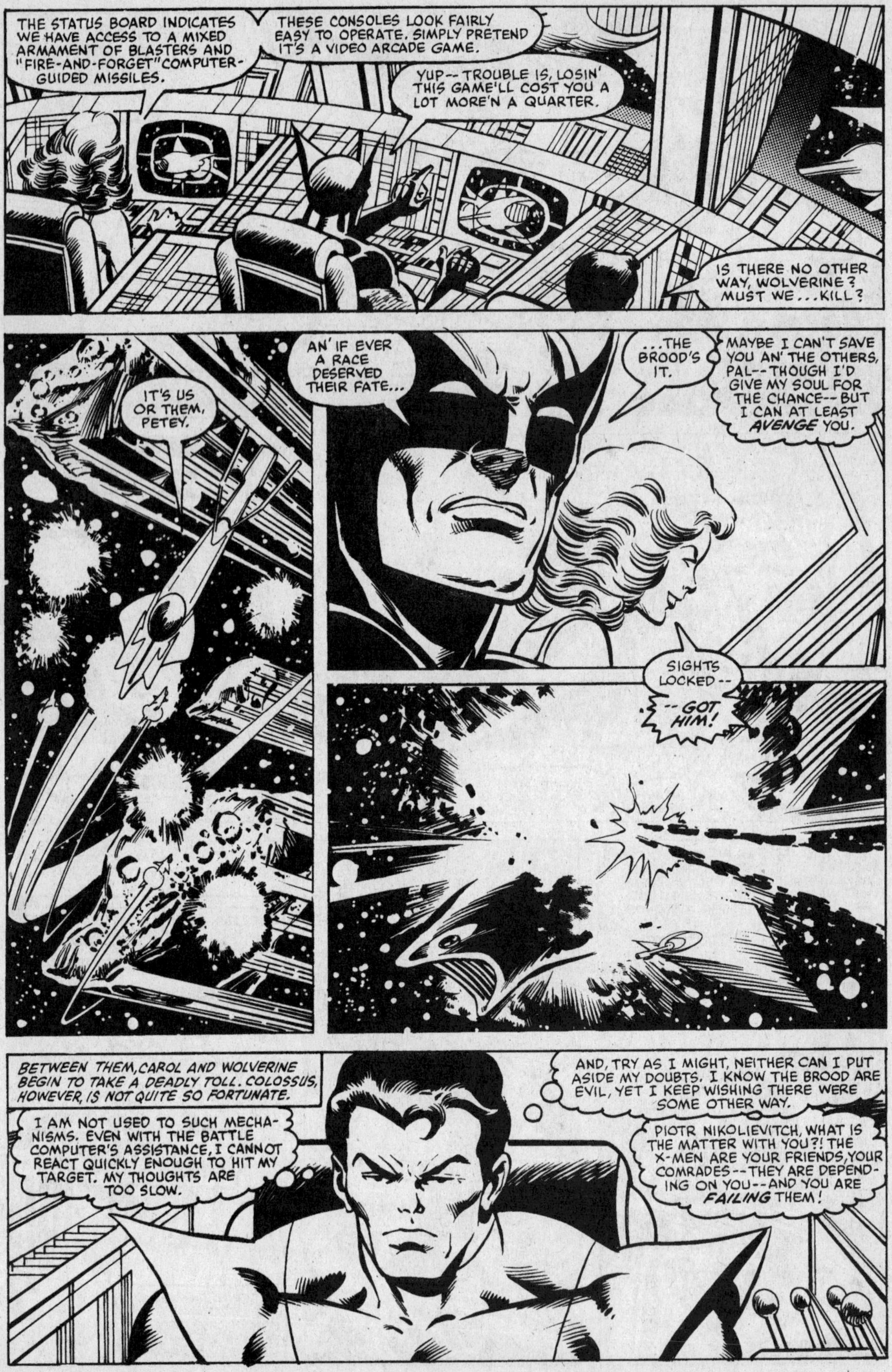
THE STATUS BOARD INDICATES WE HAVE ACCESS TO A MIXED ARMAMENT OF BLASTERS AND "FIRE-AND-FORGET" COMPUTER-GUIDED MISSILES.
THESE CONSOLES LOOK FAIRLY EASY TO OPERATE. SIMPLY PRETEND IT'S A VIDEO ARCADE GAME.
YUP-- TROUBLE IS, LOSIN' THIS GAME'LL COST YOU A LOT MORE'N A QUARTER.
IS THERE NO OTHER WAY, WOLVERINE? MUST WE . . . KILL?
IT'S US OR THEM, PETEY.
AN' IF EVER A RACE DESERVED THEIR FATE...
. . . THE BROOD'S IT.
MAYBE I CAN'T SAVE YOU AN' THE OTHERS, PAL-- THOUGH I'D GIVE MY SOUL FOR THE CHANCE-- BUT I CAN AT LEAST AVENGE YOU.
SIGHTS LOCKED --
-- GOT HIM!
BETWEEN THEM, CAROL AND WOLVERINE BEGIN TO TAKE A DEADLY TOLL. COLOSSUS, HOWEVER, IS NOT QUITE SO FORTUNATE.
I AM NOT USED TO SUCH MECHANISMS. EVEN WITH THE BATTLE COMPUTER'S ASSISTANCE, I CANNOT REACT QUICKLY ENOUGH TO HIT MY TARGET. MY THOUGHTS ARE TOO SLOW.
AND, TRY AS I MIGHT, NEITHER CAN I PUT ASIDE MY DOUBTS. I KNOW THE BROOD ARE EVIL, YET I KEEP WISHING THERE WERE SOME OTHER WAY.
PIOTR NIKOLIEVITCH, WHAT IS THE MATTER WITH YOU?! THE X-MEN ARE YOUR FRIENDS, YOUR COMRADES -- THEY ARE DEPENDING ON YOU -- AND YOU ARE FAILING THEM!

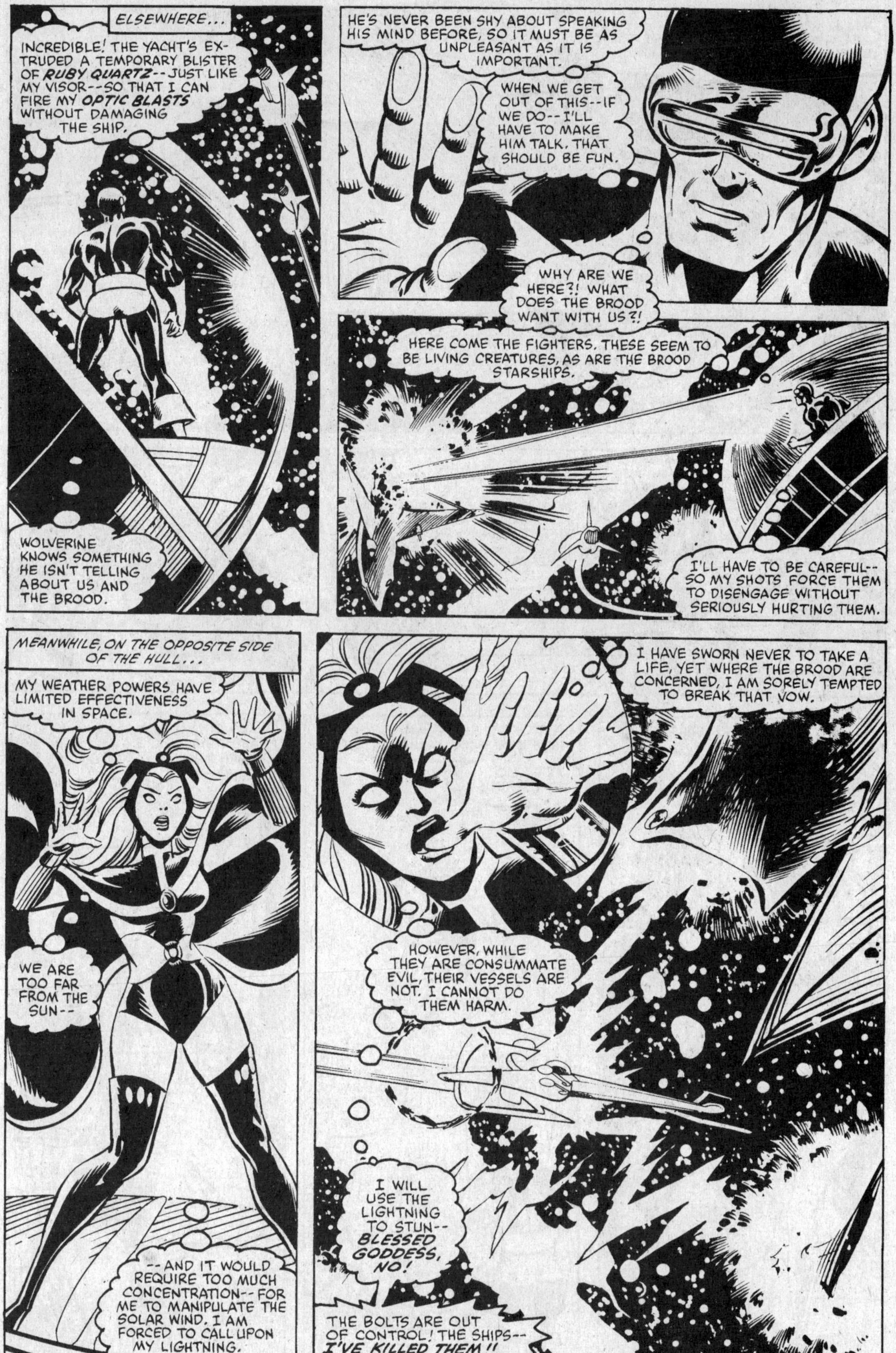
ELSEWHERE...
INCREDIBLE! THE YACHT'S EXTRUDED A TEMPORARY BLISTER OF RUBY QUARTZ--JUST LIKE MY VISOR--SO THAT I CAN FIRE MY OPTIC BLASTS WITHOUT DAMAGING THE SHIP.
WOLVERINE KNOWS SOMETHING HE ISN'T TELLING ABOUT US AND THE BROOD.
HE'S NEVER BEEN SHY ABOUT SPEAKING HIS MIND BEFORE, SO IT MUST BE AS UNPLEASANT AS IT IS IMPORTANT.
WHEN WE GET OUT OF THIS--IF WE DO--I'LL HAVE TO MAKE HIM TALK. THAT SHOULD BE FUN.
WHY ARE WE HERE?! WHAT DOES THE BROOD WANT WITH US?!
HERE COME THE FIGHTERS. THESE SEEM TO BE LIVING CREATURES, AS ARE THE BROOD STARSHIPS.
I'LL HAVE TO BE CAREFUL--SO MY SHOTS FORCE THEM TO DISENGAGE WITHOUT SERIOUSLY HURTING THEM.
MEANWHILE, ON THE OPPOSITE SIDE OF THE HULL...
MY WEATHER POWERS HAVE LIMITED EFFECTIVENESS IN SPACE.
WE ARE TOO FAR FROM THE SUN--
--AND IT WOULD REQUIRE TOO MUCH CONCENTRATION--FOR ME TO MANIPULATE THE SOLAR WIND. I AM FORCED TO CALL UPON MY LIGHTNING.
I HAVE SWORN NEVER TO TAKE A LIFE, YET WHERE THE BROOD ARE CONCERNED, I AM SORELY TEMPTED TO BREAK THAT VOW.
HOWEVER, WHILE THEY ARE CONSUMMATE EVIL, THEIR VESSELS ARE NOT. I CANNOT DO THEM HARM.
I WILL USE THE LIGHTNING TO STUN--BLESSED GODDESS, NO!
THE BOLTS ARE OUT OF CONTROL! THE SHIPS--I'VE KILLED THEM!!

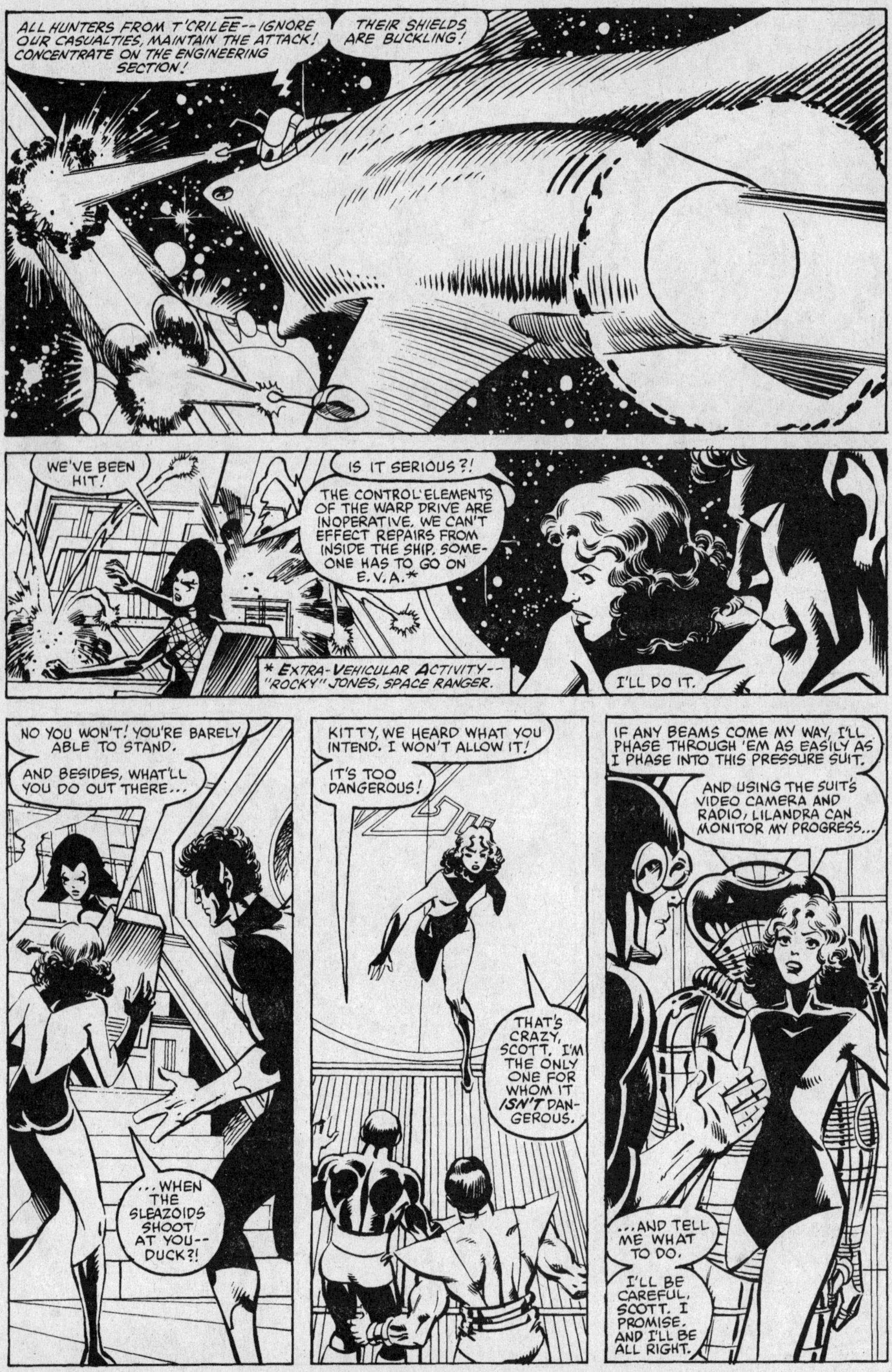

ALL HUNTERS FROM T'CRILÉE-- IGNORE OUR CASUALTIES, MAINTAIN THE ATTACK! CONCENTRATE ON THE ENGINEERING SECTION!
THEIR SHIELDS ARE BUCKLING!
WE'VE BEEN HIT!
IS IT SERIOUS?!
THE CONTROL ELEMENTS OF THE WARP DRIVE ARE INOPERATIVE. WE CAN'T EFFECT REPAIRS FROM INSIDE THE SHIP. SOMEONE HAS TO GO ON E.V.A.*
* EXTRA-VEHICULAR ACTIVITY-- "ROCKY" JONES, SPACE RANGER.
I'LL DO IT.
NO YOU WON'T! YOU'RE BARELY ABLE TO STAND.
AND BESIDES, WHAT'LL YOU DO OUT THERE...
...WHEN THE SLEAZOIDS SHOOT AT YOU-- DUCK?!
KITTY, WE HEARD WHAT YOU INTEND. I WON'T ALLOW IT!
IT'S TOO DANGEROUS!
THAT'S CRAZY, SCOTT. I'M THE ONLY ONE FOR WHOM IT ISN'T DANGEROUS.
IF ANY BEAMS COME MY WAY, I'LL PHASE THROUGH 'EM AS EASILY AS I PHASE INTO THIS PRESSURE SUIT.
AND USING THE SUIT'S VIDEO CAMERA AND RADIO, LILANDRA CAN MONITOR MY PROGRESS...
...AND TELL ME WHAT TO DO.
I'LL BE CAREFUL, SCOTT. I PROMISE. AND I'LL BE ALL RIGHT.

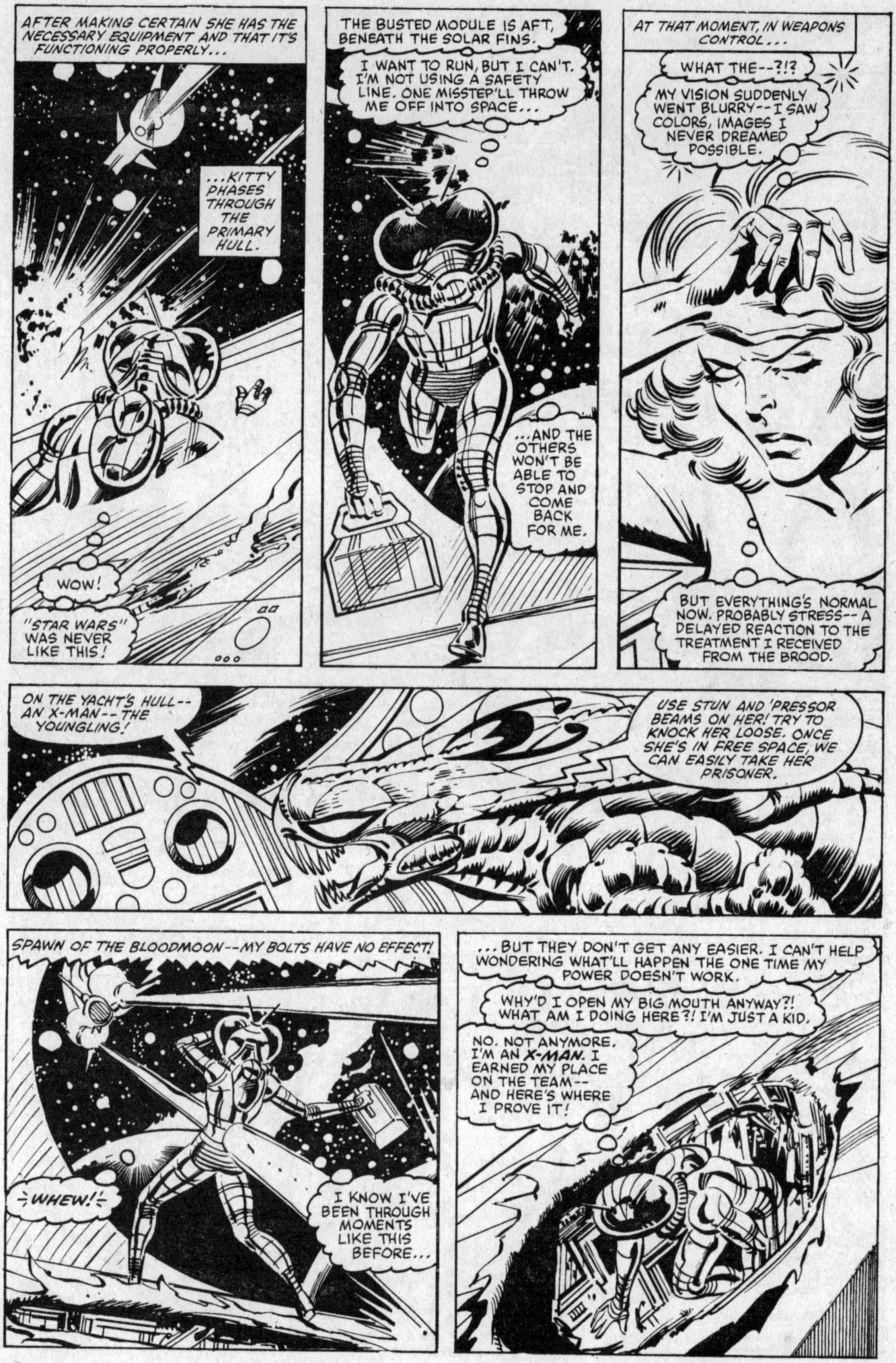
AFTER MAKING CERTAIN SHE HAS THE NECESSARY EQUIPMENT AND THAT IT'S FUNCTIONING PROPERLY...
...KITTY PHASES THROUGH THE PRIMARY HULL.
WOW!
"STAR WARS" WAS NEVER LIKE THIS!
THE BUSTED MODULE IS AFT, BENEATH THE SOLAR FINS.
I WANT TO RUN, BUT I CAN'T. I'M NOT USING A SAFETY LINE. ONE MISSTEP'LL THROW ME OFF INTO SPACE...
...AND THE OTHERS WON'T BE ABLE TO STOP AND COME BACK FOR ME.
AT THAT MOMENT, IN WEAPONS CONTROL...
WHAT THE--?!?
MY VISION SUDDENLY WENT BLURRY--I SAW COLORS, IMAGES I NEVER DREAMED POSSIBLE.
BUT EVERYTHING'S NORMAL NOW. PROBABLY STRESS--A DELAYED REACTION TO THE TREATMENT I RECEIVED FROM THE BROOD.
ON THE YACHT'S HULL--AN X-MAN--THE YOUNGLING!
USE STUN AND 'PRESSOR BEAMS ON HER! TRY TO KNOCK HER LOOSE. ONCE SHE'S IN FREE SPACE, WE CAN EASILY TAKE HER PRISONER.
SPAWN OF THE BLOODMOON--MY BOLTS HAVE NO EFFECT!
WHEW!
I KNOW I'VE BEEN THROUGH MOMENTS LIKE THIS BEFORE...
...BUT THEY DON'T GET ANY EASIER. I CAN'T HELP WONDERING WHAT'LL HAPPEN THE ONE TIME MY POWER DOESN'T WORK.
WHY'D I OPEN MY BIG MOUTH ANYWAY?! WHAT AM I DOING HERE?! I'M JUST A KID.
NO. NOT ANYMORE. I'M AN X-MAN. I EARNED MY PLACE ON THE TEAM--AND HERE'S WHERE I PROVE IT!

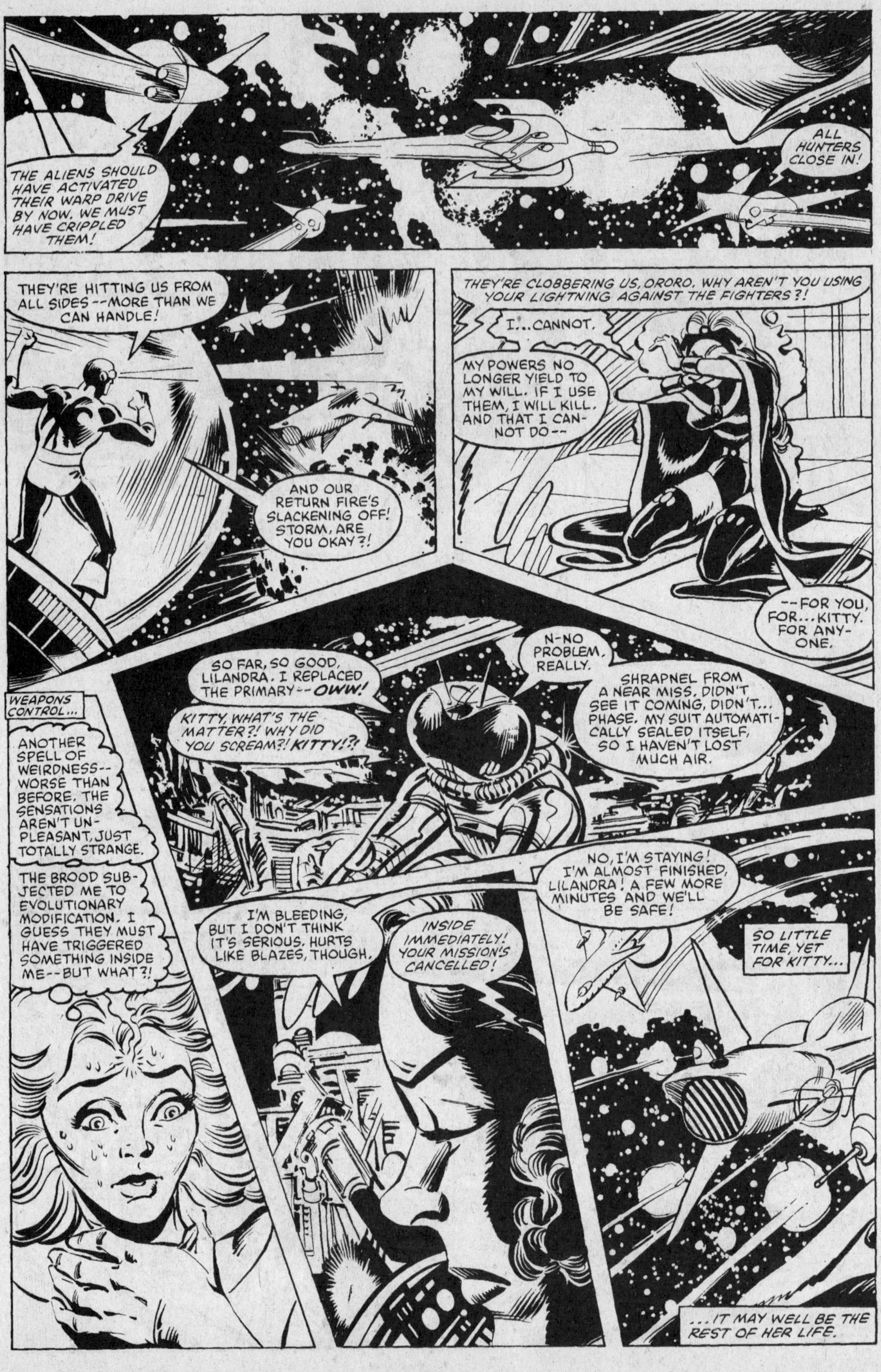
THE ALIENS SHOULD HAVE ACTIVATED THEIR WARP DRIVE BY NOW. WE MUST HAVE CRIPPLED THEM!
ALL HUNTERS CLOSE IN!
THEY'RE HITTING US FROM ALL SIDES--MORE THAN WE CAN HANDLE!
AND OUR RETURN FIRE'S SLACKENING OFF! STORM, ARE YOU OKAY?!
THEY'RE CLOBBERING US, ORORO. WHY AREN'T YOU USING YOUR LIGHTNING AGAINST THE FIGHTERS?!
I...CANNOT.
MY POWERS NO LONGER YIELD TO MY WILL. IF I USE THEM, I WILL KILL. AND THAT I CAN-NOT DO--
--FOR YOU, FOR...KITTY. FOR ANY-ONE.
WEAPONS CONTROL...
SO FAR, SO GOOD, LILANDRA. I REPLACED THE PRIMARY--OWW!
KITTY, WHAT'S THE MATTER?! WHY DID YOU SCREAM?! KITTY!?!
N-NO PROBLEM, REALLY.
SHRAPNEL FROM A NEAR MISS. DIDN'T SEE IT COMING, DIDN'T... PHASE. MY SUIT AUTOMATI-CALLY SEALED ITSELF, SO I HAVEN'T LOST MUCH AIR.
ANOTHER SPELL OF WEIRDNESS-- WORSE THAN BEFORE. THE SENSATIONS AREN'T UN-PLEASANT, JUST TOTALLY STRANGE.
THE BROOD SUB-JECTED ME TO EVOLUTIONARY MODIFICATION. I GUESS THEY MUST HAVE TRIGGERED SOMETHING INSIDE ME--BUT WHAT?!
I'M BLEEDING, BUT I DON'T THINK IT'S SERIOUS. HURTS LIKE BLAZES, THOUGH.
INSIDE IMMEDIATELY! YOUR MISSION'S CANCELLED!
NO, I'M STAYING! I'M ALMOST FINISHED, LILANDRA! A FEW MORE MINUTES AND WE'LL BE SAFE!
SO LITTLE TIME, YET FOR KITTY...
...IT MAY WELL BE THE REST OF HER LIFE.

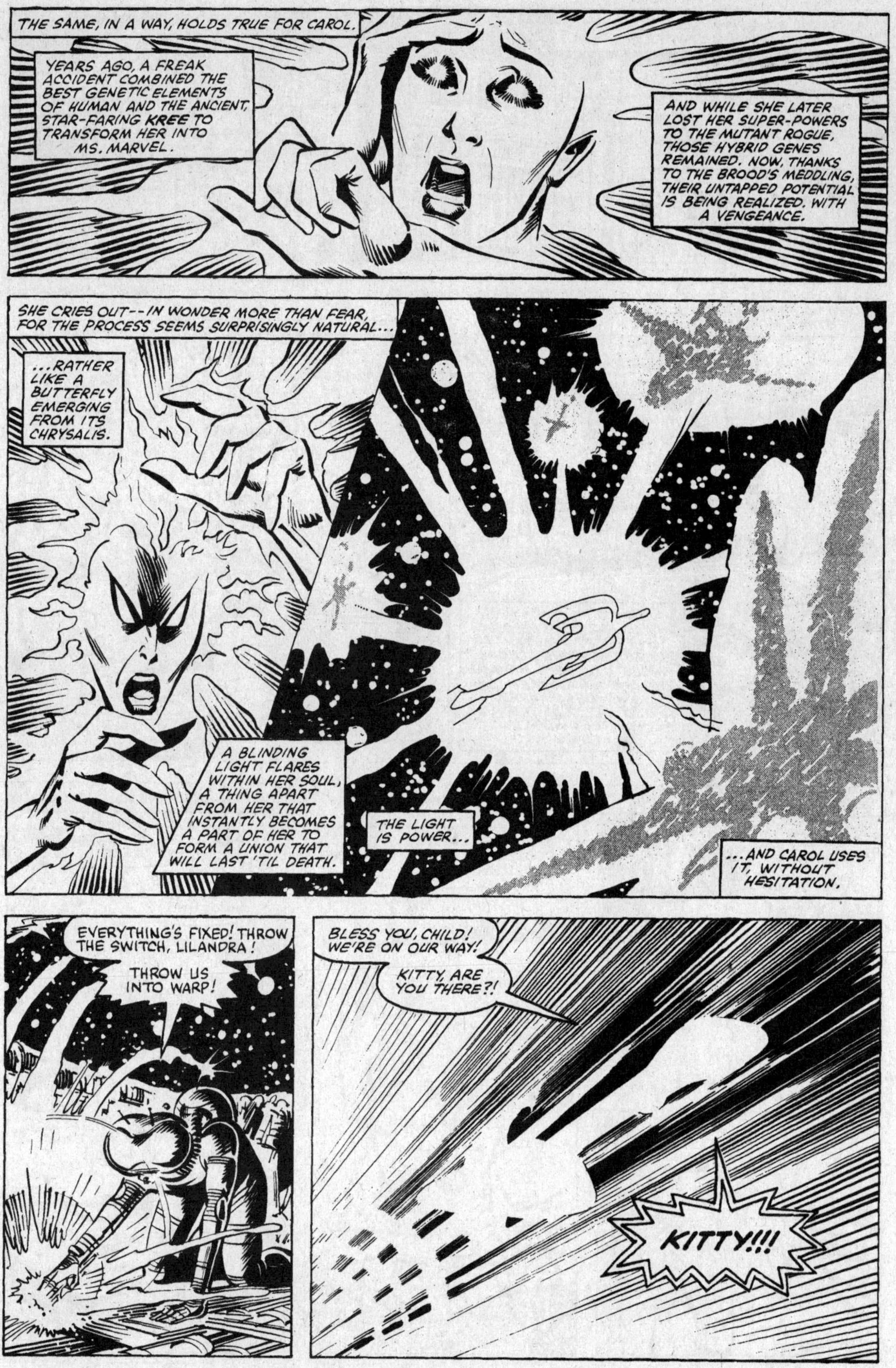

THE SAME, IN A WAY, HOLDS TRUE FOR CAROL.
YEARS AGO, A FREAK ACCIDENT COMBINED THE BEST GENETIC ELEMENTS OF HUMAN AND THE ANCIENT, STAR-FARING KREE TO TRANSFORM HER INTO MS. MARVEL.
AND WHILE SHE LATER LOST HER SUPER-POWERS TO THE MUTANT ROGUE, THOSE HYBRID GENES REMAINED. NOW, THANKS TO THE BROOD'S MEDDLING, THEIR UNTAPPED POTENTIAL IS BEING REALIZED. WITH A VENGEANCE.
SHE CRIES OUT--IN WONDER MORE THAN FEAR, FOR THE PROCESS SEEMS SURPRISINGLY NATURAL...
...RATHER LIKE A BUTTERFLY EMERGING FROM ITS CHRYSALIS.
A BLINDING LIGHT FLARES WITHIN HER SOUL, A THING APART FROM HER THAT INSTANTLY BECOMES A PART OF HER TO FORM A UNION THAT WILL LAST 'TIL DEATH.
THE LIGHT IS POWER...
...AND CAROL USES IT, WITHOUT HESITATION.
EVERYTHING'S FIXED! THROW THE SWITCH, LILANDRA!
THROW US INTO WARP!
BLESS YOU, CHILD! WE'RE ON OUR WAY!
KITTY, ARE YOU THERE?!
KITTY!!!

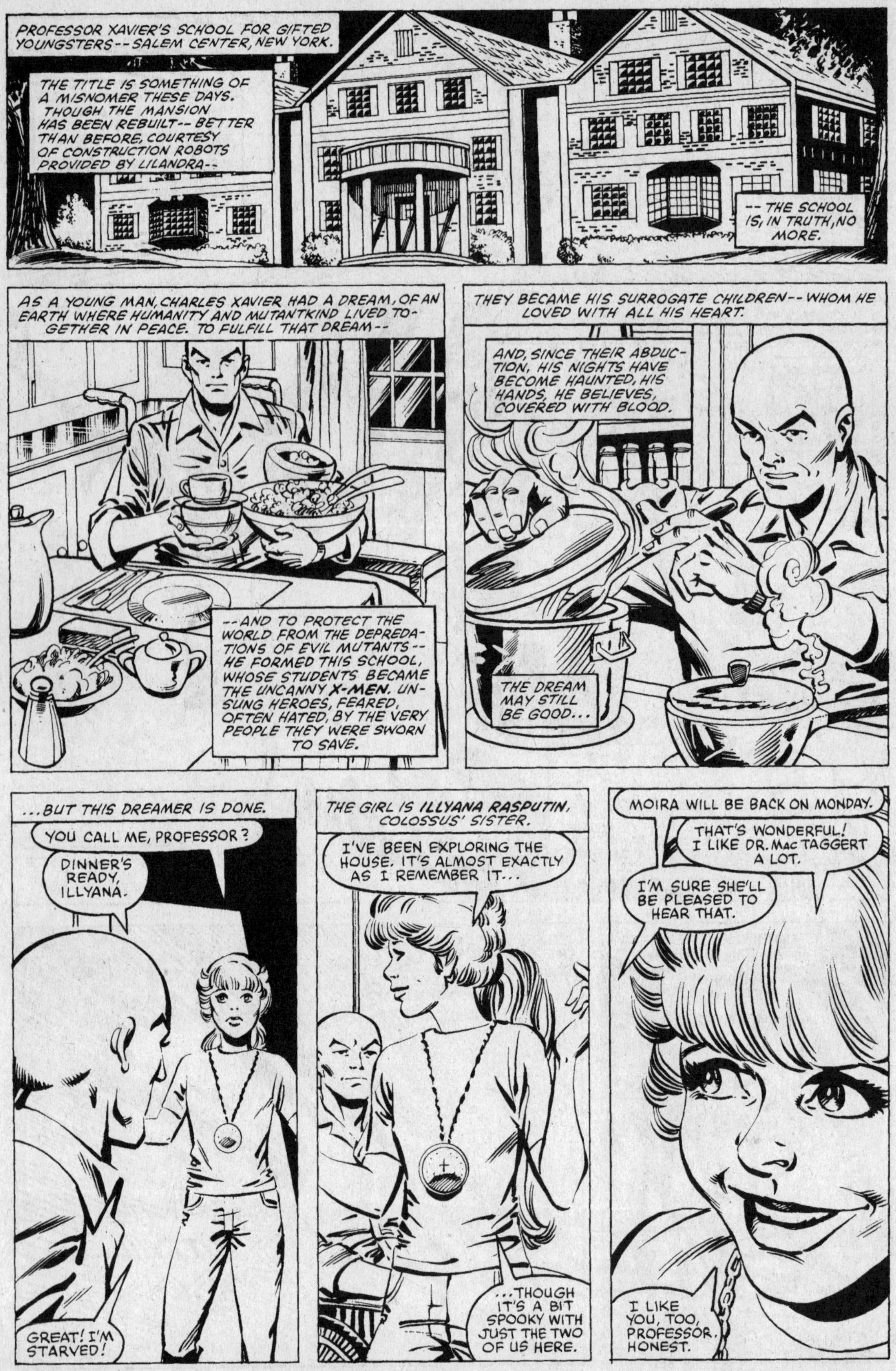
PROFESSOR XAVIER'S SCHOOL FOR GIFTED YOUNGSTERS--SALEM CENTER, NEW YORK.
THE TITLE IS SOMETHING OF A MISNOMER THESE DAYS. THOUGH THE MANSION HAS BEEN REBUILT-- BETTER THAN BEFORE, COURTESY OF CONSTRUCTION ROBOTS PROVIDED BY LILANDRA--
--THE SCHOOL IS, IN TRUTH, NO MORE.
AS A YOUNG MAN, CHARLES XAVIER HAD A DREAM, OF AN EARTH WHERE HUMANITY AND MUTANTKIND LIVED TOGETHER IN PEACE. TO FULFILL THAT DREAM--
--AND TO PROTECT THE WORLD FROM THE DEPREDATIONS OF EVIL MUTANTS--HE FORMED THIS SCHOOL, WHOSE STUDENTS BECAME THE UNCANNY X-MEN. UNSUNG HEROES, FEARED, OFTEN HATED, BY THE VERY PEOPLE THEY WERE SWORN TO SAVE.
THEY BECAME HIS SURROGATE CHILDREN--WHOM HE LOVED WITH ALL HIS HEART.
AND, SINCE THEIR ABDUCTION, HIS NIGHTS HAVE BECOME HAUNTED, HIS HANDS, HE BELIEVES, COVERED WITH BLOOD.
THE DREAM MAY STILL BE GOOD...
...BUT THIS DREAMER IS DONE.
YOU CALL ME, PROFESSOR?
DINNER'S READY, ILLYANA.
GREAT! I'M STARVED!
THE GIRL IS ILLYANA RASPUTIN, COLOSSUS' SISTER.
I'VE BEEN EXPLORING THE HOUSE. IT'S ALMOST EXACTLY AS I REMEMBER IT...
...THOUGH IT'S A BIT SPOOKY WITH JUST THE TWO OF US HERE.
MOIRA WILL BE BACK ON MONDAY.
THAT'S WONDERFUL! I LIKE DR. MacTAGGERT A LOT.
I'M SURE SHE'LL BE PLEASED TO HEAR THAT.
I LIKE YOU, TOO, PROFESSOR. HONEST.

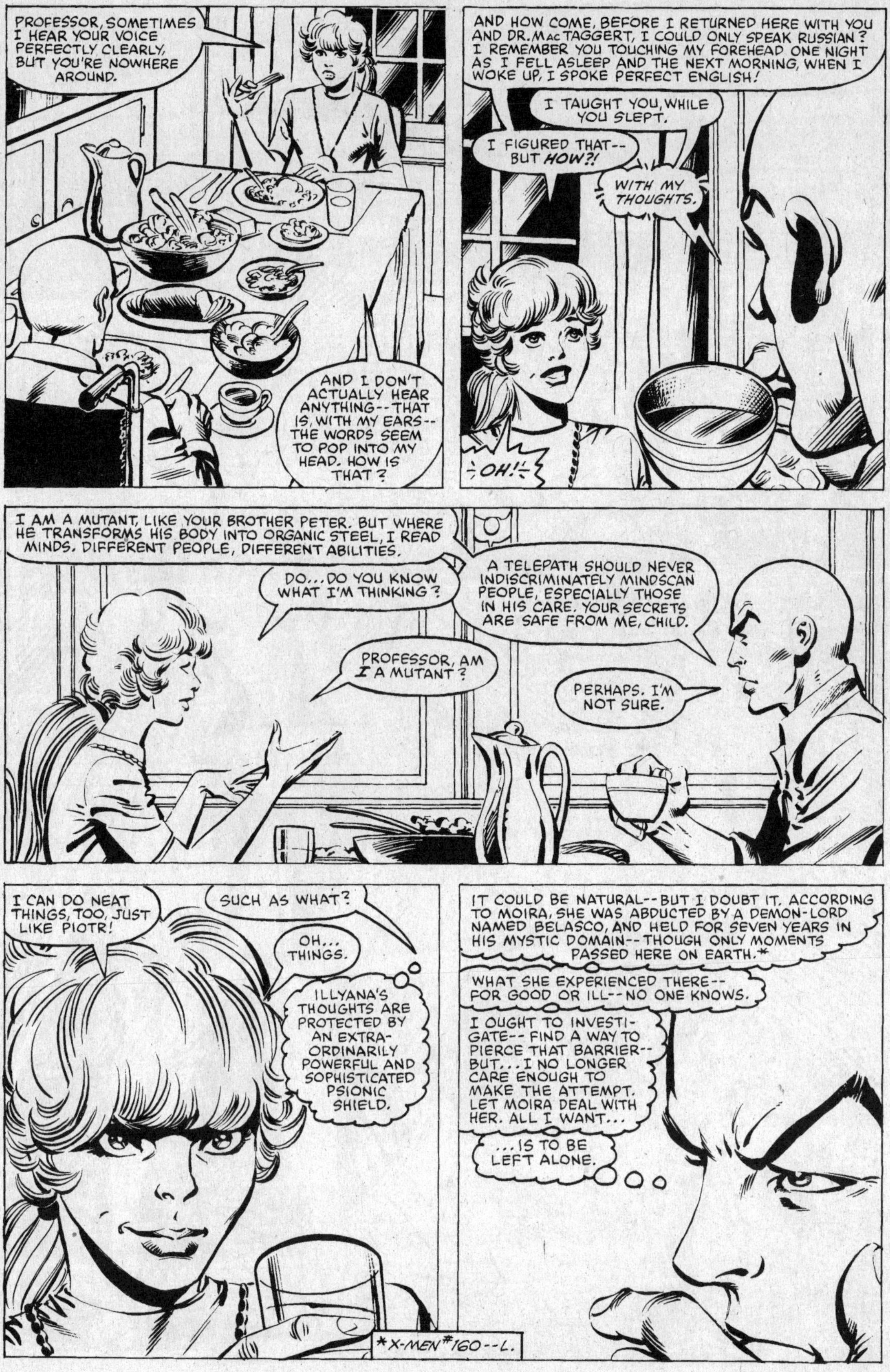
PROFESSOR, SOMETIMES I HEAR YOUR VOICE PERFECTLY CLEARLY, BUT YOU'RE NOWHERE AROUND.
AND I DON'T ACTUALLY HEAR ANYTHING--THAT IS, WITH MY EARS--THE WORDS SEEM TO POP INTO MY HEAD. HOW IS THAT?
AND HOW COME, BEFORE I RETURNED HERE WITH YOU AND DR. MacTAGGERT, I COULD ONLY SPEAK RUSSIAN? I REMEMBER YOU TOUCHING MY FOREHEAD ONE NIGHT AS I FELL ASLEEP AND THE NEXT MORNING, WHEN I WOKE UP, I SPOKE PERFECT ENGLISH!
I TAUGHT YOU, WHILE YOU SLEPT.
I FIGURED THAT--BUT HOW?!
WITH MY THOUGHTS.
OH!
I AM A MUTANT, LIKE YOUR BROTHER PETER. BUT WHERE HE TRANSFORMS HIS BODY INTO ORGANIC STEEL, I READ MINDS. DIFFERENT PEOPLE, DIFFERENT ABILITIES.
DO... DO YOU KNOW WHAT I'M THINKING?
A TELEPATH SHOULD NEVER INDISCRIMINATELY MINDSCAN PEOPLE, ESPECIALLY THOSE IN HIS CARE. YOUR SECRETS ARE SAFE FROM ME, CHILD.
PROFESSOR, AM I A MUTANT?
PERHAPS. I'M NOT SURE.
I CAN DO NEAT THINGS, TOO, JUST LIKE PIOTR!
SUCH AS WHAT?
OH... THINGS.
ILLYANA'S THOUGHTS ARE PROTECTED BY AN EXTRA-ORDINARILY POWERFUL AND SOPHISTICATED PSIONIC SHIELD.
IT COULD BE NATURAL--BUT I DOUBT IT. ACCORDING TO MOIRA, SHE WAS ABDUCTED BY A DEMON-LORD NAMED BELASCO, AND HELD FOR SEVEN YEARS IN HIS MYSTIC DOMAIN--THOUGH ONLY MOMENTS PASSED HERE ON EARTH.*
WHAT SHE EXPERIENCED THERE--FOR GOOD OR ILL--NO ONE KNOWS.
I OUGHT TO INVESTI-GATE--FIND A WAY TO PIERCE THAT BARRIER--BUT... I NO LONGER CARE ENOUGH TO MAKE THE ATTEMPT. LET MOIRA DEAL WITH HER. ALL I WANT...
...IS TO BE LEFT ALONE.
*X-MEN #160--L.

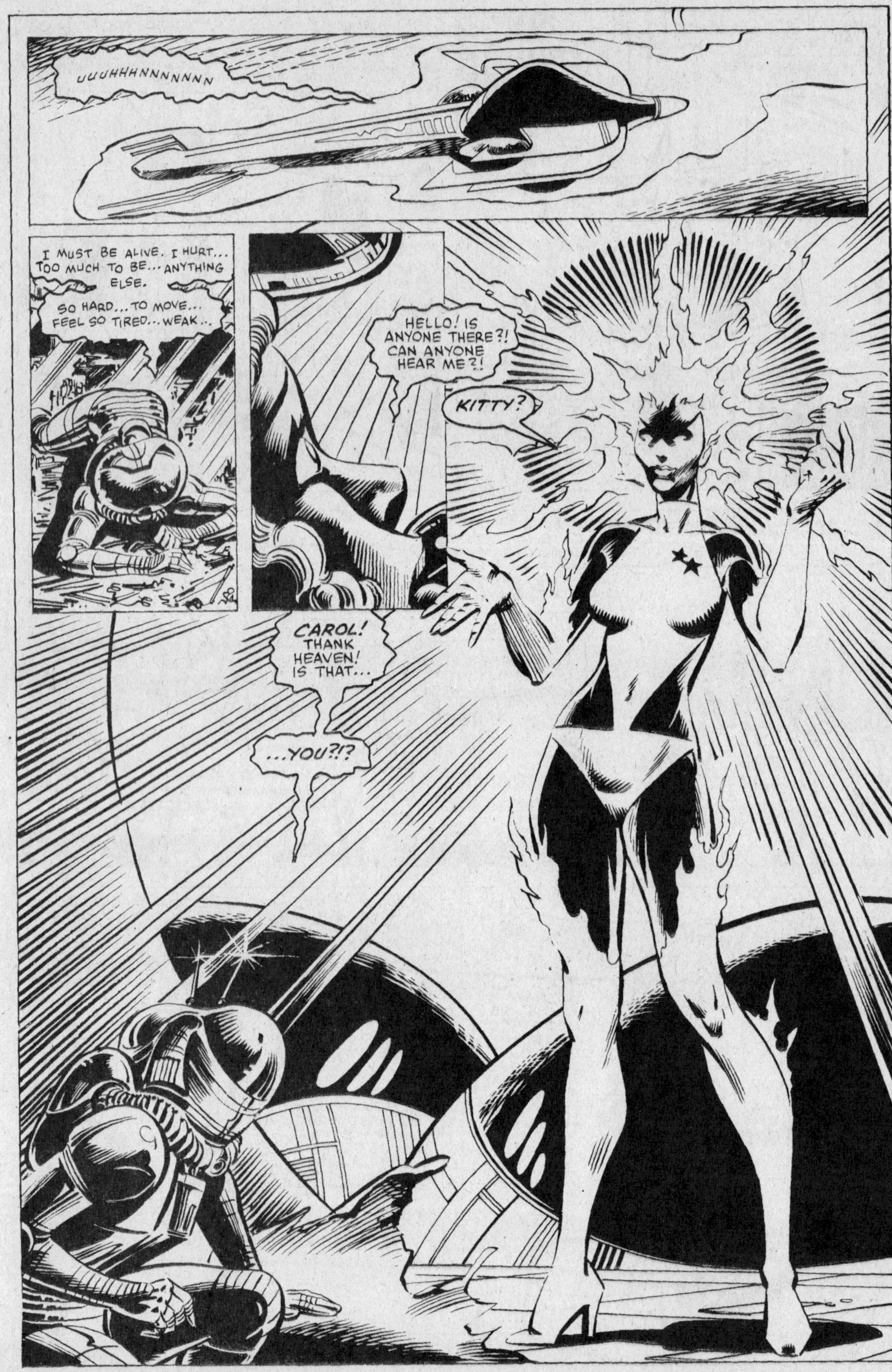
UUUHHHNNNNNNN
I MUST BE ALIVE. I HURT... TOO MUCH TO BE... ANYTHING ELSE.
SO HARD... TO MOVE... FEEL SO TIRED... WEAK...
HELLO! IS ANYONE THERE?! CAN ANYONE HEAR ME?!
KITTY?
CAROL! THANK HEAVEN! IS THAT...
...YOU?!?

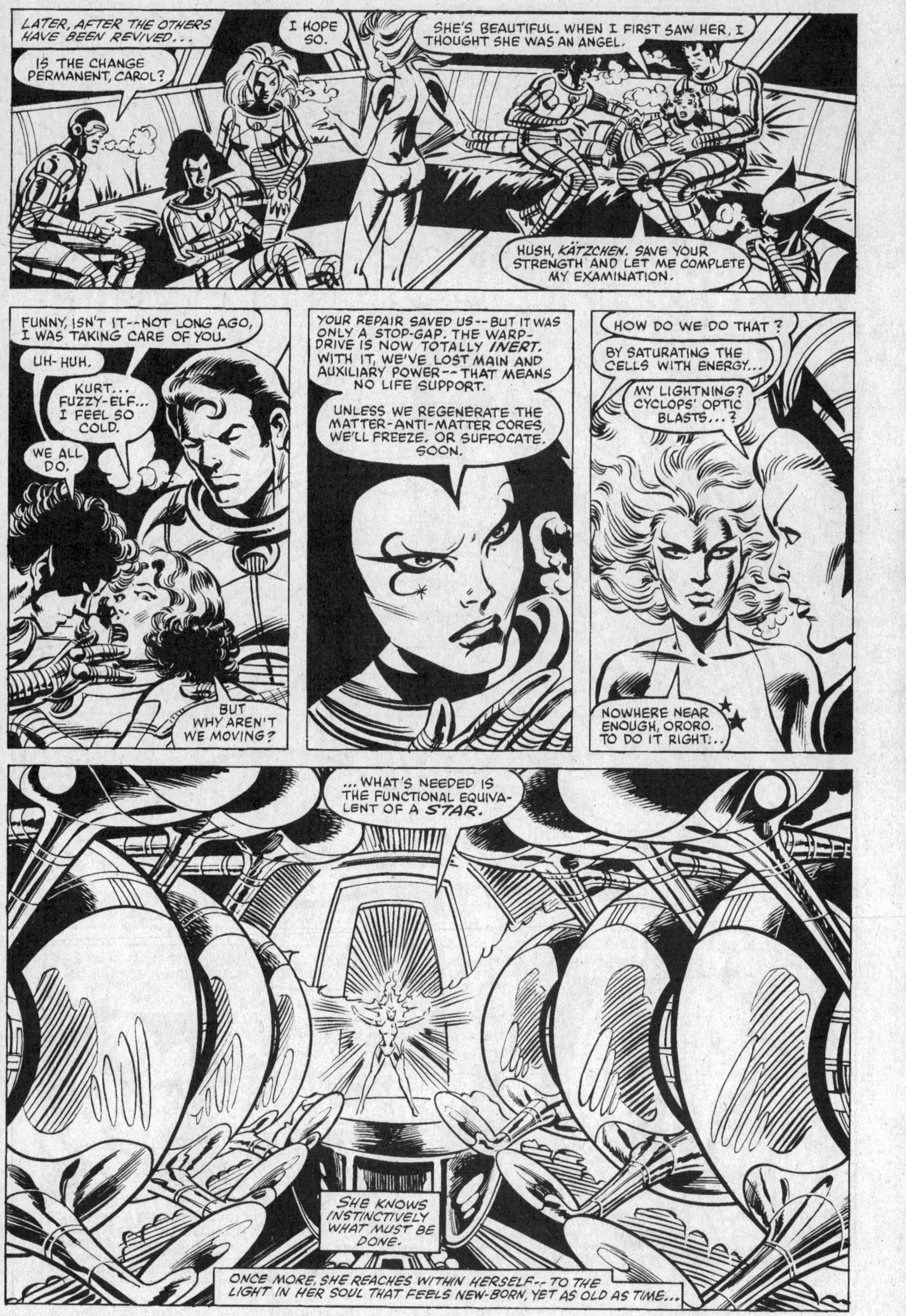
LATER, AFTER THE OTHERS HAVE BEEN REVIVED...
IS THE CHANGE PERMANENT, CAROL?
I HOPE SO.
SHE'S BEAUTIFUL. WHEN I FIRST SAW HER, I THOUGHT SHE WAS AN ANGEL.
HUSH, KÄTZCHEN. SAVE YOUR STRENGTH AND LET ME COMPLETE MY EXAMINATION.
FUNNY, ISN'T IT--NOT LONG AGO, I WAS TAKING CARE OF YOU.
UH-HUH.
KURT... FUZZY-ELF... I FEEL SO COLD.
WE ALL DO.
BUT WHY AREN'T WE MOVING?
YOUR REPAIR SAVED US--BUT IT WAS ONLY A STOP-GAP. THE WARP-DRIVE IS NOW TOTALLY INERT. WITH IT, WE'VE LOST MAIN AND AUXILIARY POWER--THAT MEANS NO LIFE SUPPORT.
UNLESS WE REGENERATE THE MATTER-ANTI-MATTER CORES, WE'LL FREEZE. OR SUFFOCATE. SOON.
HOW DO WE DO THAT?
BY SATURATING THE CELLS WITH ENERGY...
MY LIGHTNING? CYCLOPS' OPTIC BLASTS...?
NOWHERE NEAR ENOUGH, ORORO. TO DO IT RIGHT...
...WHAT'S NEEDED IS THE FUNCTIONAL EQUIVALENT OF A STAR.
SHE KNOWS INSTINCTIVELY WHAT MUST BE DONE.
ONCE MORE, SHE REACHES WITHIN HERSELF--TO THE LIGHT IN HER SOUL THAT FEELS NEW-BORN, YET AS OLD AS TIME...

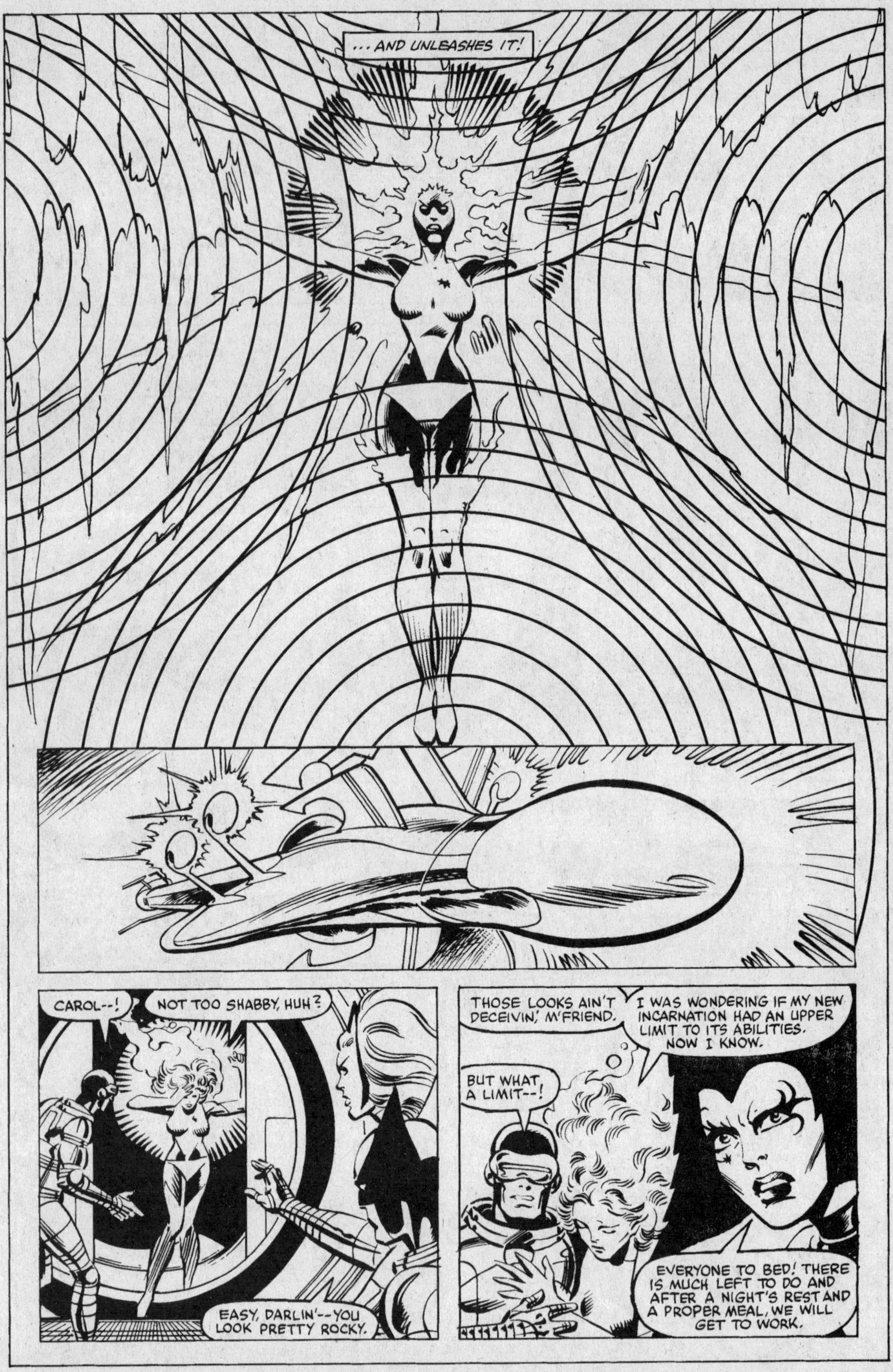
...AND UNLEASHES IT!
CAROL--!
NOT TOO SHABBY, HUH?
EASY, DARLIN'--YOU LOOK PRETTY ROCKY.
THOSE LOOKS AIN'T DECEIVIN,' M'FRIEND.
I WAS WONDERING IF MY NEW INCARNATION HAD AN UPPER LIMIT TO ITS ABILITIES. NOW I KNOW.
BUT WHAT A LIMIT--!
EVERYONE TO BED! THERE IS MUCH LEFT TO DO AND AFTER A NIGHT'S REST AND A PROPER MEAL, WE WILL GET TO WORK.

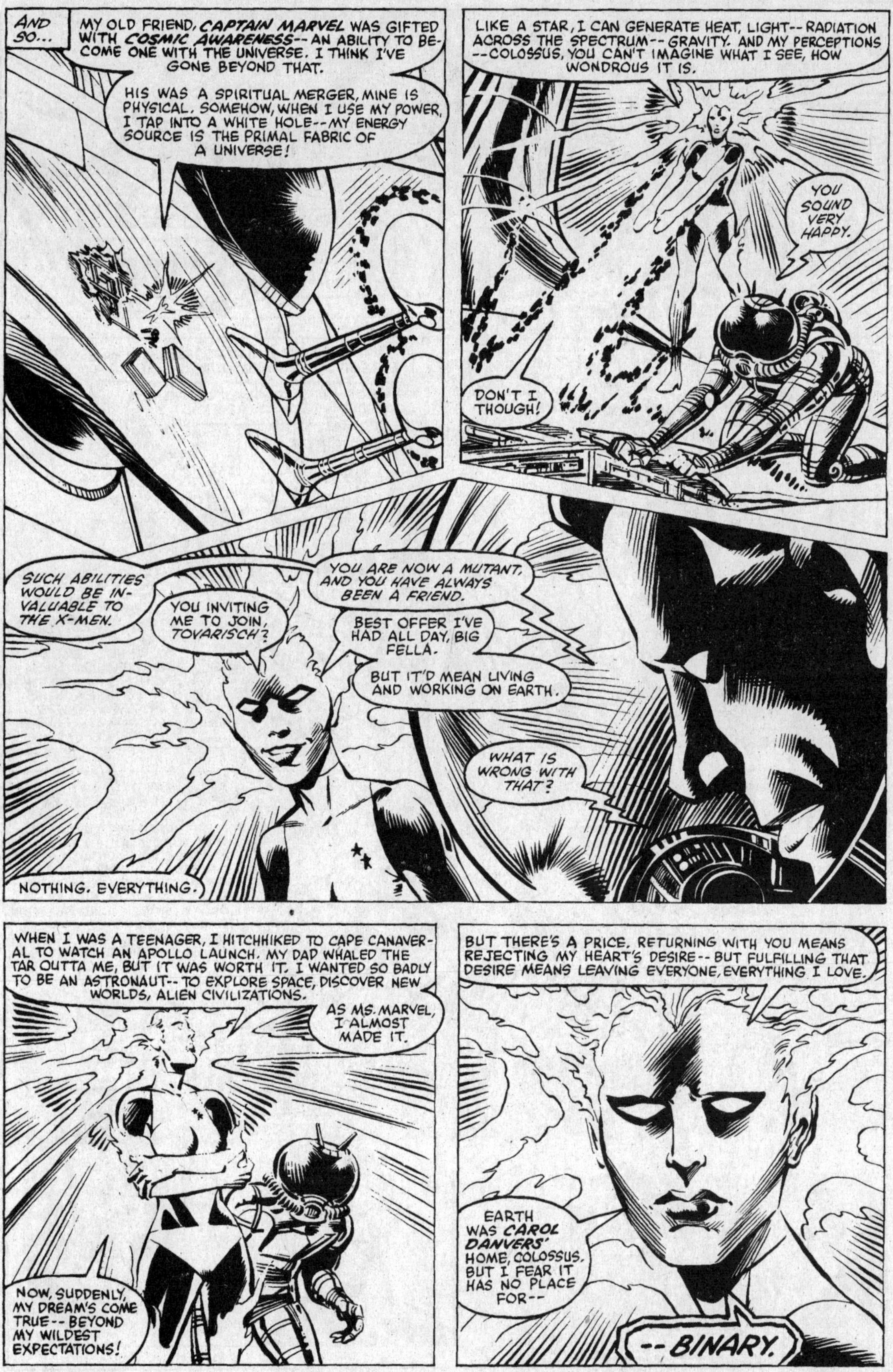

AND SO...
MY OLD FRIEND, CAPTAIN MARVEL WAS GIFTED WITH COSMIC AWARENESS-- AN ABILITY TO BECOME ONE WITH THE UNIVERSE. I THINK I'VE GONE BEYOND THAT.
HIS WAS A SPIRITUAL MERGER, MINE IS PHYSICAL. SOMEHOW, WHEN I USE MY POWER, I TAP INTO A WHITE HOLE--MY ENERGY SOURCE IS THE PRIMAL FABRIC OF A UNIVERSE!
LIKE A STAR, I CAN GENERATE HEAT, LIGHT-- RADIATION ACROSS THE SPECTRUM-- GRAVITY. AND MY PERCEPTIONS --COLOSSUS, YOU CAN'T IMAGINE WHAT I SEE, HOW WONDROUS IT IS.
YOU SOUND VERY HAPPY.
DON'T I THOUGH!
SUCH ABILITIES WOULD BE INVALUABLE TO THE X-MEN.
YOU ARE NOW A MUTANT, AND YOU HAVE ALWAYS BEEN A FRIEND.
YOU INVITING ME TO JOIN, TOVARISCH?
BEST OFFER I'VE HAD ALL DAY, BIG FELLA.
BUT IT'D MEAN LIVING AND WORKING ON EARTH.
WHAT IS WRONG WITH THAT?
NOTHING. EVERYTHING.
WHEN I WAS A TEENAGER, I HITCHHIKED TO CAPE CANAVERAL TO WATCH AN APOLLO LAUNCH. MY DAD WHALED THE TAR OUTTA ME, BUT IT WAS WORTH IT. I WANTED SO BADLY TO BE AN ASTRONAUT-- TO EXPLORE SPACE, DISCOVER NEW WORLDS, ALIEN CIVILIZATIONS.
AS MS. MARVEL, I ALMOST MADE IT.
NOW, SUDDENLY, MY DREAM'S COME TRUE-- BEYOND MY WILDEST EXPECTATIONS!
BUT THERE'S A PRICE. RETURNING WITH YOU MEANS REJECTING MY HEART'S DESIRE-- BUT FULFILLING THAT DESIRE MEANS LEAVING EVERYONE, EVERYTHING I LOVE.
EARTH WAS CAROL DANVERS' HOME, COLOSSUS. BUT I FEAR IT HAS NO PLACE FOR--
--BINARY.

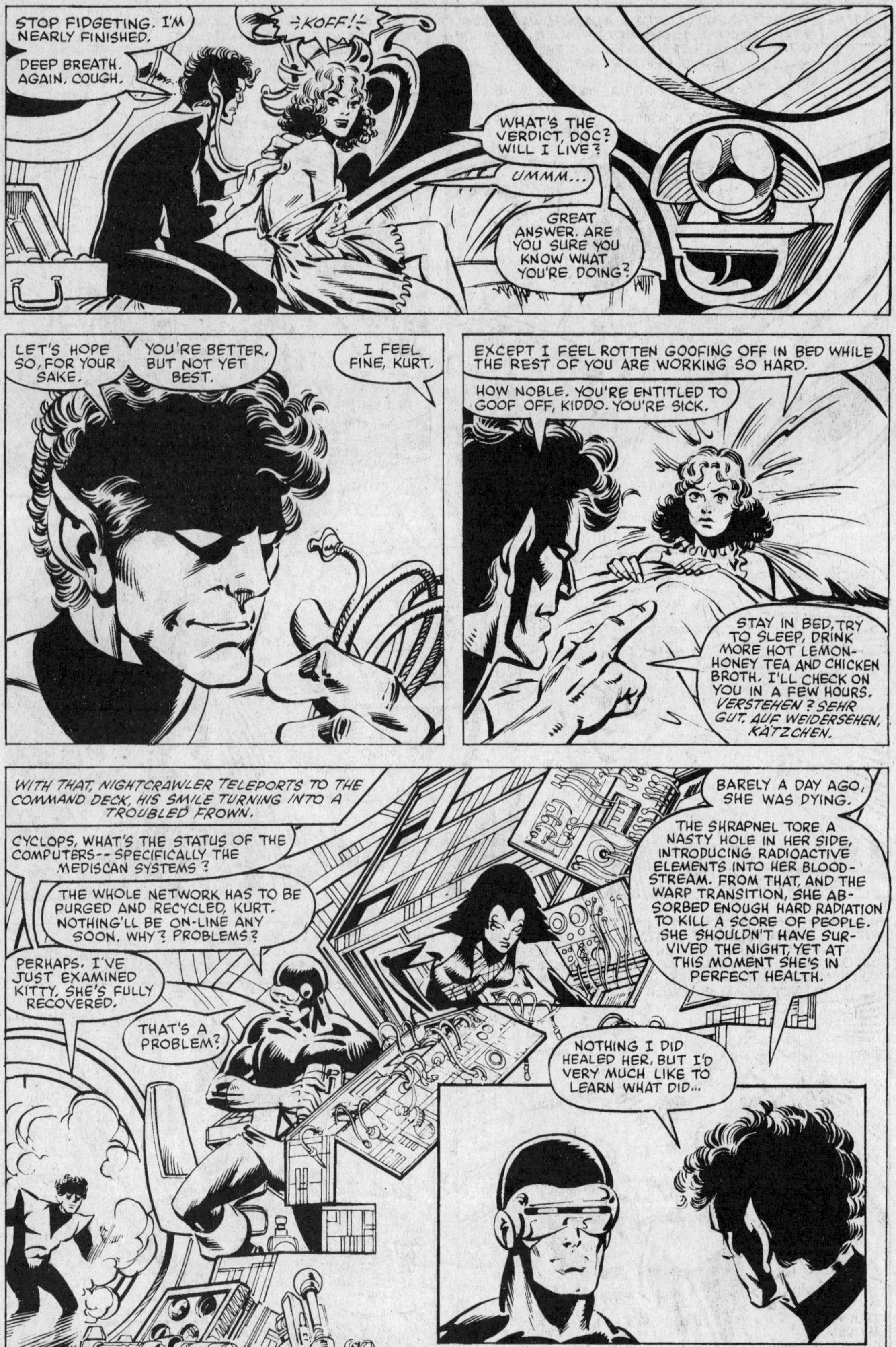
STOP FIDGETING. I'M NEARLY FINISHED.
DEEP BREATH. AGAIN. COUGH.
-KOFF!-
WHAT'S THE VERDICT, DOC? WILL I LIVE?
UMMM...
GREAT ANSWER. ARE YOU SURE YOU KNOW WHAT YOU'RE DOING?
LET'S HOPE SO, FOR YOUR SAKE.
YOU'RE BETTER, BUT NOT YET BEST.
I FEEL FINE, KURT.
EXCEPT I FEEL ROTTEN GOOFING OFF IN BED WHILE THE REST OF YOU ARE WORKING SO HARD.
HOW NOBLE. YOU'RE ENTITLED TO GOOF OFF, KIDDO. YOU'RE SICK.
STAY IN BED, TRY TO SLEEP, DRINK MORE HOT LEMON-HONEY TEA AND CHICKEN BROTH. I'LL CHECK ON YOU IN A FEW HOURS. VERSTEHEN? SEHR GUT. AUF WEIDERSEHEN, KÄTZCHEN.
WITH THAT, NIGHTCRAWLER TELEPORTS TO THE COMMAND DECK, HIS SMILE TURNING INTO A TROUBLED FROWN.
CYCLOPS, WHAT'S THE STATUS OF THE COMPUTERS-- SPECIFICALLY THE MEDISCAN SYSTEMS?
THE WHOLE NETWORK HAS TO BE PURGED AND RECYCLED, KURT. NOTHING'LL BE ON-LINE ANY SOON. WHY? PROBLEMS?
PERHAPS. I'VE JUST EXAMINED KITTY. SHE'S FULLY RECOVERED.
THAT'S A PROBLEM?
BARELY A DAY AGO, SHE WAS DYING.
THE SHRAPNEL TORE A NASTY HOLE IN HER SIDE, INTRODUCING RADIOACTIVE ELEMENTS INTO HER BLOOD-STREAM. FROM THAT, AND THE WARP TRANSITION, SHE ABSORBED ENOUGH HARD RADIATION TO KILL A SCORE OF PEOPLE. SHE SHOULDN'T HAVE SURVIVED THE NIGHT, YET AT THIS MOMENT SHE'S IN PERFECT HEALTH.
NOTHING I DID HEALED HER, BUT I'D VERY MUCH LIKE TO LEARN WHAT DID...

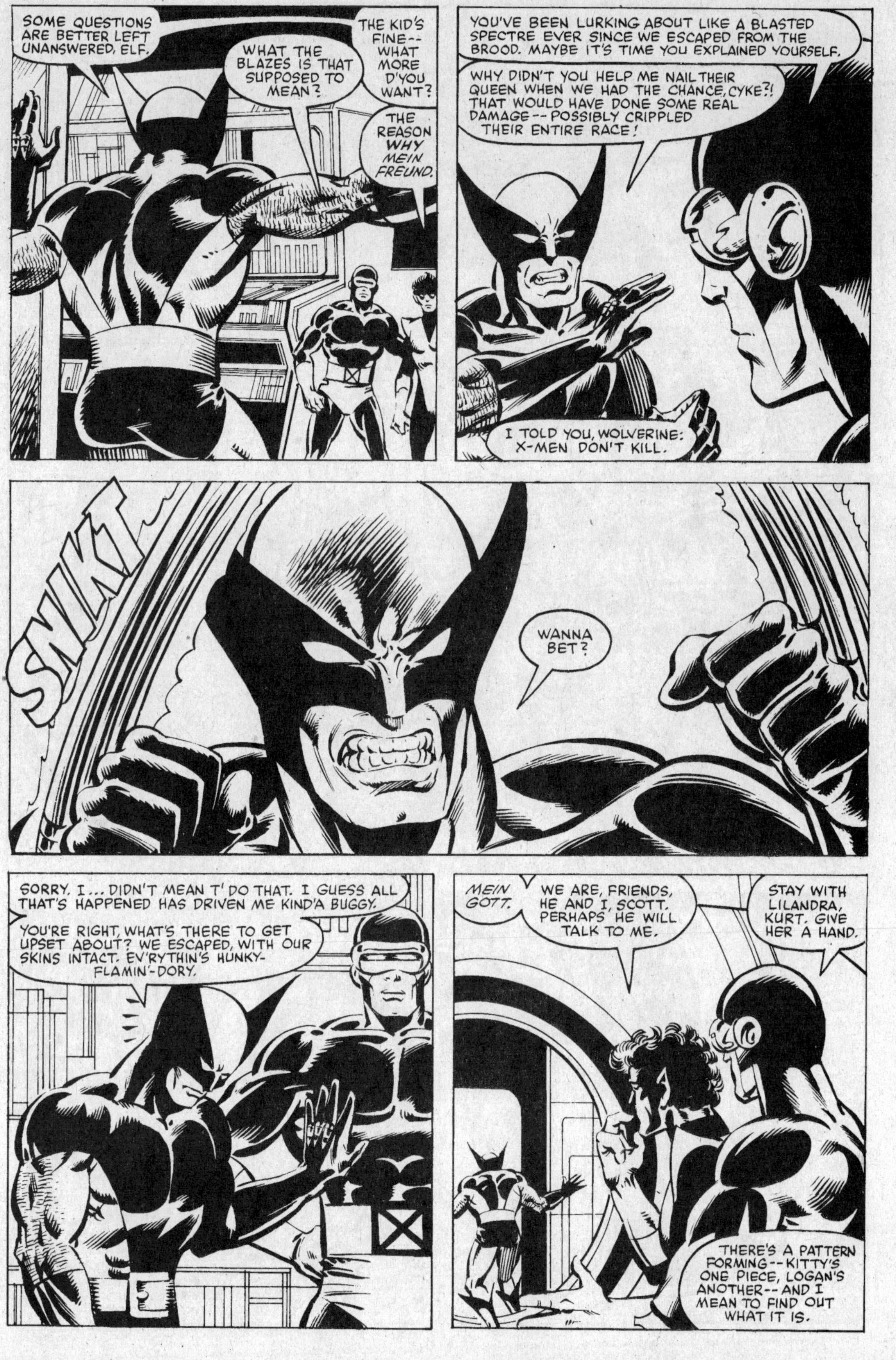

SOME QUESTIONS ARE BETTER LEFT UNANSWERED, ELF.
WHAT THE BLAZES IS THAT SUPPOSED TO MEAN?
THE KID'S FINE-- WHAT MORE D'YOU WANT?
THE REASON WHY MEIN FREUND.
YOU'VE BEEN LURKING ABOUT LIKE A BLASTED SPECTRE EVER SINCE WE ESCAPED FROM THE BROOD. MAYBE IT'S TIME YOU EXPLAINED YOURSELF.
WHY DIDN'T YOU HELP ME NAIL THEIR QUEEN WHEN WE HAD THE CHANCE, CYKE?! THAT WOULD HAVE DONE SOME REAL DAMAGE -- POSSIBLY CRIPPLED THEIR ENTIRE RACE!
I TOLD YOU, WOLVERINE: X-MEN DON'T KILL.
SNIKT
WANNA BET?
SORRY. I... DIDN'T MEAN T' DO THAT. I GUESS ALL THAT'S HAPPENED HAS DRIVEN ME KIND'A BUGGY.
YOU'RE RIGHT, WHAT'S THERE TO GET UPSET ABOUT? WE ESCAPED, WITH OUR SKINS INTACT. EV'RYTHIN'S HUNKY-FLAMIN'-DORY.
MEIN GOTT.
WE ARE, FRIENDS, HE AND I, SCOTT. PERHAPS HE WILL TALK TO ME.
STAY WITH LILANDRA, KURT. GIVE HER A HAND.
THERE'S A PATTERN FORMING--KITTY'S ONE PIECE, LOGAN'S ANOTHER-- AND I MEAN TO FIND OUT WHAT IT IS.

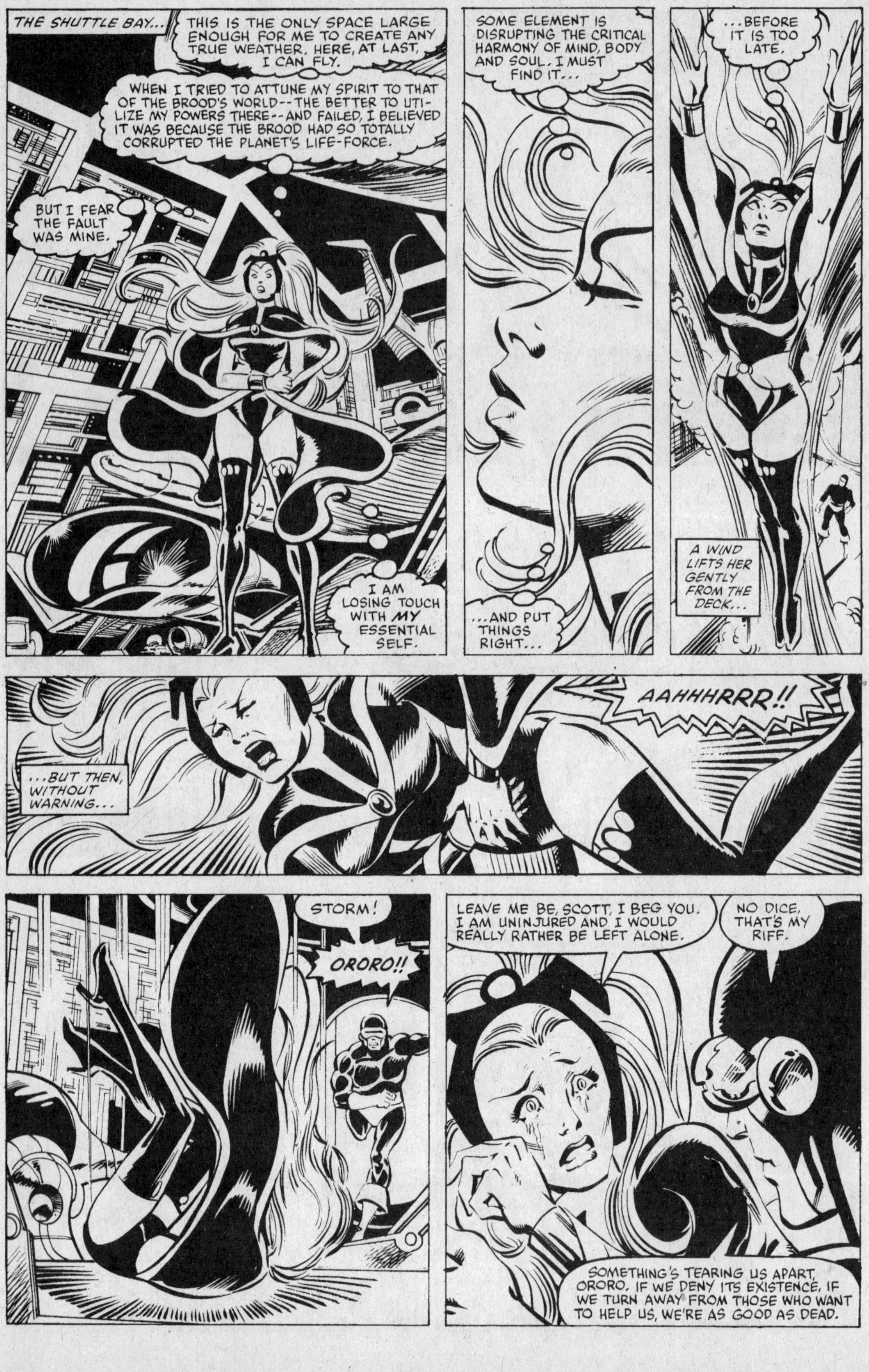
THE SHUTTLE BAY...
THIS IS THE ONLY SPACE LARGE ENOUGH FOR ME TO CREATE ANY TRUE WEATHER. HERE, AT LAST, I CAN FLY.
WHEN I TRIED TO ATTUNE MY SPIRIT TO THAT OF THE BROOD'S WORLD--THE BETTER TO UTILIZE MY POWERS THERE--AND FAILED, I BELIEVED IT WAS BECAUSE THE BROOD HAD SO TOTALLY CORRUPTED THE PLANET'S LIFE-FORCE.
BUT I FEAR THE FAULT WAS MINE.
I AM LOSING TOUCH WITH MY ESSENTIAL SELF.
SOME ELEMENT IS DISRUPTING THE CRITICAL HARMONY OF MIND, BODY AND SOUL. I MUST FIND IT...
...AND PUT THINGS RIGHT...
...BEFORE IT IS TOO LATE.
A WIND LIFTS HER GENTLY FROM THE DECK...
...BUT THEN, WITHOUT WARNING...
AAHHHRRR!!
STORM!
ORORO!!
LEAVE ME BE, SCOTT, I BEG YOU. I AM UNINJURED AND I WOULD REALLY RATHER BE LEFT ALONE.
NO DICE, THAT'S MY RIFF.
SOMETHING'S TEARING US APART, ORORO. IF WE DENY ITS EXISTENCE, IF WE TURN AWAY FROM THOSE WHO WANT TO HELP US, WE'RE AS GOOD AS DEAD.

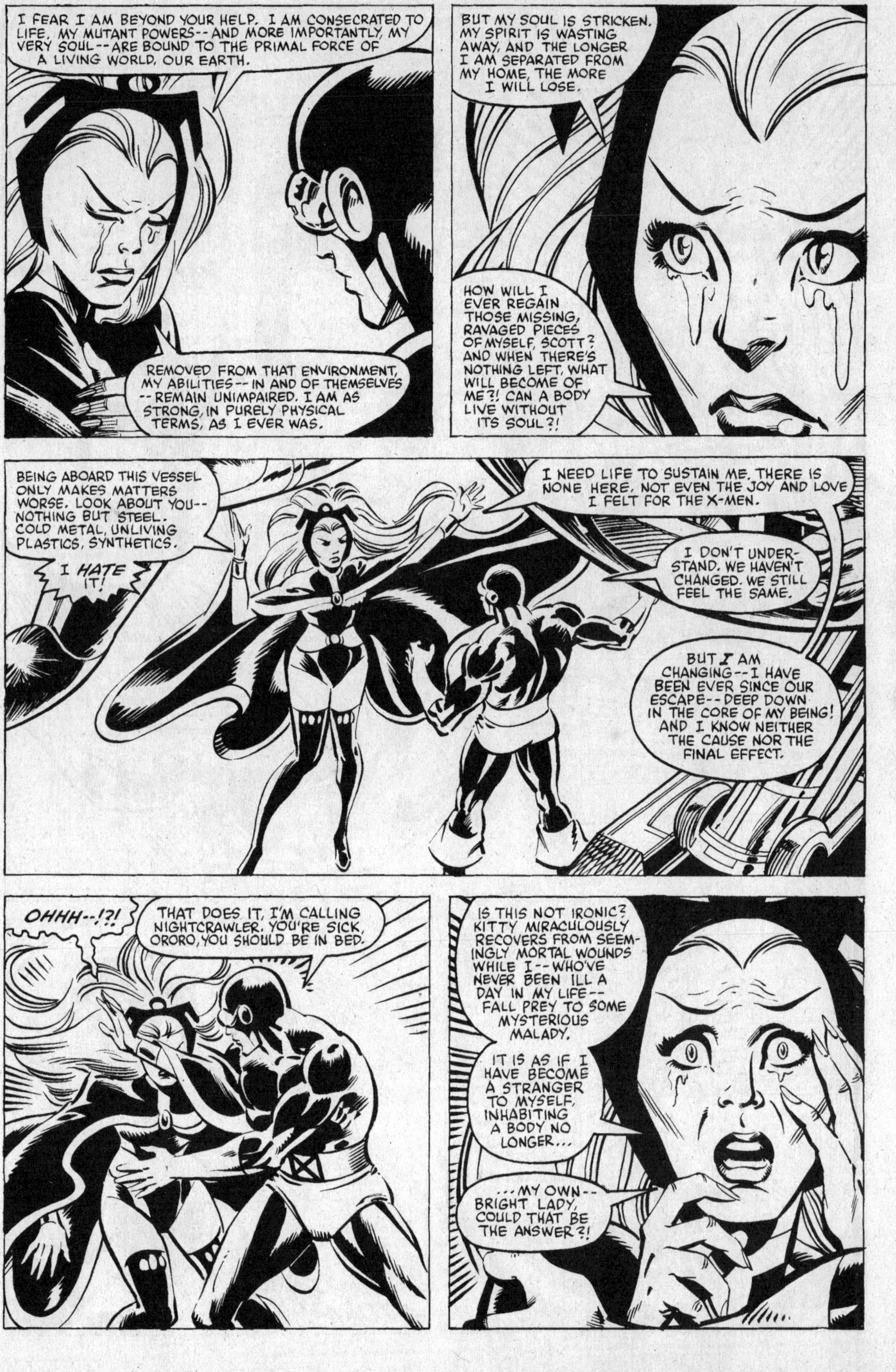
I FEAR I AM BEYOND YOUR HELP. I AM CONSECRATED TO LIFE. MY MUTANT POWERS--AND MORE IMPORTANTLY, MY VERY SOUL--ARE BOUND TO THE PRIMAL FORCE OF A LIVING WORLD, OUR EARTH.
REMOVED FROM THAT ENVIRONMENT, MY ABILITIES--IN AND OF THEMSELVES--REMAIN UNIMPAIRED. I AM AS STRONG, IN PURELY PHYSICAL TERMS, AS I EVER WAS.
BUT MY SOUL IS STRICKEN. MY SPIRIT IS WASTING AWAY, AND THE LONGER I AM SEPARATED FROM MY HOME, THE MORE I WILL LOSE.
HOW WILL I EVER REGAIN THOSE MISSING, RAVAGED PIECES OF MYSELF, SCOTT? AND WHEN THERE'S NOTHING LEFT, WHAT WILL BECOME OF ME?! CAN A BODY LIVE WITHOUT ITS SOUL?!
BEING ABOARD THIS VESSEL ONLY MAKES MATTERS WORSE. LOOK ABOUT YOU--NOTHING BUT STEEL. COLD METAL, UNLIVING PLASTICS, SYNTHETICS.
I *HATE* IT!
I NEED LIFE TO SUSTAIN ME. THERE IS NONE HERE. NOT EVEN THE JOY AND LOVE I FELT FOR THE X-MEN.
I DON'T UNDERSTAND. WE HAVEN'T CHANGED. WE STILL FEEL THE SAME.
BUT *I* AM CHANGING--I HAVE BEEN EVER SINCE OUR ESCAPE--DEEP DOWN IN THE CORE OF MY BEING! AND I KNOW NEITHER THE CAUSE NOR THE FINAL EFFECT.
OHHH--!?!
THAT DOES IT, I'M CALLING NIGHTCRAWLER. YOU'RE SICK, ORORO, YOU SHOULD BE IN BED.
IS THIS NOT IRONIC? KITTY MIRACULOUSLY RECOVERS FROM SEEMINGLY MORTAL WOUNDS WHILE I--WHO'VE NEVER BEEN ILL A DAY IN MY LIFE--FALL PREY TO SOME MYSTERIOUS MALADY.
IT IS AS IF I HAVE BECOME A STRANGER TO MYSELF, INHABITING A BODY NO LONGER...
...MY OWN--BRIGHT LADY, COULD THAT BE THE ANSWER?!

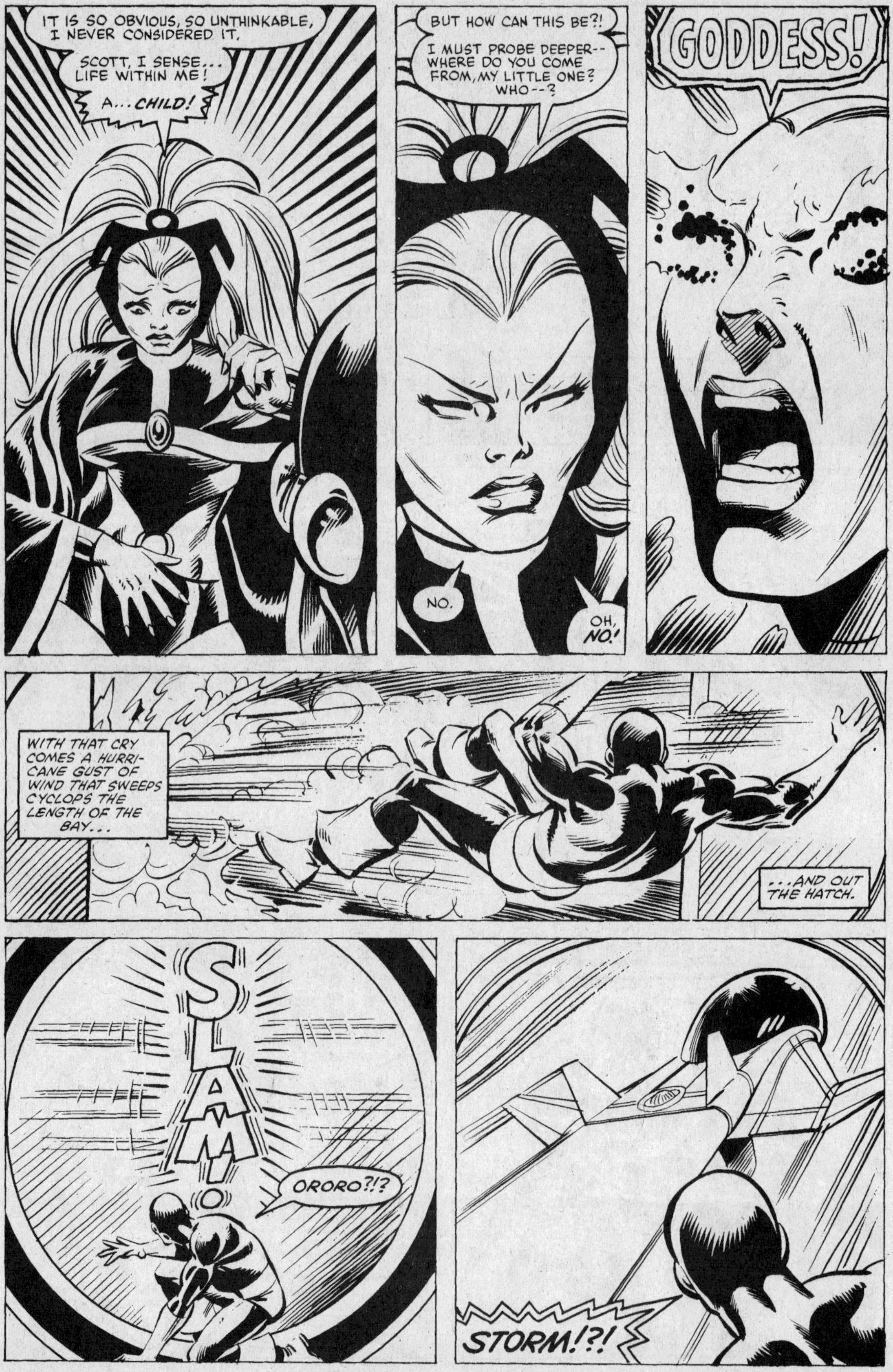
IT IS SO OBVIOUS, SO UNTHINKABLE, I NEVER CONSIDERED IT.
SCOTT, I SENSE... LIFE WITHIN ME!
A... CHILD!
BUT HOW CAN THIS BE?!
I MUST PROBE DEEPER-- WHERE DO YOU COME FROM, MY LITTLE ONE? WHO--?
NO.
OH, NO!
GODDESS!
WITH THAT CRY COMES A HURRICANE GUST OF WIND THAT SWEEPS CYCLOPS THE LENGTH OF THE BAY...
...AND OUT THE HATCH.
SLAM
ORORO?!?
STORM!?!

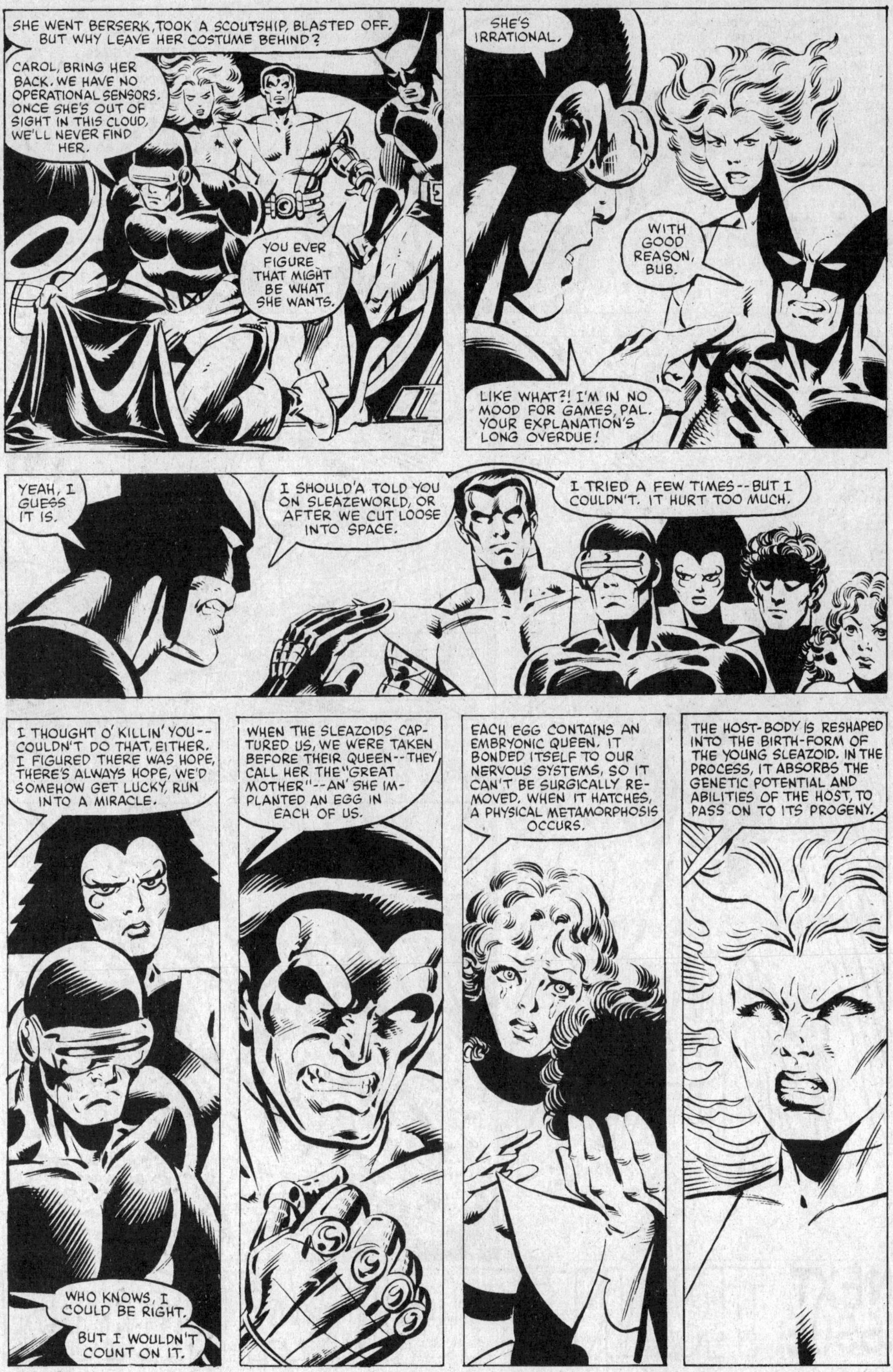

SHE WENT BERSERK, TOOK A SCOUTSHIP, BLASTED OFF. BUT WHY LEAVE HER COSTUME BEHIND?
CAROL, BRING HER BACK. WE HAVE NO OPERATIONAL SENSORS. ONCE SHE'S OUT OF SIGHT IN THIS CLOUD, WE'LL NEVER FIND HER.
YOU EVER FIGURE THAT MIGHT BE WHAT SHE WANTS.
SHE'S IRRATIONAL.
WITH GOOD REASON, BUB.
LIKE WHAT?! I'M IN NO MOOD FOR GAMES, PAL. YOUR EXPLANATION'S LONG OVERDUE!
YEAH, I GUESS IT IS.
I SHOULD'A TOLD YOU ON SLEAZEWORLD, OR AFTER WE CUT LOOSE INTO SPACE.
I TRIED A FEW TIMES--BUT I COULDN'T. IT HURT TOO MUCH.
I THOUGHT O' KILLIN' YOU--COULDN'T DO THAT, EITHER. I FIGURED THERE WAS HOPE, THERE'S ALWAYS HOPE, WE'D SOMEHOW GET LUCKY, RUN INTO A MIRACLE.
WHO KNOWS, I COULD BE RIGHT.
BUT I WOULDN'T COUNT ON IT.
WHEN THE SLEAZOIDS CAPTURED US, WE WERE TAKEN BEFORE THEIR QUEEN--THEY CALL HER THE "GREAT MOTHER"--AN' SHE IMPLANTED AN EGG IN EACH OF US.
EACH EGG CONTAINS AN EMBRYONIC QUEEN. IT BONDED ITSELF TO OUR NERVOUS SYSTEMS, SO IT CAN'T BE SURGICALLY REMOVED. WHEN IT HATCHES, A PHYSICAL METAMORPHOSIS OCCURS.
THE HOST-BODY IS RESHAPED INTO THE BIRTH-FORM OF THE YOUNG SLEAZOID. IN THE PROCESS, IT ABSORBS THE GENETIC POTENTIAL AND ABILITIES OF THE HOST, TO PASS ON TO ITS PROGENY.

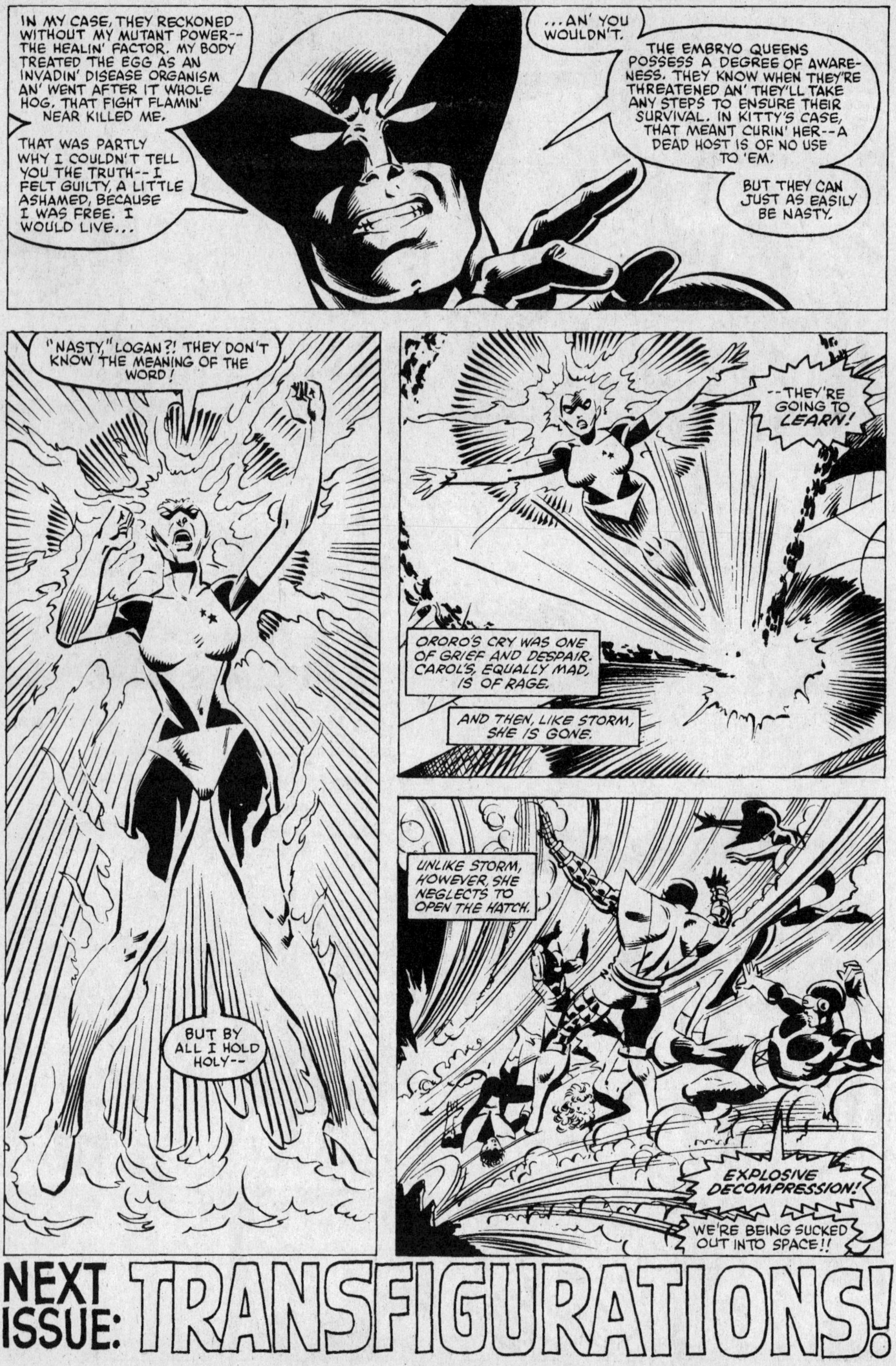
IN MY CASE, THEY RECKONED WITHOUT MY MUTANT POWER-- THE HEALIN' FACTOR. MY BODY TREATED THE EGG AS AN INVADIN' DISEASE ORGANISM AN' WENT AFTER IT WHOLE HOG. THAT FIGHT FLAMIN' NEAR KILLED ME.
THAT WAS PARTLY WHY I COULDN'T TELL YOU THE TRUTH-- I FELT GUILTY, A LITTLE ASHAMED, BECAUSE I WAS FREE. I WOULD LIVE...
...AN' YOU WOULDN'T.
THE EMBRYO QUEENS POSSESS A DEGREE OF AWARENESS. THEY KNOW WHEN THEY'RE THREATENED AN' THEY'LL TAKE ANY STEPS TO ENSURE THEIR SURVIVAL. IN KITTY'S CASE, THAT MEANT CURIN' HER--A DEAD HOST IS OF NO USE TO 'EM.
BUT THEY CAN JUST AS EASILY BE NASTY.
"NASTY," LOGAN?! THEY DON'T KNOW THE MEANING OF THE WORD!
BUT BY ALL I HOLD HOLY--
--THEY'RE GOING TO LEARN!
ORORO'S CRY WAS ONE OF GRIEF AND DESPAIR. CAROL'S, EQUALLY MAD, IS OF RAGE.
AND THEN, LIKE STORM, SHE IS GONE.
UNLIKE STORM, HOWEVER, SHE NEGLECTS TO OPEN THE HATCH.
EXPLOSIVE DECOMPRESSION!
WE'RE BEING SUCKED OUT INTO SPACE!!

NEXT ISSUE: TRANSFIGURATIONS!

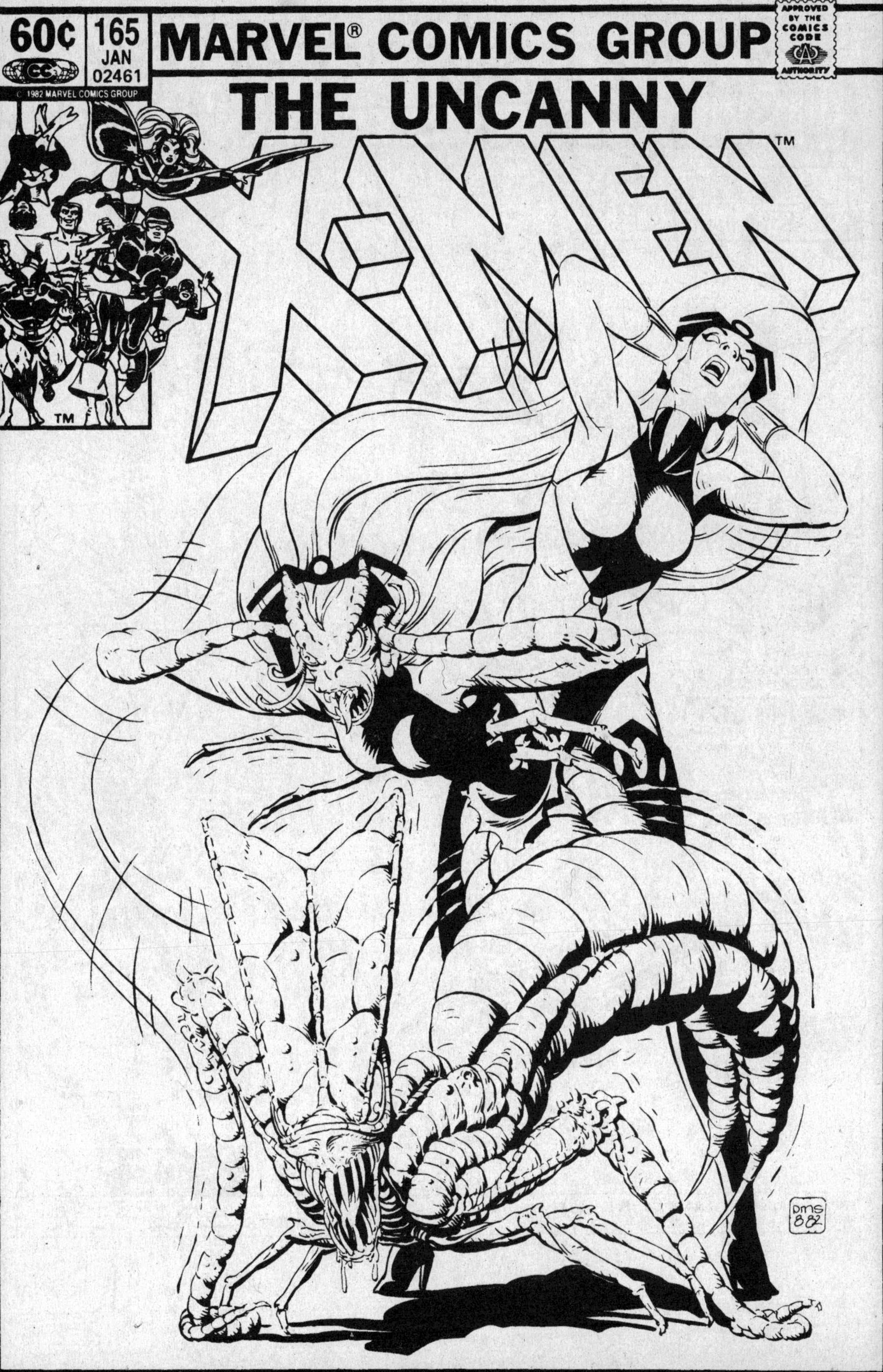
60¢
165
JAN
02461
MARVEL® COMICS GROUP
APPROVED BY THE COMICS CODE AUTHORITY
© 1982 MARVEL COMICS GROUP
THE UNCANNY
X-MEN™
TM
DMS 82

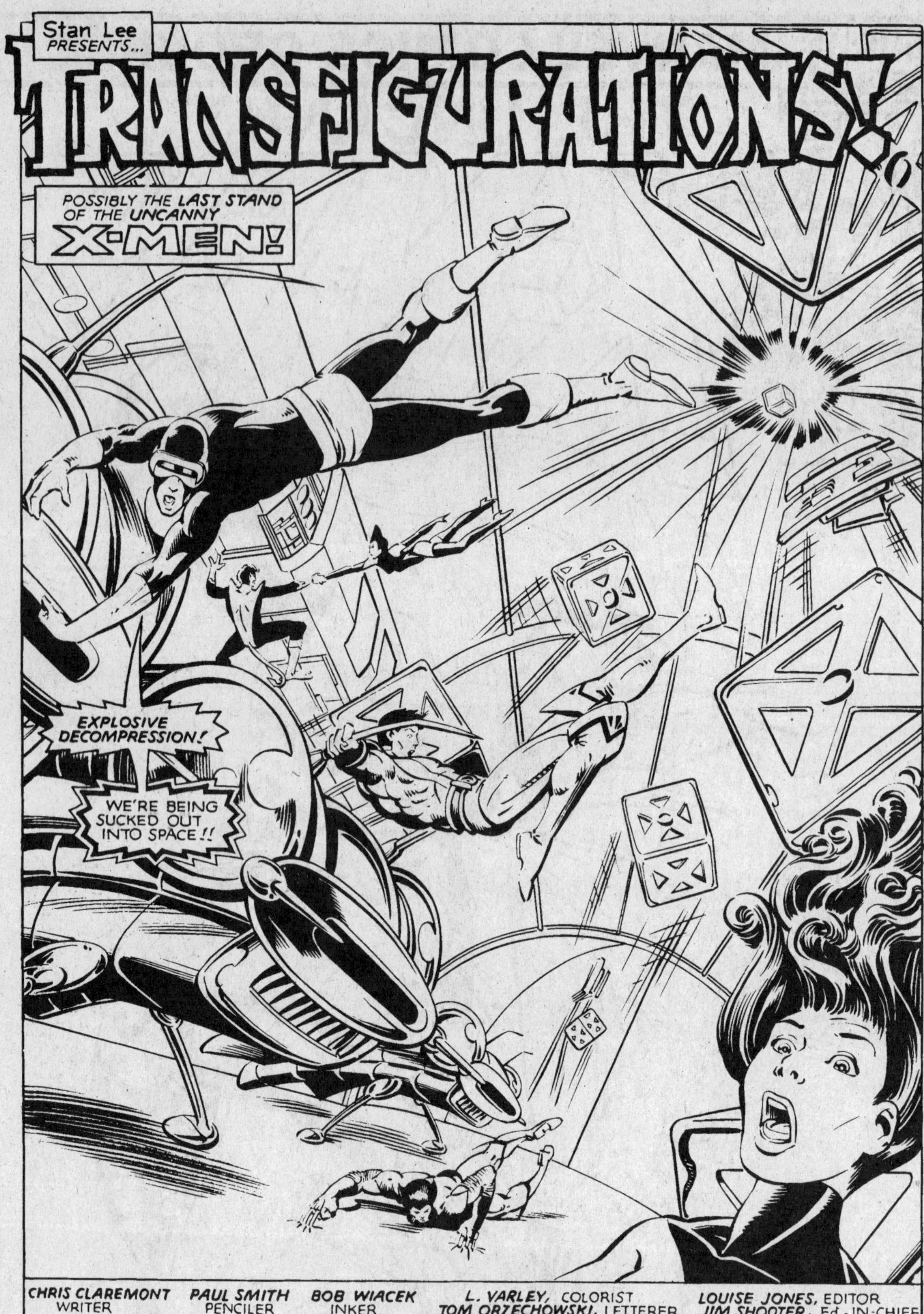
Stan Lee PRESENTS...
TRANSFIGURATIONS!
POSSIBLY THE LAST STAND OF THE UNCANNY X-MEN!
EXPLOSIVE DECOMPRESSION!
WE'RE BEING SUCKED OUT INTO SPACE!!

CHRIS CLAREMONT WRITER · PAUL SMITH PENCILER · BOB WIACEK INKER · L. VARLEY, COLORIST · TOM ORZECHOWSKI, LETTERER · LOUISE JONES, EDITOR · JIM SHOOTER, Ed.-IN-CHIEF

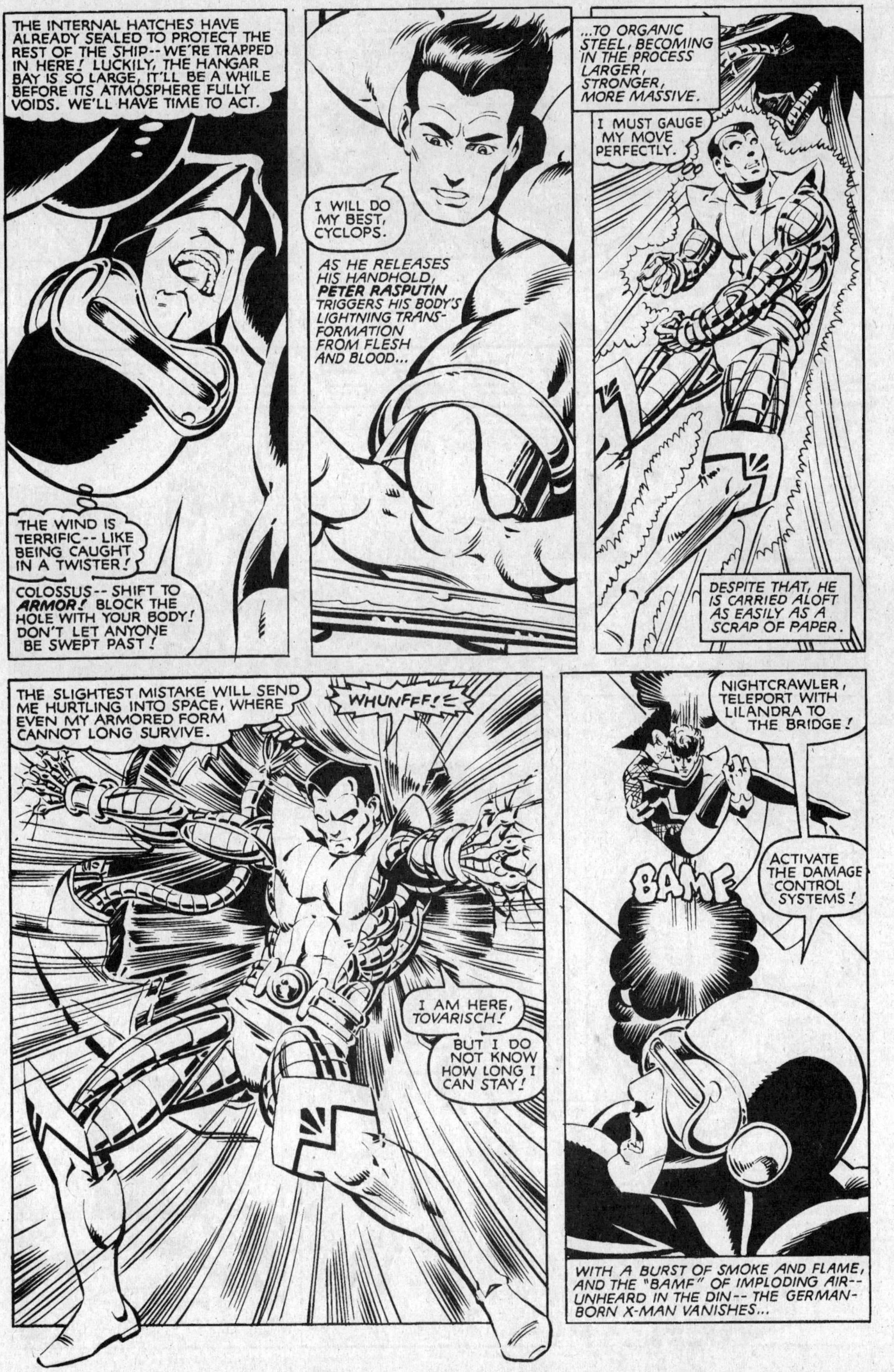
THE INTERNAL HATCHES HAVE ALREADY SEALED TO PROTECT THE REST OF THE SHIP-- WE'RE TRAPPED IN HERE! LUCKILY, THE HANGAR BAY IS SO LARGE, IT'LL BE A WHILE BEFORE ITS ATMOSPHERE FULLY VOIDS. WE'LL HAVE TIME TO ACT.
THE WIND IS TERRIFIC-- LIKE BEING CAUGHT IN A TWISTER!
COLOSSUS-- SHIFT TO ARMOR! BLOCK THE HOLE WITH YOUR BODY! DON'T LET ANYONE BE SWEPT PAST!
I WILL DO MY BEST, CYCLOPS.
AS HE RELEASES HIS HANDHOLD, PETER RASPUTIN TRIGGERS HIS BODY'S LIGHTNING TRANSFORMATION FROM FLESH AND BLOOD...
...TO ORGANIC STEEL, BECOMING IN THE PROCESS LARGER, STRONGER, MORE MASSIVE.
I MUST GAUGE MY MOVE PERFECTLY.
DESPITE THAT, HE IS CARRIED ALOFT AS EASILY AS A SCRAP OF PAPER.
THE SLIGHTEST MISTAKE WILL SEND ME HURTLING INTO SPACE, WHERE EVEN MY ARMORED FORM CANNOT LONG SURVIVE.
WHUNFFF!
I AM HERE, TOVARISCH!
BUT I DO NOT KNOW HOW LONG I CAN STAY!
NIGHTCRAWLER, TELEPORT WITH LILANDRA TO THE BRIDGE!
ACTIVATE THE DAMAGE CONTROL SYSTEMS!
BAMF
WITH A BURST OF SMOKE AND FLAME, AND THE "BAMF" OF IMPLODING AIR-- UNHEARD IN THE DIN-- THE GERMAN-BORN X-MAN VANISHES...

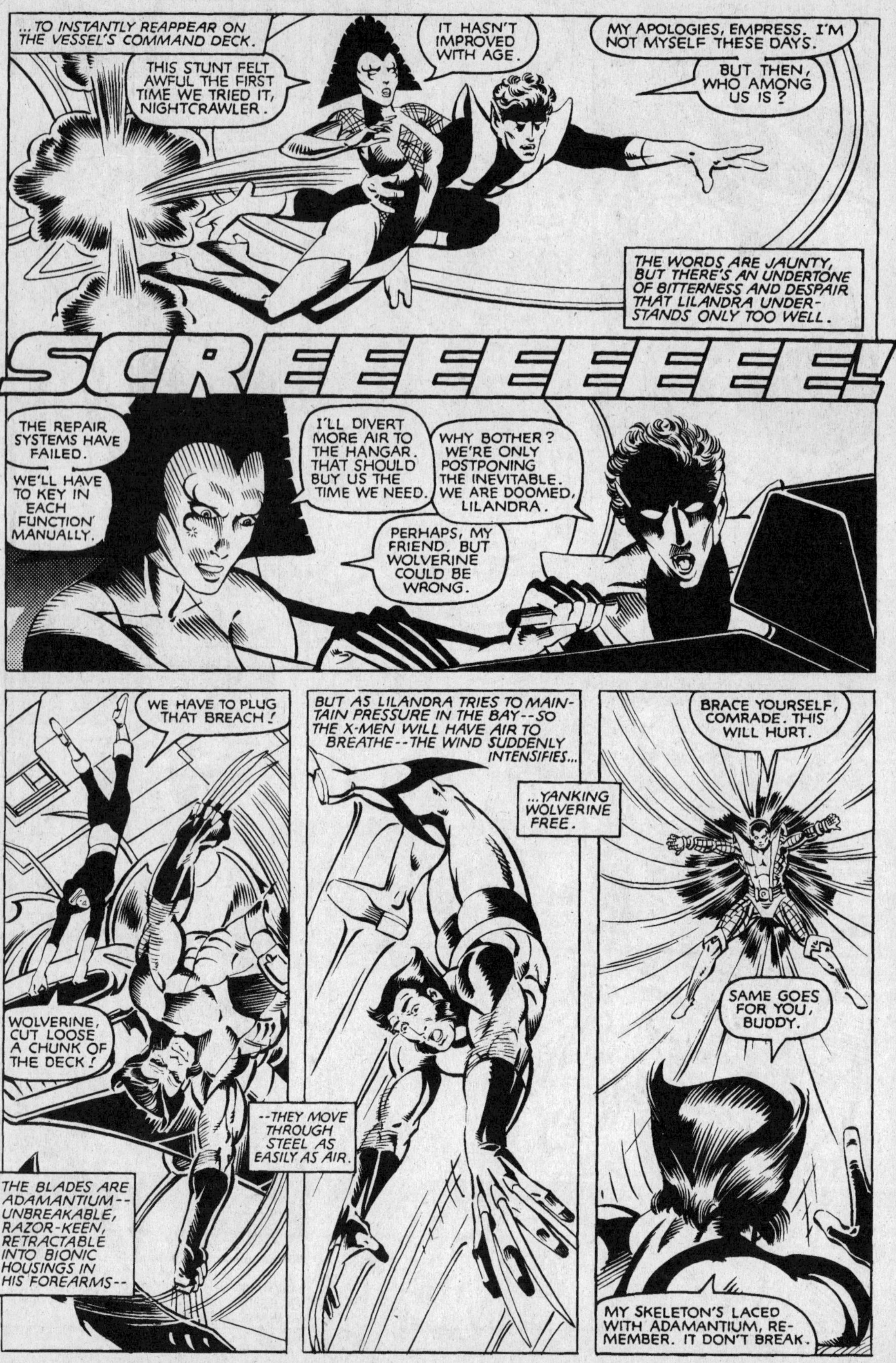
...TO INSTANTLY REAPPEAR ON THE VESSEL'S COMMAND DECK.
THIS STUNT FELT AWFUL THE FIRST TIME WE TRIED IT, NIGHTCRAWLER.
IT HASN'T IMPROVED WITH AGE.
MY APOLOGIES, EMPRESS. I'M NOT MYSELF THESE DAYS.
BUT THEN, WHO AMONG US IS?
THE WORDS ARE JAUNTY, BUT THERE'S AN UNDERTONE OF BITTERNESS AND DESPAIR THAT LILANDRA UNDERSTANDS ONLY TOO WELL.
SCREEEEEEEE!
THE REPAIR SYSTEMS HAVE FAILED.
WE'LL HAVE TO KEY IN EACH FUNCTION MANUALLY.
I'LL DIVERT MORE AIR TO THE HANGAR. THAT SHOULD BUY US THE TIME WE NEED.
WHY BOTHER? WE'RE ONLY POSTPONING THE INEVITABLE. WE ARE DOOMED, LILANDRA.
PERHAPS, MY FRIEND. BUT WOLVERINE COULD BE WRONG.
WE HAVE TO PLUG THAT BREACH!
WOLVERINE, CUT LOOSE A CHUNK OF THE DECK!
THE BLADES ARE ADAMANTIUM--UNBREAKABLE, RAZOR-KEEN, RETRACTABLE INTO BIONIC HOUSINGS IN HIS FOREARMS--
--THEY MOVE THROUGH STEEL AS EASILY AS AIR.
BUT AS LILANDRA TRIES TO MAINTAIN PRESSURE IN THE BAY--SO THE X-MEN WILL HAVE AIR TO BREATHE--THE WIND SUDDENLY INTENSIFIES...
...YANKING WOLVERINE FREE.
BRACE YOURSELF, COMRADE. THIS WILL HURT.
SAME GOES FOR YOU, BUDDY.
MY SKELETON'S LACED WITH ADAMANTIUM, REMEMBER. IT DON'T BREAK.

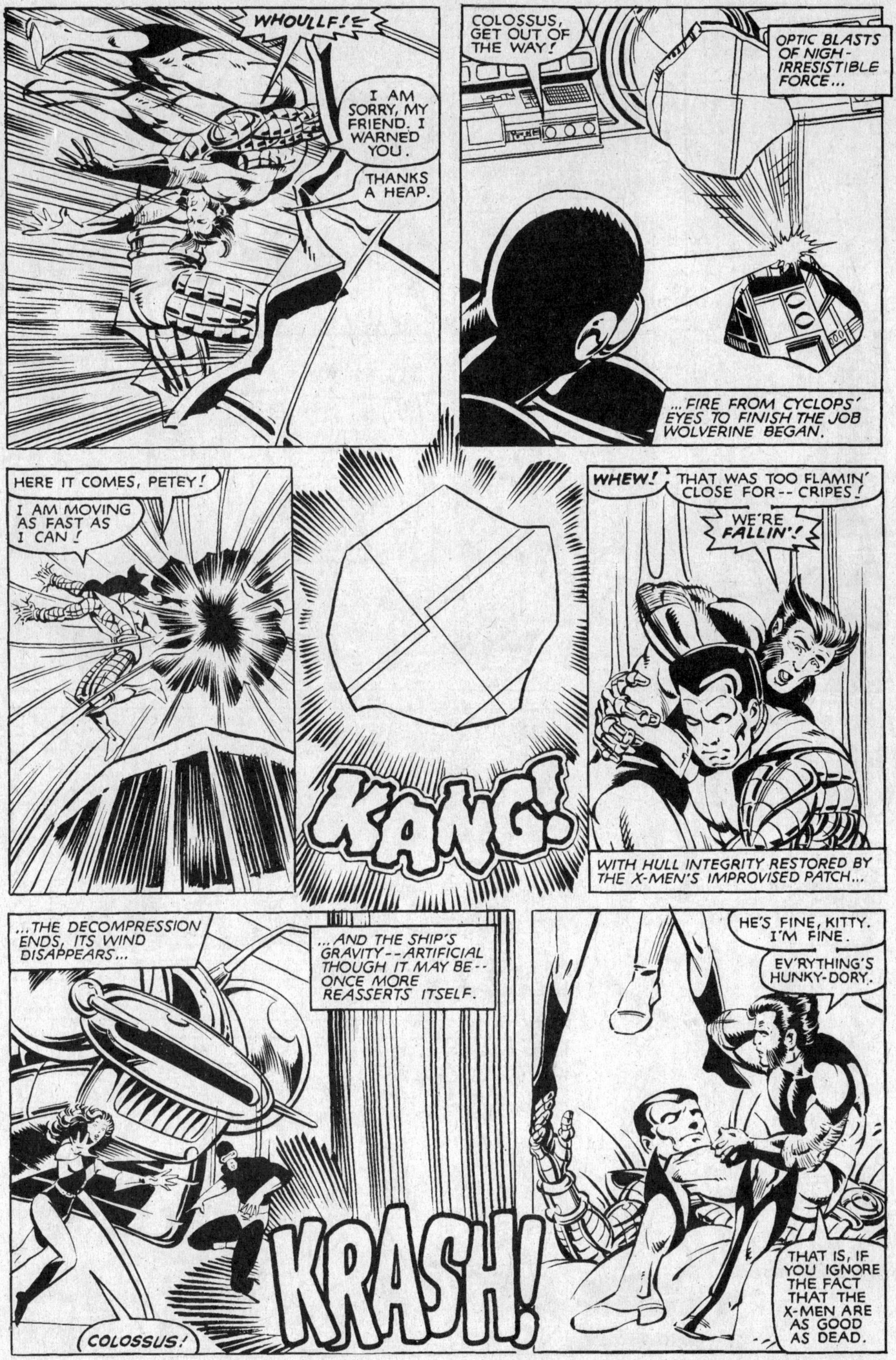
WHOULLF!
I AM SORRY, MY FRIEND. I WARNED YOU.
THANKS A HEAP.
COLOSSUS, GET OUT OF THE WAY!
OPTIC BLASTS OF NIGH-IRRESISTIBLE FORCE...
...FIRE FROM CYCLOPS' EYES TO FINISH THE JOB WOLVERINE BEGAN.
HERE IT COMES, PETEY!
I AM MOVING AS FAST AS I CAN!
KANG!
WHEW!
THAT WAS TOO FLAMIN' CLOSE FOR--CRIPES!
WE'RE FALLIN'!
WITH HULL INTEGRITY RESTORED BY THE X-MEN'S IMPROVISED PATCH...
...THE DECOMPRESSION ENDS, ITS WIND DISAPPEARS...
...AND THE SHIP'S GRAVITY--ARTIFICIAL THOUGH IT MAY BE--ONCE MORE REASSERTS ITSELF.
KRASH!
COLOSSUS!
HE'S FINE, KITTY. I'M FINE.
EV'RYTHING'S HUNKY-DORY.
THAT IS, IF YOU IGNORE THE FACT THAT THE X-MEN ARE AS GOOD AS DEAD.

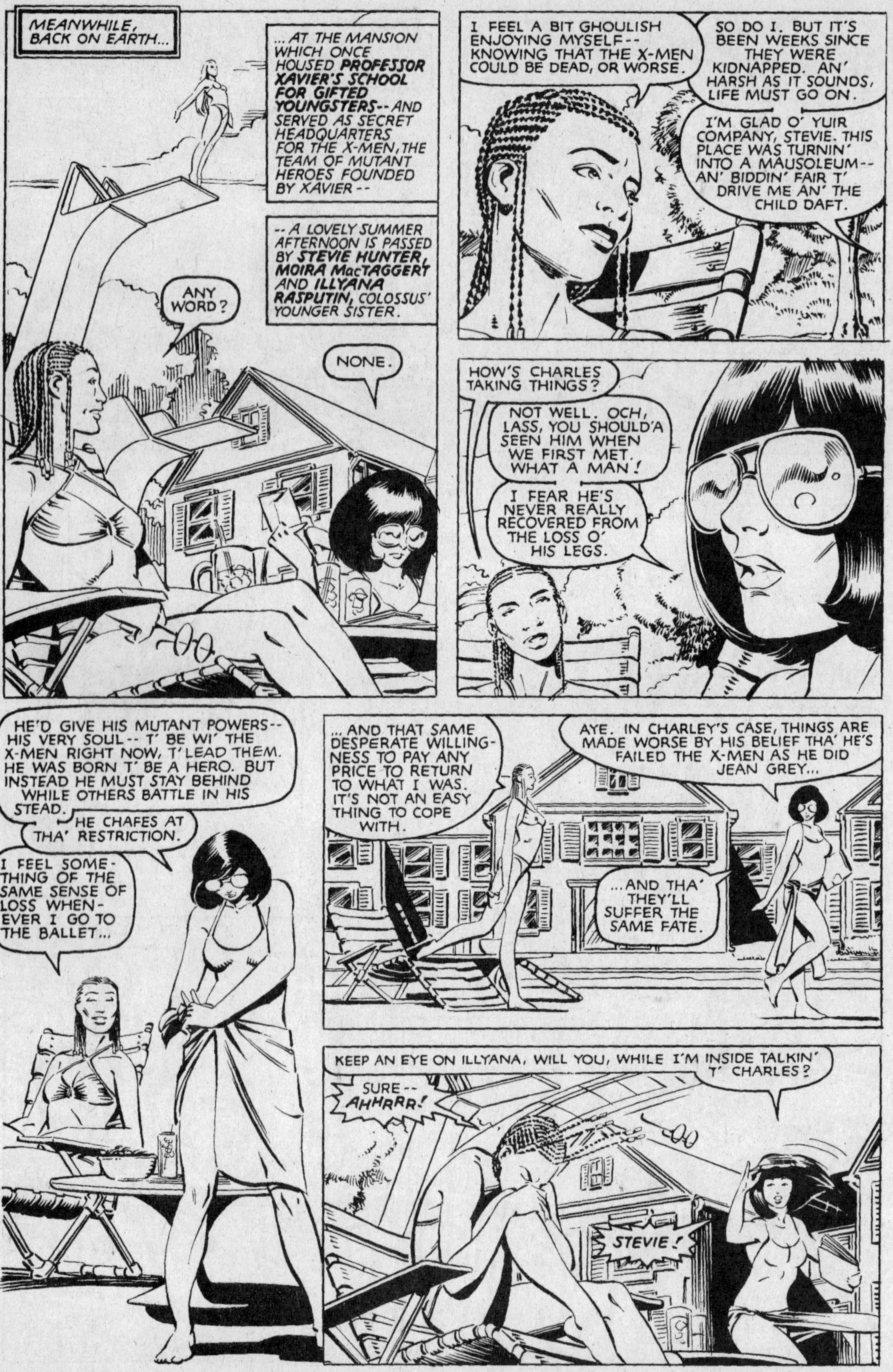

MEANWHILE, BACK ON EARTH...
...AT THE MANSION WHICH ONCE HOUSED PROFESSOR XAVIER'S SCHOOL FOR GIFTED YOUNGSTERS-- AND SERVED AS SECRET HEADQUARTERS FOR THE X-MEN, THE TEAM OF MUTANT HEROES FOUNDED BY XAVIER--
--A LOVELY SUMMER AFTERNOON IS PASSED BY STEVIE HUNTER, MOIRA MacTAGGERT AND ILLYANA RASPUTIN, COLOSSUS' YOUNGER SISTER.
ANY WORD?
NONE.
I FEEL A BIT GHOULISH ENJOYING MYSELF-- KNOWING THAT THE X-MEN COULD BE DEAD, OR WORSE.
SO DO I. BUT IT'S BEEN WEEKS SINCE THEY WERE KIDNAPPED. AN' HARSH AS IT SOUNDS, LIFE MUST GO ON.
I'M GLAD O' YUIR COMPANY, STEVIE. THIS PLACE WAS TURNIN' INTO A MAUSOLEUM-- AN' BIDDIN' FAIR T' DRIVE ME AN' THE CHILD DAFT.
HOW'S CHARLES TAKING THINGS?
NOT WELL. OCH, LASS, YOU SHOULD'A SEEN HIM WHEN WE FIRST MET. WHAT A MAN!
I FEAR HE'S NEVER REALLY RECOVERED FROM THE LOSS O' HIS LEGS.
HE'D GIVE HIS MUTANT POWERS-- HIS VERY SOUL-- T' BE WI' THE X-MEN RIGHT NOW, T' LEAD THEM. HE WAS BORN T' BE A HERO. BUT INSTEAD HE MUST STAY BEHIND WHILE OTHERS BATTLE IN HIS STEAD.
HE CHAFES AT THA' RESTRICTION.
I FEEL SOMETHING OF THE SAME SENSE OF LOSS WHENEVER I GO TO THE BALLET...
...AND THAT SAME DESPERATE WILLINGNESS TO PAY ANY PRICE TO RETURN TO WHAT I WAS. IT'S NOT AN EASY THING TO COPE WITH.
AYE. IN CHARLEY'S CASE, THINGS ARE MADE WORSE BY HIS BELIEF THA' HE'S FAILED THE X-MEN AS HE DID JEAN GREY...
...AND THA' THEY'LL SUFFER THE SAME FATE.
KEEP AN EYE ON ILLYANA, WILL YOU, WHILE I'M INSIDE TALKIN' T' CHARLES?
SURE-- AHHRRR!
STEVIE!

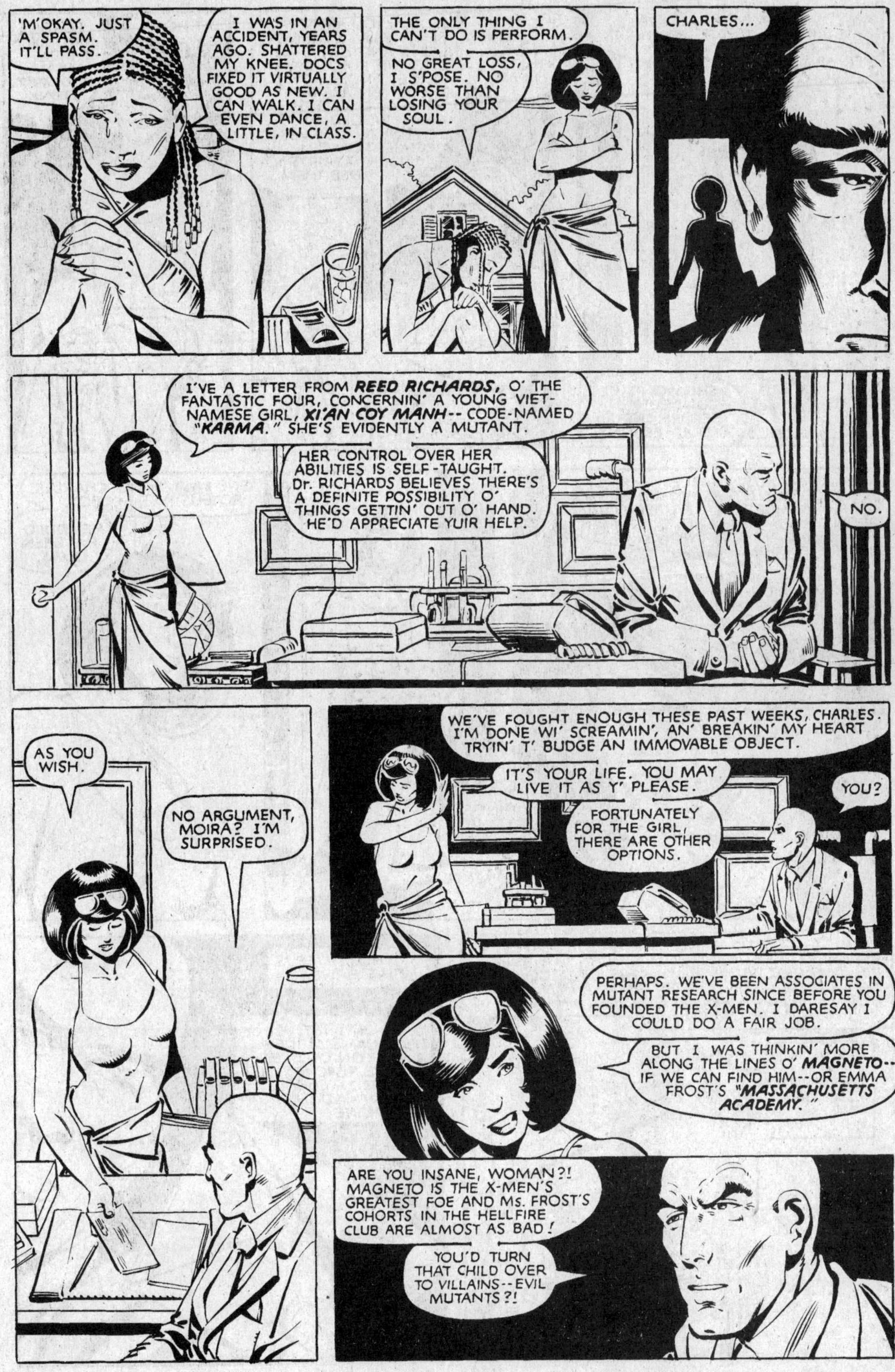
'M'OKAY. JUST A SPASM. IT'LL PASS.
I WAS IN AN ACCIDENT, YEARS AGO. SHATTERED MY KNEE. DOCS FIXED IT VIRTUALLY GOOD AS NEW. I CAN WALK. I CAN EVEN DANCE, A LITTLE, IN CLASS.
THE ONLY THING I CAN'T DO IS PERFORM.
NO GREAT LOSS, I S'POSE. NO WORSE THAN LOSING YOUR SOUL.
CHARLES...
I'VE A LETTER FROM REED RICHARDS, O' THE FANTASTIC FOUR, CONCERNIN' A YOUNG VIET-NAMESE GIRL, XI'AN COY MANH-- CODE-NAMED "KARMA." SHE'S EVIDENTLY A MUTANT.
HER CONTROL OVER HER ABILITIES IS SELF-TAUGHT. Dr. RICHARDS BELIEVES THERE'S A DEFINITE POSSIBILITY O' THINGS GETTIN' OUT O' HAND. HE'D APPRECIATE YUIR HELP.
NO.
AS YOU WISH.
NO ARGUMENT, MOIRA? I'M SURPRISED.
WE'VE FOUGHT ENOUGH THESE PAST WEEKS, CHARLES. I'M DONE WI' SCREAMIN', AN' BREAKIN' MY HEART TRYIN' T' BUDGE AN IMMOVABLE OBJECT.
IT'S YOUR LIFE. YOU MAY LIVE IT AS Y' PLEASE.
FORTUNATELY FOR THE GIRL, THERE ARE OTHER OPTIONS.
YOU?
PERHAPS. WE'VE BEEN ASSOCIATES IN MUTANT RESEARCH SINCE BEFORE YOU FOUNDED THE X-MEN. I DARESAY I COULD DO A FAIR JOB.
BUT I WAS THINKIN' MORE ALONG THE LINES O' MAGNETO-- IF WE CAN FIND HIM--OR EMMA FROST'S "MASSACHUSETTS ACADEMY."
ARE YOU INSANE, WOMAN?! MAGNETO IS THE X-MEN'S GREATEST FOE AND Ms. FROST'S COHORTS IN THE HELLFIRE CLUB ARE ALMOST AS BAD!
YOU'D TURN THAT CHILD OVER TO VILLAINS--EVIL MUTANTS?!

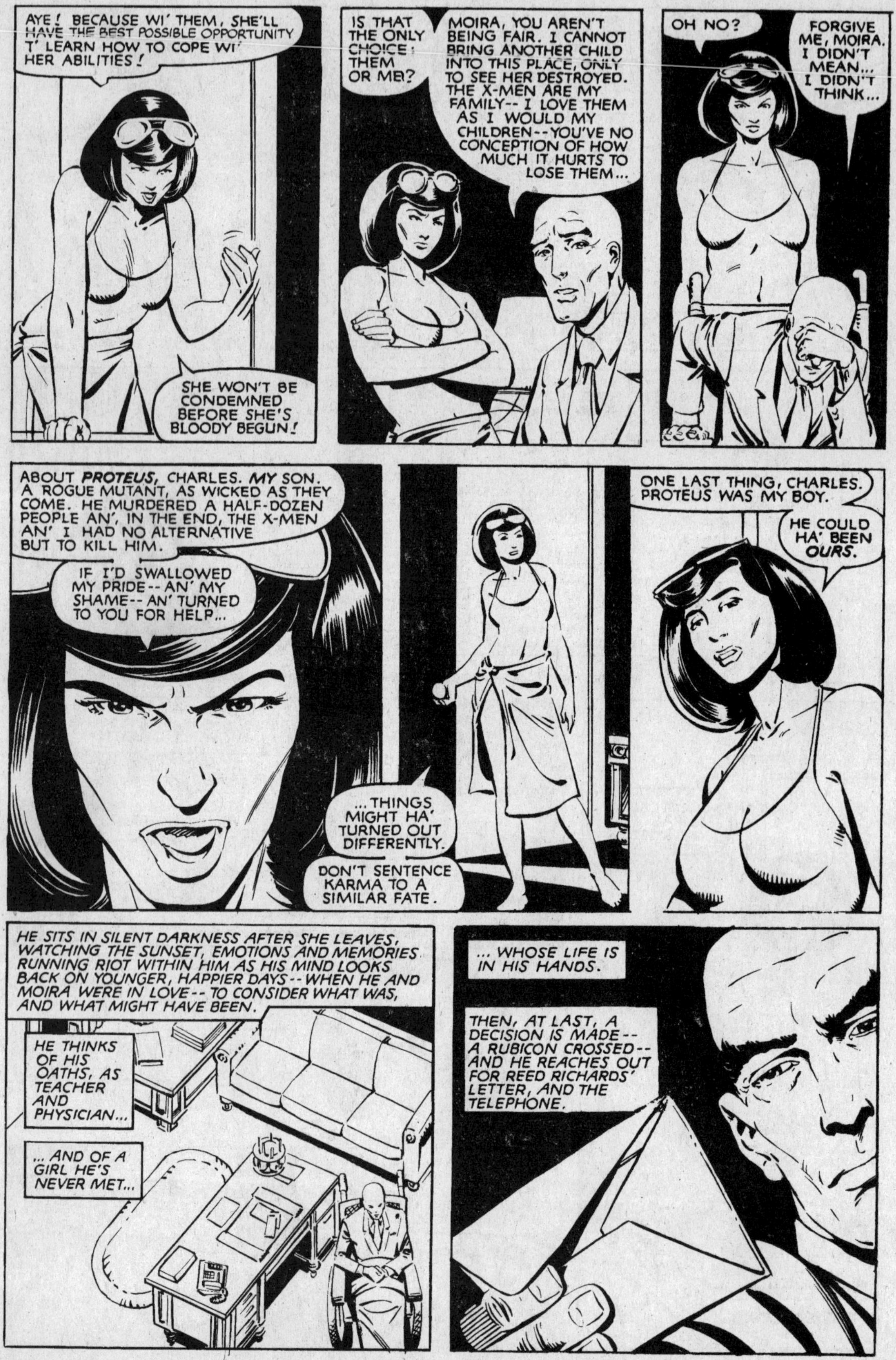

AYE! BECAUSE WI' THEM, SHE'LL HAVE THE BEST POSSIBLE OPPORTUNITY T' LEARN HOW TO COPE WI' HER ABILITIES!
SHE WON'T BE CONDEMNED BEFORE SHE'S BLOODY BEGUN!
IS THAT THE ONLY CHOICE: THEM OR ME?
MOIRA, YOU AREN'T BEING FAIR. I CANNOT BRING ANOTHER CHILD INTO THIS PLACE, ONLY TO SEE HER DESTROYED. THE X-MEN ARE MY FAMILY-- I LOVE THEM AS I WOULD MY CHILDREN--YOU'VE NO CONCEPTION OF HOW MUCH IT HURTS TO LOSE THEM...
OH NO?
FORGIVE ME, MOIRA. I DIDN'T MEAN... I DIDN'T THINK...
ABOUT PROTEUS, CHARLES. MY SON. A ROGUE MUTANT, AS WICKED AS THEY COME. HE MURDERED A HALF-DOZEN PEOPLE AN', IN THE END, THE X-MEN AN' I HAD NO ALTERNATIVE BUT TO KILL HIM.
IF I'D SWALLOWED MY PRIDE--AN' MY SHAME--AN' TURNED TO YOU FOR HELP...
...THINGS MIGHT HA' TURNED OUT DIFFERENTLY.
DON'T SENTENCE KARMA TO A SIMILAR FATE.
ONE LAST THING, CHARLES. PROTEUS WAS MY BOY.
HE COULD HA' BEEN OURS.
HE SITS IN SILENT DARKNESS AFTER SHE LEAVES, WATCHING THE SUNSET, EMOTIONS AND MEMORIES RUNNING RIOT WITHIN HIM AS HIS MIND LOOKS BACK ON YOUNGER, HAPPIER DAYS--WHEN HE AND MOIRA WERE IN LOVE--TO CONSIDER WHAT WAS, AND WHAT MIGHT HAVE BEEN.
HE THINKS OF HIS OATHS, AS TEACHER AND PHYSICIAN...
...AND OF A GIRL HE'S NEVER MET...
...WHOSE LIFE IS IN HIS HANDS.
THEN, AT LAST, A DECISION IS MADE--A RUBICON CROSSED--AND HE REACHES OUT FOR REED RICHARDS' LETTER, AND THE TELEPHONE.

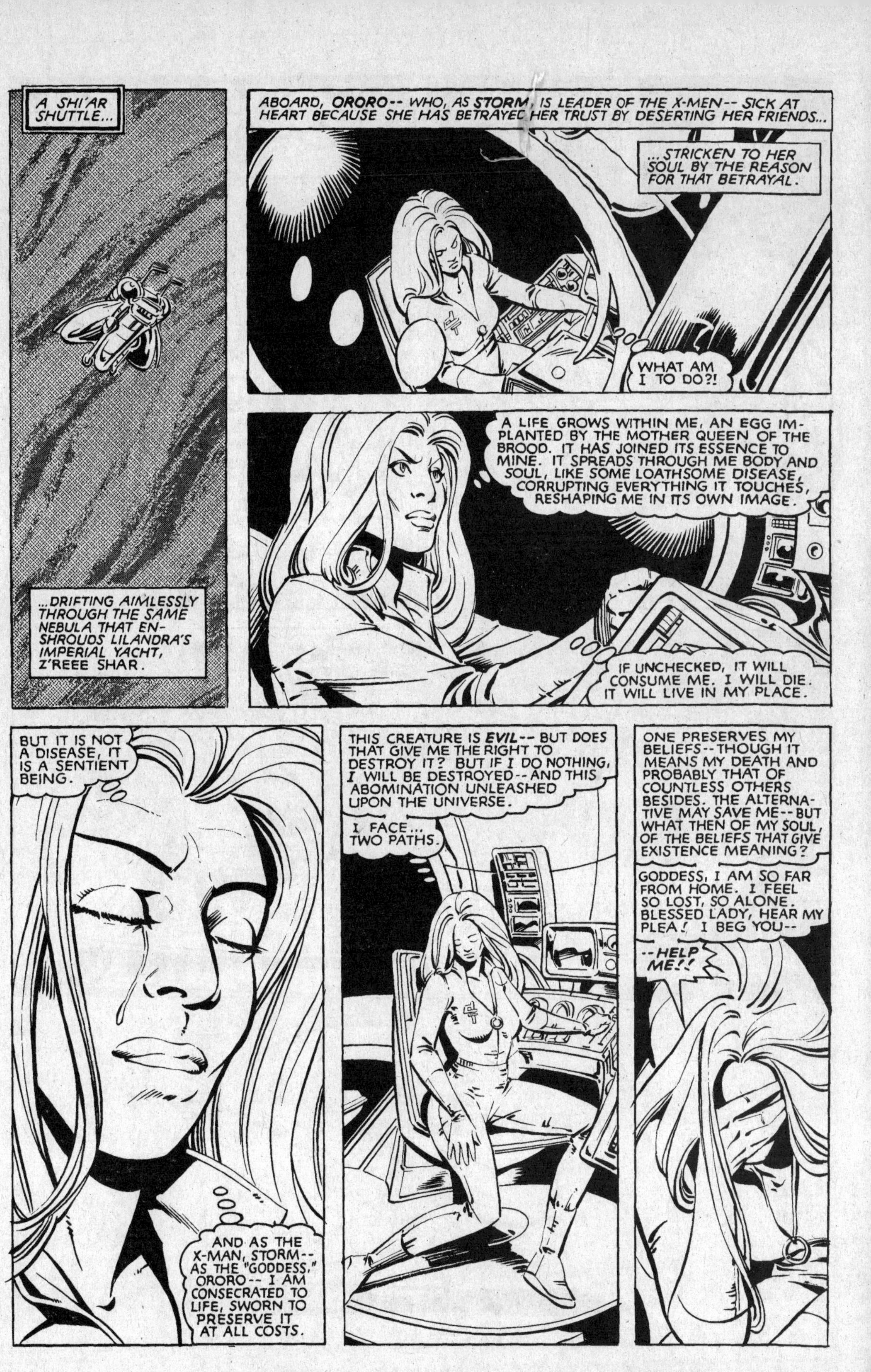
A SHI'AR SHUTTLE...
...DRIFTING AIMLESSLY THROUGH THE SAME NEBULA THAT EN-SHROUDS LILANDRA'S IMPERIAL YACHT, Z'REEE SHAR.
ABOARD, ORORO-- WHO, AS STORM, IS LEADER OF THE X-MEN-- SICK AT HEART BECAUSE SHE HAS BETRAYED HER TRUST BY DESERTING HER FRIENDS...
...STRICKEN TO HER SOUL BY THE REASON FOR THAT BETRAYAL.
WHAT AM I TO DO?!
A LIFE GROWS WITHIN ME, AN EGG IM-PLANTED BY THE MOTHER QUEEN OF THE BROOD. IT HAS JOINED ITS ESSENCE TO MINE. IT SPREADS THROUGH ME BODY AND SOUL, LIKE SOME LOATHSOME DISEASE, CORRUPTING EVERYTHING IT TOUCHES, RESHAPING ME IN ITS OWN IMAGE.
IF UNCHECKED, IT WILL CONSUME ME. I WILL DIE. IT WILL LIVE IN MY PLACE.
BUT IT IS NOT A DISEASE, IT IS A SENTIENT BEING.
AND AS THE X-MAN, STORM-- AS THE "GODDESS," ORORO-- I AM CONSECRATED TO LIFE, SWORN TO PRESERVE IT AT ALL COSTS.
THIS CREATURE IS EVIL-- BUT DOES THAT GIVE ME THE RIGHT TO DESTROY IT? BUT IF I DO NOTHING, I WILL BE DESTROYED-- AND THIS ABOMINATION UNLEASHED UPON THE UNIVERSE.
I FACE... TWO PATHS.
ONE PRESERVES MY BELIEFS-- THOUGH IT MEANS MY DEATH AND PROBABLY THAT OF COUNTLESS OTHERS BESIDES. THE ALTERNA-TIVE MAY SAVE ME-- BUT WHAT THEN OF MY SOUL, OF THE BELIEFS THAT GIVE EXISTENCE MEANING?
GODDESS, I AM SO FAR FROM HOME. I FEEL SO LOST, SO ALONE. BLESSED LADY, HEAR MY PLEA! I BEG YOU--
--HELP ME!!

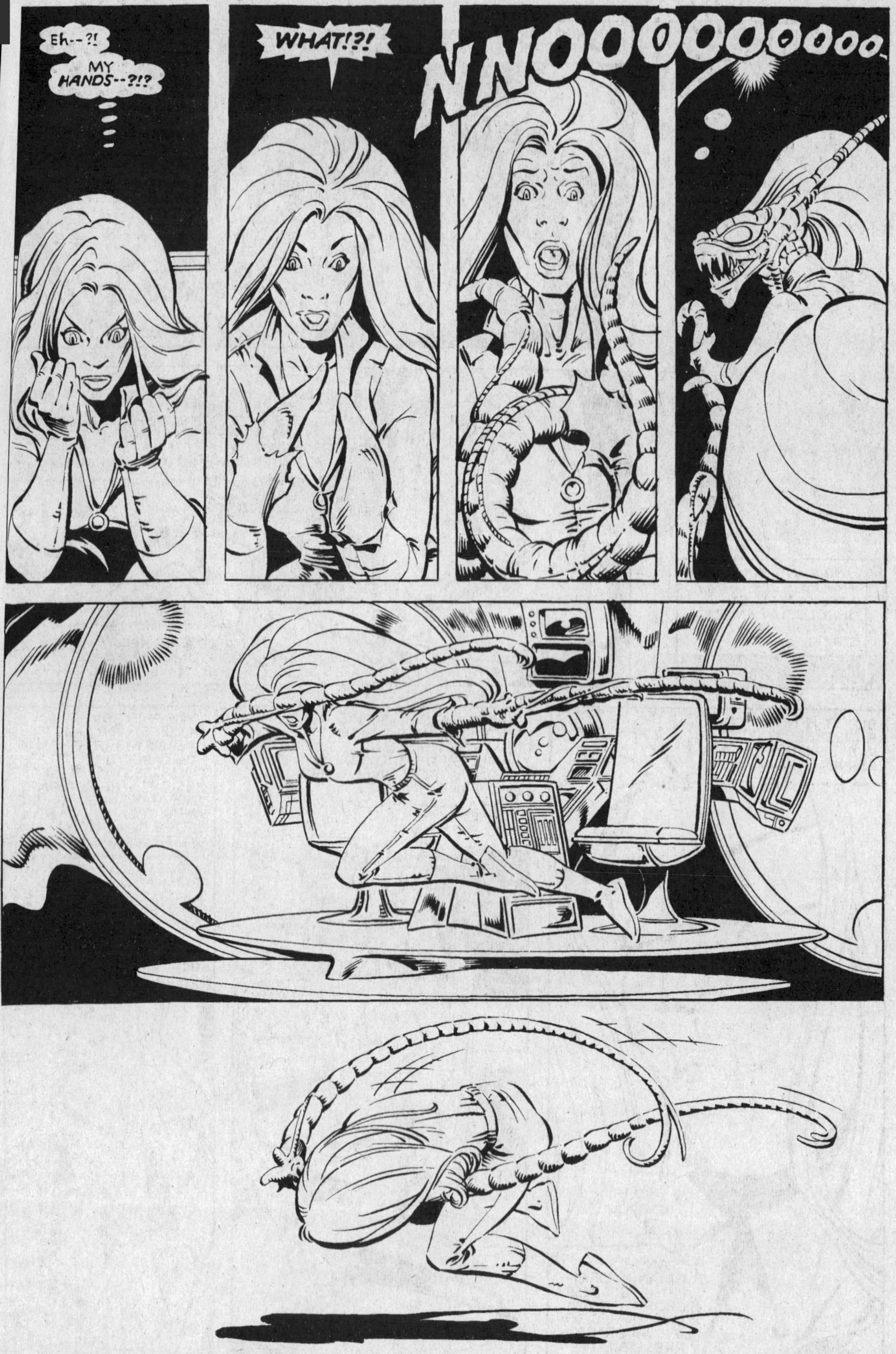
Eh--?!
MY HANDS--?!?
WHAT!?!
NNOOOOOOOooo-

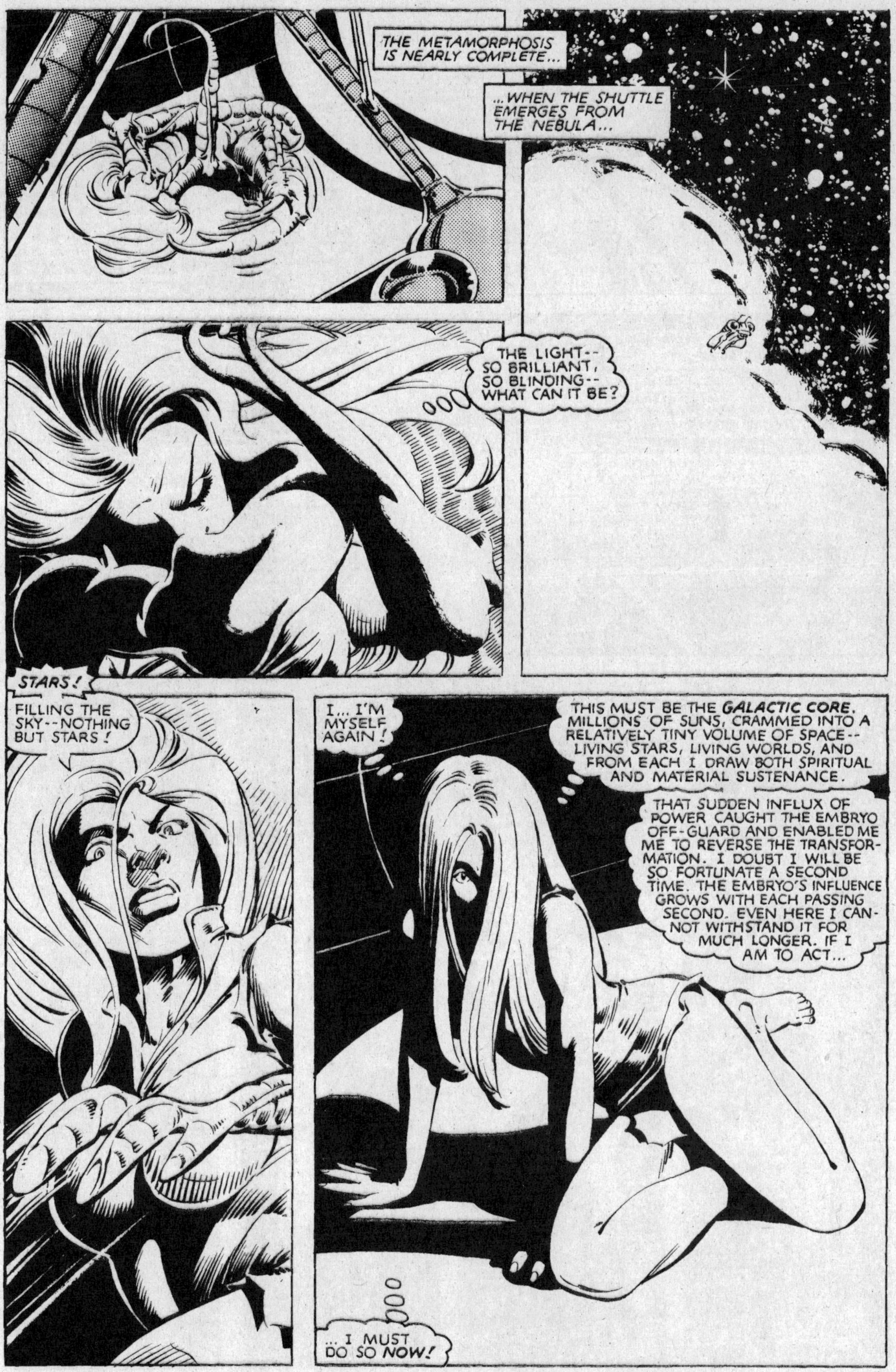
THE METAMORPHOSIS IS NEARLY COMPLETE...
...WHEN THE SHUTTLE EMERGES FROM THE NEBULA...
THE LIGHT-- SO BRILLIANT, SO BLINDING-- WHAT CAN IT BE?
STARS!
FILLING THE SKY--NOTHING BUT STARS!
I... I'M MYSELF AGAIN!
THIS MUST BE THE GALACTIC CORE. MILLIONS OF SUNS, CRAMMED INTO A RELATIVELY TINY VOLUME OF SPACE-- LIVING STARS, LIVING WORLDS, AND FROM EACH I DRAW BOTH SPIRITUAL AND MATERIAL SUSTENANCE.
THAT SUDDEN INFLUX OF POWER CAUGHT THE EMBRYO OFF-GUARD AND ENABLED ME ME TO REVERSE THE TRANSFORMATION. I DOUBT I WILL BE SO FORTUNATE A SECOND TIME. THE EMBRYO'S INFLUENCE GROWS WITH EACH PASSING SECOND. EVEN HERE I CANNOT WITHSTAND IT FOR MUCH LONGER. IF I AM TO ACT...
... I MUST DO SO NOW!

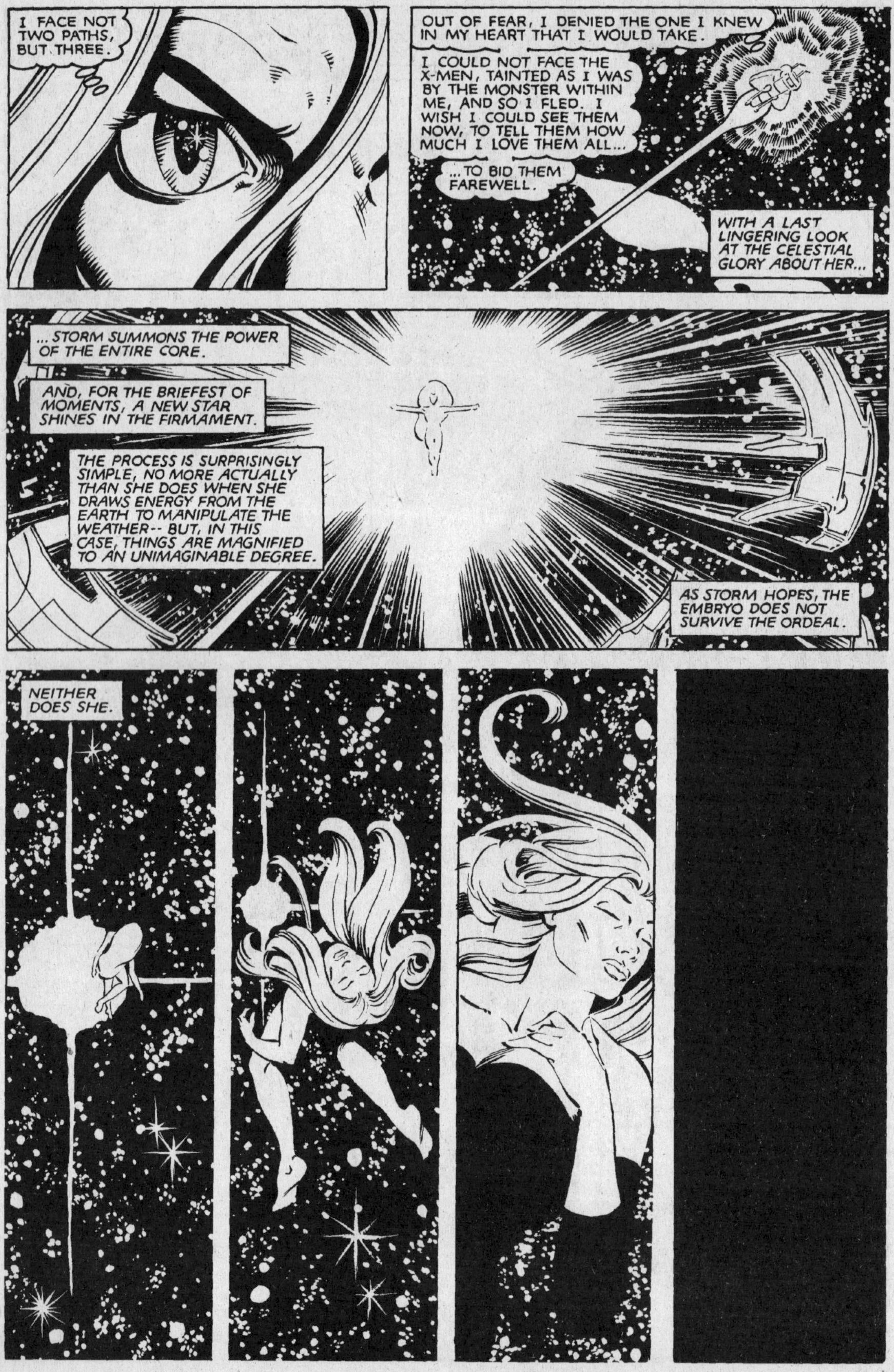
I FACE NOT TWO PATHS, BUT THREE.
OUT OF FEAR, I DENIED THE ONE I KNEW IN MY HEART THAT I WOULD TAKE.
I COULD NOT FACE THE X-MEN, TAINTED AS I WAS BY THE MONSTER WITHIN ME, AND SO I FLED. I WISH I COULD SEE THEM NOW, TO TELL THEM HOW MUCH I LOVE THEM ALL...
...TO BID THEM FAREWELL.
WITH A LAST LINGERING LOOK AT THE CELESTIAL GLORY ABOUT HER...
...STORM SUMMONS THE POWER OF THE ENTIRE CORE.
AND, FOR THE BRIEFEST OF MOMENTS, A NEW STAR SHINES IN THE FIRMAMENT.
THE PROCESS IS SURPRISINGLY SIMPLE, NO MORE ACTUALLY THAN SHE DOES WHEN SHE DRAWS ENERGY FROM THE EARTH TO MANIPULATE THE WEATHER-- BUT, IN THIS CASE, THINGS ARE MAGNIFIED TO AN UNIMAGINABLE DEGREE.
AS STORM HOPES, THE EMBRYO DOES NOT SURVIVE THE ORDEAL.
NEITHER DOES SHE.

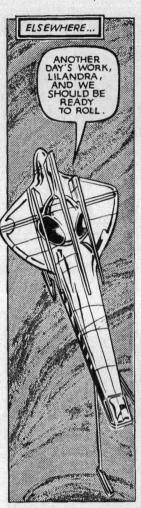

ELSEWHERE...

ANOTHER DAY'S WORK, LILANDRA, AND WE SHOULD BE READY TO ROLL.

THE QUESTION IS, WHERE DO WE GO?

HOW 'BOUT BACK THE WAY WE CAME, TA FINISH WHAT WE STARTED.

TO SLEAZEWORLD? TO TAKE ON THE BROOD? SIX PEOPLE IN AN ARMED YACHT VERSUS AN ENTIRE RACE?! YOU'RE TALKING SUICIDE, LOGAN.

WHAT'VE WE GOT TO LOSE? THE X-MEN ARE LIVIN' ON BORROWED TIME, ANYWAY. THE MOTHER QUEEN IMPLANTED AN EGG IN EACH O' US. BECAUSE O' MY MUTANT POWER-- MY BODY'S ABILITY TA HEAL ANY WOUND OR ILLNESS-- THE ONE I GOT WAS ZAPPED.

BUT YOURS'RE HEALTHY, GROWIN'. SOONER OR LATER, THEY'LL MATURE. D'YOU WANT TO SIT AROUND AN' WAIT FOR THAT TA HAPPEN...

...OR PAY THE BROOD BACK FOR WHAT THEY'VE DONE?

I AM *MAJESTRIX SHI'AR*-- EMPRESS OF A WARRIOR RACE! I WILL SHOW THE BROOD THE IDENTICAL MERCY THEY HAVE GRANTED US.

FROM THIS MOMENT ON, WHEREVER, WHENEVER I FIND THEM-- BE THEY HIGH-BORN OR LOW, ADULT OR CHILD--

--THEIR LIVES ARE *MINE!*

SOUNDS GOOD TA ME, DARLIN'.

AND... TO ME.

GOD HELP US ALL.

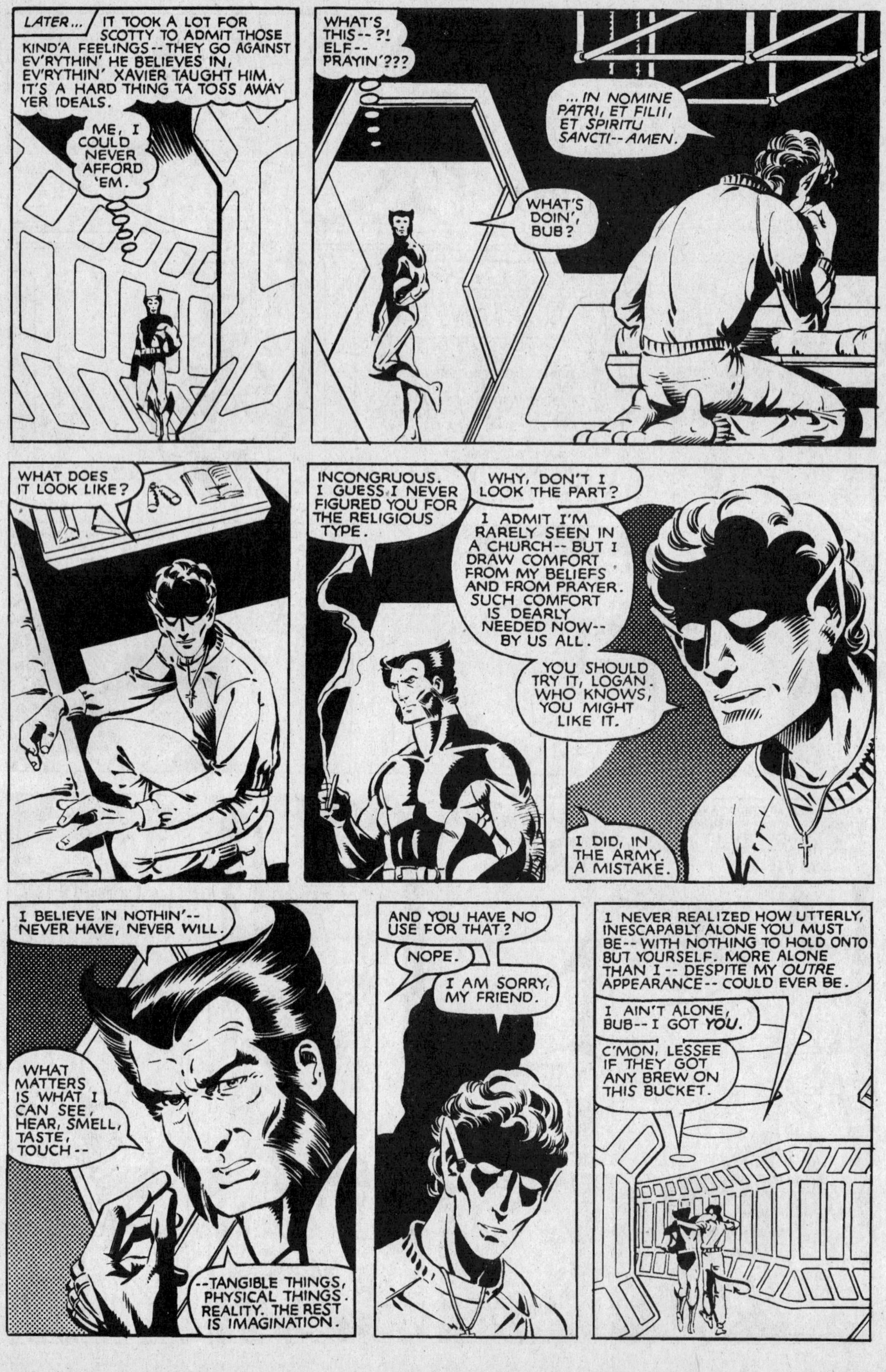
LATER...
IT TOOK A LOT FOR SCOTTY TO ADMIT THOSE KIND'A FEELINGS-- THEY GO AGAINST EV'RYTHIN' HE BELIEVES IN, EV'RYTHIN' XAVIER TAUGHT HIM. IT'S A HARD THING TA TOSS AWAY YER IDEALS.
ME, I COULD NEVER AFFORD 'EM.
WHAT'S THIS--?! ELF-- PRAYIN'???
...IN NOMINE PATRI, ET FILII, ET SPIRITU SANCTI--AMEN.
WHAT'S DOIN', BUB?
WHAT DOES IT LOOK LIKE?
INCONGRUOUS. I GUESS I NEVER FIGURED YOU FOR THE RELIGIOUS TYPE.
WHY, DON'T I LOOK THE PART?
I ADMIT I'M RARELY SEEN IN A CHURCH-- BUT I DRAW COMFORT FROM MY BELIEFS AND FROM PRAYER. SUCH COMFORT IS DEARLY NEEDED NOW-- BY US ALL.
YOU SHOULD TRY IT, LOGAN. WHO KNOWS, YOU MIGHT LIKE IT.
I DID, IN THE ARMY. A MISTAKE.
I BELIEVE IN NOTHIN'-- NEVER HAVE, NEVER WILL.
WHAT MATTERS IS WHAT I CAN SEE, HEAR, SMELL, TASTE, TOUCH--
--TANGIBLE THINGS, PHYSICAL THINGS. REALITY. THE REST IS IMAGINATION.
AND YOU HAVE NO USE FOR THAT?
NOPE.
I AM SORRY, MY FRIEND.
I NEVER REALIZED HOW UTTERLY, INESCAPABLY ALONE YOU MUST BE-- WITH NOTHING TO HOLD ONTO BUT YOURSELF. MORE ALONE THAN I -- DESPITE MY OUTRE APPEARANCE-- COULD EVER BE.
I AIN'T ALONE, BUB-- I GOT YOU.
C'MON, LESSEE IF THEY GOT ANY BREW ON THIS BUCKET.

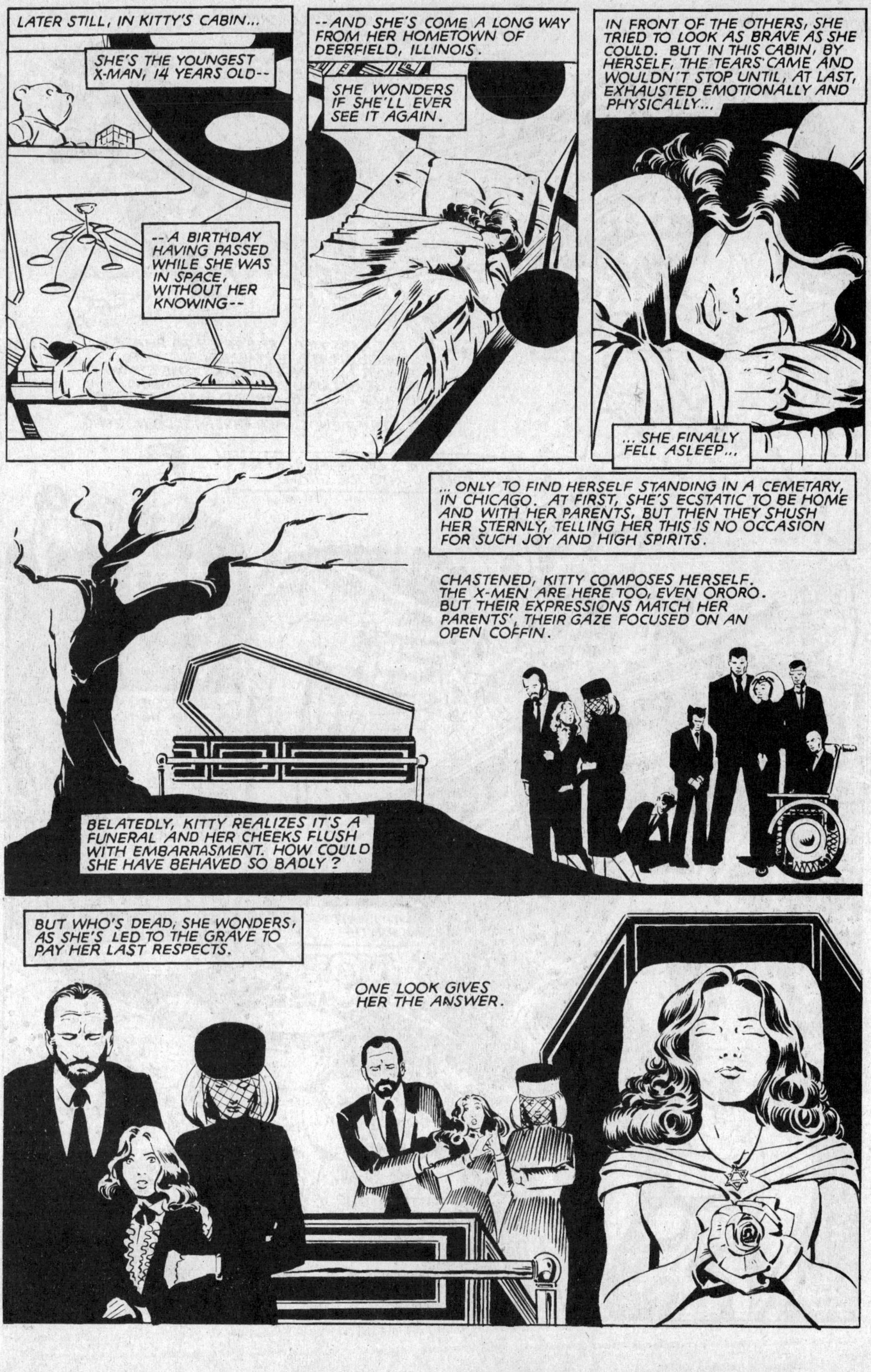
LATER STILL, IN KITTY'S CABIN...
SHE'S THE YOUNGEST X-MAN, 14 YEARS OLD--
--A BIRTHDAY HAVING PASSED WHILE SHE WAS IN SPACE, WITHOUT HER KNOWING--
--AND SHE'S COME A LONG WAY FROM HER HOMETOWN OF DEERFIELD, ILLINOIS.
SHE WONDERS IF SHE'LL EVER SEE IT AGAIN.
IN FRONT OF THE OTHERS, SHE TRIED TO LOOK AS BRAVE AS SHE COULD. BUT IN THIS CABIN, BY HERSELF, THE TEARS CAME AND WOULDN'T STOP UNTIL, AT LAST, EXHAUSTED EMOTIONALLY AND PHYSICALLY...
... SHE FINALLY FELL ASLEEP...
... ONLY TO FIND HERSELF STANDING IN A CEMETARY, IN CHICAGO. AT FIRST, SHE'S ECSTATIC TO BE HOME AND WITH HER PARENTS, BUT THEN THEY SHUSH HER STERNLY, TELLING HER THIS IS NO OCCASION FOR SUCH JOY AND HIGH SPIRITS.
CHASTENED, KITTY COMPOSES HERSELF. THE X-MEN ARE HERE TOO, EVEN ORORO. BUT THEIR EXPRESSIONS MATCH HER PARENTS', THEIR GAZE FOCUSED ON AN OPEN COFFIN.
BELATEDLY, KITTY REALIZES IT'S A FUNERAL AND HER CHEEKS FLUSH WITH EMBARRASMENT. HOW COULD SHE HAVE BEHAVED SO BADLY?
BUT WHO'S DEAD, SHE WONDERS, AS SHE'S LED TO THE GRAVE TO PAY HER LAST RESPECTS.
ONE LOOK GIVES HER THE ANSWER.

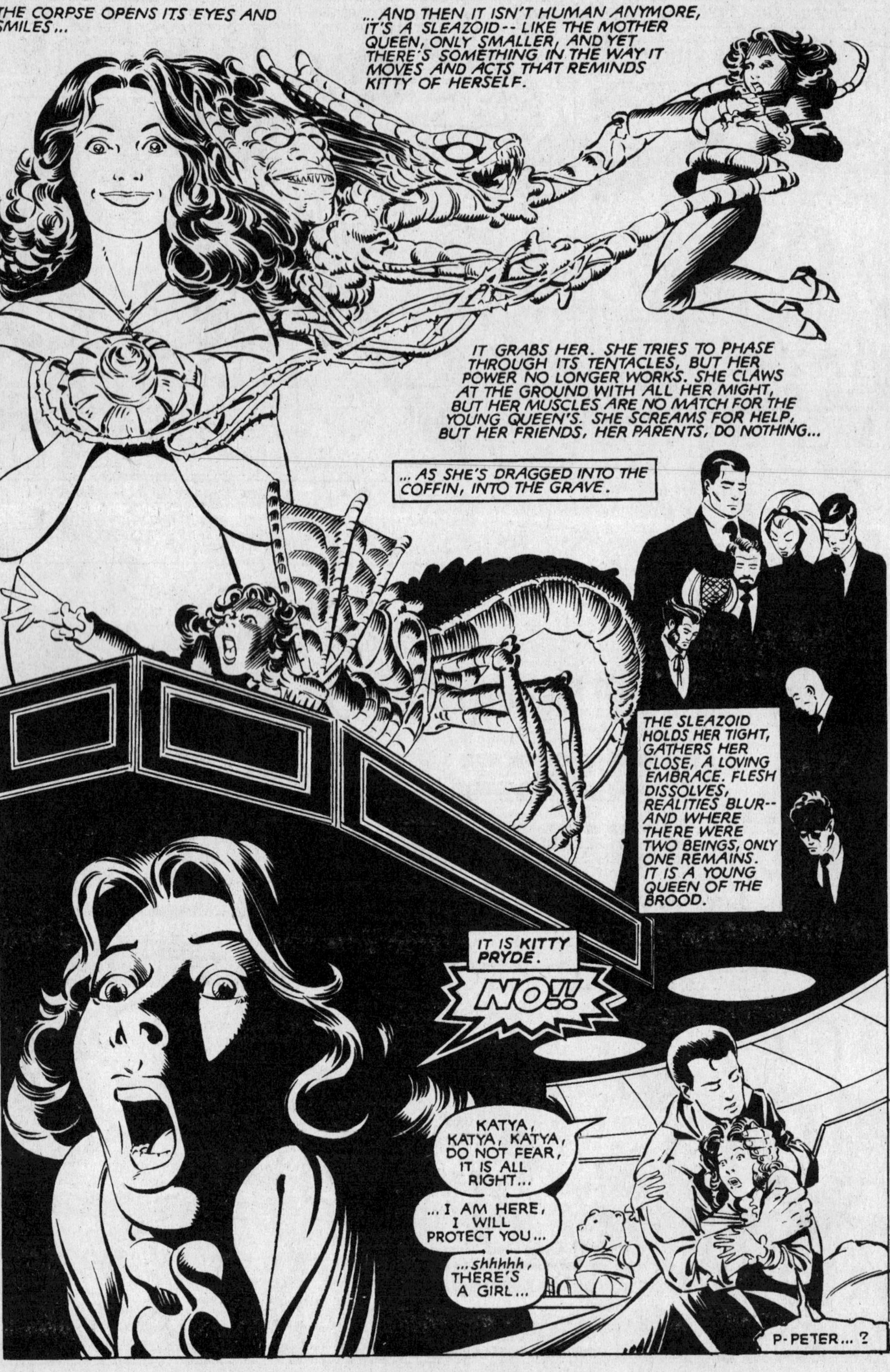
THE CORPSE OPENS ITS EYES AND SMILES...
...AND THEN IT ISN'T HUMAN ANYMORE, IT'S A SLEAZOID -- LIKE THE MOTHER QUEEN, ONLY SMALLER, AND YET THERE'S SOMETHING IN THE WAY IT MOVES AND ACTS THAT REMINDS KITTY OF HERSELF.
IT GRABS HER. SHE TRIES TO PHASE THROUGH ITS TENTACLES, BUT HER POWER NO LONGER WORKS. SHE CLAWS AT THE GROUND WITH ALL HER MIGHT, BUT HER MUSCLES ARE NO MATCH FOR THE YOUNG QUEEN'S. SHE SCREAMS FOR HELP, BUT HER FRIENDS, HER PARENTS, DO NOTHING...
...AS SHE'S DRAGGED INTO THE COFFIN, INTO THE GRAVE.
THE SLEAZOID HOLDS HER TIGHT, GATHERS HER CLOSE, A LOVING EMBRACE. FLESH DISSOLVES, REALITIES BLUR-- AND WHERE THERE WERE TWO BEINGS, ONLY ONE REMAINS. IT IS A YOUNG QUEEN OF THE BROOD.
IT IS KITTY PRYDE.
NO!!
KATYA, KATYA, KATYA, DO NOT FEAR, IT IS ALL RIGHT...
...I AM HERE, I WILL PROTECT YOU...
...shhhhh, THERE'S A GIRL...
P-PETER...?

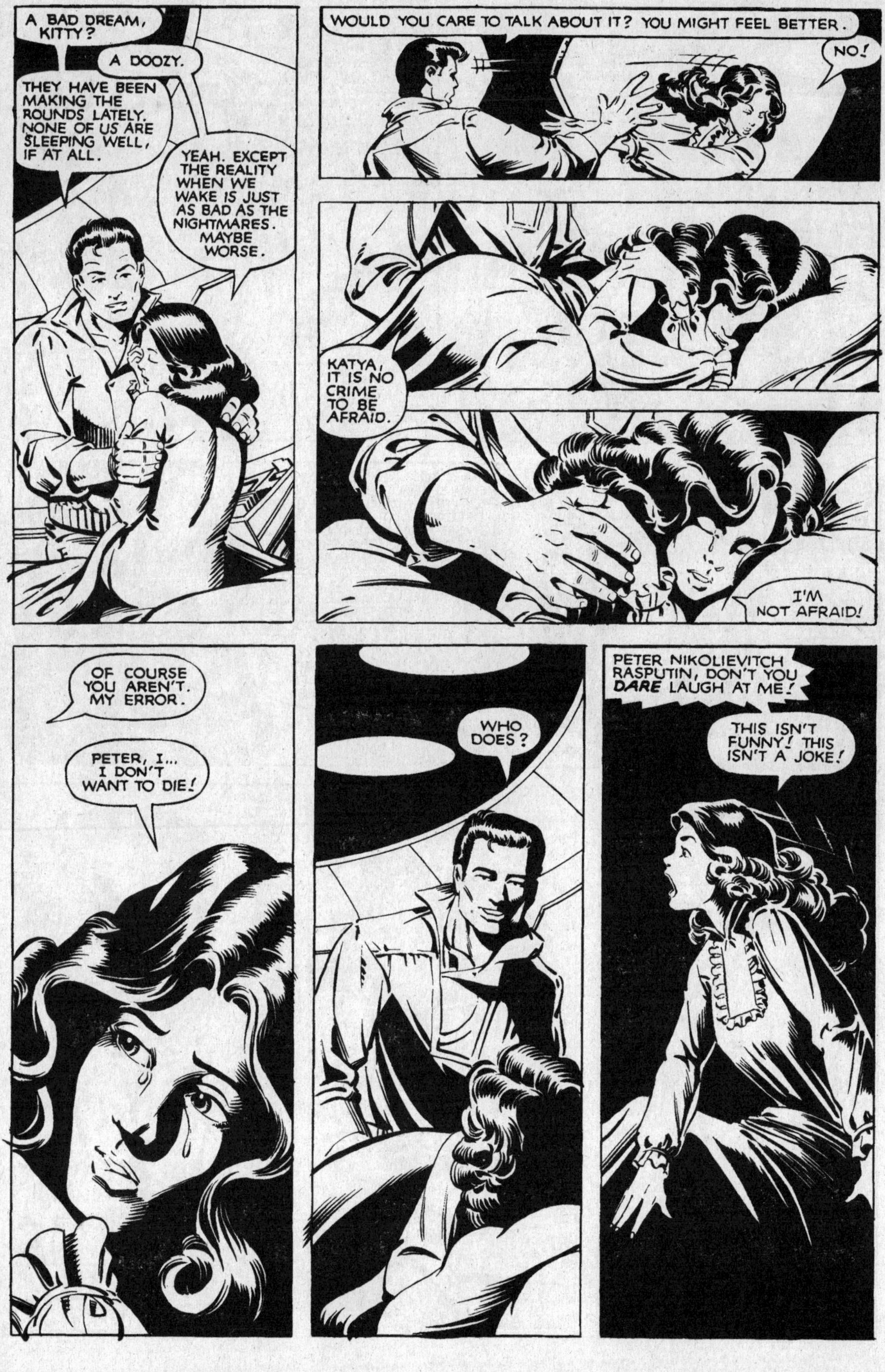
A BAD DREAM, KITTY?
A DOOZY.
THEY HAVE BEEN MAKING THE ROUNDS LATELY. NONE OF US ARE SLEEPING WELL, IF AT ALL.
YEAH. EXCEPT THE REALITY WHEN WE WAKE IS JUST AS BAD AS THE NIGHTMARES. MAYBE WORSE.
WOULD YOU CARE TO TALK ABOUT IT? YOU MIGHT FEEL BETTER.
NO!
KATYA, IT IS NO CRIME TO BE AFRAID.
I'M NOT AFRAID!
OF COURSE YOU AREN'T. MY ERROR.
PETER, I... I DON'T WANT TO DIE!
WHO DOES?
PETER NIKOLIEVITCH RASPUTIN, DON'T YOU DARE LAUGH AT ME!
THIS ISN'T FUNNY! THIS ISN'T A JOKE!

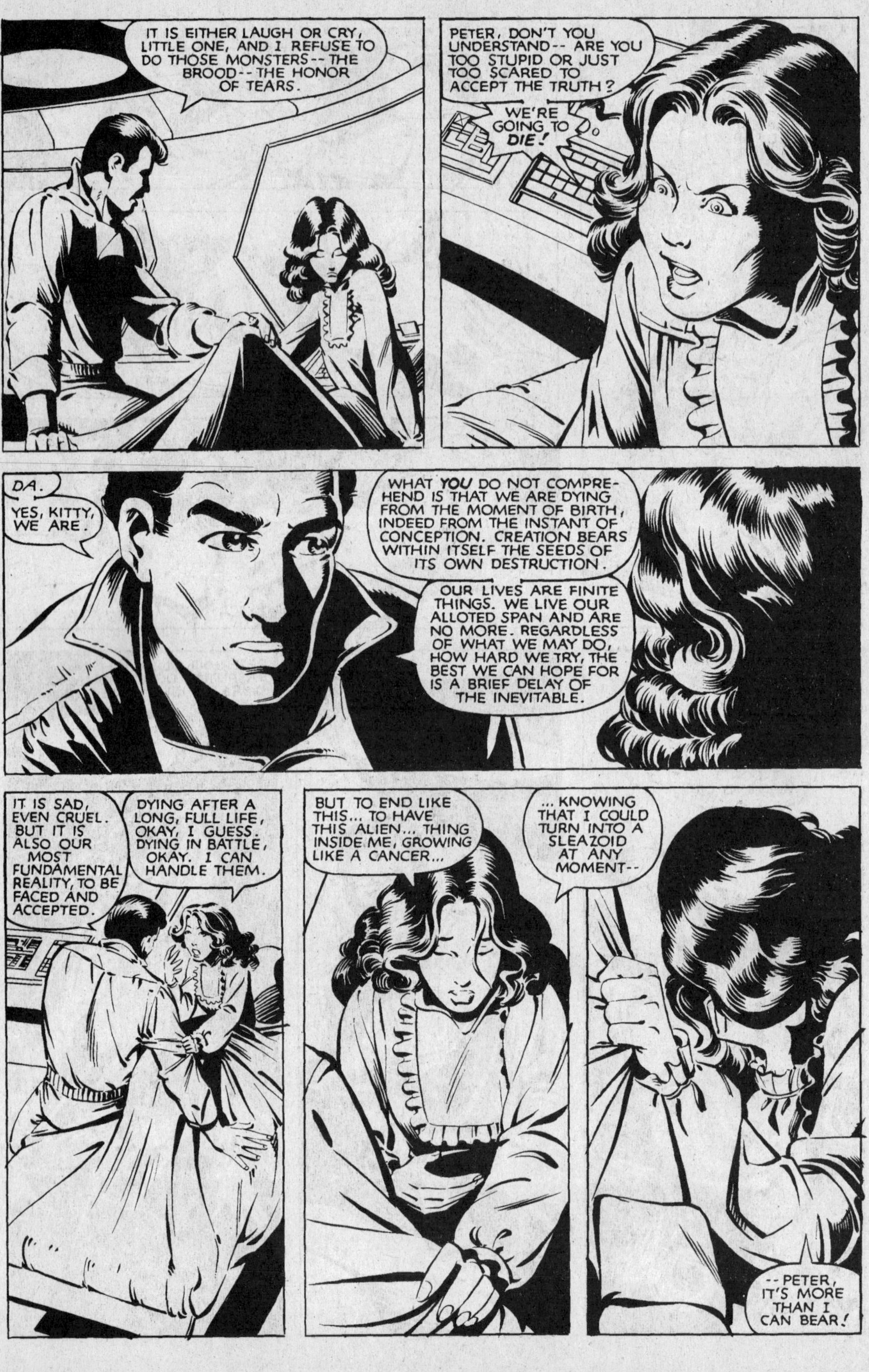

IT IS EITHER LAUGH OR CRY, LITTLE ONE, AND I REFUSE TO DO THOSE MONSTERS-- THE BROOD-- THE HONOR OF TEARS.
PETER, DON'T YOU UNDERSTAND-- ARE YOU TOO STUPID OR JUST TOO SCARED TO ACCEPT THE TRUTH?
WE'RE GOING TO DIE!
DA.
YES, KITTY, WE ARE.
WHAT YOU DO NOT COMPREHEND IS THAT WE ARE DYING FROM THE MOMENT OF BIRTH, INDEED FROM THE INSTANT OF CONCEPTION. CREATION BEARS WITHIN ITSELF THE SEEDS OF ITS OWN DESTRUCTION.
OUR LIVES ARE FINITE THINGS. WE LIVE OUR ALLOTED SPAN AND ARE NO MORE. REGARDLESS OF WHAT WE MAY DO, HOW HARD WE TRY, THE BEST WE CAN HOPE FOR IS A BRIEF DELAY OF THE INEVITABLE.
IT IS SAD, EVEN CRUEL. BUT IT IS ALSO OUR MOST FUNDAMENTAL REALITY, TO BE FACED AND ACCEPTED.
DYING AFTER A LONG, FULL LIFE, OKAY, I GUESS. DYING IN BATTLE, OKAY. I CAN HANDLE THEM.
BUT TO END LIKE THIS... TO HAVE THIS ALIEN... THING INSIDE ME, GROWING LIKE A CANCER...
... KNOWING THAT I COULD TURN INTO A SLEAZOID AT ANY MOMENT--
--PETER, IT'S MORE THAN I CAN BEAR!

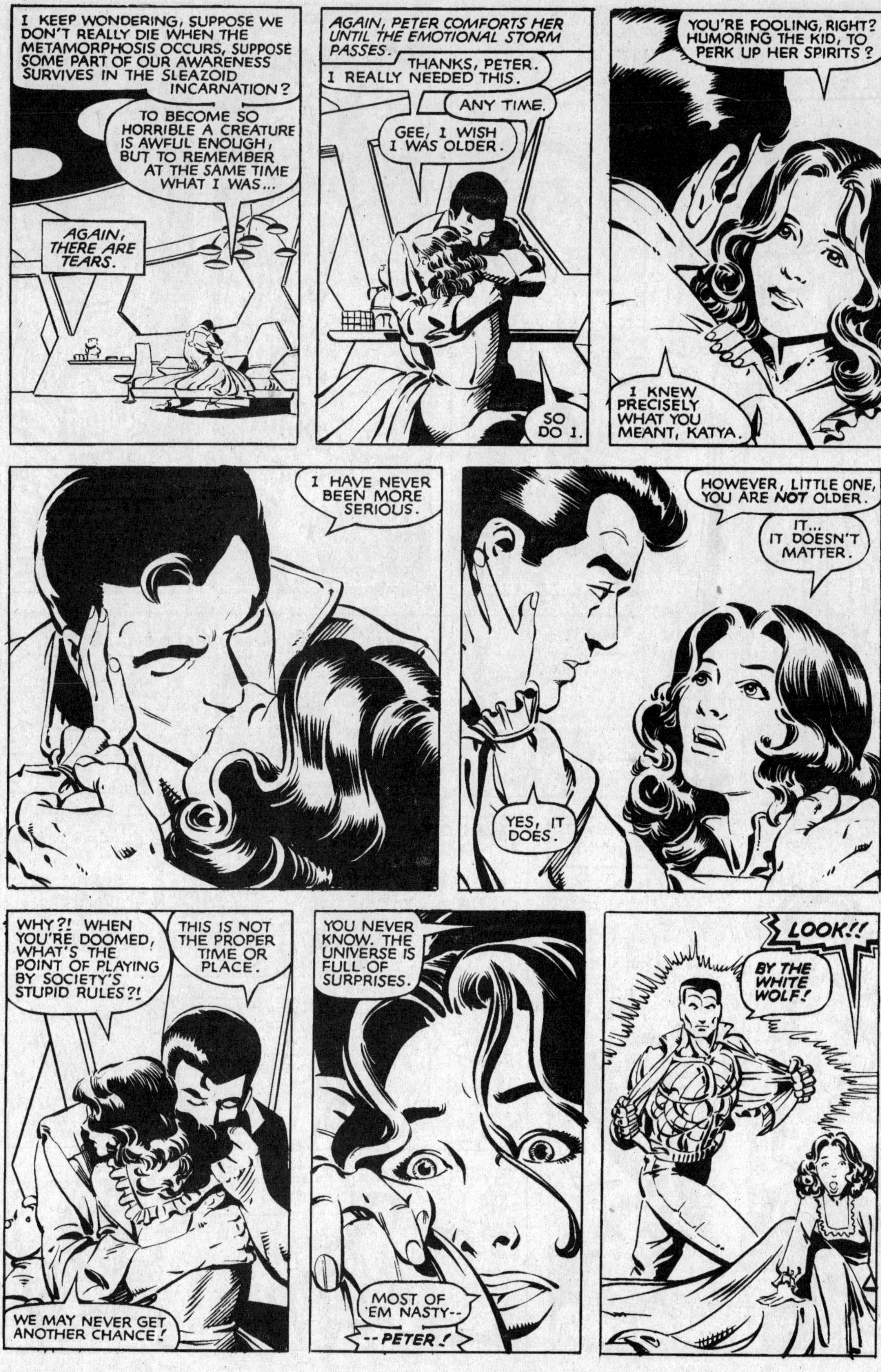
I KEEP WONDERING, SUPPOSE WE DON'T REALLY DIE WHEN THE METAMORPHOSIS OCCURS, SUPPOSE SOME PART OF OUR AWARENESS SURVIVES IN THE SLEAZOID INCARNATION?
TO BECOME SO HORRIBLE A CREATURE IS AWFUL ENOUGH, BUT TO REMEMBER AT THE SAME TIME WHAT I WAS...
AGAIN, THERE ARE TEARS.
AGAIN, PETER COMFORTS HER UNTIL THE EMOTIONAL STORM PASSES.
THANKS, PETER. I REALLY NEEDED THIS.
ANY TIME.
GEE, I WISH I WAS OLDER.
SO DO I.
YOU'RE FOOLING, RIGHT? HUMORING THE KID, TO PERK UP HER SPIRITS?
I KNEW PRECISELY WHAT YOU MEANT, KATYA.
I HAVE NEVER BEEN MORE SERIOUS.
HOWEVER, LITTLE ONE, YOU ARE NOT OLDER.
IT... IT DOESN'T MATTER.
YES, IT DOES.
WHY?! WHEN YOU'RE DOOMED, WHAT'S THE POINT OF PLAYING BY SOCIETY'S STUPID RULES?!
THIS IS NOT THE PROPER TIME OR PLACE.
WE MAY NEVER GET ANOTHER CHANCE!
YOU NEVER KNOW. THE UNIVERSE IS FULL OF SURPRISES.
MOST OF 'EM NASTY--
--PETER!
LOOK!!
BY THE WHITE WOLF!

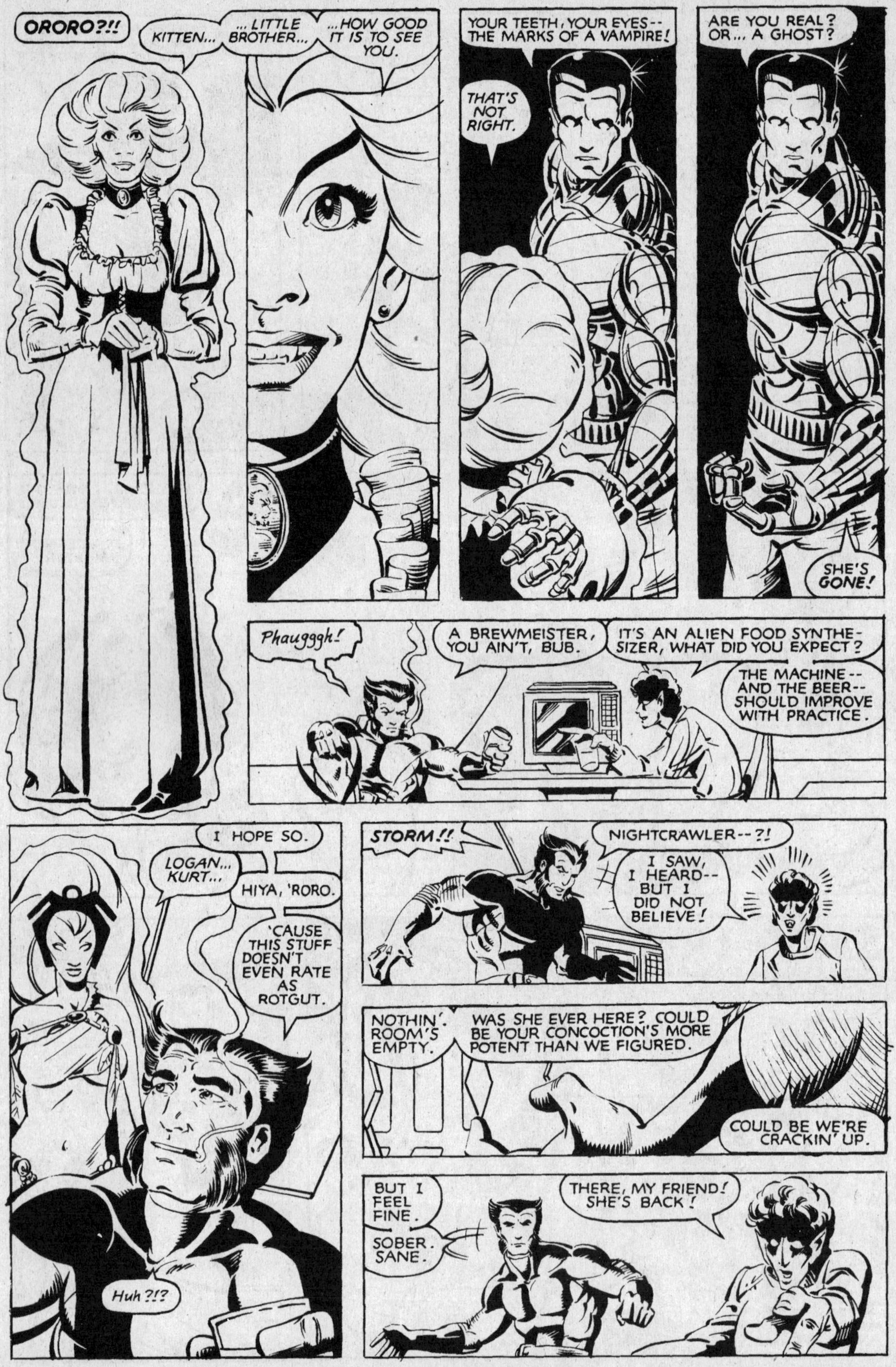

ORORO?!!
KITTEN...
...LITTLE BROTHER...
...HOW GOOD IT IS TO SEE YOU.
YOUR TEETH, YOUR EYES-- THE MARKS OF A VAMPIRE!
THAT'S NOT RIGHT.
ARE YOU REAL? OR... A GHOST?
SHE'S GONE!
Phauggghh!
A BREWMEISTER, YOU AIN'T, BUB.
IT'S AN ALIEN FOOD SYNTHESIZER, WHAT DID YOU EXPECT?
THE MACHINE-- AND THE BEER-- SHOULD IMPROVE WITH PRACTICE.
I HOPE SO.
'CAUSE THIS STUFF DOESN'T EVEN RATE AS ROTGUT.
LOGAN... KURT...
HIYA, 'RORO.
Huh?!?
STORM!!
NIGHTCRAWLER--?!
I SAW, I HEARD-- BUT I DID NOT BELIEVE!
NOTHIN'. ROOM'S EMPTY.
WAS SHE EVER HERE? COULD BE YOUR CONCOCTION'S MORE POTENT THAN WE FIGURED.
COULD BE WE'RE CRACKIN' UP.
BUT I FEEL FINE.
SOBER. SANE.
THERE, MY FRIEND! SHE'S BACK!

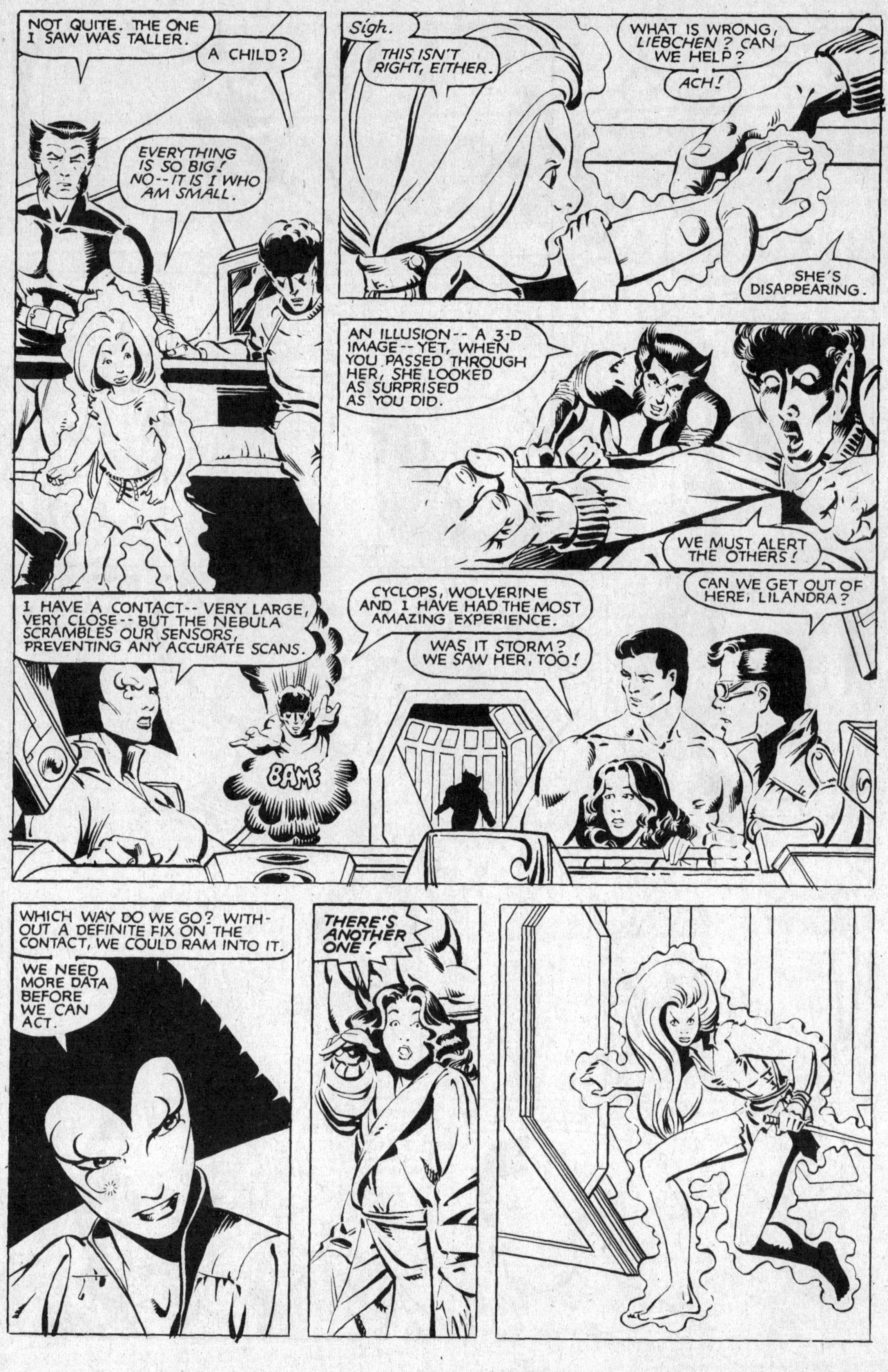
NOT QUITE. THE ONE I SAW WAS TALLER.
A CHILD?
EVERYTHING IS SO BIG! NO--IT IS I WHO AM SMALL.
Sigh.
THIS ISN'T RIGHT, EITHER.
WHAT IS WRONG, LIEBCHEN? CAN WE HELP?
ACH!
SHE'S DISAPPEARING.
AN ILLUSION--A 3-D IMAGE--YET, WHEN YOU PASSED THROUGH HER, SHE LOOKED AS SURPRISED AS YOU DID.
WE MUST ALERT THE OTHERS!
I HAVE A CONTACT--VERY LARGE, VERY CLOSE--BUT THE NEBULA SCRAMBLES OUR SENSORS, PREVENTING ANY ACCURATE SCANS.
BAMF
CYCLOPS, WOLVERINE AND I HAVE HAD THE MOST AMAZING EXPERIENCE.
WAS IT STORM? WE SAW HER, TOO!
CAN WE GET OUT OF HERE, LILANDRA?
WHICH WAY DO WE GO? WITHOUT A DEFINITE FIX ON THE CONTACT, WE COULD RAM INTO IT.
WE NEED MORE DATA BEFORE WE CAN ACT.
THERE'S ANOTHER ONE!

'RORO? RELAX, BABE, YOU'RE AMONG FRIENDS.

NO NEED TA BE SCARED.

WOLVERINE, IT'S A HOLOGRAPHIC PROJECTION, IT ISN'T REAL.

WRONG, BUB.

I THOUGHT SO TOO BUT MY SENSES TELL ME IT'S STORM. I'M FOLLOWIN' THEIR LEAD.

CRIPES, HER FEATURES ARE CHANGIN'-- GETTIN' OLDER!

MY BELOVED FRIENDS, FORGIVE THESE CLUMSY ATTEMPTS TO CONTACT YOU. I AM IMPROVING MY CONTROL WITH EXPERIENCE...

...BUT IT IS PROVING FAR MORE DIFFICULT THAN I IMAGINED.

VISUAL CONTACT!

CYCLOPS, IT'S ONE OF THE BROOD'S LIVING STAR-SHIPS!

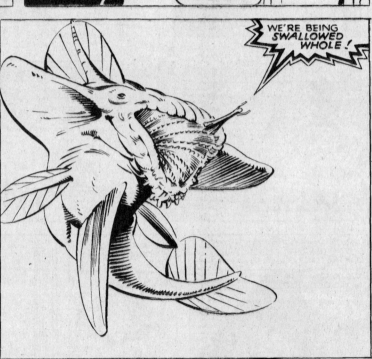

WE'RE BEING SWALLOWED WHOLE!

FULL POWER TO THE ENGINES! THE REST OF YOU, ACTIVATE THE SHIP'S COMBAT SYSTEMS!

LET'S PUNCH OUR WAY OUT OF HERE, PRONTO!

TOO LATE. THE CREATURE BROADCASTS A POWER FIELD THAT DAMPENS THE MATTER-ANTI-MATTER CORE. THE DRIVE IS INERT. SHIP'S WEAPONRY HAS BEEN RENDERED INOPERATIVE AS WELL.

THAT WAS FOR MY PROTECTION AS MUCH AS YOURS, LILANDRA.

I COULD NOT RISK YOUR INJURING THE ACANTI BEFORE I HAD AN OPPORTUNITY TO EXPLAIN.

AH! PRACTICE MAKES PERFECT, AT LAST. I MEANT TO LOOK LIKE THIS FROM THE START.

THERE IS NO CAUSE FOR ALARM.

STORM? ORORO-- IT IS YOU!

PLEASED TO SEE ME, KITTEN?

YES-- OH, YES!

I'D LIKE AN EXPLANATION, ORORO. WHAT HAPPENED TO YOU?

A GREAT DEAL, NOT ALL OF IT PLEASANT.

I AM NOT THE STORM YOU KNEW.

HOW CAN YOU BE SO SURE THIS STARBEAST-- "ACANTI," YOU CALLED IT-- WON'T HARM US?

WOW.

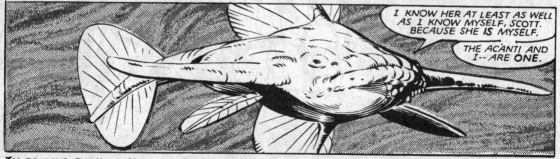

I KNOW HER AT LEAST AS WELL AS I KNOW MYSELF, SCOTT. BECAUSE SHE IS MYSELF.

THE ACANTI AND I-- ARE ONE.

IN 30 DAYS, THE X-MEN'S FINAL CONFRONTATION WITH THE BROOD, WHEREIN THEY'LL EITHER...

LIVE FREE, OR DIE!

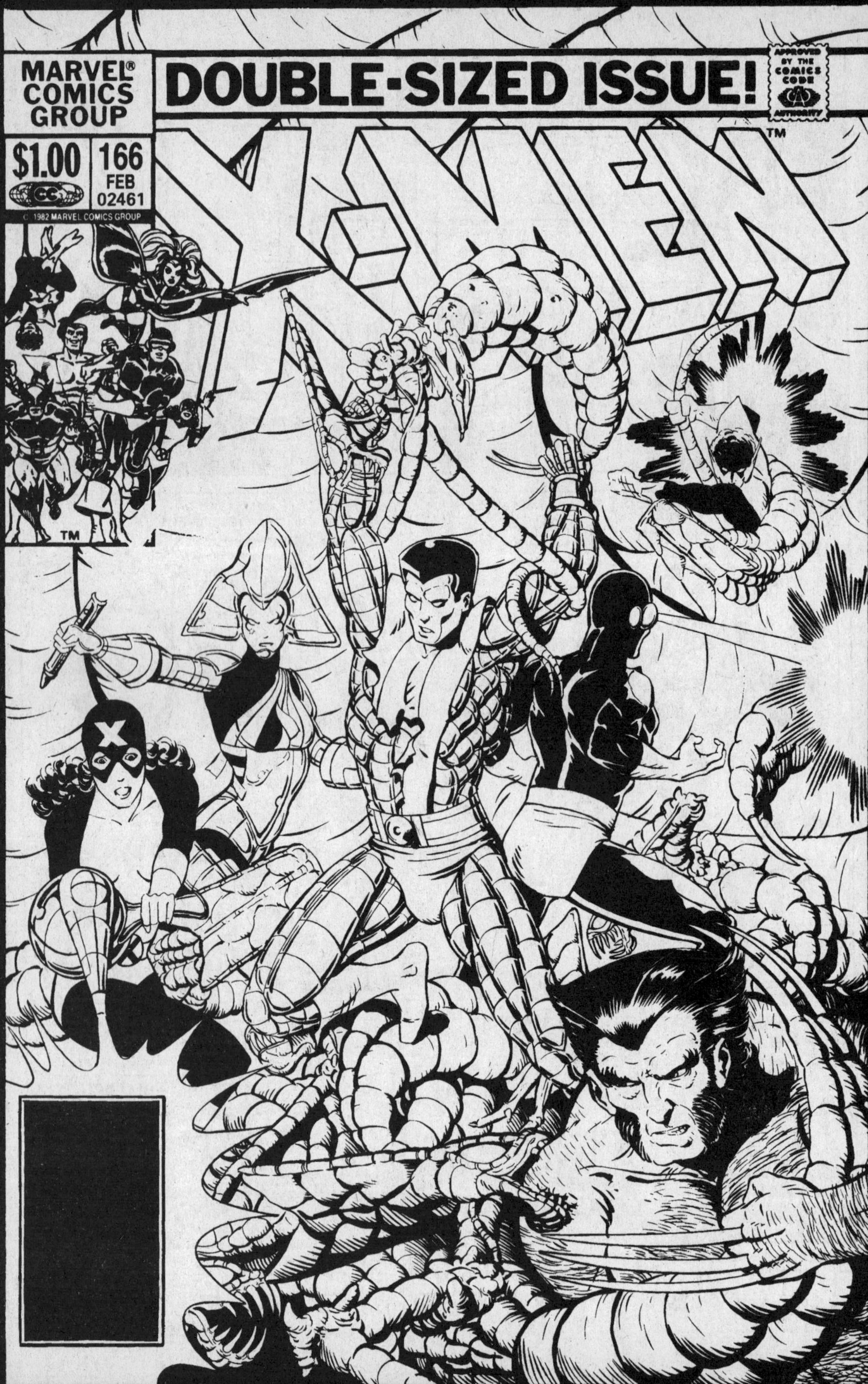

MARVEL® COMICS GROUP
DOUBLE-SIZED ISSUE!
APPROVED BY THE COMICS CODE AUTHORITY
$1.00
166
FEB
02461
© 1982 MARVEL COMICS GROUP
X-MEN™

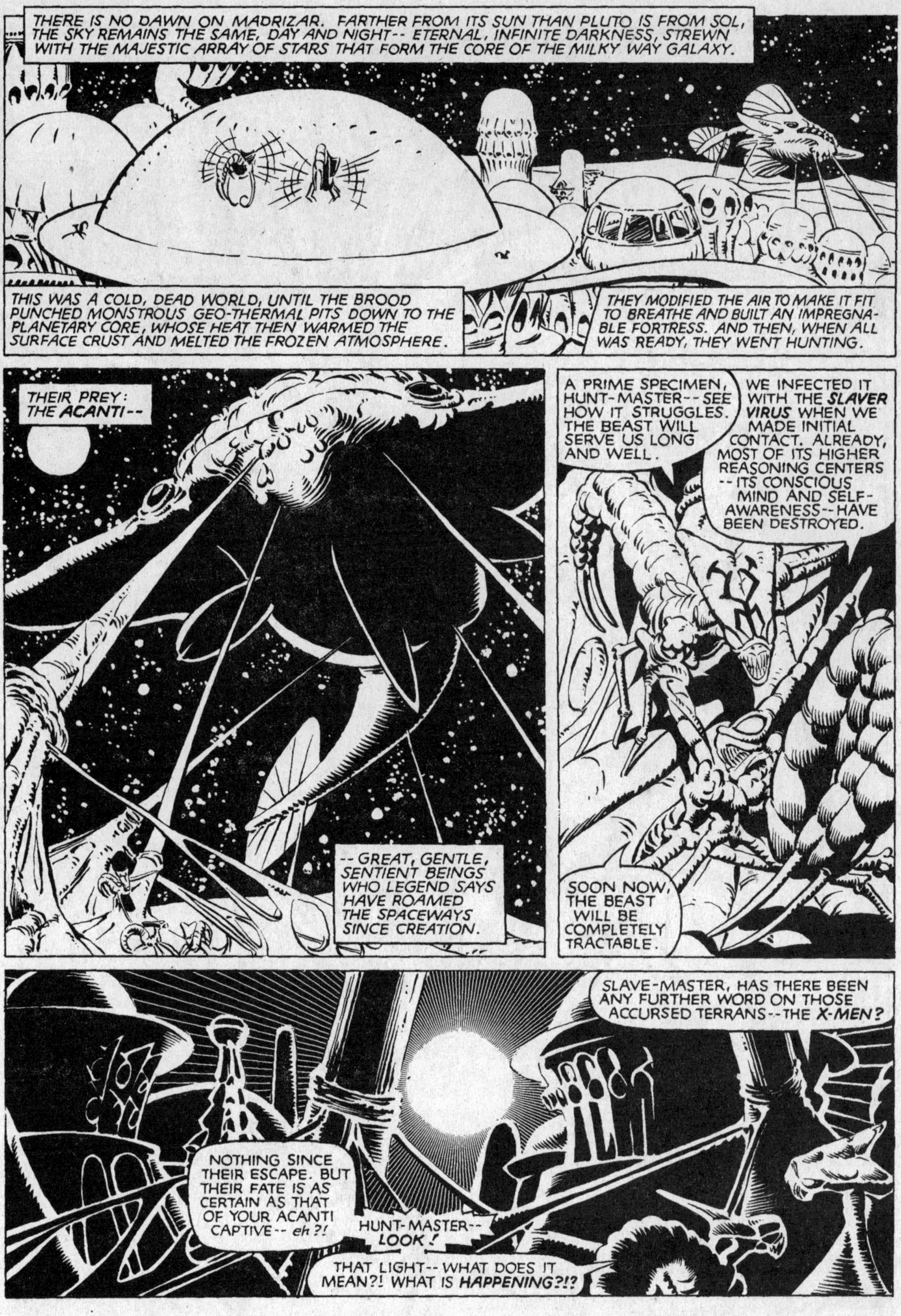
THERE IS NO DAWN ON MADRIZAR. FARTHER FROM ITS SUN THAN PLUTO IS FROM SOL, THE SKY REMAINS THE SAME, DAY AND NIGHT-- ETERNAL, INFINITE DARKNESS, STREWN WITH THE MAJESTIC ARRAY OF STARS THAT FORM THE CORE OF THE MILKY WAY GALAXY.
THIS WAS A COLD, DEAD WORLD, UNTIL THE BROOD PUNCHED MONSTROUS GEO-THERMAL PITS DOWN TO THE PLANETARY CORE, WHOSE HEAT THEN WARMED THE SURFACE CRUST AND MELTED THE FROZEN ATMOSPHERE.
THEY MODIFIED THE AIR TO MAKE IT FIT TO BREATHE AND BUILT AN IMPREGNABLE FORTRESS. AND THEN, WHEN ALL WAS READY, THEY WENT HUNTING.
THEIR PREY: THE ACANTI--
--GREAT, GENTLE, SENTIENT BEINGS WHO LEGEND SAYS HAVE ROAMED THE SPACEWAYS SINCE CREATION.
A PRIME SPECIMEN, HUNT-MASTER--SEE HOW IT STRUGGLES. THE BEAST WILL SERVE US LONG AND WELL.
WE INFECTED IT WITH THE SLAVER VIRUS WHEN WE MADE INITIAL CONTACT. ALREADY, MOST OF ITS HIGHER REASONING CENTERS --ITS CONSCIOUS MIND AND SELF-AWARENESS--HAVE BEEN DESTROYED.
SOON NOW, THE BEAST WILL BE COMPLETELY TRACTABLE.
SLAVE-MASTER, HAS THERE BEEN ANY FURTHER WORD ON THOSE ACCURSED TERRANS--THE X-MEN?
NOTHING SINCE THEIR ESCAPE. BUT THEIR FATE IS AS CERTAIN AS THAT OF YOUR ACANTI CAPTIVE-- eh?!
HUNT-MASTER-- LOOK!
THAT LIGHT--WHAT DOES IT MEAN?! WHAT IS HAPPENING?!?

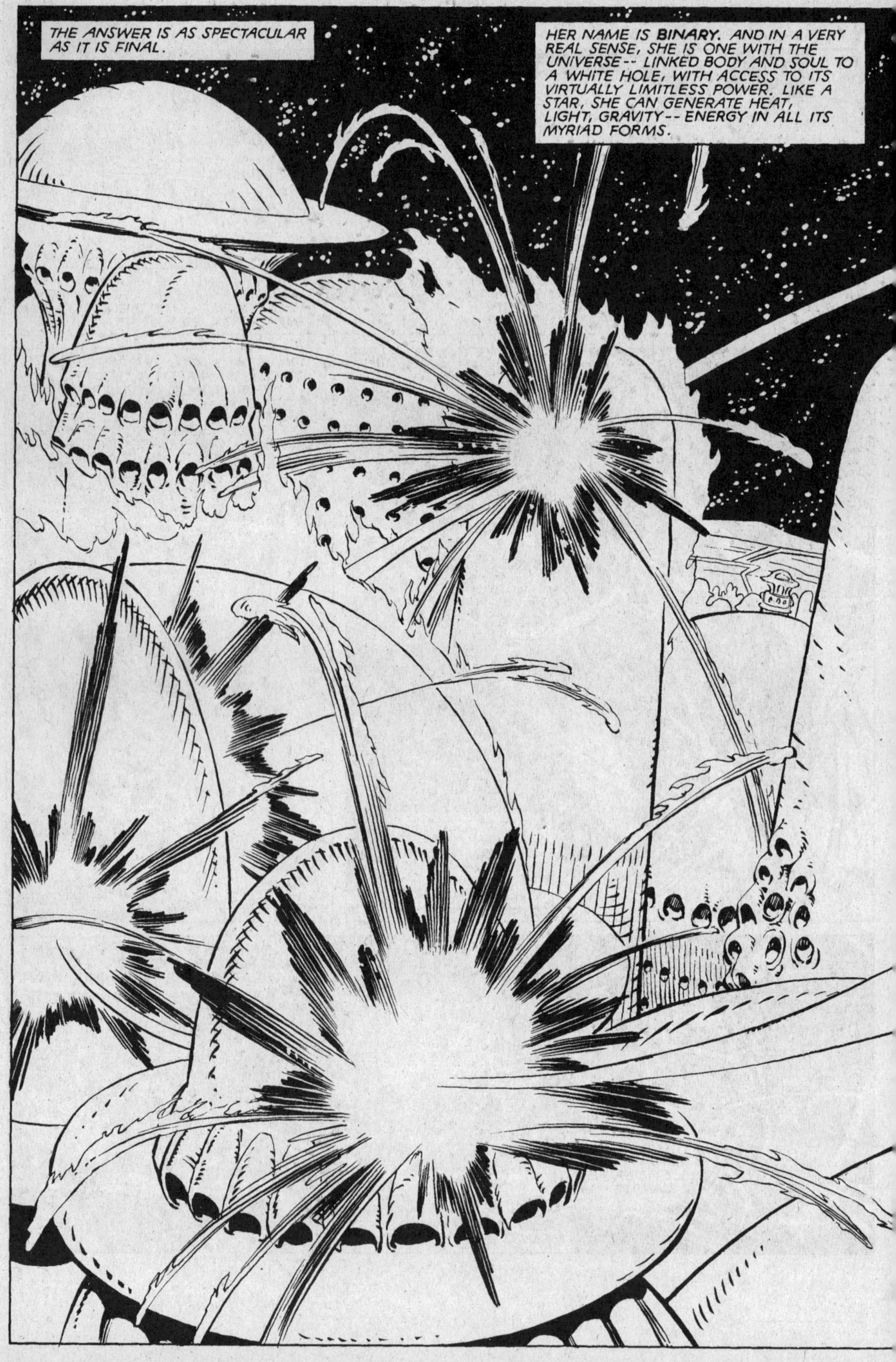
THE ANSWER IS AS SPECTACULAR AS IT IS FINAL.
HER NAME IS **BINARY.** AND IN A VERY REAL SENSE, SHE IS ONE WITH THE UNIVERSE-- LINKED BODY AND SOUL TO A WHITE HOLE, WITH ACCESS TO ITS VIRTUALLY LIMITLESS POWER. LIKE A STAR, SHE CAN GENERATE HEAT, LIGHT, GRAVITY-- ENERGY IN ALL ITS MYRIAD FORMS.

SHE IS A FRIEND OF THOSE SELFSAME X-MEN. SHE IS HERE TO *AVENGE* THEM.

STAN LEE PRESENTS THE UNCANNY **X-MEN** -- WHO THIS DAY WILL EITHER...

LIVE FREE or DIE!

| CHRIS CLAREMONT SCRIPTER | PAUL SMITH PENCILER | BOB WIACEK INKER | TOM ORZECHOWSKI LETTERER | GLYNIS WEIN COLORIST | LOUISE JONES EDITOR | JIM SHOOTER EDITOR-IN-CHIEF |

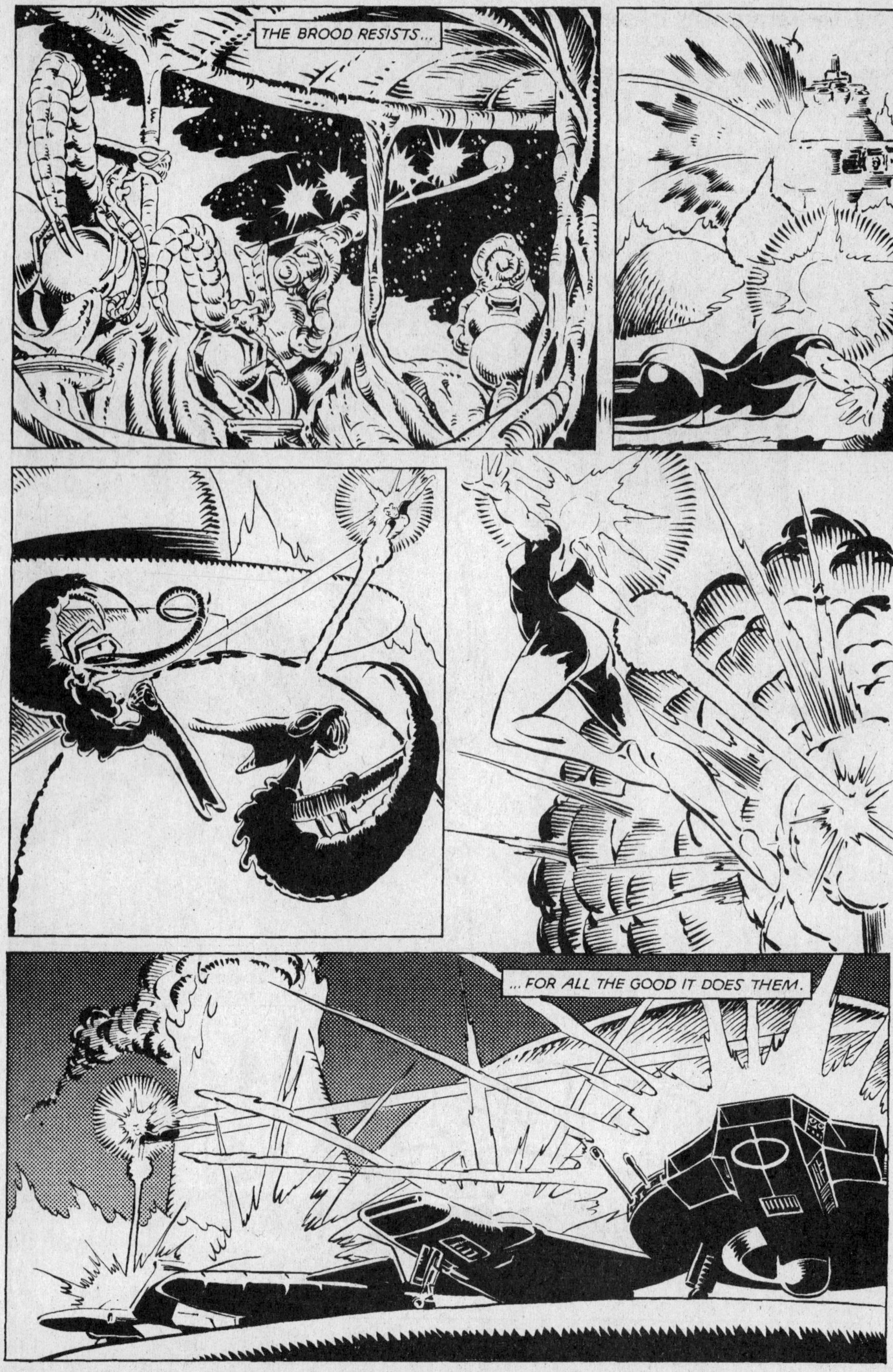
THE BROOD RESISTS...
...FOR ALL THE GOOD IT DOES THEM.

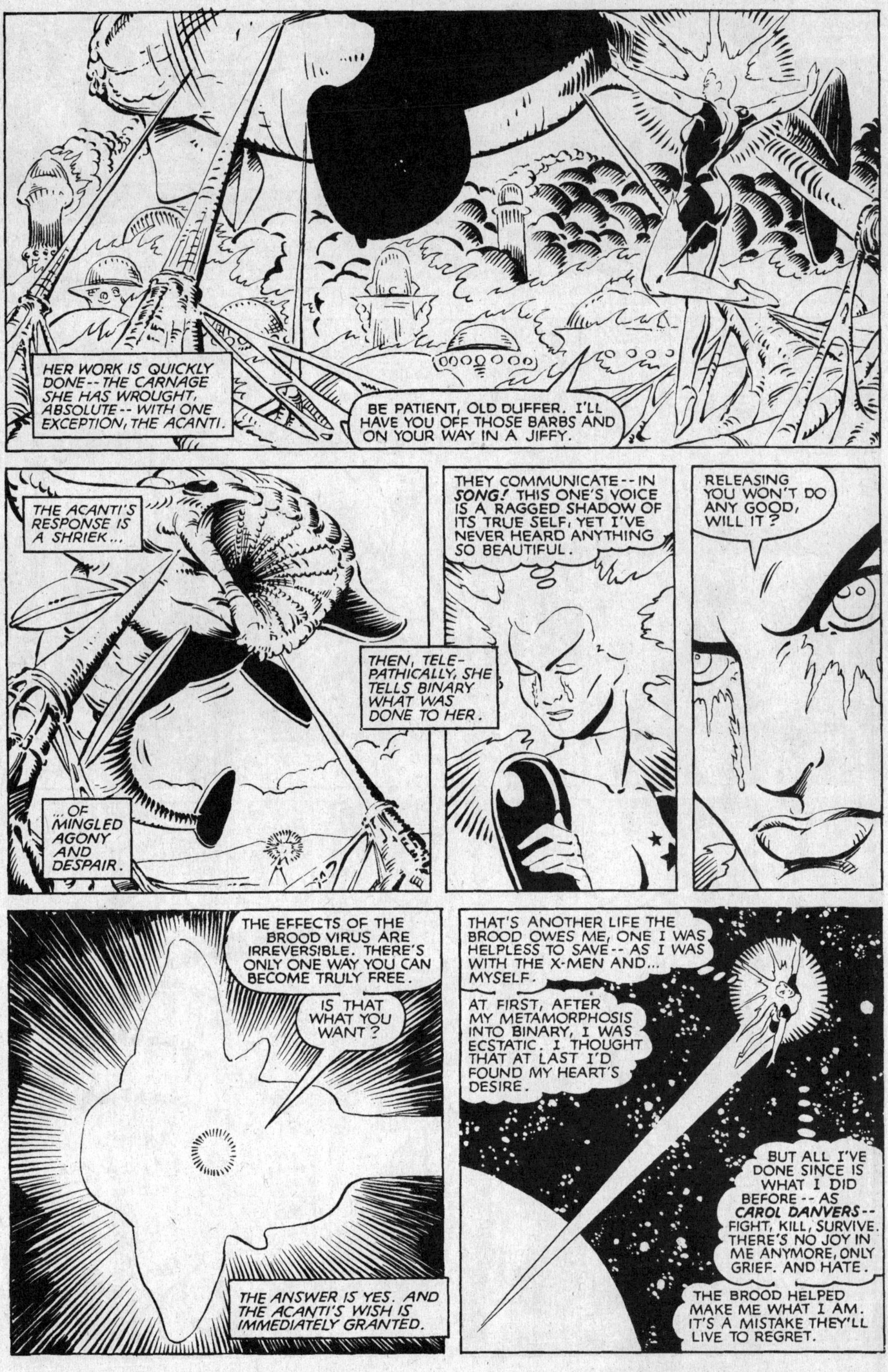
HER WORK IS QUICKLY DONE--THE CARNAGE SHE HAS WROUGHT, ABSOLUTE--WITH ONE EXCEPTION, THE ACANTI.
BE PATIENT, OLD DUFFER. I'LL HAVE YOU OFF THOSE BARBS AND ON YOUR WAY IN A JIFFY.
THE ACANTI'S RESPONSE IS A SHRIEK...
...OF MINGLED AGONY AND DESPAIR.
THEN, TELEPATHICALLY, SHE TELLS BINARY WHAT WAS DONE TO HER.
THEY COMMUNICATE--IN SONG! THIS ONE'S VOICE IS A RAGGED SHADOW OF ITS TRUE SELF, YET I'VE NEVER HEARD ANYTHING SO BEAUTIFUL.
RELEASING YOU WON'T DO ANY GOOD, WILL IT?
THE EFFECTS OF THE BROOD VIRUS ARE IRREVERSIBLE. THERE'S ONLY ONE WAY YOU CAN BECOME TRULY FREE.
IS THAT WHAT YOU WANT?
THE ANSWER IS YES. AND THE ACANTI'S WISH IS IMMEDIATELY GRANTED.
THAT'S ANOTHER LIFE THE BROOD OWES ME, ONE I WAS HELPLESS TO SAVE--AS I WAS WITH THE X-MEN AND... MYSELF.
AT FIRST, AFTER MY METAMORPHOSIS INTO BINARY, I WAS ECSTATIC. I THOUGHT THAT AT LAST I'D FOUND MY HEART'S DESIRE.
BUT ALL I'VE DONE SINCE IS WHAT I DID BEFORE--AS CAROL DANVERS--FIGHT, KILL, SURVIVE. THERE'S NO JOY IN ME ANYMORE, ONLY GRIEF. AND HATE.
THE BROOD HELPED MAKE ME WHAT I AM. IT'S A MISTAKE THEY'LL LIVE TO REGRET.

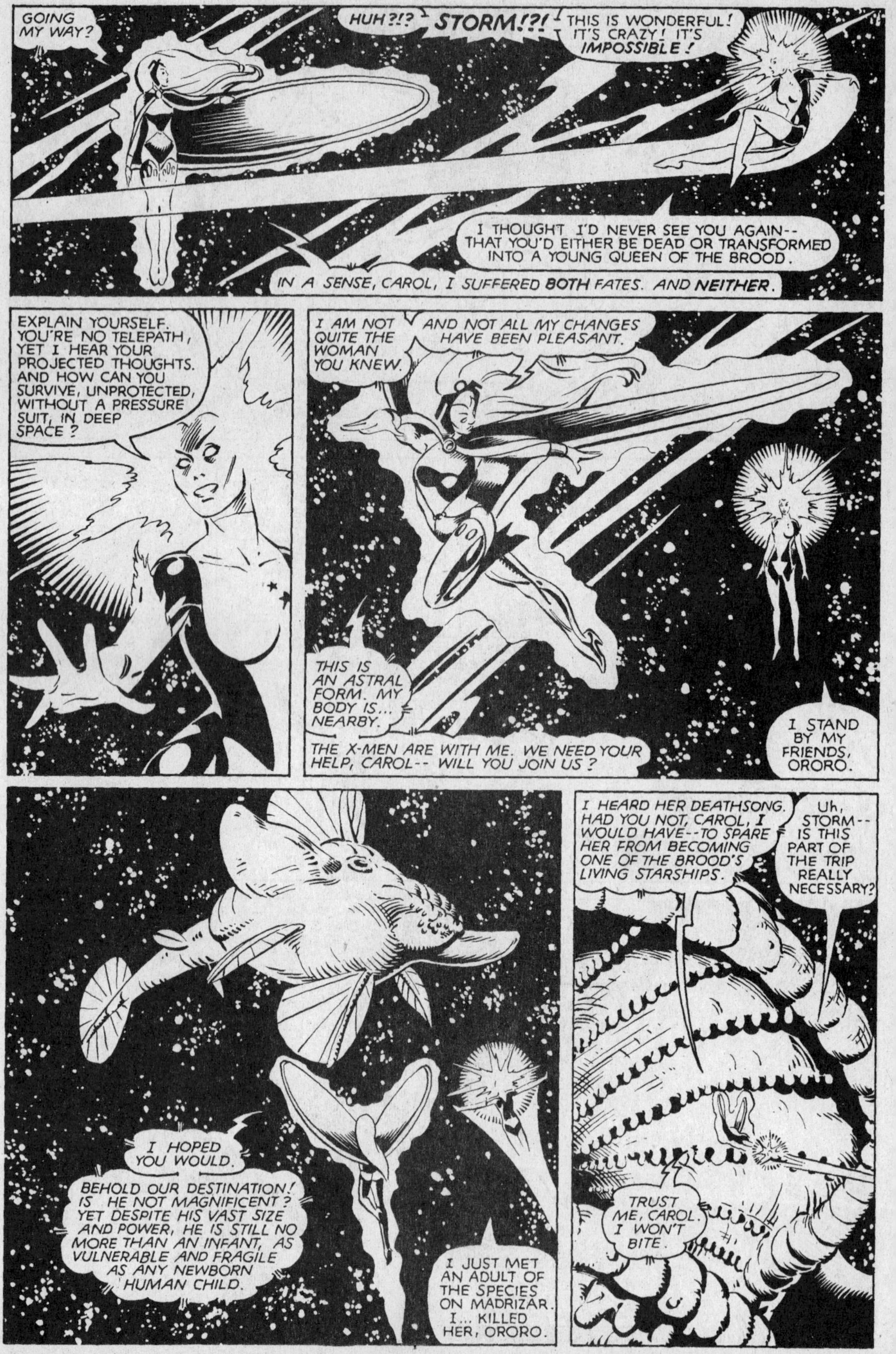

GOING MY WAY?
HUH?!?
STORM!?!
THIS IS WONDERFUL! IT'S CRAZY! IT'S IMPOSSIBLE!
I THOUGHT I'D NEVER SEE YOU AGAIN-- THAT YOU'D EITHER BE DEAD OR TRANSFORMED INTO A YOUNG QUEEN OF THE BROOD.
IN A SENSE, CAROL, I SUFFERED BOTH FATES. AND NEITHER.
EXPLAIN YOURSELF. YOU'RE NO TELEPATH, YET I HEAR YOUR PROJECTED THOUGHTS. AND HOW CAN YOU SURVIVE, UNPROTECTED, WITHOUT A PRESSURE SUIT, IN DEEP SPACE?
I AM NOT QUITE THE WOMAN YOU KNEW.
AND NOT ALL MY CHANGES HAVE BEEN PLEASANT.
THIS IS AN ASTRAL FORM. MY BODY IS... NEARBY.
THE X-MEN ARE WITH ME. WE NEED YOUR HELP, CAROL-- WILL YOU JOIN US?
I STAND BY MY FRIENDS, ORORO.
I HOPED YOU WOULD.
BEHOLD OUR DESTINATION! IS HE NOT MAGNIFICENT? YET DESPITE HIS VAST SIZE AND POWER, HE IS STILL NO MORE THAN AN INFANT, AS VULNERABLE AND FRAGILE AS ANY NEWBORN HUMAN CHILD.
I JUST MET AN ADULT OF THE SPECIES ON MADRIZAR. I... KILLED HER, ORORO.
I HEARD HER DEATHSONG. HAD YOU NOT, CAROL, I WOULD HAVE--TO SPARE HER FROM BECOMING ONE OF THE BROOD'S LIVING STARSHIPS.
Uh, STORM-- IS THIS PART OF THE TRIP REALLY NECESSARY?
TRUST ME, CAROL. I WON'T BITE.

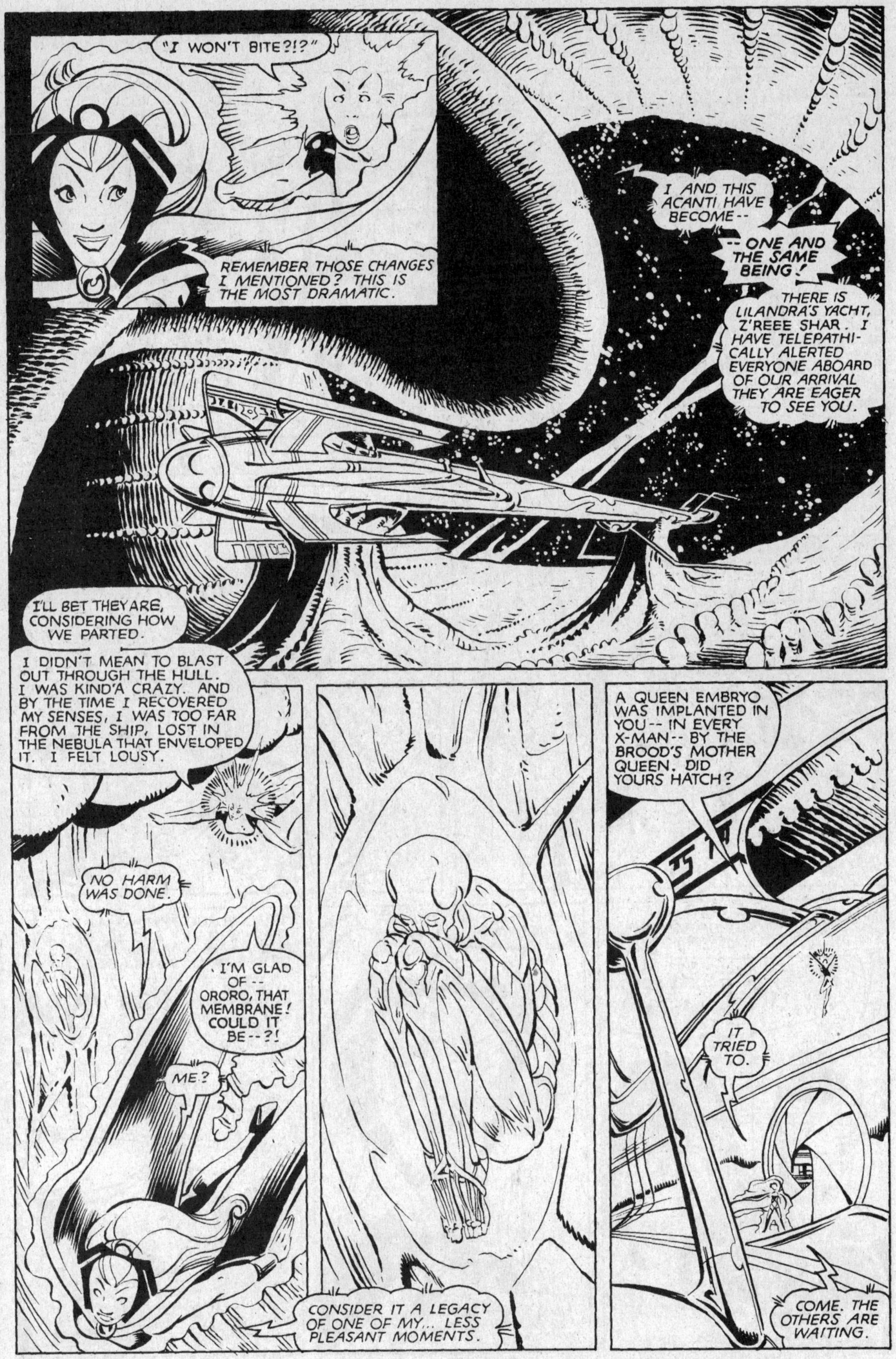
"I WON'T BITE?!?"
REMEMBER THOSE CHANGES I MENTIONED? THIS IS THE MOST DRAMATIC.
I AND THIS ACANTI HAVE BECOME--
-- ONE AND THE SAME BEING!
THERE IS LILANDRA'S YACHT, Z'REEE SHAR. I HAVE TELEPATHICALLY ALERTED EVERYONE ABOARD OF OUR ARRIVAL THEY ARE EAGER TO SEE YOU.
I'LL BET THEY ARE, CONSIDERING HOW WE PARTED.
I DIDN'T MEAN TO BLAST OUT THROUGH THE HULL. I WAS KIND'A CRAZY. AND BY THE TIME I RECOVERED MY SENSES, I WAS TOO FAR FROM THE SHIP, LOST IN THE NEBULA THAT ENVELOPED IT. I FELT LOUSY.
NO HARM WAS DONE.
I'M GLAD OF -- ORORO, THAT MEMBRANE! COULD IT BE--?!
ME?
CONSIDER IT A LEGACY OF ONE OF MY... LESS PLEASANT MOMENTS.
A QUEEN EMBRYO WAS IMPLANTED IN YOU-- IN EVERY X-MAN-- BY THE BROOD'S MOTHER QUEEN. DID YOURS HATCH?
IT TRIED TO.
COME. THE OTHERS ARE WAITING.

SIX LOST SOULS: ONE ALIEN, **LILANDRA,** EXPATRIATE RULER OF THE GALAXY-SPANNING SHI'AR EMPIRE, AND FIVE HUMAN-- **CYCLOPS, COLOSSUS, KITTY PRYDE, WOLVERINE** AND **NIGHTCRAWLER**-- MUTANTS, GIFTED WITH ABILITIES THAT SET THEM APART FROM THE REST OF THEIR SPECIES, FORGED INTO A TEAM OF UNSUNG, OCCASIONALLY OUTLAW, HEROES KNOWN AS THE **X-MEN**.

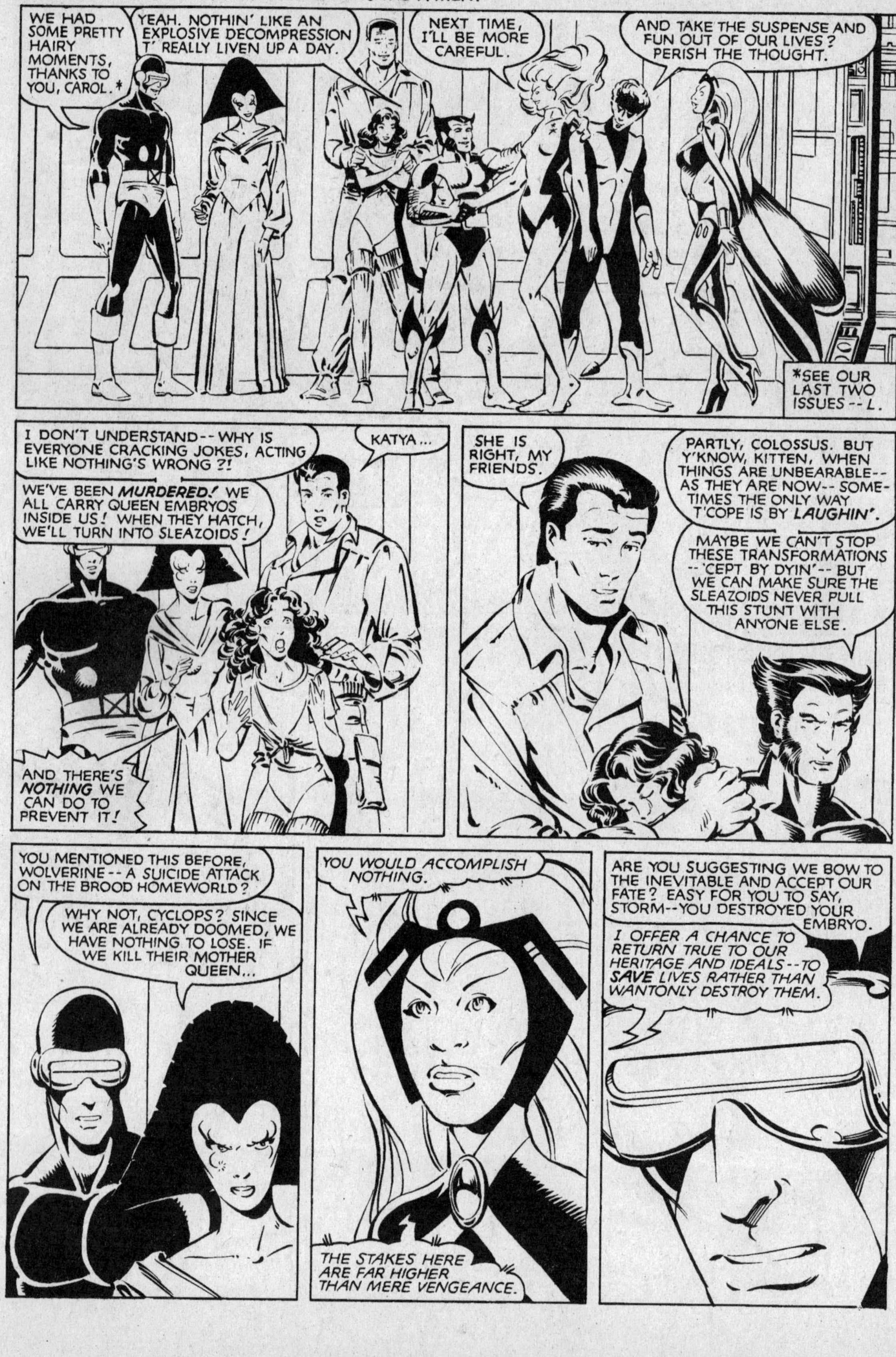

WE HAD SOME PRETTY HAIRY MOMENTS, THANKS TO YOU, CAROL.*
YEAH. NOTHIN' LIKE AN EXPLOSIVE DECOMPRESSION T' REALLY LIVEN UP A DAY.
NEXT TIME, I'LL BE MORE CAREFUL.
AND TAKE THE SUSPENSE AND FUN OUT OF OUR LIVES? PERISH THE THOUGHT.
*SEE OUR LAST TWO ISSUES -- L.
I DON'T UNDERSTAND-- WHY IS EVERYONE CRACKING JOKES, ACTING LIKE NOTHING'S WRONG?!
KATYA...
WE'VE BEEN MURDERED! WE ALL CARRY QUEEN EMBRYOS INSIDE US! WHEN THEY HATCH, WE'LL TURN INTO SLEAZOIDS!
AND THERE'S NOTHING WE CAN DO TO PREVENT IT!
SHE IS RIGHT, MY FRIENDS.
PARTLY, COLOSSUS. BUT Y'KNOW, KITTEN, WHEN THINGS ARE UNBEARABLE-- AS THEY ARE NOW-- SOMETIMES THE ONLY WAY T'COPE IS BY LAUGHIN'.
MAYBE WE CAN'T STOP THESE TRANSFORMATIONS --'CEPT BY DYIN'-- BUT WE CAN MAKE SURE THE SLEAZOIDS NEVER PULL THIS STUNT WITH ANYONE ELSE.
YOU MENTIONED THIS BEFORE, WOLVERINE-- A SUICIDE ATTACK ON THE BROOD HOMEWORLD?
WHY NOT, CYCLOPS? SINCE WE ARE ALREADY DOOMED, WE HAVE NOTHING TO LOSE. IF WE KILL THEIR MOTHER QUEEN...
YOU WOULD ACCOMPLISH NOTHING.
THE STAKES HERE ARE FAR HIGHER THAN MERE VENGEANCE.
ARE YOU SUGGESTING WE BOW TO THE INEVITABLE AND ACCEPT OUR FATE? EASY FOR YOU TO SAY, STORM--YOU DESTROYED YOUR EMBRYO.
I OFFER A CHANCE TO RETURN TRUE TO OUR HERITAGE AND IDEALS--TO SAVE LIVES RATHER THAN WANTONLY DESTROY THEM.

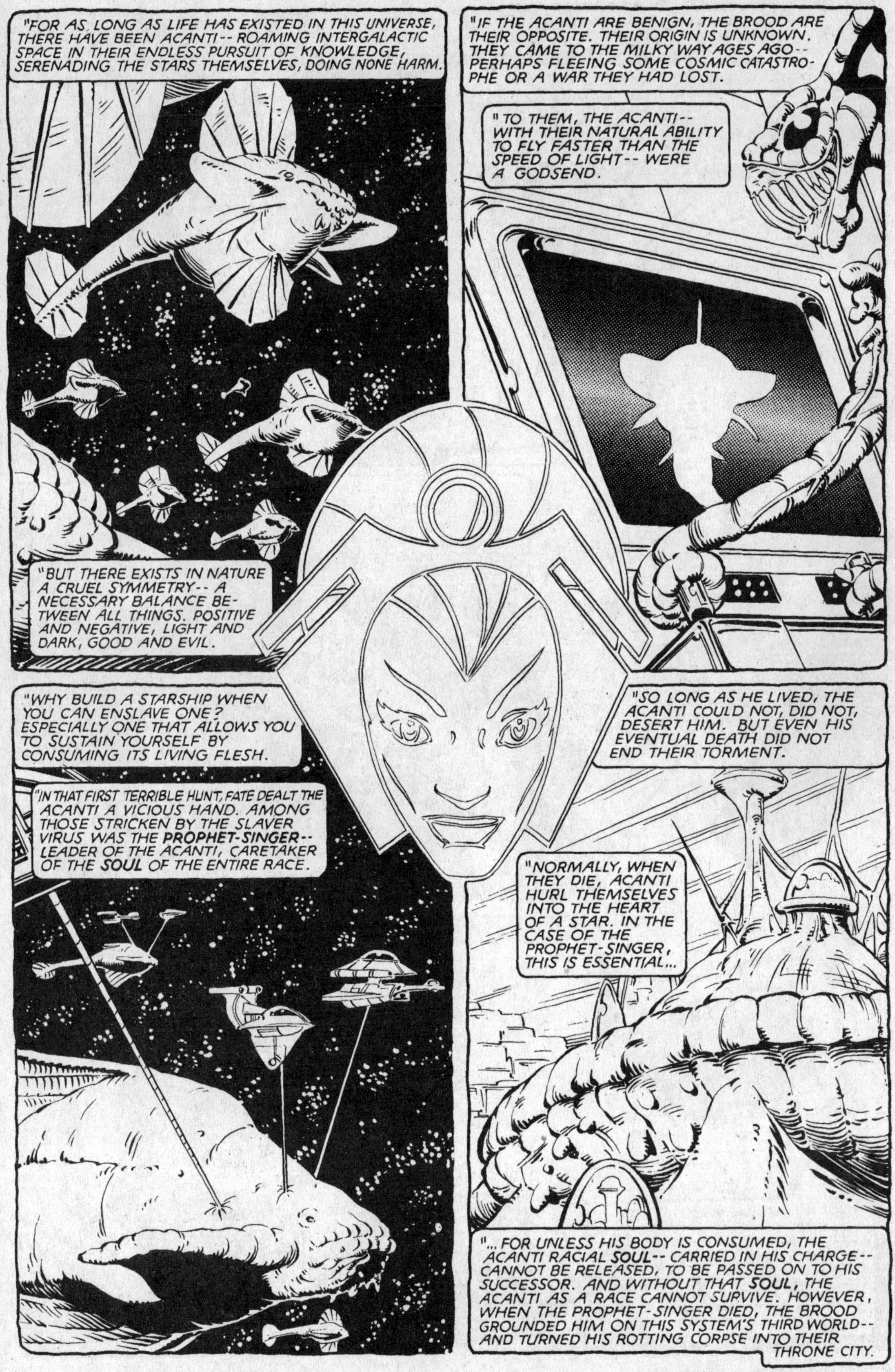
"FOR AS LONG AS LIFE HAS EXISTED IN THIS UNIVERSE, THERE HAVE BEEN ACANTI -- ROAMING INTERGALACTIC SPACE IN THEIR ENDLESS PURSUIT OF KNOWLEDGE, SERENADING THE STARS THEMSELVES, DOING NONE HARM.
"BUT THERE EXISTS IN NATURE A CRUEL SYMMETRY -- A NECESSARY BALANCE BETWEEN ALL THINGS. POSITIVE AND NEGATIVE, LIGHT AND DARK, GOOD AND EVIL.
"IF THE ACANTI ARE BENIGN, THE BROOD ARE THEIR OPPOSITE. THEIR ORIGIN IS UNKNOWN. THEY CAME TO THE MILKY WAY AGES AGO -- PERHAPS FLEEING SOME COSMIC CATASTROPHE OR A WAR THEY HAD LOST.
"TO THEM, THE ACANTI -- WITH THEIR NATURAL ABILITY TO FLY FASTER THAN THE SPEED OF LIGHT -- WERE A GODSEND.
"WHY BUILD A STARSHIP WHEN YOU CAN ENSLAVE ONE? ESPECIALLY ONE THAT ALLOWS YOU TO SUSTAIN YOURSELF BY CONSUMING ITS LIVING FLESH.
"IN THAT FIRST TERRIBLE HUNT, FATE DEALT THE ACANTI A VICIOUS HAND. AMONG THOSE STRICKEN BY THE SLAVER VIRUS WAS THE PROPHET-SINGER -- LEADER OF THE ACANTI, CARETAKER OF THE SOUL OF THE ENTIRE RACE.
"SO LONG AS HE LIVED, THE ACANTI COULD NOT, DID NOT, DESERT HIM. BUT EVEN HIS EVENTUAL DEATH DID NOT END THEIR TORMENT.
"NORMALLY, WHEN THEY DIE, ACANTI HURL THEMSELVES INTO THE HEART OF A STAR. IN THE CASE OF THE PROPHET-SINGER, THIS IS ESSENTIAL...
"... FOR UNLESS HIS BODY IS CONSUMED, THE ACANTI RACIAL SOUL -- CARRIED IN HIS CHARGE -- CANNOT BE RELEASED, TO BE PASSED ON TO HIS SUCCESSOR. AND WITHOUT THAT SOUL, THE ACANTI AS A RACE CANNOT SURVIVE. HOWEVER, WHEN THE PROPHET-SINGER DIED, THE BROOD GROUNDED HIM ON THIS SYSTEM'S THIRD WORLD -- AND TURNED HIS ROTTING CORPSE INTO THEIR THRONE CITY.

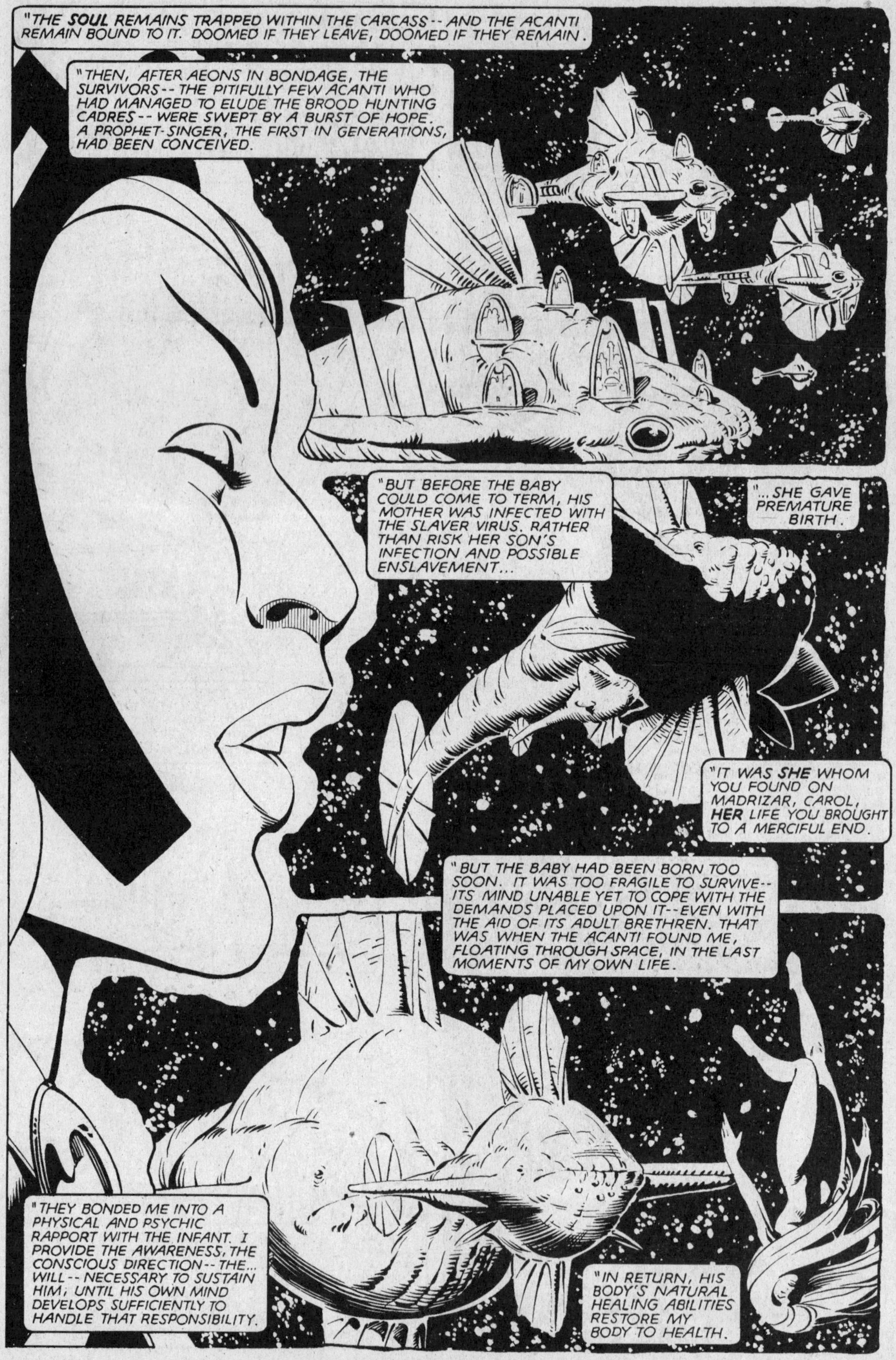
"THE SOUL REMAINS TRAPPED WITHIN THE CARCASS -- AND THE ACANTI REMAIN BOUND TO IT. DOOMED IF THEY LEAVE, DOOMED IF THEY REMAIN.
"THEN, AFTER AEONS IN BONDAGE, THE SURVIVORS -- THE PITIFULLY FEW ACANTI WHO HAD MANAGED TO ELUDE THE BROOD HUNTING CADRES -- WERE SWEPT BY A BURST OF HOPE. A PROPHET-SINGER, THE FIRST IN GENERATIONS, HAD BEEN CONCEIVED.
"BUT BEFORE THE BABY COULD COME TO TERM, HIS MOTHER WAS INFECTED WITH THE SLAVER VIRUS. RATHER THAN RISK HER SON'S INFECTION AND POSSIBLE ENSLAVEMENT...
"...SHE GAVE PREMATURE BIRTH.
"IT WAS SHE WHOM YOU FOUND ON MADRIZAR, CAROL, HER LIFE YOU BROUGHT TO A MERCIFUL END.
"BUT THE BABY HAD BEEN BORN TOO SOON. IT WAS TOO FRAGILE TO SURVIVE -- ITS MIND UNABLE YET TO COPE WITH THE DEMANDS PLACED UPON IT -- EVEN WITH THE AID OF ITS ADULT BRETHREN. THAT WAS WHEN THE ACANTI FOUND ME, FLOATING THROUGH SPACE, IN THE LAST MOMENTS OF MY OWN LIFE.
"THEY BONDED ME INTO A PHYSICAL AND PSYCHIC RAPPORT WITH THE INFANT. I PROVIDE THE AWARENESS, THE CONSCIOUS DIRECTION -- THE... WILL -- NECESSARY TO SUSTAIN HIM; UNTIL HIS OWN MIND DEVELOPS SUFFICIENTLY TO HANDLE THAT RESPONSIBILITY.
"IN RETURN, HIS BODY'S NATURAL HEALING ABILITIES RESTORE MY BODY TO HEALTH.

THUS IS A CRITICAL PERSONAL BALANCE RESTORED. AS "GODDESS" AND WOMAN, I AM CONSECRATED TO LIFE, SWORN TO PRESERVE IT. YET I DESTROYED THE QUEEN EMBRYO IMPLANTED WITHIN ME.

NOW, HOWEVER, I HAVE AN OPPORTUNITY TO *SAVE* AN EQUALLY HELPLESS LIFE. TO GIVE INSTEAD OF TAKE.

AND WHAT I DO FOR ONE, THE X-MEN MIGHT DO FOR AN ENTIRE RACE.

IF WE CAN RELEASE THE SOUL, SO THAT IT CAN BE PASSED ON TO THIS CHILD, HE CAN THEN LEAD THE ACANTI TO SAFETY.

WHERE DO WE FIND THIS SOUL, 'RORO?

IN THE HEAD OF THE SKELETON, AT ITS BASE.

FIGURES. I BEEN THERE, DARLIN'-- SOME VERY NASTY CRITTERS CLAIM THAT TURF, BEINGS EVEN THE BROOD ARE SCARED OF.

IN THAT CASE, LOGAN, WE OUGHT TO FIT RIGHT IN.

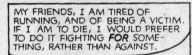

MY FRIENDS, I AM TIRED OF RUNNING, AND OF BEING A VICTIM. IF I AM TO DIE, I WOULD PREFER TO DO IT FIGHTING *FOR* SOMETHING, RATHER THAN AGAINST.

LET US SAVE THE ACANTI, IF WE CAN.

CAN WE, GUYS? PLEASE?

I THINK WE'RE AGREED ON THIS. BUT HOW TO BEST ACCOMPLISH THAT OBJECTIVE?

SUPPOSE STORM AND BINARY CREATE A DIVERSION, TO DRAW AS MUCH OF THE BROOD'S ATTENTION, AND THE BATTLE FLEET, AS POSSIBLE, AWAY FROM THE PLANET. SIMULTANEOUSLY, THE REST OF US BEAM DOWN TO THE SKELETON TO MAKE A RUN FOR THE *SOUL*.

IF WE KEEP LILANDRA'S YACHT HERE INSIDE THE BABY, THE SHIP'S SHIELDS MASKING IT FROM BROOD SENSORS, THEY'LL HAVE NO IDEA THE X-MEN ARE INVOLVED. WE COULD FINISH THE JOB BEFORE THEY'RE EVEN AWARE OF US.

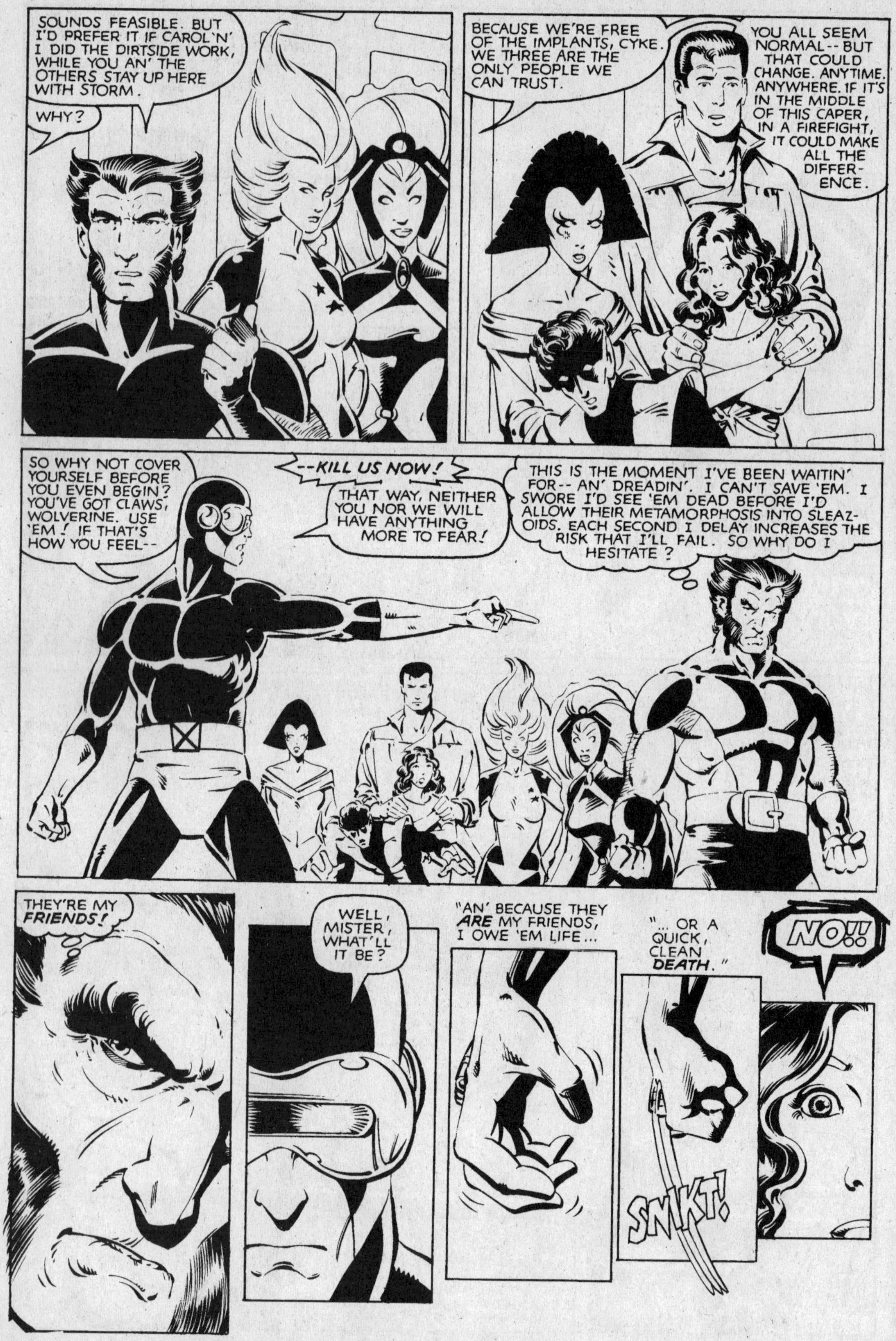

SOUNDS FEASIBLE. BUT I'D PREFER IT IF CAROL'N' I DID THE DIRTSIDE WORK, WHILE YOU AN' THE OTHERS STAY UP HERE WITH STORM.
WHY?
BECAUSE WE'RE FREE OF THE IMPLANTS, CYKE. WE THREE ARE THE ONLY PEOPLE WE CAN TRUST.
YOU ALL SEEM NORMAL-- BUT THAT COULD CHANGE. ANYTIME. ANYWHERE. IF IT'S IN THE MIDDLE OF THIS CAPER, IN A FIREFIGHT, IT COULD MAKE ALL THE DIFFERENCE.
SO WHY NOT COVER YOURSELF BEFORE YOU EVEN BEGIN? YOU'VE GOT CLAWS, WOLVERINE. USE 'EM! IF THAT'S HOW YOU FEEL--
--KILL US NOW!
THAT WAY, NEITHER YOU NOR WE WILL HAVE ANYTHING MORE TO FEAR!
THIS IS THE MOMENT I'VE BEEN WAITIN' FOR-- AN' DREADIN'. I CAN'T SAVE 'EM. I SWORE I'D SEE 'EM DEAD BEFORE I'D ALLOW THEIR METAMORPHOSIS INTO SLEAZOIDS. EACH SECOND I DELAY INCREASES THE RISK THAT I'LL FAIL. SO WHY DO I HESITATE?
THEY'RE MY FRIENDS!
WELL, MISTER, WHAT'LL IT BE?
"AN' BECAUSE THEY ARE MY FRIENDS, I OWE 'EM LIFE...
"... OR A QUICK, CLEAN DEATH."
SNIKT!
NO!!

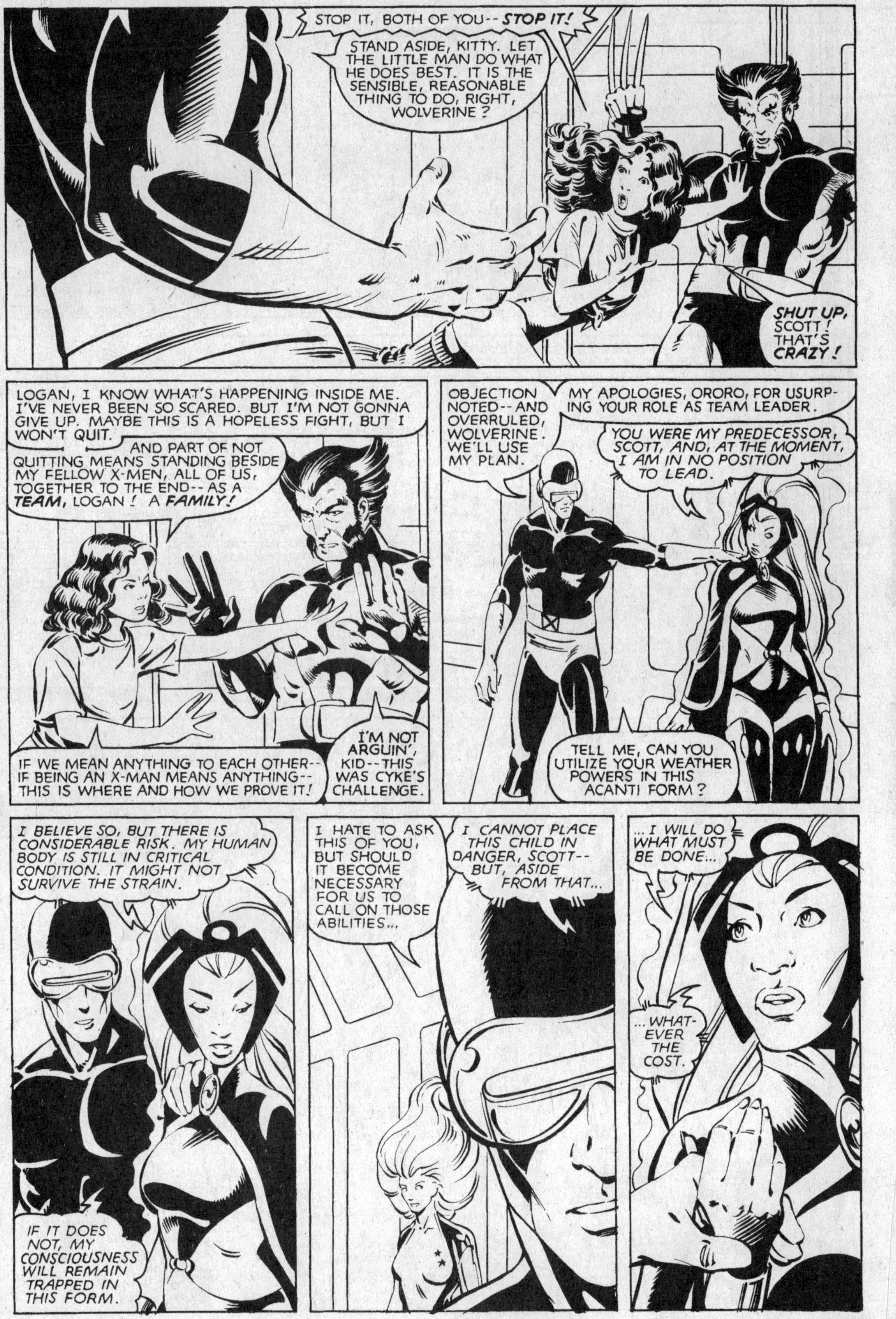
STOP IT, BOTH OF YOU-- STOP IT!
STAND ASIDE, KITTY. LET THE LITTLE MAN DO WHAT HE DOES BEST. IT IS THE SENSIBLE, REASONABLE THING TO DO, RIGHT, WOLVERINE?
SHUT UP, SCOTT! THAT'S CRAZY!
LOGAN, I KNOW WHAT'S HAPPENING INSIDE ME. I'VE NEVER BEEN SO SCARED. BUT I'M NOT GONNA GIVE UP. MAYBE THIS IS A HOPELESS FIGHT, BUT I WON'T QUIT.
AND PART OF NOT QUITTING MEANS STANDING BESIDE MY FELLOW X-MEN, ALL OF US, TOGETHER TO THE END-- AS A TEAM, LOGAN! A FAMILY!
IF WE MEAN ANYTHING TO EACH OTHER-- IF BEING AN X-MAN MEANS ANYTHING-- THIS IS WHERE AND HOW WE PROVE IT!
I'M NOT ARGUIN', KID-- THIS WAS CYKE'S CHALLENGE.
OBJECTION NOTED-- AND OVERRULED, WOLVERINE. WE'LL USE MY PLAN.
MY APOLOGIES, ORORO, FOR USURPING YOUR ROLE AS TEAM LEADER.
YOU WERE MY PREDECESSOR, SCOTT, AND, AT THE MOMENT, I AM IN NO POSITION TO LEAD.
TELL ME, CAN YOU UTILIZE YOUR WEATHER POWERS IN THIS ACANTI FORM?
I BELIEVE SO, BUT THERE IS CONSIDERABLE RISK. MY HUMAN BODY IS STILL IN CRITICAL CONDITION. IT MIGHT NOT SURVIVE THE STRAIN.
IF IT DOES NOT, MY CONSCIOUSNESS WILL REMAIN TRAPPED IN THIS FORM.
I HATE TO ASK THIS OF YOU, BUT SHOULD IT BECOME NECESSARY FOR US TO CALL ON THOSE ABILITIES...
I CANNOT PLACE THIS CHILD IN DANGER, SCOTT-- BUT, ASIDE FROM THAT...
...I WILL DO WHAT MUST BE DONE...
...WHATEVER THE COST.

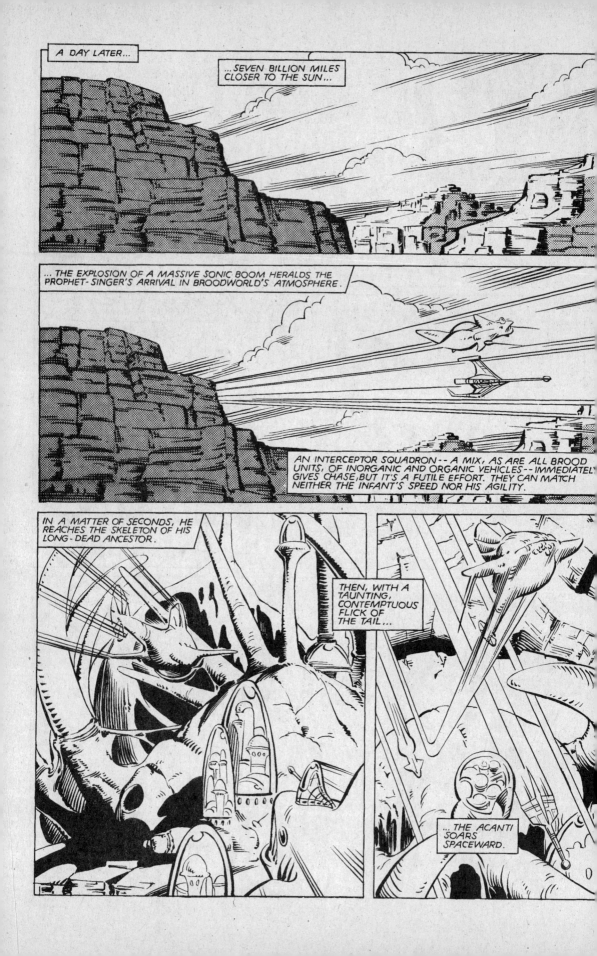

A DAY LATER...

...SEVEN BILLION MILES CLOSER TO THE SUN...

... THE EXPLOSION OF A MASSIVE SONIC BOOM HERALDS THE PROPHET-SINGER'S ARRIVAL IN BROODWORLD'S ATMOSPHERE.

AN INTERCEPTOR SQUADRON -- A MIX, AS ARE ALL BROOD UNITS, OF INORGANIC AND ORGANIC VEHICLES -- IMMEDIATELY GIVES CHASE, BUT IT'S A FUTILE EFFORT. THEY CAN MATCH NEITHER THE INFANT'S SPEED NOR HIS AGILITY.

IN A MATTER OF SECONDS, HE REACHES THE SKELETON OF HIS LONG-DEAD ANCESTOR.

THEN, WITH A TAUNTING, CONTEMPTUOUS FLICK OF THE TAIL...

... THE ACANTI SOARS SPACEWARD.

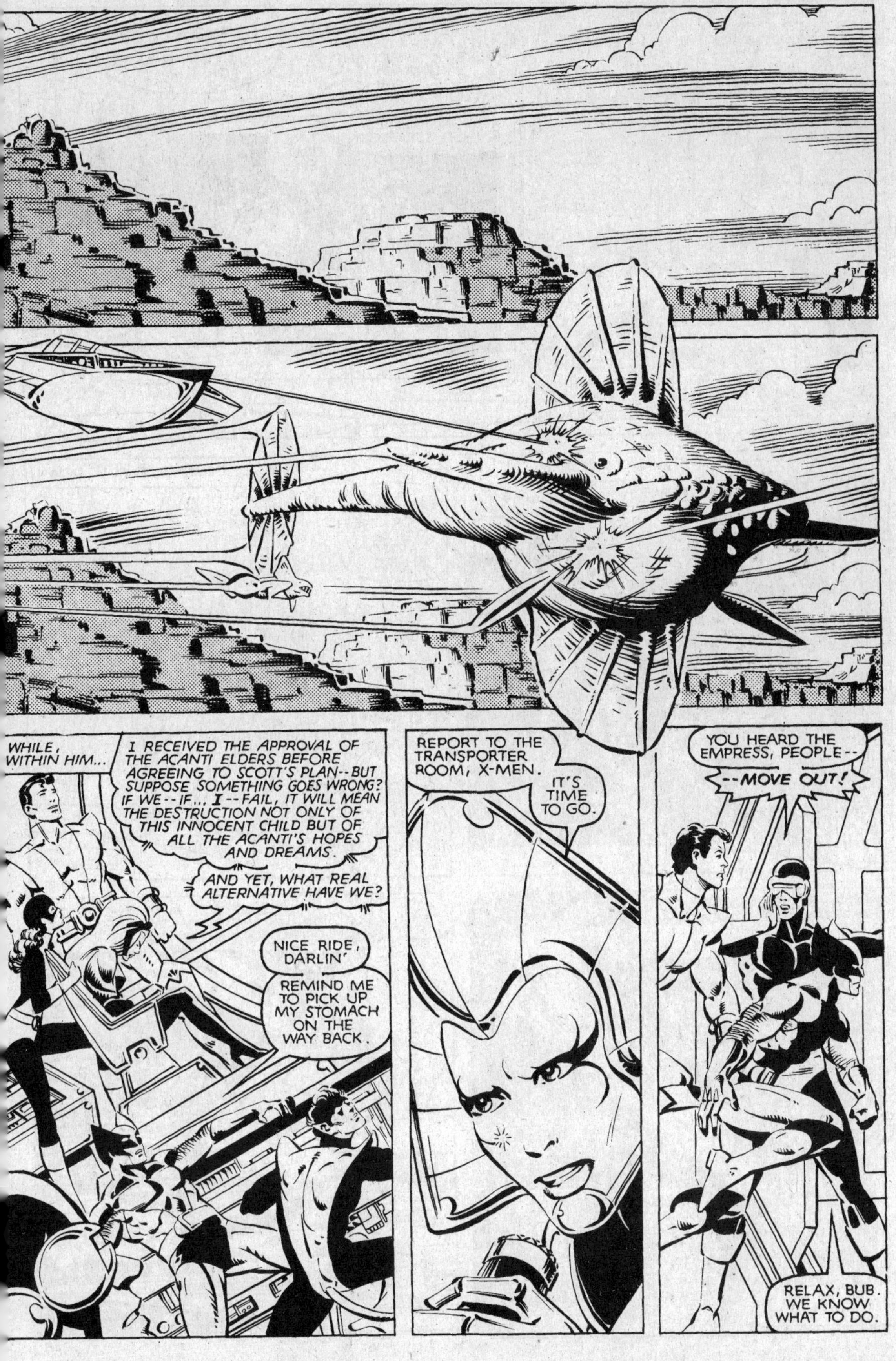
WHILE, WITHIN HIM...
I RECEIVED THE APPROVAL OF THE ACANTI ELDERS BEFORE AGREEING TO SCOTT'S PLAN--BUT SUPPOSE SOMETHING GOES WRONG? IF WE--IF... I--FAIL, IT WILL MEAN THE DESTRUCTION NOT ONLY OF THIS INNOCENT CHILD BUT OF ALL THE ACANTI'S HOPES AND DREAMS.
AND YET, WHAT REAL ALTERNATIVE HAVE WE?
NICE RIDE, DARLIN'
REMIND ME TO PICK UP MY STOMACH ON THE WAY BACK.
REPORT TO THE TRANSPORTER ROOM, X-MEN.
IT'S TIME TO GO.
YOU HEARD THE EMPRESS, PEOPLE--
--MOVE OUT!
RELAX, BUB. WE KNOW WHAT TO DO.

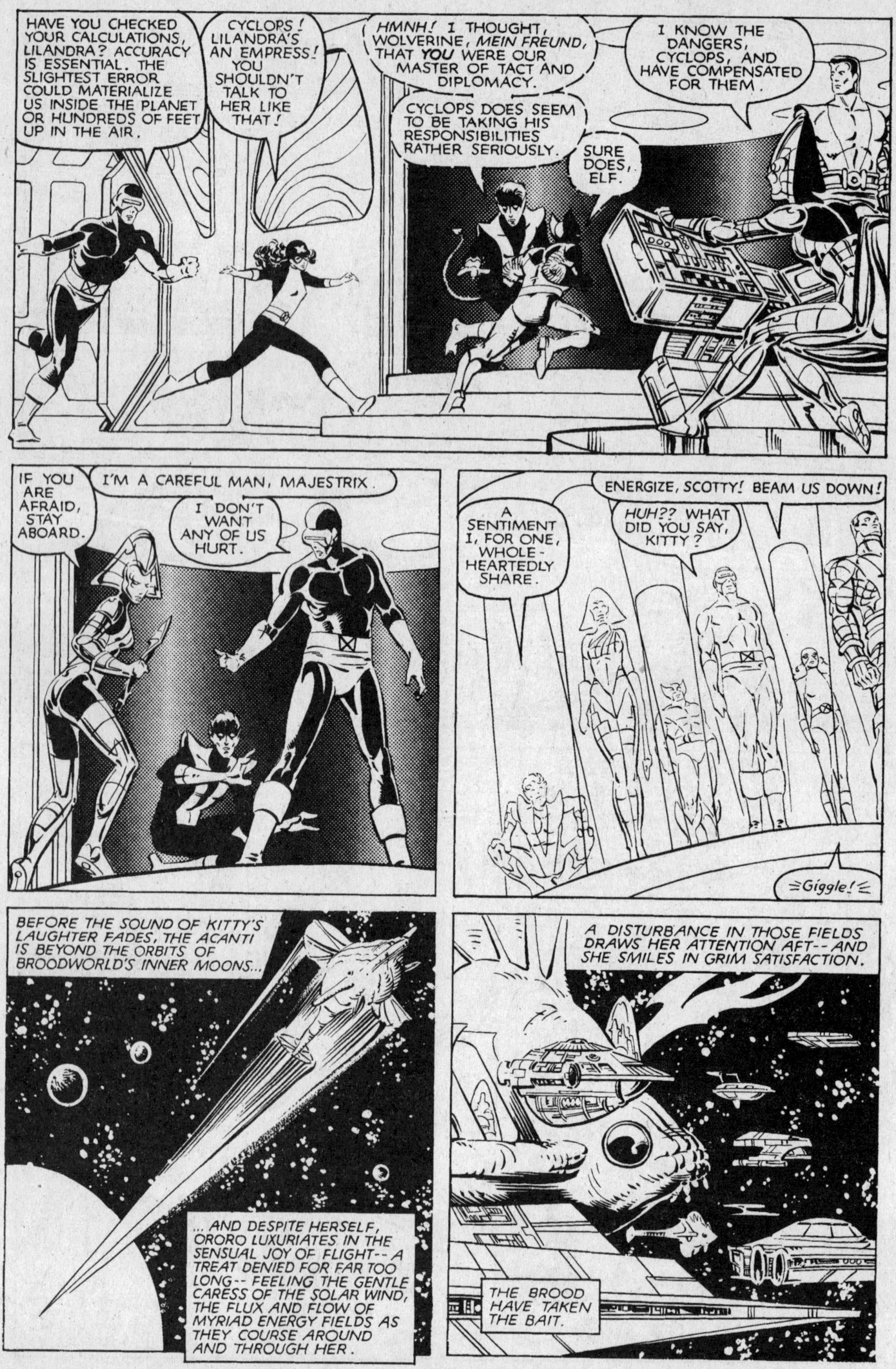
HAVE YOU CHECKED YOUR CALCULATIONS, LILANDRA? ACCURACY IS ESSENTIAL. THE SLIGHTEST ERROR COULD MATERIALIZE US INSIDE THE PLANET OR HUNDREDS OF FEET UP IN THE AIR.
CYCLOPS! LILANDRA'S AN EMPRESS! YOU SHOULDN'T TALK TO HER LIKE THAT!
HMNH! I THOUGHT, WOLVERINE, MEIN FREUND, THAT YOU WERE OUR MASTER OF TACT AND DIPLOMACY.
CYCLOPS DOES SEEM TO BE TAKING HIS RESPONSIBILITIES RATHER SERIOUSLY.
SURE DOES, ELF.
I KNOW THE DANGERS, CYCLOPS, AND HAVE COMPENSATED FOR THEM.
IF YOU ARE AFRAID, STAY ABOARD.
I'M A CAREFUL MAN, MAJESTRIX.
I DON'T WANT ANY OF US HURT.
A SENTIMENT I, FOR ONE, WHOLE-HEARTEDLY SHARE.
ENERGIZE, SCOTTY! BEAM US DOWN!
HUH?? WHAT DID YOU SAY, KITTY?
Giggle!
BEFORE THE SOUND OF KITTY'S LAUGHTER FADES, THE ACANTI IS BEYOND THE ORBITS OF BROODWORLD'S INNER MOONS...
... AND DESPITE HERSELF, ORORO LUXURIATES IN THE SENSUAL JOY OF FLIGHT-- A TREAT DENIED FOR FAR TOO LONG-- FEELING THE GENTLE CARESS OF THE SOLAR WIND, THE FLUX AND FLOW OF MYRIAD ENERGY FIELDS AS THEY COURSE AROUND AND THROUGH HER.
A DISTURBANCE IN THOSE FIELDS DRAWS HER ATTENTION AFT-- AND SHE SMILES IN GRIM SATISFACTION.
THE BROOD HAVE TAKEN THE BAIT.

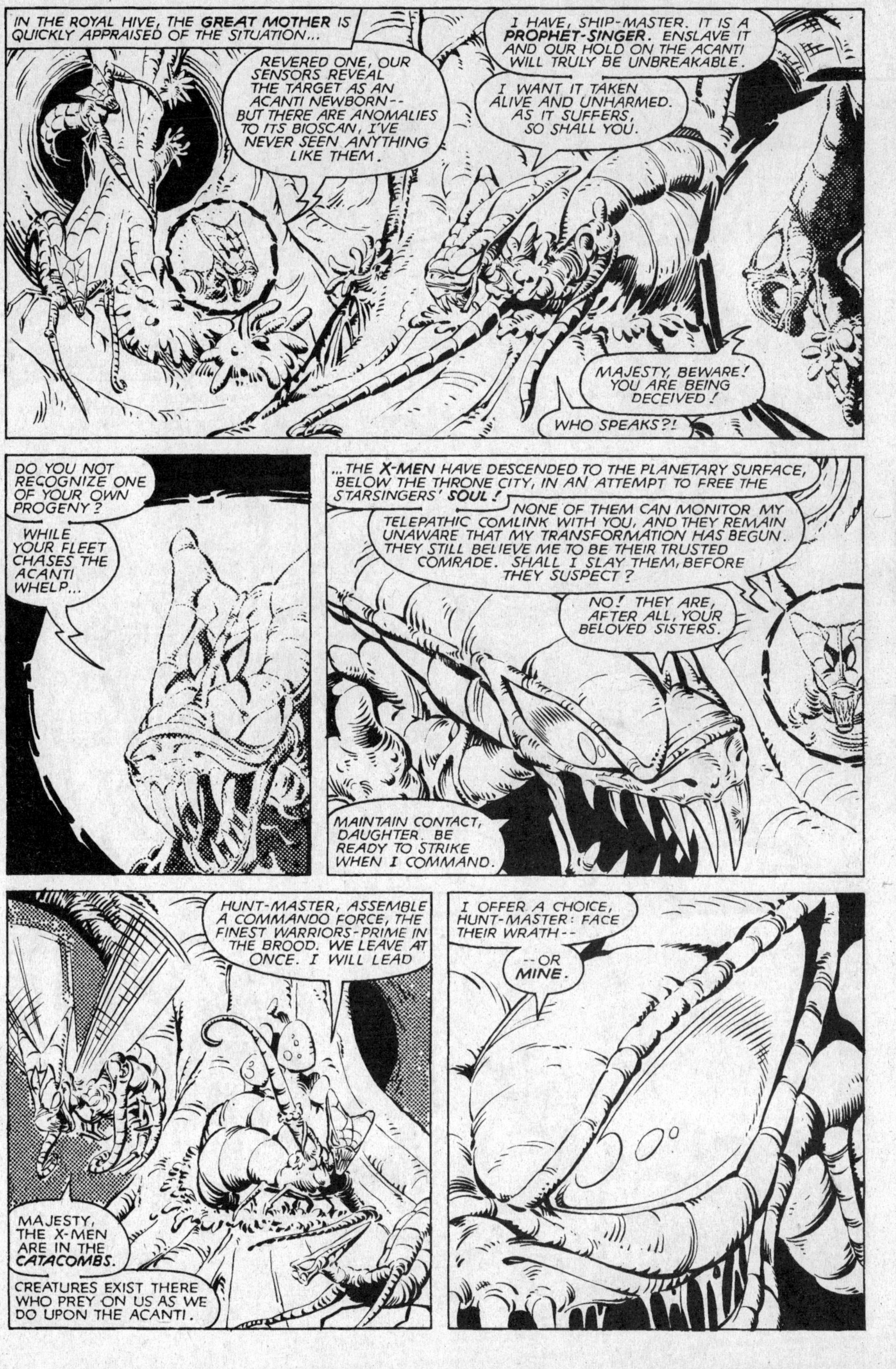
IN THE ROYAL HIVE, THE GREAT MOTHER IS QUICKLY APPRAISED OF THE SITUATION...
REVERED ONE, OUR SENSORS REVEAL THE TARGET AS AN ACANTI NEWBORN-- BUT THERE ARE ANOMALIES TO ITS BIOSCAN, I'VE NEVER SEEN ANYTHING LIKE THEM.
I HAVE, SHIP-MASTER. IT IS A PROPHET-SINGER. ENSLAVE IT AND OUR HOLD ON THE ACANTI WILL TRULY BE UNBREAKABLE.
I WANT IT TAKEN ALIVE AND UNHARMED. AS IT SUFFERS, SO SHALL YOU.
MAJESTY, BEWARE! YOU ARE BEING DECEIVED!
WHO SPEAKS?!
DO YOU NOT RECOGNIZE ONE OF YOUR OWN PROGENY?
WHILE YOUR FLEET CHASES THE ACANTI WHELP...
...THE X-MEN HAVE DESCENDED TO THE PLANETARY SURFACE, BELOW THE THRONE CITY, IN AN ATTEMPT TO FREE THE STARSINGERS' SOUL!
NONE OF THEM CAN MONITOR MY TELEPATHIC COMLINK WITH YOU, AND THEY REMAIN UNAWARE THAT MY TRANSFORMATION HAS BEGUN. THEY STILL BELIEVE ME TO BE THEIR TRUSTED COMRADE. SHALL I SLAY THEM, BEFORE THEY SUSPECT?
NO! THEY ARE, AFTER ALL, YOUR BELOVED SISTERS.
MAINTAIN CONTACT, DAUGHTER. BE READY TO STRIKE WHEN I COMMAND.
HUNT-MASTER, ASSEMBLE A COMMANDO FORCE, THE FINEST WARRIORS-PRIME IN THE BROOD. WE LEAVE AT ONCE. I WILL LEAD
MAJESTY, THE X-MEN ARE IN THE CATACOMBS.
CREATURES EXIST THERE WHO PREY ON US AS WE DO UPON THE ACANTI.
I OFFER A CHOICE, HUNT-MASTER: FACE THEIR WRATH--
--OR MINE.

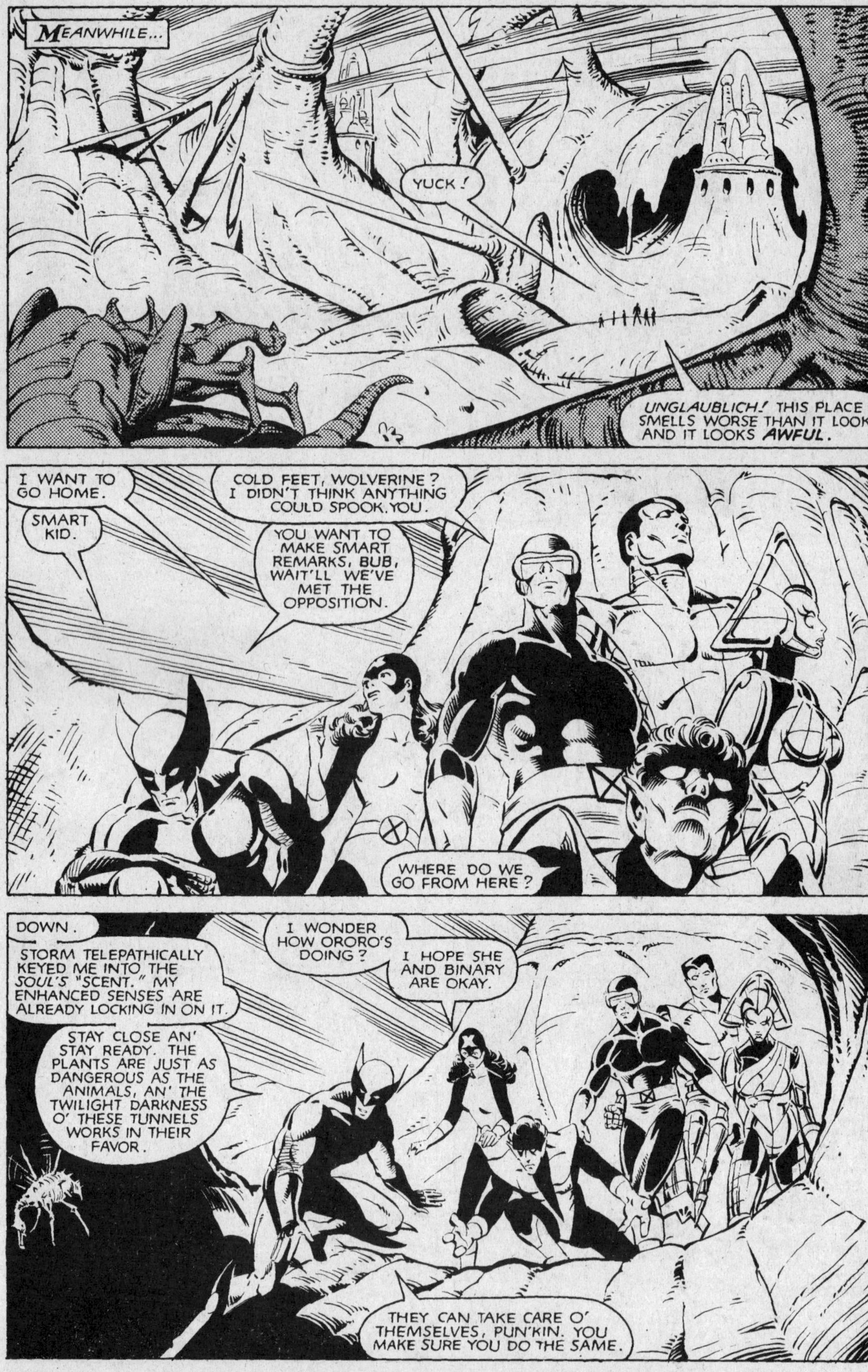
MEANWHILE...
YUCK!
UNGLAUBLICH! THIS PLACE SMELLS WORSE THAN IT LOOKS, AND IT LOOKS AWFUL.
I WANT TO GO HOME.
SMART KID.
COLD FEET, WOLVERINE? I DIDN'T THINK ANYTHING COULD SPOOK YOU.
YOU WANT TO MAKE SMART REMARKS, BUB, WAIT'LL WE'VE MET THE OPPOSITION.
WHERE DO WE GO FROM HERE?
DOWN.
STORM TELEPATHICALLY KEYED ME INTO THE SOUL'S "SCENT." MY ENHANCED SENSES ARE ALREADY LOCKING IN ON IT.
STAY CLOSE AN' STAY READY. THE PLANTS ARE JUST AS DANGEROUS AS THE ANIMALS, AN' THE TWILIGHT DARKNESS O' THESE TUNNELS WORKS IN THEIR FAVOR.
I WONDER HOW ORORO'S DOING?
I HOPE SHE AND BINARY ARE OKAY.
THEY CAN TAKE CARE O' THEMSELVES, PUN'KIN. YOU MAKE SURE YOU DO THE SAME.

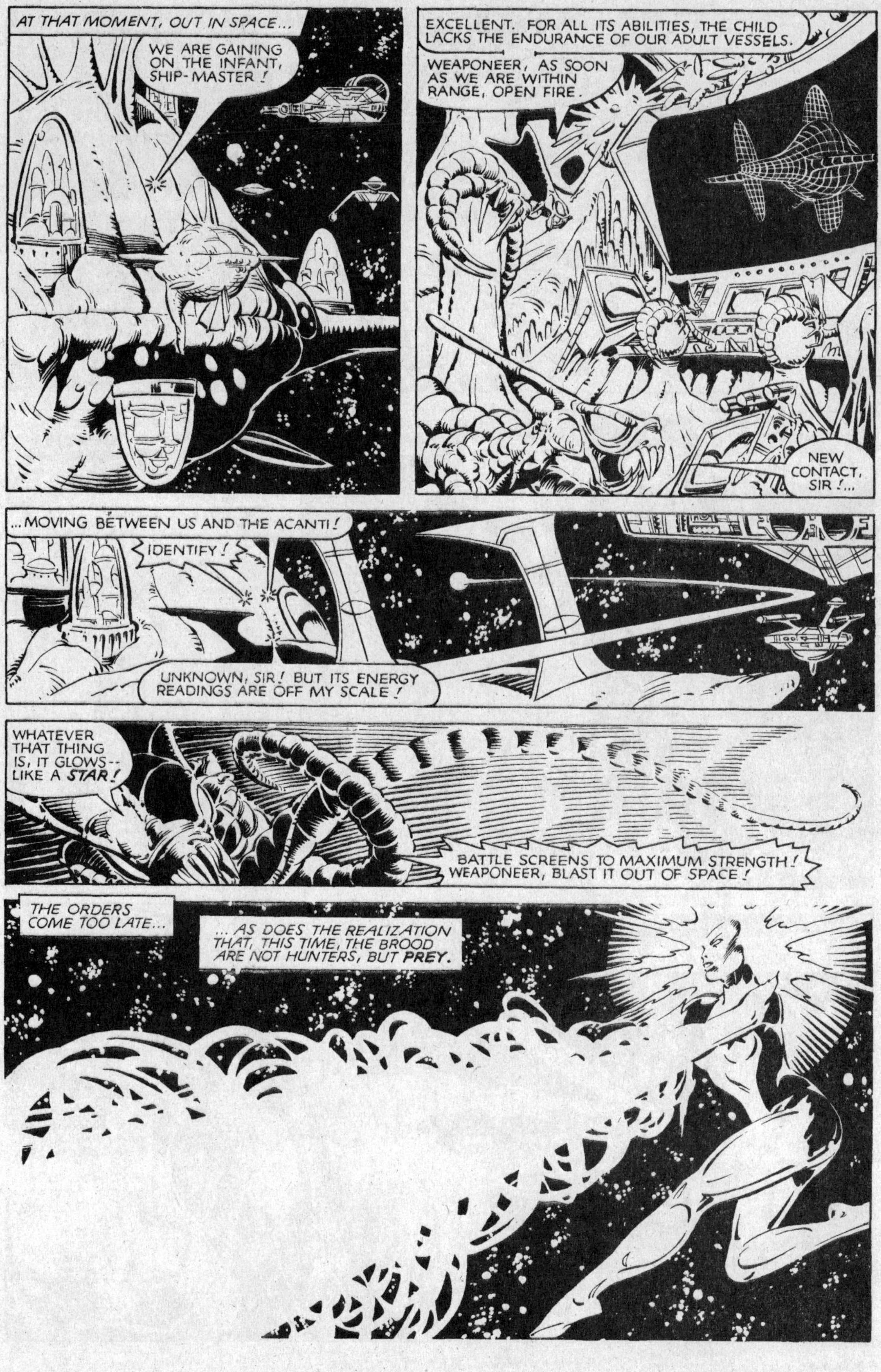
AT THAT MOMENT, OUT IN SPACE...
WE ARE GAINING ON THE INFANT, SHIP-MASTER!
EXCELLENT. FOR ALL ITS ABILITIES, THE CHILD LACKS THE ENDURANCE OF OUR ADULT VESSELS.
WEAPONEER, AS SOON AS WE ARE WITHIN RANGE, OPEN FIRE.
NEW CONTACT, SIR!...
...MOVING BETWEEN US AND THE ACANTI!
IDENTIFY!
UNKNOWN, SIR! BUT ITS ENERGY READINGS ARE OFF MY SCALE!
WHATEVER THAT THING IS, IT GLOWS-- LIKE A STAR!
BATTLE SCREENS TO MAXIMUM STRENGTH! WEAPONEER, BLAST IT OUT OF SPACE!
THE ORDERS COME TOO LATE...
...AS DOES THE REALIZATION THAT, THIS TIME, THE BROOD ARE NOT HUNTERS, BUT PREY.

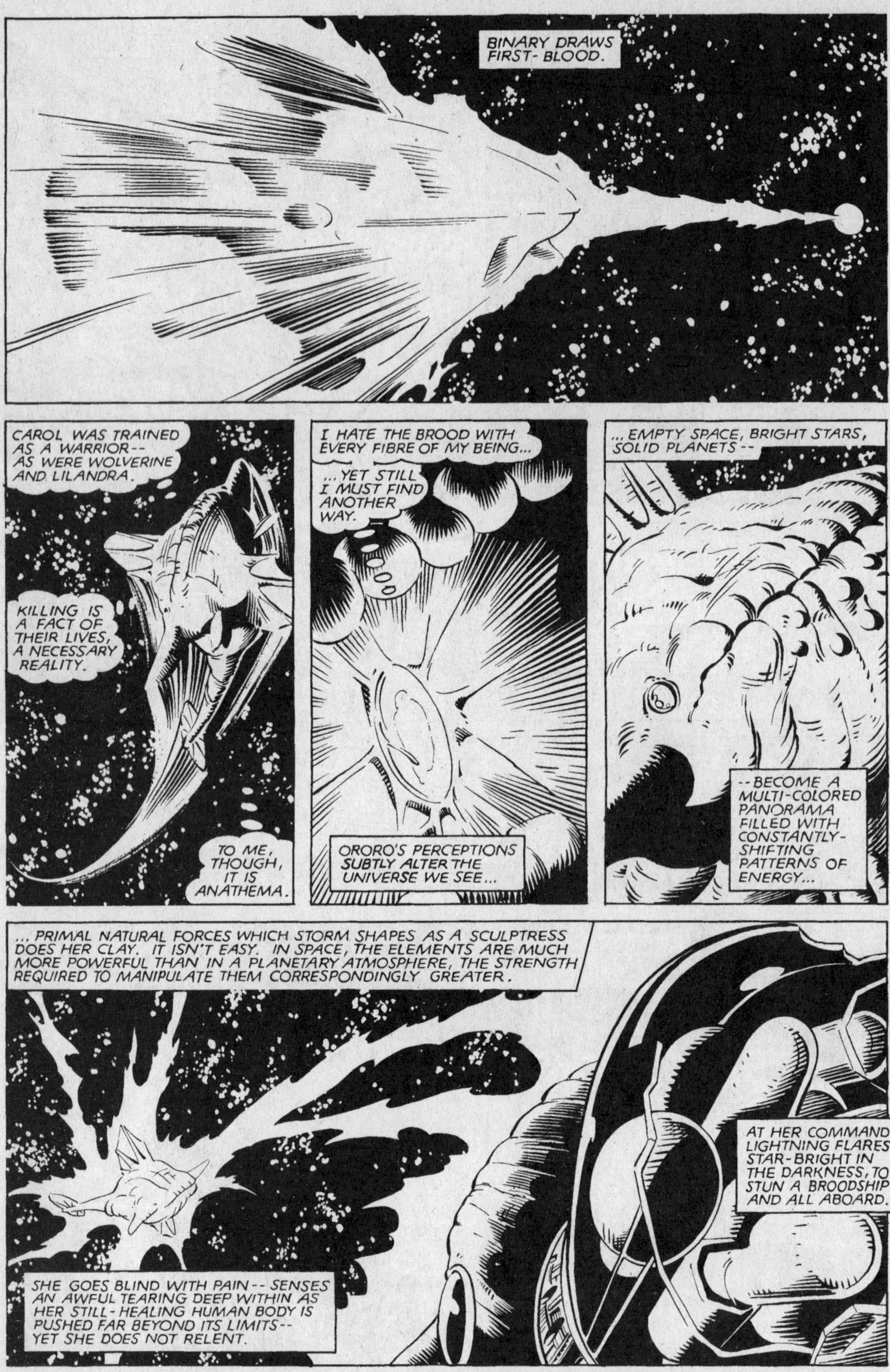
BINARY DRAWS FIRST-BLOOD.
CAROL WAS TRAINED AS A WARRIOR-- AS WERE WOLVERINE AND LILANDRA.
KILLING IS A FACT OF THEIR LIVES, A NECESSARY REALITY.
TO ME, THOUGH, IT IS ANATHEMA.
I HATE THE BROOD WITH EVERY FIBRE OF MY BEING...
...YET STILL I MUST FIND ANOTHER WAY.
ORORO'S PERCEPTIONS SUBTLY ALTER THE UNIVERSE WE SEE...
...EMPTY SPACE, BRIGHT STARS, SOLID PLANETS--
--BECOME A MULTI-COLORED PANORAMA FILLED WITH CONSTANTLY-SHIFTING PATTERNS OF ENERGY...
...PRIMAL NATURAL FORCES WHICH STORM SHAPES AS A SCULPTRESS DOES HER CLAY. IT ISN'T EASY. IN SPACE, THE ELEMENTS ARE MUCH MORE POWERFUL THAN IN A PLANETARY ATMOSPHERE, THE STRENGTH REQUIRED TO MANIPULATE THEM CORRESPONDINGLY GREATER.
AT HER COMMAND, LIGHTNING FLARES STAR-BRIGHT IN THE DARKNESS, TO STUN A BROODSHIP AND ALL ABOARD.
SHE GOES BLIND WITH PAIN-- SENSES AN AWFUL TEARING DEEP WITHIN AS HER STILL-HEALING HUMAN BODY IS PUSHED FAR BEYOND ITS LIMITS-- YET SHE DOES NOT RELENT.

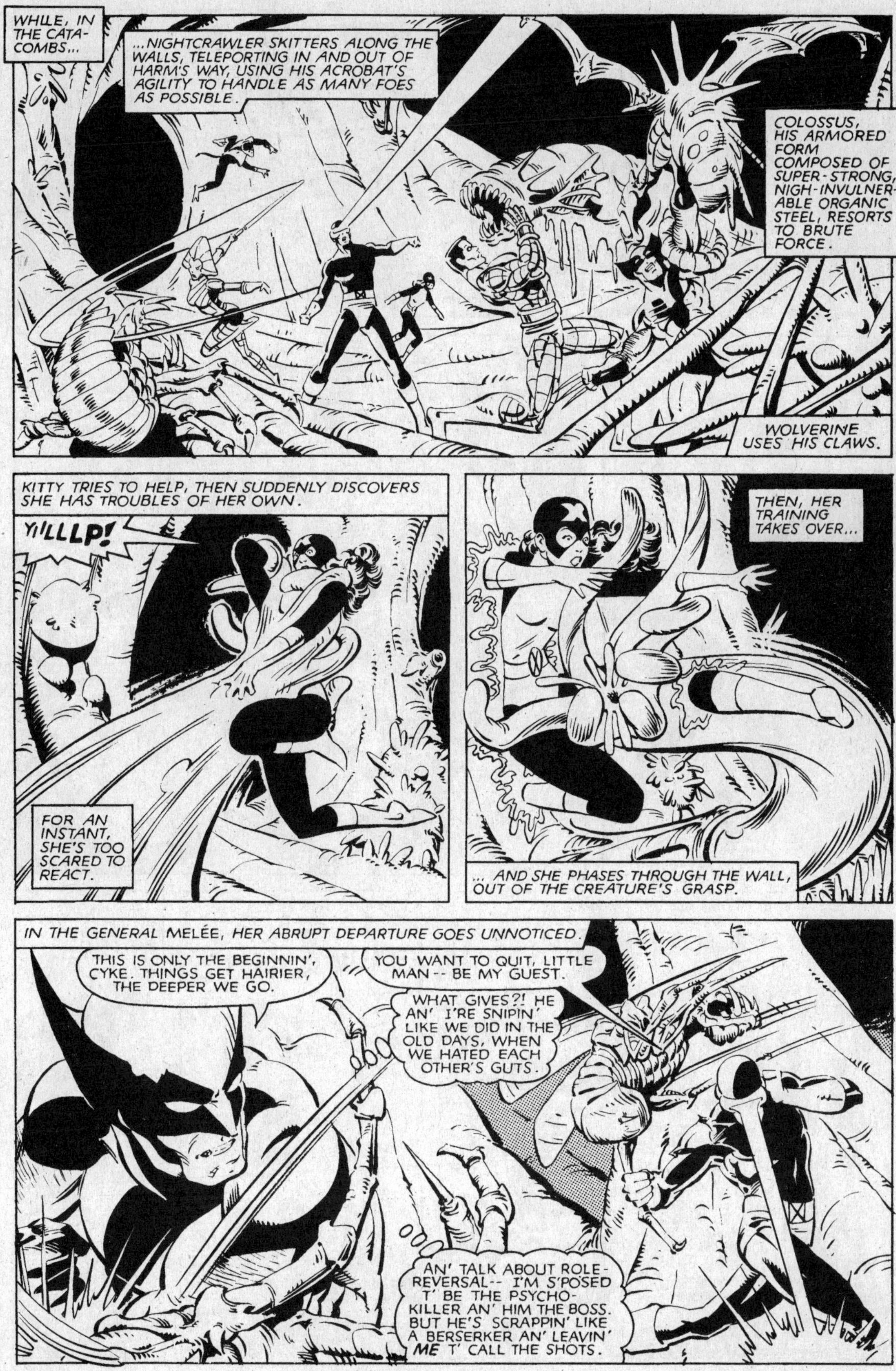
WHILE, IN THE CATA-COMBS...
...NIGHTCRAWLER SKITTERS ALONG THE WALLS, TELEPORTING IN AND OUT OF HARM'S WAY, USING HIS ACROBAT'S AGILITY TO HANDLE AS MANY FOES AS POSSIBLE.
COLOSSUS, HIS ARMORED FORM COMPOSED OF SUPER-STRONG, NIGH-INVULNERABLE ORGANIC STEEL, RESORTS TO BRUTE FORCE.
WOLVERINE USES HIS CLAWS.
KITTY TRIES TO HELP, THEN SUDDENLY DISCOVERS SHE HAS TROUBLES OF HER OWN.
YIILLLP!
FOR AN INSTANT, SHE'S TOO SCARED TO REACT.
THEN, HER TRAINING TAKES OVER...
... AND SHE PHASES THROUGH THE WALL, OUT OF THE CREATURE'S GRASP.
IN THE GENERAL MELÉE, HER ABRUPT DEPARTURE GOES UNNOTICED.
THIS IS ONLY THE BEGINNIN', CYKE. THINGS GET HAIRIER, THE DEEPER WE GO.
YOU WANT TO QUIT, LITTLE MAN -- BE MY GUEST.
WHAT GIVES?! HE AN' I'RE SNIPIN' LIKE WE DID IN THE OLD DAYS, WHEN WE HATED EACH OTHER'S GUTS.
AN' TALK ABOUT ROLE-REVERSAL-- I'M S'POSED T' BE THE PSYCHO-KILLER AN' HIM THE BOSS. BUT HE'S SCRAPPIN' LIKE A BERSERKER AN' LEAVIN' ME T' CALL THE SHOTS.

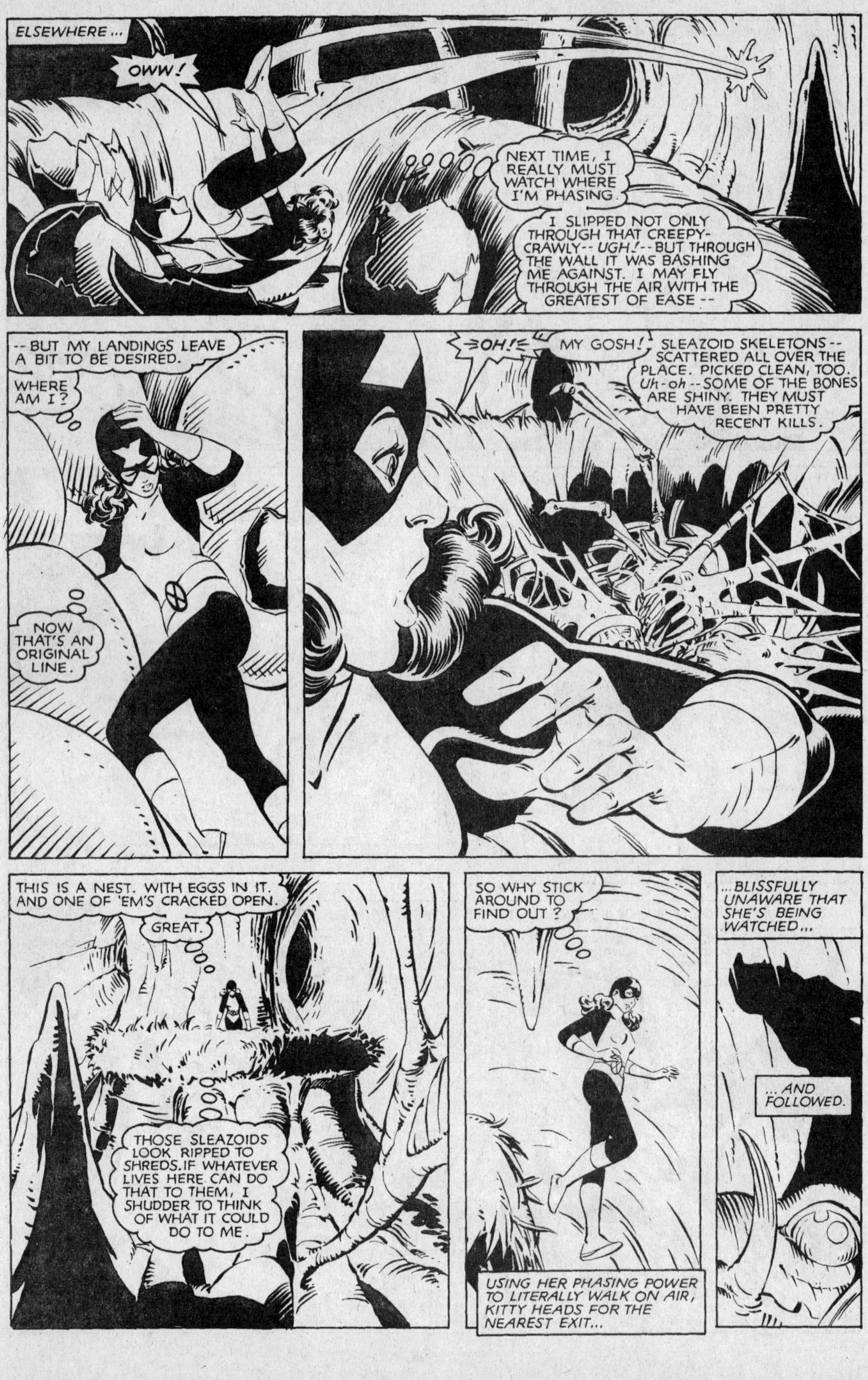
ELSEWHERE...
OWW!
NEXT TIME, I REALLY MUST WATCH WHERE I'M PHASING.
I SLIPPED NOT ONLY THROUGH THAT CREEPY-CRAWLY-- UGH!-- BUT THROUGH THE WALL IT WAS BASHING ME AGAINST. I MAY FLY THROUGH THE AIR WITH THE GREATEST OF EASE --
-- BUT MY LANDINGS LEAVE A BIT TO BE DESIRED.
WHERE AM I?
NOW THAT'S AN ORIGINAL LINE.
OH!
MY GOSH!
SLEAZOID SKELETONS-- SCATTERED ALL OVER THE PLACE. PICKED CLEAN, TOO. Uh-oh -- SOME OF THE BONES ARE SHINY. THEY MUST HAVE BEEN PRETTY RECENT KILLS.
THIS IS A NEST. WITH EGGS IN IT. AND ONE OF 'EM'S CRACKED OPEN.
GREAT.
THOSE SLEAZOIDS LOOK RIPPED TO SHREDS. IF WHATEVER LIVES HERE CAN DO THAT TO THEM, I SHUDDER TO THINK OF WHAT IT COULD DO TO ME.
SO WHY STICK AROUND TO FIND OUT?
USING HER PHASING POWER TO LITERALLY WALK ON AIR, KITTY HEADS FOR THE NEAREST EXIT...
...BLISSFULLY UNAWARE THAT SHE'S BEING WATCHED...
...AND FOLLOWED.

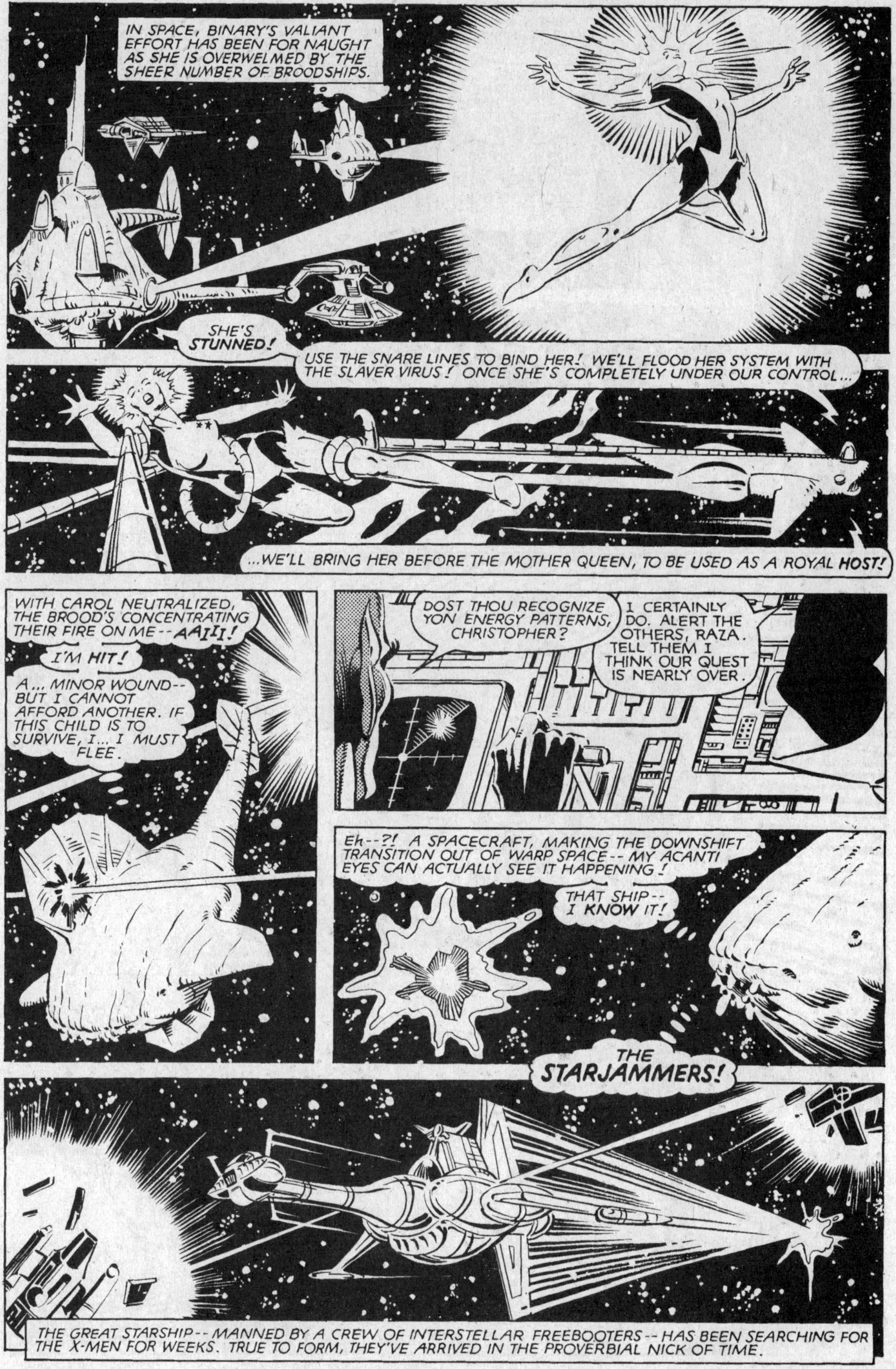

IN SPACE, BINARY'S VALIANT EFFORT HAS BEEN FOR NAUGHT AS SHE IS OVERWELMED BY THE SHEER NUMBER OF BROODSHIPS.
SHE'S STUNNED!
USE THE SNARE LINES TO BIND HER! WE'LL FLOOD HER SYSTEM WITH THE SLAVER VIRUS! ONCE SHE'S COMPLETELY UNDER OUR CONTROL...
...WE'LL BRING HER BEFORE THE MOTHER QUEEN, TO BE USED AS A ROYAL HOST!
WITH CAROL NEUTRALIZED, THE BROOD'S CONCENTRATING THEIR FIRE ON ME--AAIII!
I'M HIT!
A... MINOR WOUND--BUT I CANNOT AFFORD ANOTHER. IF THIS CHILD IS TO SURVIVE, I... I MUST FLEE.
DOST THOU RECOGNIZE YON ENERGY PATTERNS, CHRISTOPHER?
I CERTAINLY DO. ALERT THE OTHERS, RAZA. TELL THEM I THINK OUR QUEST IS NEARLY OVER.
Eh--?! A SPACECRAFT, MAKING THE DOWNSHIFT TRANSITION OUT OF WARP SPACE--MY ACANTI EYES CAN ACTUALLY SEE IT HAPPENING!
THAT SHIP--I KNOW IT!
THE STARJAMMERS!
THE GREAT STARSHIP--MANNED BY A CREW OF INTERSTELLAR FREEBOOTERS--HAS BEEN SEARCHING FOR THE X-MEN FOR WEEKS. TRUE TO FORM, THEY'VE ARRIVED IN THE PROVERBIAL NICK OF TIME.

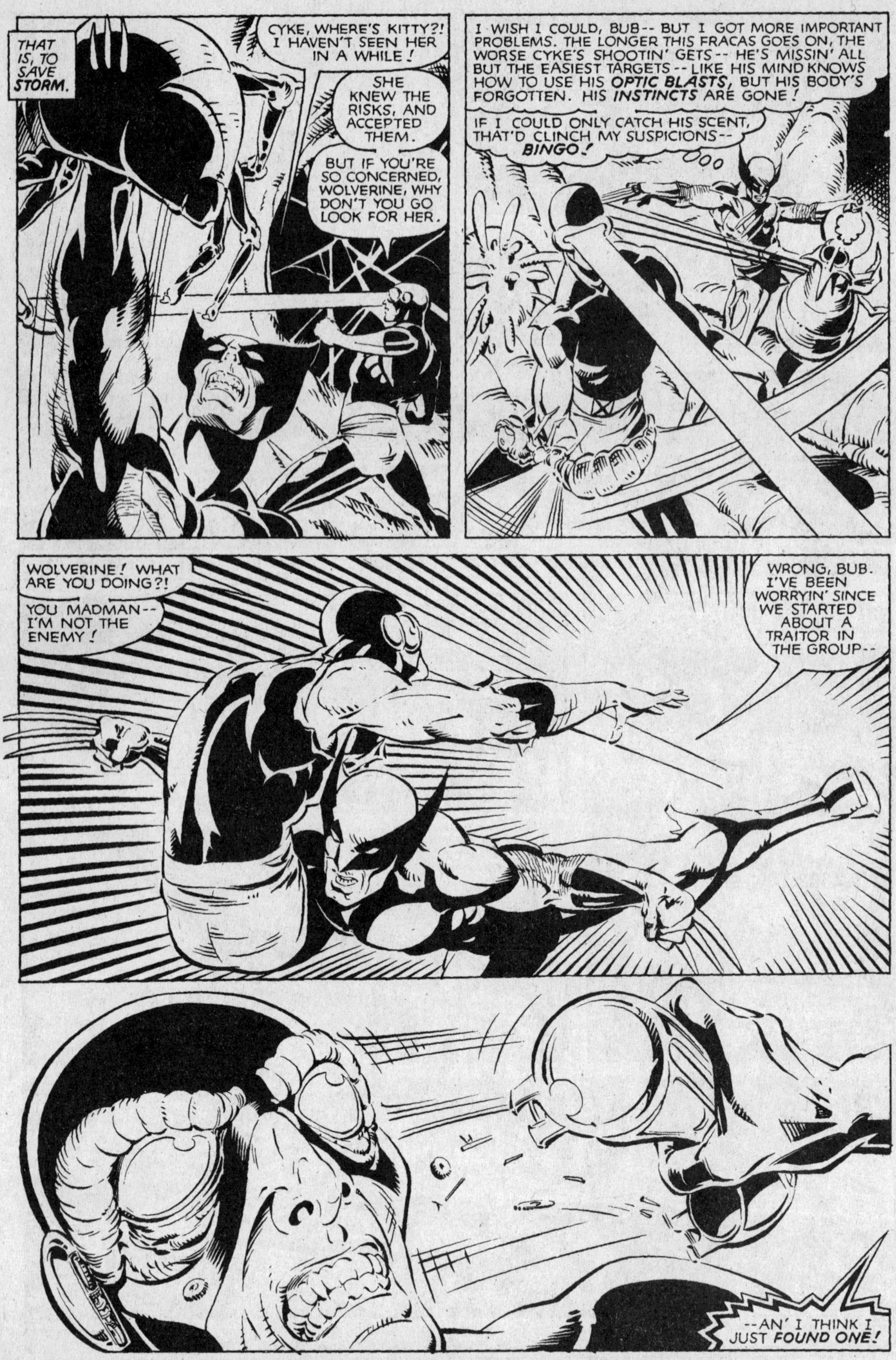
THAT IS, TO SAVE STORM.
CYKE, WHERE'S KITTY?! I HAVEN'T SEEN HER IN A WHILE!
SHE KNEW THE RISKS, AND ACCEPTED THEM.
BUT IF YOU'RE SO CONCERNED, WOLVERINE, WHY DON'T YOU GO LOOK FOR HER.
I WISH I COULD, BUB-- BUT I GOT MORE IMPORTANT PROBLEMS. THE LONGER THIS FRACAS GOES ON, THE WORSE CYKE'S SHOOTIN' GETS-- HE'S MISSIN' ALL BUT THE EASIEST TARGETS--LIKE HIS MIND KNOWS HOW TO USE HIS OPTIC BLASTS, BUT HIS BODY'S FORGOTTEN. HIS INSTINCTS ARE GONE!
IF I COULD ONLY CATCH HIS SCENT, THAT'D CLINCH MY SUSPICIONS-- BINGO!
WOLVERINE! WHAT ARE YOU DOING?!
YOU MADMAN-- I'M NOT THE ENEMY!
WRONG, BUB. I'VE BEEN WORRYIN' SINCE WE STARTED ABOUT A TRAITOR IN THE GROUP--
--AN' I THINK I JUST FOUND ONE!

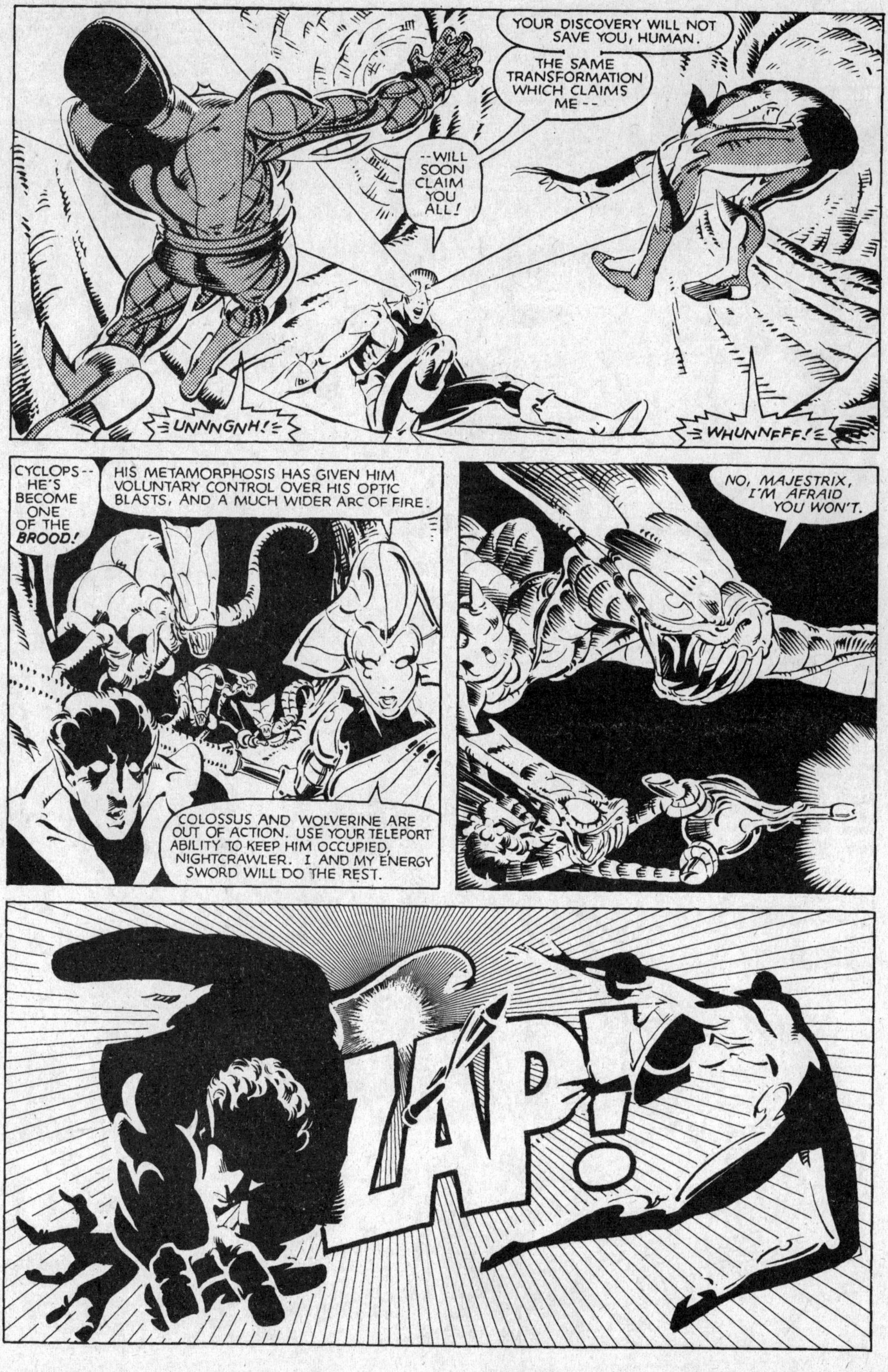
YOUR DISCOVERY WILL NOT SAVE YOU, HUMAN.
THE SAME TRANSFORMATION WHICH CLAIMS ME --
--WILL SOON CLAIM YOU ALL!
UNNNGNH!
WHUNNFFF!
CYCLOPS-- HE'S BECOME ONE OF THE BROOD!
HIS METAMORPHOSIS HAS GIVEN HIM VOLUNTARY CONTROL OVER HIS OPTIC BLASTS, AND A MUCH WIDER ARC OF FIRE.
COLOSSUS AND WOLVERINE ARE OUT OF ACTION. USE YOUR TELEPORT ABILITY TO KEEP HIM OCCUPIED, NIGHTCRAWLER. I AND MY ENERGY SWORD WILL DO THE REST.
NO, MAJESTRIX, I'M AFRAID YOU WON'T.
ZAP!

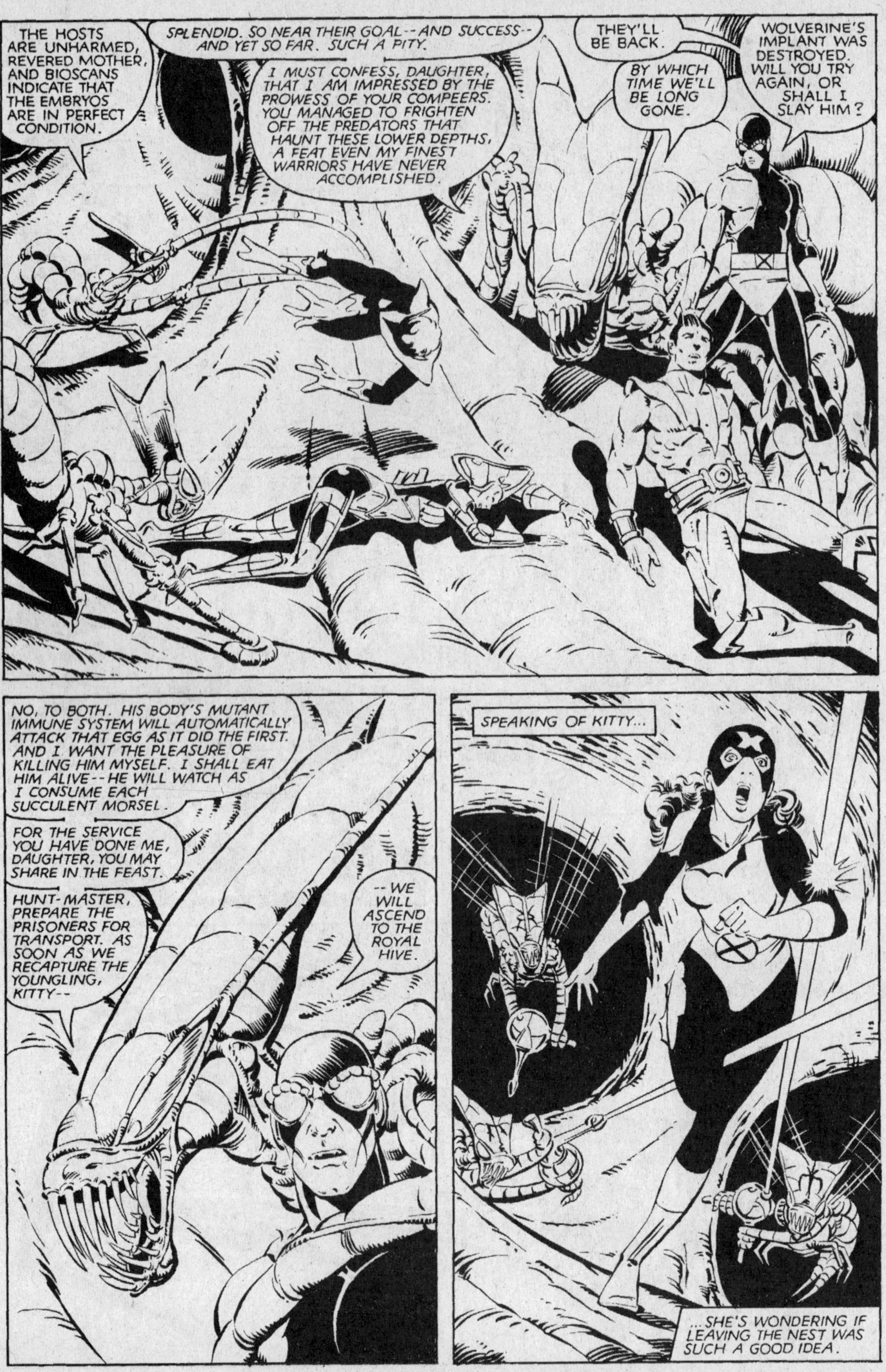
THE HOSTS ARE UNHARMED, REVERED MOTHER, AND BIOSCANS INDICATE THAT THE EMBRYOS ARE IN PERFECT CONDITION.
SPLENDID. SO NEAR THEIR GOAL--AND SUCCESS--AND YET SO FAR. SUCH A PITY.
I MUST CONFESS, DAUGHTER, THAT I AM IMPRESSED BY THE PROWESS OF YOUR COMPEERS. YOU MANAGED TO FRIGHTEN OFF THE PREDATORS THAT HAUNT THESE LOWER DEPTHS, A FEAT EVEN MY FINEST WARRIORS HAVE NEVER ACCOMPLISHED.
THEY'LL BE BACK.
BY WHICH TIME WE'LL BE LONG GONE.
WOLVERINE'S IMPLANT WAS DESTROYED. WILL YOU TRY AGAIN, OR SHALL I SLAY HIM?
NO, TO BOTH. HIS BODY'S MUTANT IMMUNE SYSTEM WILL AUTOMATICALLY ATTACK THAT EGG AS IT DID THE FIRST. AND I WANT THE PLEASURE OF KILLING HIM MYSELF. I SHALL EAT HIM ALIVE--HE WILL WATCH AS I CONSUME EACH SUCCULENT MORSEL.
FOR THE SERVICE YOU HAVE DONE ME, DAUGHTER, YOU MAY SHARE IN THE FEAST.
HUNT-MASTER, PREPARE THE PRISONERS FOR TRANSPORT. AS SOON AS WE RECAPTURE THE YOUNGLING, KITTY--
--WE WILL ASCEND TO THE ROYAL HIVE.
SPEAKING OF KITTY...
...SHE'S WONDERING IF LEAVING THE NEST WAS SUCH A GOOD IDEA.

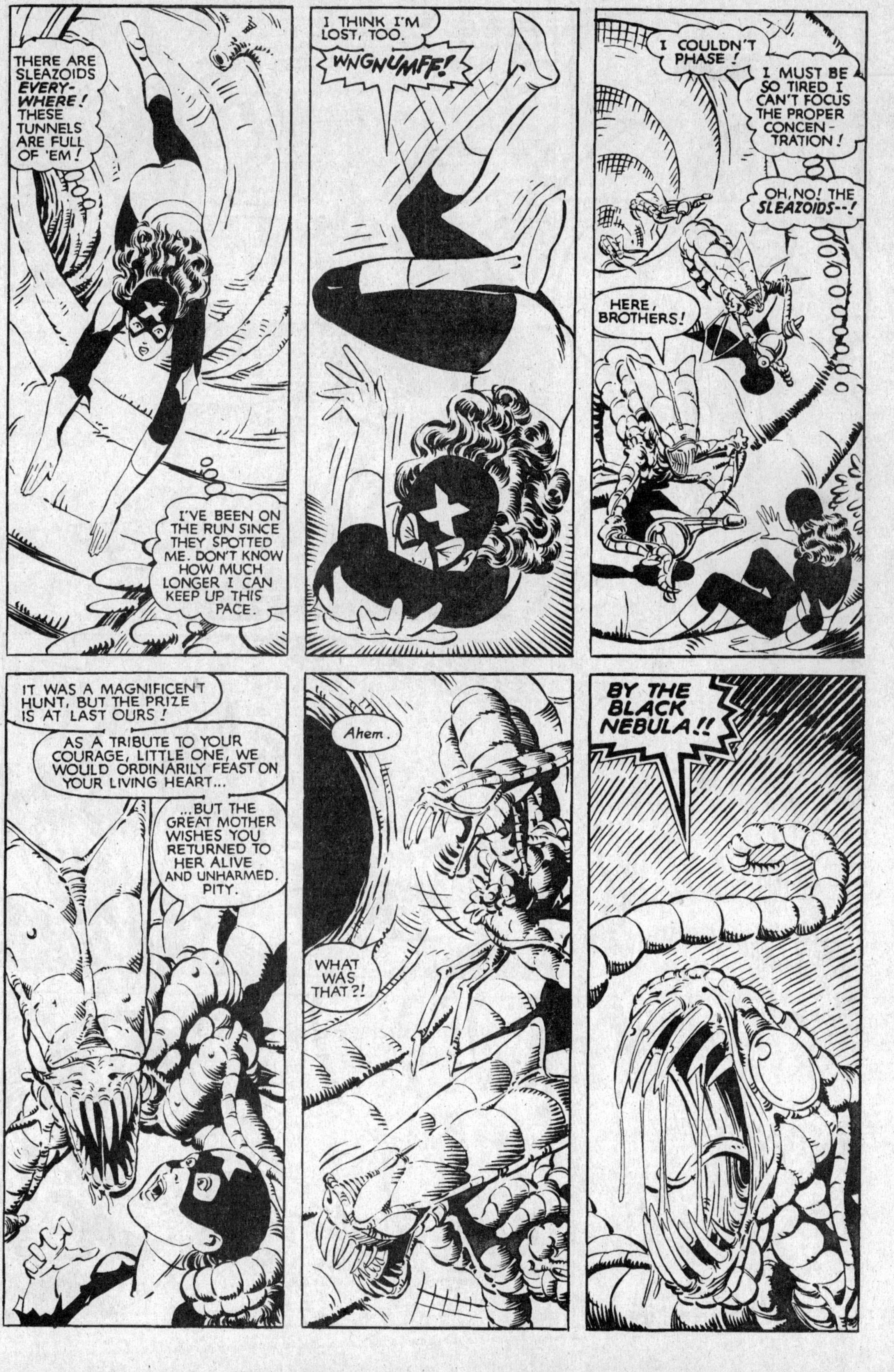
THERE ARE SLEAZOIDS EVERY-WHERE! THESE TUNNELS ARE FULL OF 'EM!
I'VE BEEN ON THE RUN SINCE THEY SPOTTED ME. DON'T KNOW HOW MUCH LONGER I CAN KEEP UP THIS PACE.
I THINK I'M LOST, TOO.
WNGNUMFF!
I COULDN'T PHASE!
I MUST BE SO TIRED I CAN'T FOCUS THE PROPER CONCEN-TRATION!
OH, NO! THE SLEAZOIDS--!
HERE, BROTHERS!
IT WAS A MAGNIFICENT HUNT, BUT THE PRIZE IS AT LAST OURS!
AS A TRIBUTE TO YOUR COURAGE, LITTLE ONE, WE WOULD ORDINARILY FEAST ON YOUR LIVING HEART...
...BUT THE GREAT MOTHER WISHES YOU RETURNED TO HER ALIVE AND UNHARMED. PITY.
Ahem.
WHAT WAS THAT?!
BY THE BLACK NEBULA!!

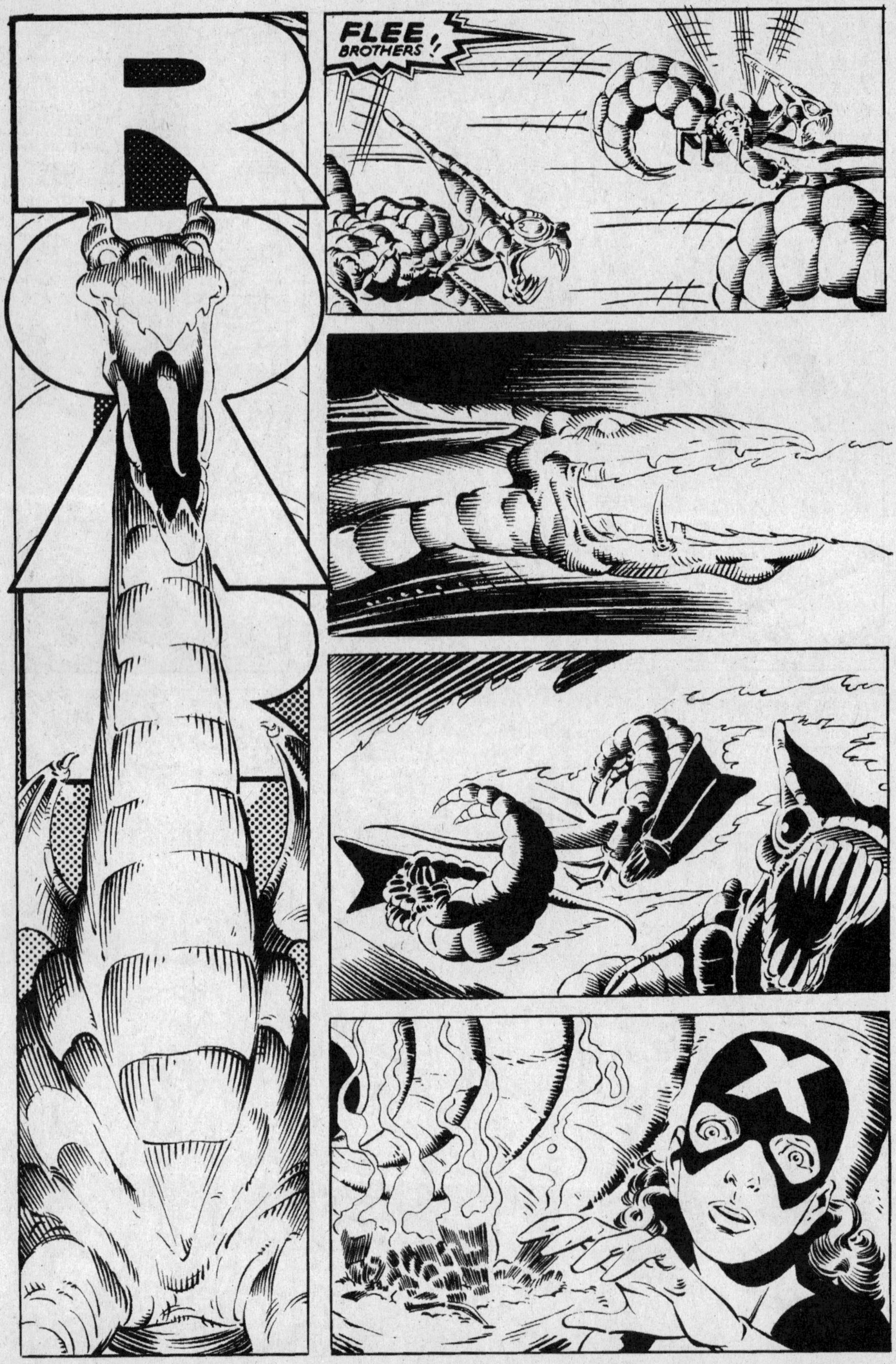
ROAR
FLEE, BROTHERS!

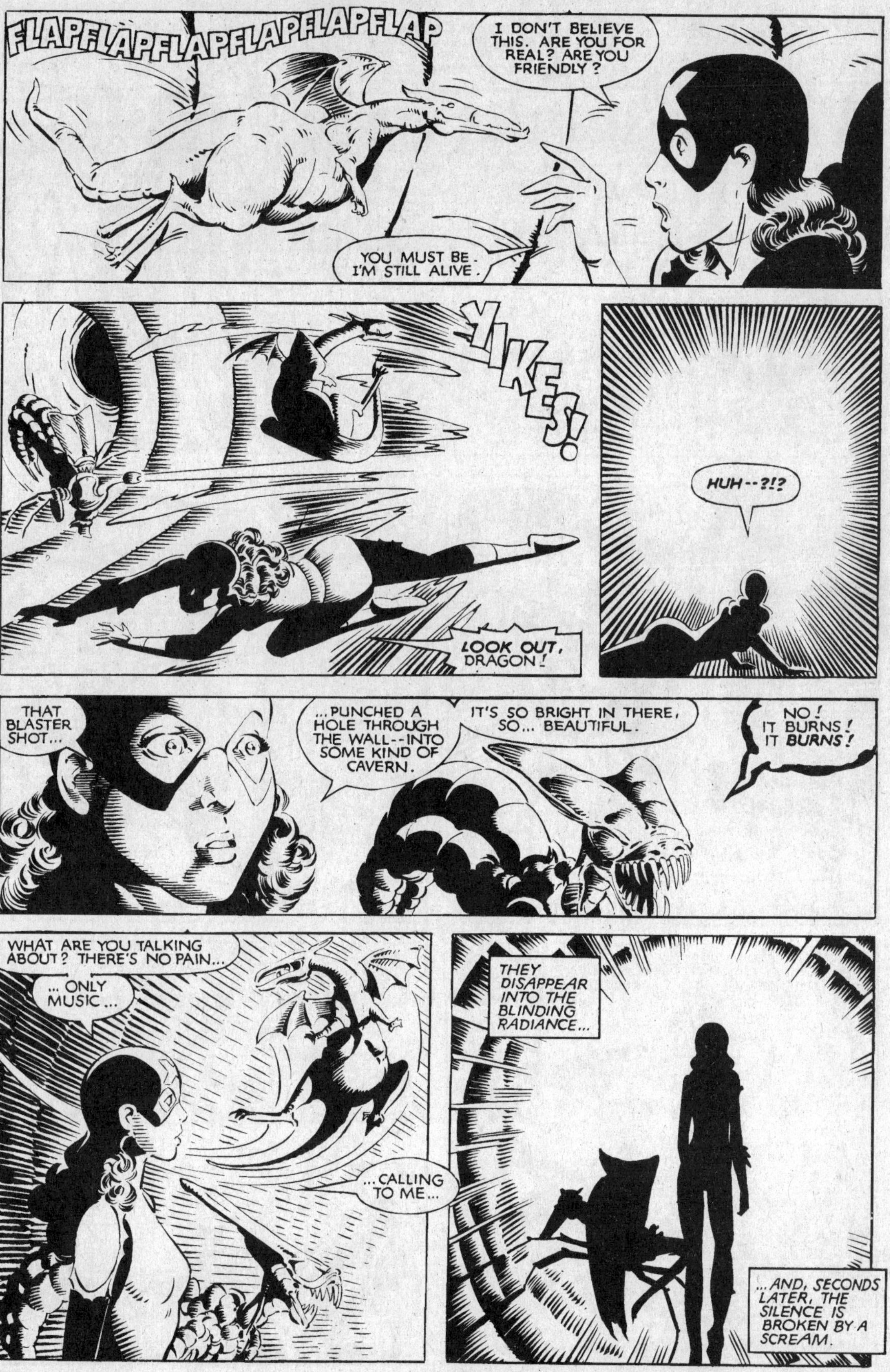
FLAPFLAPFLAPFLAPFLAPFLAP
I DON'T BELIEVE THIS. ARE YOU FOR REAL? ARE YOU FRIENDLY?
YOU MUST BE. I'M STILL ALIVE.
YIKES!
LOOK OUT, DRAGON!
HUH--?!?
THAT BLASTER SHOT...
...PUNCHED A HOLE THROUGH THE WALL--INTO SOME KIND OF CAVERN.
IT'S SO BRIGHT IN THERE, SO... BEAUTIFUL.
NO! IT BURNS! IT BURNS!
WHAT ARE YOU TALKING ABOUT? THERE'S NO PAIN...
...ONLY MUSIC...
...CALLING TO ME...
THEY DISAPPEAR INTO THE BLINDING RADIANCE...
...AND, SECONDS LATER, THE SILENCE IS BROKEN BY A SCREAM.

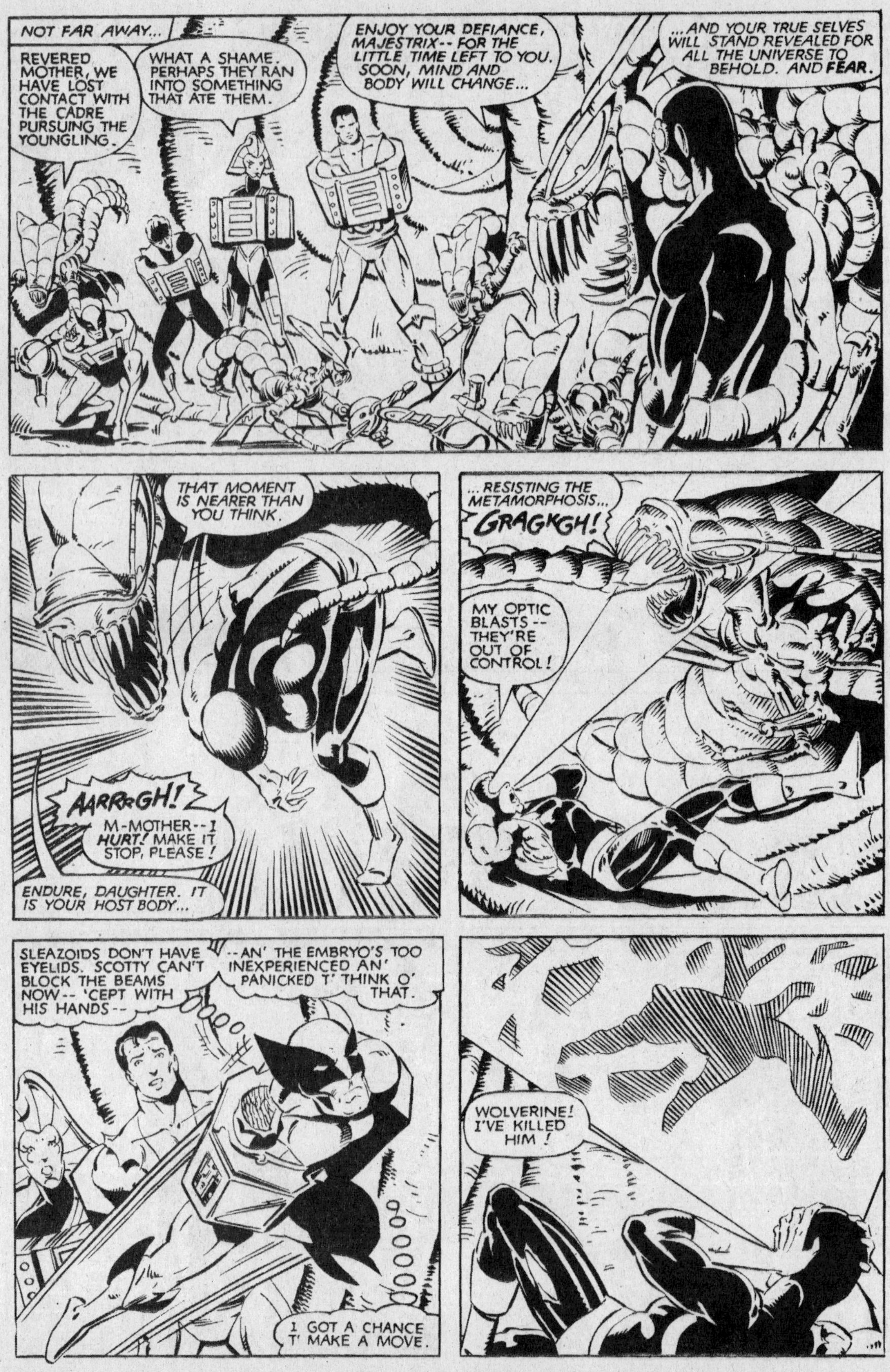
NOT FAR AWAY...
REVERED MOTHER, WE HAVE LOST CONTACT WITH THE CADRE PURSUING THE YOUNGLING.
WHAT A SHAME. PERHAPS THEY RAN INTO SOMETHING THAT ATE THEM.
ENJOY YOUR DEFIANCE, MAJESTRIX-- FOR THE LITTLE TIME LEFT TO YOU. SOON, MIND AND BODY WILL CHANGE...
...AND YOUR TRUE SELVES WILL STAND REVEALED FOR ALL THE UNIVERSE TO BEHOLD. AND FEAR.
THAT MOMENT IS NEARER THAN YOU THINK.
AARRRGH!
M-MOTHER-- I HURT! MAKE IT STOP, PLEASE!
ENDURE, DAUGHTER. IT IS YOUR HOST BODY...
...RESISTING THE METAMORPHOSIS...
GRAGKGH!
MY OPTIC BLASTS -- THEY'RE OUT OF CONTROL!
SLEAZOIDS DON'T HAVE EYELIDS. SCOTTY CAN'T BLOCK THE BEAMS NOW -- 'CEPT WITH HIS HANDS--
--AN' THE EMBRYO'S TOO INEXPERIENCED AN' PANICKED T' THINK O' THAT.
I GOT A CHANCE T' MAKE A MOVE.
WOLVERINE! I'VE KILLED HIM!

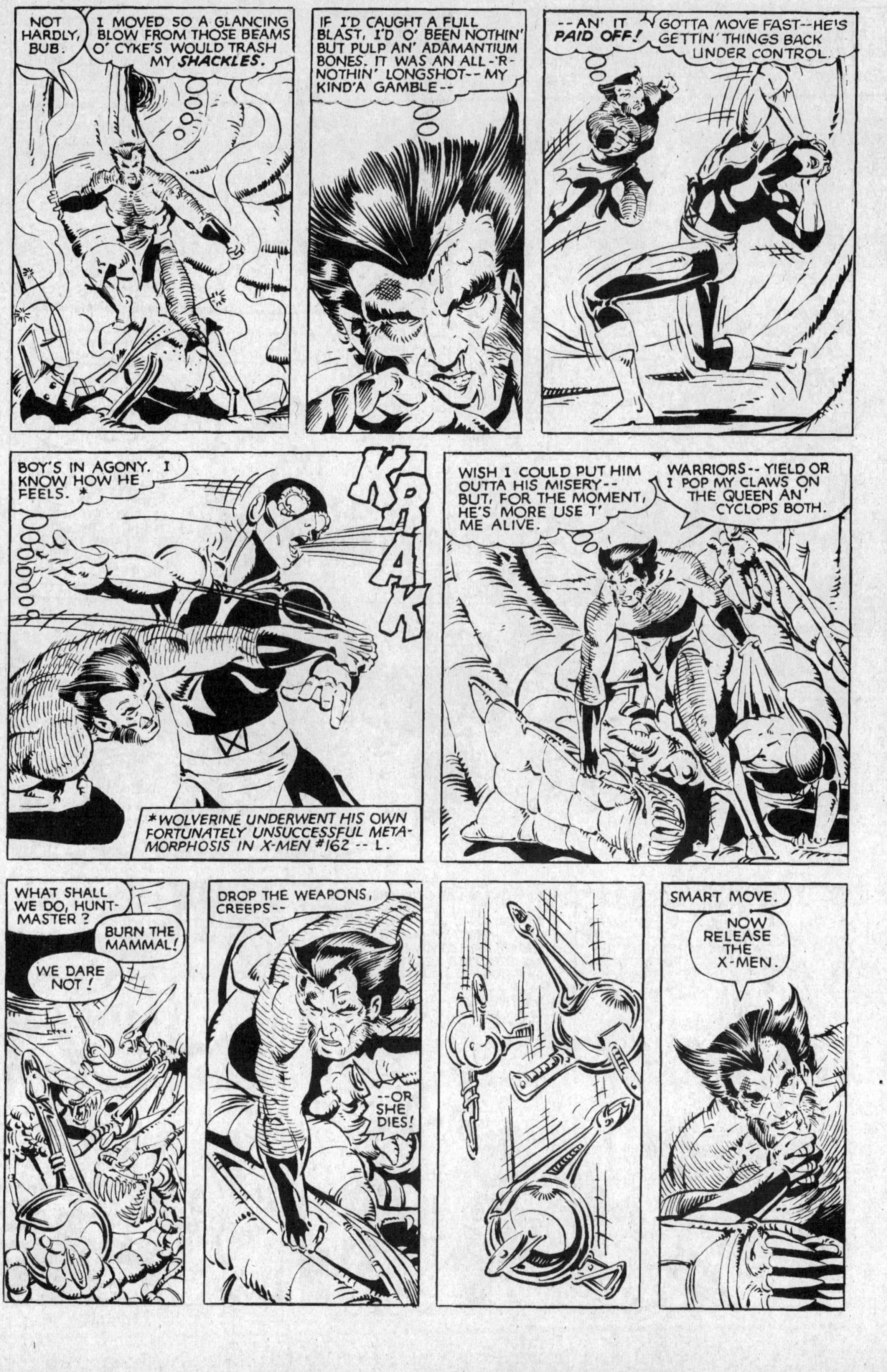
NOT HARDLY, BUB.
I MOVED SO A GLANCING BLOW FROM THOSE BEAMS O' CYKE'S WOULD TRASH MY SHACKLES.
IF I'D CAUGHT A FULL BLAST, I'D O' BEEN NOTHIN' BUT PULP AN' ADAMANTIUM BONES. IT WAS AN ALL-'R-NOTHIN' LONGSHOT-- MY KIND'A GAMBLE--
--AN' IT PAID OFF!
GOTTA MOVE FAST--HE'S GETTIN' THINGS BACK UNDER CONTROL.
BOY'S IN AGONY. I KNOW HOW HE FEELS. *
KRAK
*WOLVERINE UNDERWENT HIS OWN FORTUNATELY UNSUCCESSFUL META-MORPHOSIS IN X-MEN #162 -- L.
WISH I COULD PUT HIM OUTTA HIS MISERY-- BUT, FOR THE MOMENT, HE'S MORE USE T' ME ALIVE.
WARRIORS-- YIELD OR I POP MY CLAWS ON THE QUEEN AN' CYCLOPS BOTH.
WHAT SHALL WE DO, HUNT-MASTER?
BURN THE MAMMAL!
WE DARE NOT!
DROP THE WEAPONS, CREEPS--
--OR SHE DIES!
SMART MOVE.
NOW RELEASE THE X-MEN.

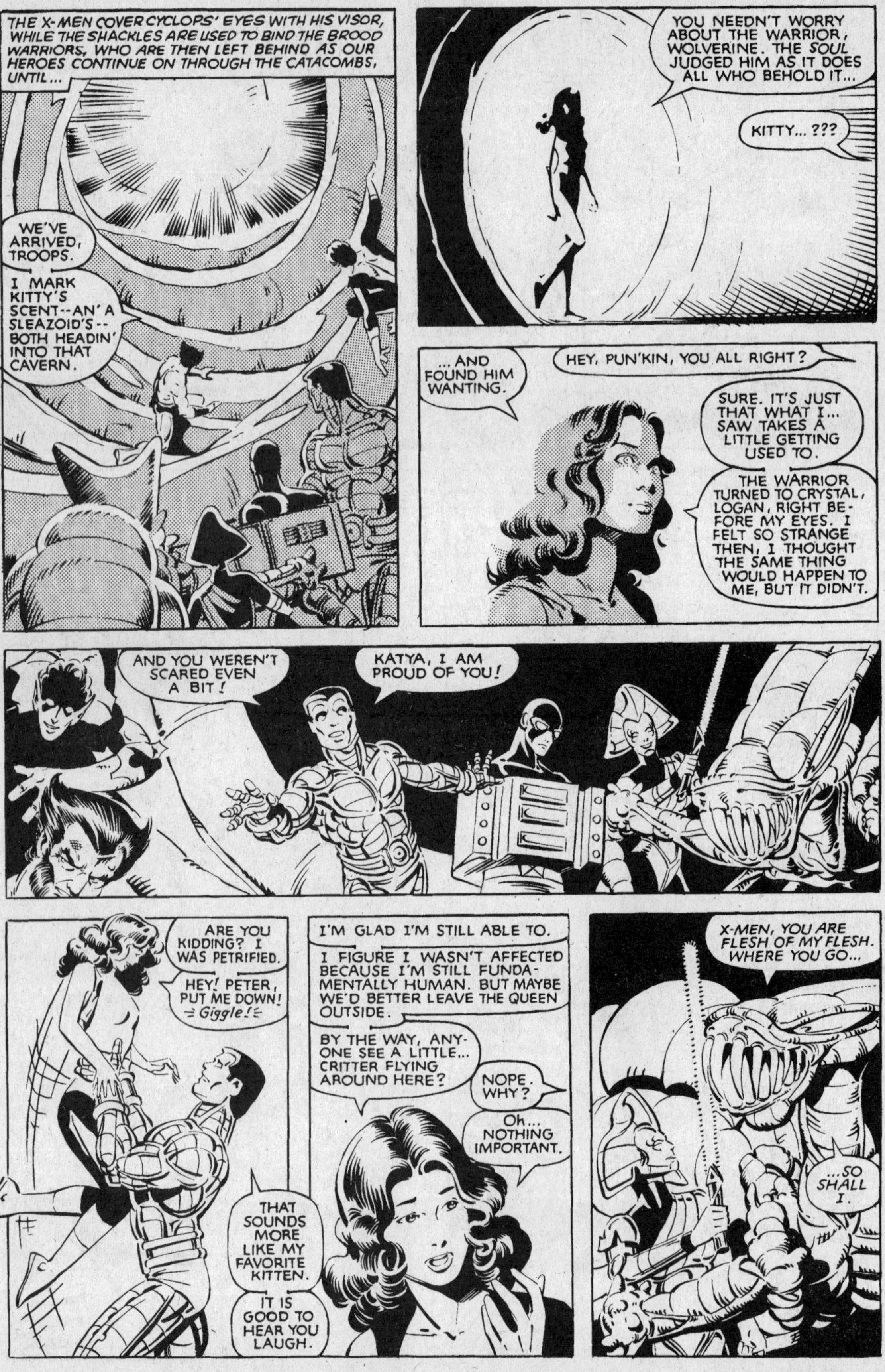
THE X-MEN COVER CYCLOPS' EYES WITH HIS VISOR, WHILE THE SHACKLES ARE USED TO BIND THE BROOD WARRIORS, WHO ARE THEN LEFT BEHIND AS OUR HEROES CONTINUE ON THROUGH THE CATACOMBS, UNTIL...
WE'VE ARRIVED, TROOPS.
I MARK KITTY'S SCENT--AN' A SLEAZOID'S--BOTH HEADIN' INTO THAT CAVERN.
YOU NEEDN'T WORRY ABOUT THE WARRIOR, WOLVERINE. THE SOUL JUDGED HIM AS IT DOES ALL WHO BEHOLD IT...
KITTY... ???
...AND FOUND HIM WANTING.
HEY, PUN'KIN, YOU ALL RIGHT?
SURE. IT'S JUST THAT WHAT I... SAW TAKES A LITTLE GETTING USED TO.
THE WARRIOR TURNED TO CRYSTAL, LOGAN, RIGHT BEFORE MY EYES. I FELT SO STRANGE THEN, I THOUGHT THE SAME THING WOULD HAPPEN TO ME, BUT IT DIDN'T.
AND YOU WEREN'T SCARED EVEN A BIT!
KATYA, I AM PROUD OF YOU!
ARE YOU KIDDING? I WAS PETRIFIED.
HEY! PETER, PUT ME DOWN! Giggle!
THAT SOUNDS MORE LIKE MY FAVORITE KITTEN.
IT IS GOOD TO HEAR YOU LAUGH.
I'M GLAD I'M STILL ABLE TO.
I FIGURE I WASN'T AFFECTED BECAUSE I'M STILL FUNDAMENTALLY HUMAN. BUT MAYBE WE'D BETTER LEAVE THE QUEEN OUTSIDE.
BY THE WAY, ANYONE SEE A LITTLE... CRITTER FLYING AROUND HERE?
NOPE. WHY?
Oh... NOTHING IMPORTANT.
X-MEN, YOU ARE FLESH OF MY FLESH. WHERE YOU GO...
...SO SHALL I.

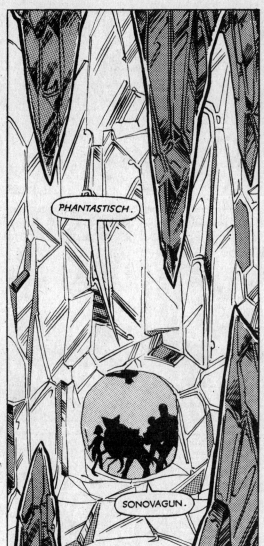

PHANTASTISCH.

SONOVAGUN.

CAN YOU FEEL THE LOVE, GUYS? WE'RE STRANGERS-- ALIENS--YET THE *SOUL* WELCOMES US.

WELCOMES *YOU*, PERHAPS, YOUNGLING--

--BUT I SENSE ONLY A HATRED AS DEEP AND ABIDING AS MY OWN.

BY THE WHITE WOLF! COMRADES, LOOK AT THE CRYSTAL BENEATH THE QUEEN!

FASCINATING. EVIDENTLY, I AM CAPABLE OF CORRUPTING EVEN THIS HOLY OF HOLIES.

AND SO, IT SEEMS, ARE MY CHILDREN.

NO!

OUTTA HERE, EVERY- BODY-- BEFORE IT'S TOO LATE!

IT IS ALREADY TOO LATE, WOLVERINE, FOR THEM--

--AND *YOU*!

AAH THPPP!

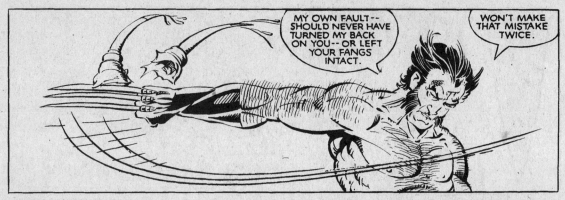

MY OWN FAULT-- SHOULD NEVER HAVE TURNED MY BACK ON YOU -- OR LEFT YOUR FANGS INTACT.

WON'T MAKE THAT MISTAKE TWICE.

TRUE, LITTLE MAN-- FOR YOU ARE ABOUT TO DIE.

NOT... YET, MAMA!

TOOK ONE HECKUVA JOLT-- MAYBE MORE VENOM THAN MY SYSTEM CAN HANDLE.

BUT I AIN'T LETTIN' THAT STOP ME. NOT 'TIL I'VE DONE...

A MAJESTIC SIGHT, IS IT NOT?

THE EMPATHIC RESONANCE OF THEIR METAMORPHOSIS ALREADY SATURATES THIS CHAMBER.

AS THEY ARE CONSUMED, SO SHALL THE ACANTI SOUL BE TRANSFORMED WITH THEM. NO LONGER WILL WE HAVE TO HUNT THE STARSINGERS, THEY WILL SERVE US WILLINGLY-- BECAUSE ACANTI AND BROOD WILL HAVE BECOME ONE!

OUR RULE WILL SPREAD ACROSS THE STARS, OUR MANIFEST DESTINY FULFILLED!

WANNA... BET?

FIRST THEM, QUEENIE.

SNIKT

THEN-- WITH MY LAST BREATH, IF NEED BE--

--YOU!

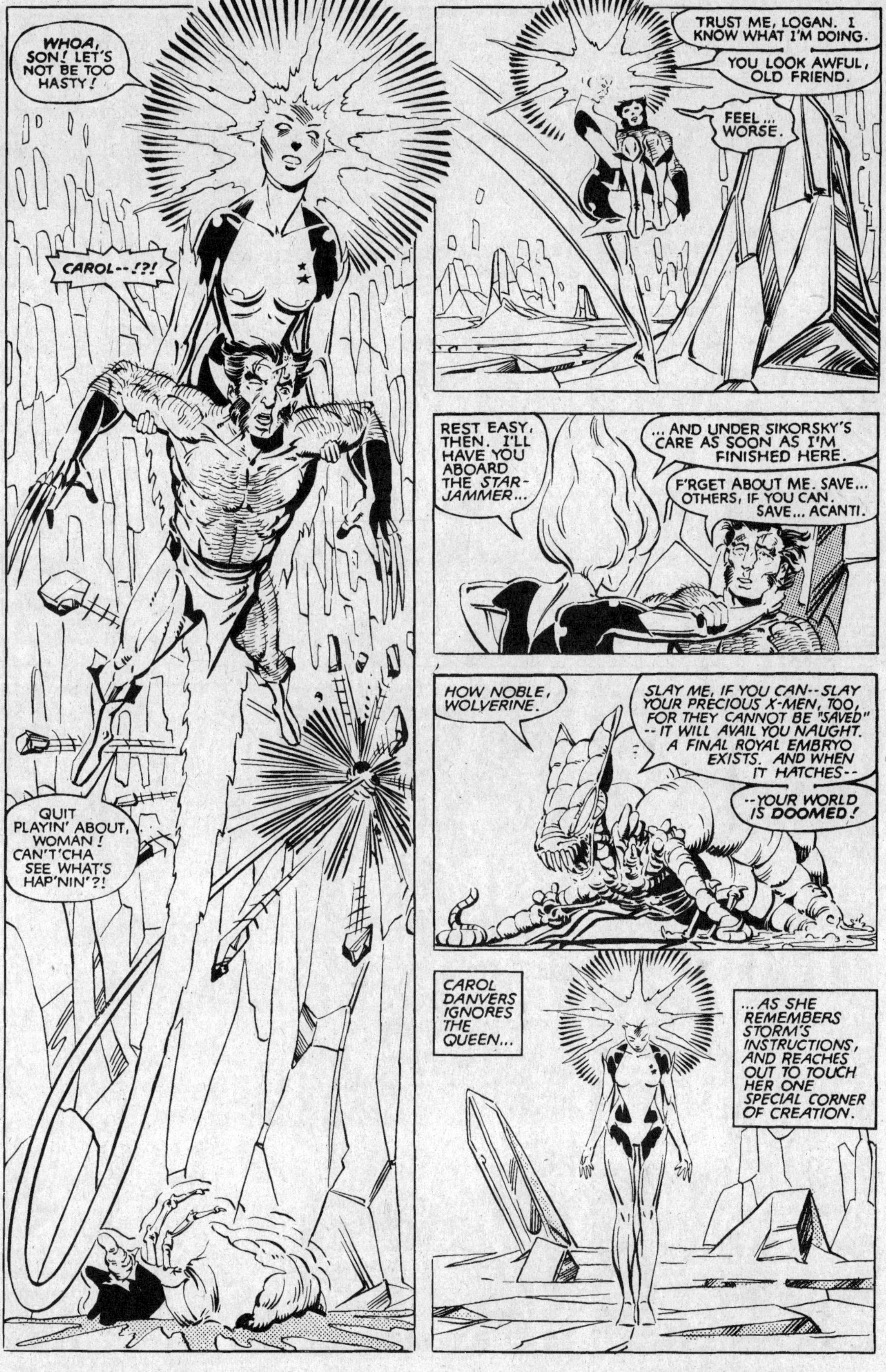
WHOA, SON! LET'S NOT BE TOO HASTY!
CAROL--!?!
QUIT PLAYIN' ABOUT, WOMAN! CAN'T'CHA SEE WHAT'S HAP'NIN'?!
TRUST ME, LOGAN. I KNOW WHAT I'M DOING.
YOU LOOK AWFUL, OLD FRIEND.
FEEL... WORSE.
REST EASY, THEN. I'LL HAVE YOU ABOARD THE STAR-JAMMER...
...AND UNDER SIKORSKY'S CARE AS SOON AS I'M FINISHED HERE.
F'RGET ABOUT ME. SAVE... OTHERS, IF YOU CAN. SAVE... ACANTI.
HOW NOBLE, WOLVERINE.
SLAY ME, IF YOU CAN--SLAY YOUR PRECIOUS X-MEN, TOO, FOR THEY CANNOT BE "SAVED" --IT WILL AVAIL YOU NAUGHT. A FINAL ROYAL EMBRYO EXISTS. AND WHEN IT HATCHES--
--YOUR WORLD IS DOOMED!
CAROL DANVERS IGNORES THE QUEEN...
...AS SHE REMEMBERS STORM'S INSTRUCTIONS, AND REACHES OUT TO TOUCH HER ONE SPECIAL CORNER OF CREATION.

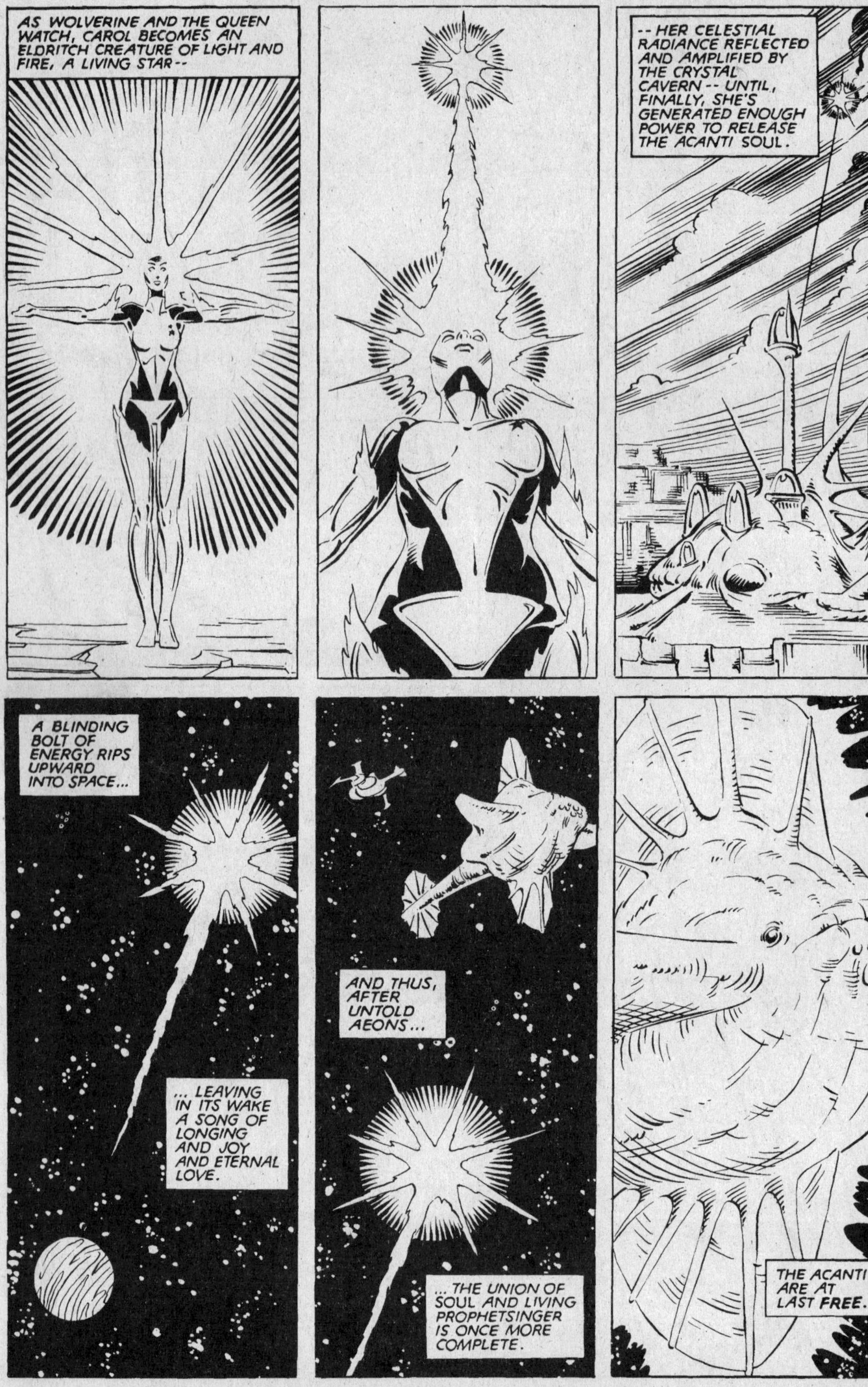
AS WOLVERINE AND THE QUEEN WATCH, CAROL BECOMES AN ELDRITCH CREATURE OF LIGHT AND FIRE, A LIVING STAR--
-- HER CELESTIAL RADIANCE REFLECTED AND AMPLIFIED BY THE CRYSTAL CAVERN -- UNTIL, FINALLY, SHE'S GENERATED ENOUGH POWER TO RELEASE THE ACANTI SOUL.
A BLINDING BOLT OF ENERGY RIPS UPWARD INTO SPACE...
... LEAVING IN ITS WAKE A SONG OF LONGING AND JOY AND ETERNAL LOVE.
AND THUS, AFTER UNTOLD AEONS...
...THE UNION OF SOUL AND LIVING PROPHETSINGER IS ONCE MORE COMPLETE.
THE ACANTI ARE AT LAST FREE.

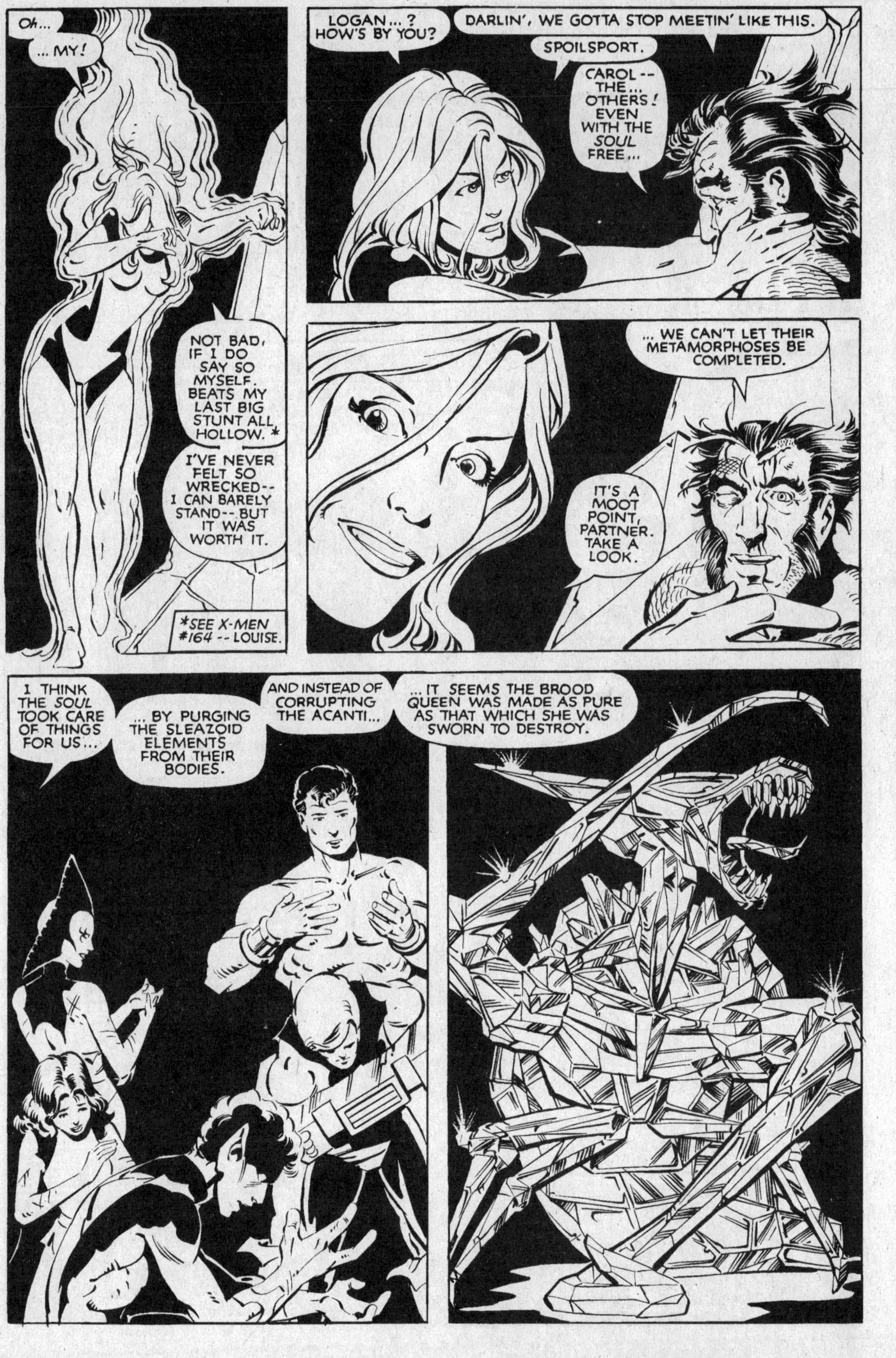
Oh...
... MY!
LOGAN...? HOW'S BY YOU?
DARLIN', WE GOTTA STOP MEETIN' LIKE THIS.
SPOILSPORT.
CAROL -- THE... OTHERS! EVEN WITH THE SOUL FREE...
NOT BAD, IF I DO SAY SO MYSELF. BEATS MY LAST BIG STUNT ALL HOLLOW.*
I'VE NEVER FELT SO WRECKED-- I CAN BARELY STAND-- BUT IT WAS WORTH IT.
*SEE X-MEN #164 -- LOUISE.
... WE CAN'T LET THEIR METAMORPHOSES BE COMPLETED.
IT'S A MOOT POINT, PARTNER. TAKE A LOOK.
I THINK THE SOUL TOOK CARE OF THINGS FOR US...
... BY PURGING THE SLEAZOID ELEMENTS FROM THEIR BODIES.
AND INSTEAD OF CORRUPTING THE ACANTI...
... IT SEEMS THE BROOD QUEEN WAS MADE AS PURE AS THAT WHICH SHE WAS SWORN TO DESTROY.

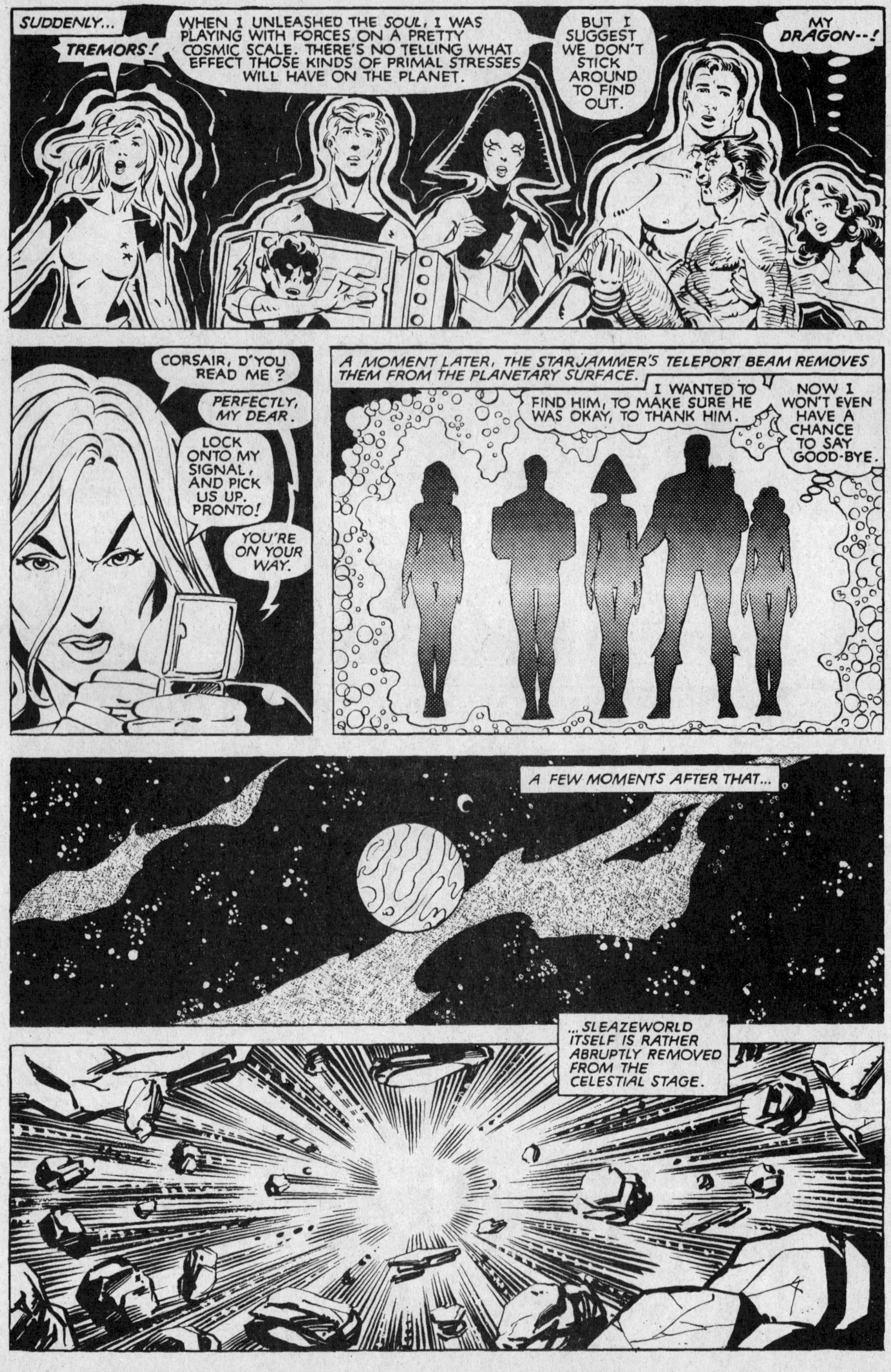
SUDDENLY...
TREMORS!
WHEN I UNLEASHED THE SOUL, I WAS PLAYING WITH FORCES ON A PRETTY COSMIC SCALE. THERE'S NO TELLING WHAT EFFECT THOSE KINDS OF PRIMAL STRESSES WILL HAVE ON THE PLANET.
BUT I SUGGEST WE DON'T STICK AROUND TO FIND OUT.
MY DRAGON--!
CORSAIR, D'YOU READ ME?
PERFECTLY, MY DEAR.
LOCK ONTO MY SIGNAL, AND PICK US UP. PRONTO!
YOU'RE ON YOUR WAY.
A MOMENT LATER, THE STARJAMMER'S TELEPORT BEAM REMOVES THEM FROM THE PLANETARY SURFACE.
I WANTED TO FIND HIM, TO MAKE SURE HE WAS OKAY, TO THANK HIM.
NOW I WON'T EVEN HAVE A CHANCE TO SAY GOOD-BYE.
A FEW MOMENTS AFTER THAT...
...SLEAZEWORLD ITSELF IS RATHER ABRUPTLY REMOVED FROM THE CELESTIAL STAGE.

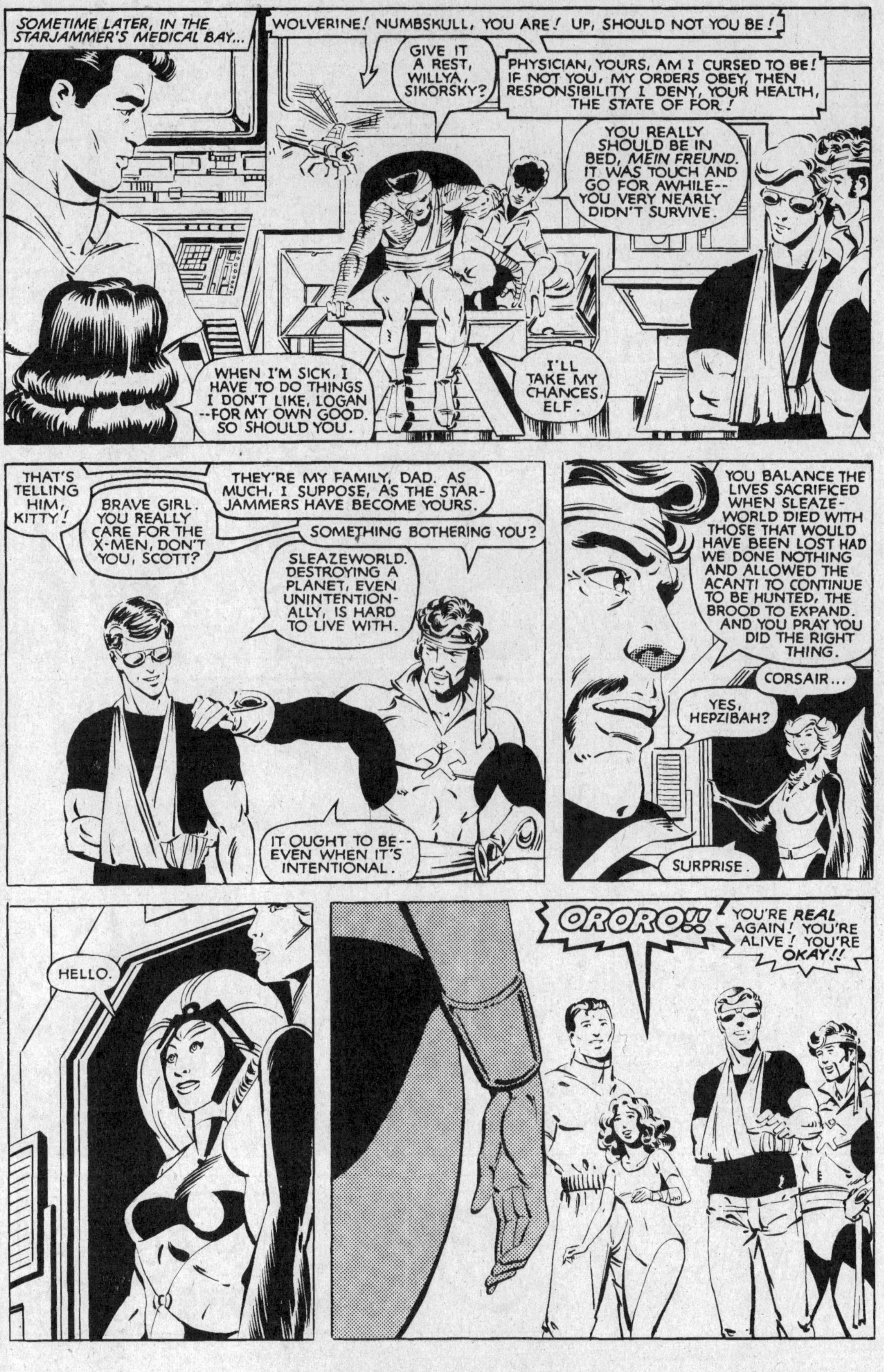

SOMETIME LATER, IN THE STARJAMMER'S MEDICAL BAY...
WOLVERINE! NUMBSKULL, YOU ARE! UP, SHOULD NOT YOU BE!
GIVE IT A REST, WILLYA, SIKORSKY?
PHYSICIAN, YOURS, AM I CURSED TO BE! IF NOT YOU, MY ORDERS OBEY, THEN RESPONSIBILITY I DENY, YOUR HEALTH, THE STATE OF FOR!
YOU REALLY SHOULD BE IN BED, MEIN FREUND. IT WAS TOUCH AND GO FOR AWHILE-- YOU VERY NEARLY DIDN'T SURVIVE.
WHEN I'M SICK, I HAVE TO DO THINGS I DON'T LIKE, LOGAN --FOR MY OWN GOOD. SO SHOULD YOU.
I'LL TAKE MY CHANCES, ELF.
THAT'S TELLING HIM, KITTY!
BRAVE GIRL. YOU REALLY CARE FOR THE X-MEN, DON'T YOU, SCOTT?
THEY'RE MY FAMILY, DAD. AS MUCH, I SUPPOSE, AS THE STAR-JAMMERS HAVE BECOME YOURS.
SOMETHING BOTHERING YOU?
SLEAZEWORLD. DESTROYING A PLANET, EVEN UNINTENTION-ALLY, IS HARD TO LIVE WITH.
IT OUGHT TO BE-- EVEN WHEN IT'S INTENTIONAL.
YOU BALANCE THE LIVES SACRIFICED WHEN SLEAZE-WORLD DIED WITH THOSE THAT WOULD HAVE BEEN LOST HAD WE DONE NOTHING AND ALLOWED THE ACANTI TO CONTINUE TO BE HUNTED, THE BROOD TO EXPAND. AND YOU PRAY YOU DID THE RIGHT THING.
CORSAIR...
YES, HEPZIBAH?
SURPRISE.
HELLO.
ORORO!!
YOU'RE REAL AGAIN! YOU'RE ALIVE! YOU'RE OKAY!!

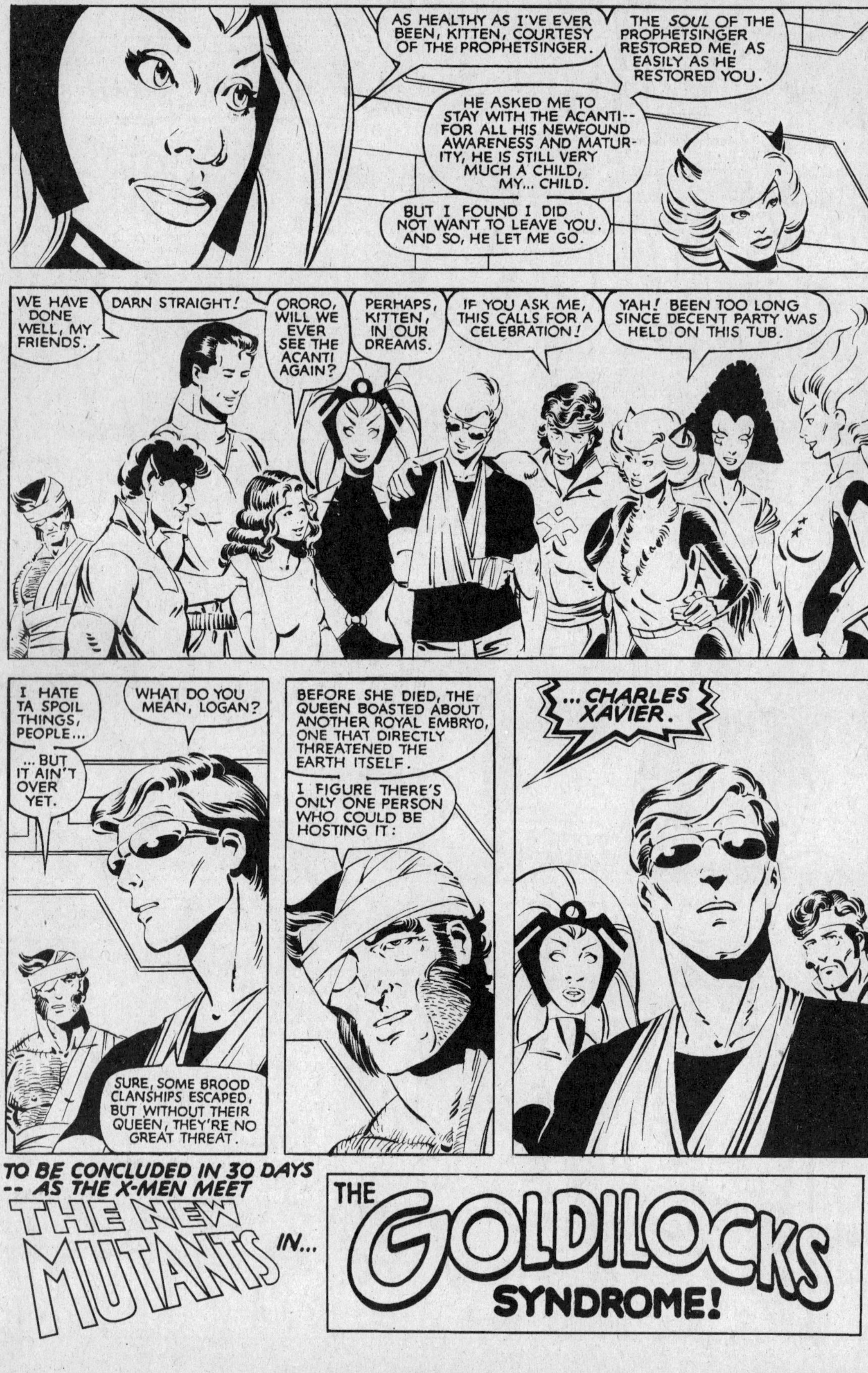
AS HEALTHY AS I'VE EVER BEEN, KITTEN, COURTESY OF THE PROPHETSINGER.
THE SOUL OF THE PROPHETSINGER RESTORED ME, AS EASILY AS HE RESTORED YOU.
HE ASKED ME TO STAY WITH THE ACANTI-- FOR ALL HIS NEWFOUND AWARENESS AND MATURITY, HE IS STILL VERY MUCH A CHILD, MY... CHILD.
BUT I FOUND I DID NOT WANT TO LEAVE YOU. AND SO, HE LET ME GO.
WE HAVE DONE WELL, MY FRIENDS.
DARN STRAIGHT!
ORORO, WILL WE EVER SEE THE ACANTI AGAIN?
PERHAPS, KITTEN, IN OUR DREAMS.
IF YOU ASK ME, THIS CALLS FOR A CELEBRATION!
YAH! BEEN TOO LONG SINCE DECENT PARTY WAS HELD ON THIS TUB.
I HATE TA SPOIL THINGS, PEOPLE...
...BUT IT AIN'T OVER YET.
WHAT DO YOU MEAN, LOGAN?
SURE, SOME BROOD CLANSHIPS ESCAPED, BUT WITHOUT THEIR QUEEN, THEY'RE NO GREAT THREAT.
BEFORE SHE DIED, THE QUEEN BOASTED ABOUT ANOTHER ROYAL EMBRYO, ONE THAT DIRECTLY THREATENED THE EARTH ITSELF.
I FIGURE THERE'S ONLY ONE PERSON WHO COULD BE HOSTING IT:
...CHARLES XAVIER.
TO BE CONCLUDED IN 30 DAYS -- AS THE X-MEN MEET
THE NEW MUTANTS IN...
THE GOLDILOCKS SYNDROME!

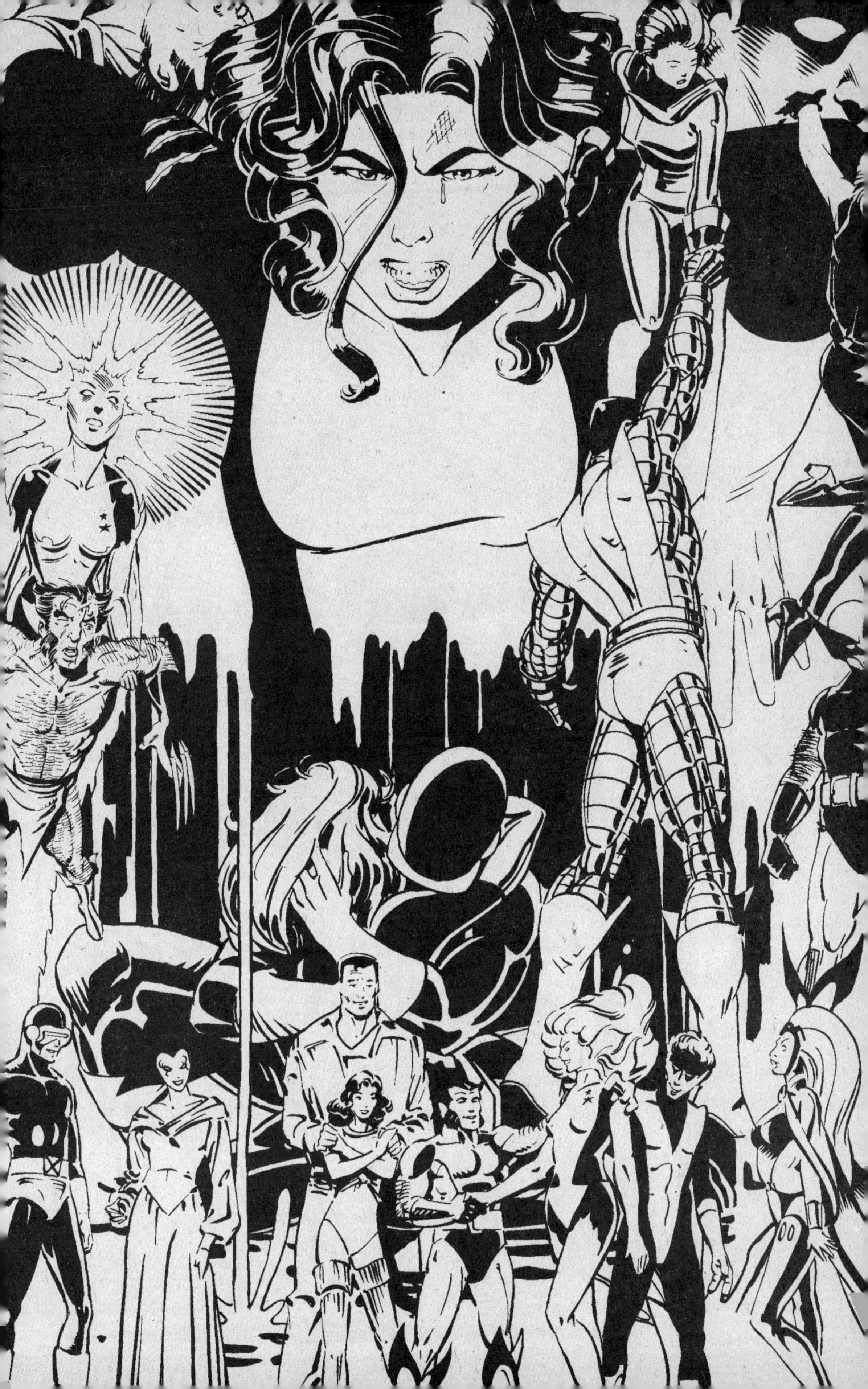

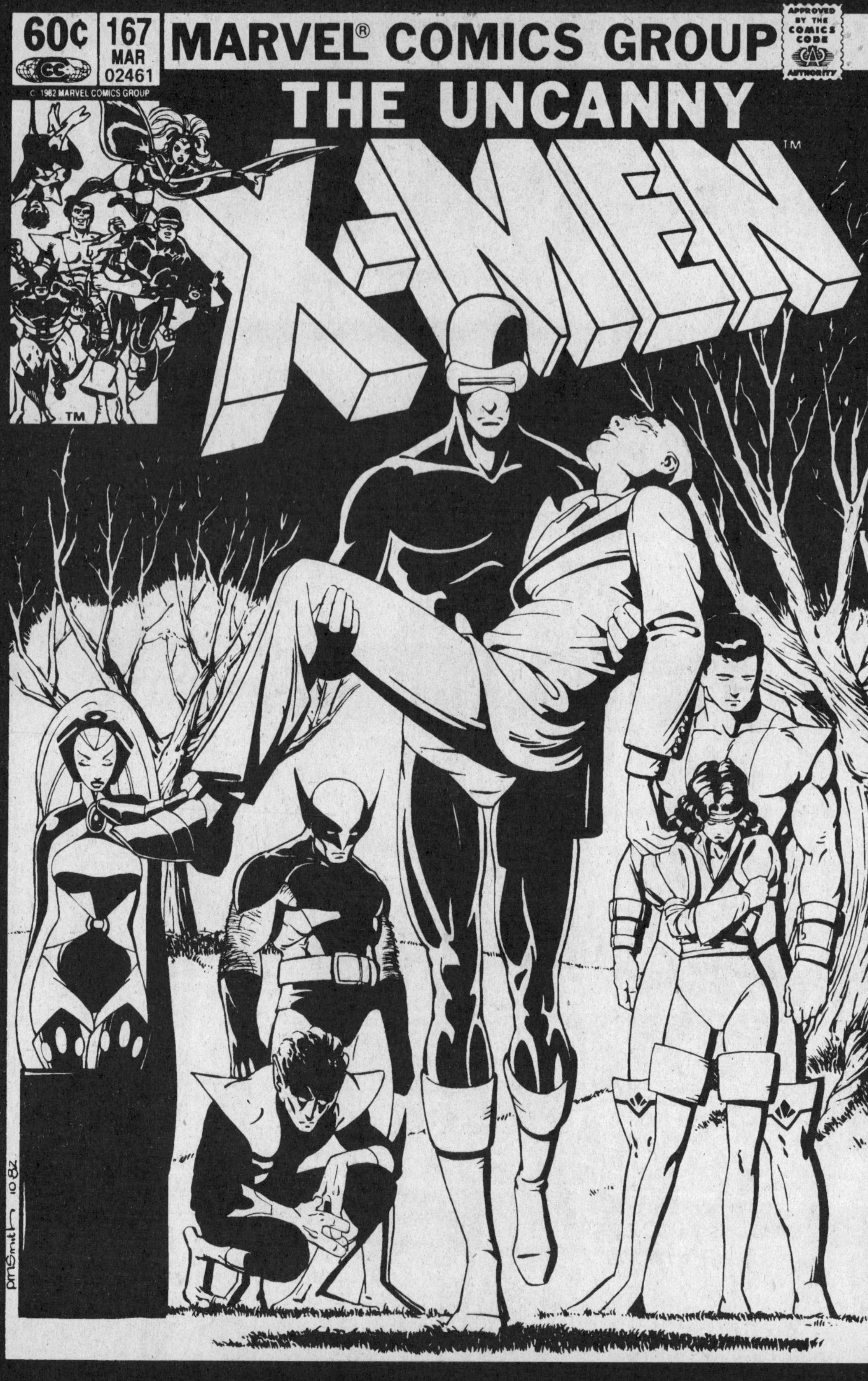
60¢
167
MAR
02461
© 1982 MARVEL COMICS GROUP
MARVEL® COMICS GROUP
APPROVED BY THE COMICS CODE AUTHORITY
THE UNCANNY
X-MEN™

JUST OUTSIDE THE TOWN OF *SALEM CENTER* -- ROUGHLY AN HOUR'S DRIVE UPSTATE FROM NEW YORK CITY -- LIES PROFESSOR CHARLES XAVIER'S SCHOOL FOR GIFTED YOUNGSTERS...

... A VERY RECLUSIVE, EXCLUSIVE, PRIVATE ACADEMY WHOSE STUDENT BODY CURRENTLY CONSISTS OF FIVE UNIQUE YOUNG INDIVIDUALS.

THEY ARE MUTANTS...

...GIFTED --OR CURSED, DEPENDING ON ONE'S POINT-OF-VIEW-- WITH POWERS AND ABILITIES THAT SET THEM APART FROM THE REST OF HUMANITY.

XAVIER ONLY RECENTLY GATHERED THEM TO TEACH THEM HOW TO COPE WITH THEIR NASCENT TALENTS, TO ENABLE THEM TO FUNCTION IN A WORLD THAT DISTRUSTS-- AND OCCASIONALLY HATES-- THEM, SIMPLY BECAUSE THEY EXIST.

SAM GUTHRIE.

WAY T' GO, MAGNUM! LOOK AT THAT MAN MOVE!

HE SURE IS CUTE.

Y' SHOULD NA' THINK SUCH THOUGHTS, DANI. THEY'RE NA' PROPER.

HE IS VERRA HANDSOME, THOUGH.

XI'AN COY MANH.

RAHNE SINCLAIR.

DANIELLE MOONSTAR.

ROBERTO da COSTA.

THEY ARE NOT THE FIRST TO BE TAUGHT BY XAVIER -- HIMSELF A TELEPATH, THE STRONGEST MUTANT MIND ON EARTH -- BUT THEY MAY WELL TURN OUT TO BE THE LAST.

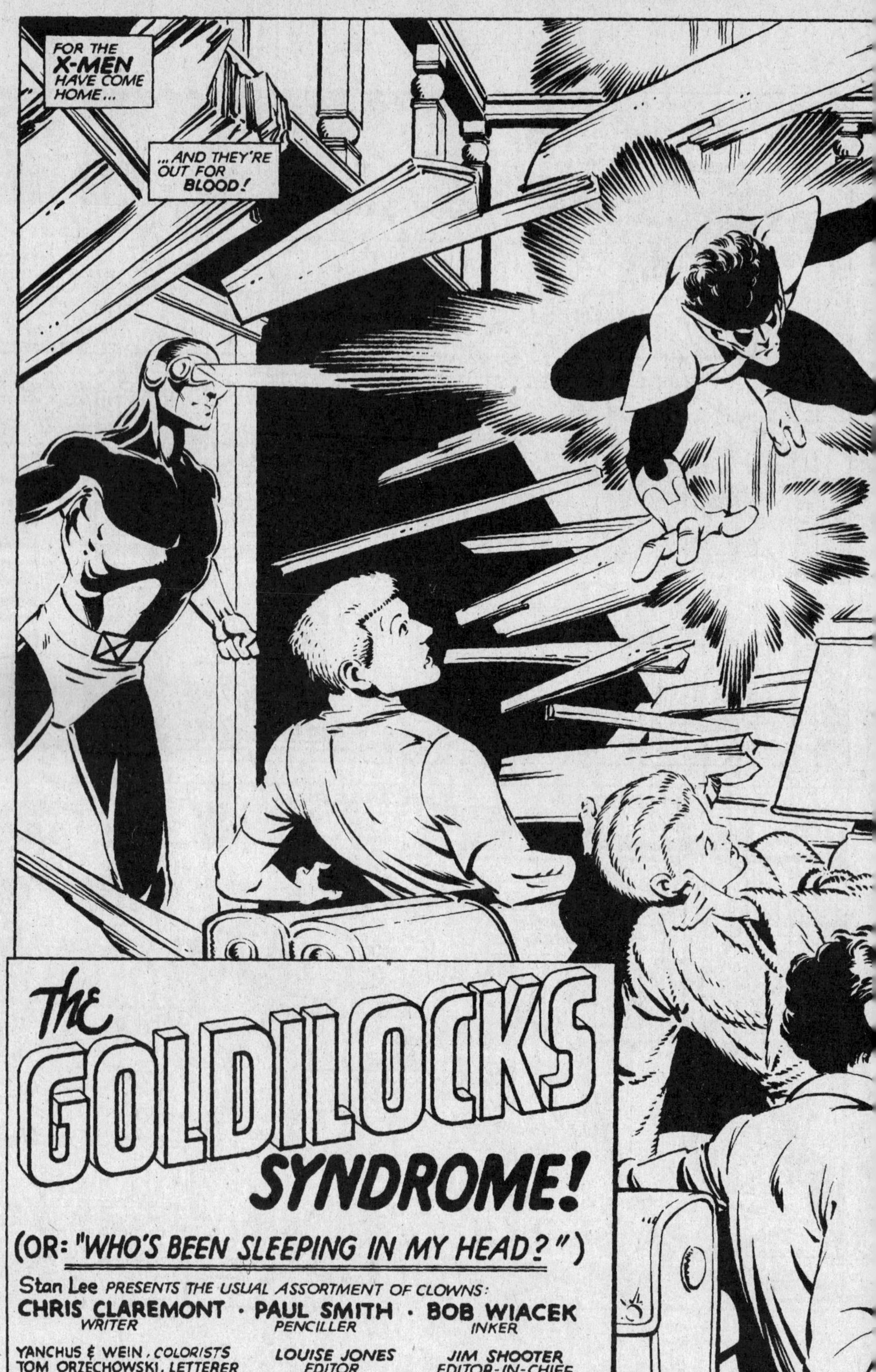
FOR THE X-MEN HAVE COME HOME...
...AND THEY'RE OUT FOR BLOOD!
THE GOLDILOCKS SYNDROME!
(OR: "WHO'S BEEN SLEEPING IN MY HEAD?")
Stan Lee PRESENTS THE USUAL ASSORTMENT OF CLOWNS:
CHRIS CLAREMONT · PAUL SMITH · BOB WIACEK
WRITER PENCILLER INKER
YANCHUS & WEIN, COLORISTS
TOM ORZECHOWSKI, LETTERER
LOUISE JONES EDITOR
JIM SHOOTER EDITOR-IN-CHIEF

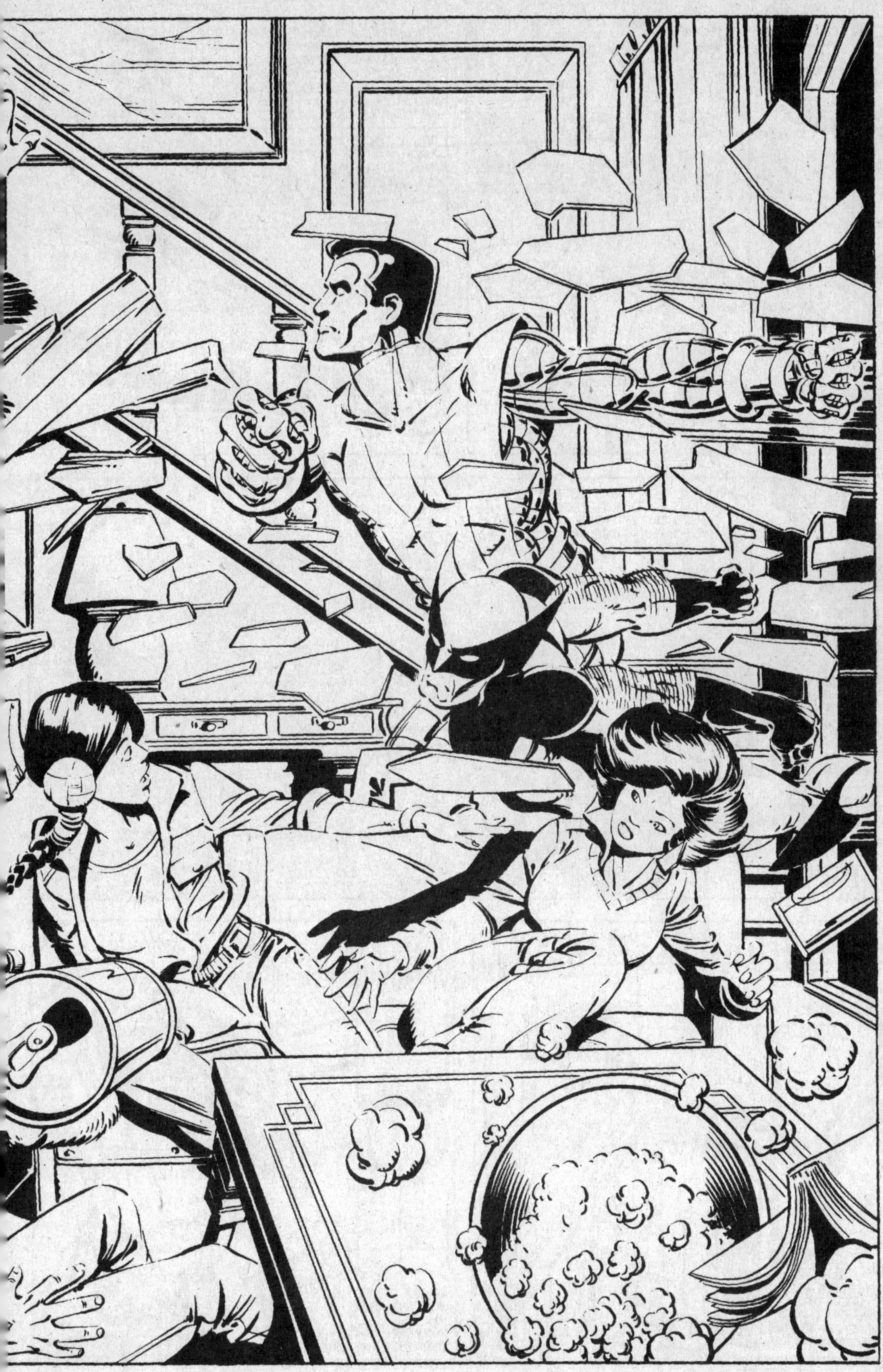

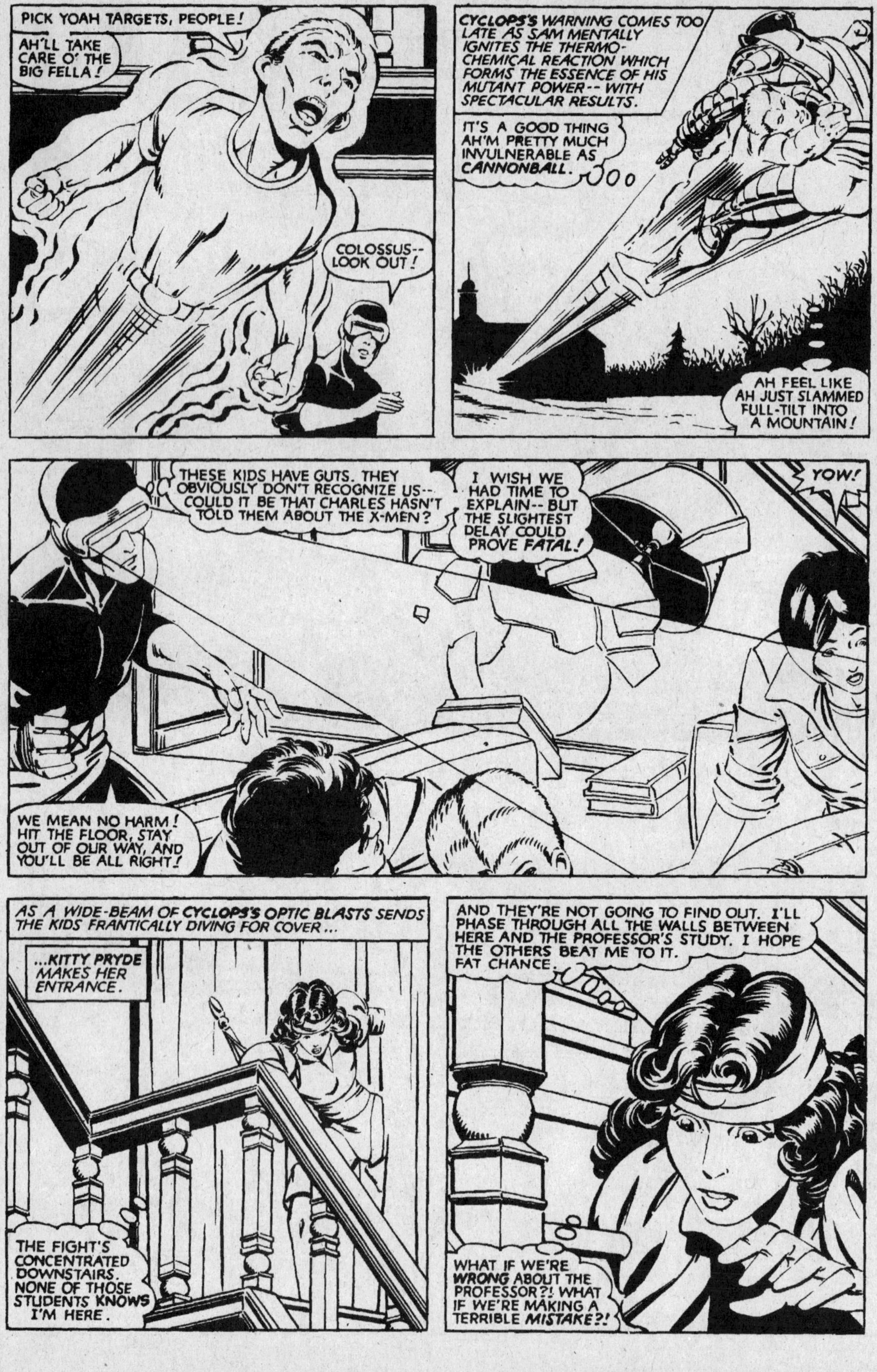
PICK YOAH TARGETS, PEOPLE!
AH'LL TAKE CARE O' THE BIG FELLA!
COLOSSUS-- LOOK OUT!
CYCLOPS'S WARNING COMES TOO LATE AS SAM MENTALLY IGNITES THE THERMO-CHEMICAL REACTION WHICH FORMS THE ESSENCE OF HIS MUTANT POWER-- WITH SPECTACULAR RESULTS.
IT'S A GOOD THING AH'M PRETTY MUCH INVULNERABLE AS CANNONBALL.
AH FEEL LIKE AH JUST SLAMMED FULL-TILT INTO A MOUNTAIN!
THESE KIDS HAVE GUTS. THEY OBVIOUSLY DON'T RECOGNIZE US-- COULD IT BE THAT CHARLES HASN'T TOLD THEM ABOUT THE X-MEN?
I WISH WE HAD TIME TO EXPLAIN-- BUT THE SLIGHTEST DELAY COULD PROVE FATAL!
YOW!
WE MEAN NO HARM! HIT THE FLOOR, STAY OUT OF OUR WAY, AND YOU'LL BE ALL RIGHT!
AS A WIDE-BEAM OF CYCLOPS'S OPTIC BLASTS SENDS THE KIDS FRANTICALLY DIVING FOR COVER...
...KITTY PRYDE MAKES HER ENTRANCE.
THE FIGHT'S CONCENTRATED DOWNSTAIRS. NONE OF THOSE STUDENTS KNOWS I'M HERE.
AND THEY'RE NOT GOING TO FIND OUT. I'LL PHASE THROUGH ALL THE WALLS BETWEEN HERE AND THE PROFESSOR'S STUDY. I HOPE THE OTHERS BEAT ME TO IT. FAT CHANCE.
WHAT IF WE'RE WRONG ABOUT THE PROFESSOR?! WHAT IF WE'RE MAKING A TERRIBLE MISTAKE?!

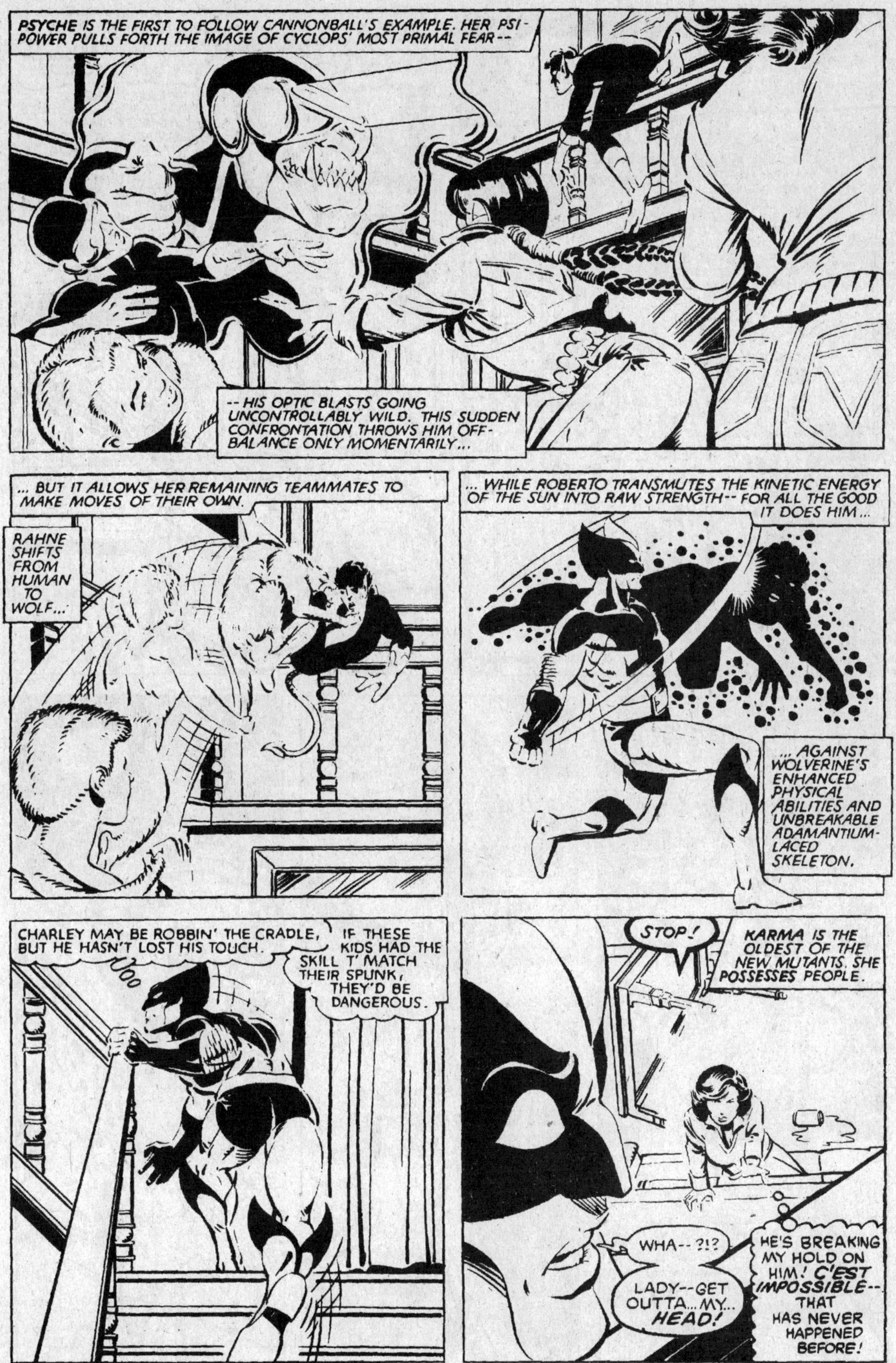
PSYCHE IS THE FIRST TO FOLLOW CANNONBALL'S EXAMPLE. HER PSI-POWER PULLS FORTH THE IMAGE OF CYCLOPS' MOST PRIMAL FEAR--
--HIS OPTIC BLASTS GOING UNCONTROLLABLY WILD. THIS SUDDEN CONFRONTATION THROWS HIM OFF-BALANCE ONLY MOMENTARILY...
... BUT IT ALLOWS HER REMAINING TEAMMATES TO MAKE MOVES OF THEIR OWN.
RAHNE SHIFTS FROM HUMAN TO WOLF...
... WHILE ROBERTO TRANSMUTES THE KINETIC ENERGY OF THE SUN INTO RAW STRENGTH-- FOR ALL THE GOOD IT DOES HIM...
... AGAINST WOLVERINE'S ENHANCED PHYSICAL ABILITIES AND UNBREAKABLE ADAMANTIUM-LACED SKELETON.
CHARLEY MAY BE ROBBIN' THE CRADLE, BUT HE HASN'T LOST HIS TOUCH.
IF THESE KIDS HAD THE SKILL T' MATCH THEIR SPUNK, THEY'D BE DANGEROUS.
STOP!
KARMA IS THE OLDEST OF THE NEW MUTANTS. SHE POSSESSES PEOPLE.
WHA--?!?
LADY--GET OUTTA...MY... HEAD!
HE'S BREAKING MY HOLD ON HIM! C'EST IMPOSSIBLE-- THAT HAS NEVER HAPPENED BEFORE!

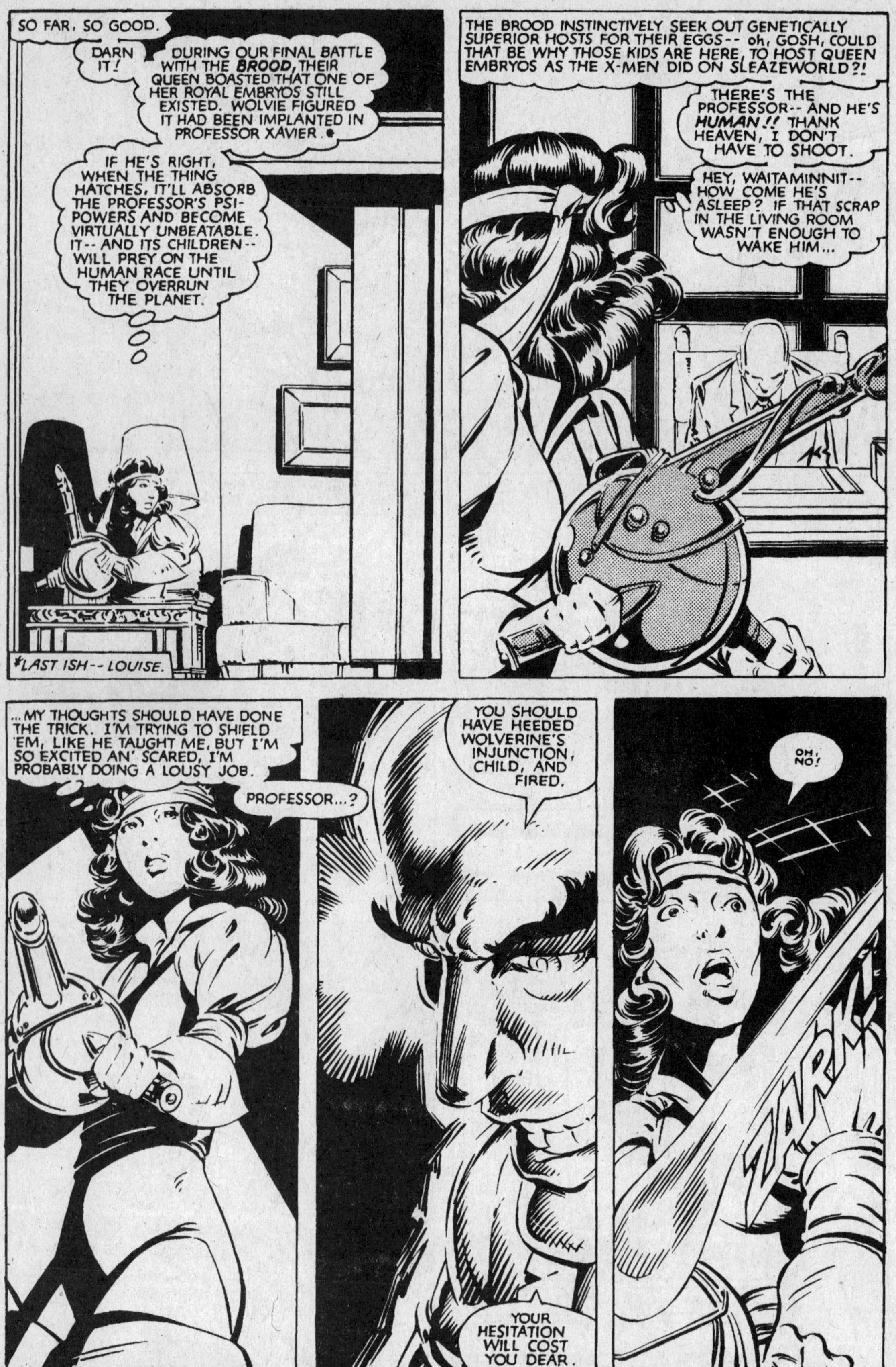
SO FAR, SO GOOD.
DARN IT!
DURING OUR FINAL BATTLE WITH THE **BROOD**, THEIR QUEEN BOASTED THAT ONE OF HER ROYAL EMBRYOS STILL EXISTED. WOLVIE FIGURED IT HAD BEEN IMPLANTED IN PROFESSOR XAVIER.*
IF HE'S RIGHT, WHEN THE THING HATCHES, IT'LL ABSORB THE PROFESSOR'S PSI-POWERS AND BECOME VIRTUALLY UNBEATABLE. IT-- AND ITS CHILDREN-- WILL PREY ON THE HUMAN RACE UNTIL THEY OVERRUN THE PLANET.
*LAST ISH-- LOUISE.
THE BROOD INSTINCTIVELY SEEK OUT GENETICALLY SUPERIOR HOSTS FOR THEIR EGGS-- oh, GOSH, COULD THAT BE WHY THOSE KIDS ARE HERE, TO HOST QUEEN EMBRYOS AS THE X-MEN DID ON SLEAZEWORLD?!
THERE'S THE PROFESSOR-- AND HE'S *HUMAN!!* THANK HEAVEN, I DON'T HAVE TO SHOOT.
HEY, WAITAMINNIT-- HOW COME HE'S ASLEEP? IF THAT SCRAP IN THE LIVING ROOM WASN'T ENOUGH TO WAKE HIM...
...MY THOUGHTS SHOULD HAVE DONE THE TRICK. I'M TRYING TO SHIELD 'EM, LIKE HE TAUGHT ME, BUT I'M SO EXCITED AN' SCARED, I'M PROBABLY DOING A LOUSY JOB.
PROFESSOR...?
YOU SHOULD HAVE HEEDED WOLVERINE'S INJUNCTION, CHILD, AND FIRED.
YOUR HESITATION WILL COST YOU DEAR.
OH, NO!
ZARK!

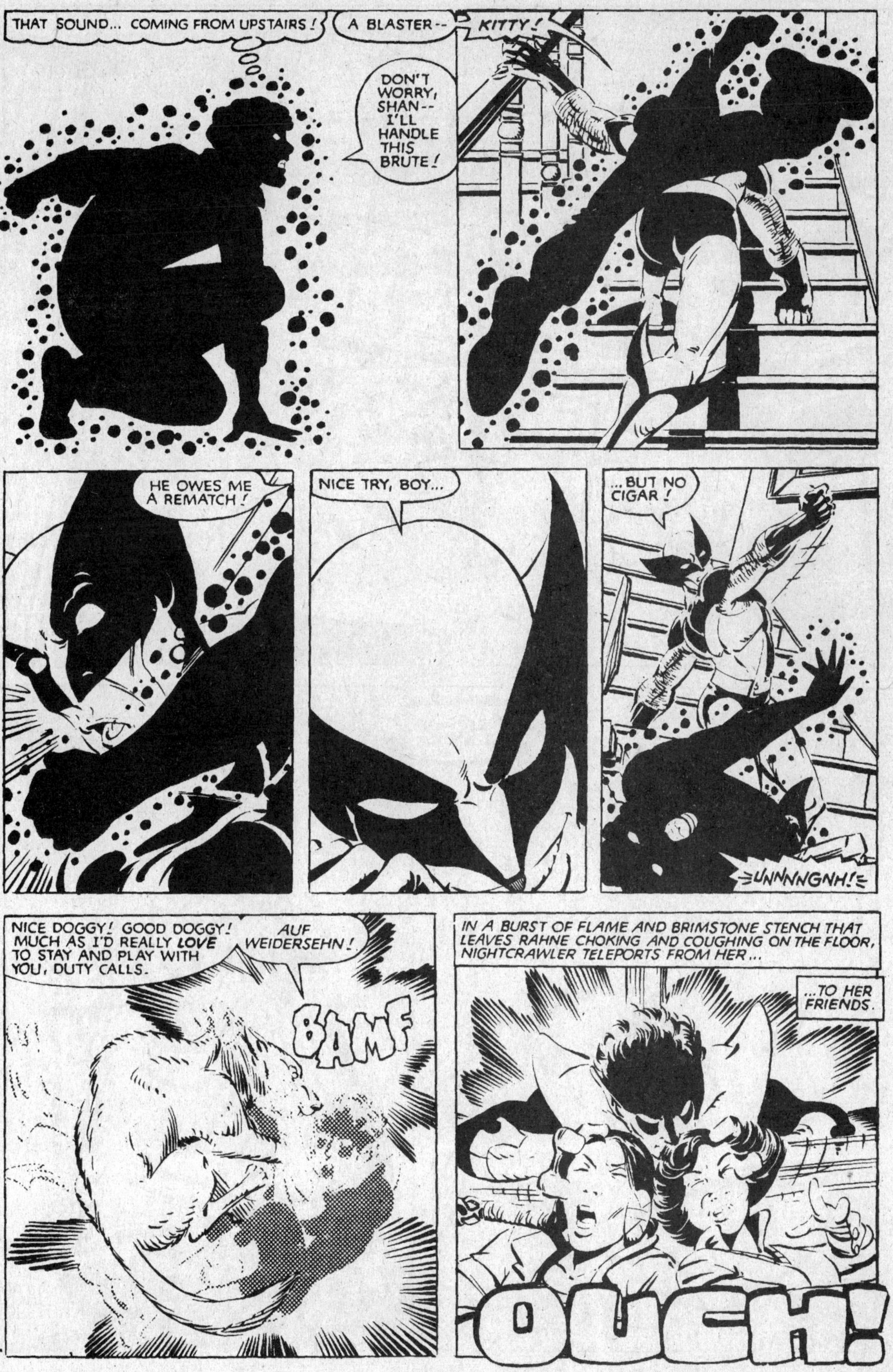
THAT SOUND... COMING FROM UPSTAIRS!
A BLASTER--
KITTY!
DON'T WORRY, SHAN-- I'LL HANDLE THIS BRUTE!
HE OWES ME A REMATCH!
NICE TRY, BOY...
...BUT NO CIGAR!
UNNNNGNH!
NICE DOGGY! GOOD DOGGY! MUCH AS I'D REALLY LOVE TO STAY AND PLAY WITH YOU, DUTY CALLS.
AUF WEIDERSEHN!
BAMF
IN A BURST OF FLAME AND BRIMSTONE STENCH THAT LEAVES RAHNE CHOKING AND COUGHING ON THE FLOOR, NIGHTCRAWLER TELEPORTS FROM HER...
...TO HER FRIENDS.
OUCH!

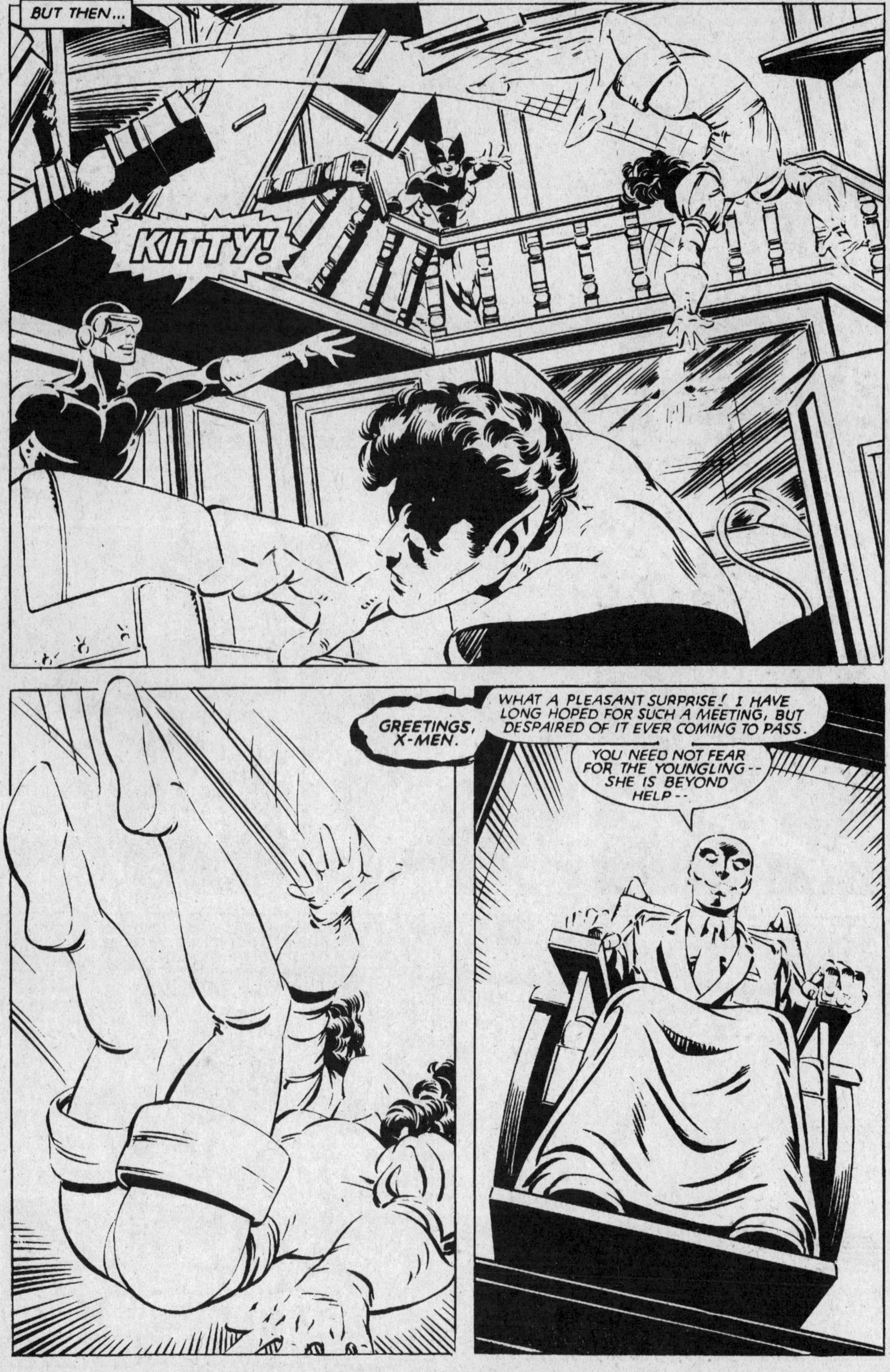
BUT THEN...
KITTY!
GREETINGS, X-MEN.
WHAT A PLEASANT SURPRISE! I HAVE LONG HOPED FOR SUCH A MEETING, BUT DESPAIRED OF IT EVER COMING TO PASS.
YOU NEED NOT FEAR FOR THE YOUNGLING-- SHE IS BEYOND HELP--

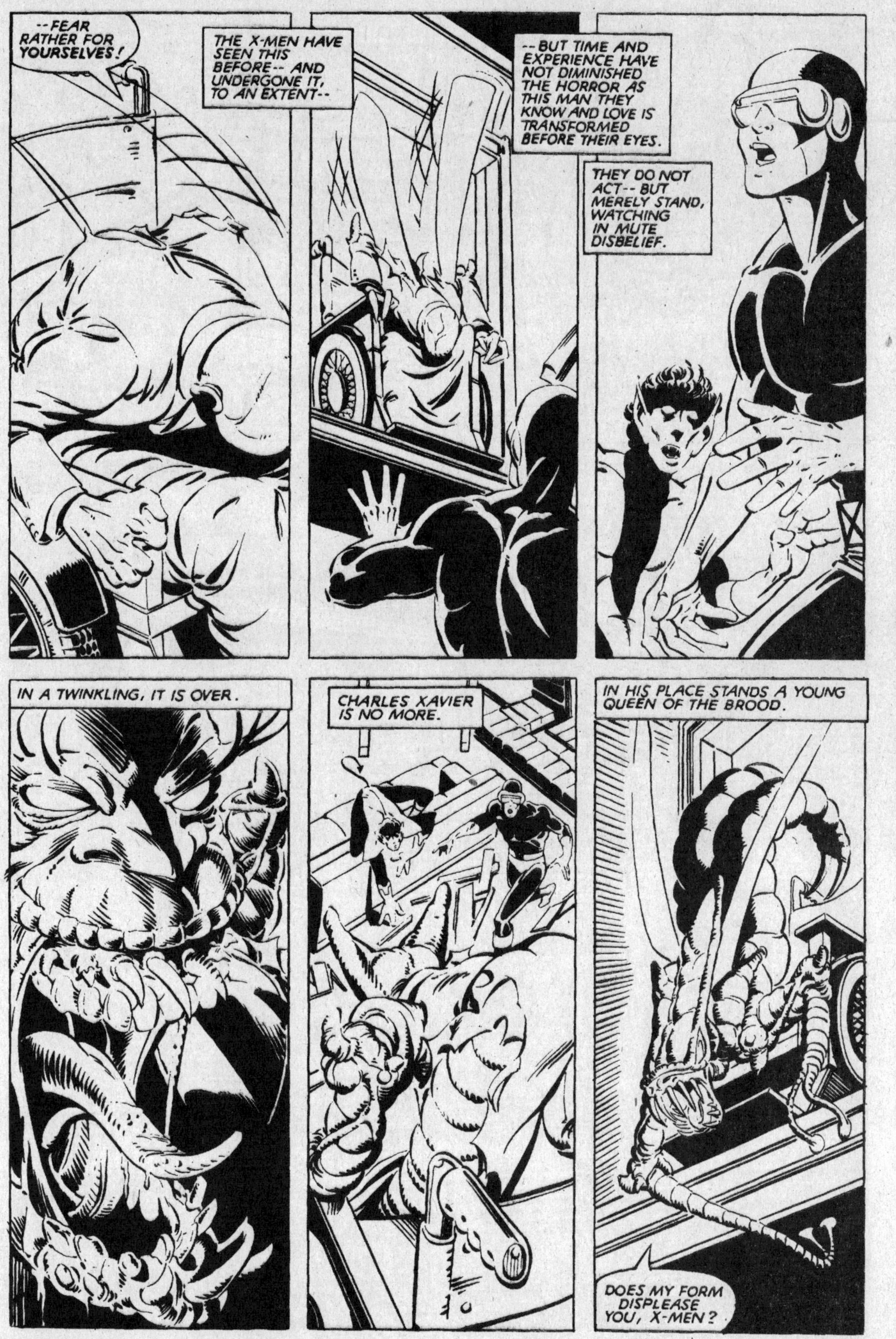
--FEAR RATHER FOR YOURSELVES!
THE X-MEN HAVE SEEN THIS BEFORE-- AND UNDERGONE IT, TO AN EXTENT--
--BUT TIME AND EXPERIENCE HAVE NOT DIMINISHED THE HORROR AS THIS MAN THEY KNOW AND LOVE IS TRANSFORMED BEFORE THEIR EYES.
THEY DO NOT ACT-- BUT MERELY STAND, WATCHING IN MUTE DISBELIEF.
IN A TWINKLING, IT IS OVER.
CHARLES XAVIER IS NO MORE.
IN HIS PLACE STANDS A YOUNG QUEEN OF THE BROOD.
DOES MY FORM DISPLEASE YOU, X-MEN?

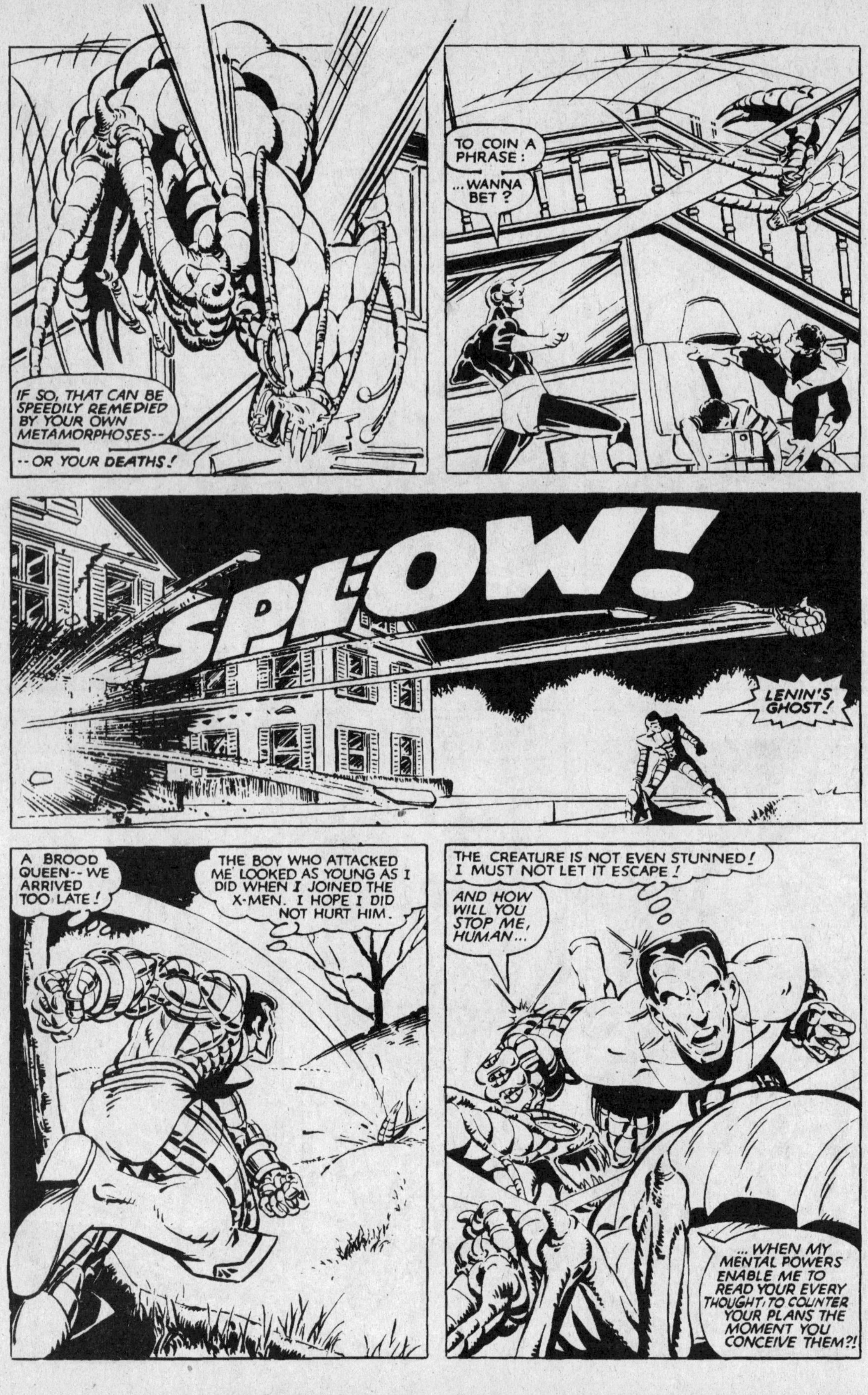
IF SO, THAT CAN BE SPEEDILY REMEDIED BY YOUR OWN METAMORPHOSES--
--OR YOUR DEATHS!
TO COIN A PHRASE:
...WANNA BET?
SPLOW!
LENIN'S GHOST!
A BROOD QUEEN-- WE ARRIVED TOO LATE!
THE BOY WHO ATTACKED ME LOOKED AS YOUNG AS I DID WHEN I JOINED THE X-MEN. I HOPE I DID NOT HURT HIM.
THE CREATURE IS NOT EVEN STUNNED! I MUST NOT LET IT ESCAPE!
AND HOW WILL YOU STOP ME, HUMAN...
...WHEN MY MENTAL POWERS ENABLE ME TO READ YOUR EVERY THOUGHT; TO COUNTER YOUR PLANS THE MOMENT YOU CONCEIVE THEM?!

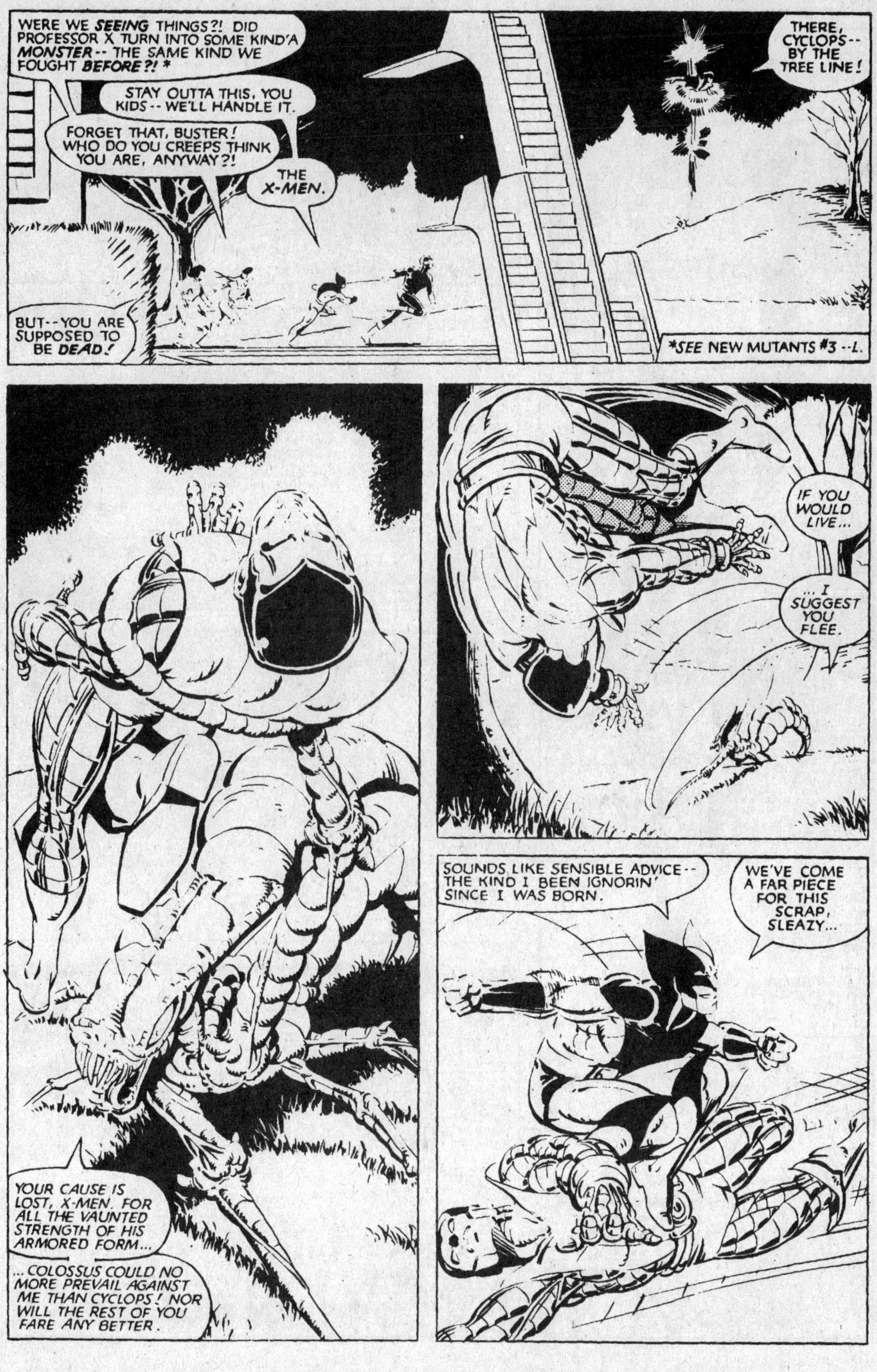
WERE WE SEEING THINGS?! DID PROFESSOR X TURN INTO SOME KIND'A MONSTER -- THE SAME KIND WE FOUGHT BEFORE?! *
STAY OUTTA THIS, YOU KIDS -- WE'LL HANDLE IT.
FORGET THAT, BUSTER! WHO DO YOU CREEPS THINK YOU ARE, ANYWAY?!
THE X-MEN.
THERE, CYCLOPS -- BY THE TREE LINE!
BUT--YOU ARE SUPPOSED TO BE DEAD!
*SEE NEW MUTANTS #3 --L.
YOUR CAUSE IS LOST, X-MEN. FOR ALL THE VAUNTED STRENGTH OF HIS ARMORED FORM...
...COLOSSUS COULD NO MORE PREVAIL AGAINST ME THAN CYCLOPS! NOR WILL THE REST OF YOU FARE ANY BETTER.
IF YOU WOULD LIVE...
...I SUGGEST YOU FLEE.
SOUNDS LIKE SENSIBLE ADVICE -- THE KIND I BEEN IGNORIN' SINCE I WAS BORN.
WE'VE COME A FAR PIECE FOR THIS SCRAP, SLEAZY...

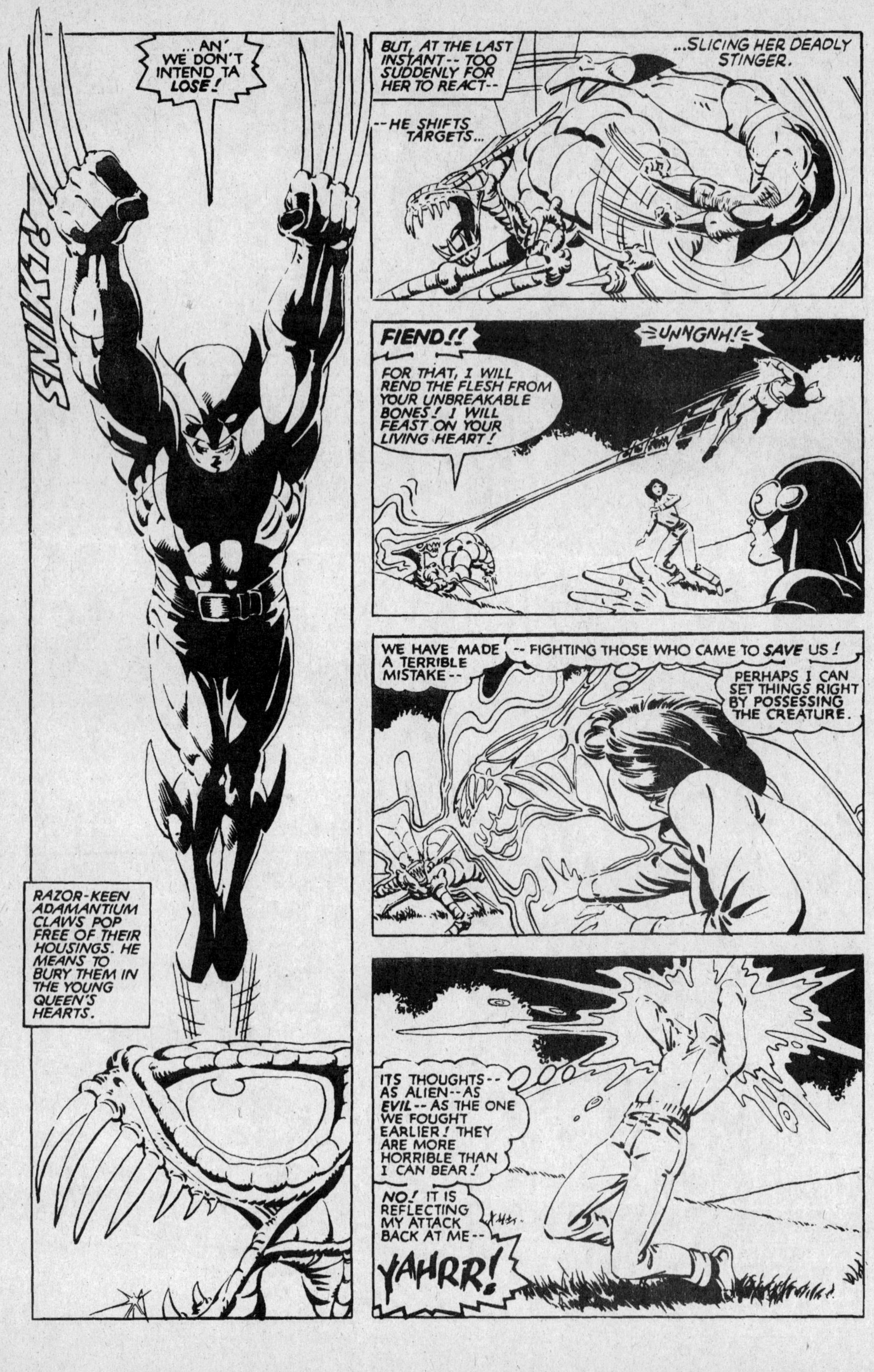
... AN' WE DON'T INTEND TA LOSE!
SNIKT!
RAZOR-KEEN ADAMANTIUM CLAWS POP FREE OF THEIR HOUSINGS. HE MEANS TO BURY THEM IN THE YOUNG QUEEN'S HEARTS.
BUT, AT THE LAST INSTANT-- TOO SUDDENLY FOR HER TO REACT--
--HE SHIFTS TARGETS...
...SLICING HER DEADLY STINGER.
FIEND!!
FOR THAT, I WILL REND THE FLESH FROM YOUR UNBREAKABLE BONES! I WILL FEAST ON YOUR LIVING HEART!
UNNGNH!
WE HAVE MADE A TERRIBLE MISTAKE--
--FIGHTING THOSE WHO CAME TO SAVE US!
PERHAPS I CAN SET THINGS RIGHT BY POSSESSING THE CREATURE.
ITS THOUGHTS-- AS ALIEN--AS EVIL-- AS THE ONE WE FOUGHT EARLIER! THEY ARE MORE HORRIBLE THAN I CAN BEAR!
NO! IT IS REFLECTING MY ATTACK BACK AT ME--
YAHRR!

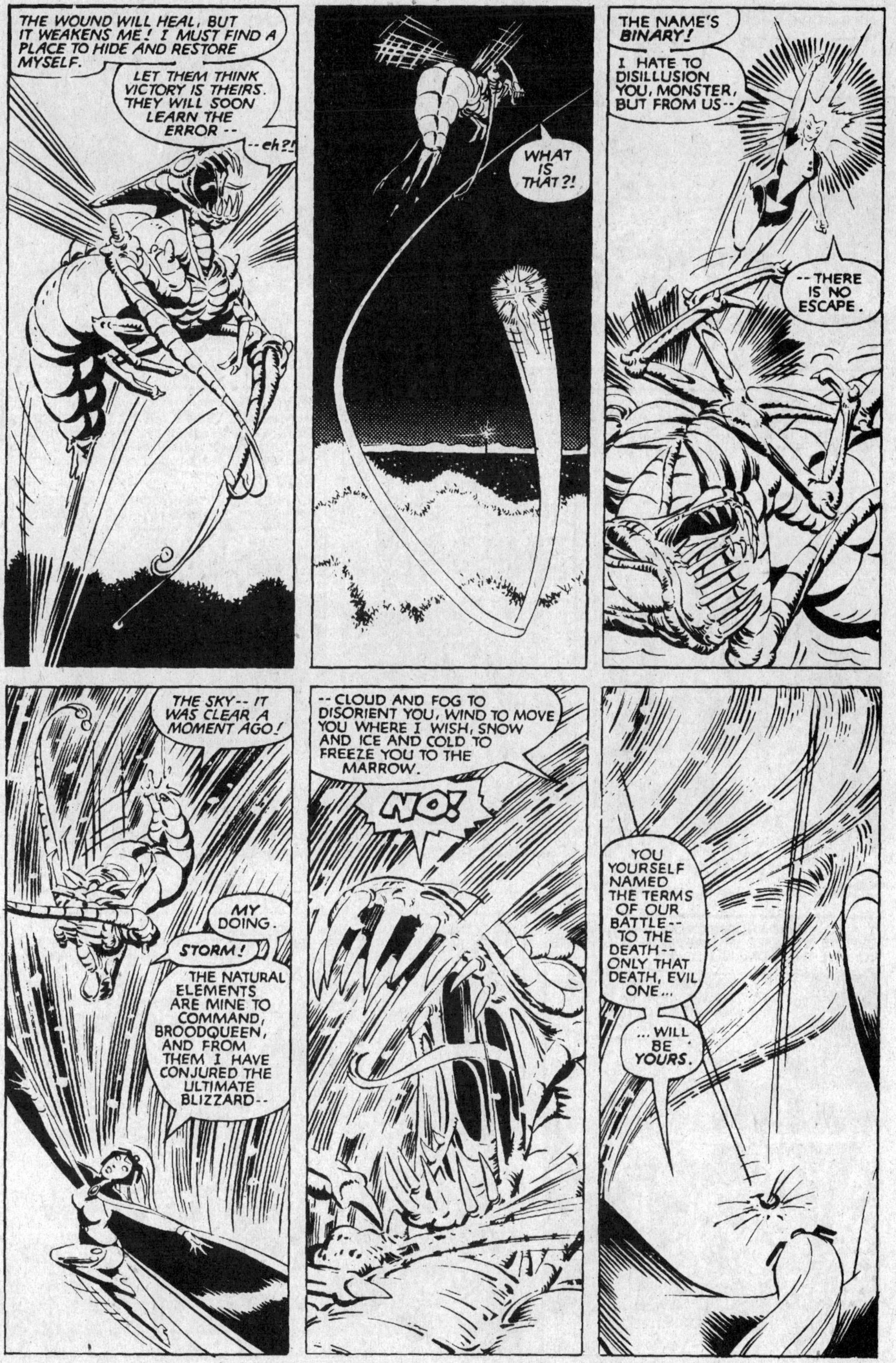
THE WOUND WILL HEAL, BUT IT WEAKENS ME! I MUST FIND A PLACE TO HIDE AND RESTORE MYSELF.
LET THEM THINK VICTORY IS THEIRS. THEY WILL SOON LEARN THE ERROR --
--eh?!
WHAT IS THAT?!
THE NAME'S BINARY!
I HATE TO DISILLUSION YOU, MONSTER, BUT FROM US--
--THERE IS NO ESCAPE.
THE SKY-- IT WAS CLEAR A MOMENT AGO!
MY DOING.
STORM!
THE NATURAL ELEMENTS ARE MINE TO COMMAND, BROODQUEEN, AND FROM THEM I HAVE CONJURED THE ULTIMATE BLIZZARD--
--CLOUD AND FOG TO DISORIENT YOU, WIND TO MOVE YOU WHERE I WISH, SNOW AND ICE AND COLD TO FREEZE YOU TO THE MARROW.
NO!
YOU YOURSELF NAMED THE TERMS OF OUR BATTLE-- TO THE DEATH-- ONLY THAT DEATH, EVIL ONE...
...WILL BE YOURS.

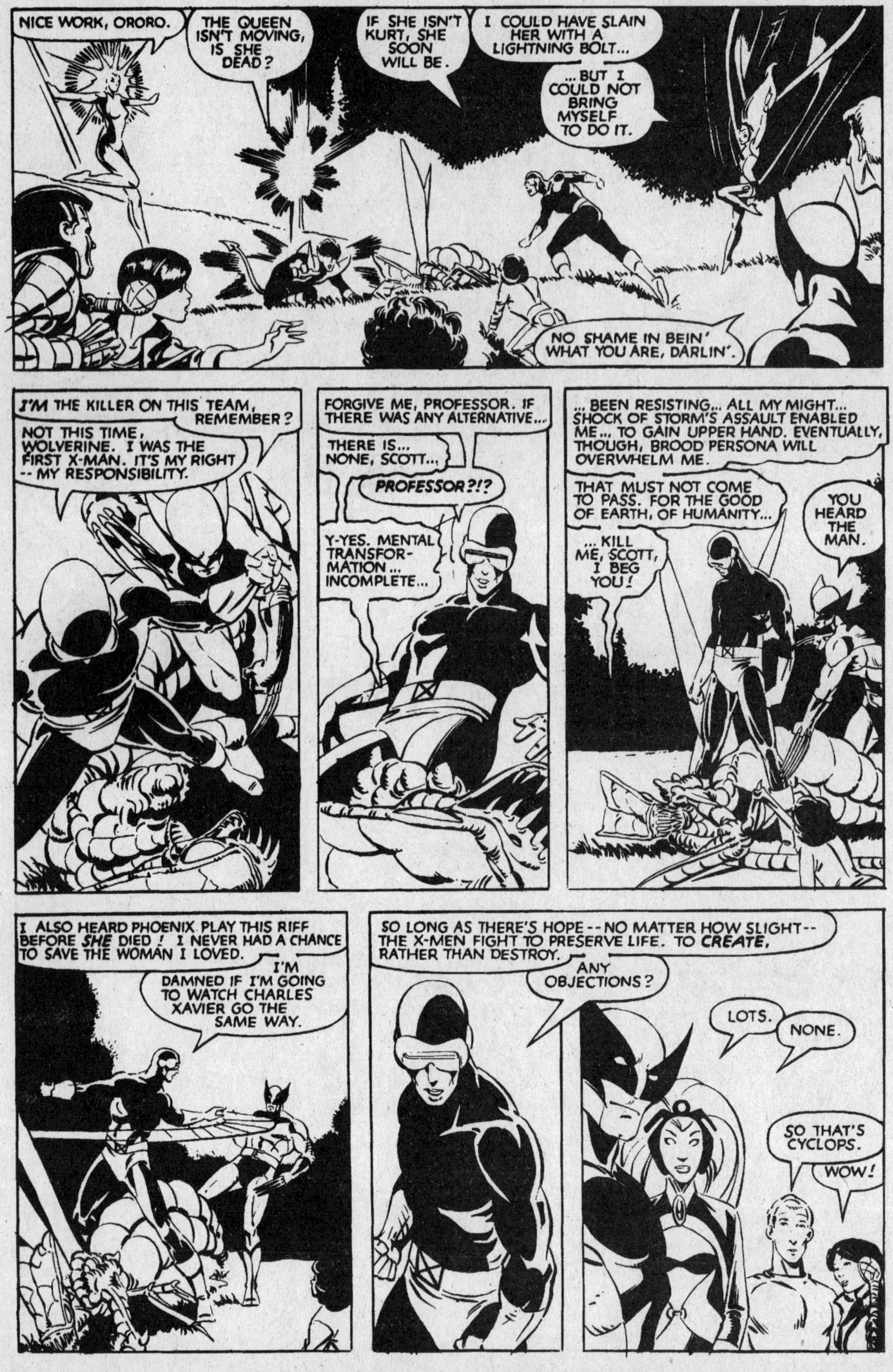
NICE WORK, ORORO.
THE QUEEN ISN'T MOVING, IS SHE DEAD?
IF SHE ISN'T KURT, SHE SOON WILL BE.
I COULD HAVE SLAIN HER WITH A LIGHTNING BOLT...
... BUT I COULD NOT BRING MYSELF TO DO IT.
NO SHAME IN BEIN' WHAT YOU ARE, DARLIN'.
I'M THE KILLER ON THIS TEAM, REMEMBER?
NOT THIS TIME, WOLVERINE. I WAS THE FIRST X-MAN. IT'S MY RIGHT -- MY RESPONSIBILITY.
FORGIVE ME, PROFESSOR. IF THERE WAS ANY ALTERNATIVE...
THERE IS... NONE, SCOTT...
PROFESSOR?!?
Y-YES. MENTAL TRANSFORMATION... INCOMPLETE...
... BEEN RESISTING... ALL MY MIGHT... SHOCK OF STORM'S ASSAULT ENABLED ME... TO GAIN UPPER HAND. EVENTUALLY, THOUGH, BROOD PERSONA WILL OVERWHELM ME.
THAT MUST NOT COME TO PASS. FOR THE GOOD OF EARTH, OF HUMANITY...
... KILL ME, SCOTT, I BEG YOU!
YOU HEARD THE MAN.
I ALSO HEARD PHOENIX PLAY THIS RIFF BEFORE SHE DIED! I NEVER HAD A CHANCE TO SAVE THE WOMAN I LOVED.
I'M DAMNED IF I'M GOING TO WATCH CHARLES XAVIER GO THE SAME WAY.
SO LONG AS THERE'S HOPE -- NO MATTER HOW SLIGHT -- THE X-MEN FIGHT TO PRESERVE LIFE. TO CREATE, RATHER THAN DESTROY.
ANY OBJECTIONS?
LOTS.
NONE.
SO THAT'S CYCLOPS.
WOW!

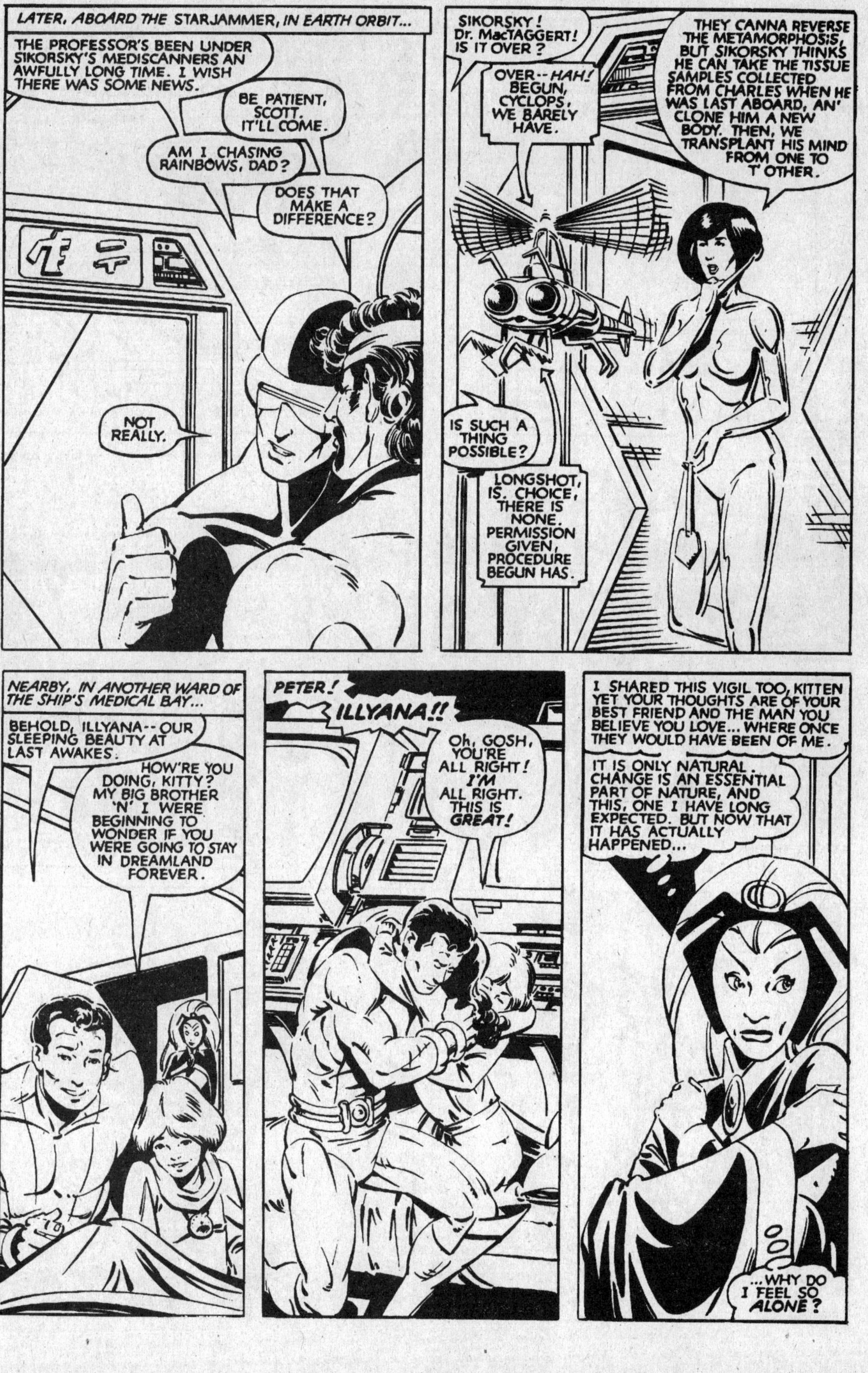
LATER, ABOARD THE STARJAMMER, IN EARTH ORBIT...
THE PROFESSOR'S BEEN UNDER SIKORSKY'S MEDISCANNERS AN AWFULLY LONG TIME. I WISH THERE WAS SOME NEWS.
BE PATIENT, SCOTT. IT'LL COME.
AM I CHASING RAINBOWS, DAD?
DOES THAT MAKE A DIFFERENCE?
NOT REALLY.
SIKORSKY! Dr. MacTAGGERT! IS IT OVER?
OVER--HAH! BEGUN, CYCLOPS, WE BARELY HAVE.
THEY CANNA REVERSE THE METAMORPHOSIS, BUT SIKORSKY THINKS HE CAN TAKE THE TISSUE SAMPLES COLLECTED FROM CHARLES WHEN HE WAS LAST ABOARD, AN' CLONE HIM A NEW BODY. THEN, WE TRANSPLANT HIS MIND FROM ONE TO T'OTHER.
IS SUCH A THING POSSIBLE?
LONGSHOT, IS. CHOICE, THERE IS NONE. PERMISSION GIVEN, PROCEDURE BEGUN HAS.
NEARBY, IN ANOTHER WARD OF THE SHIP'S MEDICAL BAY...
BEHOLD, ILLYANA--OUR SLEEPING BEAUTY AT LAST AWAKES.
HOW'RE YOU DOING, KITTY? MY BIG BROTHER 'N' I WERE BEGINNING TO WONDER IF YOU WERE GOING TO STAY IN DREAMLAND FOREVER.
PETER!
ILLYANA!!
Oh, GOSH, YOU'RE ALL RIGHT! I'M ALL RIGHT. THIS IS GREAT!
I SHARED THIS VIGIL TOO, KITTEN YET YOUR THOUGHTS ARE OF YOUR BEST FRIEND AND THE MAN YOU BELIEVE YOU LOVE... WHERE ONCE THEY WOULD HAVE BEEN OF ME.
IT IS ONLY NATURAL. CHANGE IS AN ESSENTIAL PART OF NATURE, AND THIS, ONE I HAVE LONG EXPECTED. BUT NOW THAT IT HAS ACTUALLY HAPPENED...
...WHY DO I FEEL SO ALONE?

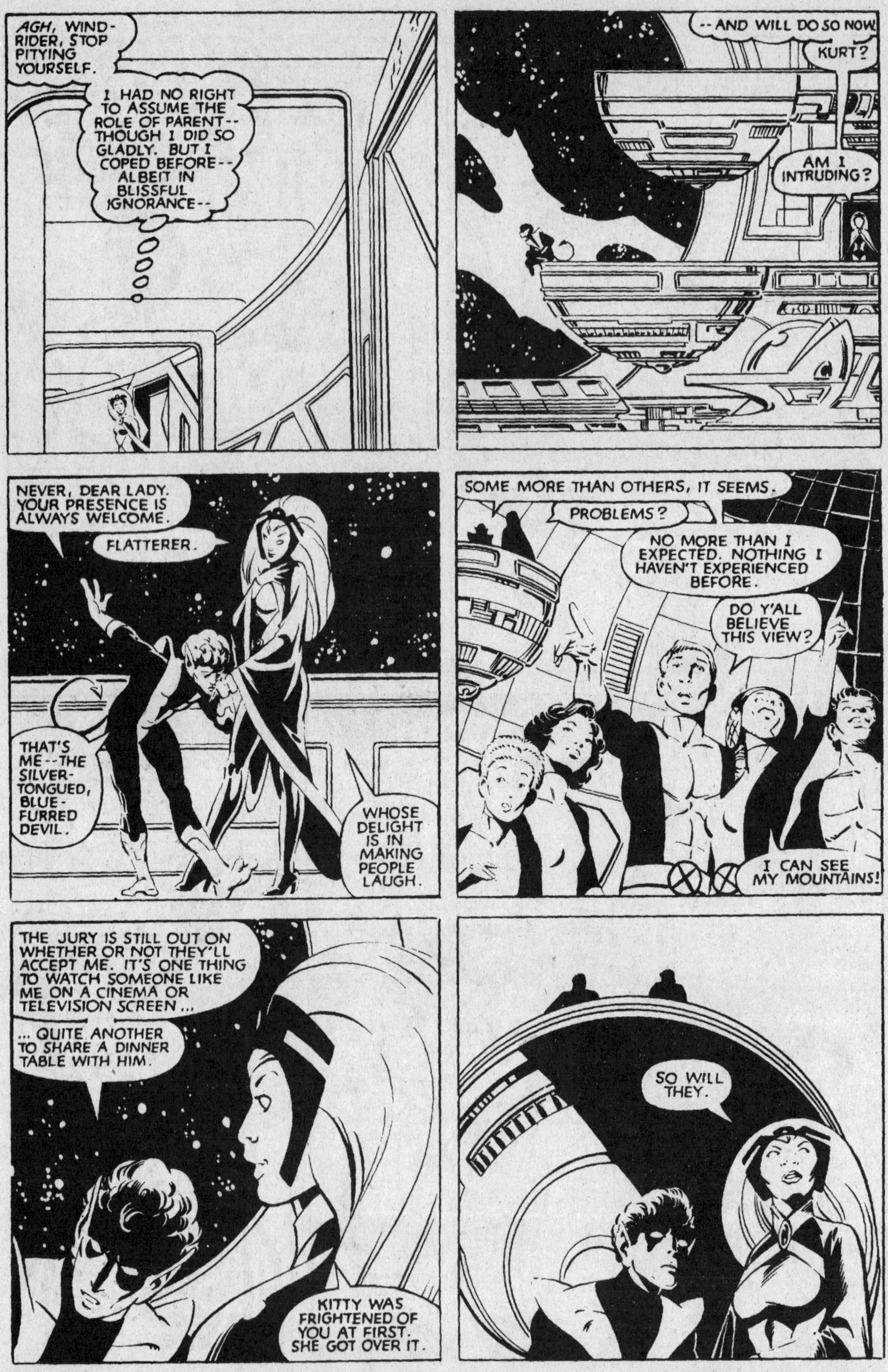
AGH, WIND-RIDER, STOP PITYING YOURSELF.
I HAD NO RIGHT TO ASSUME THE ROLE OF PARENT -- THOUGH I DID SO GLADLY. BUT I COPED BEFORE -- ALBEIT IN BLISSFUL IGNORANCE --
-- AND WILL DO SO NOW.
KURT?
AM I INTRUDING?
NEVER, DEAR LADY. YOUR PRESENCE IS ALWAYS WELCOME.
FLATTERER.
THAT'S ME -- THE SILVER-TONGUED, BLUE-FURRED DEVIL.
WHOSE DELIGHT IS IN MAKING PEOPLE LAUGH.
SOME MORE THAN OTHERS, IT SEEMS.
PROBLEMS?
NO MORE THAN I EXPECTED. NOTHING I HAVEN'T EXPERIENCED BEFORE.
DO Y'ALL BELIEVE THIS VIEW?
I CAN SEE MY MOUNTAINS!
THE JURY IS STILL OUT ON WHETHER OR NOT THEY'LL ACCEPT ME. IT'S ONE THING TO WATCH SOMEONE LIKE ME ON A CINEMA OR TELEVISION SCREEN ...
... QUITE ANOTHER TO SHARE A DINNER TABLE WITH HIM.
KITTY WAS FRIGHTENED OF YOU AT FIRST. SHE GOT OVER IT.
SO WILL THEY.

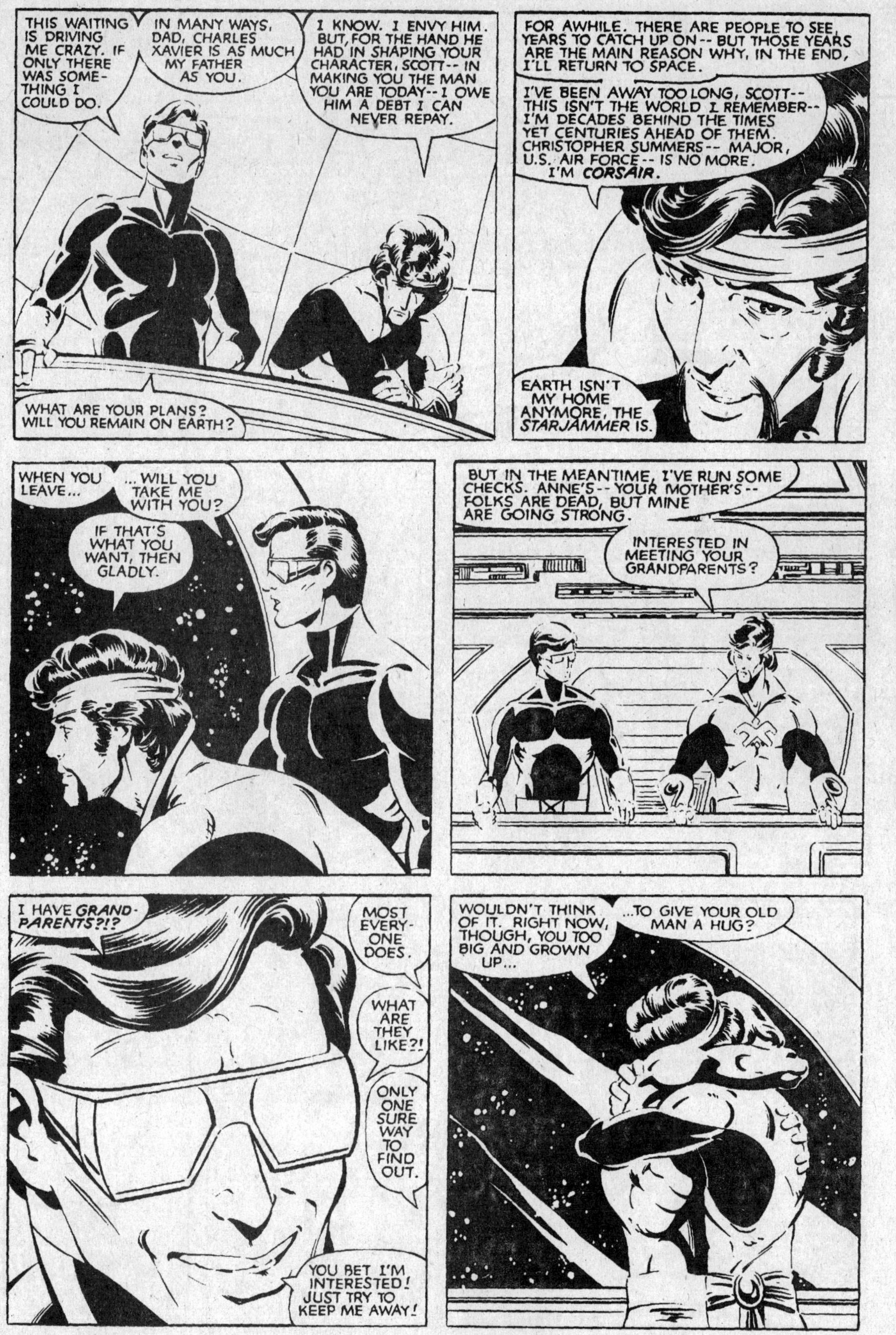
THIS WAITING IS DRIVING ME CRAZY. IF ONLY THERE WAS SOMETHING I COULD DO.
IN MANY WAYS, DAD, CHARLES XAVIER IS AS MUCH MY FATHER AS YOU.
I KNOW. I ENVY HIM. BUT, FOR THE HAND HE HAD IN SHAPING YOUR CHARACTER, SCOTT-- IN MAKING YOU THE MAN YOU ARE TODAY-- I OWE HIM A DEBT I CAN NEVER REPAY.
WHAT ARE YOUR PLANS? WILL YOU REMAIN ON EARTH?
FOR AWHILE. THERE ARE PEOPLE TO SEE, YEARS TO CATCH UP ON-- BUT THOSE YEARS ARE THE MAIN REASON WHY, IN THE END, I'LL RETURN TO SPACE.
I'VE BEEN AWAY TOO LONG, SCOTT-- THIS ISN'T THE WORLD I REMEMBER-- I'M DECADES BEHIND THE TIMES YET CENTURIES AHEAD OF THEM. CHRISTOPHER SUMMERS-- MAJOR, U.S. AIR FORCE-- IS NO MORE. I'M CORSAIR.
EARTH ISN'T MY HOME ANYMORE, THE STARJAMMER IS.
WHEN YOU LEAVE...
...WILL YOU TAKE ME WITH YOU?
IF THAT'S WHAT YOU WANT, THEN GLADLY.
BUT IN THE MEANTIME, I'VE RUN SOME CHECKS. ANNE'S-- YOUR MOTHER'S-- FOLKS ARE DEAD, BUT MINE ARE GOING STRONG.
INTERESTED IN MEETING YOUR GRANDPARENTS?
I HAVE GRANDPARENTS?!?
MOST EVERYONE DOES.
WHAT ARE THEY LIKE?!
ONLY ONE SURE WAY TO FIND OUT.
YOU BET I'M INTERESTED! JUST TRY TO KEEP ME AWAY!
WOULDN'T THINK OF IT. RIGHT NOW, THOUGH, YOU TOO BIG AND GROWN UP...
...TO GIVE YOUR OLD MAN A HUG?

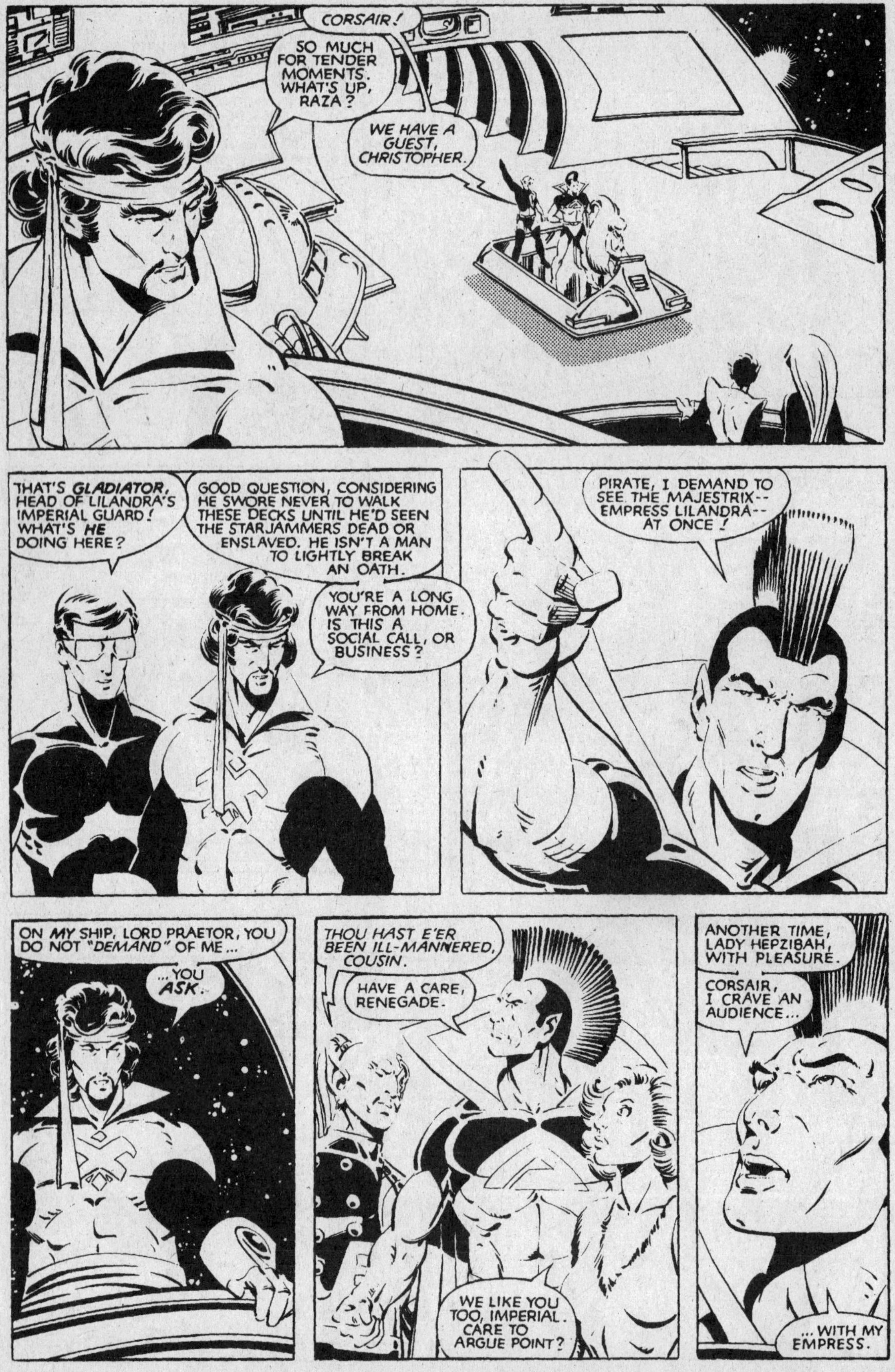
CORSAIR!
SO MUCH FOR TENDER MOMENTS. WHAT'S UP, RAZA?
WE HAVE A GUEST, CHRISTOPHER.
THAT'S GLADIATOR, HEAD OF LILANDRA'S IMPERIAL GUARD! WHAT'S HE DOING HERE?
GOOD QUESTION, CONSIDERING HE SWORE NEVER TO WALK THESE DECKS UNTIL HE'D SEEN THE STARJAMMERS DEAD OR ENSLAVED. HE ISN'T A MAN TO LIGHTLY BREAK AN OATH.
YOU'RE A LONG WAY FROM HOME. IS THIS A SOCIAL CALL, OR BUSINESS?
PIRATE, I DEMAND TO SEE THE MAJESTRIX-- EMPRESS LILANDRA-- AT ONCE!
ON MY SHIP, LORD PRAETOR, YOU DO NOT "DEMAND" OF ME...
...YOU ASK.
THOU HAST E'ER BEEN ILL-MANNERED, COUSIN.
HAVE A CARE, RENEGADE.
WE LIKE YOU TOO, IMPERIAL. CARE TO ARGUE POINT?
ANOTHER TIME, LADY HEPZIBAH, WITH PLEASURE.
CORSAIR, I CRAVE AN AUDIENCE...
...WITH MY EMPRESS.

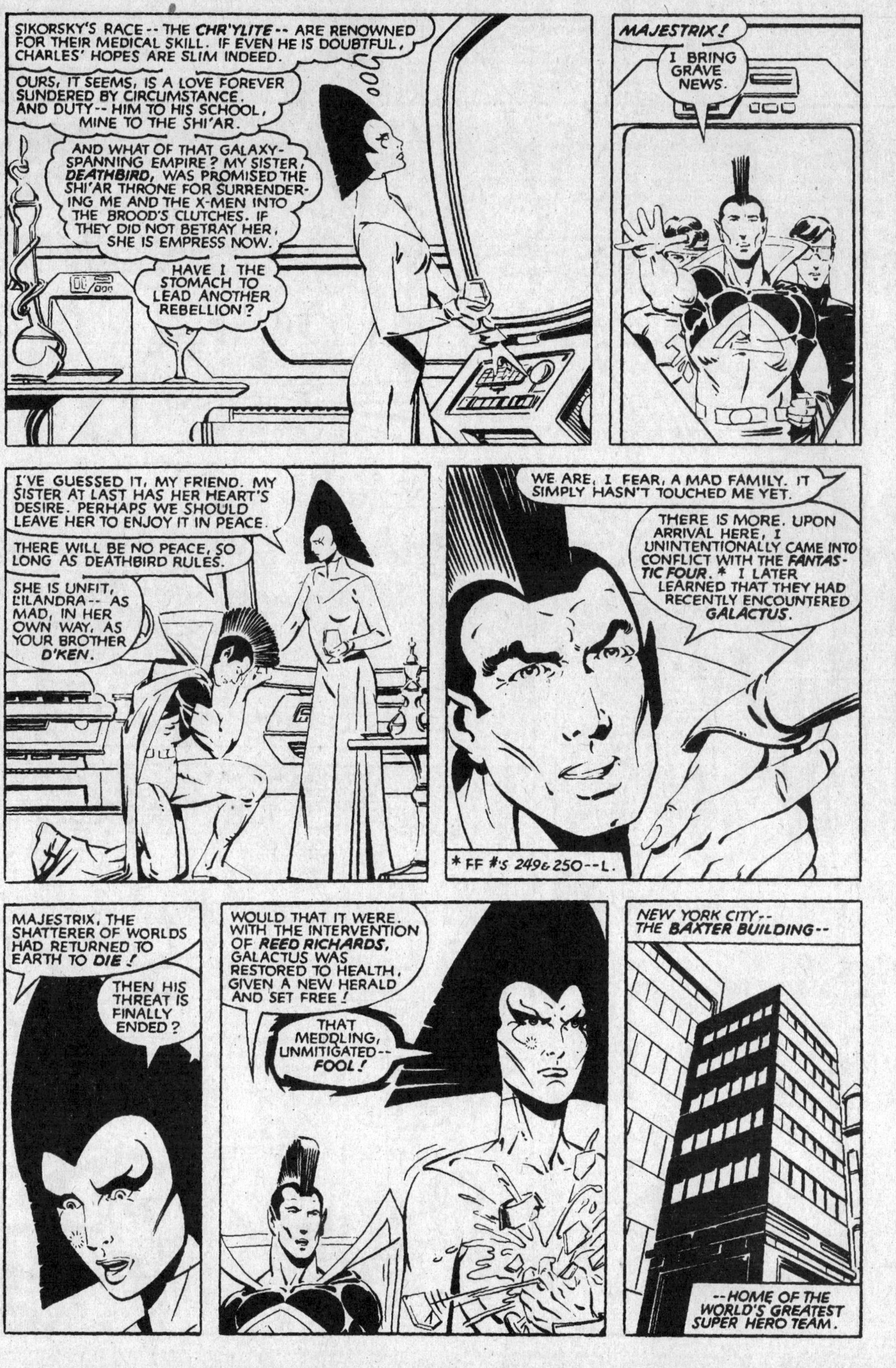
SIKORSKY'S RACE -- THE CHR'YLITE -- ARE RENOWNED FOR THEIR MEDICAL SKILL. IF EVEN HE IS DOUBTFUL, CHARLES' HOPES ARE SLIM INDEED.
OURS, IT SEEMS, IS A LOVE FOREVER SUNDERED BY CIRCUMSTANCE. AND DUTY -- HIM TO HIS SCHOOL, MINE TO THE SHI'AR.
AND WHAT OF THAT GALAXY-SPANNING EMPIRE? MY SISTER, DEATHBIRD, WAS PROMISED THE SHI'AR THRONE FOR SURRENDERING ME AND THE X-MEN INTO THE BROOD'S CLUTCHES. IF THEY DID NOT BETRAY HER, SHE IS EMPRESS NOW.
HAVE I THE STOMACH TO LEAD ANOTHER REBELLION?
MAJESTRIX!
I BRING GRAVE NEWS.
I'VE GUESSED IT, MY FRIEND. MY SISTER AT LAST HAS HER HEART'S DESIRE. PERHAPS WE SHOULD LEAVE HER TO ENJOY IT IN PEACE.
THERE WILL BE NO PEACE, SO LONG AS DEATHBIRD RULES.
SHE IS UNFIT, LILANDRA -- AS MAD, IN HER OWN WAY, AS YOUR BROTHER D'KEN.
WE ARE, I FEAR, A MAD FAMILY. IT SIMPLY HASN'T TOUCHED ME YET.
THERE IS MORE. UPON ARRIVAL HERE, I UNINTENTIONALLY CAME INTO CONFLICT WITH THE FANTASTIC FOUR.* I LATER LEARNED THAT THEY HAD RECENTLY ENCOUNTERED GALACTUS.
*FF #'S 249 & 250 -- L.
MAJESTRIX, THE SHATTERER OF WORLDS HAD RETURNED TO EARTH TO DIE!
THEN HIS THREAT IS FINALLY ENDED?
WOULD THAT IT WERE. WITH THE INTERVENTION OF REED RICHARDS, GALACTUS WAS RESTORED TO HEALTH, GIVEN A NEW HERALD AND SET FREE!
THAT MEDDLING, UNMITIGATED -- FOOL!
NEW YORK CITY -- THE BAXTER BUILDING --
-- HOME OF THE WORLD'S GREATEST SUPER HERO TEAM.

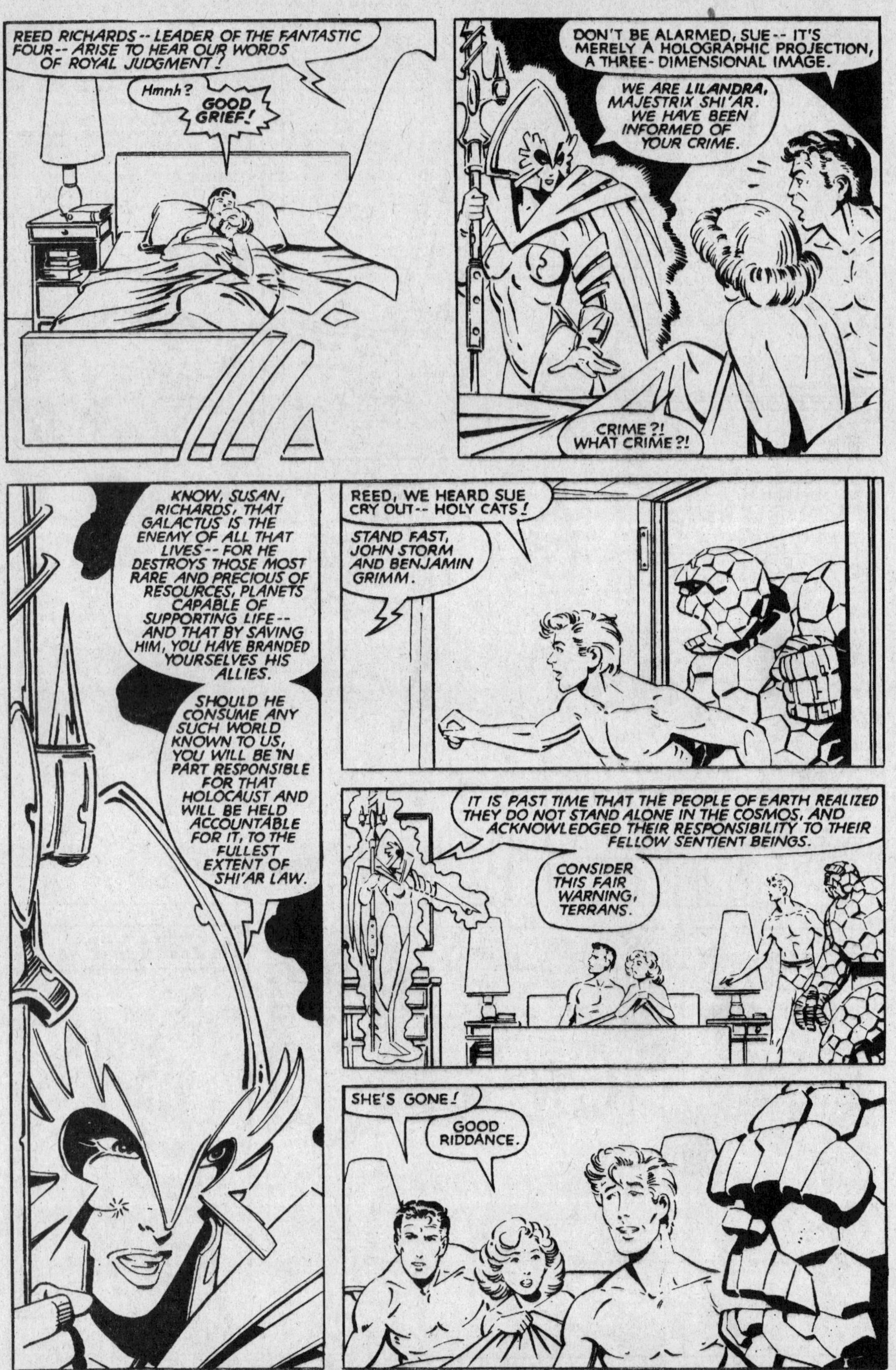

REED RICHARDS -- LEADER OF THE FANTASTIC FOUR -- ARISE TO HEAR OUR WORDS OF ROYAL JUDGMENT!
Hmnh?
GOOD GRIEF!
DON'T BE ALARMED, SUE -- IT'S MERELY A HOLOGRAPHIC PROJECTION, A THREE-DIMENSIONAL IMAGE.
WE ARE LILANDRA, MAJESTRIX SHI'AR. WE HAVE BEEN INFORMED OF YOUR CRIME.
CRIME?! WHAT CRIME?!
KNOW, SUSAN, RICHARDS, THAT GALACTUS IS THE ENEMY OF ALL THAT LIVES -- FOR HE DESTROYS THOSE MOST RARE AND PRECIOUS OF RESOURCES, PLANETS CAPABLE OF SUPPORTING LIFE -- AND THAT BY SAVING HIM, YOU HAVE BRANDED YOURSELVES HIS ALLIES.
SHOULD HE CONSUME ANY SUCH WORLD KNOWN TO US, YOU WILL BE IN PART RESPONSIBLE FOR THAT HOLOCAUST AND WILL BE HELD ACCOUNTABLE FOR IT, TO THE FULLEST EXTENT OF SHI'AR LAW.
REED, WE HEARD SUE CRY OUT -- HOLY CATS!
STAND FAST, JOHN STORM AND BENJAMIN GRIMM.
IT IS PAST TIME THAT THE PEOPLE OF EARTH REALIZED THEY DO NOT STAND ALONE IN THE COSMOS, AND ACKNOWLEDGED THEIR RESPONSIBILITY TO THEIR FELLOW SENTIENT BEINGS.
CONSIDER THIS FAIR WARNING, TERRANS.
SHE'S GONE!
GOOD RIDDANCE.

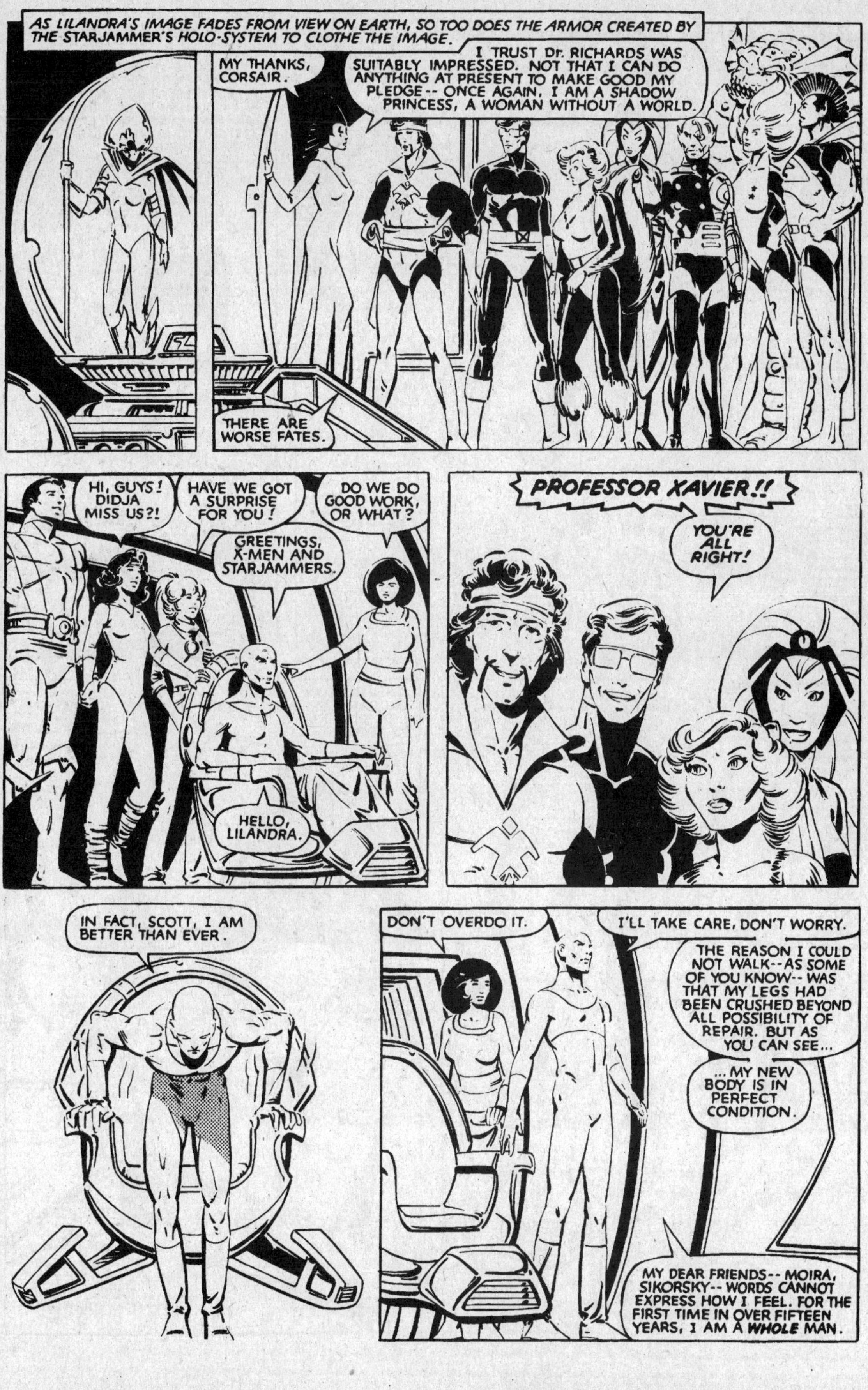

AS LILANDRA'S IMAGE FADES FROM VIEW ON EARTH, SO TOO DOES THE ARMOR CREATED BY THE STARJAMMER'S HOLO-SYSTEM TO CLOTHE THE IMAGE.
MY THANKS, CORSAIR.
I TRUST Dr. RICHARDS WAS SUITABLY IMPRESSED. NOT THAT I CAN DO ANYTHING AT PRESENT TO MAKE GOOD MY PLEDGE-- ONCE AGAIN, I AM A SHADOW PRINCESS, A WOMAN WITHOUT A WORLD.
THERE ARE WORSE FATES.
HI, GUYS! DIDJA MISS US?!
HAVE WE GOT A SURPRISE FOR YOU!
DO WE DO GOOD WORK, OR WHAT?
GREETINGS, X-MEN AND STARJAMMERS.
HELLO, LILANDRA.
PROFESSOR XAVIER!!
YOU'RE ALL RIGHT!
IN FACT, SCOTT, I AM BETTER THAN EVER.
DON'T OVERDO IT.
I'LL TAKE CARE, DON'T WORRY.
THE REASON I COULD NOT WALK--AS SOME OF YOU KNOW--WAS THAT MY LEGS HAD BEEN CRUSHED BEYOND ALL POSSIBILITY OF REPAIR. BUT AS YOU CAN SEE...
...MY NEW BODY IS IN PERFECT CONDITION.
MY DEAR FRIENDS-- MOIRA, SIKORSKY-- WORDS CANNOT EXPRESS HOW I FEEL. FOR THE FIRST TIME IN OVER FIFTEEN YEARS, I AM A WHOLE MAN.

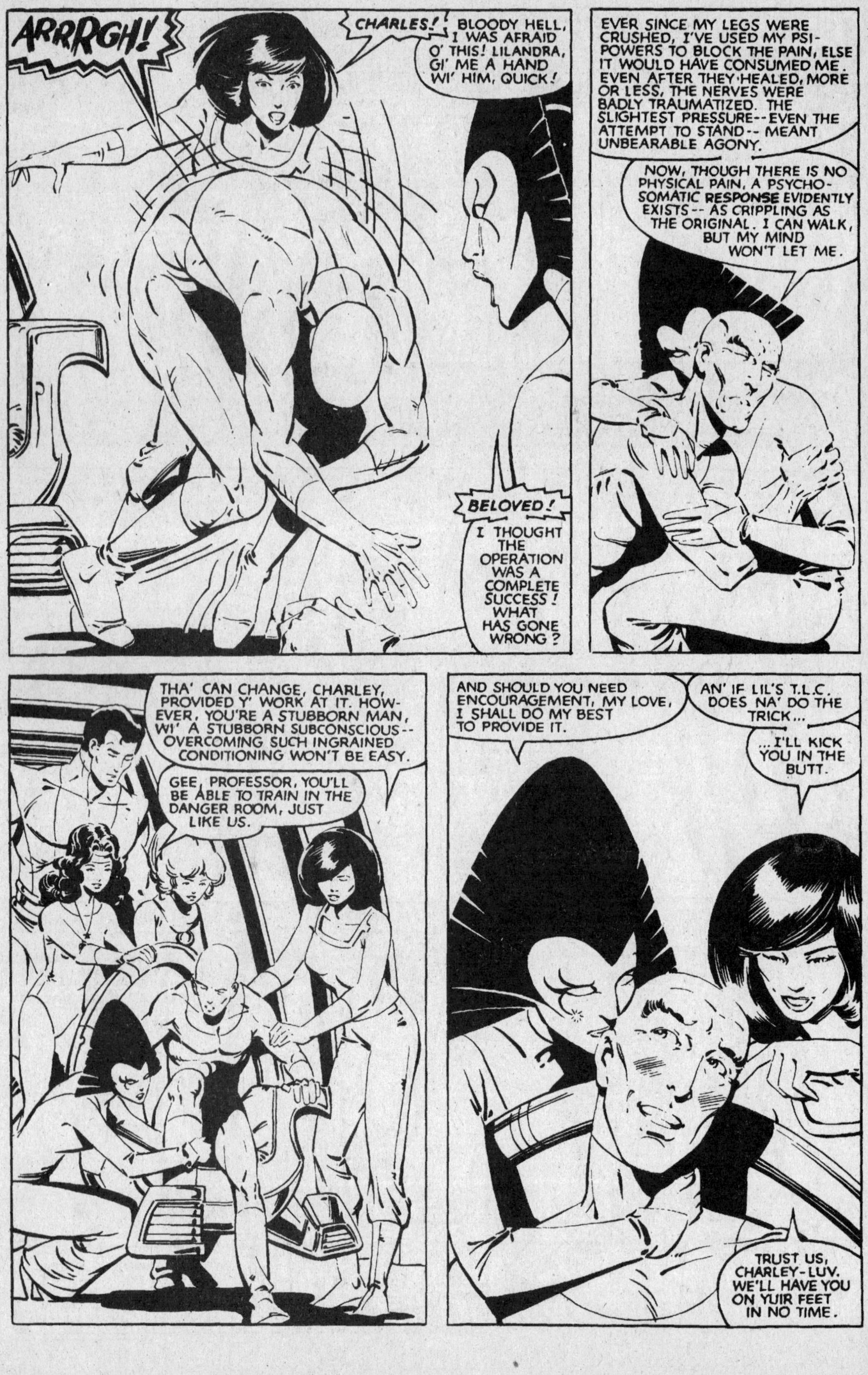
ARRRGH!
CHARLES!
BLOODY HELL, I WAS AFRAID O' THIS! LILANDRA, GI' ME A HAND WI' HIM, QUICK!
BELOVED! I THOUGHT THE OPERATION WAS A COMPLETE SUCCESS! WHAT HAS GONE WRONG?
EVER SINCE MY LEGS WERE CRUSHED, I'VE USED MY PSI-POWERS TO BLOCK THE PAIN, ELSE IT WOULD HAVE CONSUMED ME. EVEN AFTER THEY HEALED, MORE OR LESS, THE NERVES WERE BADLY TRAUMATIZED. THE SLIGHTEST PRESSURE--EVEN THE ATTEMPT TO STAND--MEANT UNBEARABLE AGONY.
NOW, THOUGH THERE IS NO PHYSICAL PAIN, A PSYCHO-SOMATIC RESPONSE EVIDENTLY EXISTS--AS CRIPPLING AS THE ORIGINAL. I CAN WALK, BUT MY MIND WON'T LET ME.
THA' CAN CHANGE, CHARLEY, PROVIDED Y' WORK AT IT. HOW-EVER, YOU'RE A STUBBORN MAN, WI' A STUBBORN SUBCONSCIOUS--OVERCOMING SUCH INGRAINED CONDITIONING WON'T BE EASY.
GEE, PROFESSOR, YOU'LL BE ABLE TO TRAIN IN THE DANGER ROOM, JUST LIKE US.
AND SHOULD YOU NEED ENCOURAGEMENT, MY LOVE, I SHALL DO MY BEST TO PROVIDE IT.
AN' IF LIL'S T.L.C. DOES NA' DO THE TRICK...
...I'LL KICK YOU IN THE BUTT.
TRUST US, CHARLEY-LUV. WE'LL HAVE YOU ON YUIR FEET IN NO TIME.

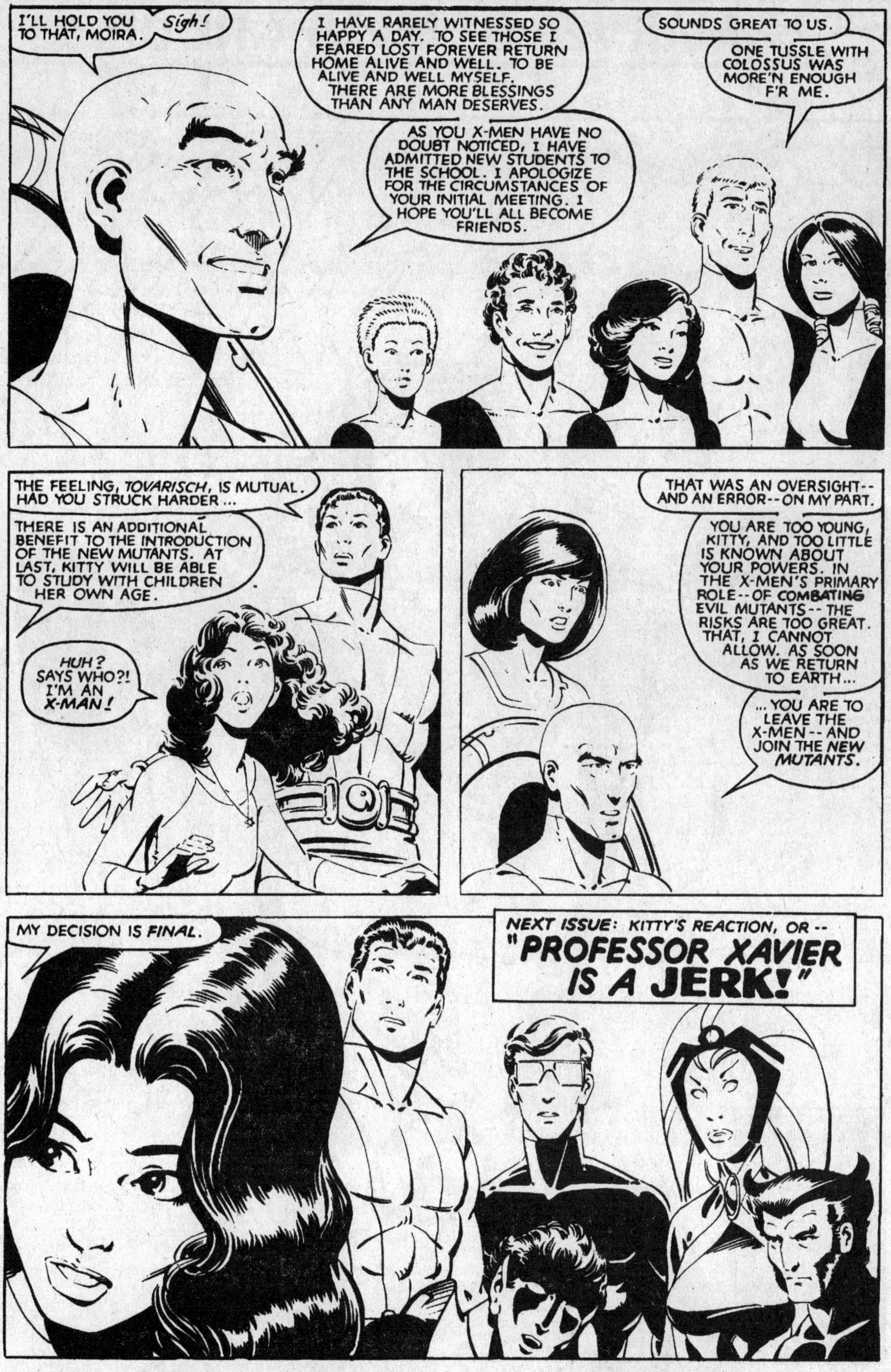

I'LL HOLD YOU TO THAT, MOIRA.
Sigh!
I HAVE RARELY WITNESSED SO HAPPY A DAY. TO SEE THOSE I FEARED LOST FOREVER RETURN HOME ALIVE AND WELL. TO BE ALIVE AND WELL MYSELF. THERE ARE MORE BLESSINGS THAN ANY MAN DESERVES.
AS YOU X-MEN HAVE NO DOUBT NOTICED, I HAVE ADMITTED NEW STUDENTS TO THE SCHOOL. I APOLOGIZE FOR THE CIRCUMSTANCES OF YOUR INITIAL MEETING. I HOPE YOU'LL ALL BECOME FRIENDS.
SOUNDS GREAT TO US.
ONE TUSSLE WITH COLOSSUS WAS MORE'N ENOUGH F'R ME.
THE FEELING, TOVARISCH, IS MUTUAL. HAD YOU STRUCK HARDER...
THERE IS AN ADDITIONAL BENEFIT TO THE INTRODUCTION OF THE NEW MUTANTS. AT LAST, KITTY WILL BE ABLE TO STUDY WITH CHILDREN HER OWN AGE.
HUH? SAYS WHO?! I'M AN X-MAN!
THAT WAS AN OVERSIGHT-- AND AN ERROR--ON MY PART.
YOU ARE TOO YOUNG, KITTY, AND TOO LITTLE IS KNOWN ABOUT YOUR POWERS. IN THE X-MEN'S PRIMARY ROLE--OF COMBATING EVIL MUTANTS--THE RISKS ARE TOO GREAT. THAT, I CANNOT ALLOW. AS SOON AS WE RETURN TO EARTH...
...YOU ARE TO LEAVE THE X-MEN--AND JOIN THE NEW MUTANTS.
MY DECISION IS FINAL.
NEXT ISSUE: KITTY'S REACTION, OR --
"PROFESSOR XAVIER IS A JERK!"

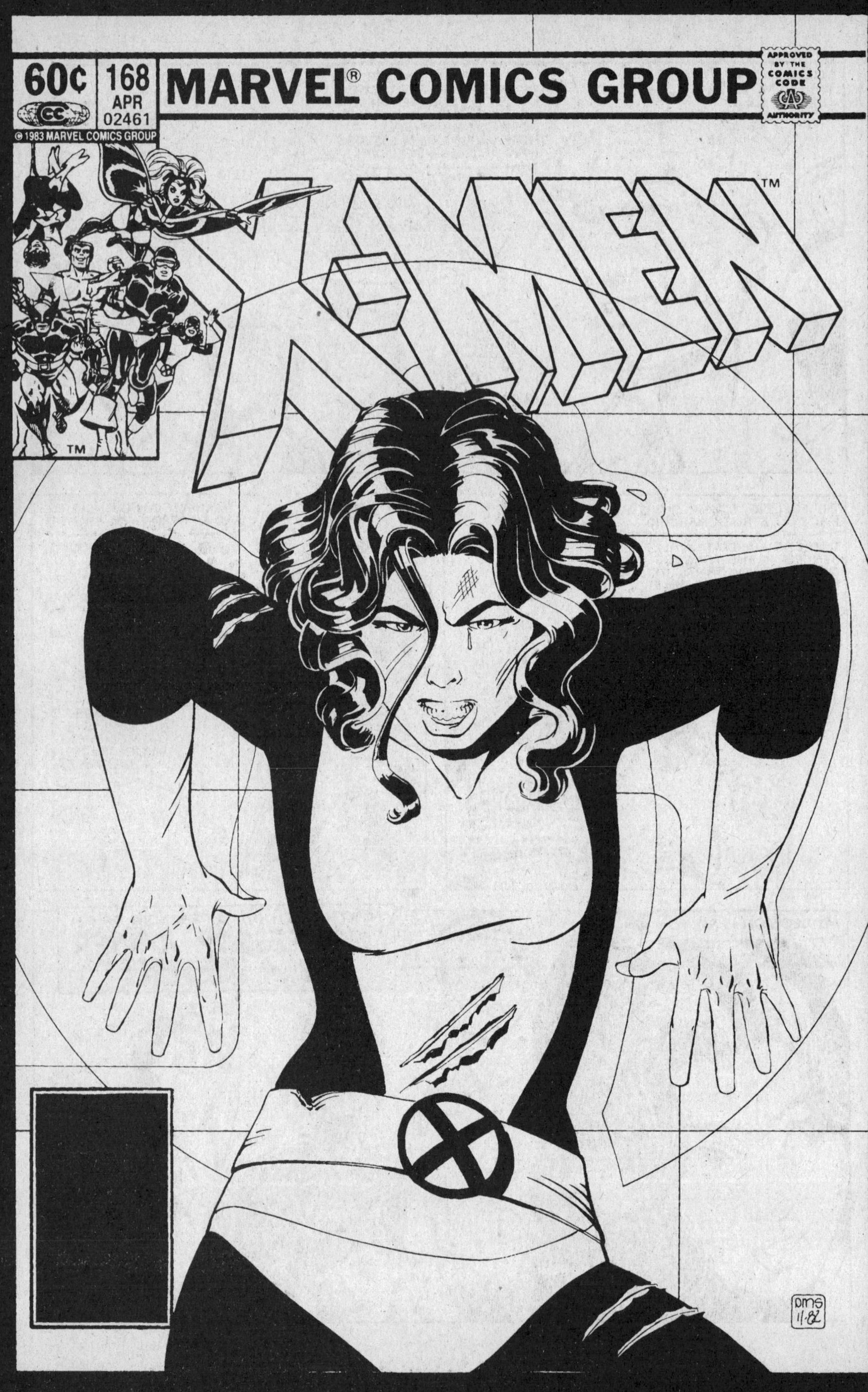

60¢
168
APR
02461
MARVEL® COMICS GROUP
APPROVED BY THE COMICS CODE AUTHORITY
© 1983 MARVEL COMICS GROUP
X-MEN™
TM

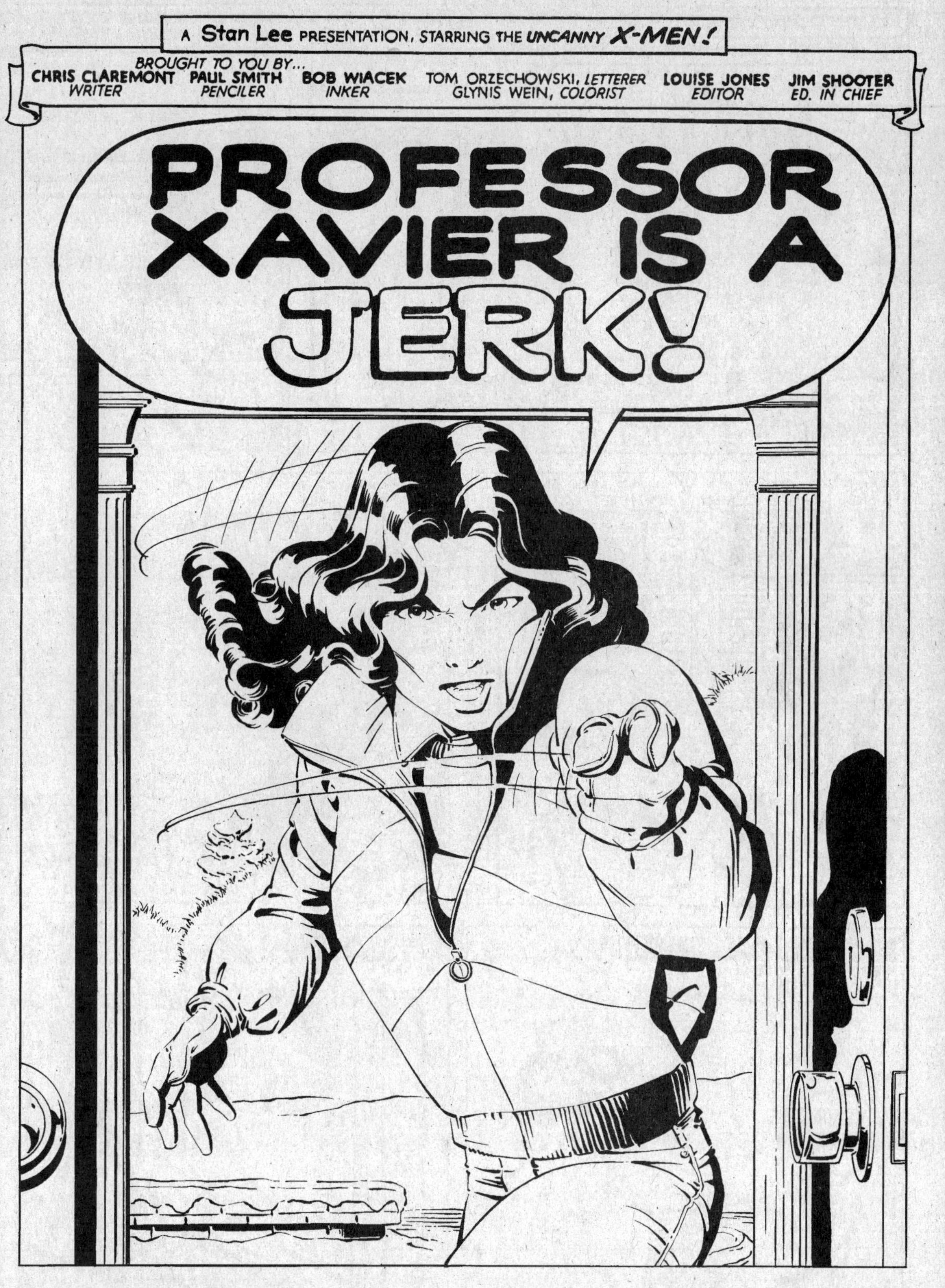
A Stan Lee PRESENTATION, STARRING THE UNCANNY X-MEN!
BROUGHT TO YOU BY... CHRIS CLAREMONT WRITER PAUL SMITH PENCILER BOB WIACEK INKER TOM ORZECHOWSKI, LETTERER GLYNIS WEIN, COLORIST LOUISE JONES EDITOR JIM SHOOTER ED. IN CHIEF
PROFESSOR XAVIER IS A JERK!

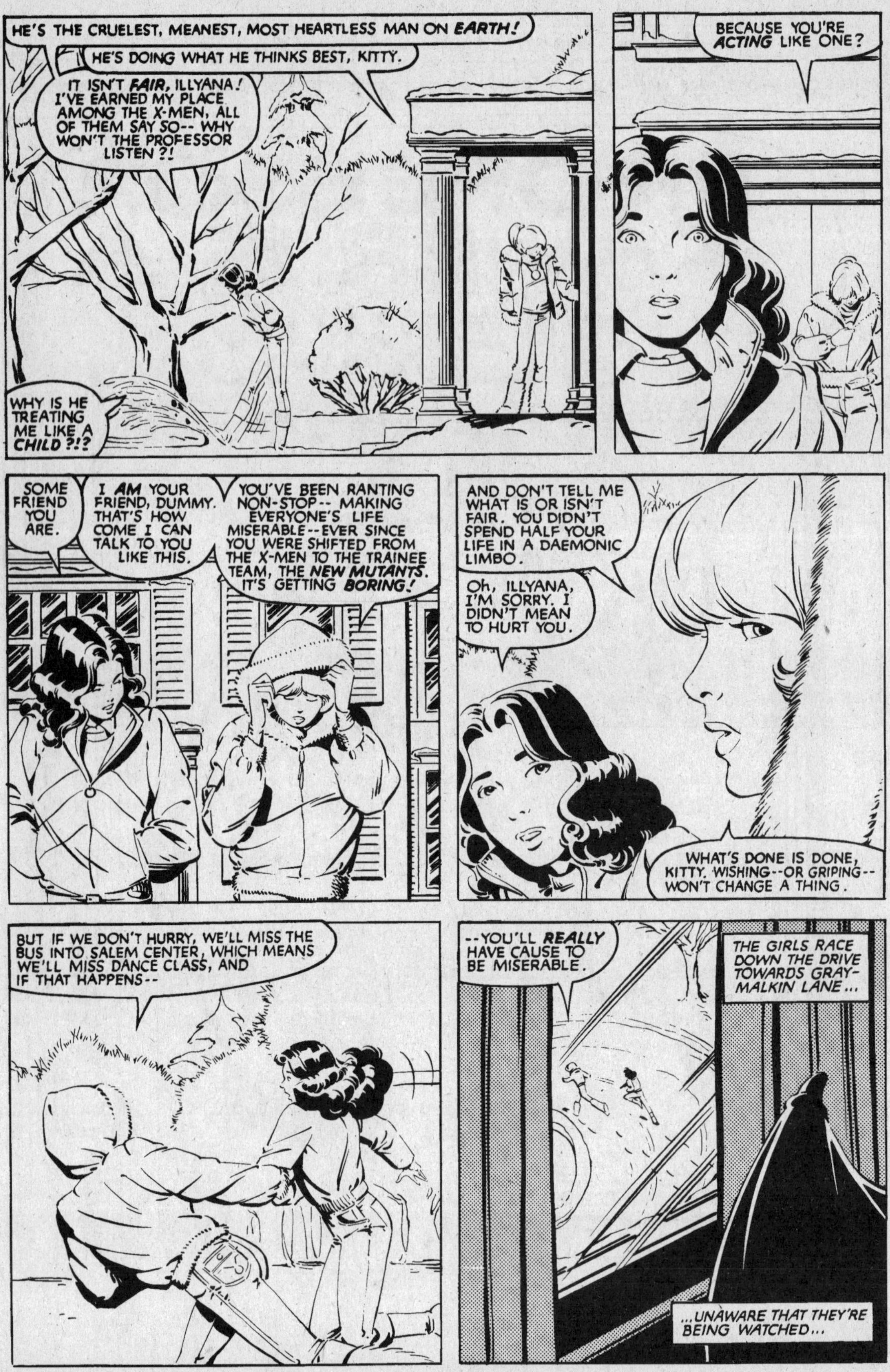

HE'S THE CRUELEST, MEANEST, MOST HEARTLESS MAN ON EARTH!
HE'S DOING WHAT HE THINKS BEST, KITTY.
IT ISN'T FAIR, ILLYANA! I'VE EARNED MY PLACE AMONG THE X-MEN, ALL OF THEM SAY SO-- WHY WON'T THE PROFESSOR LISTEN?!
WHY IS HE TREATING ME LIKE A CHILD?!?
BECAUSE YOU'RE ACTING LIKE ONE?
SOME FRIEND YOU ARE.
I AM YOUR FRIEND, DUMMY. THAT'S HOW COME I CAN TALK TO YOU LIKE THIS.
YOU'VE BEEN RANTING NON-STOP-- MAKING EVERYONE'S LIFE MISERABLE--EVER SINCE YOU WERE SHIFTED FROM THE X-MEN TO THE TRAINEE TEAM, THE NEW MUTANTS. IT'S GETTING BORING!
AND DON'T TELL ME WHAT IS OR ISN'T FAIR. YOU DIDN'T SPEND HALF YOUR LIFE IN A DAEMONIC LIMBO.
Oh, ILLYANA, I'M SORRY. I DIDN'T MEAN TO HURT YOU.
WHAT'S DONE IS DONE, KITTY. WISHING--OR GRIPING-- WON'T CHANGE A THING.
BUT IF WE DON'T HURRY, WE'LL MISS THE BUS INTO SALEM CENTER, WHICH MEANS WE'LL MISS DANCE CLASS, AND IF THAT HAPPENS--
--YOU'LL REALLY HAVE CAUSE TO BE MISERABLE.
THE GIRLS RACE DOWN THE DRIVE TOWARDS GRAYMALKIN LANE...
...UNAWARE THAT THEY'RE BEING WATCHED...

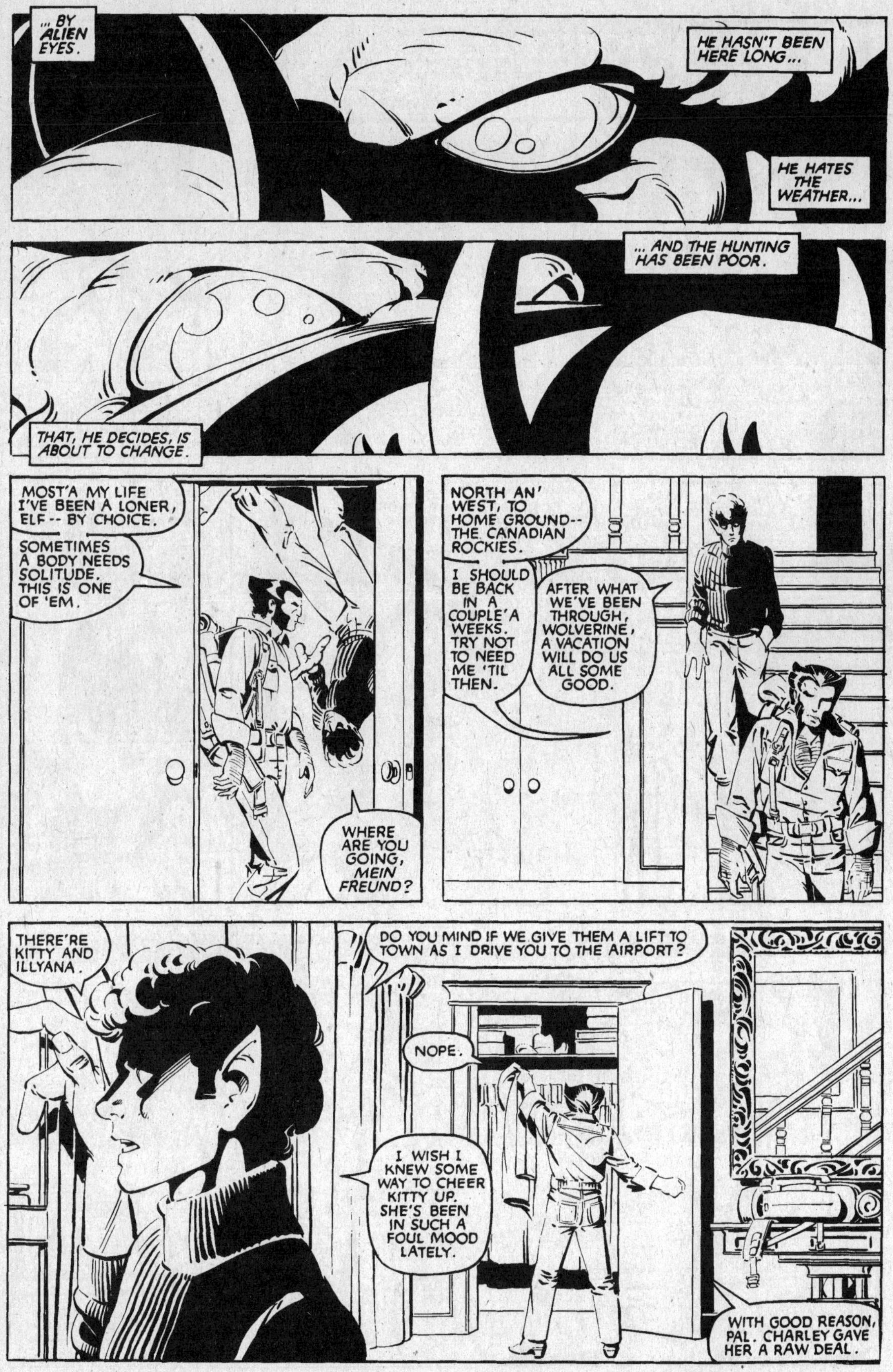

...BY ALIEN EYES.
HE HASN'T BEEN HERE LONG...
HE HATES THE WEATHER...
...AND THE HUNTING HAS BEEN POOR.
THAT, HE DECIDES, IS ABOUT TO CHANGE.
MOST'A MY LIFE I'VE BEEN A LONER, ELF -- BY CHOICE.
SOMETIMES A BODY NEEDS SOLITUDE. THIS IS ONE OF 'EM.
WHERE ARE YOU GOING, MEIN FREUND?
NORTH AN' WEST, TO HOME GROUND-- THE CANADIAN ROCKIES.
I SHOULD BE BACK IN A COUPLE'A WEEKS. TRY NOT TO NEED ME 'TIL THEN.
AFTER WHAT WE'VE BEEN THROUGH, WOLVERINE, A VACATION WILL DO US ALL SOME GOOD.
THERE'RE KITTY AND ILLYANA.
DO YOU MIND IF WE GIVE THEM A LIFT TO TOWN AS I DRIVE YOU TO THE AIRPORT?
NOPE.
I WISH I KNEW SOME WAY TO CHEER KITTY UP. SHE'S BEEN IN SUCH A FOUL MOOD LATELY.
WITH GOOD REASON, PAL. CHARLEY GAVE HER A RAW DEAL.

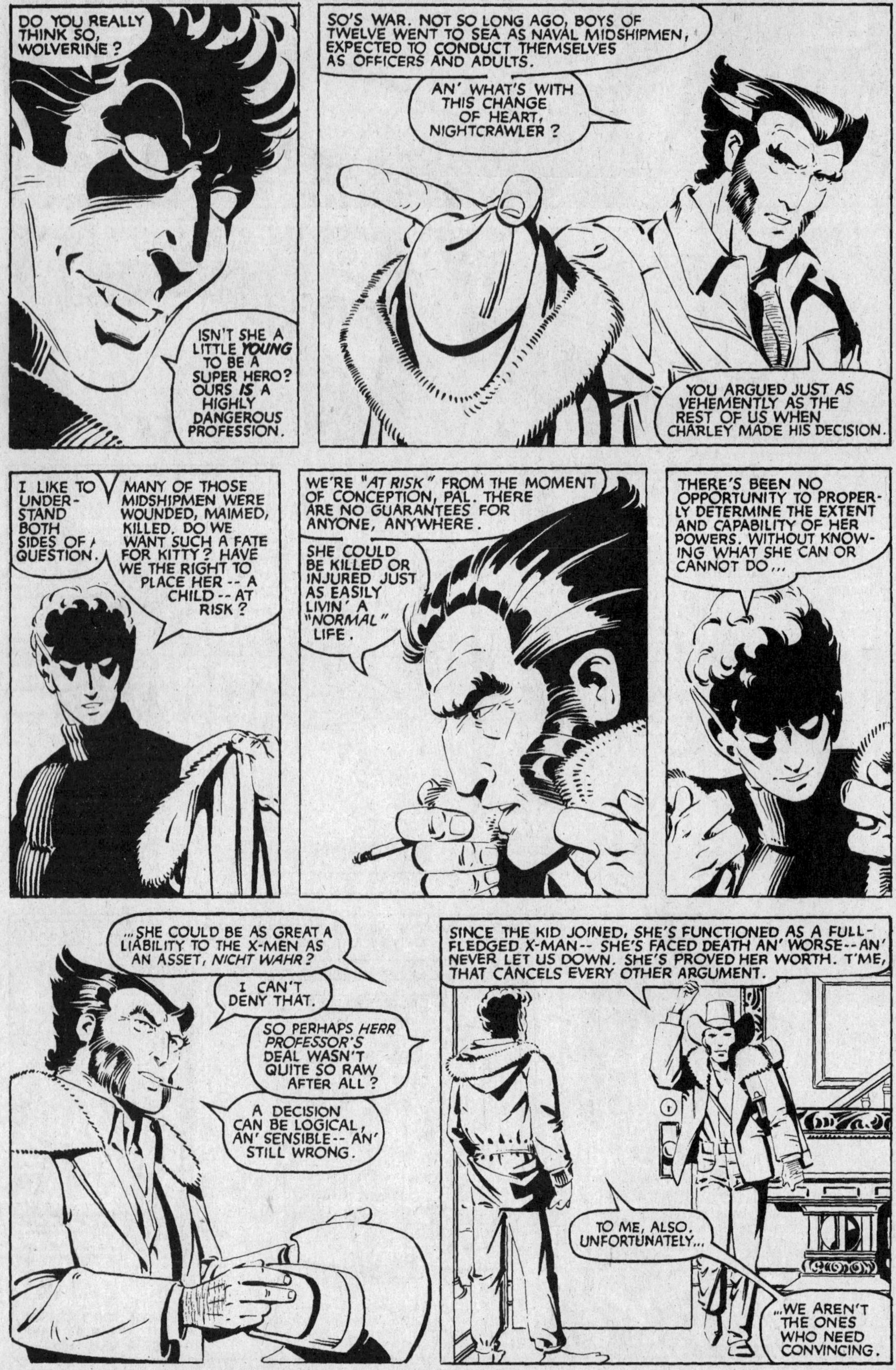
DO YOU REALLY THINK SO, WOLVERINE?
ISN'T SHE A LITTLE YOUNG TO BE A SUPER HERO? OURS IS A HIGHLY DANGEROUS PROFESSION.
SO'S WAR. NOT SO LONG AGO, BOYS OF TWELVE WENT TO SEA AS NAVAL MIDSHIPMEN, EXPECTED TO CONDUCT THEMSELVES AS OFFICERS AND ADULTS.
AN' WHAT'S WITH THIS CHANGE OF HEART, NIGHTCRAWLER?
YOU ARGUED JUST AS VEHEMENTLY AS THE REST OF US WHEN CHARLEY MADE HIS DECISION.
I LIKE TO UNDERSTAND BOTH SIDES OF A QUESTION.
MANY OF THOSE MIDSHIPMEN WERE WOUNDED, MAIMED, KILLED. DO WE WANT SUCH A FATE FOR KITTY? HAVE WE THE RIGHT TO PLACE HER -- A CHILD -- AT RISK?
WE'RE "AT RISK" FROM THE MOMENT OF CONCEPTION, PAL. THERE ARE NO GUARANTEES FOR ANYONE, ANYWHERE.
SHE COULD BE KILLED OR INJURED JUST AS EASILY LIVIN' A "NORMAL" LIFE.
THERE'S BEEN NO OPPORTUNITY TO PROPERLY DETERMINE THE EXTENT AND CAPABILITY OF HER POWERS. WITHOUT KNOWING WHAT SHE CAN OR CANNOT DO...
...SHE COULD BE AS GREAT A LIABILITY TO THE X-MEN AS AN ASSET, NICHT WAHR?
I CAN'T DENY THAT.
SO PERHAPS HERR PROFESSOR'S DEAL WASN'T QUITE SO RAW AFTER ALL?
A DECISION CAN BE LOGICAL, AN' SENSIBLE -- AN' STILL WRONG.
SINCE THE KID JOINED, SHE'S FUNCTIONED AS A FULL-FLEDGED X-MAN -- SHE'S FACED DEATH AN' WORSE -- AN' NEVER LET US DOWN. SHE'S PROVED HER WORTH. T'ME, THAT CANCELS EVERY OTHER ARGUMENT.
TO ME, ALSO. UNFORTUNATELY...
...WE AREN'T THE ONES WHO NEED CONVINCING.

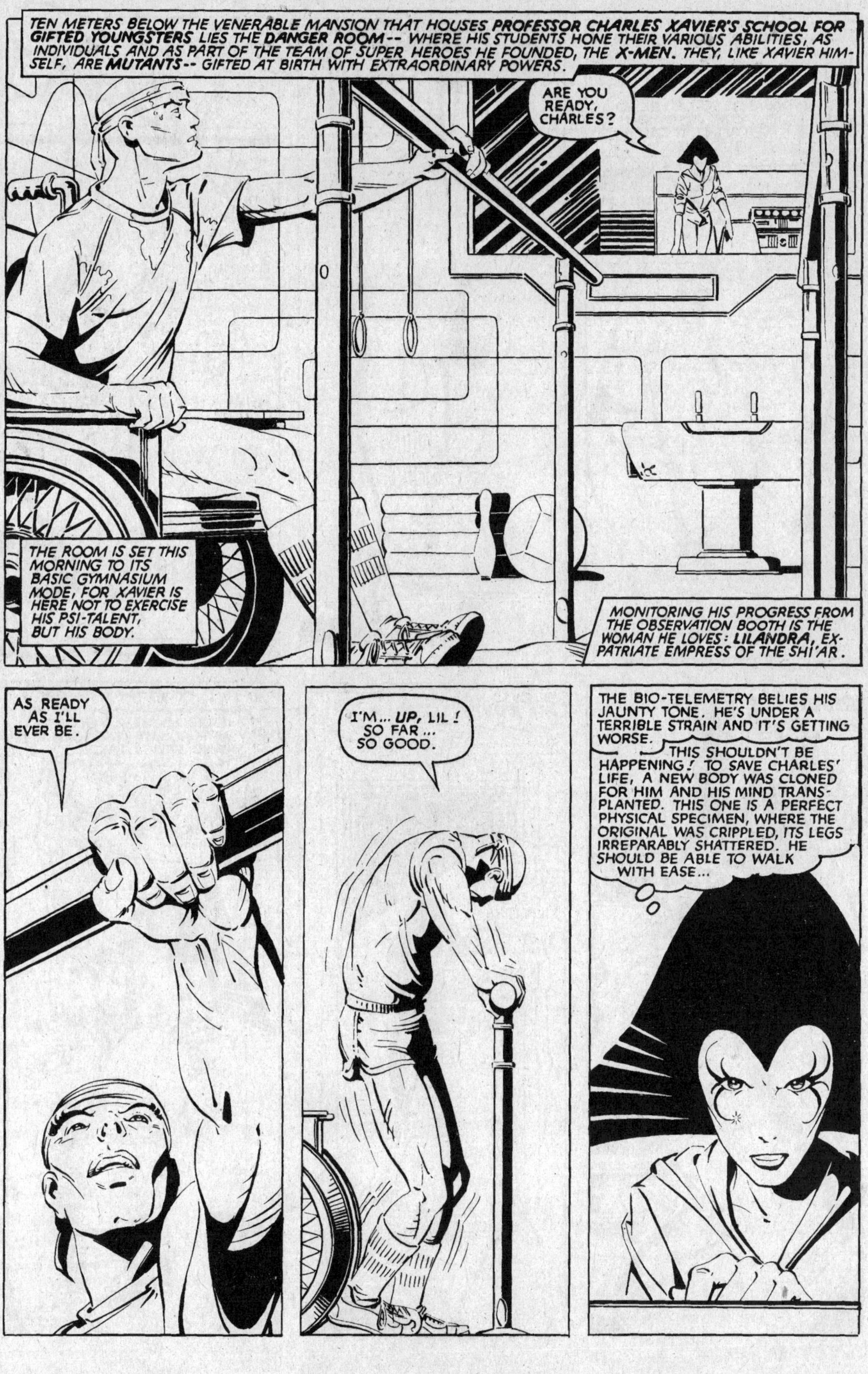
TEN METERS BELOW THE VENERABLE MANSION THAT HOUSES PROFESSOR CHARLES XAVIER'S SCHOOL FOR GIFTED YOUNGSTERS LIES THE DANGER ROOM-- WHERE HIS STUDENTS HONE THEIR VARIOUS ABILITIES, AS INDIVIDUALS AND AS PART OF THE TEAM OF SUPER HEROES HE FOUNDED, THE X-MEN. THEY, LIKE XAVIER HIMSELF, ARE MUTANTS-- GIFTED AT BIRTH WITH EXTRAORDINARY POWERS.
ARE YOU READY, CHARLES?
THE ROOM IS SET THIS MORNING TO ITS BASIC GYMNASIUM MODE, FOR XAVIER IS HERE NOT TO EXERCISE HIS PSI-TALENT, BUT HIS BODY.
MONITORING HIS PROGRESS FROM THE OBSERVATION BOOTH IS THE WOMAN HE LOVES: LILANDRA, EXPATRIATE EMPRESS OF THE SHI'AR.
AS READY AS I'LL EVER BE.
I'M... UP, LIL! SO FAR... SO GOOD.
THE BIO-TELEMETRY BELIES HIS JAUNTY TONE. HE'S UNDER A TERRIBLE STRAIN AND IT'S GETTING WORSE.
THIS SHOULDN'T BE HAPPENING! TO SAVE CHARLES' LIFE, A NEW BODY WAS CLONED FOR HIM AND HIS MIND TRANSPLANTED. THIS ONE IS A PERFECT PHYSICAL SPECIMEN, WHERE THE ORIGINAL WAS CRIPPLED, ITS LEGS IRREPARABLY SHATTERED. HE SHOULD BE ABLE TO WALK WITH EASE...

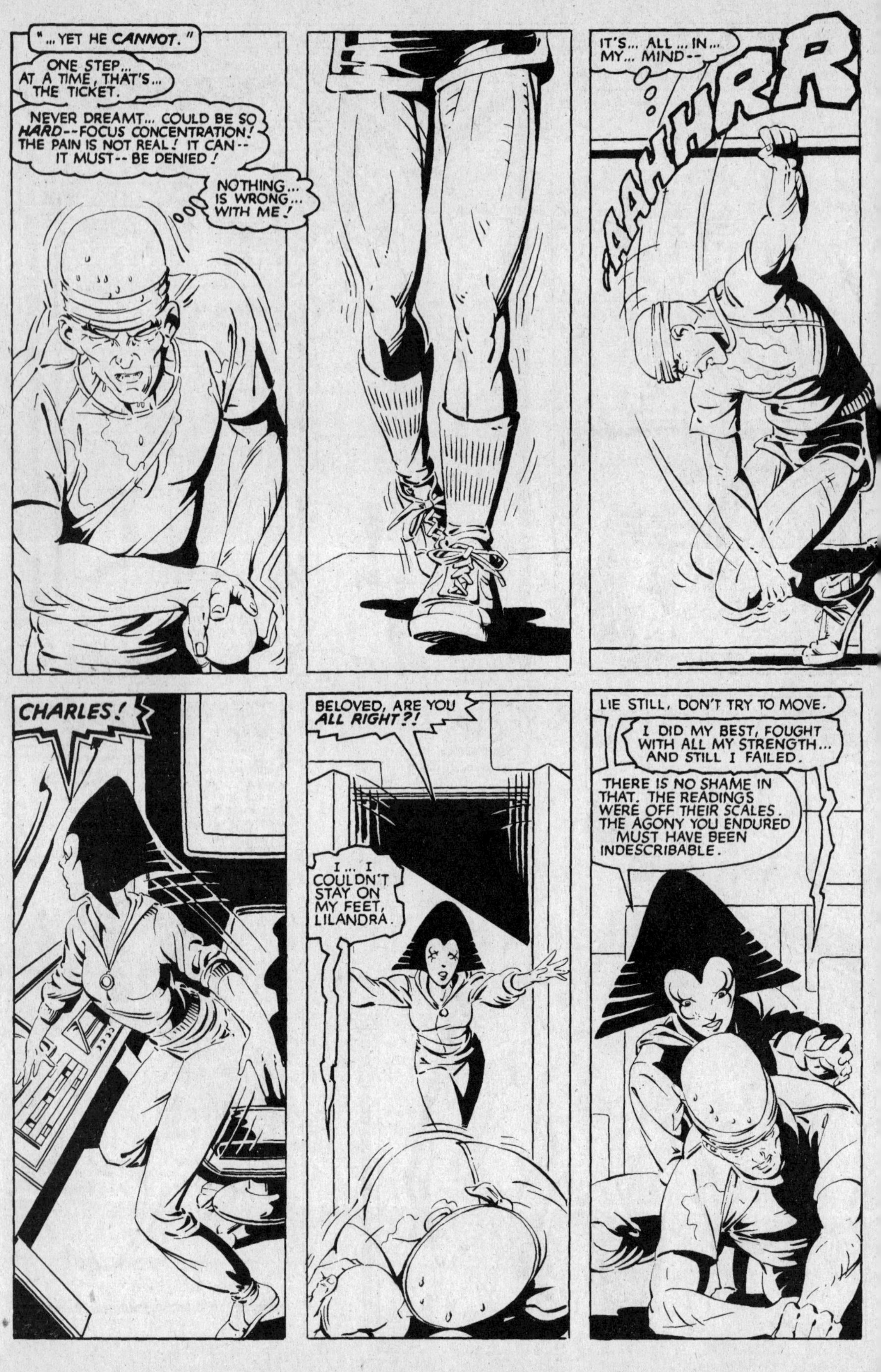
"... YET HE CANNOT."
ONE STEP... AT A TIME, THAT'S... THE TICKET.
NEVER DREAMT... COULD BE SO HARD--FOCUS CONCENTRATION! THE PAIN IS NOT REAL! IT CAN-- IT MUST-- BE DENIED!
NOTHING... IS WRONG... WITH ME!
IT'S... ALL ... IN... MY... MIND--
AAHHRR
CHARLES!
BELOVED, ARE YOU ALL RIGHT?!
I... I COULDN'T STAY ON MY FEET, LILANDRA.
LIE STILL, DON'T TRY TO MOVE.
I DID MY BEST, FOUGHT WITH ALL MY STRENGTH... AND STILL I FAILED.
THERE IS NO SHAME IN THAT. THE READINGS WERE OFF THEIR SCALES. THE AGONY YOU ENDURED MUST HAVE BEEN INDESCRIBABLE.

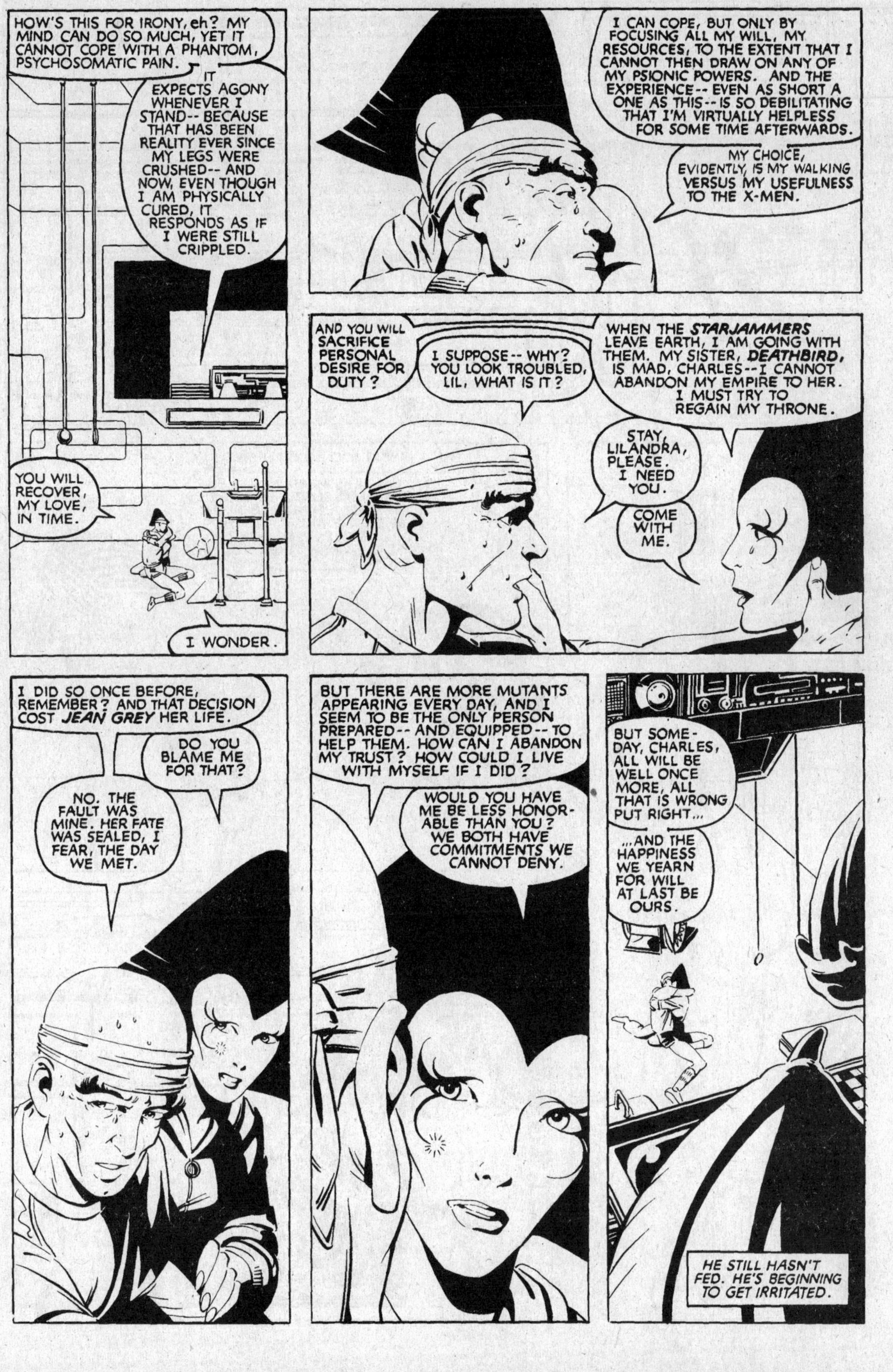

HOW'S THIS FOR IRONY, eh? MY MIND CAN DO SO MUCH, YET IT CANNOT COPE WITH A PHANTOM, PSYCHOSOMATIC PAIN.
IT EXPECTS AGONY WHENEVER I STAND-- BECAUSE THAT HAS BEEN REALITY EVER SINCE MY LEGS WERE CRUSHED-- AND NOW, EVEN THOUGH I AM PHYSICALLY CURED, IT RESPONDS AS IF I WERE STILL CRIPPLED.
YOU WILL RECOVER, MY LOVE, IN TIME.
I WONDER.
I CAN COPE, BUT ONLY BY FOCUSING ALL MY WILL, MY RESOURCES, TO THE EXTENT THAT I CANNOT THEN DRAW ON ANY OF MY PSIONIC POWERS. AND THE EXPERIENCE-- EVEN AS SHORT A ONE AS THIS-- IS SO DEBILITATING THAT I'M VIRTUALLY HELPLESS FOR SOME TIME AFTERWARDS.
MY CHOICE, EVIDENTLY, IS MY WALKING VERSUS MY USEFULNESS TO THE X-MEN.
AND YOU WILL SACRIFICE PERSONAL DESIRE FOR DUTY?
I SUPPOSE-- WHY? YOU LOOK TROUBLED, LIL. WHAT IS IT?
WHEN THE STARJAMMERS LEAVE EARTH, I AM GOING WITH THEM. MY SISTER, DEATHBIRD, IS MAD, CHARLES-- I CANNOT ABANDON MY EMPIRE TO HER. I MUST TRY TO REGAIN MY THRONE.
STAY, LILANDRA, PLEASE. I NEED YOU.
COME WITH ME.
I DID SO ONCE BEFORE, REMEMBER? AND THAT DECISION COST JEAN GREY HER LIFE.
DO YOU BLAME ME FOR THAT?
NO. THE FAULT WAS MINE. HER FATE WAS SEALED, I FEAR, THE DAY WE MET.
BUT THERE ARE MORE MUTANTS APPEARING EVERY DAY, AND I SEEM TO BE THE ONLY PERSON PREPARED-- AND EQUIPPED-- TO HELP THEM. HOW CAN I ABANDON MY TRUST? HOW COULD I LIVE WITH MYSELF IF I DID?
WOULD YOU HAVE ME BE LESS HONORABLE THAN YOU? WE BOTH HAVE COMMITMENTS WE CANNOT DENY.
BUT SOMEDAY, CHARLES, ALL WILL BE WELL ONCE MORE, ALL THAT IS WRONG PUT RIGHT...
...AND THE HAPPINESS WE YEARN FOR WILL AT LAST BE OURS.
HE STILL HASN'T FED. HE'S BEGINNING TO GET IRRITATED.

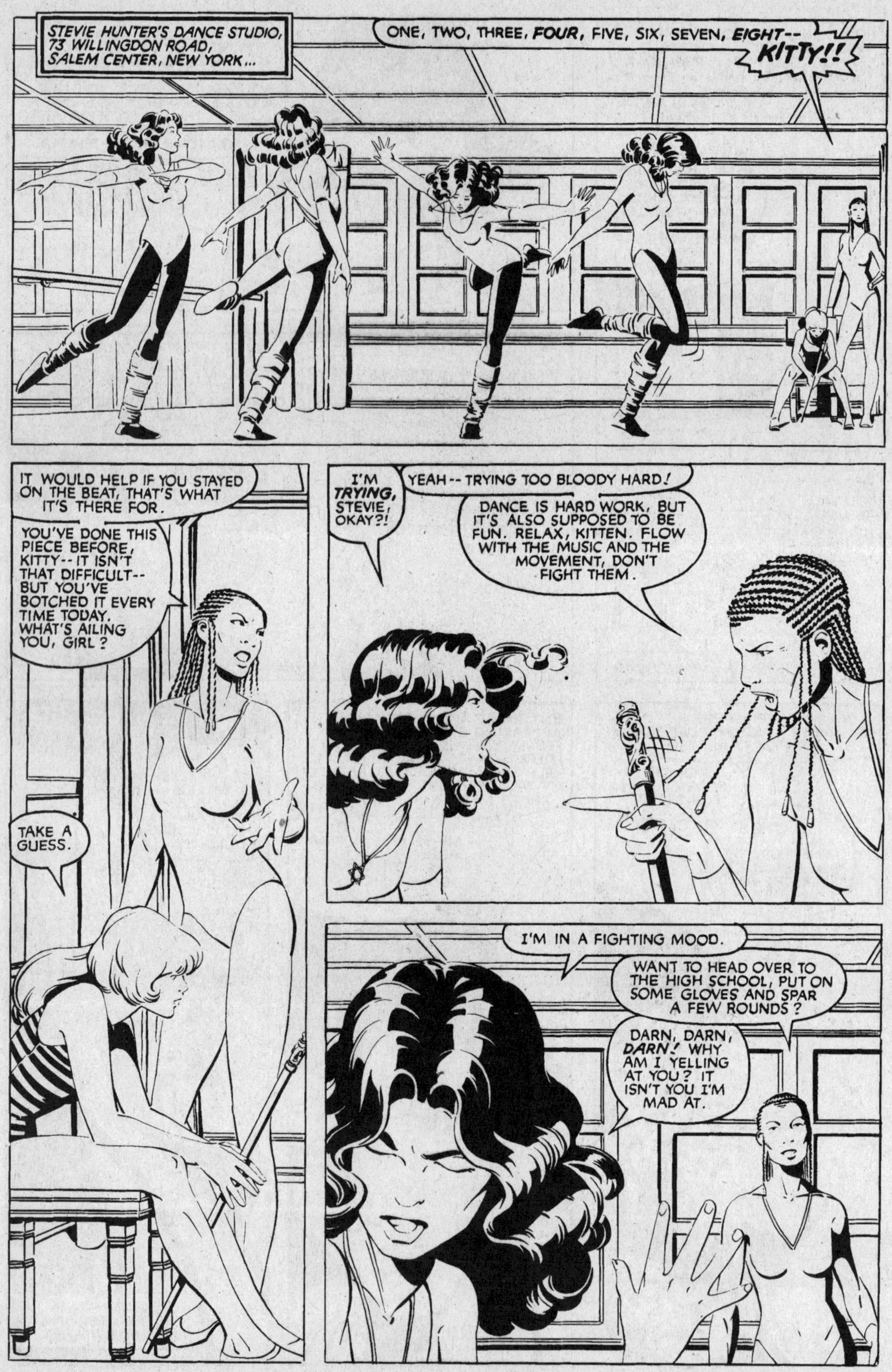

STEVIE HUNTER'S DANCE STUDIO, 73 WILLINGDON ROAD, SALEM CENTER, NEW YORK...
ONE, TWO, THREE, FOUR, FIVE, SIX, SEVEN, EIGHT--
KITTY!!
IT WOULD HELP IF YOU STAYED ON THE BEAT, THAT'S WHAT IT'S THERE FOR.
YOU'VE DONE THIS PIECE BEFORE, KITTY-- IT ISN'T THAT DIFFICULT-- BUT YOU'VE BOTCHED IT EVERY TIME TODAY. WHAT'S AILING YOU, GIRL?
TAKE A GUESS.
I'M TRYING, STEVIE, OKAY?!
YEAH -- TRYING TOO BLOODY HARD!
DANCE IS HARD WORK, BUT IT'S ALSO SUPPOSED TO BE FUN. RELAX, KITTEN. FLOW WITH THE MUSIC AND THE MOVEMENT, DON'T FIGHT THEM.
I'M IN A FIGHTING MOOD.
WANT TO HEAD OVER TO THE HIGH SCHOOL, PUT ON SOME GLOVES AND SPAR A FEW ROUNDS?
DARN, DARN, DARN! WHY AM I YELLING AT YOU? IT ISN'T YOU I'M MAD AT.

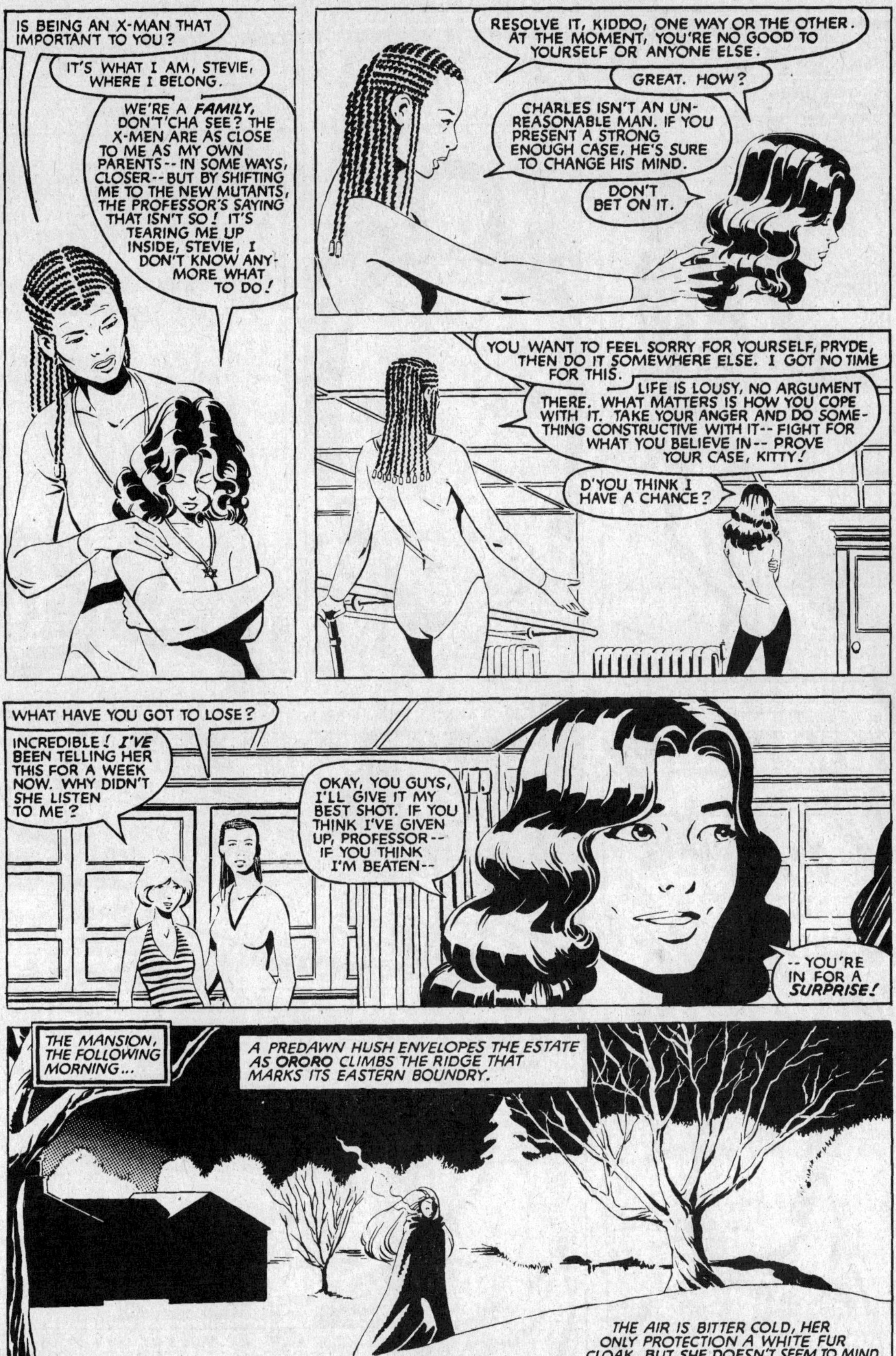
IS BEING AN X-MAN THAT IMPORTANT TO YOU?
IT'S WHAT I AM, STEVIE, WHERE I BELONG.
WE'RE A FAMILY, DON'T'CHA SEE? THE X-MEN ARE AS CLOSE TO ME AS MY OWN PARENTS -- IN SOME WAYS, CLOSER -- BUT BY SHIFTING ME TO THE NEW MUTANTS, THE PROFESSOR'S SAYING THAT ISN'T SO! IT'S TEARING ME UP INSIDE, STEVIE, I DON'T KNOW ANY-MORE WHAT TO DO!
RESOLVE IT, KIDDO, ONE WAY OR THE OTHER. AT THE MOMENT, YOU'RE NO GOOD TO YOURSELF OR ANYONE ELSE.
GREAT. HOW?
CHARLES ISN'T AN UN-REASONABLE MAN. IF YOU PRESENT A STRONG ENOUGH CASE, HE'S SURE TO CHANGE HIS MIND.
DON'T BET ON IT.
YOU WANT TO FEEL SORRY FOR YOURSELF, PRYDE, THEN DO IT SOMEWHERE ELSE. I GOT NO TIME FOR THIS.
LIFE IS LOUSY, NO ARGUMENT THERE. WHAT MATTERS IS HOW YOU COPE WITH IT. TAKE YOUR ANGER AND DO SOME-THING CONSTRUCTIVE WITH IT -- FIGHT FOR WHAT YOU BELIEVE IN -- PROVE YOUR CASE, KITTY!
D'YOU THINK I HAVE A CHANCE?
WHAT HAVE YOU GOT TO LOSE?
INCREDIBLE! I'VE BEEN TELLING HER THIS FOR A WEEK NOW. WHY DIDN'T SHE LISTEN TO ME?
OKAY, YOU GUYS, I'LL GIVE IT MY BEST SHOT. IF YOU THINK I'VE GIVEN UP, PROFESSOR -- IF YOU THINK I'M BEATEN --
-- YOU'RE IN FOR A SURPRISE!
THE MANSION, THE FOLLOWING MORNING...
A PREDAWN HUSH ENVELOPES THE ESTATE AS ORORO CLIMBS THE RIDGE THAT MARKS ITS EASTERN BOUNDRY.
THE AIR IS BITTER COLD, HER ONLY PROTECTION A WHITE FUR CLOAK, BUT SHE DOESN'T SEEM TO MIND.

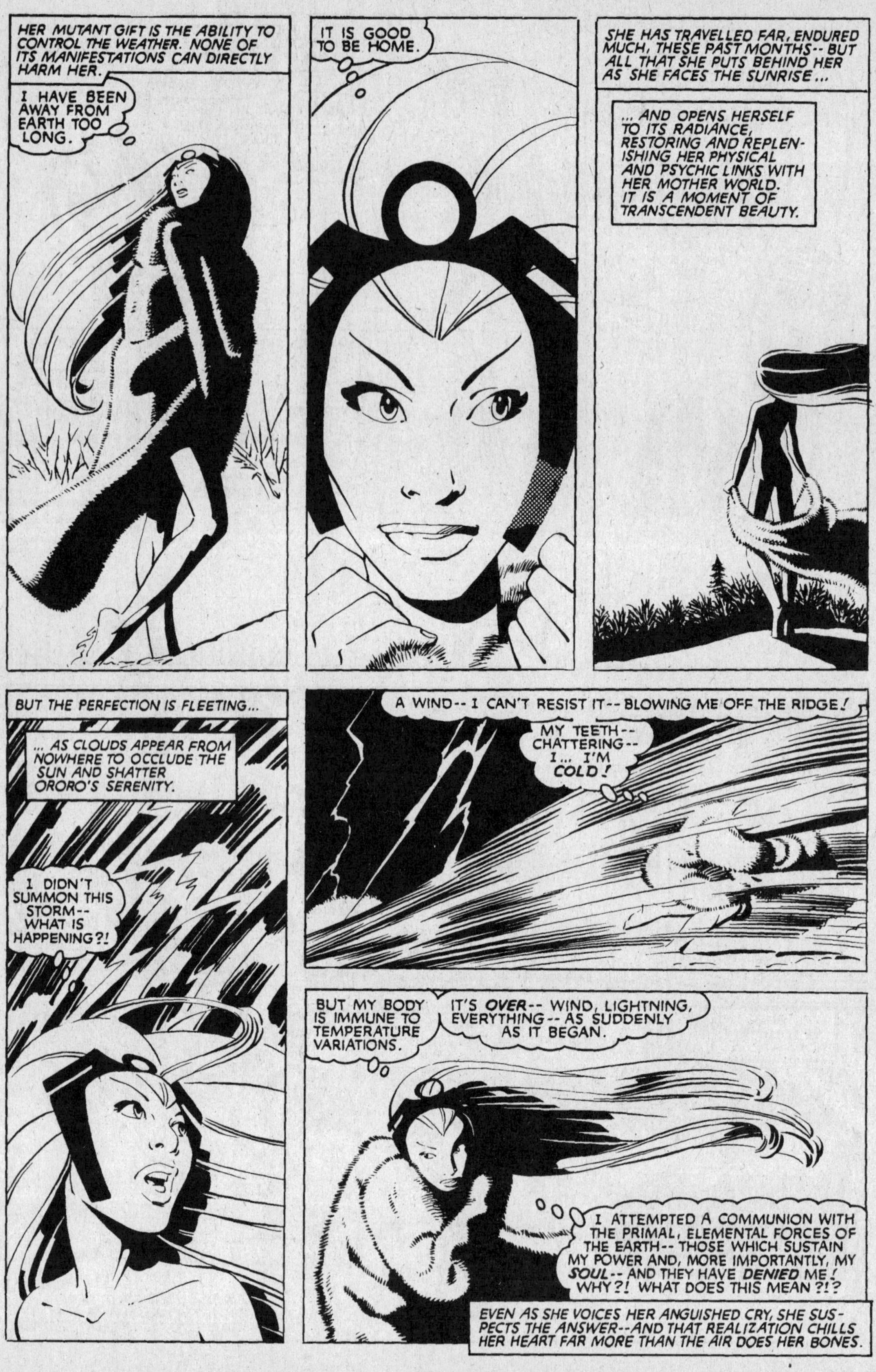
HER MUTANT GIFT IS THE ABILITY TO CONTROL THE WEATHER. NONE OF ITS MANIFESTATIONS CAN DIRECTLY HARM HER.
I HAVE BEEN AWAY FROM EARTH TOO LONG.
IT IS GOOD TO BE HOME.
SHE HAS TRAVELLED FAR, ENDURED MUCH, THESE PAST MONTHS-- BUT ALL THAT SHE PUTS BEHIND HER AS SHE FACES THE SUNRISE...
... AND OPENS HERSELF TO ITS RADIANCE, RESTORING AND REPLENISHING HER PHYSICAL AND PSYCHIC LINKS WITH HER MOTHER WORLD. IT IS A MOMENT OF TRANSCENDENT BEAUTY.
BUT THE PERFECTION IS FLEETING...
... AS CLOUDS APPEAR FROM NOWHERE TO OCCLUDE THE SUN AND SHATTER ORORO'S SERENITY.
I DIDN'T SUMMON THIS STORM-- WHAT IS HAPPENING?!
A WIND-- I CAN'T RESIST IT-- BLOWING ME OFF THE RIDGE!
MY TEETH-- CHATTERING-- I... I'M COLD!
BUT MY BODY IS IMMUNE TO TEMPERATURE VARIATIONS.
IT'S OVER-- WIND, LIGHTNING, EVERYTHING-- AS SUDDENLY AS IT BEGAN.
I ATTEMPTED A COMMUNION WITH THE PRIMAL, ELEMENTAL FORCES OF THE EARTH-- THOSE WHICH SUSTAIN MY POWER AND, MORE IMPORTANTLY, MY SOUL-- AND THEY HAVE DENIED ME! WHY?! WHAT DOES THIS MEAN?!?
EVEN AS SHE VOICES HER ANGUISHED CRY, SHE SUSPECTS THE ANSWER--AND THAT REALIZATION CHILLS HER HEART FAR MORE THAN THE AIR DOES HER BONES.

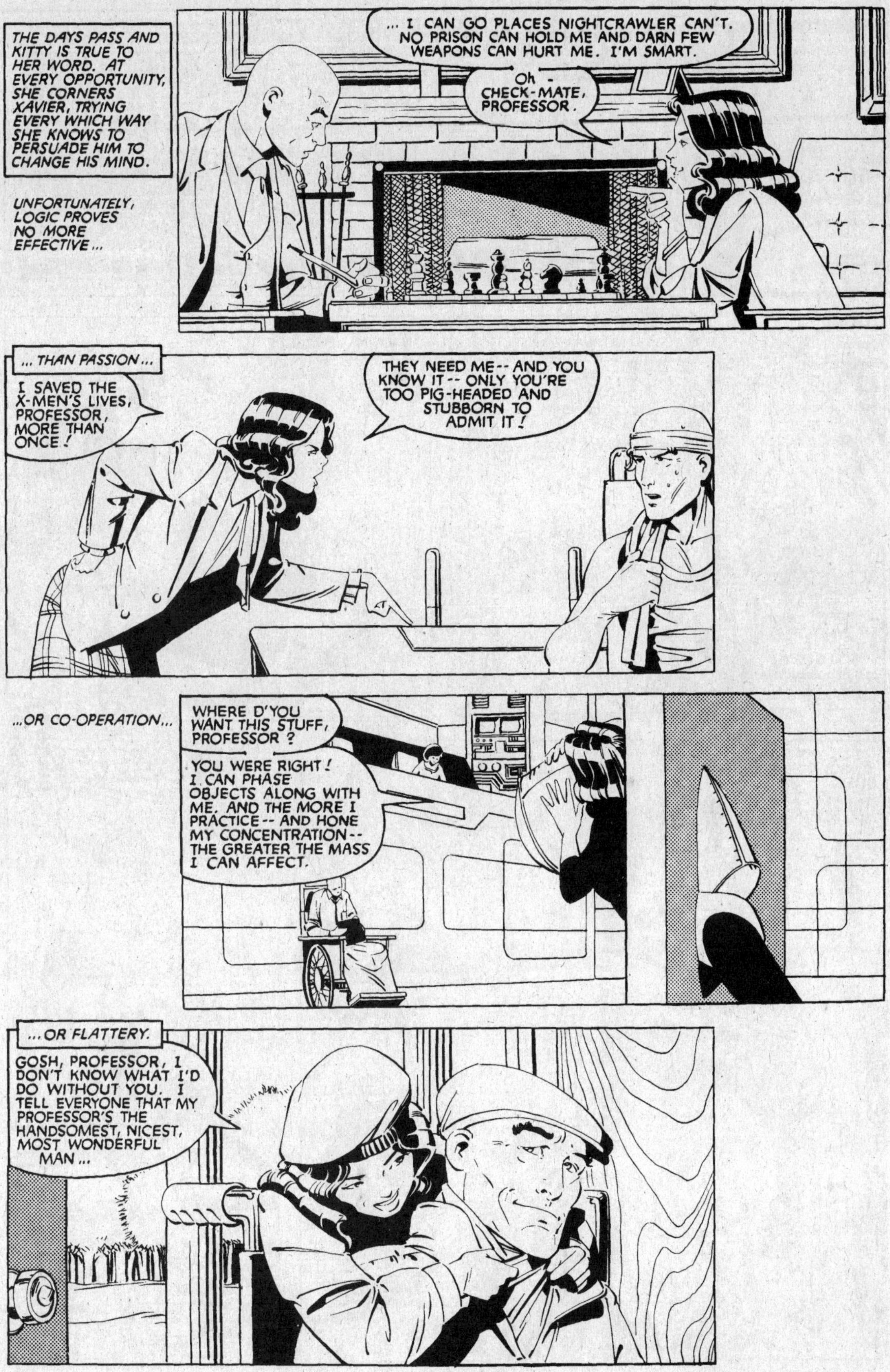
THE DAYS PASS AND KITTY IS TRUE TO HER WORD. AT EVERY OPPORTUNITY, SHE CORNERS XAVIER, TRYING EVERY WHICH WAY SHE KNOWS TO PERSUADE HIM TO CHANGE HIS MIND.
UNFORTUNATELY, LOGIC PROVES NO MORE EFFECTIVE...
... I CAN GO PLACES NIGHTCRAWLER CAN'T. NO PRISON CAN HOLD ME AND DARN FEW WEAPONS CAN HURT ME. I'M SMART.
Oh - CHECK-MATE, PROFESSOR.
... THAN PASSION...
I SAVED THE X-MEN'S LIVES, PROFESSOR, MORE THAN ONCE!
THEY NEED ME -- AND YOU KNOW IT -- ONLY YOU'RE TOO PIG-HEADED AND STUBBORN TO ADMIT IT!
...OR CO-OPERATION...
WHERE D'YOU WANT THIS STUFF, PROFESSOR ?
YOU WERE RIGHT! I CAN PHASE OBJECTS ALONG WITH ME. AND THE MORE I PRACTICE -- AND HONE MY CONCENTRATION -- THE GREATER THE MASS I CAN AFFECT.
... OR FLATTERY.
GOSH, PROFESSOR, I DON'T KNOW WHAT I'D DO WITHOUT YOU. I TELL EVERYONE THAT MY PROFESSOR'S THE HANDSOMEST, NICEST, MOST WONDERFUL MAN ...

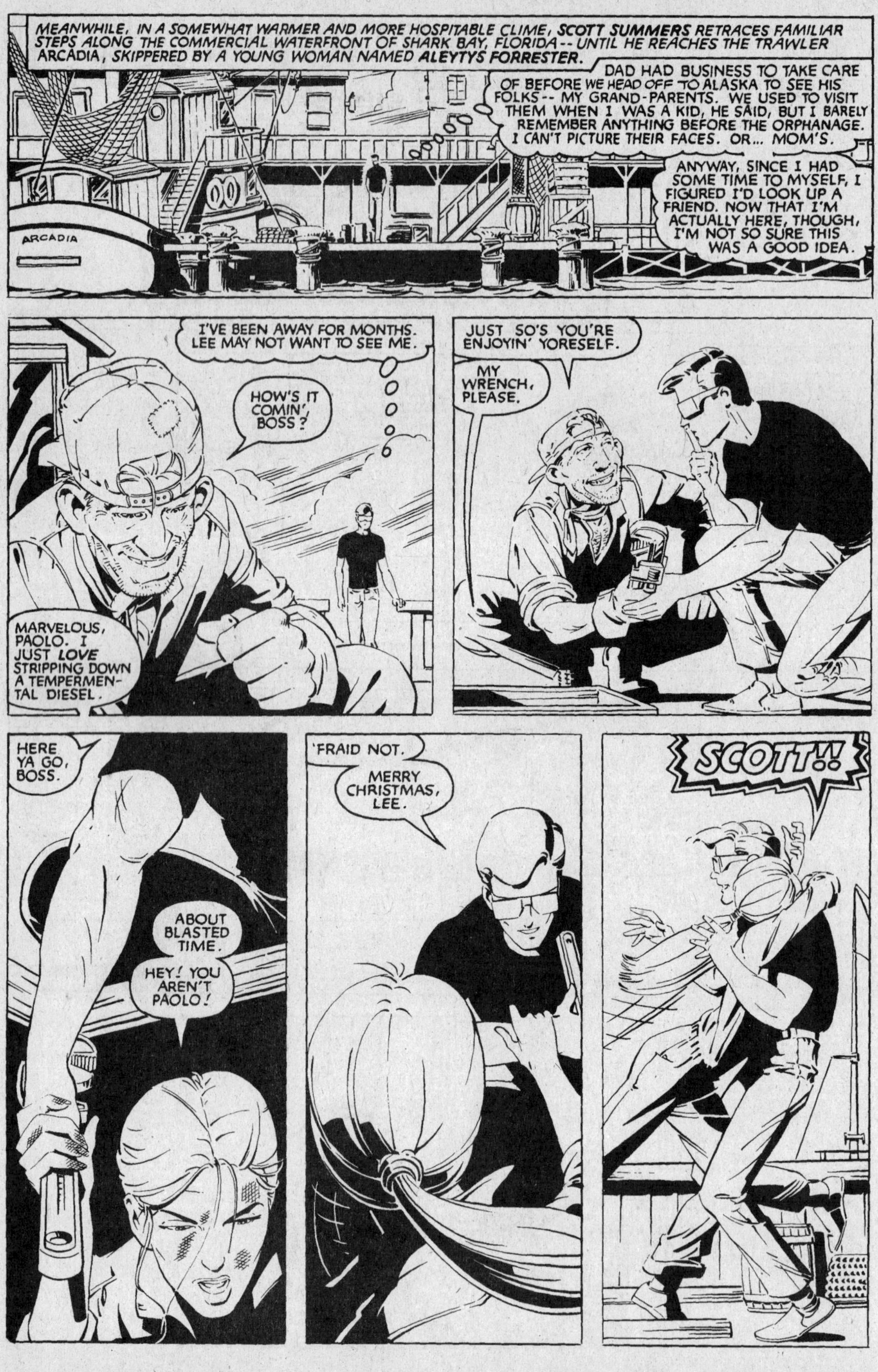
MEANWHILE, IN A SOMEWHAT WARMER AND MORE HOSPITABLE CLIME, SCOTT SUMMERS RETRACES FAMILIAR STEPS ALONG THE COMMERCIAL WATERFRONT OF SHARK BAY, FLORIDA -- UNTIL HE REACHES THE TRAWLER ARCADIA, SKIPPERED BY A YOUNG WOMAN NAMED ALEYTYS FORRESTER.
DAD HAD BUSINESS TO TAKE CARE OF BEFORE WE HEAD OFF TO ALASKA TO SEE HIS FOLKS -- MY GRAND-PARENTS. WE USED TO VISIT THEM WHEN I WAS A KID, HE SAID, BUT I BARELY REMEMBER ANYTHING BEFORE THE ORPHANAGE. I CAN'T PICTURE THEIR FACES. OR... MOM'S.
ANYWAY, SINCE I HAD SOME TIME TO MYSELF, I FIGURED I'D LOOK UP A FRIEND. NOW THAT I'M ACTUALLY HERE, THOUGH, I'M NOT SO SURE THIS WAS A GOOD IDEA.
ARCADIA
I'VE BEEN AWAY FOR MONTHS. LEE MAY NOT WANT TO SEE ME.
HOW'S IT COMIN', BOSS?
MARVELOUS, PAOLO. I JUST LOVE STRIPPING DOWN A TEMPERMENTAL DIESEL.
JUST SO'S YOU'RE ENJOYIN' YORESELF.
MY WRENCH, PLEASE.
HERE YA GO, BOSS.
ABOUT BLASTED TIME.
HEY! YOU AREN'T PAOLO!
'FRAID NOT.
MERRY CHRISTMAS, LEE.
SCOTT!!

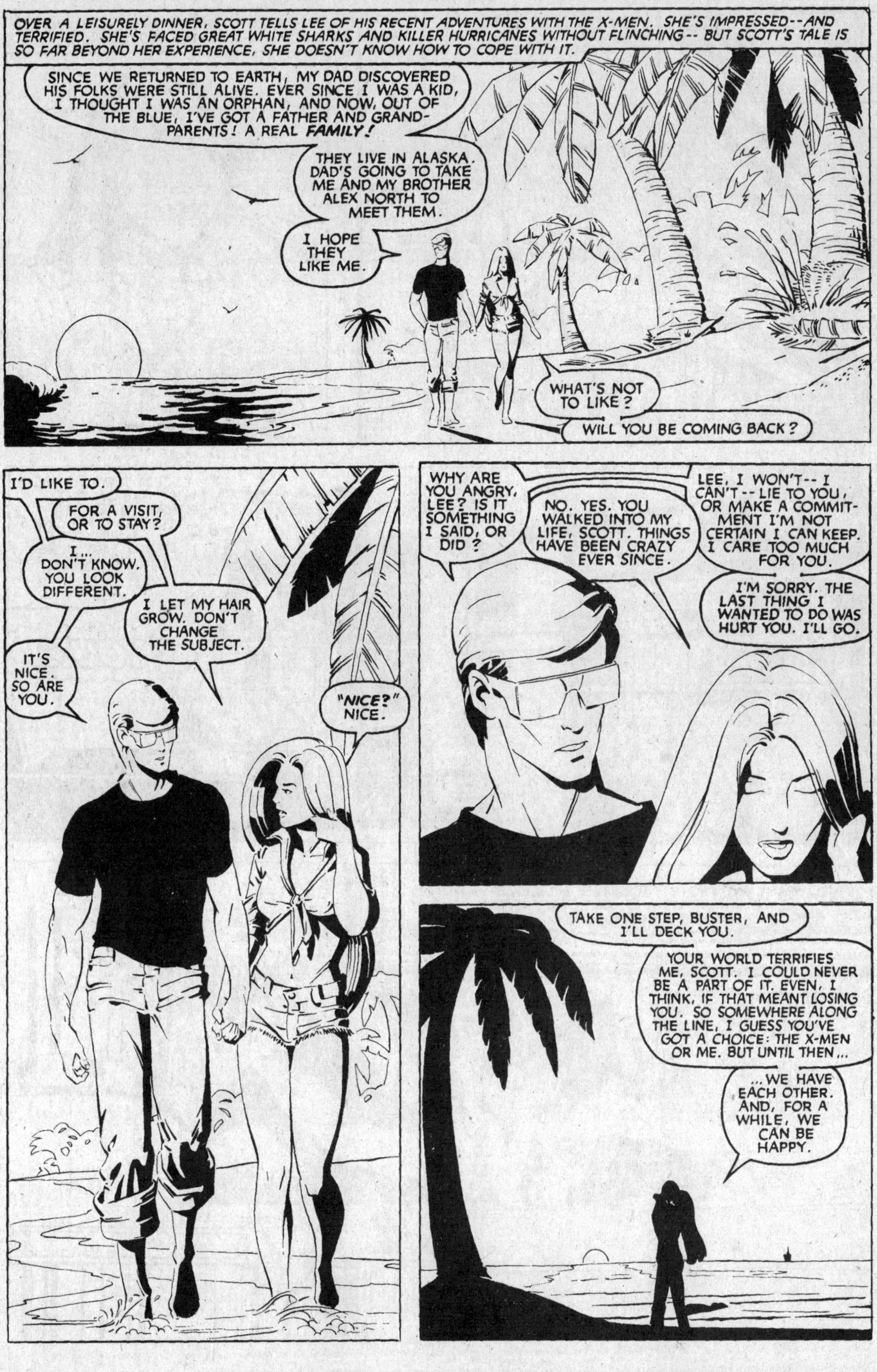

OVER A LEISURELY DINNER, SCOTT TELLS LEE OF HIS RECENT ADVENTURES WITH THE X-MEN. SHE'S IMPRESSED--AND TERRIFIED. SHE'S FACED GREAT WHITE SHARKS AND KILLER HURRICANES WITHOUT FLINCHING-- BUT SCOTT'S TALE IS SO FAR BEYOND HER EXPERIENCE, SHE DOESN'T KNOW HOW TO COPE WITH IT.
SINCE WE RETURNED TO EARTH, MY DAD DISCOVERED HIS FOLKS WERE STILL ALIVE. EVER SINCE I WAS A KID, I THOUGHT I WAS AN ORPHAN, AND NOW, OUT OF THE BLUE, I'VE GOT A FATHER AND GRAND-PARENTS! A REAL FAMILY!
THEY LIVE IN ALASKA. DAD'S GOING TO TAKE ME AND MY BROTHER ALEX NORTH TO MEET THEM.
I HOPE THEY LIKE ME.
WHAT'S NOT TO LIKE?
WILL YOU BE COMING BACK?
I'D LIKE TO.
FOR A VISIT, OR TO STAY?
I... DON'T KNOW. YOU LOOK DIFFERENT.
I LET MY HAIR GROW. DON'T CHANGE THE SUBJECT.
IT'S NICE. SO ARE YOU.
"NICE?" NICE.
WHY ARE YOU ANGRY, LEE? IS IT SOMETHING I SAID, OR DID?
NO. YES. YOU WALKED INTO MY LIFE, SCOTT. THINGS HAVE BEEN CRAZY EVER SINCE.
LEE, I WON'T-- I CAN'T--LIE TO YOU, OR MAKE A COMMIT-MENT I'M NOT CERTAIN I CAN KEEP. I CARE TOO MUCH FOR YOU.
I'M SORRY. THE LAST THING I WANTED TO DO WAS HURT YOU. I'LL GO.
TAKE ONE STEP, BUSTER, AND I'LL DECK YOU.
YOUR WORLD TERRIFIES ME, SCOTT. I COULD NEVER BE A PART OF IT. EVEN, I THINK, IF THAT MEANT LOSING YOU. SO SOMEWHERE ALONG THE LINE, I GUESS YOU'VE GOT A CHOICE: THE X-MEN OR ME. BUT UNTIL THEN...
...WE HAVE EACH OTHER. AND, FOR A WHILE, WE CAN BE HAPPY.

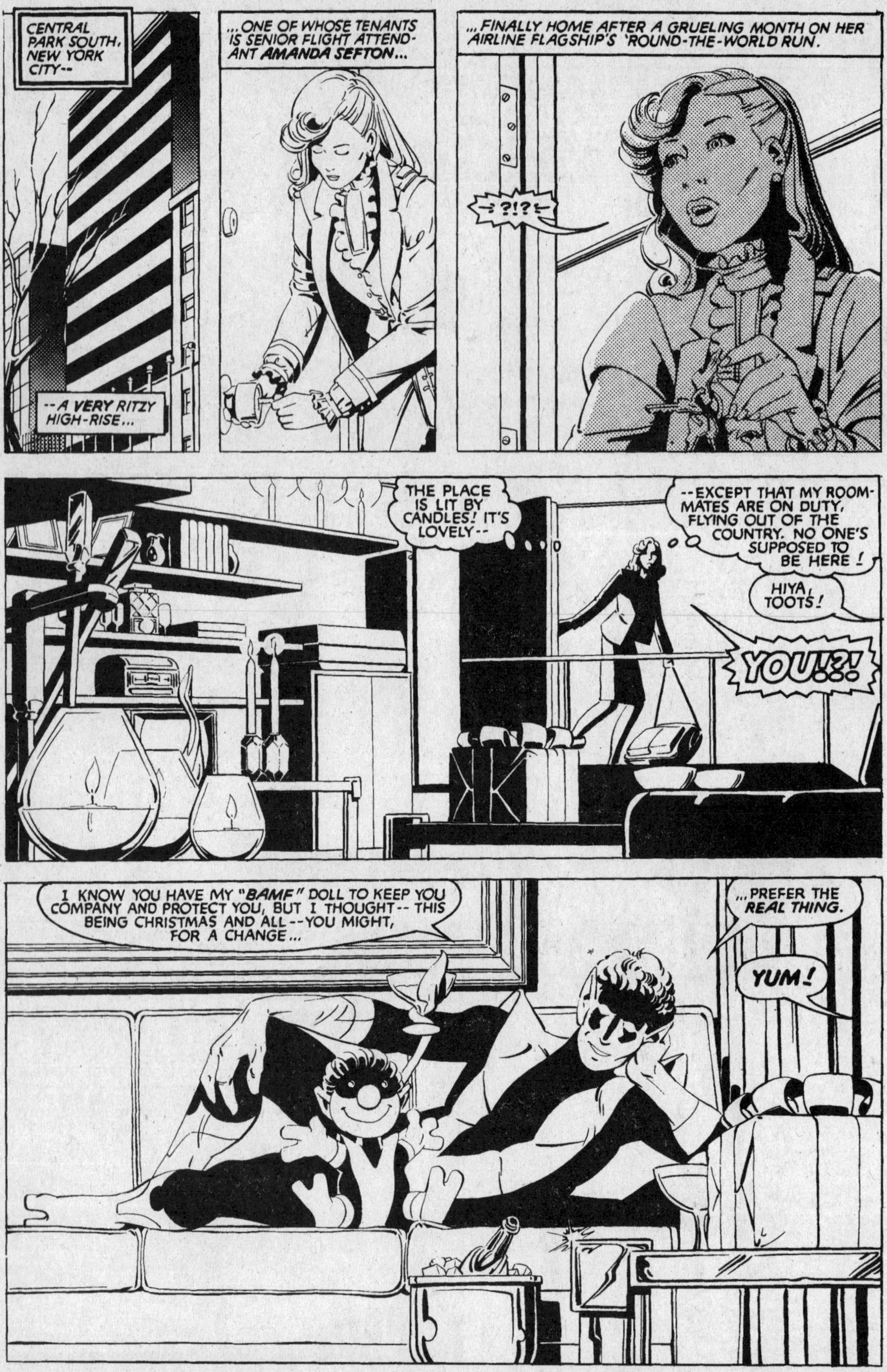
CENTRAL PARK SOUTH, NEW YORK CITY--
--A VERY RITZY HIGH-RISE...
...ONE OF WHOSE TENANTS IS SENIOR FLIGHT ATTENDANT AMANDA SEFTON...
...FINALLY HOME AFTER A GRUELING MONTH ON HER AIRLINE FLAGSHIP'S 'ROUND-THE-WORLD RUN.
?!?
THE PLACE IS LIT BY CANDLES! IT'S LOVELY--
--EXCEPT THAT MY ROOMMATES ARE ON DUTY, FLYING OUT OF THE COUNTRY. NO ONE'S SUPPOSED TO BE HERE!
HIYA, TOOTS!
YOU!?!
I KNOW YOU HAVE MY "BAMF" DOLL TO KEEP YOU COMPANY AND PROTECT YOU, BUT I THOUGHT-- THIS BEING CHRISTMAS AND ALL--YOU MIGHT, FOR A CHANGE...
...PREFER THE REAL THING.
YUM!

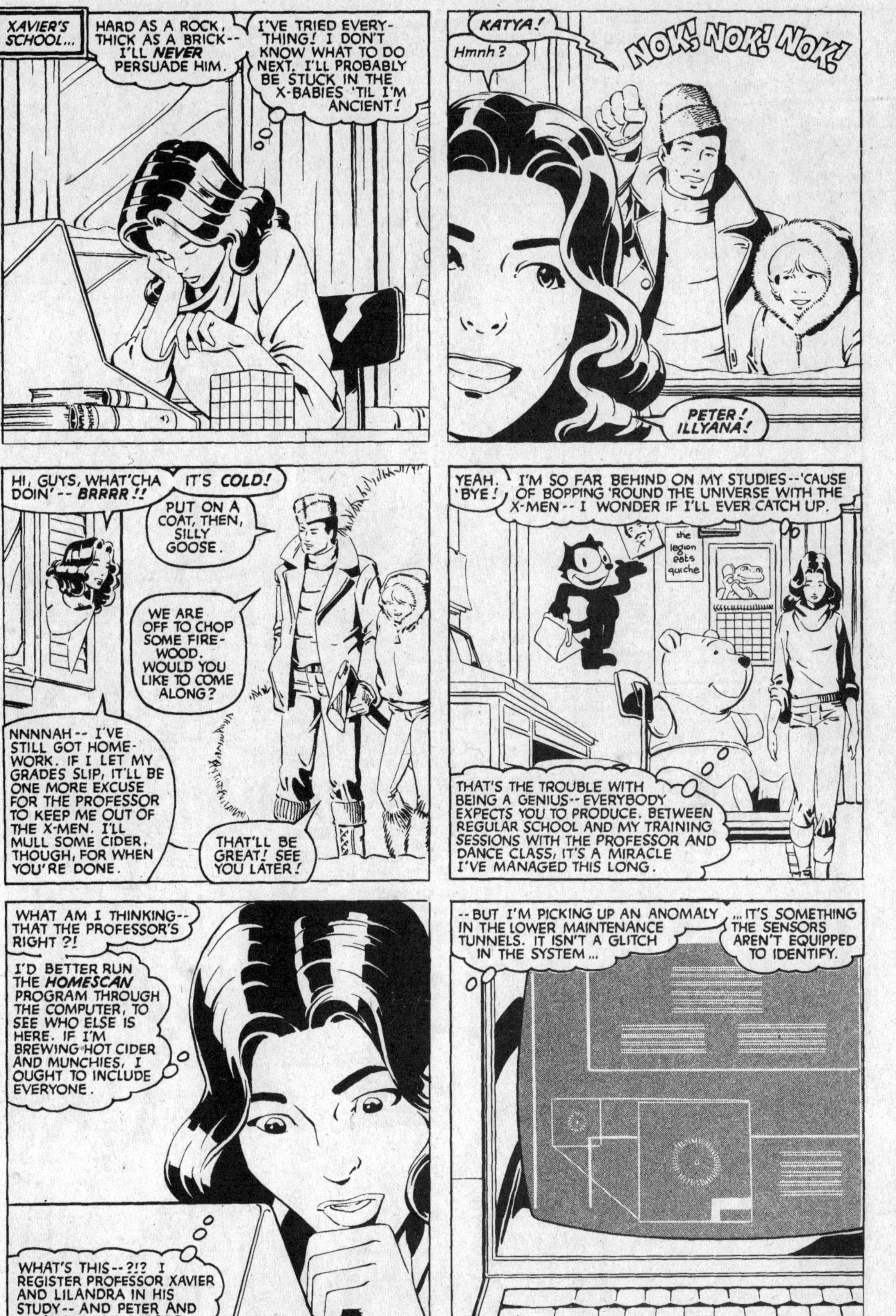
XAVIER'S SCHOOL...
HARD AS A ROCK, THICK AS A BRICK-- I'LL NEVER PERSUADE HIM.
I'VE TRIED EVERYTHING! I DON'T KNOW WHAT TO DO NEXT. I'LL PROBABLY BE STUCK IN THE X-BABIES 'TIL I'M ANCIENT!
KATYA!
Hmnh?
NOK! NOK! NOK!
PETER! ILLYANA!
HI, GUYS, WHAT'CHA DOIN' -- BRRRR!!
IT'S COLD!
PUT ON A COAT, THEN, SILLY GOOSE.
WE ARE OFF TO CHOP SOME FIREWOOD. WOULD YOU LIKE TO COME ALONG?
NNNNAH -- I'VE STILL GOT HOMEWORK. IF I LET MY GRADES SLIP, IT'LL BE ONE MORE EXCUSE FOR THE PROFESSOR TO KEEP ME OUT OF THE X-MEN. I'LL MULL SOME CIDER, THOUGH, FOR WHEN YOU'RE DONE.
THAT'LL BE GREAT! SEE YOU LATER!
YEAH. 'BYE!
I'M SO FAR BEHIND ON MY STUDIES--'CAUSE OF BOPPING 'ROUND THE UNIVERSE WITH THE X-MEN-- I WONDER IF I'LL EVER CATCH UP.
the legion eats quiche
THAT'S THE TROUBLE WITH BEING A GENIUS-- EVERYBODY EXPECTS YOU TO PRODUCE. BETWEEN REGULAR SCHOOL AND MY TRAINING SESSIONS WITH THE PROFESSOR AND DANCE CLASS, IT'S A MIRACLE I'VE MANAGED THIS LONG.
WHAT AM I THINKING-- THAT THE PROFESSOR'S RIGHT?!
I'D BETTER RUN THE HOMESCAN PROGRAM THROUGH THE COMPUTER, TO SEE WHO ELSE IS HERE. IF I'M BREWING HOT CIDER AND MUNCHIES, I OUGHT TO INCLUDE EVERYONE.
WHAT'S THIS--?!? I REGISTER PROFESSOR XAVIER AND LILANDRA IN HIS STUDY-- AND PETER AND ILLYANA IN THE WOODS--
--BUT I'M PICKING UP AN ANOMALY IN THE LOWER MAINTENANCE TUNNELS. IT ISN'T A GLITCH IN THE SYSTEM...
...IT'S SOMETHING THE SENSORS AREN'T EQUIPPED TO IDENTIFY.

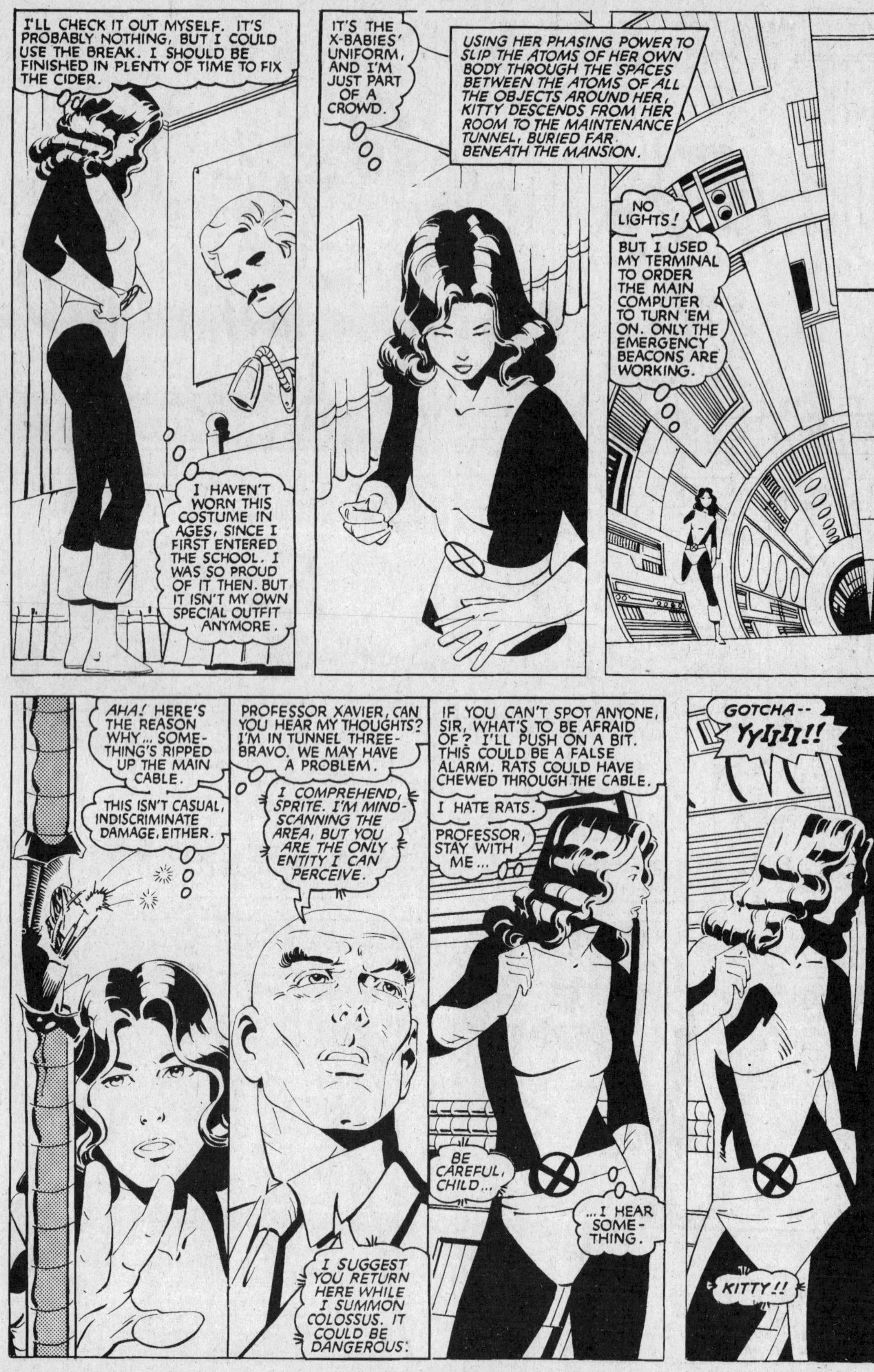
I'LL CHECK IT OUT MYSELF. IT'S PROBABLY NOTHING, BUT I COULD USE THE BREAK. I SHOULD BE FINISHED IN PLENTY OF TIME TO FIX THE CIDER.
I HAVEN'T WORN THIS COSTUME IN AGES, SINCE I FIRST ENTERED THE SCHOOL. I WAS SO PROUD OF IT THEN. BUT IT ISN'T MY OWN SPECIAL OUTFIT ANYMORE.
IT'S THE X-BABIES' UNIFORM, AND I'M JUST PART OF A CROWD.
USING HER PHASING POWER TO SLIP THE ATOMS OF HER OWN BODY THROUGH THE SPACES BETWEEN THE ATOMS OF ALL THE OBJECTS AROUND HER, KITTY DESCENDS FROM HER ROOM TO THE MAINTENANCE TUNNEL, BURIED FAR BENEATH THE MANSION.
NO LIGHTS!
BUT I USED MY TERMINAL TO ORDER THE MAIN COMPUTER TO TURN 'EM ON. ONLY THE EMERGENCY BEACONS ARE WORKING.
AHA! HERE'S THE REASON WHY... SOMETHING'S RIPPED UP THE MAIN CABLE.
THIS ISN'T CASUAL, INDISCRIMINATE DAMAGE, EITHER.
PROFESSOR XAVIER, CAN YOU HEAR MY THOUGHTS? I'M IN TUNNEL THREE-BRAVO. WE MAY HAVE A PROBLEM.
I COMPREHEND, SPRITE. I'M MIND-SCANNING THE AREA, BUT YOU ARE THE ONLY ENTITY I CAN PERCEIVE.
I SUGGEST YOU RETURN HERE WHILE I SUMMON COLOSSUS. IT COULD BE DANGEROUS.
IF YOU CAN'T SPOT ANYONE, SIR, WHAT'S TO BE AFRAID OF? I'LL PUSH ON A BIT. THIS COULD BE A FALSE ALARM. RATS COULD HAVE CHEWED THROUGH THE CABLE.
I HATE RATS.
PROFESSOR, STAY WITH ME...
BE CAREFUL, CHILD...
...I HEAR SOMETHING.
GOTCHA--
YYIIII!!
KITTY!!

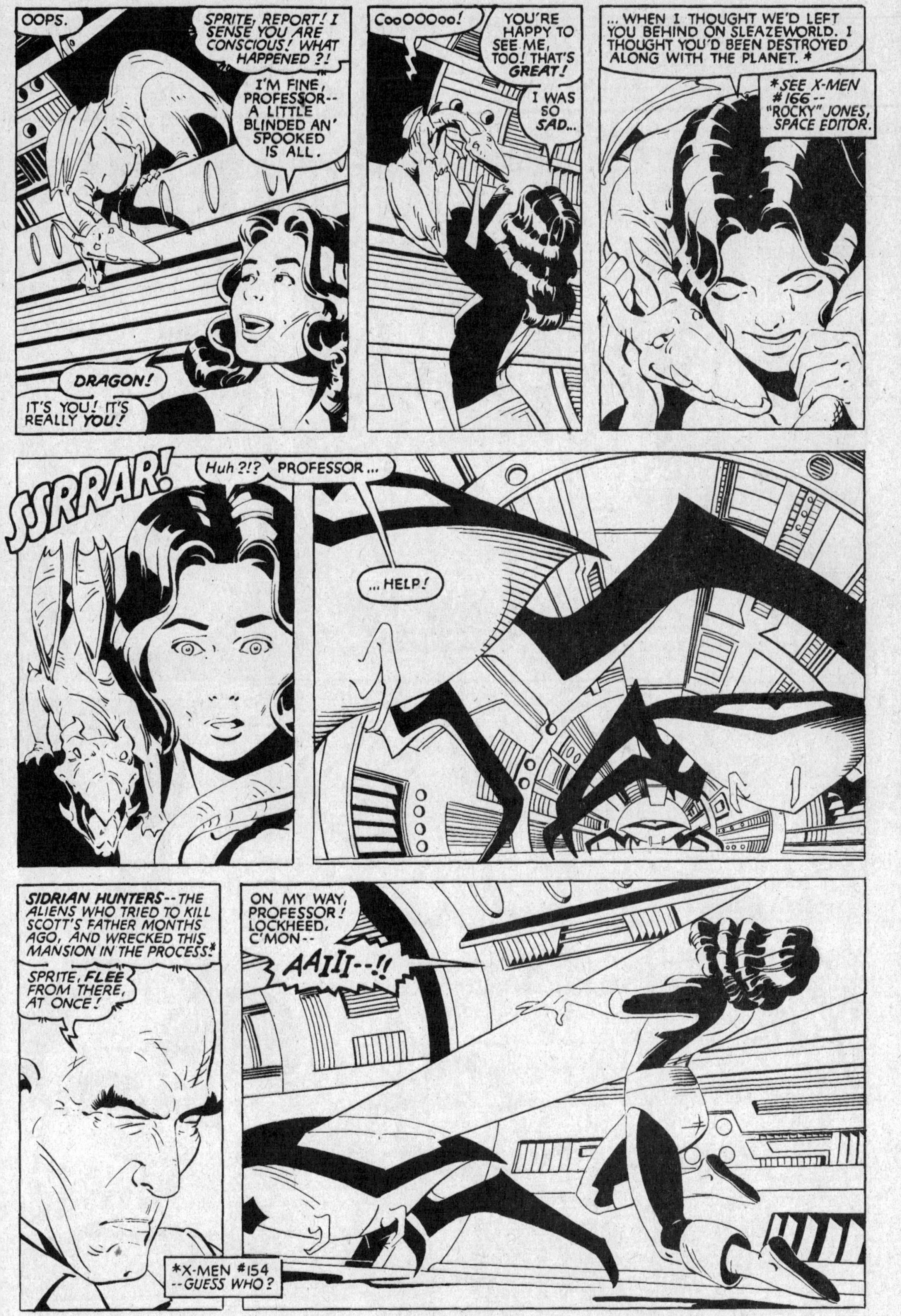
OOPS.
SPRITE, REPORT! I SENSE YOU ARE CONSCIOUS! WHAT HAPPENED ?!
I'M FINE, PROFESSOR-- A LITTLE BLINDED AN' SPOOKED IS ALL.
DRAGON!
IT'S YOU! IT'S REALLY YOU!
CooOOOoo!
YOU'RE HAPPY TO SEE ME, TOO! THAT'S GREAT!
I WAS SO SAD...
... WHEN I THOUGHT WE'D LEFT YOU BEHIND ON SLEAZEWORLD. I THOUGHT YOU'D BEEN DESTROYED ALONG WITH THE PLANET. *
*SEE X-MEN #166 -- "ROCKY" JONES, SPACE EDITOR.
SSRRAR!
Huh ?!?
PROFESSOR ...
... HELP!
SIDRIAN HUNTERS--THE ALIENS WHO TRIED TO KILL SCOTT'S FATHER MONTHS AGO, AND WRECKED THIS MANSION IN THE PROCESS.*
SPRITE, FLEE FROM THERE, AT ONCE!
ON MY WAY, PROFESSOR! LOCKHEED, C'MON--
AAIII--!!
*X-MEN #154 --GUESS WHO?

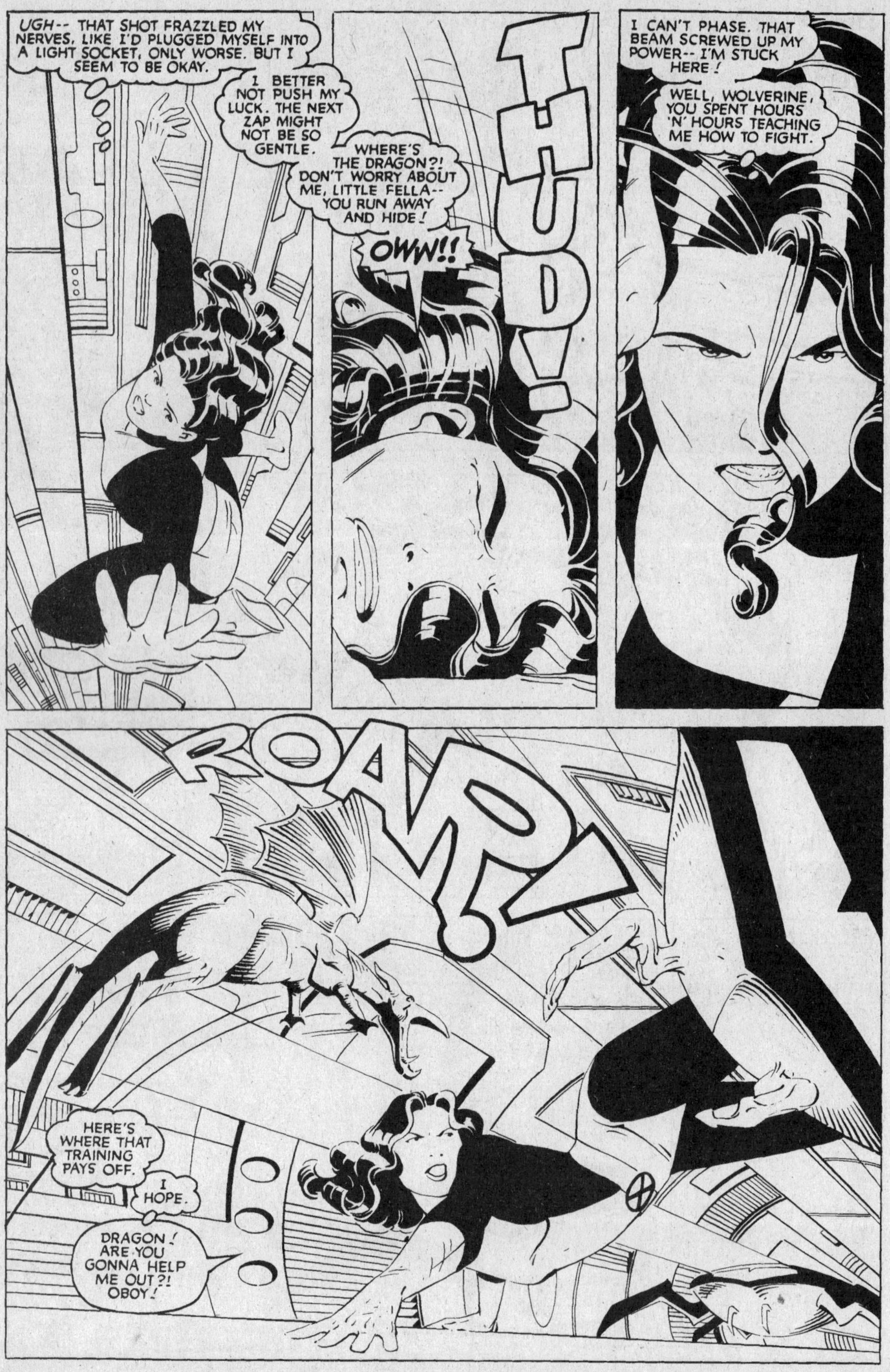
UGH-- THAT SHOT FRAZZLED MY NERVES, LIKE I'D PLUGGED MYSELF INTO A LIGHT SOCKET, ONLY WORSE. BUT I SEEM TO BE OKAY.
I BETTER NOT PUSH MY LUCK. THE NEXT ZAP MIGHT NOT BE SO GENTLE.
WHERE'S THE DRAGON?! DON'T WORRY ABOUT ME, LITTLE FELLA-- YOU RUN AWAY AND HIDE!
THUD!
OWW!!
I CAN'T PHASE. THAT BEAM SCREWED UP MY POWER-- I'M STUCK HERE!
WELL, WOLVERINE, YOU SPENT HOURS 'N' HOURS TEACHING ME HOW TO FIGHT.
ROAR!
HERE'S WHERE THAT TRAINING PAYS OFF.
I HOPE.
DRAGON! ARE YOU GONNA HELP ME OUT?! OBOY!

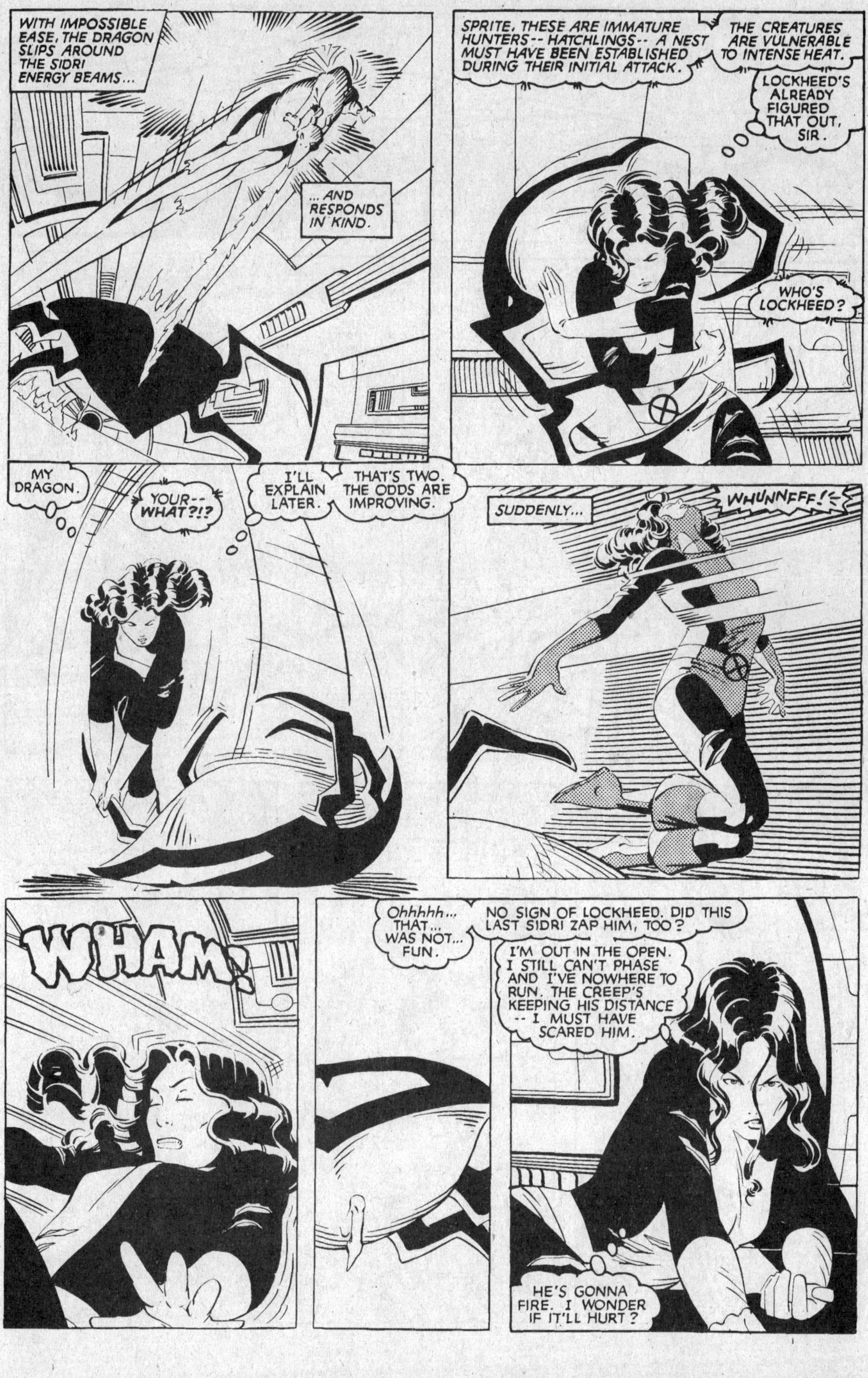
WITH IMPOSSIBLE EASE, THE DRAGON SLIPS AROUND THE SIDRI ENERGY BEAMS...
...AND RESPONDS IN KIND.
SPRITE, THESE ARE IMMATURE HUNTERS-- HATCHLINGS-- A NEST MUST HAVE BEEN ESTABLISHED DURING THEIR INITIAL ATTACK.
THE CREATURES ARE VULNERABLE TO INTENSE HEAT.
LOCKHEED'S ALREADY FIGURED THAT OUT, SIR.
WHO'S LOCKHEED?
MY DRAGON.
YOUR-- WHAT?!?
I'LL EXPLAIN LATER.
THAT'S TWO. THE ODDS ARE IMPROVING.
SUDDENLY...
WHUNNFFF!
WHAM!
Ohhhhh... THAT... WAS NOT... FUN.
NO SIGN OF LOCKHEED. DID THIS LAST SIDRI ZAP HIM, TOO?
I'M OUT IN THE OPEN. I STILL CAN'T PHASE AND I'VE NOWHERE TO RUN. THE CREEP'S KEEPING HIS DISTANCE -- I MUST HAVE SCARED HIM.
HE'S GONNA FIRE. I WONDER IF IT'LL HURT?

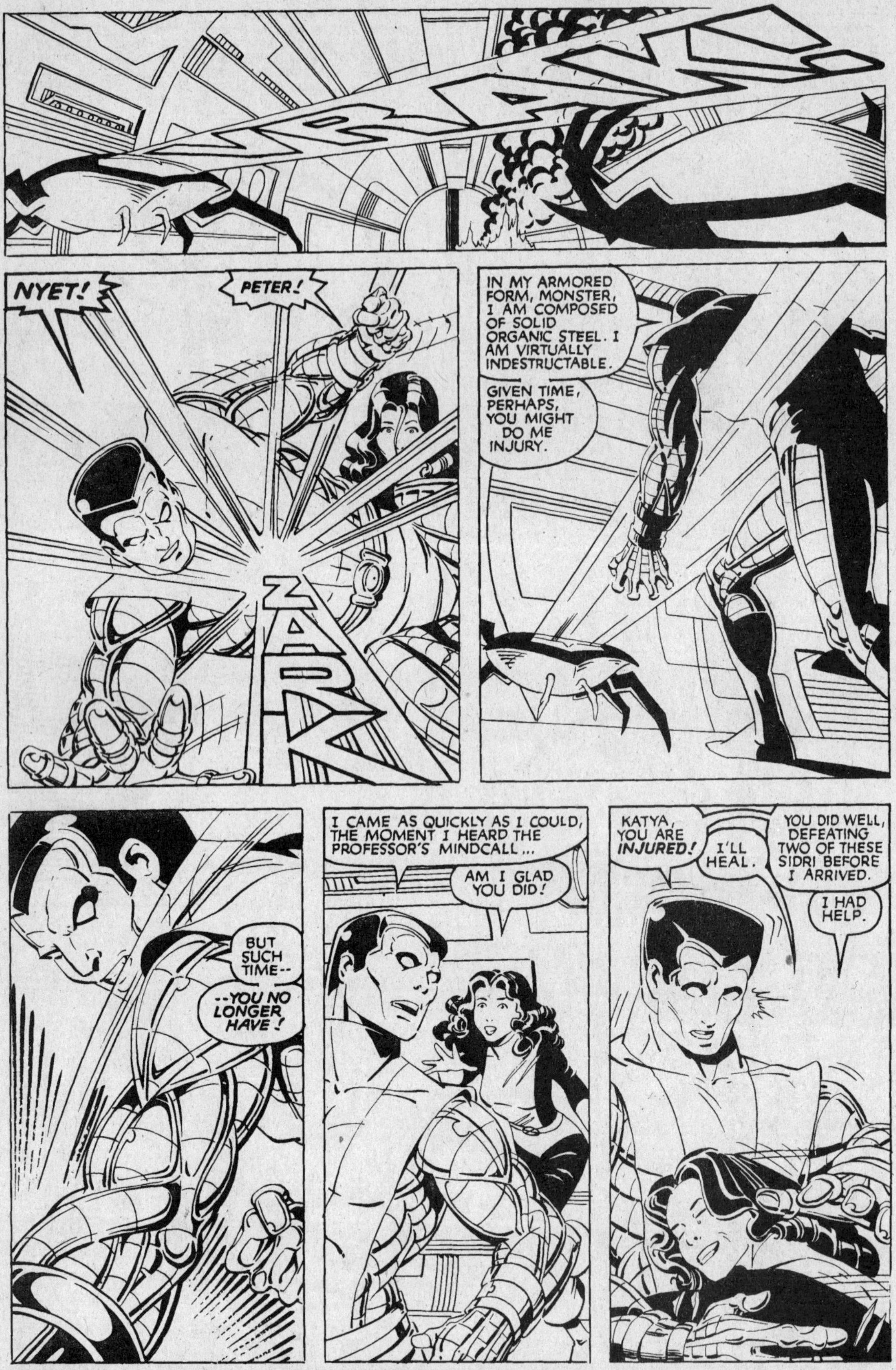
NYET!
PETER!
IN MY ARMORED FORM, MONSTER, I AM COMPOSED OF SOLID ORGANIC STEEL. I AM VIRTUALLY INDESTRUCTABLE.
GIVEN TIME, PERHAPS, YOU MIGHT DO ME INJURY.
BUT SUCH TIME--
--YOU NO LONGER HAVE!
I CAME AS QUICKLY AS I COULD, THE MOMENT I HEARD THE PROFESSOR'S MINDCALL...
AM I GLAD YOU DID!
KATYA, YOU ARE INJURED!
I'LL HEAL.
YOU DID WELL, DEFEATING TWO OF THESE SIDRI BEFORE I ARRIVED.
I HAD HELP.

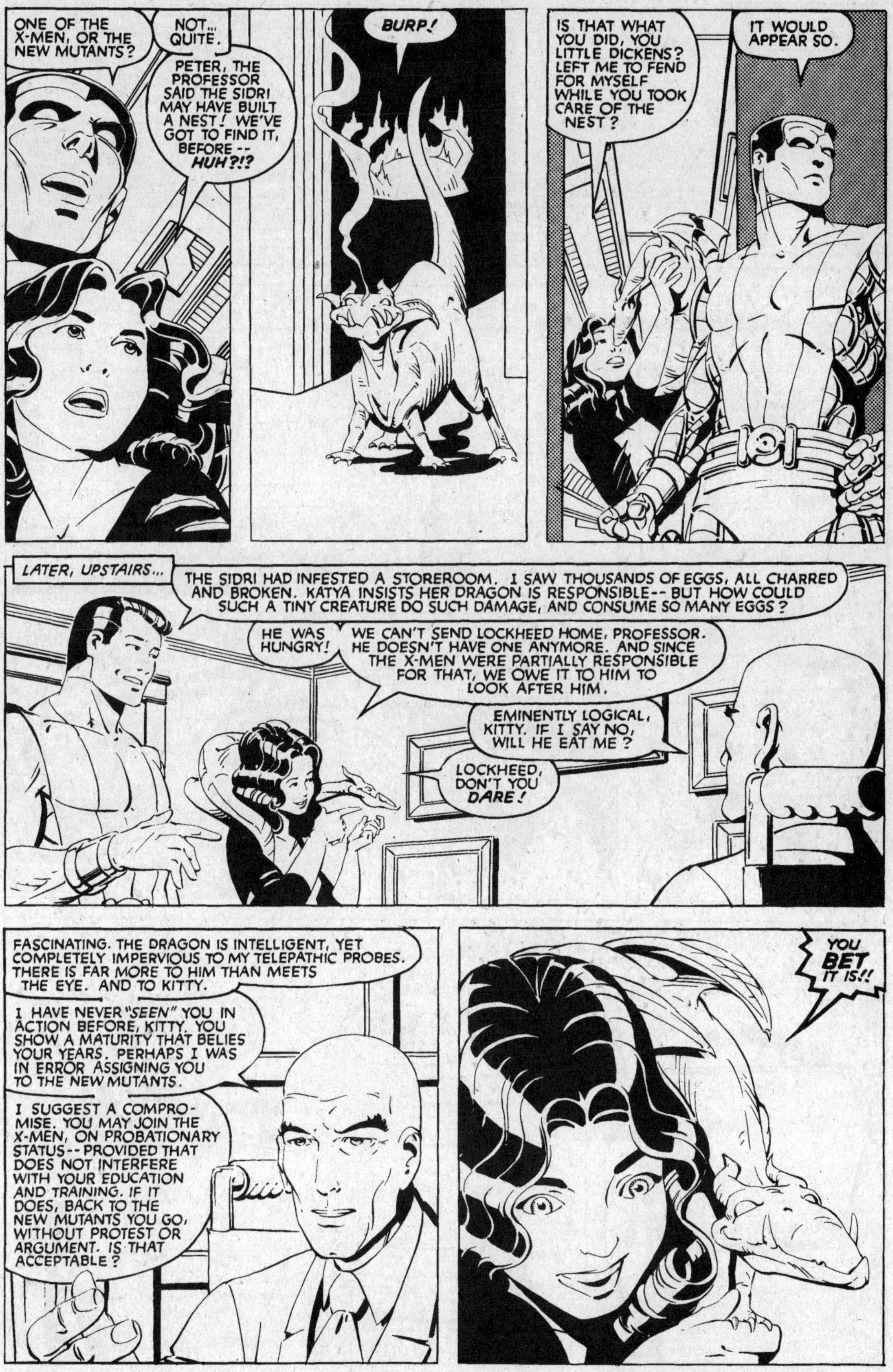
ONE OF THE X-MEN, OR THE NEW MUTANTS?
NOT... QUITE.
PETER, THE PROFESSOR SAID THE SIDRI MAY HAVE BUILT A NEST! WE'VE GOT TO FIND IT, BEFORE -- HUH?!?
BURP!
IS THAT WHAT YOU DID, YOU LITTLE DICKENS? LEFT ME TO FEND FOR MYSELF WHILE YOU TOOK CARE OF THE NEST?
IT WOULD APPEAR SO.
LATER, UPSTAIRS...
THE SIDRI HAD INFESTED A STOREROOM. I SAW THOUSANDS OF EGGS, ALL CHARRED AND BROKEN. KATYA INSISTS HER DRAGON IS RESPONSIBLE-- BUT HOW COULD SUCH A TINY CREATURE DO SUCH DAMAGE, AND CONSUME SO MANY EGGS?
HE WAS HUNGRY!
WE CAN'T SEND LOCKHEED HOME, PROFESSOR. HE DOESN'T HAVE ONE ANYMORE. AND SINCE THE X-MEN WERE PARTIALLY RESPONSIBLE FOR THAT, WE OWE IT TO HIM TO LOOK AFTER HIM.
EMINENTLY LOGICAL, KITTY. IF I SAY NO, WILL HE EAT ME?
LOCKHEED, DON'T YOU DARE!
FASCINATING. THE DRAGON IS INTELLIGENT, YET COMPLETELY IMPERVIOUS TO MY TELEPATHIC PROBES. THERE IS FAR MORE TO HIM THAN MEETS THE EYE. AND TO KITTY.
I HAVE NEVER "SEEN" YOU IN ACTION BEFORE, KITTY. YOU SHOW A MATURITY THAT BELIES YOUR YEARS. PERHAPS I WAS IN ERROR ASSIGNING YOU TO THE NEW MUTANTS.
I SUGGEST A COMPROMISE. YOU MAY JOIN THE X-MEN, ON PROBATIONARY STATUS-- PROVIDED THAT DOES NOT INTERFERE WITH YOUR EDUCATION AND TRAINING. IF IT DOES, BACK TO THE NEW MUTANTS YOU GO, WITHOUT PROTEST OR ARGUMENT. IS THAT ACCEPTABLE?
YOU BET IT IS!!

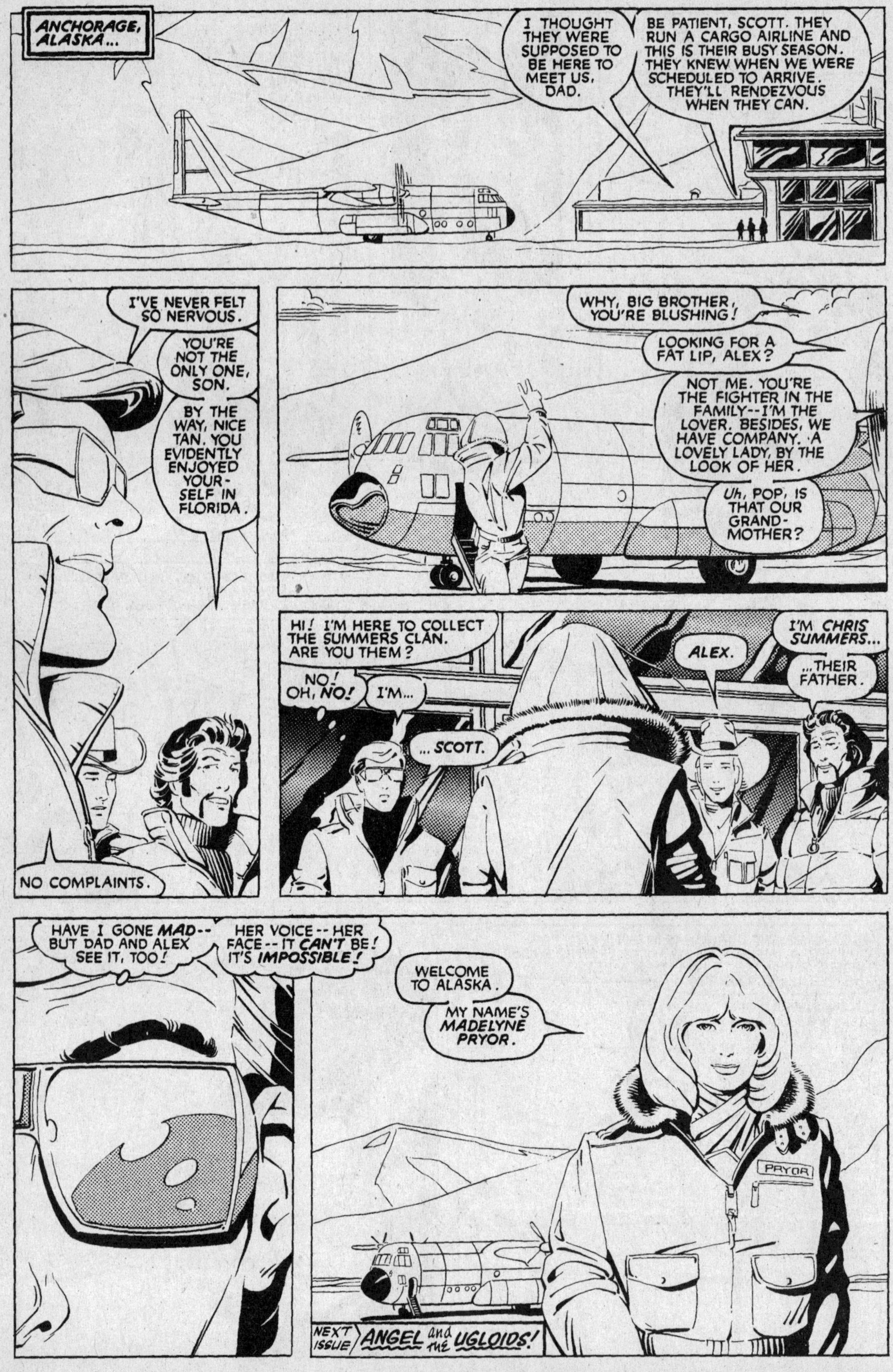

ANCHORAGE, ALASKA...
I THOUGHT THEY WERE SUPPOSED TO BE HERE TO MEET US, DAD.
BE PATIENT, SCOTT. THEY RUN A CARGO AIRLINE AND THIS IS THEIR BUSY SEASON. THEY KNEW WHEN WE WERE SCHEDULED TO ARRIVE. THEY'LL RENDEZVOUS WHEN THEY CAN.
I'VE NEVER FELT SO NERVOUS.
YOU'RE NOT THE ONLY ONE, SON.
BY THE WAY, NICE TAN. YOU EVIDENTLY ENJOYED YOURSELF IN FLORIDA.
NO COMPLAINTS.
WHY, BIG BROTHER, YOU'RE BLUSHING!
LOOKING FOR A FAT LIP, ALEX?
NOT ME. YOU'RE THE FIGHTER IN THE FAMILY--I'M THE LOVER. BESIDES, WE HAVE COMPANY. A LOVELY LADY, BY THE LOOK OF HER.
Uh, POP, IS THAT OUR GRANDMOTHER?
HI! I'M HERE TO COLLECT THE SUMMERS CLAN. ARE YOU THEM?
NO! OH, NO!
I'M...
...SCOTT.
ALEX.
I'M CHRIS SUMMERS...
...THEIR FATHER.
HAVE I GONE MAD-- BUT DAD AND ALEX SEE IT, TOO!
HER VOICE--HER FACE--IT CAN'T BE! IT'S IMPOSSIBLE!
WELCOME TO ALASKA.
MY NAME'S MADELYNE PRYOR.
PRYOR
NEXT ISSUE ANGEL and the UGLOIDS!

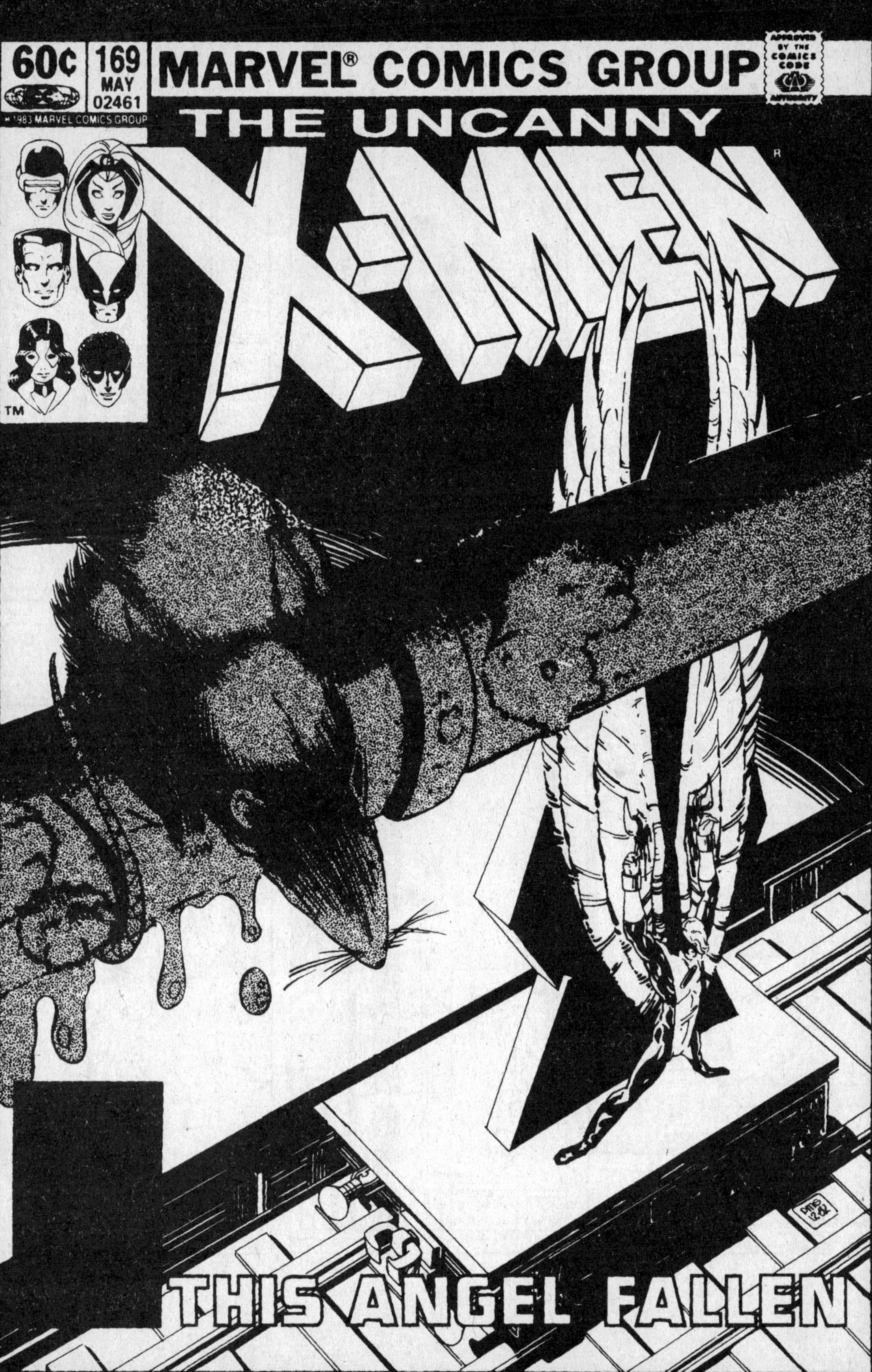
60¢
169
MAY
02461
MARVEL® COMICS GROUP
APPROVED BY THE COMICS CODE AUTHORITY
© 1983 MARVEL COMICS GROUP
THE UNCANNY
X-MEN
TM
THIS ANGEL FALLEN

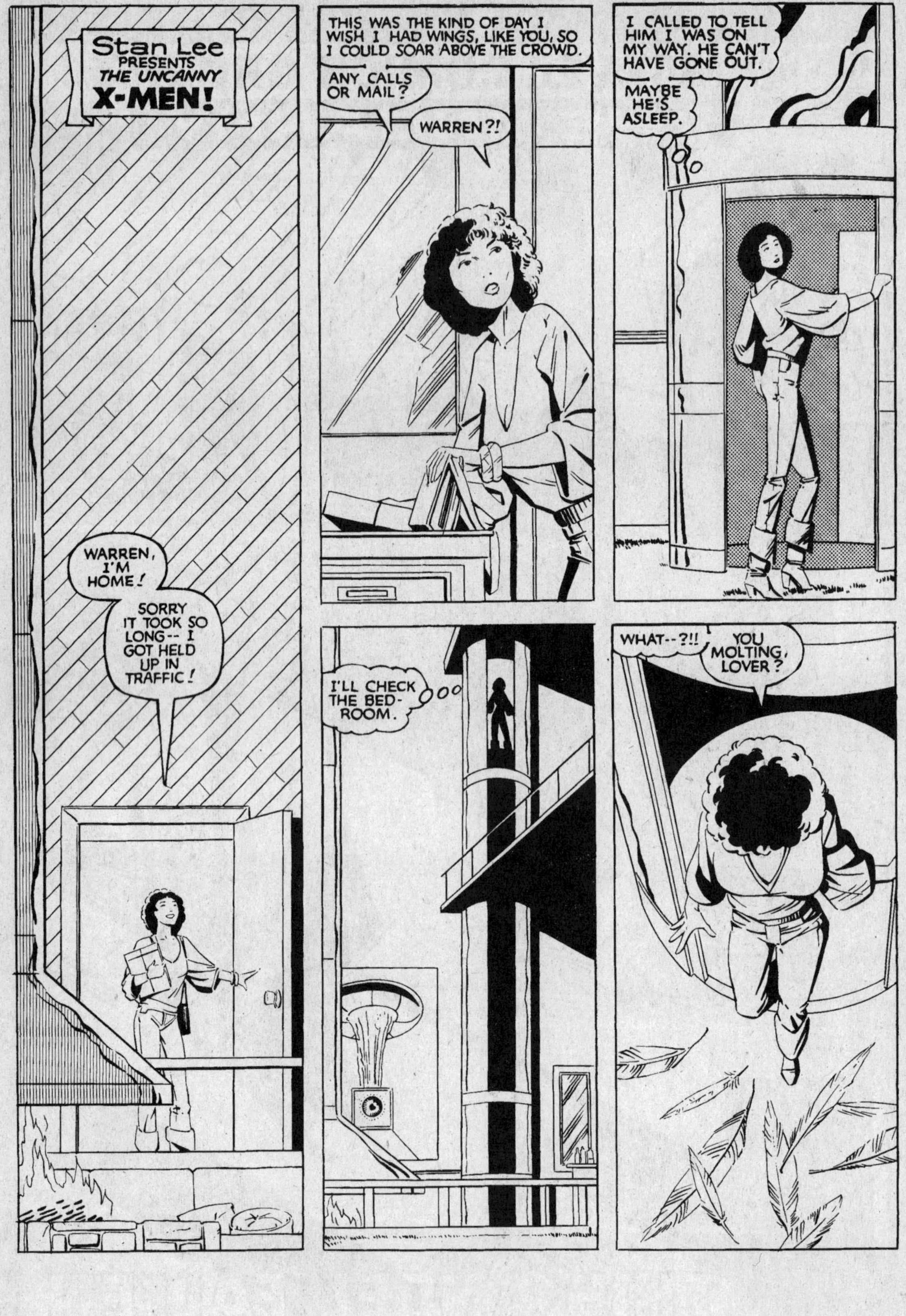
Stan Lee PRESENTS THE UNCANNY X-MEN!
WARREN, I'M HOME!
SORRY IT TOOK SO LONG-- I GOT HELD UP IN TRAFFIC!
THIS WAS THE KIND OF DAY I WISH I HAD WINGS, LIKE YOU, SO I COULD SOAR ABOVE THE CROWD.
ANY CALLS OR MAIL?
WARREN?!
I CALLED TO TELL HIM I WAS ON MY WAY. HE CAN'T HAVE GONE OUT.
MAYBE HE'S ASLEEP.
I'LL CHECK THE BED-ROOM.
WHAT--?!!
YOU MOLTING, LOVER?

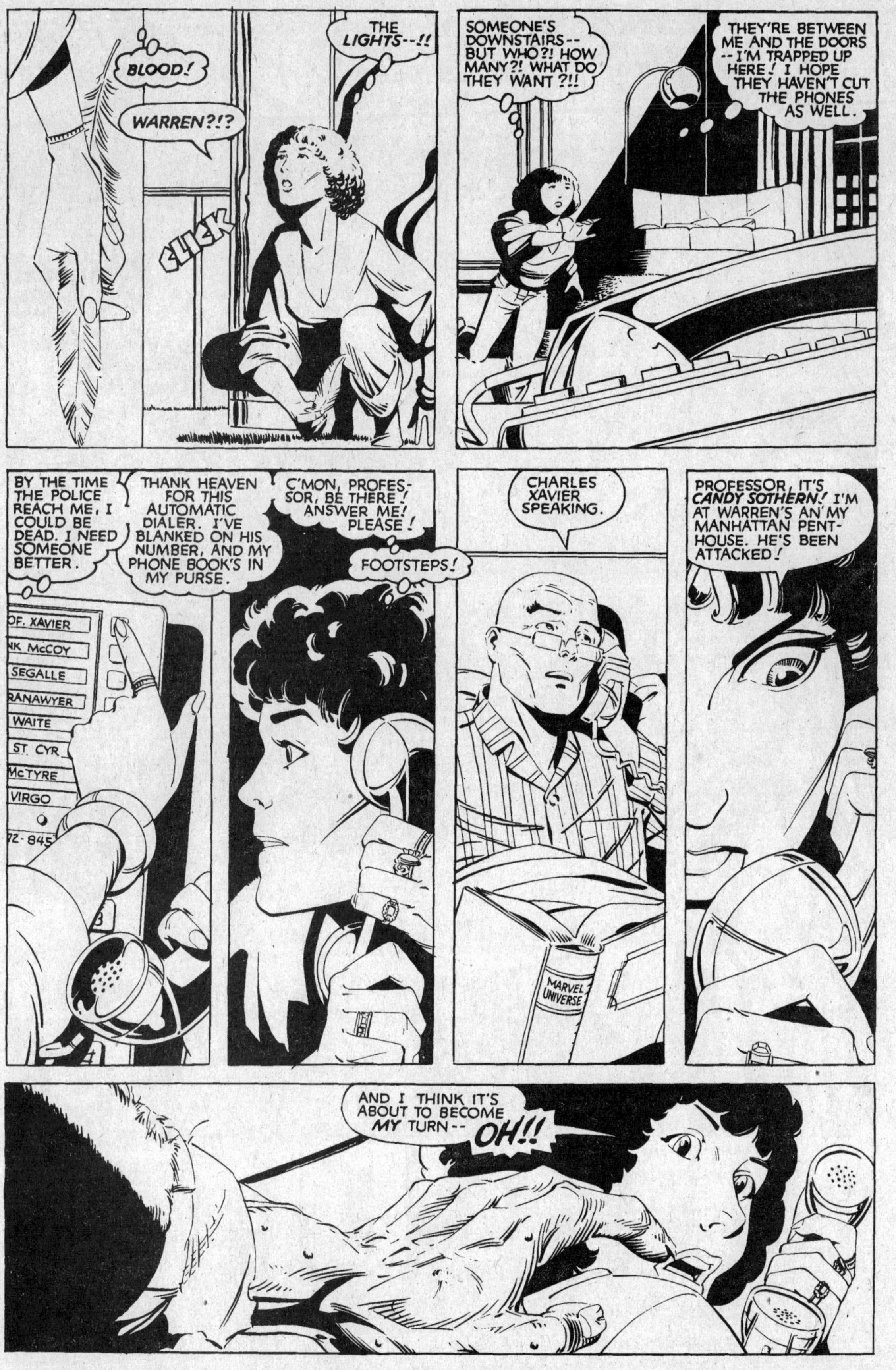
BLOOD!
WARREN?!?
CLICK
THE LIGHTS--!!
SOMEONE'S DOWNSTAIRS-- BUT WHO?! HOW MANY?! WHAT DO THEY WANT?!!
THEY'RE BETWEEN ME AND THE DOORS -- I'M TRAPPED UP HERE! I HOPE THEY HAVEN'T CUT THE PHONES AS WELL.
BY THE TIME THE POLICE REACH ME, I COULD BE DEAD. I NEED SOMEONE BETTER.
THANK HEAVEN FOR THIS AUTOMATIC DIALER. I'VE BLANKED ON HIS NUMBER, AND MY PHONE BOOK'S IN MY PURSE.
OF. XAVIER
NK McCOY
SEGALLE
RANAWYER
WAITE
ST CYR
McTYRE
VIRGO
C'MON, PROFESSOR, BE THERE! ANSWER ME! PLEASE!
FOOTSTEPS!
CHARLES XAVIER SPEAKING.
MARVEL UNIVERSE
PROFESSOR, IT'S CANDY SOTHERN! I'M AT WARREN'S AN' MY MANHATTAN PENTHOUSE. HE'S BEEN ATTACKED!
AND I THINK IT'S ABOUT TO BECOME MY TURN-- OH!!

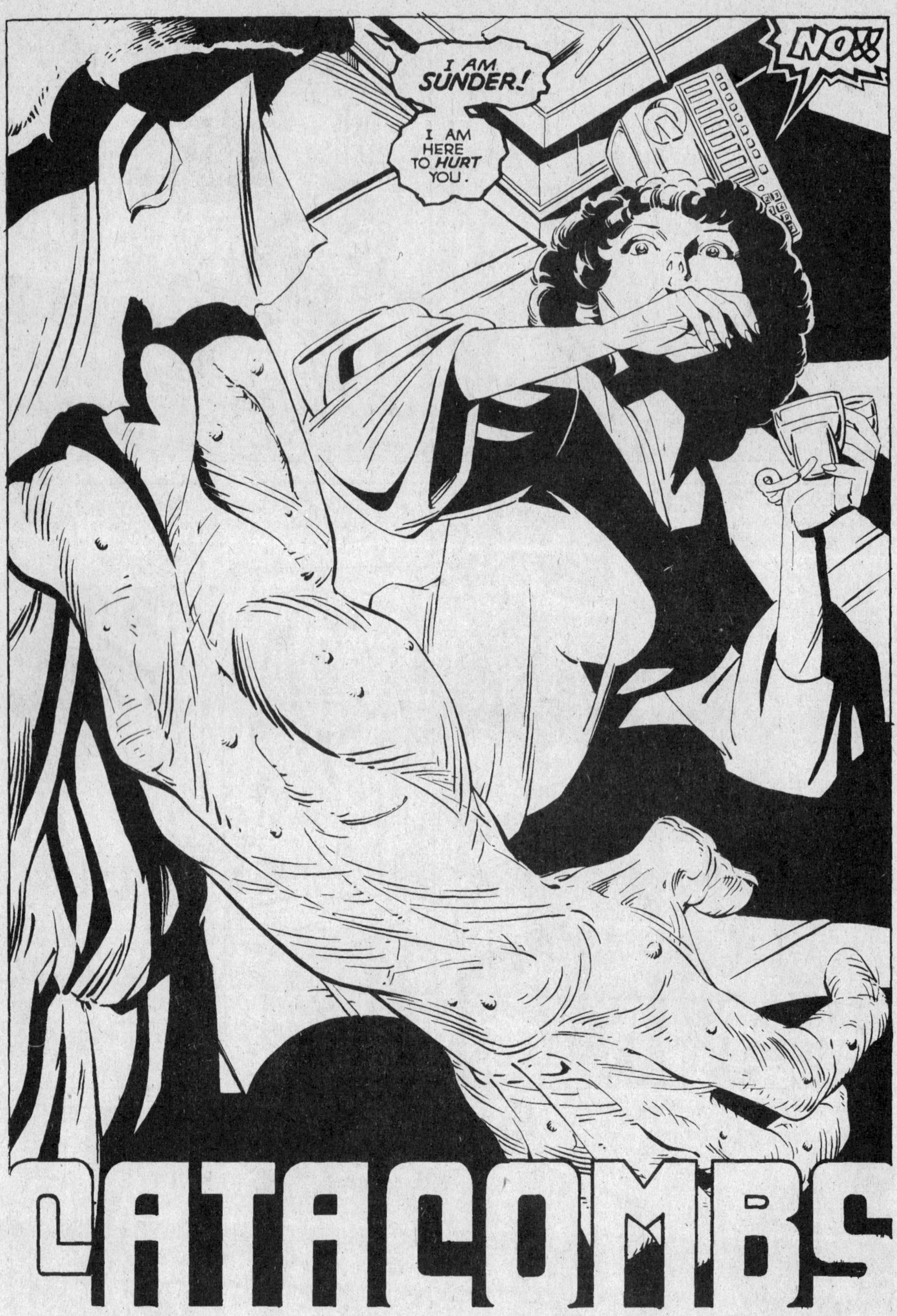
I AM SUNDER!
I AM HERE TO HURT YOU.
NO!!
CATACOMBS

CHRIS CLAREMONT *WRITER* · PAUL SMITH *PENCILLER* · BOB WIACEK *INKER* · BOB SHAREN *COLORIST* · TOM ORZECHOWSKI *LETTERER* · LOUISE JONES *EDITOR* · JIM SHOOTER *EDITOR-IN-CHIEF*

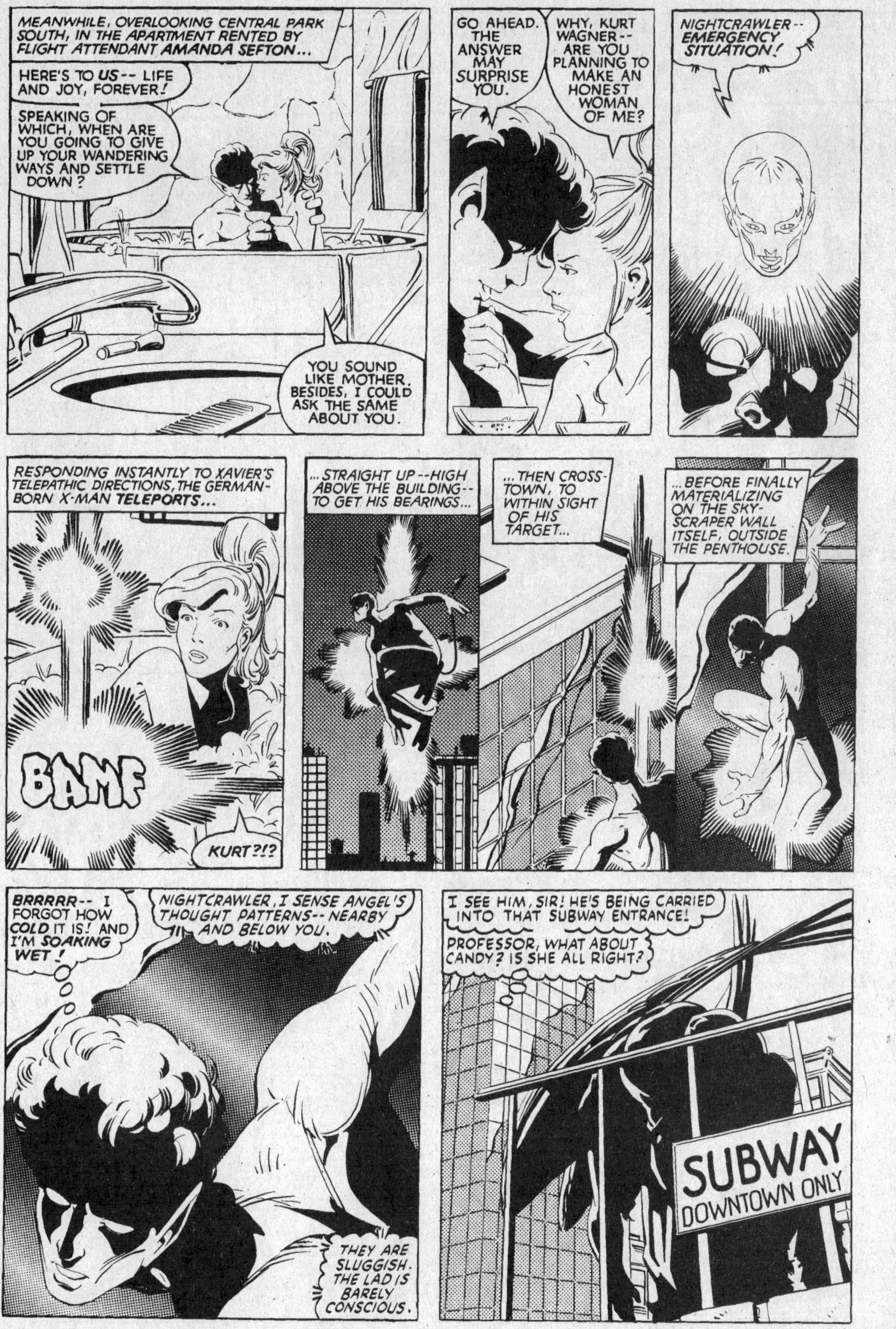
MEANWHILE, OVERLOOKING CENTRAL PARK SOUTH, IN THE APARTMENT RENTED BY FLIGHT ATTENDANT AMANDA SEFTON...
HERE'S TO US -- LIFE AND JOY, FOREVER!
SPEAKING OF WHICH, WHEN ARE YOU GOING TO GIVE UP YOUR WANDERING WAYS AND SETTLE DOWN?
YOU SOUND LIKE MOTHER. BESIDES, I COULD ASK THE SAME ABOUT YOU.
WHY, KURT WAGNER -- ARE YOU PLANNING TO MAKE AN HONEST WOMAN OF ME?
GO AHEAD. THE ANSWER MAY SURPRISE YOU.
NIGHTCRAWLER -- EMERGENCY SITUATION!
RESPONDING INSTANTLY TO XAVIER'S TELEPATHIC DIRECTIONS, THE GERMAN-BORN X-MAN TELEPORTS...
BAMF
KURT?!?
...STRAIGHT UP -- HIGH ABOVE THE BUILDING -- TO GET HIS BEARINGS...
...THEN CROSS-TOWN, TO WITHIN SIGHT OF HIS TARGET...
...BEFORE FINALLY MATERIALIZING ON THE SKY-SCRAPER WALL ITSELF, OUTSIDE THE PENTHOUSE.
BRRRRR -- I FORGOT HOW COLD IT IS! AND I'M SOAKING WET!
NIGHTCRAWLER, I SENSE ANGEL'S THOUGHT PATTERNS -- NEARBY AND BELOW YOU.
THEY ARE SLUGGISH. THE LAD IS BARELY CONSCIOUS.
I SEE HIM, SIR! HE'S BEING CARRIED INTO THAT SUBWAY ENTRANCE!
PROFESSOR, WHAT ABOUT CANDY? IS SHE ALL RIGHT?
SUBWAY
DOWNTOWN ONLY

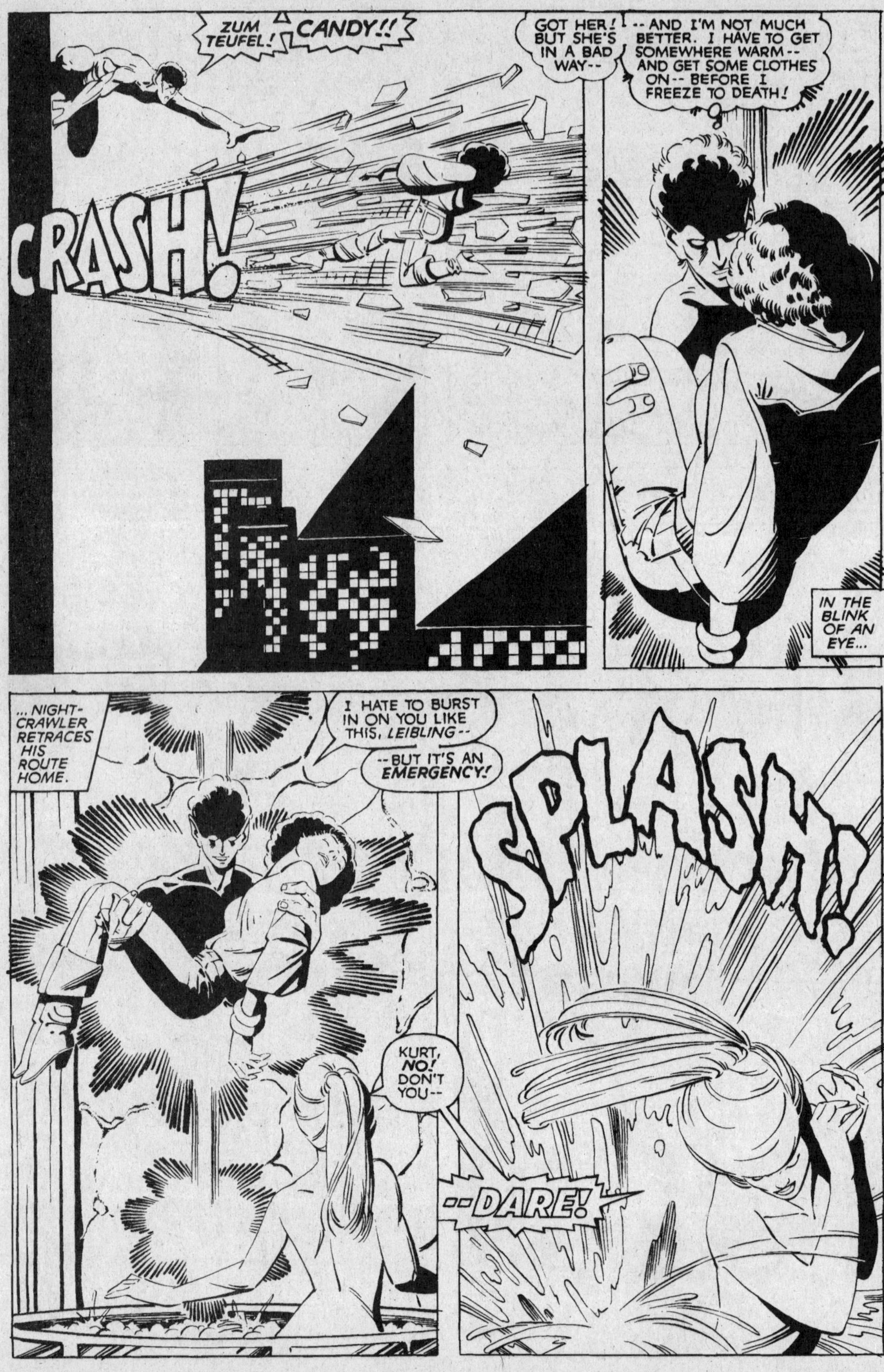
ZUM TEUFEL!
CANDY!!
CRASH!
GOT HER! BUT SHE'S IN A BAD WAY--
--AND I'M NOT MUCH BETTER. I HAVE TO GET SOMEWHERE WARM--AND GET SOME CLOTHES ON--BEFORE I FREEZE TO DEATH!
IN THE BLINK OF AN EYE...
...NIGHT-CRAWLER RETRACES HIS ROUTE HOME.
I HATE TO BURST IN ON YOU LIKE THIS, *LEIBLING*--
--BUT IT'S AN *EMERGENCY!*
KURT, **NO!** DON'T YOU--
--DARE!
SPLASH!

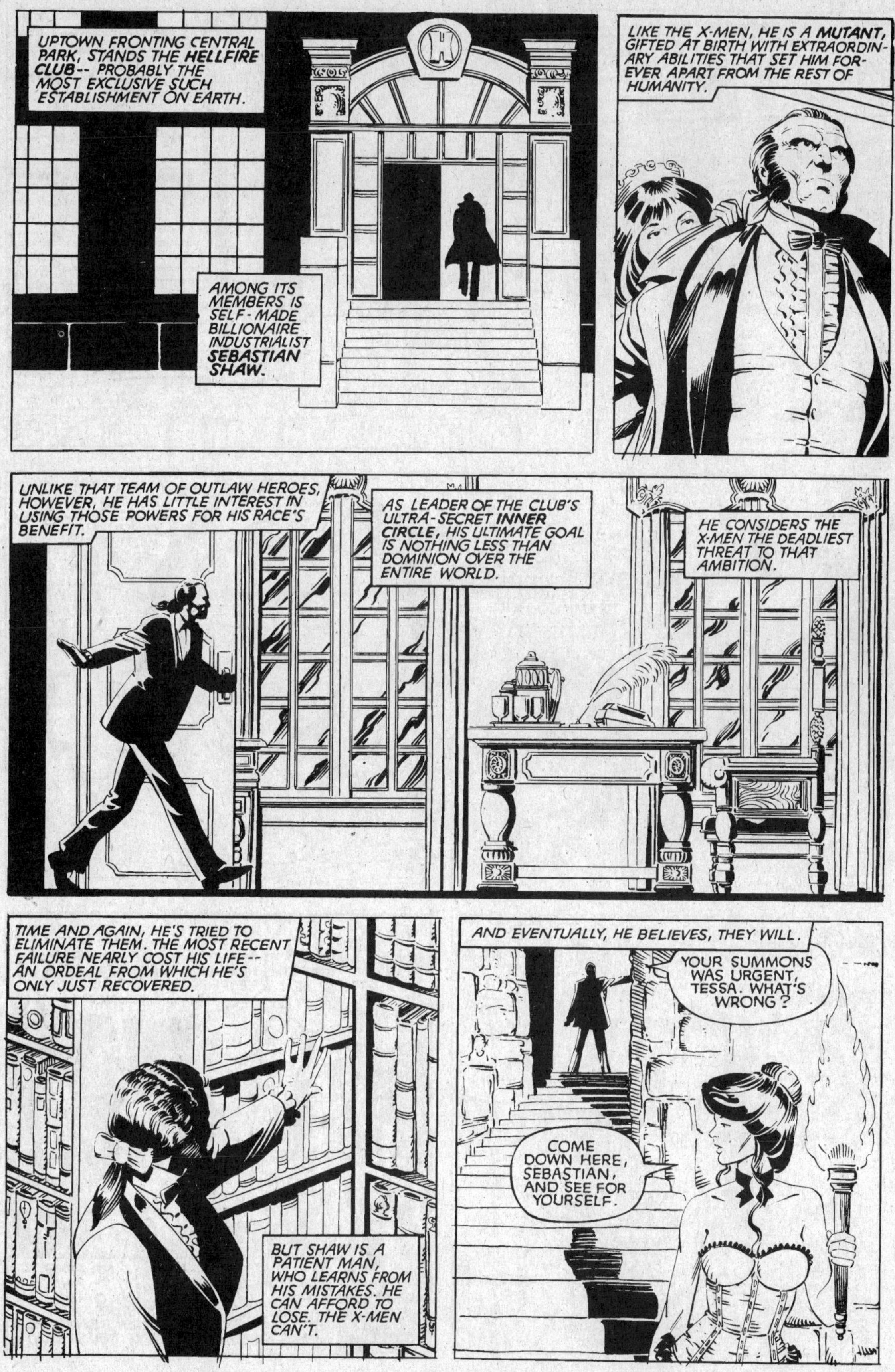
UPTOWN FRONTING CENTRAL PARK, STANDS THE HELLFIRE CLUB-- PROBABLY THE MOST EXCLUSIVE SUCH ESTABLISHMENT ON EARTH.
AMONG ITS MEMBERS IS SELF-MADE BILLIONAIRE INDUSTRIALIST SEBASTIAN SHAW.
LIKE THE X-MEN, HE IS A MUTANT, GIFTED AT BIRTH WITH EXTRAORDINARY ABILITIES THAT SET HIM FOREVER APART FROM THE REST OF HUMANITY.
UNLIKE THAT TEAM OF OUTLAW HEROES, HOWEVER, HE HAS LITTLE INTEREST IN USING THOSE POWERS FOR HIS RACE'S BENEFIT.
AS LEADER OF THE CLUB'S ULTRA-SECRET INNER CIRCLE, HIS ULTIMATE GOAL IS NOTHING LESS THAN DOMINION OVER THE ENTIRE WORLD.
HE CONSIDERS THE X-MEN THE DEADLIEST THREAT TO THAT AMBITION.
TIME AND AGAIN, HE'S TRIED TO ELIMINATE THEM. THE MOST RECENT FAILURE NEARLY COST HIS LIFE-- AN ORDEAL FROM WHICH HE'S ONLY JUST RECOVERED.
BUT SHAW IS A PATIENT MAN, WHO LEARNS FROM HIS MISTAKES. HE CAN AFFORD TO LOSE. THE X-MEN CAN'T.
AND EVENTUALLY, HE BELIEVES, THEY WILL.
YOUR SUMMONS WAS URGENT, TESSA. WHAT'S WRONG?
COME DOWN HERE, SEBASTIAN, AND SEE FOR YOURSELF.

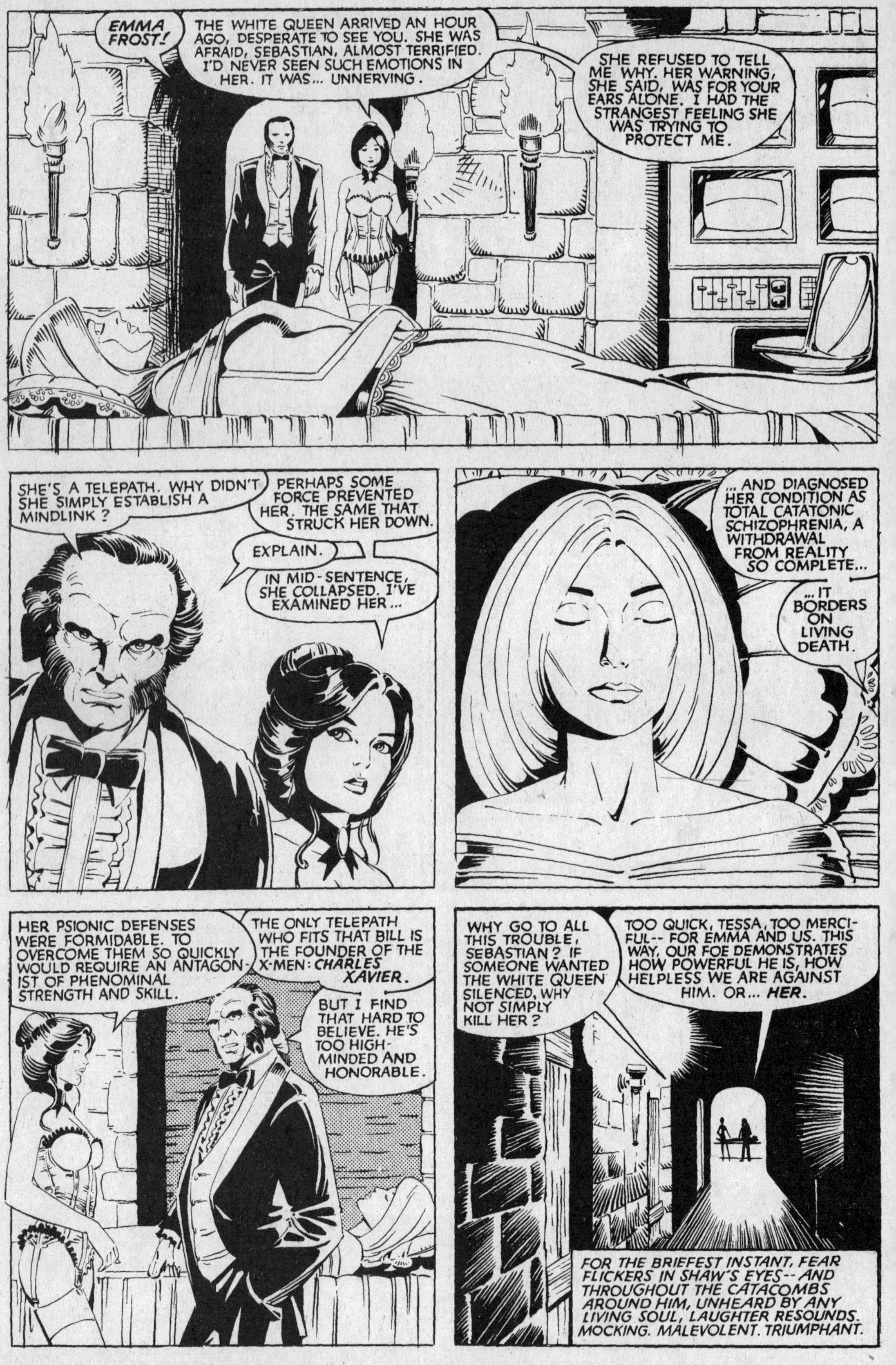
EMMA FROST!
THE WHITE QUEEN ARRIVED AN HOUR AGO, DESPERATE TO SEE YOU. SHE WAS AFRAID, SEBASTIAN, ALMOST TERRIFIED. I'D NEVER SEEN SUCH EMOTIONS IN HER. IT WAS... UNNERVING.
SHE REFUSED TO TELL ME WHY. HER WARNING, SHE SAID, WAS FOR YOUR EARS ALONE. I HAD THE STRANGEST FEELING SHE WAS TRYING TO PROTECT ME.
SHE'S A TELEPATH. WHY DIDN'T SHE SIMPLY ESTABLISH A MINDLINK?
PERHAPS SOME FORCE PREVENTED HER. THE SAME THAT STRUCK HER DOWN.
EXPLAIN.
IN MID-SENTENCE, SHE COLLAPSED. I'VE EXAMINED HER...
... AND DIAGNOSED HER CONDITION AS TOTAL CATATONIC SCHIZOPHRENIA, A WITHDRAWAL FROM REALITY SO COMPLETE...
... IT BORDERS ON LIVING DEATH.
HER PSIONIC DEFENSES WERE FORMIDABLE. TO OVERCOME THEM SO QUICKLY WOULD REQUIRE AN ANTAGONIST OF PHENOMINAL STRENGTH AND SKILL.
THE ONLY TELEPATH WHO FITS THAT BILL IS THE FOUNDER OF THE X-MEN: CHARLES XAVIER.
BUT I FIND THAT HARD TO BELIEVE. HE'S TOO HIGH-MINDED AND HONORABLE.
WHY GO TO ALL THIS TROUBLE, SEBASTIAN? IF SOMEONE WANTED THE WHITE QUEEN SILENCED, WHY NOT SIMPLY KILL HER?
TOO QUICK, TESSA, TOO MERCIFUL-- FOR EMMA AND US. THIS WAY, OUR FOE DEMONSTRATES HOW POWERFUL HE IS, HOW HELPLESS WE ARE AGAINST HIM. OR... HER.
FOR THE BRIEFEST INSTANT, FEAR FLICKERS IN SHAW'S EYES-- AND THROUGHOUT THE CATACOMBS AROUND HIM, UNHEARD BY ANY LIVING SOUL, LAUGHTER RESOUNDS. MOCKING. MALEVOLENT. TRIUMPHANT.

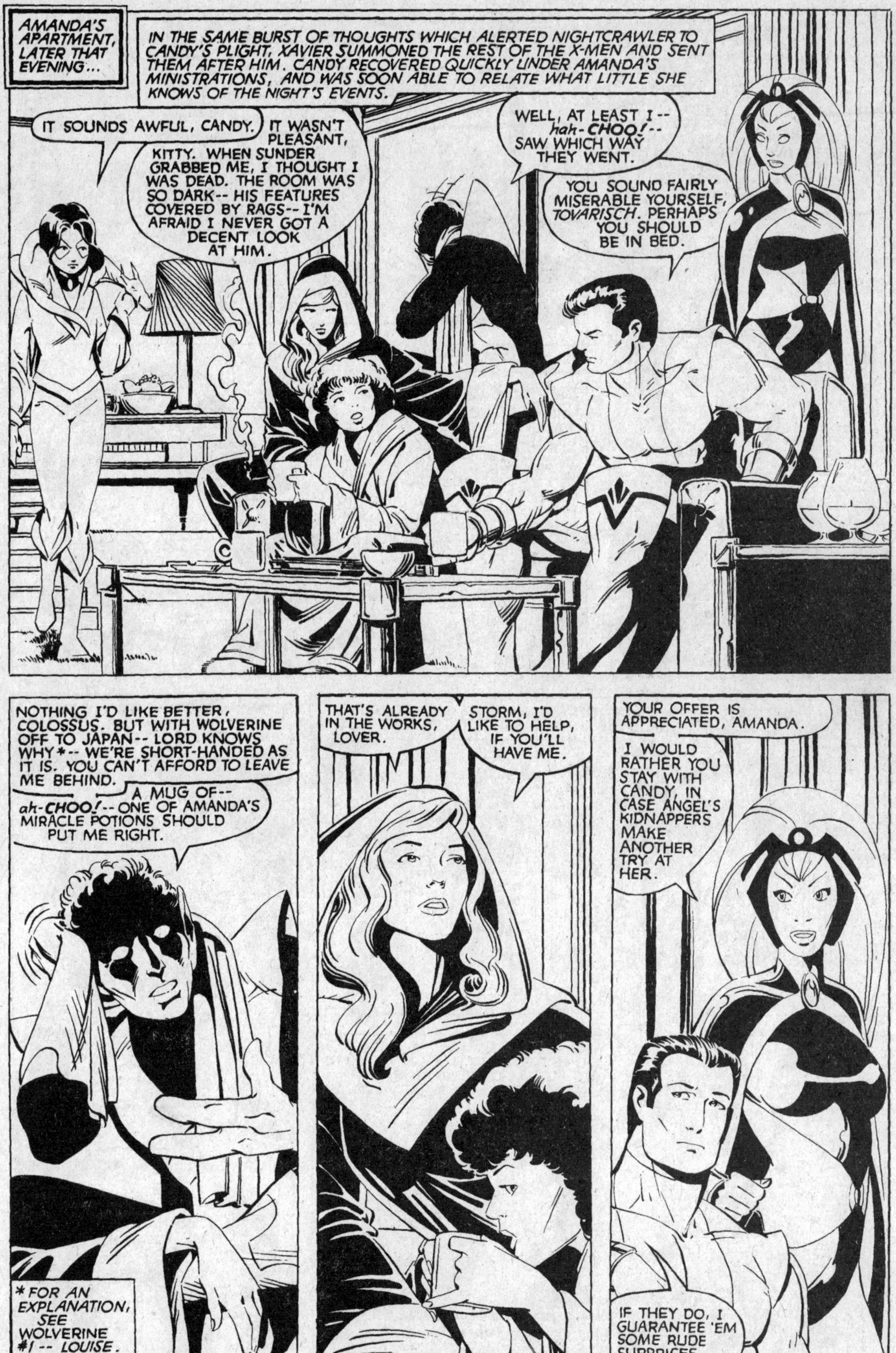
AMANDA'S APARTMENT, LATER THAT EVENING...
IN THE SAME BURST OF THOUGHTS WHICH ALERTED NIGHTCRAWLER TO CANDY'S PLIGHT, XAVIER SUMMONED THE REST OF THE X-MEN AND SENT THEM AFTER HIM. CANDY RECOVERED QUICKLY UNDER AMANDA'S MINISTRATIONS, AND WAS SOON ABLE TO RELATE WHAT LITTLE SHE KNOWS OF THE NIGHT'S EVENTS.
IT SOUNDS AWFUL, CANDY.
IT WASN'T PLEASANT, KITTY. WHEN SUNDER GRABBED ME, I THOUGHT I WAS DEAD. THE ROOM WAS SO DARK-- HIS FEATURES COVERED BY RAGS-- I'M AFRAID I NEVER GOT A DECENT LOOK AT HIM.
WELL, AT LEAST I -- hah-CHOO! -- SAW WHICH WAY THEY WENT.
YOU SOUND FAIRLY MISERABLE YOURSELF, TOVARISCH. PERHAPS YOU SHOULD BE IN BED.
NOTHING I'D LIKE BETTER, COLOSSUS. BUT WITH WOLVERINE OFF TO JAPAN-- LORD KNOWS WHY*-- WE'RE SHORT-HANDED AS IT IS. YOU CAN'T AFFORD TO LEAVE ME BEHIND.
A MUG OF-- ah-CHOO!-- ONE OF AMANDA'S MIRACLE POTIONS SHOULD PUT ME RIGHT.
* FOR AN EXPLANATION, SEE WOLVERINE #1 -- LOUISE.
THAT'S ALREADY IN THE WORKS, LOVER.
STORM, I'D LIKE TO HELP, IF YOU'LL HAVE ME.
YOUR OFFER IS APPRECIATED, AMANDA.
I WOULD RATHER YOU STAY WITH CANDY, IN CASE ANGEL'S KIDNAPPERS MAKE ANOTHER TRY AT HER.
IF THEY DO, I GUARANTEE 'EM SOME RUDE SURPRISES.

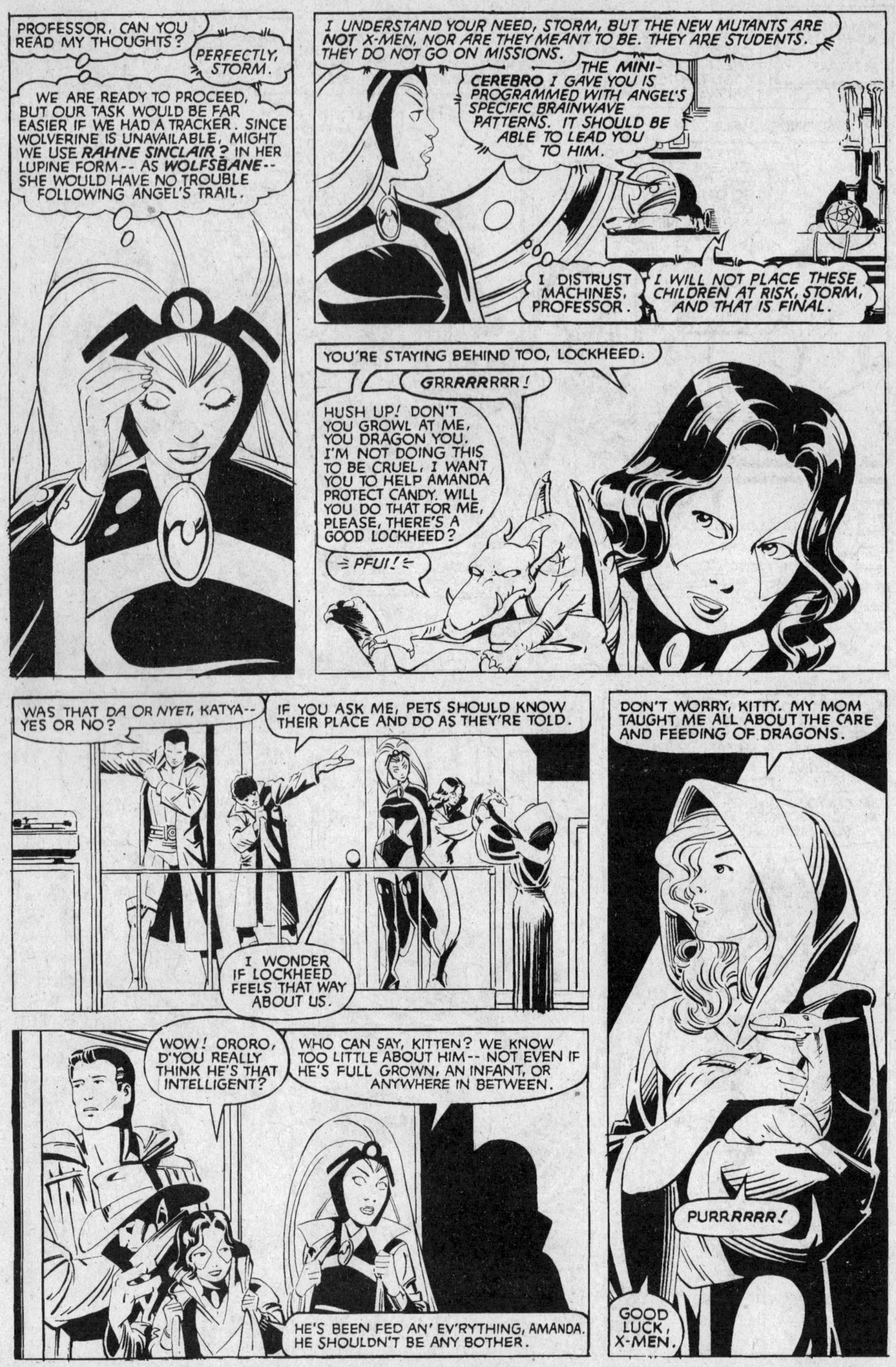
PROFESSOR, CAN YOU READ MY THOUGHTS?
PERFECTLY, STORM.
WE ARE READY TO PROCEED, BUT OUR TASK WOULD BE FAR EASIER IF WE HAD A TRACKER. SINCE WOLVERINE IS UNAVAILABLE, MIGHT WE USE RAHNE SINCLAIR? IN HER LUPINE FORM -- AS WOLFSBANE -- SHE WOULD HAVE NO TROUBLE FOLLOWING ANGEL'S TRAIL.
I UNDERSTAND YOUR NEED, STORM, BUT THE NEW MUTANTS ARE NOT X-MEN, NOR ARE THEY MEANT TO BE. THEY ARE STUDENTS. THEY DO NOT GO ON MISSIONS.
THE MINI-CEREBRO I GAVE YOU IS PROGRAMMED WITH ANGEL'S SPECIFIC BRAINWAVE PATTERNS. IT SHOULD BE ABLE TO LEAD YOU TO HIM.
I DISTRUST MACHINES, PROFESSOR.
I WILL NOT PLACE THESE CHILDREN AT RISK, STORM, AND THAT IS FINAL.
YOU'RE STAYING BEHIND TOO, LOCKHEED.
GRRRRRRRR!
HUSH UP! DON'T YOU GROWL AT ME, YOU DRAGON YOU. I'M NOT DOING THIS TO BE CRUEL, I WANT YOU TO HELP AMANDA PROTECT CANDY. WILL YOU DO THAT FOR ME, PLEASE, THERE'S A GOOD LOCKHEED?
PFUI!
WAS THAT DA OR NYET, KATYA -- YES OR NO?
IF YOU ASK ME, PETS SHOULD KNOW THEIR PLACE AND DO AS THEY'RE TOLD.
I WONDER IF LOCKHEED FEELS THAT WAY ABOUT US.
WOW! ORORO, D'YOU REALLY THINK HE'S THAT INTELLIGENT?
WHO CAN SAY, KITTEN? WE KNOW TOO LITTLE ABOUT HIM -- NOT EVEN IF HE'S FULL GROWN, AN INFANT, OR ANYWHERE IN BETWEEN.
HE'S BEEN FED AN' EV'RYTHING, AMANDA. HE SHOULDN'T BE ANY BOTHER.
DON'T WORRY, KITTY. MY MOM TAUGHT ME ALL ABOUT THE CARE AND FEEDING OF DRAGONS.
PURRRRRR!
GOOD LUCK, X-MEN.

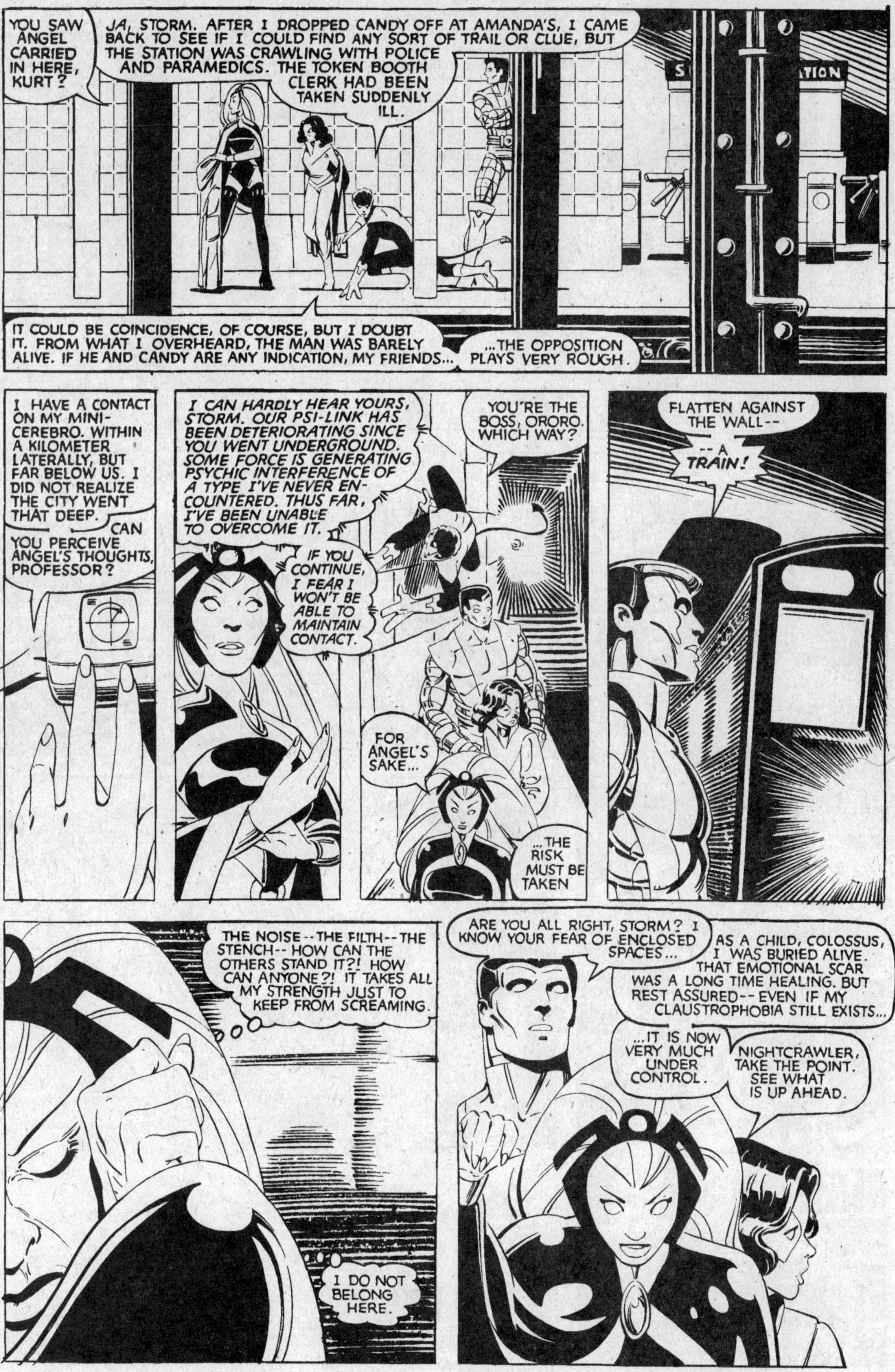

YOU SAW ANGEL CARRIED IN HERE, KURT?
JA, STORM. AFTER I DROPPED CANDY OFF AT AMANDA'S, I CAME BACK TO SEE IF I COULD FIND ANY SORT OF TRAIL OR CLUE, BUT THE STATION WAS CRAWLING WITH POLICE AND PARAMEDICS. THE TOKEN BOOTH CLERK HAD BEEN TAKEN SUDDENLY ILL.
IT COULD BE COINCIDENCE, OF COURSE, BUT I DOUBT IT. FROM WHAT I OVERHEARD, THE MAN WAS BARELY ALIVE. IF HE AND CANDY ARE ANY INDICATION, MY FRIENDS...
...THE OPPOSITION PLAYS VERY ROUGH.
I HAVE A CONTACT ON MY MINI-CEREBRO. WITHIN A KILOMETER LATERALLY, BUT FAR BELOW US. I DID NOT REALIZE THE CITY WENT THAT DEEP.
CAN YOU PERCEIVE ANGEL'S THOUGHTS, PROFESSOR?
I CAN HARDLY HEAR YOURS, STORM. OUR PSI-LINK HAS BEEN DETERIORATING SINCE YOU WENT UNDERGROUND. SOME FORCE IS GENERATING PSYCHIC INTERFERENCE OF A TYPE I'VE NEVER ENCOUNTERED. THUS FAR, I'VE BEEN UNABLE TO OVERCOME IT.
IF YOU CONTINUE, I FEAR I WON'T BE ABLE TO MAINTAIN CONTACT.
YOU'RE THE BOSS, ORORO. WHICH WAY?
FOR ANGEL'S SAKE...
...THE RISK MUST BE TAKEN
FLATTEN AGAINST THE WALL--
--A TRAIN!
THE NOISE--THE FILTH--THE STENCH--HOW CAN THE OTHERS STAND IT?! HOW CAN ANYONE?! IT TAKES ALL MY STRENGTH JUST TO KEEP FROM SCREAMING.
I DO NOT BELONG HERE.
ARE YOU ALL RIGHT, STORM? I KNOW YOUR FEAR OF ENCLOSED SPACES...
AS A CHILD, COLOSSUS, I WAS BURIED ALIVE. THAT EMOTIONAL SCAR WAS A LONG TIME HEALING. BUT REST ASSURED--EVEN IF MY CLAUSTROPHOBIA STILL EXISTS...
...IT IS NOW VERY MUCH UNDER CONTROL.
NIGHTCRAWLER, TAKE THE POINT. SEE WHAT IS UP AHEAD.

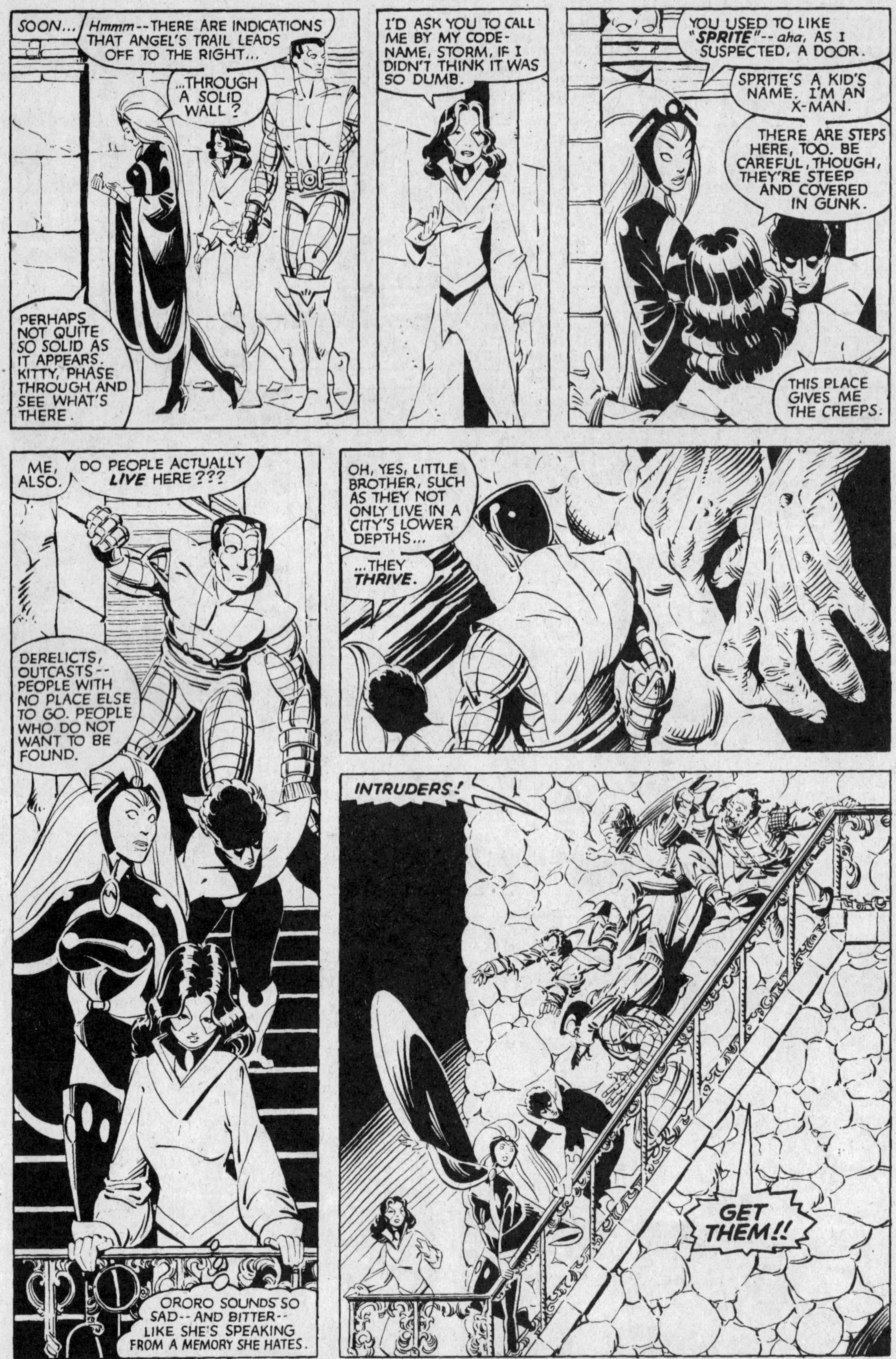
SOON...
Hmmm--THERE ARE INDICATIONS THAT ANGEL'S TRAIL LEADS OFF TO THE RIGHT...
...THROUGH A SOLID WALL?
PERHAPS NOT QUITE SO SOLID AS IT APPEARS. KITTY, PHASE THROUGH AND SEE WHAT'S THERE.
I'D ASK YOU TO CALL ME BY MY CODE-NAME, STORM, IF I DIDN'T THINK IT WAS SO DUMB.
YOU USED TO LIKE "SPRITE"-- aha, AS I SUSPECTED, A DOOR.
SPRITE'S A KID'S NAME. I'M AN X-MAN.
THERE ARE STEPS HERE, TOO. BE CAREFUL, THOUGH, THEY'RE STEEP AND COVERED IN GUNK.
THIS PLACE GIVES ME THE CREEPS.
ME, ALSO.
DO PEOPLE ACTUALLY LIVE HERE???
DERELICTS, OUTCASTS-- PEOPLE WITH NO PLACE ELSE TO GO. PEOPLE WHO DO NOT WANT TO BE FOUND.
ORORO SOUNDS SO SAD-- AND BITTER-- LIKE SHE'S SPEAKING FROM A MEMORY SHE HATES.
OH, YES, LITTLE BROTHER, SUCH AS THEY NOT ONLY LIVE IN A CITY'S LOWER DEPTHS...
...THEY THRIVE.
INTRUDERS!
GET THEM!!

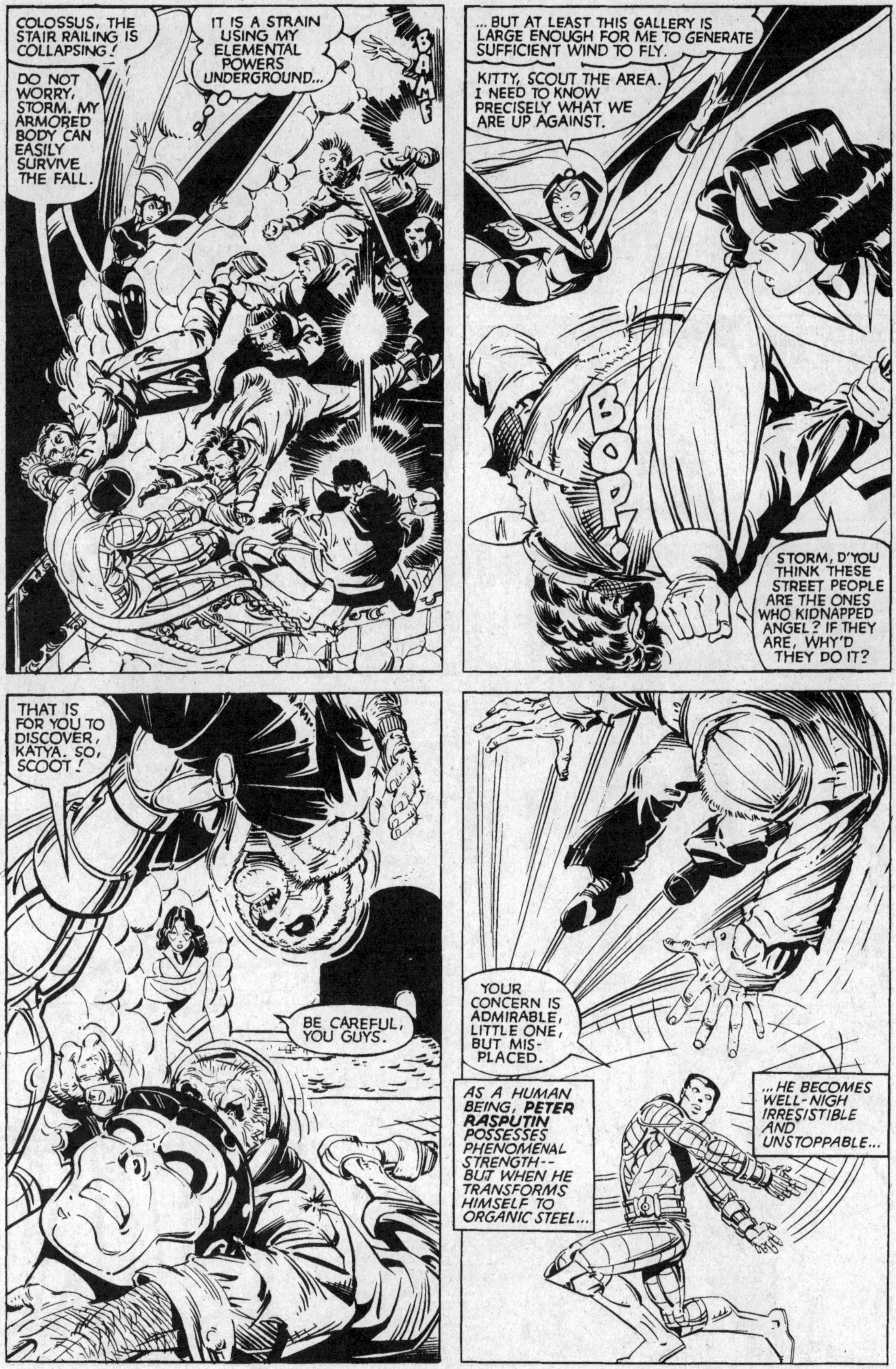

COLOSSUS, THE STAIR RAILING IS COLLAPSING!
IT IS A STRAIN USING MY ELEMENTAL POWERS UNDERGROUND...
BAMF
DO NOT WORRY, STORM. MY ARMORED BODY CAN EASILY SURVIVE THE FALL.
...BUT AT LEAST THIS GALLERY IS LARGE ENOUGH FOR ME TO GENERATE SUFFICIENT WIND TO FLY.
KITTY, SCOUT THE AREA. I NEED TO KNOW PRECISELY WHAT WE ARE UP AGAINST.
BOP!
STORM, D'YOU THINK THESE STREET PEOPLE ARE THE ONES WHO KIDNAPPED ANGEL? IF THEY ARE, WHY'D THEY DO IT?
THAT IS FOR YOU TO DISCOVER, KATYA. SO, SCOOT!
BE CAREFUL, YOU GUYS.
YOUR CONCERN IS ADMIRABLE, LITTLE ONE, BUT MISPLACED.
AS A HUMAN BEING, PETER RASPUTIN POSSESSES PHENOMENAL STRENGTH--BUT WHEN HE TRANSFORMS HIMSELF TO ORGANIC STEEL...
...HE BECOMES WELL-NIGH IRRESISTIBLE AND UNSTOPPABLE...

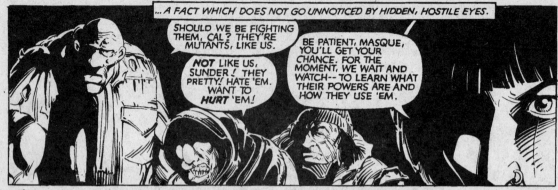

...A FACT WHICH DOES NOT GO UNNOTICED BY HIDDEN, HOSTILE EYES.

SHOULD WE BE FIGHTING THEM, CAL? THEY'RE MUTANTS, LIKE US.

NOT LIKE US, SUNDER! THEY PRETTY! HATE 'EM! WANT TO HURT 'EM!

BE PATIENT, MASQUE, YOU'LL GET YOUR CHANCE. FOR THE MOMENT, WE WAIT AND WATCH-- TO LEARN WHAT THEIR POWERS ARE AND HOW THEY USE 'EM.

WE'LL LURE OUR GUESTS DEEPER-- INTO THE ALLEY-- THEN WE'LL NAIL 'EM.

PAYDIRT! WOW-- FROM CANDY'S DESCRIPTION, THAT BIG CREEP HAS TO BE SUNDER. HE'S HUGE!

WHY AREN'T THEY JOINING THE FIGHT? ARE THEY PLANNING A TRAP?! I'LL EDGE CLOSER-- TO HEAR ALL I CAN-- BEFORE WARNING STORM.

A SCENT--

--GIRL, YOUNG, CLEAN--

--OUT-SIDER!

UH-OH! I'VE BEEN SPOTTED-- BUT HOW?!

PLAGUE-- SHE'S YOURS!

I DON'T KNOW IF THESE PEOPLE CAN HURT ME, BUT WITH NAMES LIKE THEIRS, I DON'T WANNA FIND OUT!

MY ARM-- I WAS PHASING, BUT IT TINGLED WHEN THAT OLD LADY PASSED THROUGH ME-- WHAT DID SHE DO TO IT?!!

I CAN'T TOUCH HER! THE GIRL'S A GHOST!

THAT WALL WON'T KEEP US FROM HER.

STAND ASIDE, PLAGUE!

SHUNK

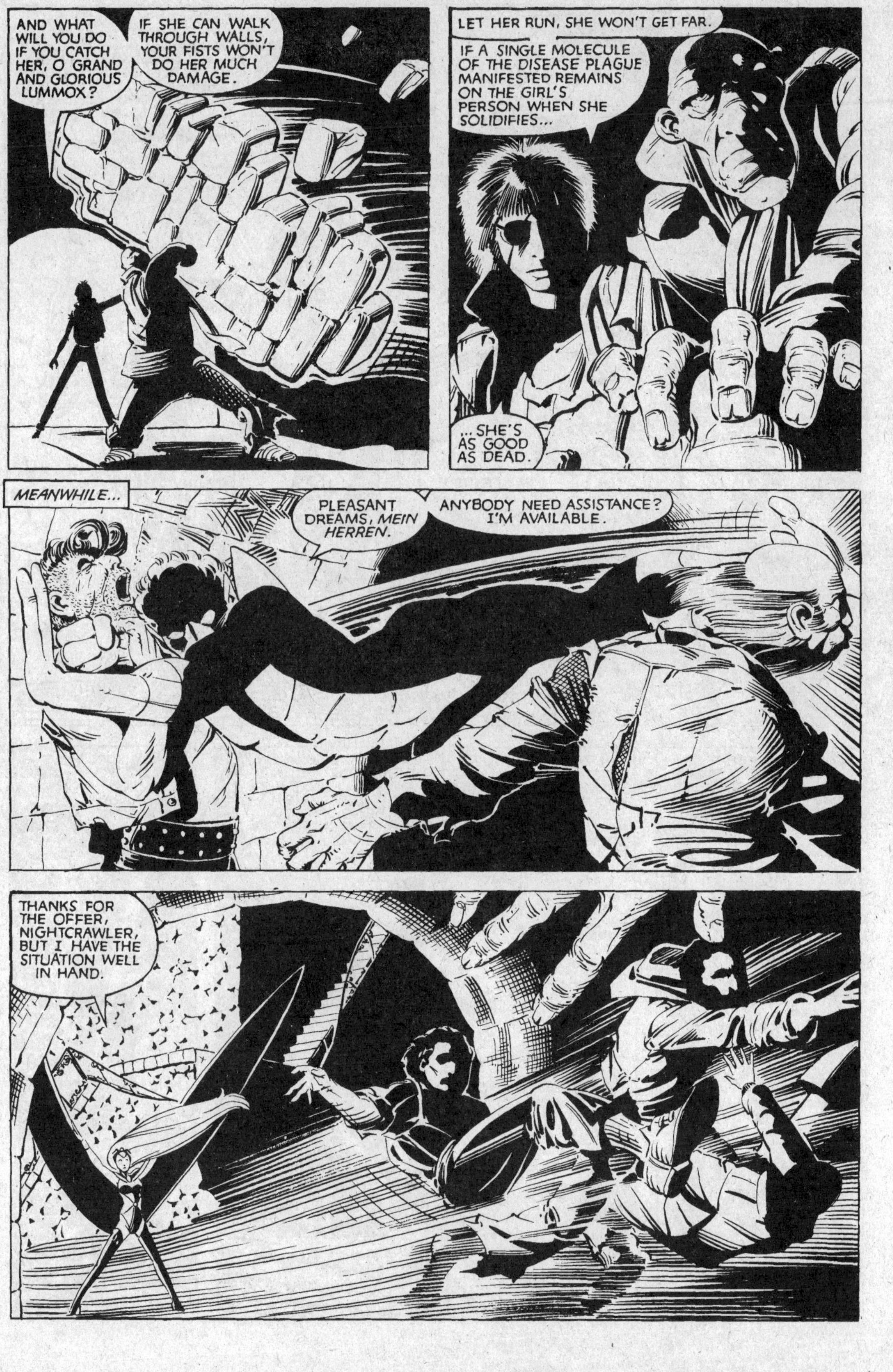
AND WHAT WILL YOU DO IF YOU CATCH HER, O GRAND AND GLORIOUS LUMMOX?
IF SHE CAN WALK THROUGH WALLS, YOUR FISTS WON'T DO HER MUCH DAMAGE.
LET HER RUN, SHE WON'T GET FAR.
IF A SINGLE MOLECULE OF THE DISEASE PLAGUE MANIFESTED REMAINS ON THE GIRL'S PERSON WHEN SHE SOLIDIFIES...
...SHE'S AS GOOD AS DEAD.
MEANWHILE...
PLEASANT DREAMS, MEIN HERREN.
ANYBODY NEED ASSISTANCE? I'M AVAILABLE.
THANKS FOR THE OFFER, NIGHTCRAWLER, BUT I HAVE THE SITUATION WELL IN HAND.

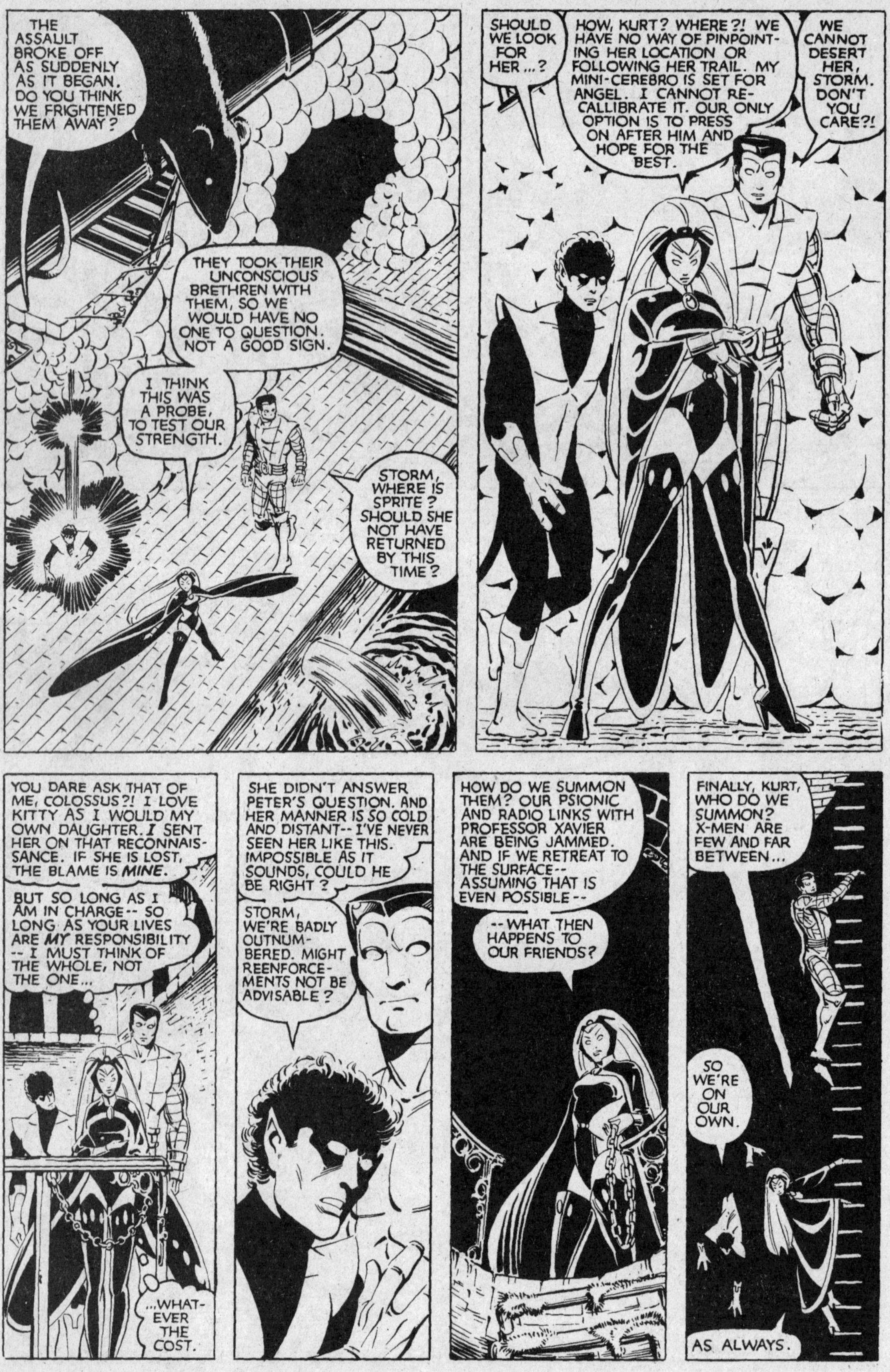
THE ASSAULT BROKE OFF AS SUDDENLY AS IT BEGAN. DO YOU THINK WE FRIGHTENED THEM AWAY?
THEY TOOK THEIR UNCONSCIOUS BRETHREN WITH THEM, SO WE WOULD HAVE NO ONE TO QUESTION. NOT A GOOD SIGN.
I THINK THIS WAS A PROBE, TO TEST OUR STRENGTH.
STORM, WHERE IS SPRITE? SHOULD SHE NOT HAVE RETURNED BY THIS TIME?
SHOULD WE LOOK FOR HER...?
HOW, KURT? WHERE?! WE HAVE NO WAY OF PINPOINTING HER LOCATION OR FOLLOWING HER TRAIL. MY MINI-CEREBRO IS SET FOR ANGEL. I CANNOT RECALLIBRATE IT. OUR ONLY OPTION IS TO PRESS ON AFTER HIM AND HOPE FOR THE BEST.
WE CANNOT DESERT HER, STORM. DON'T YOU CARE?!
YOU DARE ASK THAT OF ME, COLOSSUS?! I LOVE KITTY AS I WOULD MY OWN DAUGHTER. I SENT HER ON THAT RECONNAISSANCE. IF SHE IS LOST, THE BLAME IS MINE.
BUT SO LONG AS I AM IN CHARGE -- SO LONG AS YOUR LIVES ARE MY RESPONSIBILITY -- I MUST THINK OF THE WHOLE, NOT THE ONE...
...WHATEVER THE COST.
SHE DIDN'T ANSWER PETER'S QUESTION. AND HER MANNER IS SO COLD AND DISTANT -- I'VE NEVER SEEN HER LIKE THIS. IMPOSSIBLE AS IT SOUNDS, COULD HE BE RIGHT?
STORM, WE'RE BADLY OUTNUMBERED. MIGHT REENFORCEMENTS NOT BE ADVISABLE?
HOW DO WE SUMMON THEM? OUR PSIONIC AND RADIO LINKS WITH PROFESSOR XAVIER ARE BEING JAMMED. AND IF WE RETREAT TO THE SURFACE -- ASSUMING THAT IS EVEN POSSIBLE --
-- WHAT THEN HAPPENS TO OUR FRIENDS?
FINALLY, KURT, WHO DO WE SUMMON? X-MEN ARE FEW AND FAR BETWEEN...
SO WE'RE ON OUR OWN.
AS ALWAYS.

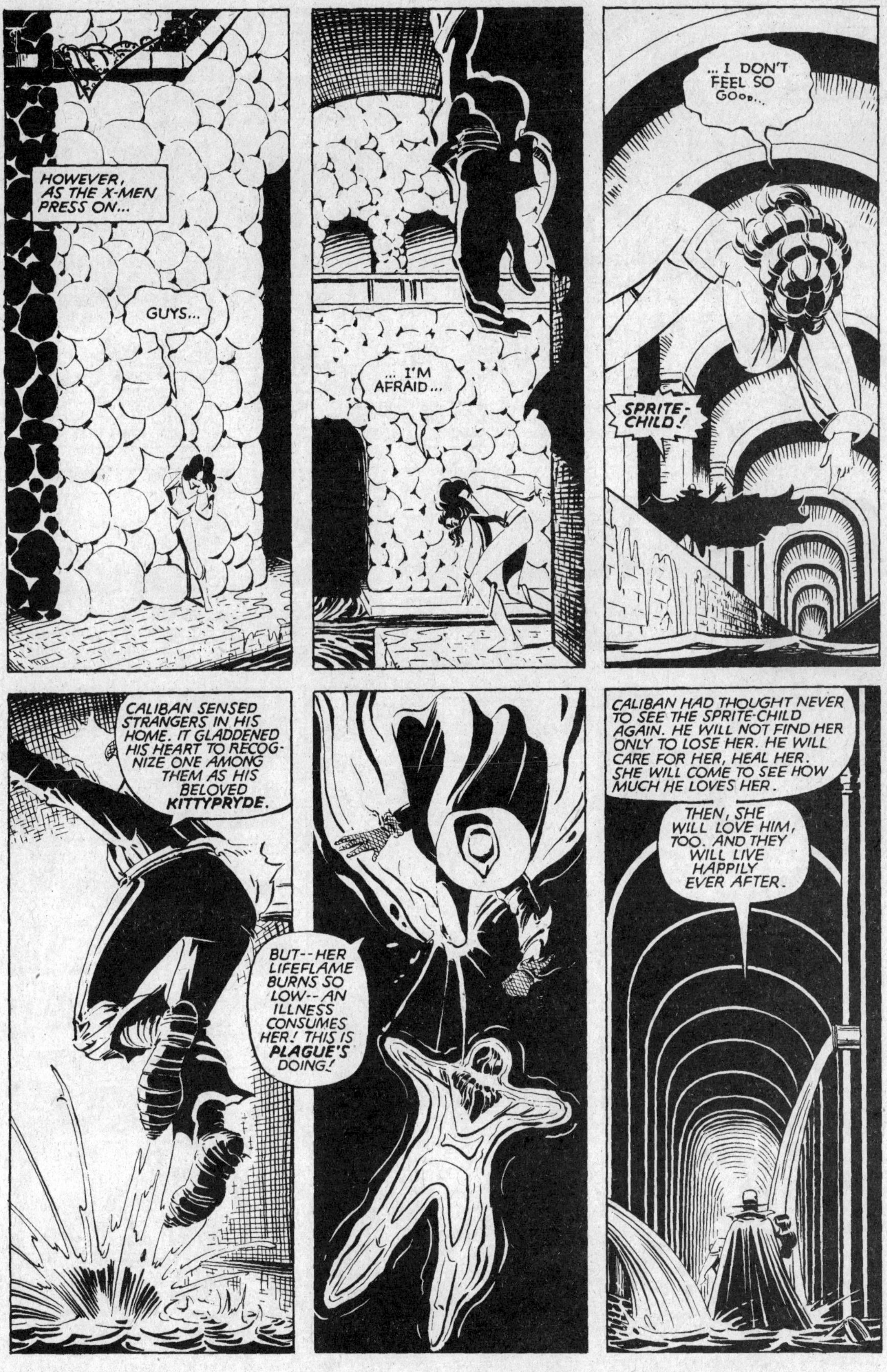
HOWEVER, AS THE X-MEN PRESS ON...
GUYS...
... I'M AFRAID...
... I DON'T FEEL SO GOOD...
SPRITE-CHILD!
CALIBAN SENSED STRANGERS IN HIS HOME. IT GLADDENED HIS HEART TO RECOGNIZE ONE AMONG THEM AS HIS BELOVED KITTYPRYDE.
BUT--HER LIFEFLAME BURNS SO LOW--AN ILLNESS CONSUMES HER! THIS IS PLAGUE'S DOING!
CALIBAN HAD THOUGHT NEVER TO SEE THE SPRITE-CHILD AGAIN. HE WILL NOT FIND HER ONLY TO LOSE HER. HE WILL CARE FOR HER, HEAL HER. SHE WILL COME TO SEE HOW MUCH HE LOVES HER.
THEN, SHE WILL LOVE HIM, TOO. AND THEY WILL LIVE HAPPILY EVER AFTER.

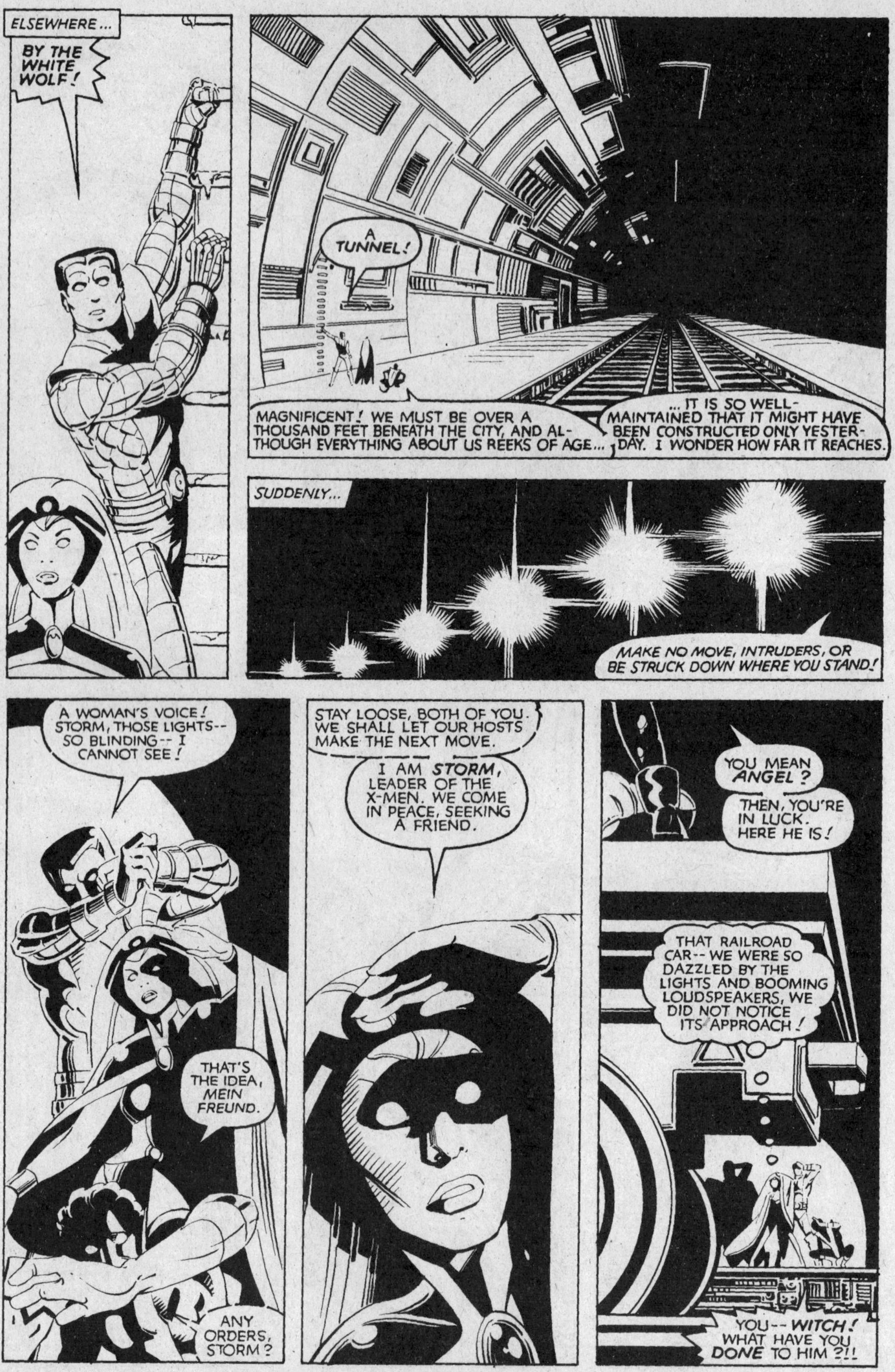
ELSEWHERE...
BY THE WHITE WOLF!
A TUNNEL!
MAGNIFICENT! WE MUST BE OVER A THOUSAND FEET BENEATH THE CITY, AND ALTHOUGH EVERYTHING ABOUT US REEKS OF AGE...
... IT IS SO WELL-MAINTAINED THAT IT MIGHT HAVE BEEN CONSTRUCTED ONLY YESTERDAY. I WONDER HOW FAR IT REACHES.
SUDDENLY...
MAKE NO MOVE, INTRUDERS, OR BE STRUCK DOWN WHERE YOU STAND!
A WOMAN'S VOICE! STORM, THOSE LIGHTS-- SO BLINDING-- I CANNOT SEE!
THAT'S THE IDEA, MEIN FREUND.
ANY ORDERS, STORM?
STAY LOOSE, BOTH OF YOU. WE SHALL LET OUR HOSTS MAKE THE NEXT MOVE.
I AM STORM, LEADER OF THE X-MEN. WE COME IN PEACE, SEEKING A FRIEND.
YOU MEAN ANGEL?
THEN, YOU'RE IN LUCK. HERE HE IS!
THAT RAILROAD CAR-- WE WERE SO DAZZLED BY THE LIGHTS AND BOOMING LOUDSPEAKERS, WE DID NOT NOTICE ITS APPROACH!
YOU-- WITCH! WHAT HAVE YOU DONE TO HIM?!!

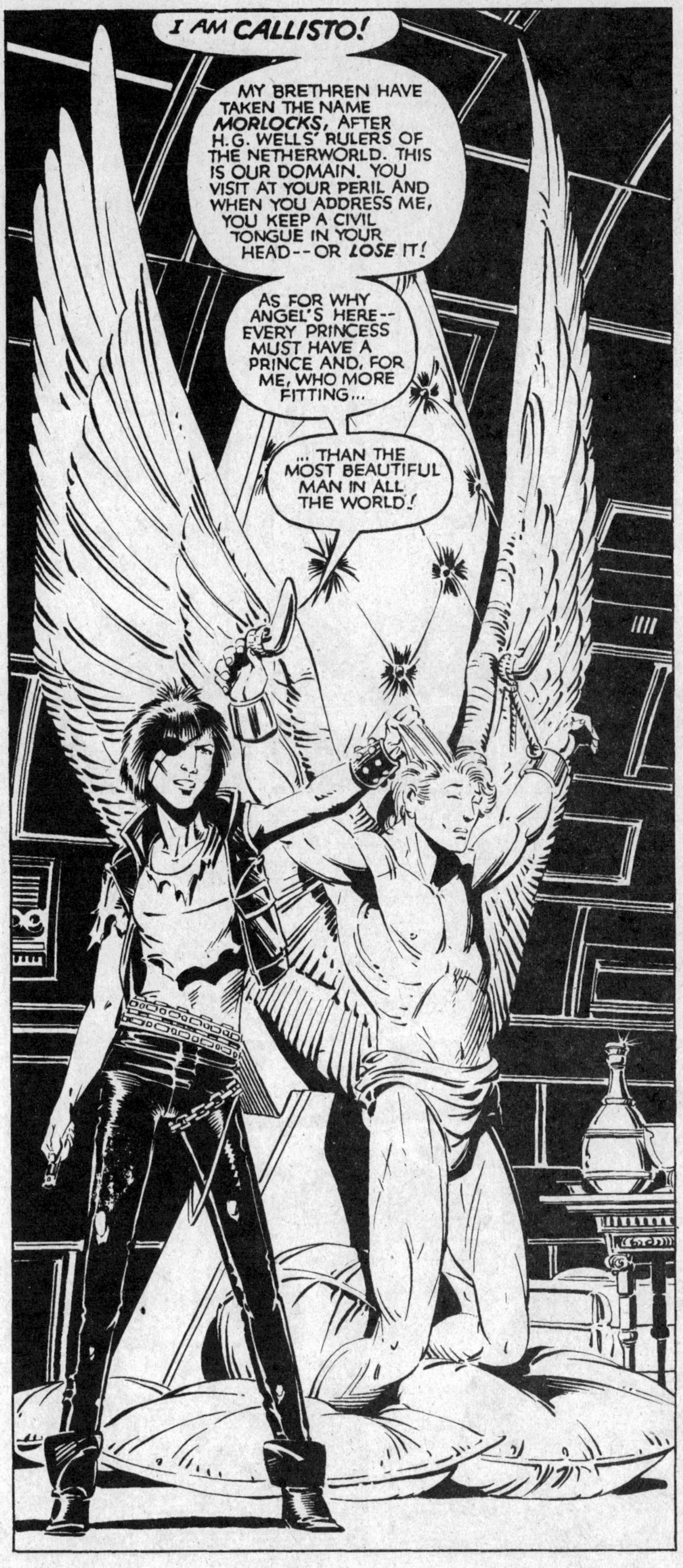
I AM CALLISTO!
MY BRETHREN HAVE TAKEN THE NAME MORLOCKS, AFTER H.G. WELLS' RULERS OF THE NETHERWORLD. THIS IS OUR DOMAIN. YOU VISIT AT YOUR PERIL AND WHEN YOU ADDRESS ME, YOU KEEP A CIVIL TONGUE IN YOUR HEAD--OR LOSE IT!
AS FOR WHY ANGEL'S HERE-- EVERY PRINCESS MUST HAVE A PRINCE AND, FOR ME, WHO MORE FITTING...
... THAN THE MOST BEAUTIFUL MAN IN ALL THE WORLD!

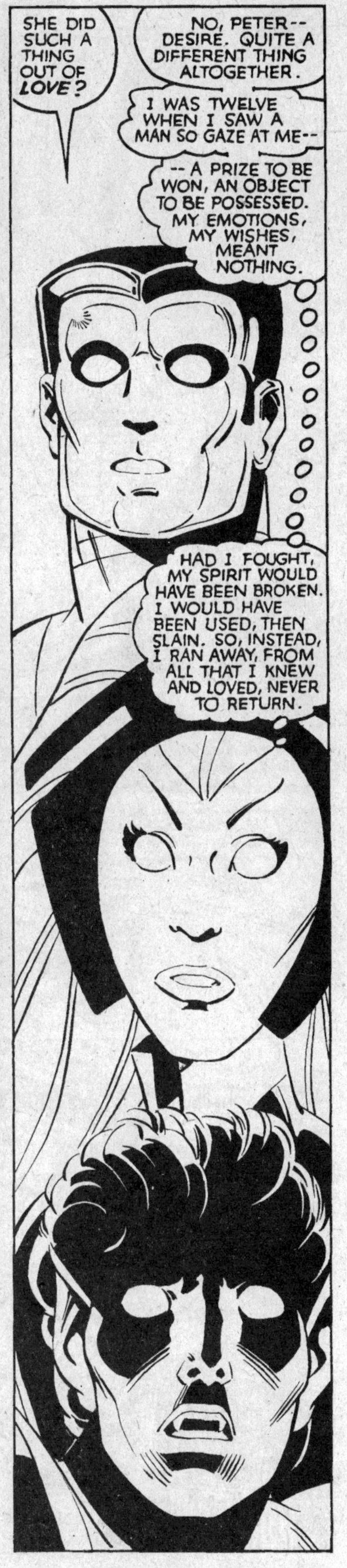
SHE DID SUCH A THING OUT OF LOVE?
NO, PETER-- DESIRE. QUITE A DIFFERENT THING ALTOGETHER.
I WAS TWELVE WHEN I SAW A MAN SO GAZE AT ME--
-- A PRIZE TO BE WON, AN OBJECT TO BE POSSESSED. MY EMOTIONS, MY WISHES, MEANT NOTHING.
HAD I FOUGHT, MY SPIRIT WOULD HAVE BEEN BROKEN. I WOULD HAVE BEEN USED, THEN SLAIN. SO, INSTEAD, I RAN AWAY, FROM ALL THAT I KNEW AND LOVED, NEVER TO RETURN.

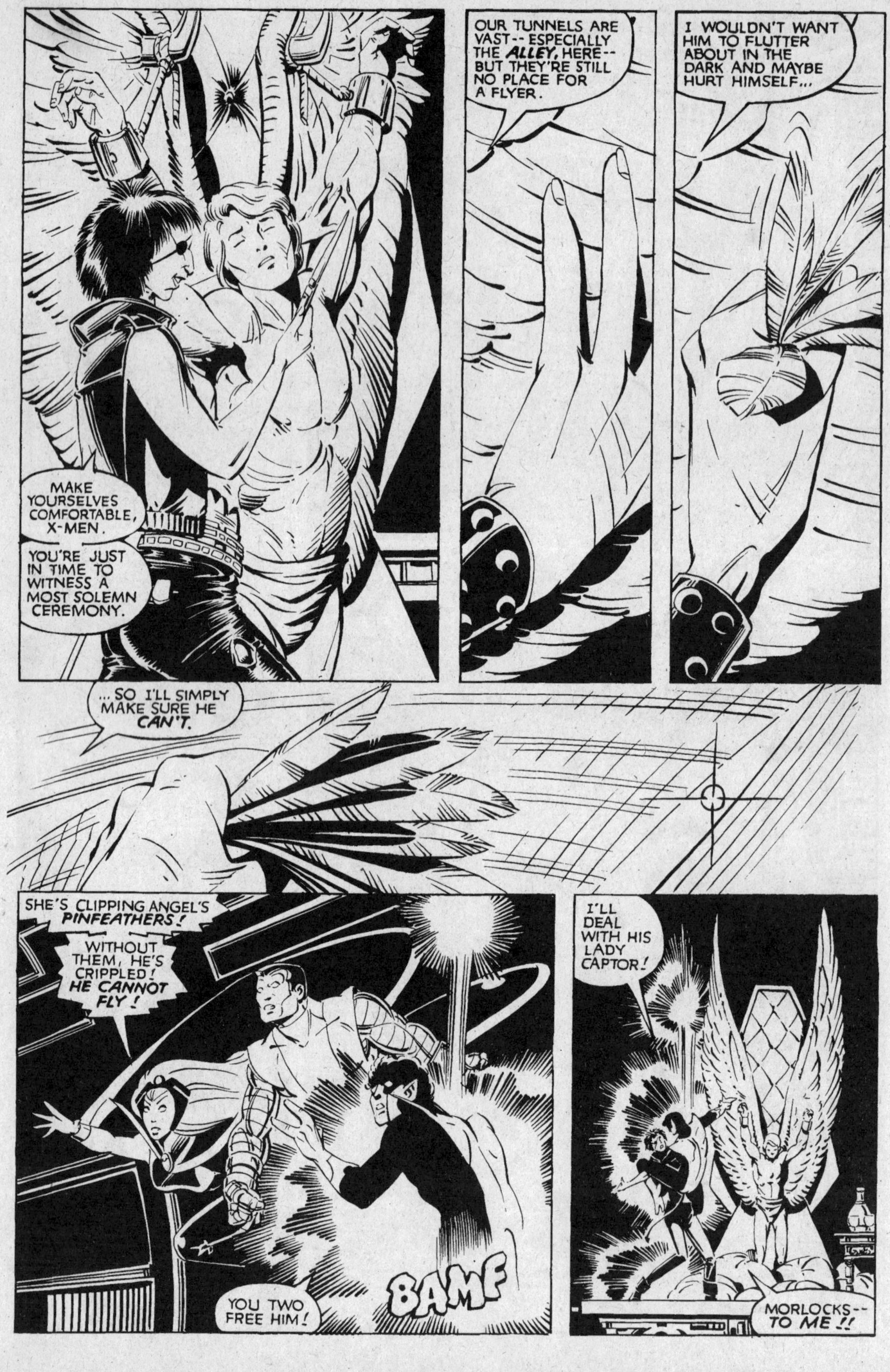

MAKE YOURSELVES COMFORTABLE, X-MEN.
YOU'RE JUST IN TIME TO WITNESS A MOST SOLEMN CEREMONY.
OUR TUNNELS ARE VAST-- ESPECIALLY THE ALLEY, HERE-- BUT THEY'RE STILL NO PLACE FOR A FLYER.
I WOULDN'T WANT HIM TO FLUTTER ABOUT IN THE DARK AND MAYBE HURT HIMSELF...
...SO I'LL SIMPLY MAKE SURE HE CAN'T.
SHE'S CLIPPING ANGEL'S PINFEATHERS!
WITHOUT THEM, HE'S CRIPPLED! HE CANNOT FLY!
YOU TWO FREE HIM!
BAMF
I'LL DEAL WITH HIS LADY CAPTOR!
MORLOCKS-- TO ME!!

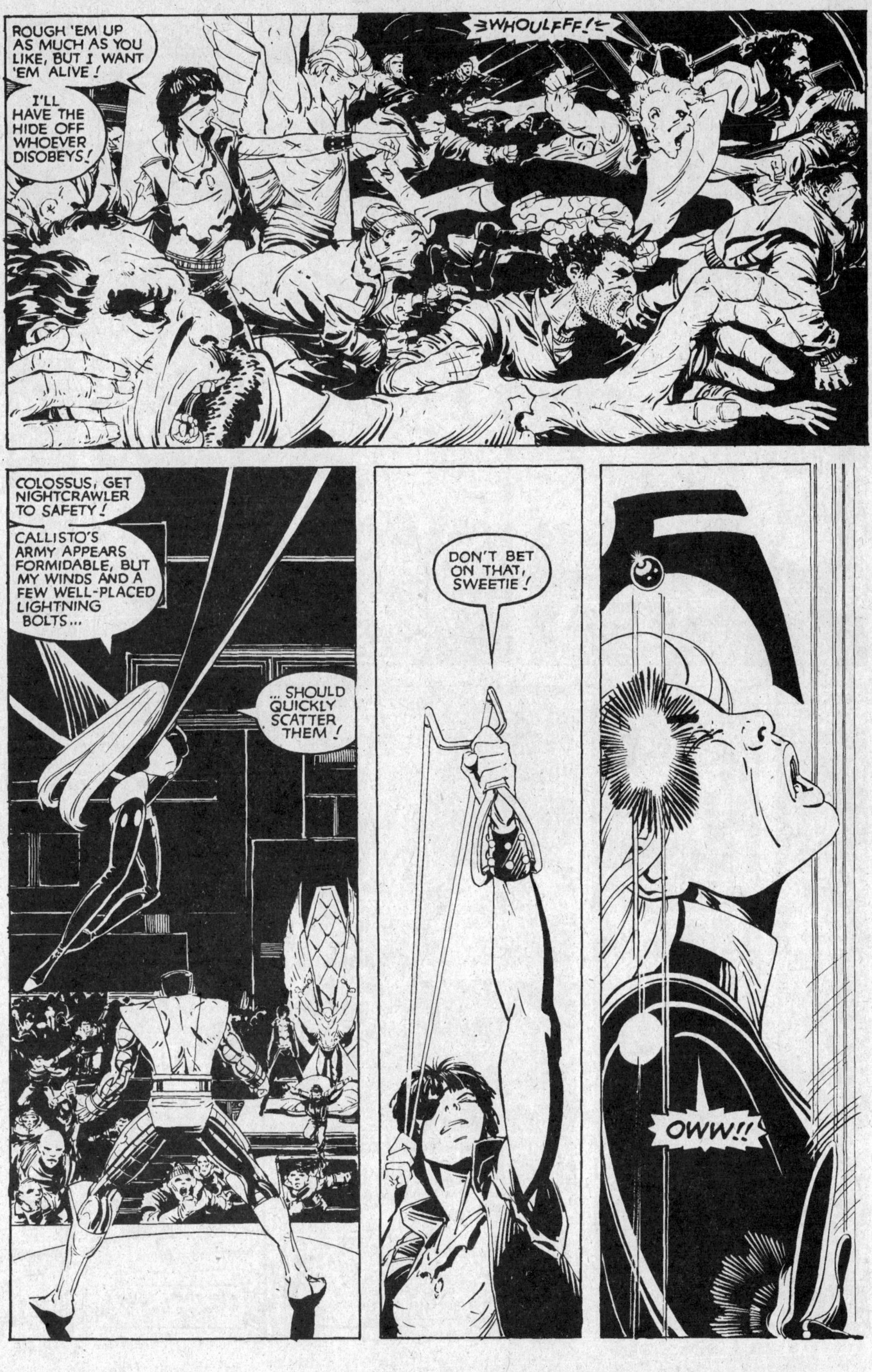
ROUGH 'EM UP AS MUCH AS YOU LIKE, BUT I WANT 'EM ALIVE!
I'LL HAVE THE HIDE OFF WHOEVER DISOBEYS!
WHOULFFF!
COLOSSUS, GET NIGHTCRAWLER TO SAFETY!
CALLISTO'S ARMY APPEARS FORMIDABLE, BUT MY WINDS AND A FEW WELL-PLACED LIGHTNING BOLTS...
...SHOULD QUICKLY SCATTER THEM!
DON'T BET ON THAT, SWEETIE!
OWW!!

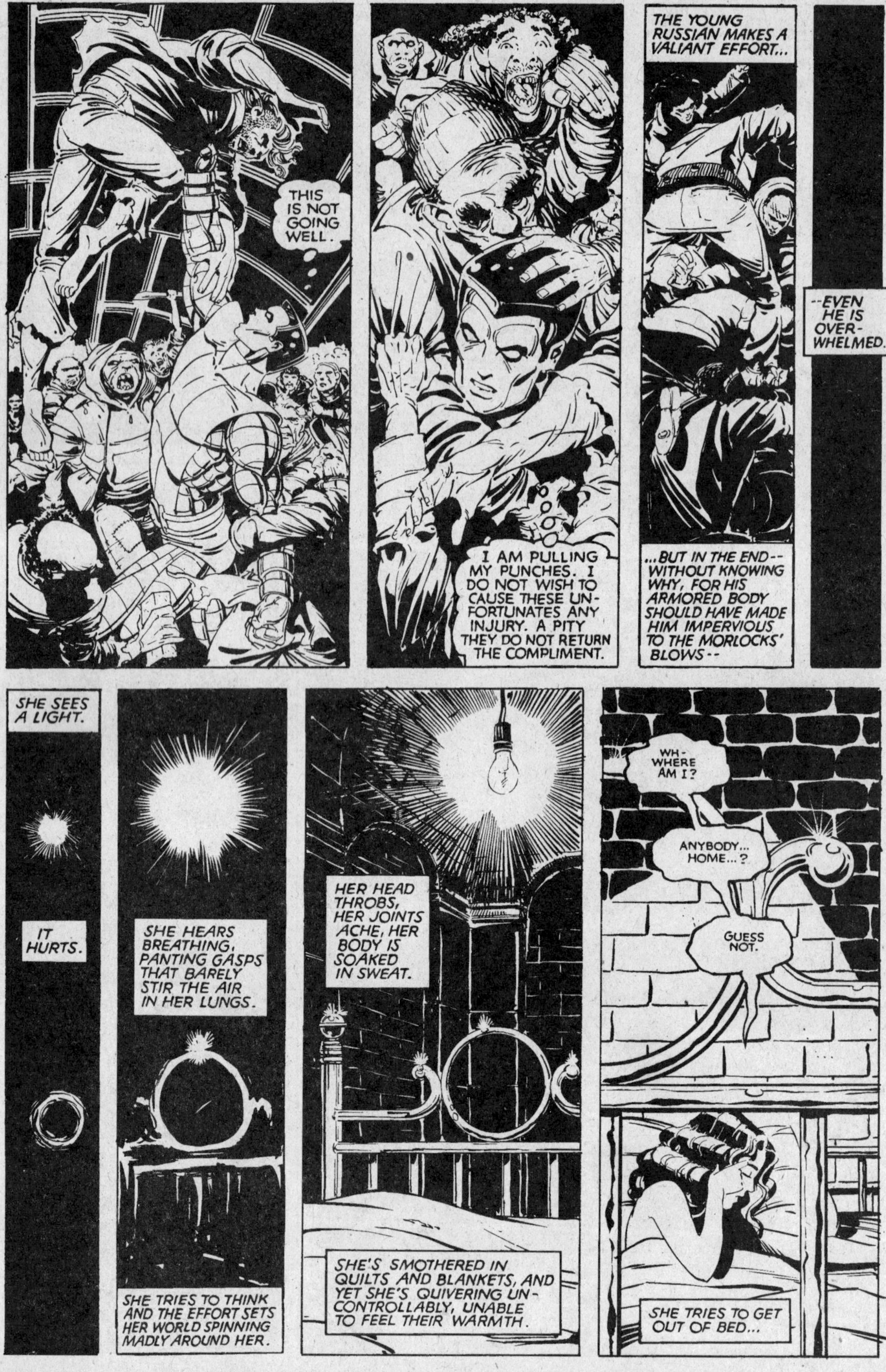
THIS IS NOT GOING WELL.
I AM PULLING MY PUNCHES. I DO NOT WISH TO CAUSE THESE UNFORTUNATES ANY INJURY. A PITY THEY DO NOT RETURN THE COMPLIMENT.
THE YOUNG RUSSIAN MAKES A VALIANT EFFORT...
...BUT IN THE END--WITHOUT KNOWING WHY, FOR HIS ARMORED BODY SHOULD HAVE MADE HIM IMPERVIOUS TO THE MORLOCKS' BLOWS--
--EVEN HE IS OVERWHELMED.
SHE SEES A LIGHT.
IT HURTS.
SHE HEARS BREATHING, PANTING GASPS THAT BARELY STIR THE AIR IN HER LUNGS.
SHE TRIES TO THINK AND THE EFFORT SETS HER WORLD SPINNING MADLY AROUND HER.
HER HEAD THROBS, HER JOINTS ACHE, HER BODY IS SOAKED IN SWEAT.
SHE'S SMOTHERED IN QUILTS AND BLANKETS, AND YET SHE'S QUIVERING UNCONTROLLABLY, UNABLE TO FEEL THEIR WARMTH.
WH-WHERE AM I?
ANYBODY... HOME...?
GUESS NOT.
SHE TRIES TO GET OUT OF BED...

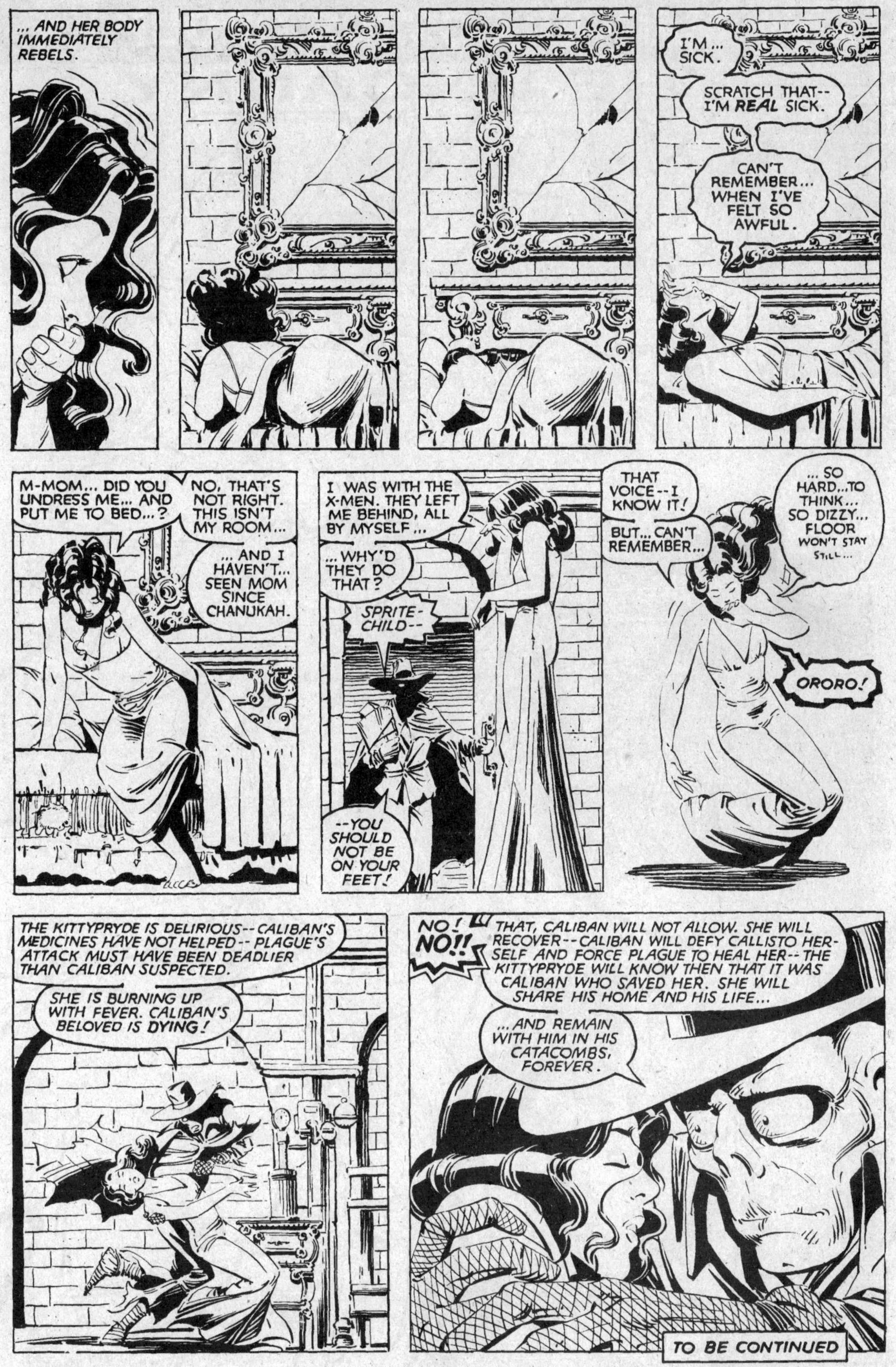
...AND HER BODY IMMEDIATELY REBELS.
I'M... SICK.
SCRATCH THAT-- I'M REAL SICK.
CAN'T REMEMBER... WHEN I'VE FELT SO AWFUL.
M-MOM... DID YOU UNDRESS ME... AND PUT ME TO BED...?
NO, THAT'S NOT RIGHT. THIS ISN'T MY ROOM...
...AND I HAVEN'T... SEEN MOM SINCE CHANUKAH.
I WAS WITH THE X-MEN. THEY LEFT ME BEHIND, ALL BY MYSELF...
...WHY'D THEY DO THAT?
SPRITE-CHILD--
--YOU SHOULD NOT BE ON YOUR FEET!
THAT VOICE--I KNOW IT!
BUT... CAN'T REMEMBER...
...SO HARD...TO THINK... SO DIZZY... FLOOR WON'T STAY STILL...
ORORO!
THE KITTYPRYDE IS DELIRIOUS--CALIBAN'S MEDICINES HAVE NOT HELPED--PLAGUE'S ATTACK MUST HAVE BEEN DEADLIER THAN CALIBAN SUSPECTED.
SHE IS BURNING UP WITH FEVER. CALIBAN'S BELOVED IS DYING!
NO! NO!!
THAT, CALIBAN WILL NOT ALLOW. SHE WILL RECOVER--CALIBAN WILL DEFY CALLISTO HER-SELF AND FORCE PLAGUE TO HEAL HER--THE KITTYPRYDE WILL KNOW THEN THAT IT WAS CALIBAN WHO SAVED HER. SHE WILL SHARE HIS HOME AND HIS LIFE...
...AND REMAIN WITH HIM IN HIS CATACOMBS, FOREVER.
TO BE CONTINUED

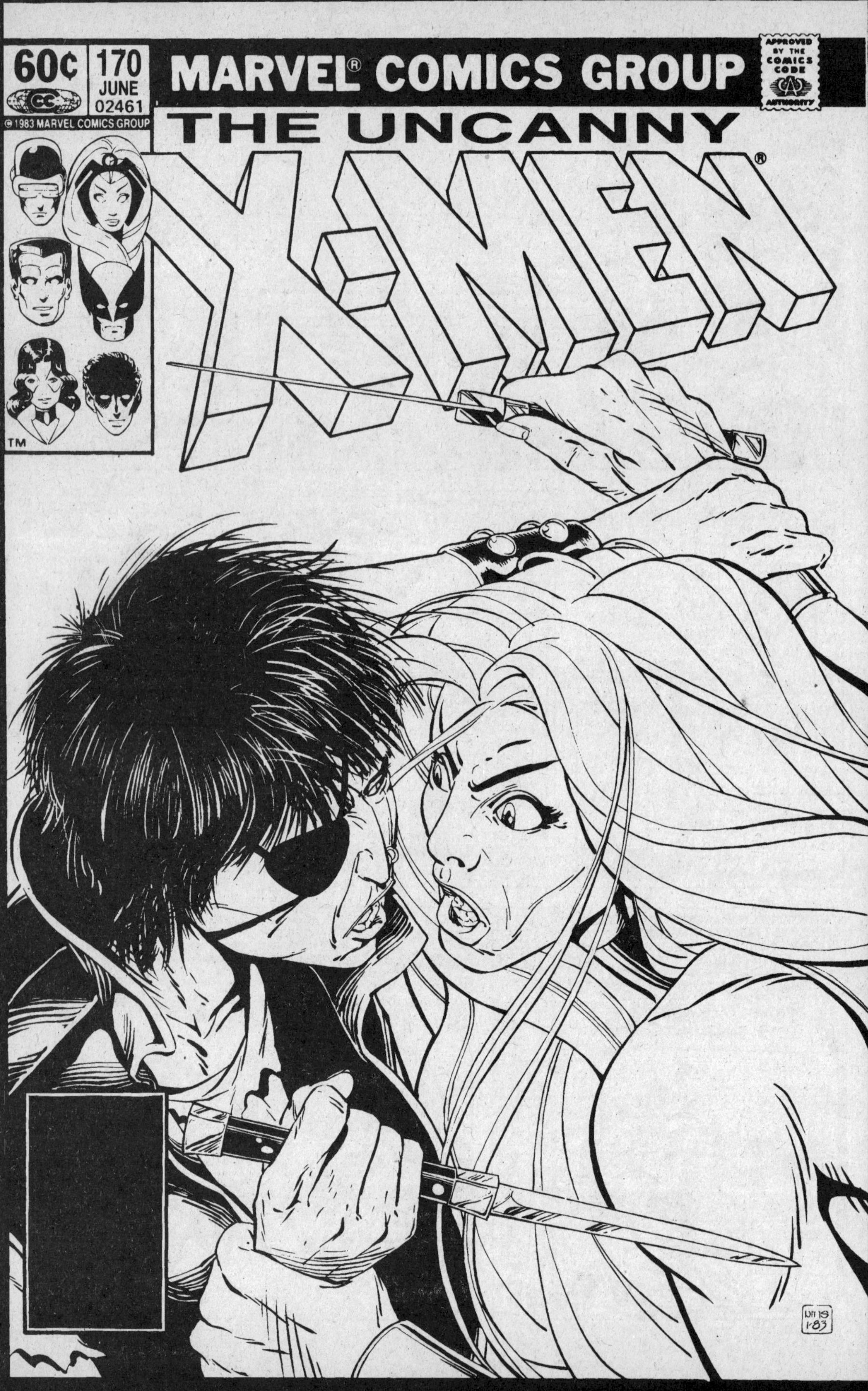
60¢
170
JUNE
02461
© 1983 MARVEL COMICS GROUP
MARVEL® COMICS GROUP
APPROVED BY THE COMICS CODE AUTHORITY
THE UNCANNY
X-MEN®
TM

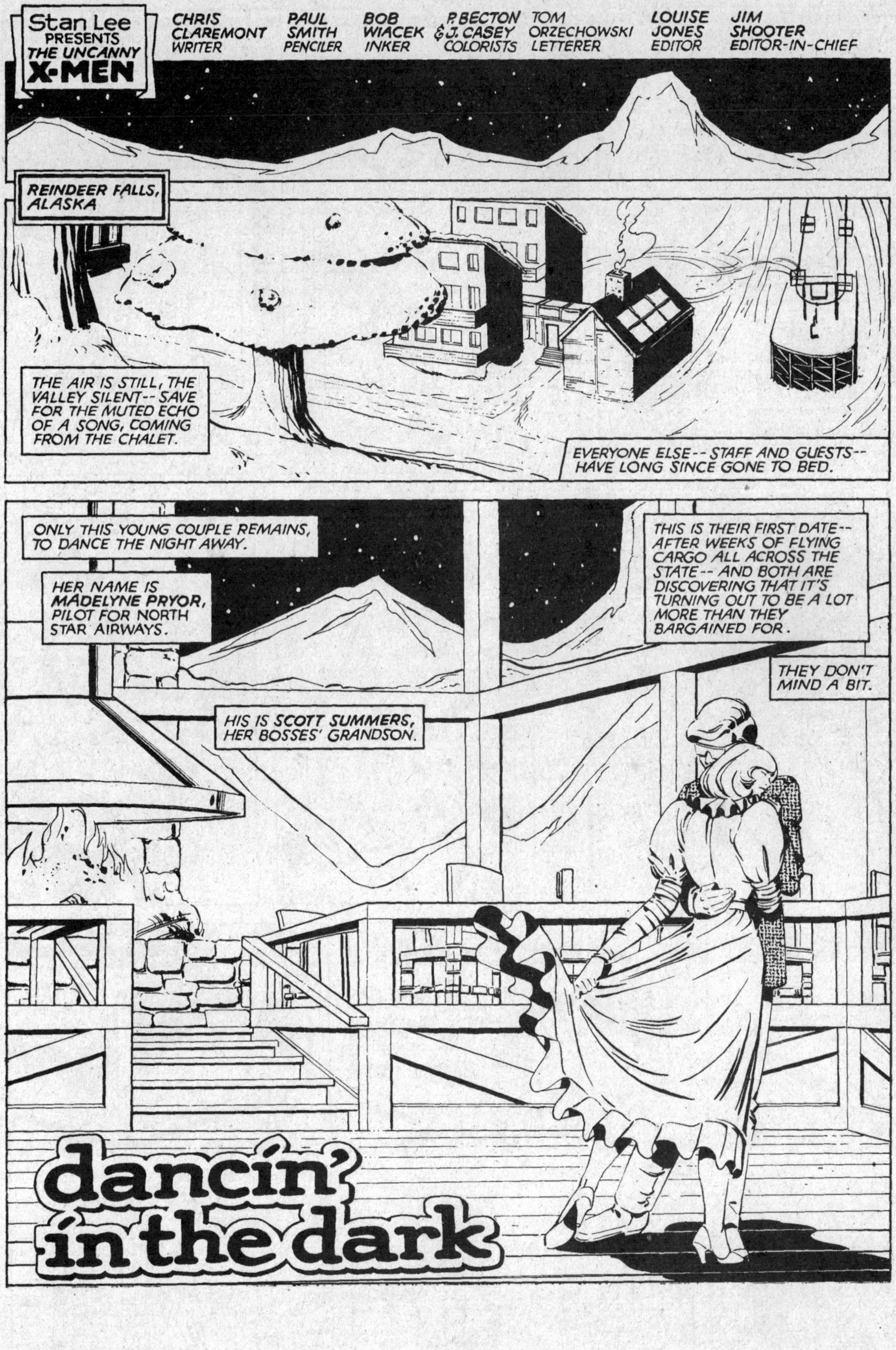

Stan Lee PRESENTS THE UNCANNY X-MEN
CHRIS CLAREMONT WRITER
PAUL SMITH PENCILER
BOB WIACEK INKER
P. BECTON & J. CASEY COLORISTS
TOM ORZECHOWSKI LETTERER
LOUISE JONES EDITOR
JIM SHOOTER EDITOR-IN-CHIEF
REINDEER FALLS, ALASKA
THE AIR IS STILL, THE VALLEY SILENT-- SAVE FOR THE MUTED ECHO OF A SONG, COMING FROM THE CHALET.
EVERYONE ELSE-- STAFF AND GUESTS-- HAVE LONG SINCE GONE TO BED.
ONLY THIS YOUNG COUPLE REMAINS, TO DANCE THE NIGHT AWAY.
HER NAME IS MADELYNE PRYOR, PILOT FOR NORTH STAR AIRWAYS.
HIS IS SCOTT SUMMERS, HER BOSSES' GRANDSON.
THIS IS THEIR FIRST DATE-- AFTER WEEKS OF FLYING CARGO ALL ACROSS THE STATE-- AND BOTH ARE DISCOVERING THAT IT'S TURNING OUT TO BE A LOT MORE THAN THEY BARGAINED FOR.
THEY DON'T MIND A BIT.
dancin' in the dark

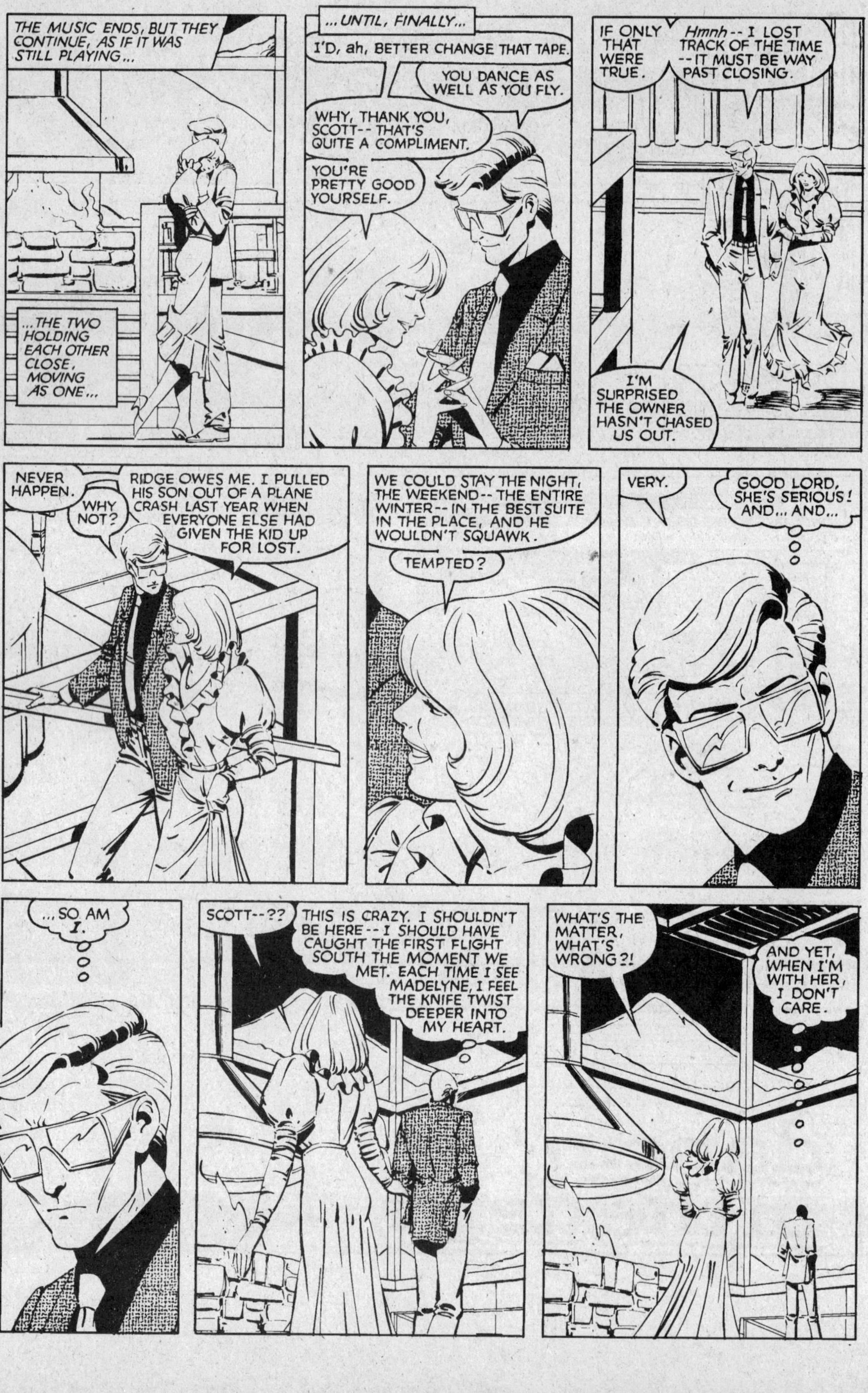
THE MUSIC ENDS, BUT THEY CONTINUE, AS IF IT WAS STILL PLAYING...
...THE TWO HOLDING EACH OTHER CLOSE, MOVING AS ONE...
...UNTIL, FINALLY...
I'D, ah, BETTER CHANGE THAT TAPE.
YOU DANCE AS WELL AS YOU FLY.
WHY, THANK YOU, SCOTT-- THAT'S QUITE A COMPLIMENT.
YOU'RE PRETTY GOOD YOURSELF.
Hmnh-- I LOST TRACK OF THE TIME --IT MUST BE WAY PAST CLOSING.
IF ONLY THAT WERE TRUE.
I'M SURPRISED THE OWNER HASN'T CHASED US OUT.
NEVER HAPPEN.
WHY NOT?
RIDGE OWES ME. I PULLED HIS SON OUT OF A PLANE CRASH LAST YEAR WHEN EVERYONE ELSE HAD GIVEN THE KID UP FOR LOST.
WE COULD STAY THE NIGHT, THE WEEKEND-- THE ENTIRE WINTER-- IN THE BEST SUITE IN THE PLACE, AND HE WOULDN'T SQUAWK.
TEMPTED?
VERY.
GOOD LORD, SHE'S SERIOUS! AND... AND...
...SO AM I.
SCOTT--??
THIS IS CRAZY. I SHOULDN'T BE HERE-- I SHOULD HAVE CAUGHT THE FIRST FLIGHT SOUTH THE MOMENT WE MET. EACH TIME I SEE MADELYNE, I FEEL THE KNIFE TWIST DEEPER INTO MY HEART.
WHAT'S THE MATTER, WHAT'S WRONG?!
AND YET, WHEN I'M WITH HER, I DON'T CARE.

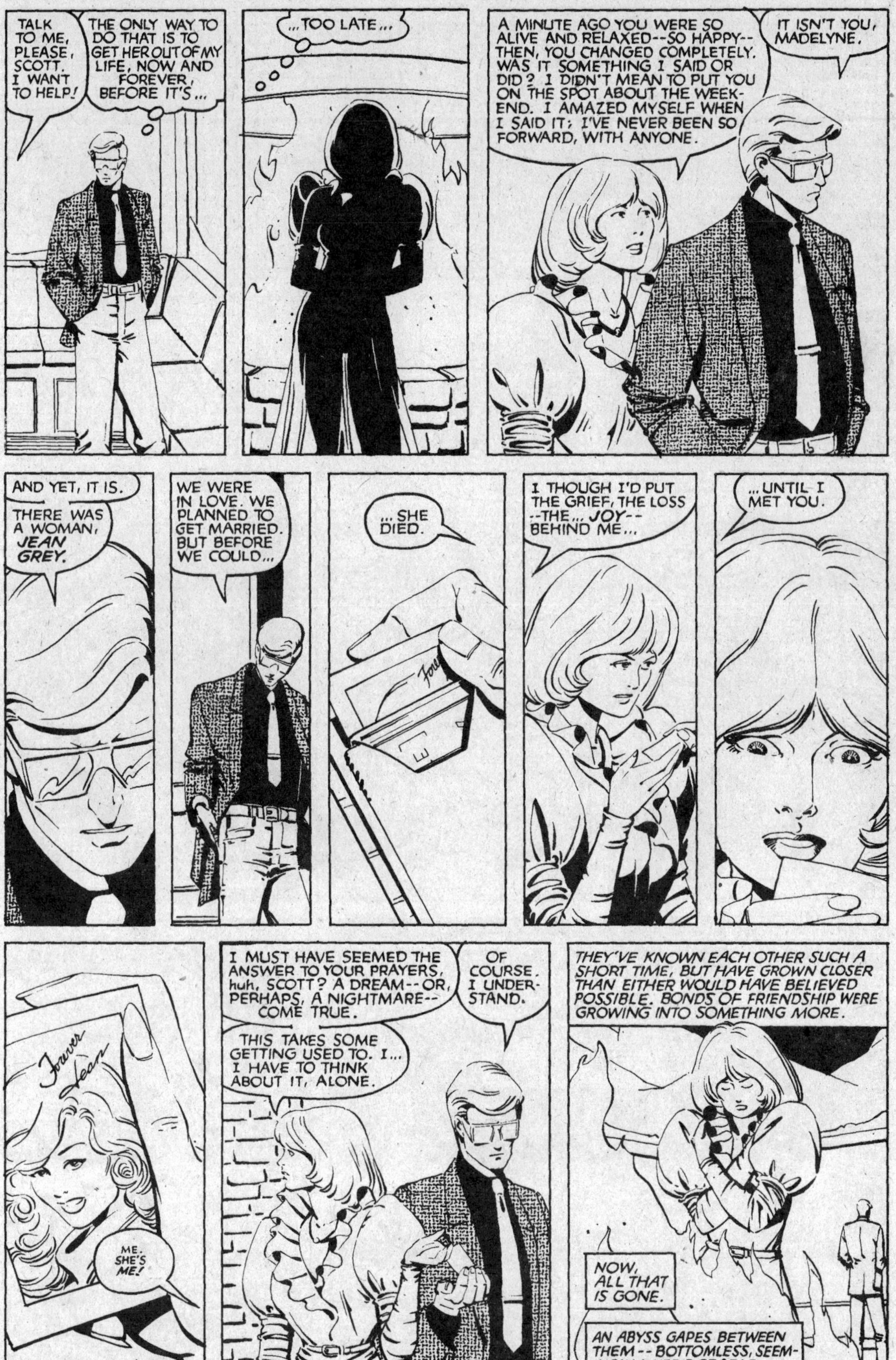
TALK TO ME, PLEASE, SCOTT. I WANT TO HELP!
THE ONLY WAY TO DO THAT IS TO GET HER OUT OF MY LIFE, NOW AND FOREVER, BEFORE IT'S...
...TOO LATE...
A MINUTE AGO YOU WERE SO ALIVE AND RELAXED--SO HAPPY--THEN, YOU CHANGED COMPLETELY. WAS IT SOMETHING I SAID OR DID? I DIDN'T MEAN TO PUT YOU ON THE SPOT ABOUT THE WEEK-END. I AMAZED MYSELF WHEN I SAID IT; I'VE NEVER BEEN SO FORWARD, WITH ANYONE.
IT ISN'T YOU, MADELYNE.
AND YET, IT IS.
THERE WAS A WOMAN, JEAN GREY.
WE WERE IN LOVE. WE PLANNED TO GET MARRIED. BUT BEFORE WE COULD...
...SHE DIED.
I THOUGH I'D PUT THE GRIEF, THE LOSS --THE... JOY-- BEHIND ME...
...UNTIL I MET YOU.
Forever Jean
ME. SHE'S ME!
I MUST HAVE SEEMED THE ANSWER TO YOUR PRAYERS, huh, SCOTT? A DREAM--OR, PERHAPS, A NIGHTMARE--COME TRUE.
OF COURSE. I UNDERSTAND.
THIS TAKES SOME GETTING USED TO. I... I HAVE TO THINK ABOUT IT, ALONE.
THEY'VE KNOWN EACH OTHER SUCH A SHORT TIME, BUT HAVE GROWN CLOSER THAN EITHER WOULD HAVE BELIEVED POSSIBLE. BONDS OF FRIENDSHIP WERE GROWING INTO SOMETHING MORE.
NOW, ALL THAT IS GONE.
AN ABYSS GAPES BETWEEN THEM -- BOTTOMLESS, SEEMINGLY UNBRIDGEABLE.

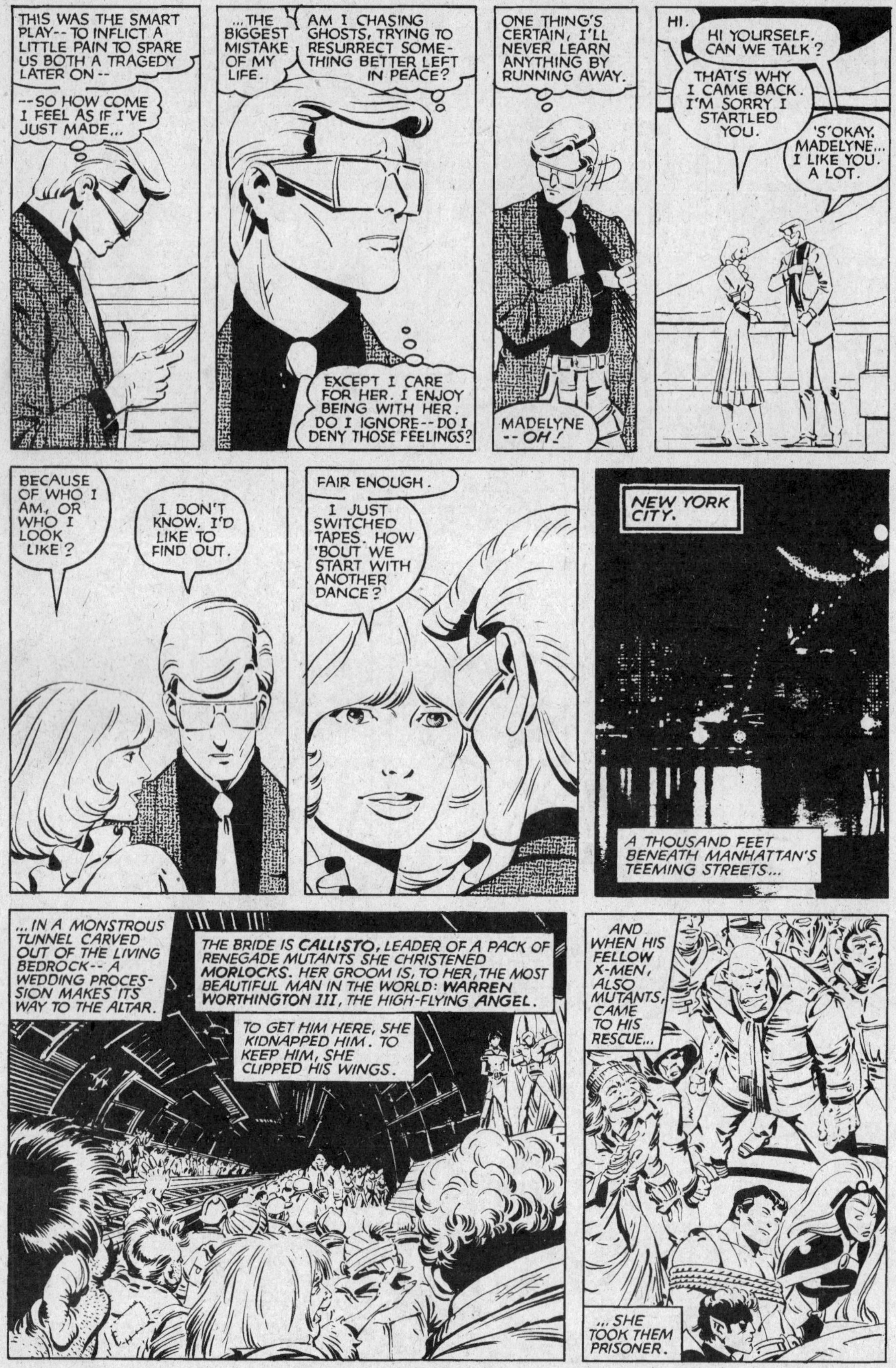
THIS WAS THE SMART PLAY-- TO INFLICT A LITTLE PAIN TO SPARE US BOTH A TRAGEDY LATER ON --
--SO HOW COME I FEEL AS IF I'VE JUST MADE...
...THE BIGGEST MISTAKE OF MY LIFE.
AM I CHASING GHOSTS, TRYING TO RESURRECT SOMETHING BETTER LEFT IN PEACE?
EXCEPT I CARE FOR HER. I ENJOY BEING WITH HER. DO I IGNORE--DO I DENY THOSE FEELINGS?
ONE THING'S CERTAIN, I'LL NEVER LEARN ANYTHING BY RUNNING AWAY.
MADELYNE --OH!
HI.
HI YOURSELF. CAN WE TALK?
THAT'S WHY I CAME BACK. I'M SORRY I STARTLED YOU.
'S'OKAY, MADELYNE... I LIKE YOU. A LOT.
BECAUSE OF WHO I AM, OR WHO I LOOK LIKE?
I DON'T KNOW. I'D LIKE TO FIND OUT.
FAIR ENOUGH.
I JUST SWITCHED TAPES. HOW 'BOUT WE START WITH ANOTHER DANCE?
NEW YORK CITY.
A THOUSAND FEET BENEATH MANHATTAN'S TEEMING STREETS...
...IN A MONSTROUS TUNNEL CARVED OUT OF THE LIVING BEDROCK-- A WEDDING PROCESSION MAKES ITS WAY TO THE ALTAR.
THE BRIDE IS CALLISTO, LEADER OF A PACK OF RENEGADE MUTANTS SHE CHRISTENED MORLOCKS. HER GROOM IS, TO HER, THE MOST BEAUTIFUL MAN IN THE WORLD: WARREN WORTHINGTON III, THE HIGH-FLYING ANGEL.
TO GET HIM HERE, SHE KIDNAPPED HIM. TO KEEP HIM, SHE CLIPPED HIS WINGS.
AND WHEN HIS FELLOW X-MEN, ALSO MUTANTS, CAME TO HIS RESCUE...
...SHE TOOK THEM PRISONER.

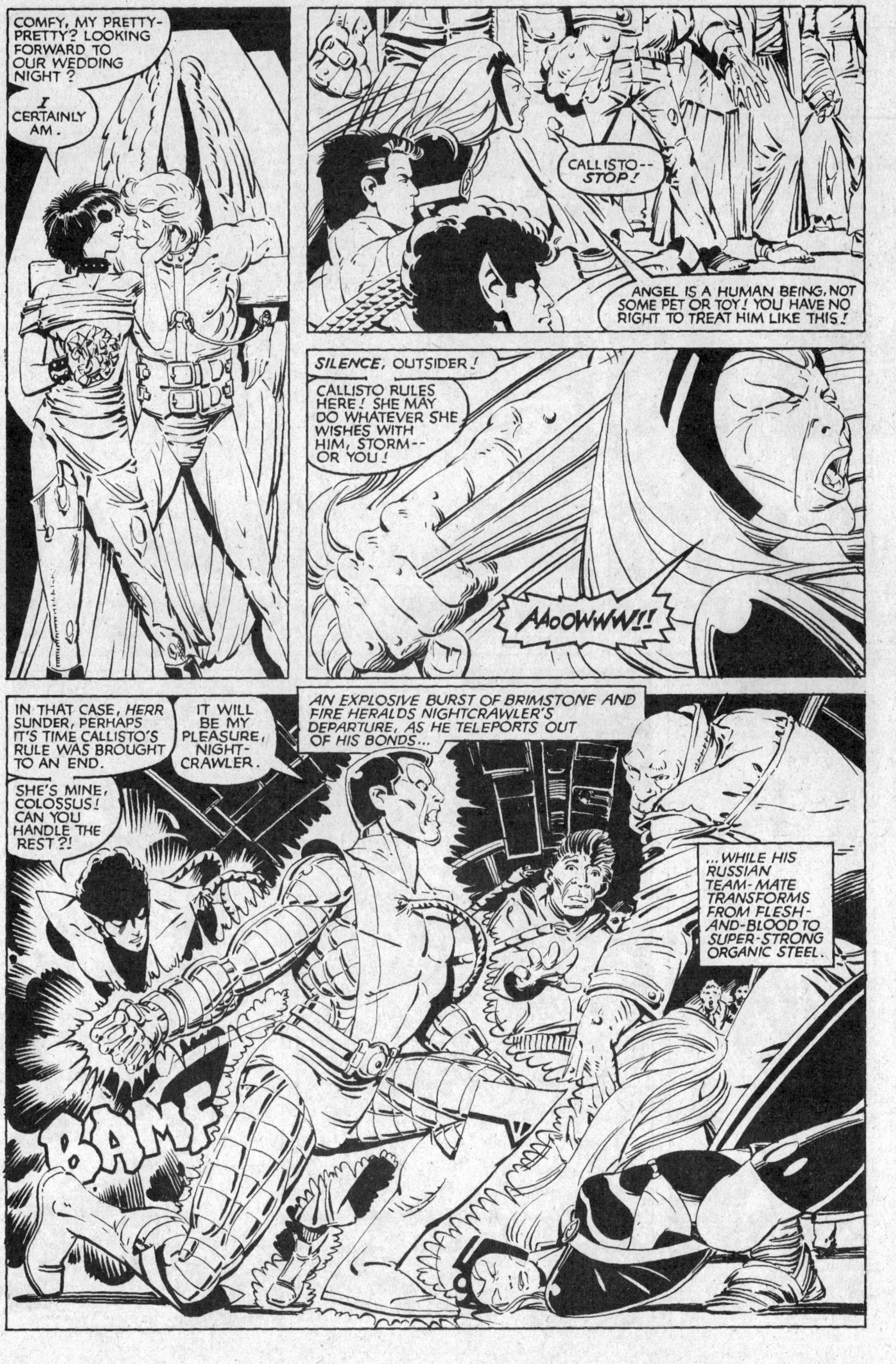

COMFY, MY PRETTY-PRETTY? LOOKING FORWARD TO OUR WEDDING NIGHT?
I CERTAINLY AM.
CALLISTO-- STOP!
ANGEL IS A HUMAN BEING, NOT SOME PET OR TOY! YOU HAVE NO RIGHT TO TREAT HIM LIKE THIS!
SILENCE, OUTSIDER!
CALLISTO RULES HERE! SHE MAY DO WHATEVER SHE WISHES WITH HIM, STORM-- OR YOU!
AAOOWWW!!
IN THAT CASE, HERR SUNDER, PERHAPS IT'S TIME CALLISTO'S RULE WAS BROUGHT TO AN END.
IT WILL BE MY PLEASURE, NIGHT-CRAWLER.
AN EXPLOSIVE BURST OF BRIMSTONE AND FIRE HERALDS NIGHTCRAWLER'S DEPARTURE, AS HE TELEPORTS OUT OF HIS BONDS...
SHE'S MINE, COLOSSUS! CAN YOU HANDLE THE REST?!
...WHILE HIS RUSSIAN TEAM-MATE TRANSFORMS FROM FLESH-AND-BLOOD TO SUPER-STRONG ORGANIC STEEL.
BAMF

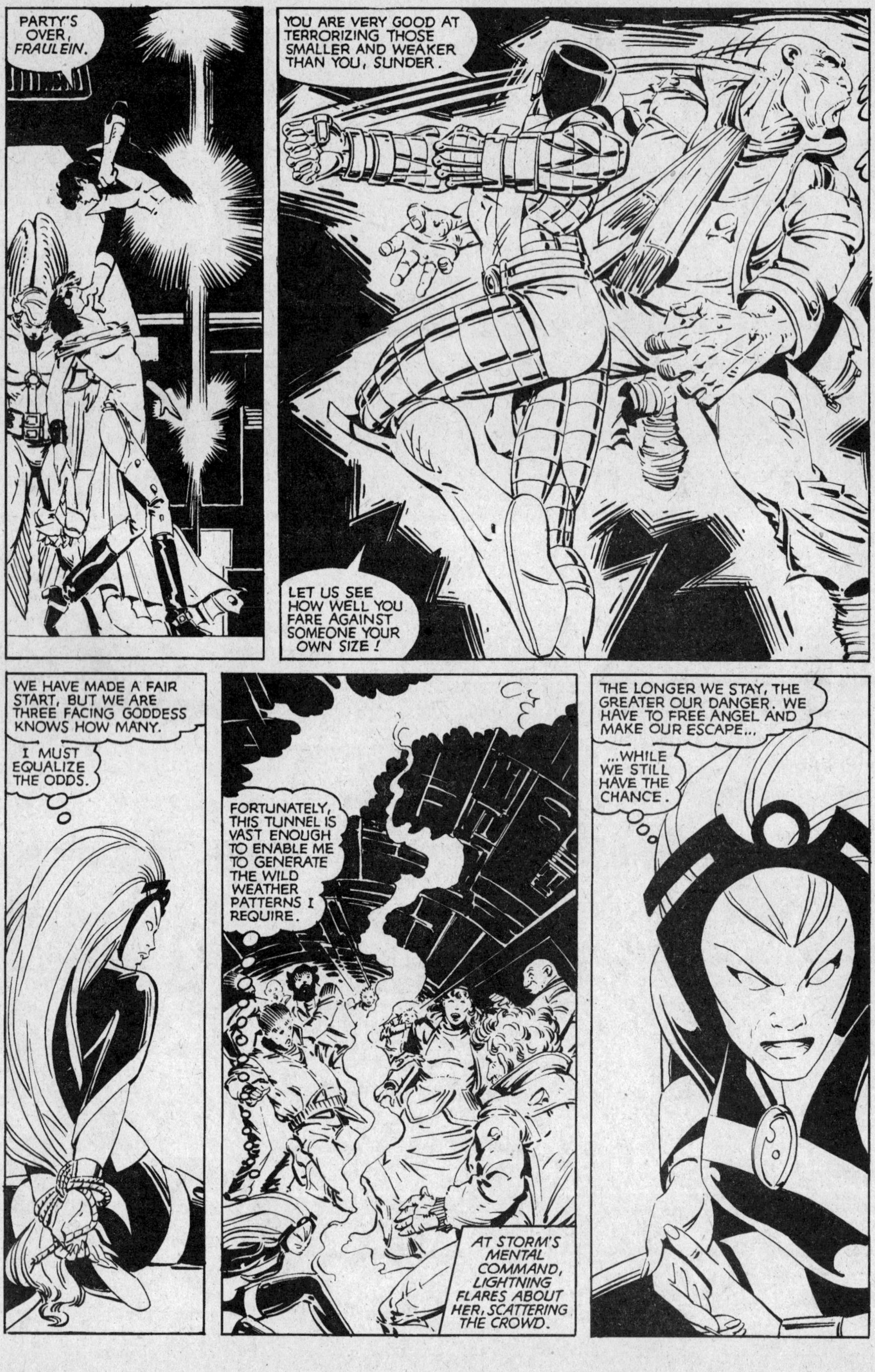

PARTY'S OVER, FRAULEIN.
YOU ARE VERY GOOD AT TERRORIZING THOSE SMALLER AND WEAKER THAN YOU, SUNDER.
LET US SEE HOW WELL YOU FARE AGAINST SOMEONE YOUR OWN SIZE!
WE HAVE MADE A FAIR START, BUT WE ARE THREE FACING GODDESS KNOWS HOW MANY.
I MUST EQUALIZE THE ODDS.
FORTUNATELY, THIS TUNNEL IS VAST ENOUGH TO ENABLE ME TO GENERATE THE WILD WEATHER PATTERNS I REQUIRE.
AT STORM'S MENTAL COMMAND, LIGHTNING FLARES ABOUT HER, SCATTERING THE CROWD.
THE LONGER WE STAY, THE GREATER OUR DANGER. WE HAVE TO FREE ANGEL AND MAKE OUR ESCAPE...
...WHILE WE STILL HAVE THE CHANCE.

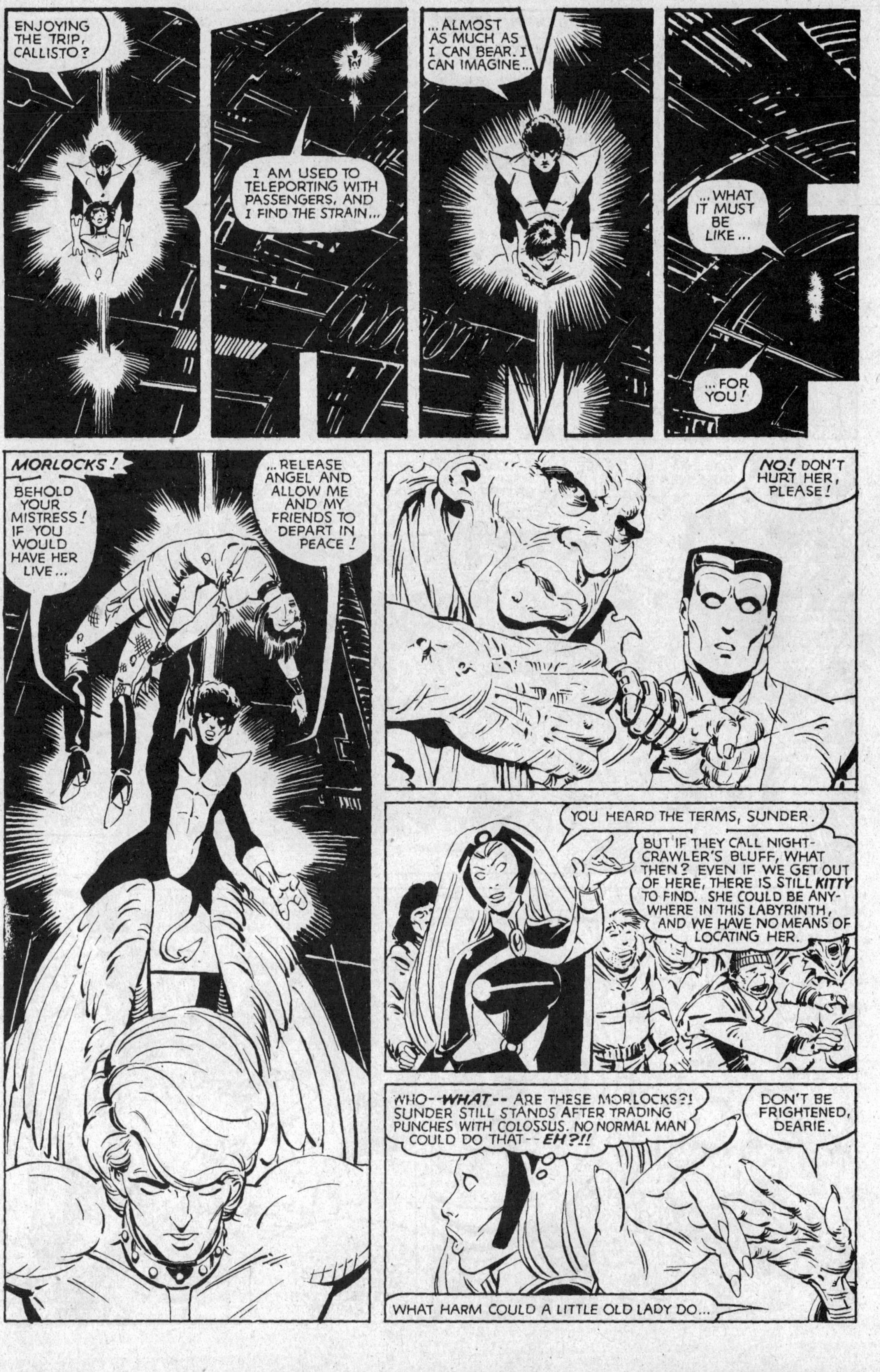
ENJOYING THE TRIP, CALLISTO?
I AM USED TO TELEPORTING WITH PASSENGERS, AND I FIND THE STRAIN...
...ALMOST AS MUCH AS I CAN BEAR. I CAN IMAGINE...
...WHAT IT MUST BE LIKE...
...FOR YOU!
BAMF
MORLOCKS!
BEHOLD YOUR MISTRESS! IF YOU WOULD HAVE HER LIVE...
...RELEASE ANGEL AND ALLOW ME AND MY FRIENDS TO DEPART IN PEACE!
NO! DON'T HURT HER, PLEASE!
YOU HEARD THE TERMS, SUNDER.
BUT IF THEY CALL NIGHT-CRAWLER'S BLUFF, WHAT THEN? EVEN IF WE GET OUT OF HERE, THERE IS STILL KITTY TO FIND. SHE COULD BE ANY-WHERE IN THIS LABYRINTH, AND WE HAVE NO MEANS OF LOCATING HER.
WHO--WHAT--ARE THESE MORLOCKS?! SUNDER STILL STANDS AFTER TRADING PUNCHES WITH COLOSSUS. NO NORMAL MAN COULD DO THAT--EH?!!
DON'T BE FRIGHTENED, DEARIE.
WHAT HARM COULD A LITTLE OLD LADY DO...

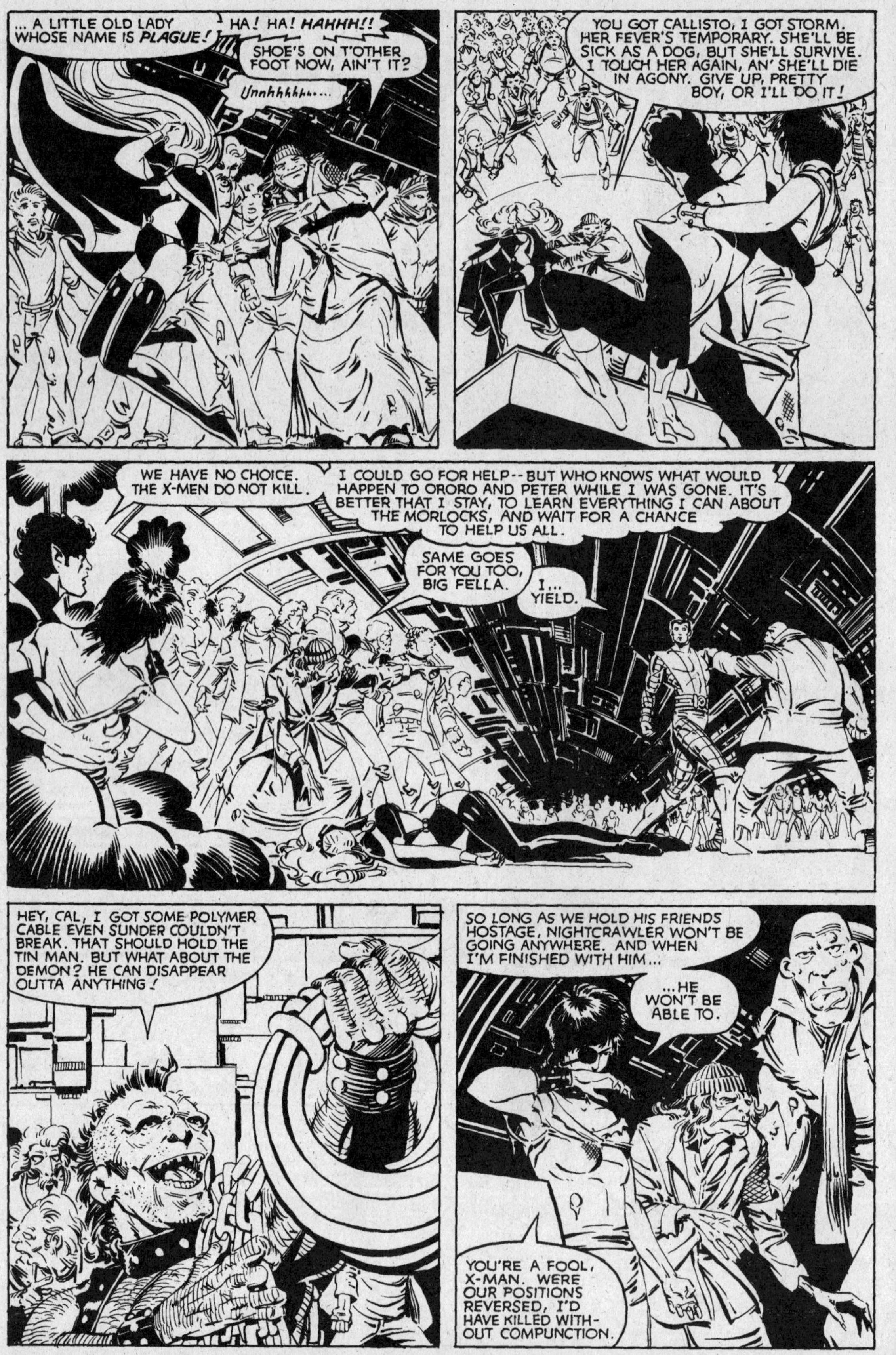
... A LITTLE OLD LADY WHOSE NAME IS *PLAGUE*!
HA! HA! *HAHHH!!*
SHOE'S ON T'OTHER FOOT NOW, AIN'T IT?
Unnhhhhhh....
YOU GOT CALLISTO, I GOT STORM. HER FEVER'S TEMPORARY. SHE'LL BE SICK AS A DOG, BUT SHE'LL SURVIVE. I TOUCH HER AGAIN, AN' SHE'LL DIE IN AGONY. GIVE UP, PRETTY BOY, OR I'LL DO IT!
WE HAVE NO CHOICE. THE X-MEN DO NOT KILL.
I COULD GO FOR HELP-- BUT WHO KNOWS WHAT WOULD HAPPEN TO ORORO AND PETER WHILE I WAS GONE. IT'S BETTER THAT I STAY, TO LEARN EVERYTHING I CAN ABOUT THE MORLOCKS, AND WAIT FOR A CHANCE TO HELP US ALL.
SAME GOES FOR YOU TOO, BIG FELLA.
I... YIELD.
HEY, CAL, I GOT SOME POLYMER CABLE EVEN SUNDER COULDN'T BREAK. THAT SHOULD HOLD THE TIN MAN. BUT WHAT ABOUT THE DEMON? HE CAN DISAPPEAR OUTTA ANYTHING!
SO LONG AS WE HOLD HIS FRIENDS HOSTAGE, NIGHTCRAWLER WON'T BE GOING ANYWHERE. AND WHEN I'M FINISHED WITH HIM...
...HE WON'T BE ABLE TO.
YOU'RE A FOOL, X-MAN. WERE OUR POSITIONS REVERSED, I'D HAVE KILLED WITH-OUT COMPUNCTION.

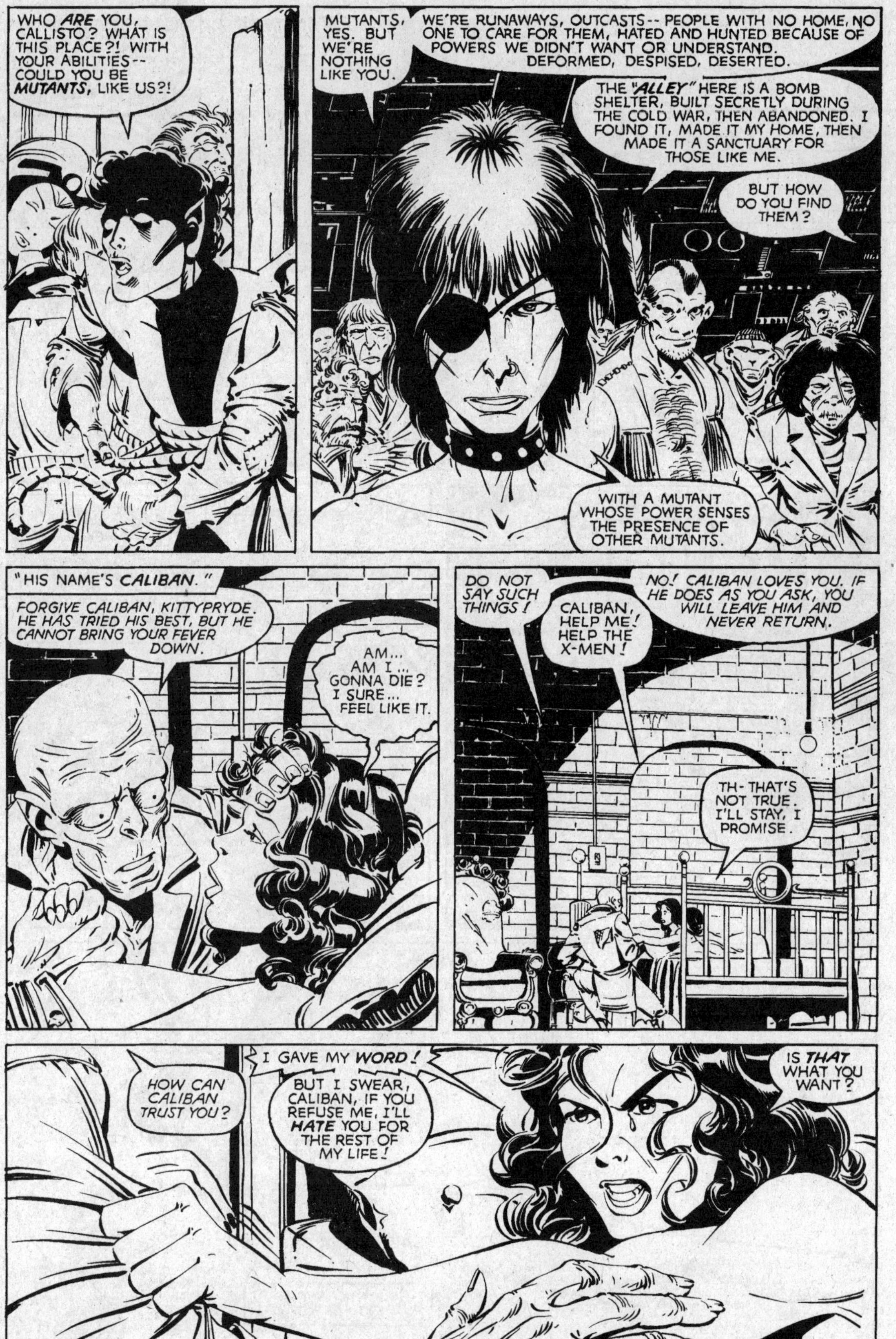

WHO ARE YOU, CALLISTO? WHAT IS THIS PLACE?! WITH YOUR ABILITIES-- COULD YOU BE MUTANTS, LIKE US?!
MUTANTS, YES. BUT WE'RE NOTHING LIKE YOU.
WE'RE RUNAWAYS, OUTCASTS-- PEOPLE WITH NO HOME, NO ONE TO CARE FOR THEM, HATED AND HUNTED BECAUSE OF POWERS WE DIDN'T WANT OR UNDERSTAND. DEFORMED, DESPISED, DESERTED.
THE "ALLEY" HERE IS A BOMB SHELTER, BUILT SECRETLY DURING THE COLD WAR, THEN ABANDONED. I FOUND IT, MADE IT MY HOME, THEN MADE IT A SANCTUARY FOR THOSE LIKE ME.
BUT HOW DO YOU FIND THEM?
WITH A MUTANT WHOSE POWER SENSES THE PRESENCE OF OTHER MUTANTS.
"HIS NAME'S CALIBAN."
FORGIVE CALIBAN, KITTYPRYDE. HE HAS TRIED HIS BEST, BUT HE CANNOT BRING YOUR FEVER DOWN.
AM... AM I... GONNA DIE? I SURE... FEEL LIKE IT.
DO NOT SAY SUCH THINGS!
CALIBAN, HELP ME! HELP THE X-MEN!
NO! CALIBAN LOVES YOU. IF HE DOES AS YOU ASK, YOU WILL LEAVE HIM AND NEVER RETURN.
TH- THAT'S NOT TRUE. I'LL STAY, I PROMISE.
HOW CAN CALIBAN TRUST YOU?
I GAVE MY WORD!
BUT I SWEAR, CALIBAN, IF YOU REFUSE ME, I'LL HATE YOU FOR THE REST OF MY LIFE!
IS THAT WHAT YOU WANT?

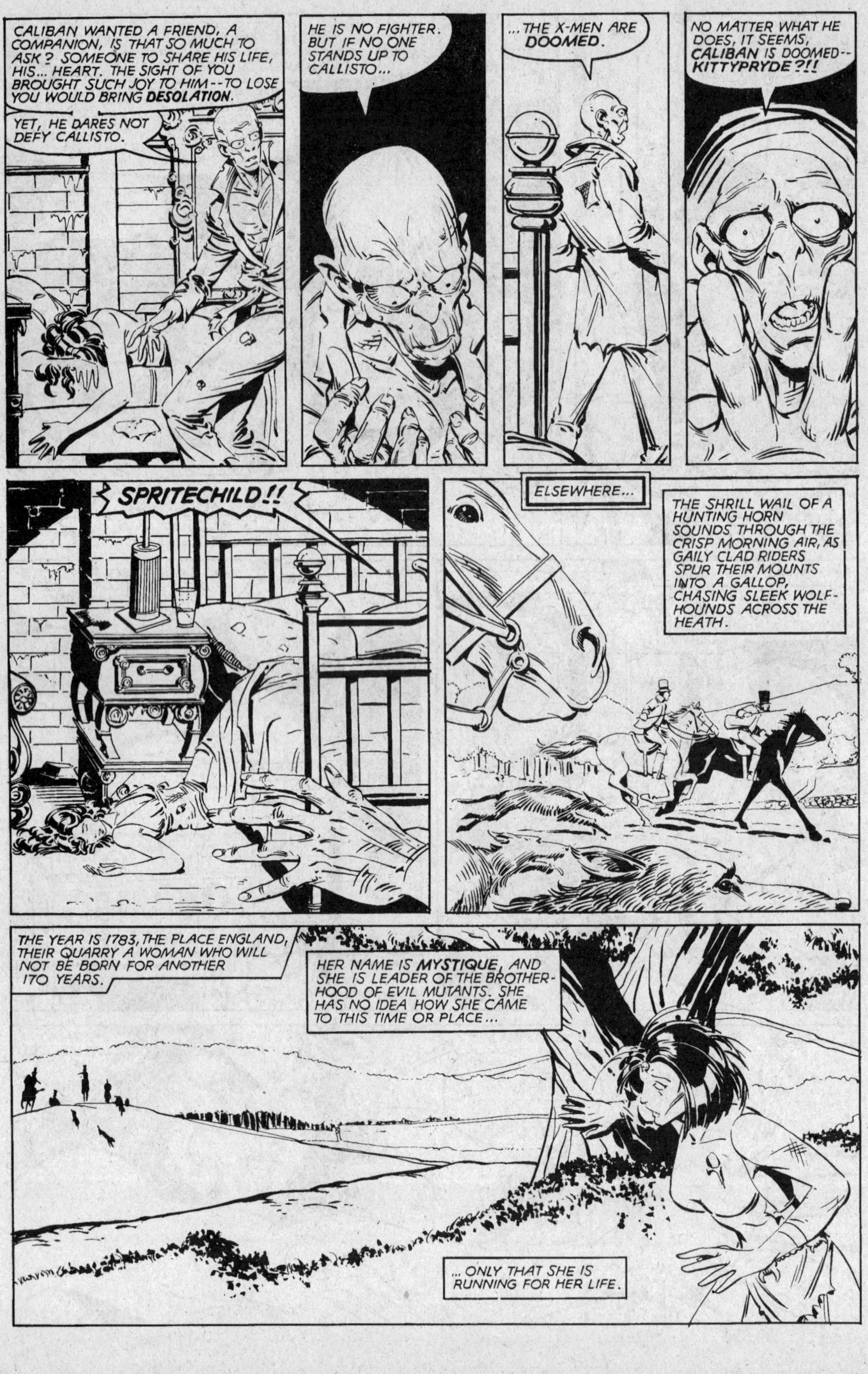
CALIBAN WANTED A FRIEND, A COMPANION, IS THAT SO MUCH TO ASK? SOMEONE TO SHARE HIS LIFE, HIS... HEART. THE SIGHT OF YOU BROUGHT SUCH JOY TO HIM--TO LOSE YOU WOULD BRING DESOLATION.
YET, HE DARES NOT DEFY CALLISTO.
HE IS NO FIGHTER. BUT IF NO ONE STANDS UP TO CALLISTO...
...THE X-MEN ARE DOOMED.
NO MATTER WHAT HE DOES, IT SEEMS, CALIBAN IS DOOMED-- KITTYPRYDE?!!
SPRITECHILD!!
ELSEWHERE...
THE SHRILL WAIL OF A HUNTING HORN SOUNDS THROUGH THE CRISP MORNING AIR, AS GAILY CLAD RIDERS SPUR THEIR MOUNTS INTO A GALLOP, CHASING SLEEK WOLF-HOUNDS ACROSS THE HEATH.
THE YEAR IS 1783, THE PLACE ENGLAND, THEIR QUARRY A WOMAN WHO WILL NOT BE BORN FOR ANOTHER 170 YEARS.
HER NAME IS MYSTIQUE, AND SHE IS LEADER OF THE BROTHER-HOOD OF EVIL MUTANTS. SHE HAS NO IDEA HOW SHE CAME TO THIS TIME OR PLACE...
...ONLY THAT SHE IS RUNNING FOR HER LIFE.

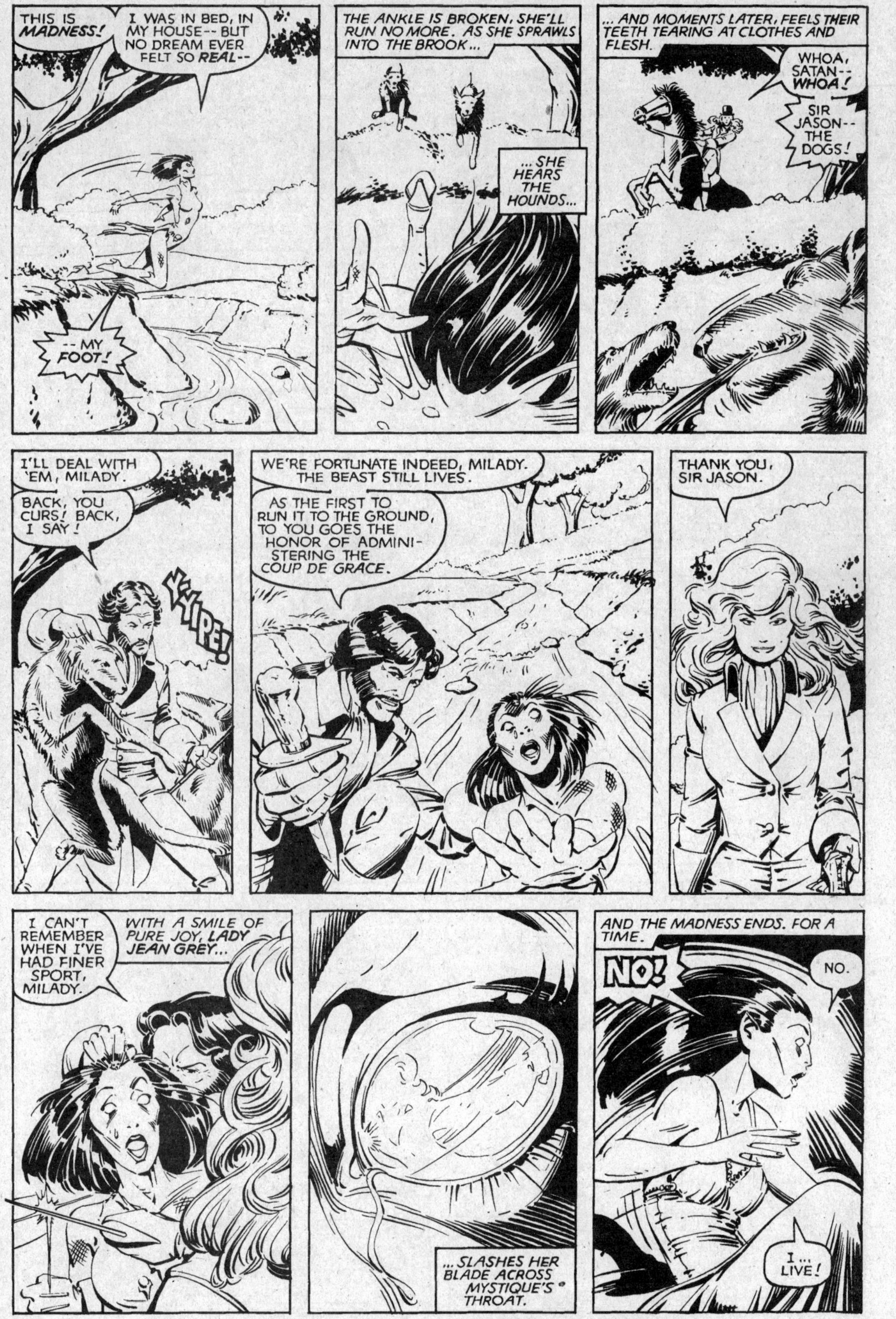

THIS IS MADNESS!
I WAS IN BED, IN MY HOUSE-- BUT NO DREAM EVER FELT SO REAL--
--MY FOOT!
THE ANKLE IS BROKEN. SHE'LL RUN NO MORE. AS SHE SPRAWLS INTO THE BROOK...
...SHE HEARS THE HOUNDS...
...AND MOMENTS LATER, FEELS THEIR TEETH TEARING AT CLOTHES AND FLESH.
WHOA, SATAN-- WHOA!
SIR JASON-- THE DOGS!
I'LL DEAL WITH 'EM, MILADY.
BACK, YOU CURS! BACK, I SAY!
Y-YIPE!
WE'RE FORTUNATE INDEED, MILADY. THE BEAST STILL LIVES.
AS THE FIRST TO RUN IT TO THE GROUND, TO YOU GOES THE HONOR OF ADMINISTERING THE COUP DE GRACE.
THANK YOU, SIR JASON.
I CAN'T REMEMBER WHEN I'VE HAD FINER SPORT, MILADY.
WITH A SMILE OF PURE JOY, LADY JEAN GREY...
...SLASHES HER BLADE ACROSS MYSTIQUE'S THROAT.
AND THE MADNESS ENDS. FOR A TIME.
NO!
NO.
I... LIVE!

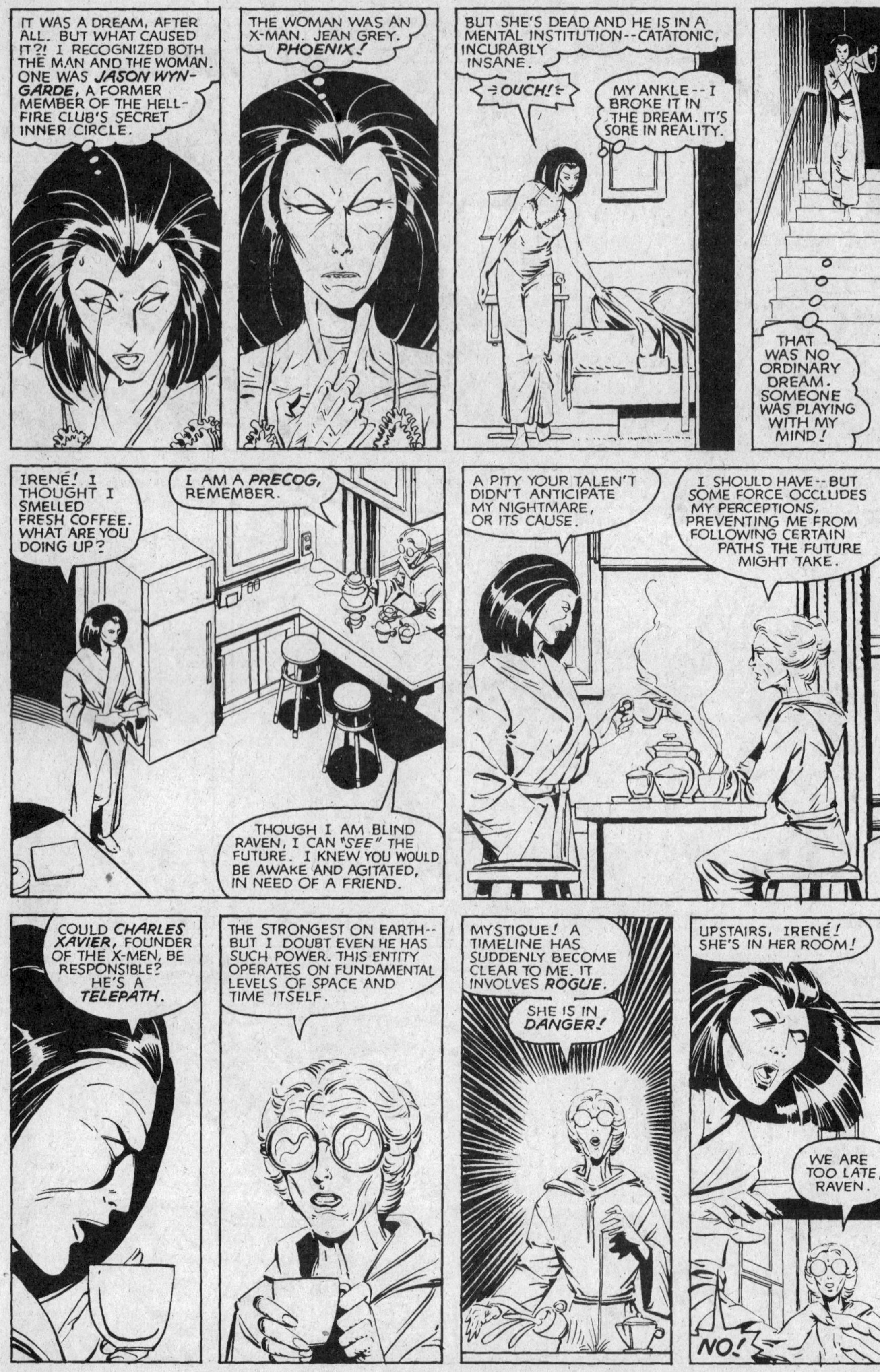
IT WAS A DREAM, AFTER ALL. BUT WHAT CAUSED IT?! I RECOGNIZED BOTH THE MAN AND THE WOMAN. ONE WAS JASON WYNGARDE, A FORMER MEMBER OF THE HELL-FIRE CLUB'S SECRET INNER CIRCLE.
THE WOMAN WAS AN X-MAN. JEAN GREY. PHOENIX!
BUT SHE'S DEAD AND HE IS IN A MENTAL INSTITUTION--CATATONIC, INCURABLY INSANE.
OUCH!
MY ANKLE--I BROKE IT IN THE DREAM. IT'S SORE IN REALITY.
THAT WAS NO ORDINARY DREAM. SOMEONE WAS PLAYING WITH MY MIND!
IRENÉ! I THOUGHT I SMELLED FRESH COFFEE. WHAT ARE YOU DOING UP?
I AM A PRECOG, REMEMBER.
THOUGH I AM BLIND RAVEN, I CAN "SEE" THE FUTURE. I KNEW YOU WOULD BE AWAKE AND AGITATED, IN NEED OF A FRIEND.
A PITY YOUR TALEN'T DIDN'T ANTICIPATE MY NIGHTMARE, OR ITS CAUSE.
I SHOULD HAVE--BUT SOME FORCE OCCLUDES MY PERCEPTIONS, PREVENTING ME FROM FOLLOWING CERTAIN PATHS THE FUTURE MIGHT TAKE.
COULD CHARLES XAVIER, FOUNDER OF THE X-MEN, BE RESPONSIBLE? HE'S A TELEPATH.
THE STRONGEST ON EARTH--BUT I DOUBT EVEN HE HAS SUCH POWER. THIS ENTITY OPERATES ON FUNDAMENTAL LEVELS OF SPACE AND TIME ITSELF.
MYSTIQUE! A TIMELINE HAS SUDDENLY BECOME CLEAR TO ME. IT INVOLVES ROGUE.
SHE IS IN DANGER!
UPSTAIRS, IRENÉ! SHE'S IN HER ROOM!
WE ARE TOO LATE, RAVEN.
NO!

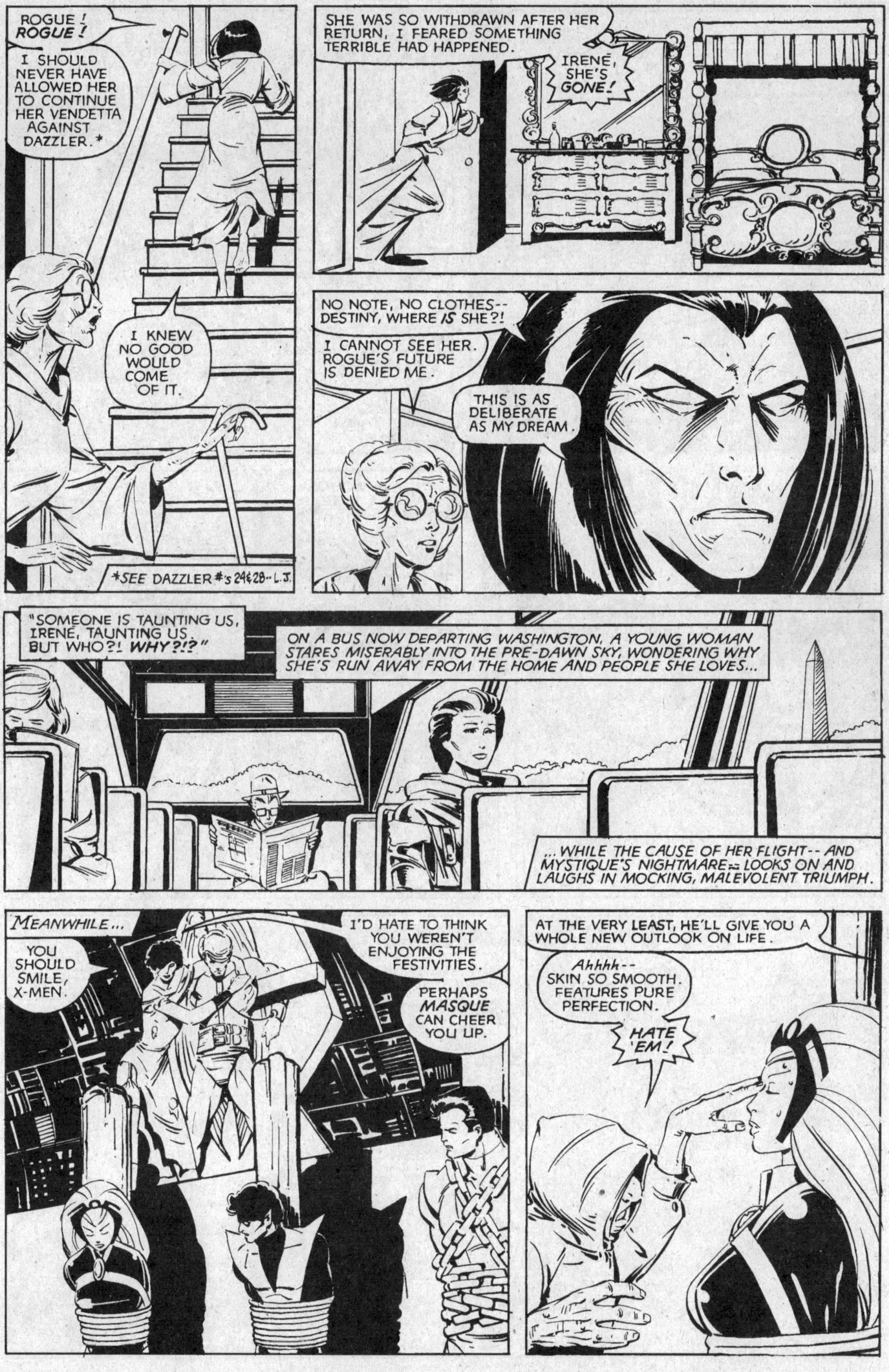
ROGUE! ROGUE!
I SHOULD NEVER HAVE ALLOWED HER TO CONTINUE HER VENDETTA AGAINST DAZZLER.*
I KNEW NO GOOD WOULD COME OF IT.
*SEE DAZZLER #'s 24 & 28 -- L.J.
SHE WAS SO WITHDRAWN AFTER HER RETURN, I FEARED SOMETHING TERRIBLE HAD HAPPENED.
IRENÉ, SHE'S GONE!
NO NOTE, NO CLOTHES-- DESTINY, WHERE IS SHE?!
I CANNOT SEE HER. ROGUE'S FUTURE IS DENIED ME.
THIS IS AS DELIBERATE AS MY DREAM.
"SOMEONE IS TAUNTING US, IRENÉ, TAUNTING US. BUT WHO?! WHY?!?"
ON A BUS NOW DEPARTING WASHINGTON, A YOUNG WOMAN STARES MISERABLY INTO THE PRE-DAWN SKY, WONDERING WHY SHE'S RUN AWAY FROM THE HOME AND PEOPLE SHE LOVES...
...WHILE THE CAUSE OF HER FLIGHT-- AND MYSTIQUE'S NIGHTMARE-- LOOKS ON AND LAUGHS IN MOCKING, MALEVOLENT TRIUMPH.
MEANWHILE...
YOU SHOULD SMILE, X-MEN.
I'D HATE TO THINK YOU WEREN'T ENJOYING THE FESTIVITIES.
PERHAPS MASQUE CAN CHEER YOU UP.
AT THE VERY LEAST, HE'LL GIVE YOU A WHOLE NEW OUTLOOK ON LIFE.
Ahhhh-- SKIN SO SMOOTH. FEATURES PURE PERFECTION.
HATE 'EM!

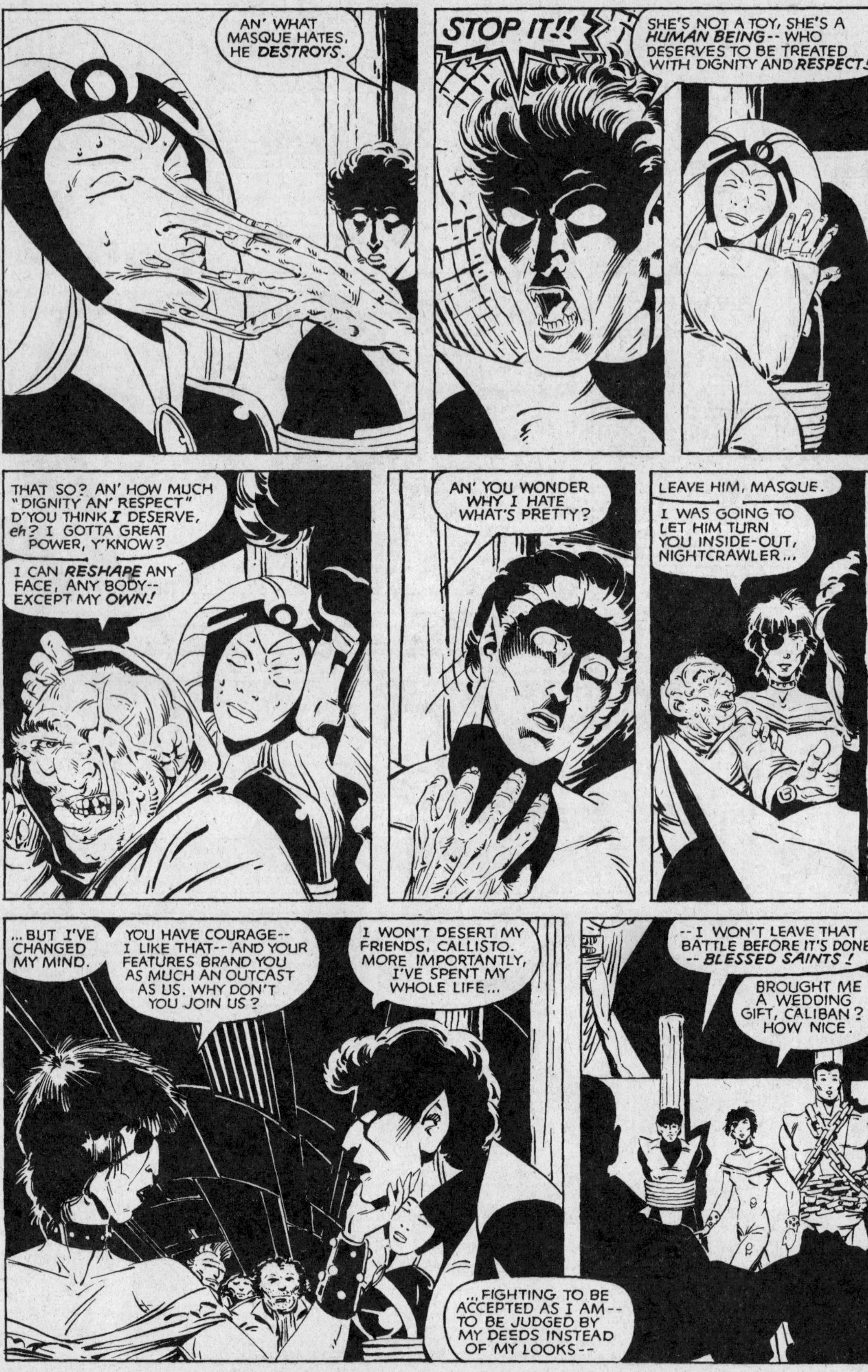

AN' WHAT MASQUE HATES, HE DESTROYS.
STOP IT!!
SHE'S NOT A TOY, SHE'S A HUMAN BEING -- WHO DESERVES TO BE TREATED WITH DIGNITY AND RESPECT!
THAT SO? AN' HOW MUCH "DIGNITY AN' RESPECT" D'YOU THINK I DESERVE, eh? I GOTTA GREAT POWER, Y'KNOW?
I CAN RESHAPE ANY FACE, ANY BODY-- EXCEPT MY OWN!
AN' YOU WONDER WHY I HATE WHAT'S PRETTY?
LEAVE HIM, MASQUE.
I WAS GOING TO LET HIM TURN YOU INSIDE-OUT, NIGHTCRAWLER...
...BUT I'VE CHANGED MY MIND.
YOU HAVE COURAGE-- I LIKE THAT-- AND YOUR FEATURES BRAND YOU AS MUCH AN OUTCAST AS US. WHY DON'T YOU JOIN US?
I WON'T DESERT MY FRIENDS, CALLISTO. MORE IMPORTANTLY, I'VE SPENT MY WHOLE LIFE...
...FIGHTING TO BE ACCEPTED AS I AM-- TO BE JUDGED BY MY DEEDS INSTEAD OF MY LOOKS--
--I WON'T LEAVE THAT BATTLE BEFORE IT'S DONE -- BLESSED SAINTS!
BROUGHT ME A WEDDING GIFT, CALIBAN? HOW NICE.

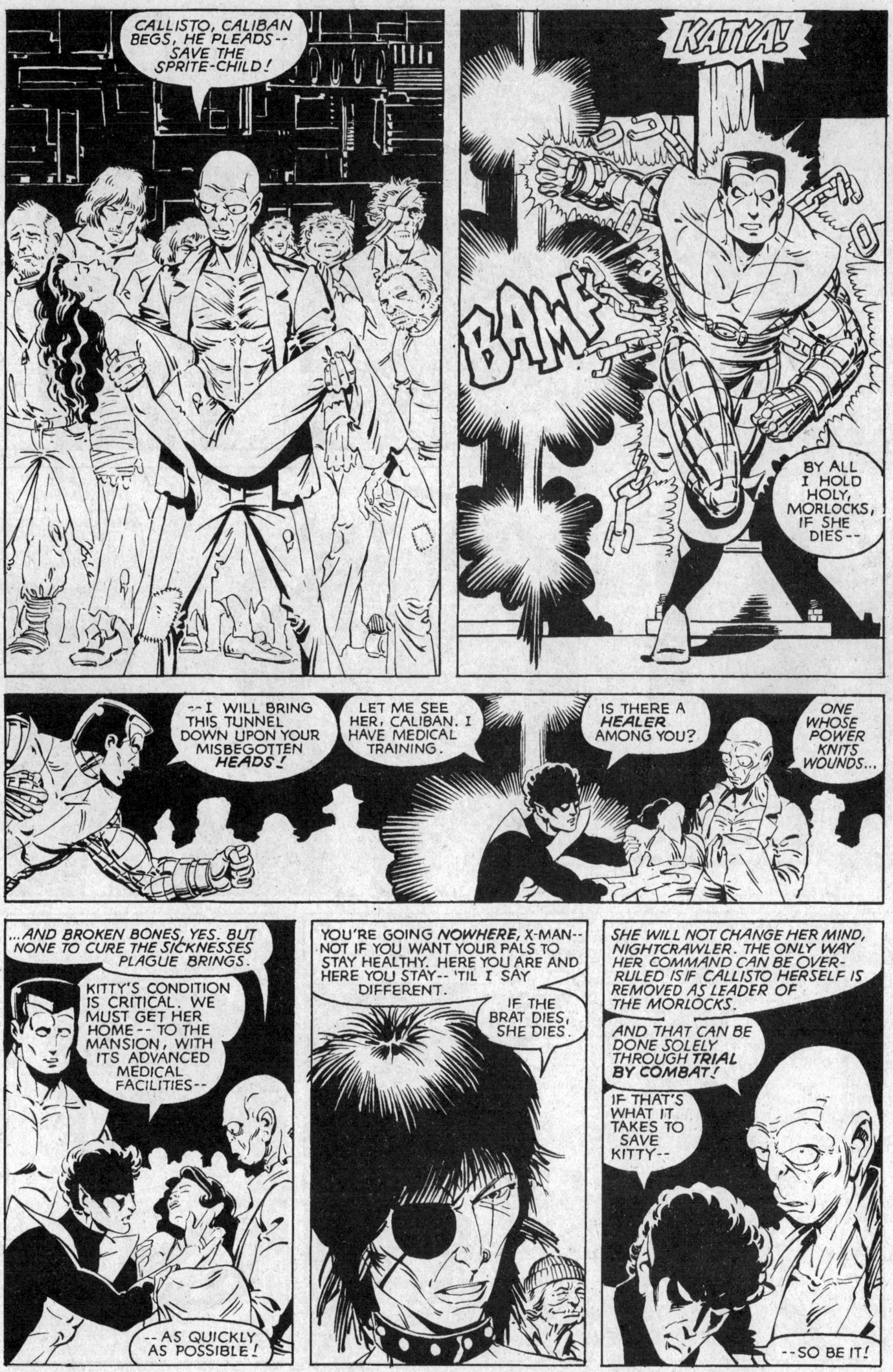
CALLISTO, CALIBAN BEGS, HE PLEADS-- SAVE THE SPRITE-CHILD!
KATYA!
BAMF
BY ALL I HOLD HOLY, MORLOCKS, IF SHE DIES--
--I WILL BRING THIS TUNNEL DOWN UPON YOUR MISBEGOTTEN HEADS!
LET ME SEE HER, CALIBAN. I HAVE MEDICAL TRAINING.
IS THERE A HEALER AMONG YOU?
ONE WHOSE POWER KNITS WOUNDS...
...AND BROKEN BONES, YES. BUT NONE TO CURE THE SICKNESSES PLAGUE BRINGS.
KITTY'S CONDITION IS CRITICAL. WE MUST GET HER HOME-- TO THE MANSION, WITH ITS ADVANCED MEDICAL FACILITIES--
--AS QUICKLY AS POSSIBLE!
YOU'RE GOING NOWHERE, X-MAN-- NOT IF YOU WANT YOUR PALS TO STAY HEALTHY. HERE YOU ARE AND HERE YOU STAY-- 'TIL I SAY DIFFERENT.
IF THE BRAT DIES, SHE DIES.
SHE WILL NOT CHANGE HER MIND, NIGHTCRAWLER. THE ONLY WAY HER COMMAND CAN BE OVER-RULED IS IF CALLISTO HERSELF IS REMOVED AS LEADER OF THE MORLOCKS.
AND THAT CAN BE DONE SOLELY THROUGH TRIAL BY COMBAT!
IF THAT'S WHAT IT TAKES TO SAVE KITTY--
--SO BE IT!

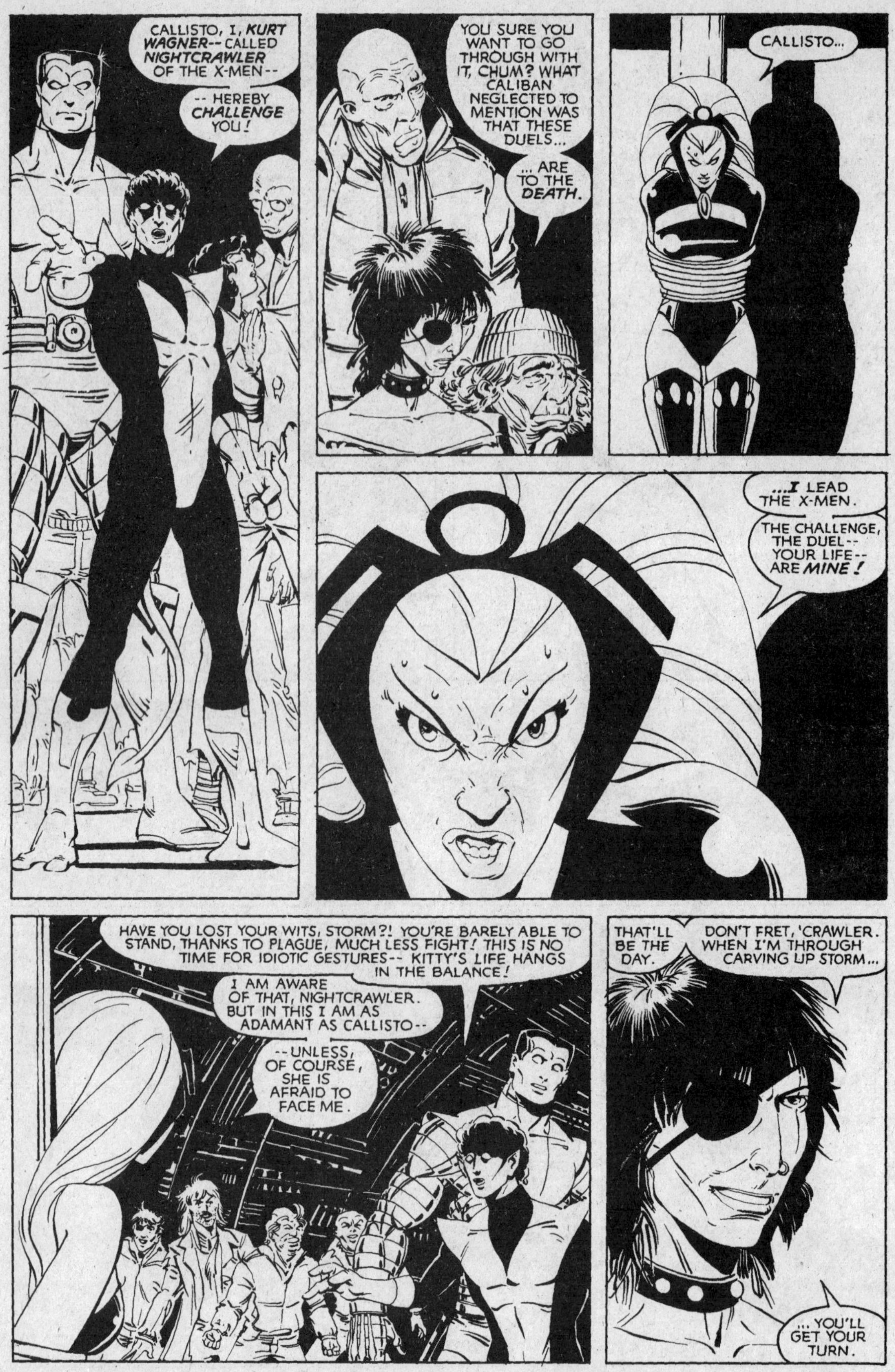
CALLISTO, I, KURT WAGNER-- CALLED NIGHTCRAWLER OF THE X-MEN--
-- HEREBY CHALLENGE YOU!
YOU SURE YOU WANT TO GO THROUGH WITH IT, CHUM? WHAT CALIBAN NEGLECTED TO MENTION WAS THAT THESE DUELS...
... ARE TO THE DEATH.
CALLISTO...
...I LEAD THE X-MEN.
THE CHALLENGE, THE DUEL-- YOUR LIFE-- ARE MINE!
HAVE YOU LOST YOUR WITS, STORM?! YOU'RE BARELY ABLE TO STAND, THANKS TO PLAGUE, MUCH LESS FIGHT! THIS IS NO TIME FOR IDIOTIC GESTURES-- KITTY'S LIFE HANGS IN THE BALANCE!
I AM AWARE OF THAT, NIGHTCRAWLER. BUT IN THIS I AM AS ADAMANT AS CALLISTO--
--UNLESS, OF COURSE, SHE IS AFRAID TO FACE ME.
THAT'LL BE THE DAY.
DON'T FRET, 'CRAWLER. WHEN I'M THROUGH CARVING UP STORM...
... YOU'LL GET YOUR TURN.

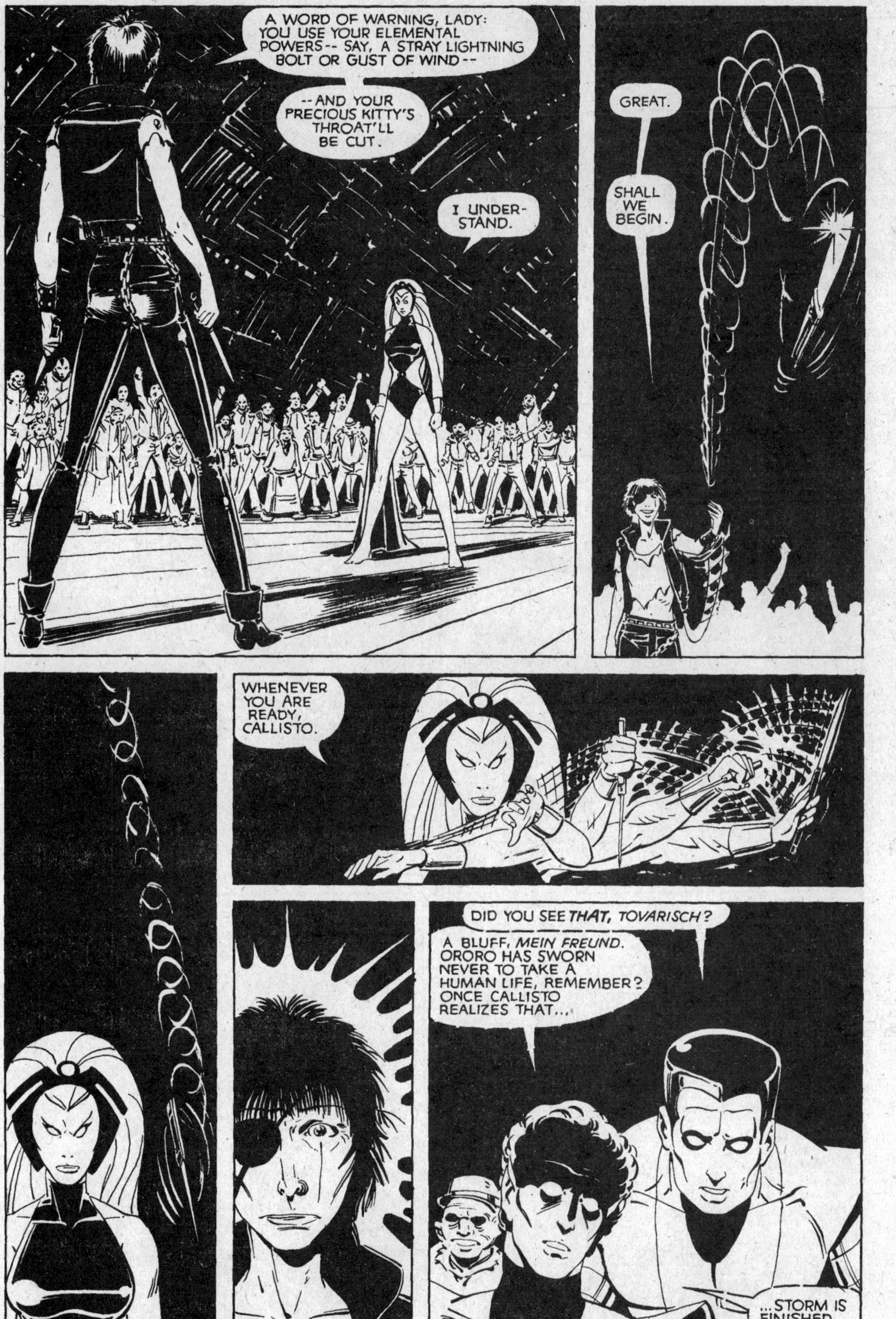
A WORD OF WARNING, LADY: YOU USE YOUR ELEMENTAL POWERS-- SAY, A STRAY LIGHTNING BOLT OR GUST OF WIND--
--AND YOUR PRECIOUS KITTY'S THROAT'LL BE CUT.
I UNDER-STAND.
GREAT.
SHALL WE BEGIN.
WHENEVER YOU ARE READY, CALLISTO.
DID YOU SEE *THAT, TOVARISCH*?
A BLUFF, *MEIN FREUND*. ORORO HAS SWORN NEVER TO TAKE A HUMAN LIFE, REMEMBER? ONCE CALLISTO REALIZES THAT...
...STORM IS FINISHED.

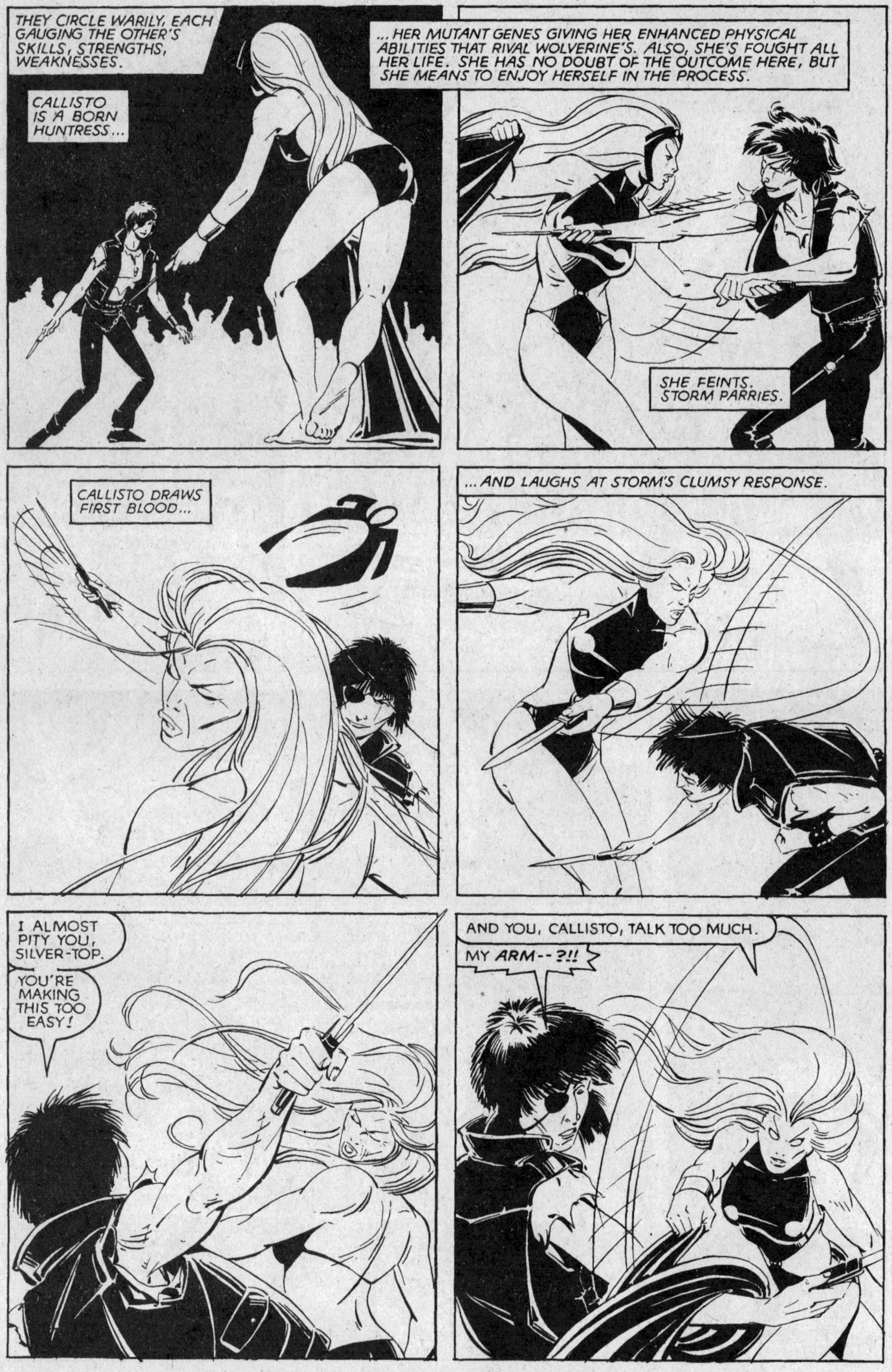
THEY CIRCLE WARILY, EACH GAUGING THE OTHER'S SKILLS, STRENGTHS, WEAKNESSES.
CALLISTO IS A BORN HUNTRESS...
...HER MUTANT GENES GIVING HER ENHANCED PHYSICAL ABILITIES THAT RIVAL WOLVERINE'S. ALSO, SHE'S FOUGHT ALL HER LIFE. SHE HAS NO DOUBT OF THE OUTCOME HERE, BUT SHE MEANS TO ENJOY HERSELF IN THE PROCESS.
SHE FEINTS. STORM PARRIES.
CALLISTO DRAWS FIRST BLOOD...
...AND LAUGHS AT STORM'S CLUMSY RESPONSE.
I ALMOST PITY YOU, SILVER-TOP.
YOU'RE MAKING THIS TOO EASY!
AND YOU, CALLISTO, TALK TOO MUCH.
MY ARM--?!!

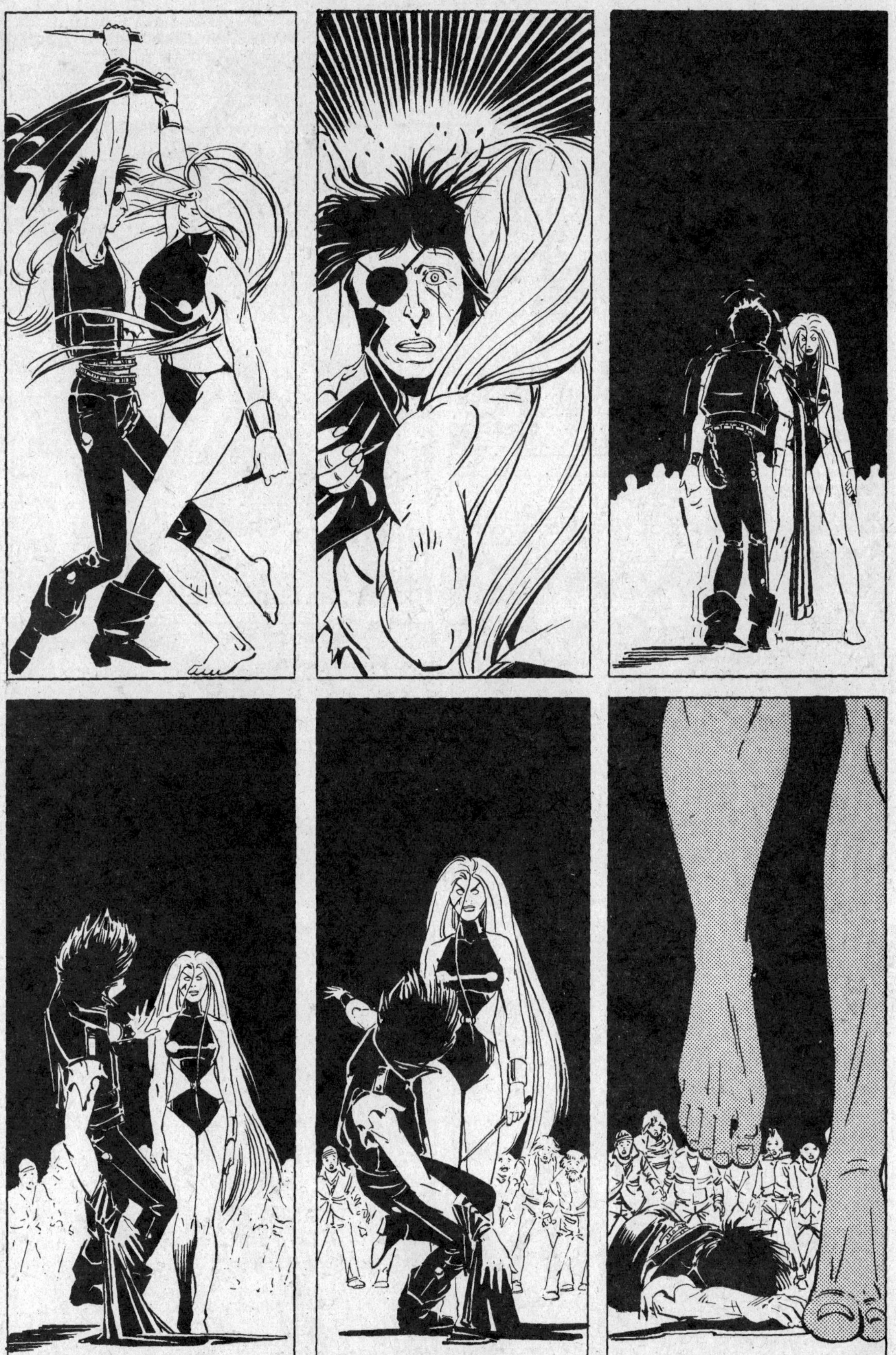

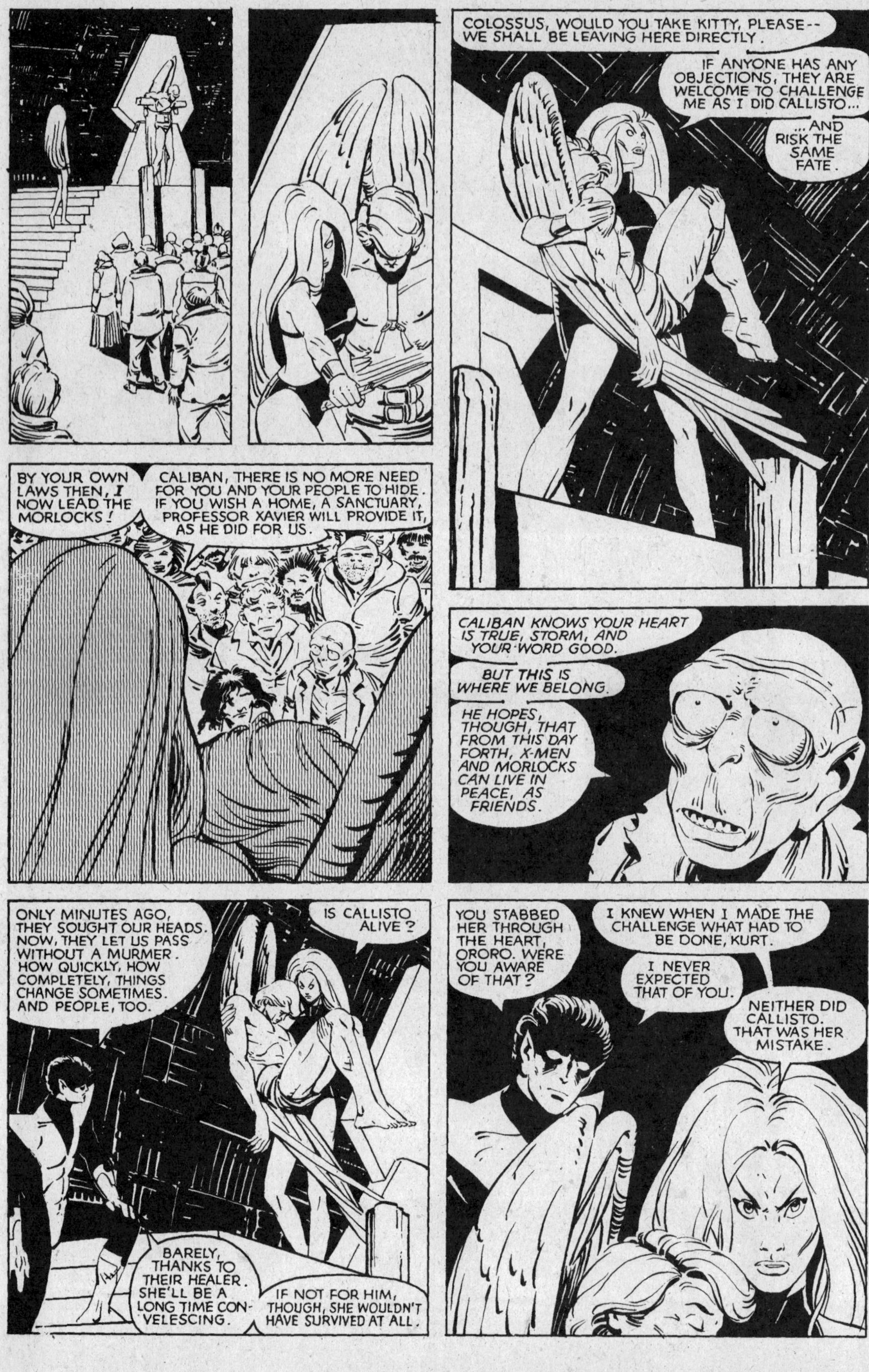
COLOSSUS, WOULD YOU TAKE KITTY, PLEASE-- WE SHALL BE LEAVING HERE DIRECTLY.
IF ANYONE HAS ANY OBJECTIONS, THEY ARE WELCOME TO CHALLENGE ME AS I DID CALLISTO...
...AND RISK THE SAME FATE.
BY YOUR OWN LAWS THEN, I NOW LEAD THE MORLOCKS!
CALIBAN, THERE IS NO MORE NEED FOR YOU AND YOUR PEOPLE TO HIDE. IF YOU WISH A HOME, A SANCTUARY, PROFESSOR XAVIER WILL PROVIDE IT, AS HE DID FOR US.
CALIBAN KNOWS YOUR HEART IS TRUE, STORM, AND YOUR WORD GOOD.
BUT THIS IS WHERE WE BELONG.
HE HOPES, THOUGH, THAT FROM THIS DAY FORTH, X-MEN AND MORLOCKS CAN LIVE IN PEACE, AS FRIENDS.
ONLY MINUTES AGO, THEY SOUGHT OUR HEADS. NOW, THEY LET US PASS WITHOUT A MURMER. HOW QUICKLY, HOW COMPLETELY, THINGS CHANGE SOMETIMES. AND PEOPLE, TOO.
IS CALLISTO ALIVE?
BARELY, THANKS TO THEIR HEALER. SHE'LL BE A LONG TIME CONVELESCING.
IF NOT FOR HIM, THOUGH, SHE WOULDN'T HAVE SURVIVED AT ALL.
YOU STABBED HER THROUGH THE HEART, ORORO. WERE YOU AWARE OF THAT?
I KNEW WHEN I MADE THE CHALLENGE WHAT HAD TO BE DONE, KURT.
I NEVER EXPECTED THAT OF YOU.
NEITHER DID CALLISTO. THAT WAS HER MISTAKE.

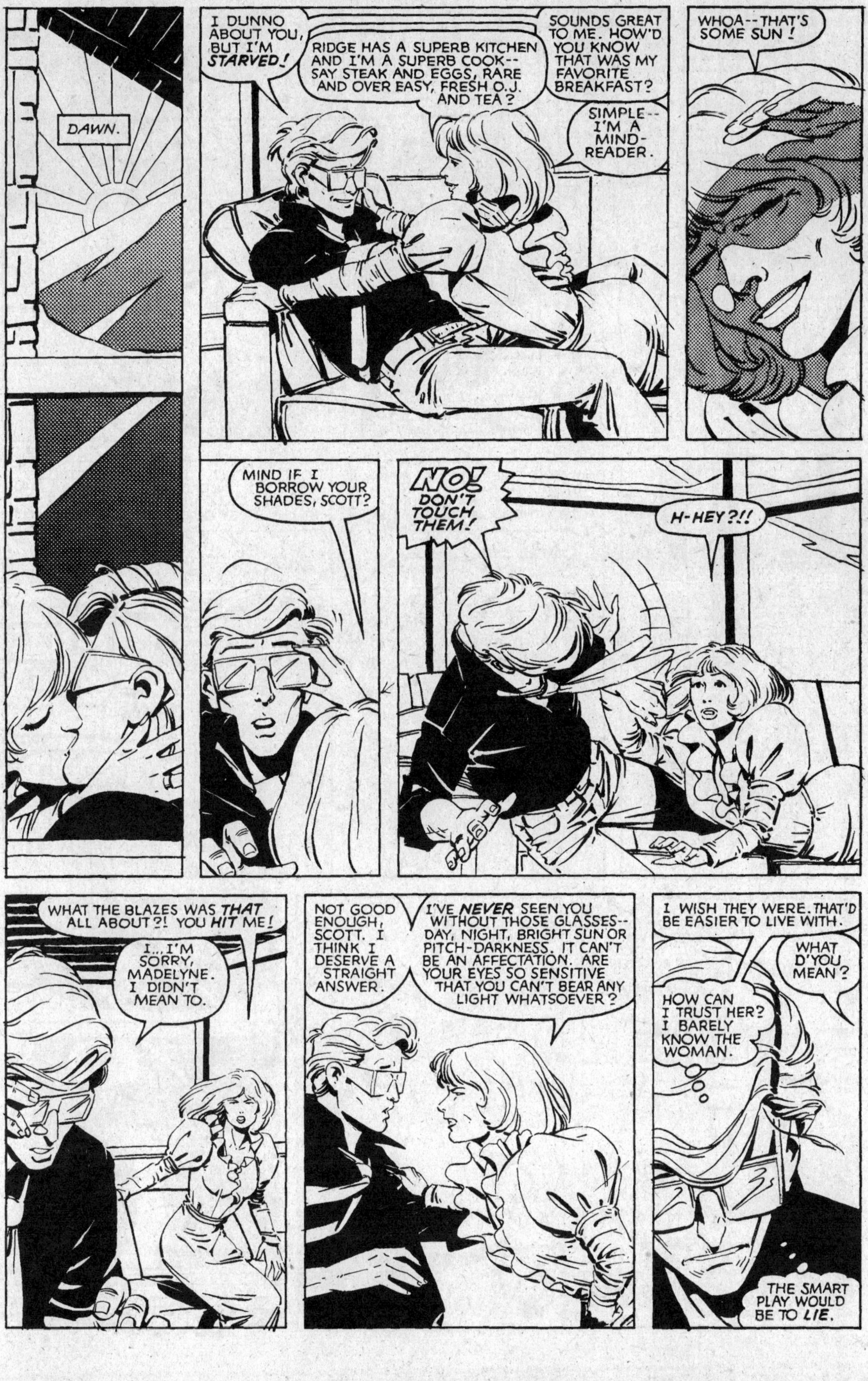
DAWN.
I DUNNO ABOUT YOU, BUT I'M STARVED!
RIDGE HAS A SUPERB KITCHEN AND I'M A SUPERB COOK-- SAY STEAK AND EGGS, RARE AND OVER EASY, FRESH O.J. AND TEA?
SOUNDS GREAT TO ME. HOW'D YOU KNOW THAT WAS MY FAVORITE BREAKFAST?
SIMPLE-- I'M A MIND-READER.
WHOA--THAT'S SOME SUN!
MIND IF I BORROW YOUR SHADES, SCOTT?
NO! DON'T TOUCH THEM!
H-HEY?!!
WHAT THE BLAZES WAS THAT ALL ABOUT?! YOU HIT ME!
I...I'M SORRY, MADELYNE. I DIDN'T MEAN TO.
NOT GOOD ENOUGH, SCOTT. I THINK I DESERVE A STRAIGHT ANSWER.
I'VE NEVER SEEN YOU WITHOUT THOSE GLASSES-- DAY, NIGHT, BRIGHT SUN OR PITCH-DARKNESS. IT CAN'T BE AN AFFECTATION. ARE YOUR EYES SO SENSITIVE THAT YOU CAN'T BEAR ANY LIGHT WHATSOEVER?
I WISH THEY WERE. THAT'D BE EASIER TO LIVE WITH.
WHAT D'YOU MEAN?
HOW CAN I TRUST HER? I BARELY KNOW THE WOMAN.
THE SMART PLAY WOULD BE TO LIE.

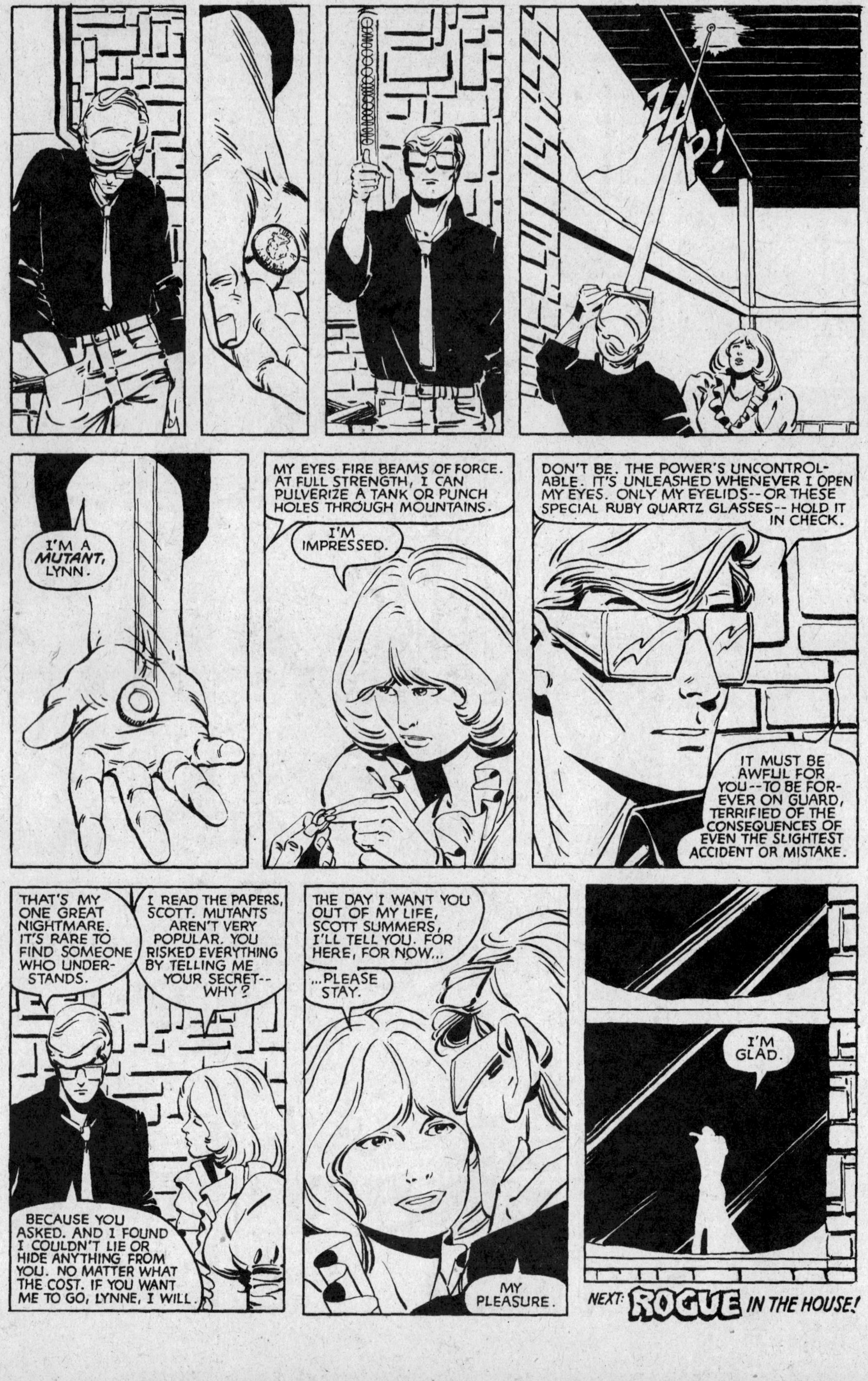

ZAP!
I'M A MUTANT, LYNN.
MY EYES FIRE BEAMS OF FORCE. AT FULL STRENGTH, I CAN PULVERIZE A TANK OR PUNCH HOLES THROUGH MOUNTAINS.
I'M IMPRESSED.
DON'T BE. THE POWER'S UNCONTROLABLE. IT'S UNLEASHED WHENEVER I OPEN MY EYES. ONLY MY EYELIDS-- OR THESE SPECIAL RUBY QUARTZ GLASSES-- HOLD IT IN CHECK.
IT MUST BE AWFUL FOR YOU--TO BE FOREVER ON GUARD, TERRIFIED OF THE CONSEQUENCES OF EVEN THE SLIGHTEST ACCIDENT OR MISTAKE.
THAT'S MY ONE GREAT NIGHTMARE. IT'S RARE TO FIND SOMEONE WHO UNDERSTANDS.
I READ THE PAPERS, SCOTT. MUTANTS AREN'T VERY POPULAR. YOU RISKED EVERYTHING BY TELLING ME YOUR SECRET-- WHY?
BECAUSE YOU ASKED. AND I FOUND I COULDN'T LIE OR HIDE ANYTHING FROM YOU. NO MATTER WHAT THE COST. IF YOU WANT ME TO GO, LYNNE, I WILL.
THE DAY I WANT YOU OUT OF MY LIFE, SCOTT SUMMERS, I'LL TELL YOU. FOR HERE, FOR NOW...
...PLEASE STAY.
MY PLEASURE.
I'M GLAD.
NEXT: ROGUE IN THE HOUSE!

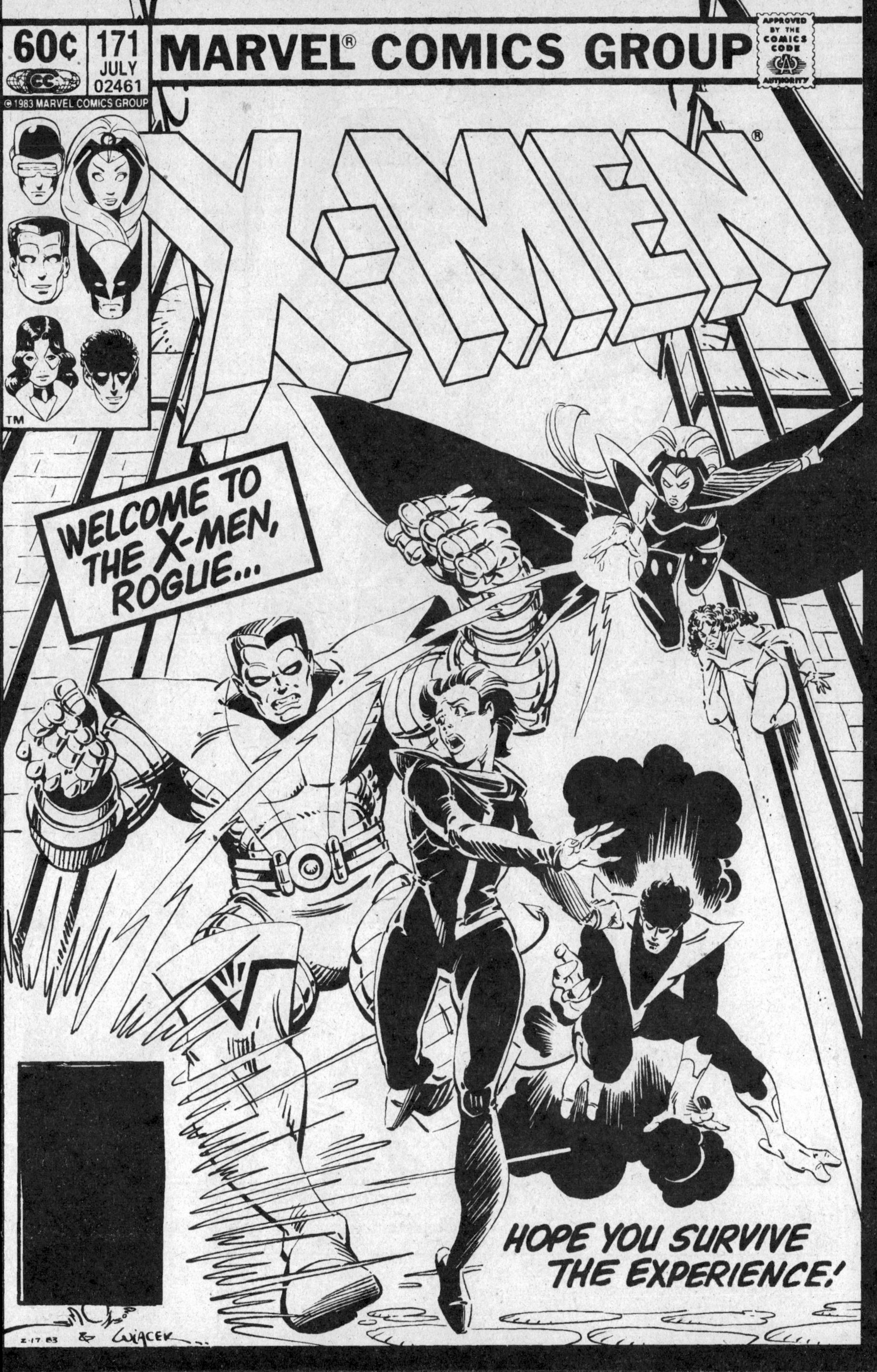
60¢
171
JULY
02461
© 1983 MARVEL COMICS GROUP
MARVEL® COMICS GROUP
APPROVED BY THE COMICS CODE AUTHORITY
X-MEN®
TM
WELCOME TO THE X-MEN, ROGUE...
HOPE YOU SURVIVE THE EXPERIENCE!

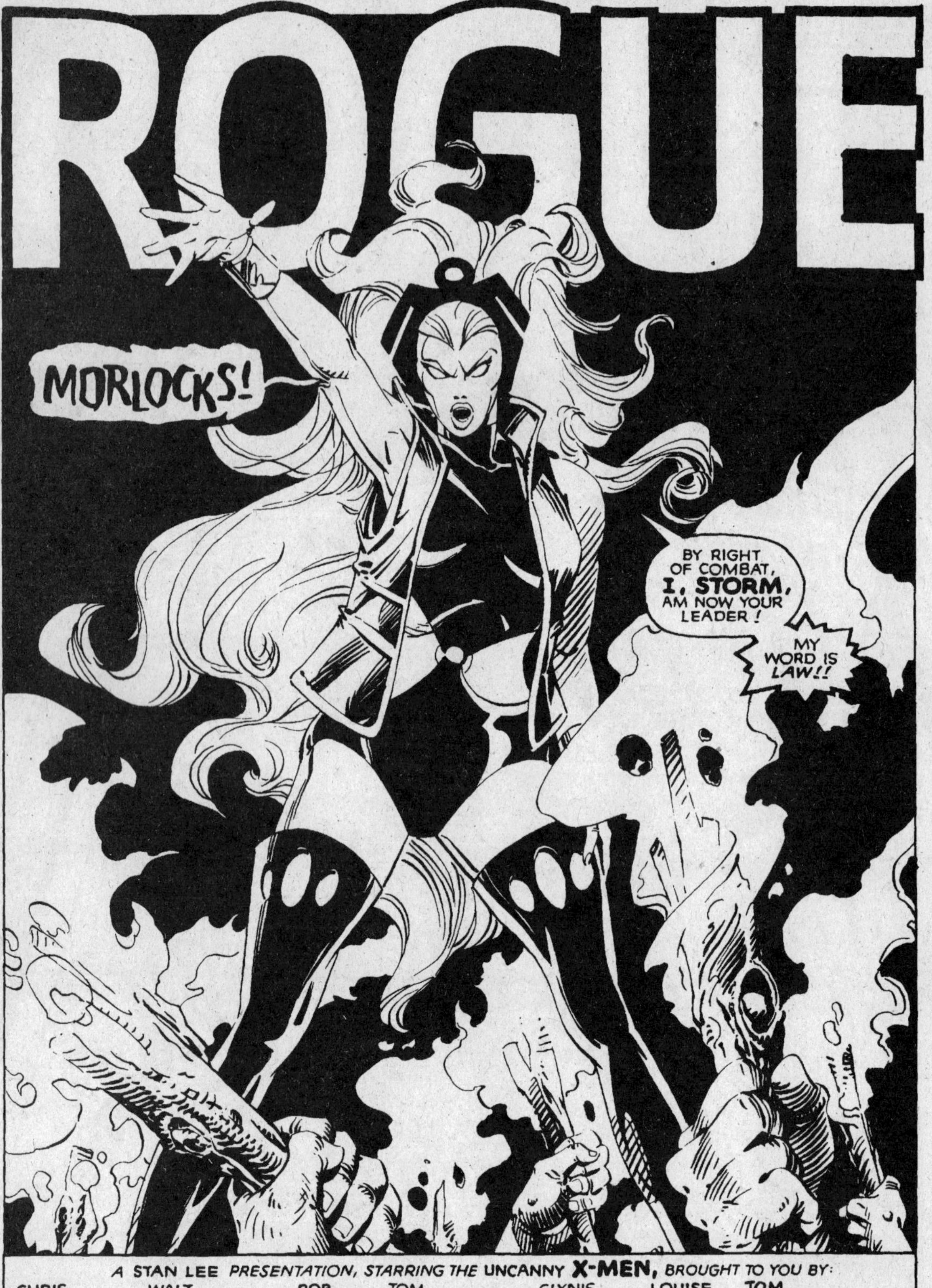
ROGUE
MORLOCKS!
BY RIGHT OF COMBAT, I, STORM, AM NOW YOUR LEADER!
MY WORD IS LAW!!

A STAN LEE *PRESENTATION, STARRING THE* UNCANNY **X-MEN,** *BROUGHT TO YOU BY:*

CHRIS CLAREMONT	WALT SIMONSON	BOB WIACEK,	TOM ORZECHOWSKI	GLYNIS WEIN	LOUISE JONES	TOM DEFALCO
SCRIPTER	*GUEST PENCILER*	*FINISHER*	*LETTERER*	*COLORIST*	*EDITOR*	*EDITOR-IN-CHIEF*

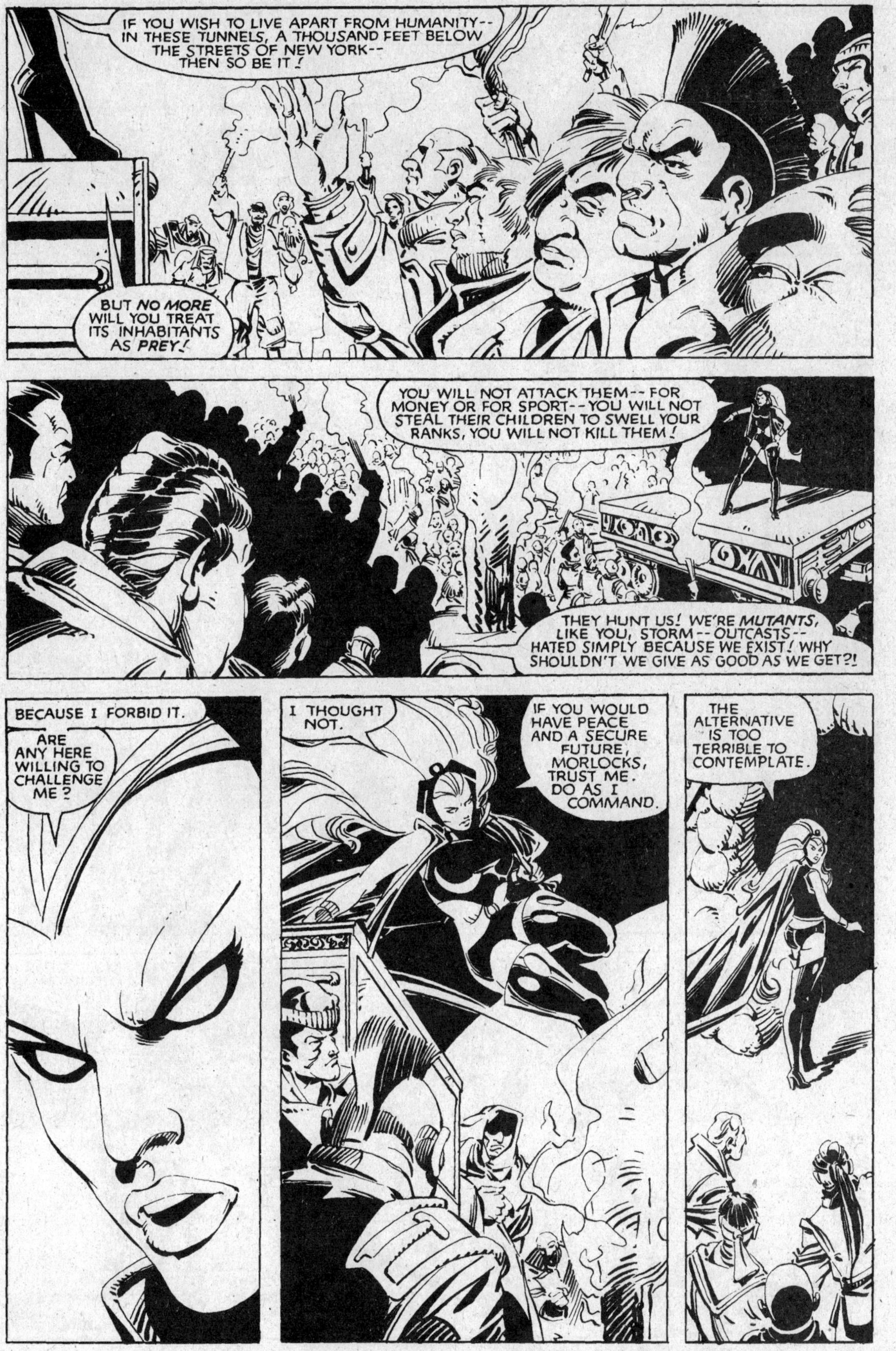

IF YOU WISH TO LIVE APART FROM HUMANITY-- IN THESE TUNNELS, A THOUSAND FEET BELOW THE STREETS OF NEW YORK-- THEN SO BE IT!
BUT NO MORE WILL YOU TREAT ITS INHABITANTS AS PREY!
YOU WILL NOT ATTACK THEM-- FOR MONEY OR FOR SPORT-- YOU WILL NOT STEAL THEIR CHILDREN TO SWELL YOUR RANKS, YOU WILL NOT KILL THEM!
THEY HUNT US! WE'RE MUTANTS, LIKE YOU, STORM-- OUTCASTS-- HATED SIMPLY BECAUSE WE EXIST! WHY SHOULDN'T WE GIVE AS GOOD AS WE GET?!
BECAUSE I FORBID IT.
ARE ANY HERE WILLING TO CHALLENGE ME?
I THOUGHT NOT.
IF YOU WOULD HAVE PEACE AND A SECURE FUTURE, MORLOCKS, TRUST ME. DO AS I COMMAND.
THE ALTERNATIVE IS TOO TERRIBLE TO CONTEMPLATE.

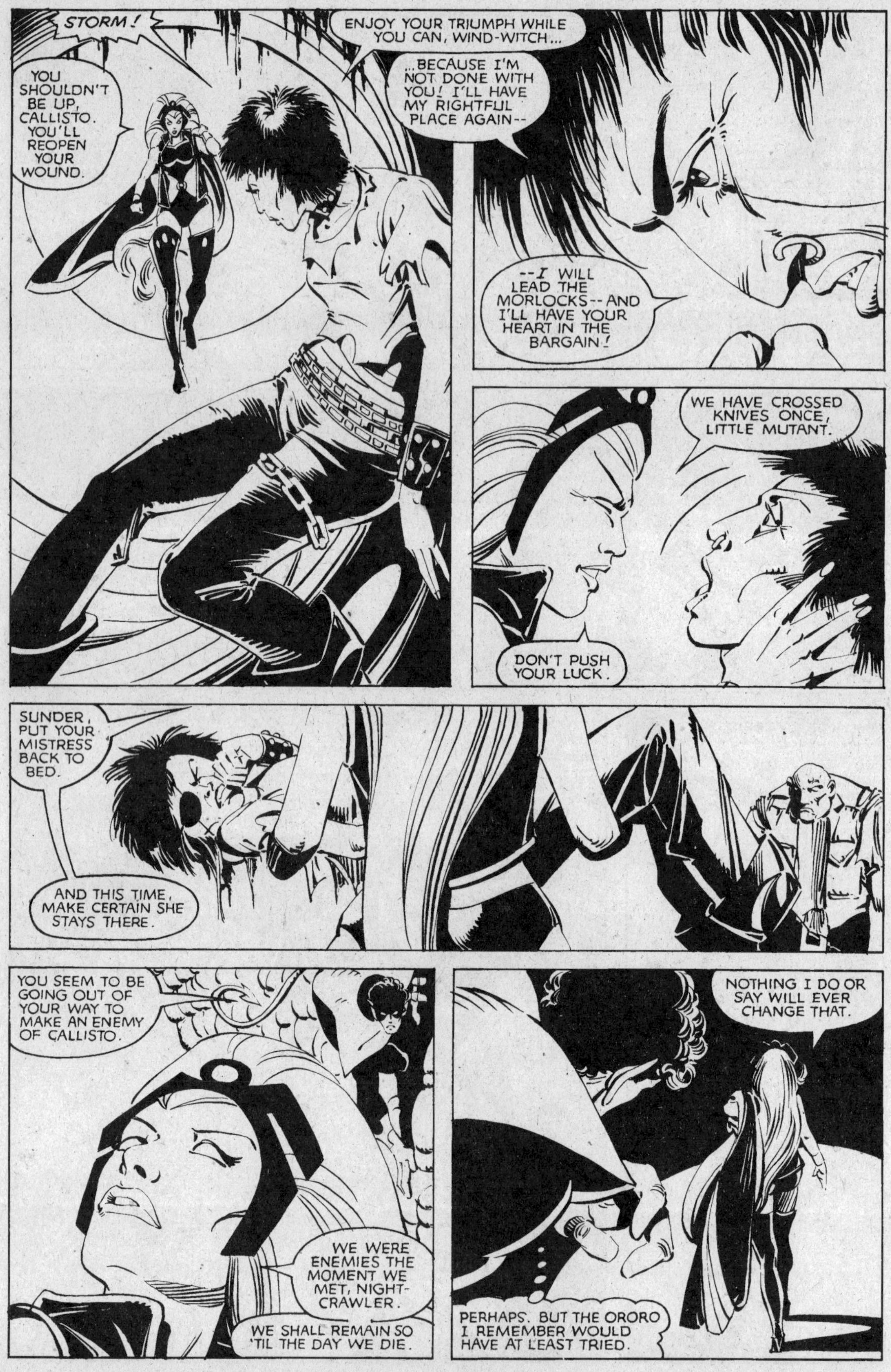
STORM!
YOU SHOULDN'T BE UP, CALLISTO. YOU'LL REOPEN YOUR WOUND.
ENJOY YOUR TRIUMPH WHILE YOU CAN, WIND-WITCH...
...BECAUSE I'M NOT DONE WITH YOU! I'LL HAVE MY RIGHTFUL PLACE AGAIN--
--I WILL LEAD THE MORLOCKS--AND I'LL HAVE YOUR HEART IN THE BARGAIN!
WE HAVE CROSSED KNIVES ONCE, LITTLE MUTANT.
DON'T PUSH YOUR LUCK.
SUNDER, PUT YOUR MISTRESS BACK TO BED.
AND THIS TIME, MAKE CERTAIN SHE STAYS THERE.
YOU SEEM TO BE GOING OUT OF YOUR WAY TO MAKE AN ENEMY OF CALLISTO.
WE WERE ENEMIES THE MOMENT WE MET, NIGHT-CRAWLER.
WE SHALL REMAIN SO 'TIL THE DAY WE DIE.
NOTHING I DO OR SAY WILL EVER CHANGE THAT.
PERHAPS. BUT THE ORORO I REMEMBER WOULD HAVE AT LEAST TRIED.

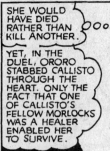

SHE WOULD HAVE DIED RATHER THAN KILL ANOTHER.

YET, IN THE DUEL, ORORO STABBED CALLISTO THROUGH THE HEART. ONLY THE FACT THAT ONE OF CALLISTO'S FELLOW MORLOCKS WAS A HEALER ENABLED HER TO SURVIVE.

ORORO IS CHANGING-- BEFORE MY EYES-- BUT WHAT TRULY TERRIFIES ME IS THAT SHE DOESN'T SEEM TO MIND.

ANCHORAGE, ALASKA.

OUTSIDE, THE AIR IS BITTER COLD, THOUGH IT'S TECHNICALLY SPRING.

WITHIN THE HOUSE, THOUGH, A FIRE WARMS THE BEDROOM...

...ITS FLAMES CASTING A CHEERY GLOW...

...ACROSS THE SLEEPING FIGURE OF MADELYNE PRYOR.

SHE IS DEEP IN DREAMLAND...

...AND THE VISIT ISN'T PLEASANT.

NO! DEAR LORD IN HEAVEN--

--NO!

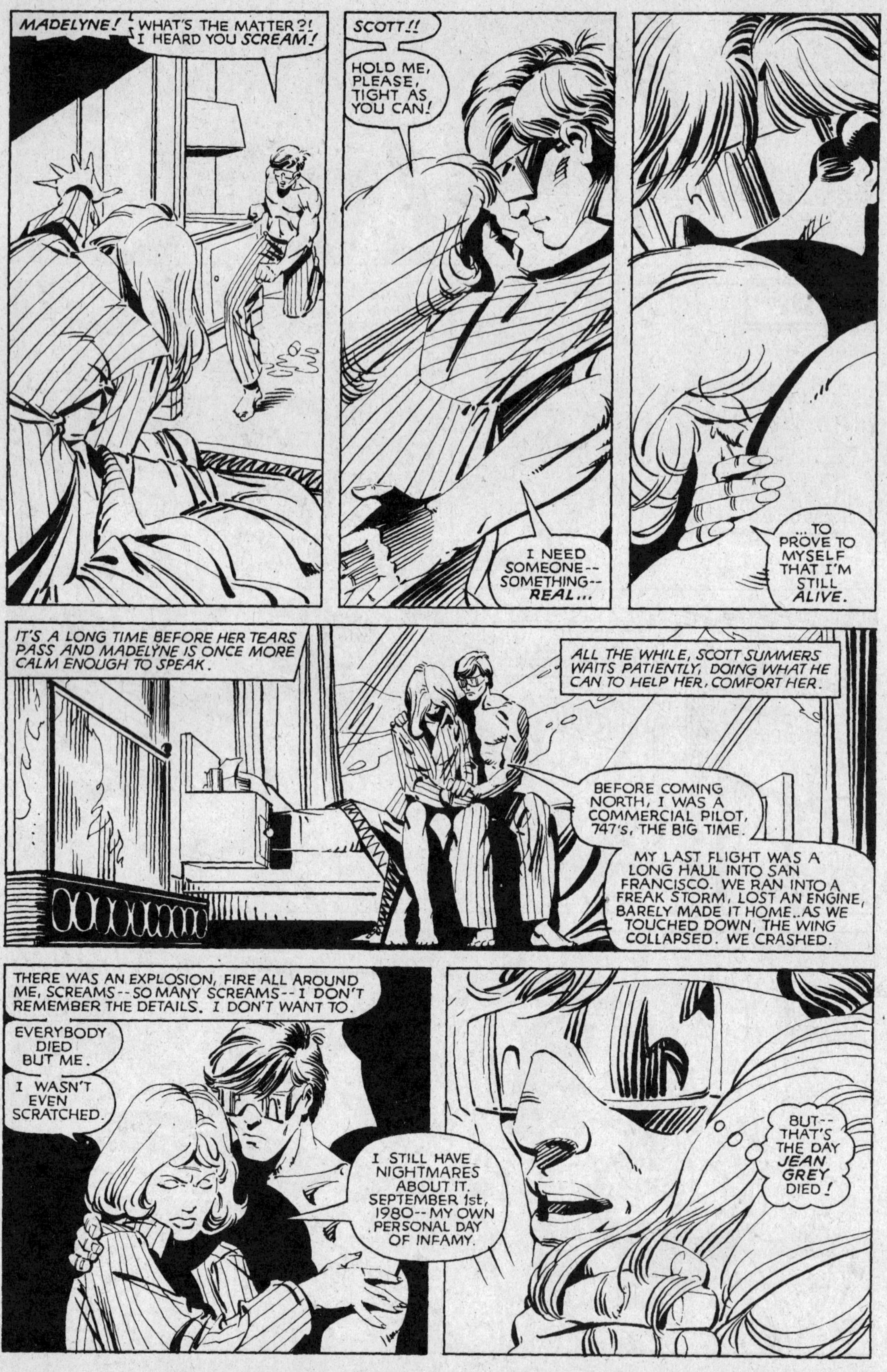
MADELYNE!
WHAT'S THE MATTER?! I HEARD YOU SCREAM!
SCOTT!!
HOLD ME, PLEASE, TIGHT AS YOU CAN!
I NEED SOMEONE-- SOMETHING-- REAL...
...TO PROVE TO MYSELF THAT I'M STILL ALIVE.
IT'S A LONG TIME BEFORE HER TEARS PASS AND MADELYNE IS ONCE MORE CALM ENOUGH TO SPEAK.
ALL THE WHILE, SCOTT SUMMERS WAITS PATIENTLY, DOING WHAT HE CAN TO HELP HER, COMFORT HER.
BEFORE COMING NORTH, I WAS A COMMERCIAL PILOT, 747'S, THE BIG TIME.
MY LAST FLIGHT WAS A LONG HAUL INTO SAN FRANCISCO. WE RAN INTO A FREAK STORM, LOST AN ENGINE, BARELY MADE IT HOME..AS WE TOUCHED DOWN, THE WING COLLAPSED. WE CRASHED.
THERE WAS AN EXPLOSION, FIRE ALL AROUND ME, SCREAMS--SO MANY SCREAMS--I DON'T REMEMBER THE DETAILS. I DON'T WANT TO.
EVERYBODY DIED BUT ME.
I WASN'T EVEN SCRATCHED.
I STILL HAVE NIGHTMARES ABOUT IT. SEPTEMBER 1st, 1980--MY OWN PERSONAL DAY OF INFAMY.
BUT-- THAT'S THE DAY JEAN GREY DIED!

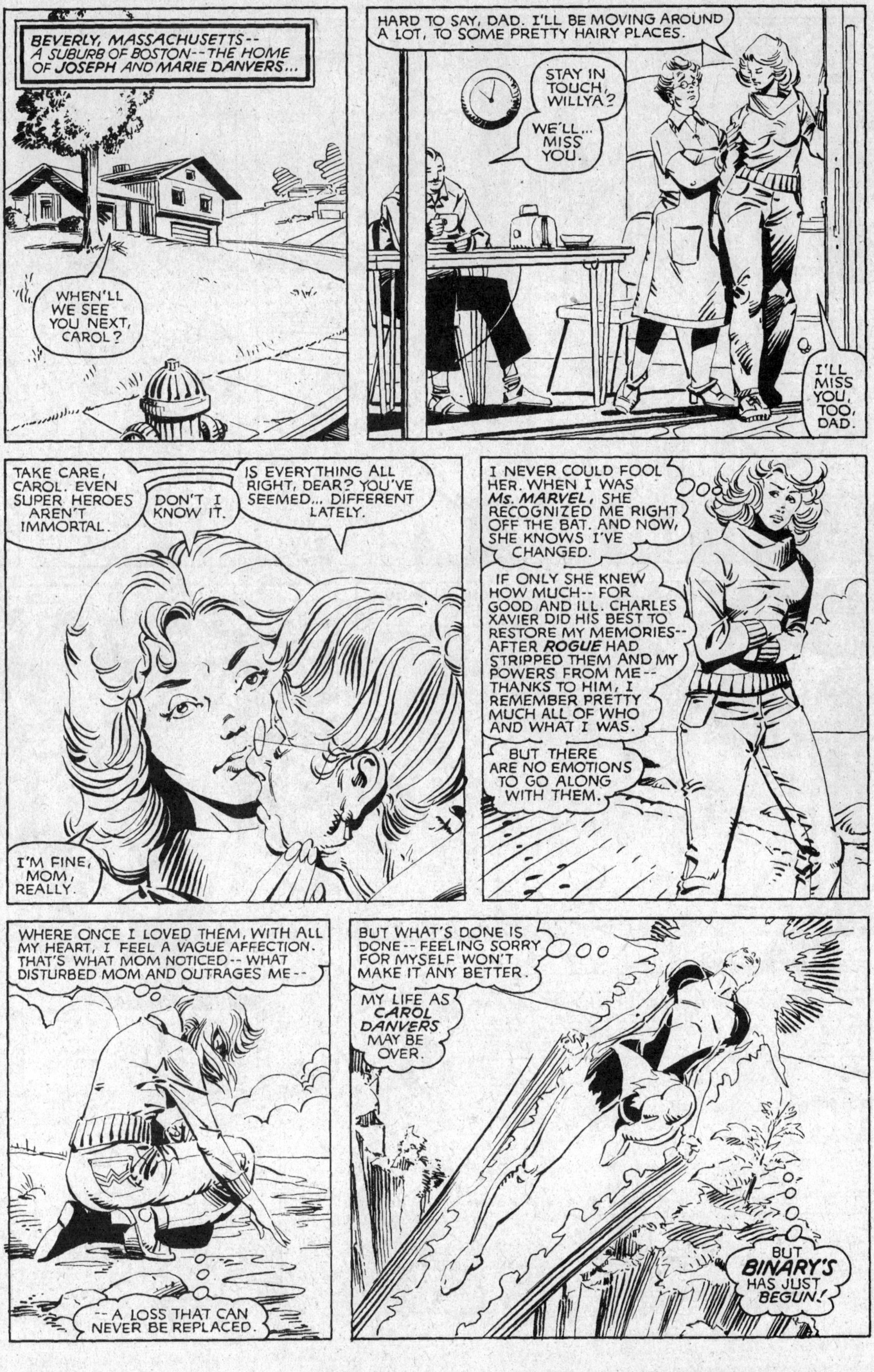
BEVERLY, MASSACHUSETTS-- A SUBURB OF BOSTON--THE HOME OF JOSEPH AND MARIE DANVERS...
WHEN'LL WE SEE YOU NEXT, CAROL?
HARD TO SAY, DAD. I'LL BE MOVING AROUND A LOT, TO SOME PRETTY HAIRY PLACES.
STAY IN TOUCH, WILLYA?
WE'LL... MISS YOU.
I'LL MISS YOU, TOO, DAD.
TAKE CARE, CAROL. EVEN SUPER HEROES AREN'T IMMORTAL.
DON'T I KNOW IT.
IS EVERYTHING ALL RIGHT, DEAR? YOU'VE SEEMED... DIFFERENT LATELY.
I'M FINE, MOM, REALLY.
I NEVER COULD FOOL HER. WHEN I WAS Ms. MARVEL, SHE RECOGNIZED ME RIGHT OFF THE BAT. AND NOW, SHE KNOWS I'VE CHANGED.
IF ONLY SHE KNEW HOW MUCH-- FOR GOOD AND ILL. CHARLES XAVIER DID HIS BEST TO RESTORE MY MEMORIES-- AFTER ROGUE HAD STRIPPED THEM AND MY POWERS FROM ME-- THANKS TO HIM, I REMEMBER PRETTY MUCH ALL OF WHO AND WHAT I WAS.
BUT THERE ARE NO EMOTIONS TO GO ALONG WITH THEM.
WHERE ONCE I LOVED THEM, WITH ALL MY HEART, I FEEL A VAGUE AFFECTION. THAT'S WHAT MOM NOTICED -- WHAT DISTURBED MOM AND OUTRAGES ME --
-- A LOSS THAT CAN NEVER BE REPLACED.
BUT WHAT'S DONE IS DONE -- FEELING SORRY FOR MYSELF WON'T MAKE IT ANY BETTER.
MY LIFE AS CAROL DANVERS MAY BE OVER.
BUT BINARY'S HAS JUST BEGUN!

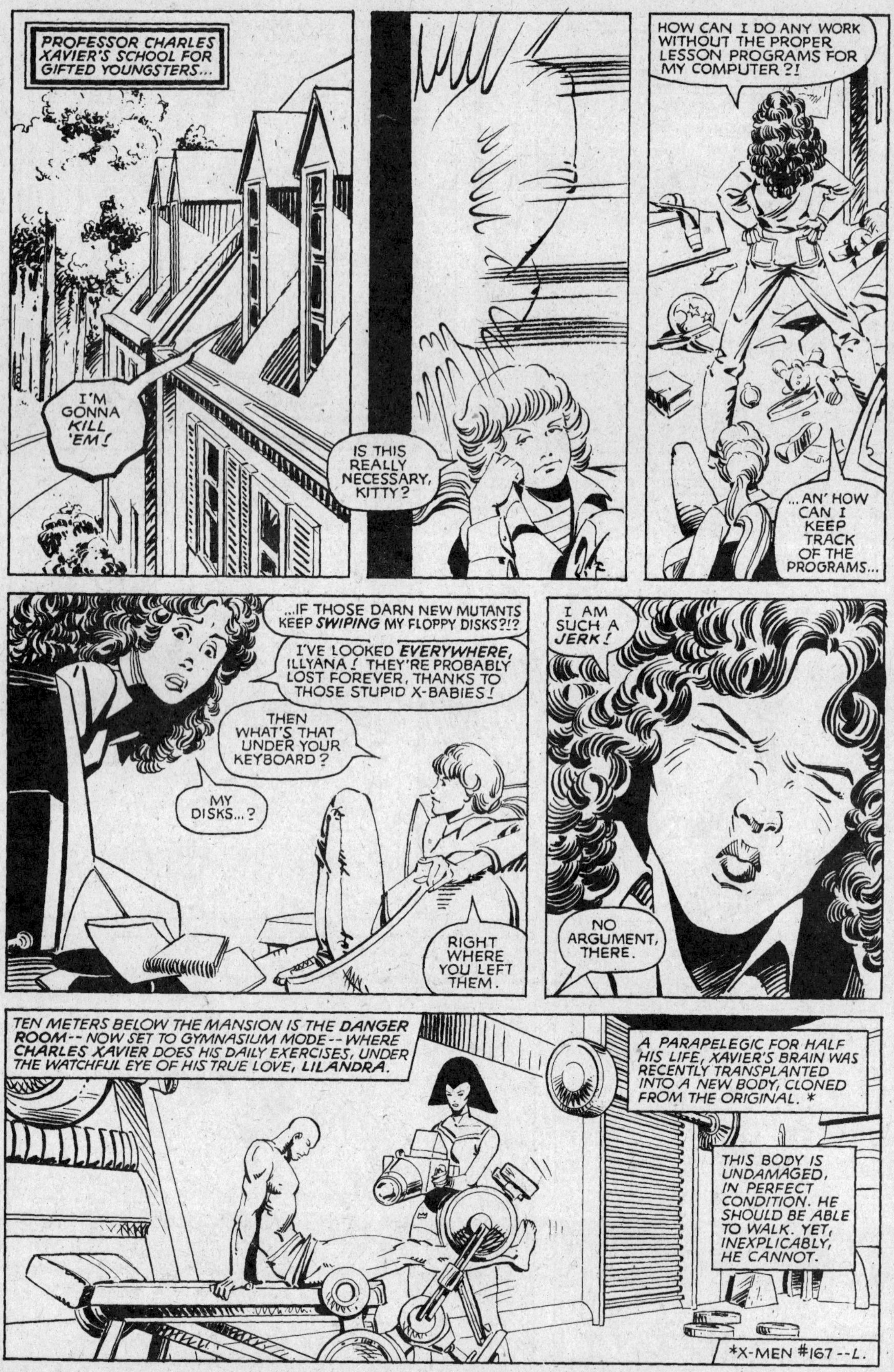
PROFESSOR CHARLES XAVIER'S SCHOOL FOR GIFTED YOUNGSTERS...
I'M GONNA KILL 'EM!
IS THIS REALLY NECESSARY, KITTY?
HOW CAN I DO ANY WORK WITHOUT THE PROPER LESSON PROGRAMS FOR MY COMPUTER?!
...AN' HOW CAN I KEEP TRACK OF THE PROGRAMS...
...IF THOSE DARN NEW MUTANTS KEEP SWIPING MY FLOPPY DISKS?!?
I'VE LOOKED EVERYWHERE, ILLYANA! THEY'RE PROBABLY LOST FOREVER, THANKS TO THOSE STUPID X-BABIES!
THEN WHAT'S THAT UNDER YOUR KEYBOARD?
MY DISKS...?
RIGHT WHERE YOU LEFT THEM.
I AM SUCH A JERK!
NO ARGUMENT, THERE.
TEN METERS BELOW THE MANSION IS THE DANGER ROOM-- NOW SET TO GYMNASIUM MODE-- WHERE CHARLES XAVIER DOES HIS DAILY EXERCISES, UNDER THE WATCHFUL EYE OF HIS TRUE LOVE, LILANDRA.
A PARAPELEGIC FOR HALF HIS LIFE, XAVIER'S BRAIN WAS RECENTLY TRANSPLANTED INTO A NEW BODY, CLONED FROM THE ORIGINAL. *
THIS BODY IS UNDAMAGED, IN PERFECT CONDITION. HE SHOULD BE ABLE TO WALK. YET, INEXPLICABLY, HE CANNOT.
*X-MEN #167 --L.

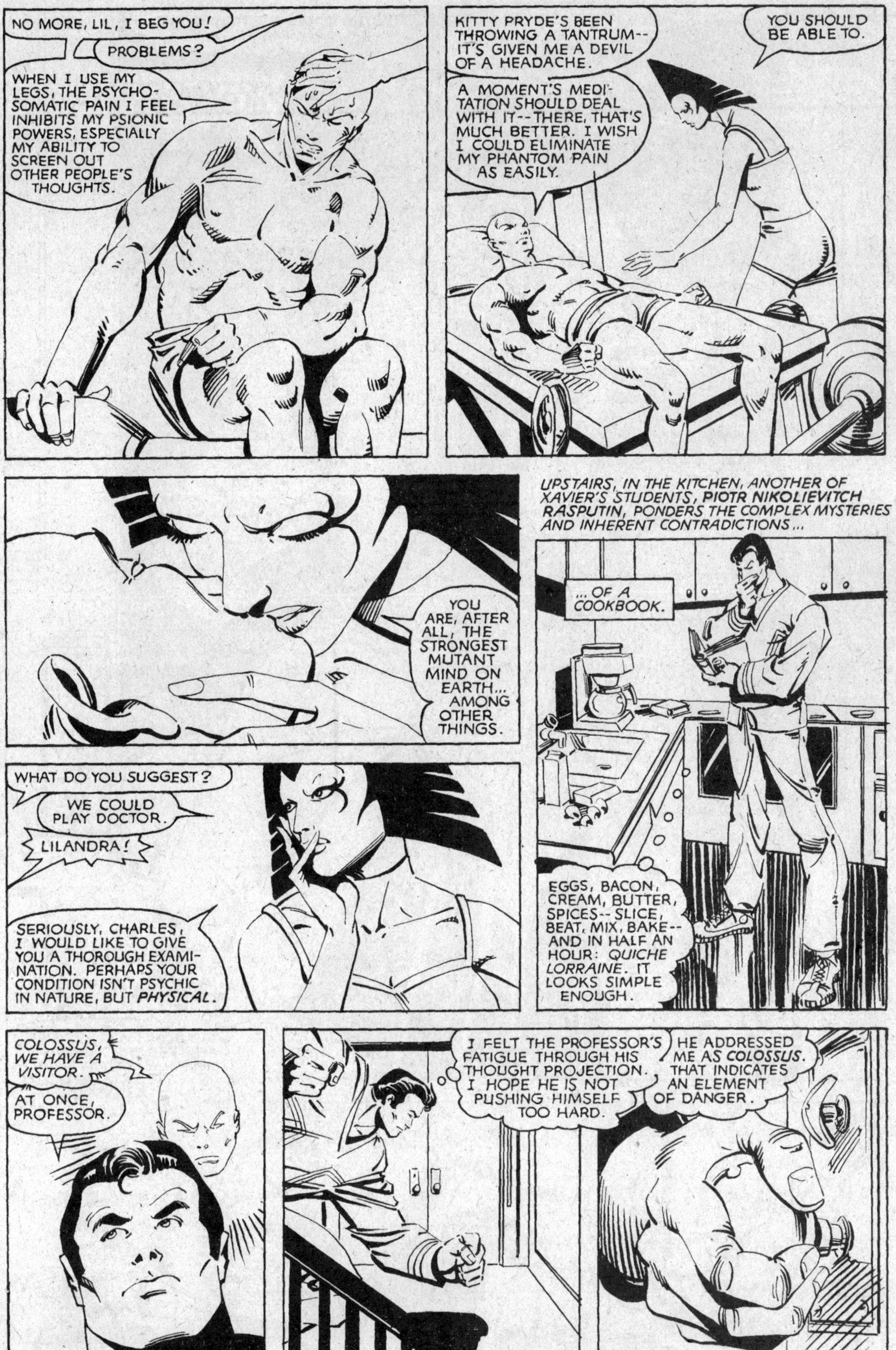
NO MORE, LIL, I BEG YOU!
PROBLEMS?
WHEN I USE MY LEGS, THE PSYCHO-SOMATIC PAIN I FEEL INHIBITS MY PSIONIC POWERS, ESPECIALLY MY ABILITY TO SCREEN OUT OTHER PEOPLE'S THOUGHTS.
KITTY PRYDE'S BEEN THROWING A TANTRUM-- IT'S GIVEN ME A DEVIL OF A HEADACHE.
YOU SHOULD BE ABLE TO.
A MOMENT'S MEDITATION SHOULD DEAL WITH IT--THERE, THAT'S MUCH BETTER. I WISH I COULD ELIMINATE MY PHANTOM PAIN AS EASILY.
YOU ARE, AFTER ALL, THE STRONGEST MUTANT MIND ON EARTH... AMONG OTHER THINGS.
WHAT DO YOU SUGGEST?
WE COULD PLAY DOCTOR.
LILANDRA!
SERIOUSLY, CHARLES, I WOULD LIKE TO GIVE YOU A THOROUGH EXAMINATION. PERHAPS YOUR CONDITION ISN'T PSYCHIC IN NATURE, BUT PHYSICAL.
UPSTAIRS, IN THE KITCHEN, ANOTHER OF XAVIER'S STUDENTS, PIOTR NIKOLIEVITCH RASPUTIN, PONDERS THE COMPLEX MYSTERIES AND INHERENT CONTRADICTIONS...
...OF A COOKBOOK.
EGGS, BACON, CREAM, BUTTER, SPICES-- SLICE, BEAT, MIX, BAKE-- AND IN HALF AN HOUR: QUICHE LORRAINE. IT LOOKS SIMPLE ENOUGH.
COLOSSUS, WE HAVE A VISITOR.
AT ONCE, PROFESSOR.
I FELT THE PROFESSOR'S FATIGUE THROUGH HIS THOUGHT PROJECTION. I HOPE HE IS NOT PUSHING HIMSELF TOO HARD.
HE ADDRESSED ME AS COLOSSUS. THAT INDICATES AN ELEMENT OF DANGER.

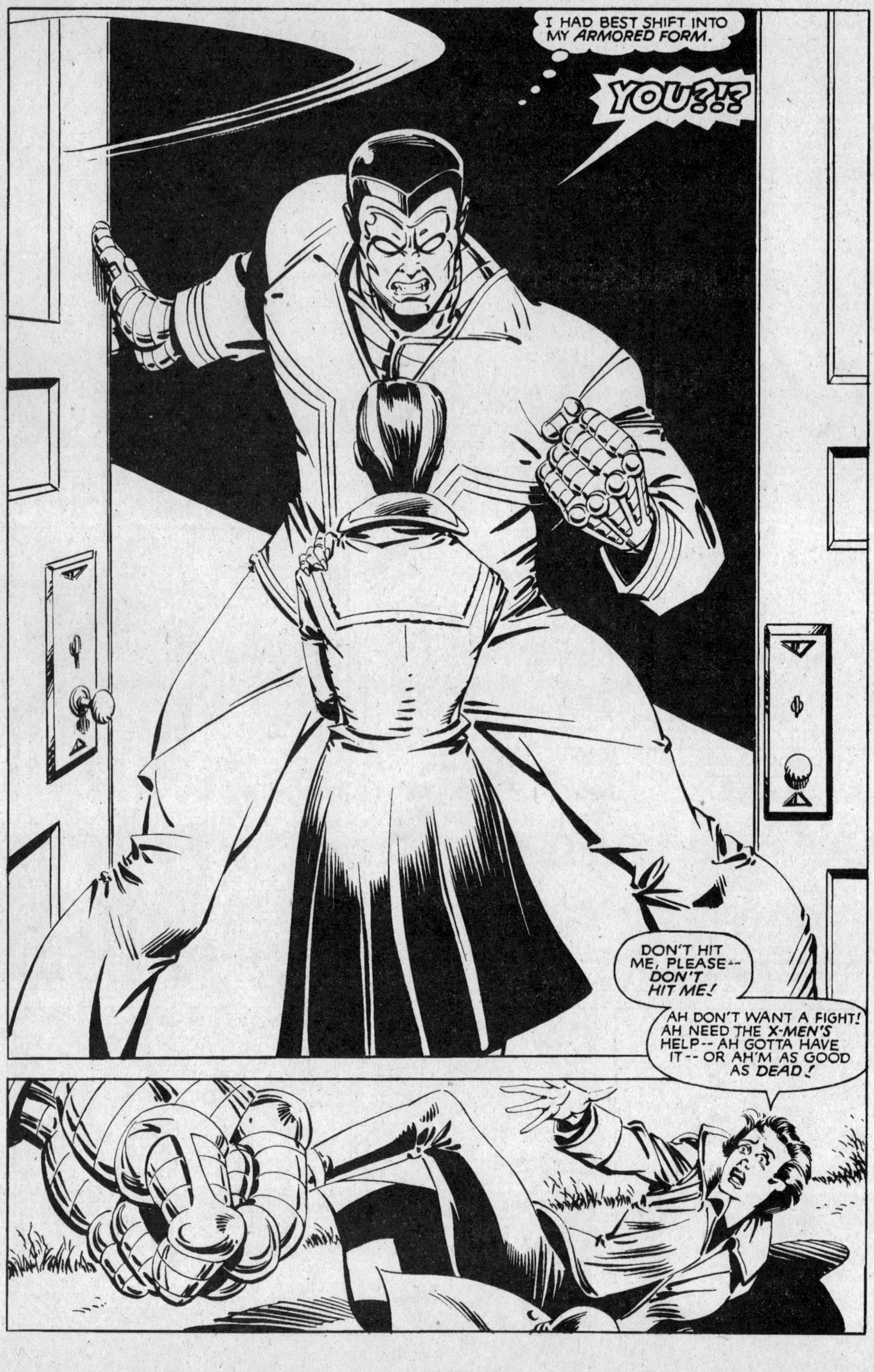
I HAD BEST SHIFT INTO MY ARMORED FORM.
YOU?!?
DON'T HIT ME, PLEASE-- DON'T HIT ME!
AH DON'T WANT A FIGHT! AH NEED THE X-MEN'S HELP-- AH GOTTA HAVE IT-- OR AH'M AS GOOD AS DEAD!

LATER...

HER NAME IS *ROGUE*, A MEMBER OF THE *BROTHERHOOD OF EVIL MUTANTS*.

THROUGH DIRECT PHYSICAL CONTACT, SHE ABSORBS THE ABILITIES AND MEMORIES OF OTHERS.

COULD THIS BE A DIVERSION-- THE PRELUDE TO AN ATTACK?

I'VE PSI-SCANNED THE ESTATE, NIGHTCRAWLER. SHE IS QUITE ALONE.

WHY ARE YOU HERE, CHILD? WHAT DO YOU WANT?

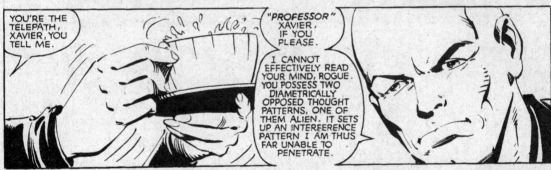

YOU'RE THE TELEPATH, XAVIER, YOU TELL ME.

"*PROFESSOR*" XAVIER, IF YOU PLEASE.

I CANNOT EFFECTIVELY READ YOUR MIND, ROGUE. YOU POSSESS TWO DIAMETRICALLY OPPOSED THOUGHT PATTERNS, ONE OF THEM ALIEN. IT SETS UP AN INTERFERENCE PATTERN I AM THUS FAR UNABLE TO PENETRATE.

THAT'S THE PERSONA AH ABSORBED FROM *CAROL DANVERS* WHEN AH ABSORBED HER POWERS, LAST YEAR.

AH DIDN'T INTEND THE TRANSFER TO BE PERMANENT. IT WAS AN ACCIDENT!

IT'S DRIVING ME CRAZY, PROFESSOR. YOU'VE GOTTA HELP ME!

YOU'VE GOT SOME NERVE, ROGUE, ASKIN' THAT AFTER ALL YOU'VE DONE!

HUSH, KITTY!

GO ON, ROGUE.

MAH POWERS ARE OUT OF CONTROL. THE SLIGHTEST TOUCH TRIGGERS THE TRANSFER. IT'S GETTIN' SO AH DON'T KNOW ANYMORE WHICH THOUGHTS-- OR MEM'RIES, OR FEELIN'S-- ARE MINE!

AH LOOK INTO A MIRROR, AN' SEE A *STRANGER'S* FACE!

IF YOU ASK ME, A MOST APT PUNISHMENT FOR YOUR CRIMES.

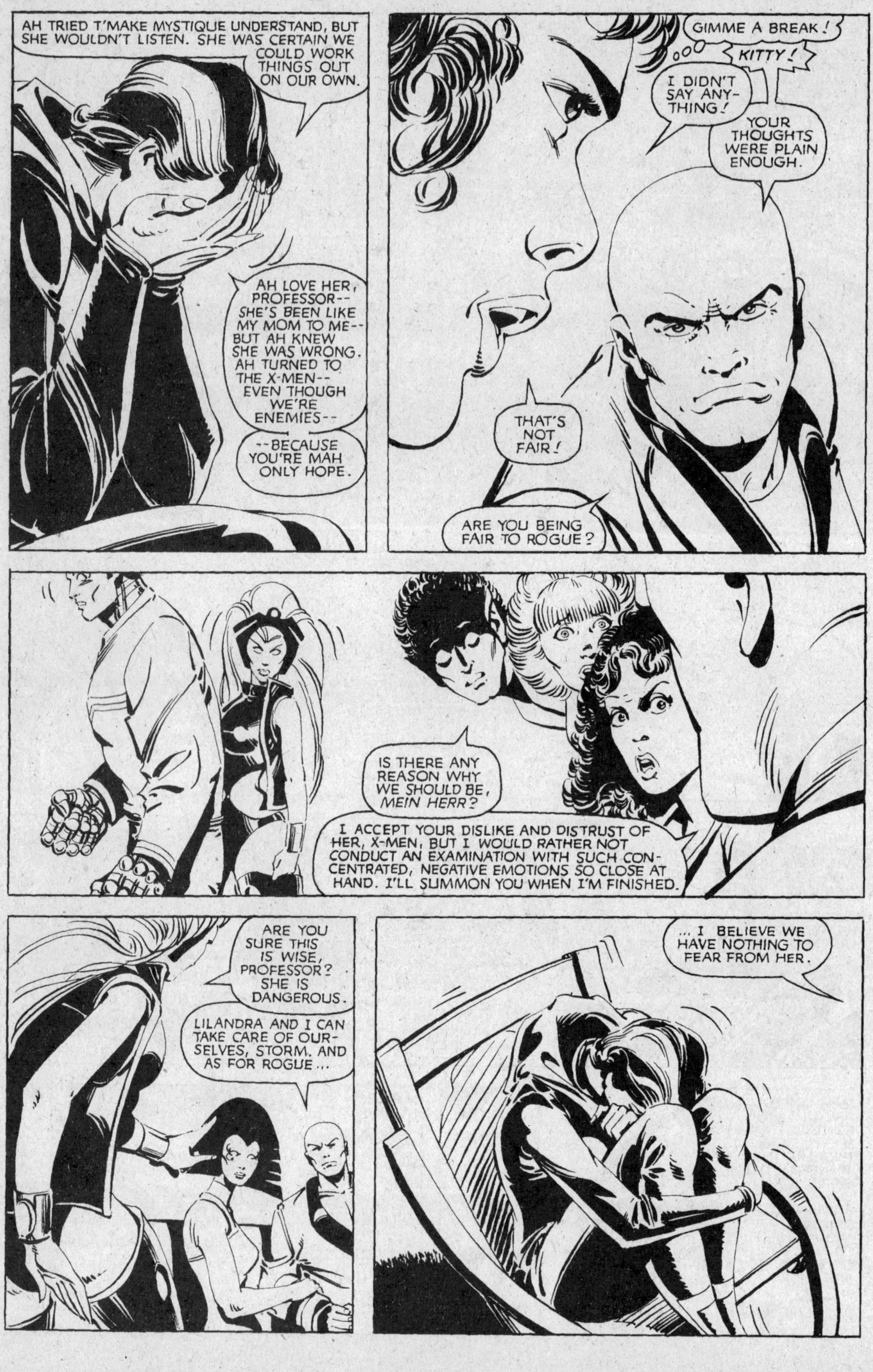
AH TRIED T'MAKE MYSTIQUE UNDERSTAND, BUT SHE WOULDN'T LISTEN. SHE WAS CERTAIN WE COULD WORK THINGS OUT ON OUR OWN.
AH LOVE HER, PROFESSOR-- SHE'S BEEN LIKE MY MOM TO ME-- BUT AH KNEW SHE WAS WRONG. AH TURNED TO THE X-MEN-- EVEN THOUGH WE'RE ENEMIES--
--BECAUSE YOU'RE MAH ONLY HOPE.
GIMME A BREAK!
KITTY!
I DIDN'T SAY ANYTHING!
YOUR THOUGHTS WERE PLAIN ENOUGH.
THAT'S NOT FAIR!
ARE YOU BEING FAIR TO ROGUE?
IS THERE ANY REASON WHY WE SHOULD BE, MEIN HERR?
I ACCEPT YOUR DISLIKE AND DISTRUST OF HER, X-MEN, BUT I WOULD RATHER NOT CONDUCT AN EXAMINATION WITH SUCH CONCENTRATED, NEGATIVE EMOTIONS SO CLOSE AT HAND. I'LL SUMMON YOU WHEN I'M FINISHED.
ARE YOU SURE THIS IS WISE, PROFESSOR? SHE IS DANGEROUS.
LILANDRA AND I CAN TAKE CARE OF OURSELVES, STORM. AND AS FOR ROGUE...
... I BELIEVE WE HAVE NOTHING TO FEAR FROM HER.

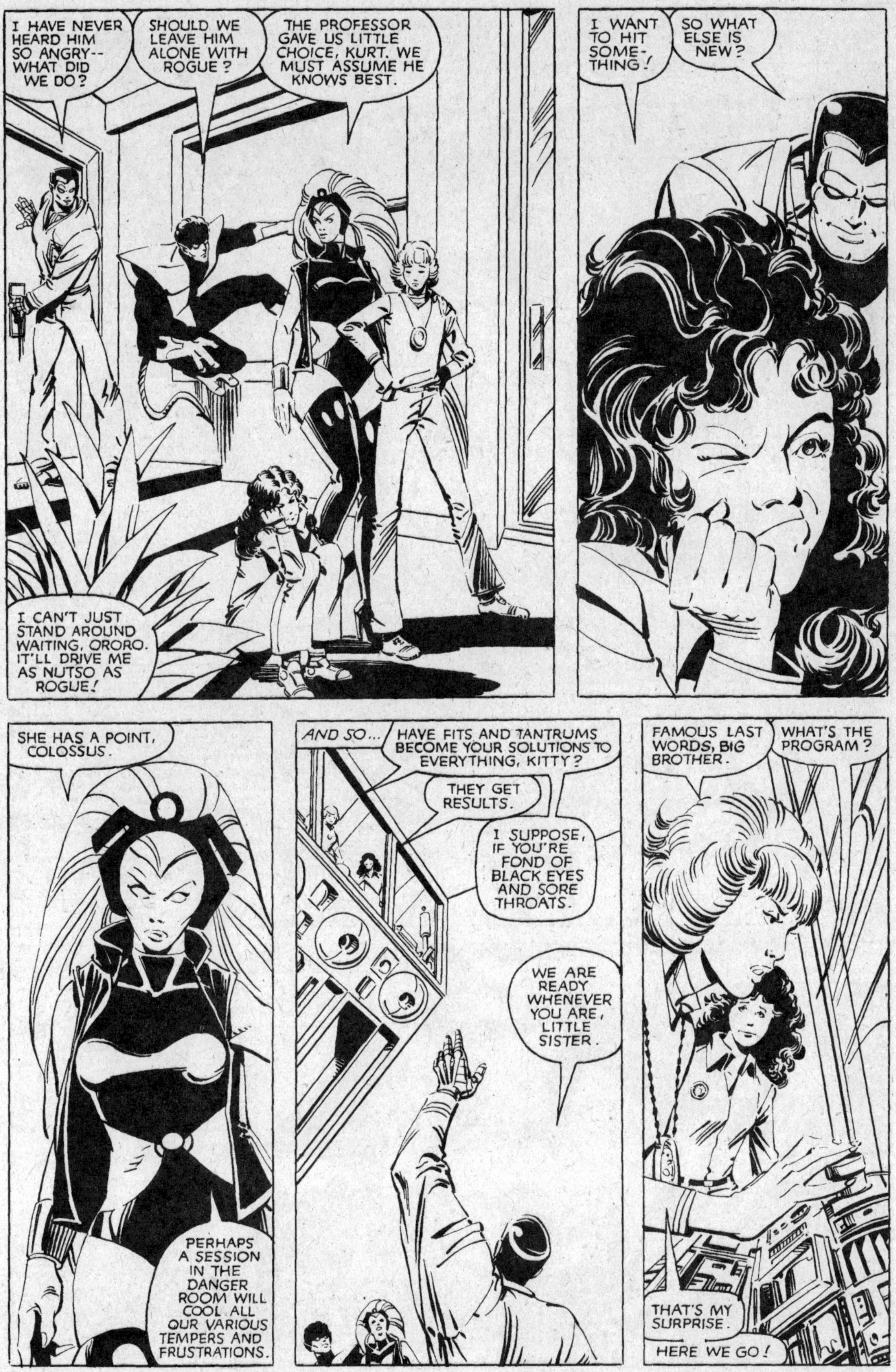
I HAVE NEVER HEARD HIM SO ANGRY-- WHAT DID WE DO?
SHOULD WE LEAVE HIM ALONE WITH ROGUE?
THE PROFESSOR GAVE US LITTLE CHOICE, KURT. WE MUST ASSUME HE KNOWS BEST.
I CAN'T JUST STAND AROUND WAITING, ORORO. IT'LL DRIVE ME AS NUTSO AS ROGUE!
I WANT TO HIT SOME-THING!
SO WHAT ELSE IS NEW?
SHE HAS A POINT, COLOSSUS.
PERHAPS A SESSION IN THE DANGER ROOM WILL COOL ALL OUR VARIOUS TEMPERS AND FRUSTRATIONS.
AND SO...
HAVE FITS AND TANTRUMS BECOME YOUR SOLUTIONS TO EVERYTHING, KITTY?
THEY GET RESULTS.
I SUPPOSE, IF YOU'RE FOND OF BLACK EYES AND SORE THROATS.
WE ARE READY WHENEVER YOU ARE, LITTLE SISTER.
FAMOUS LAST WORDS, BIG BROTHER.
WHAT'S THE PROGRAM?
THAT'S MY SURPRISE.
HERE WE GO!

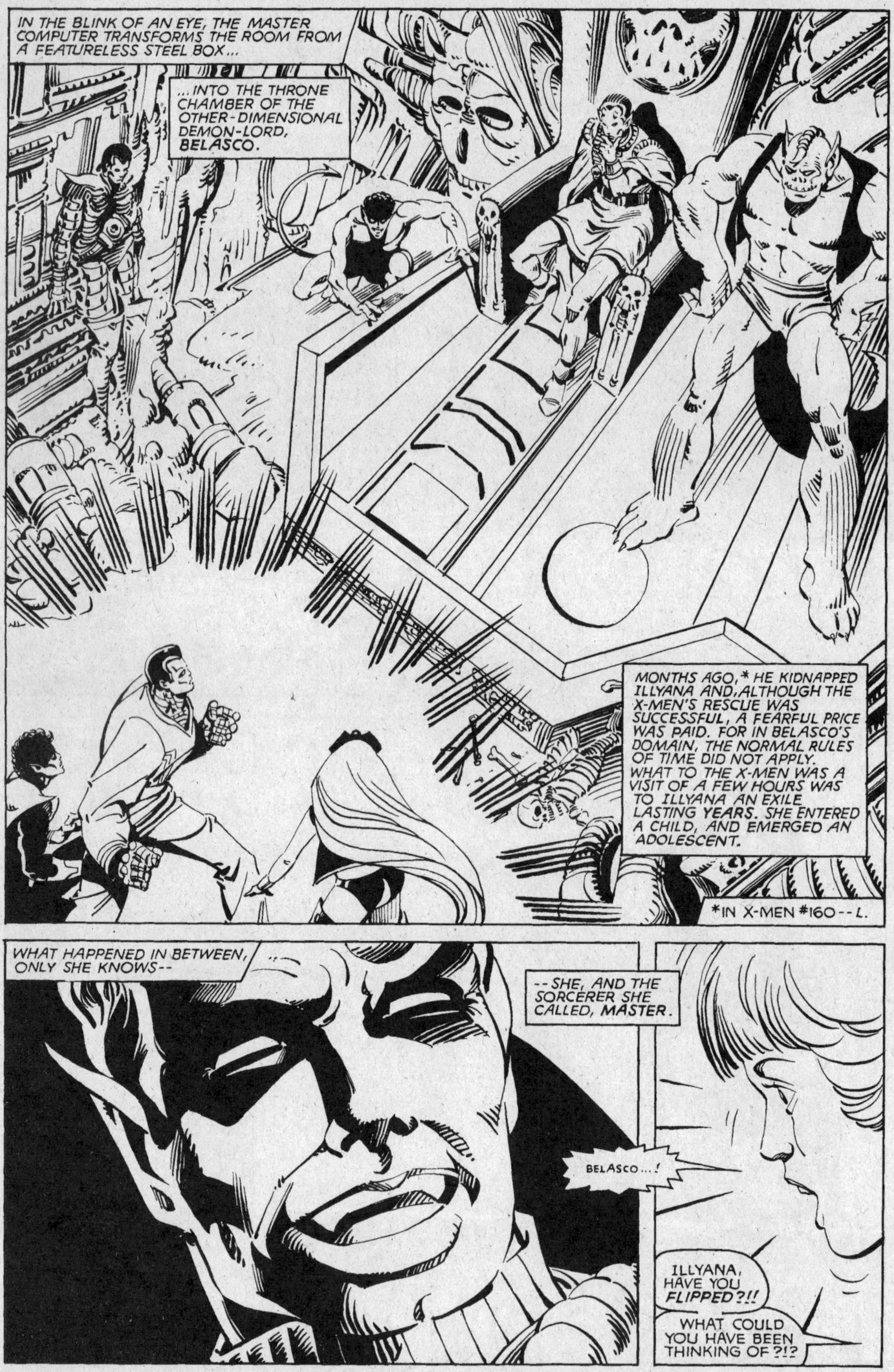

IN THE BLINK OF AN EYE, THE MASTER COMPUTER TRANSFORMS THE ROOM FROM A FEATURELESS STEEL BOX...
...INTO THE THRONE CHAMBER OF THE OTHER-DIMENSIONAL DEMON-LORD, BELASCO.
MONTHS AGO,* HE KIDNAPPED ILLYANA AND, ALTHOUGH THE X-MEN'S RESCUE WAS SUCCESSFUL, A FEARFUL PRICE WAS PAID. FOR IN BELASCO'S DOMAIN, THE NORMAL RULES OF TIME DID NOT APPLY. WHAT TO THE X-MEN WAS A VISIT OF A FEW HOURS WAS TO ILLYANA AN EXILE LASTING YEARS. SHE ENTERED A CHILD, AND EMERGED AN ADOLESCENT.
*IN X-MEN #160 -- L.
WHAT HAPPENED IN BETWEEN, ONLY SHE KNOWS--
--SHE, AND THE SORCERER SHE CALLED, MASTER.
BELASCO...!
ILLYANA, HAVE YOU FLIPPED?!!
WHAT COULD YOU HAVE BEEN THINKING OF?!?

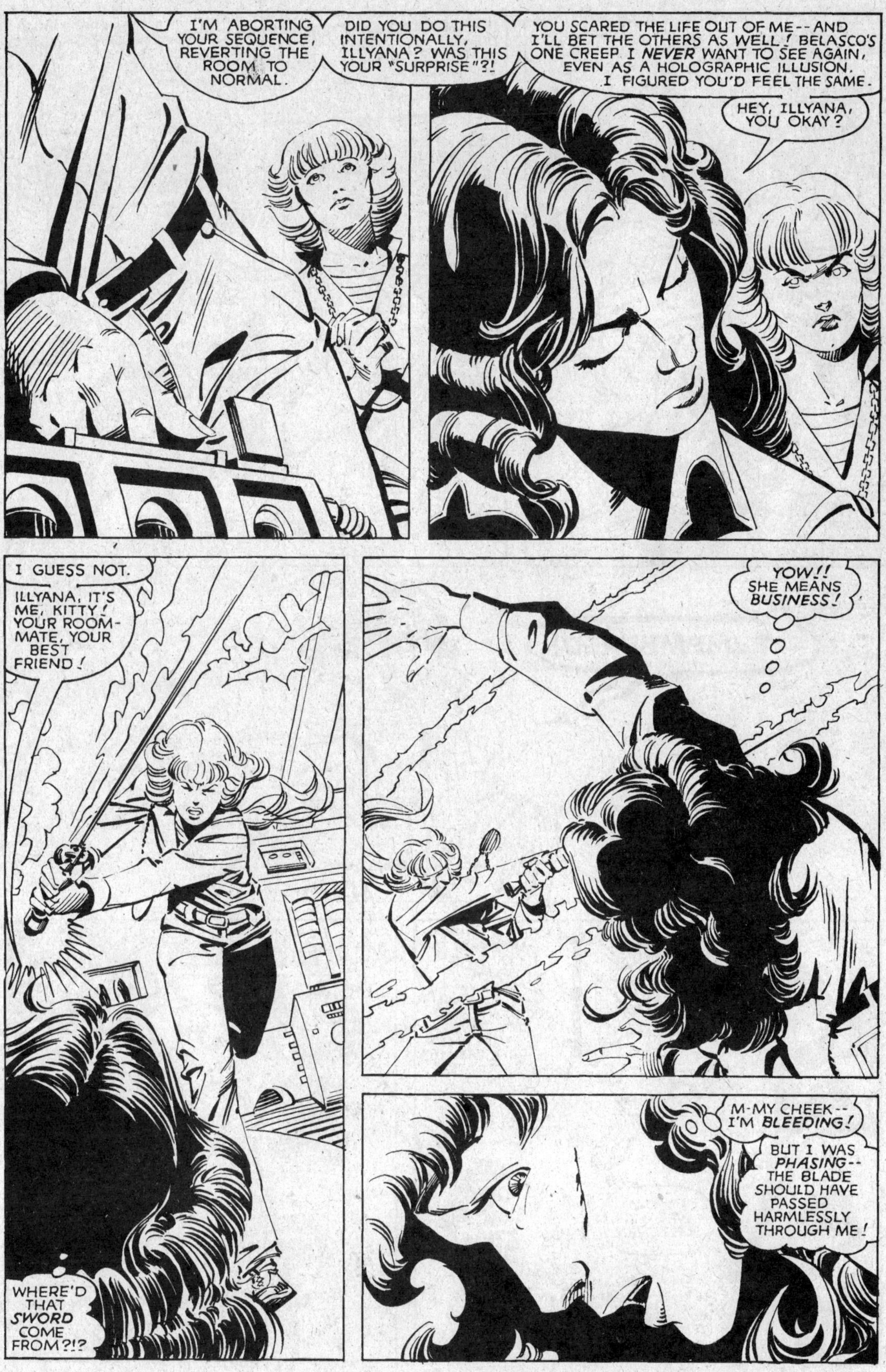
I'M ABORTING YOUR SEQUENCE, REVERTING THE ROOM TO NORMAL.
DID YOU DO THIS INTENTIONALLY, ILLYANA? WAS THIS YOUR "SURPRISE"?!
YOU SCARED THE LIFE OUT OF ME-- AND I'LL BET THE OTHERS AS WELL! BELASCO'S ONE CREEP I NEVER WANT TO SEE AGAIN, EVEN AS A HOLOGRAPHIC ILLUSION. I FIGURED YOU'D FEEL THE SAME.
HEY, ILLYANA, YOU OKAY?
I GUESS NOT.
ILLYANA, IT'S ME, KITTY! YOUR ROOMMATE, YOUR BEST FRIEND!
WHERE'D THAT SWORD COME FROM?!?
YOW!! SHE MEANS BUSINESS!
M-MY CHEEK-- I'M BLEEDING!
BUT I WAS PHASING-- THE BLADE SHOULD HAVE PASSED HARMLESSLY THROUGH ME!

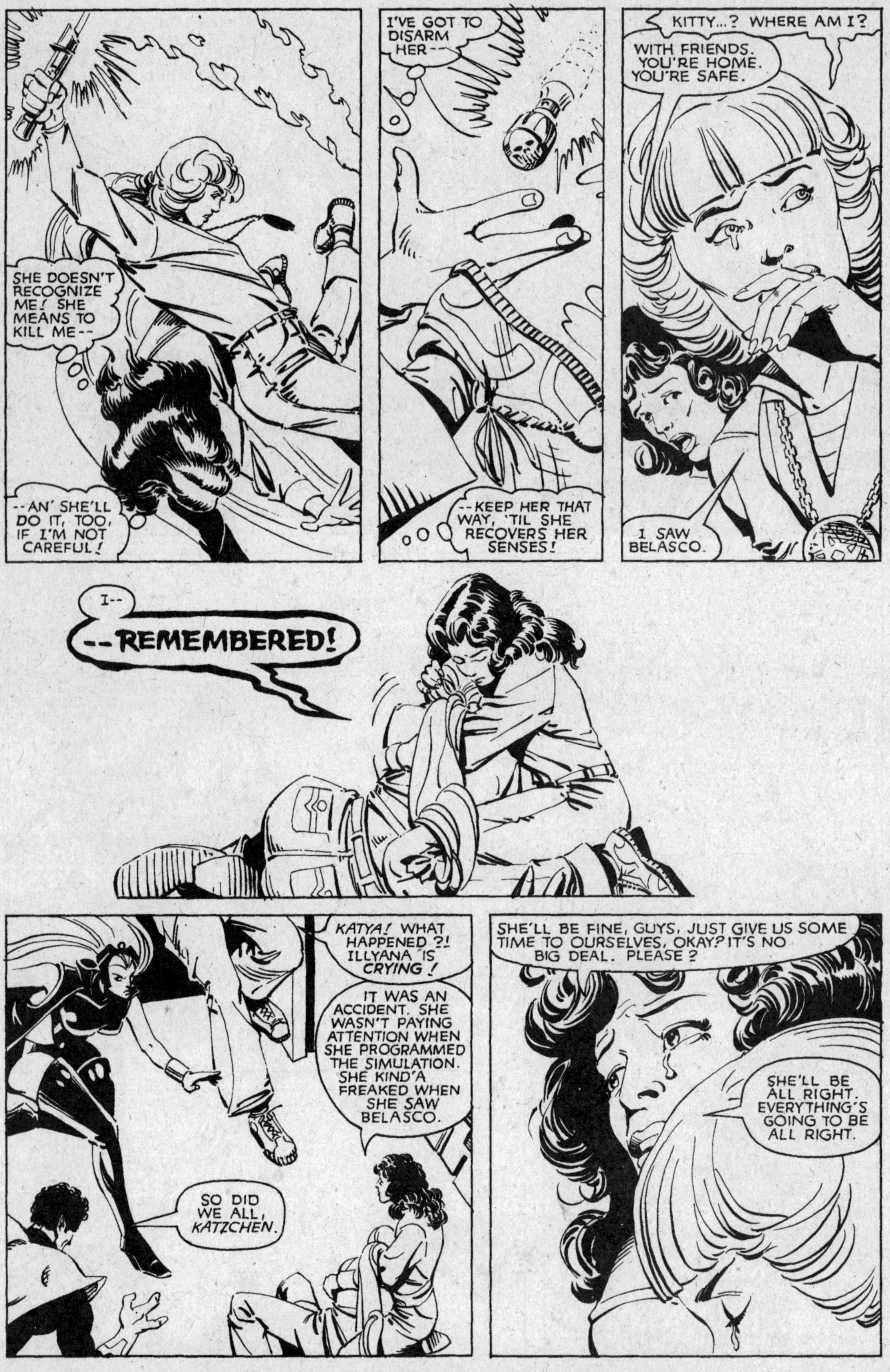
SHE DOESN'T RECOGNIZE ME! SHE MEANS TO KILL ME--
--AN' SHE'LL DO IT, TOO, IF I'M NOT CAREFUL!
I'VE GOT TO DISARM HER--
--KEEP HER THAT WAY, 'TIL SHE RECOVERS HER SENSES!
KITTY...? WHERE AM I?
WITH FRIENDS. YOU'RE HOME. YOU'RE SAFE.
I SAW BELASCO.
I--
--REMEMBERED!
KATYA! WHAT HAPPENED?! ILLYANA IS CRYING!
IT WAS AN ACCIDENT. SHE WASN'T PAYING ATTENTION WHEN SHE PROGRAMMED THE SIMULATION. SHE KIND'A FREAKED WHEN SHE SAW BELASCO.
SO DID WE ALL, KATZCHEN.
SHE'LL BE FINE, GUYS, JUST GIVE US SOME TIME TO OURSELVES, OKAY? IT'S NO BIG DEAL. PLEASE?
SHE'LL BE ALL RIGHT. EVERYTHING'S GOING TO BE ALL RIGHT.

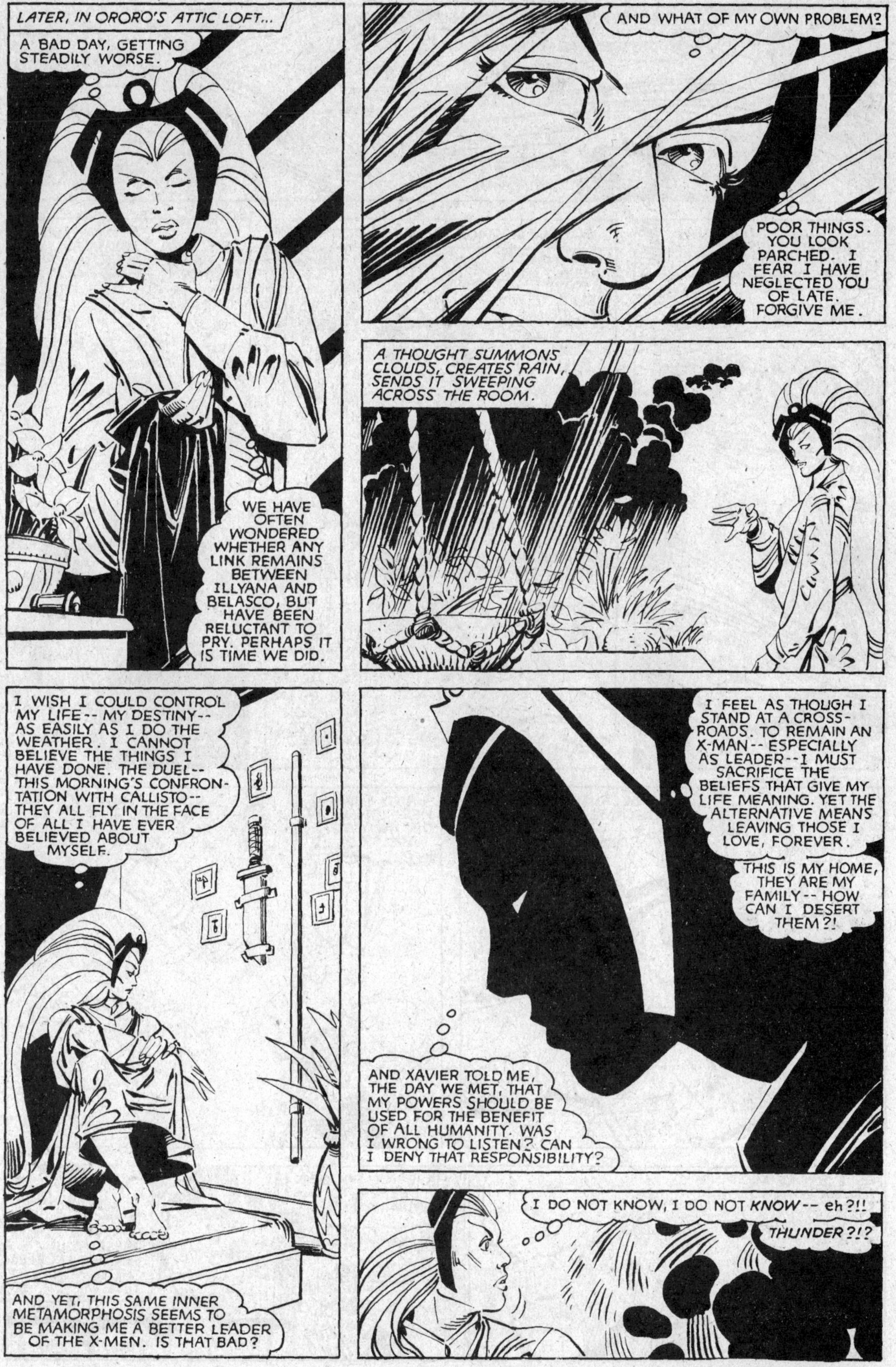
LATER, IN ORORO'S ATTIC LOFT...
A BAD DAY, GETTING STEADILY WORSE.
WE HAVE OFTEN WONDERED WHETHER ANY LINK REMAINS BETWEEN ILLYANA AND BELASCO, BUT HAVE BEEN RELUCTANT TO PRY. PERHAPS IT IS TIME WE DID.
AND WHAT OF MY OWN PROBLEM?
POOR THINGS. YOU LOOK PARCHED. I FEAR I HAVE NEGLECTED YOU OF LATE. FORGIVE ME.
A THOUGHT SUMMONS CLOUDS, CREATES RAIN, SENDS IT SWEEPING ACROSS THE ROOM.
I WISH I COULD CONTROL MY LIFE-- MY DESTINY-- AS EASILY AS I DO THE WEATHER. I CANNOT BELIEVE THE THINGS I HAVE DONE. THE DUEL-- THIS MORNING'S CONFRONTATION WITH CALLISTO-- THEY ALL FLY IN THE FACE OF ALL I HAVE EVER BELIEVED ABOUT MYSELF.
AND YET, THIS SAME INNER METAMORPHOSIS SEEMS TO BE MAKING ME A BETTER LEADER OF THE X-MEN. IS THAT BAD?
I FEEL AS THOUGH I STAND AT A CROSS-ROADS. TO REMAIN AN X-MAN-- ESPECIALLY AS LEADER--I MUST SACRIFICE THE BELIEFS THAT GIVE MY LIFE MEANING. YET THE ALTERNATIVE MEANS LEAVING THOSE I LOVE, FOREVER.
THIS IS MY HOME, THEY ARE MY FAMILY-- HOW CAN I DESERT THEM?!
AND XAVIER TOLD ME, THE DAY WE MET, THAT MY POWERS SHOULD BE USED FOR THE BENEFIT OF ALL HUMANITY. WAS I WRONG TO LISTEN? CAN I DENY THAT RESPONSIBILITY?
I DO NOT KNOW, I DO NOT KNOW-- eh?!!
THUNDER?!?

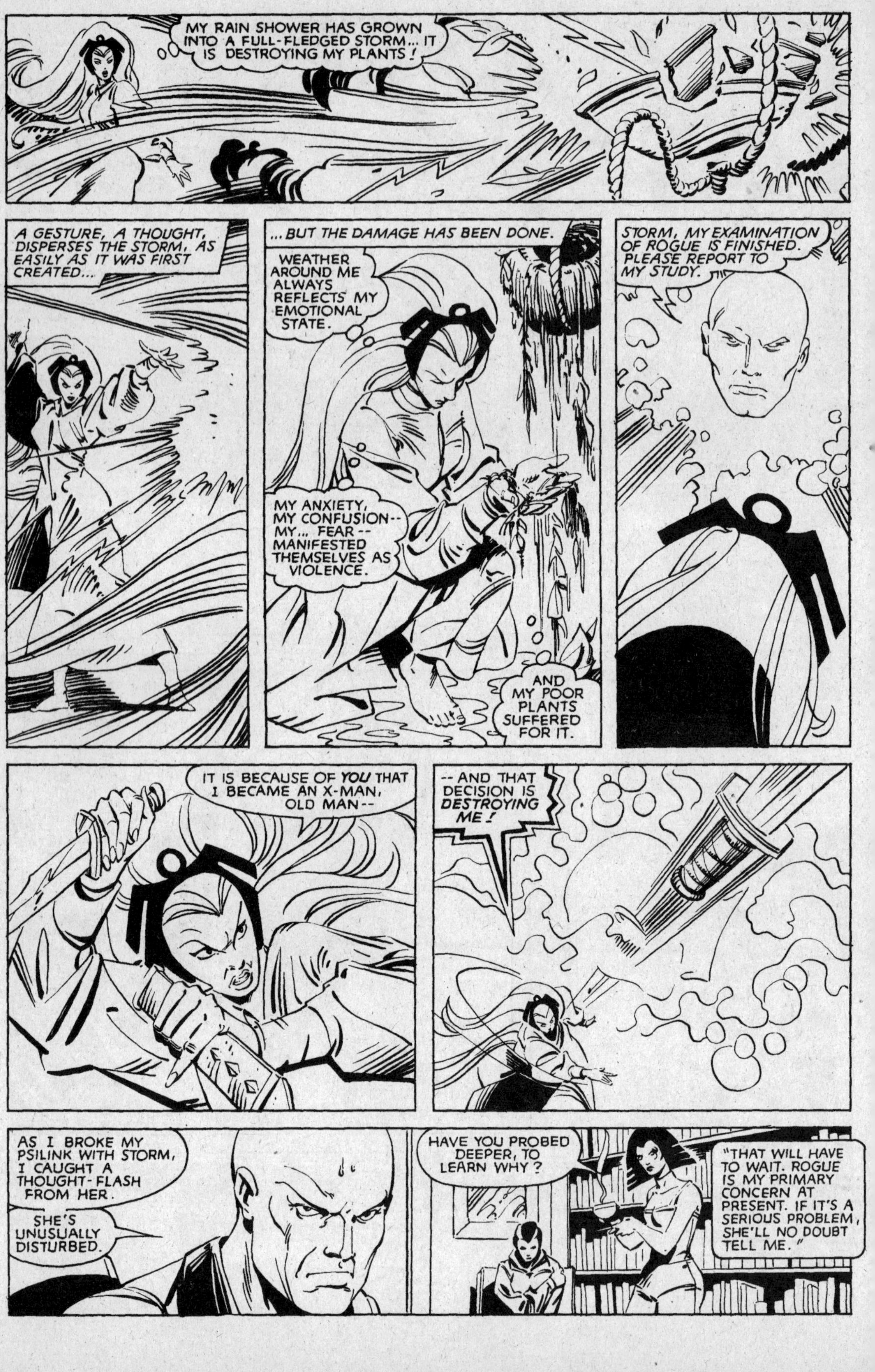
MY RAIN SHOWER HAS GROWN INTO A FULL-FLEDGED STORM... IT IS DESTROYING MY PLANTS!
A GESTURE, A THOUGHT, DISPERSES THE STORM, AS EASILY AS IT WAS FIRST CREATED...
...BUT THE DAMAGE HAS BEEN DONE.
WEATHER AROUND ME ALWAYS REFLECTS MY EMOTIONAL STATE.
MY ANXIETY, MY CONFUSION-- MY... FEAR -- MANIFESTED THEMSELVES AS VIOLENCE.
AND MY POOR PLANTS SUFFERED FOR IT.
STORM, MY EXAMINATION OF ROGUE IS FINISHED. PLEASE REPORT TO MY STUDY.
IT IS BECAUSE OF YOU THAT I BECAME AN X-MAN, OLD MAN--
--AND THAT DECISION IS DESTROYING ME!
AS I BROKE MY PSILINK WITH STORM, I CAUGHT A THOUGHT-FLASH FROM HER.
SHE'S UNUSUALLY DISTURBED.
HAVE YOU PROBED DEEPER, TO LEARN WHY?
"THAT WILL HAVE TO WAIT. ROGUE IS MY PRIMARY CONCERN AT PRESENT. IF IT'S A SERIOUS PROBLEM, SHE'LL NO DOUBT TELL ME."

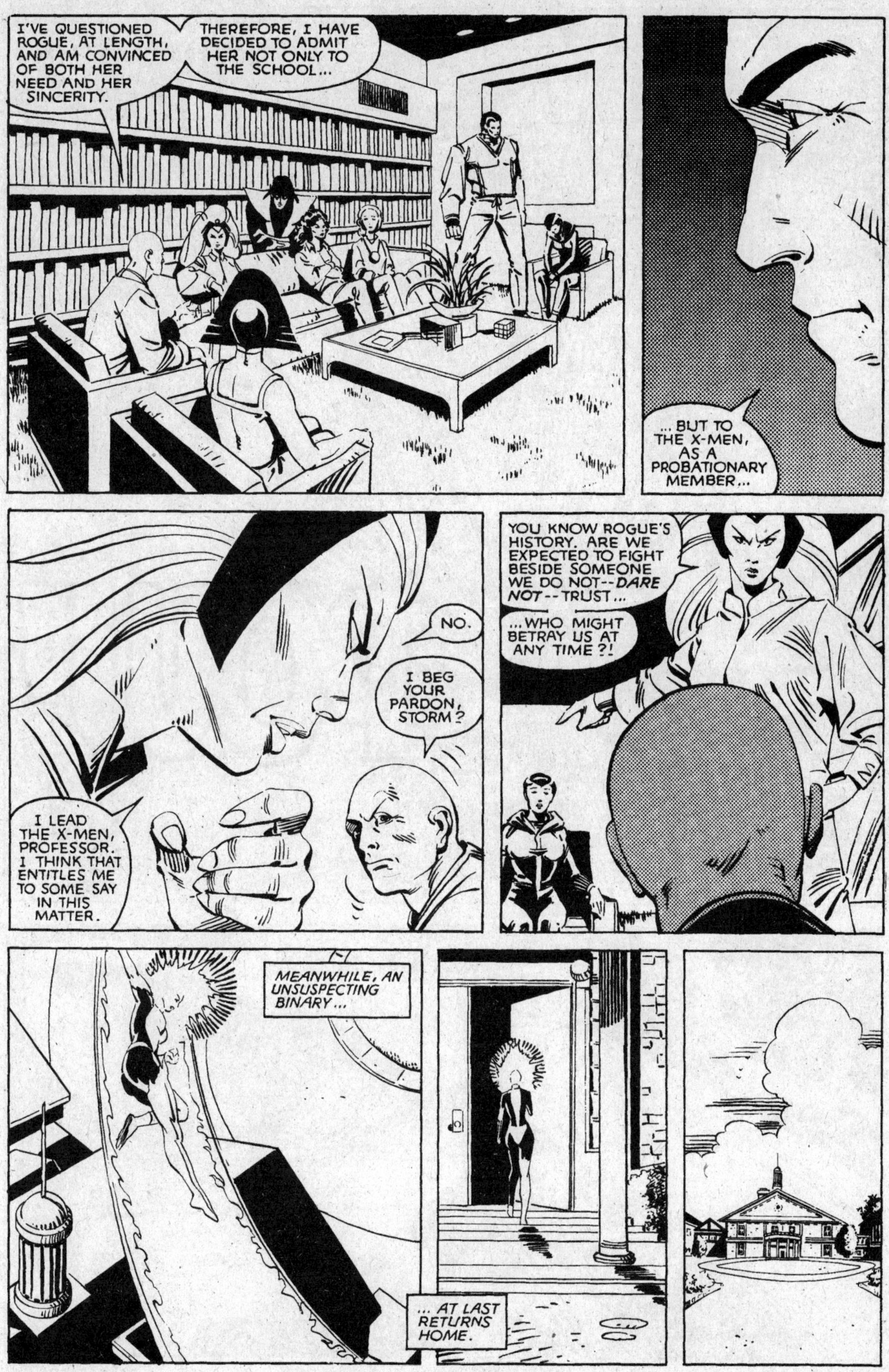
I'VE QUESTIONED ROGUE, AT LENGTH, AND AM CONVINCED OF BOTH HER NEED AND HER SINCERITY.
THEREFORE, I HAVE DECIDED TO ADMIT HER NOT ONLY TO THE SCHOOL...
... BUT TO THE X-MEN, AS A PROBATIONARY MEMBER...
NO.
I BEG YOUR PARDON, STORM?
I LEAD THE X-MEN, PROFESSOR. I THINK THAT ENTITLES ME TO SOME SAY IN THIS MATTER.
YOU KNOW ROGUE'S HISTORY. ARE WE EXPECTED TO FIGHT BESIDE SOMEONE WE DO NOT--*DARE NOT*--TRUST...
...WHO MIGHT BETRAY US AT ANY TIME?!
MEANWHILE, AN UNSUSPECTING BINARY...
... AT LAST RETURNS HOME.

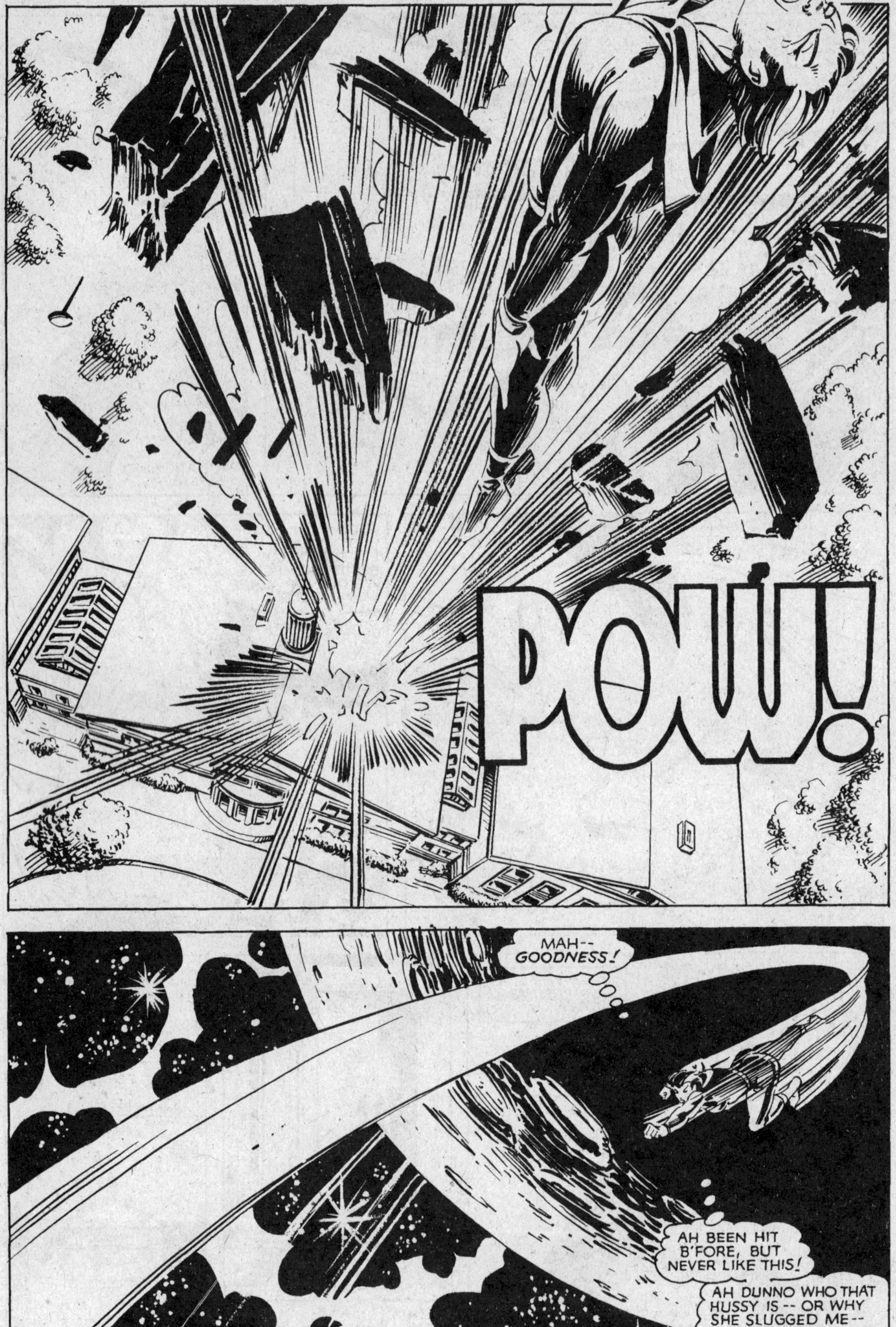
POW!
MAH-- GOODNESS!
AH BEEN HIT B'FORE, BUT NEVER LIKE THIS!
AH DUNNO WHO THAT HUSSY IS -- OR WHY SHE SLUGGED ME -- BUT AH AIM TO MAKE HER REGRET IT!

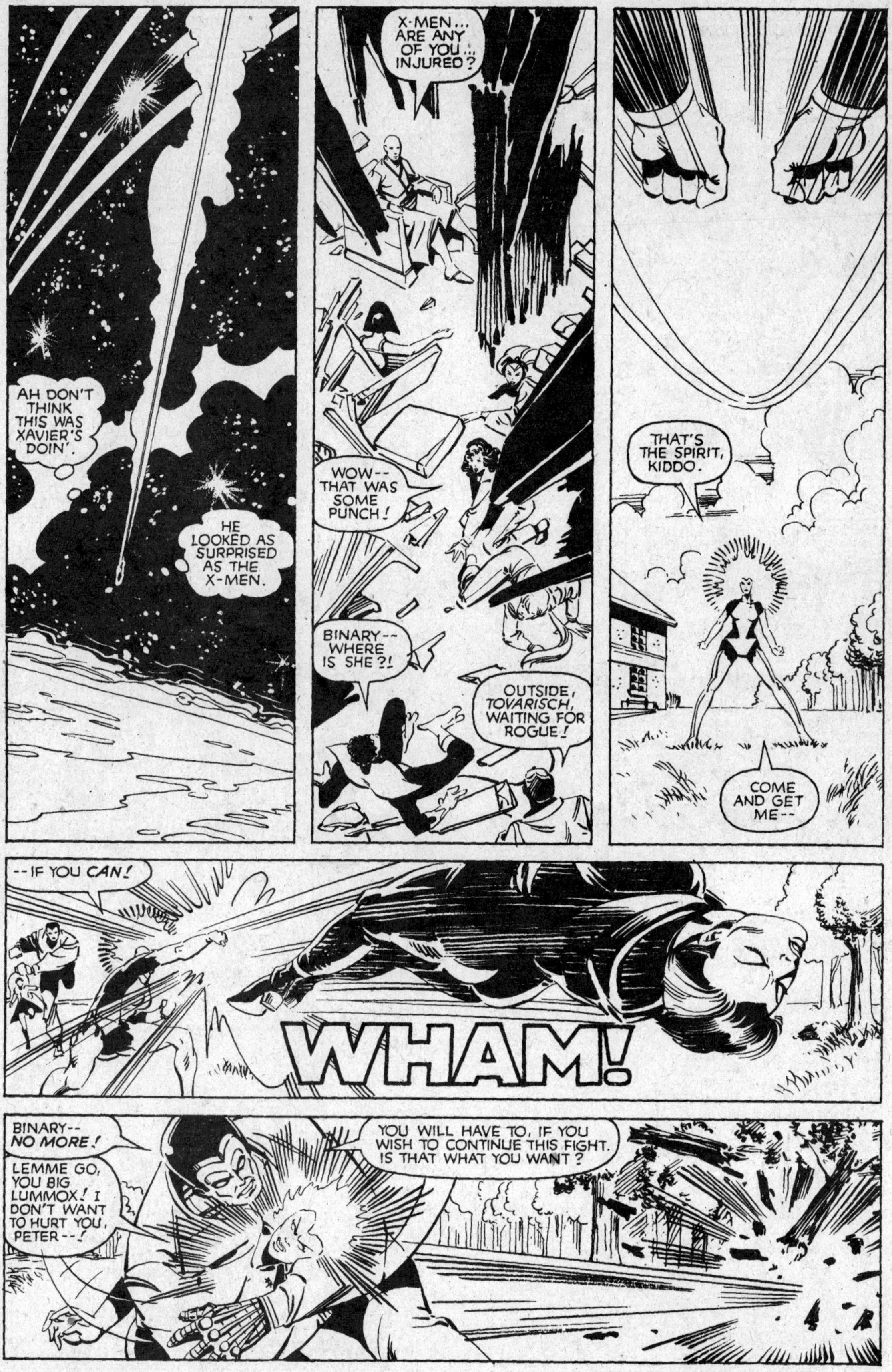
AH DON'T THINK THIS WAS XAVIER'S DOIN'.
HE LOOKED AS SURPRISED AS THE X-MEN.
X-MEN... ARE ANY OF YOU... INJURED?
WOW-- THAT WAS SOME PUNCH!
BINARY-- WHERE IS SHE?!
OUTSIDE, *TOVARISCH*, WAITING FOR ROGUE!
THAT'S THE SPIRIT, KIDDO.
COME AND GET ME--
--IF YOU *CAN!*
WHAM!
BINARY-- *NO MORE!*
YOU WILL HAVE TO, IF YOU WISH TO CONTINUE THIS FIGHT. IS THAT WHAT YOU WANT?
LEMME GO, YOU BIG LUMMOX! I DON'T WANT TO HURT YOU, PETER--!

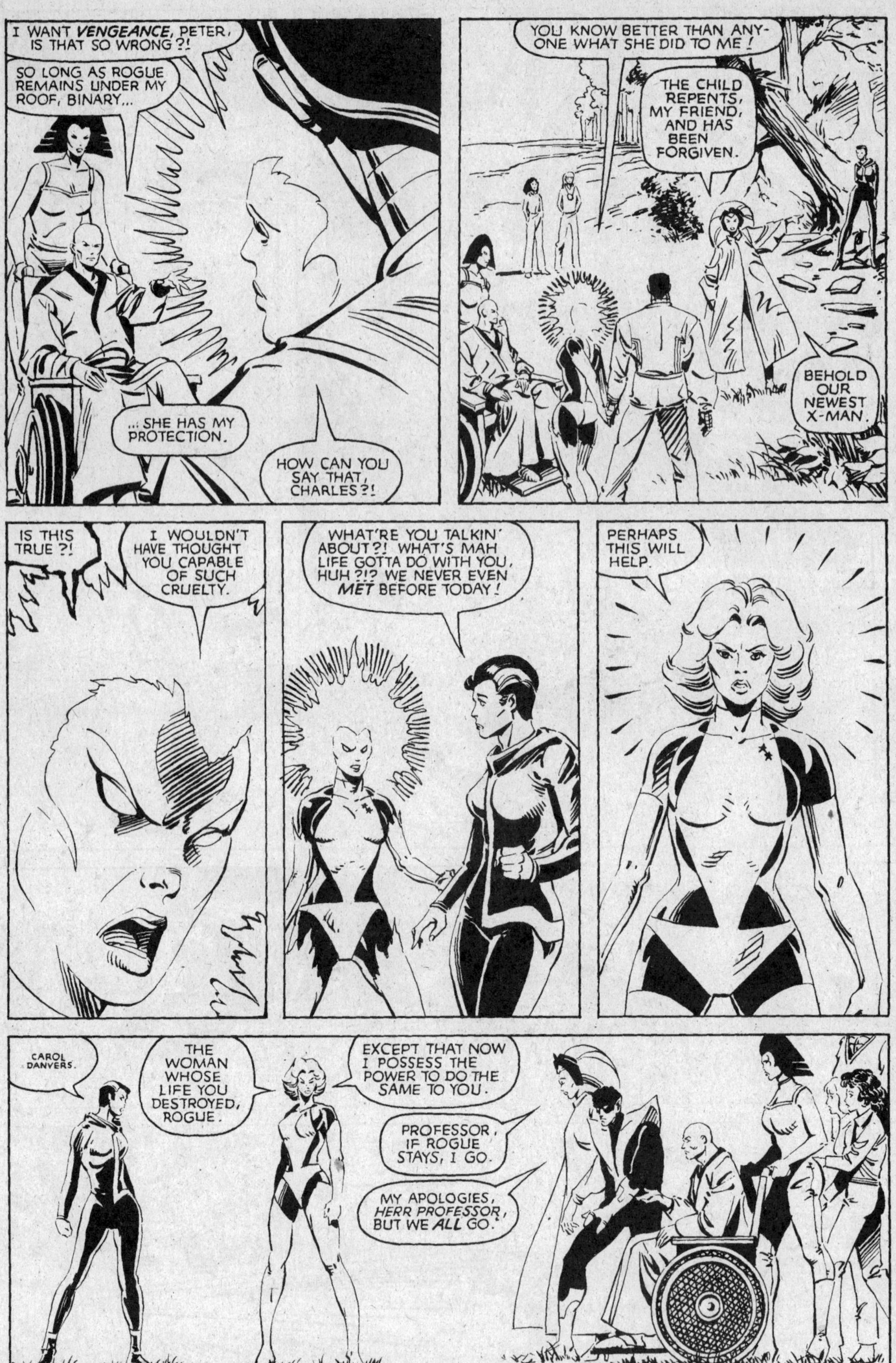
I WANT VENGEANCE, PETER. IS THAT SO WRONG?!
SO LONG AS ROGUE REMAINS UNDER MY ROOF, BINARY...
...SHE HAS MY PROTECTION.
HOW CAN YOU SAY THAT, CHARLES?!
YOU KNOW BETTER THAN ANYONE WHAT SHE DID TO ME!
THE CHILD REPENTS, MY FRIEND, AND HAS BEEN FORGIVEN.
BEHOLD OUR NEWEST X-MAN.
IS THIS TRUE?!
I WOULDN'T HAVE THOUGHT YOU CAPABLE OF SUCH CRUELTY.
WHAT'RE YOU TALKIN' ABOUT?! WHAT'S MAH LIFE GOTTA DO WITH YOU, HUH?!? WE NEVER EVEN MET BEFORE TODAY!
PERHAPS THIS WILL HELP.
CAROL DANVERS.
THE WOMAN WHOSE LIFE YOU DESTROYED, ROGUE.
EXCEPT THAT NOW I POSSESS THE POWER TO DO THE SAME TO YOU.
PROFESSOR, IF ROGUE STAYS, I GO.
MY APOLOGIES, HERR PROFESSOR, BUT WE ALL GO.

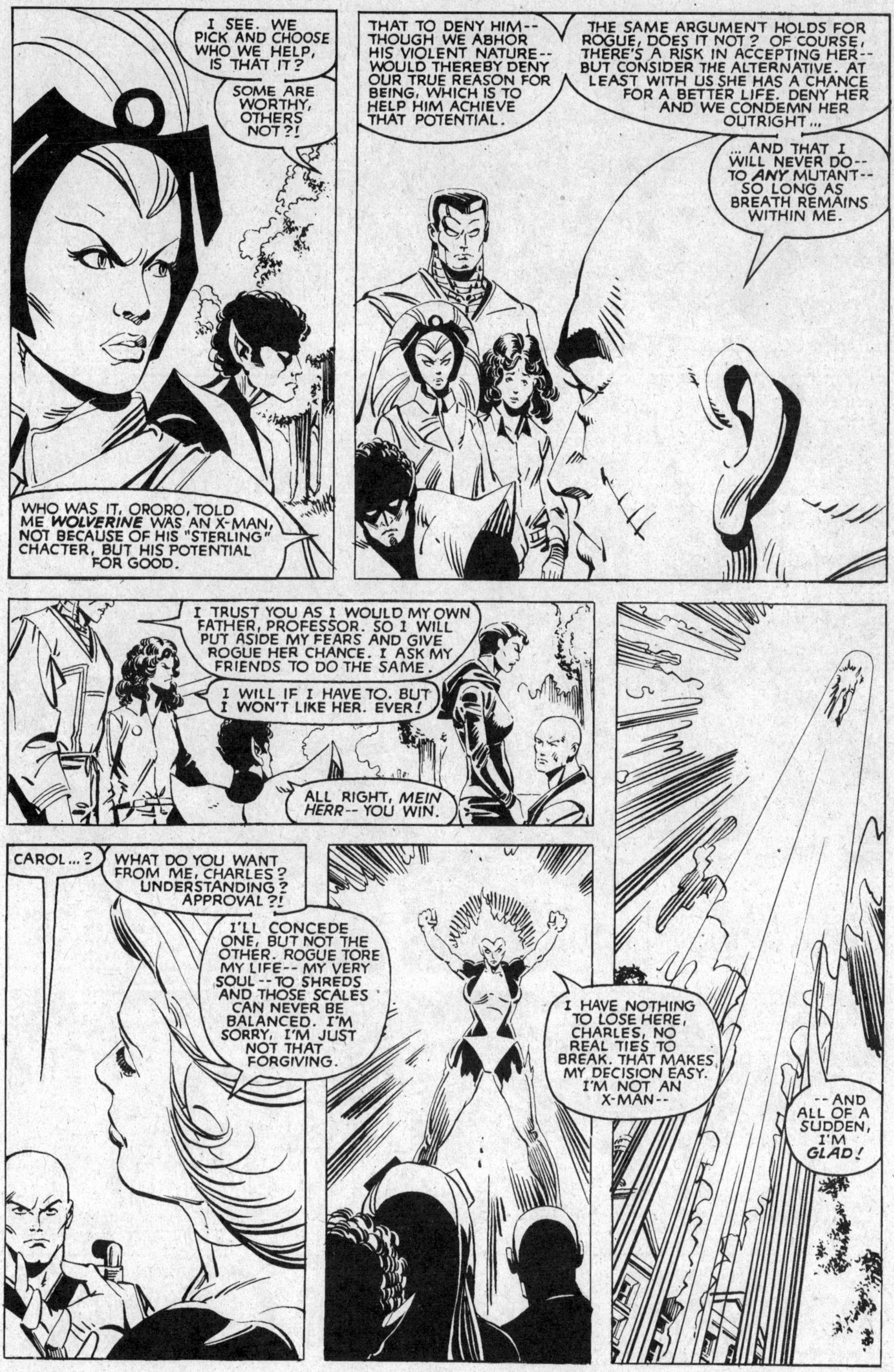
I SEE. WE PICK AND CHOOSE WHO WE HELP, IS THAT IT?
SOME ARE WORTHY, OTHERS NOT?!
WHO WAS IT, ORORO, TOLD ME WOLVERINE WAS AN X-MAN, NOT BECAUSE OF HIS "STERLING" CHACTER, BUT HIS POTENTIAL FOR GOOD.
THAT TO DENY HIM-- THOUGH WE ABHOR HIS VIOLENT NATURE-- WOULD THEREBY DENY OUR TRUE REASON FOR BEING, WHICH IS TO HELP HIM ACHIEVE THAT POTENTIAL.
THE SAME ARGUMENT HOLDS FOR ROGUE, DOES IT NOT? OF COURSE, THERE'S A RISK IN ACCEPTING HER-- BUT CONSIDER THE ALTERNATIVE. AT LEAST WITH US SHE HAS A CHANCE FOR A BETTER LIFE. DENY HER AND WE CONDEMN HER OUTRIGHT...
... AND THAT I WILL NEVER DO-- TO ANY MUTANT-- SO LONG AS BREATH REMAINS WITHIN ME.
I TRUST YOU AS I WOULD MY OWN FATHER, PROFESSOR. SO I WILL PUT ASIDE MY FEARS AND GIVE ROGUE HER CHANCE. I ASK MY FRIENDS TO DO THE SAME.
I WILL IF I HAVE TO. BUT I WON'T LIKE HER. EVER!
ALL RIGHT, MEIN HERR-- YOU WIN.
CAROL...?
WHAT DO YOU WANT FROM ME, CHARLES? UNDERSTANDING? APPROVAL?!
I'LL CONCEDE ONE, BUT NOT THE OTHER. ROGUE TORE MY LIFE-- MY VERY SOUL-- TO SHREDS AND THOSE SCALES CAN NEVER BE BALANCED. I'M SORRY, I'M JUST NOT THAT FORGIVING.
I HAVE NOTHING TO LOSE HERE, CHARLES, NO REAL TIES TO BREAK. THAT MAKES MY DECISION EASY. I'M NOT AN X-MAN--
--AND ALL OF A SUDDEN, I'M GLAD!

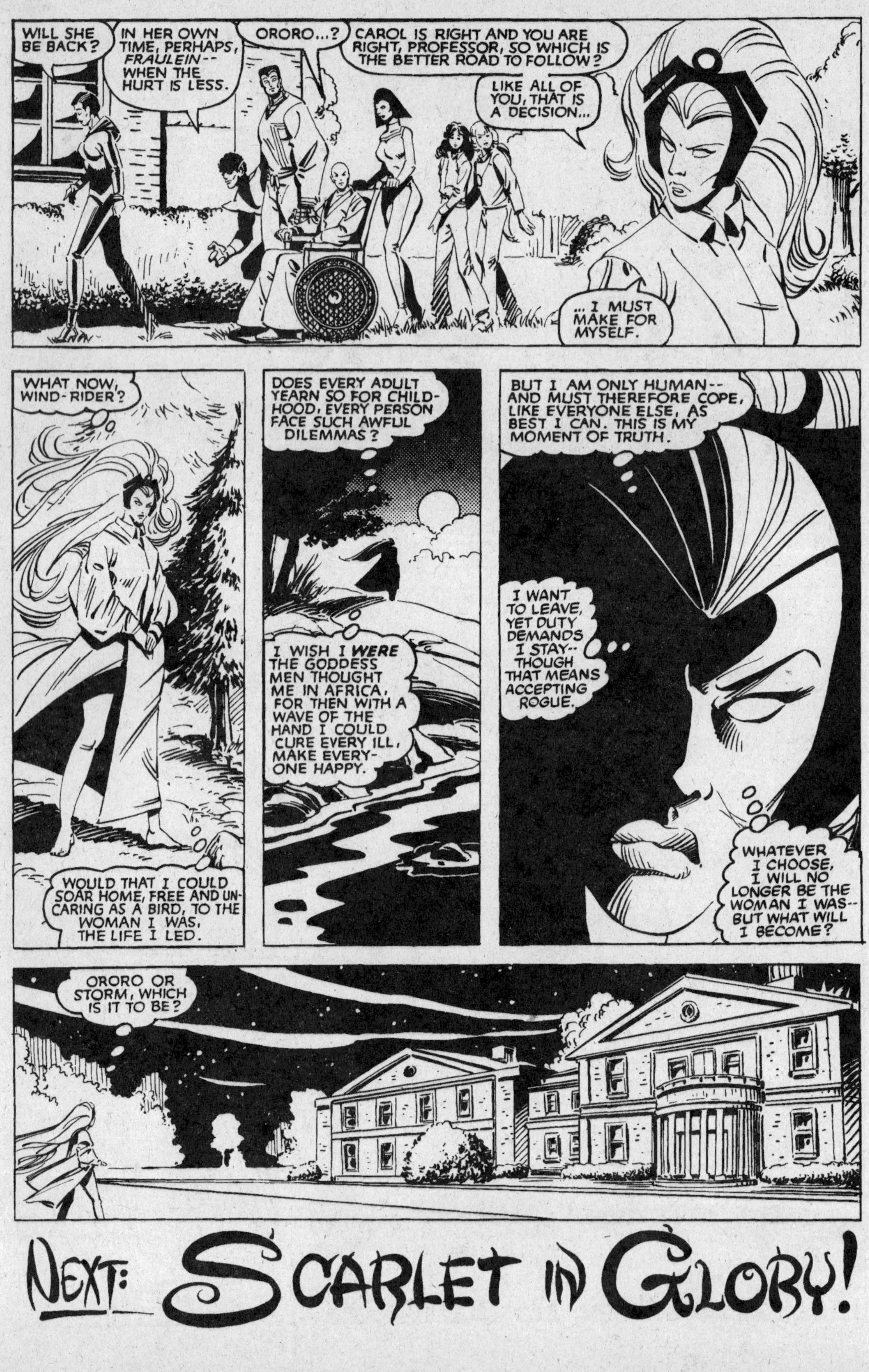
WILL SHE BE BACK?
IN HER OWN TIME, PERHAPS, *FRAULEIN*-- WHEN THE HURT IS LESS.
ORORO...?
CAROL IS RIGHT AND YOU ARE RIGHT, PROFESSOR, SO WHICH IS THE BETTER ROAD TO FOLLOW?
LIKE ALL OF YOU, THAT IS A DECISION...
...I MUST MAKE FOR MYSELF.
WHAT NOW, WIND-RIDER?
WOULD THAT I COULD SOAR HOME, FREE AND UNCARING AS A BIRD, TO THE WOMAN I WAS, THE LIFE I LED.
DOES EVERY ADULT YEARN SO FOR CHILDHOOD, EVERY PERSON FACE SUCH AWFUL DILEMMAS?
I WISH I ***WERE*** THE GODDESS MEN THOUGHT ME IN AFRICA, FOR THEN WITH A WAVE OF THE HAND I COULD CURE EVERY ILL, MAKE EVERYONE HAPPY.
BUT I AM ONLY HUMAN-- AND MUST THEREFORE COPE, LIKE EVERYONE ELSE, AS BEST I CAN. THIS IS MY MOMENT OF TRUTH.
I WANT TO LEAVE, YET DUTY DEMANDS I STAY-- THOUGH THAT MEANS ACCEPTING ROGUE.
WHATEVER I CHOOSE, I WILL NO LONGER BE THE WOMAN I WAS-- BUT WHAT WILL I BECOME?
ORORO OR STORM, WHICH IS IT TO BE?
NEXT: SCARLET IN GLORY!

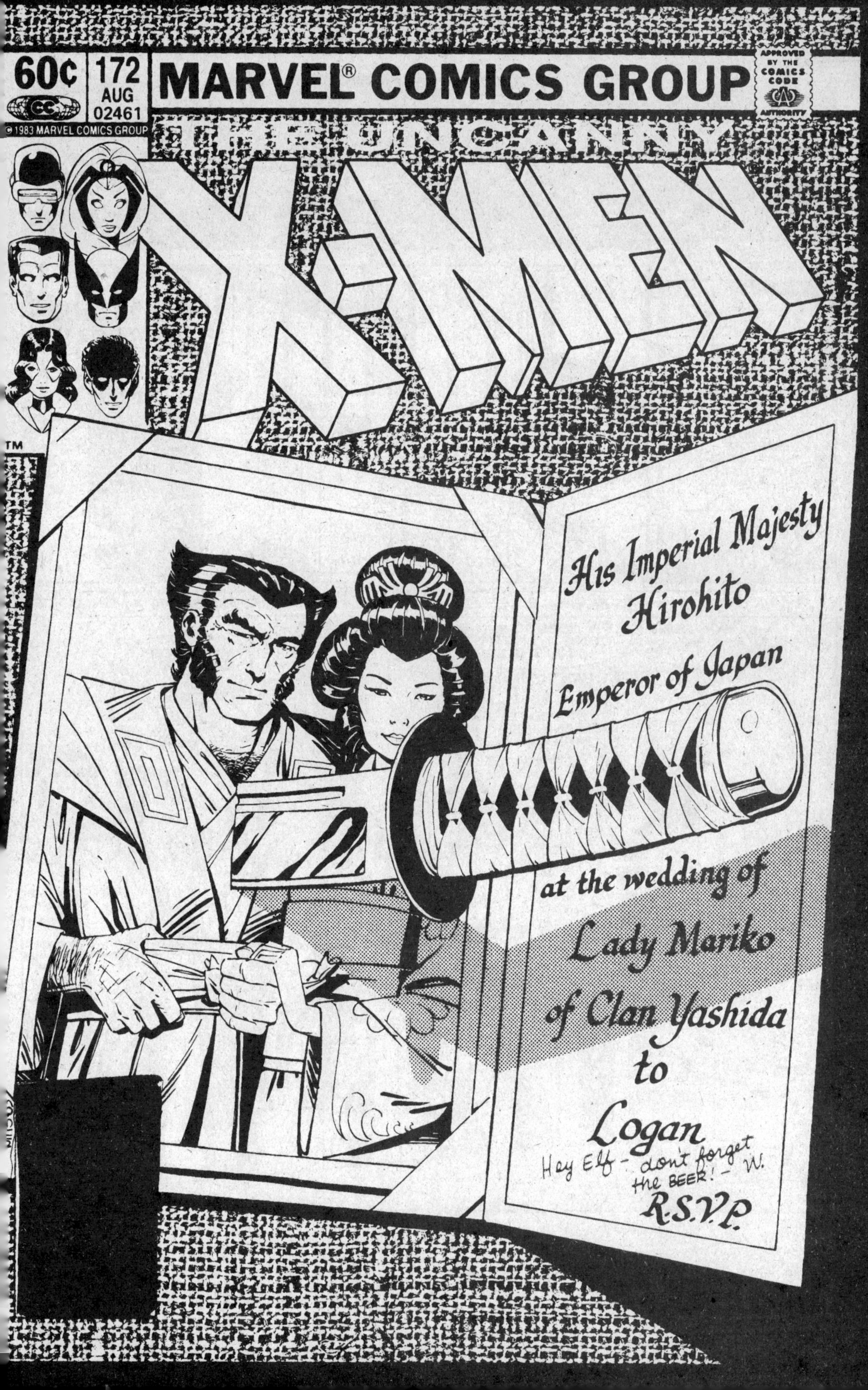
60¢
172
AUG
02461
© 1983 MARVEL COMICS GROUP
MARVEL® COMICS GROUP
APPROVED BY THE COMICS CODE AUTHORITY
THE UNCANNY
X-MEN
TM
His Imperial Majesty
Hirohito
Emperor of Japan
at the wedding of
Lady Mariko
of Clan Yashida
to
Logan
Hey Elf - don't forget the BEER! - W.
R.S.V.P.

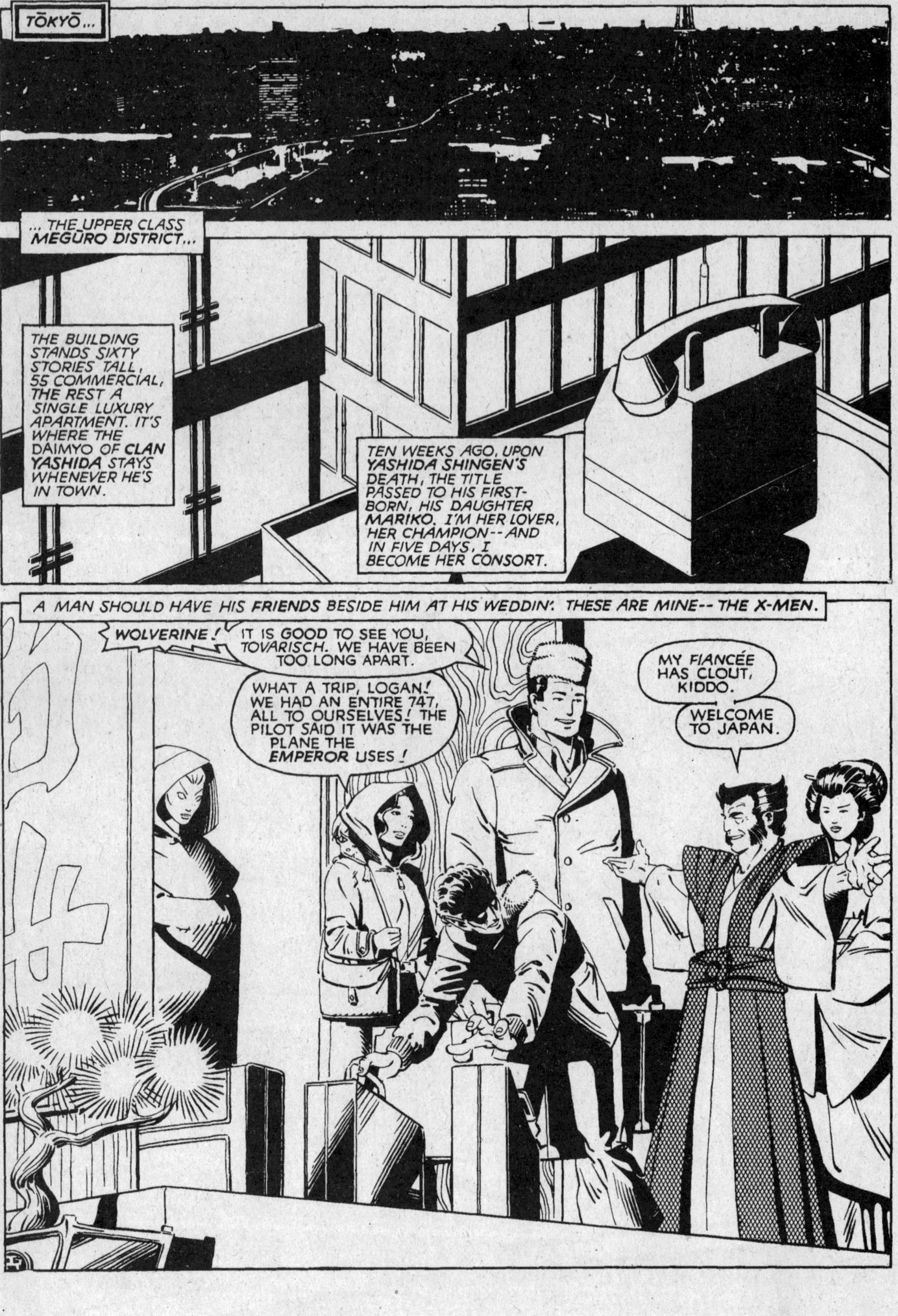
TŌKYŌ...
... THE UPPER CLASS MEGŪRO DISTRICT...
THE BUILDING STANDS SIXTY STORIES TALL, 55 COMMERCIAL, THE REST A SINGLE LUXURY APARTMENT. IT'S WHERE THE DAIMYO OF CLAN YASHIDA STAYS WHENEVER HE'S IN TOWN.
TEN WEEKS AGO, UPON YASHIDA SHINGEN'S DEATH, THE TITLE PASSED TO HIS FIRST-BORN, HIS DAUGHTER MARIKO. I'M HER LOVER, HER CHAMPION-- AND IN FIVE DAYS, I BECOME HER CONSORT.
A MAN SHOULD HAVE HIS FRIENDS BESIDE HIM AT HIS WEDDIN'. THESE ARE MINE-- THE X-MEN.
WOLVERINE!
IT IS GOOD TO SEE YOU, TOVARISCH. WE HAVE BEEN TOO LONG APART.
WHAT A TRIP, LOGAN! WE HAD AN ENTIRE 747, ALL TO OURSELVES! THE PILOT SAID IT WAS THE PLANE THE EMPEROR USES!
MY FIANCÉE HAS CLOUT, KIDDO.
WELCOME TO JAPAN.

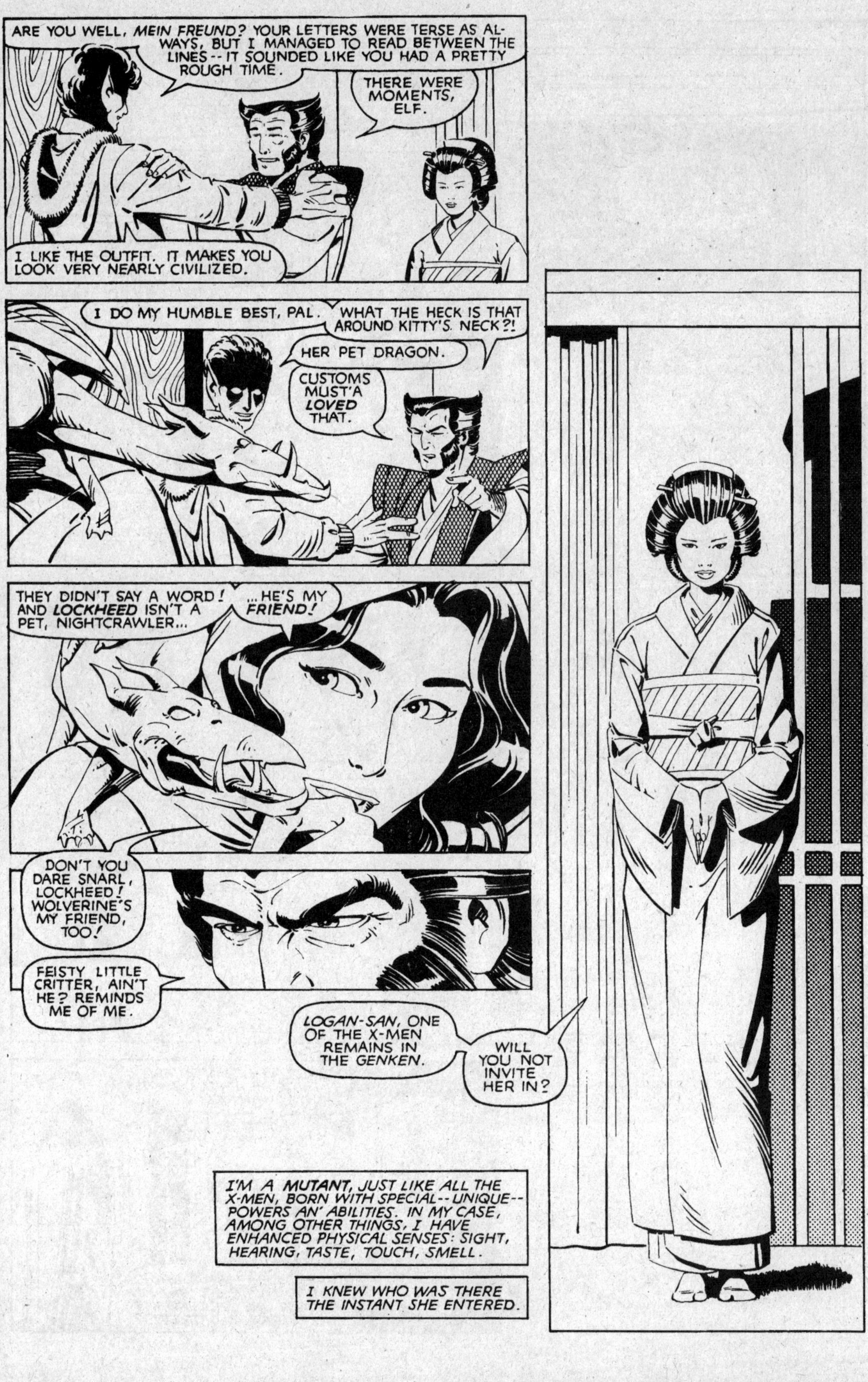
ARE YOU WELL, MEIN FREUND? YOUR LETTERS WERE TERSE AS ALWAYS, BUT I MANAGED TO READ BETWEEN THE LINES -- IT SOUNDED LIKE YOU HAD A PRETTY ROUGH TIME.
THERE WERE MOMENTS, ELF.
I LIKE THE OUTFIT. IT MAKES YOU LOOK VERY NEARLY CIVILIZED.
I DO MY HUMBLE BEST, PAL.
WHAT THE HECK IS THAT AROUND KITTY'S NECK?!
HER PET DRAGON.
CUSTOMS MUST'A LOVED THAT.
THEY DIDN'T SAY A WORD! AND LOCKHEED ISN'T A PET, NIGHTCRAWLER...
...HE'S MY FRIEND!
DON'T YOU DARE SNARL, LOCKHEED! WOLVERINE'S MY FRIEND, TOO!
FEISTY LITTLE CRITTER, AIN'T HE? REMINDS ME OF ME.
LOGAN-SAN, ONE OF THE X-MEN REMAINS IN THE GENKEN.
WILL YOU NOT INVITE HER IN?
I'M A MUTANT, JUST LIKE ALL THE X-MEN, BORN WITH SPECIAL-- UNIQUE-- POWERS AN' ABILITIES. IN MY CASE, AMONG OTHER THINGS, I HAVE ENHANCED PHYSICAL SENSES: SIGHT, HEARING, TASTE, TOUCH, SMELL.
I KNEW WHO WAS THERE THE INSTANT SHE ENTERED.

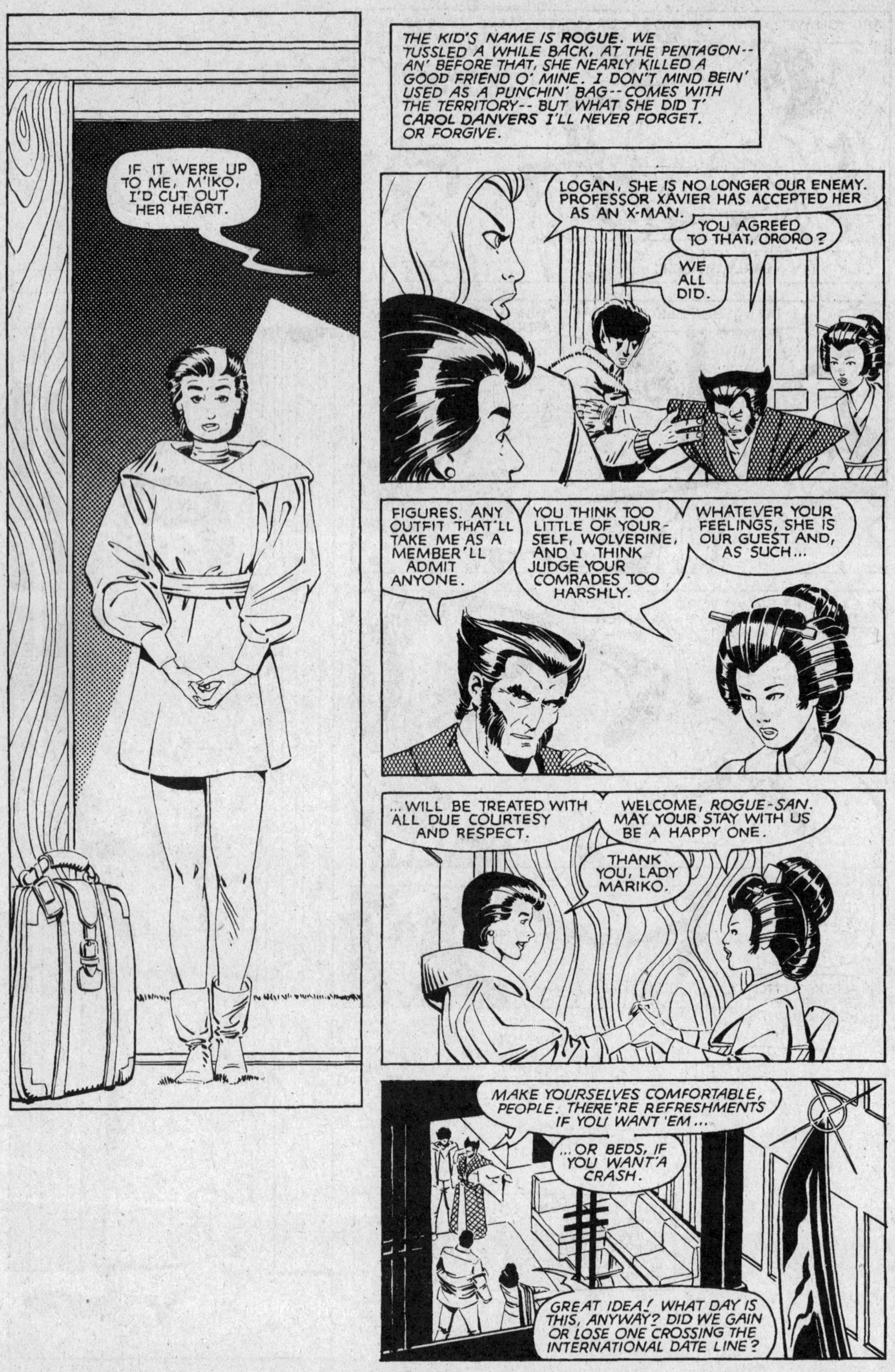
IF IT WERE UP TO ME, M'IKO, I'D CUT OUT HER HEART.
THE KID'S NAME IS ROGUE. WE TUSSLED A WHILE BACK, AT THE PENTAGON-- AN' BEFORE THAT, SHE NEARLY KILLED A GOOD FRIEND O' MINE. I DON'T MIND BEIN' USED AS A PUNCHIN' BAG--COMES WITH THE TERRITORY-- BUT WHAT SHE DID T' CAROL DANVERS I'LL NEVER FORGET. OR FORGIVE.
LOGAN, SHE IS NO LONGER OUR ENEMY. PROFESSOR XAVIER HAS ACCEPTED HER AS AN X-MAN.
YOU AGREED TO THAT, ORORO?
WE ALL DID.
FIGURES. ANY OUTFIT THAT'LL TAKE ME AS A MEMBER'LL ADMIT ANYONE.
YOU THINK TOO LITTLE OF YOURSELF, WOLVERINE, AND I THINK JUDGE YOUR COMRADES TOO HARSHLY.
WHATEVER YOUR FEELINGS, SHE IS OUR GUEST AND, AS SUCH...
...WILL BE TREATED WITH ALL DUE COURTESY AND RESPECT.
WELCOME, ROGUE-SAN. MAY YOUR STAY WITH US BE A HAPPY ONE.
THANK YOU, LADY MARIKO.
MAKE YOURSELVES COMFORTABLE, PEOPLE. THERE'RE REFRESHMENTS IF YOU WANT 'EM...
...OR BEDS, IF YOU WANT'A CRASH.
GREAT IDEA! WHAT DAY IS THIS, ANYWAY? DID WE GAIN OR LOSE ONE CROSSING THE INTERNATIONAL DATE LINE?

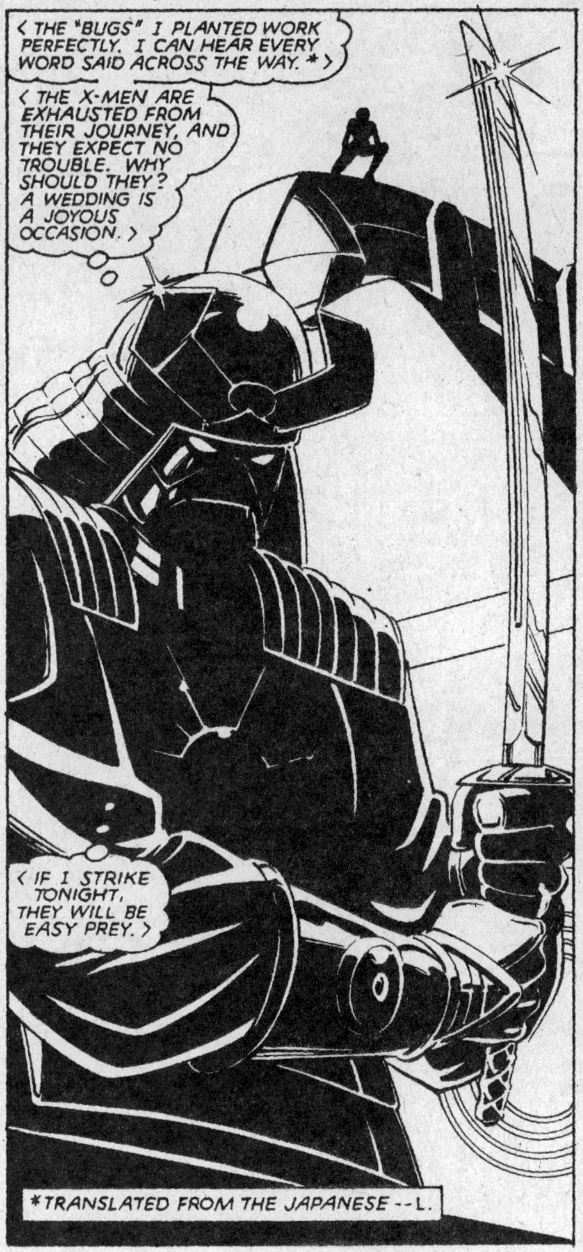

< THE "BUGS" I PLANTED WORK PERFECTLY. I CAN HEAR EVERY WORD SAID ACROSS THE WAY. * >
< THE X-MEN ARE EXHAUSTED FROM THEIR JOURNEY, AND THEY EXPECT NO TROUBLE. WHY SHOULD THEY? A WEDDING IS A JOYOUS OCCASION. >
< IF I STRIKE TONIGHT, THEY WILL BE EASY PREY. >
*TRANSLATED FROM THE JAPANESE --L.

Stan Lee PRESENTS...

Scarlet IN GLORY

CHRIS CLAREMONT WRITER · PAUL SMITH PENCILER · BOB WIACEK INKER

GLYNIS WEIN, colorist • TOM ORZECHOWSKI, letterer

LOUISE JONES EDITOR · JIM SHOOTER EDITOR-IN-CHIEF

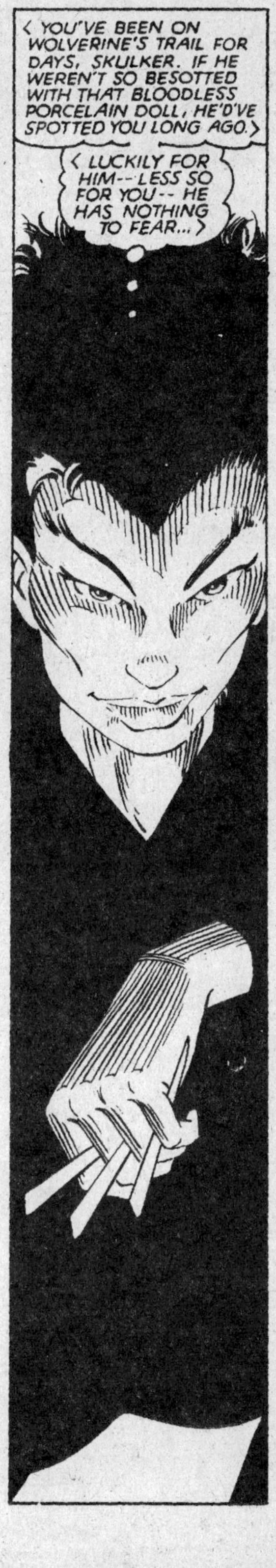

< YOU'VE BEEN ON WOLVERINE'S TRAIL FOR DAYS, SKULKER. IF HE WEREN'T SO BESOTTED WITH THAT BLOODLESS PORCELAIN DOLL, HE'D'VE SPOTTED YOU LONG AGO. >
< LUCKILY FOR HIM--LESS SO FOR YOU-- HE HAS NOTHING TO FEAR... >

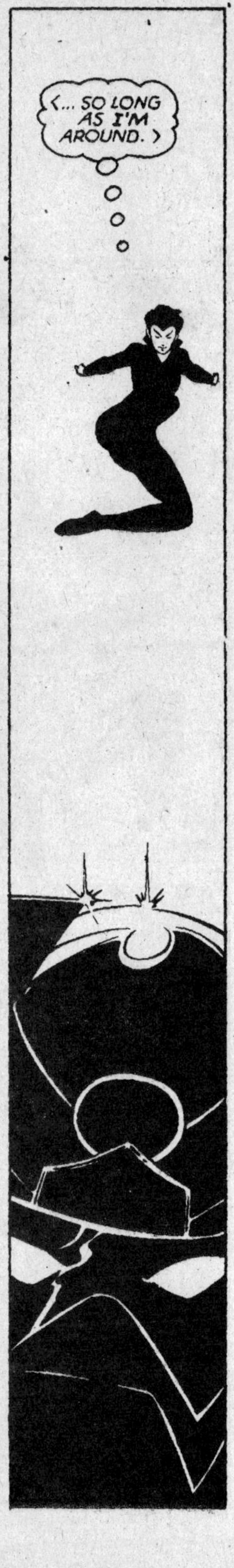

<... SO LONG AS I'M AROUND. >

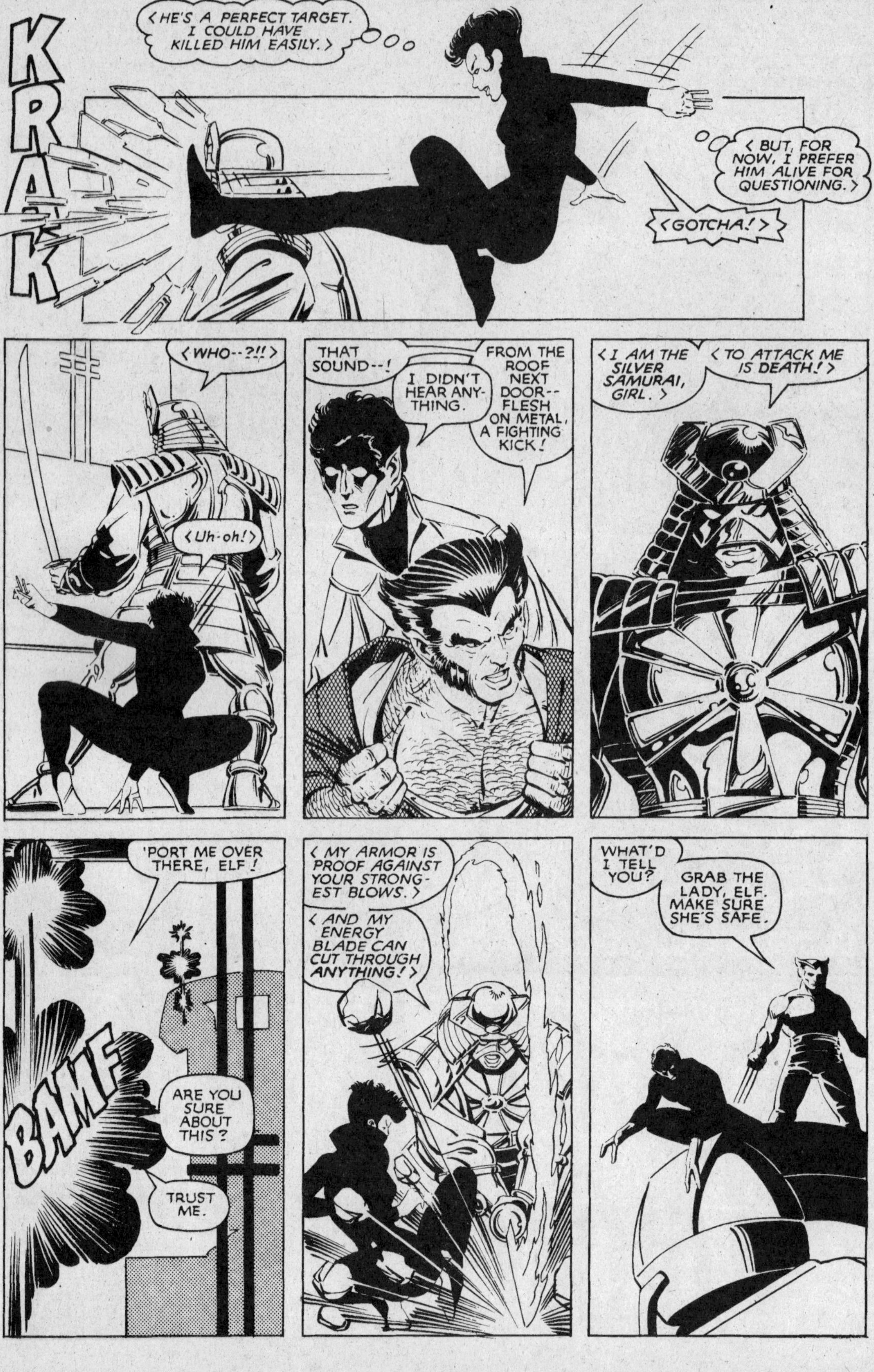

KRAKK
< HE'S A PERFECT TARGET. I COULD HAVE KILLED HIM EASILY. >
< BUT, FOR NOW, I PREFER HIM ALIVE FOR QUESTIONING. >
< GOTCHA! >
< WHO--?!! >
< Uh-oh! >
THAT SOUND--!
I DIDN'T HEAR ANY-THING.
FROM THE ROOF NEXT DOOR--FLESH ON METAL, A FIGHTING KICK!
< I AM THE SILVER SAMURAI, GIRL. >
< TO ATTACK ME IS DEATH! >
'PORT ME OVER THERE, ELF!
BAMF
ARE YOU SURE ABOUT THIS?
TRUST ME.
< MY ARMOR IS PROOF AGAINST YOUR STRONG-EST BLOWS. >
< AND MY ENERGY BLADE CAN CUT THROUGH ANYTHING! >
WHAT'D I TELL YOU?
GRAB THE LADY, ELF. MAKE SURE SHE'S SAFE.

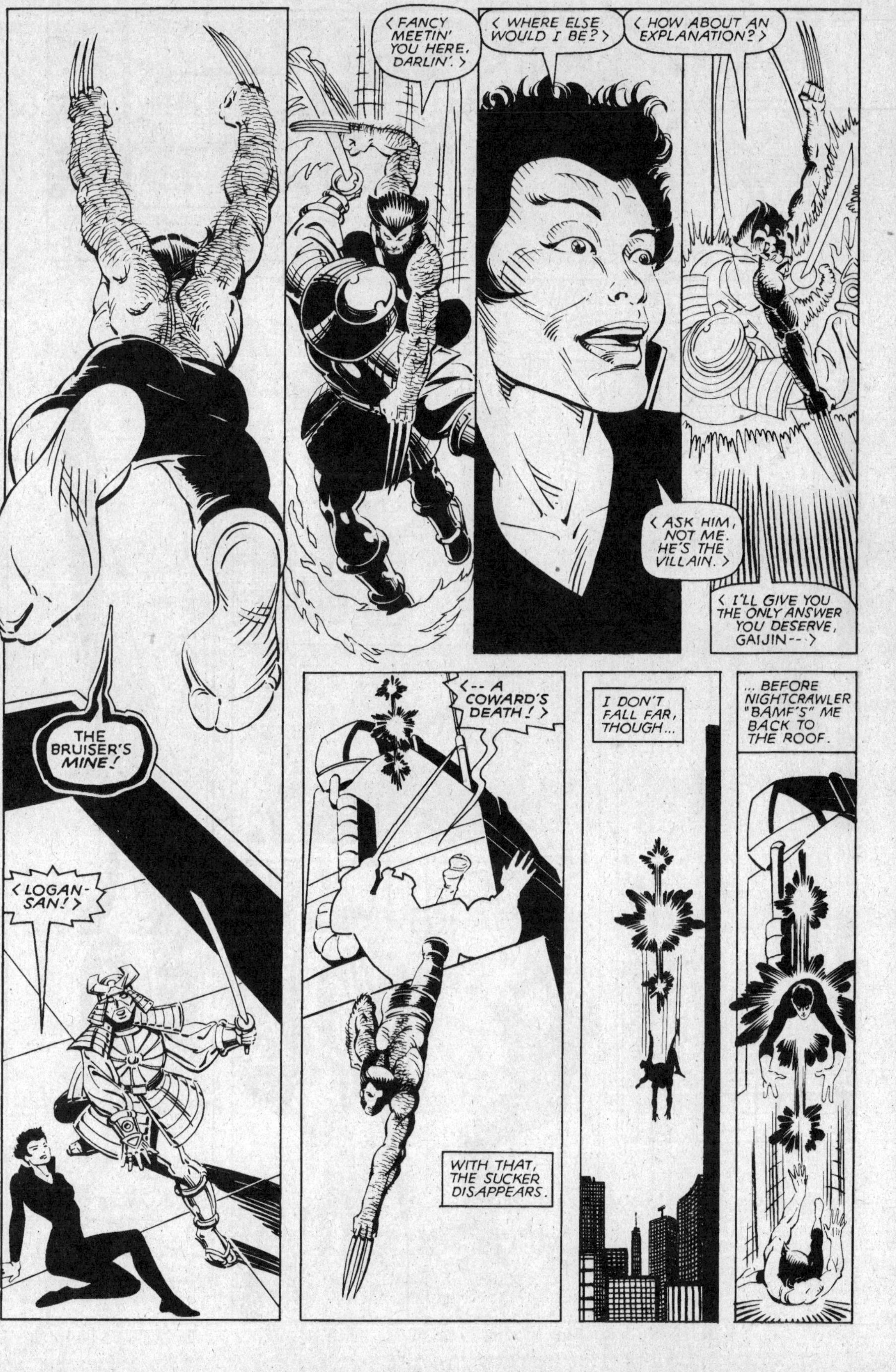
THE BRUISER'S MINE!
< LOGAN-SAN! >
< FANCY MEETIN' YOU HERE, DARLIN'. >
< WHERE ELSE WOULD I BE? >
< HOW ABOUT AN EXPLANATION? >
< ASK HIM, NOT ME. HE'S THE VILLAIN. >
< I'LL GIVE YOU THE ONLY ANSWER YOU DESERVE, GAIJIN-- >
<-- A COWARD'S DEATH! >
WITH THAT, THE SUCKER DISAPPEARS.
I DON'T FALL FAR, THOUGH...
... BEFORE NIGHTCRAWLER "BAMF'S" ME BACK TO THE ROOF.

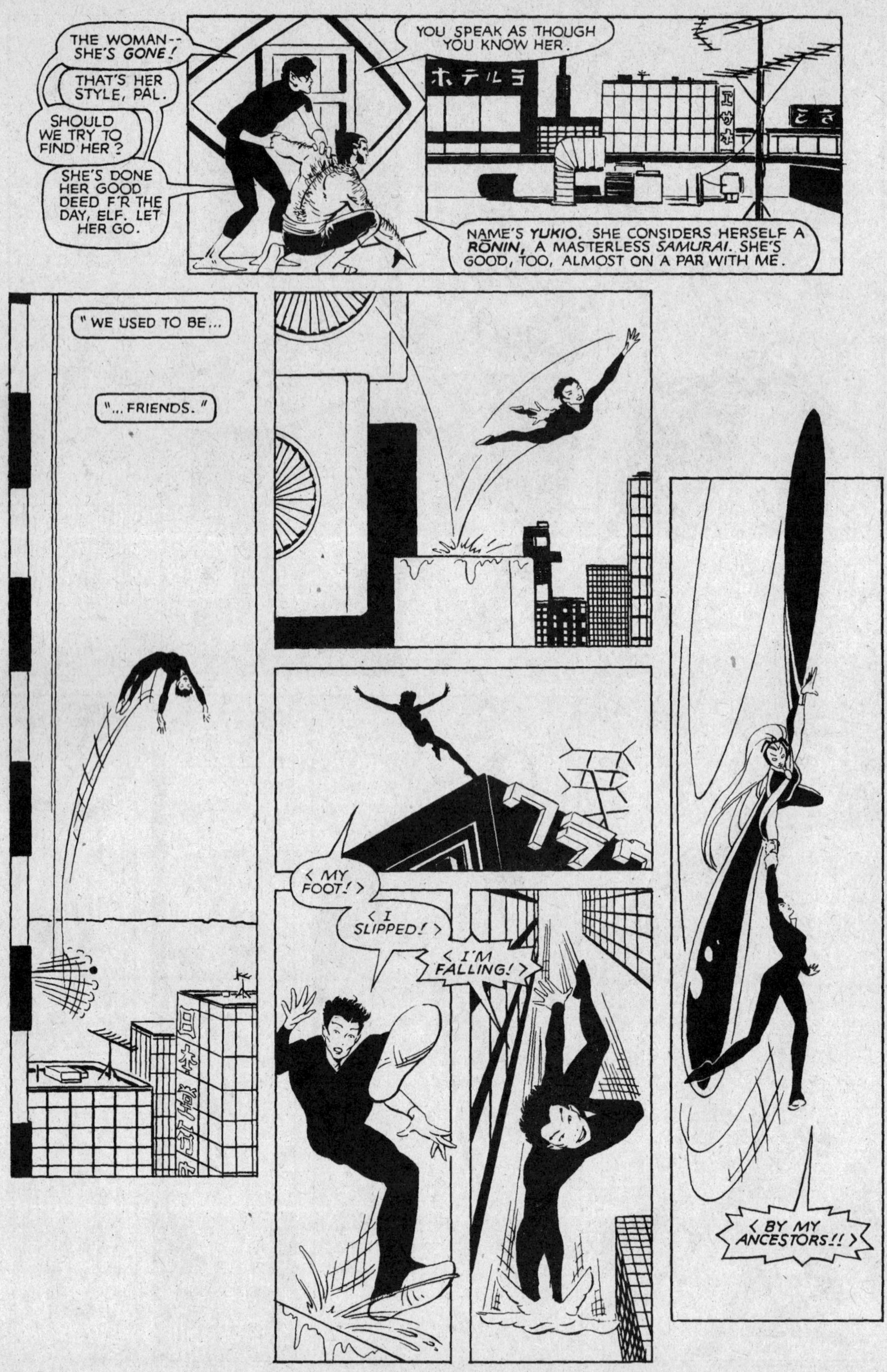
THE WOMAN-- SHE'S GONE!
YOU SPEAK AS THOUGH YOU KNOW HER.
THAT'S HER STYLE, PAL.
SHOULD WE TRY TO FIND HER?
SHE'S DONE HER GOOD DEED F'R THE DAY, ELF. LET HER GO.
NAME'S YUKIO. SHE CONSIDERS HERSELF A RŌNIN, A MASTERLESS SAMURAI. SHE'S GOOD, TOO, ALMOST ON A PAR WITH ME.
"WE USED TO BE...
"...FRIENDS."
< MY FOOT! >
< I SLIPPED! >
< I'M FALLING! >
< BY MY ANCESTORS!! >

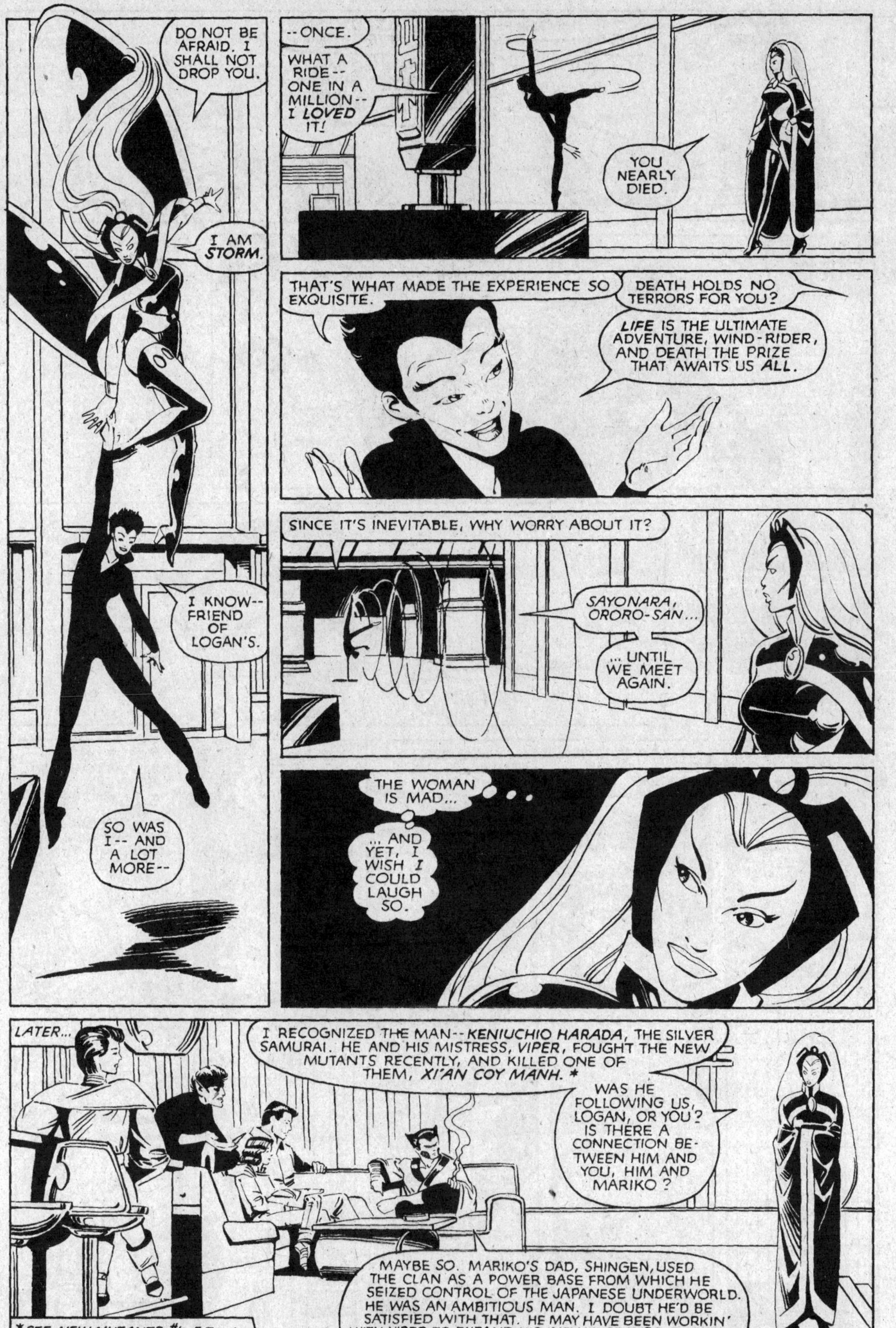
DO NOT BE AFRAID. I SHALL NOT DROP YOU.
I AM STORM.
I KNOW-- FRIEND OF LOGAN'S.
SO WAS I -- AND A LOT MORE--
--ONCE.
WHAT A RIDE -- ONE IN A MILLION -- I LOVED IT!
YOU NEARLY DIED.
THAT'S WHAT MADE THE EXPERIENCE SO EXQUISITE.
DEATH HOLDS NO TERRORS FOR YOU?
LIFE IS THE ULTIMATE ADVENTURE, WIND-RIDER, AND DEATH THE PRIZE THAT AWAITS US ALL.
SINCE IT'S INEVITABLE, WHY WORRY ABOUT IT?
SAYONARA, ORORO-SAN...
... UNTIL WE MEET AGAIN.
THE WOMAN IS MAD...
... AND YET, I WISH I COULD LAUGH SO.
LATER...
I RECOGNIZED THE MAN--KENIUCHIO HARADA, THE SILVER SAMURAI. HE AND HIS MISTRESS, VIPER, FOUGHT THE NEW MUTANTS RECENTLY, AND KILLED ONE OF THEM, XI'AN COY MANH. *
WAS HE FOLLOWING US, LOGAN, OR YOU? IS THERE A CONNECTION BE-TWEEN HIM AND YOU, HIM AND MARIKO?
MAYBE SO. MARIKO'S DAD, SHINGEN, USED THE CLAN AS A POWER BASE FROM WHICH HE SEIZED CONTROL OF THE JAPANESE UNDERWORLD. HE WAS AN AMBITIOUS MAN. I DOUBT HE'D BE SATISFIED WITH THAT. HE MAY HAVE BEEN WORKIN' WITH VIPER TO EXPAND HIS INFLUENCE WORLD-WIDE.
*SEE NEW MUTANTS #'s 5-7 --L.

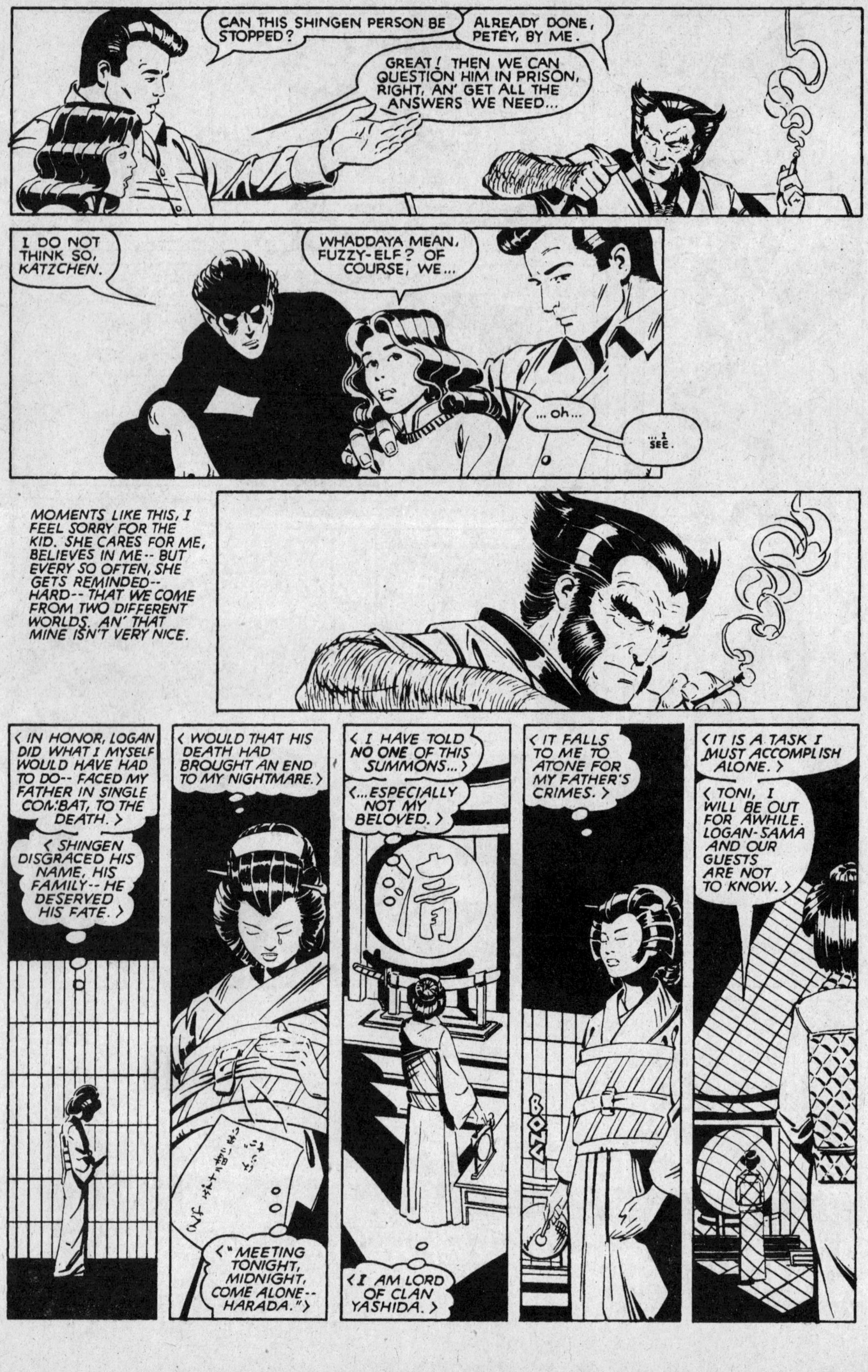
CAN THIS SHINGEN PERSON BE STOPPED?
ALREADY DONE, PETEY, BY ME.
GREAT! THEN WE CAN QUESTION HIM IN PRISON, RIGHT, AN' GET ALL THE ANSWERS WE NEED...
I DO NOT THINK SO, KATZCHEN.
WHADDAYA MEAN, FUZZY-ELF? OF COURSE, WE...
...oh...
...I SEE.
MOMENTS LIKE THIS, I FEEL SORRY FOR THE KID. SHE CARES FOR ME, BELIEVES IN ME-- BUT EVERY SO OFTEN, SHE GETS REMINDED-- HARD-- THAT WE COME FROM TWO DIFFERENT WORLDS. AN' THAT MINE ISN'T VERY NICE.
< IN HONOR, LOGAN DID WHAT I MYSELF WOULD HAVE HAD TO DO-- FACED MY FATHER IN SINGLE COMBAT, TO THE DEATH. >
< SHINGEN DISGRACED HIS NAME, HIS FAMILY-- HE DESERVED HIS FATE. >
< WOULD THAT HIS DEATH HAD BROUGHT AN END TO MY NIGHTMARE. >
< "MEETING TONIGHT, MIDNIGHT. COME ALONE-- HARADA." >
< I HAVE TOLD NO ONE OF THIS SUMMONS... >
< ...ESPECIALLY NOT MY BELOVED. >
< I AM LORD OF CLAN YASHIDA. >
< IT FALLS TO ME TO ATONE FOR MY FATHER'S CRIMES. >
BONG
< IT IS A TASK I MUST ACCOMPLISH ALONE. >
< TONI, I WILL BE OUT FOR AWHILE. LOGAN-SAMA AND OUR GUESTS ARE NOT TO KNOW. >

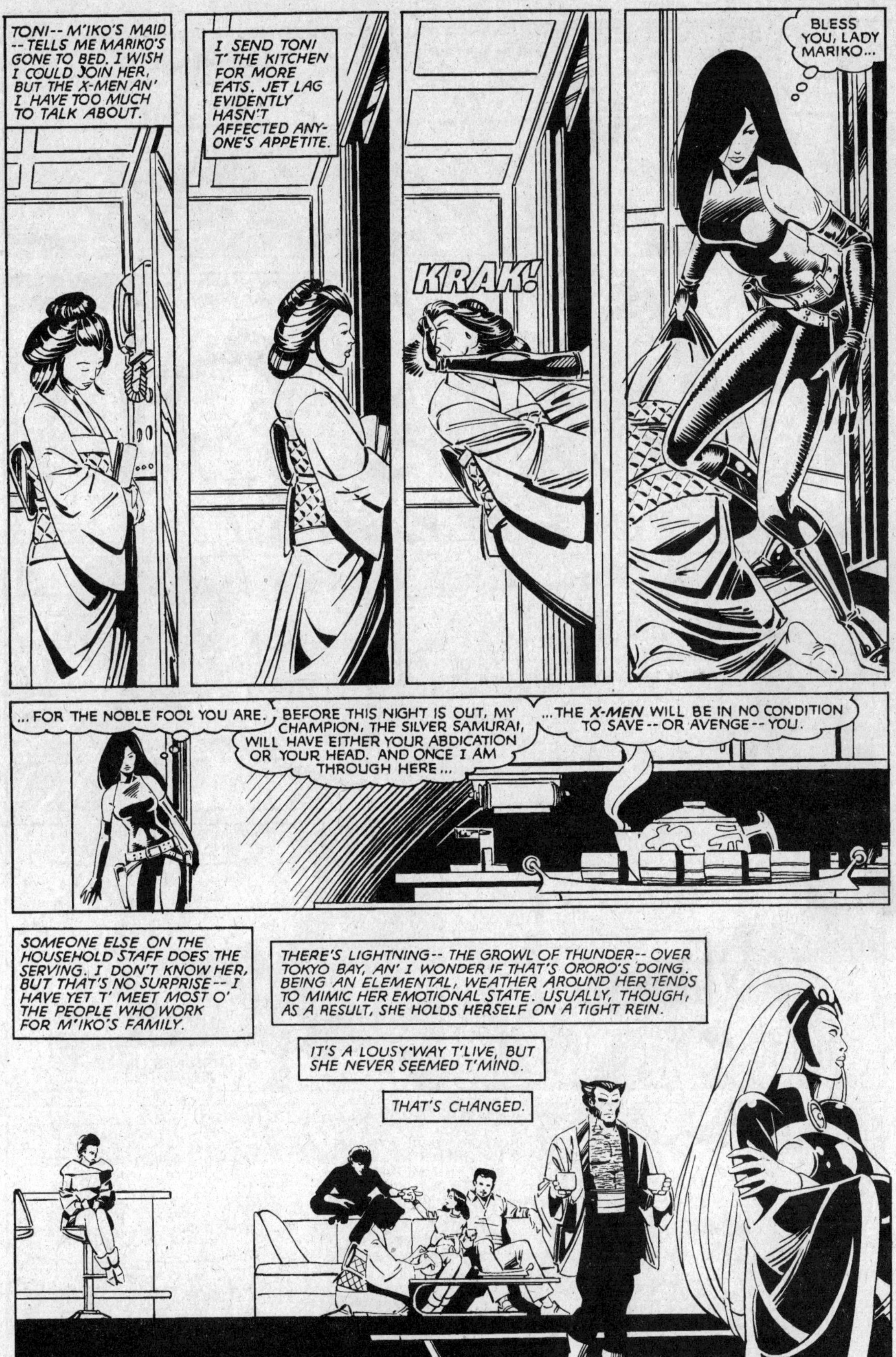

TONI-- M'IKO'S MAID --TELLS ME MARIKO'S GONE TO BED. I WISH I COULD JOIN HER, BUT THE X-MEN AN' I HAVE TOO MUCH TO TALK ABOUT.
I SEND TONI T' THE KITCHEN FOR MORE EATS. JET LAG EVIDENTLY HASN'T AFFECTED ANYONE'S APPETITE.
KRAK!
BLESS YOU, LADY MARIKO...
... FOR THE NOBLE FOOL YOU ARE.
BEFORE THIS NIGHT IS OUT, MY CHAMPION, THE SILVER SAMURAI, WILL HAVE EITHER YOUR ABDICATION OR YOUR HEAD. AND ONCE I AM THROUGH HERE...
...THE X-MEN WILL BE IN NO CONDITION TO SAVE--OR AVENGE--YOU.
SOMEONE ELSE ON THE HOUSEHOLD STAFF DOES THE SERVING. I DON'T KNOW HER, BUT THAT'S NO SURPRISE-- I HAVE YET T' MEET MOST O' THE PEOPLE WHO WORK FOR M'IKO'S FAMILY.
THERE'S LIGHTNING-- THE GROWL OF THUNDER-- OVER TOKYO BAY, AN' I WONDER IF THAT'S ORORO'S DOING. BEING AN ELEMENTAL, WEATHER AROUND HER TENDS TO MIMIC HER EMOTIONAL STATE. USUALLY, THOUGH, AS A RESULT, SHE HOLDS HERSELF ON A TIGHT REIN.
IT'S A LOUSY WAY T'LIVE, BUT SHE NEVER SEEMED T'MIND.
THAT'S CHANGED.

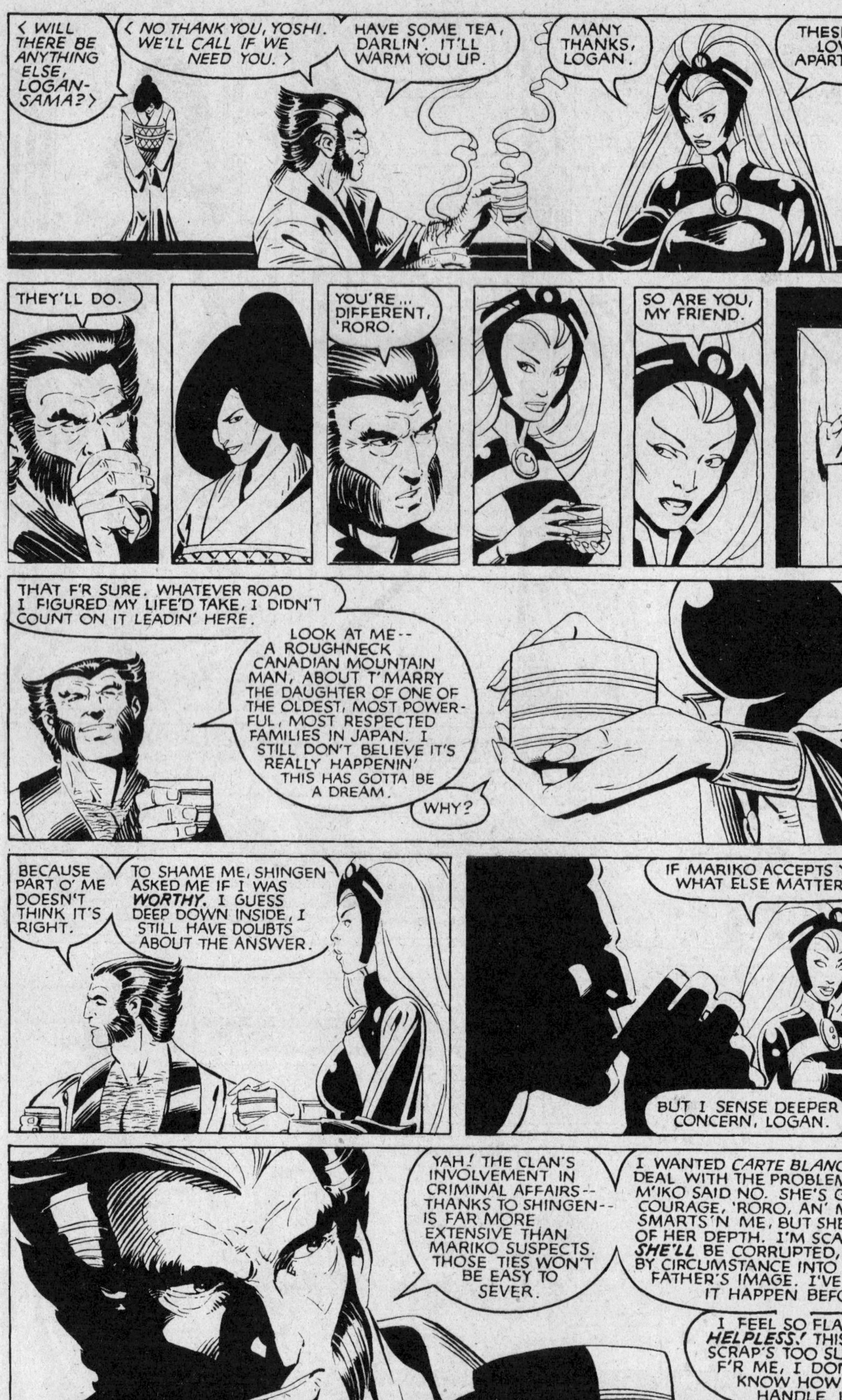

< WILL THERE BE ANYTHING ELSE, LOGAN-SAMA? >
< NO THANK YOU, YOSHI. WE'LL CALL IF WE NEED YOU. >
HAVE SOME TEA, DARLIN'. IT'LL WARM YOU UP.
MANY THANKS, LOGAN.
THESE ARE LOVELY APARTMENTS.
THEY'LL DO.
YOU'RE... DIFFERENT, 'RORO.
SO ARE YOU, MY FRIEND.
THAT F'R SURE. WHATEVER ROAD I FIGURED MY LIFE'D TAKE, I DIDN'T COUNT ON IT LEADIN' HERE.
LOOK AT ME-- A ROUGHNECK CANADIAN MOUNTAIN MAN, ABOUT T'MARRY THE DAUGHTER OF ONE OF THE OLDEST, MOST POWERFUL, MOST RESPECTED FAMILIES IN JAPAN. I STILL DON'T BELIEVE IT'S REALLY HAPPENIN' THIS HAS GOTTA BE A DREAM.
WHY?
BECAUSE PART O' ME DOESN'T THINK IT'S RIGHT.
TO SHAME ME, SHINGEN ASKED ME IF I WAS WORTHY. I GUESS DEEP DOWN INSIDE, I STILL HAVE DOUBTS ABOUT THE ANSWER.
IF MARIKO ACCEPTS YOU, WHAT ELSE MATTERS?
BUT I SENSE DEEPER CONCERN, LOGAN.
YAH! THE CLAN'S INVOLVEMENT IN CRIMINAL AFFAIRS-- THANKS TO SHINGEN-- IS FAR MORE EXTENSIVE THAN MARIKO SUSPECTS. THOSE TIES WON'T BE EASY TO SEVER.
I WANTED CARTE BLANCHE TO DEAL WITH THE PROBLEM, BUT M'IKO SAID NO. SHE'S GOT COURAGE, 'RORO, AN' MORE SMARTS 'N ME, BUT SHE'S OUT OF HER DEPTH. I'M SCARED SHE'LL BE CORRUPTED, SHAPED BY CIRCUMSTANCE INTO HER FATHER'S IMAGE. I'VE SEEN IT HAPPEN BEFORE.
I FEEL SO FLAMIN' HELPLESS! THIS KIND'A SCRAP'S TOO SUBTLE F'R ME, I DON'T KNOW HOW TO HANDLE IT.

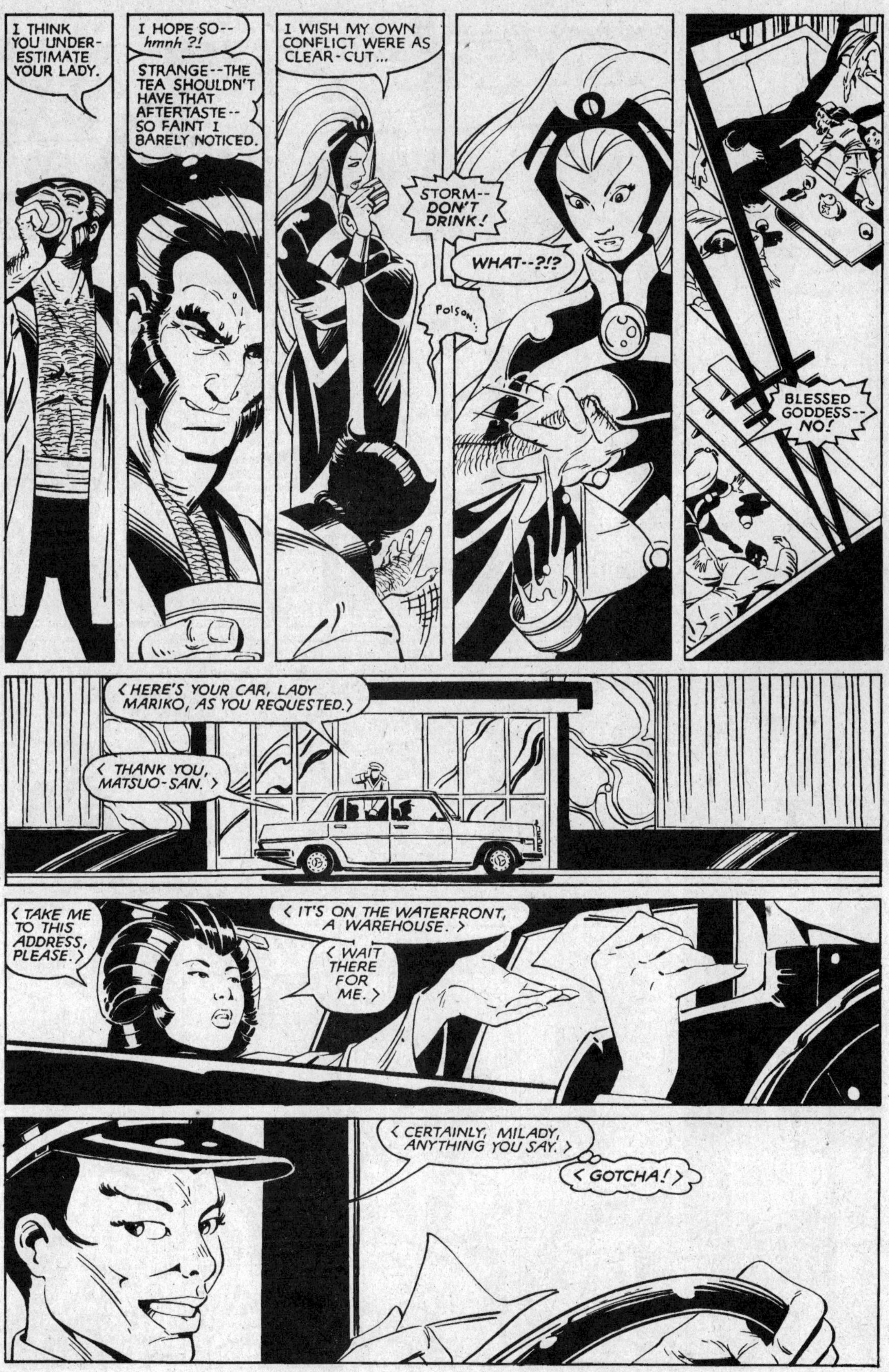
I THINK YOU UNDER-ESTIMATE YOUR LADY.
I HOPE SO-- hmnh ?!
STRANGE--THE TEA SHOULDN'T HAVE THAT AFTERTASTE-- SO FAINT I BARELY NOTICED.
I WISH MY OWN CONFLICT WERE AS CLEAR-CUT...
STORM-- DON'T DRINK!
WHAT--?!?
POISON...
BLESSED GODDESS-- NO!
< HERE'S YOUR CAR, LADY MARIKO, AS YOU REQUESTED. >
< THANK YOU, MATSUO-SAN. >
< TAKE ME TO THIS ADDRESS, PLEASE. >
< IT'S ON THE WATERFRONT, A WAREHOUSE. >
< WAIT THERE FOR ME. >
< CERTAINLY, MILADY, ANYTHING YOU SAY. >
< GOTCHA! >

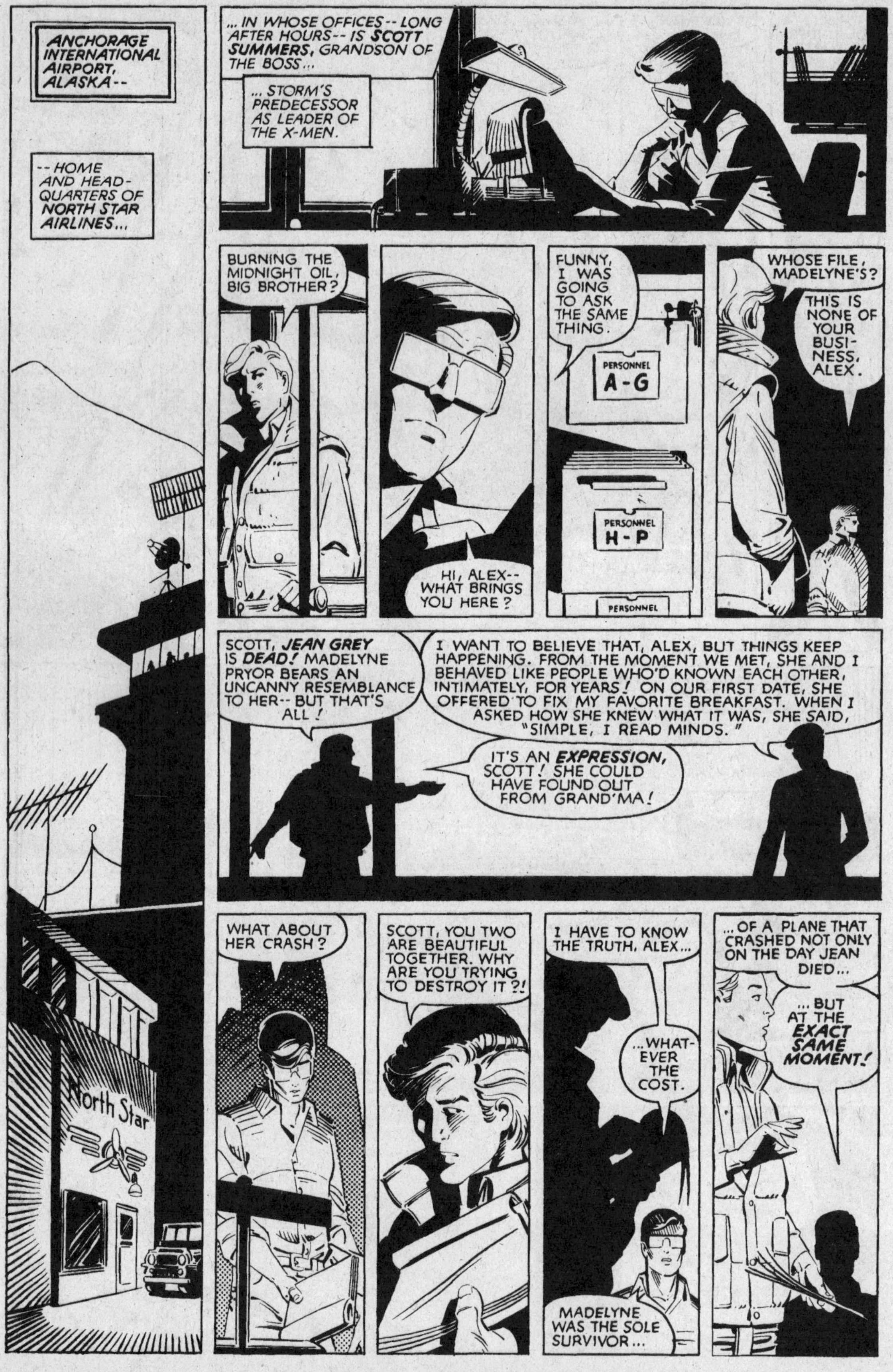
ANCHORAGE INTERNATIONAL AIRPORT, ALASKA--
--HOME AND HEAD-QUARTERS OF NORTH STAR AIRLINES...
...IN WHOSE OFFICES--LONG AFTER HOURS--IS SCOTT SUMMERS, GRANDSON OF THE BOSS...
...STORM'S PREDECESSOR AS LEADER OF THE X-MEN.
BURNING THE MIDNIGHT OIL, BIG BROTHER?
HI, ALEX--WHAT BRINGS YOU HERE?
FUNNY, I WAS GOING TO ASK THE SAME THING.
PERSONNEL A-G
PERSONNEL H-P
PERSONNEL
WHOSE FILE, MADELYNE'S?
THIS IS NONE OF YOUR BUSI-NESS, ALEX.
SCOTT, JEAN GREY IS DEAD! MADELYNE PRYOR BEARS AN UNCANNY RESEMBLANCE TO HER--BUT THAT'S ALL!
I WANT TO BELIEVE THAT, ALEX, BUT THINGS KEEP HAPPENING. FROM THE MOMENT WE MET, SHE AND I BEHAVED LIKE PEOPLE WHO'D KNOWN EACH OTHER, INTIMATELY, FOR YEARS! ON OUR FIRST DATE, SHE OFFERED TO FIX MY FAVORITE BREAKFAST. WHEN I ASKED HOW SHE KNEW WHAT IT WAS, SHE SAID, "SIMPLE, I READ MINDS."
IT'S AN EXPRESSION, SCOTT! SHE COULD HAVE FOUND OUT FROM GRAND'MA!
North Star
WHAT ABOUT HER CRASH?
SCOTT, YOU TWO ARE BEAUTIFUL TOGETHER. WHY ARE YOU TRYING TO DESTROY IT?!
I HAVE TO KNOW THE TRUTH, ALEX...
...WHAT-EVER THE COST.
MADELYNE WAS THE SOLE SURVIVOR...
...OF A PLANE THAT CRASHED NOT ONLY ON THE DAY JEAN DIED...
...BUT AT THE EXACT SAME MOMENT!

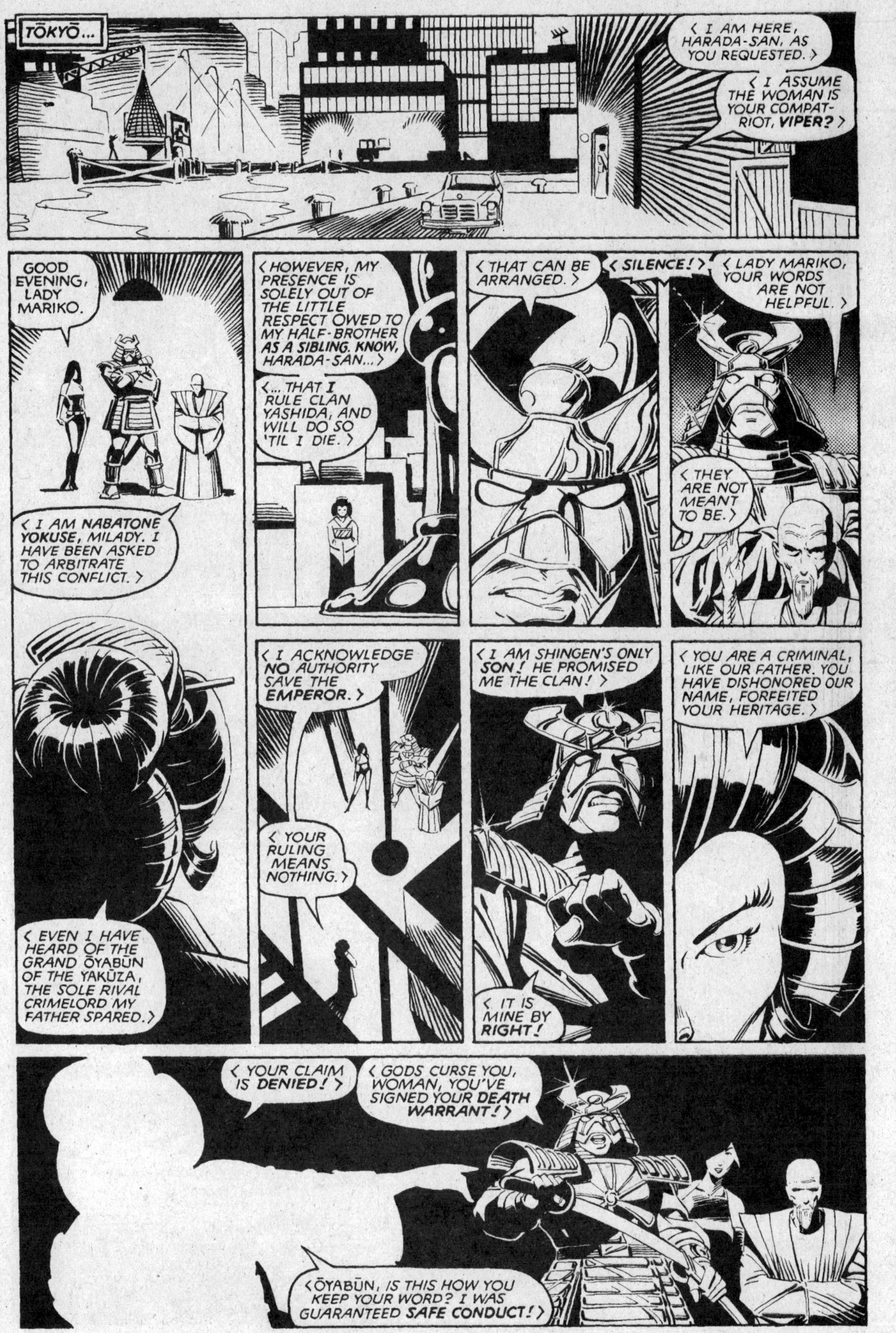
TŌKYŌ...
< I AM HERE, HARADA-SAN, AS YOU REQUESTED. >
< I ASSUME THE WOMAN IS YOUR COMPATRIOT, VIPER? >
GOOD EVENING, LADY MARIKO.
< I AM NABATONE YOKUSE, MILADY. I HAVE BEEN ASKED TO ARBITRATE THIS CONFLICT. >
< HOWEVER, MY PRESENCE IS SOLELY OUT OF THE LITTLE RESPECT OWED TO MY HALF-BROTHER AS A SIBLING. KNOW, HARADA-SAN... >
< ...THAT I RULE CLAN YASHIDA, AND WILL DO SO 'TIL I DIE. >
< THAT CAN BE ARRANGED. >
< SILENCE! >
< LADY MARIKO, YOUR WORDS ARE NOT HELPFUL. >
< THEY ARE NOT MEANT TO BE. >
< EVEN I HAVE HEARD OF THE GRAND ŌYABŪN OF THE YAKŪZA, THE SOLE RIVAL CRIMELORD MY FATHER SPARED. >
< I ACKNOWLEDGE NO AUTHORITY SAVE THE EMPEROR. >
< YOUR RULING MEANS NOTHING. >
< I AM SHINGEN'S ONLY SON! HE PROMISED ME THE CLAN! >
< IT IS MINE BY RIGHT! >
< YOU ARE A CRIMINAL, LIKE OUR FATHER. YOU HAVE DISHONORED OUR NAME, FORFEITED YOUR HERITAGE. >
< YOUR CLAIM IS DENIED! >
< GODS CURSE YOU, WOMAN, YOU'VE SIGNED YOUR DEATH WARRANT! >
< ŌYABŪN, IS THIS HOW YOU KEEP YOUR WORD? I WAS GUARANTEED SAFE CONDUCT! >

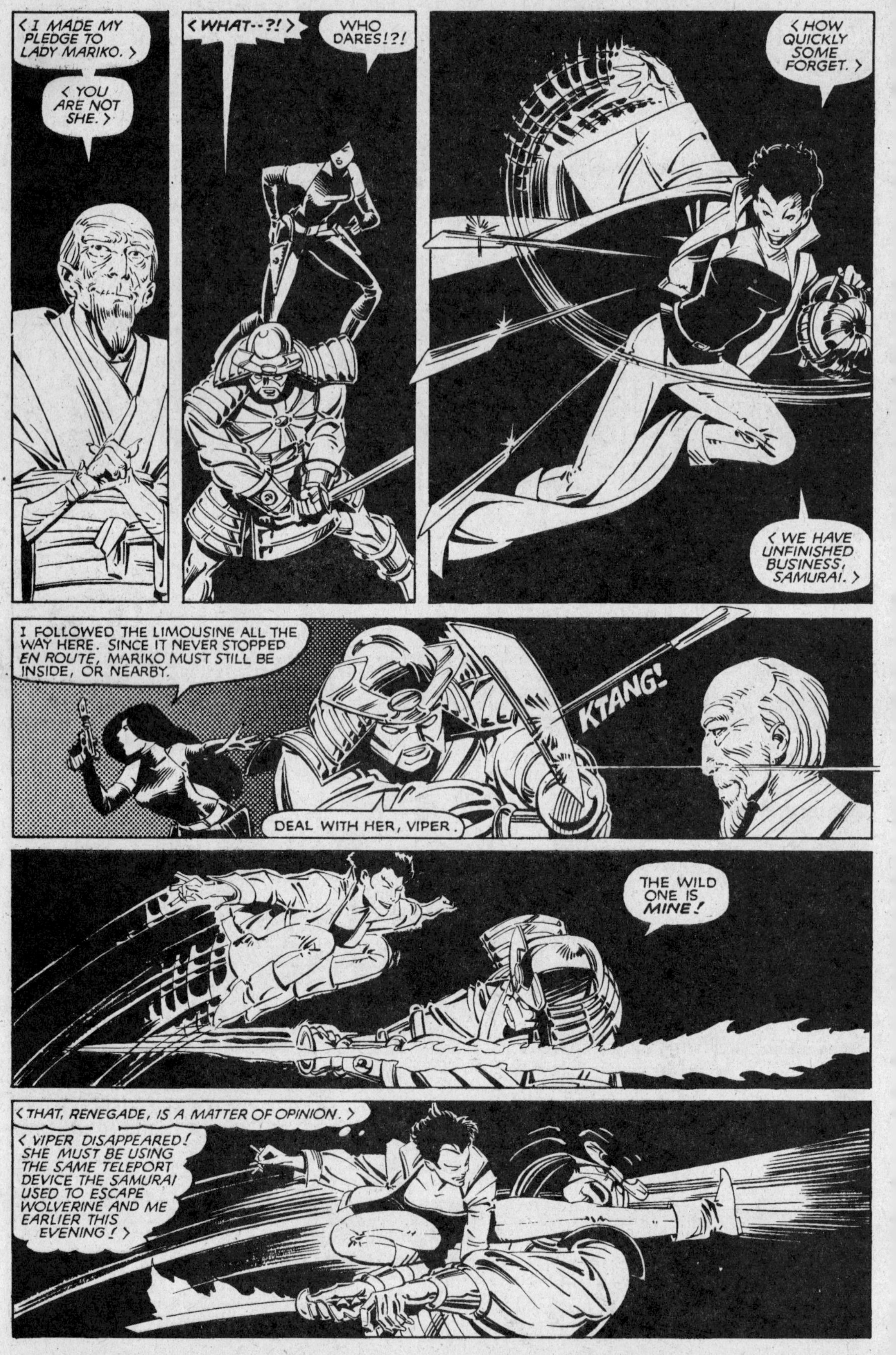

< I MADE MY PLEDGE TO LADY MARIKO. >
< YOU ARE NOT SHE. >
< WHAT--?! >
WHO DARES!?!
< HOW QUICKLY SOME FORGET. >
< WE HAVE UNFINISHED BUSINESS, SAMURAI. >
I FOLLOWED THE LIMOUSINE ALL THE WAY HERE. SINCE IT NEVER STOPPED EN ROUTE, MARIKO MUST STILL BE INSIDE, OR NEARBY.
KTANG!
DEAL WITH HER, VIPER.
THE WILD ONE IS MINE!
< THAT, RENEGADE, IS A MATTER OF OPINION. >
< VIPER DISAPPEARED! SHE MUST BE USING THE SAME TELEPORT DEVICE THE SAMURAI USED TO ESCAPE WOLVERINE AND ME EARLIER THIS EVENING! >

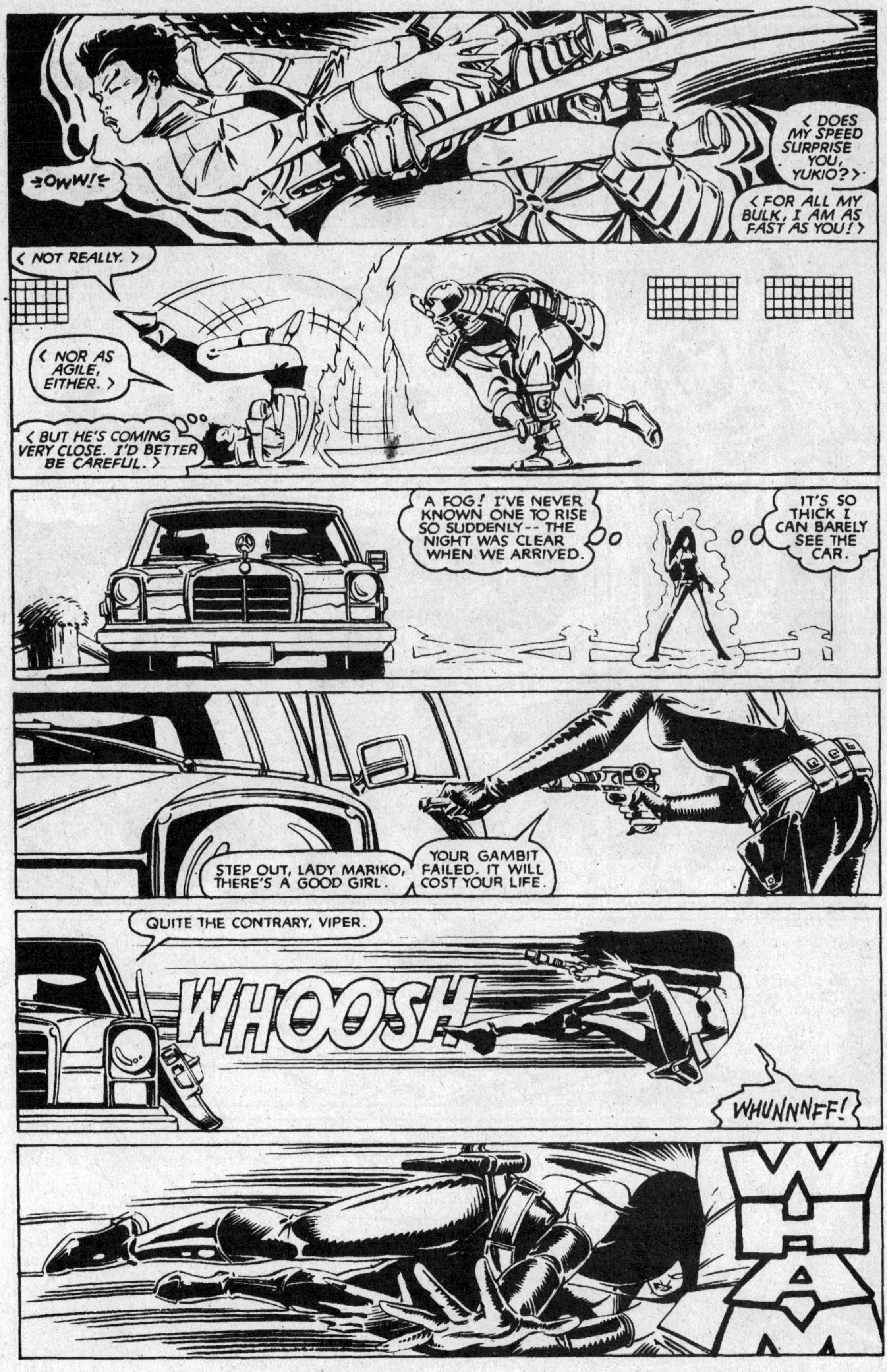
OWW!
< DOES MY SPEED SURPRISE YOU, YUKIO? >
< FOR ALL MY BULK, I AM AS FAST AS YOU! >
< NOT REALLY. >
< NOR AS AGILE, EITHER. >
< BUT HE'S COMING VERY CLOSE. I'D BETTER BE CAREFUL. >
A FOG! I'VE NEVER KNOWN ONE TO RISE SO SUDDENLY -- THE NIGHT WAS CLEAR WHEN WE ARRIVED.
IT'S SO THICK I CAN BARELY SEE THE CAR.
STEP OUT, LADY MARIKO, THERE'S A GOOD GIRL.
YOUR GAMBIT FAILED. IT WILL COST YOUR LIFE.
QUITE THE CONTRARY, VIPER.
WHOOSH
WHUNNNFF!
WHAM

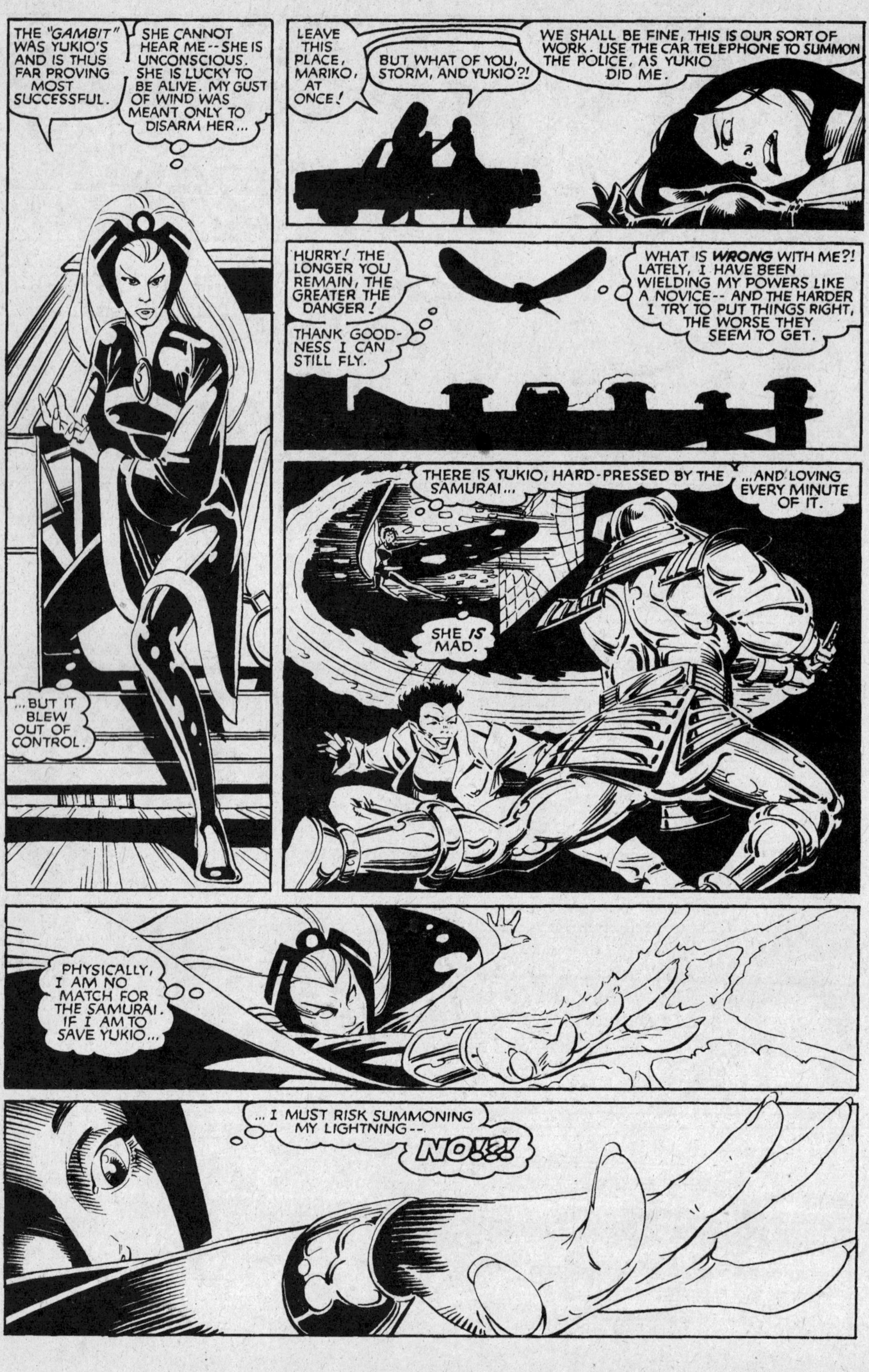
THE "GAMBIT" WAS YUKIO'S AND IS THUS FAR PROVING MOST SUCCESSFUL.
SHE CANNOT HEAR ME-- SHE IS UNCONSCIOUS. SHE IS LUCKY TO BE ALIVE. MY GUST OF WIND WAS MEANT ONLY TO DISARM HER...
...BUT IT BLEW OUT OF CONTROL.
LEAVE THIS PLACE, MARIKO, AT ONCE!
BUT WHAT OF YOU, STORM, AND YUKIO?!
WE SHALL BE FINE, THIS IS OUR SORT OF WORK. USE THE CAR TELEPHONE TO SUMMON THE POLICE, AS YUKIO DID ME.
HURRY! THE LONGER YOU REMAIN, THE GREATER THE DANGER!
THANK GOODNESS I CAN STILL FLY.
WHAT IS WRONG WITH ME?! LATELY, I HAVE BEEN WIELDING MY POWERS LIKE A NOVICE-- AND THE HARDER I TRY TO PUT THINGS RIGHT, THE WORSE THEY SEEM TO GET.
THERE IS YUKIO, HARD-PRESSED BY THE SAMURAI...
...AND LOVING EVERY MINUTE OF IT.
SHE IS MAD.
PHYSICALLY, I AM NO MATCH FOR THE SAMURAI. IF I AM TO SAVE YUKIO...
...I MUST RISK SUMMONING MY LIGHTNING--
NO!?!

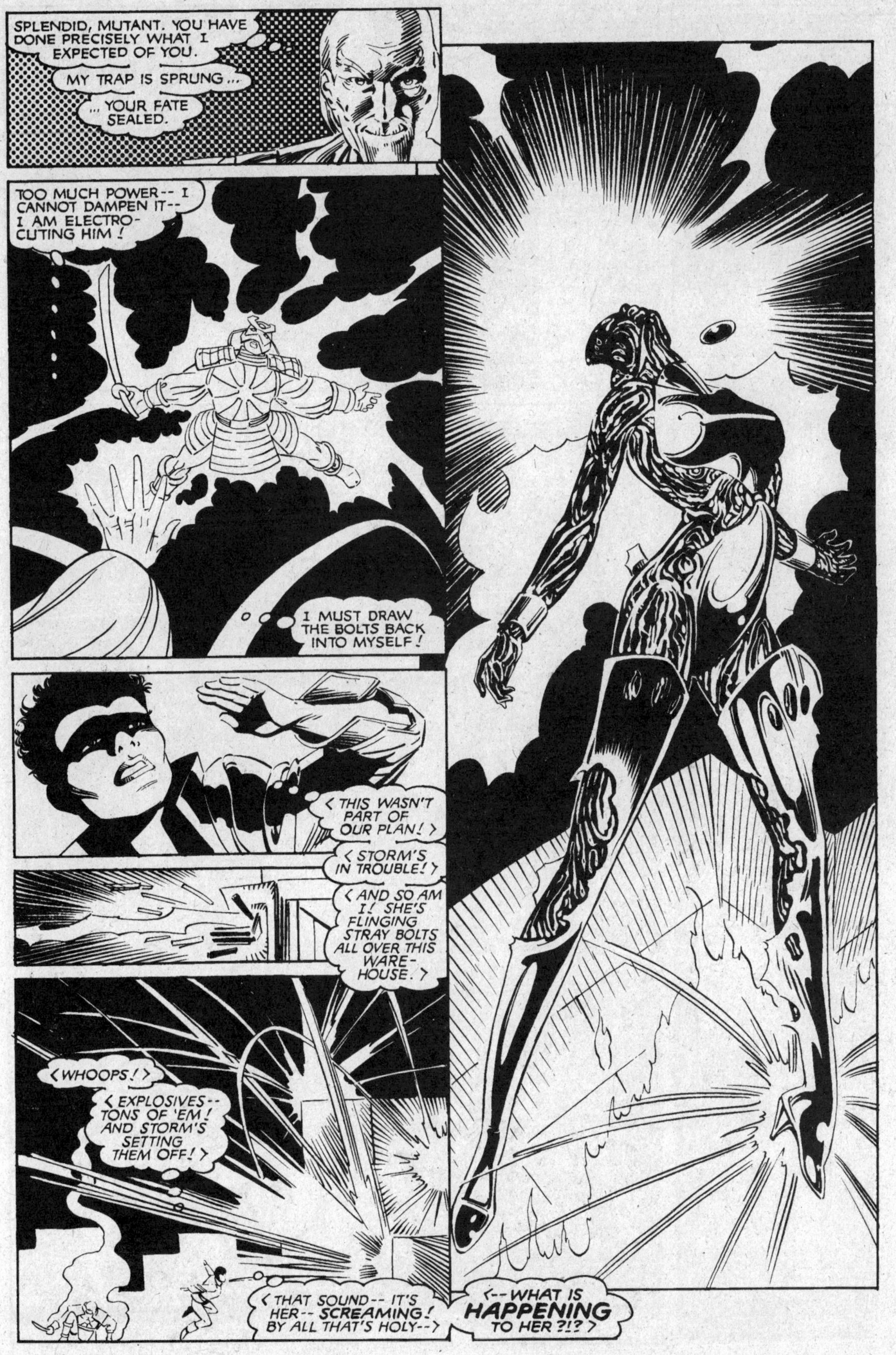
SPLENDID, MUTANT. YOU HAVE DONE PRECISELY WHAT I EXPECTED OF YOU.
MY TRAP IS SPRUNG...
... YOUR FATE SEALED.
TOO MUCH POWER-- I CANNOT DAMPEN IT-- I AM ELECTROCUTING HIM!
I MUST DRAW THE BOLTS BACK INTO MYSELF!
< THIS WASN'T PART OF OUR PLAN! >
< STORM'S IN TROUBLE! >
< AND SO AM I! SHE'S FLINGING STRAY BOLTS ALL OVER THIS WAREHOUSE. >
< WHOOPS! >
< EXPLOSIVES-- TONS OF 'EM! AND STORM'S SETTING THEM OFF! >
< THAT SOUND-- IT'S HER-- SCREAMING! BY ALL THAT'S HOLY-- >
< --WHAT IS HAPPENING TO HER ?!? >

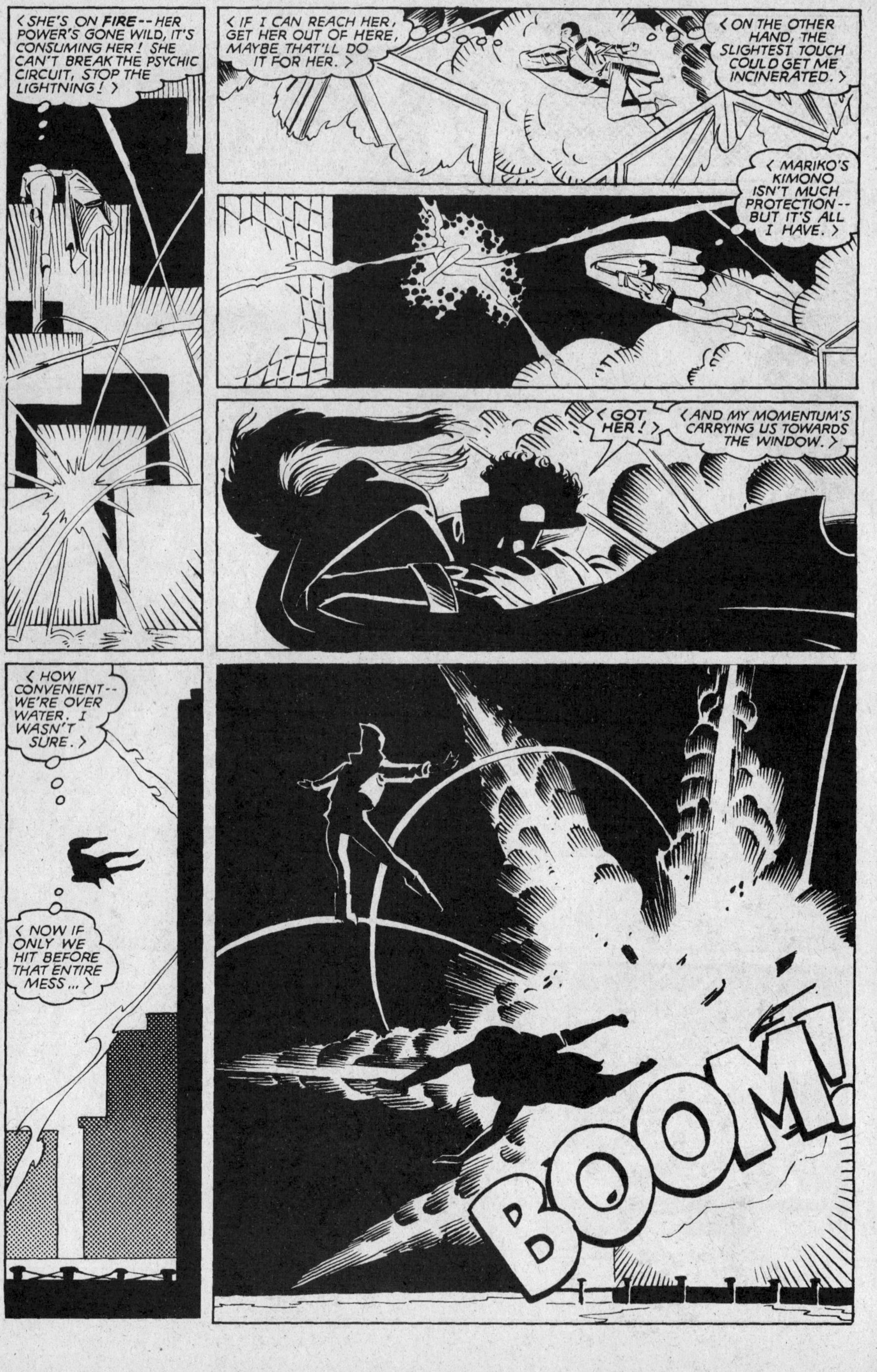
< SHE'S ON FIRE -- HER POWER'S GONE WILD, IT'S CONSUMING HER! SHE CAN'T BREAK THE PSYCHIC CIRCUIT, STOP THE LIGHTNING! >
< IF I CAN REACH HER, GET HER OUT OF HERE, MAYBE THAT'LL DO IT FOR HER. >
< ON THE OTHER HAND, THE SLIGHTEST TOUCH COULD GET ME INCINERATED. >
< MARIKO'S KIMONO ISN'T MUCH PROTECTION -- BUT IT'S ALL I HAVE. >
< GOT HER! >
< AND MY MOMENTUM'S CARRYING US TOWARDS THE WINDOW. >
< HOW CONVENIENT -- WE'RE OVER WATER. I WASN'T SURE. >
< NOW IF ONLY WE HIT BEFORE THAT ENTIRE MESS ... >
BOOOM!

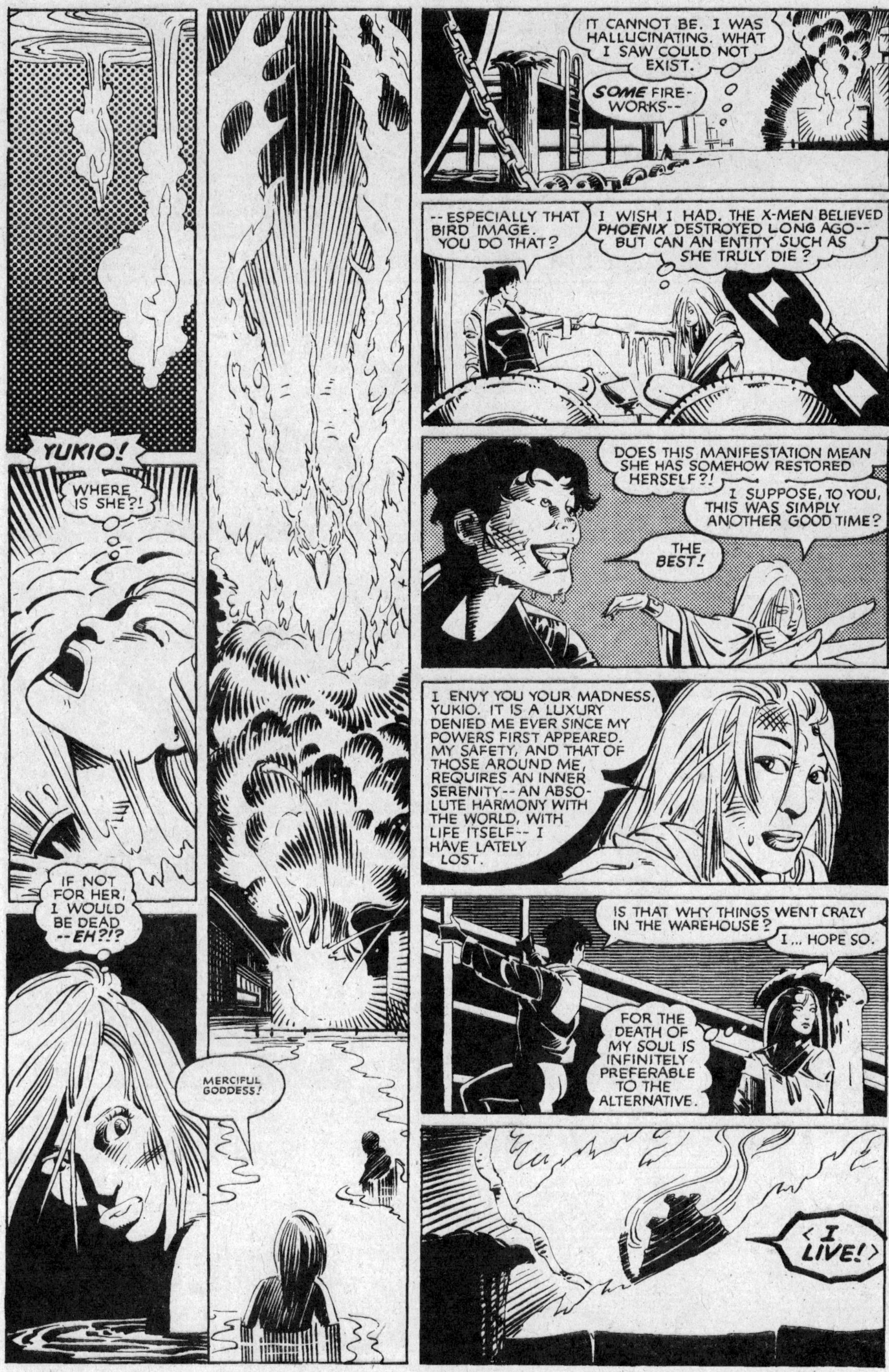
YUKIO!
WHERE IS SHE?!
IF NOT FOR HER, I WOULD BE DEAD --EH?!?
MERCIFUL GODDESS!
IT CANNOT BE. I WAS HALLUCINATING. WHAT I SAW COULD NOT EXIST.
SOME FIRE-WORKS--
--ESPECIALLY THAT BIRD IMAGE. YOU DO THAT?
I WISH I HAD. THE X-MEN BELIEVED PHOENIX DESTROYED LONG AGO-- BUT CAN AN ENTITY SUCH AS SHE TRULY DIE?
DOES THIS MANIFESTATION MEAN SHE HAS SOMEHOW RESTORED HERSELF?!
I SUPPOSE, TO YOU, THIS WAS SIMPLY ANOTHER GOOD TIME?
THE BEST!
I ENVY YOU YOUR MADNESS, YUKIO. IT IS A LUXURY DENIED ME EVER SINCE MY POWERS FIRST APPEARED. MY SAFETY, AND THAT OF THOSE AROUND ME, REQUIRES AN INNER SERENITY-- AN ABSOLUTE HARMONY WITH THE WORLD, WITH LIFE ITSELF-- I HAVE LATELY LOST.
IS THAT WHY THINGS WENT CRAZY IN THE WAREHOUSE?
I... HOPE SO.
FOR THE DEATH OF MY SOUL IS INFINITELY PREFERABLE TO THE ALTERNATIVE.
<I LIVE!>

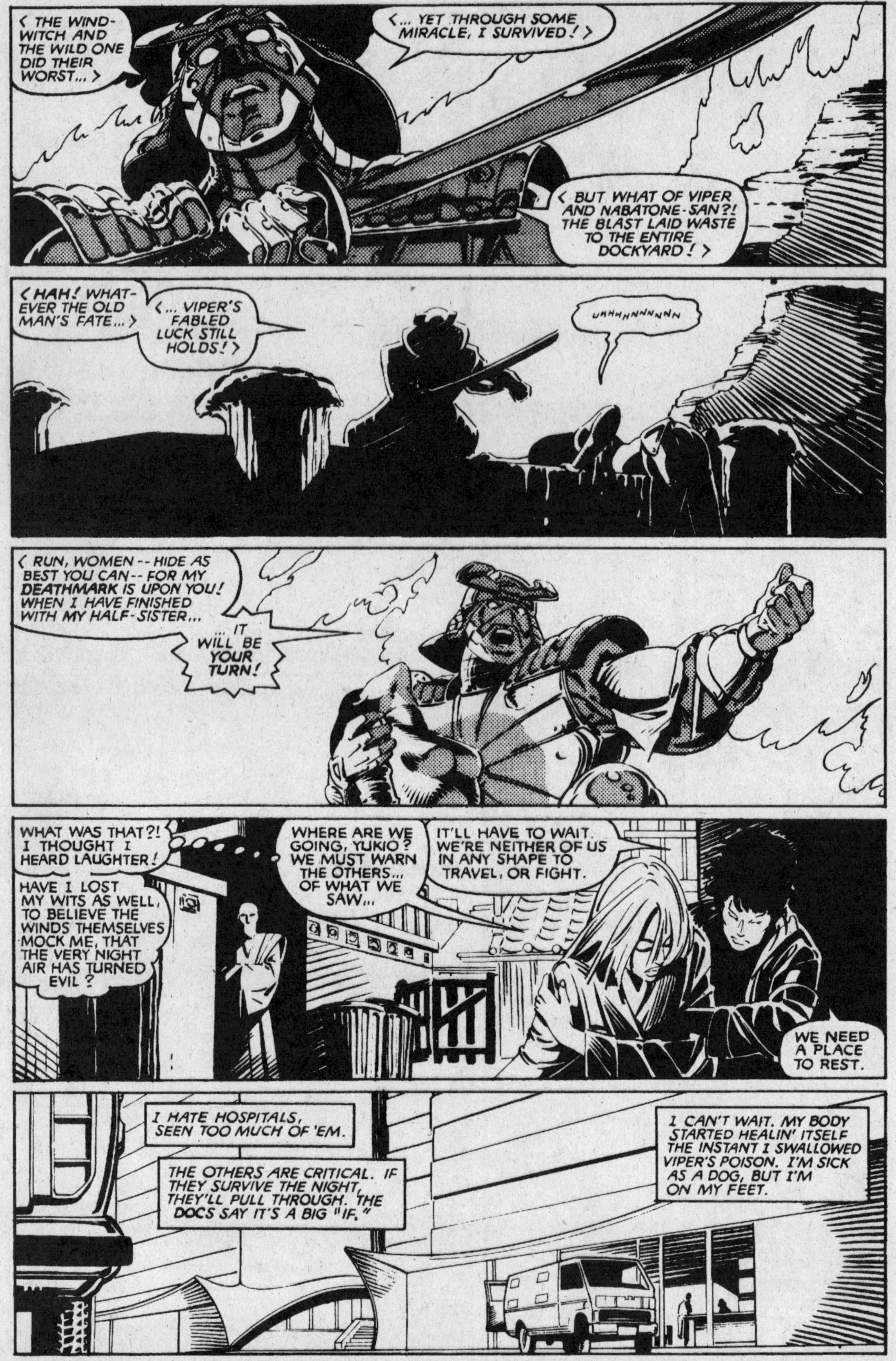
< THE WIND-WITCH AND THE WILD ONE DID THEIR WORST... >
<... YET THROUGH SOME MIRACLE, I SURVIVED! >
< BUT WHAT OF VIPER AND NABATONE-SAN?! THE BLAST LAID WASTE TO THE ENTIRE DOCKYARD! >
< HAH! WHATEVER THE OLD MAN'S FATE... >
<... VIPER'S FABLED LUCK STILL HOLDS! >
UHHHHNNNNNN
< RUN, WOMEN -- HIDE AS BEST YOU CAN -- FOR MY DEATHMARK IS UPON YOU! WHEN I HAVE FINISHED WITH MY HALF-SISTER...
... IT WILL BE YOUR TURN!
WHAT WAS THAT?! I THOUGHT I HEARD LAUGHTER!
HAVE I LOST MY WITS AS WELL, TO BELIEVE THE WINDS THEMSELVES MOCK ME, THAT THE VERY NIGHT AIR HAS TURNED EVIL?
WHERE ARE WE GOING, YUKIO? WE MUST WARN THE OTHERS... OF WHAT WE SAW...
IT'LL HAVE TO WAIT. WE'RE NEITHER OF US IN ANY SHAPE TO TRAVEL, OR FIGHT.
WE NEED A PLACE TO REST.
I HATE HOSPITALS, SEEN TOO MUCH OF 'EM.
THE OTHERS ARE CRITICAL. IF THEY SURVIVE THE NIGHT, THEY'LL PULL THROUGH. THE DOCS SAY IT'S A BIG "IF."
I CAN'T WAIT. MY BODY STARTED HEALIN' ITSELF THE INSTANT I SWALLOWED VIPER'S POISON. I'M SICK AS A DOG, BUT I'M ON MY FEET.

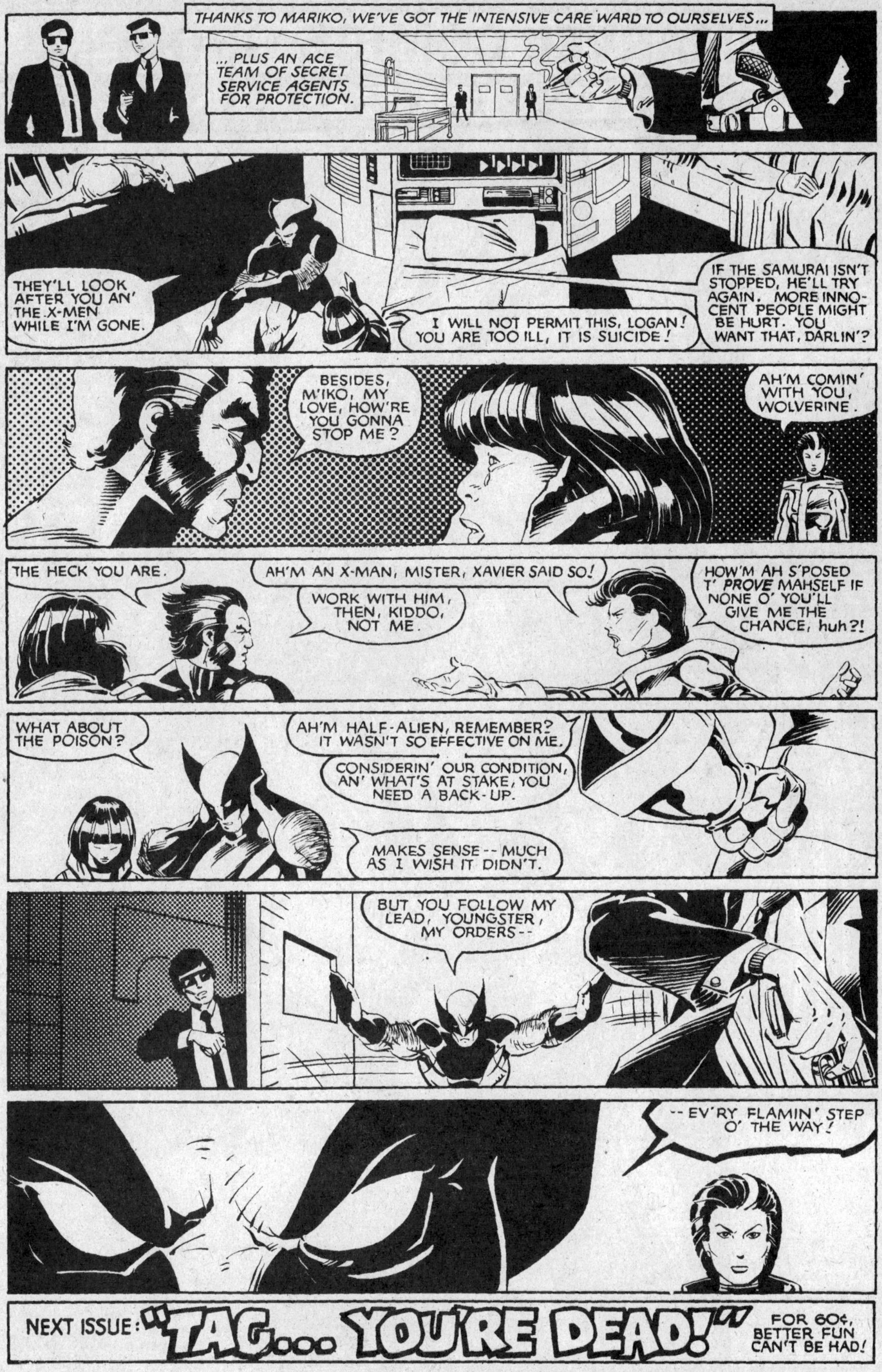
THANKS TO MARIKO, WE'VE GOT THE INTENSIVE CARE WARD TO OURSELVES...
..., PLUS AN ACE TEAM OF SECRET SERVICE AGENTS FOR PROTECTION.
THEY'LL LOOK AFTER YOU AN' THE X-MEN WHILE I'M GONE.
I WILL NOT PERMIT THIS, LOGAN! YOU ARE TOO ILL, IT IS SUICIDE!
IF THE SAMURAI ISN'T STOPPED, HE'LL TRY AGAIN. MORE INNOCENT PEOPLE MIGHT BE HURT. YOU WANT THAT, DARLIN'?
BESIDES, M'IKO, MY LOVE, HOW'RE YOU GONNA STOP ME?
AH'M COMIN' WITH YOU, WOLVERINE.
THE HECK YOU ARE.
AH'M AN X-MAN, MISTER, XAVIER SAID SO!
WORK WITH HIM, THEN, KIDDO, NOT ME.
HOW'M AH S'POSED T' *PROVE* MAHSELF IF NONE O' YOU'LL GIVE ME THE CHANCE, huh?!
WHAT ABOUT THE POISON?
AH'M HALF-ALIEN, REMEMBER? IT WASN'T SO EFFECTIVE ON ME.
CONSIDERIN' OUR CONDITION, AN' WHAT'S AT STAKE, YOU NEED A BACK-UP.
MAKES SENSE -- MUCH AS I WISH IT DIDN'T.
BUT YOU FOLLOW MY LEAD, YOUNGSTER, MY ORDERS--
-- EV'RY FLAMIN' STEP O' THE WAY!
NEXT ISSUE: "TAG... YOU'RE DEAD!"
FOR 60¢, BETTER FUN CAN'T BE HAD!

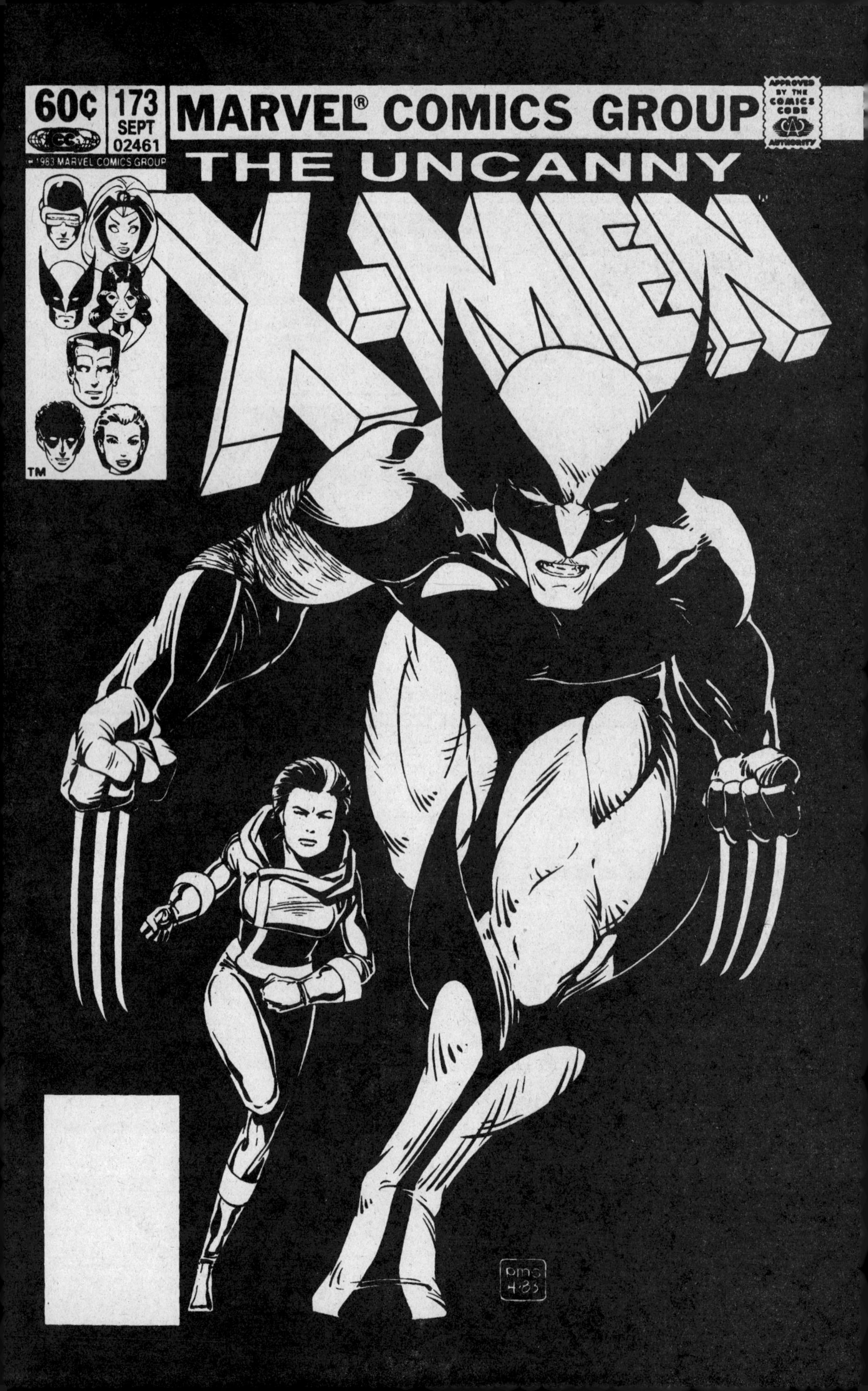
60¢
173
SEPT
02461
© 1983 MARVEL COMICS GROUP
MARVEL® COMICS GROUP
APPROVED BY THE COMICS CODE AUTHORITY
THE UNCANNY
X-MEN
TM
pms 4·83

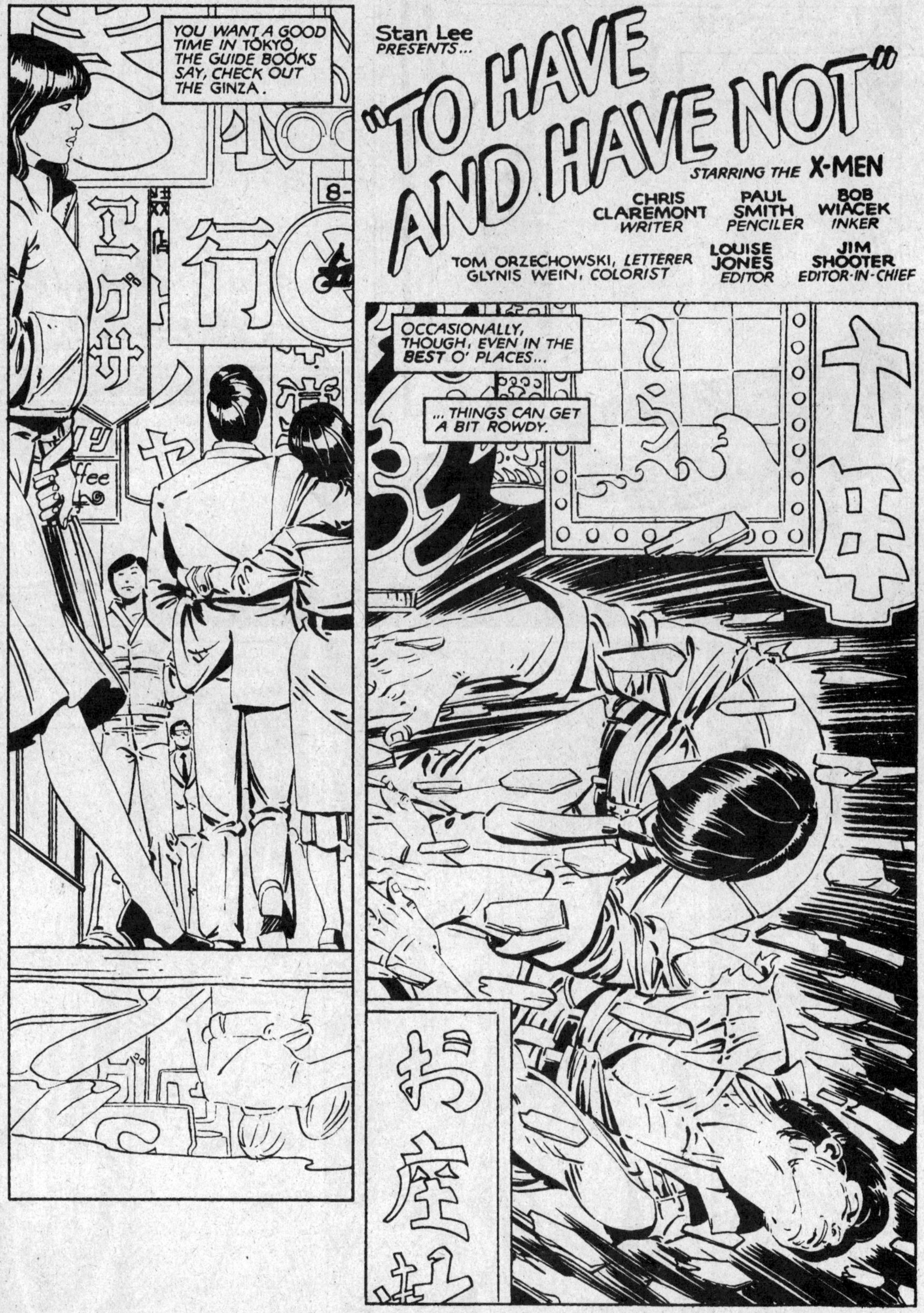
YOU WANT A GOOD TIME IN TOKYO, THE GUIDE BOOKS SAY, CHECK OUT THE GINZA.
Stan Lee PRESENTS...
"TO HAVE AND HAVE NOT"
STARRING THE X-MEN
CHRIS CLAREMONT WRITER
PAUL SMITH PENCILER
BOB WIACEK INKER
TOM ORZECHOWSKI, LETTERER
GLYNIS WEIN, COLORIST
LOUISE JONES EDITOR
JIM SHOOTER EDITOR-IN-CHIEF
OCCASIONALLY, THOUGH, EVEN IN THE BEST O' PLACES...
...THINGS CAN GET A BIT ROWDY.

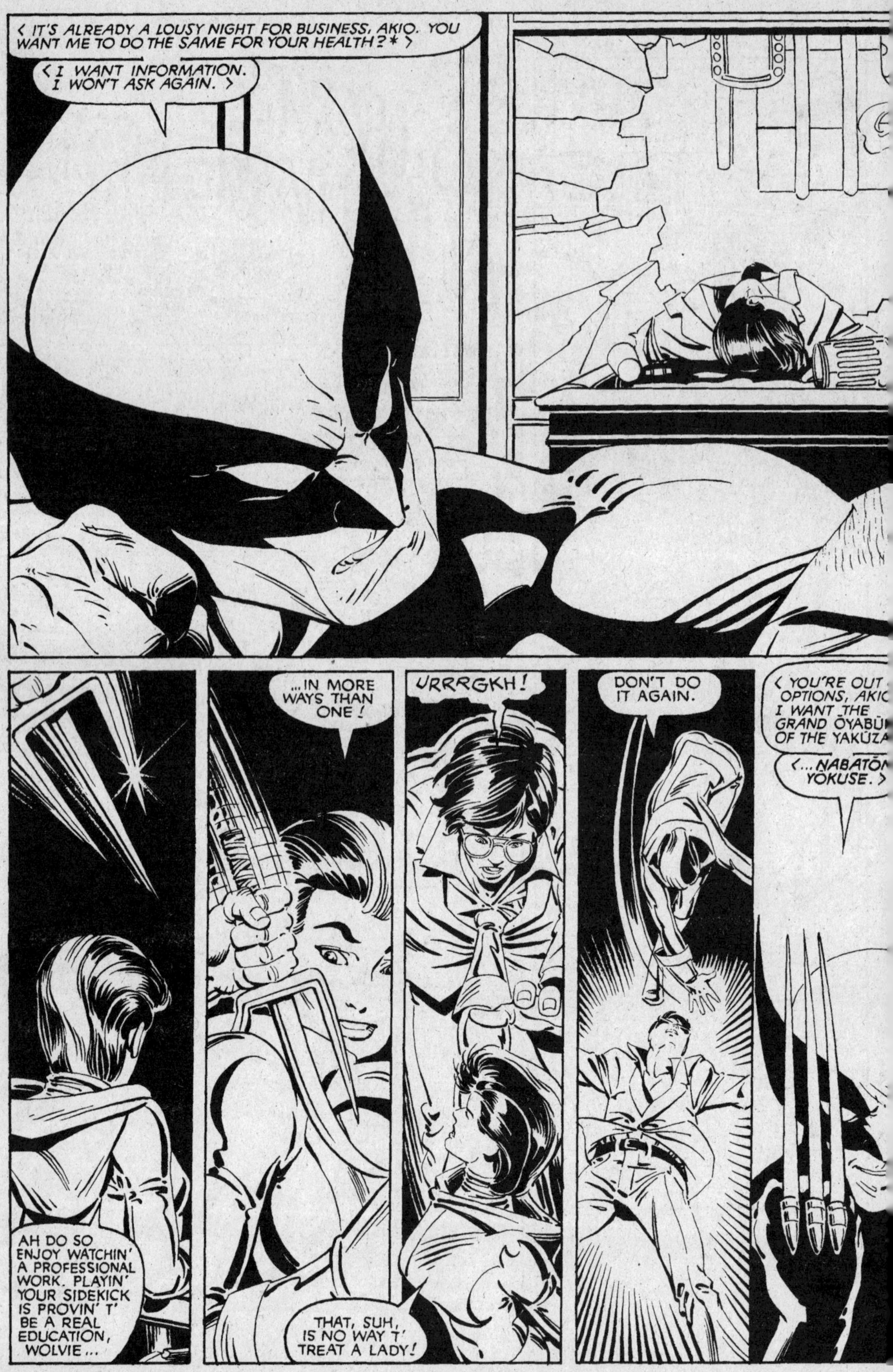
< IT'S ALREADY A LOUSY NIGHT FOR BUSINESS, AKIO. YOU WANT ME TO DO THE SAME FOR YOUR HEALTH?* >
< I WANT INFORMATION. I WON'T ASK AGAIN. >
AH DO SO ENJOY WATCHIN' A PROFESSIONAL WORK. PLAYIN' YOUR SIDEKICK IS PROVIN' T' BE A REAL EDUCATION, WOLVIE...
...IN MORE WAYS THAN ONE!
URRRGKH!
THAT, SUH, IS NO WAY T' TREAT A LADY!
DON'T DO IT AGAIN.
< YOU'RE OUT
OPTIONS, AKI
I WANT THE
GRAND ŌYABŪ
OF THE YAKŪZA
<...NABATŌ
YŌKUSE. >

Y'ALL BETTER COOPERATE, SUGAH. WE BEEN GETTIN' THE RUNAROUND ALL EVENIN' AN' IT'S MAKIN' *WOLVERINE* A WEE BIT *TESTY*.

< I DARE NOT BETRAY MY OATH OF SILENCE. IT WOULD MEAN MY LIFE! >

< IN THAT CASE, BUB, YOU GOT A PROBLEM. >

*TRANSLATED FROM THE JAPANESE -- LOUISE.

YOU'LL NEVER REACH HIM, GAIJIN. NABATÔNE-SAN IS DEFENDED BY A VERITABLE ARMY, THE FINEST MARTIAL ARTISTS IN NIPPON! >

THAT'S *MY* PROBLEM. >

YOURS IS MORE IMMEDIATE. >

PUNK'S A SURVIVOR. HE TALKS, FIGURING WHATEVER HAPPENS, HE'LL COME OUT AHEAD.

EITHER I'LL NAIL THE OLD MAN...

...OR VICE VERSA.

WHAT'S OUR NEXT MOVE, WOLVIE?

NABATÔNE. HE'LL LEAD US TO *VIPER* AN' THE *SILVER SAMURAI*.

AND THEN?

THINGS GET NASTY.

I INVITED THE X-MEN TO JAPAN FOR MY WEDDING. INSTEAD, THERE'S A GOOD CHANCE THEY'LL BE ATTENDIN' THEIR OWN *FUNERALS*.

MY FIANCÉE -- *MARIKO YASHIDA'S*-- DAD WAS A CRIME-LORD. HER HALF-BROTHER, THE SILVER SAMURAI, WANTS CONTROL O' THAT EMPIRE. HE MEANS TO GET IT BY KILLING HER. TO KEEP ME AN' MY FELLOW MUTANTS OUTTA THE PICTURE, VIPER POISONED ALL OF US 'CEPT FOR *STORM*.

ROGUE AN' I RECOVERED. WE'VE BEEN ON THE SAMURAI'S TRAIL EVER SINCE. THE OTHERS ARE IN THE HOSPITAL, INTENSIVE CARE, CRITICAL CONDITION.

STORM'S DISAPPEARED.

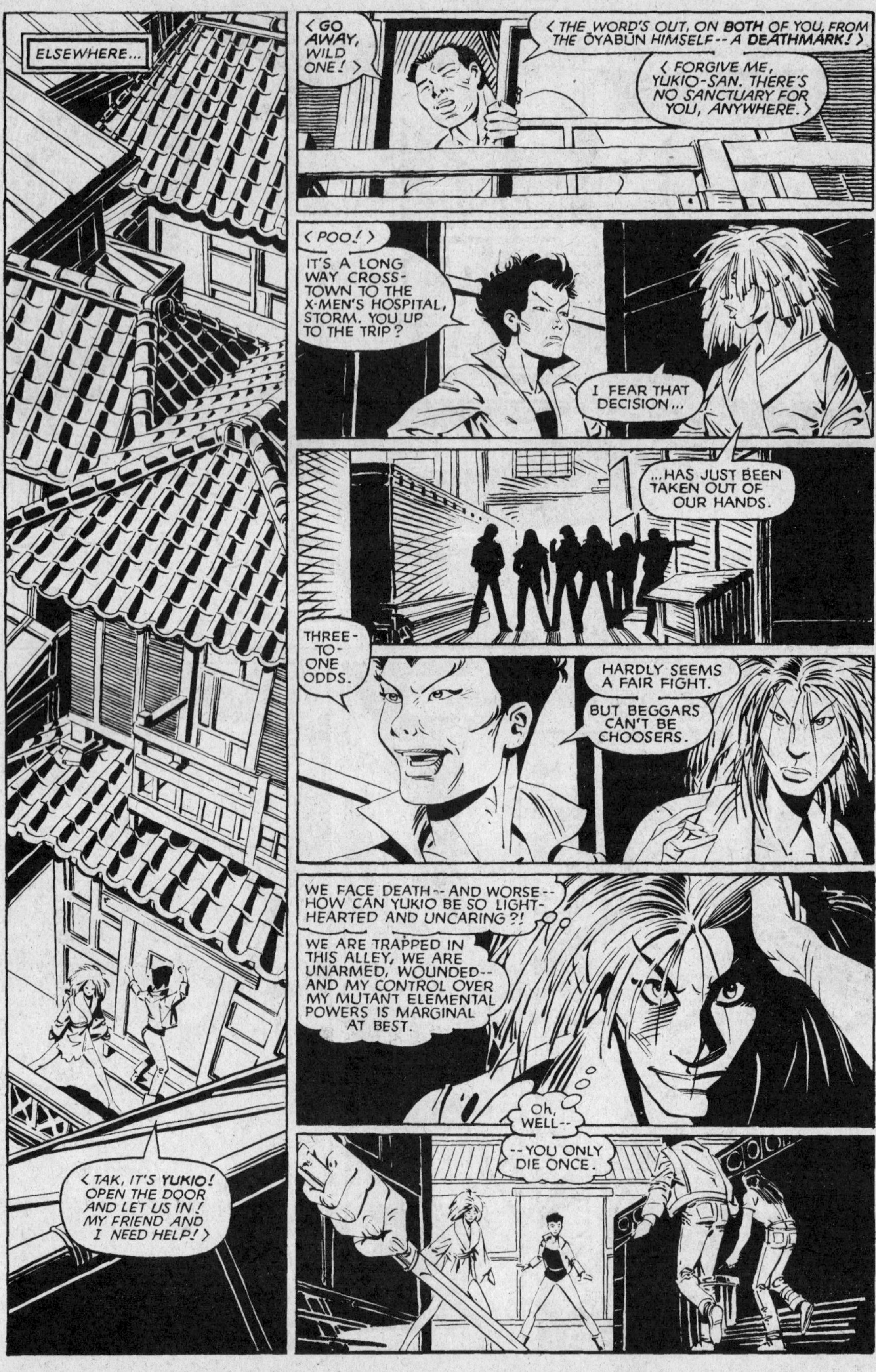
ELSEWHERE...
< TAK, IT'S YUKIO! OPEN THE DOOR AND LET US IN! MY FRIEND AND I NEED HELP! >
< GO AWAY, WILD ONE! >
< THE WORD'S OUT, ON BOTH OF YOU, FROM THE ŌYABŪN HIMSELF-- A DEATHMARK! >
< FORGIVE ME, YUKIO-SAN. THERE'S NO SANCTUARY FOR YOU, ANYWHERE. >
< POO! >
IT'S A LONG WAY CROSS-TOWN TO THE X-MEN'S HOSPITAL, STORM. YOU UP TO THE TRIP?
I FEAR THAT DECISION...
...HAS JUST BEEN TAKEN OUT OF OUR HANDS.
THREE-TO-ONE ODDS.
HARDLY SEEMS A FAIR FIGHT.
BUT BEGGARS CAN'T BE CHOOSERS.
WE FACE DEATH-- AND WORSE-- HOW CAN YUKIO BE SO LIGHT-HEARTED AND UNCARING?!
WE ARE TRAPPED IN THIS ALLEY, WE ARE UNARMED, WOUNDED-- AND MY CONTROL OVER MY MUTANT ELEMENTAL POWERS IS MARGINAL AT BEST.
Oh, WELL--
--YOU ONLY DIE ONCE.

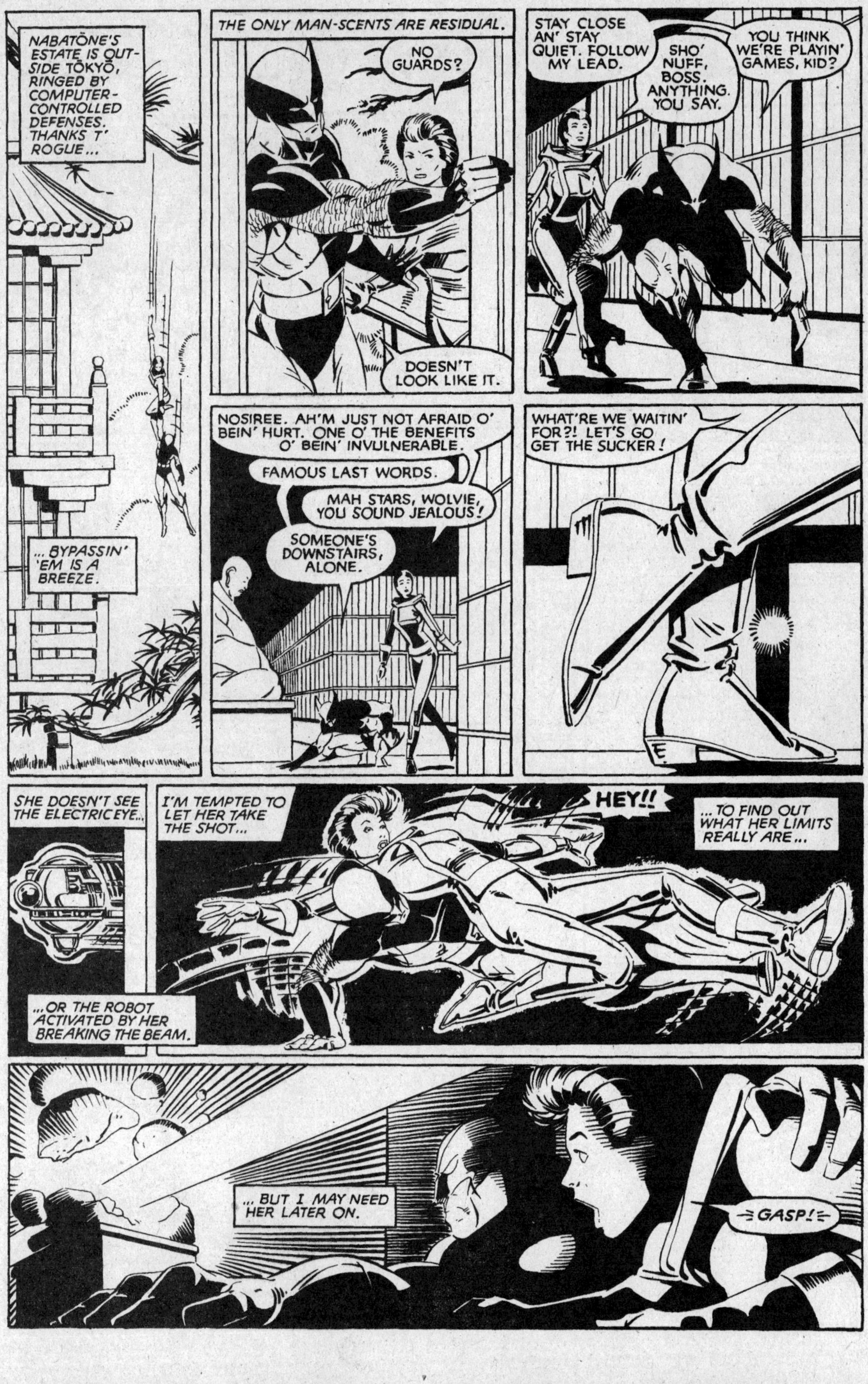
NABATŌNE'S ESTATE IS OUTSIDE TŌKYŌ, RINGED BY COMPUTER-CONTROLLED DEFENSES. THANKS T' ROGUE...
...BYPASSIN' 'EM IS A BREEZE.
THE ONLY MAN-SCENTS ARE RESIDUAL.
NO GUARDS?
DOESN'T LOOK LIKE IT.
STAY CLOSE AN' STAY QUIET. FOLLOW MY LEAD.
SHO' NUFF, BOSS. ANYTHING. YOU SAY.
YOU THINK WE'RE PLAYIN' GAMES, KID?
NOSIREE. AH'M JUST NOT AFRAID O' BEIN' HURT. ONE O' THE BENEFITS O' BEIN' INVULNERABLE.
FAMOUS LAST WORDS.
MAH STARS, WOLVIE, YOU SOUND JEALOUS!
SOMEONE'S DOWNSTAIRS, ALONE.
WHAT'RE WE WAITIN' FOR?! LET'S GO GET THE SUCKER!
SHE DOESN'T SEE THE ELECTRIC EYE...
...OR THE ROBOT ACTIVATED BY HER BREAKING THE BEAM.
I'M TEMPTED TO LET HER TAKE THE SHOT...
HEY!!
...TO FIND OUT WHAT HER LIMITS REALLY ARE...
...BUT I MAY NEED HER LATER ON.
GASP!

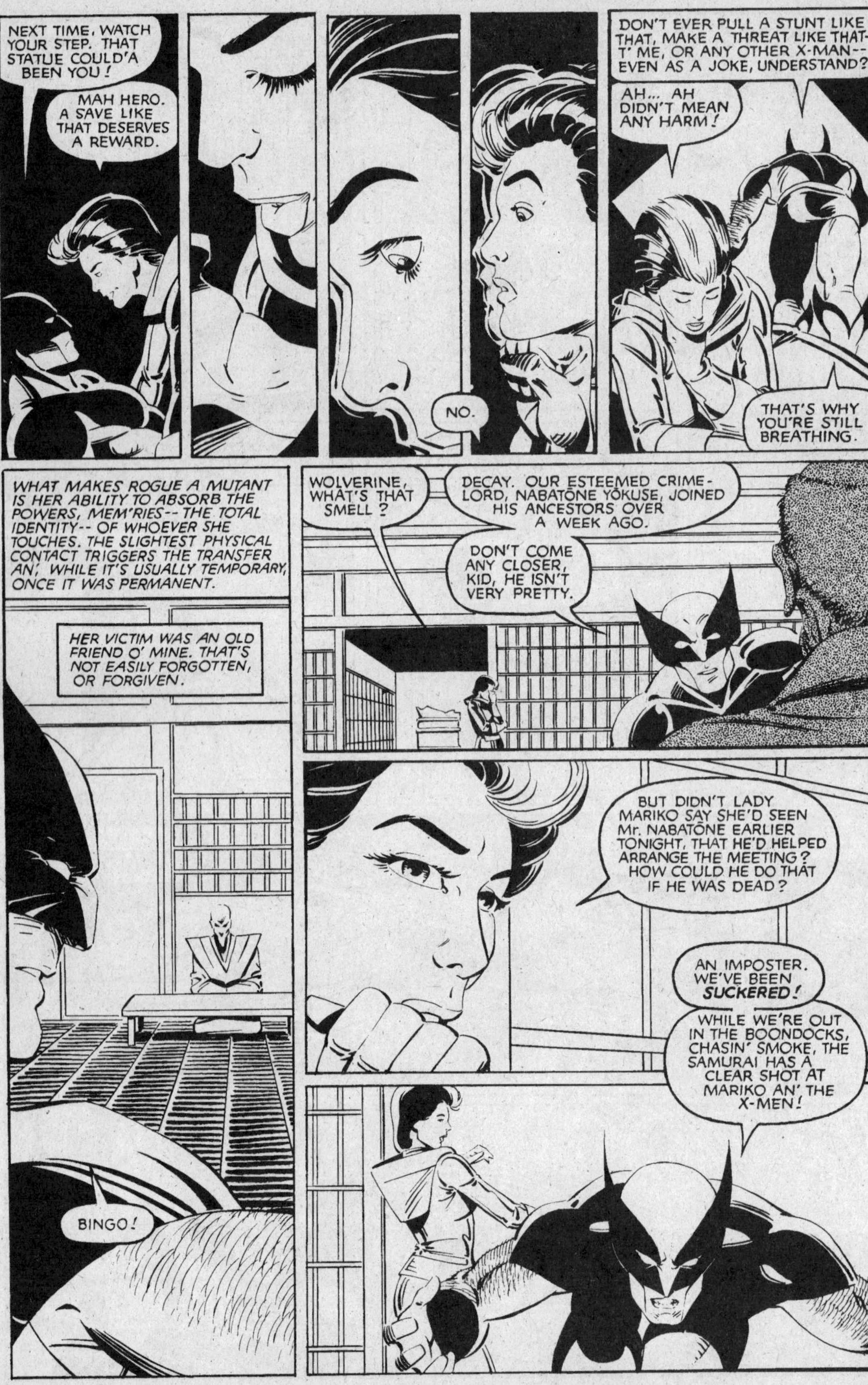
NEXT TIME, WATCH YOUR STEP. THAT STATUE COULD'A BEEN YOU!
MAH HERO. A SAVE LIKE THAT DESERVES A REWARD.
NO.
DON'T EVER PULL A STUNT LIKE THAT, MAKE A THREAT LIKE THAT-- T' ME, OR ANY OTHER X-MAN-- EVEN AS A JOKE, UNDERSTAND?!
AH... AH DIDN'T MEAN ANY HARM!
THAT'S WHY YOU'RE STILL BREATHING.
WHAT MAKES ROGUE A MUTANT IS HER ABILITY TO ABSORB THE POWERS, MEM'RIES-- THE TOTAL IDENTITY-- OF WHOEVER SHE TOUCHES. THE SLIGHTEST PHYSICAL CONTACT TRIGGERS THE TRANSFER AN,' WHILE IT'S USUALLY TEMPORARY, ONCE IT WAS PERMANENT.
HER VICTIM WAS AN OLD FRIEND O' MINE. THAT'S NOT EASILY FORGOTTEN, OR FORGIVEN.
BINGO!
WOLVERINE, WHAT'S THAT SMELL?
DECAY. OUR ESTEEMED CRIME-LORD, NABATŌNE YŌKUSE, JOINED HIS ANCESTORS OVER A WEEK AGO.
DON'T COME ANY CLOSER, KID, HE ISN'T VERY PRETTY.
BUT DIDN'T LADY MARIKO SAY SHE'D SEEN Mr. NABATŌNE EARLIER TONIGHT, THAT HE'D HELPED ARRANGE THE MEETING? HOW COULD HE DO THAT IF HE WAS DEAD?
AN IMPOSTER. WE'VE BEEN SUCKERED!
WHILE WE'RE OUT IN THE BOONDOCKS, CHASIN' SMOKE, THE SAMURAI HAS A CLEAR SHOT AT MARIKO AN' THE X-MEN!

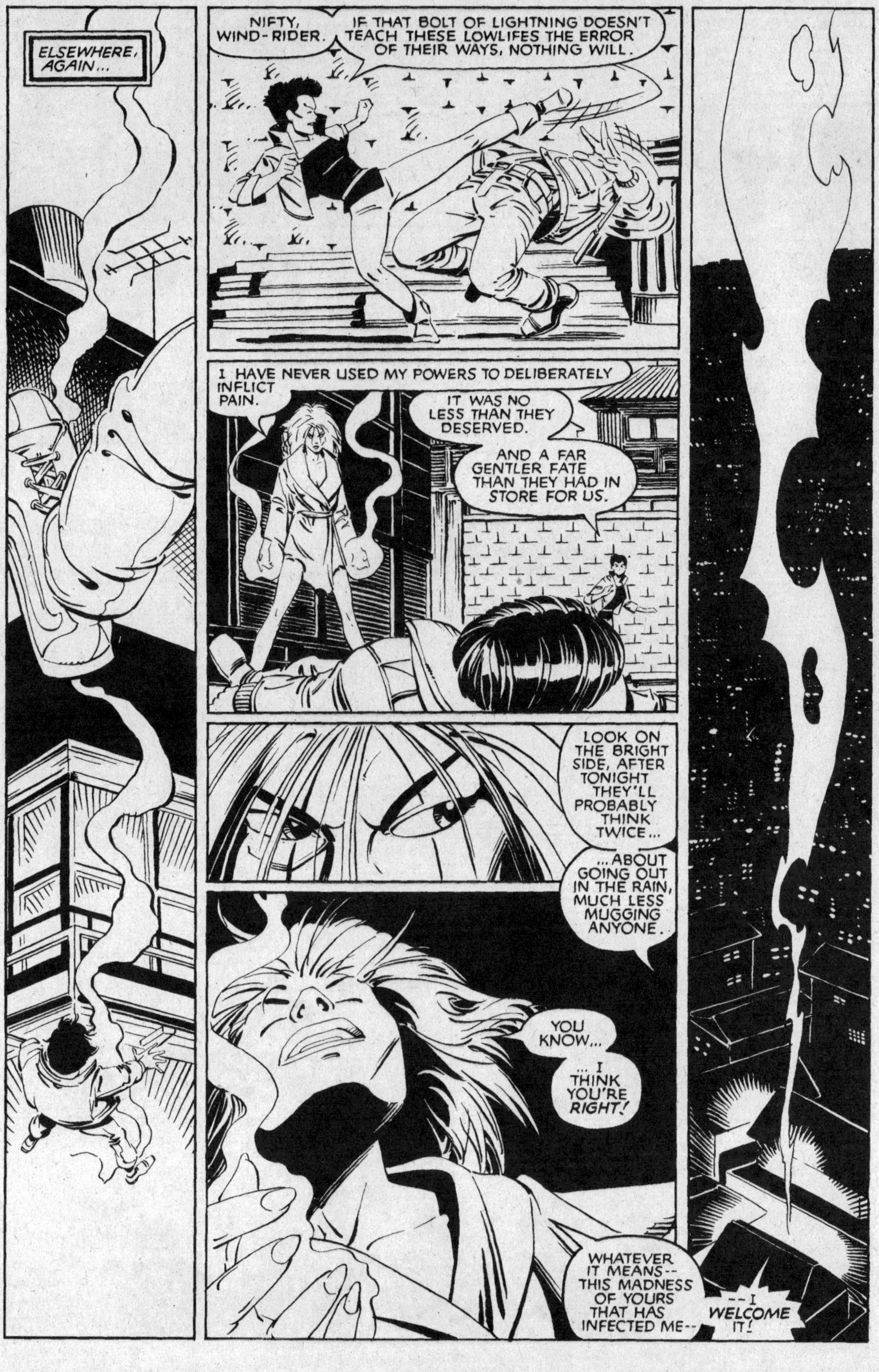

ELSEWHERE, AGAIN...
NIFTY, WIND-RIDER.
IF THAT BOLT OF LIGHTNING DOESN'T TEACH THESE LOWLIFES THE ERROR OF THEIR WAYS, NOTHING WILL.
I HAVE NEVER USED MY POWERS TO DELIBERATELY INFLICT PAIN.
IT WAS NO LESS THAN THEY DESERVED.
AND A FAR GENTLER FATE THAN THEY HAD IN STORE FOR US.
LOOK ON THE BRIGHT SIDE, AFTER TONIGHT THEY'LL PROBABLY THINK TWICE...
...ABOUT GOING OUT IN THE RAIN, MUCH LESS MUGGING ANYONE.
YOU KNOW...
...I THINK YOU'RE RIGHT!
WHATEVER IT MEANS-- THIS MADNESS OF YOURS THAT HAS INFECTED ME--
--I WELCOME IT!

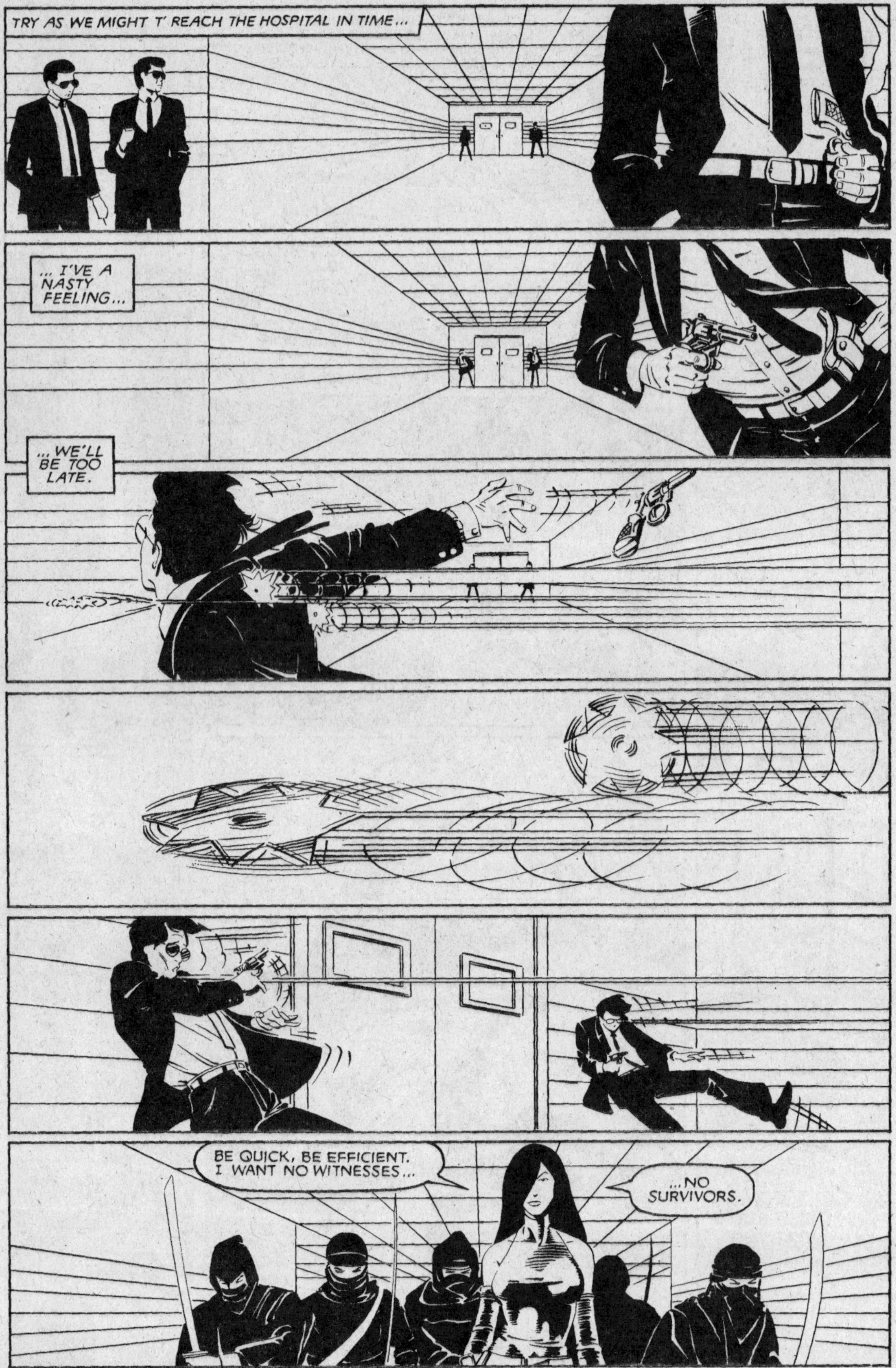
TRY AS WE MIGHT T' REACH THE HOSPITAL IN TIME...
... I'VE A NASTY FEELING...
... WE'LL BE TOO LATE.
BE QUICK, BE EFFICIENT. I WANT NO WITNESSES...
...NO SURVIVORS.

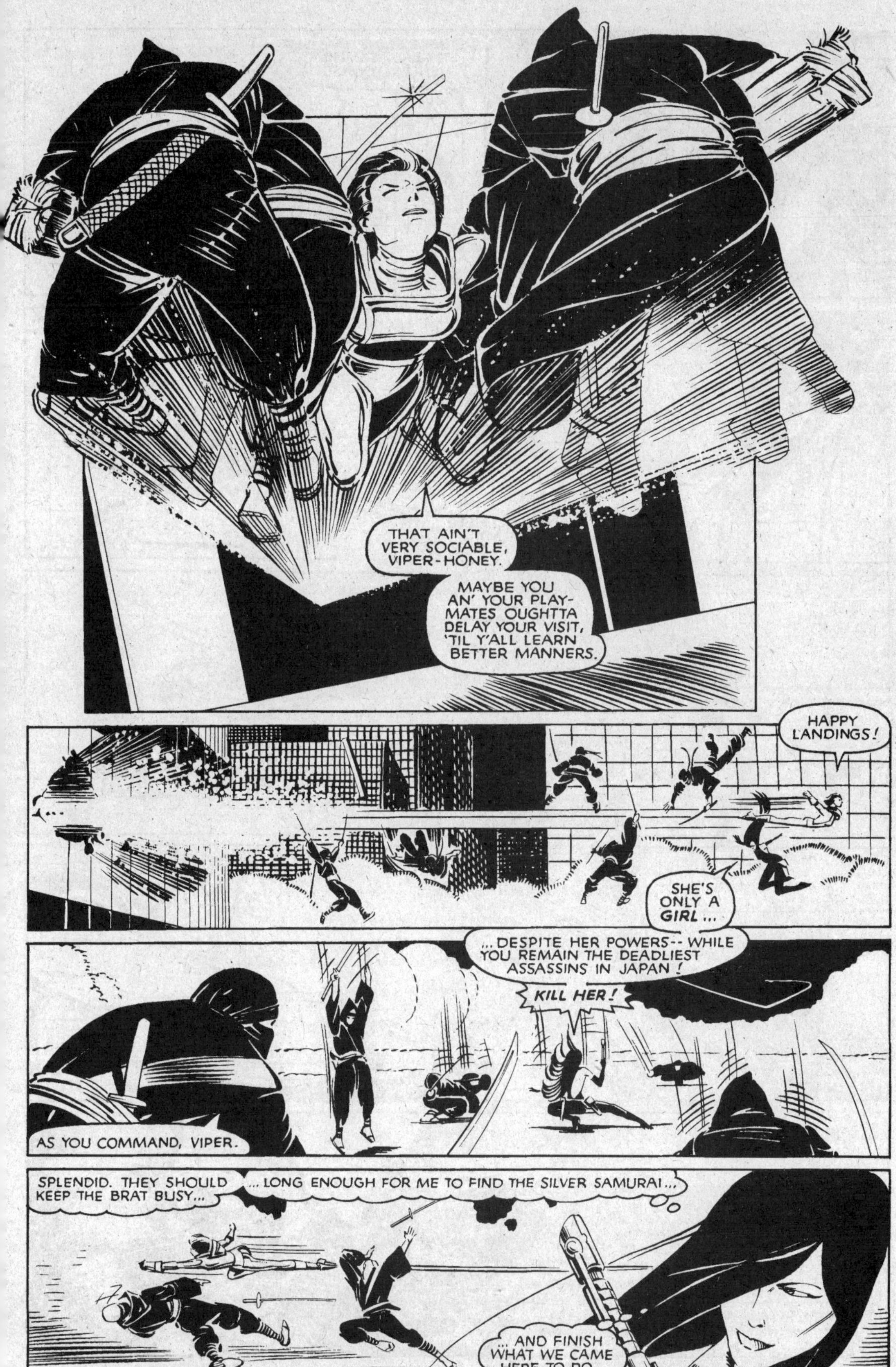
THAT AIN'T VERY SOCIABLE, VIPER-HONEY.
MAYBE YOU AN' YOUR PLAY-MATES OUGHTTA DELAY YOUR VISIT, 'TIL Y'ALL LEARN BETTER MANNERS.
HAPPY LANDINGS!
SHE'S ONLY A GIRL...
...DESPITE HER POWERS-- WHILE YOU REMAIN THE DEADLIEST ASSASSINS IN JAPAN!
KILL HER!
AS YOU COMMAND, VIPER.
SPLENDID. THEY SHOULD KEEP THE BRAT BUSY...
...LONG ENOUGH FOR ME TO FIND THE SILVER SAMURAI...
...AND FINISH WHAT WE CAME HERE TO DO.

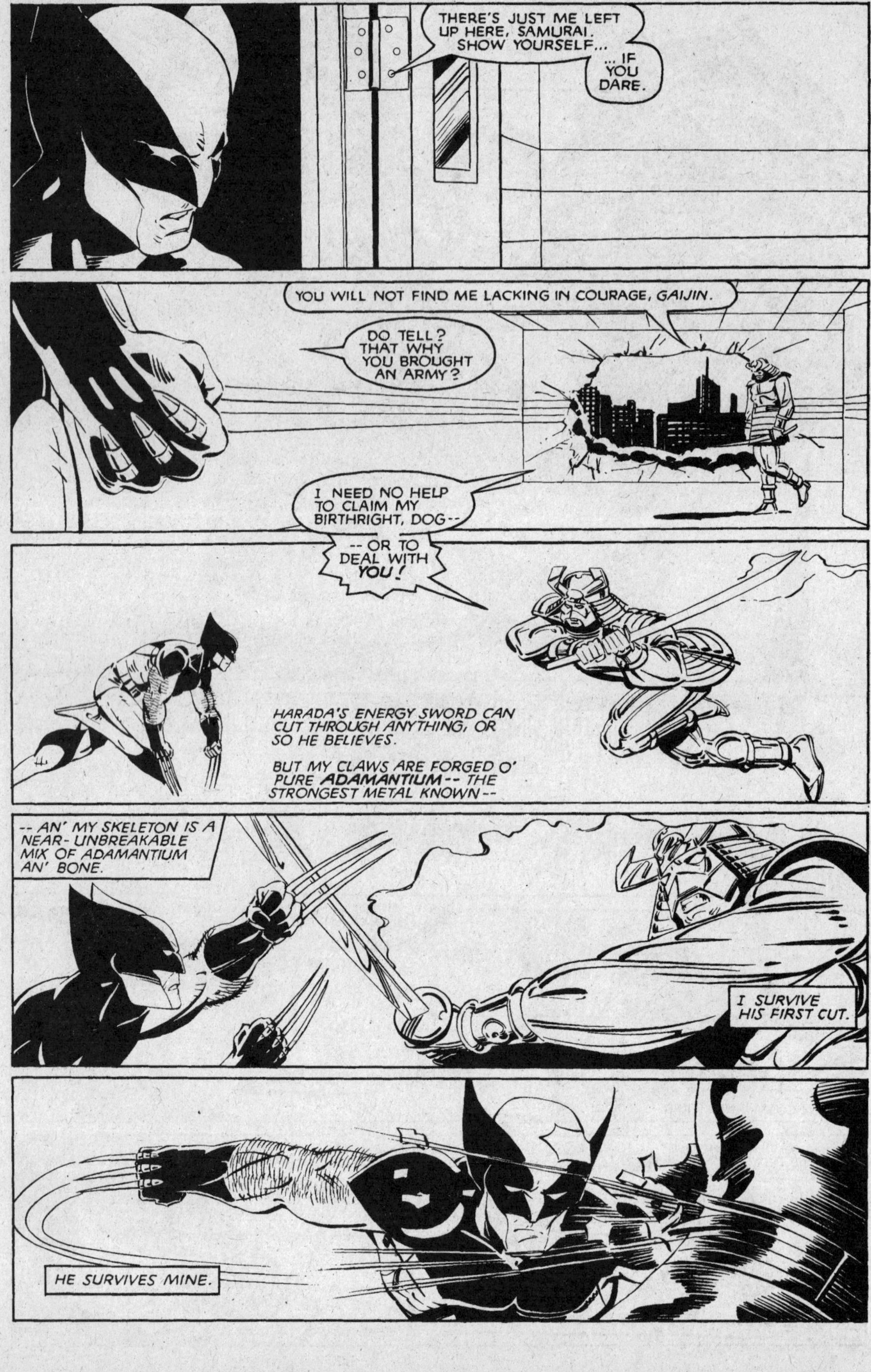
THERE'S JUST ME LEFT UP HERE, SAMURAI. SHOW YOURSELF...
... IF YOU DARE.
YOU WILL NOT FIND ME LACKING IN COURAGE, GAIJIN.
DO TELL? THAT WHY YOU BROUGHT AN ARMY?
I NEED NO HELP TO CLAIM MY BIRTHRIGHT, DOG--
-- OR TO DEAL WITH YOU!
HARADA'S ENERGY SWORD CAN CUT THROUGH ANYTHING, OR SO HE BELIEVES.
BUT MY CLAWS ARE FORGED O' PURE ADAMANTIUM -- THE STRONGEST METAL KNOWN--
-- AN' MY SKELETON IS A NEAR-UNBREAKABLE MIX OF ADAMANTIUM AN' BONE.
I SURVIVE HIS FIRST CUT.
HE SURVIVES MINE.

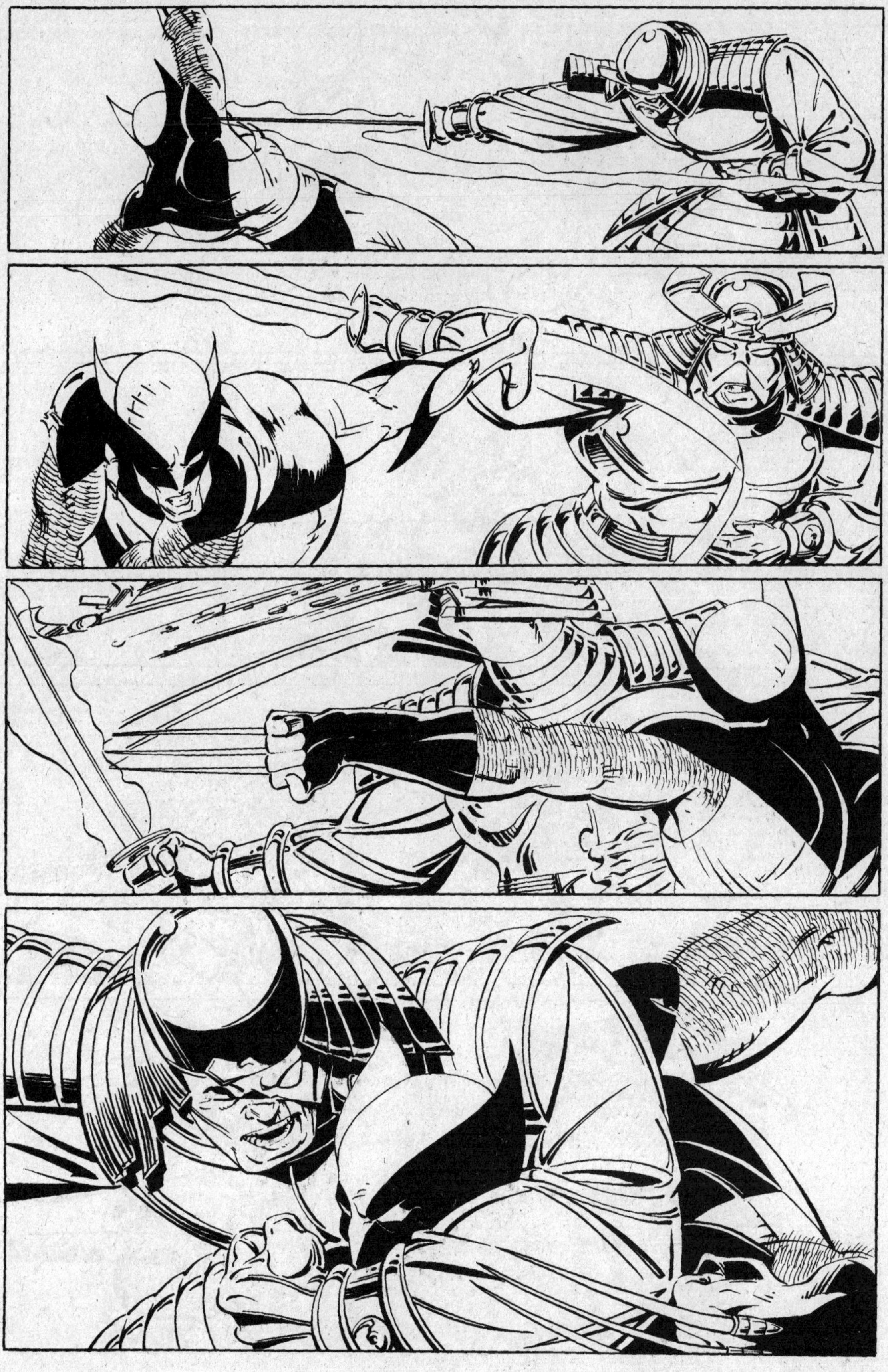

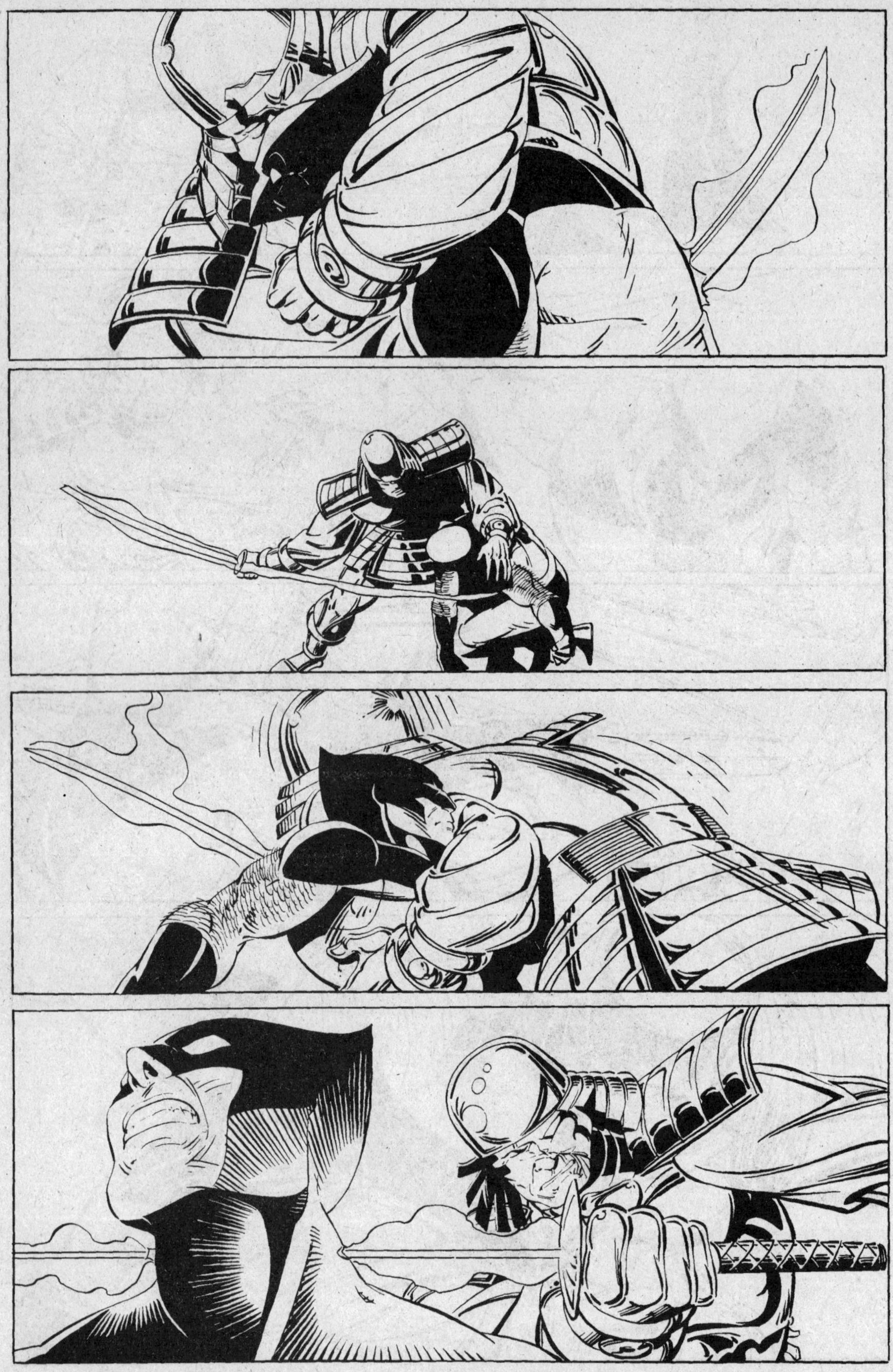

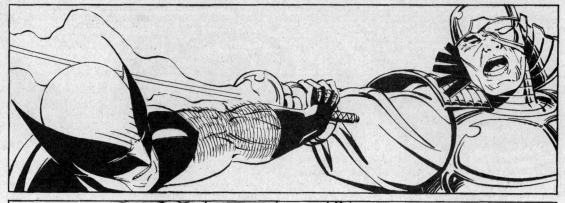

SNAP!

IIE, LOGAN-SAN-- **NO!!**

ENOUGH BLOOD HAS BEEN SPILLED, BELOVED. LET THIS BE AN END TO IT!

MY HALF-BROTHER HAS LOST. GRANT HIM HIS LIFE!

I DO THAT, M'IKO, THIS'LL **NEVER** BE OVER. HE'LL KEEP COMIN' BACK, 'TIL ONE OF YOU IS **DEAD!**

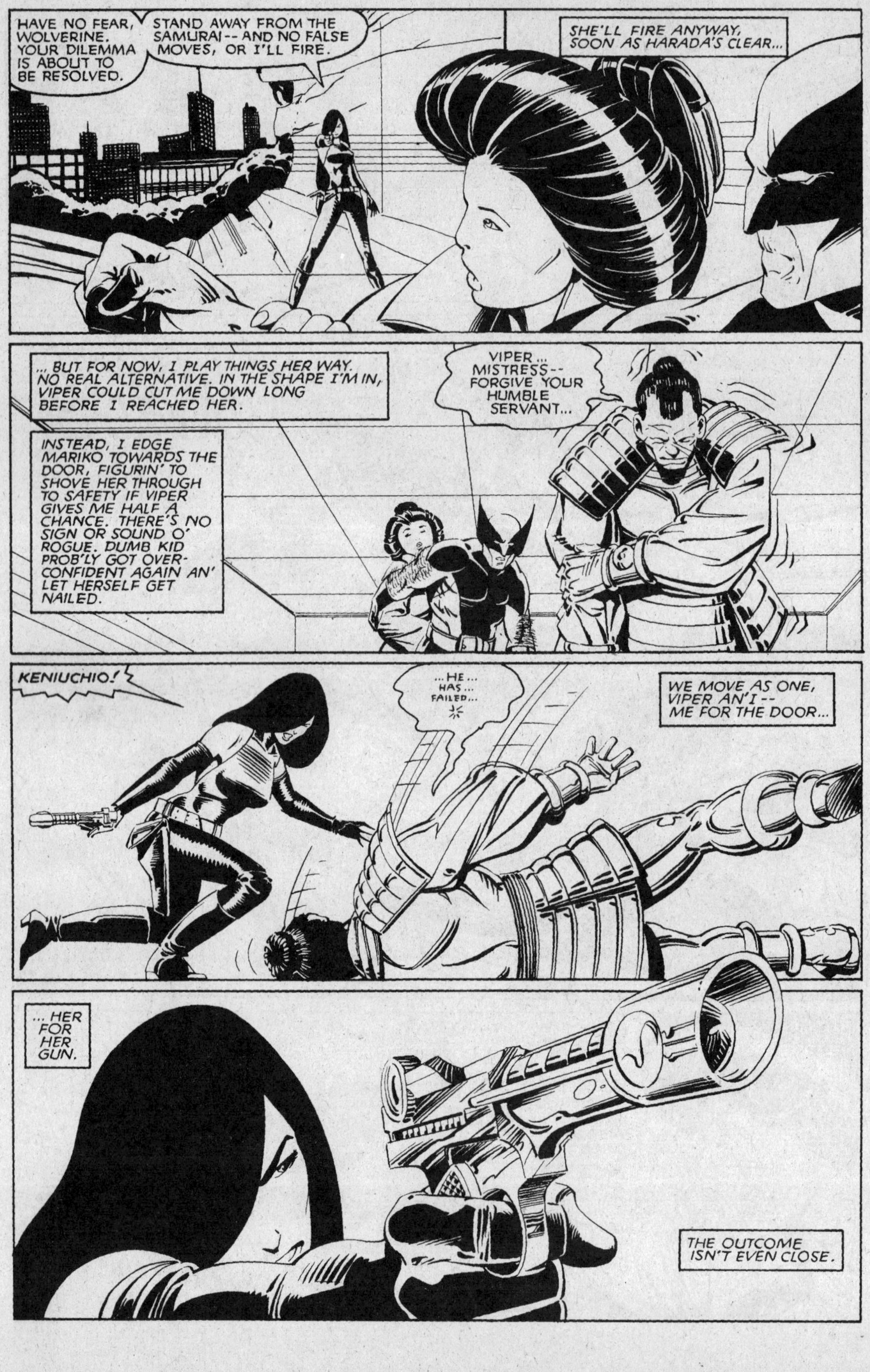

HAVE NO FEAR, WOLVERINE. YOUR DILEMMA IS ABOUT TO BE RESOLVED.
STAND AWAY FROM THE SAMURAI -- AND NO FALSE MOVES, OR I'LL FIRE.
SHE'LL FIRE ANYWAY, SOON AS HARADA'S CLEAR...
... BUT FOR NOW, I PLAY THINGS HER WAY. NO REAL ALTERNATIVE. IN THE SHAPE I'M IN, VIPER COULD CUT ME DOWN LONG BEFORE I REACHED HER.
INSTEAD, I EDGE MARIKO TOWARDS THE DOOR, FIGURIN' TO SHOVE HER THROUGH TO SAFETY IF VIPER GIVES ME HALF A CHANCE. THERE'S NO SIGN OR SOUND O' ROGUE. DUMB KID PROB'LY GOT OVER-CONFIDENT AGAIN AN' LET HERSELF GET NAILED.
VIPER... MISTRESS-- FORGIVE YOUR HUMBLE SERVANT...
KENIUCHIO!
...HE... HAS... FAILED...
WE MOVE AS ONE, VIPER AN' I -- ME FOR THE DOOR...
... HER FOR HER GUN.
THE OUTCOME ISN'T EVEN CLOSE.

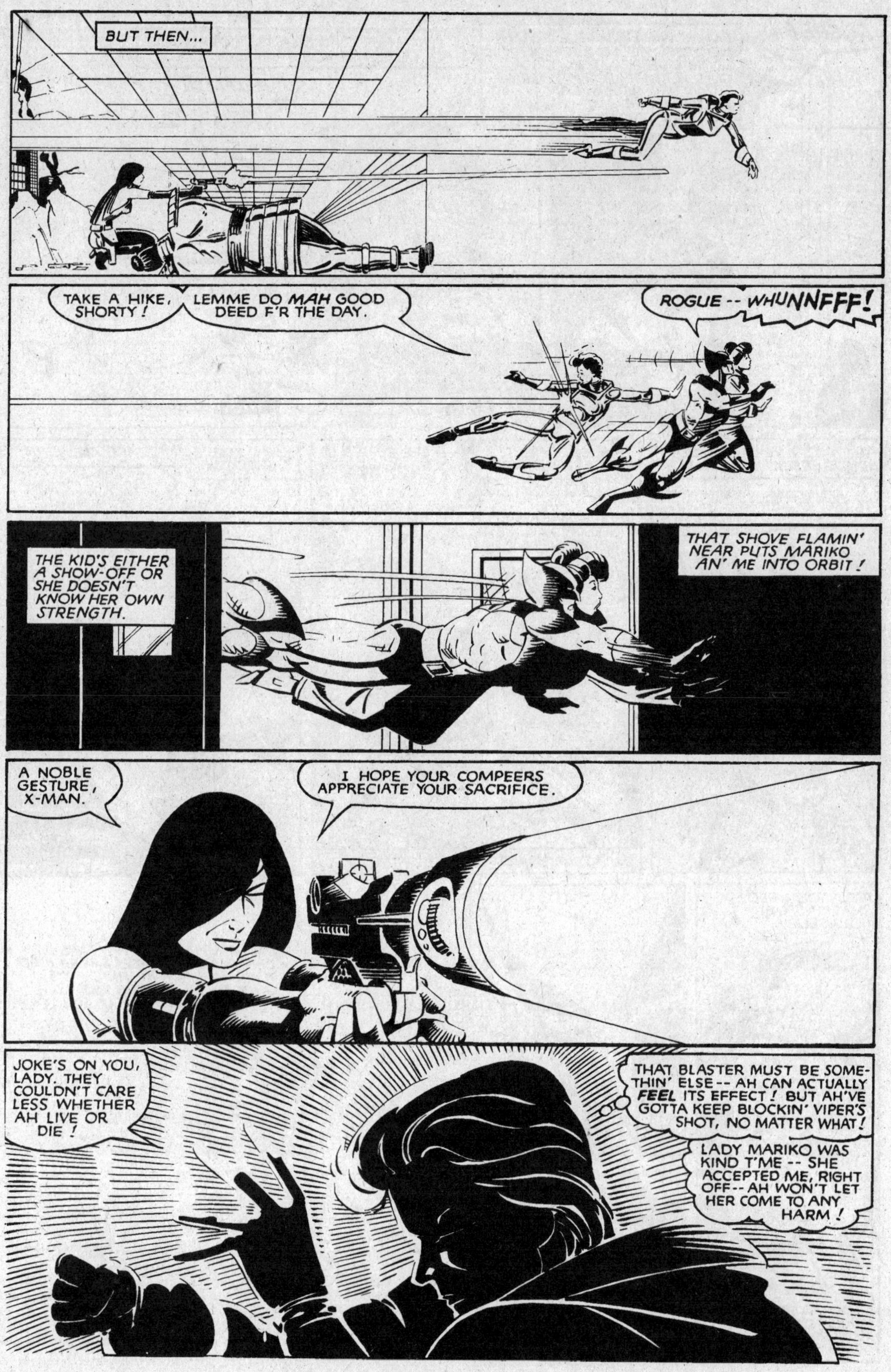
BUT THEN...
TAKE A HIKE, SHORTY!
LEMME DO MAH GOOD DEED F'R THE DAY.
ROGUE -- WHUNNFFF!
THE KID'S EITHER A SHOW-OFF OR SHE DOESN'T KNOW HER OWN STRENGTH.
THAT SHOVE FLAMIN' NEAR PUTS MARIKO AN' ME INTO ORBIT!
A NOBLE GESTURE, X-MAN.
I HOPE YOUR COMPEERS APPRECIATE YOUR SACRIFICE.
JOKE'S ON YOU, LADY. THEY COULDN'T CARE LESS WHETHER AH LIVE OR DIE!
THAT BLASTER MUST BE SOMETHIN' ELSE -- AH CAN ACTUALLY FEEL ITS EFFECT! BUT AH'VE GOTTA KEEP BLOCKIN' VIPER'S SHOT, NO MATTER WHAT!
LADY MARIKO WAS KIND T'ME -- SHE ACCEPTED ME, RIGHT OFF -- AH WON'T LET HER COME TO ANY HARM!

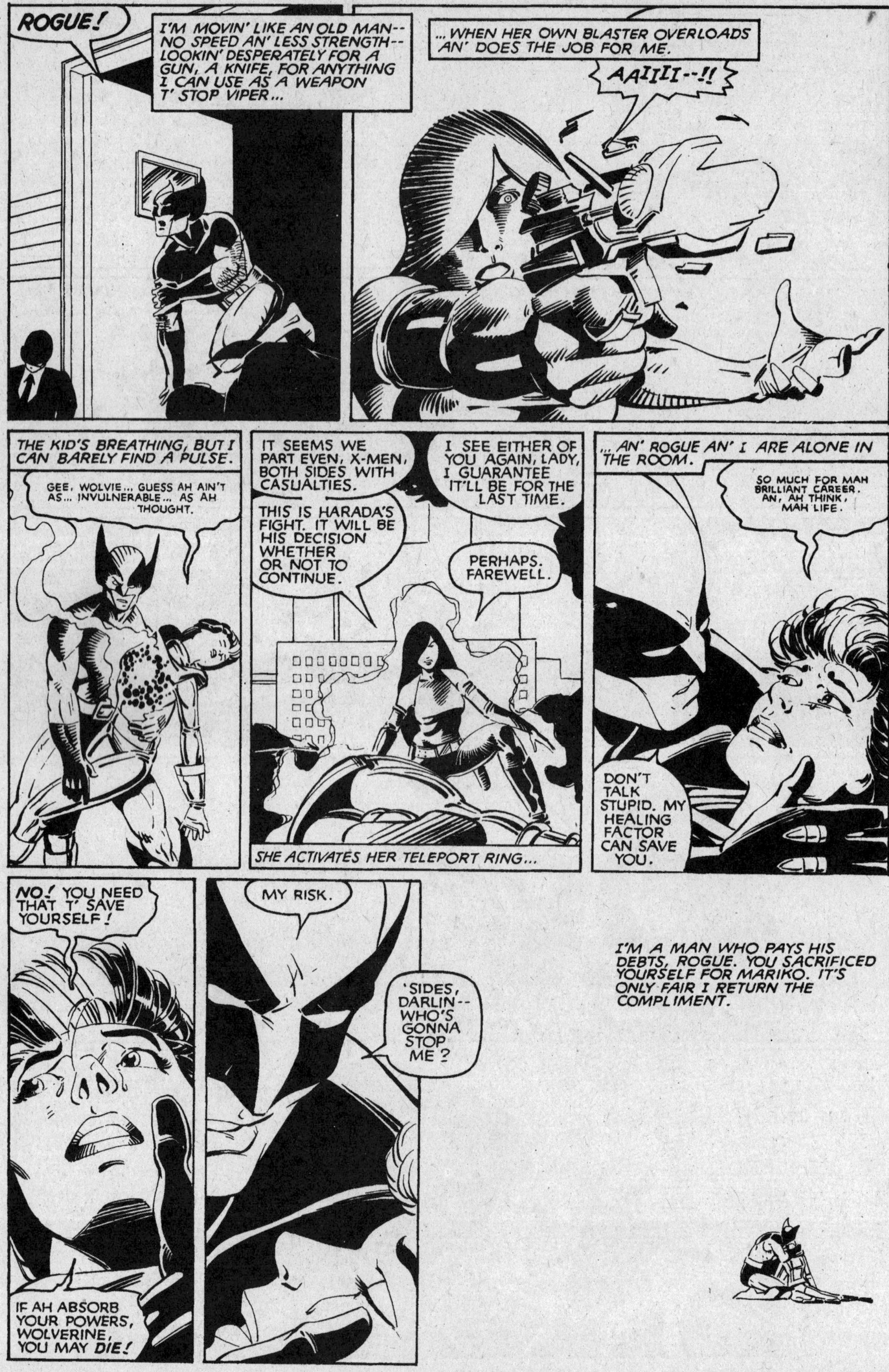
ROGUE!
I'M MOVIN' LIKE AN OLD MAN--NO SPEED AN' LESS STRENGTH--LOOKIN' DESPERATELY FOR A GUN, A KNIFE, FOR ANYTHING I CAN USE AS A WEAPON T' STOP VIPER...
...WHEN HER OWN BLASTER OVERLOADS AN' DOES THE JOB FOR ME.
AAIIII--!!
THE KID'S BREATHING, BUT I CAN BARELY FIND A PULSE.
GEE, WOLVIE... GUESS AH AIN'T AS... INVULNERABLE... AS AH THOUGHT.
IT SEEMS WE PART EVEN, X-MEN, BOTH SIDES WITH CASUALTIES.
THIS IS HARADA'S FIGHT. IT WILL BE HIS DECISION WHETHER OR NOT TO CONTINUE.
I SEE EITHER OF YOU AGAIN, LADY, I GUARANTEE IT'LL BE FOR THE LAST TIME.
PERHAPS. FAREWELL.
SHE ACTIVATES HER TELEPORT RING...
...AN' ROGUE AN' I ARE ALONE IN THE ROOM.
SO MUCH FOR MAH BRILLIANT CAREER. AN, AH THINK, MAH LIFE.
DON'T TALK STUPID. MY HEALING FACTOR CAN SAVE YOU.
NO! YOU NEED THAT T' SAVE YOURSELF!
IF AH ABSORB YOUR POWERS, WOLVERINE, YOU MAY DIE!
MY RISK.
'SIDES, DARLIN--WHO'S GONNA STOP ME?
I'M A MAN WHO PAYS HIS DEBTS, ROGUE. YOU SACRIFICED YOURSELF FOR MARIKO. IT'S ONLY FAIR I RETURN THE COMPLIMENT.

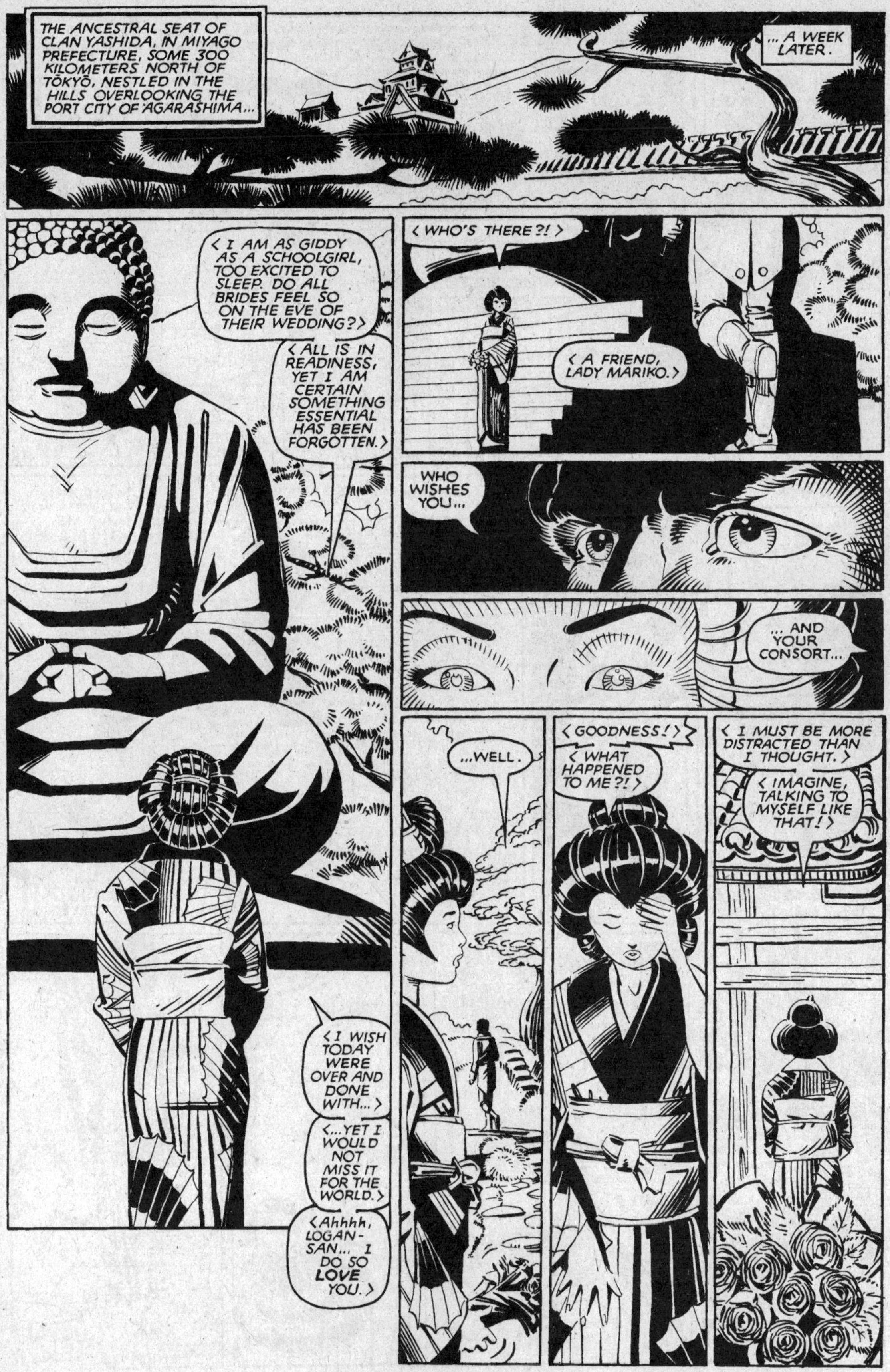
THE ANCESTRAL SEAT OF CLAN YASHIDA, IN MIYAGO PREFECTURE, SOME 300 KILOMETERS NORTH OF TŌKYŌ, NESTLED IN THE HILLS OVERLOOKING THE PORT CITY OF AGARASHIMA...
... A WEEK LATER.
< I AM AS GIDDY AS A SCHOOLGIRL, TOO EXCITED TO SLEEP. DO ALL BRIDES FEEL SO ON THE EVE OF THEIR WEDDING? >
< ALL IS IN READINESS, YET I AM CERTAIN SOMETHING ESSENTIAL HAS BEEN FORGOTTEN. >
< I WISH TODAY WERE OVER AND DONE WITH... >
<...YET I WOULD NOT MISS IT FOR THE WORLD. >
< Ahhhh, LOGAN-SAN... I DO SO LOVE YOU. >
< WHO'S THERE?! >
< A FRIEND, LADY MARIKO. >
WHO WISHES YOU...
... AND YOUR CONSORT...
...WELL.
< GOODNESS! >
< WHAT HAPPENED TO ME?! >
< I MUST BE MORE DISTRACTED THAN I THOUGHT. >
< IMAGINE, TALKING TO MYSELF LIKE THAT! >

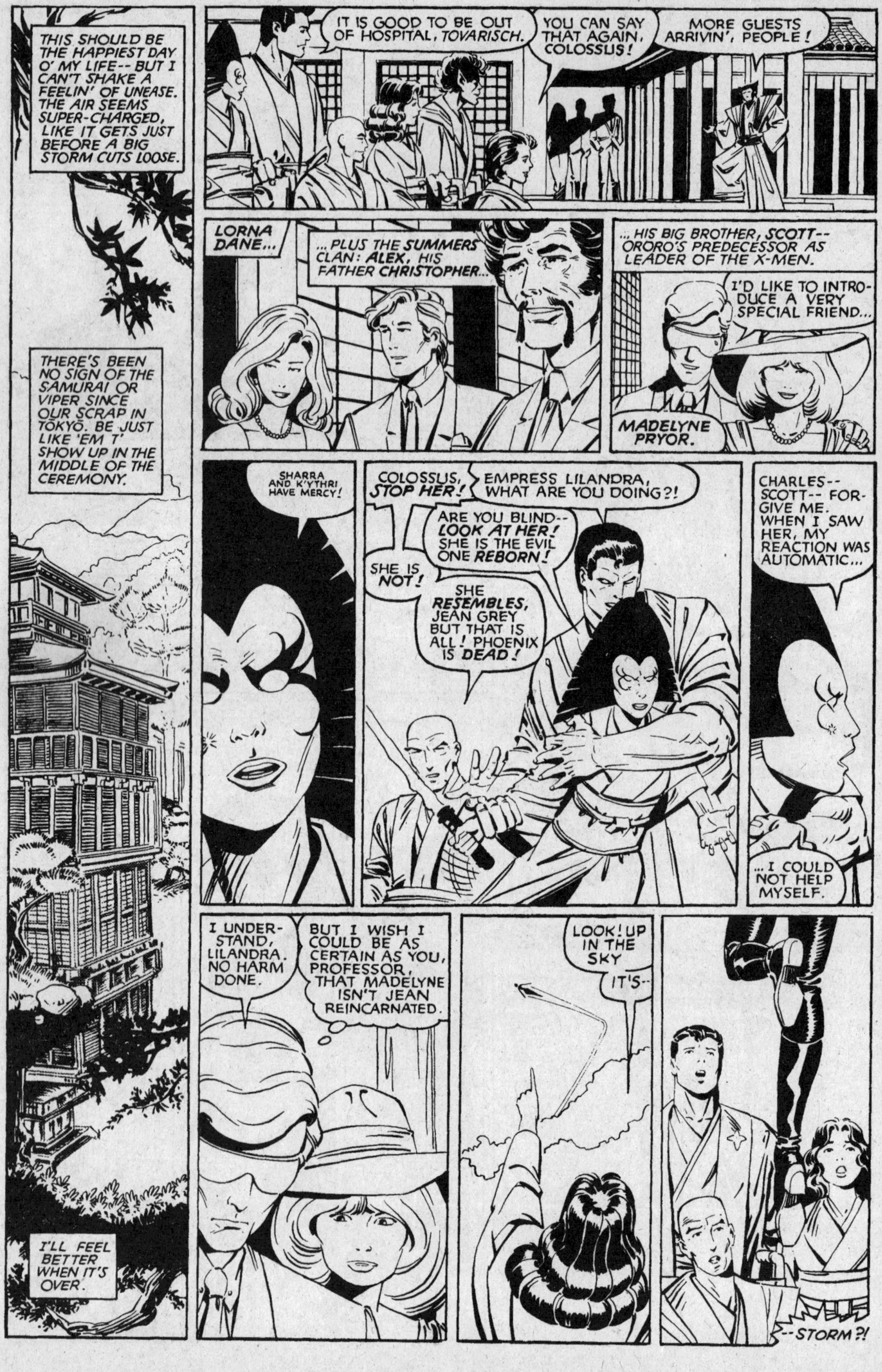
THIS SHOULD BE THE HAPPIEST DAY O' MY LIFE-- BUT I CAN'T SHAKE A FEELIN' OF UNEASE. THE AIR SEEMS SUPER-CHARGED, LIKE IT GETS JUST BEFORE A BIG STORM CUTS LOOSE.
IT IS GOOD TO BE OUT OF HOSPITAL, TOVARISCH.
YOU CAN SAY THAT AGAIN, COLOSSUS!
MORE GUESTS ARRIVIN', PEOPLE!
THERE'S BEEN NO SIGN OF THE SAMURAI OR VIPER SINCE OUR SCRAP IN TOKYO. BE JUST LIKE 'EM T' SHOW UP IN THE MIDDLE OF THE CEREMONY.
LORNA DANE...
...PLUS THE SUMMERS CLAN: ALEX, HIS FATHER CHRISTOPHER...
...HIS BIG BROTHER, SCOTT-- ORORO'S PREDECESSOR AS LEADER OF THE X-MEN.
I'D LIKE TO INTRODUCE A VERY SPECIAL FRIEND...
MADELYNE PRYOR.
SHARRA AND K'YTHRI HAVE MERCY!
COLOSSUS, STOP HER!
EMPRESS LILANDRA, WHAT ARE YOU DOING?!
ARE YOU BLIND-- LOOK AT HER! SHE IS THE EVIL ONE REBORN!
SHE IS NOT!
SHE RESEMBLES, JEAN GREY BUT THAT IS ALL! PHOENIX IS DEAD!
CHARLES-- SCOTT-- FORGIVE ME. WHEN I SAW HER, MY REACTION WAS AUTOMATIC...
...I COULD NOT HELP MYSELF.
I UNDERSTAND, LILANDRA. NO HARM DONE.
BUT I WISH I COULD BE AS CERTAIN AS YOU, PROFESSOR, THAT MADELYNE ISN'T JEAN REINCARNATED.
I'LL FEEL BETTER WHEN IT'S OVER.
LOOK! UP IN THE SKY
IT'S--
--STORM?!

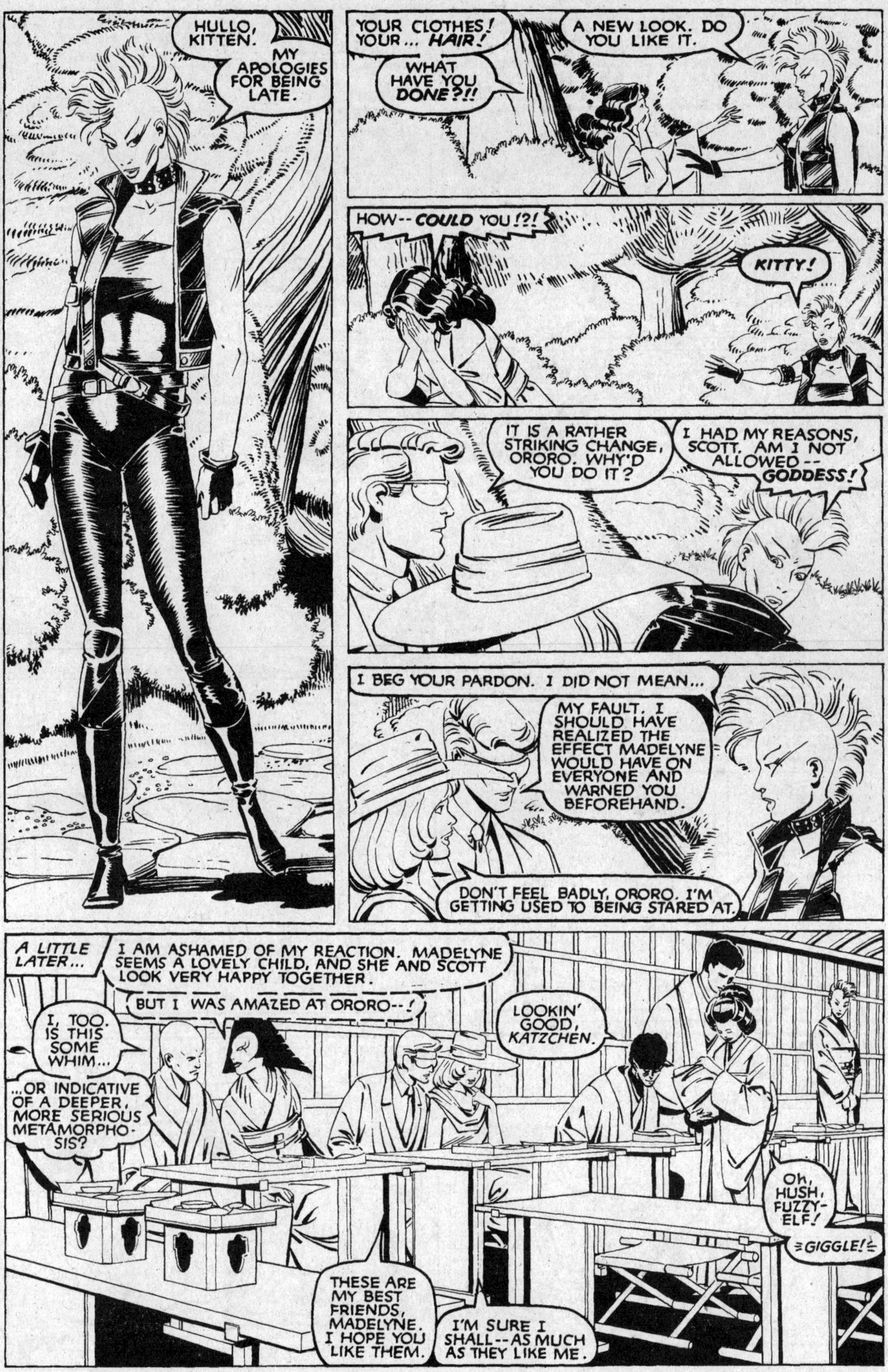
HULLO, KITTEN.
MY APOLOGIES FOR BEING LATE.
YOUR CLOTHES! YOUR... HAIR!
WHAT HAVE YOU DONE?!!
A NEW LOOK. DO YOU LIKE IT.
HOW--COULD YOU!?!
KITTY!
IT IS A RATHER STRIKING CHANGE, ORORO. WHY'D YOU DO IT?
I HAD MY REASONS, SCOTT. AM I NOT ALLOWED--GODDESS!
I BEG YOUR PARDON. I DID NOT MEAN...
MY FAULT. I SHOULD HAVE REALIZED THE EFFECT MADELYNE WOULD HAVE ON EVERYONE AND WARNED YOU BEFOREHAND.
DON'T FEEL BADLY, ORORO. I'M GETTING USED TO BEING STARED AT.
A LITTLE LATER...
I AM ASHAMED OF MY REACTION. MADELYNE SEEMS A LOVELY CHILD, AND SHE AND SCOTT LOOK VERY HAPPY TOGETHER.
BUT I WAS AMAZED AT ORORO--!
I, TOO. IS THIS SOME WHIM...
...OR INDICATIVE OF A DEEPER, MORE SERIOUS METAMORPHOSIS?
LOOKIN' GOOD, KATZCHEN.
Oh, HUSH, FUZZY-ELF!
GIGGLE!
THESE ARE MY BEST FRIENDS, MADELYNE. I HOPE YOU LIKE THEM.
I'M SURE I SHALL--AS MUCH AS THEY LIKE ME.

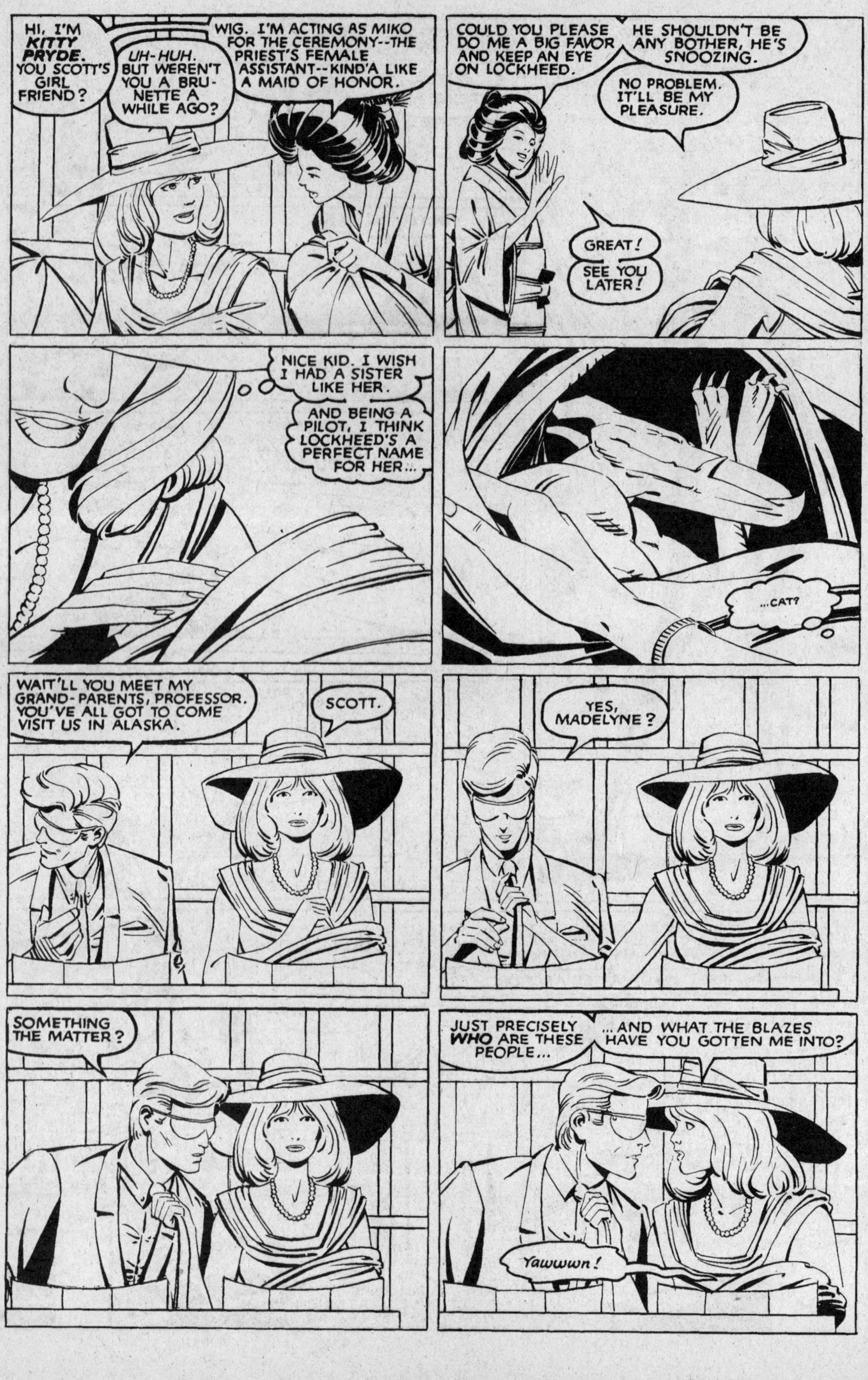

HI, I'M **KITTY PRYDE**. YOU SCOTT'S GIRL FRIEND?
UH-HUH. BUT WEREN'T YOU A BRU-NETTE A WHILE AGO?
WIG. I'M ACTING AS MIKO FOR THE CEREMONY--THE PRIEST'S FEMALE ASSISTANT--KIND'A LIKE A MAID OF HONOR.
COULD YOU PLEASE DO ME A BIG FAVOR AND KEEP AN EYE ON LOCKHEED.
HE SHOULDN'T BE ANY BOTHER, HE'S SNOOZING.
NO PROBLEM. IT'LL BE MY PLEASURE.
GREAT!
SEE YOU LATER!
NICE KID. I WISH I HAD A SISTER LIKE HER.
AND BEING A PILOT, I THINK LOCKHEED'S A PERFECT NAME FOR HER...
...CAT?
WAIT'LL YOU MEET MY GRAND-PARENTS, PROFESSOR. YOU'VE ALL GOT TO COME VISIT US IN ALASKA.
SCOTT.
YES, MADELYNE?
SOMETHING THE MATTER?
JUST PRECISELY **WHO** ARE THESE PEOPLE...
...AND WHAT THE BLAZES HAVE YOU GOTTEN ME INTO?
Yawwwn!

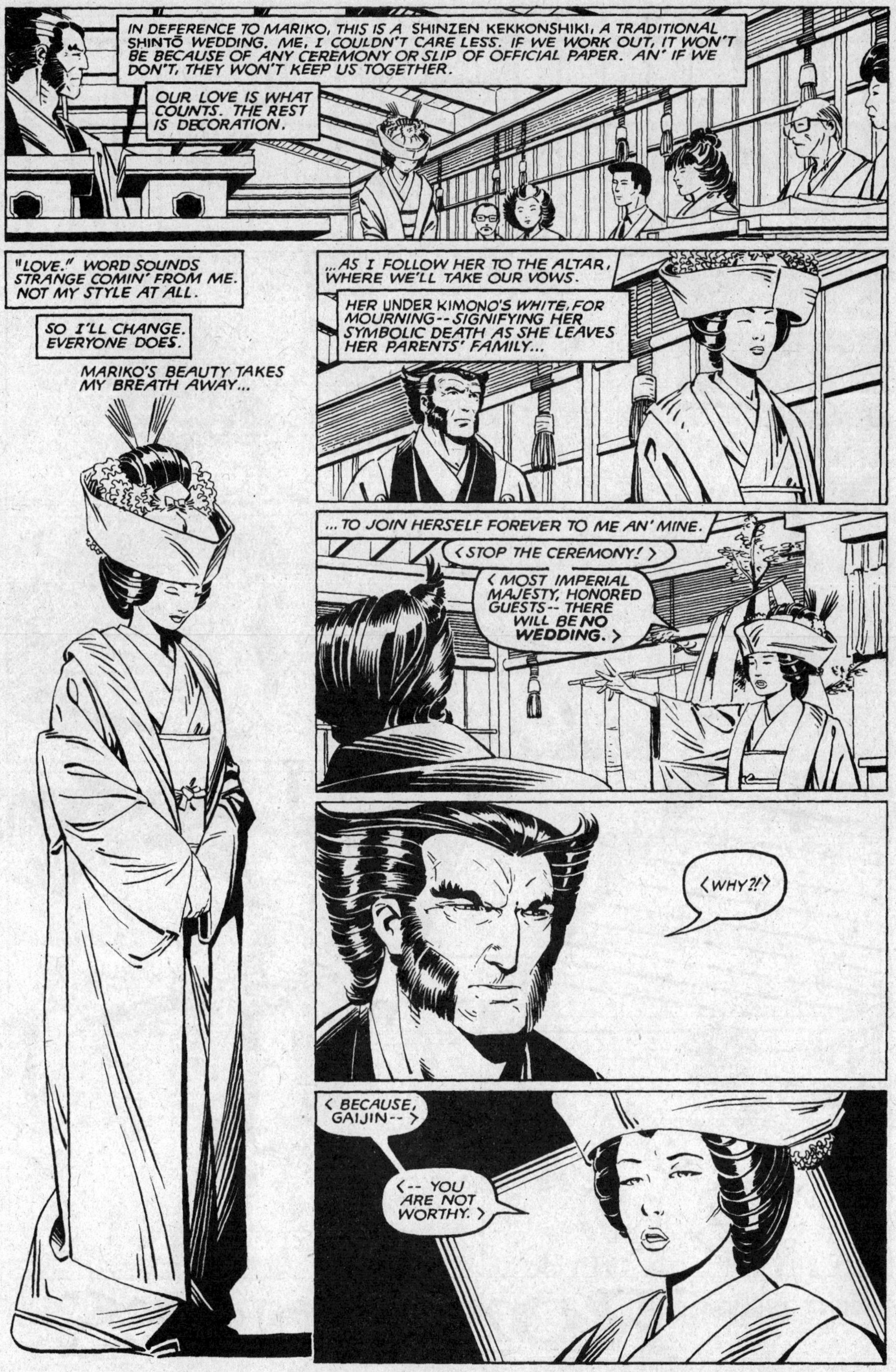
IN DEFERENCE TO MARIKO, THIS IS A SHINZEN KEKKONSHIKI, A TRADITIONAL SHINTŌ WEDDING. ME, I COULDN'T CARE LESS. IF WE WORK OUT, IT WON'T BE BECAUSE OF ANY CEREMONY OR SLIP OF OFFICIAL PAPER. AN' IF WE DON'T, THEY WON'T KEEP US TOGETHER.
OUR LOVE IS WHAT COUNTS. THE REST IS DECORATION.
"LOVE." WORD SOUNDS STRANGE COMIN' FROM ME. NOT MY STYLE AT ALL.
SO I'LL CHANGE. EVERYONE DOES.
MARIKO'S BEAUTY TAKES MY BREATH AWAY...
...AS I FOLLOW HER TO THE ALTAR, WHERE WE'LL TAKE OUR VOWS.
HER UNDER KIMONO'S WHITE, FOR MOURNING--SIGNIFYING HER SYMBOLIC DEATH AS SHE LEAVES HER PARENTS' FAMILY...
...TO JOIN HERSELF FOREVER TO ME AN' MINE.
‹STOP THE CEREMONY!›
‹MOST IMPERIAL MAJESTY, HONORED GUESTS-- THERE WILL BE NO WEDDING.›
‹WHY?!›
‹BECAUSE, GAIJIN--›
‹-- YOU ARE NOT WORTHY.›

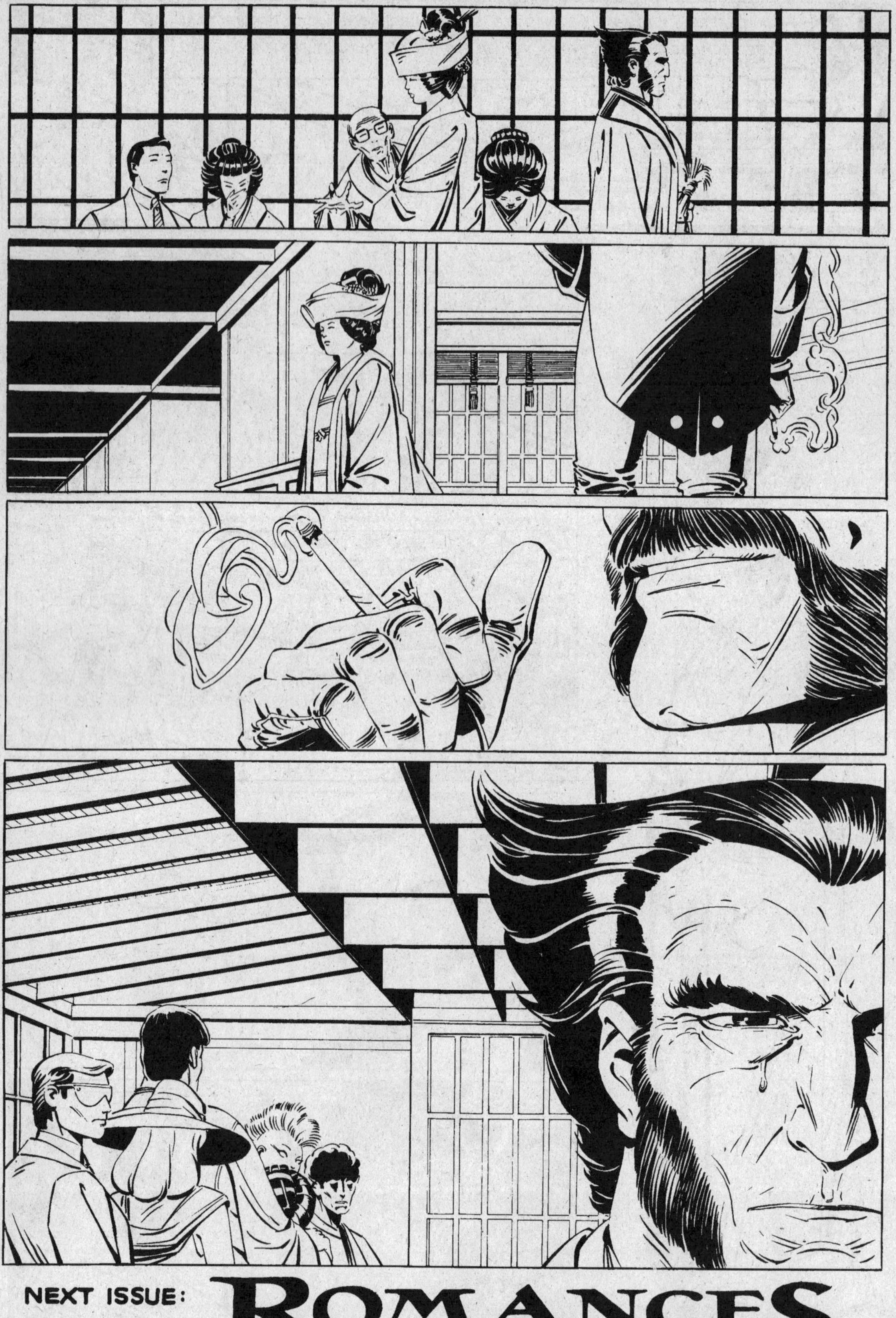

NEXT ISSUE: ROMANCES

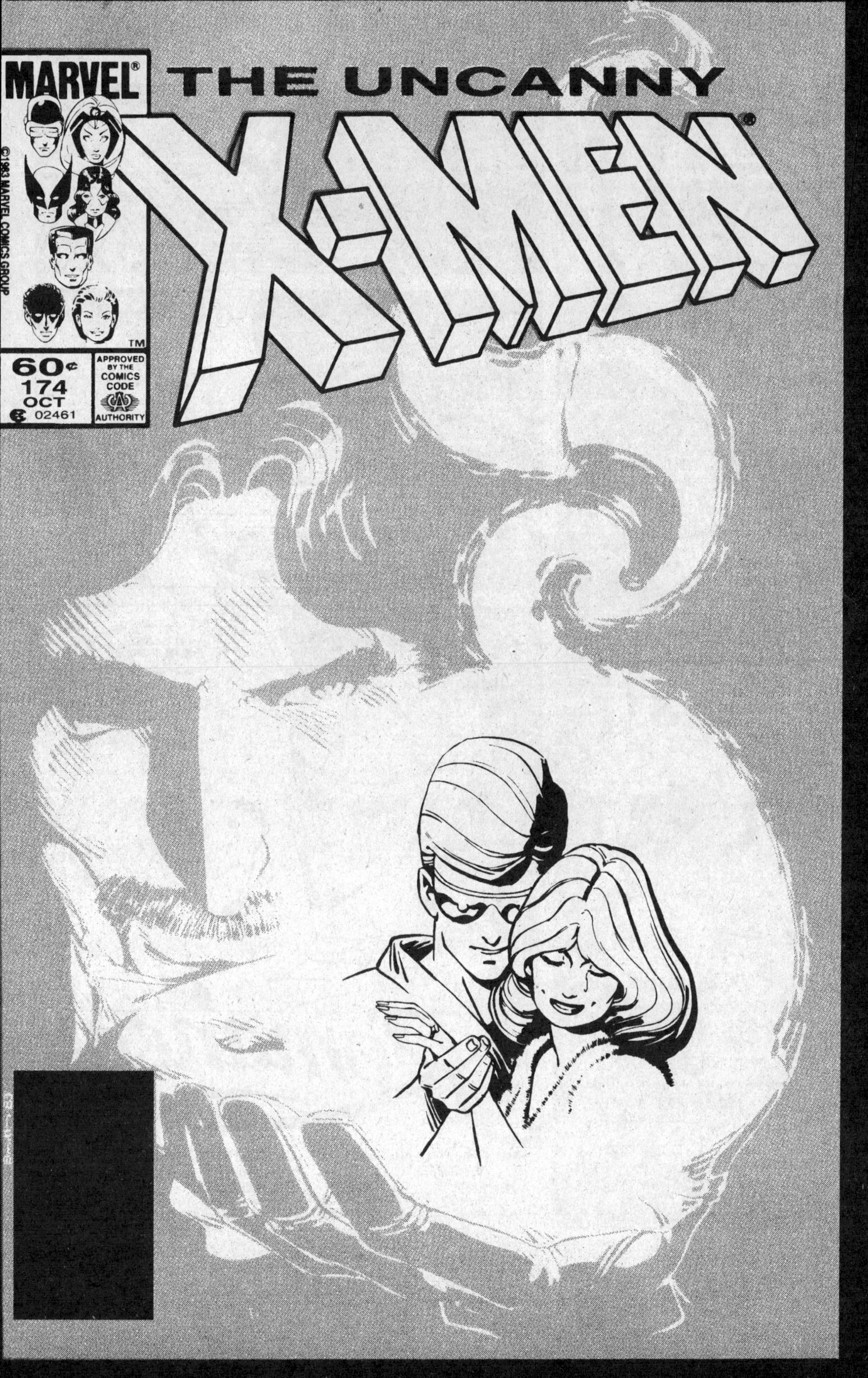
MARVEL®
THE UNCANNY
X-MEN®
©1983 MARVEL COMICS GROUP
TM
60¢
174
OCT
02461
APPROVED BY THE COMICS CODE AUTHORITY

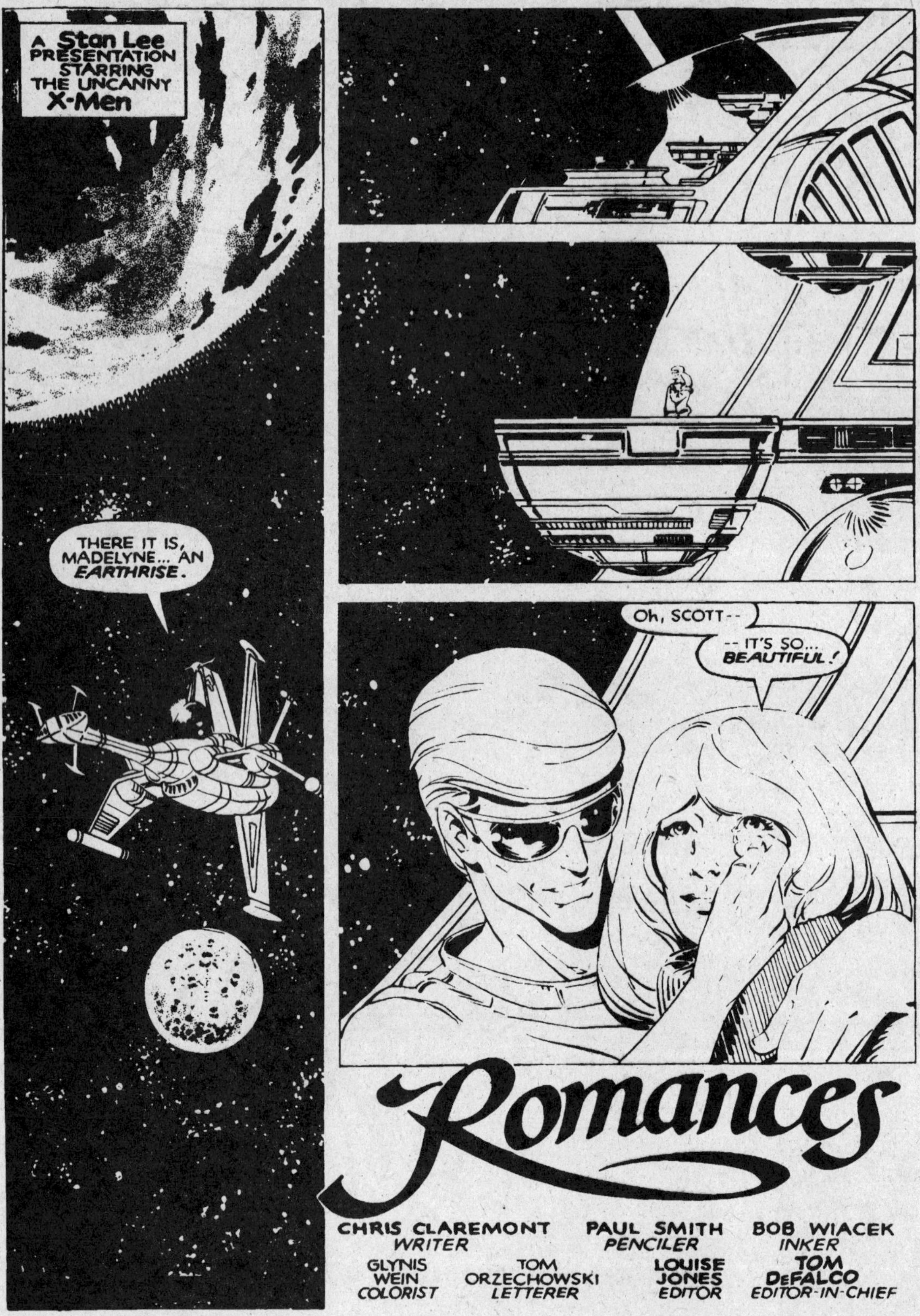
A Stan Lee PRESENTATION STARRING THE UNCANNY X-Men
THERE IT IS, MADELYNE... AN EARTHRISE.
Oh, SCOTT--
-- IT'S SO... BEAUTIFUL!
Romances
CHRIS CLAREMONT WRITER
PAUL SMITH PENCILER
BOB WIACEK INKER
GLYNIS WEIN COLORIST
TOM ORZECHOWSKI LETTERER
LOUISE JONES EDITOR
TOM DeFALCO EDITOR-IN-CHIEF

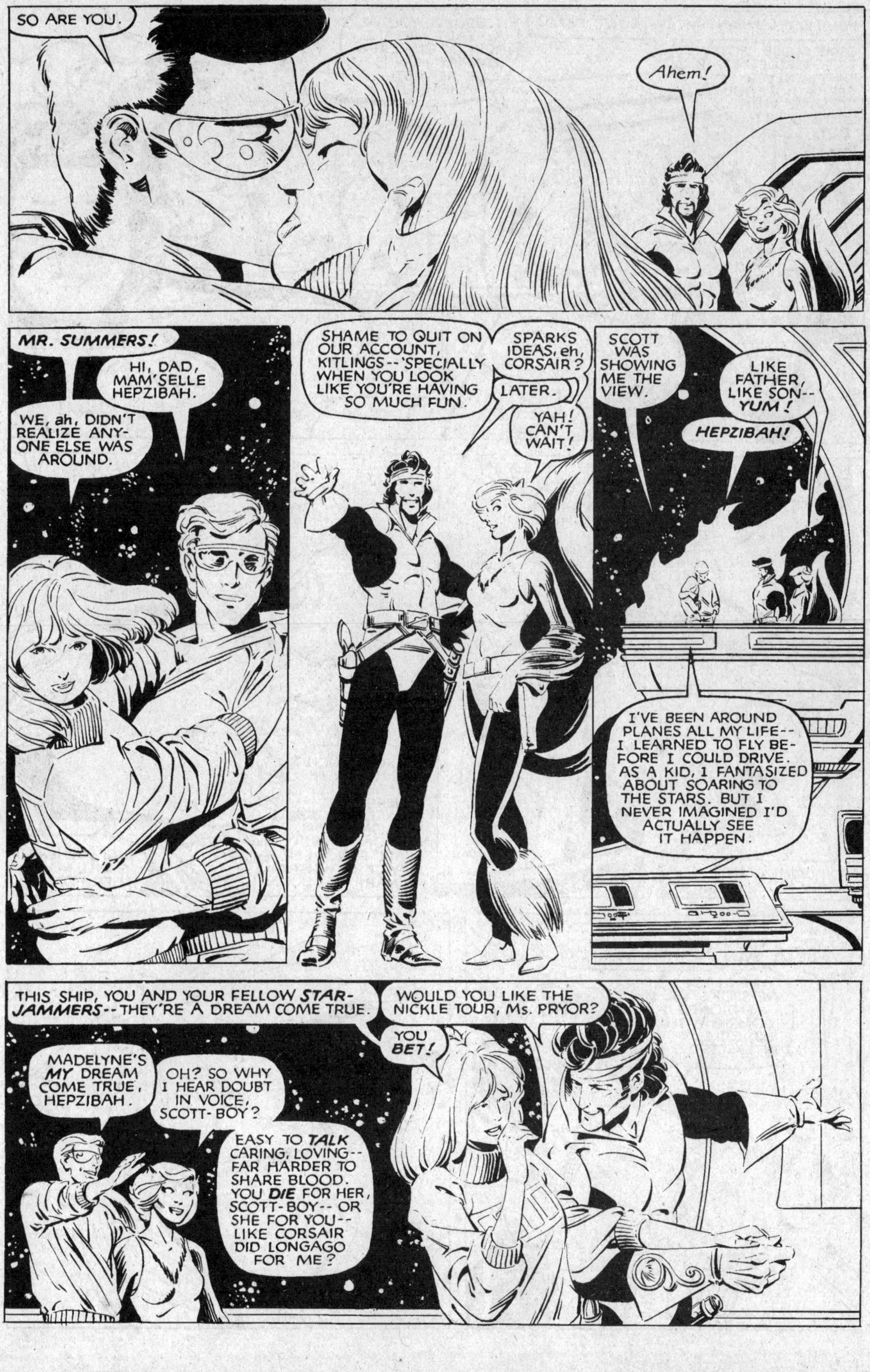
SO ARE YOU.
Ahem!
MR. SUMMERS!
HI, DAD, MAM'SELLE HEPZIBAH.
WE, ah, DIDN'T REALIZE ANY-ONE ELSE WAS AROUND.
SHAME TO QUIT ON OUR ACCOUNT, KITLINGS--'SPECIALLY WHEN YOU LOOK LIKE YOU'RE HAVING SO MUCH FUN.
SPARKS IDEAS, eh, CORSAIR?
LATER.
YAH! CAN'T WAIT!
SCOTT WAS SHOWING ME THE VIEW.
LIKE FATHER, LIKE SON--YUM!
HEPZIBAH!
I'VE BEEN AROUND PLANES ALL MY LIFE-- I LEARNED TO FLY BEFORE I COULD DRIVE. AS A KID, I FANTASIZED ABOUT SOARING TO THE STARS. BUT I NEVER IMAGINED I'D ACTUALLY SEE IT HAPPEN.
THIS SHIP, YOU AND YOUR FELLOW STAR-JAMMERS--THEY'RE A DREAM COME TRUE.
WOULD YOU LIKE THE NICKLE TOUR, Ms. PRYOR?
YOU BET!
MADELYNE'S MY DREAM COME TRUE, HEPZIBAH.
OH? SO WHY I HEAR DOUBT IN VOICE, SCOTT-BOY?
EASY TO TALK CARING, LOVING--FAR HARDER TO SHARE BLOOD. YOU DIE FOR HER, SCOTT-BOY--OR SHE FOR YOU--LIKE CORSAIR DID LONGAGO FOR ME?

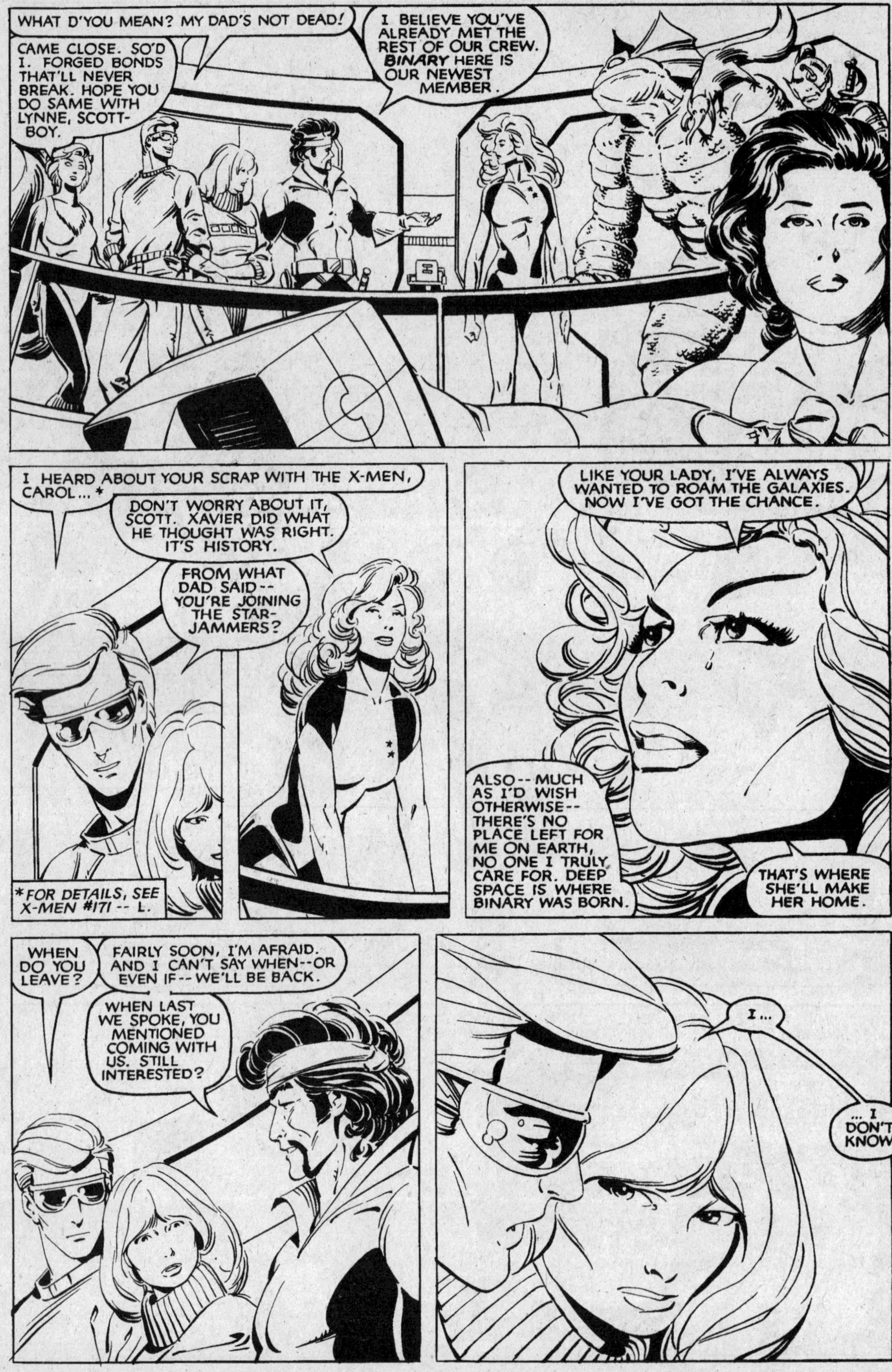
WHAT D'YOU MEAN? MY DAD'S NOT DEAD!
CAME CLOSE. SO'D I. FORGED BONDS THAT'LL NEVER BREAK. HOPE YOU DO SAME WITH LYNNE, SCOTT-BOY.
I BELIEVE YOU'VE ALREADY MET THE REST OF OUR CREW. BINARY HERE IS OUR NEWEST MEMBER.
I HEARD ABOUT YOUR SCRAP WITH THE X-MEN, CAROL... *
DON'T WORRY ABOUT IT, SCOTT. XAVIER DID WHAT HE THOUGHT WAS RIGHT. IT'S HISTORY.
FROM WHAT DAD SAID-- YOU'RE JOINING THE STAR-JAMMERS?
*FOR DETAILS, SEE X-MEN #171 -- L.
LIKE YOUR LADY, I'VE ALWAYS WANTED TO ROAM THE GALAXIES. NOW I'VE GOT THE CHANCE.
ALSO--MUCH AS I'D WISH OTHERWISE-- THERE'S NO PLACE LEFT FOR ME ON EARTH, NO ONE I TRULY CARE FOR. DEEP SPACE IS WHERE BINARY WAS BORN.
THAT'S WHERE SHE'LL MAKE HER HOME.
WHEN DO YOU LEAVE?
FAIRLY SOON, I'M AFRAID. AND I CAN'T SAY WHEN--OR EVEN IF--WE'LL BE BACK.
WHEN LAST WE SPOKE, YOU MENTIONED COMING WITH US. STILL INTERESTED?
I...
...I DON'T KNOW.

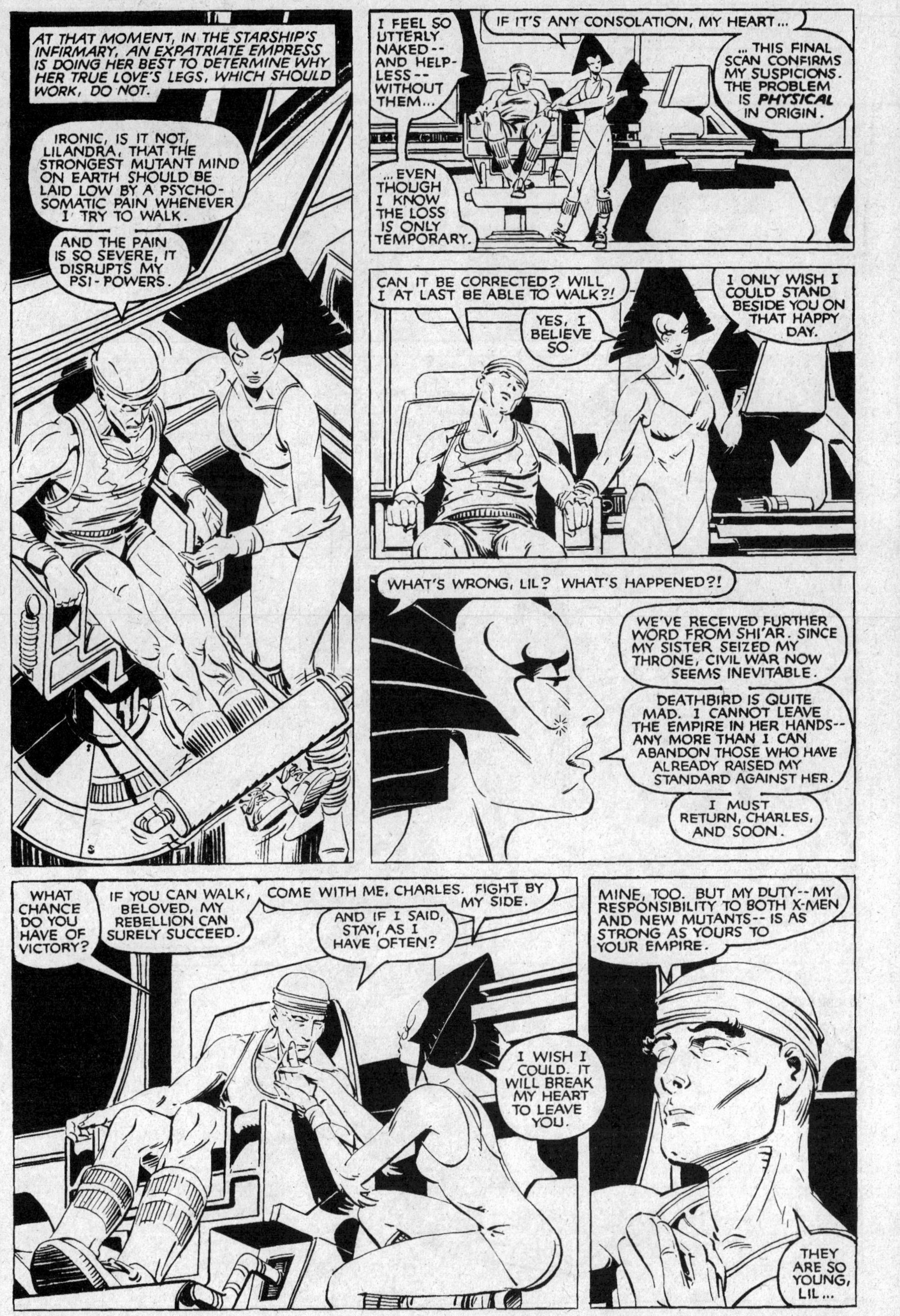
AT THAT MOMENT, IN THE STARSHIP'S INFIRMARY, AN EXPATRIATE EMPRESS IS DOING HER BEST TO DETERMINE WHY HER TRUE LOVE'S LEGS, WHICH SHOULD WORK, DO NOT.
IRONIC, IS IT NOT, LILANDRA, THAT THE STRONGEST MUTANT MIND ON EARTH SHOULD BE LAID LOW BY A PSYCHOSOMATIC PAIN WHENEVER I TRY TO WALK.
AND THE PAIN IS SO SEVERE, IT DISRUPTS MY PSI-POWERS.
I FEEL SO UTTERLY NAKED-- AND HELPLESS-- WITHOUT THEM...
...EVEN THOUGH I KNOW THE LOSS IS ONLY TEMPORARY.
IF IT'S ANY CONSOLATION, MY HEART...
...THIS FINAL SCAN CONFIRMS MY SUSPICIONS. THE PROBLEM IS PHYSICAL IN ORIGIN.
CAN IT BE CORRECTED? WILL I AT LAST BE ABLE TO WALK?!
YES, I BELIEVE SO.
I ONLY WISH I COULD STAND BESIDE YOU ON THAT HAPPY DAY.
WHAT'S WRONG, LIL? WHAT'S HAPPENED?!
WE'VE RECEIVED FURTHER WORD FROM SHI'AR. SINCE MY SISTER SEIZED MY THRONE, CIVIL WAR NOW SEEMS INEVITABLE.
DEATHBIRD IS QUITE MAD. I CANNOT LEAVE THE EMPIRE IN HER HANDS-- ANY MORE THAN I CAN ABANDON THOSE WHO HAVE ALREADY RAISED MY STANDARD AGAINST HER.
I MUST RETURN, CHARLES, AND SOON.
COME WITH ME, CHARLES. FIGHT BY MY SIDE.
WHAT CHANCE DO YOU HAVE OF VICTORY?
IF YOU CAN WALK, BELOVED, MY REBELLION CAN SURELY SUCCEED.
AND IF I SAID, STAY, AS I HAVE OFTEN?
I WISH I COULD. IT WILL BREAK MY HEART TO LEAVE YOU.
MINE, TOO. BUT MY DUTY--MY RESPONSIBILITY TO BOTH X-MEN AND NEW MUTANTS-- IS AS STRONG AS YOURS TO YOUR EMPIRE.
THEY ARE SO YOUNG, LIL...

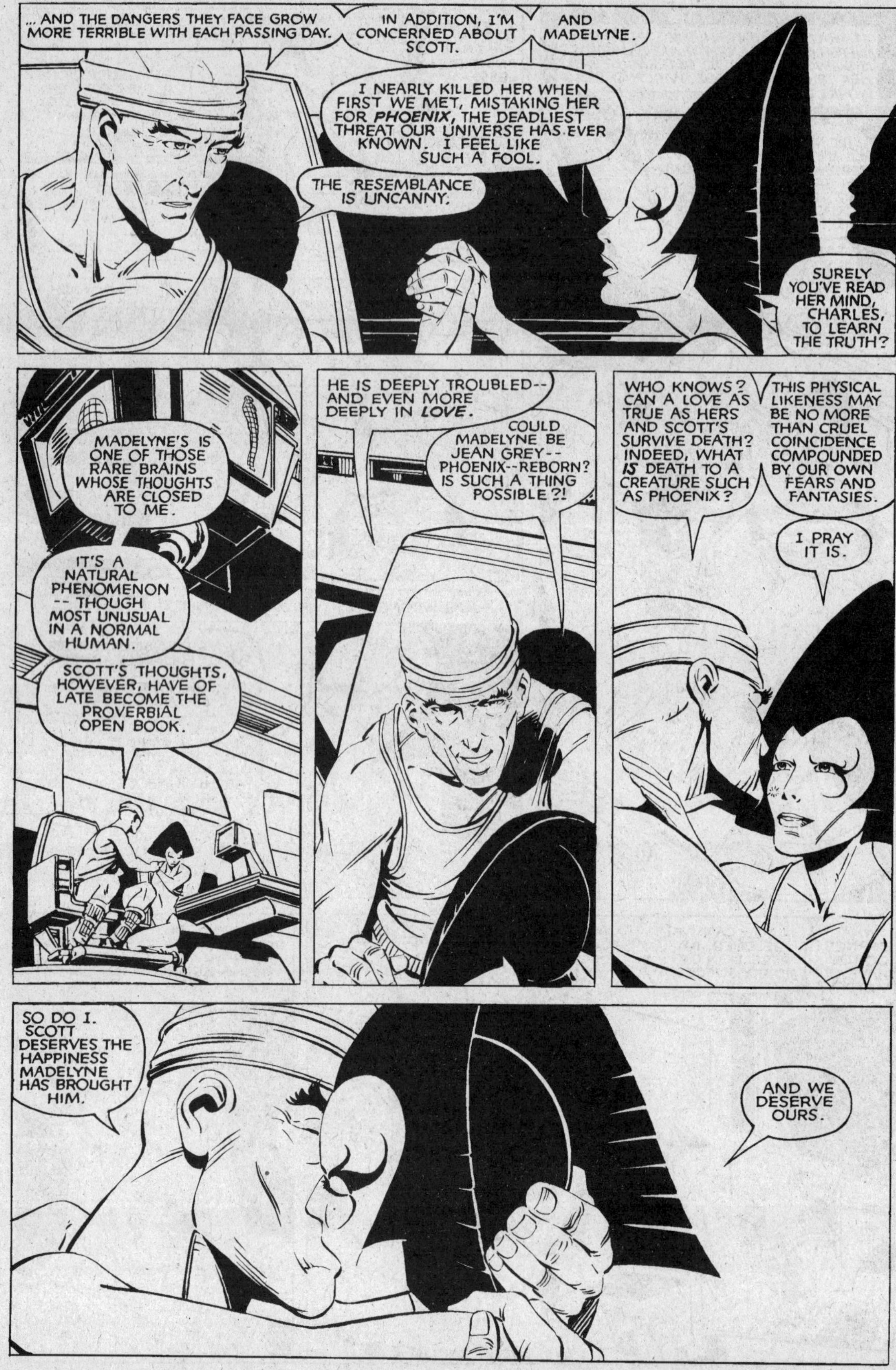
...AND THE DANGERS THEY FACE GROW MORE TERRIBLE WITH EACH PASSING DAY.
IN ADDITION, I'M CONCERNED ABOUT SCOTT.
AND MADELYNE.
I NEARLY KILLED HER WHEN FIRST WE MET, MISTAKING HER FOR PHOENIX, THE DEADLIEST THREAT OUR UNIVERSE HAS EVER KNOWN. I FEEL LIKE SUCH A FOOL.
THE RESEMBLANCE IS UNCANNY.
SURELY YOU'VE READ HER MIND, CHARLES, TO LEARN THE TRUTH?
MADELYNE'S IS ONE OF THOSE RARE BRAINS WHOSE THOUGHTS ARE CLOSED TO ME.
IT'S A NATURAL PHENOMENON -- THOUGH MOST UNUSUAL IN A NORMAL HUMAN.
SCOTT'S THOUGHTS, HOWEVER, HAVE OF LATE BECOME THE PROVERBIAL OPEN BOOK.
HE IS DEEPLY TROUBLED-- AND EVEN MORE DEEPLY IN LOVE.
COULD MADELYNE BE JEAN GREY-- PHOENIX--REBORN? IS SUCH A THING POSSIBLE?!
WHO KNOWS? CAN A LOVE AS TRUE AS HERS AND SCOTT'S SURVIVE DEATH? INDEED, WHAT IS DEATH TO A CREATURE SUCH AS PHOENIX?
THIS PHYSICAL LIKENESS MAY BE NO MORE THAN CRUEL COINCIDENCE COMPOUNDED BY OUR OWN FEARS AND FANTASIES.
I PRAY IT IS.
SO DO I. SCOTT DESERVES THE HAPPINESS MADELYNE HAS BROUGHT HIM.
AND WE DESERVE OURS.

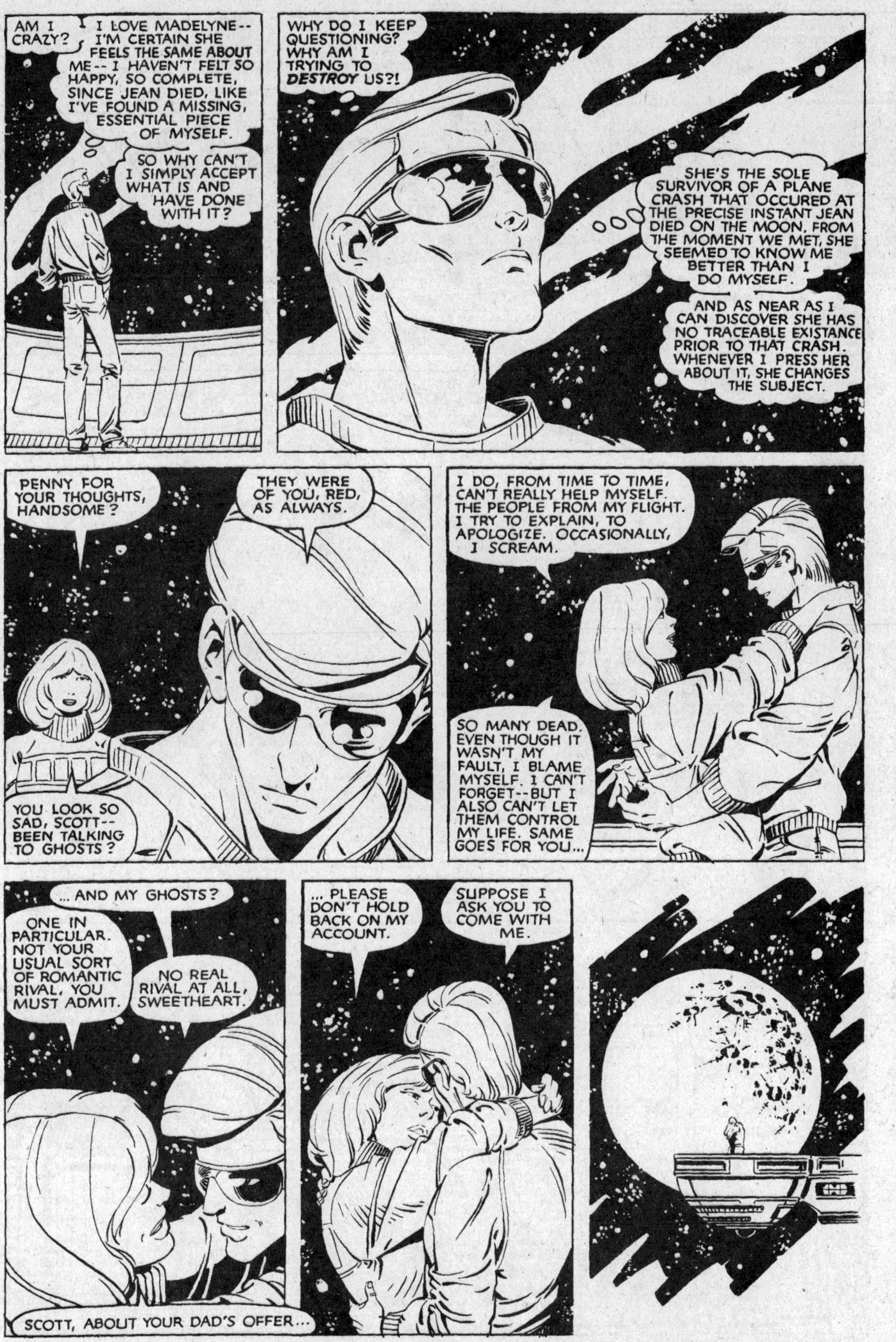
AM I CRAZY?
I LOVE MADELYNE-- I'M CERTAIN SHE FEELS THE SAME ABOUT ME-- I HAVEN'T FELT SO HAPPY, SO COMPLETE, SINCE JEAN DIED, LIKE I'VE FOUND A MISSING, ESSENTIAL PIECE OF MYSELF.
SO WHY CAN'T I SIMPLY ACCEPT WHAT IS AND HAVE DONE WITH IT?
WHY DO I KEEP QUESTIONING? WHY AM I TRYING TO DESTROY US?!
SHE'S THE SOLE SURVIVOR OF A PLANE CRASH THAT OCCURED AT THE PRECISE INSTANT JEAN DIED ON THE MOON. FROM THE MOMENT WE MET, SHE SEEMED TO KNOW ME BETTER THAN I DO MYSELF.
AND AS NEAR AS I CAN DISCOVER SHE HAS NO TRACEABLE EXISTANCE PRIOR TO THAT CRASH. WHENEVER I PRESS HER ABOUT IT, SHE CHANGES THE SUBJECT.
PENNY FOR YOUR THOUGHTS, HANDSOME?
THEY WERE OF YOU, RED, AS ALWAYS.
YOU LOOK SO SAD, SCOTT-- BEEN TALKING TO GHOSTS?
I DO, FROM TIME TO TIME, CAN'T REALLY HELP MYSELF. THE PEOPLE FROM MY FLIGHT. I TRY TO EXPLAIN, TO APOLOGIZE. OCCASIONALLY, I SCREAM.
SO MANY DEAD. EVEN THOUGH IT WASN'T MY FAULT, I BLAME MYSELF. I CAN'T FORGET--BUT I ALSO CAN'T LET THEM CONTROL MY LIFE. SAME GOES FOR YOU...
... AND MY GHOSTS?
ONE IN PARTICULAR. NOT YOUR USUAL SORT OF ROMANTIC RIVAL, YOU MUST ADMIT.
NO REAL RIVAL AT ALL, SWEETHEART.
SCOTT, ABOUT YOUR DAD'S OFFER...
... PLEASE DON'T HOLD BACK ON MY ACCOUNT.
SUPPOSE I ASK YOU TO COME WITH ME.

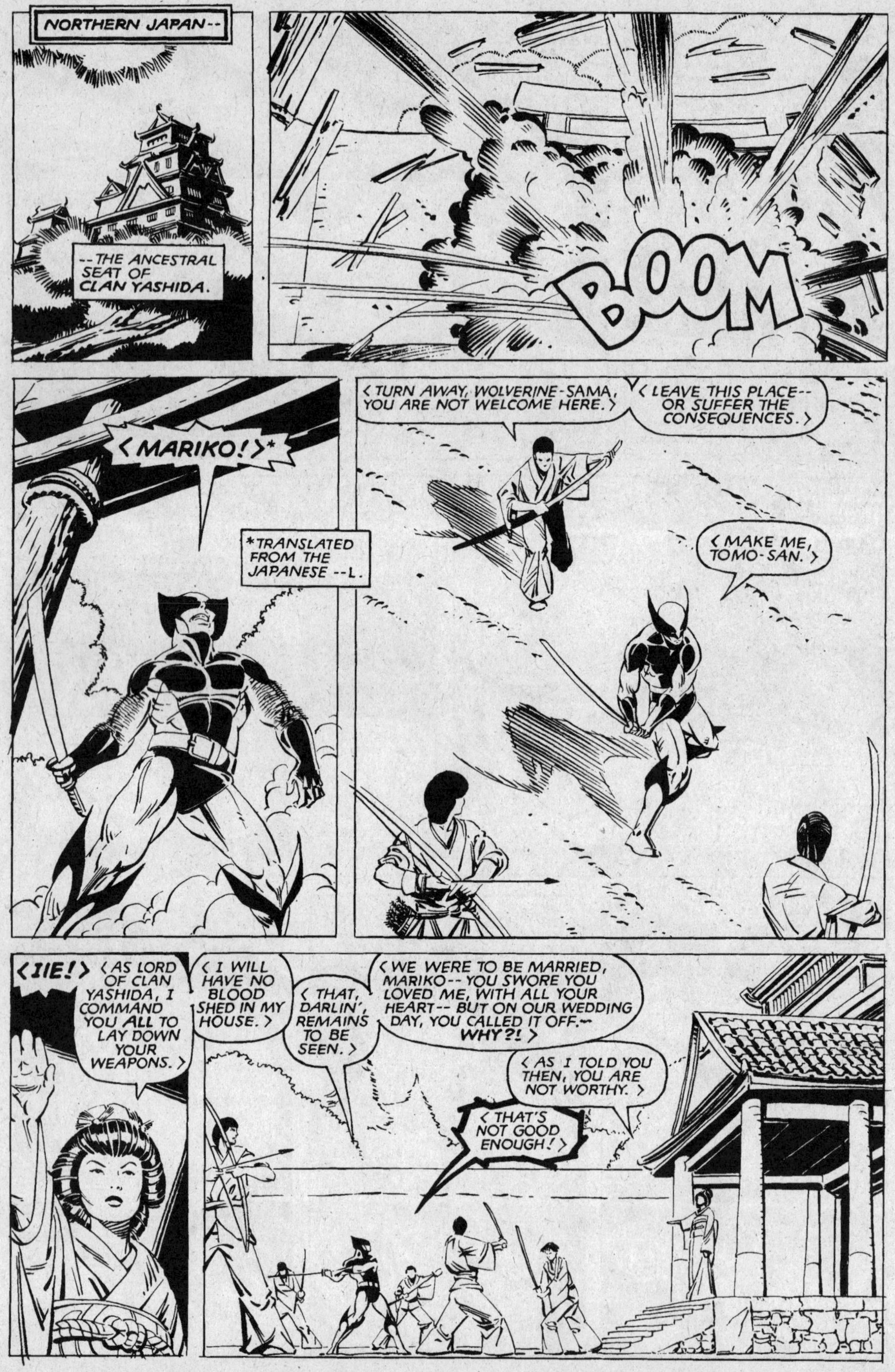
NORTHERN JAPAN--
--THE ANCESTRAL SEAT OF CLAN YASHIDA.
BOOM
<MARIKO!>*
*TRANSLATED FROM THE JAPANESE --L.
<TURN AWAY, WOLVERINE-SAMA, YOU ARE NOT WELCOME HERE.>
<LEAVE THIS PLACE-- OR SUFFER THE CONSEQUENCES.>
<MAKE ME, TOMO-SAN.>
<IIE!>
<AS LORD OF CLAN YASHIDA, I COMMAND YOU ALL TO LAY DOWN YOUR WEAPONS.>
<I WILL HAVE NO BLOOD SHED IN MY HOUSE.>
<THAT, DARLIN', REMAINS TO BE SEEN.>
<WE WERE TO BE MARRIED, MARIKO-- YOU SWORE YOU LOVED ME, WITH ALL YOUR HEART-- BUT ON OUR WEDDING DAY, YOU CALLED IT OFF.-- WHY?!>
<AS I TOLD YOU THEN, YOU ARE NOT WORTHY.>
<THAT'S NOT GOOD ENOUGH!>

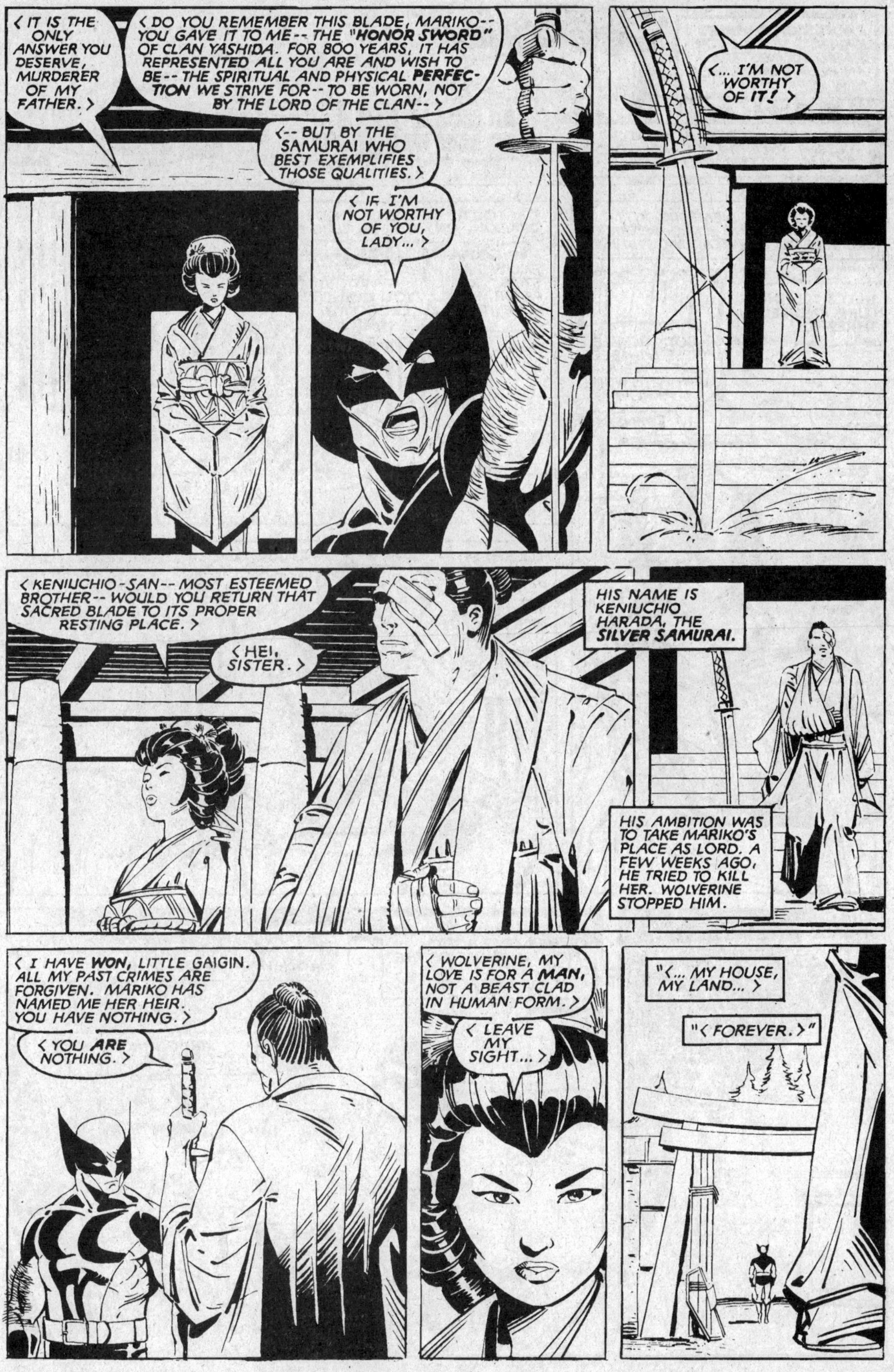
< IT IS THE ONLY ANSWER YOU DESERVE, MURDERER OF MY FATHER. >
< DO YOU REMEMBER THIS BLADE, MARIKO-- YOU GAVE IT TO ME-- THE "HONOR SWORD" OF CLAN YASHIDA. FOR 800 YEARS, IT HAS REPRESENTED ALL YOU ARE AND WISH TO BE-- THE SPIRITUAL AND PHYSICAL PERFECTION WE STRIVE FOR-- TO BE WORN, NOT BY THE LORD OF THE CLAN-- >
<-- BUT BY THE SAMURAI WHO BEST EXEMPLIFIES THOSE QUALITIES. >
< IF I'M NOT WORTHY OF YOU, LADY... >
<... I'M NOT WORTHY OF IT! >
< KENIUCHIO-SAN-- MOST ESTEEMED BROTHER-- WOULD YOU RETURN THAT SACRED BLADE TO ITS PROPER RESTING PLACE. >
< HEI, SISTER. >
HIS NAME IS KENIUCHIO HARADA, THE SILVER SAMURAI.
HIS AMBITION WAS TO TAKE MARIKO'S PLACE AS LORD. A FEW WEEKS AGO, HE TRIED TO KILL HER. WOLVERINE STOPPED HIM.
< I HAVE WON, LITTLE GAIGIN. ALL MY PAST CRIMES ARE FORGIVEN. MARIKO HAS NAMED ME HER HEIR. YOU HAVE NOTHING. >
< YOU ARE NOTHING. >
< WOLVERINE, MY LOVE IS FOR A MAN, NOT A BEAST CLAD IN HUMAN FORM. >
< LEAVE MY SIGHT... >
"<... MY HOUSE, MY LAND... >
"< FOREVER. >"

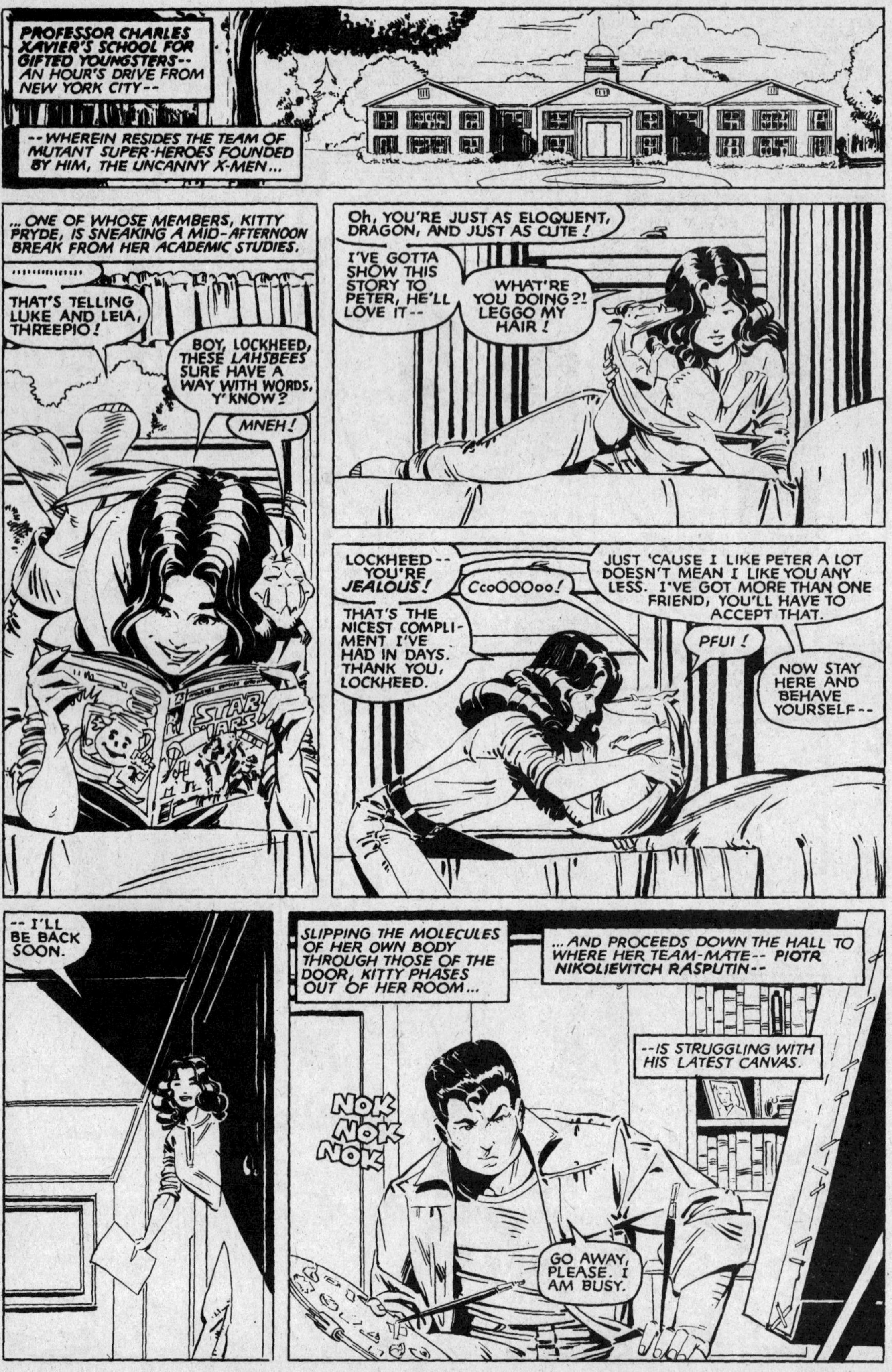
PROFESSOR CHARLES XAVIER'S SCHOOL FOR GIFTED YOUNGSTERS-- AN HOUR'S DRIVE FROM NEW YORK CITY--
--WHEREIN RESIDES THE TEAM OF MUTANT SUPER-HEROES FOUNDED BY HIM, THE UNCANNY X-MEN...
...ONE OF WHOSE MEMBERS, KITTY PRYDE, IS SNEAKING A MID-AFTERNOON BREAK FROM HER ACADEMIC STUDIES.
....
THAT'S TELLING LUKE AND LEIA, THREEPIO!
BOY, LOCKHEED, THESE LAHSBEES SURE HAVE A WAY WITH WORDS, Y'KNOW?
MNEH!
Oh, YOU'RE JUST AS ELOQUENT, DRAGON, AND JUST AS CUTE!
I'VE GOTTA SHOW THIS STORY TO PETER, HE'LL LOVE IT--
WHAT'RE YOU DOING?! LEGGO MY HAIR!
LOCKHEED-- YOU'RE JEALOUS!
CcoOOOoo!
THAT'S THE NICEST COMPLIMENT I'VE HAD IN DAYS. THANK YOU, LOCKHEED.
JUST 'CAUSE I LIKE PETER A LOT DOESN'T MEAN I LIKE YOU ANY LESS. I'VE GOT MORE THAN ONE FRIEND, YOU'LL HAVE TO ACCEPT THAT.
PFUI!
NOW STAY HERE AND BEHAVE YOURSELF--
-- I'LL BE BACK SOON.
SLIPPING THE MOLECULES OF HER OWN BODY THROUGH THOSE OF THE DOOR, KITTY PHASES OUT OF HER ROOM...
...AND PROCEEDS DOWN THE HALL TO WHERE HER TEAM-MATE-- PIOTR NIKOLIEVITCH RASPUTIN--
--IS STRUGGLING WITH HIS LATEST CANVAS.
NOK NOK NOK
GO AWAY, PLEASE. I AM BUSY.

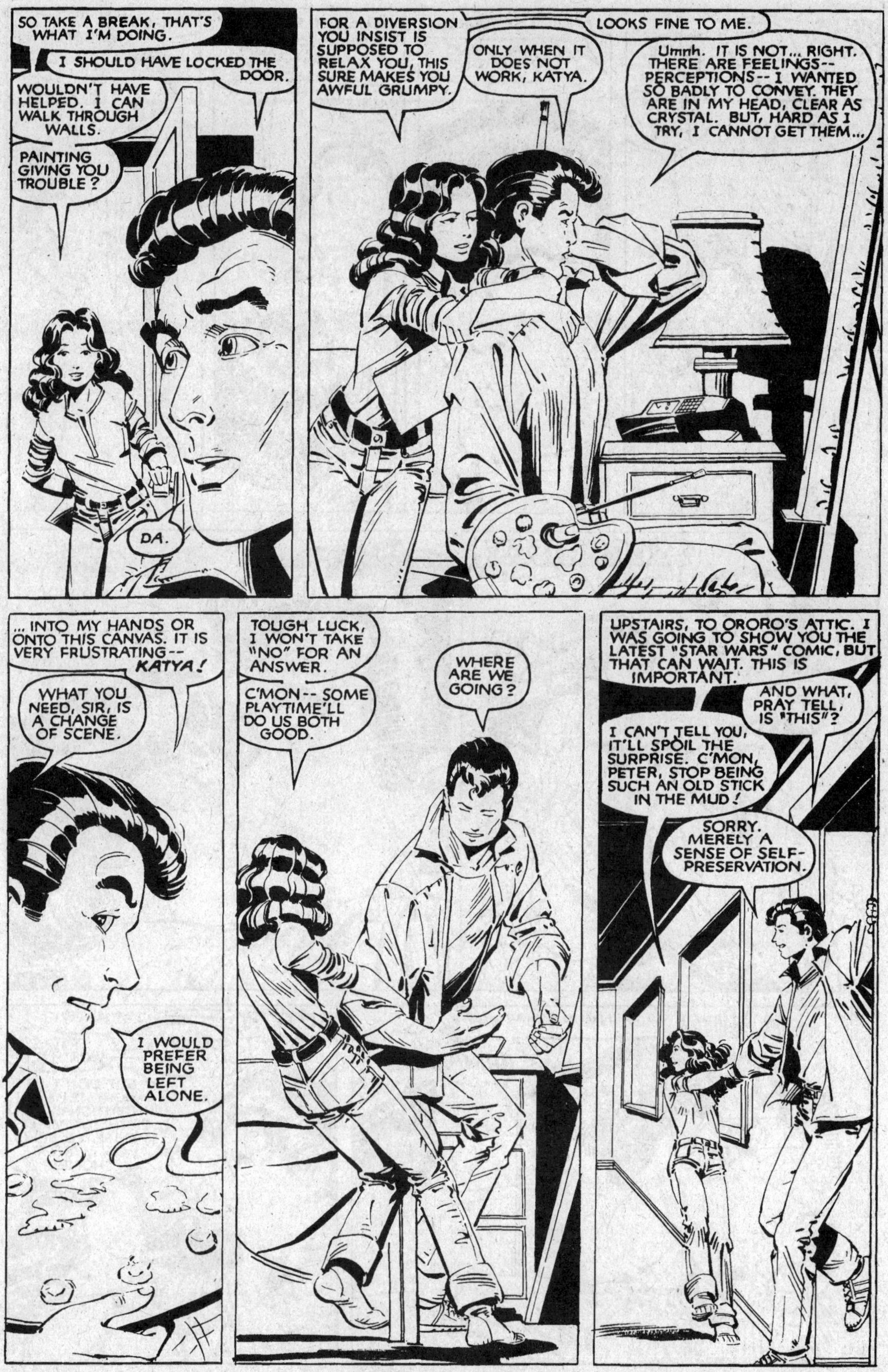
SO TAKE A BREAK, THAT'S WHAT I'M DOING.
I SHOULD HAVE LOCKED THE DOOR.
WOULDN'T HAVE HELPED. I CAN WALK THROUGH WALLS.
PAINTING GIVING YOU TROUBLE?
DA.
FOR A DIVERSION YOU INSIST IS SUPPOSED TO RELAX YOU, THIS SURE MAKES YOU AWFUL GRUMPY.
LOOKS FINE TO ME.
ONLY WHEN IT DOES NOT WORK, KATYA.
Umnh. IT IS NOT... RIGHT. THERE ARE FEELINGS-- PERCEPTIONS-- I WANTED SO BADLY TO CONVEY. THEY ARE IN MY HEAD, CLEAR AS CRYSTAL. BUT, HARD AS I TRY, I CANNOT GET THEM...
...INTO MY HANDS OR ONTO THIS CANVAS. IT IS VERY FRUSTRATING-- KATYA!
WHAT YOU NEED, SIR, IS A CHANGE OF SCENE.
I WOULD PREFER BEING LEFT ALONE.
TOUGH LUCK, I WON'T TAKE "NO" FOR AN ANSWER.
C'MON-- SOME PLAYTIME'LL DO US BOTH GOOD.
WHERE ARE WE GOING?
UPSTAIRS, TO ORORO'S ATTIC. I WAS GOING TO SHOW YOU THE LATEST "STAR WARS" COMIC, BUT THAT CAN WAIT. THIS IS IMPORTANT.
AND WHAT, PRAY TELL, IS "THIS"?
I CAN'T TELL YOU, IT'LL SPOIL THE SURPRISE. C'MON, PETER, STOP BEING SUCH AN OLD STICK IN THE MUD!
SORRY. MERELY A SENSE OF SELF-PRESERVATION.

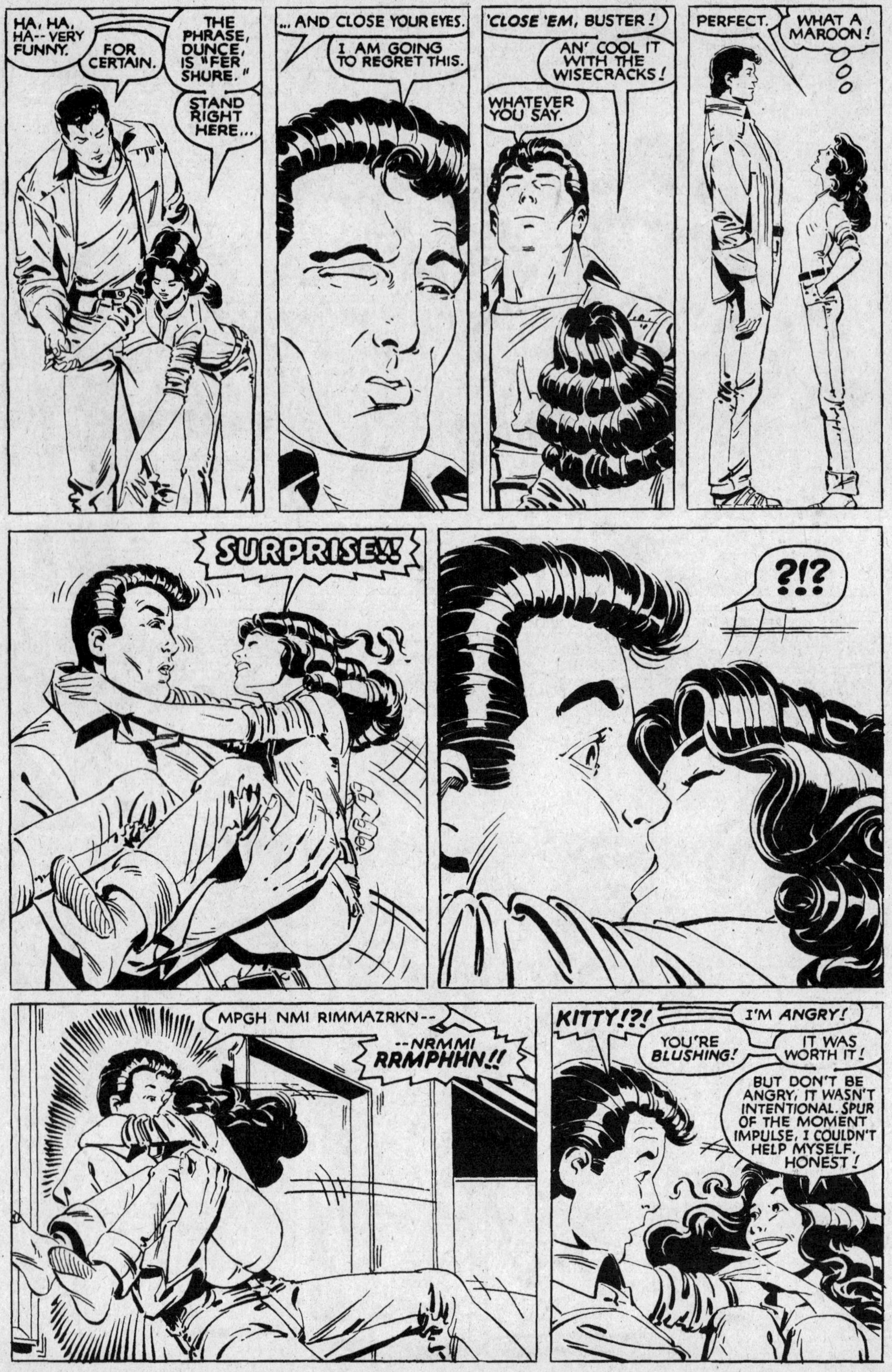
HA, HA, HA-- VERY FUNNY.
FOR CERTAIN.
THE PHRASE, DUNCE, IS "FER SHURE."
STAND RIGHT HERE...
... AND CLOSE YOUR EYES.
I AM GOING TO REGRET THIS.
'CLOSE 'EM, BUSTER!
AN' COOL IT WITH THE WISECRACKS!
WHATEVER YOU SAY.
PERFECT.
WHAT A MAROON!
SURPRISE!!
?!?
MPGH NMI RIMMAZRKN--
--NRMMI RRMPHHN!!
KITTY!?!
I'M ANGRY!
YOU'RE BLUSHING!
IT WAS WORTH IT!
BUT DON'T BE ANGRY, IT WASN'T INTENTIONAL. SPUR OF THE MOMENT IMPULSE, I COULDN'T HELP MYSELF. HONEST!

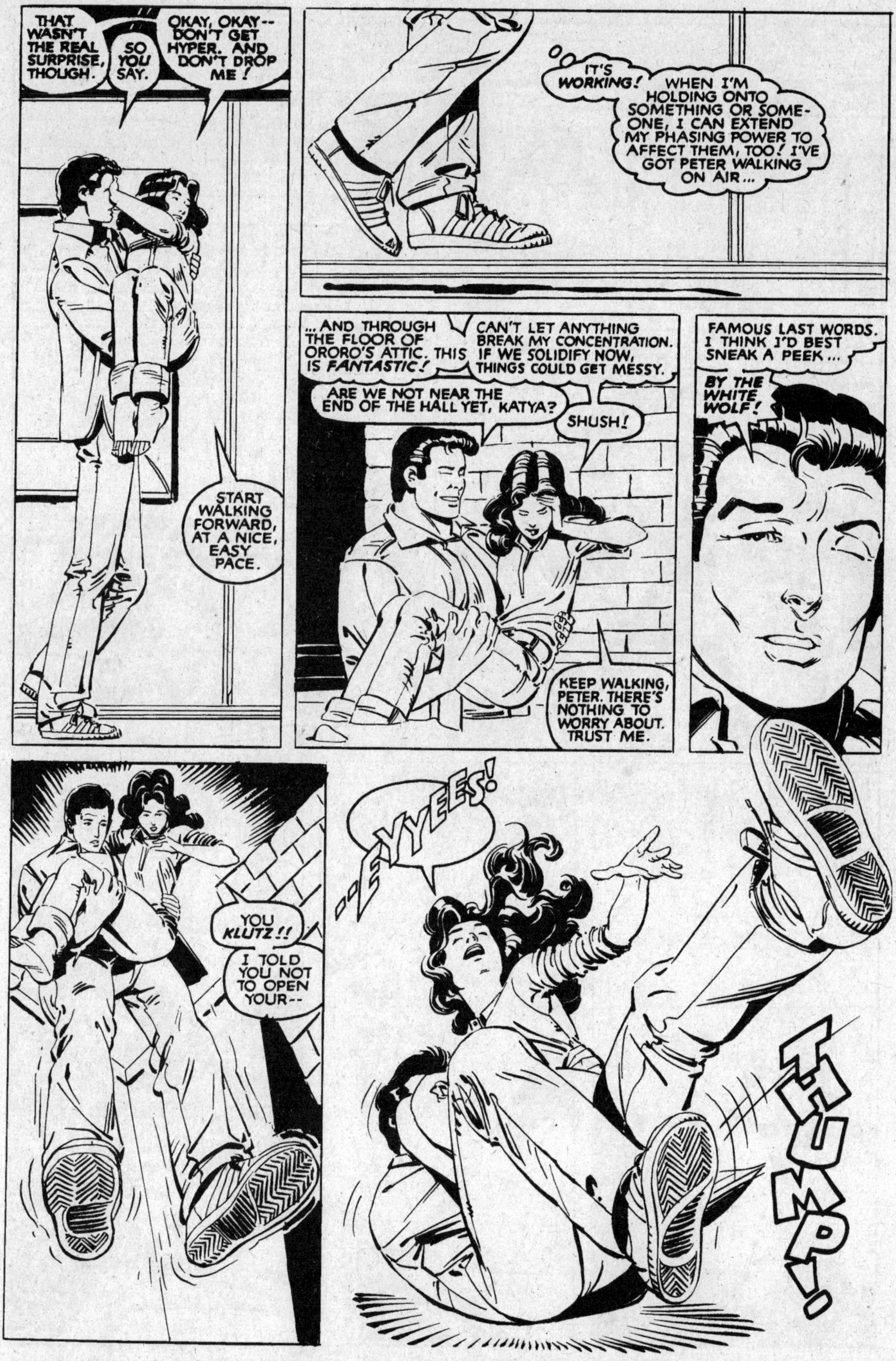
THAT WASN'T THE REAL SURPRISE, THOUGH.
SO YOU SAY.
OKAY, OKAY-- DON'T GET HYPER. AND DON'T DROP ME!
START WALKING FORWARD, AT A NICE, EASY PACE.
IT'S WORKING! WHEN I'M HOLDING ONTO SOMETHING OR SOMEONE, I CAN EXTEND MY PHASING POWER TO AFFECT THEM, TOO! I'VE GOT PETER WALKING ON AIR...
...AND THROUGH THE FLOOR OF ORORO'S ATTIC. THIS IS FANTASTIC!
CAN'T LET ANYTHING BREAK MY CONCENTRATION. IF WE SOLIDIFY NOW, THINGS COULD GET MESSY.
ARE WE NOT NEAR THE END OF THE HALL YET, KATYA?
SHUSH!
KEEP WALKING, PETER. THERE'S NOTHING TO WORRY ABOUT. TRUST ME.
FAMOUS LAST WORDS. I THINK I'D BEST SNEAK A PEEK...
BY THE WHITE WOLF!
YOU KLUTZ!! I TOLD YOU NOT TO OPEN YOUR--
--EYYEES!
THUMP!

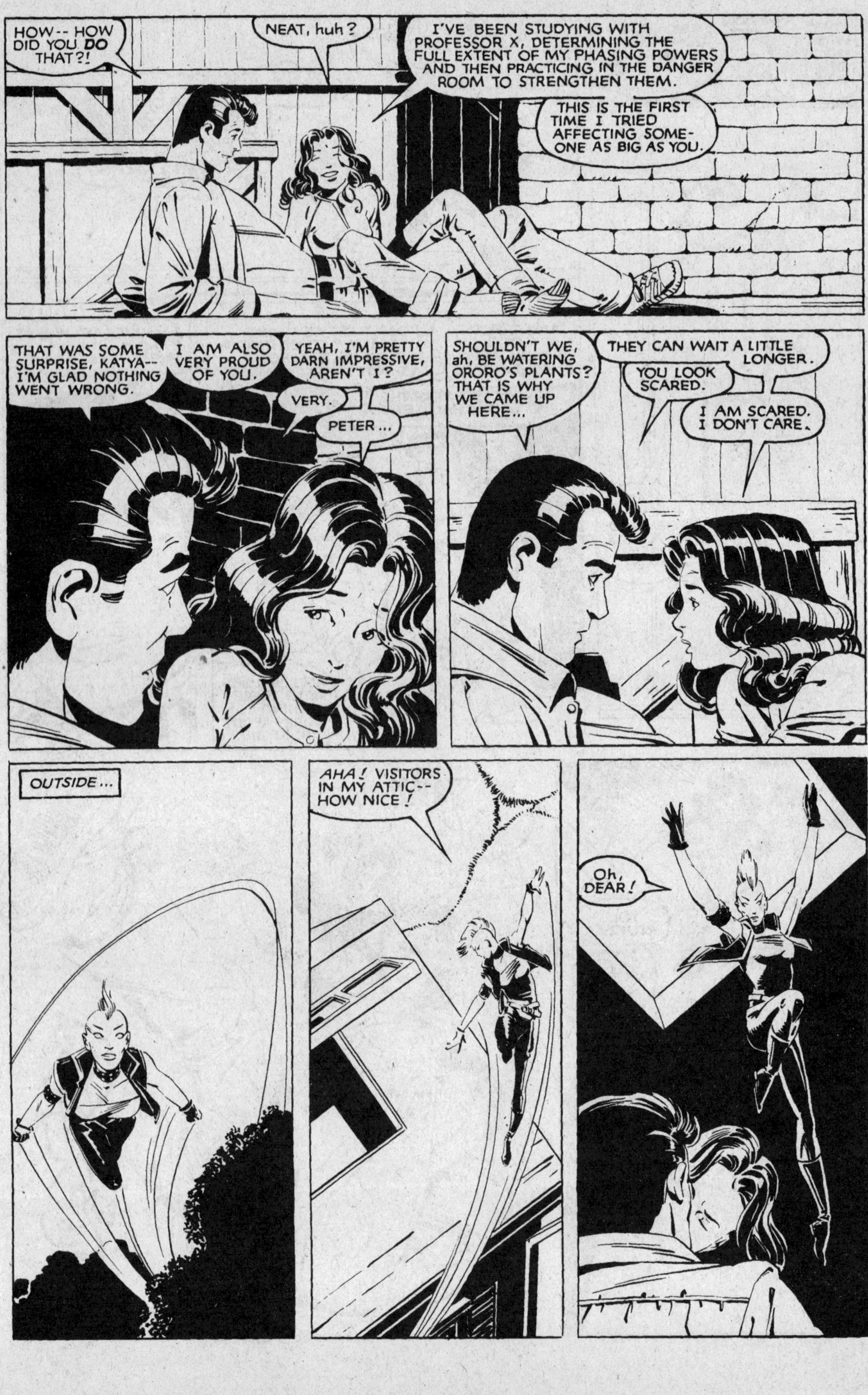

HOW-- HOW DID YOU DO THAT?!
NEAT, huh?
I'VE BEEN STUDYING WITH PROFESSOR X, DETERMINING THE FULL EXTENT OF MY PHASING POWERS AND THEN PRACTICING IN THE DANGER ROOM TO STRENGTHEN THEM.
THIS IS THE FIRST TIME I TRIED AFFECTING SOME-ONE AS BIG AS YOU.
THAT WAS SOME SURPRISE, KATYA-- I'M GLAD NOTHING WENT WRONG.
I AM ALSO VERY PROUD OF YOU.
YEAH, I'M PRETTY DARN IMPRESSIVE, AREN'T I?
VERY.
PETER...
SHOULDN'T WE, ah, BE WATERING ORORO'S PLANTS? THAT IS WHY WE CAME UP HERE...
THEY CAN WAIT A LITTLE LONGER.
YOU LOOK SCARED.
I AM SCARED. I DON'T CARE.
OUTSIDE...
AHA! VISITORS IN MY ATTIC-- HOW NICE!
Oh, DEAR!

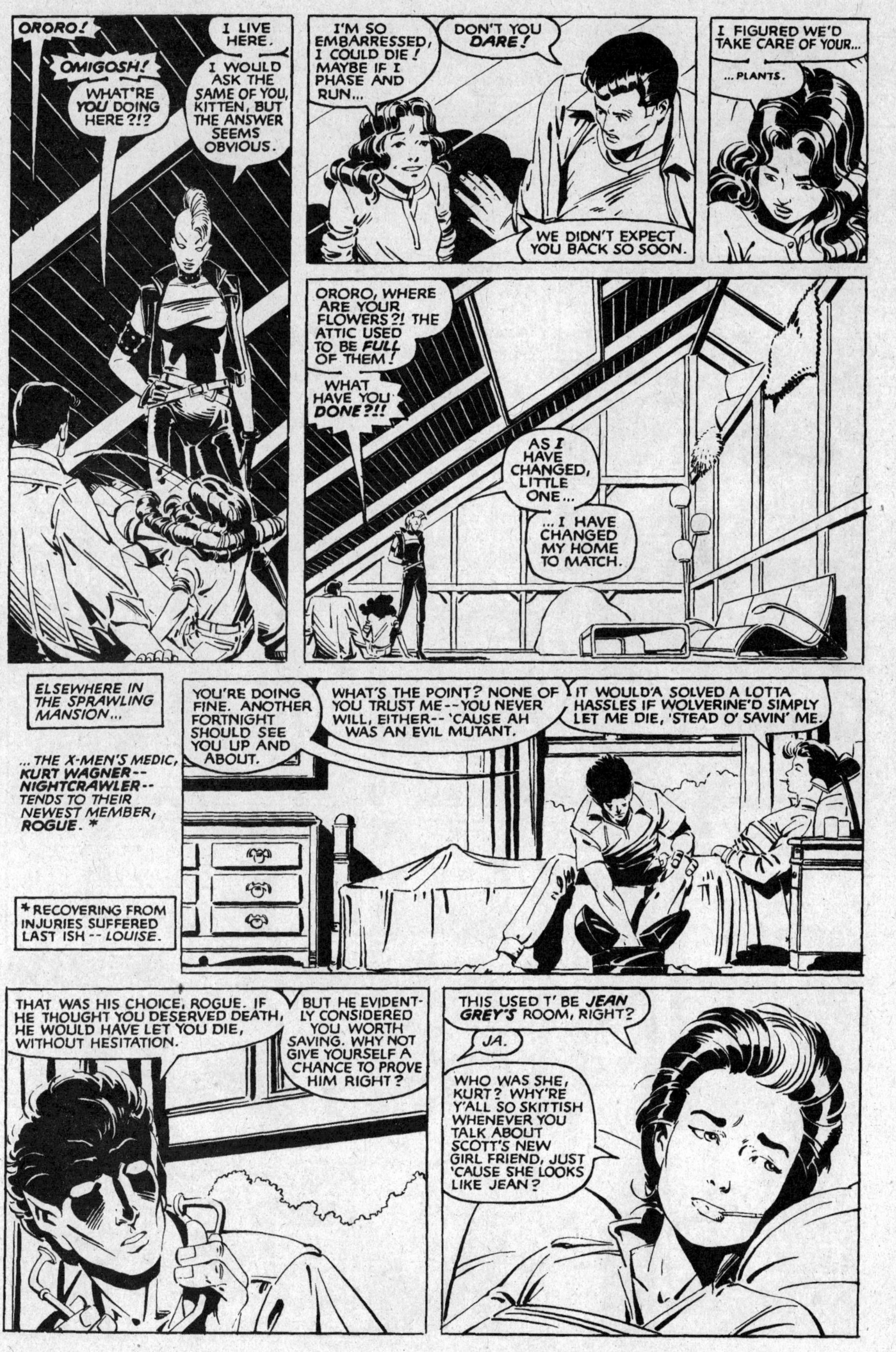

ORORO!
OMIGOSH!
WHAT'RE YOU DOING HERE?!?
I LIVE HERE.
I WOULD ASK THE SAME OF YOU, KITTEN, BUT THE ANSWER SEEMS OBVIOUS.
I'M SO EMBARRESSED, I COULD DIE! MAYBE IF I PHASE AND RUN...
DON'T YOU DARE!
WE DIDN'T EXPECT YOU BACK SO SOON.
I FIGURED WE'D TAKE CARE OF YOUR...
...PLANTS.
ORORO, WHERE ARE YOUR FLOWERS?! THE ATTIC USED TO BE FULL OF THEM!
WHAT HAVE YOU DONE?!!
AS I HAVE CHANGED, LITTLE ONE...
...I HAVE CHANGED MY HOME TO MATCH.
ELSEWHERE IN THE SPRAWLING MANSION...
...THE X-MEN'S MEDIC, KURT WAGNER--NIGHTCRAWLER--TENDS TO THEIR NEWEST MEMBER, ROGUE.*
*RECOVERING FROM INJURIES SUFFERED LAST ISH--LOUISE.
YOU'RE DOING FINE. ANOTHER FORTNIGHT SHOULD SEE YOU UP AND ABOUT.
WHAT'S THE POINT? NONE OF YOU TRUST ME--YOU NEVER WILL, EITHER--'CAUSE AH WAS AN EVIL MUTANT.
IT WOULD'A SOLVED A LOTTA HASSLES IF WOLVERINE'D SIMPLY LET ME DIE, 'STEAD O' SAVIN' ME.
THAT WAS HIS CHOICE, ROGUE. IF HE THOUGHT YOU DESERVED DEATH, HE WOULD HAVE LET YOU DIE, WITHOUT HESITATION.
BUT HE EVIDENTLY CONSIDERED YOU WORTH SAVING. WHY NOT GIVE YOURSELF A CHANCE TO PROVE HIM RIGHT?
THIS USED T' BE JEAN GREY'S ROOM, RIGHT?
JA.
WHO WAS SHE, KURT? WHY'RE Y'ALL SO SKITTISH WHENEVER YOU TALK ABOUT SCOTT'S NEW GIRL FRIEND, JUST 'CAUSE SHE LOOKS LIKE JEAN?

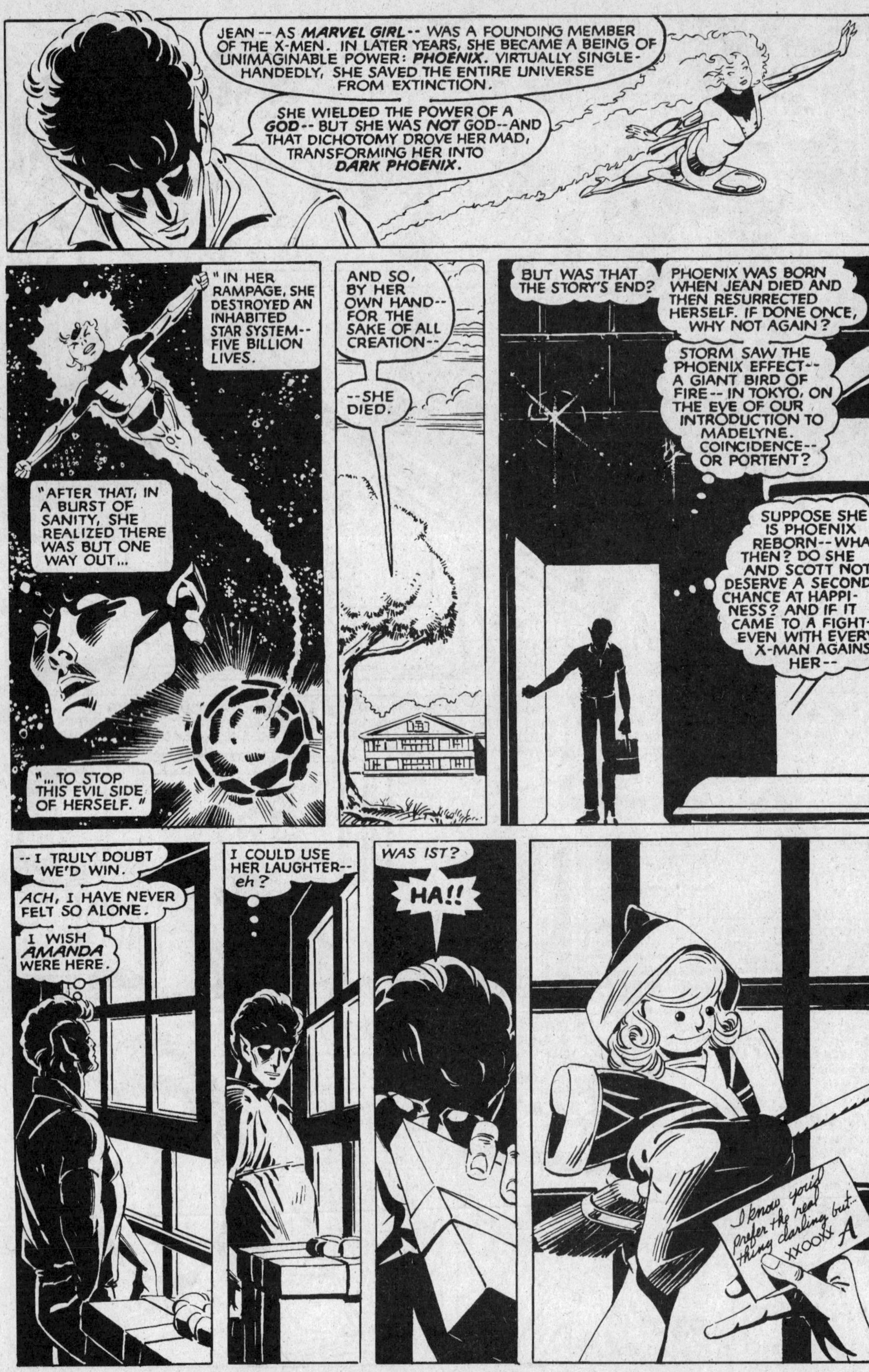
JEAN -- AS MARVEL GIRL -- WAS A FOUNDING MEMBER OF THE X-MEN. IN LATER YEARS, SHE BECAME A BEING OF UNIMAGINABLE POWER: PHOENIX. VIRTUALLY SINGLE-HANDEDLY, SHE SAVED THE ENTIRE UNIVERSE FROM EXTINCTION.
SHE WIELDED THE POWER OF A GOD -- BUT SHE WAS NOT GOD -- AND THAT DICHOTOMY DROVE HER MAD, TRANSFORMING HER INTO DARK PHOENIX.
"IN HER RAMPAGE, SHE DESTROYED AN INHABITED STAR SYSTEM -- FIVE BILLION LIVES.
"AFTER THAT, IN A BURST OF SANITY, SHE REALIZED THERE WAS BUT ONE WAY OUT...
"...TO STOP THIS EVIL SIDE OF HERSELF."
AND SO, BY HER OWN HAND -- FOR THE SAKE OF ALL CREATION --
-- SHE DIED.
BUT WAS THAT THE STORY'S END?
PHOENIX WAS BORN WHEN JEAN DIED AND THEN RESURRECTED HERSELF. IF DONE ONCE, WHY NOT AGAIN?
STORM SAW THE PHOENIX EFFECT -- A GIANT BIRD OF FIRE -- IN TOKYO, ON THE EVE OF OUR INTRODUCTION TO MADELYNE. COINCIDENCE -- OR PORTENT?
SUPPOSE SHE IS PHOENIX REBORN -- WHAT THEN? DO SHE AND SCOTT NOT DESERVE A SECOND CHANCE AT HAPPINESS? AND IF IT CAME TO A FIGHT -- EVEN WITH EVERY X-MAN AGAINST HER --
-- I TRULY DOUBT WE'D WIN.
ACH, I HAVE NEVER FELT SO ALONE.
I WISH AMANDA WERE HERE.
I COULD USE HER LAUGHTER -- eh?
WAS IST?
HA!!
I know you'd prefer the real thing darling but...
XXOOXX A

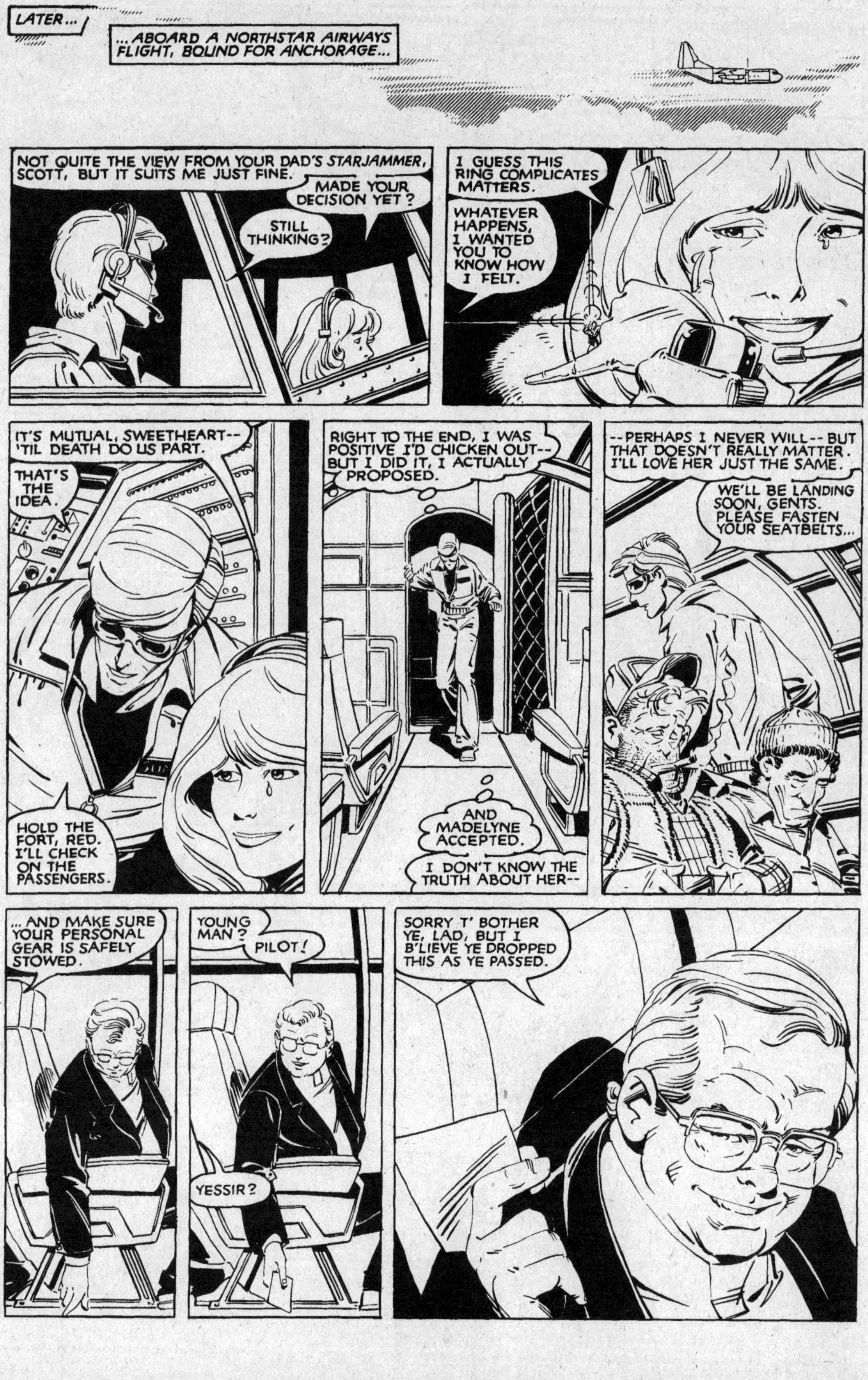
LATER...
...ABOARD A NORTHSTAR AIRWAYS FLIGHT, BOUND FOR ANCHORAGE...
NOT QUITE THE VIEW FROM YOUR DAD'S STARJAMMER, SCOTT, BUT IT SUITS ME JUST FINE.
MADE YOUR DECISION YET?
STILL THINKING?
I GUESS THIS RING COMPLICATES MATTERS.
WHATEVER HAPPENS, I WANTED YOU TO KNOW HOW I FELT.
IT'S MUTUAL, SWEETHEART-- 'TIL DEATH DO US PART.
THAT'S THE IDEA.
HOLD THE FORT, RED. I'LL CHECK ON THE PASSENGERS.
RIGHT TO THE END, I WAS POSITIVE I'D CHICKEN OUT-- BUT I DID IT, I ACTUALLY PROPOSED.
AND MADELYNE ACCEPTED.
I DON'T KNOW THE TRUTH ABOUT HER--
--PERHAPS I NEVER WILL-- BUT THAT DOESN'T REALLY MATTER. I'LL LOVE HER JUST THE SAME.
WE'LL BE LANDING SOON, GENTS. PLEASE FASTEN YOUR SEATBELTS...
...AND MAKE SURE YOUR PERSONAL GEAR IS SAFELY STOWED.
YOUNG MAN?
PILOT!
YESSIR?
SORRY T' BOTHER YE, LAD, BUT I B'LIEVE YE DROPPED THIS AS YE PASSED.

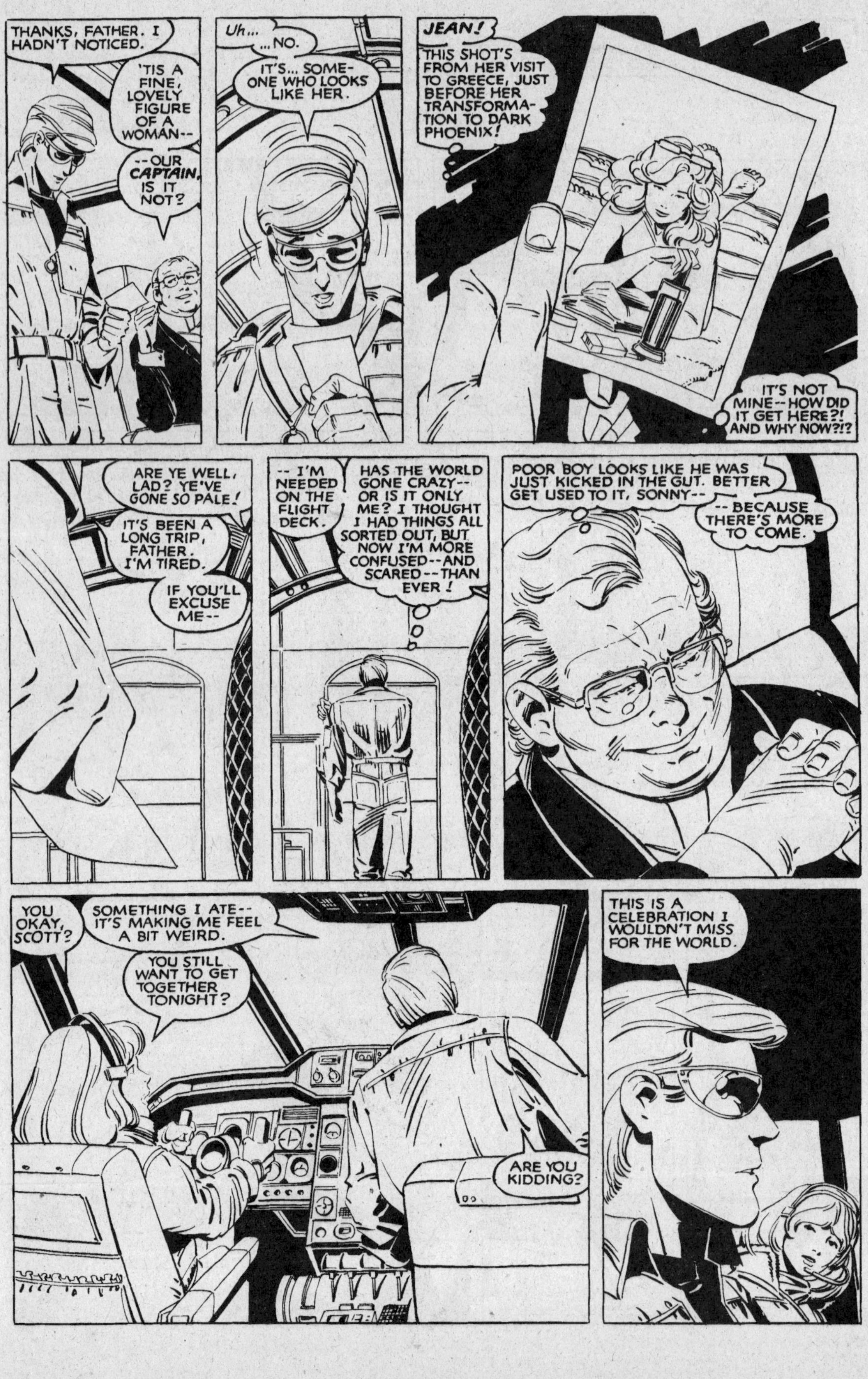
THANKS, FATHER. I HADN'T NOTICED.
'TIS A FINE, LOVELY FIGURE OF A WOMAN--
--OUR CAPTAIN, IS IT NOT?
Uh...
...NO.
IT'S... SOME-ONE WHO LOOKS LIKE HER.
JEAN!
THIS SHOT'S FROM HER VISIT TO GREECE, JUST BEFORE HER TRANSFORMA-TION TO DARK PHOENIX!
IT'S NOT MINE--HOW DID IT GET HERE?! AND WHY NOW?!?
ARE YE WELL, LAD? YE'VE GONE SO PALE!
IT'S BEEN A LONG TRIP, FATHER. I'M TIRED.
IF YOU'LL EXCUSE ME--
--I'M NEEDED ON THE FLIGHT DECK.
HAS THE WORLD GONE CRAZY--OR IS IT ONLY ME? I THOUGHT I HAD THINGS ALL SORTED OUT, BUT NOW I'M MORE CONFUSED--AND SCARED--THAN EVER!
POOR BOY LOOKS LIKE HE WAS JUST KICKED IN THE GUT. BETTER GET USED TO IT, SONNY--
--BECAUSE THERE'S MORE TO COME.
YOU OKAY, SCOTT?
SOMETHING I ATE--IT'S MAKING ME FEEL A BIT WEIRD.
YOU STILL WANT TO GET TOGETHER TONIGHT?
ARE YOU KIDDING?
THIS IS A CELEBRATION I WOULDN'T MISS FOR THE WORLD.

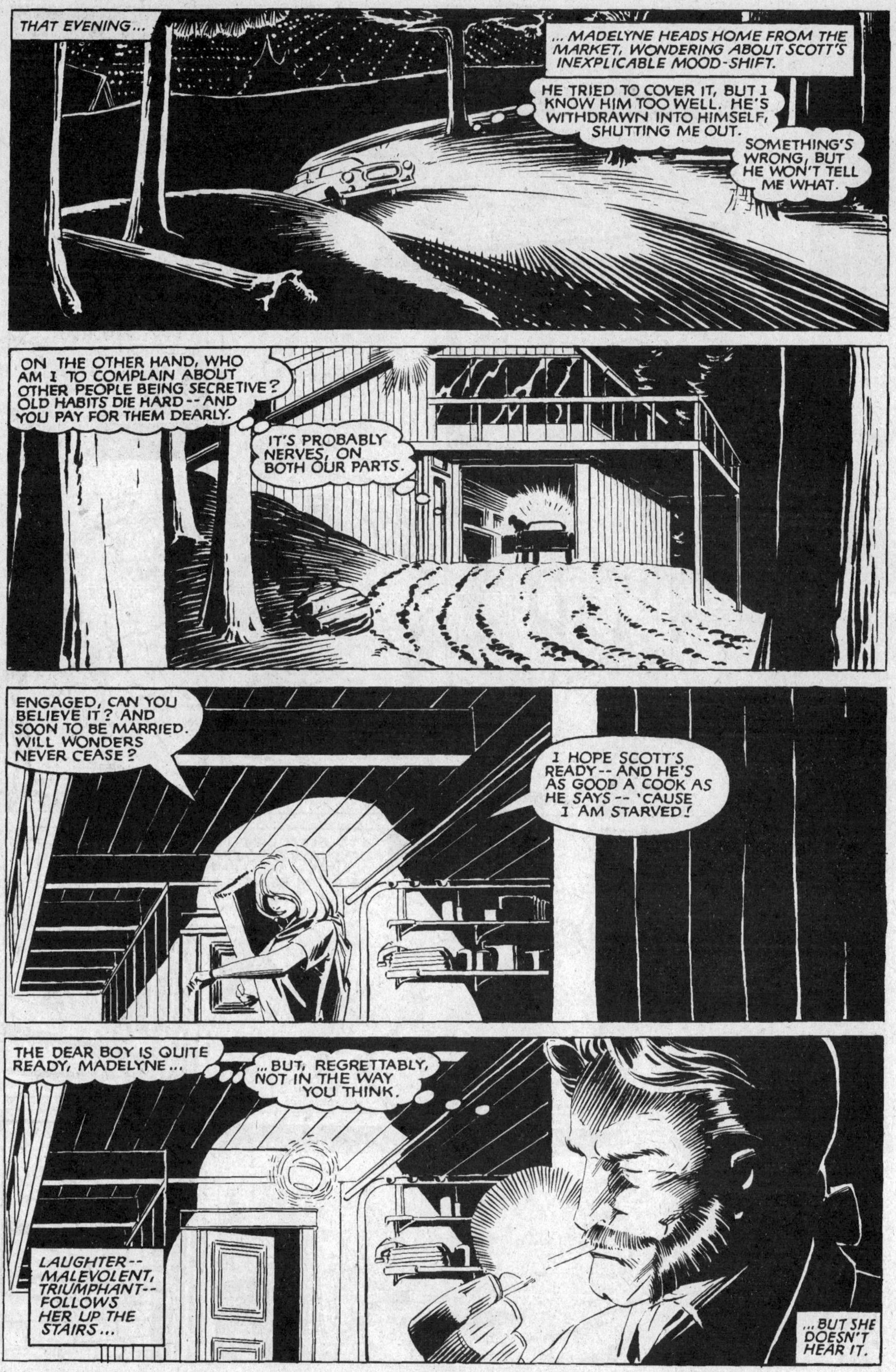
THAT EVENING...
...MADELYNE HEADS HOME FROM THE MARKET, WONDERING ABOUT SCOTT'S INEXPLICABLE MOOD-SHIFT.
HE TRIED TO COVER IT, BUT I KNOW HIM TOO WELL. HE'S WITHDRAWN INTO HIMSELF, SHUTTING ME OUT.
SOMETHING'S WRONG, BUT HE WON'T TELL ME WHAT.
ON THE OTHER HAND, WHO AM I TO COMPLAIN ABOUT OTHER PEOPLE BEING SECRETIVE? OLD HABITS DIE HARD-- AND YOU PAY FOR THEM DEARLY.
IT'S PROBABLY NERVES, ON BOTH OUR PARTS.
ENGAGED, CAN YOU BELIEVE IT? AND SOON TO BE MARRIED. WILL WONDERS NEVER CEASE?
I HOPE SCOTT'S READY-- AND HE'S AS GOOD A COOK AS HE SAYS-- 'CAUSE I AM STARVED!
THE DEAR BOY IS QUITE READY, MADELYNE...
...BUT, REGRETTABLY, NOT IN THE WAY YOU THINK.
LAUGHTER-- MALEVOLENT, TRIUMPHANT-- FOLLOWS HER UP THE STAIRS...
...BUT SHE DOESN'T HEAR IT.

I'M HOME, SWEETHEART!

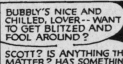

BUBBLY'S NICE AND CHILLED, LOVER-- WANT TO GET BLITZED AND FOOL AROUND?

SCOTT? IS ANYTHING THE MATTER? HAS SOMETHING HAPPENED TO YOUR DAD OR THE X-MEN?!

NO, NOTHING LIKE THAT.

I'VE BEEN THINKING.

I NEED AN ANSWER TO A VERY IMPORTANT QUESTION.

WE PLAYED THIS SCENE THIS MORNING, REMEMBER?

I SAID, YES.

MADELYNE, I'M SERIOUS!

I'VE BEEN WRESTLING WITH THIS ALL DAY, TRYING TO EXPLAIN AWAY MY DOUBTS-- AND FEARS-- TELLING MY-SELF I'M BEING A FOOL, BUT IT'S NO GOOD. I CAN'T. I HAVE TO KNOW.

ARE YOU THE *REINCARNATION* OF JEAN GREY?

ARE YOU *PHOENIX*?

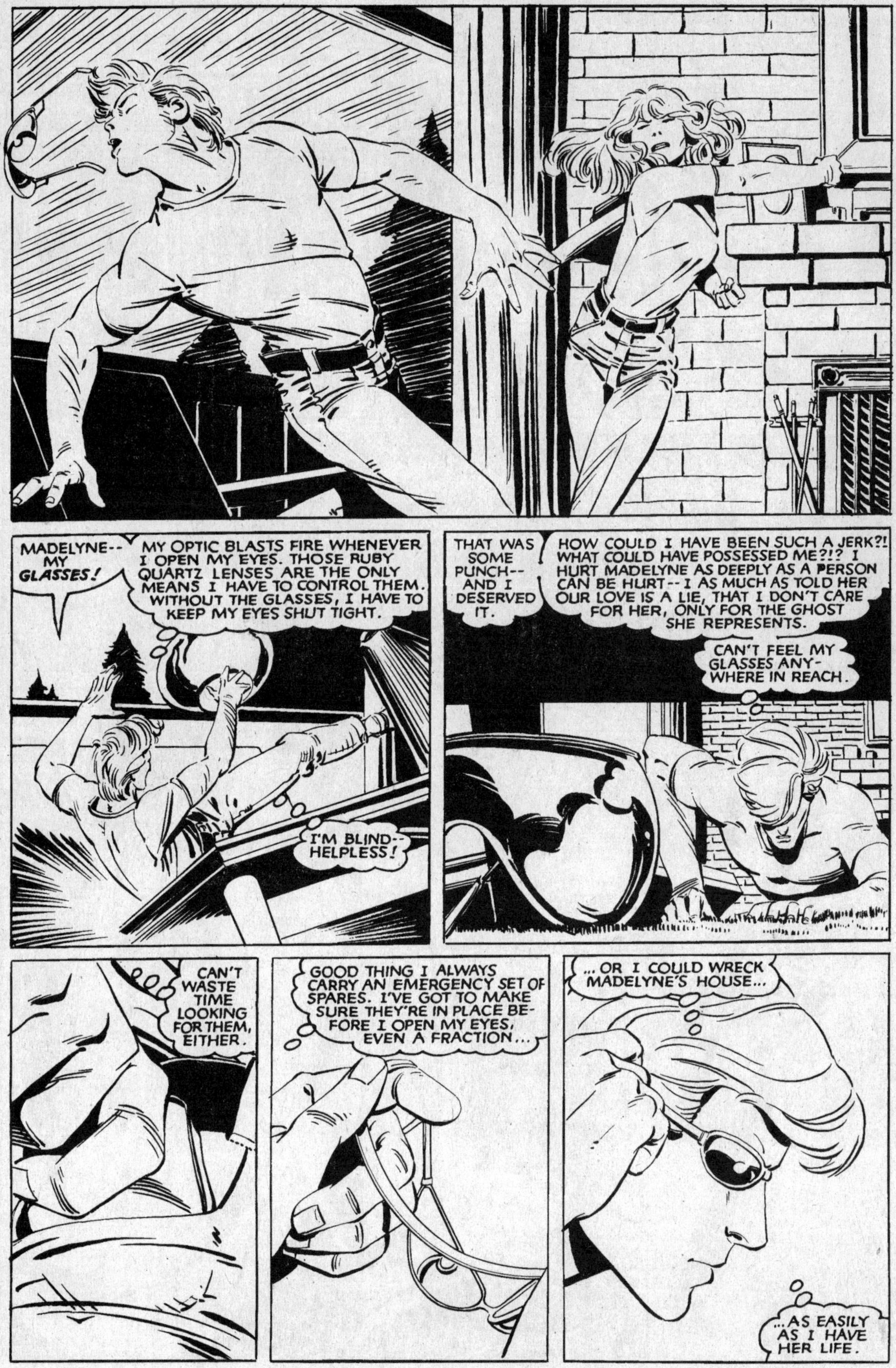

MADELYNE-- MY GLASSES!
MY OPTIC BLASTS FIRE WHENEVER I OPEN MY EYES. THOSE RUBY QUARTZ LENSES ARE THE ONLY MEANS I HAVE TO CONTROL THEM. WITHOUT THE GLASSES, I HAVE TO KEEP MY EYES SHUT TIGHT.
I'M BLIND-- HELPLESS!
THAT WAS SOME PUNCH-- AND I DESERVED IT.
HOW COULD I HAVE BEEN SUCH A JERK?! WHAT COULD HAVE POSSESSED ME?!? I HURT MADELYNE AS DEEPLY AS A PERSON CAN BE HURT-- I AS MUCH AS TOLD HER OUR LOVE IS A LIE, THAT I DON'T CARE FOR HER, ONLY FOR THE GHOST SHE REPRESENTS.
CAN'T FEEL MY GLASSES ANY-WHERE IN REACH.
CAN'T WASTE TIME LOOKING FOR THEM, EITHER.
GOOD THING I ALWAYS CARRY AN EMERGENCY SET OF SPARES. I'VE GOT TO MAKE SURE THEY'RE IN PLACE BE-FORE I OPEN MY EYES, EVEN A FRACTION...
...OR I COULD WRECK MADELYNE'S HOUSE...
...AS EASILY AS I HAVE HER LIFE.

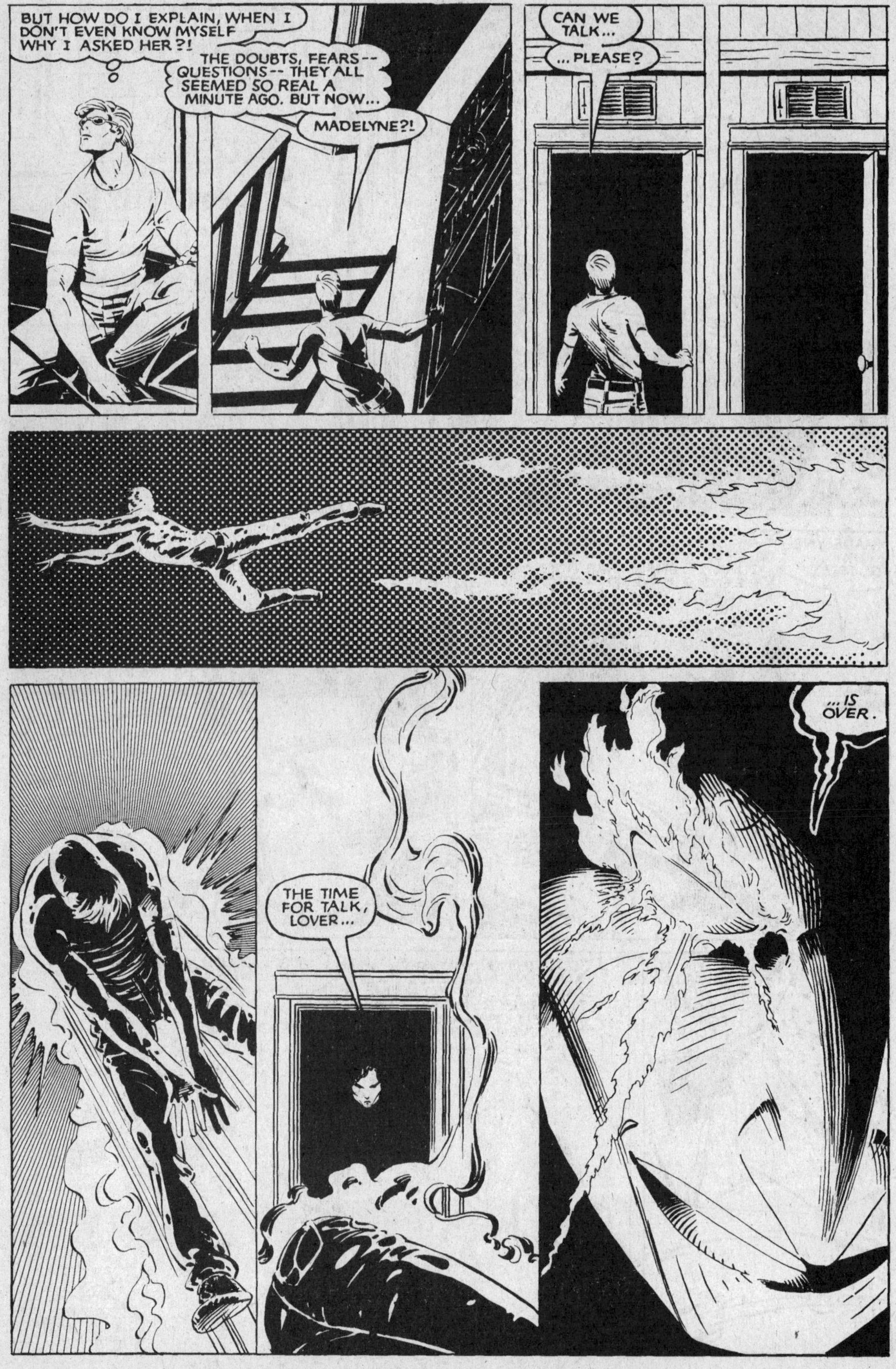
BUT HOW DO I EXPLAIN, WHEN I DON'T EVEN KNOW MYSELF WHY I ASKED HER?!
THE DOUBTS, FEARS-- QUESTIONS-- THEY ALL SEEMED SO REAL A MINUTE AGO. BUT NOW...
MADELYNE?!
CAN WE TALK...
...PLEASE?
THE TIME FOR TALK, LOVER...
...IS OVER.

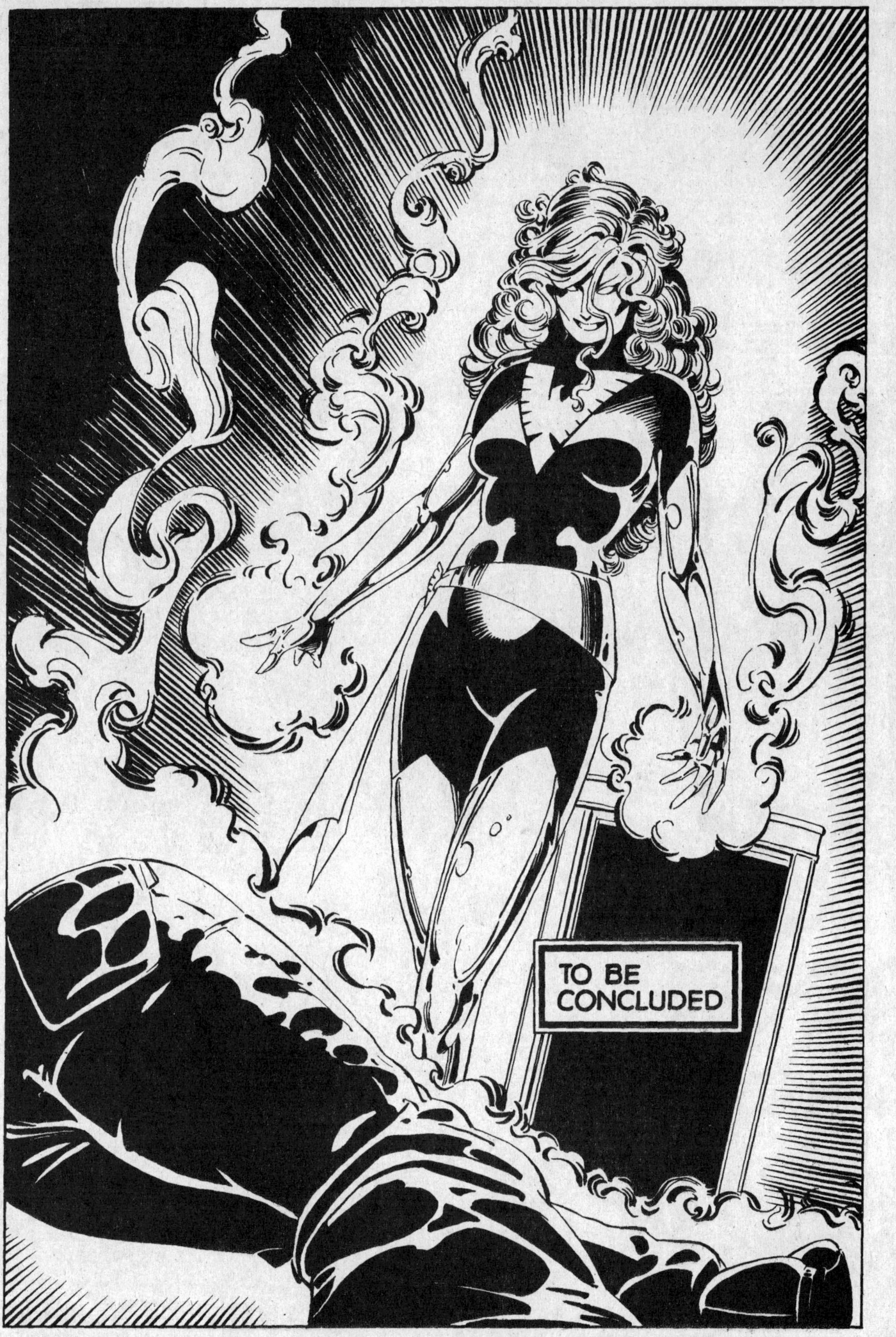
TO BE CONCLUDED

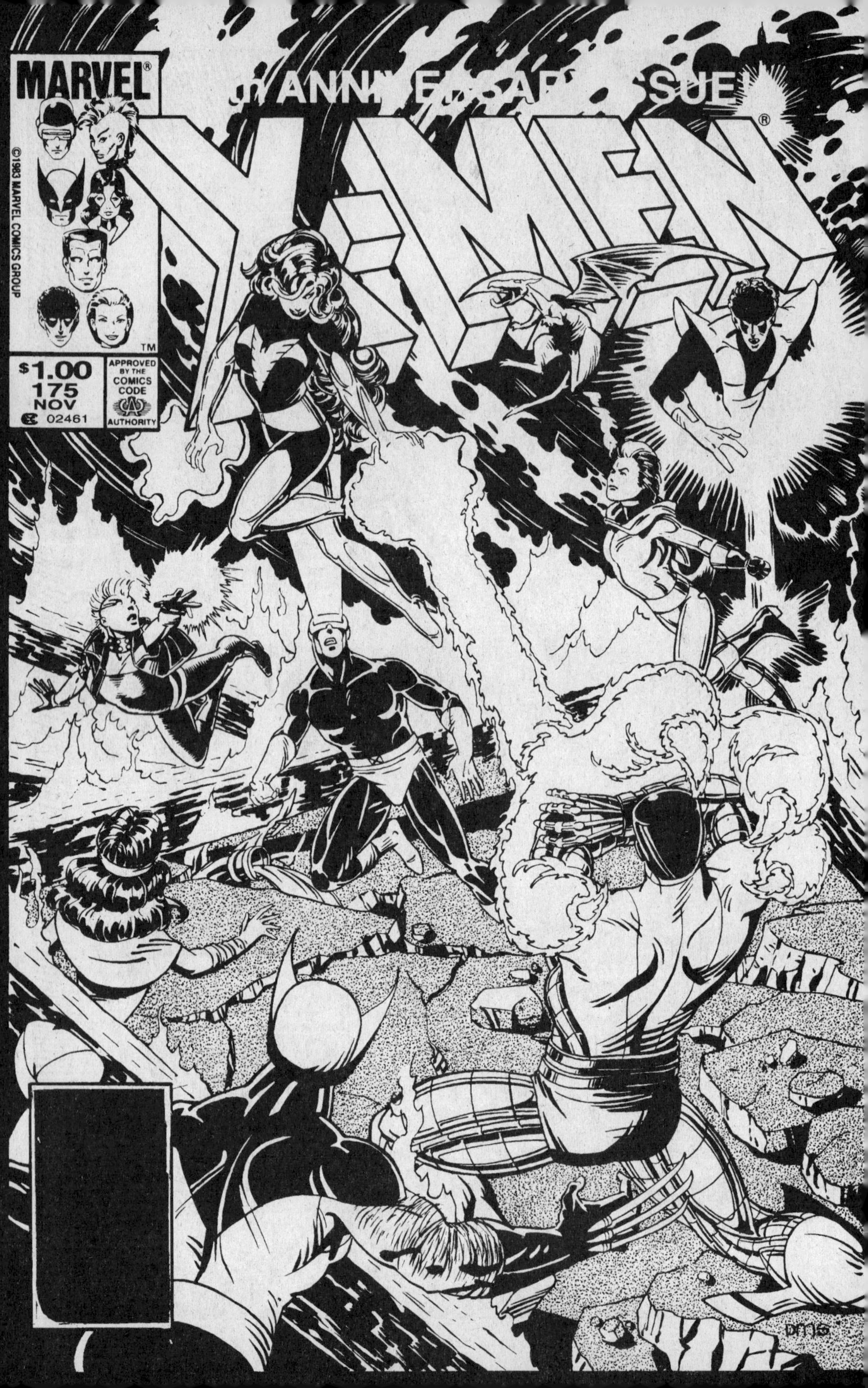
MARVEL®
X-MEN®
©1983 MARVEL COMICS GROUP
TM
$1.00
175
NOV
02461
APPROVED BY THE COMICS CODE AUTHORITY

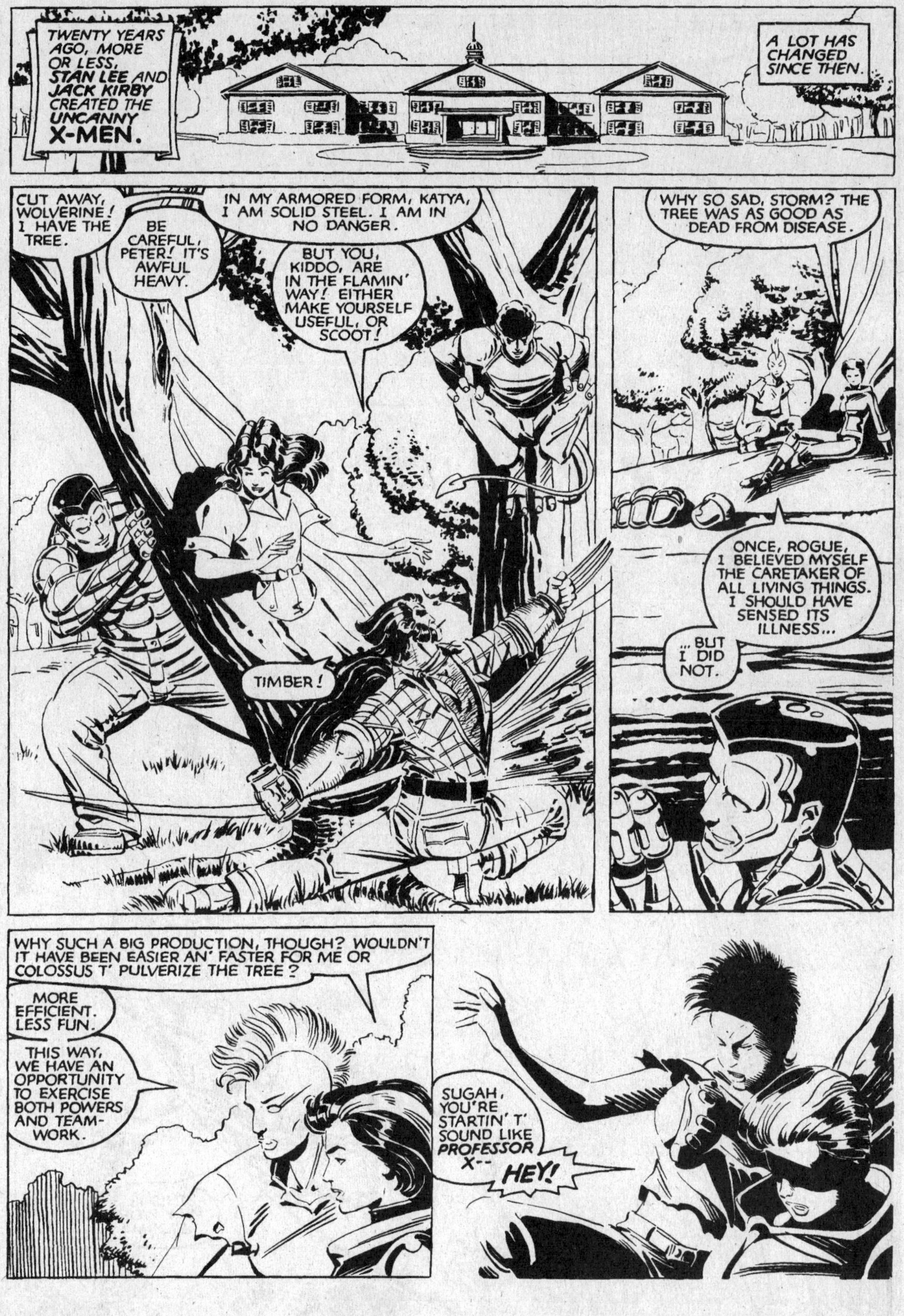
TWENTY YEARS AGO, MORE OR LESS, STAN LEE AND JACK KIRBY CREATED THE UNCANNY X-MEN.
A LOT HAS CHANGED SINCE THEN.
CUT AWAY, WOLVERINE! I HAVE THE TREE.
BE CAREFUL, PETER! IT'S AWFUL HEAVY.
IN MY ARMORED FORM, KATYA, I AM SOLID STEEL. I AM IN NO DANGER.
BUT YOU, KIDDO, ARE IN THE FLAMIN' WAY! EITHER MAKE YOURSELF USEFUL, OR SCOOT!
TIMBER!
WHY SO SAD, STORM? THE TREE WAS AS GOOD AS DEAD FROM DISEASE.
ONCE, ROGUE, I BELIEVED MYSELF THE CARETAKER OF ALL LIVING THINGS. I SHOULD HAVE SENSED ITS ILLNESS...
...BUT I DID NOT.
WHY SUCH A BIG PRODUCTION, THOUGH? WOULDN'T IT HAVE BEEN EASIER AN' FASTER FOR ME OR COLOSSUS T' PULVERIZE THE TREE?
MORE EFFICIENT. LESS FUN.
THIS WAY, WE HAVE AN OPPORTUNITY TO EXERCISE BOTH POWERS AND TEAM-WORK.
SUGAH, YOU'RE STARTIN' T' SOUND LIKE PROFESSOR X--
HEY!

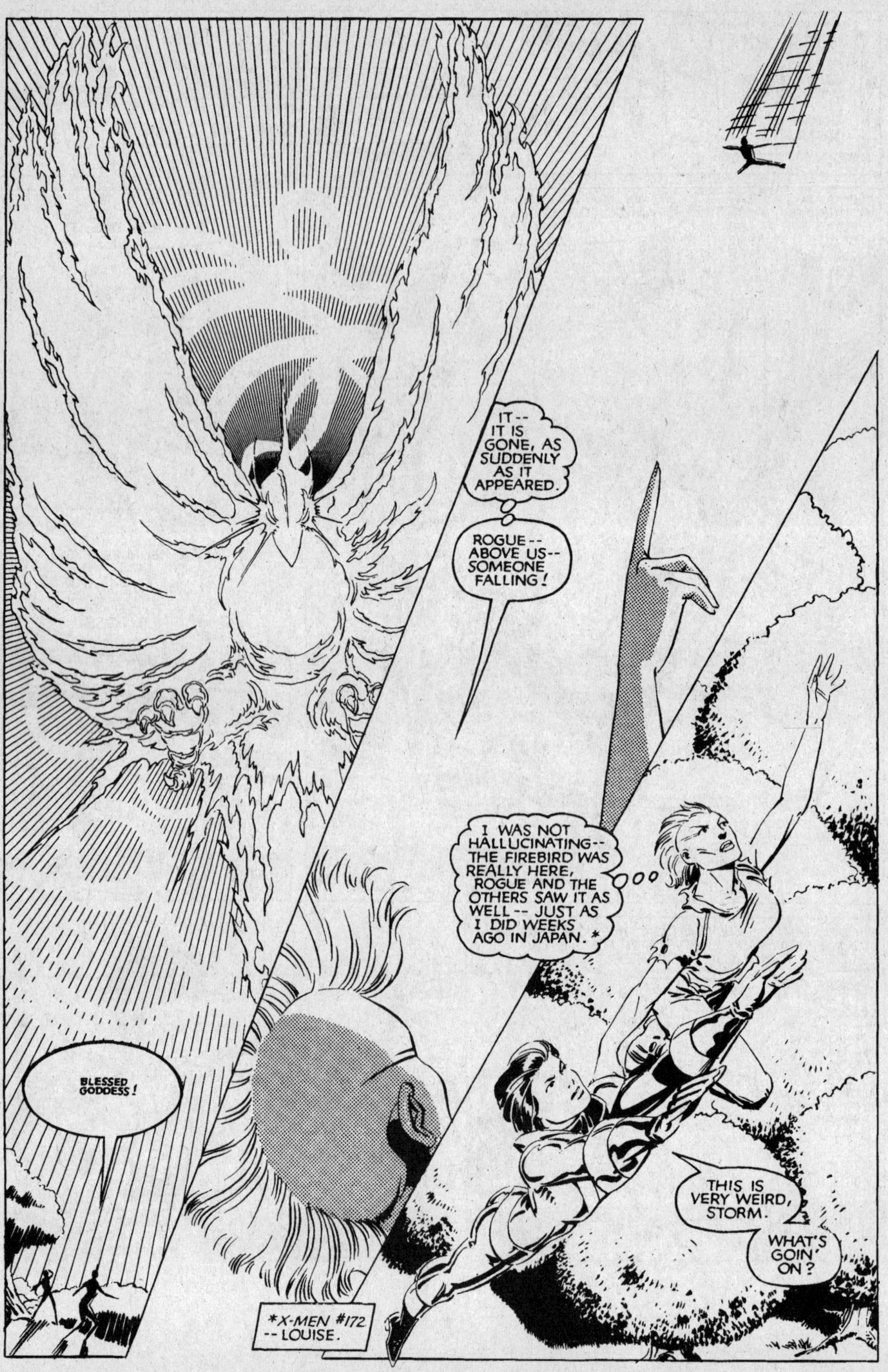
IT-- IT IS GONE, AS SUDDENLY AS IT APPEARED.
ROGUE-- ABOVE US-- SOMEONE FALLING!
BLESSED GODDESS!
I WAS NOT HALLUCINATING-- THE FIREBIRD WAS REALLY HERE, ROGUE AND THE OTHERS SAW IT AS WELL -- JUST AS I DID WEEKS AGO IN JAPAN.*
*X-MEN #172 --LOUISE.
THIS IS VERY WEIRD, STORM.
WHAT'S GOIN' ON?

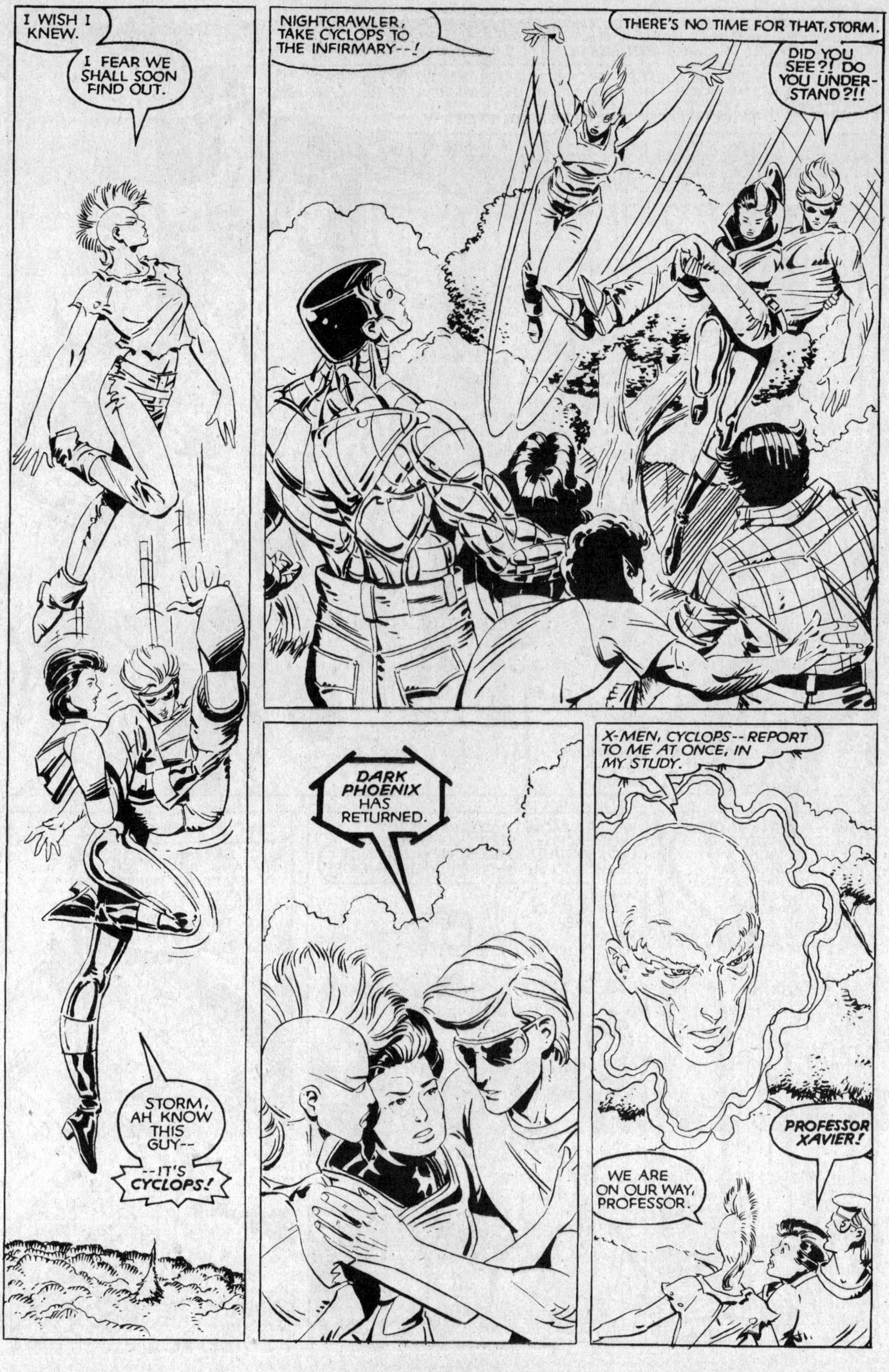
I WISH I KNEW.
I FEAR WE SHALL SOON FIND OUT.
STORM, AH KNOW THIS GUY--
--IT'S CYCLOPS!
NIGHTCRAWLER, TAKE CYCLOPS TO THE INFIRMARY--!
THERE'S NO TIME FOR THAT, STORM.
DID YOU SEE?! DO YOU UNDER-STAND?!!
DARK PHOENIX HAS RETURNED.
X-MEN, CYCLOPS--REPORT TO ME AT ONCE, IN MY STUDY.
PROFESSOR XAVIER!
WE ARE ON OUR WAY, PROFESSOR.

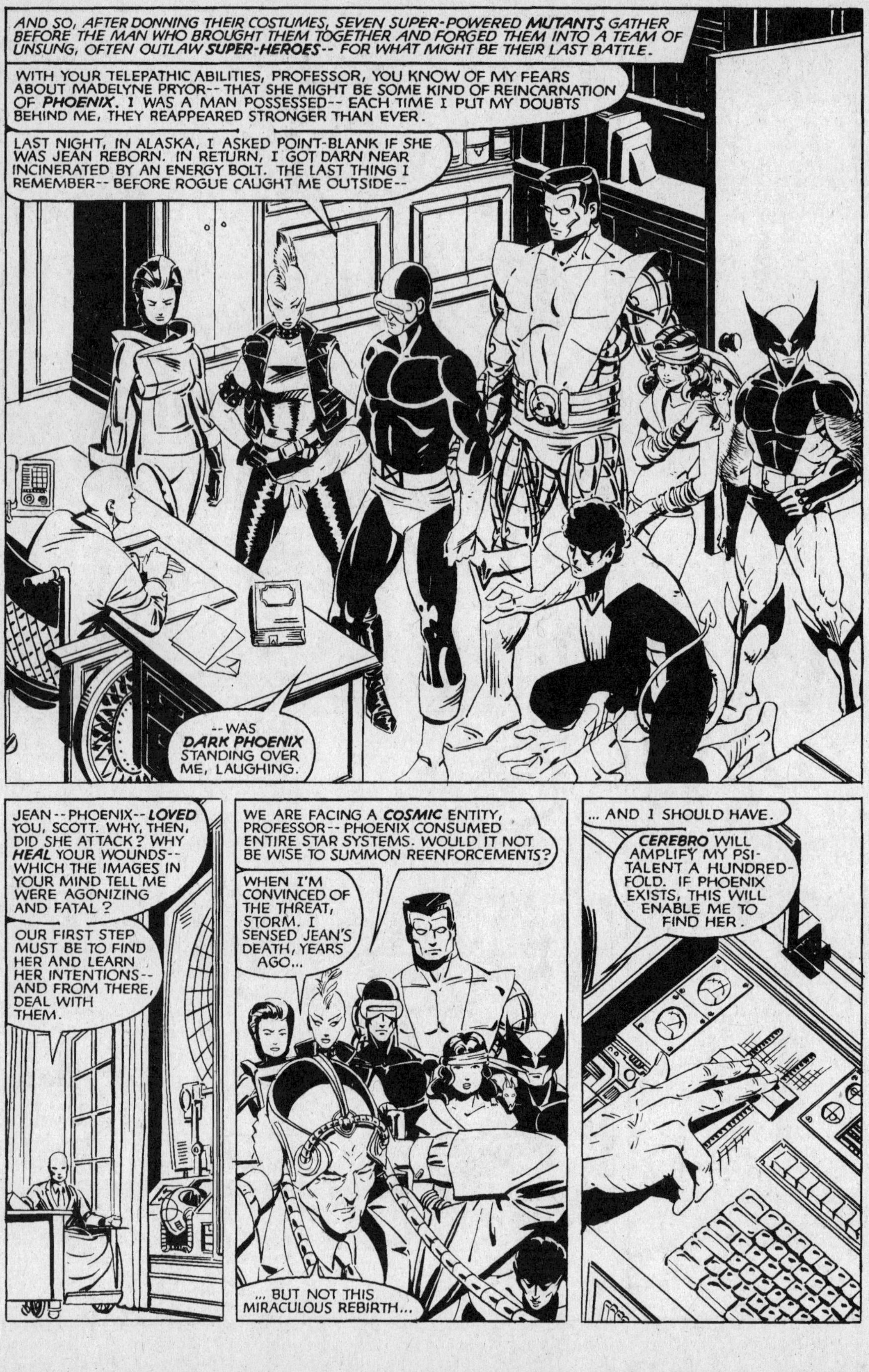
AND SO, AFTER DONNING THEIR COSTUMES, SEVEN SUPER-POWERED MUTANTS GATHER BEFORE THE MAN WHO BROUGHT THEM TOGETHER AND FORGED THEM INTO A TEAM OF UNSUNG, OFTEN OUTLAW SUPER-HEROES-- FOR WHAT MIGHT BE THEIR LAST BATTLE.
WITH YOUR TELEPATHIC ABILITIES, PROFESSOR, YOU KNOW OF MY FEARS ABOUT MADELYNE PRYOR-- THAT SHE MIGHT BE SOME KIND OF REINCARNATION OF PHOENIX. I WAS A MAN POSSESSED-- EACH TIME I PUT MY DOUBTS BEHIND ME, THEY REAPPEARED STRONGER THAN EVER.
LAST NIGHT, IN ALASKA, I ASKED POINT-BLANK IF SHE WAS JEAN REBORN. IN RETURN, I GOT DARN NEAR INCINERATED BY AN ENERGY BOLT. THE LAST THING I REMEMBER-- BEFORE ROGUE CAUGHT ME OUTSIDE--
--WAS DARK PHOENIX STANDING OVER ME, LAUGHING.
JEAN--PHOENIX--LOVED YOU, SCOTT. WHY, THEN, DID SHE ATTACK? WHY HEAL YOUR WOUNDS-- WHICH THE IMAGES IN YOUR MIND TELL ME WERE AGONIZING AND FATAL?
OUR FIRST STEP MUST BE TO FIND HER AND LEARN HER INTENTIONS-- AND FROM THERE, DEAL WITH THEM.
WE ARE FACING A COSMIC ENTITY, PROFESSOR-- PHOENIX CONSUMED ENTIRE STAR SYSTEMS. WOULD IT NOT BE WISE TO SUMMON REENFORCEMENTS?
WHEN I'M CONVINCED OF THE THREAT, STORM. I SENSED JEAN'S DEATH, YEARS AGO...
... BUT NOT THIS MIRACULOUS REBIRTH...
... AND I SHOULD HAVE.
CEREBRO WILL AMPLIFY MY PSI-TALENT A HUNDRED-FOLD. IF PHOENIX EXISTS, THIS WILL ENABLE ME TO FIND HER.

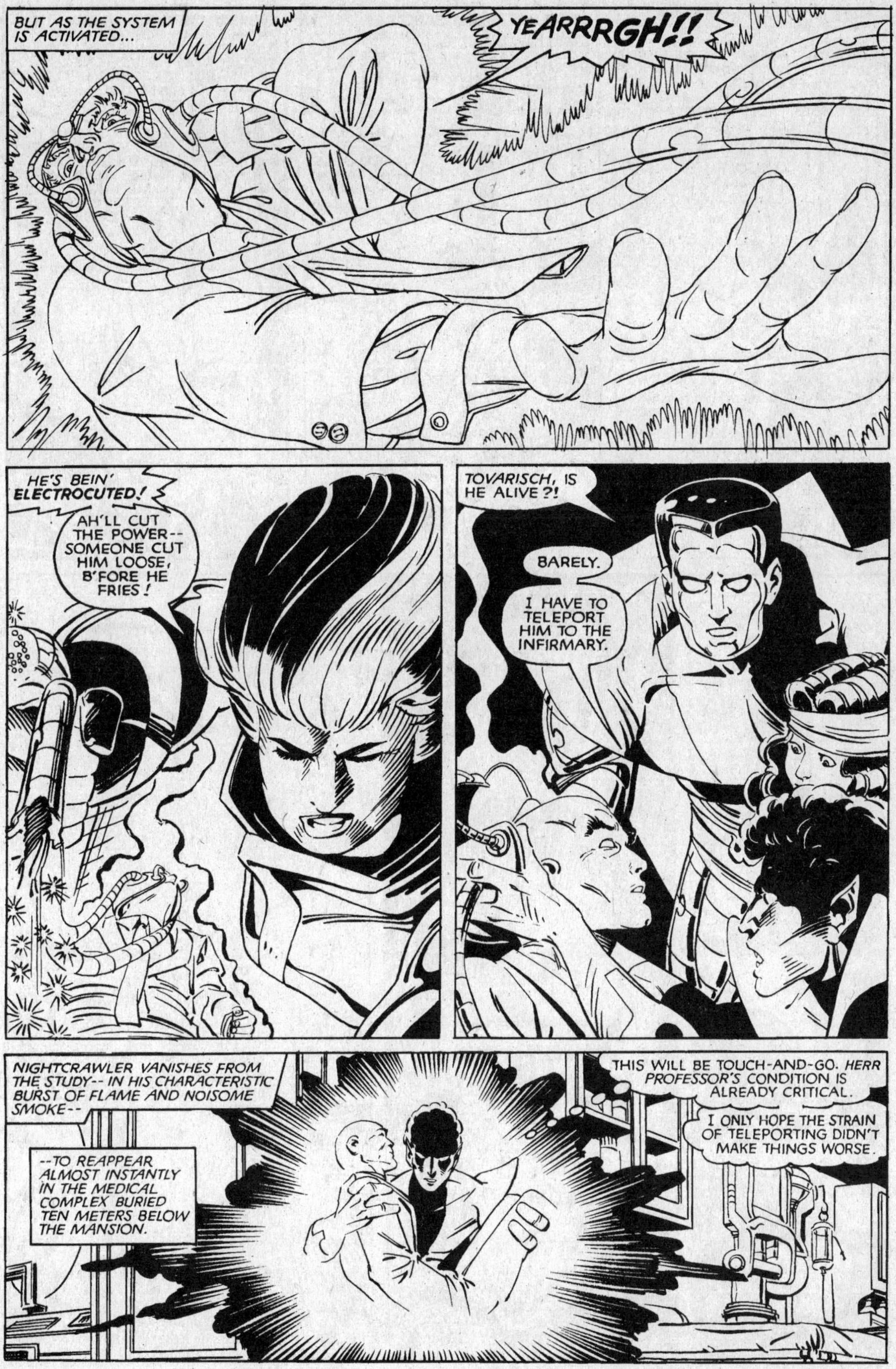
BUT AS THE SYSTEM IS ACTIVATED...
YEARRRGH!!
HE'S BEIN' ELECTROCUTED!
AH'LL CUT THE POWER-- SOMEONE CUT HIM LOOSE, B'FORE HE FRIES!
TOVARISCH, IS HE ALIVE?!
BARELY.
I HAVE TO TELEPORT HIM TO THE INFIRMARY.
NIGHTCRAWLER VANISHES FROM THE STUDY-- IN HIS CHARACTERISTIC BURST OF FLAME AND NOISOME SMOKE--
--TO REAPPEAR ALMOST INSTANTLY IN THE MEDICAL COMPLEX BURIED TEN METERS BELOW THE MANSION.
THIS WILL BE TOUCH-AND-GO. HERR PROFESSOR'S CONDITION IS ALREADY CRITICAL.
I ONLY HOPE THE STRAIN OF TELEPORTING DIDN'T MAKE THINGS WORSE.

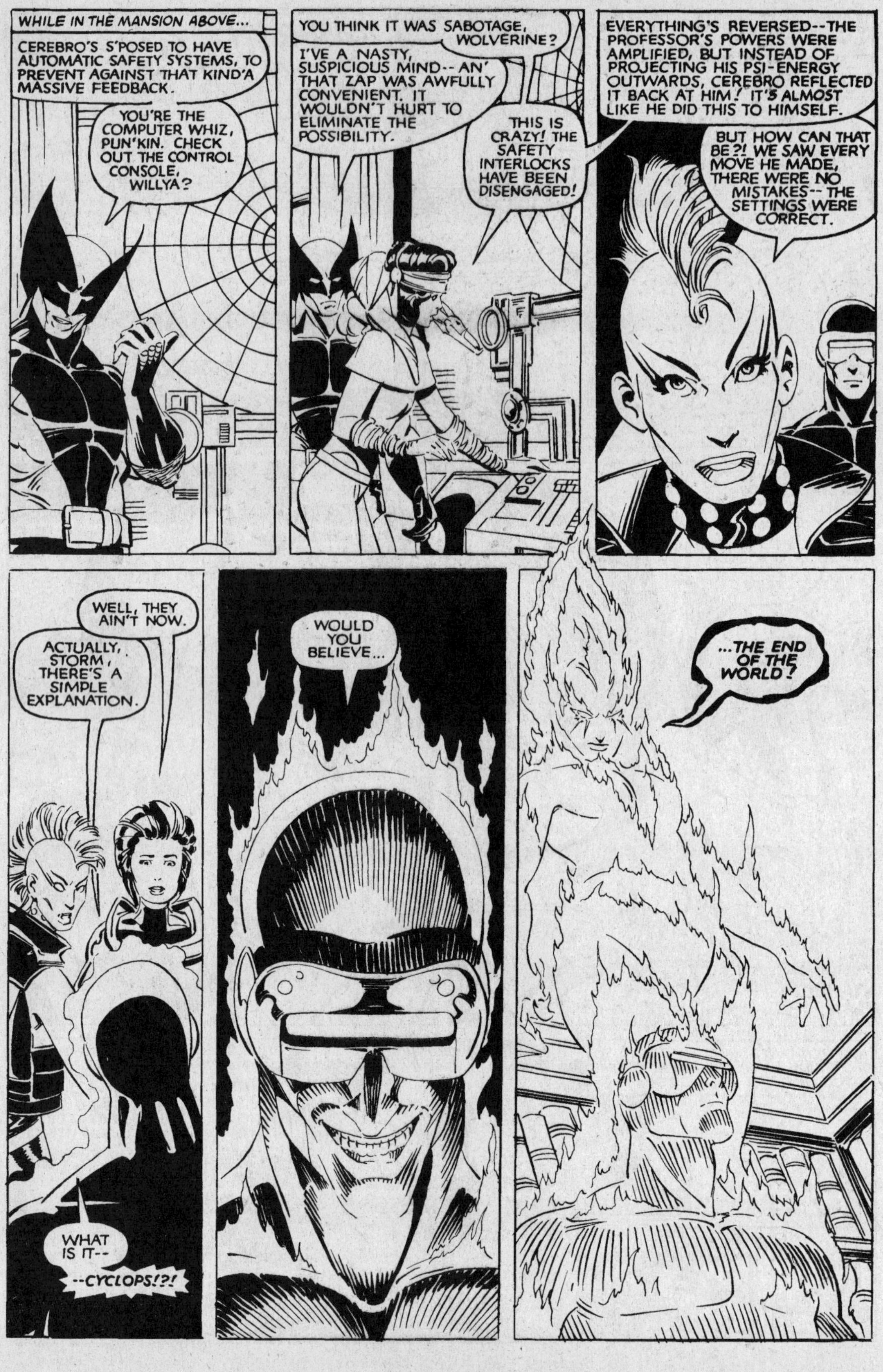
WHILE IN THE MANSION ABOVE...
CEREBRO'S S'POSED TO HAVE AUTOMATIC SAFETY SYSTEMS, TO PREVENT AGAINST THAT KIND'A MASSIVE FEEDBACK.
YOU'RE THE COMPUTER WHIZ, PUN'KIN. CHECK OUT THE CONTROL CONSOLE, WILLYA?
YOU THINK IT WAS SABOTAGE, WOLVERINE?
I'VE A NASTY, SUSPICIOUS MIND-- AN' THAT ZAP WAS AWFULLY CONVENIENT. IT WOULDN'T HURT TO ELIMINATE THE POSSIBILITY.
THIS IS CRAZY! THE SAFETY INTERLOCKS HAVE BEEN DISENGAGED!
EVERYTHING'S REVERSED--THE PROFESSOR'S POWERS WERE AMPLIFIED, BUT INSTEAD OF PROJECTING HIS PSI-ENERGY OUTWARDS, CEREBRO REFLECTED IT BACK AT HIM! IT'S ALMOST LIKE HE DID THIS TO HIMSELF.
BUT HOW CAN THAT BE?! WE SAW EVERY MOVE HE MADE, THERE WERE NO MISTAKES-- THE SETTINGS WERE CORRECT.
WELL, THEY AIN'T NOW.
ACTUALLY, STORM, THERE'S A SIMPLE EXPLANATION.
WHAT IS IT--
--CYCLOPS!?!
WOULD YOU BELIEVE...
...THE END OF THE WORLD?

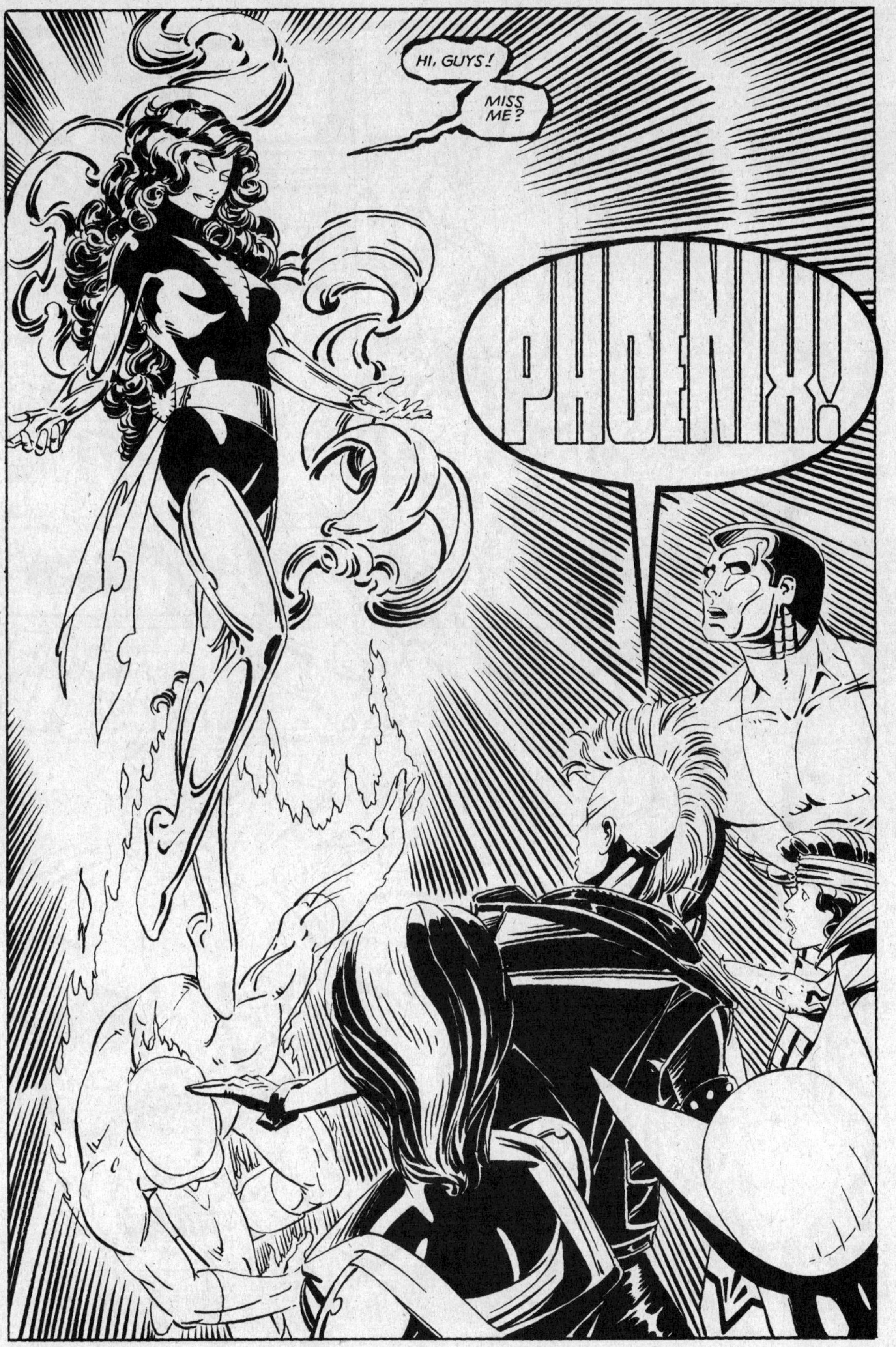
HI, GUYS!
MISS ME?
PHOENIX!

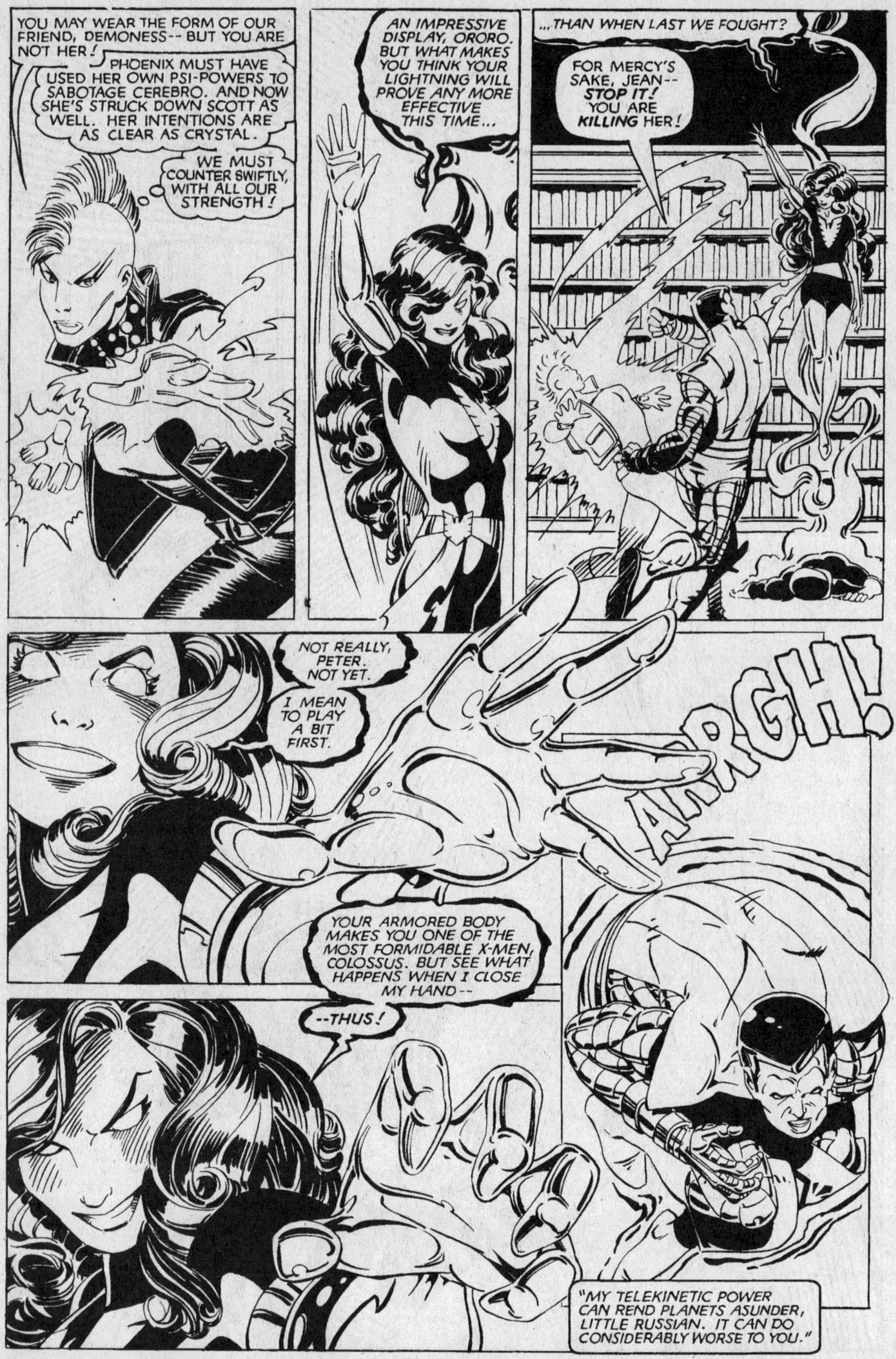
YOU MAY WEAR THE FORM OF OUR FRIEND, DEMONESS-- BUT YOU ARE NOT HER!
PHOENIX MUST HAVE USED HER OWN PSI-POWERS TO SABOTAGE CEREBRO. AND NOW SHE'S STRUCK DOWN SCOTT AS WELL. HER INTENTIONS ARE AS CLEAR AS CRYSTAL.
WE MUST COUNTER SWIFTLY, WITH ALL OUR STRENGTH!
AN IMPRESSIVE DISPLAY, ORORO. BUT WHAT MAKES YOU THINK YOUR LIGHTNING WILL PROVE ANY MORE EFFECTIVE THIS TIME...
...THAN WHEN LAST WE FOUGHT?
FOR MERCY'S SAKE, JEAN-- STOP IT! YOU ARE KILLING HER!
NOT REALLY, PETER. NOT YET.
I MEAN TO PLAY A BIT FIRST.
AARRGH!
YOUR ARMORED BODY MAKES YOU ONE OF THE MOST FORMIDABLE X-MEN, COLOSSUS. BUT SEE WHAT HAPPENS WHEN I CLOSE MY HAND--
--THUS!
"MY TELEKINETIC POWER CAN REND PLANETS ASUNDER, LITTLE RUSSIAN. IT CAN DO CONSIDERABLY WORSE TO YOU."

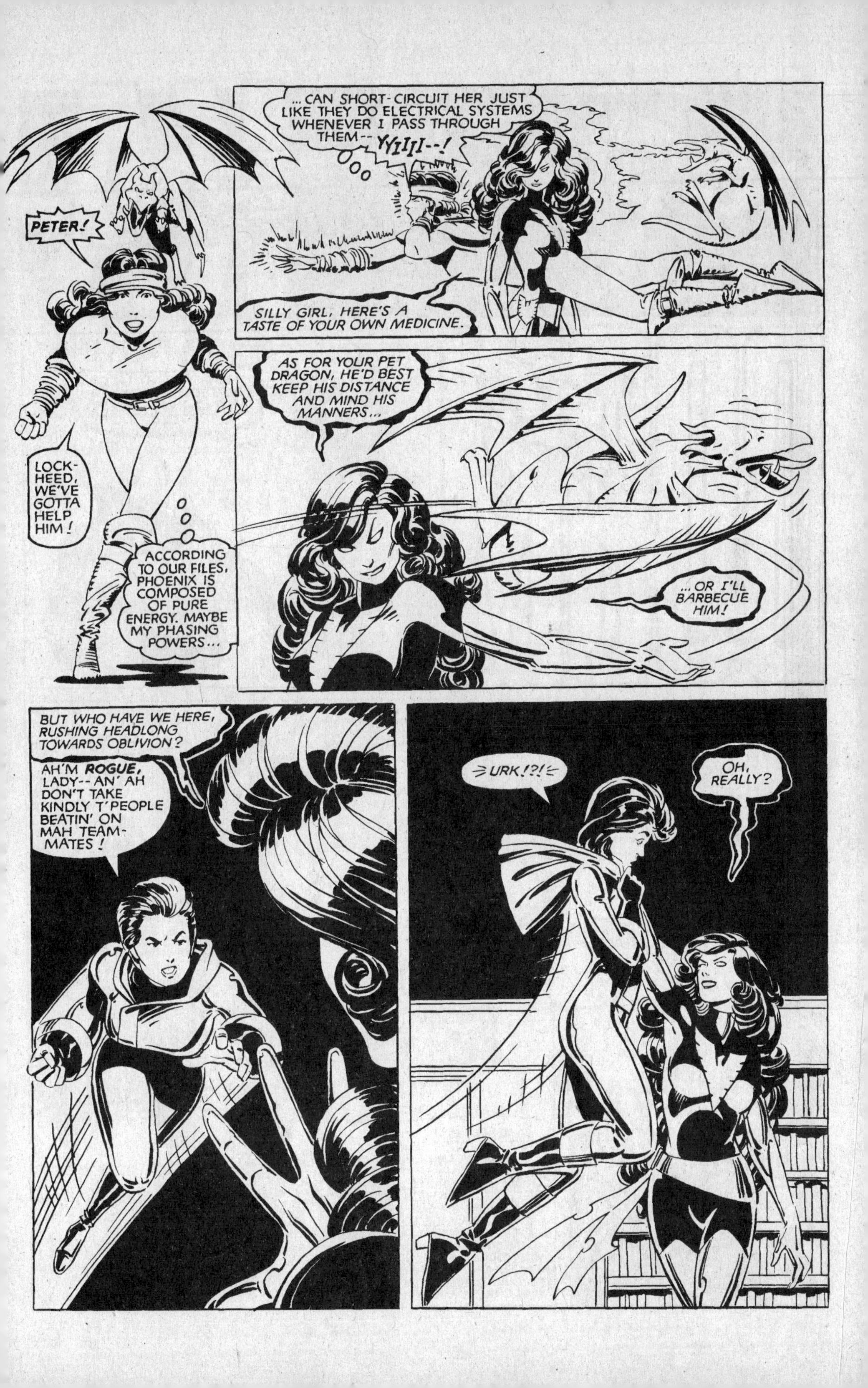
PETER!
LOCK-HEED, WE'VE GOTTA HELP HIM!
ACCORDING TO OUR FILES, PHOENIX IS COMPOSED OF PURE ENERGY. MAYBE MY PHASING POWERS...
...CAN SHORT-CIRCUIT HER JUST LIKE THEY DO ELECTRICAL SYSTEMS WHENEVER I PASS THROUGH THEM-- YYIIII--!
SILLY GIRL, HERE'S A TASTE OF YOUR OWN MEDICINE.
AS FOR YOUR PET DRAGON, HE'D BEST KEEP HIS DISTANCE AND MIND HIS MANNERS...
...OR I'LL BARBECUE HIM!
BUT WHO HAVE WE HERE, RUSHING HEADLONG TOWARDS OBLIVION?
AH'M ROGUE, LADY-- AN' AH DON'T TAKE KINDLY T'PEOPLE BEATIN' ON MAH TEAM-MATES!
URK!?!
OH, REALLY?

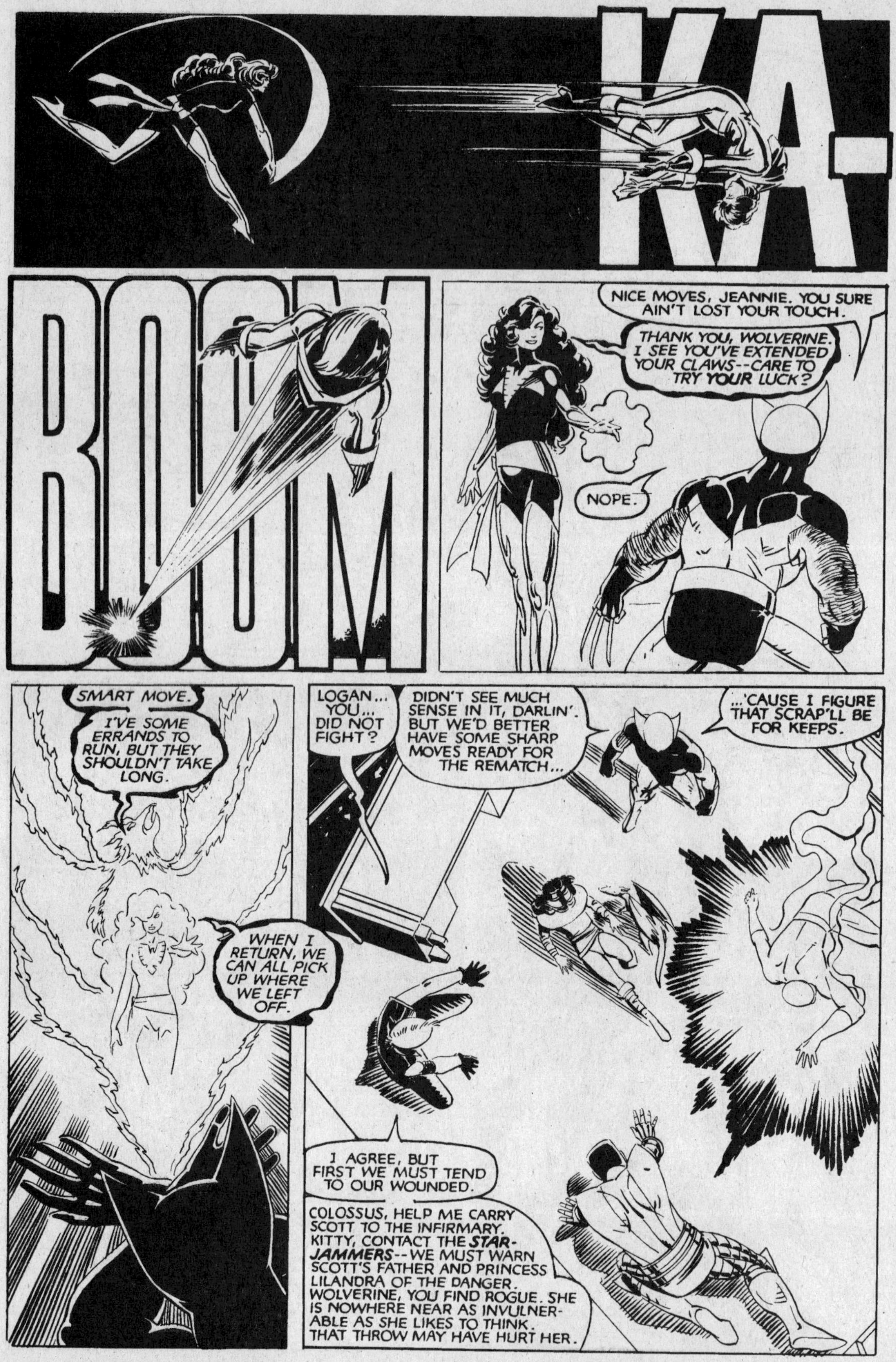
KA-
BOOM
NICE MOVES, JEANNIE. YOU SURE AIN'T LOST YOUR TOUCH.
THANK YOU, WOLVERINE. I SEE YOU'VE EXTENDED YOUR CLAWS--CARE TO TRY YOUR LUCK?
NOPE.
SMART MOVE.
I'VE SOME ERRANDS TO RUN, BUT THEY SHOULDN'T TAKE LONG.
WHEN I RETURN, WE CAN ALL PICK UP WHERE WE LEFT OFF.
LOGAN... YOU... DID NOT FIGHT?
DIDN'T SEE MUCH SENSE IN IT, DARLIN'. BUT WE'D BETTER HAVE SOME SHARP MOVES READY FOR THE REMATCH...
...'CAUSE I FIGURE THAT SCRAP'LL BE FOR KEEPS.
I AGREE, BUT FIRST WE MUST TEND TO OUR WOUNDED.
COLOSSUS, HELP ME CARRY SCOTT TO THE INFIRMARY. KITTY, CONTACT THE STAR-JAMMERS--WE MUST WARN SCOTT'S FATHER AND PRINCESS LILANDRA OF THE DANGER. WOLVERINE, YOU FIND ROGUE. SHE IS NOWHERE NEAR AS INVULNERABLE AS SHE LIKES TO THINK. THAT THROW MAY HAVE HURT HER.

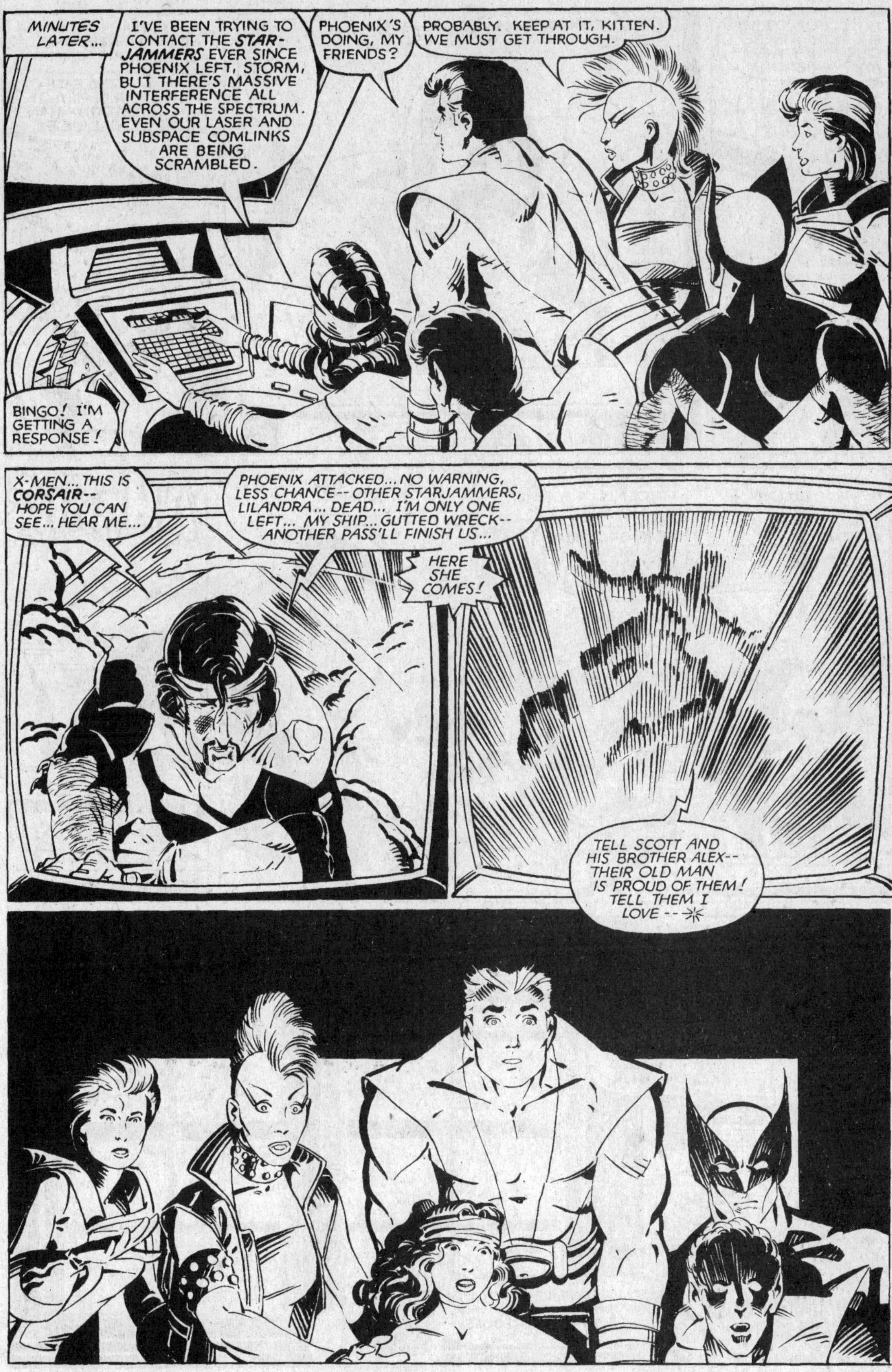
MINUTES LATER...
I'VE BEEN TRYING TO CONTACT THE STAR-JAMMERS EVER SINCE PHOENIX LEFT, STORM, BUT THERE'S MASSIVE INTERFERENCE ALL ACROSS THE SPECTRUM. EVEN OUR LASER AND SUBSPACE COMLINKS ARE BEING SCRAMBLED.
PHOENIX'S DOING, MY FRIENDS?
PROBABLY. KEEP AT IT, KITTEN. WE MUST GET THROUGH.
BINGO! I'M GETTING A RESPONSE!
X-MEN... THIS IS CORSAIR-- HOPE YOU CAN SEE... HEAR ME...
PHOENIX ATTACKED... NO WARNING, LESS CHANCE-- OTHER STARJAMMERS, LILANDRA... DEAD... I'M ONLY ONE LEFT... MY SHIP... GUTTED WRECK-- ANOTHER PASS'LL FINISH US...
HERE SHE COMES!
TELL SCOTT AND HIS BROTHER ALEX-- THEIR OLD MAN IS PROUD OF THEM! TELL THEM I LOVE --

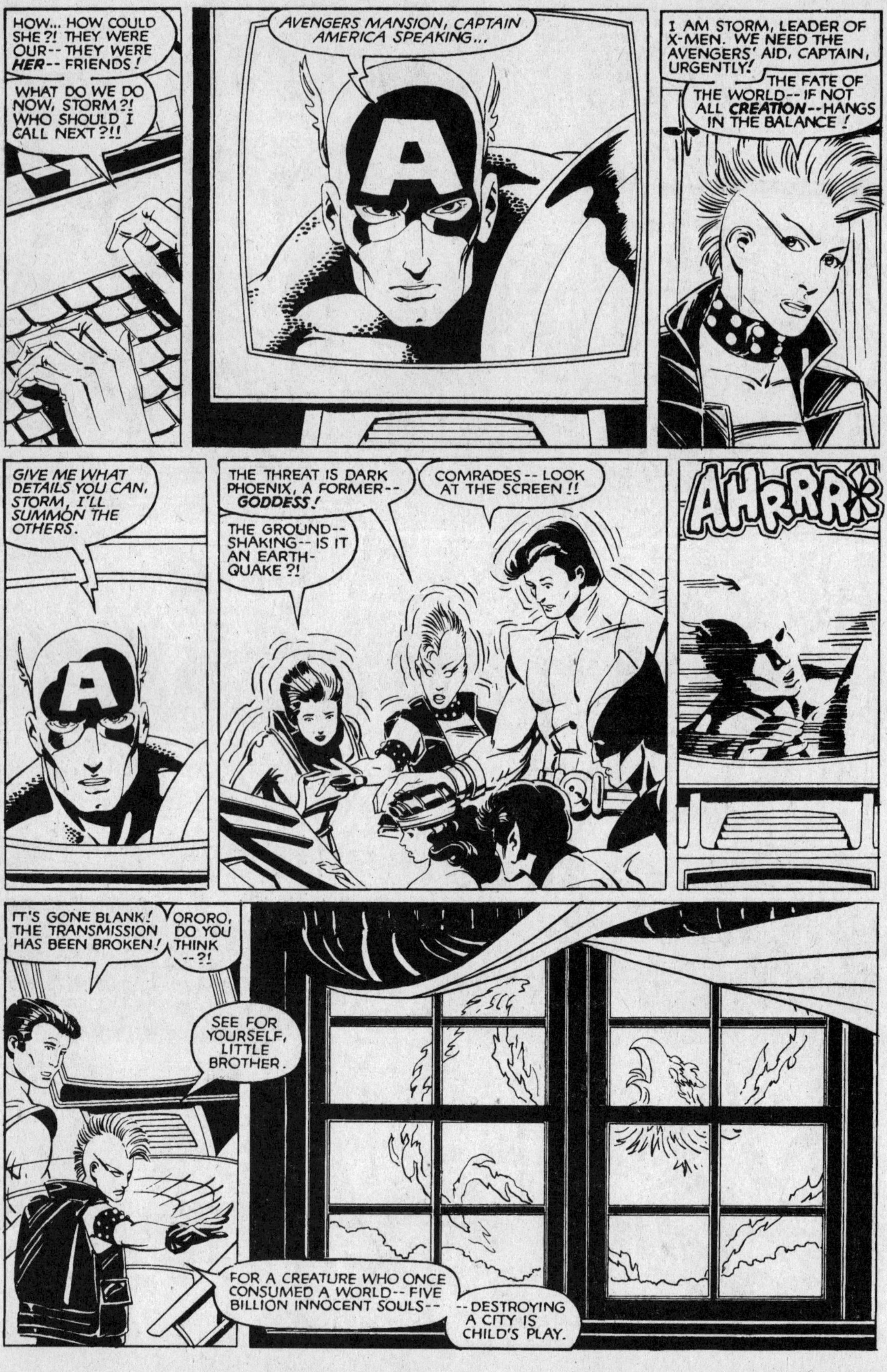
HOW... HOW COULD SHE?! THEY WERE OUR-- THEY WERE HER-- FRIENDS!
WHAT DO WE DO NOW, STORM?! WHO SHOULD I CALL NEXT?!!
AVENGERS MANSION, CAPTAIN AMERICA SPEAKING...
I AM STORM, LEADER OF X-MEN. WE NEED THE AVENGERS' AID, CAPTAIN, URGENTLY!
THE FATE OF THE WORLD-- IF NOT ALL CREATION--HANGS IN THE BALANCE!
GIVE ME WHAT DETAILS YOU CAN, STORM, I'LL SUMMON THE OTHERS.
THE THREAT IS DARK PHOENIX, A FORMER-- GODDESS!
THE GROUND-- SHAKING-- IS IT AN EARTH-QUAKE?!
COMRADES -- LOOK AT THE SCREEN!!
AHRRR!
IT'S GONE BLANK! THE TRANSMISSION HAS BEEN BROKEN!
ORORO, DO YOU THINK --?!
SEE FOR YOURSELF, LITTLE BROTHER.
FOR A CREATURE WHO ONCE CONSUMED A WORLD-- FIVE BILLION INNOCENT SOULS--
--DESTROYING A CITY IS CHILD'S PLAY.

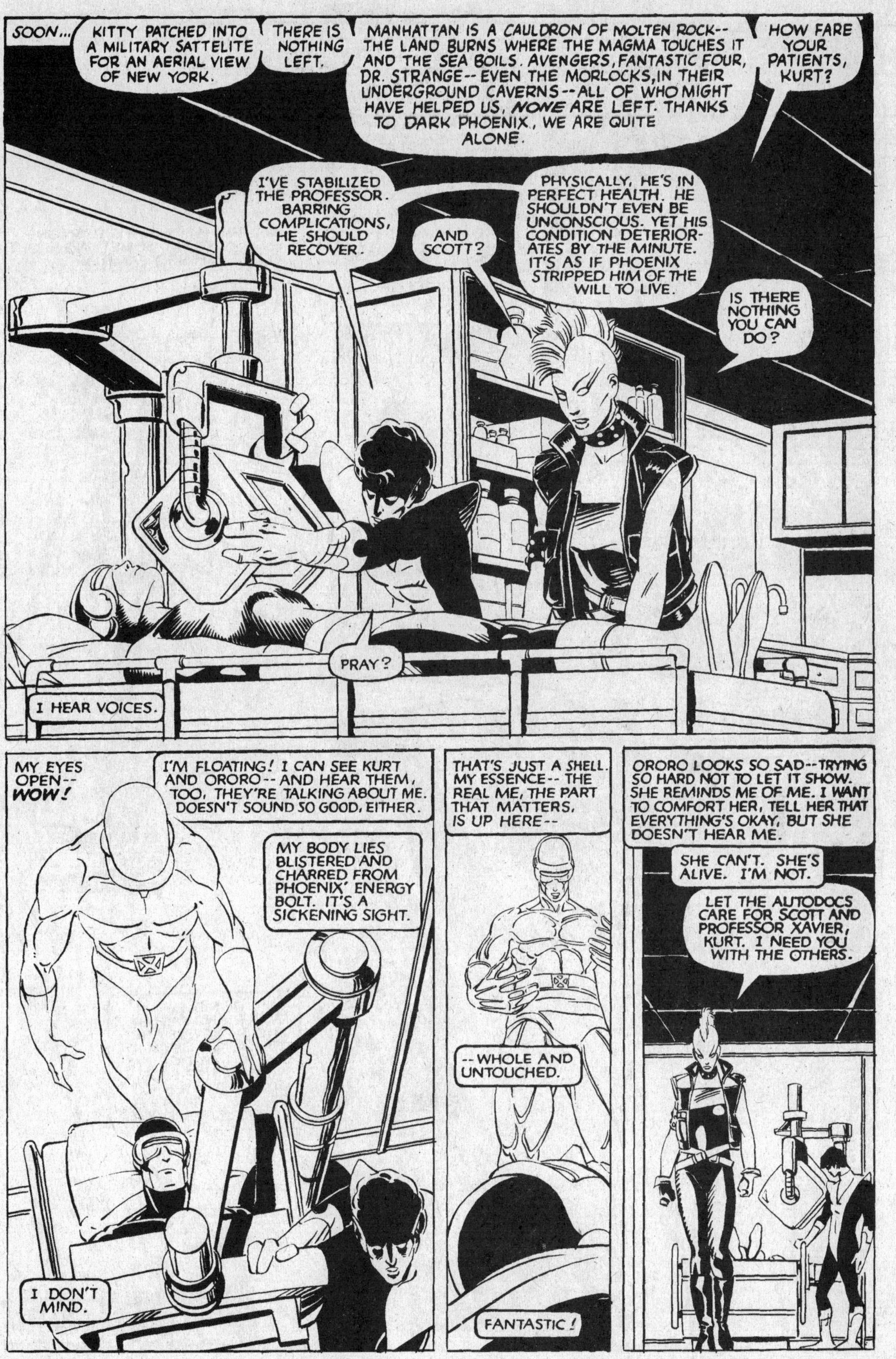

SOON...
KITTY PATCHED INTO A MILITARY SATTELITE FOR AN AERIAL VIEW OF NEW YORK.
THERE IS NOTHING LEFT.
MANHATTAN IS A CAULDRON OF MOLTEN ROCK-- THE LAND BURNS WHERE THE MAGMA TOUCHES IT AND THE SEA BOILS. AVENGERS, FANTASTIC FOUR, DR. STRANGE-- EVEN THE MORLOCKS, IN THEIR UNDERGROUND CAVERNS--ALL OF WHO MIGHT HAVE HELPED US, NONE ARE LEFT. THANKS TO DARK PHOENIX, WE ARE QUITE ALONE.
HOW FARE YOUR PATIENTS, KURT?
I'VE STABILIZED THE PROFESSOR. BARRING COMPLICATIONS, HE SHOULD RECOVER.
AND SCOTT?
PHYSICALLY, HE'S IN PERFECT HEALTH. HE SHOULDN'T EVEN BE UNCONSCIOUS. YET HIS CONDITION DETERIORATES BY THE MINUTE. IT'S AS IF PHOENIX STRIPPED HIM OF THE WILL TO LIVE.
IS THERE NOTHING YOU CAN DO?
PRAY?
I HEAR VOICES.
MY EYES OPEN-- WOW!
I'M FLOATING! I CAN SEE KURT AND ORORO-- AND HEAR THEM, TOO. THEY'RE TALKING ABOUT ME. DOESN'T SOUND SO GOOD, EITHER.
MY BODY LIES BLISTERED AND CHARRED FROM PHOENIX' ENERGY BOLT. IT'S A SICKENING SIGHT.
I DON'T MIND.
THAT'S JUST A SHELL. MY ESSENCE-- THE REAL ME, THE PART THAT MATTERS, IS UP HERE--
--WHOLE AND UNTOUCHED.
FANTASTIC!
ORORO LOOKS SO SAD--TRYING SO HARD NOT TO LET IT SHOW. SHE REMINDS ME OF ME. I WANT TO COMFORT HER, TELL HER THAT EVERYTHING'S OKAY, BUT SHE DOESN'T HEAR ME.
SHE CAN'T. SHE'S ALIVE. I'M NOT.
LET THE AUTODOCS CARE FOR SCOTT AND PROFESSOR XAVIER, KURT. I NEED YOU WITH THE OTHERS.

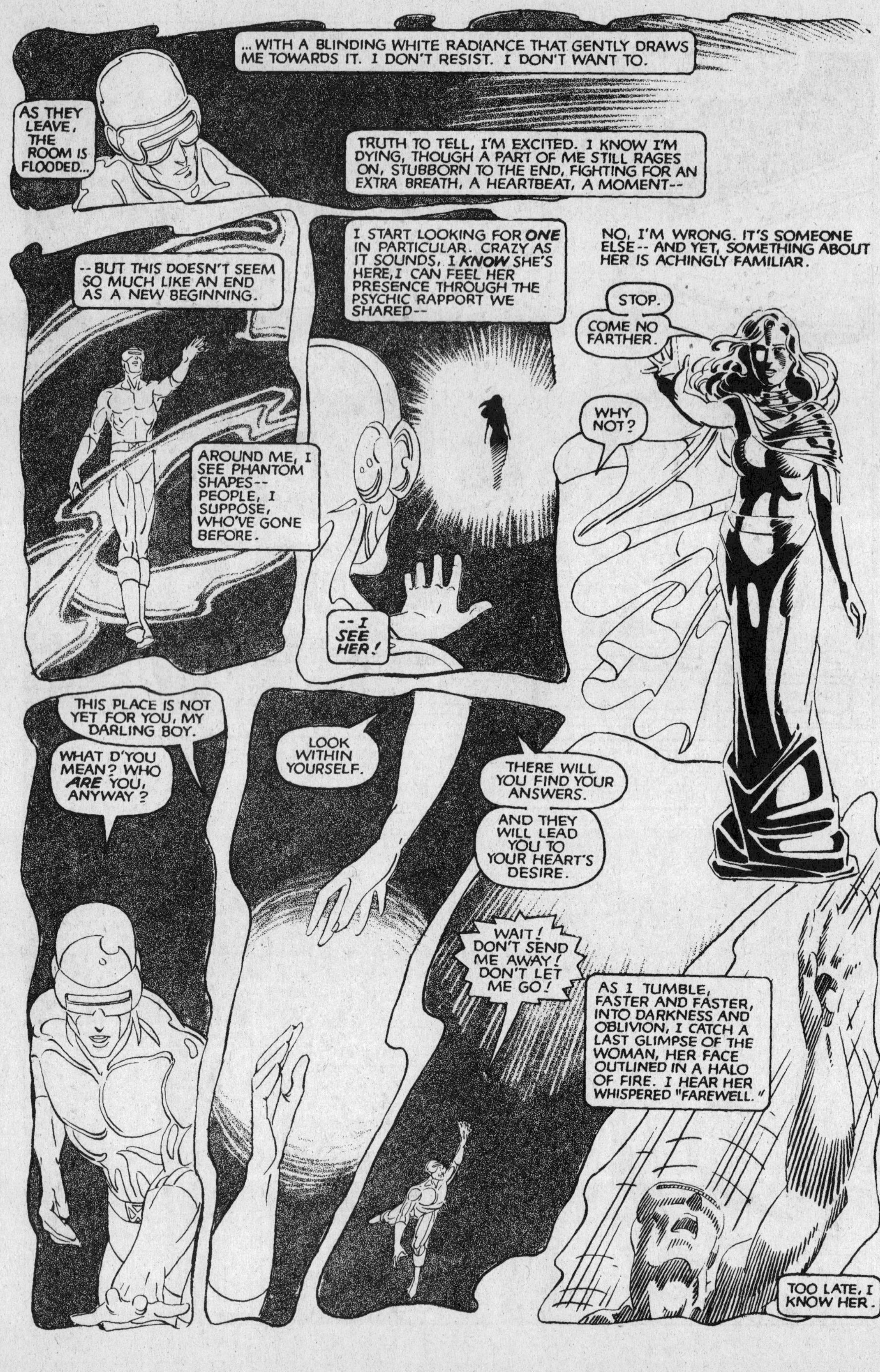
...WITH A BLINDING WHITE RADIANCE THAT GENTLY DRAWS ME TOWARDS IT. I DON'T RESIST. I DON'T WANT TO.
AS THEY LEAVE, THE ROOM IS FLOODED...
TRUTH TO TELL, I'M EXCITED. I KNOW I'M DYING, THOUGH A PART OF ME STILL RAGES ON, STUBBORN TO THE END, FIGHTING FOR AN EXTRA BREATH, A HEARTBEAT, A MOMENT--
--BUT THIS DOESN'T SEEM SO MUCH LIKE AN END AS A NEW BEGINNING.
AROUND ME, I SEE PHANTOM SHAPES--PEOPLE, I SUPPOSE, WHO'VE GONE BEFORE.
I START LOOKING FOR ONE IN PARTICULAR. CRAZY AS IT SOUNDS, I KNOW SHE'S HERE, I CAN FEEL HER PRESENCE THROUGH THE PSYCHIC RAPPORT WE SHARED--
--I SEE HER!
NO, I'M WRONG. IT'S SOMEONE ELSE-- AND YET, SOMETHING ABOUT HER IS ACHINGLY FAMILIAR.
STOP.
COME NO FARTHER.
WHY NOT?
THIS PLACE IS NOT YET FOR YOU, MY DARLING BOY.
WHAT D'YOU MEAN? WHO ARE YOU, ANYWAY?
LOOK WITHIN YOURSELF.
THERE WILL YOU FIND YOUR ANSWERS.
AND THEY WILL LEAD YOU TO YOUR HEART'S DESIRE.
WAIT! DON'T SEND ME AWAY! DON'T LET ME GO!
AS I TUMBLE, FASTER AND FASTER, INTO DARKNESS AND OBLIVION, I CATCH A LAST GLIMPSE OF THE WOMAN, HER FACE OUTLINED IN A HALO OF FIRE. I HEAR HER WHISPERED "FAREWELL."
TOO LATE, I KNOW HER.

MOM!

I'M AWAKE.

I'M CRYING, REMEMBERING WHO I WAS LOOKING FOR. HOW CERTAIN I WAS I'D FIND HER. I SUPPOSE, NO MATTER WHAT I SAID OR DID, I NEVER REALLY ACCEPTED WHAT HAPPENED YEARS AGO. BUT NOW, I HAVE NO CHOICE.

JEAN IS DEAD.

BUT IF THAT'S SO, THEN WHO -- OR WHAT -- ARE WE UP AGAINST?

LAST NIGHT, MADELYNE TRANSFORMED TO PHOENIX, BLASTED ME, HEALED ME. TODAY, PHOENIX EMERGES FROM ME, AND I GET BURNED AGAIN.

BUT LOOK AT ME, NOT A SCRATCH!

SUPPOSE I WASN'T BURNED AT ALL, BUT ONLY THOUGHT I WAS?

SUPPOSE THERE'S NO PHOENIX, EITHER -- AND WE'RE JUST BEING TRICKED INTO BELIEVING SHE'S RETURNED.

THAT'D EXPLAIN WHY CHARLES WAS ZAPPED... TO PREVENT HIM LEARNING THE TRUTH. IT'D ALSO EXPLAIN THE TIME THAT PASSED BETWEEN MANIFESTATIONS. PHOENIX COULD COVER THE DISTANCE FROM ALASKA TO HERE IN AN INSTANT.

SO WHY A TWELVE-HOUR DELAY -- UNLESS SOMEONE HAD TO FLY FROM ANCHORAGE TO NEW YORK?

BUT WHO? THAT "SOMEONE'S" GOING TO AN AWFUL LOT OF TROUBLE. AND FROM ALL INDICATIONS, HIS KNOWLEDGE OF THE X-MEN IS AS DEEP AS HIS HATE.

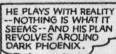

HE PLAYS WITH REALITY --NOTHING IS WHAT IT SEEMS-- AND HIS PLAN REVOLVES AROUND DARK PHOENIX.

ONLY ONE PERSON IT CAN BE.

I HAVE TO WARN THE X-MEN, AND THEN FLUSH HIM INTO THE OPEN -- WITH NO IDEA OF WHEN, WHERE OR HOW HE'LL STRIKE NEXT. FOR THE MOMENT, I HAVE THE ADVANTAGE OF SURPRISE-- HE MUST BELIEVE THAT I'M DYING.

BUT ONCE I SHOW MYSELF, HE'LL DO ANYTHING TO PREVENT MY UNMASKING HIM. I'D BETTER RIG SOME ACES IN THE HOLE TO EVEN THE ODDS.

LORD KNOWS WHAT HE'S DONE TO MADELYNE. IT DOESN'T MATTER. THIS TIME, I PLAY BY HIS RULES. WHEN I CATCH HIM -- HE'S A DEAD MAN.

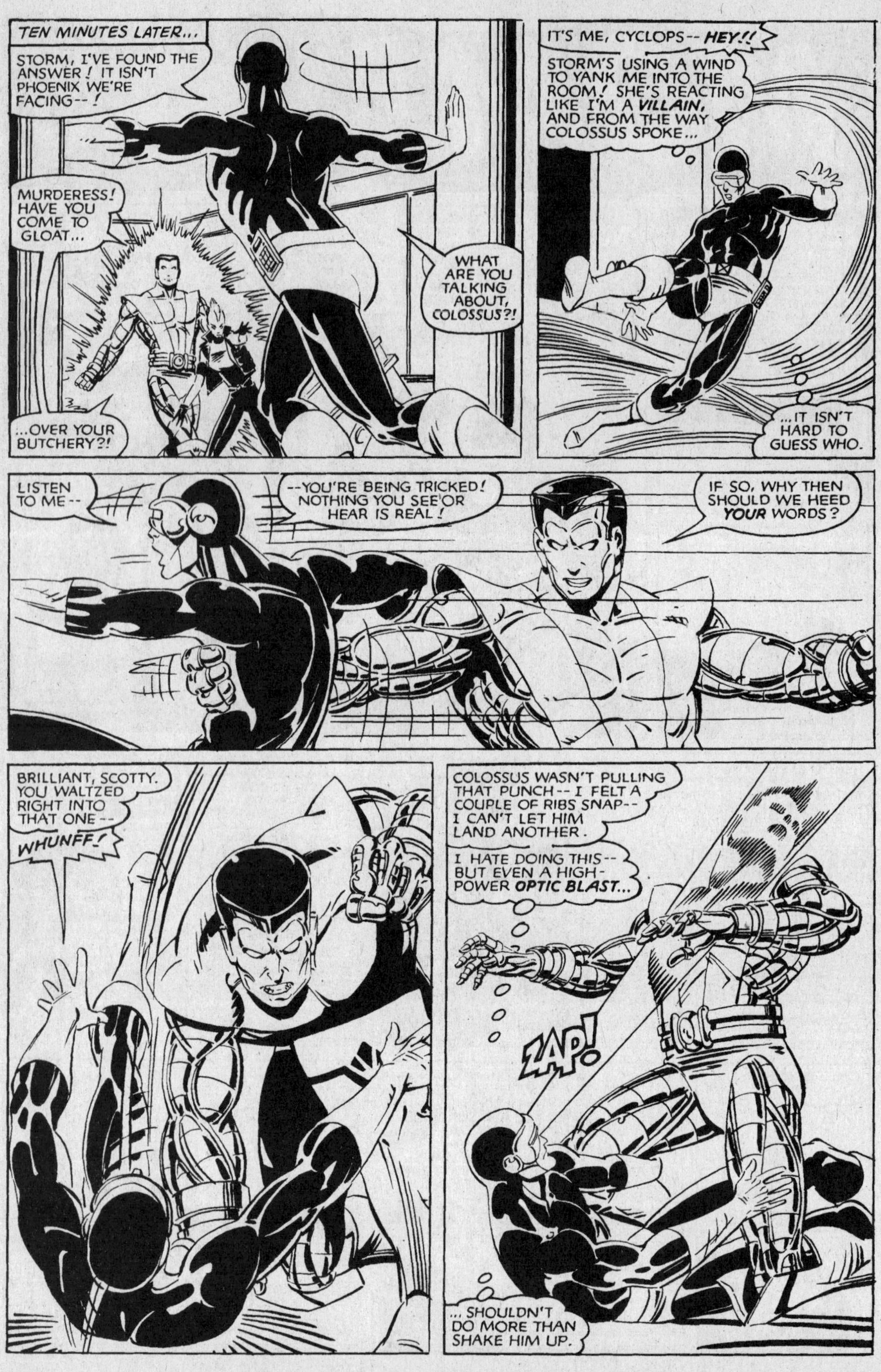
TEN MINUTES LATER...
STORM, I'VE FOUND THE ANSWER! IT ISN'T PHOENIX WE'RE FACING--!
MURDERESS! HAVE YOU COME TO GLOAT...
...OVER YOUR BUTCHERY?!
WHAT ARE YOU TALKING ABOUT, COLOSSUS?!
IT'S ME, CYCLOPS-- HEY!!
STORM'S USING A WIND TO YANK ME INTO THE ROOM! SHE'S REACTING LIKE I'M A VILLAIN, AND FROM THE WAY COLOSSUS SPOKE...
...IT ISN'T HARD TO GUESS WHO.
LISTEN TO ME--
--YOU'RE BEING TRICKED! NOTHING YOU SEE OR HEAR IS REAL!
IF SO, WHY THEN SHOULD WE HEED YOUR WORDS?
BRILLIANT, SCOTTY. YOU WALTZED RIGHT INTO THAT ONE--
WHUNFF!
COLOSSUS WASN'T PULLING THAT PUNCH-- I FELT A COUPLE OF RIBS SNAP-- I CAN'T LET HIM LAND ANOTHER.
I HATE DOING THIS-- BUT EVEN A HIGH-POWER OPTIC BLAST...
ZAP!
...SHOULDN'T DO MORE THAN SHAKE HIM UP.

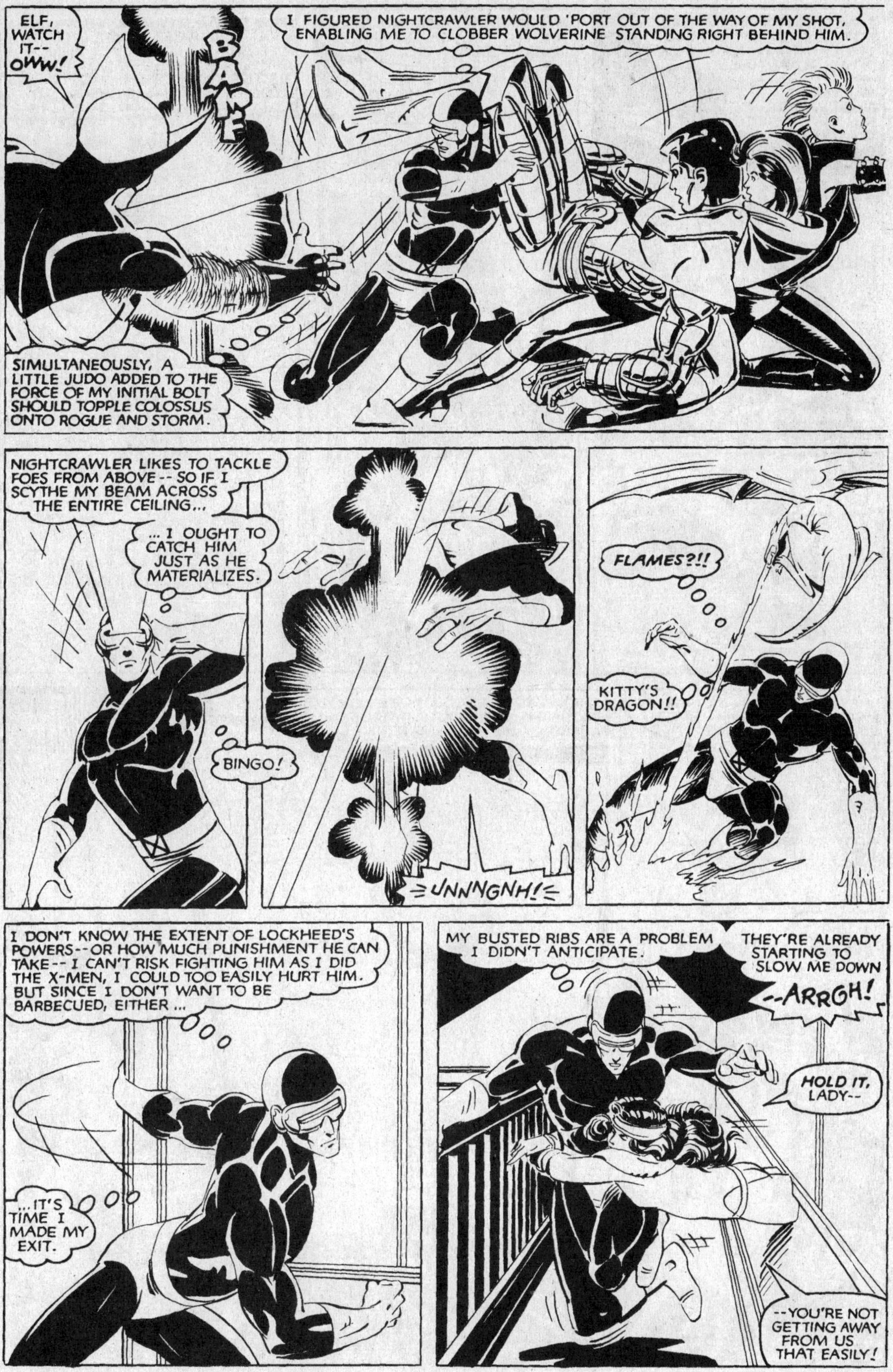
ELF, WATCH IT-- OWW!
BAMF
I FIGURED NIGHTCRAWLER WOULD 'PORT OUT OF THE WAY OF MY SHOT, ENABLING ME TO CLOBBER WOLVERINE STANDING RIGHT BEHIND HIM.
SIMULTANEOUSLY, A LITTLE JUDO ADDED TO THE FORCE OF MY INITIAL BOLT SHOULD TOPPLE COLOSSUS ONTO ROGUE AND STORM.
NIGHTCRAWLER LIKES TO TACKLE FOES FROM ABOVE -- SO IF I SCYTHE MY BEAM ACROSS THE ENTIRE CEILING...
... I OUGHT TO CATCH HIM JUST AS HE MATERIALIZES.
BINGO!
UNNNGNH!
FLAMES?!!
KITTY'S DRAGON!!
I DON'T KNOW THE EXTENT OF LOCKHEED'S POWERS -- OR HOW MUCH PUNISHMENT HE CAN TAKE -- I CAN'T RISK FIGHTING HIM AS I DID THE X-MEN, I COULD TOO EASILY HURT HIM. BUT SINCE I DON'T WANT TO BE BARBECUED, EITHER ...
... IT'S TIME I MADE MY EXIT.
MY BUSTED RIBS ARE A PROBLEM I DIDN'T ANTICIPATE.
THEY'RE ALREADY STARTING TO SLOW ME DOWN
--ARRGH!
HOLD IT, LADY--
--YOU'RE NOT GETTING AWAY FROM US THAT EASILY!

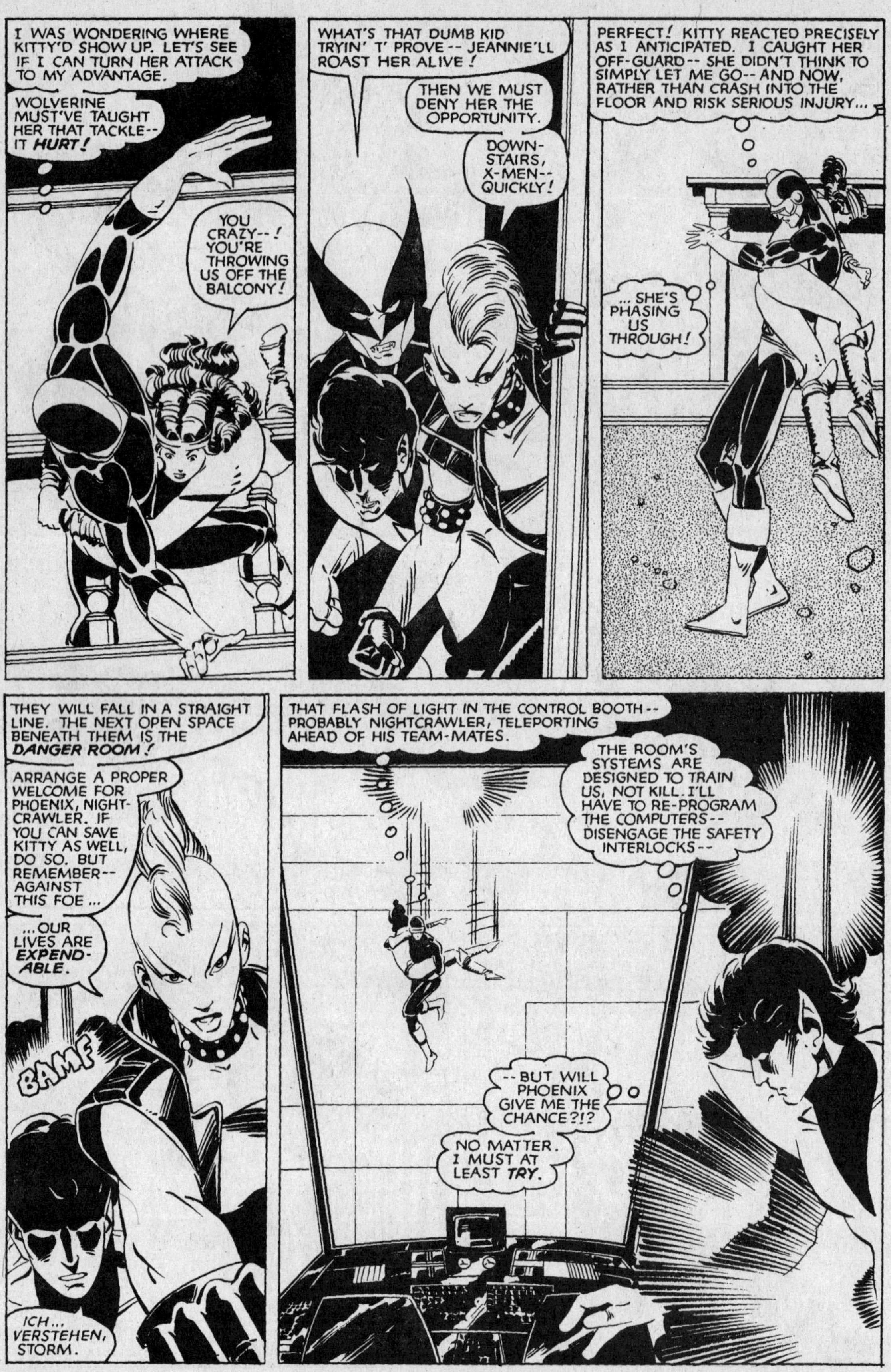

I WAS WONDERING WHERE KITTY'D SHOW UP. LET'S SEE IF I CAN TURN HER ATTACK TO MY ADVANTAGE.
WOLVERINE MUST'VE TAUGHT HER THAT TACKLE-- IT HURT!
YOU CRAZY--! YOU'RE THROWING US OFF THE BALCONY!
WHAT'S THAT DUMB KID TRYIN' T' PROVE -- JEANNIE'LL ROAST HER ALIVE!
THEN WE MUST DENY HER THE OPPORTUNITY.
DOWN-STAIRS, X-MEN-- QUICKLY!
PERFECT! KITTY REACTED PRECISELY AS I ANTICIPATED. I CAUGHT HER OFF-GUARD-- SHE DIDN'T THINK TO SIMPLY LET ME GO-- AND NOW, RATHER THAN CRASH INTO THE FLOOR AND RISK SERIOUS INJURY...
... SHE'S PHASING US THROUGH!
THEY WILL FALL IN A STRAIGHT LINE. THE NEXT OPEN SPACE BENEATH THEM IS THE DANGER ROOM!
ARRANGE A PROPER WELCOME FOR PHOENIX, NIGHT-CRAWLER. IF YOU CAN SAVE KITTY AS WELL, DO SO. BUT REMEMBER-- AGAINST THIS FOE ...
...OUR LIVES ARE EXPEND-ABLE.
BAMF
ICH... VERSTEHEN, STORM.
THAT FLASH OF LIGHT IN THE CONTROL BOOTH -- PROBABLY NIGHTCRAWLER, TELEPORTING AHEAD OF HIS TEAM-MATES.
THE ROOM'S SYSTEMS ARE DESIGNED TO TRAIN US, NOT KILL. I'LL HAVE TO RE-PROGRAM THE COMPUTERS -- DISENGAGE THE SAFETY INTERLOCKS --
-- BUT WILL PHOENIX GIVE ME THE CHANCE?!?
NO MATTER. I MUST AT LEAST TRY.

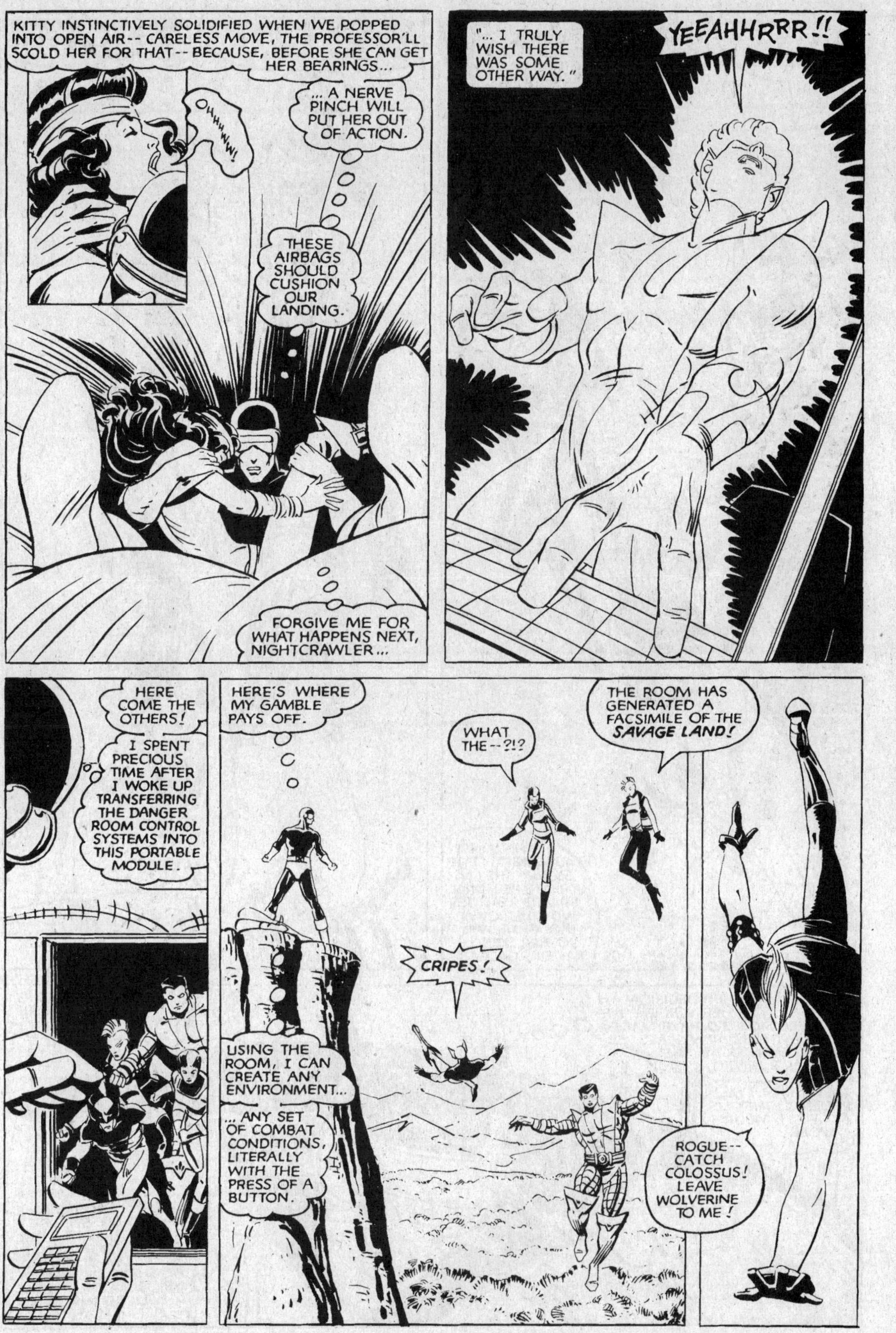
KITTY INSTINCTIVELY SOLIDIFIED WHEN WE POPPED INTO OPEN AIR-- CARELESS MOVE, THE PROFESSOR'LL SCOLD HER FOR THAT-- BECAUSE, BEFORE SHE CAN GET HER BEARINGS...
OHHHWW!
...A NERVE PINCH WILL PUT HER OUT OF ACTION.
THESE AIRBAGS SHOULD CUSHION OUR LANDING.
FORGIVE ME FOR WHAT HAPPENS NEXT, NIGHTCRAWLER...
"... I TRULY WISH THERE WAS SOME OTHER WAY."
YEEAHHRRR!!
HERE COME THE OTHERS!
I SPENT PRECIOUS TIME AFTER I WOKE UP TRANSFERRING THE DANGER ROOM CONTROL SYSTEMS INTO THIS PORTABLE MODULE.
HERE'S WHERE MY GAMBLE PAYS OFF.
USING THE ROOM, I CAN CREATE ANY ENVIRONMENT...
...ANY SET OF COMBAT CONDITIONS, LITERALLY WITH THE PRESS OF A BUTTON.
WHAT THE--?!?
THE ROOM HAS GENERATED A FACSIMILE OF THE SAVAGE LAND!
CRIPES!
ROGUE-- CATCH COLOSSUS! LEAVE WOLVERINE TO ME!

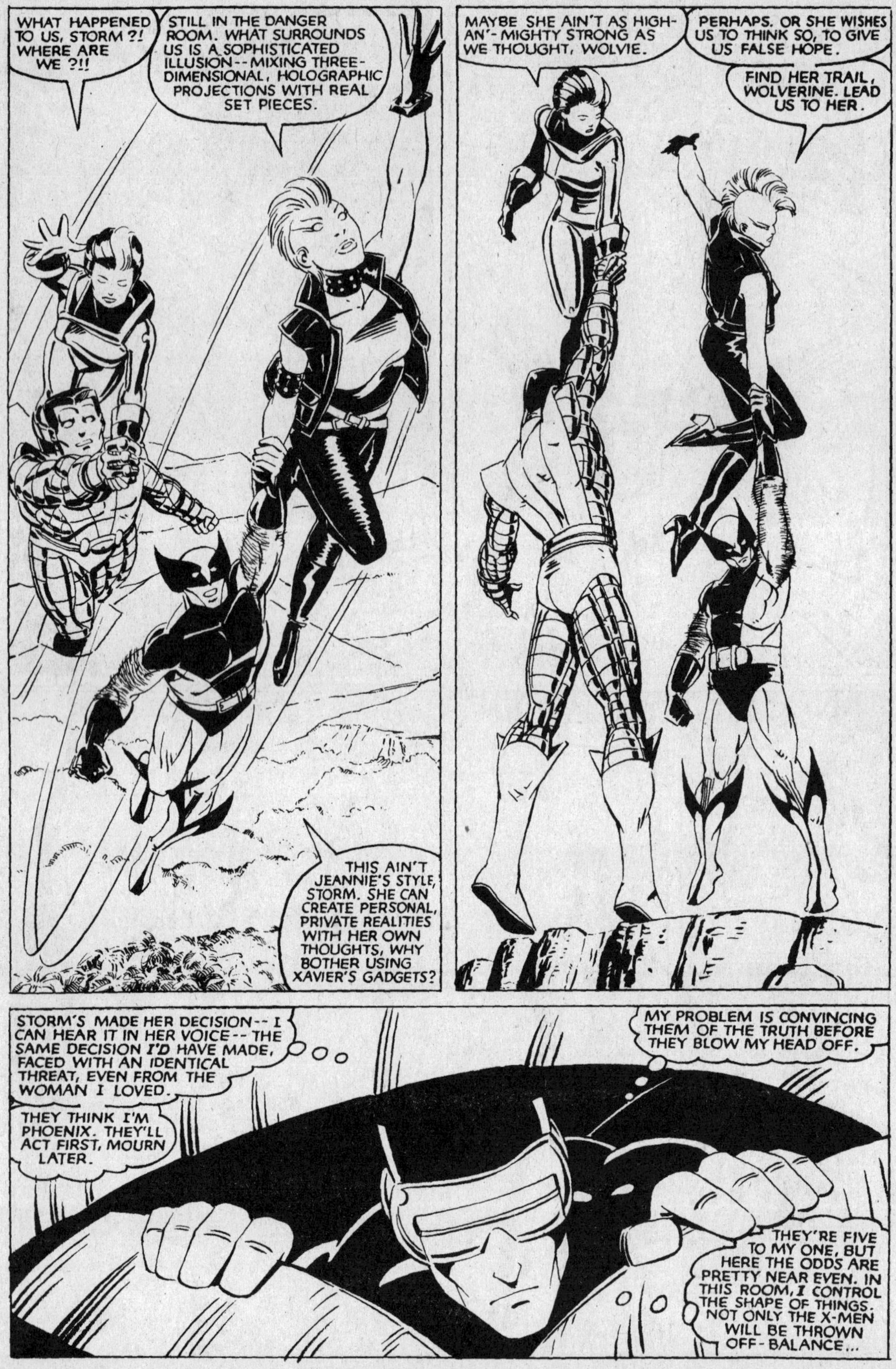
WHAT HAPPENED TO US, STORM ?! WHERE ARE WE ?!!
STILL IN THE DANGER ROOM. WHAT SURROUNDS US IS A SOPHISTICATED ILLUSION -- MIXING THREE-DIMENSIONAL, HOLOGRAPHIC PROJECTIONS WITH REAL SET PIECES.
THIS AIN'T JEANNIE'S STYLE, STORM. SHE CAN CREATE PERSONAL, PRIVATE REALITIES WITH HER OWN THOUGHTS, WHY BOTHER USING XAVIER'S GADGETS?
MAYBE SHE AIN'T AS HIGH-AN'-MIGHTY STRONG AS WE THOUGHT, WOLVIE.
PERHAPS. OR SHE WISHES US TO THINK SO, TO GIVE US FALSE HOPE.
FIND HER TRAIL, WOLVERINE. LEAD US TO HER.
STORM'S MADE HER DECISION -- I CAN HEAR IT IN HER VOICE -- THE SAME DECISION I'D HAVE MADE, FACED WITH AN IDENTICAL THREAT, EVEN FROM THE WOMAN I LOVED.
THEY THINK I'M PHOENIX. THEY'LL ACT FIRST, MOURN LATER.
MY PROBLEM IS CONVINCING THEM OF THE TRUTH BEFORE THEY BLOW MY HEAD OFF.
THEY'RE FIVE TO MY ONE, BUT HERE THE ODDS ARE PRETTY NEAR EVEN. IN THIS ROOM, I CONTROL THE SHAPE OF THINGS. NOT ONLY THE X-MEN WILL BE THROWN OFF-BALANCE...

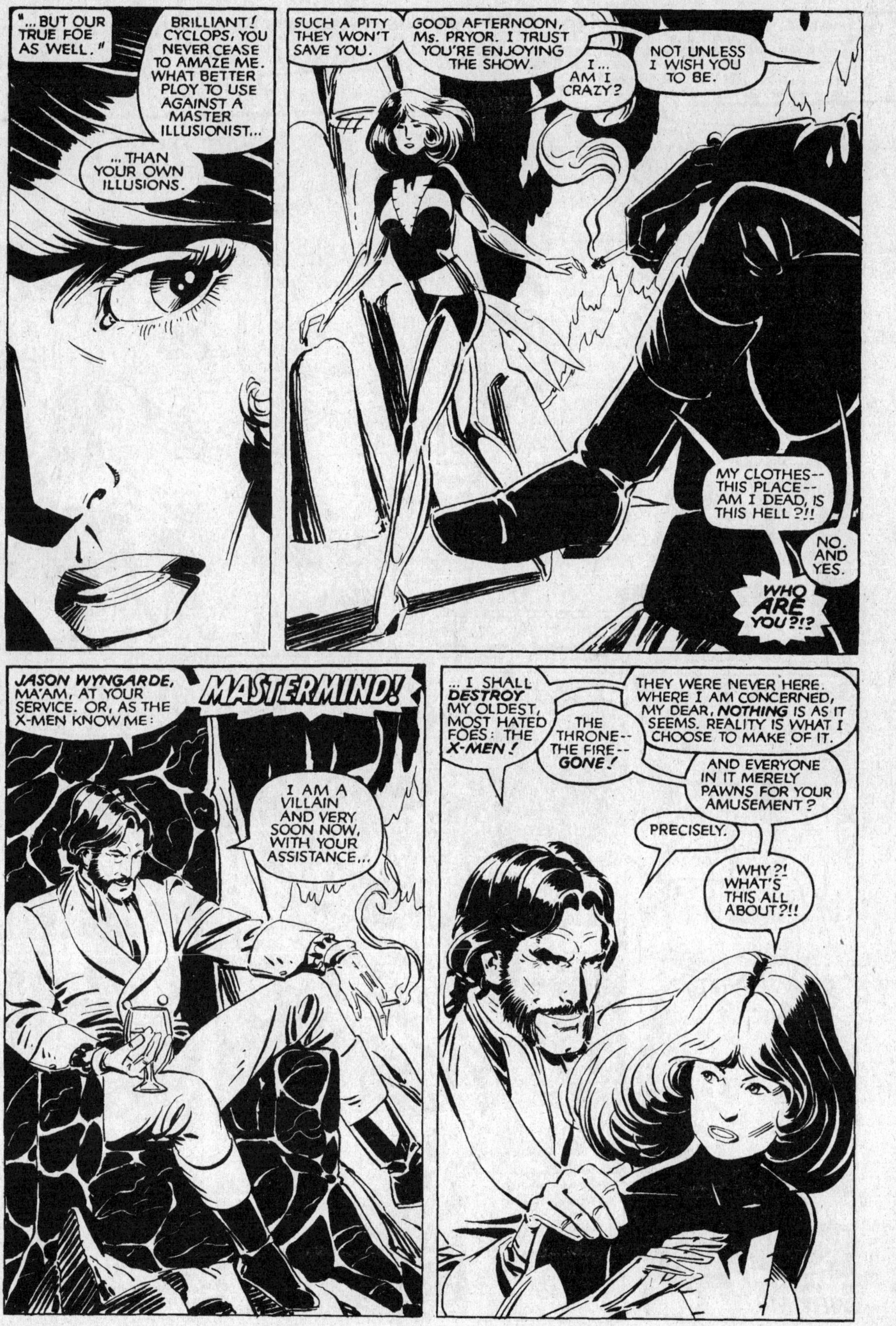
"...BUT OUR TRUE FOE AS WELL."
BRILLIANT! CYCLOPS, YOU NEVER CEASE TO AMAZE ME. WHAT BETTER PLOY TO USE AGAINST A MASTER ILLUSIONIST...
...THAN YOUR OWN ILLUSIONS.
SUCH A PITY THEY WON'T SAVE YOU.
GOOD AFTERNOON, Ms. PRYOR. I TRUST YOU'RE ENJOYING THE SHOW.
I... AM I CRAZY?
NOT UNLESS I WISH YOU TO BE.
MY CLOTHES-- THIS PLACE-- AM I DEAD, IS THIS HELL?!!
NO. AND YES.
WHO ARE YOU?!?
JASON WYNGARDE, MA'AM, AT YOUR SERVICE. OR, AS THE X-MEN KNOW ME:
MASTERMIND!
I AM A VILLAIN AND VERY SOON NOW, WITH YOUR ASSISTANCE...
...I SHALL DESTROY MY OLDEST, MOST HATED FOES: THE X-MEN!
THE THRONE-- THE FIRE-- GONE!
THEY WERE NEVER HERE. WHERE I AM CONCERNED, MY DEAR, NOTHING IS AS IT SEEMS. REALITY IS WHAT I CHOOSE TO MAKE OF IT.
AND EVERYONE IN IT MERELY PAWNS FOR YOUR AMUSEMENT?
PRECISELY.
WHY?! WHAT'S THIS ALL ABOUT?!!

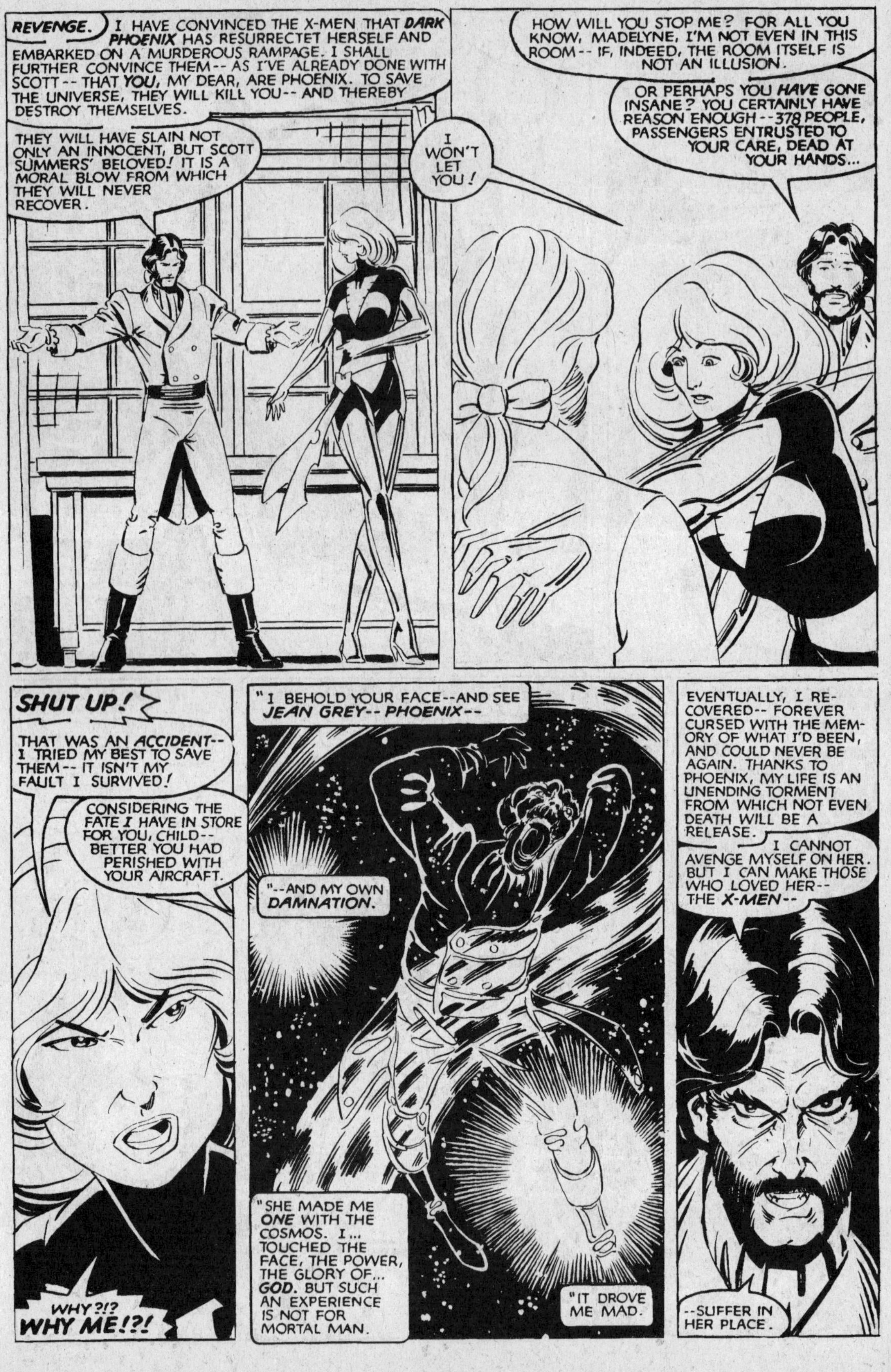
REVENGE. I HAVE CONVINCED THE X-MEN THAT DARK PHOENIX HAS RESURRECTET HERSELF AND EMBARKED ON A MURDEROUS RAMPAGE. I SHALL FURTHER CONVINCE THEM -- AS I'VE ALREADY DONE WITH SCOTT -- THAT YOU, MY DEAR, ARE PHOENIX. TO SAVE THE UNIVERSE, THEY WILL KILL YOU -- AND THEREBY DESTROY THEMSELVES.
THEY WILL HAVE SLAIN NOT ONLY AN INNOCENT, BUT SCOTT SUMMERS' BELOVED! IT IS A MORAL BLOW FROM WHICH THEY WILL NEVER RECOVER.
I WON'T LET YOU!
HOW WILL YOU STOP ME? FOR ALL YOU KNOW, MADELYNE, I'M NOT EVEN IN THIS ROOM -- IF, INDEED, THE ROOM ITSELF IS NOT AN ILLUSION.
OR PERHAPS YOU HAVE GONE INSANE? YOU CERTAINLY HAVE REASON ENOUGH -- 378 PEOPLE, PASSENGERS ENTRUSTED TO YOUR CARE, DEAD AT YOUR HANDS...
SHUT UP!
THAT WAS AN ACCIDENT -- I TRIED MY BEST TO SAVE THEM -- IT ISN'T MY FAULT I SURVIVED!
CONSIDERING THE FATE I HAVE IN STORE FOR YOU, CHILD -- BETTER YOU HAD PERISHED WITH YOUR AIRCRAFT.
WHY?!? WHY ME!?!
"I BEHOLD YOUR FACE -- AND SEE JEAN GREY -- PHOENIX --
"-- AND MY OWN DAMNATION.
"SHE MADE ME ONE WITH THE COSMOS. I... TOUCHED THE FACE, THE POWER, THE GLORY OF... GOD. BUT SUCH AN EXPERIENCE IS NOT FOR MORTAL MAN.
"IT DROVE ME MAD.
EVENTUALLY, I RECOVERED -- FOREVER CURSED WITH THE MEMORY OF WHAT I'D BEEN, AND COULD NEVER BE AGAIN. THANKS TO PHOENIX, MY LIFE IS AN UNENDING TORMENT FROM WHICH NOT EVEN DEATH WILL BE A RELEASE.
I CANNOT AVENGE MYSELF ON HER. BUT I CAN MAKE THOSE WHO LOVED HER -- THE X-MEN --
-- SUFFER IN HER PLACE.

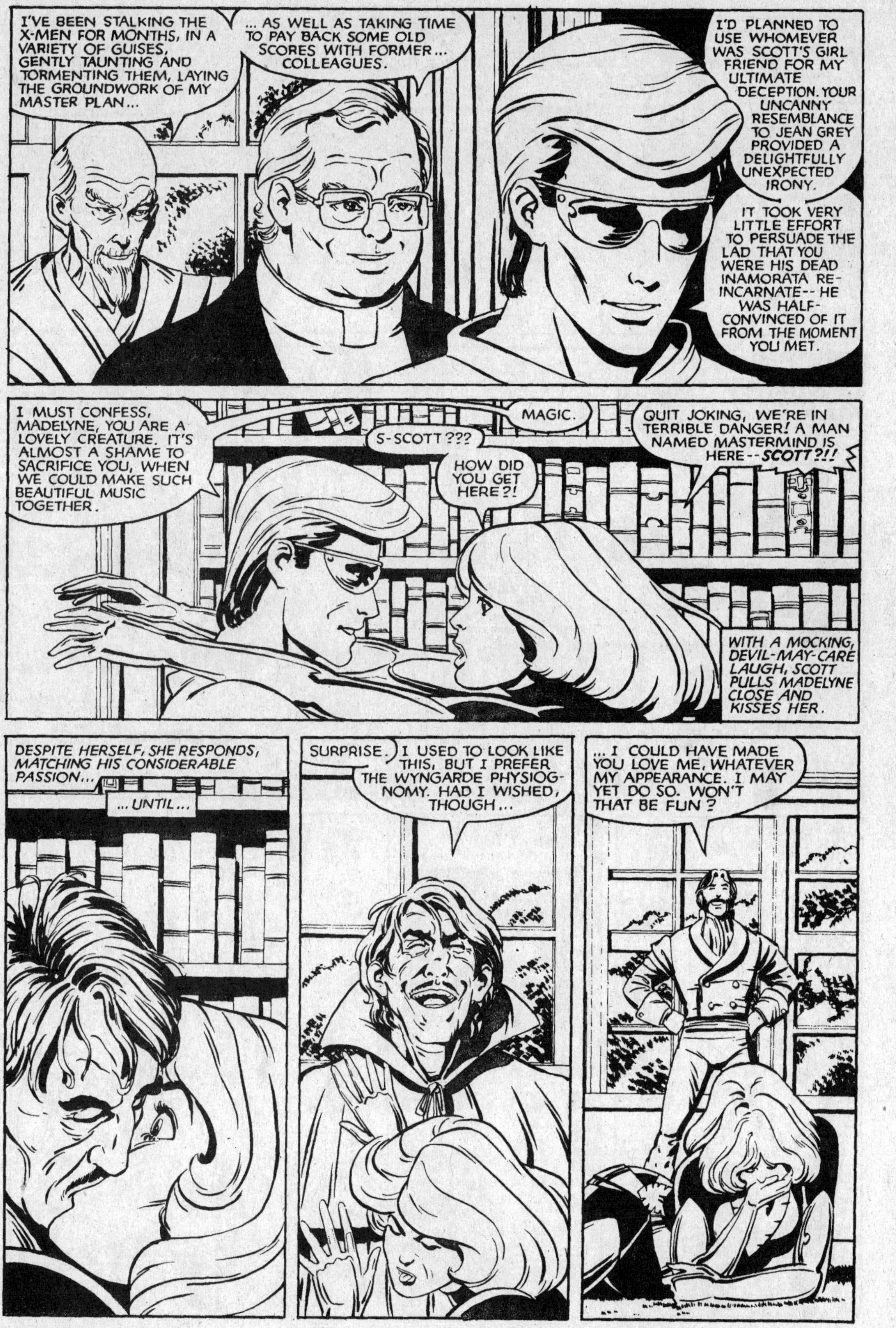
I'VE BEEN STALKING THE X-MEN FOR MONTHS, IN A VARIETY OF GUISES, GENTLY TAUNTING AND TORMENTING THEM, LAYING THE GROUNDWORK OF MY MASTER PLAN...
... AS WELL AS TAKING TIME TO PAY BACK SOME OLD SCORES WITH FORMER... COLLEAGUES.
I'D PLANNED TO USE WHOMEVER WAS SCOTT'S GIRL FRIEND FOR MY ULTIMATE DECEPTION. YOUR UNCANNY RESEMBLANCE TO JEAN GREY PROVIDED A DELIGHTFULLY UNEXPECTED IRONY.
IT TOOK VERY LITTLE EFFORT TO PERSUADE THE LAD THAT YOU WERE HIS DEAD INAMORATA RE-INCARNATE-- HE WAS HALF-CONVINCED OF IT FROM THE MOMENT YOU MET.
I MUST CONFESS, MADELYNE, YOU ARE A LOVELY CREATURE. IT'S ALMOST A SHAME TO SACRIFICE YOU, WHEN WE COULD MAKE SUCH BEAUTIFUL MUSIC TOGETHER.
S-SCOTT???
MAGIC.
HOW DID YOU GET HERE?!
QUIT JOKING, WE'RE IN TERRIBLE DANGER! A MAN NAMED MASTERMIND IS HERE--SCOTT?!!
WITH A MOCKING, DEVIL-MAY-CARE LAUGH, SCOTT PULLS MADELYNE CLOSE AND KISSES HER.
DESPITE HERSELF, SHE RESPONDS, MATCHING HIS CONSIDERABLE PASSION...
... UNTIL...
SURPRISE.
I USED TO LOOK LIKE THIS, BUT I PREFER THE WYNGARDE PHYSIOGNOMY. HAD I WISHED, THOUGH...
... I COULD HAVE MADE YOU LOVE ME, WHATEVER MY APPEARANCE. I MAY YET DO SO. WON'T THAT BE FUN?

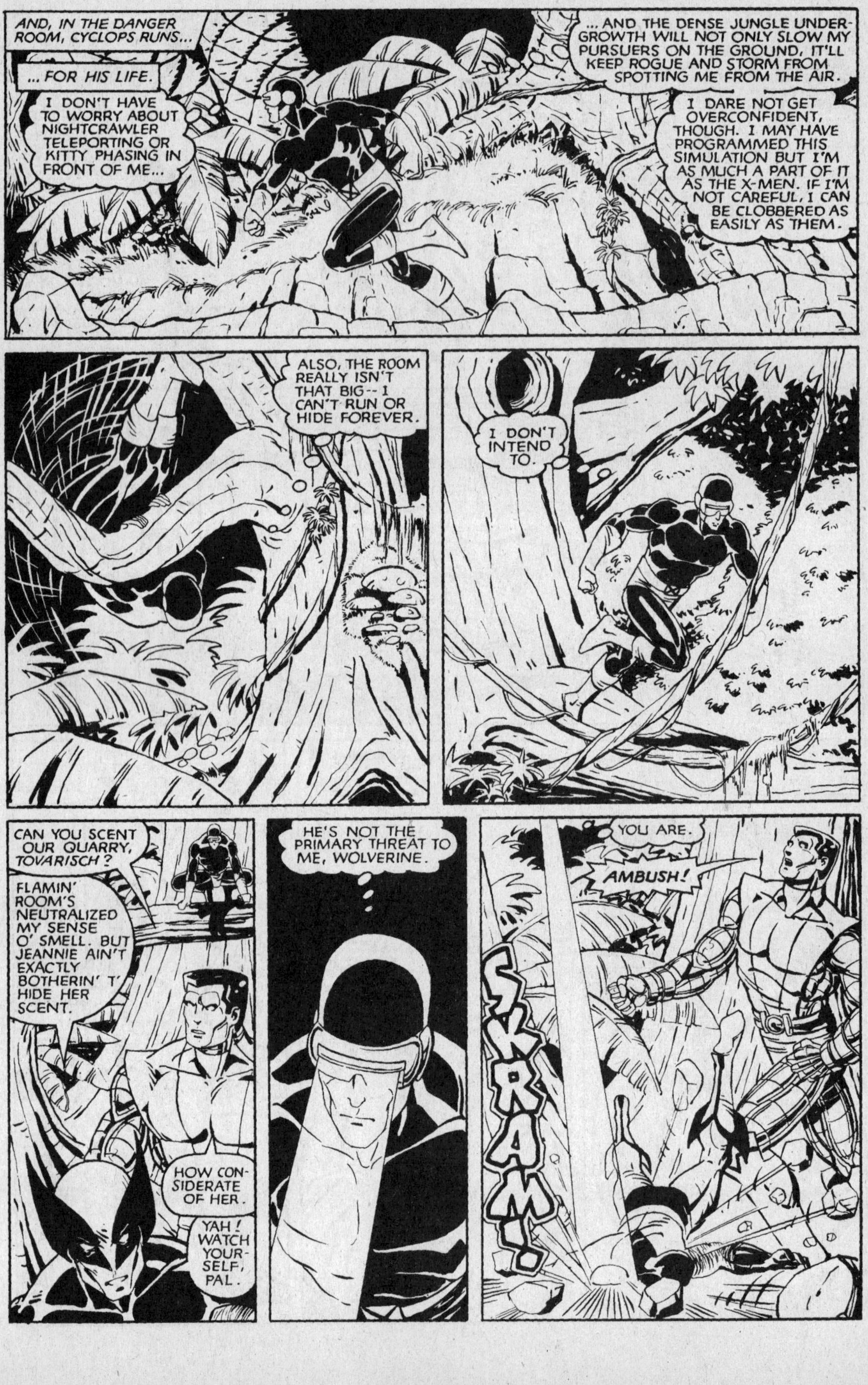
AND, IN THE DANGER ROOM, CYCLOPS RUNS...
... FOR HIS LIFE.
I DON'T HAVE TO WORRY ABOUT NIGHTCRAWLER TELEPORTING OR KITTY PHASING IN FRONT OF ME...
... AND THE DENSE JUNGLE UNDERGROWTH WILL NOT ONLY SLOW MY PURSUERS ON THE GROUND, IT'LL KEEP ROGUE AND STORM FROM SPOTTING ME FROM THE AIR.
I DARE NOT GET OVERCONFIDENT, THOUGH. I MAY HAVE PROGRAMMED THIS SIMULATION BUT I'M AS MUCH A PART OF IT AS THE X-MEN. IF I'M NOT CAREFUL, I CAN BE CLOBBERED AS EASILY AS THEM.
ALSO, THE ROOM REALLY ISN'T THAT BIG-- I CAN'T RUN OR HIDE FOREVER.
I DON'T INTEND TO.
CAN YOU SCENT OUR QUARRY, *TOVARISCH*?
FLAMIN' ROOM'S NEUTRALIZED MY SENSE O' SMELL. BUT JEANNIE AIN'T EXACTLY BOTHERIN' T' HIDE HER SCENT.
HOW CONSIDERATE OF HER.
YAH! WATCH YOURSELF, PAL.
HE'S NOT THE PRIMARY THREAT TO ME, WOLVERINE.
YOU ARE.
AMBUSH!
SKRAM!

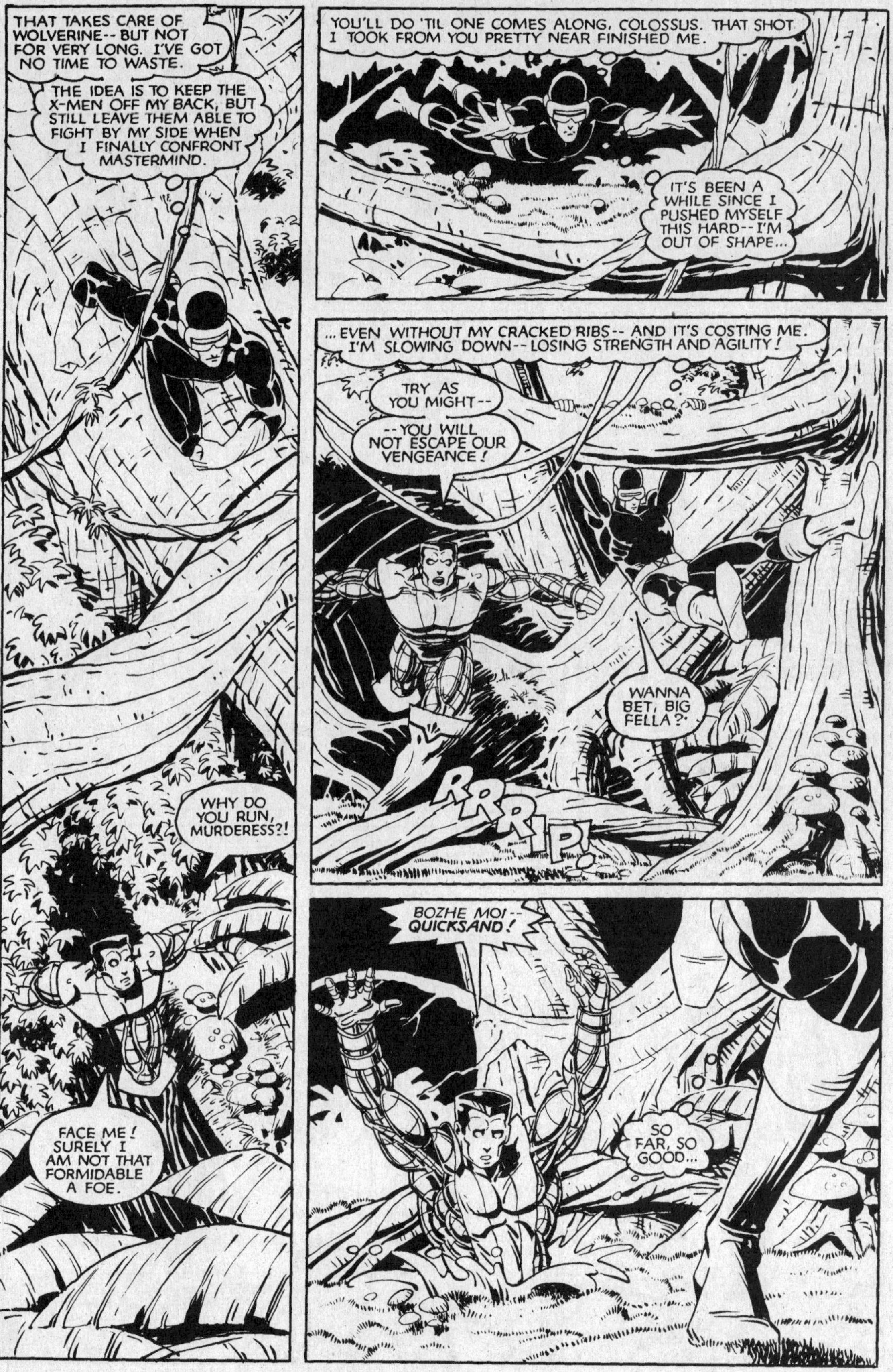
THAT TAKES CARE OF WOLVERINE-- BUT NOT FOR VERY LONG. I'VE GOT NO TIME TO WASTE.
THE IDEA IS TO KEEP THE X-MEN OFF MY BACK, BUT STILL LEAVE THEM ABLE TO FIGHT BY MY SIDE WHEN I FINALLY CONFRONT MASTERMIND.
WHY DO YOU RUN, MURDERESS?!
FACE ME! SURELY I AM NOT THAT FORMIDABLE A FOE.
YOU'LL DO 'TIL ONE COMES ALONG, COLOSSUS. THAT SHOT I TOOK FROM YOU PRETTY NEAR FINISHED ME.
IT'S BEEN A WHILE SINCE I PUSHED MYSELF THIS HARD--I'M OUT OF SHAPE...
... EVEN WITHOUT MY CRACKED RIBS-- AND IT'S COSTING ME. I'M SLOWING DOWN-- LOSING STRENGTH AND AGILITY!
TRY AS YOU MIGHT--
--YOU WILL NOT ESCAPE OUR VENGEANCE!
WANNA BET, BIG FELLA?
RRRIP!
BOZHE MOI-- QUICKSAND!
SO FAR, SO GOOD...

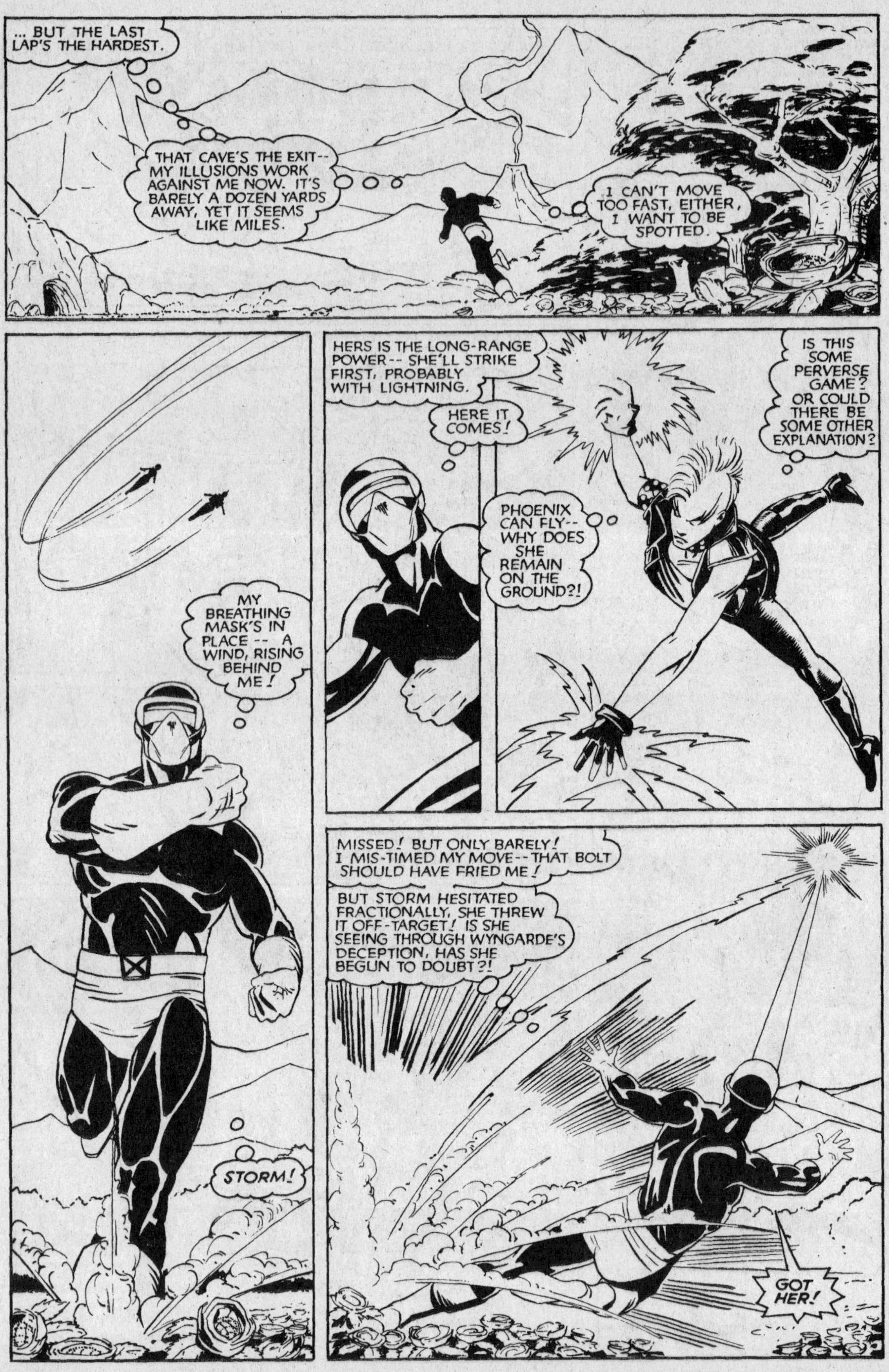
... BUT THE LAST LAP'S THE HARDEST.
THAT CAVE'S THE EXIT-- MY ILLUSIONS WORK AGAINST ME NOW. IT'S BARELY A DOZEN YARDS AWAY, YET IT SEEMS LIKE MILES.
I CAN'T MOVE TOO FAST, EITHER, I WANT TO BE SPOTTED.
MY BREATHING MASK'S IN PLACE -- A WIND, RISING BEHIND ME!
STORM!
HERS IS THE LONG-RANGE POWER-- SHE'LL STRIKE FIRST, PROBABLY WITH LIGHTNING.
HERE IT COMES!
PHOENIX CAN FLY-- WHY DOES SHE REMAIN ON THE GROUND?!
IS THIS SOME PERVERSE GAME? OR COULD THERE BE SOME OTHER EXPLANATION?
MISSED! BUT ONLY BARELY! I MIS-TIMED MY MOVE--THAT BOLT SHOULD HAVE FRIED ME!
BUT STORM HESITATED FRACTIONALLY, SHE THREW IT OFF-TARGET! IS SHE SEEING THROUGH WYNGARDE'S DECEPTION, HAS SHE BEGUN TO DOUBT?!
GOT HER!

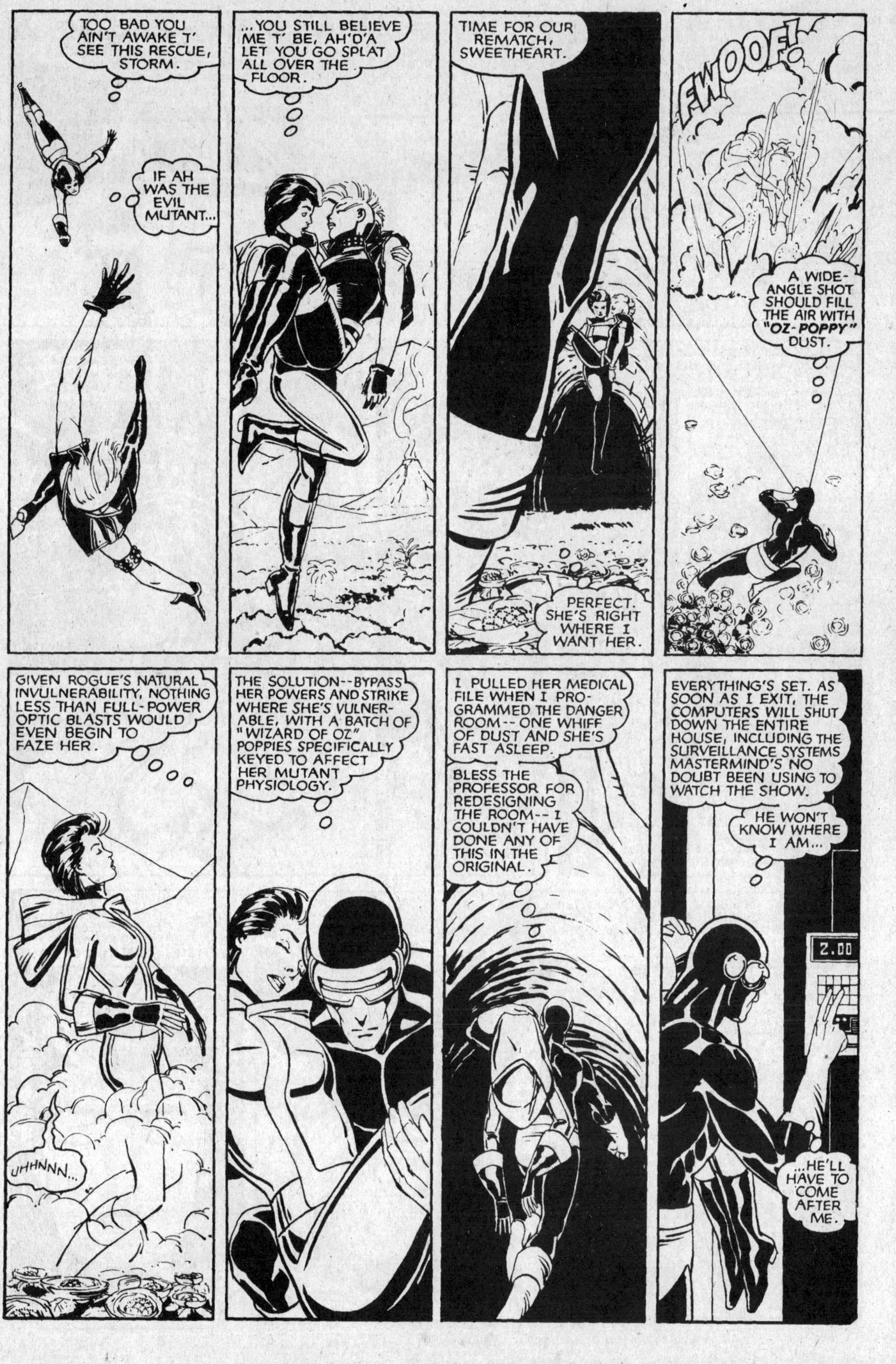
TOO BAD YOU AIN'T AWAKE T' SEE THIS RESCUE, STORM.
IF AH WAS THE EVIL MUTANT...
...YOU STILL BELIEVE ME T' BE, AH'D'A LET YOU GO SPLAT ALL OVER THE FLOOR.
TIME FOR OUR REMATCH, SWEETHEART.
PERFECT. SHE'S RIGHT WHERE I WANT HER.
FWOOF!
A WIDE-ANGLE SHOT SHOULD FILL THE AIR WITH "OZ-POPPY" DUST.
GIVEN ROGUE'S NATURAL INVULNERABILITY, NOTHING LESS THAN FULL-POWER OPTIC BLASTS WOULD EVEN BEGIN TO FAZE HER.
UHHNNN...
THE SOLUTION--BYPASS HER POWERS AND STRIKE WHERE SHE'S VULNERABLE, WITH A BATCH OF "WIZARD OF OZ" POPPIES SPECIFICALLY KEYED TO AFFECT HER MUTANT PHYSIOLOGY.
I PULLED HER MEDICAL FILE WHEN I PROGRAMMED THE DANGER ROOM-- ONE WHIFF OF DUST AND SHE'S FAST ASLEEP.
BLESS THE PROFESSOR FOR REDESIGNING THE ROOM-- I COULDN'T HAVE DONE ANY OF THIS IN THE ORIGINAL.
EVERYTHING'S SET. AS SOON AS I EXIT, THE COMPUTERS WILL SHUT DOWN THE ENTIRE HOUSE, INCLUDING THE SURVEILLANCE SYSTEMS MASTERMIND'S NO DOUBT BEEN USING TO WATCH THE SHOW.
HE WON'T KNOW WHERE I AM...
2.00
...HE'LL HAVE TO COME AFTER ME.

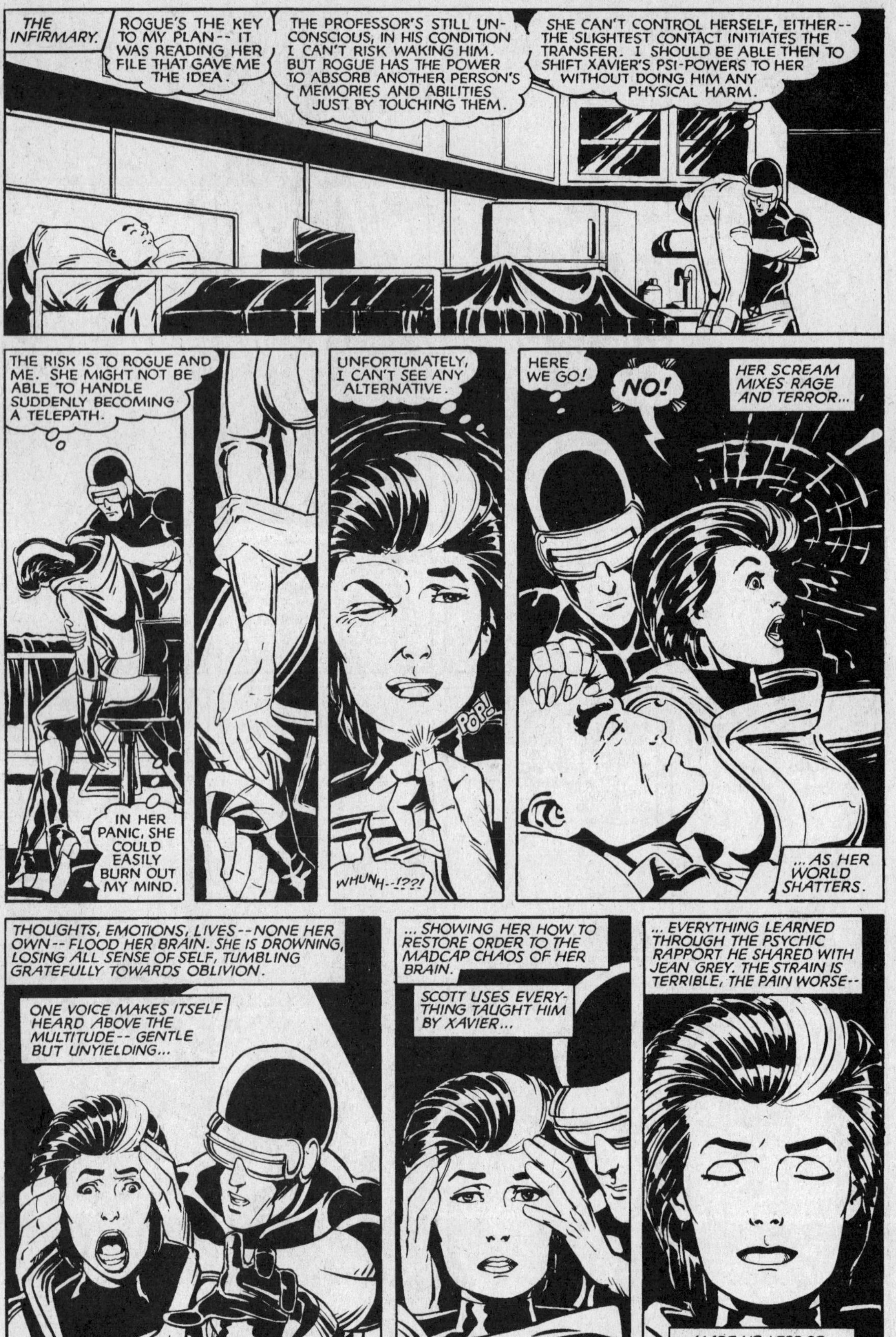
THE INFIRMARY.
ROGUE'S THE KEY TO MY PLAN-- IT WAS READING HER FILE THAT GAVE ME THE IDEA.
THE PROFESSOR'S STILL UNCONSCIOUS; IN HIS CONDITION I CAN'T RISK WAKING HIM. BUT ROGUE HAS THE POWER TO ABSORB ANOTHER PERSON'S MEMORIES AND ABILITIES JUST BY TOUCHING THEM.
SHE CAN'T CONTROL HERSELF, EITHER-- THE SLIGHTEST CONTACT INITIATES THE TRANSFER. I SHOULD BE ABLE THEN TO SHIFT XAVIER'S PSI-POWERS TO HER WITHOUT DOING HIM ANY PHYSICAL HARM.
THE RISK IS TO ROGUE AND ME. SHE MIGHT NOT BE ABLE TO HANDLE SUDDENLY BECOMING A TELEPATH.
IN HER PANIC, SHE COULD EASILY BURN OUT MY MIND.
UNFORTUNATELY, I CAN'T SEE ANY ALTERNATIVE.
POP!
WHUNH--!??!
HERE WE GO!
NO!
HER SCREAM MIXES RAGE AND TERROR...
...AS HER WORLD SHATTERS.
THOUGHTS, EMOTIONS, LIVES--NONE HER OWN--FLOOD HER BRAIN. SHE IS DROWNING, LOSING ALL SENSE OF SELF, TUMBLING GRATEFULLY TOWARDS OBLIVION.
ONE VOICE MAKES ITSELF HEARD ABOVE THE MULTITUDE-- GENTLE BUT UNYIELDING...
...SHOWING HER HOW TO RESTORE ORDER TO THE MADCAP CHAOS OF HER BRAIN.
SCOTT USES EVERYTHING TAUGHT HIM BY XAVIER...
...EVERYTHING LEARNED THROUGH THE PSYCHIC RAPPORT HE SHARED WITH JEAN GREY. THE STRAIN IS TERRIBLE, THE PAIN WORSE--
--MADE NO LESS SO BECAUSE IT IS SHARED.

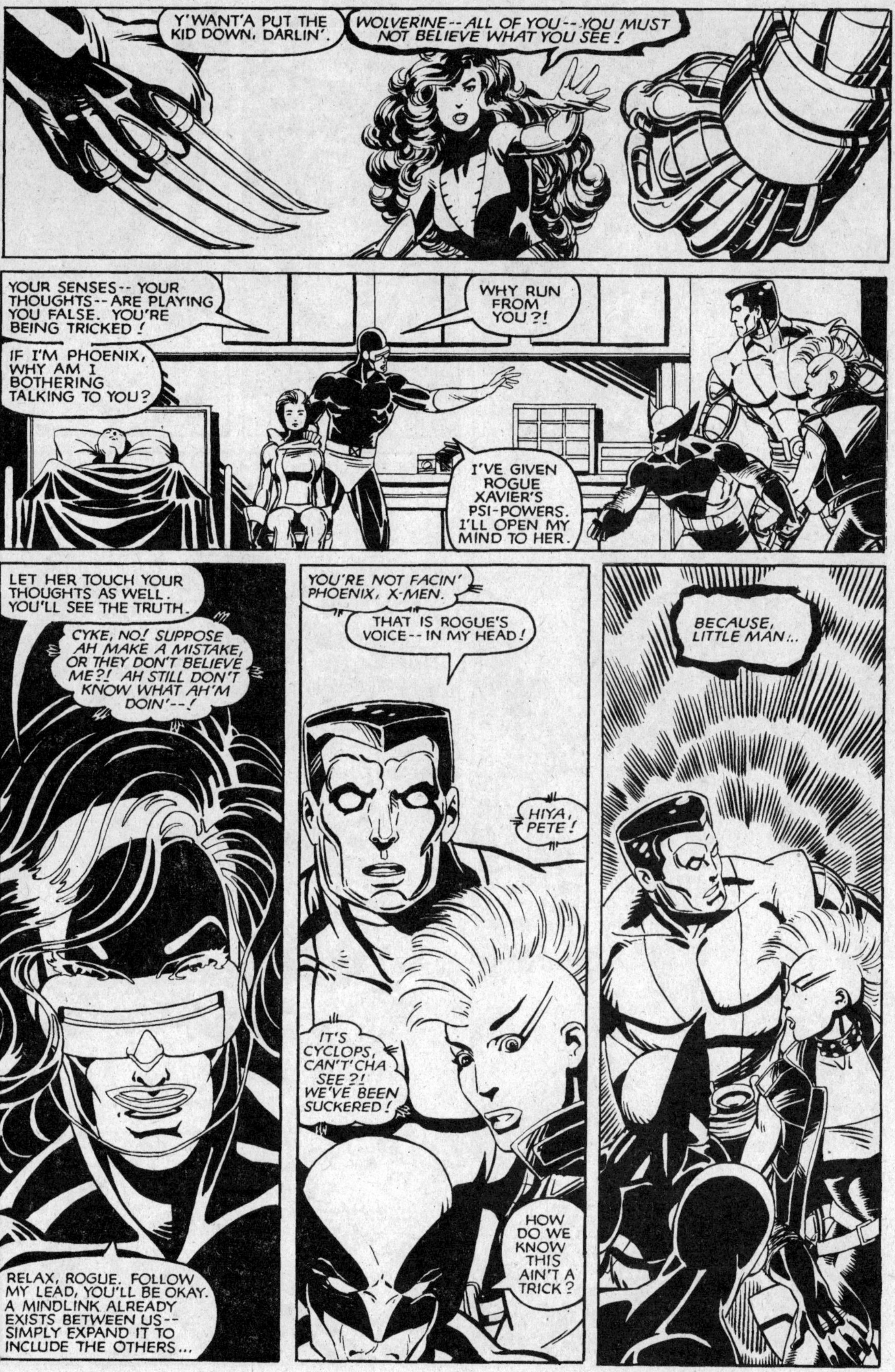

Y'WANT'A PUT THE KID DOWN, DARLIN'.
WOLVERINE--ALL OF YOU--YOU MUST NOT BELIEVE WHAT YOU SEE!
YOUR SENSES--YOUR THOUGHTS--ARE PLAYING YOU FALSE. YOU'RE BEING TRICKED!
IF I'M PHOENIX, WHY AM I BOTHERING TALKING TO YOU?
WHY RUN FROM YOU?!
I'VE GIVEN ROGUE XAVIER'S PSI-POWERS. I'LL OPEN MY MIND TO HER.
LET HER TOUCH YOUR THOUGHTS AS WELL. YOU'LL SEE THE TRUTH.
CYKE, NO! SUPPOSE AH MAKE A MISTAKE, OR THEY DON'T BELIEVE ME?! AH STILL DON'T KNOW WHAT AH'M DOIN'--!
RELAX, ROGUE. FOLLOW MY LEAD, YOU'LL BE OKAY. A MINDLINK ALREADY EXISTS BETWEEN US--SIMPLY EXPAND IT TO INCLUDE THE OTHERS...
YOU'RE NOT FACIN' PHOENIX, X-MEN.
THAT IS ROGUE'S VOICE--IN MY HEAD!
HIYA, PETE!
IT'S CYCLOPS, CAN'T'CHA SEE?! WE'VE BEEN SUCKERED!
HOW DO WE KNOW THIS AIN'T A TRICK?
BECAUSE, LITTLE MAN...

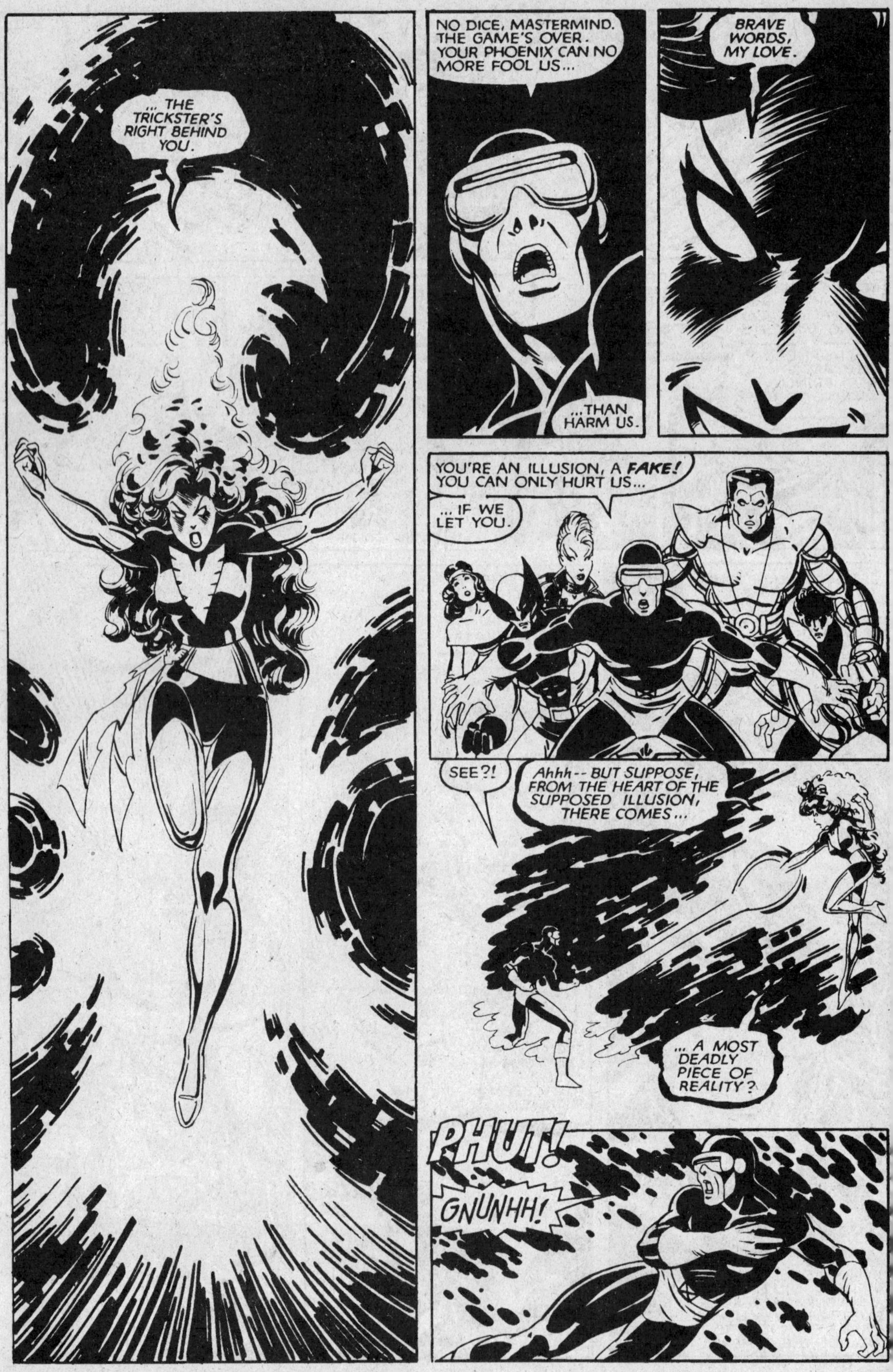
... THE TRICKSTER'S RIGHT BEHIND YOU.
NO DICE, MASTERMIND. THE GAME'S OVER. YOUR PHOENIX CAN NO MORE FOOL US...
...THAN HARM US.
BRAVE WORDS, MY LOVE.
YOU'RE AN ILLUSION, A FAKE! YOU CAN ONLY HURT US...
... IF WE LET YOU.
SEE?!
Ahhh-- BUT SUPPOSE, FROM THE HEART OF THE SUPPOSED ILLUSION, THERE COMES...
... A MOST DEADLY PIECE OF REALITY?
PHUT!
GNUNHH!

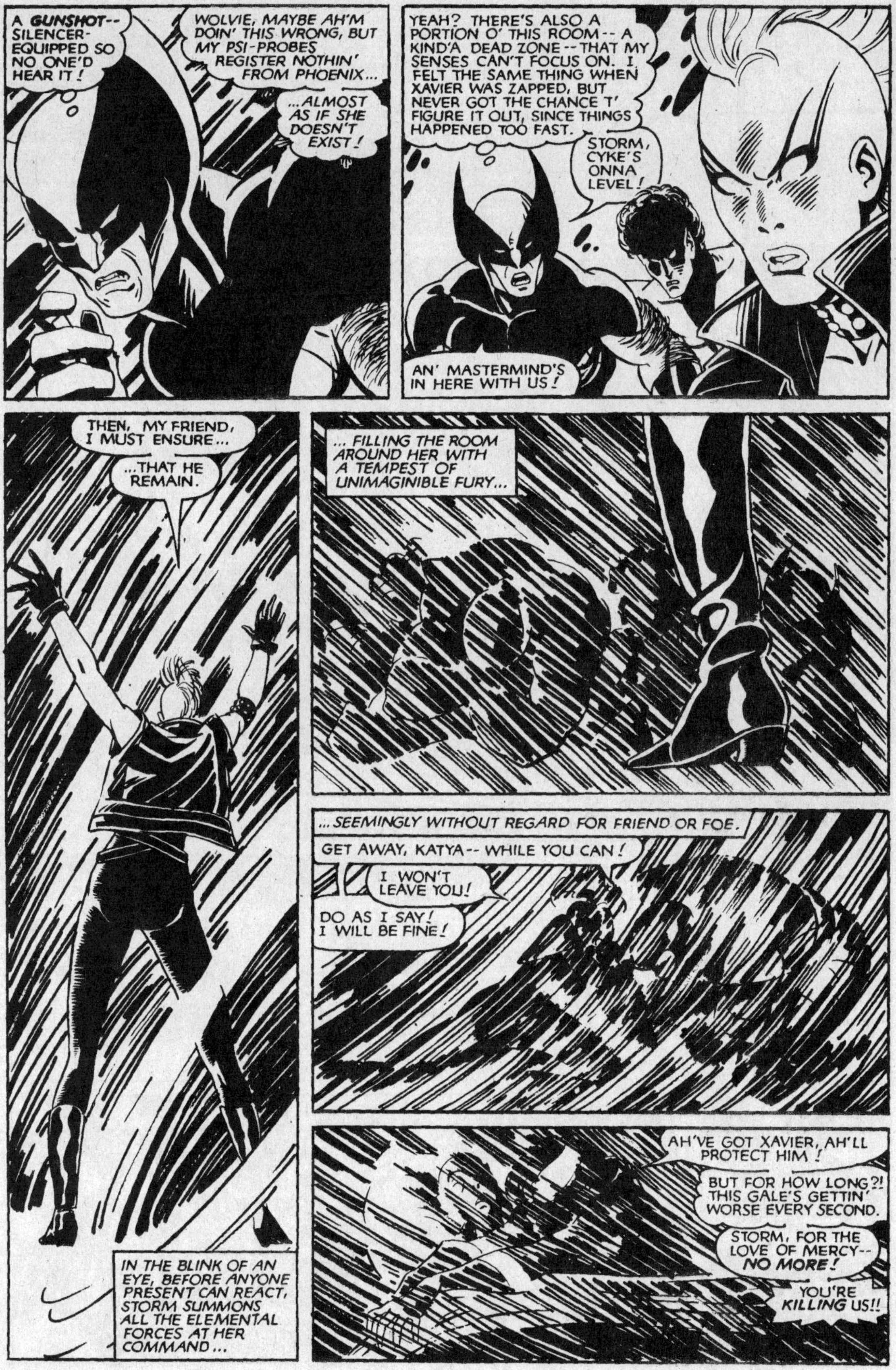
A GUNSHOT-- SILENCER-EQUIPPED SO NO ONE'D HEAR IT!
WOLVIE, MAYBE AH'M DOIN' THIS WRONG, BUT MY PSI-PROBES REGISTER NOTHIN' FROM PHOENIX...
...ALMOST AS IF SHE DOESN'T EXIST!
YEAH? THERE'S ALSO A PORTION O' THIS ROOM -- A KIND'A DEAD ZONE -- THAT MY SENSES CAN'T FOCUS ON. I FELT THE SAME THING WHEN XAVIER WAS ZAPPED, BUT NEVER GOT THE CHANCE T' FIGURE IT OUT, SINCE THINGS HAPPENED TOO FAST.
STORM, CYKE'S ONNA LEVEL!
AN' MASTERMIND'S IN HERE WITH US!
THEN, MY FRIEND, I MUST ENSURE...
...THAT HE REMAIN.
IN THE BLINK OF AN EYE, BEFORE ANYONE PRESENT CAN REACT, STORM SUMMONS ALL THE ELEMENTAL FORCES AT HER COMMAND...
... FILLING THE ROOM AROUND HER WITH A TEMPEST OF UNIMAGINIBLE FURY...
...SEEMINGLY WITHOUT REGARD FOR FRIEND OR FOE.
GET AWAY, KATYA -- WHILE YOU CAN!
I WON'T LEAVE YOU!
DO AS I SAY! I WILL BE FINE!
AH'VE GOT XAVIER, AH'LL PROTECT HIM!
BUT FOR HOW LONG?! THIS GALE'S GETTIN' WORSE EVERY SECOND.
STORM, FOR THE LOVE OF MERCY-- NO MORE!
YOU'RE KILLING US!!

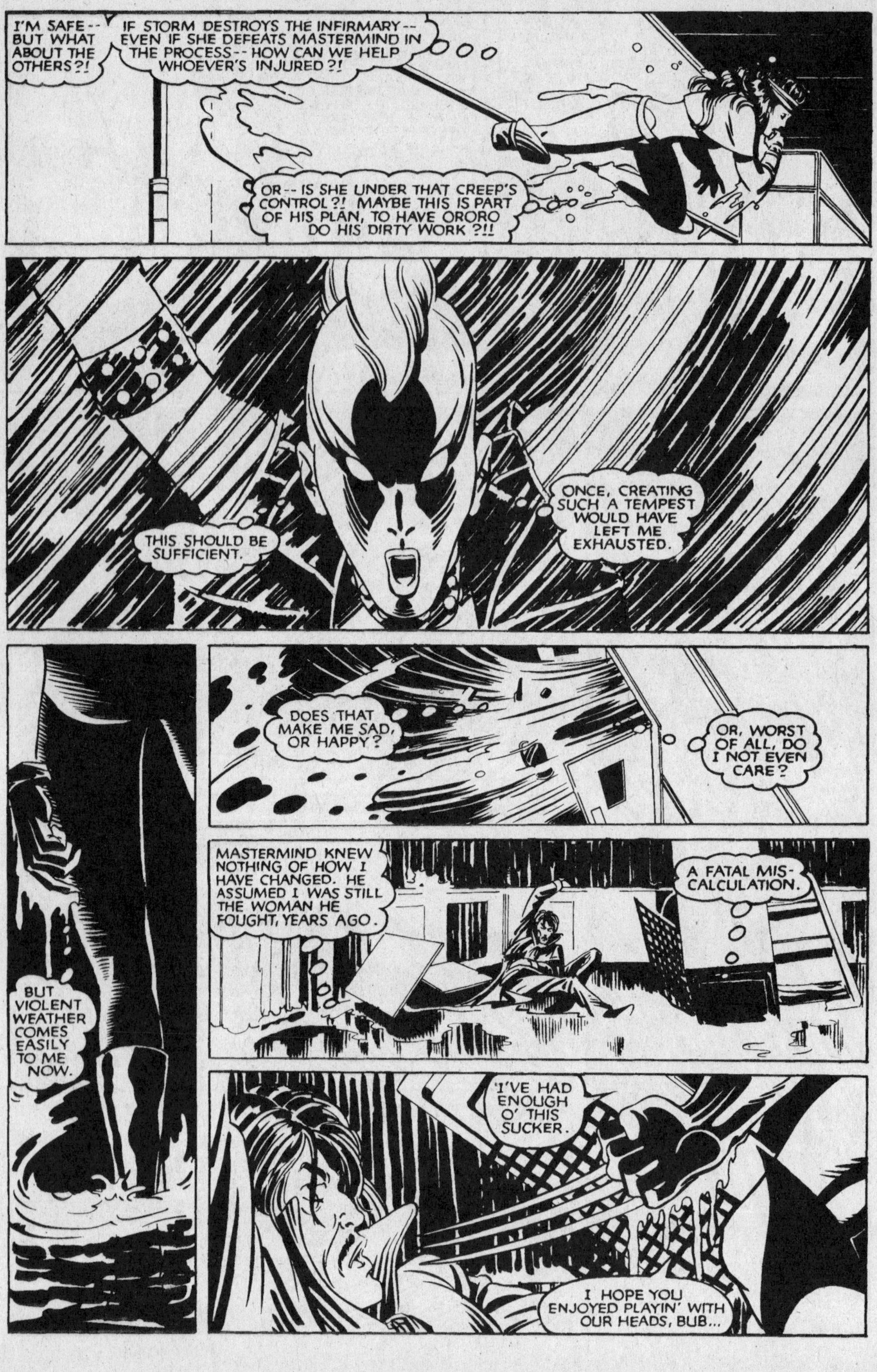

I'M SAFE-- BUT WHAT ABOUT THE OTHERS?!
IF STORM DESTROYS THE INFIRMARY-- EVEN IF SHE DEFEATS MASTERMIND IN THE PROCESS-- HOW CAN WE HELP WHOEVER'S INJURED?!
OR-- IS SHE UNDER THAT CREEP'S CONTROL?! MAYBE THIS IS PART OF HIS PLAN, TO HAVE ORORO DO HIS DIRTY WORK?!!
THIS SHOULD BE SUFFICIENT.
ONCE, CREATING SUCH A TEMPEST WOULD HAVE LEFT ME EXHAUSTED.
BUT VIOLENT WEATHER COMES EASILY TO ME NOW.
DOES THAT MAKE ME SAD, OR HAPPY?
OR, WORST OF ALL, DO I NOT EVEN CARE?
MASTERMIND KNEW NOTHING OF HOW I HAVE CHANGED. HE ASSUMED I WAS STILL THE WOMAN HE FOUGHT, YEARS AGO.
A FATAL MIS-CALCULATION.
'I'VE HAD ENOUGH O' THIS SUCKER.
I HOPE YOU ENJOYED PLAYIN' WITH OUR HEADS, BUB...

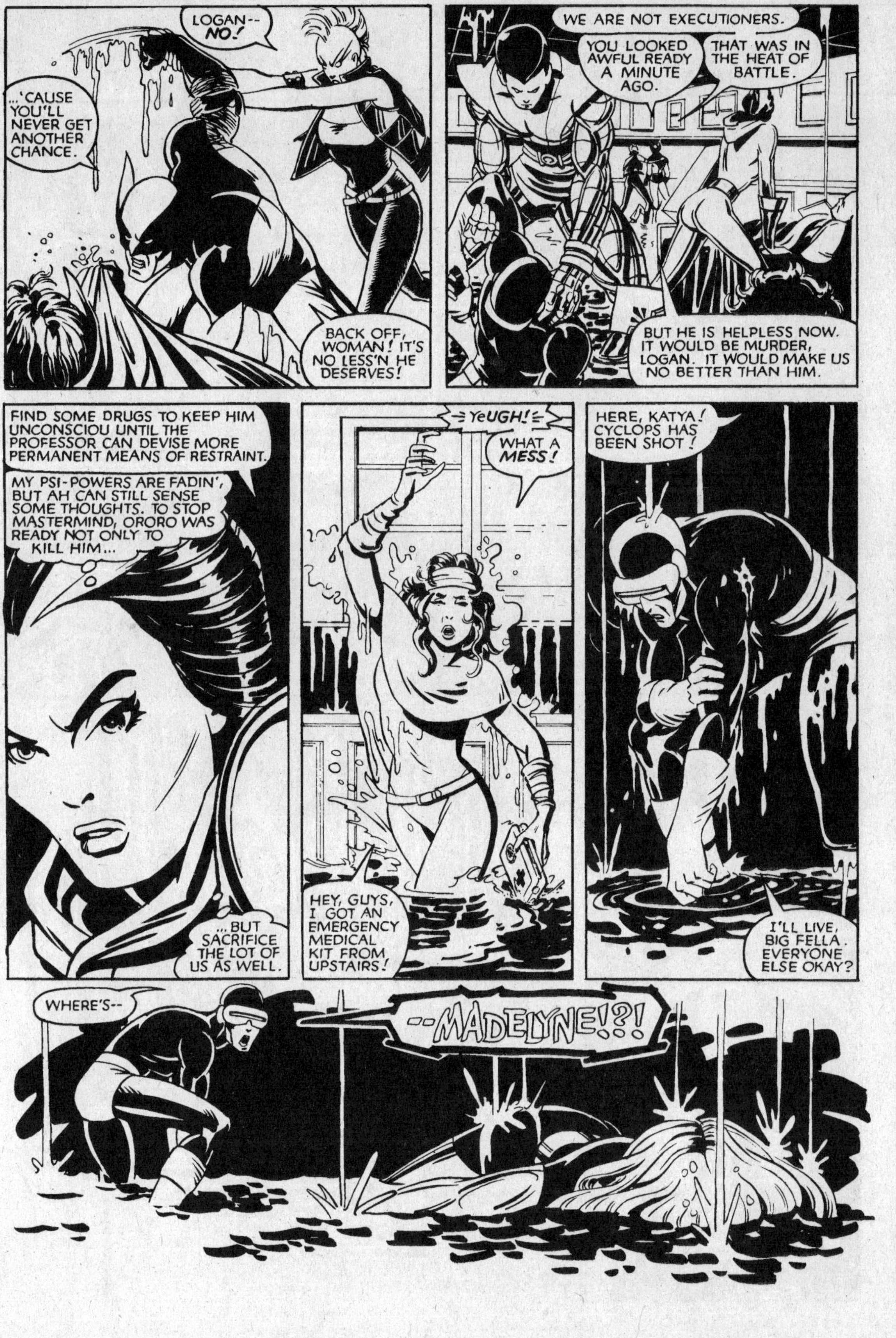
LOGAN-- NO!
...'CAUSE YOU'LL NEVER GET ANOTHER CHANCE.
BACK OFF, WOMAN! IT'S NO LESS'N HE DESERVES!
WE ARE NOT EXECUTIONERS.
YOU LOOKED AWFUL READY A MINUTE AGO.
THAT WAS IN THE HEAT OF BATTLE.
BUT HE IS HELPLESS NOW. IT WOULD BE MURDER, LOGAN. IT WOULD MAKE US NO BETTER THAN HIM.
FIND SOME DRUGS TO KEEP HIM UNCONSCIOU UNTIL THE PROFESSOR CAN DEVISE MORE PERMANENT MEANS OF RESTRAINT.
MY PSI-POWERS ARE FADIN', BUT AH CAN STILL SENSE SOME THOUGHTS. TO STOP MASTERMIND, ORORO WAS READY NOT ONLY TO KILL HIM...
...BUT SACRIFICE THE LOT OF US AS WELL.
YeUGH!
WHAT A MESS!
HEY, GUYS, I GOT AN EMERGENCY MEDICAL KIT FROM UPSTAIRS!
HERE, KATYA! CYCLOPS HAS BEEN SHOT!
I'LL LIVE, BIG FELLA. EVERYONE ELSE OKAY?
WHERE'S--
--MADELYNE!?!

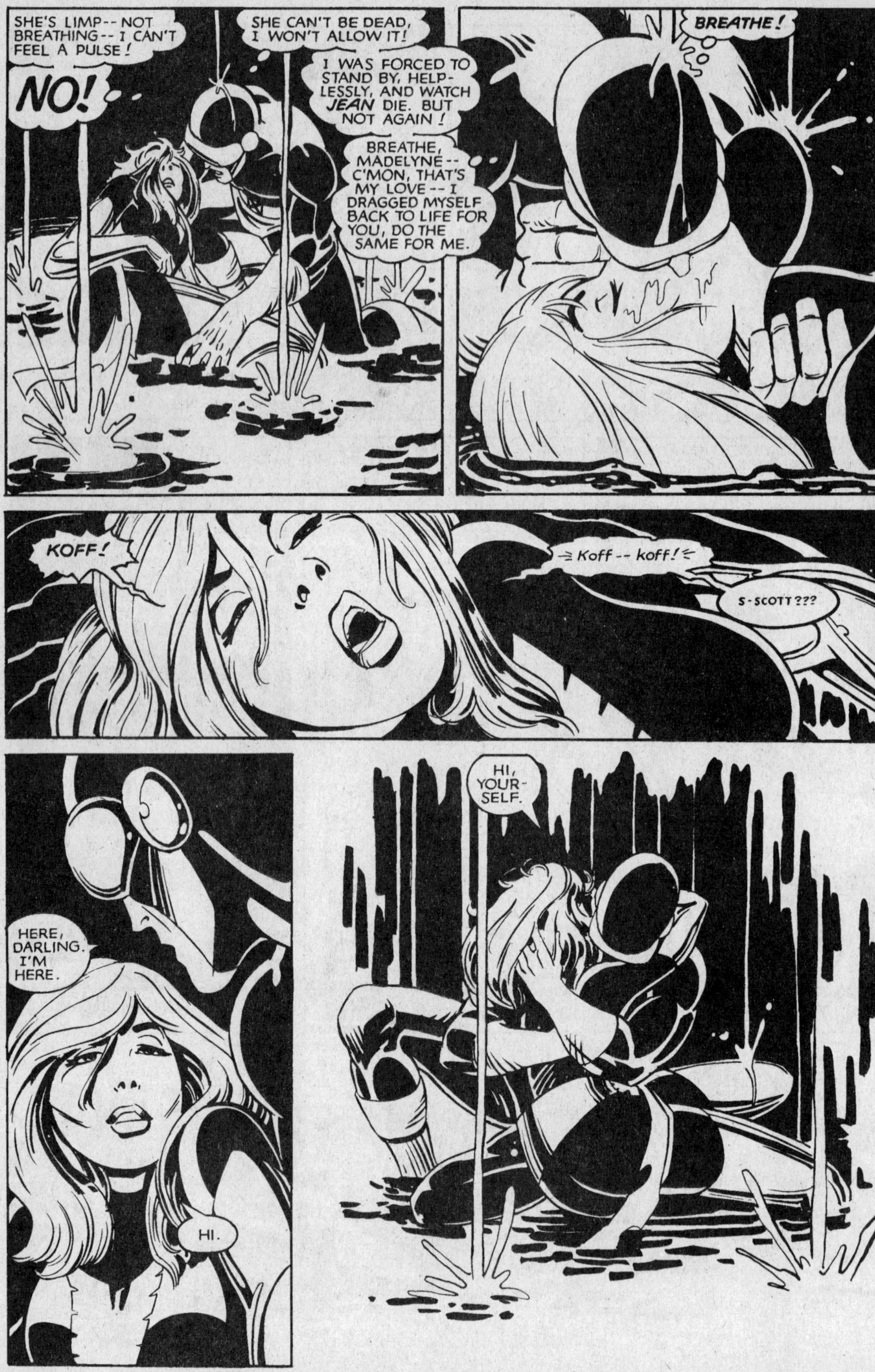
SHE'S LIMP-- NOT BREATHING-- I CAN'T FEEL A PULSE!
NO!
SHE CAN'T BE DEAD, I WON'T ALLOW IT!
I WAS FORCED TO STAND BY, HELP-LESSLY, AND WATCH JEAN DIE. BUT NOT AGAIN!
BREATHE, MADELYNE-- C'MON, THAT'S MY LOVE-- I DRAGGED MYSELF BACK TO LIFE FOR YOU, DO THE SAME FOR ME.
BREATHE!
KOFF!
Koff-- koff!
S-SCOTT???
HERE, DARLING. I'M HERE.
HI.
HI, YOUR-SELF.

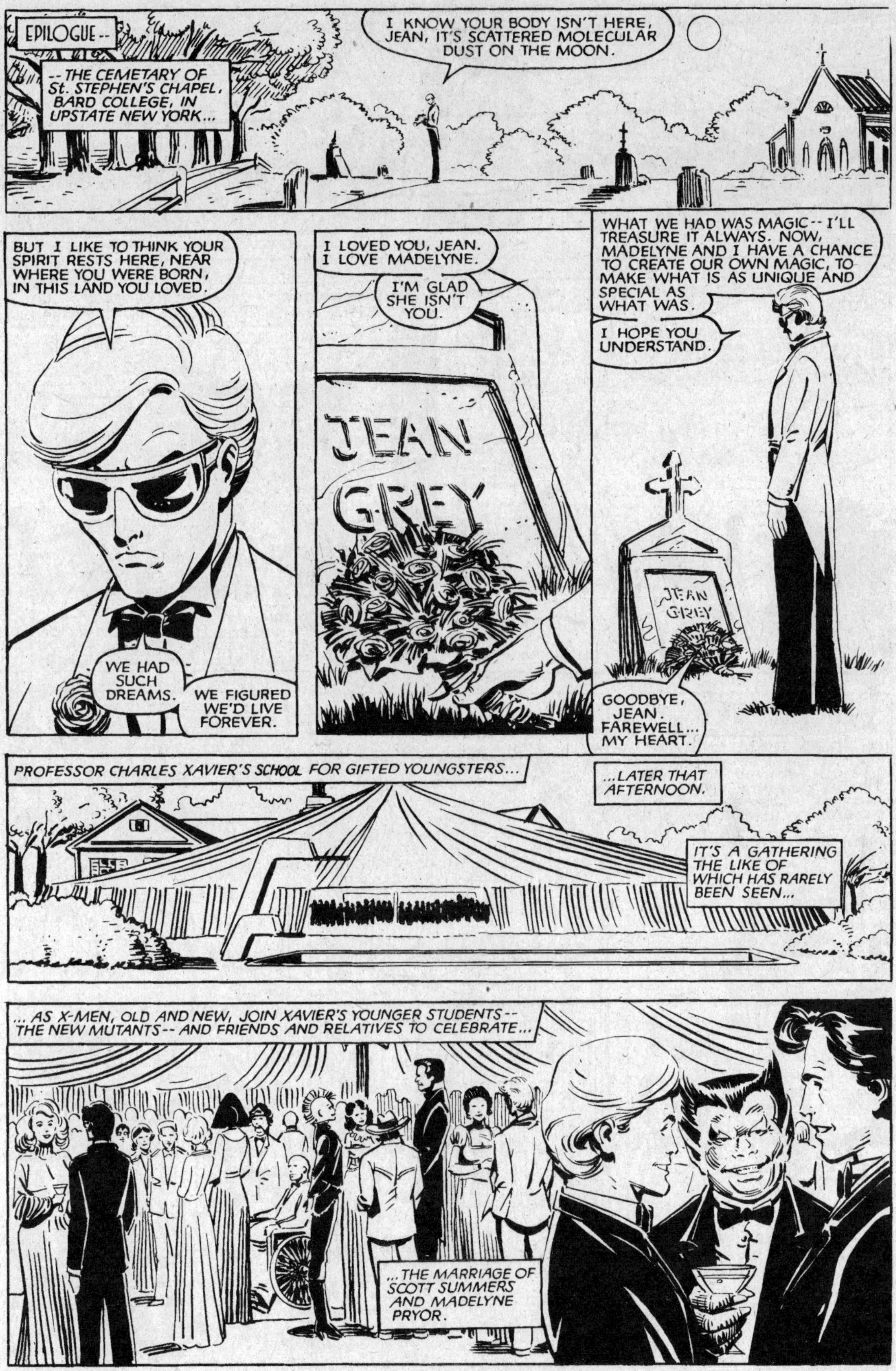
EPILOGUE--
--THE CEMETARY OF St. STEPHEN'S CHAPEL, BARD COLLEGE, IN UPSTATE NEW YORK...
I KNOW YOUR BODY ISN'T HERE, JEAN, IT'S SCATTERED MOLECULAR DUST ON THE MOON.
BUT I LIKE TO THINK YOUR SPIRIT RESTS HERE, NEAR WHERE YOU WERE BORN, IN THIS LAND YOU LOVED.
WE HAD SUCH DREAMS.
WE FIGURED WE'D LIVE FOREVER.
I LOVED YOU, JEAN. I LOVE MADELYNE.
I'M GLAD SHE ISN'T YOU.
JEAN GREY
WHAT WE HAD WAS MAGIC--I'LL TREASURE IT ALWAYS. NOW, MADELYNE AND I HAVE A CHANCE TO CREATE OUR OWN MAGIC, TO MAKE WHAT IS AS UNIQUE AND SPECIAL AS WHAT WAS.
I HOPE YOU UNDERSTAND.
JEAN GREY
GOODBYE, JEAN. FAREWELL... MY HEART.
PROFESSOR CHARLES XAVIER'S SCHOOL FOR GIFTED YOUNGSTERS...
...LATER THAT AFTERNOON.
IT'S A GATHERING THE LIKE OF WHICH HAS RARELY BEEN SEEN...
...AS X-MEN, OLD AND NEW, JOIN XAVIER'S YOUNGER STUDENTS--THE NEW MUTANTS--AND FRIENDS AND RELATIVES TO CELEBRATE...
...THE MARRIAGE OF SCOTT SUMMERS AND MADELYNE PRYOR.

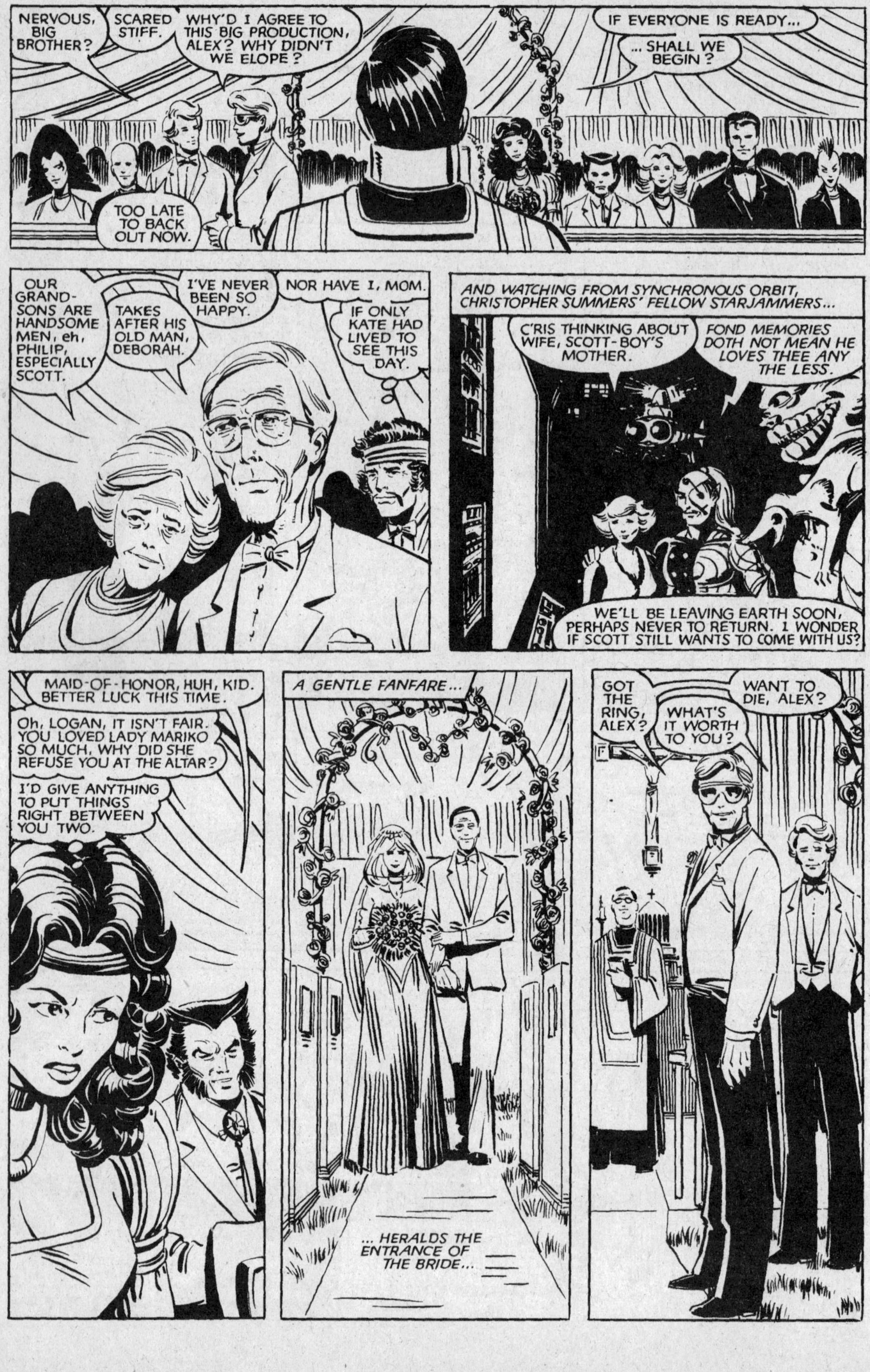
NERVOUS, BIG BROTHER?
SCARED STIFF.
WHY'D I AGREE TO THIS BIG PRODUCTION, ALEX? WHY DIDN'T WE ELOPE?
TOO LATE TO BACK OUT NOW.
IF EVERYONE IS READY...
... SHALL WE BEGIN?
OUR GRANDSONS ARE HANDSOME MEN, eh, PHILIP, ESPECIALLY SCOTT.
TAKES AFTER HIS OLD MAN, DEBORAH.
I'VE NEVER BEEN SO HAPPY.
NOR HAVE I, MOM.
IF ONLY KATE HAD LIVED TO SEE THIS DAY.
AND WATCHING FROM SYNCHRONOUS ORBIT, CHRISTOPHER SUMMERS' FELLOW STARJAMMERS...
C'RIS THINKING ABOUT WIFE, SCOTT-BOY'S MOTHER.
FOND MEMORIES DOTH NOT MEAN HE LOVES THEE ANY THE LESS.
WE'LL BE LEAVING EARTH SOON, PERHAPS NEVER TO RETURN. I WONDER IF SCOTT STILL WANTS TO COME WITH US?
MAID-OF-HONOR, HUH, KID. BETTER LUCK THIS TIME.
Oh, LOGAN, IT ISN'T FAIR. YOU LOVED LADY MARIKO SO MUCH, WHY DID SHE REFUSE YOU AT THE ALTAR?
I'D GIVE ANYTHING TO PUT THINGS RIGHT BETWEEN YOU TWO.
A GENTLE FANFARE...
... HERALDS THE ENTRANCE OF THE BRIDE...
GOT THE RING, ALEX?
WHAT'S IT WORTH TO YOU?
WANT TO DIE, ALEX?

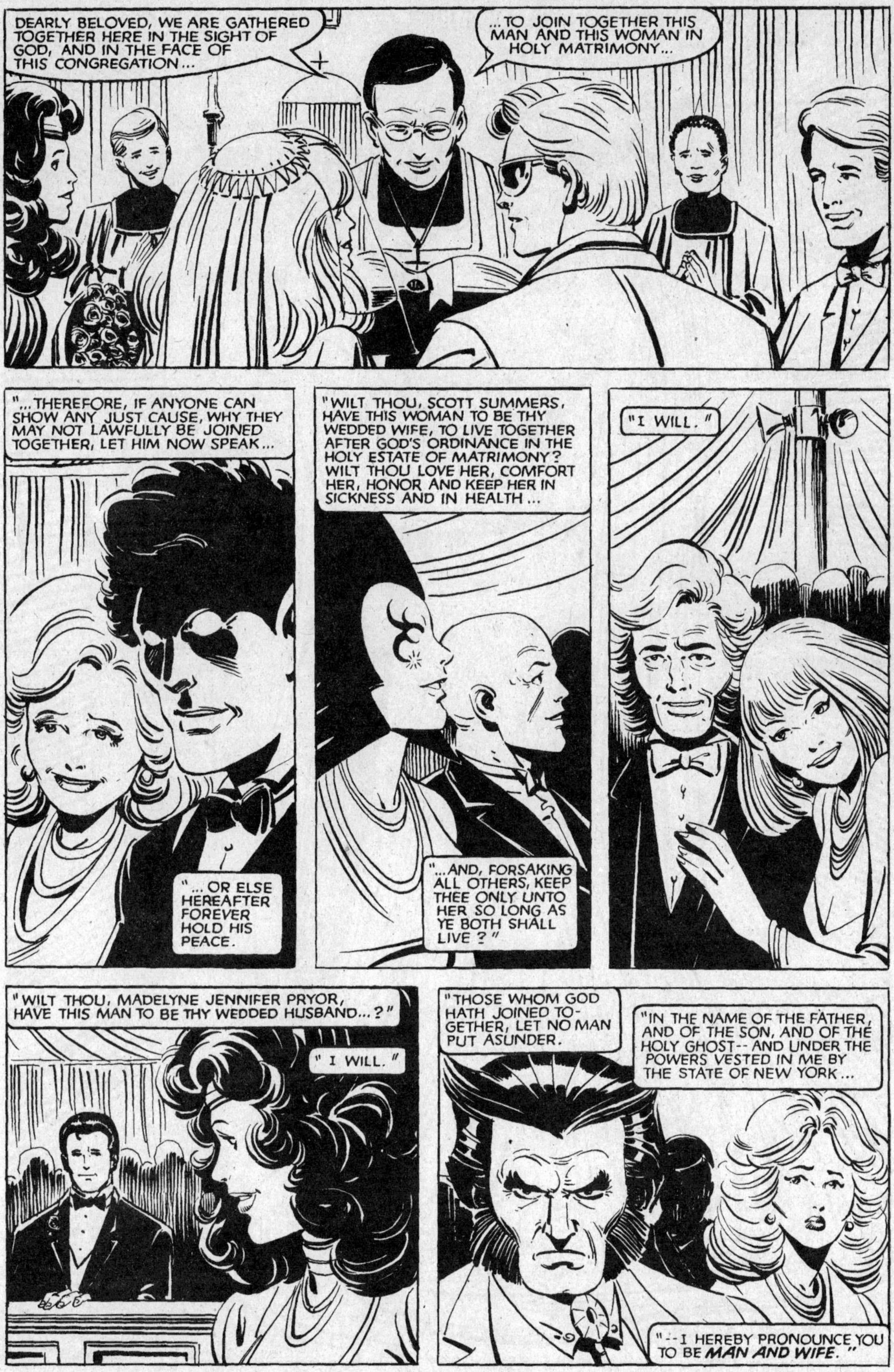
DEARLY BELOVED, WE ARE GATHERED TOGETHER HERE IN THE SIGHT OF GOD, AND IN THE FACE OF THIS CONGREGATION...
...TO JOIN TOGETHER THIS MAN AND THIS WOMAN IN HOLY MATRIMONY...
"...THEREFORE, IF ANYONE CAN SHOW ANY JUST CAUSE, WHY THEY MAY NOT LAWFULLY BE JOINED TOGETHER, LET HIM NOW SPEAK...
"...OR ELSE HEREAFTER FOREVER HOLD HIS PEACE.
"WILT THOU, SCOTT SUMMERS, HAVE THIS WOMAN TO BE THY WEDDED WIFE, TO LIVE TOGETHER AFTER GOD'S ORDINANCE IN THE HOLY ESTATE OF MATRIMONY? WILT THOU LOVE HER, COMFORT HER, HONOR AND KEEP HER IN SICKNESS AND IN HEALTH...
"...AND, FORSAKING ALL OTHERS, KEEP THEE ONLY UNTO HER SO LONG AS YE BOTH SHALL LIVE?"
"I WILL."
"WILT THOU, MADELYNE JENNIFER PRYOR, HAVE THIS MAN TO BE THY WEDDED HUSBAND...?"
"I WILL."
"THOSE WHOM GOD HATH JOINED TOGETHER, LET NO MAN PUT ASUNDER.
"IN THE NAME OF THE FATHER, AND OF THE SON, AND OF THE HOLY GHOST-- AND UNDER THE POWERS VESTED IN ME BY THE STATE OF NEW YORK...
"--I HEREBY PRONOUNCE YOU TO BE MAN AND WIFE."

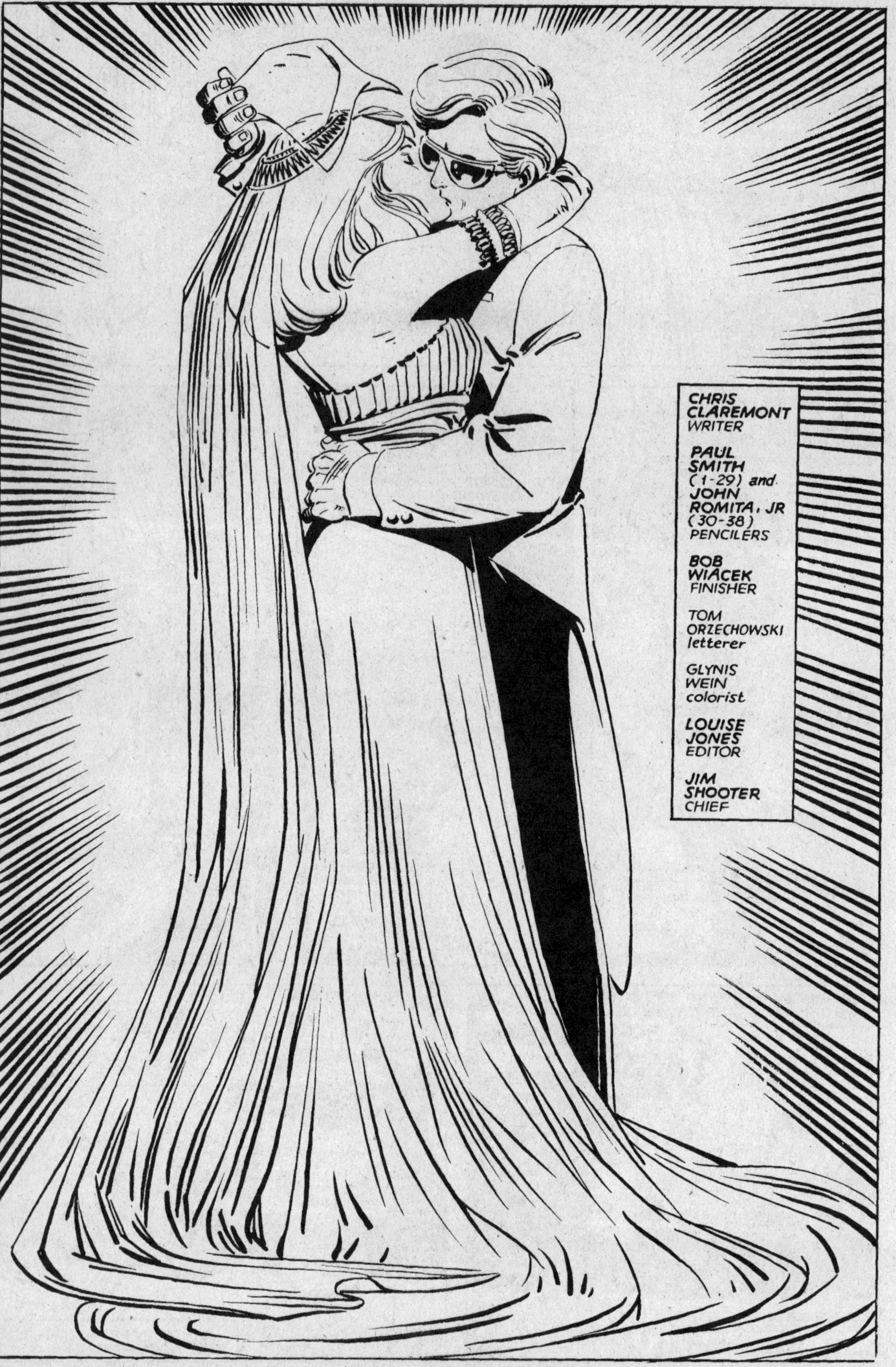
CHRIS CLAREMONT WRITER
PAUL SMITH (1-29) and JOHN ROMITA, JR (30-38) PENCILERS
BOB WIACEK FINISHER
TOM ORZECHOWSKI letterer
GLYNIS WEIN colorist
LOUISE JONES EDITOR
JIM SHOOTER CHIEF

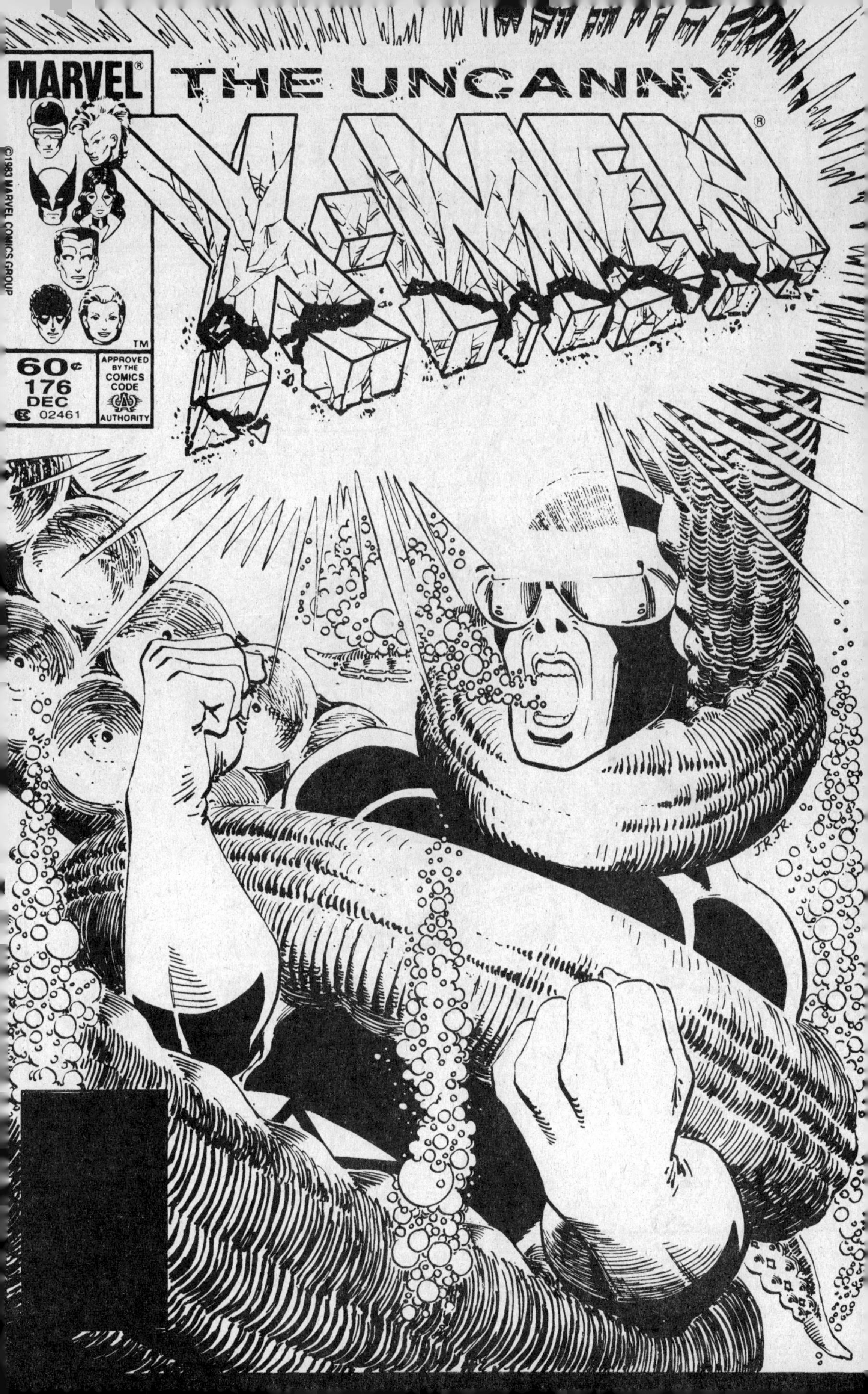
MARVEL®
THE UNCANNY
X-MEN®
TM
60¢
176
DEC
02461
APPROVED BY THE COMICS CODE AUTHORITY
©1983 MARVEL COMICS GROUP
J.R.JR.

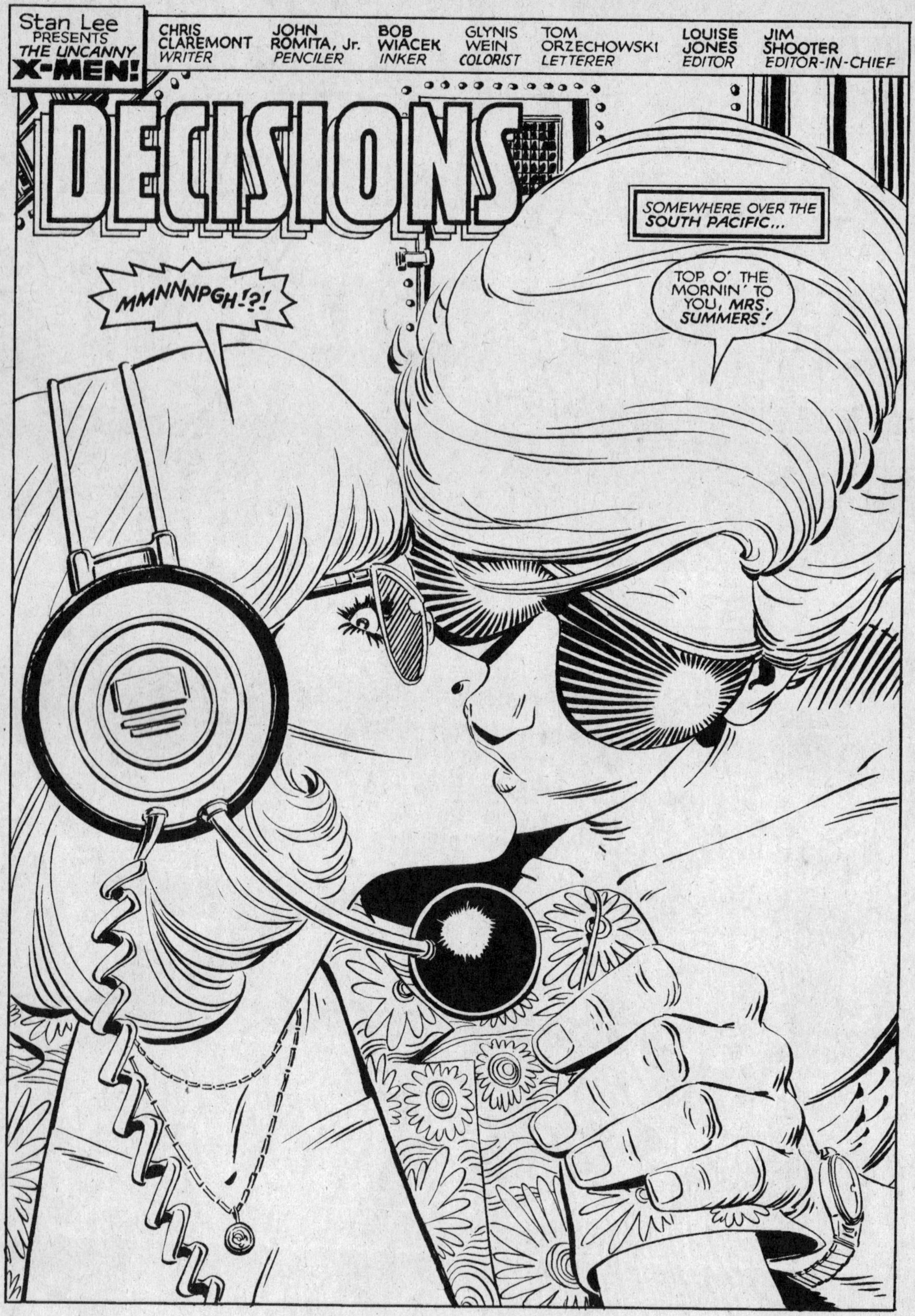
Stan Lee PRESENTS THE UNCANNY X-MEN!
CHRIS CLAREMONT WRITER
JOHN ROMITA, Jr. PENCILER
BOB WIACEK INKER
GLYNIS WEIN COLORIST
TOM ORZECHOWSKI LETTERER
LOUISE JONES EDITOR
JIM SHOOTER EDITOR-IN-CHIEF
DECISIONS
SOMEWHERE OVER THE SOUTH PACIFIC...
TOP O' THE MORNIN' TO YOU, MRS. SUMMERS!
MMNNNPGH!?!

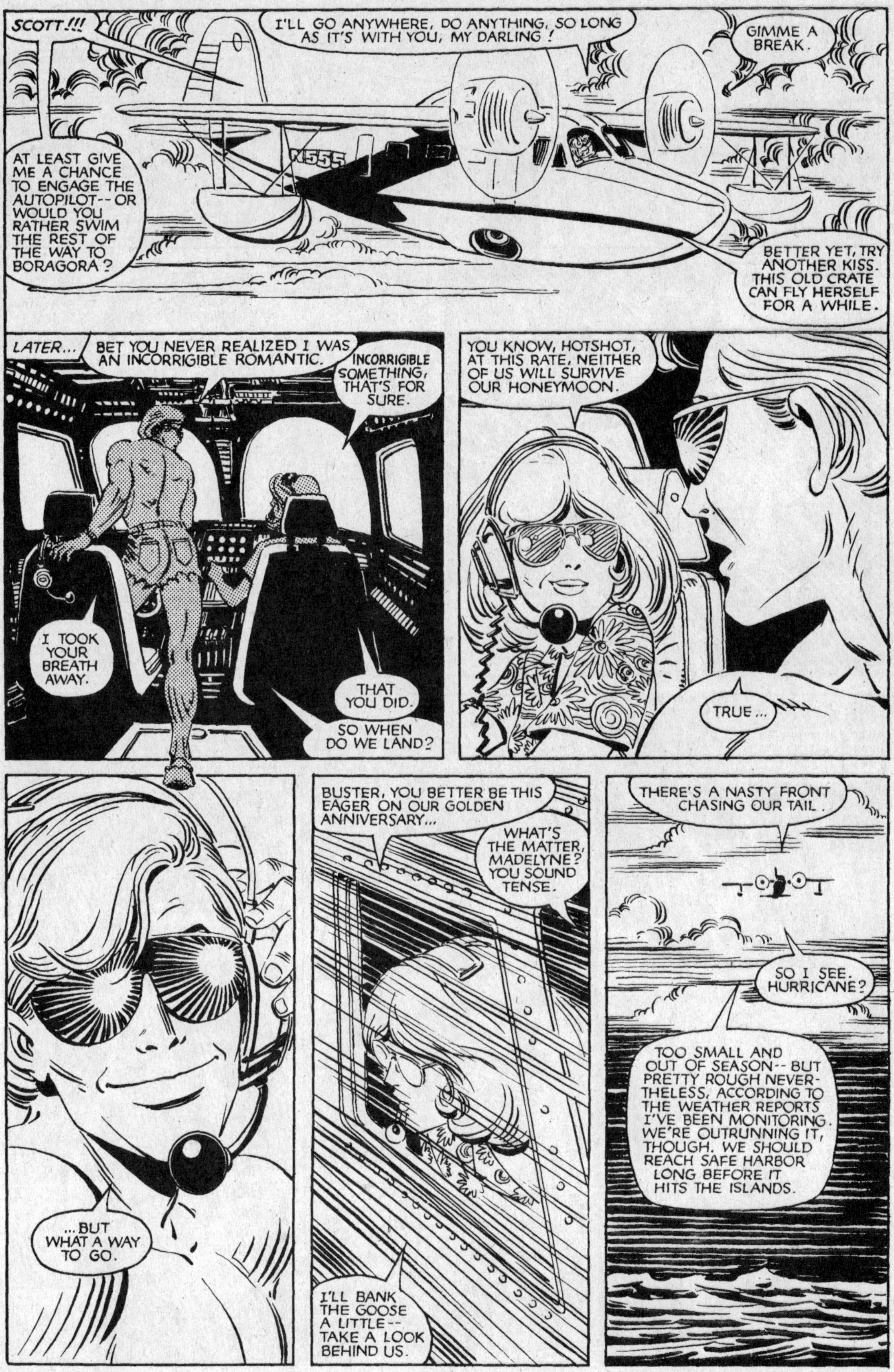
SCOTT!!!
I'LL GO ANYWHERE, DO ANYTHING, SO LONG AS IT'S WITH YOU, MY DARLING!
GIMME A BREAK.
AT LEAST GIVE ME A CHANCE TO ENGAGE THE AUTOPILOT-- OR WOULD YOU RATHER SWIM THE REST OF THE WAY TO BORAGORA?
BETTER YET, TRY ANOTHER KISS. THIS OLD CRATE CAN FLY HERSELF FOR A WHILE.
LATER...
BET YOU NEVER REALIZED I WAS AN INCORRIGIBLE ROMANTIC.
INCORRIGIBLE SOMETHING, THAT'S FOR SURE.
I TOOK YOUR BREATH AWAY.
THAT YOU DID.
SO WHEN DO WE LAND?
YOU KNOW, HOTSHOT, AT THIS RATE, NEITHER OF US WILL SURVIVE OUR HONEYMOON.
TRUE...
...BUT WHAT A WAY TO GO.
BUSTER, YOU BETTER BE THIS EAGER ON OUR GOLDEN ANNIVERSARY...
WHAT'S THE MATTER, MADELYNE? YOU SOUND TENSE.
I'LL BANK THE GOOSE A LITTLE-- TAKE A LOOK BEHIND US.
THERE'S A NASTY FRONT CHASING OUR TAIL.
SO I SEE. HURRICANE?
TOO SMALL AND OUT OF SEASON-- BUT PRETTY ROUGH NEVERTHELESS, ACCORDING TO THE WEATHER REPORTS I'VE BEEN MONITORING. WE'RE OUTRUNNING IT, THOUGH. WE SHOULD REACH SAFE HARBOR LONG BEFORE IT HITS THE ISLANDS.

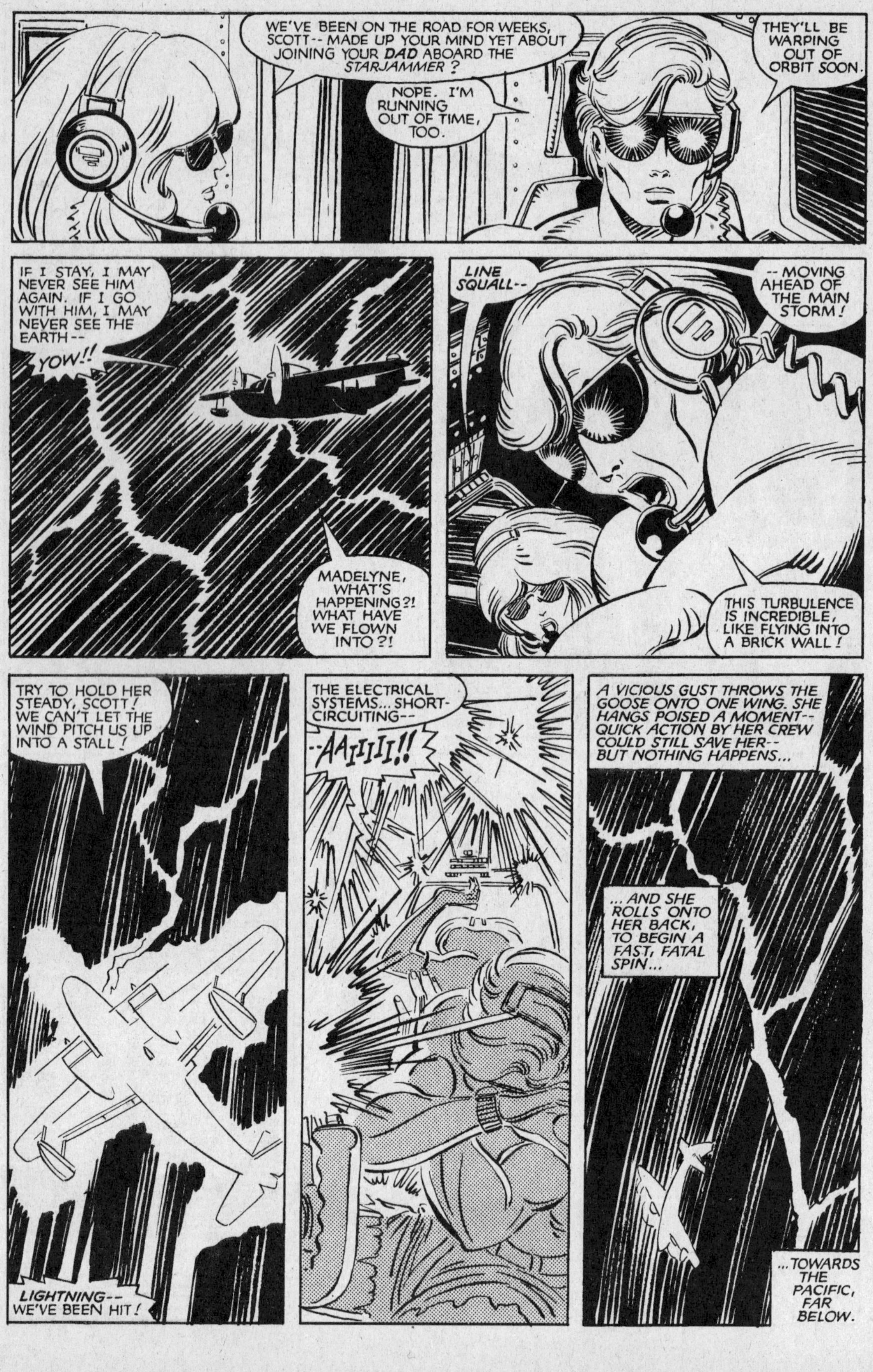
WE'VE BEEN ON THE ROAD FOR WEEKS, SCOTT-- MADE UP YOUR MIND YET ABOUT JOINING YOUR DAD ABOARD THE STARJAMMER?
NOPE. I'M RUNNING OUT OF TIME, TOO.
THEY'LL BE WARPING OUT OF ORBIT SOON.
IF I STAY, I MAY NEVER SEE HIM AGAIN. IF I GO WITH HIM, I MAY NEVER SEE THE EARTH--
YOW!!
MADELYNE, WHAT'S HAPPENING?! WHAT HAVE WE FLOWN INTO?!
LINE SQUALL--
--MOVING AHEAD OF THE MAIN STORM!
THIS TURBULENCE IS INCREDIBLE, LIKE FLYING INTO A BRICK WALL!
TRY TO HOLD HER STEADY, SCOTT! WE CAN'T LET THE WIND PITCH US UP INTO A STALL!
LIGHTNING-- WE'VE BEEN HIT!
THE ELECTRICAL SYSTEMS... SHORT-CIRCUITING--
--AAIIIII!!
A VICIOUS GUST THROWS THE GOOSE ONTO ONE WING. SHE HANGS POISED A MOMENT-- QUICK ACTION BY HER CREW COULD STILL SAVE HER-- BUT NOTHING HAPPENS...
...AND SHE ROLLS ONTO HER BACK, TO BEGIN A FAST, FATAL SPIN...
...TOWARDS THE PACIFIC, FAR BELOW.

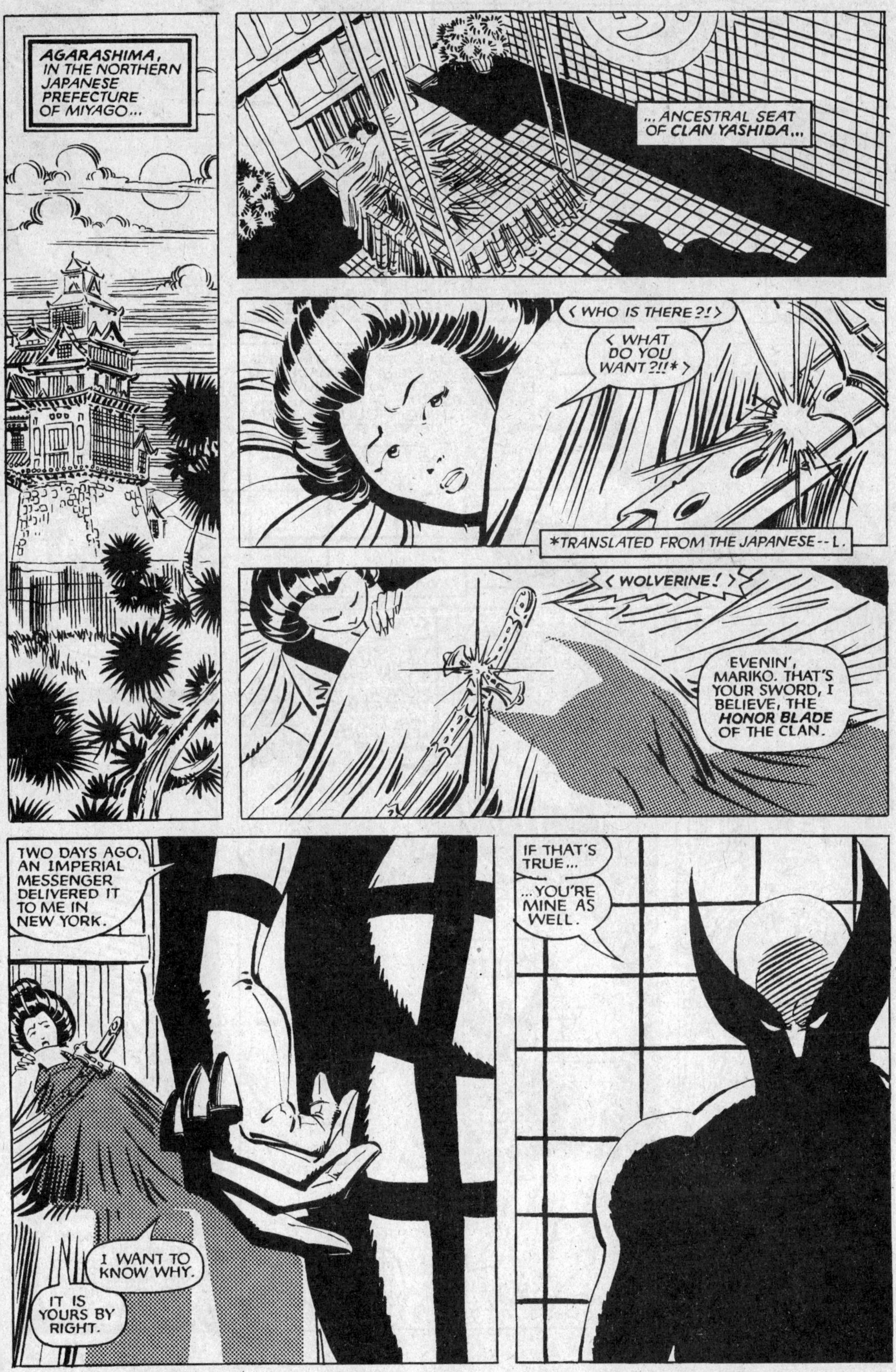
AGARASHIMA, IN THE NORTHERN JAPANESE PREFECTURE OF MIYAGO...
...ANCESTRAL SEAT OF CLAN YASHIDA...
< WHO IS THERE?! >
< WHAT DO YOU WANT?!!* >
*TRANSLATED FROM THE JAPANESE--L.
< WOLVERINE! >
EVENIN', MARIKO. THAT'S YOUR SWORD, I BELIEVE, THE HONOR BLADE OF THE CLAN.
TWO DAYS AGO, AN IMPERIAL MESSENGER DELIVERED IT TO ME IN NEW YORK.
I WANT TO KNOW WHY.
IT IS YOURS BY RIGHT.
IF THAT'S TRUE...
...YOU'RE MINE AS WELL.

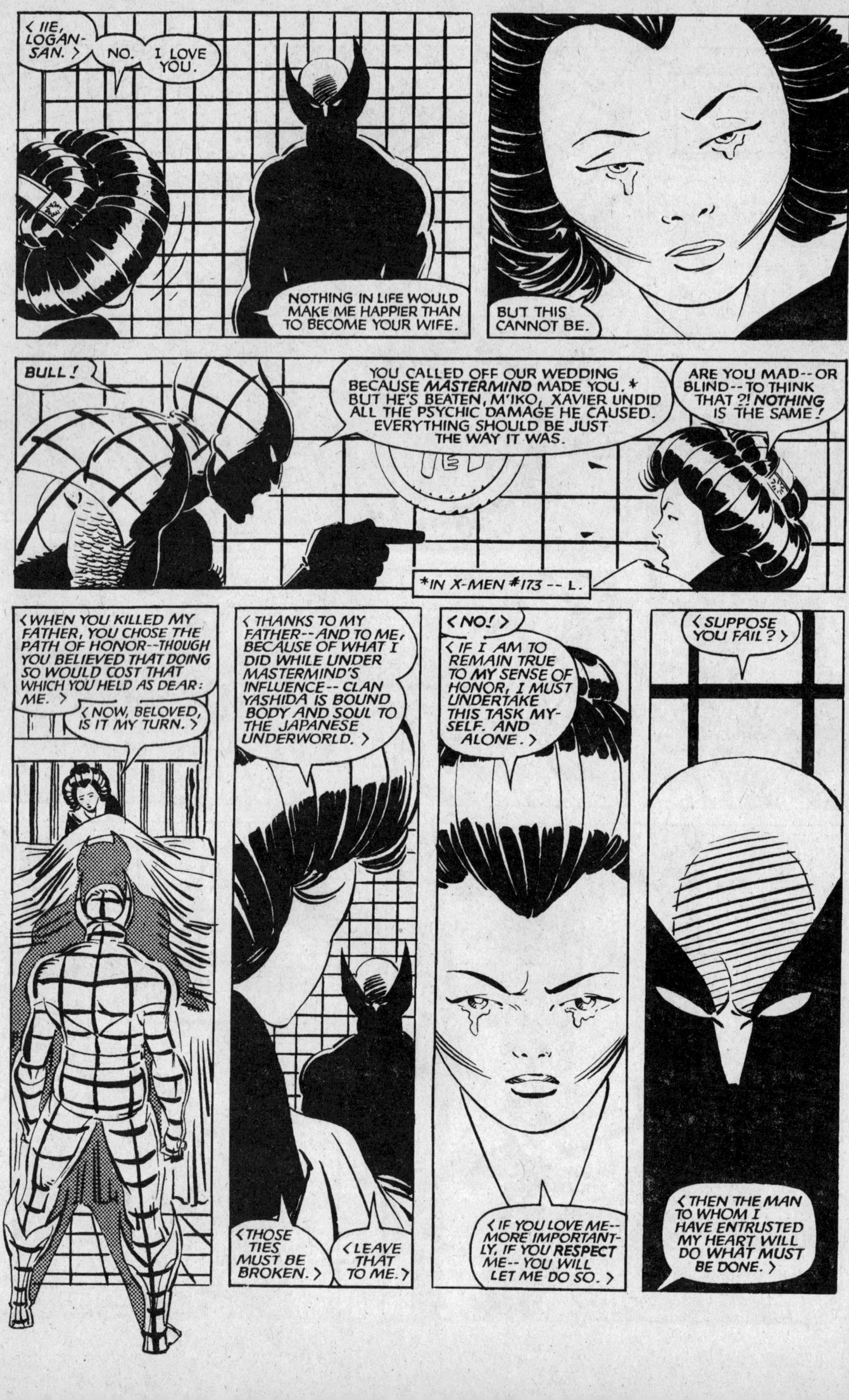

< IIE, LOGAN-SAN. >
NO.
I LOVE YOU.
NOTHING IN LIFE WOULD MAKE ME HAPPIER THAN TO BECOME YOUR WIFE.
BUT THIS CANNOT BE.
BULL!
YOU CALLED OFF OUR WEDDING BECAUSE MASTERMIND MADE YOU.* BUT HE'S BEATEN, M'IKO, XAVIER UNDID ALL THE PSYCHIC DAMAGE HE CAUSED. EVERYTHING SHOULD BE JUST THE WAY IT WAS.
ARE YOU MAD--OR BLIND--TO THINK THAT?! NOTHING IS THE SAME!
*IN X-MEN #173 -- L.
< WHEN YOU KILLED MY FATHER, YOU CHOSE THE PATH OF HONOR--THOUGH YOU BELIEVED THAT DOING SO WOULD COST THAT WHICH YOU HELD AS DEAR: ME. >
< NOW, BELOVED, IS IT MY TURN. >
< THANKS TO MY FATHER--AND TO ME, BECAUSE OF WHAT I DID WHILE UNDER MASTERMIND'S INFLUENCE-- CLAN YASHIDA IS BOUND BODY AND SOUL TO THE JAPANESE UNDERWORLD. >
< THOSE TIES MUST BE BROKEN. >
< LEAVE THAT TO ME. >
< NO! >
< IF I AM TO REMAIN TRUE TO MY SENSE OF HONOR, I MUST UNDERTAKE THIS TASK MYSELF. AND ALONE. >
< IF YOU LOVE ME-- MORE IMPORTANTLY, IF YOU RESPECT ME-- YOU WILL LET ME DO SO. >
< SUPPOSE YOU FAIL? >
< THEN THE MAN TO WHOM I HAVE ENTRUSTED MY HEART WILL DO WHAT MUST BE DONE. >

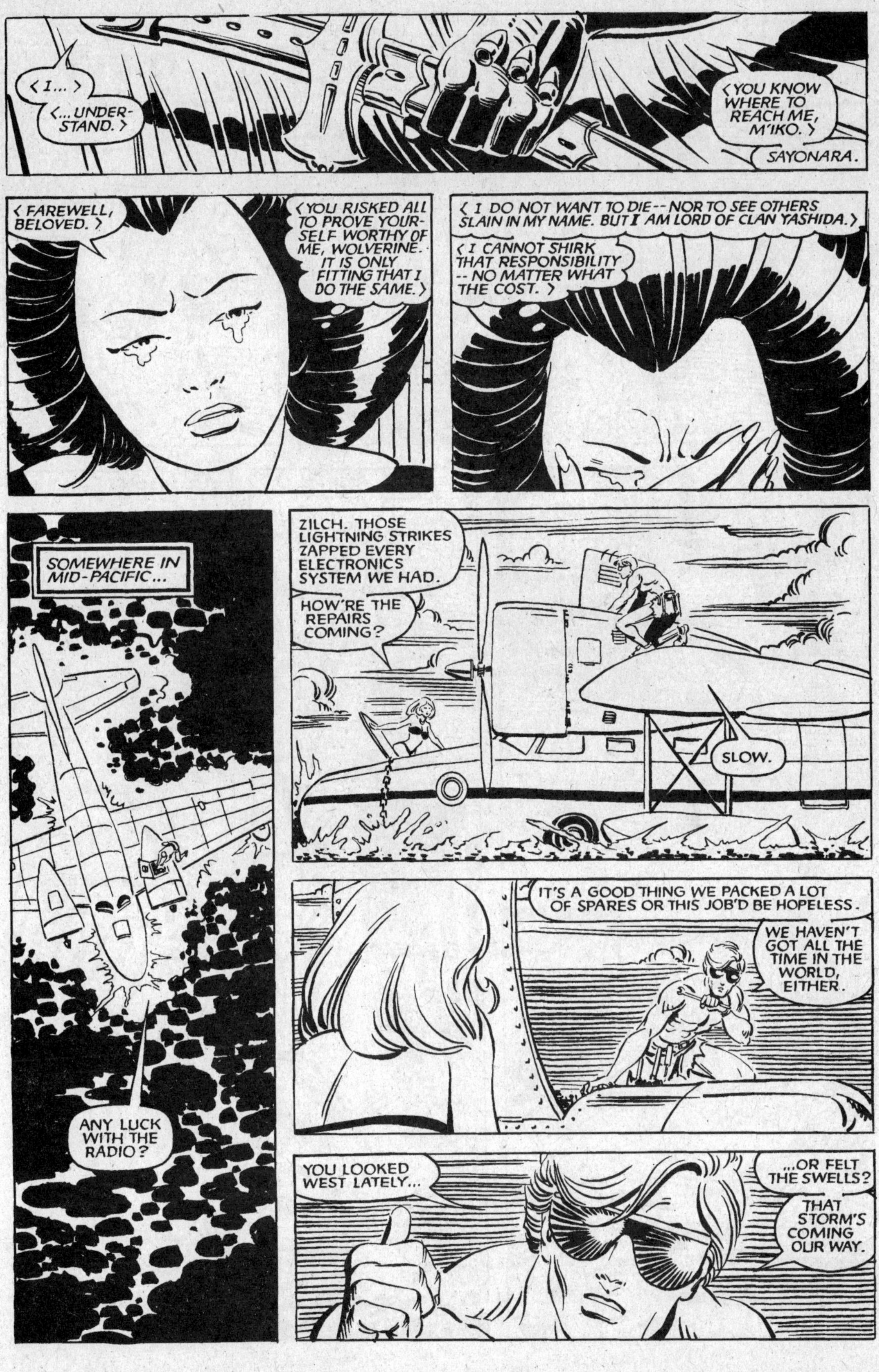

‹ I... ›
‹ ...UNDERSTAND. ›
‹ YOU KNOW WHERE TO REACH ME, M'IKO. ›
SAYONARA.
‹ FAREWELL, BELOVED. ›
‹ YOU RISKED ALL TO PROVE YOURSELF WORTHY OF ME, WOLVERINE. IT IS ONLY FITTING THAT I DO THE SAME. ›
‹ I DO NOT WANT TO DIE-- NOR TO SEE OTHERS SLAIN IN MY NAME. BUT I AM LORD OF CLAN YASHIDA. ›
‹ I CANNOT SHIRK THAT RESPONSIBILITY -- NO MATTER WHAT THE COST. ›
SOMEWHERE IN MID-PACIFIC...
ANY LUCK WITH THE RADIO?
ZILCH. THOSE LIGHTNING STRIKES ZAPPED EVERY ELECTRONICS SYSTEM WE HAD.
HOW'RE THE REPAIRS COMING?
SLOW.
IT'S A GOOD THING WE PACKED A LOT OF SPARES OR THIS JOB'D BE HOPELESS.
WE HAVEN'T GOT ALL THE TIME IN THE WORLD, EITHER.
YOU LOOKED WEST LATELY...
...OR FELT THE SWELLS?
THAT STORM'S COMING OUR WAY.

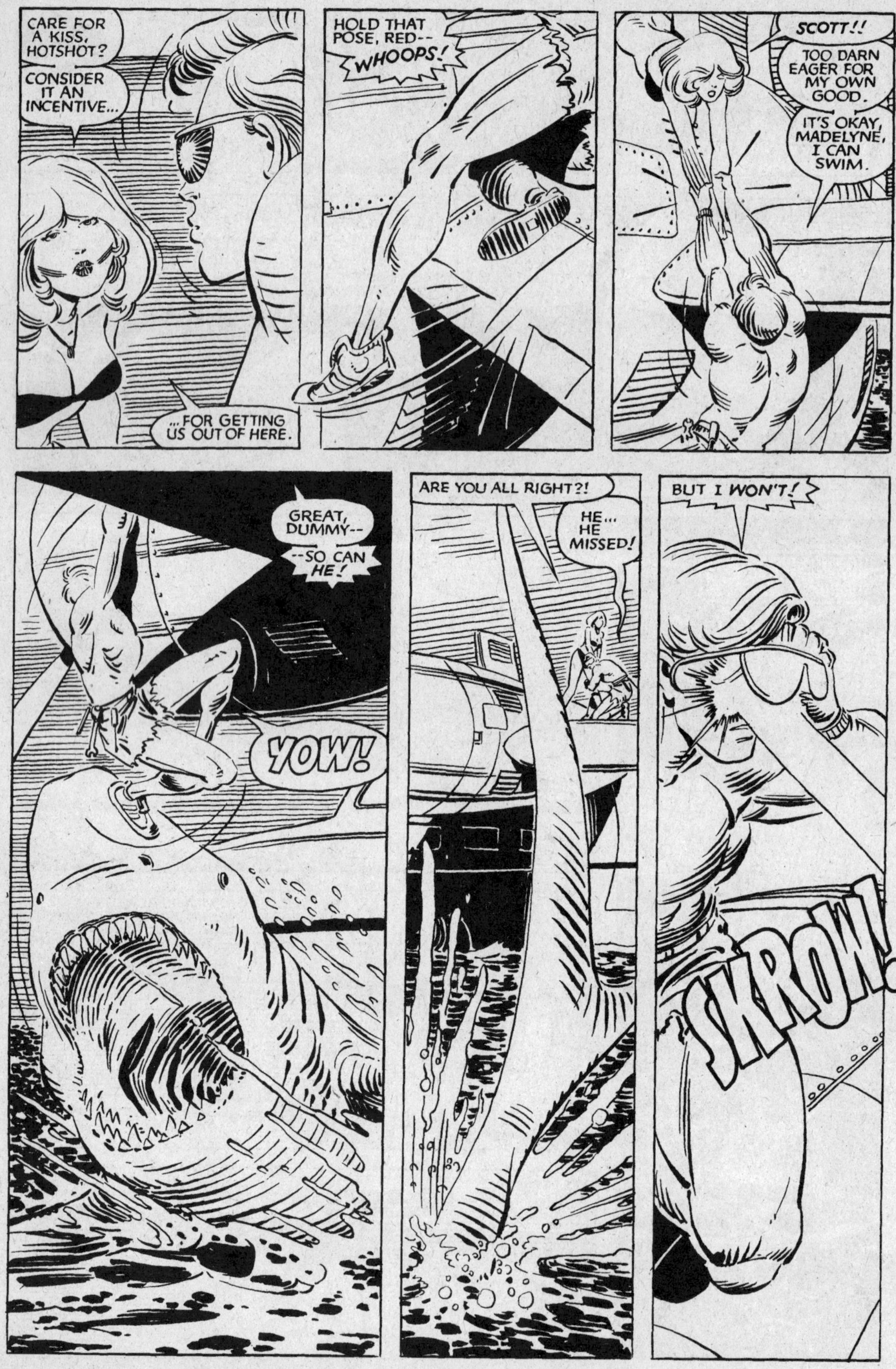
CARE FOR A KISS, HOTSHOT?
CONSIDER IT AN INCENTIVE...
...FOR GETTING US OUT OF HERE.
HOLD THAT POSE, RED--
WHOOPS!
SCOTT!!
TOO DARN EAGER FOR MY OWN GOOD.
IT'S OKAY, MADELYNE, I CAN SWIM.
GREAT, DUMMY--
--SO CAN HE!
YOW!
ARE YOU ALL RIGHT?!
HE... HE MISSED!
BUT I WON'T!
SKROW!

YOU'RE SHAKING!

I'M SCARED!

I MEAN, AFTER ALL I'VE BEEN THROUGH AS AN *X-MAN*...

...TO GET EATEN BY A SHARK ON MY HONEYMOON IS A BIT MUCH.

SO HOW 'BOUT WE FIX THE ENGINES AND BLOW THIS JOINT...

...BEFORE THE STORM ARRIVES TO GIVE THAT CRITTER ANOTHER CHANCE?

GOOD POINT.

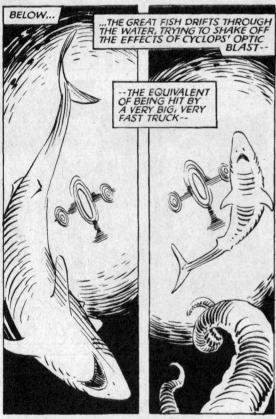

BELOW...

...THE GREAT FISH DRIFTS THROUGH THE WATER, TRYING TO SHAKE OFF THE EFFECTS OF CYCLOPS' OPTIC BLAST--

--THE EQUIVALENT OF BEING HIT BY A VERY BIG, VERY FAST TRUCK--

--UNAWARE UNTIL IT'S TOO LATE THAT IT'S ROLE HAS CHANGED...

...FROM HUNTER TO PREY.

WASHINGTON, D.C...

YOUR IDENTIFICATION, SIR?

HENRY PETER GYRICH, NATIONAL SECURITY COUNCIL. I'M EXPECTED.

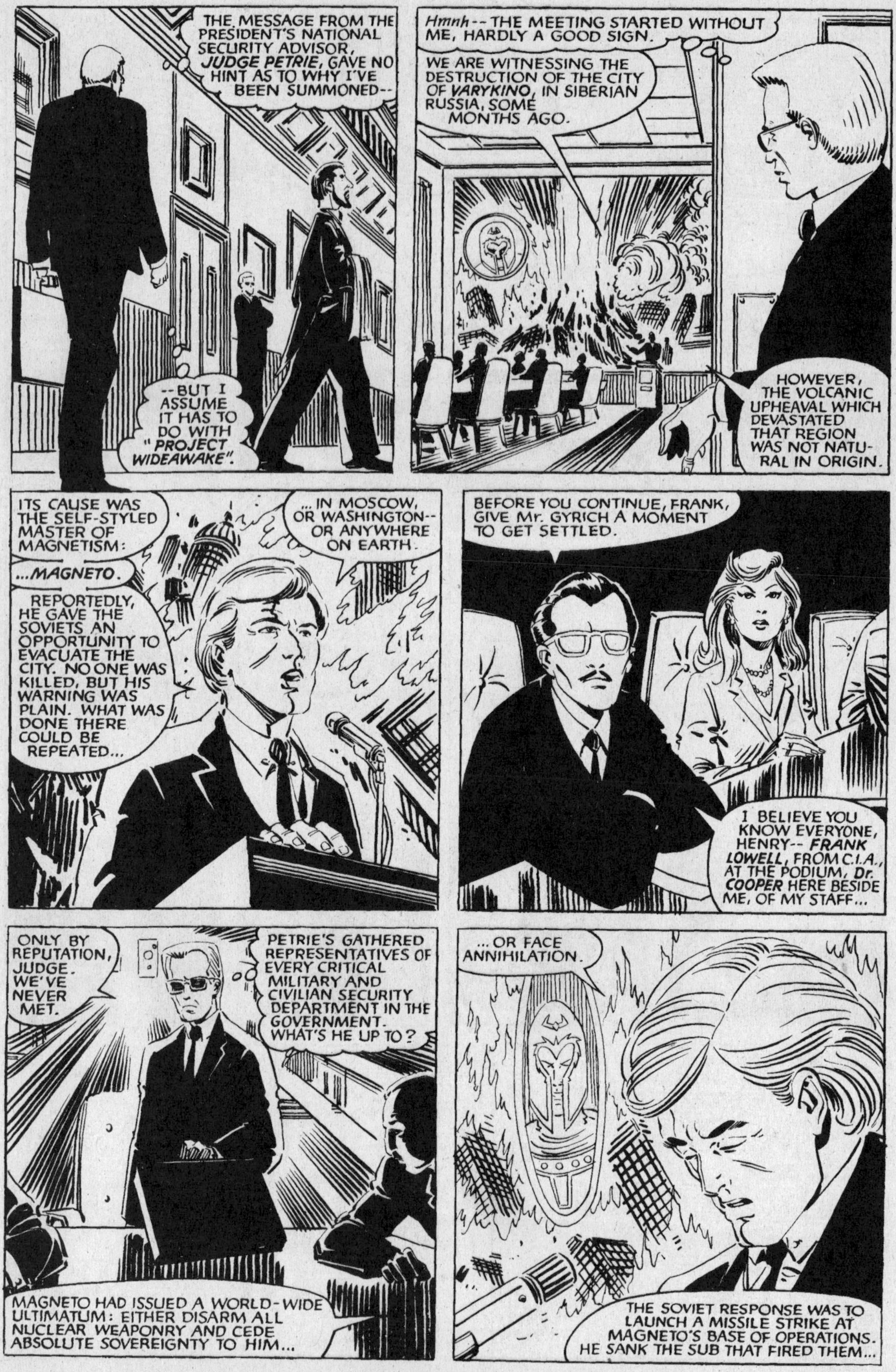
THE MESSAGE FROM THE PRESIDENT'S NATIONAL SECURITY ADVISOR, JUDGE PETRIE, GAVE NO HINT AS TO WHY I'VE BEEN SUMMONED--
--BUT I ASSUME IT HAS TO DO WITH "PROJECT WIDEAWAKE".
Hmnh--THE MEETING STARTED WITHOUT ME, HARDLY A GOOD SIGN.
WE ARE WITNESSING THE DESTRUCTION OF THE CITY OF VARYKINO, IN SIBERIAN RUSSIA, SOME MONTHS AGO.
HOWEVER, THE VOLCANIC UPHEAVAL WHICH DEVASTATED THAT REGION WAS NOT NATURAL IN ORIGIN.
ITS CAUSE WAS THE SELF-STYLED MASTER OF MAGNETISM: ...MAGNETO.
REPORTEDLY, HE GAVE THE SOVIETS AN OPPORTUNITY TO EVACUATE THE CITY. NO ONE WAS KILLED, BUT HIS WARNING WAS PLAIN. WHAT WAS DONE THERE COULD BE REPEATED...
...IN MOSCOW, OR WASHINGTON--OR ANYWHERE ON EARTH.
BEFORE YOU CONTINUE, FRANK, GIVE Mr. GYRICH A MOMENT TO GET SETTLED.
I BELIEVE YOU KNOW EVERYONE, HENRY-- FRANK LOWELL, FROM C.I.A., AT THE PODIUM, Dr. COOPER HERE BESIDE ME, OF MY STAFF...
ONLY BY REPUTATION, JUDGE. WE'VE NEVER MET.
PETRIE'S GATHERED REPRESENTATIVES OF EVERY CRITICAL MILITARY AND CIVILIAN SECURITY DEPARTMENT IN THE GOVERNMENT. WHAT'S HE UP TO?
MAGNETO HAD ISSUED A WORLD-WIDE ULTIMATUM: EITHER DISARM ALL NUCLEAR WEAPONRY AND CEDE ABSOLUTE SOVEREIGNTY TO HIM...
...OR FACE ANNIHILATION.
THE SOVIET RESPONSE WAS TO LAUNCH A MISSILE STRIKE AT MAGNETO'S BASE OF OPERATIONS. HE SANK THE SUB THAT FIRED THEM...

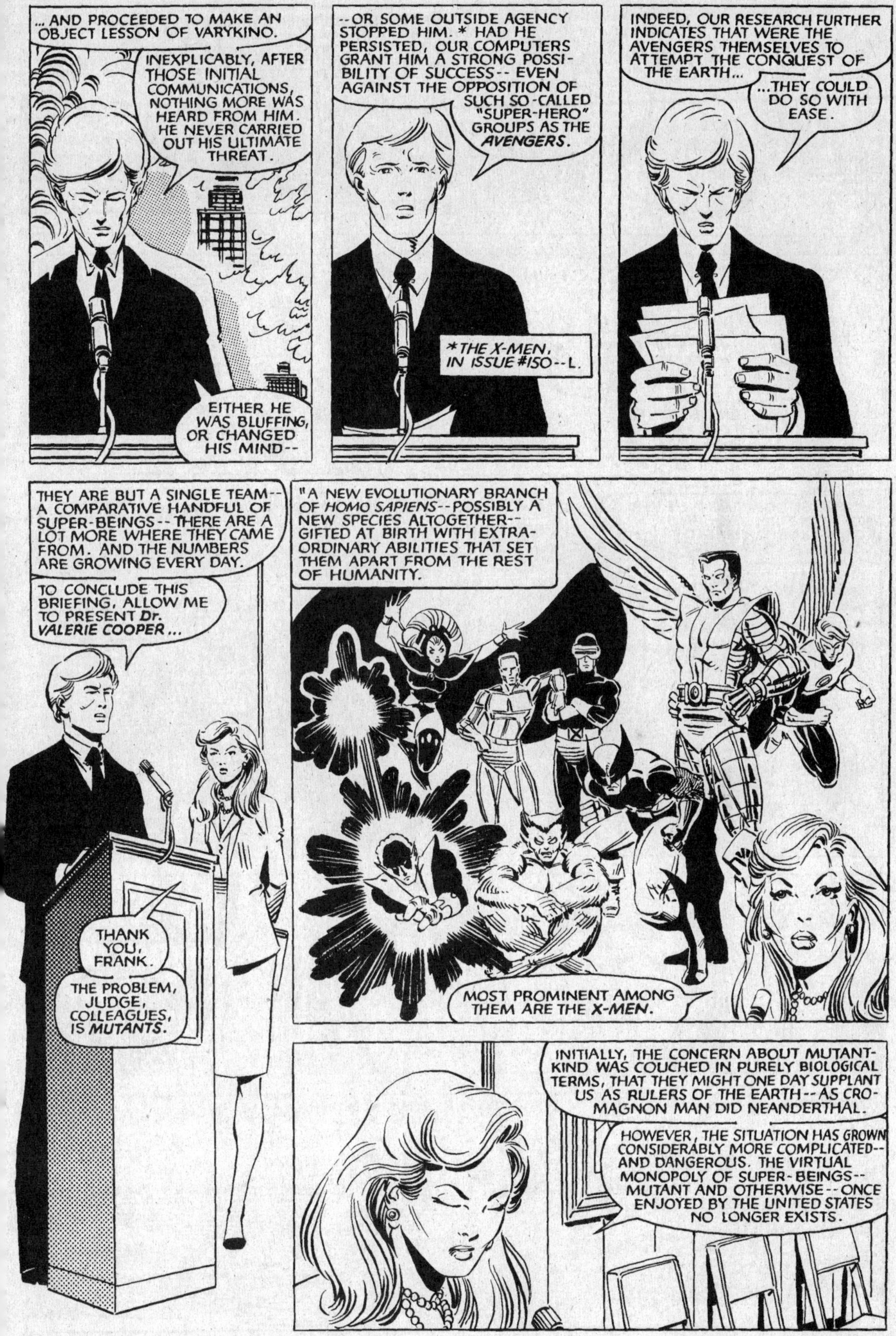
...AND PROCEEDED TO MAKE AN OBJECT LESSON OF VARYKINO.
INEXPLICABLY, AFTER THOSE INITIAL COMMUNICATIONS, NOTHING MORE WAS HEARD FROM HIM. HE NEVER CARRIED OUT HIS ULTIMATE THREAT.
EITHER HE WAS BLUFFING, OR CHANGED HIS MIND--
--OR SOME OUTSIDE AGENCY STOPPED HIM. * HAD HE PERSISTED, OUR COMPUTERS GRANT HIM A STRONG POSSIBILITY OF SUCCESS-- EVEN AGAINST THE OPPOSITION OF SUCH SO-CALLED "SUPER-HERO" GROUPS AS THE AVENGERS.
*THE X-MEN, IN ISSUE #150--L.
INDEED, OUR RESEARCH FURTHER INDICATES THAT WERE THE AVENGERS THEMSELVES TO ATTEMPT THE CONQUEST OF THE EARTH...
...THEY COULD DO SO WITH EASE.
THEY ARE BUT A SINGLE TEAM-- A COMPARATIVE HANDFUL OF SUPER-BEINGS-- THERE ARE A LOT MORE WHERE THEY CAME FROM. AND THE NUMBERS ARE GROWING EVERY DAY.
TO CONCLUDE THIS BRIEFING, ALLOW ME TO PRESENT Dr. VALERIE COOPER...
THANK YOU, FRANK.
THE PROBLEM, JUDGE, COLLEAGUES, IS MUTANTS.
"A NEW EVOLUTIONARY BRANCH OF HOMO SAPIENS--POSSIBLY A NEW SPECIES ALTOGETHER-- GIFTED AT BIRTH WITH EXTRA-ORDINARY ABILITIES THAT SET THEM APART FROM THE REST OF HUMANITY.
MOST PROMINENT AMONG THEM ARE THE X-MEN.
INITIALLY, THE CONCERN ABOUT MUTANT-KIND WAS COUCHED IN PURELY BIOLOGICAL TERMS, THAT THEY MIGHT ONE DAY SUPPLANT US AS RULERS OF THE EARTH--AS CRO-MAGNON MAN DID NEANDERTHAL.
HOWEVER, THE SITUATION HAS GROWN CONSIDERABLY MORE COMPLICATED-- AND DANGEROUS. THE VIRTUAL MONOPOLY OF SUPER-BEINGS-- MUTANT AND OTHERWISE--ONCE ENJOYED BY THE UNITED STATES NO LONGER EXISTS.

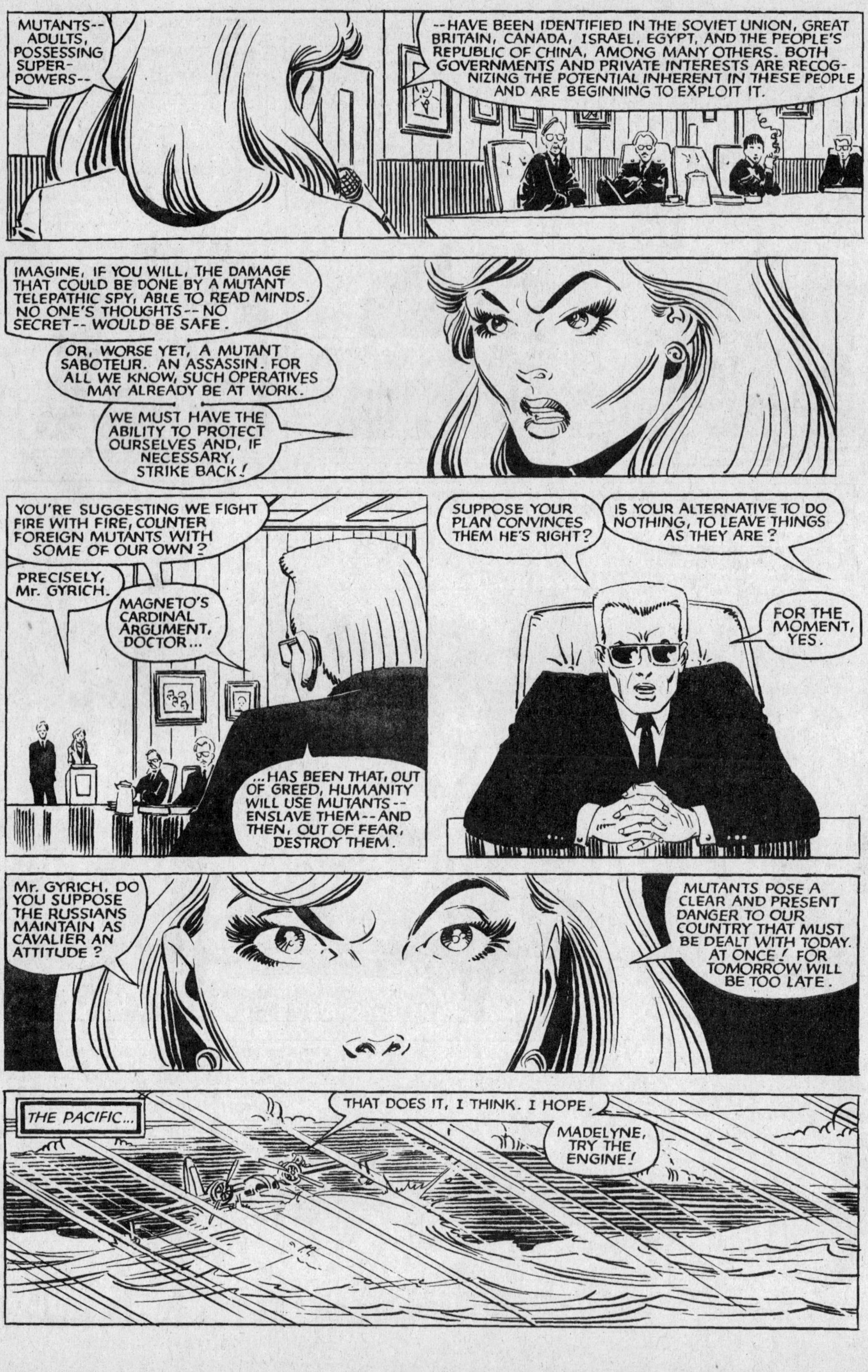
MUTANTS-- ADULTS, POSSESSING SUPER-POWERS--
--HAVE BEEN IDENTIFIED IN THE SOVIET UNION, GREAT BRITAIN, CANADA, ISRAEL, EGYPT, AND THE PEOPLE'S REPUBLIC OF CHINA, AMONG MANY OTHERS. BOTH GOVERNMENTS AND PRIVATE INTERESTS ARE RECOGNIZING THE POTENTIAL INHERENT IN THESE PEOPLE AND ARE BEGINNING TO EXPLOIT IT.
IMAGINE, IF YOU WILL, THE DAMAGE THAT COULD BE DONE BY A MUTANT TELEPATHIC SPY, ABLE TO READ MINDS. NO ONE'S THOUGHTS-- NO SECRET-- WOULD BE SAFE.
OR, WORSE YET, A MUTANT SABOTEUR. AN ASSASSIN. FOR ALL WE KNOW, SUCH OPERATIVES MAY ALREADY BE AT WORK.
WE MUST HAVE THE ABILITY TO PROTECT OURSELVES AND, IF NECESSARY, STRIKE BACK!
YOU'RE SUGGESTING WE FIGHT FIRE WITH FIRE, COUNTER FOREIGN MUTANTS WITH SOME OF OUR OWN?
PRECISELY, Mr. GYRICH.
MAGNETO'S CARDINAL ARGUMENT, DOCTOR...
...HAS BEEN THAT, OUT OF GREED, HUMANITY WILL USE MUTANTS-- ENSLAVE THEM--AND THEN, OUT OF FEAR, DESTROY THEM.
SUPPOSE YOUR PLAN CONVINCES THEM HE'S RIGHT?
IS YOUR ALTERNATIVE TO DO NOTHING, TO LEAVE THINGS AS THEY ARE?
FOR THE MOMENT, YES.
Mr. GYRICH, DO YOU SUPPOSE THE RUSSIANS MAINTAIN AS CAVALIER AN ATTITUDE?
MUTANTS POSE A CLEAR AND PRESENT DANGER TO OUR COUNTRY THAT MUST BE DEALT WITH TODAY. AT ONCE! FOR TOMORROW WILL BE TOO LATE.
THE PACIFIC...
THAT DOES IT, I THINK. I HOPE.
MADELYNE, TRY THE ENGINE!

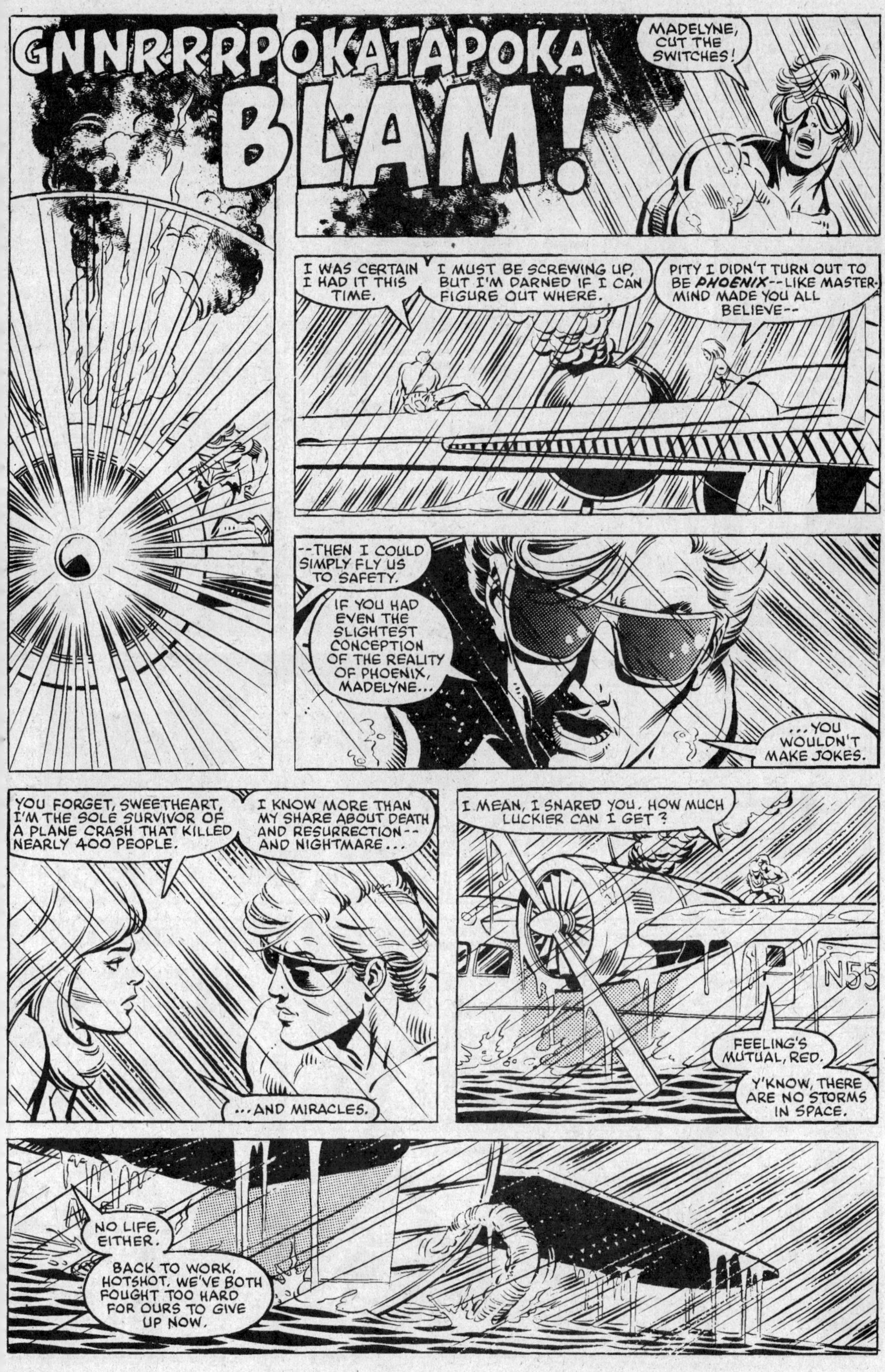
GNNRRRPOKATAPOKA
BLAM!
MADELYNE, CUT THE SWITCHES!
I WAS CERTAIN I HAD IT THIS TIME.
I MUST BE SCREWING UP, BUT I'M DARNED IF I CAN FIGURE OUT WHERE.
PITY I DIDN'T TURN OUT TO BE PHOENIX--LIKE MASTERMIND MADE YOU ALL BELIEVE--
--THEN I COULD SIMPLY FLY US TO SAFETY.
IF YOU HAD EVEN THE SLIGHTEST CONCEPTION OF THE REALITY OF PHOENIX, MADELYNE...
...YOU WOULDN'T MAKE JOKES.
YOU FORGET, SWEETHEART, I'M THE SOLE SURVIVOR OF A PLANE CRASH THAT KILLED NEARLY 400 PEOPLE.
I KNOW MORE THAN MY SHARE ABOUT DEATH AND RESURRECTION--AND NIGHTMARE...
...AND MIRACLES.
I MEAN, I SNARED YOU. HOW MUCH LUCKIER CAN I GET?
N55
FEELING'S MUTUAL, RED.
Y'KNOW, THERE ARE NO STORMS IN SPACE.
NO LIFE, EITHER.
BACK TO WORK, HOTSHOT, WE'VE BOTH FOUGHT TOO HARD FOR OURS TO GIVE UP NOW.

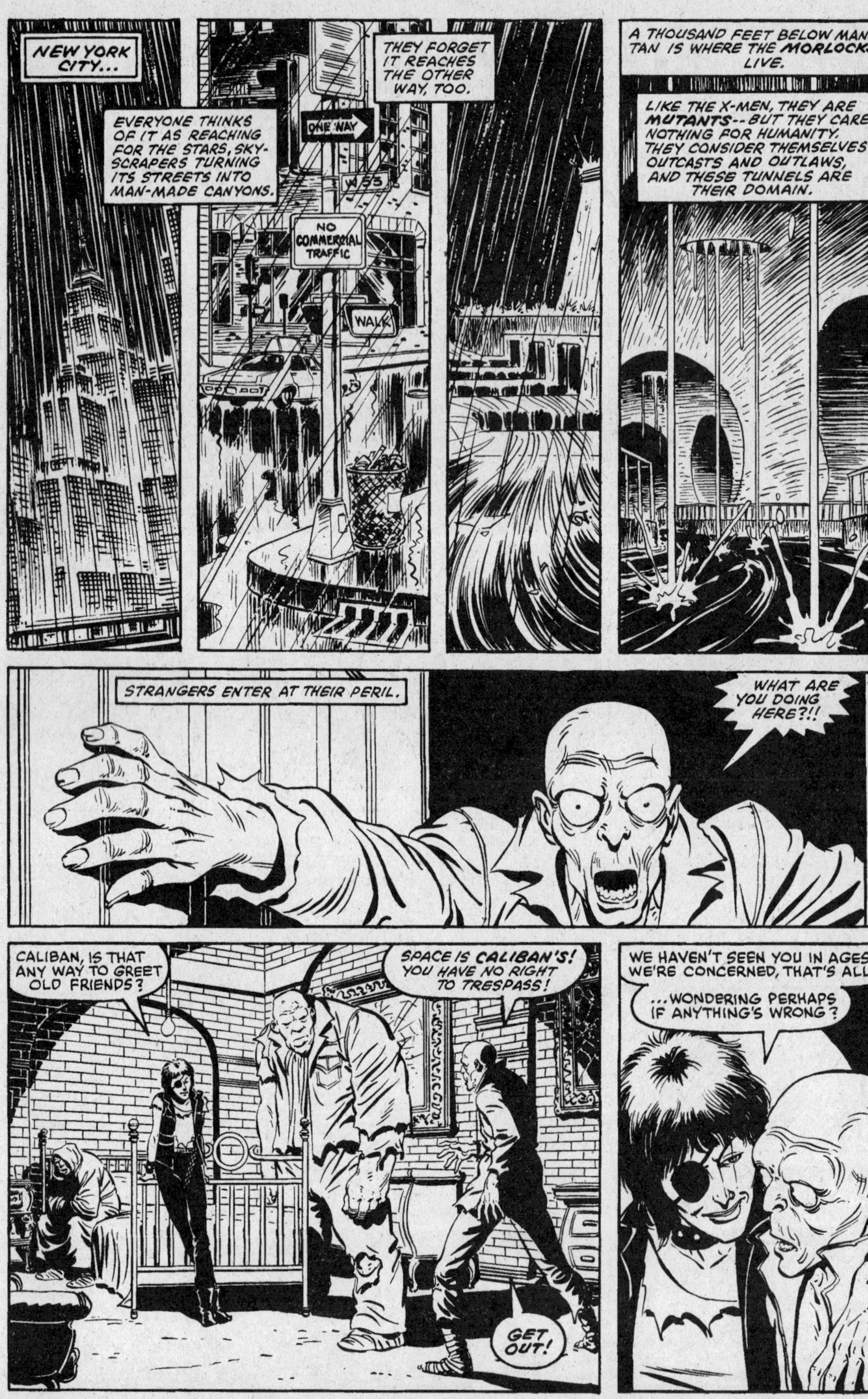
NEW YORK CITY...
EVERYONE THINKS OF IT AS REACHING FOR THE STARS, SKY-SCRAPERS TURNING ITS STREETS INTO MAN-MADE CANYONS.
ONE WAY
W 53
NO COMMERCIAL TRAFFIC
WALK
THEY FORGET IT REACHES THE OTHER WAY, TOO.
A THOUSAND FEET BELOW MANHAT-TAN IS WHERE THE MORLOCKS LIVE.
LIKE THE X-MEN, THEY ARE MUTANTS-- BUT THEY CARE NOTHING FOR HUMANITY. THEY CONSIDER THEMSELVES OUTCASTS AND OUTLAWS, AND THESE TUNNELS ARE THEIR DOMAIN.
STRANGERS ENTER AT THEIR PERIL.
WHAT ARE YOU DOING HERE?!!
CALIBAN, IS THAT ANY WAY TO GREET OLD FRIENDS?
SPACE IS CALIBAN'S! YOU HAVE NO RIGHT TO TRESPASS!
GET OUT!
WE HAVEN'T SEEN YOU IN AGES. WE'RE CONCERNED, THAT'S ALL...
...WONDERING PERHAPS IF ANYTHING'S WRONG?

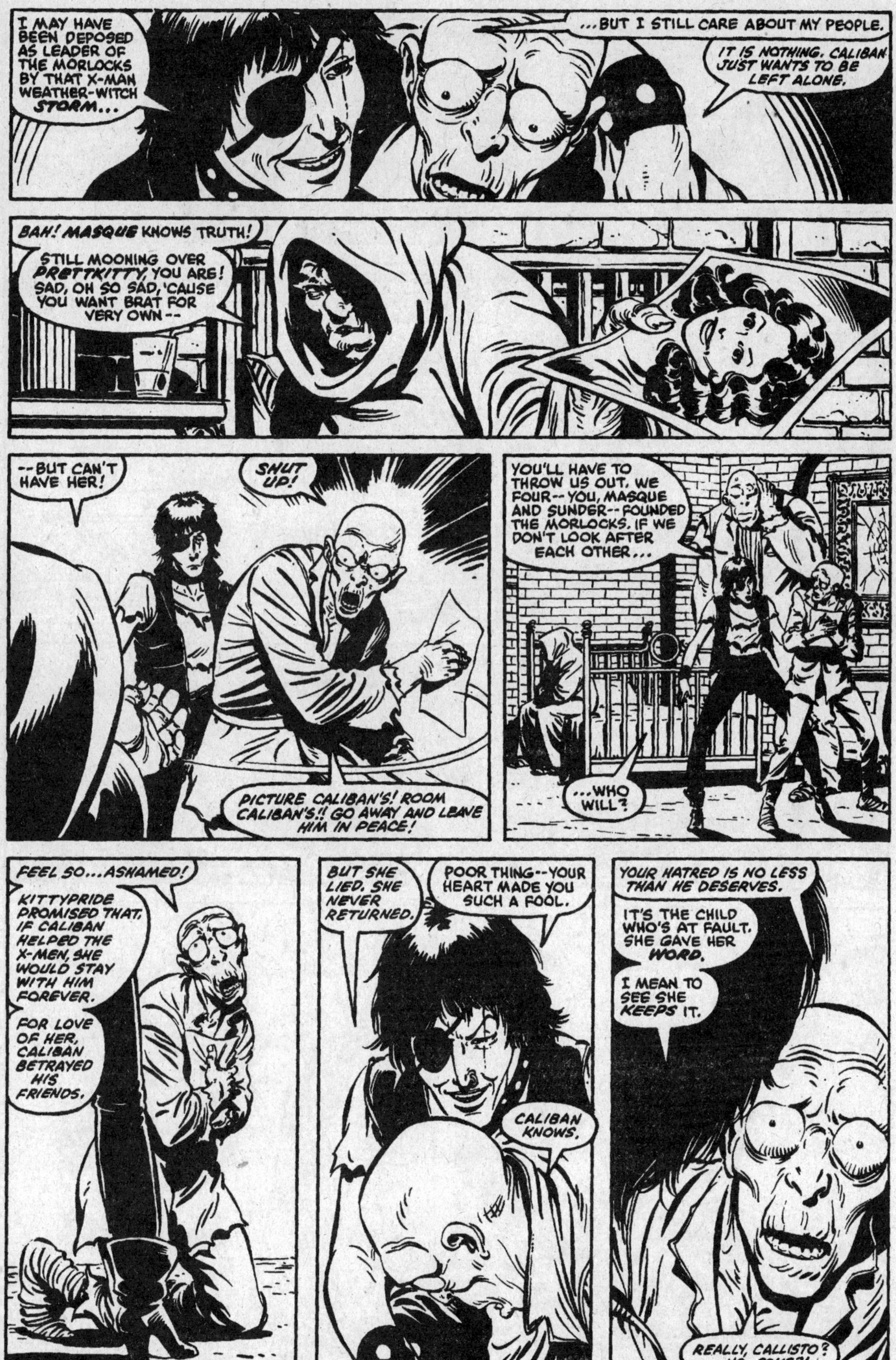
I MAY HAVE BEEN DEPOSED AS LEADER OF THE MORLOCKS BY THAT X-MAN WEATHER-WITCH STORM...
...BUT I STILL CARE ABOUT MY PEOPLE.
IT IS NOTHING. CALIBAN JUST WANTS TO BE LEFT ALONE.
BAH! MASQUE KNOWS TRUTH!
STILL MOONING OVER PRETTKITTY, YOU ARE! SAD, OH SO SAD, 'CAUSE YOU WANT BRAT FOR VERY OWN--
--BUT CAN'T HAVE HER!
SHUT UP!
PICTURE CALIBAN'S! ROOM CALIBAN'S!! GO AWAY AND LEAVE HIM IN PEACE!
YOU'LL HAVE TO THROW US OUT. WE FOUR--YOU, MASQUE AND SUNDER--FOUNDED THE MORLOCKS. IF WE DON'T LOOK AFTER EACH OTHER...
...WHO WILL?
FEEL SO...ASHAMED!
KITTYPRIDE PROMISED THAT, IF CALIBAN HELPED THE X-MEN, SHE WOULD STAY WITH HIM FOREVER.
FOR LOVE OF HER, CALIBAN BETRAYED HIS FRIENDS.
BUT SHE LIED. SHE NEVER RETURNED.
POOR THING--YOUR HEART MADE YOU SUCH A FOOL.
CALIBAN KNOWS.
YOUR HATRED IS NO LESS THAN HE DESERVES.
IT'S THE CHILD WHO'S AT FAULT. SHE GAVE HER WORD.
I MEAN TO SEE SHE KEEPS IT.
REALLY, CALLISTO? NO JOKE?!

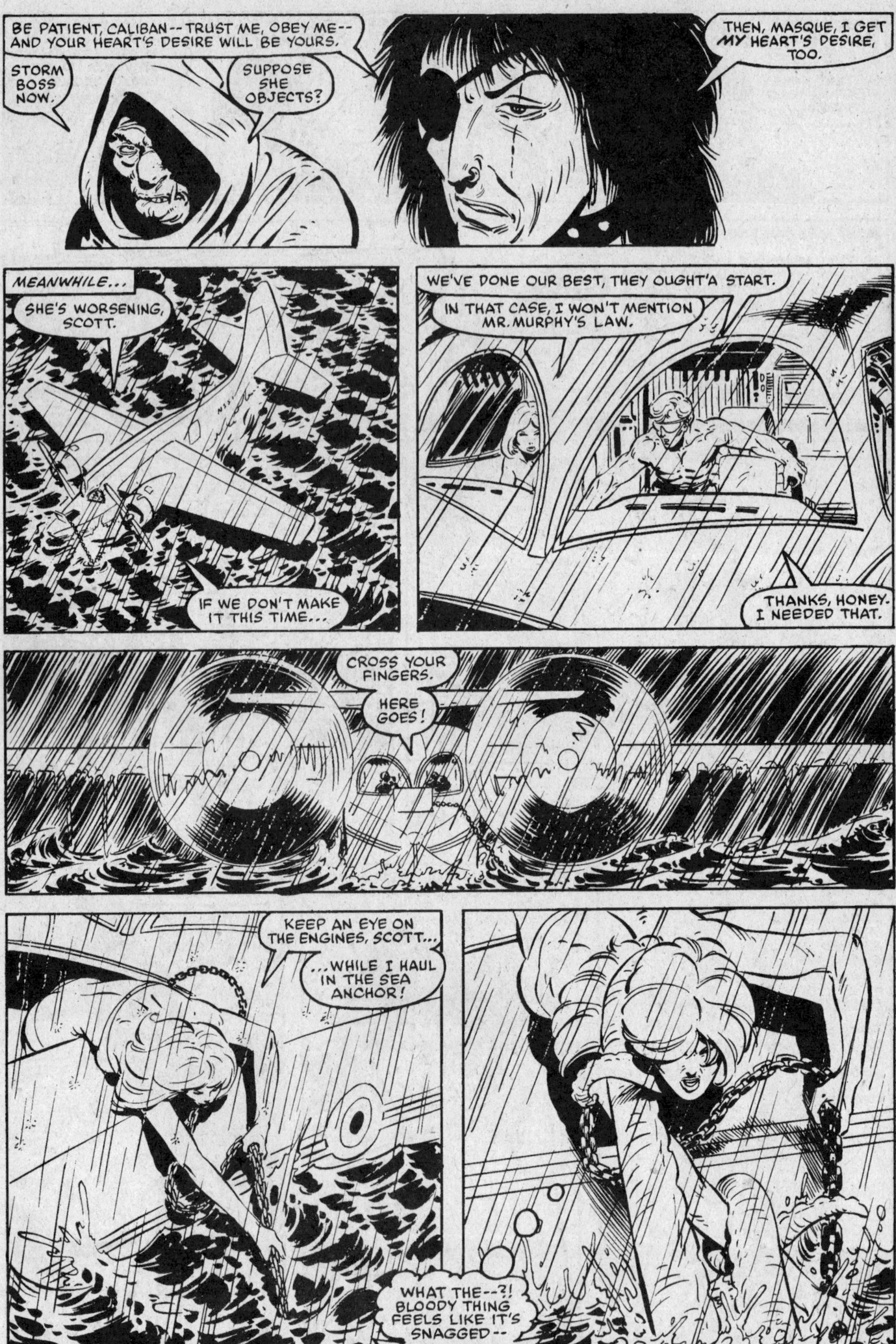
BE PATIENT, CALIBAN--TRUST ME, OBEY ME--AND YOUR HEART'S DESIRE WILL BE YOURS.
STORM BOSS NOW.
SUPPOSE SHE OBJECTS?
THEN, MASQUE, I GET MY HEART'S DESIRE, TOO.
MEANWHILE...
SHE'S WORSENING, SCOTT.
IF WE DON'T MAKE IT THIS TIME...
WE'VE DONE OUR BEST, THEY OUGHT'A START.
IN THAT CASE, I WON'T MENTION MR. MURPHY'S LAW.
THANKS, HONEY. I NEEDED THAT.
CROSS YOUR FINGERS.
HERE GOES!
KEEP AN EYE ON THE ENGINES, SCOTT...
...WHILE I HAUL IN THE SEA ANCHOR!
WHAT THE--?! BLOODY THING FEELS LIKE IT'S SNAGGED--
AYYIII!!

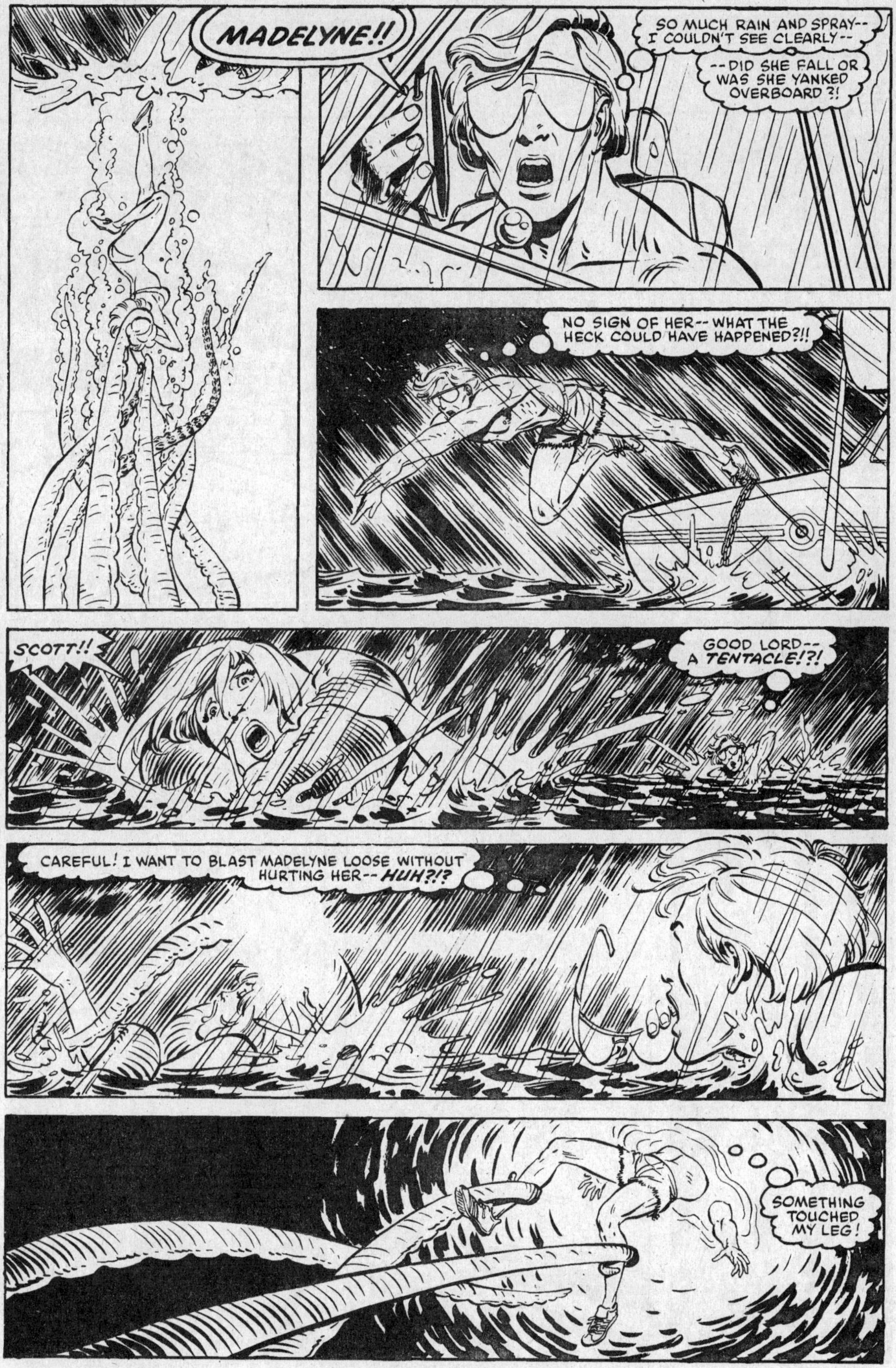
MADELYNE!!
SO MUCH RAIN AND SPRAY-- I COULDN'T SEE CLEARLY--
--DID SHE FALL OR WAS SHE YANKED OVERBOARD?!
NO SIGN OF HER-- WHAT THE HECK COULD HAVE HAPPENED?!!
SCOTT!!
GOOD LORD-- A TENTACLE!?!
CAREFUL! I WANT TO BLAST MADELYNE LOOSE WITHOUT HURTING HER-- HUH?!?
SOMETHING TOUCHED MY LEG!

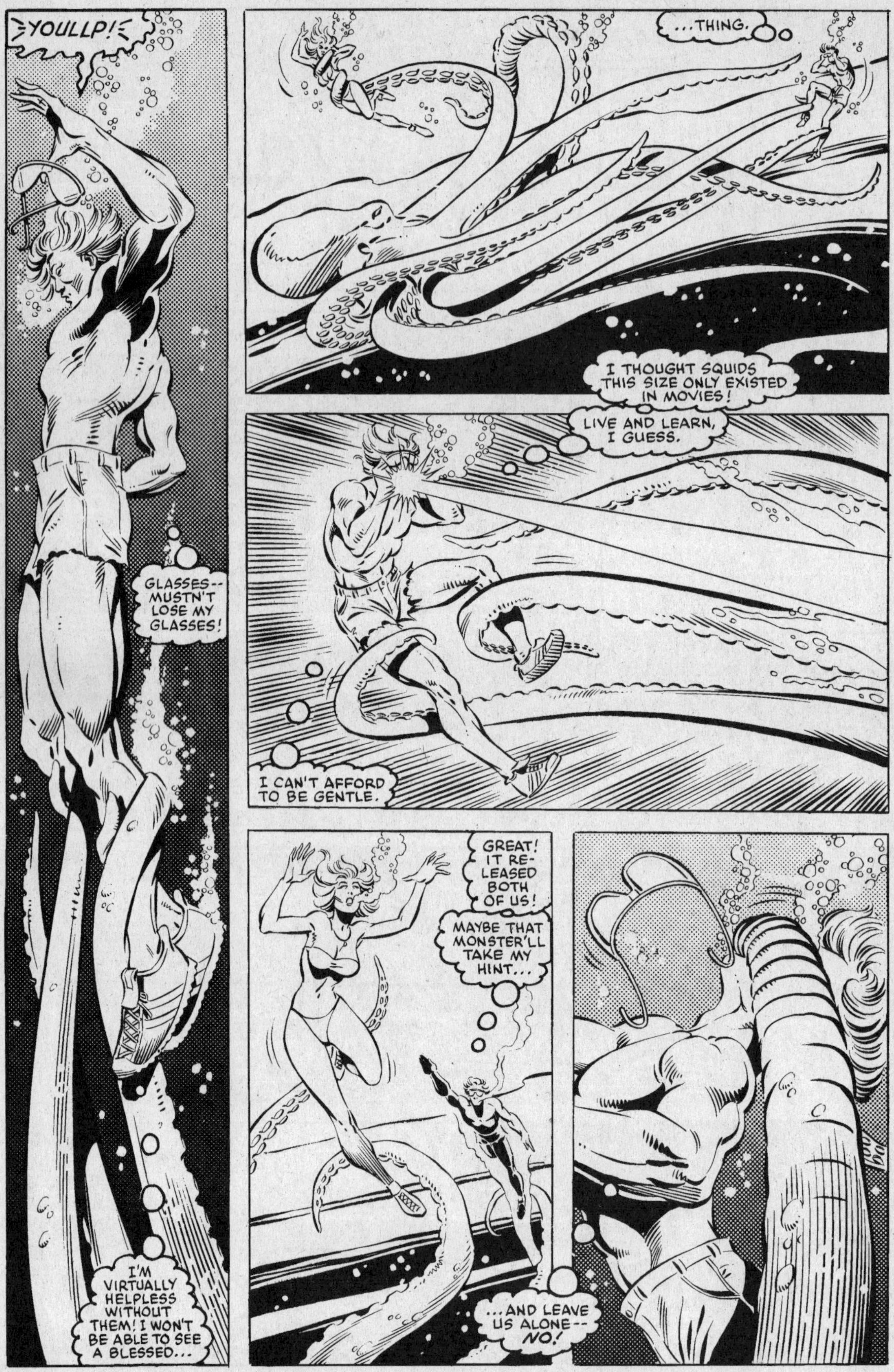
YOULLP!
GLASSES-- MUSTN'T LOSE MY GLASSES!
I'M VIRTUALLY HELPLESS WITHOUT THEM! I WON'T BE ABLE TO SEE A BLESSED...
...THING.
I THOUGHT SQUIDS THIS SIZE ONLY EXISTED IN MOVIES!
LIVE AND LEARN, I GUESS.
I CAN'T AFFORD TO BE GENTLE.
GREAT! IT RELEASED BOTH OF US!
MAYBE THAT MONSTER'LL TAKE MY HINT...
...AND LEAVE US ALONE-- NO!

BAD MOVE, BUSTER! AT THIS RANGE, MY *OPTIC BLASTS* CAN PUNCH THROUGH STEEL ARMOUR PLATE!

TROUBLE IS, BUSTING FREE IS THE LEAST OF MY PROBLEMS.

MADELYNE--!

OVER HERE! BEHIND YOU!

KEEP YELLING! USE YOUR VOICE TO GUIDE ME!

I LOST MY GLASSES. THE ONLY WAY TO PREVENT MY OPTIC BLASTS FROM FIRING...

...IS TO KEEP MY EYES SHUT TIGHT!

I SAW YOU ZAP THE SQUID. DID YOU KILL IT?

THE WATER BLUNTED THE FORCE OF THE BEAM. I DOUBT I EVEN HURT IT MUCH--EXCEPT TO MAKE IT MAD.

SWIM STRAIGHT AHEAD! THE PLANE ISN'T FAR!

OH, NO!

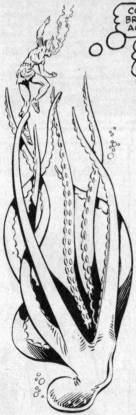

COULDN'T GRAB...DECENT BREATH...ONLY SECONDS TO ACT BEFORE I DROWN.

SQUID'S PULLING ME STRAIGHT DOWN, IT MUST BE DIRECTLY BELOW. MADELYNE'S STILL ON THE SURFACE--OUT OF MY LINE OF FIRE--I DON'T HAVE TO WORRY ABOUT HER.

LET'S SEE HOW WELL THIS MONSTER HANDLES A FULL POWER BLAST!

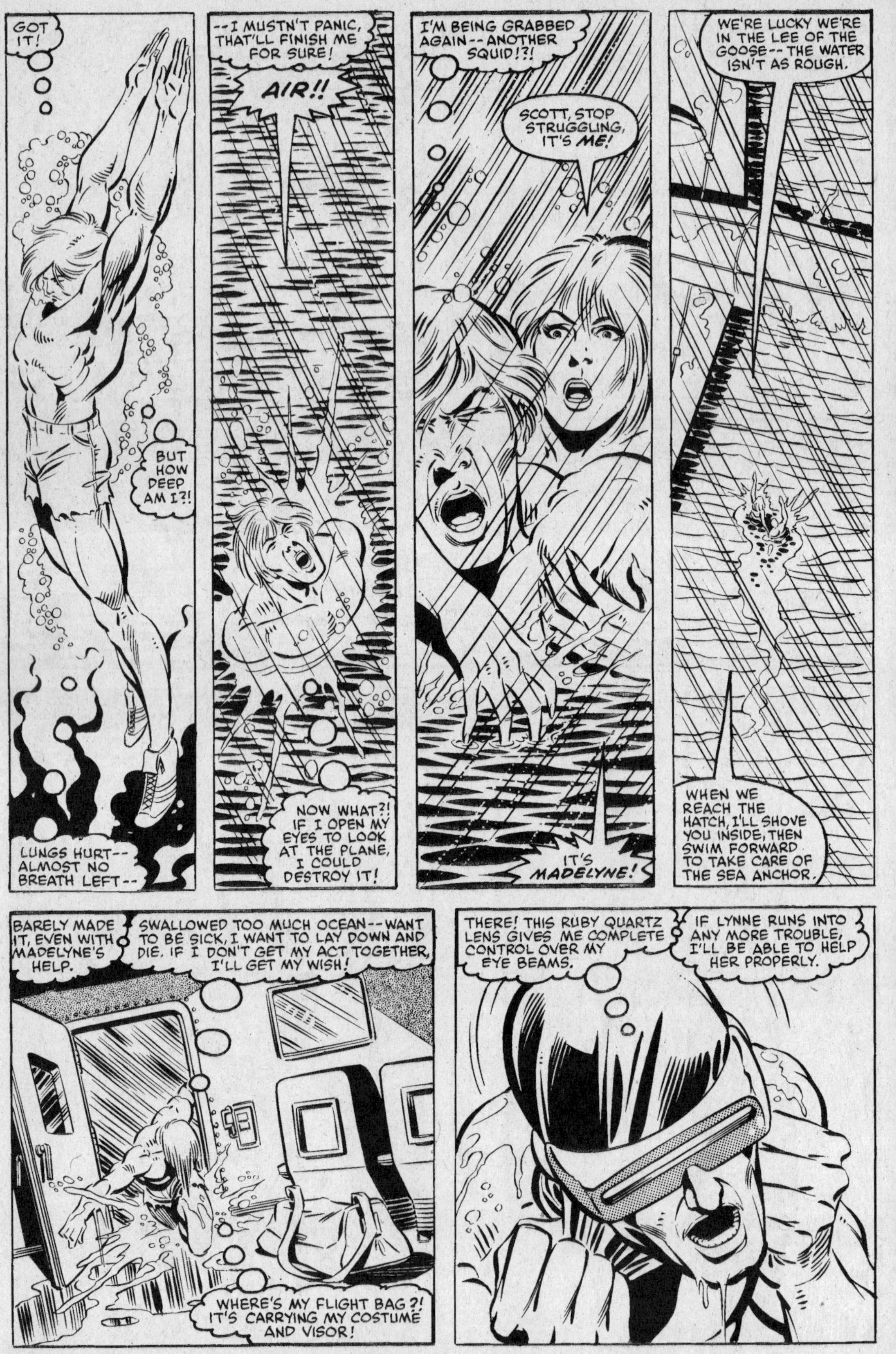
GOT IT!
BUT HOW DEEP AM I?!
LUNGS HURT-- ALMOST NO BREATH LEFT--
--I MUSTN'T PANIC, THAT'LL FINISH ME FOR SURE!
AIR!!
NOW WHAT?! IF I OPEN MY EYES TO LOOK AT THE PLANE, I COULD DESTROY IT!
I'M BEING GRABBED AGAIN-- ANOTHER SQUID!?!
SCOTT, STOP STRUGGLING, IT'S ME!
IT'S MADELYNE!
WE'RE LUCKY WE'RE IN THE LEE OF THE GOOSE-- THE WATER ISN'T AS ROUGH.
WHEN WE REACH THE HATCH, I'LL SHOVE YOU INSIDE, THEN SWIM FORWARD TO TAKE CARE OF THE SEA ANCHOR.
BARELY MADE IT, EVEN WITH MADELYNE'S HELP.
SWALLOWED TOO MUCH OCEAN-- WANT TO BE SICK, I WANT TO LAY DOWN AND DIE. IF I DON'T GET MY ACT TOGETHER, I'LL GET MY WISH!
WHERE'S MY FLIGHT BAG?! IT'S CARRYING MY COSTUME AND VISOR!
THERE! THIS RUBY QUARTZ LENS GIVES ME COMPLETE CONTROL OVER MY EYE BEAMS.
IF LYNNE RUNS INTO ANY MORE TROUBLE, I'LL BE ABLE TO HELP HER PROPERLY.

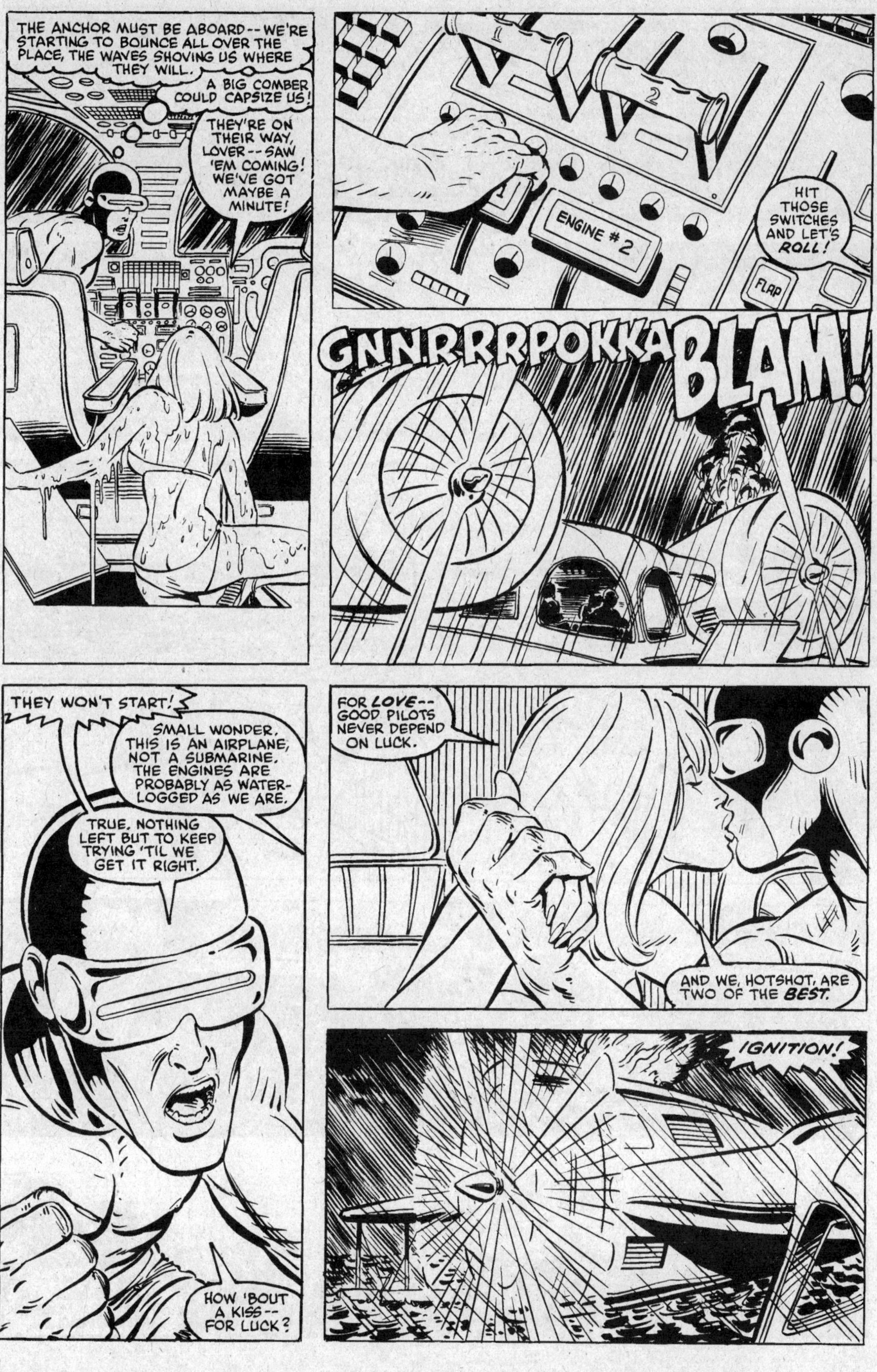
THE ANCHOR MUST BE ABOARD--WE'RE STARTING TO BOUNCE ALL OVER THE PLACE, THE WAVES SHOVING US WHERE THEY WILL.
A BIG COMBER COULD CAPSIZE US!
THEY'RE ON THEIR WAY, LOVER--SAW 'EM COMING! WE'VE GOT MAYBE A MINUTE!
ENGINE #2
HIT THOSE SWITCHES AND LET'S ROLL!
FLAP
GNNRRRPOKKA BLAM!
THEY WON'T START!
SMALL WONDER. THIS IS AN AIRPLANE, NOT A SUBMARINE. THE ENGINES ARE PROBABLY AS WATER-LOGGED AS WE ARE.
TRUE. NOTHING LEFT BUT TO KEEP TRYING 'TIL WE GET IT RIGHT.
HOW 'BOUT A KISS--FOR LUCK?
FOR LOVE--GOOD PILOTS NEVER DEPEND ON LUCK.
AND WE, HOTSHOT, ARE TWO OF THE BEST.
IGNITION!

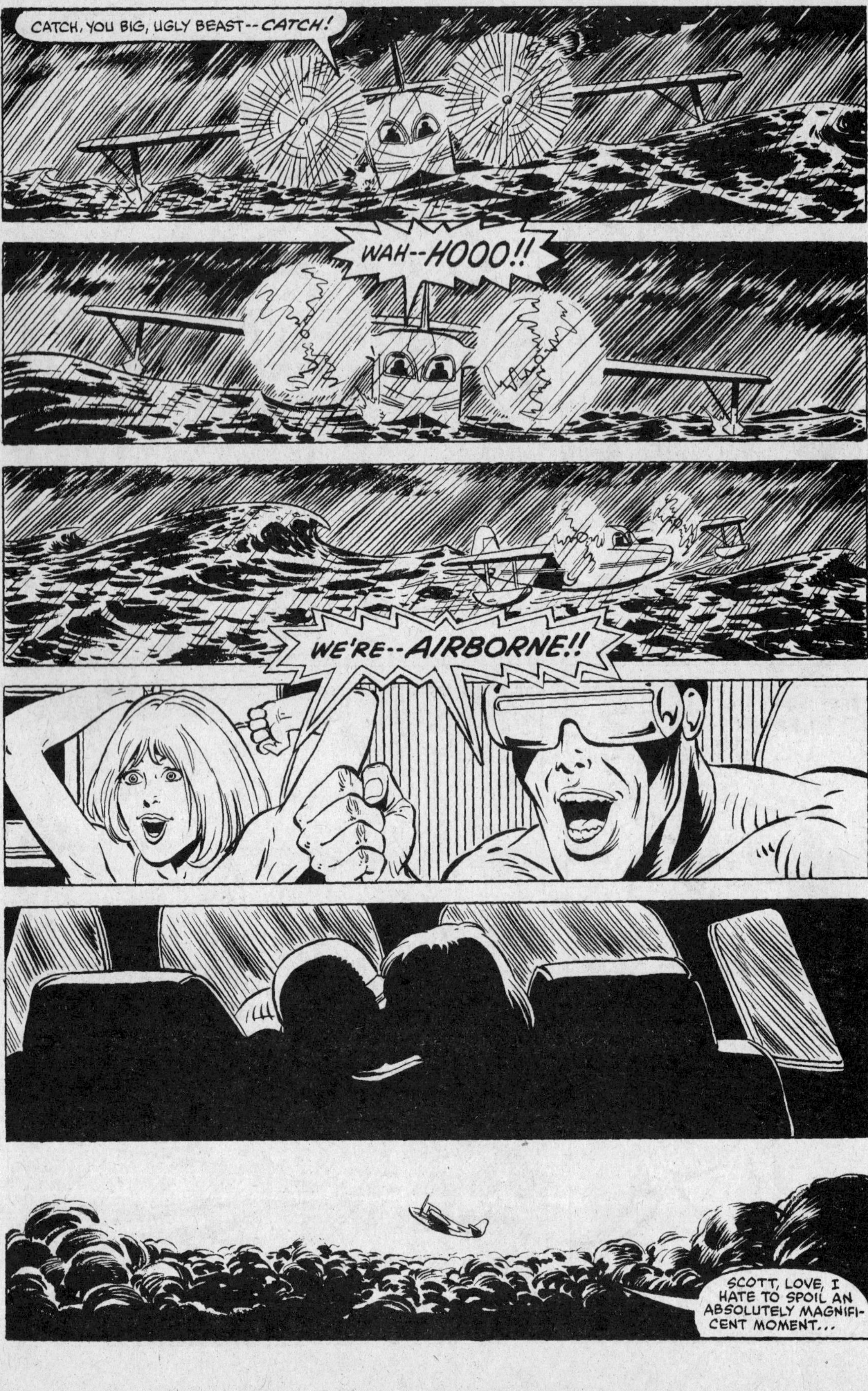
CATCH, YOU BIG, UGLY BEAST--CATCH!
WAH--HOOO!!
WE'RE--AIRBORNE!!
SCOTT, LOVE, I HATE TO SPOIL AN ABSOLUTELY MAGNIFI- CENT MOMENT...

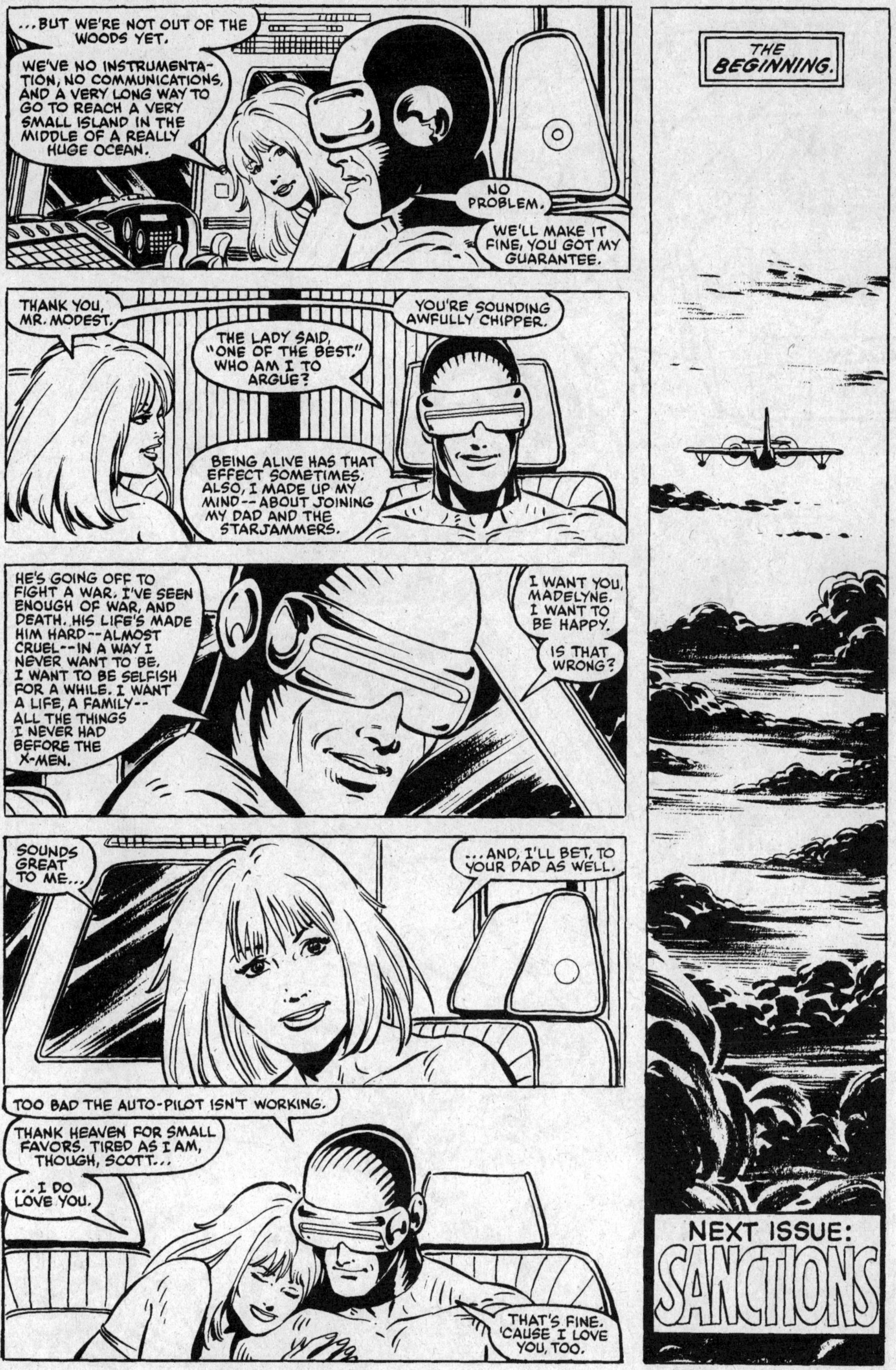
...BUT WE'RE NOT OUT OF THE WOODS YET.
WE'VE NO INSTRUMENTATION, NO COMMUNICATIONS, AND A VERY LONG WAY TO GO TO REACH A VERY SMALL ISLAND IN THE MIDDLE OF A REALLY HUGE OCEAN.
NO PROBLEM.
WE'LL MAKE IT FINE, YOU GOT MY GUARANTEE.
THANK YOU, MR. MODEST.
YOU'RE SOUNDING AWFULLY CHIPPER.
THE LADY SAID, "ONE OF THE BEST." WHO AM I TO ARGUE?
BEING ALIVE HAS THAT EFFECT SOMETIMES. ALSO, I MADE UP MY MIND--ABOUT JOINING MY DAD AND THE STARJAMMERS.
HE'S GOING OFF TO FIGHT A WAR. I'VE SEEN ENOUGH OF WAR, AND DEATH. HIS LIFE'S MADE HIM HARD--ALMOST CRUEL--IN A WAY I NEVER WANT TO BE. I WANT TO BE SELFISH FOR A WHILE. I WANT A LIFE, A FAMILY--ALL THE THINGS I NEVER HAD BEFORE THE X-MEN.
I WANT YOU, MADELYNE. I WANT TO BE HAPPY.
IS THAT WRONG?
SOUNDS GREAT TO ME...
...AND, I'LL BET, TO YOUR DAD AS WELL.
TOO BAD THE AUTO-PILOT ISN'T WORKING.
THANK HEAVEN FOR SMALL FAVORS. TIRED AS I AM, THOUGH, SCOTT...
...I DO LOVE YOU.
THAT'S FINE. 'CAUSE I LOVE YOU, TOO.
THE BEGINNING.
NEXT ISSUE:
SANCTIONS

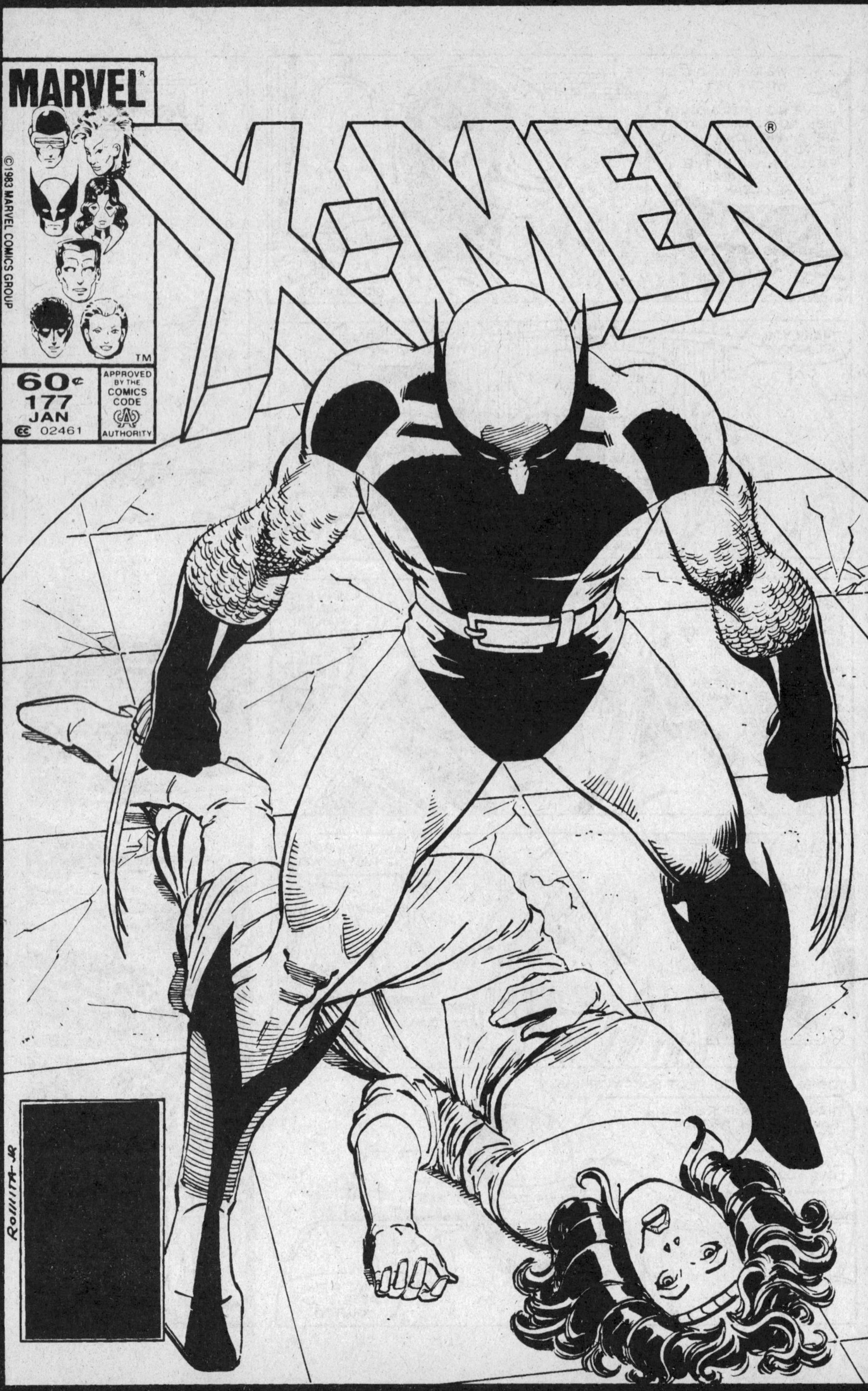
MARVEL
X-MEN
©1983 MARVEL COMICS GROUP
60¢
177
JAN
02461
APPROVED BY THE COMICS CODE AUTHORITY
ROMITA JR

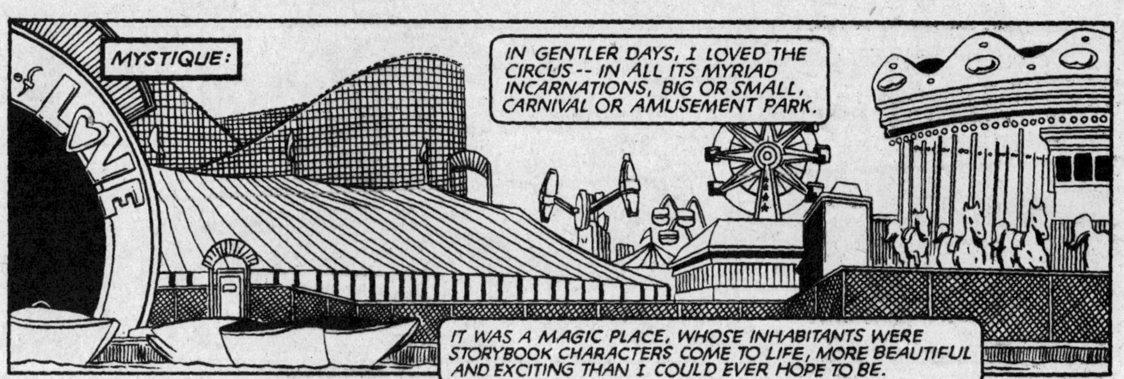
MYSTIQUE:
IN GENTLER DAYS, I LOVED THE CIRCUS -- IN ALL ITS MYRIAD INCARNATIONS, BIG OR SMALL, CARNIVAL OR AMUSEMENT PARK.
LOVE
IT WAS A MAGIC PLACE, WHOSE INHABITANTS WERE STORYBOOK CHARACTERS COME TO LIFE, MORE BEAUTIFUL AND EXCITING THAN I COULD EVER HOPE TO BE.

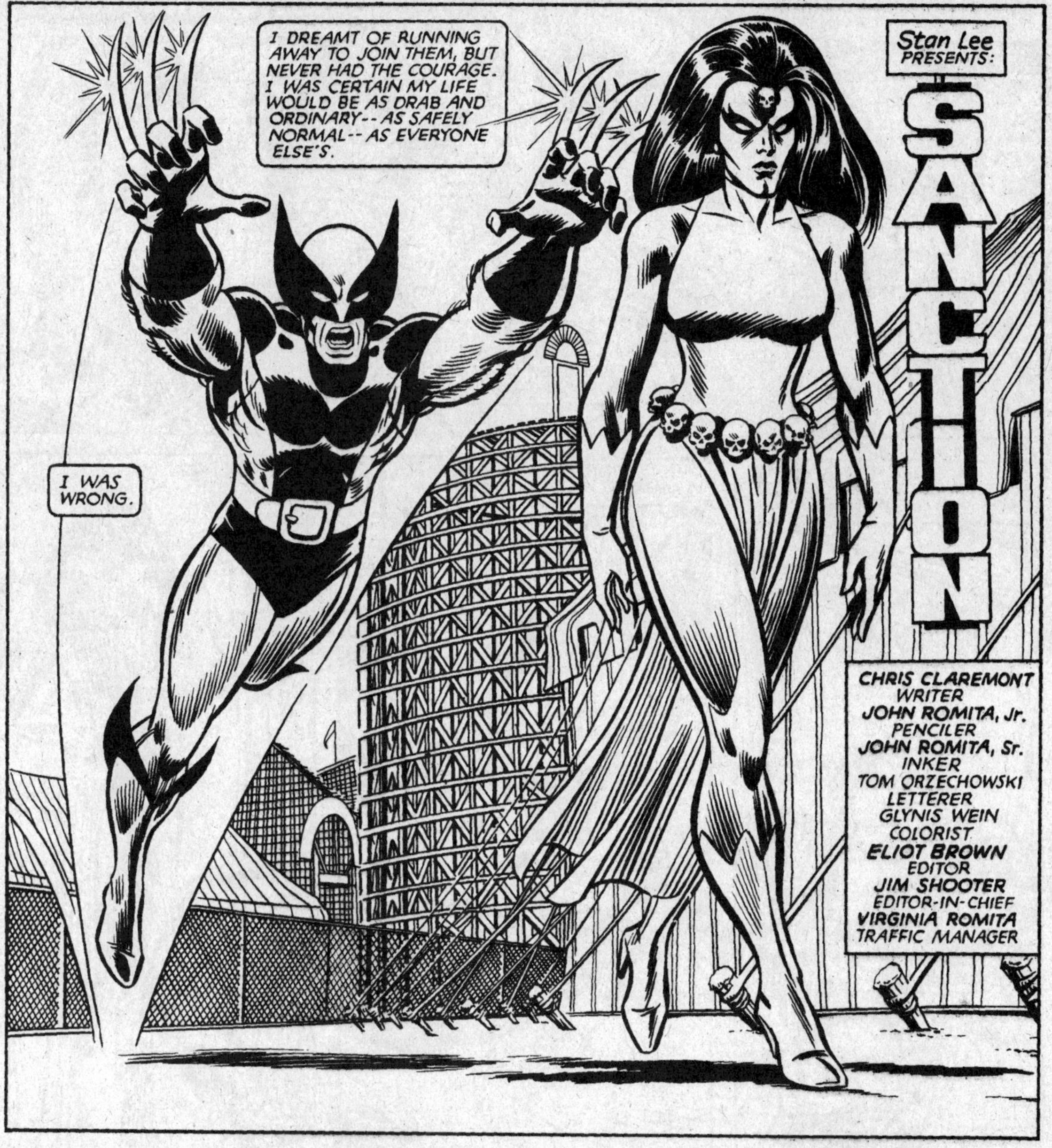
I DREAMT OF RUNNING AWAY TO JOIN THEM, BUT NEVER HAD THE COURAGE. I WAS CERTAIN MY LIFE WOULD BE AS DRAB AND ORDINARY -- AS SAFELY NORMAL -- AS EVERYONE ELSE'S.
Stan Lee PRESENTS:
SANCTION
I WAS WRONG.
CHRIS CLAREMONT WRITER
JOHN ROMITA, Jr. PENCILER
JOHN ROMITA, Sr. INKER
TOM ORZECHOWSKI LETTERER
GLYNIS WEIN COLORIST
ELIOT BROWN EDITOR
JIM SHOOTER EDITOR-IN-CHIEF
VIRGINIA ROMITA TRAFFIC MANAGER

FAST AS I REACT TO WOLVERINE'S ATTACK...

...HE STILL DRAWS BLOOD.

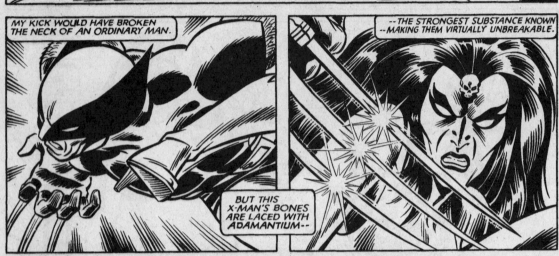

MY KICK WOULD HAVE BROKEN THE NECK OF AN ORDINARY MAN.

BUT THIS X-MAN'S BONES ARE LACED WITH ADAMANTIUM--

--THE STRONGEST SUBSTANCE KNOWN --MAKING THEM VIRTUALLY UNBREAKABLE.

HIS CLAWS ARE FORGED OF THE PURE METAL. RAZOR-KEEN, THEY CAN CUT STEEL GIRDERS WITH EASE.

TICKETS 50¢

BUT FOR ALL HIS POWER AND SKILL...

... HE IS STILL VULNERABLE...

...TO A SLIT THROAT.

NO BONES TO STOP MY BLADE.

AND EVEN YOUR MUTANT HEALING FACTOR WON'T PREVENT YOUR BLEEDING TO DEATH.

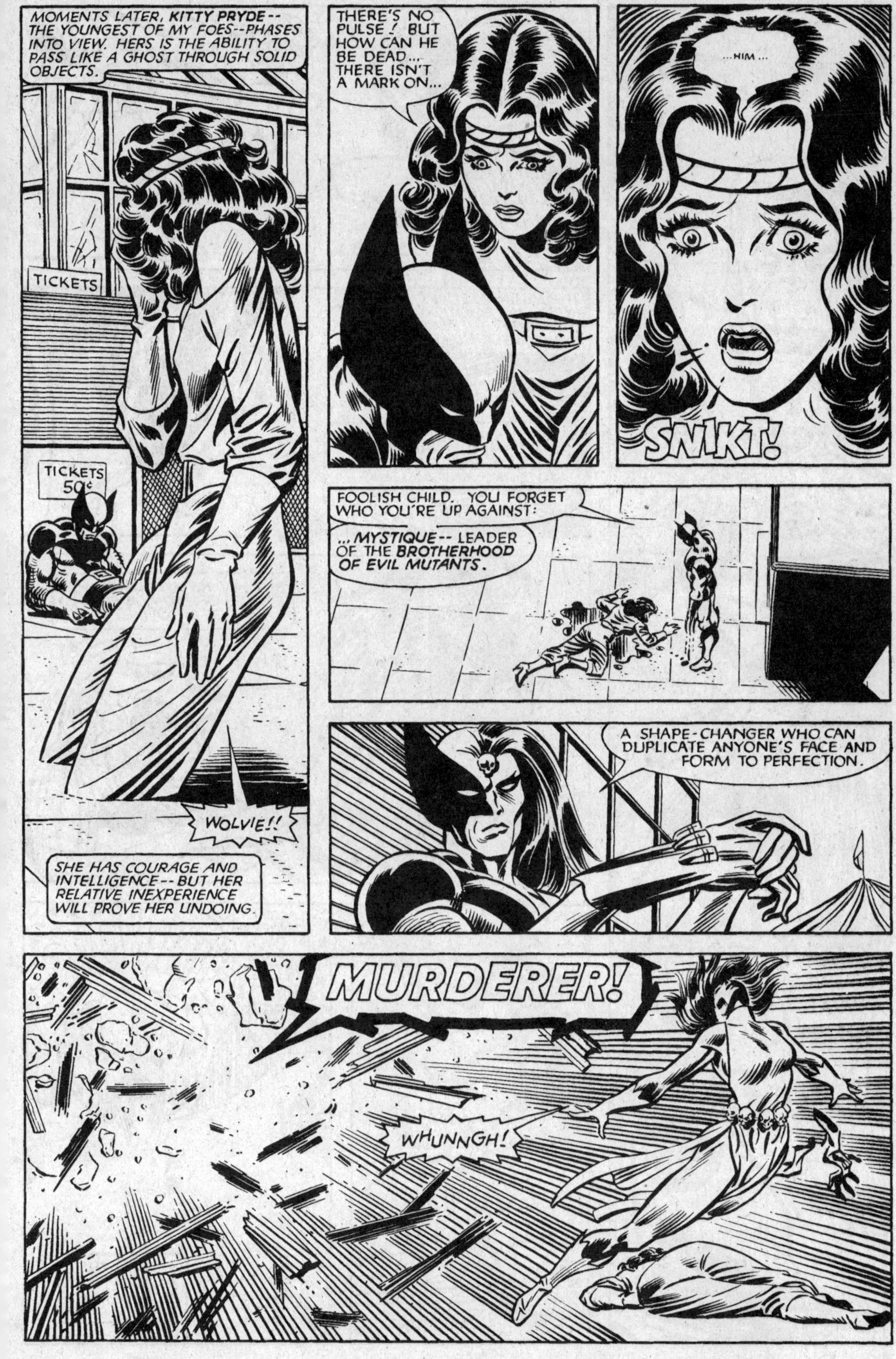
MOMENTS LATER, KITTY PRYDE-- THE YOUNGEST OF MY FOES--PHASES INTO VIEW. HERS IS THE ABILITY TO PASS LIKE A GHOST THROUGH SOLID OBJECTS.
TICKETS
TICKETS 50¢
WOLVIE!!
SHE HAS COURAGE AND INTELLIGENCE-- BUT HER RELATIVE INEXPERIENCE WILL PROVE HER UNDOING.
THERE'S NO PULSE! BUT HOW CAN HE BE DEAD... THERE ISN'T A MARK ON...
...HIM...
SNIKT!
FOOLISH CHILD. YOU FORGET WHO YOU'RE UP AGAINST:
...MYSTIQUE-- LEADER OF THE BROTHERHOOD OF EVIL MUTANTS.
A SHAPE-CHANGER WHO CAN DUPLICATE ANYONE'S FACE AND FORM TO PERFECTION.
MURDERER!
WHUNNGH!

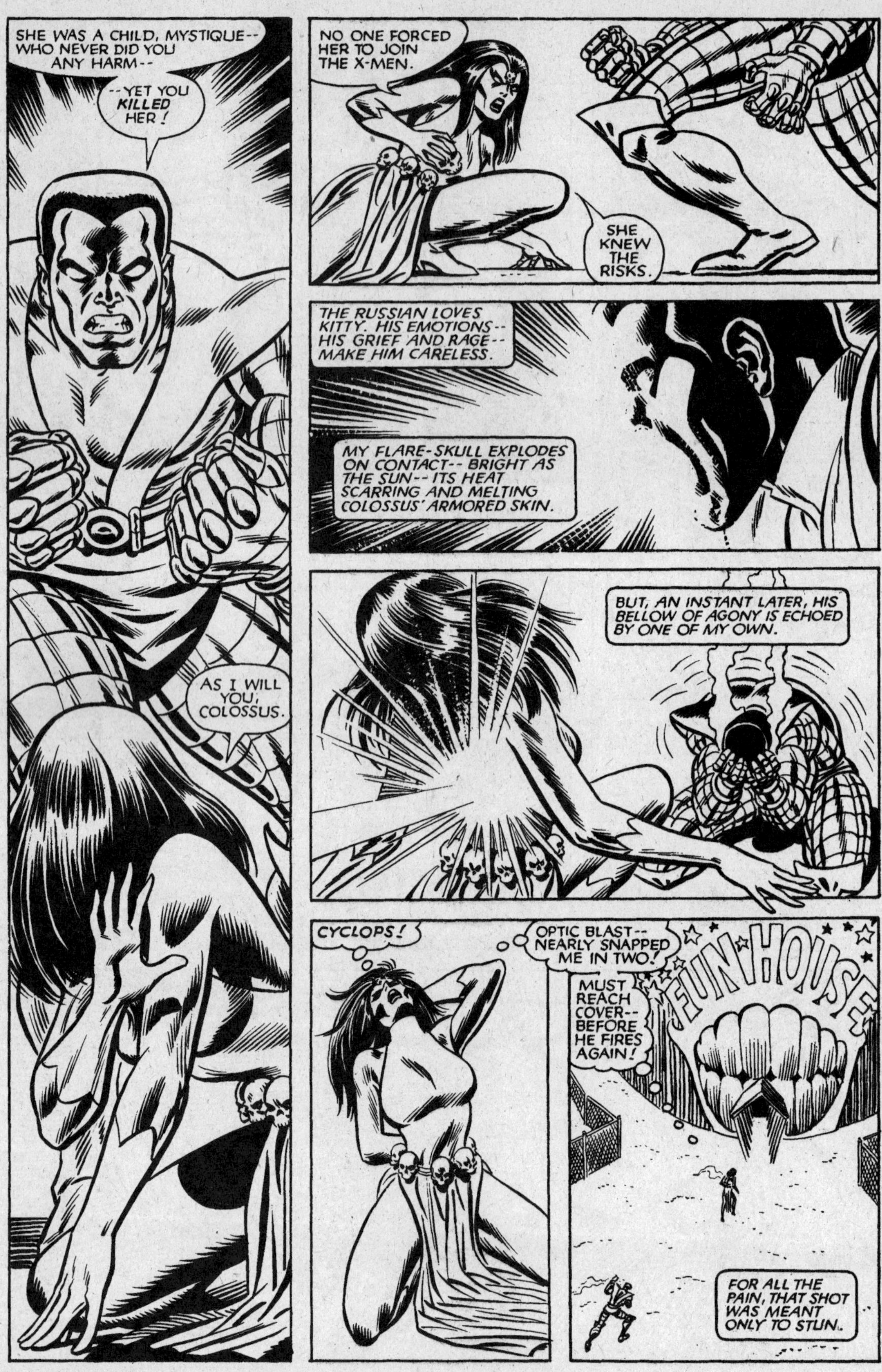
SHE WAS A CHILD, MYSTIQUE-- WHO NEVER DID YOU ANY HARM--
--YET YOU KILLED HER!
AS I WILL YOU, COLOSSUS.
NO ONE FORCED HER TO JOIN THE X-MEN.
SHE KNEW THE RISKS.
THE RUSSIAN LOVES KITTY. HIS EMOTIONS-- HIS GRIEF AND RAGE-- MAKE HIM CARELESS.
MY FLARE-SKULL EXPLODES ON CONTACT-- BRIGHT AS THE SUN-- ITS HEAT SCARRING AND MELTING COLOSSUS' ARMORED SKIN.
BUT, AN INSTANT LATER, HIS BELLOW OF AGONY IS ECHOED BY ONE OF MY OWN.
CYCLOPS!
OPTIC BLAST-- NEARLY SNAPPED ME IN TWO!
FUN HOUSE
MUST REACH COVER-- BEFORE HE FIRES AGAIN!
FOR ALL THE PAIN, THAT SHOT WAS MEANT ONLY TO STUN.

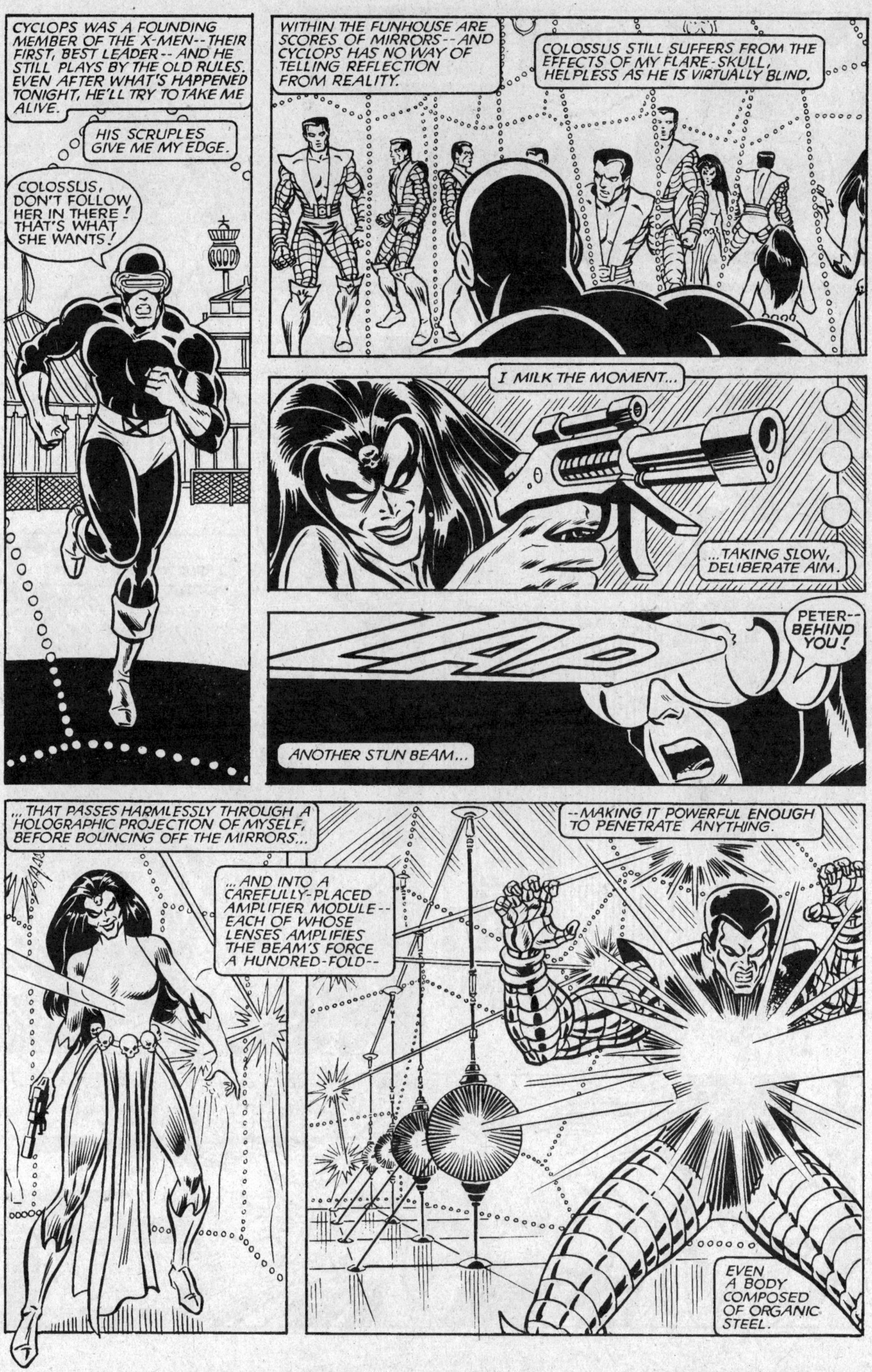
CYCLOPS WAS A FOUNDING MEMBER OF THE X-MEN--THEIR FIRST, BEST LEADER -- AND HE STILL PLAYS BY THE OLD RULES. EVEN AFTER WHAT'S HAPPENED TONIGHT, HE'LL TRY TO TAKE ME ALIVE.
HIS SCRUPLES GIVE ME MY EDGE.
COLOSSUS, DON'T FOLLOW HER IN THERE! THAT'S WHAT SHE WANTS!
WITHIN THE FUNHOUSE ARE SCORES OF MIRRORS-- AND CYCLOPS HAS NO WAY OF TELLING REFLECTION FROM REALITY.
COLOSSUS STILL SUFFERS FROM THE EFFECTS OF MY FLARE-SKULL, HELPLESS AS HE IS VIRTUALLY BLIND.
I MILK THE MOMENT...
...TAKING SLOW, DELIBERATE AIM.
ANOTHER STUN BEAM...
PETER-- BEHIND YOU!
...THAT PASSES HARMLESSLY THROUGH A HOLOGRAPHIC PROJECTION OF MYSELF, BEFORE BOUNCING OFF THE MIRRORS...
...AND INTO A CAREFULLY-PLACED AMPLIFIER MODULE-- EACH OF WHOSE LENSES AMPLIFIES THE BEAM'S FORCE A HUNDRED-FOLD--
--MAKING IT POWERFUL ENOUGH TO PENETRATE ANYTHING.
EVEN A BODY COMPOSED OF ORGANIC STEEL.

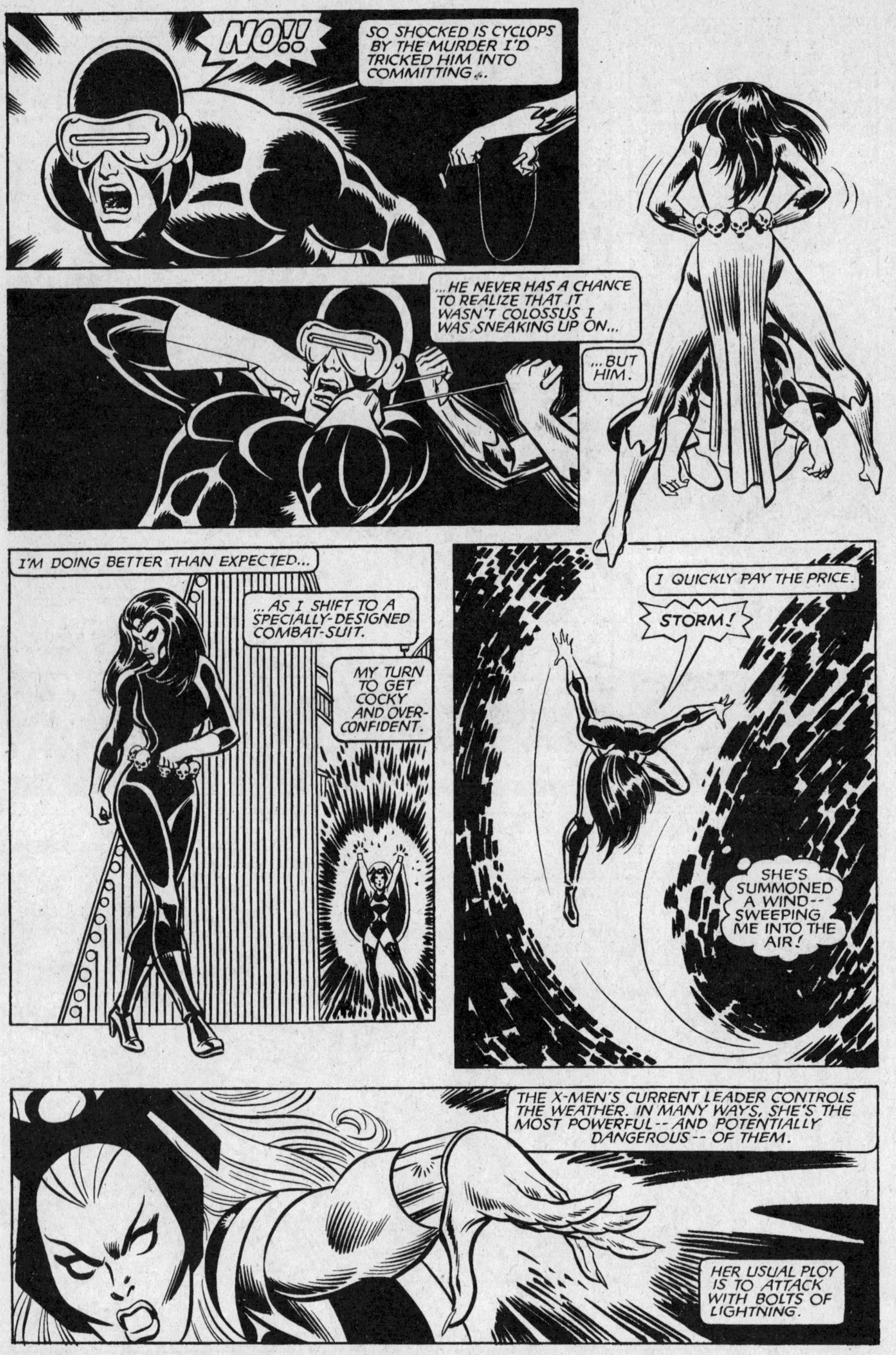
NO!!
SO SHOCKED IS CYCLOPS BY THE MURDER I'D TRICKED HIM INTO COMMITTING...
...HE NEVER HAS A CHANCE TO REALIZE THAT IT WASN'T COLOSSUS I WAS SNEAKING UP ON...
...BUT HIM.
I'M DOING BETTER THAN EXPECTED...
...AS I SHIFT TO A SPECIALLY-DESIGNED COMBAT-SUIT.
MY TURN TO GET COCKY AND OVER-CONFIDENT.
I QUICKLY PAY THE PRICE.
STORM!
SHE'S SUMMONED A WIND--SWEEPING ME INTO THE AIR!
THE X-MEN'S CURRENT LEADER CONTROLS THE WEATHER. IN MANY WAYS, SHE'S THE MOST POWERFUL-- AND POTENTIALLY DANGEROUS-- OF THEM.
HER USUAL PLOY IS TO ATTACK WITH BOLTS OF LIGHTNING.

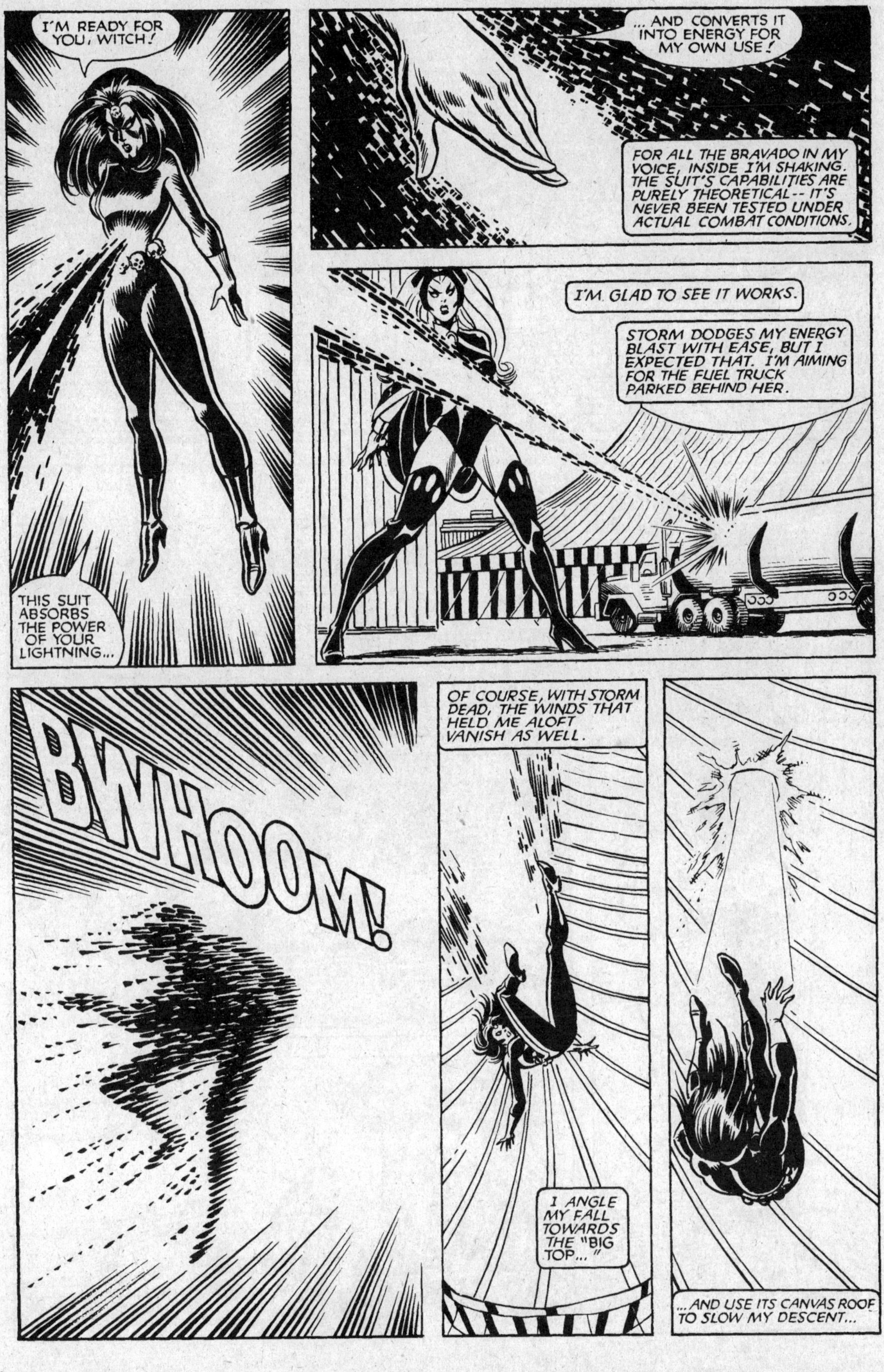
I'M READY FOR YOU, WITCH!
THIS SUIT ABSORBS THE POWER OF YOUR LIGHTNING...
...AND CONVERTS IT INTO ENERGY FOR MY OWN USE!
FOR ALL THE BRAVADO IN MY VOICE, INSIDE I'M SHAKING. THE SUIT'S CAPABILITIES ARE PURELY THEORETICAL -- IT'S NEVER BEEN TESTED UNDER ACTUAL COMBAT CONDITIONS.
I'M GLAD TO SEE IT WORKS.
STORM DODGES MY ENERGY BLAST WITH EASE, BUT I EXPECTED THAT. I'M AIMING FOR THE FUEL TRUCK PARKED BEHIND HER.
BWHOOM!
OF COURSE, WITH STORM DEAD, THE WINDS THAT HELD ME ALOFT VANISH AS WELL.
I ANGLE MY FALL TOWARDS THE "BIG TOP..."
...AND USE ITS CANVAS ROOF TO SLOW MY DESCENT...

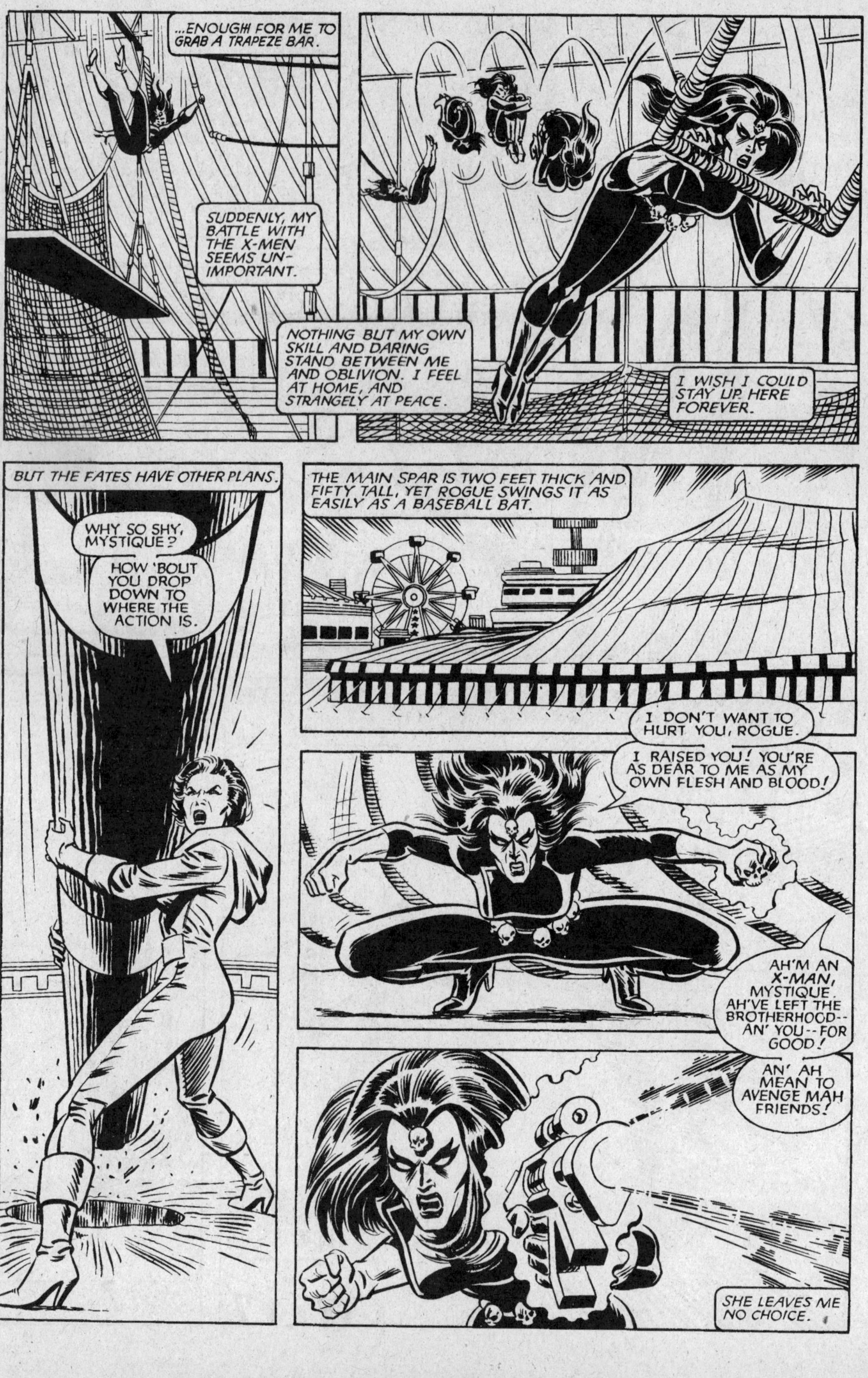
...ENOUGH FOR ME TO GRAB A TRAPEZE BAR.
SUDDENLY, MY BATTLE WITH THE X-MEN SEEMS UN-IMPORTANT.
NOTHING BUT MY OWN SKILL AND DARING STAND BETWEEN ME AND OBLIVION. I FEEL AT HOME, AND STRANGELY AT PEACE.
I WISH I COULD STAY UP HERE FOREVER.
BUT THE FATES HAVE OTHER PLANS.
WHY SO SHY, MYSTIQUE?
HOW 'BOUT YOU DROP DOWN TO WHERE THE ACTION IS.
THE MAIN SPAR IS TWO FEET THICK AND FIFTY TALL, YET ROGUE SWINGS IT AS EASILY AS A BASEBALL BAT.
I DON'T WANT TO HURT YOU, ROGUE.
I RAISED YOU! YOU'RE AS DEAR TO ME AS MY OWN FLESH AND BLOOD!
AH'M AN X-MAN, MYSTIQUE. AH'VE LEFT THE BROTHERHOOD-- AN' YOU--FOR GOOD!
AN' AH MEAN TO AVENGE MAH FRIENDS!
SHE LEAVES ME NO CHOICE.

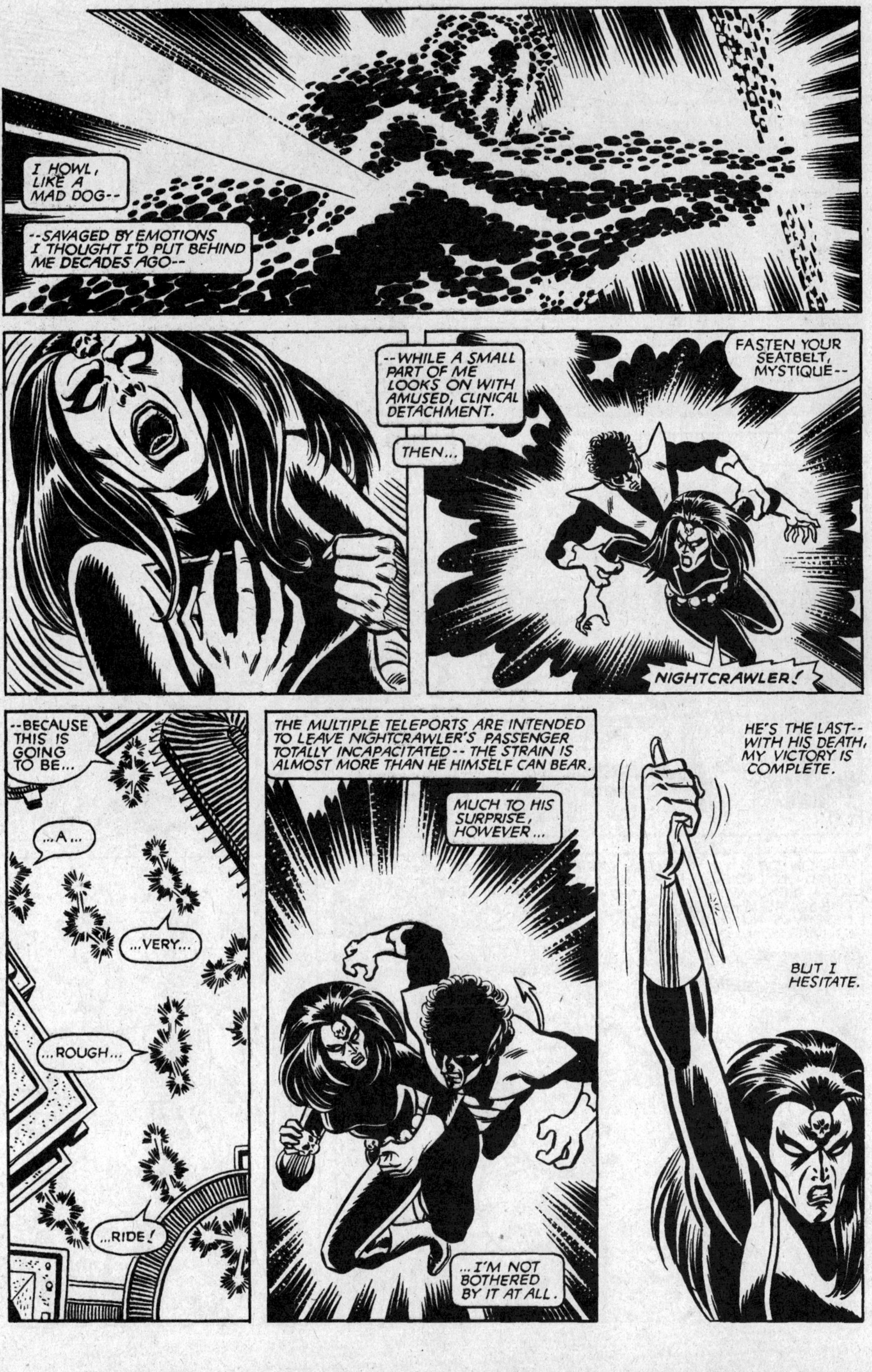

I HOWL, LIKE A MAD DOG--
--SAVAGED BY EMOTIONS I THOUGHT I'D PUT BEHIND ME DECADES AGO--
--WHILE A SMALL PART OF ME LOOKS ON WITH AMUSED, CLINICAL DETACHMENT.
THEN...
FASTEN YOUR SEATBELT, MYSTIQUE--
NIGHTCRAWLER!
--BECAUSE THIS IS GOING TO BE...
...A...
...VERY...
...ROUGH...
...RIDE!
THE MULTIPLE TELEPORTS ARE INTENDED TO LEAVE NIGHTCRAWLER'S PASSENGER TOTALLY INCAPACITATED-- THE STRAIN IS ALMOST MORE THAN HE HIMSELF CAN BEAR.
MUCH TO HIS SURPRISE, HOWEVER...
...I'M NOT BOTHERED BY IT AT ALL.
HE'S THE LAST-- WITH HIS DEATH, MY VICTORY IS COMPLETE.
BUT I HESITATE.

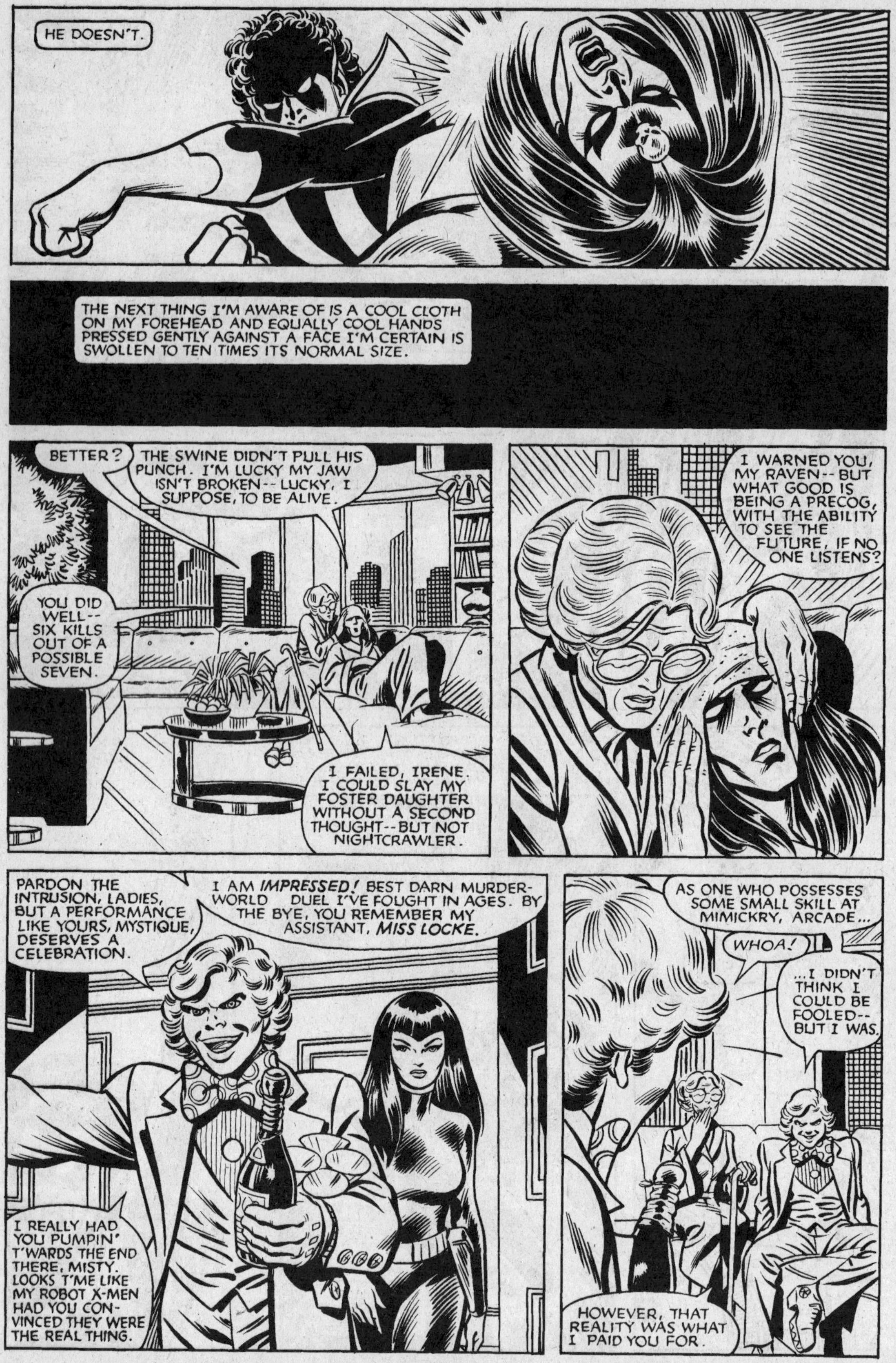

HE DOESN'T.
THE NEXT THING I'M AWARE OF IS A COOL CLOTH ON MY FOREHEAD AND EQUALLY COOL HANDS PRESSED GENTLY AGAINST A FACE I'M CERTAIN IS SWOLLEN TO TEN TIMES ITS NORMAL SIZE.
BETTER?
THE SWINE DIDN'T PULL HIS PUNCH. I'M LUCKY MY JAW ISN'T BROKEN-- LUCKY, I SUPPOSE, TO BE ALIVE.
YOU DID WELL-- SIX KILLS OUT OF A POSSIBLE SEVEN.
I FAILED, IRENE. I COULD SLAY MY FOSTER DAUGHTER WITHOUT A SECOND THOUGHT--BUT NOT NIGHTCRAWLER.
I WARNED YOU, MY RAVEN-- BUT WHAT GOOD IS BEING A PRECOG, WITH THE ABILITY TO SEE THE FUTURE, IF NO ONE LISTENS?
PARDON THE INTRUSION, LADIES, BUT A PERFORMANCE LIKE YOURS, MYSTIQUE, DESERVES A CELEBRATION.
I AM *IMPRESSED!* BEST DARN MURDER-WORLD DUEL I'VE FOUGHT IN AGES. BY THE BYE, YOU REMEMBER MY ASSISTANT, *MISS LOCKE*.
I REALLY HAD YOU PUMPIN' T'WARDS THE END THERE, MISTY. LOOKS T'ME LIKE MY ROBOT X-MEN HAD YOU CONVINCED THEY WERE THE REAL THING.
AS ONE WHO POSSESSES SOME SMALL SKILL AT MIMICKRY, ARCADE...
WHOA!
...I DIDN'T THINK I COULD BE FOOLED-- BUT I WAS.
HOWEVER, THAT REALITY WAS WHAT I PAID YOU FOR.

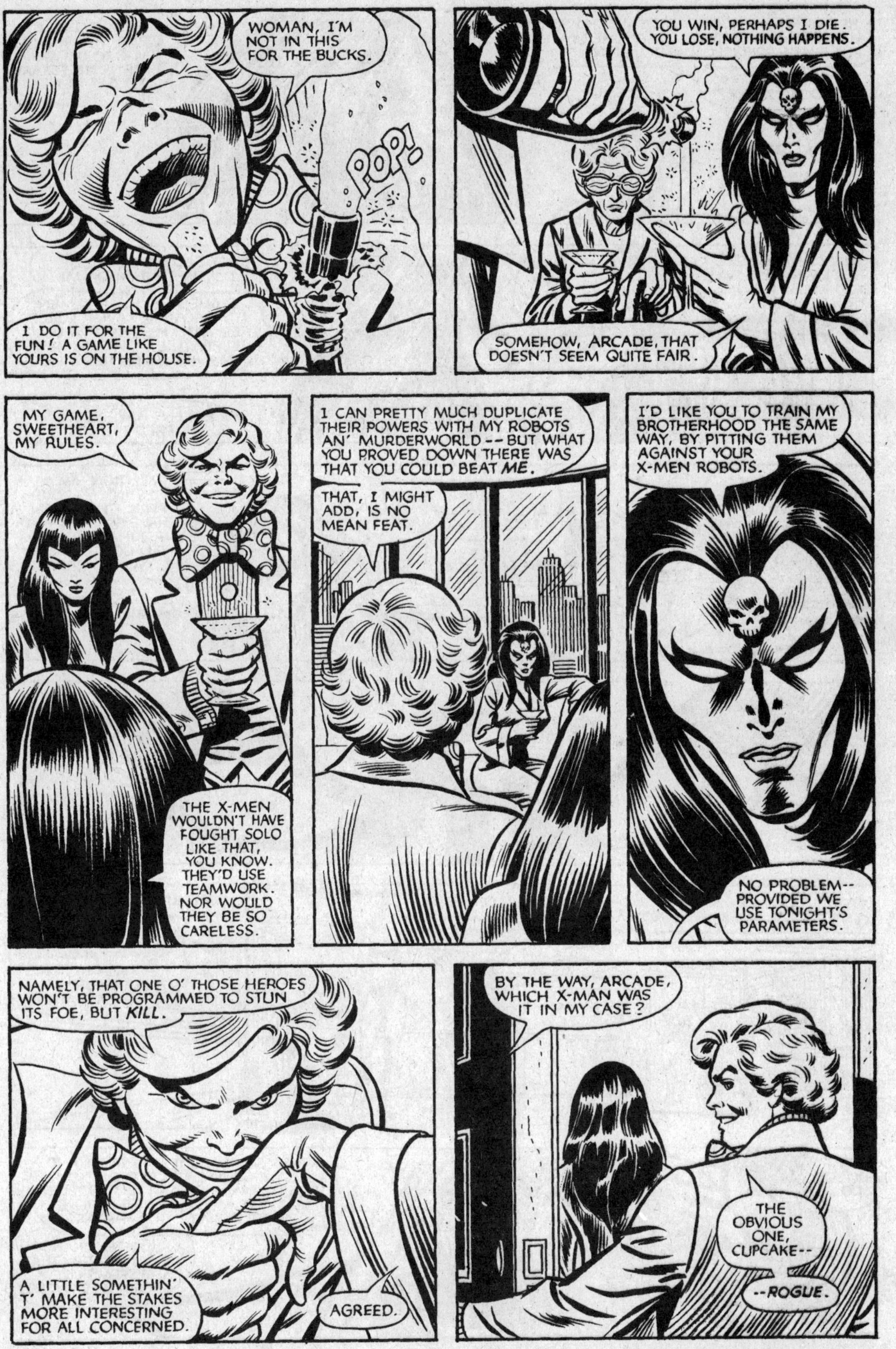
WOMAN, I'M NOT IN THIS FOR THE BUCKS.
POP!
I DO IT FOR THE FUN! A GAME LIKE YOURS IS ON THE HOUSE.
YOU WIN, PERHAPS I DIE. YOU LOSE, NOTHING HAPPENS.
SOMEHOW, ARCADE, THAT DOESN'T SEEM QUITE FAIR.
MY GAME, SWEETHEART, MY RULES.
THE X-MEN WOULDN'T HAVE FOUGHT SOLO LIKE THAT, YOU KNOW. THEY'D USE TEAMWORK. NOR WOULD THEY BE SO CARELESS.
I CAN PRETTY MUCH DUPLICATE THEIR POWERS WITH MY ROBOTS AN' MURDERWORLD -- BUT WHAT YOU PROVED DOWN THERE WAS THAT YOU COULD BEAT ME.
THAT, I MIGHT ADD, IS NO MEAN FEAT.
I'D LIKE YOU TO TRAIN MY BROTHERHOOD THE SAME WAY, BY PITTING THEM AGAINST YOUR X-MEN ROBOTS.
NO PROBLEM-- PROVIDED WE USE TONIGHT'S PARAMETERS.
NAMELY, THAT ONE O' THOSE HEROES WON'T BE PROGRAMMED TO STUN ITS FOE, BUT KILL.
A LITTLE SOMETHIN' T' MAKE THE STAKES MORE INTERESTING FOR ALL CONCERNED.
AGREED.
BY THE WAY, ARCADE, WHICH X-MAN WAS IT IN MY CASE?
THE OBVIOUS ONE, CUPCAKE--
--ROGUE.

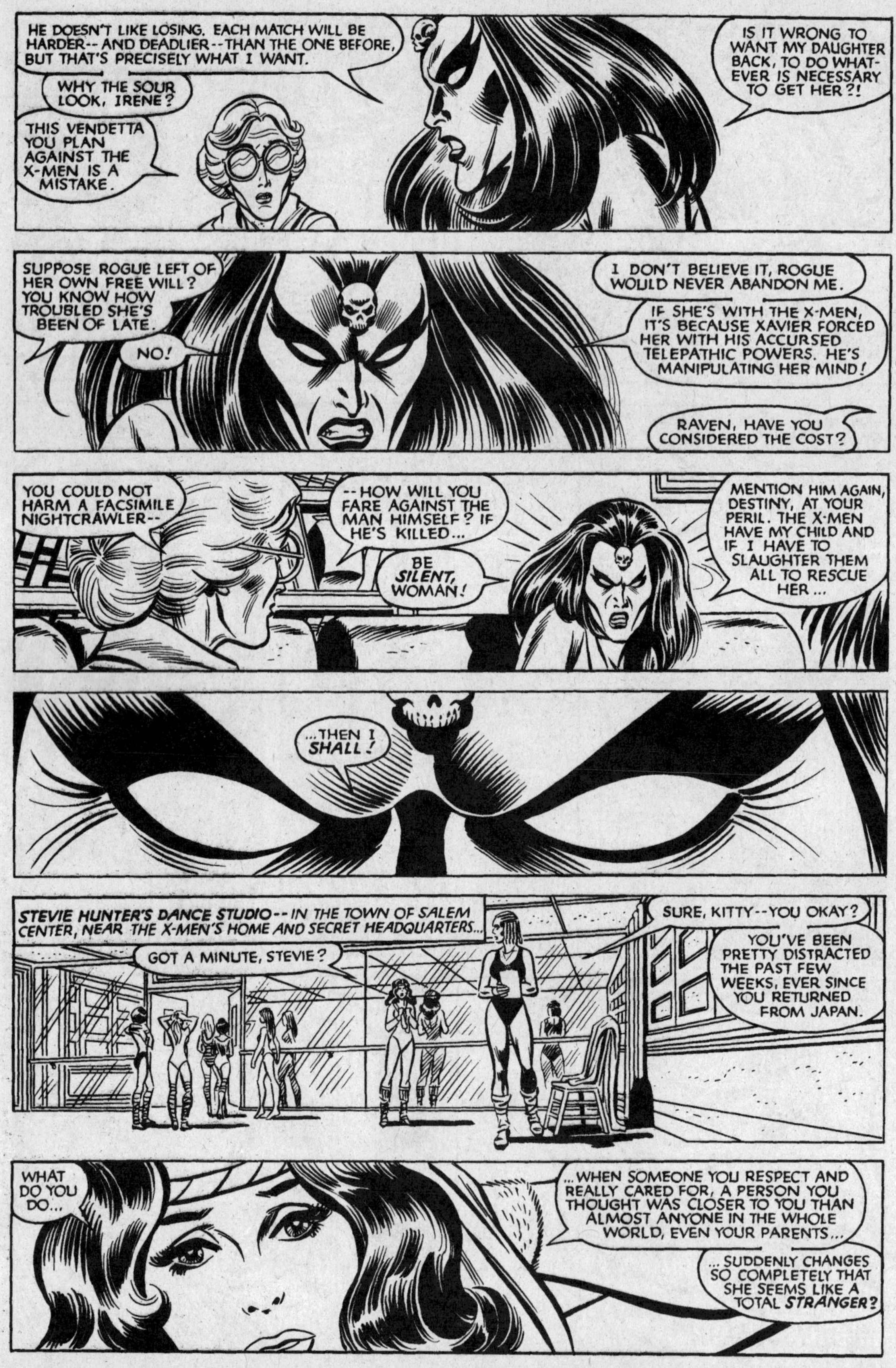
HE DOESN'T LIKE LOSING. EACH MATCH WILL BE HARDER-- AND DEADLIER--THAN THE ONE BEFORE, BUT THAT'S PRECISELY WHAT I WANT.
WHY THE SOUR LOOK, IRENE?
THIS VENDETTA YOU PLAN AGAINST THE X-MEN IS A MISTAKE.
IS IT WRONG TO WANT MY DAUGHTER BACK, TO DO WHATEVER IS NECESSARY TO GET HER?!
SUPPOSE ROGUE LEFT OF HER OWN FREE WILL? YOU KNOW HOW TROUBLED SHE'S BEEN OF LATE.
NO!
I DON'T BELIEVE IT. ROGUE WOULD NEVER ABANDON ME.
IF SHE'S WITH THE X-MEN, IT'S BECAUSE XAVIER FORCED HER WITH HIS ACCURSED TELEPATHIC POWERS. HE'S MANIPULATING HER MIND!
RAVEN, HAVE YOU CONSIDERED THE COST?
YOU COULD NOT HARM A FACSIMILE NIGHTCRAWLER--
--HOW WILL YOU FARE AGAINST THE MAN HIMSELF? IF HE'S KILLED...
BE SILENT, WOMAN!
MENTION HIM AGAIN, DESTINY, AT YOUR PERIL. THE X-MEN HAVE MY CHILD AND IF I HAVE TO SLAUGHTER THEM ALL TO RESCUE HER...
...THEN I SHALL!
STEVIE HUNTER'S DANCE STUDIO-- IN THE TOWN OF SALEM CENTER, NEAR THE X-MEN'S HOME AND SECRET HEADQUARTERS...
GOT A MINUTE, STEVIE?
SURE, KITTY--YOU OKAY?
YOU'VE BEEN PRETTY DISTRACTED THE PAST FEW WEEKS, EVER SINCE YOU RETURNED FROM JAPAN.
WHAT DO YOU DO...
...WHEN SOMEONE YOU RESPECT AND REALLY CARED FOR, A PERSON YOU THOUGHT WAS CLOSER TO YOU THAN ALMOST ANYONE IN THE WHOLE WORLD, EVEN YOUR PARENTS...
...SUDDENLY CHANGES SO COMPLETELY THAT SHE SEEMS LIKE A TOTAL STRANGER?

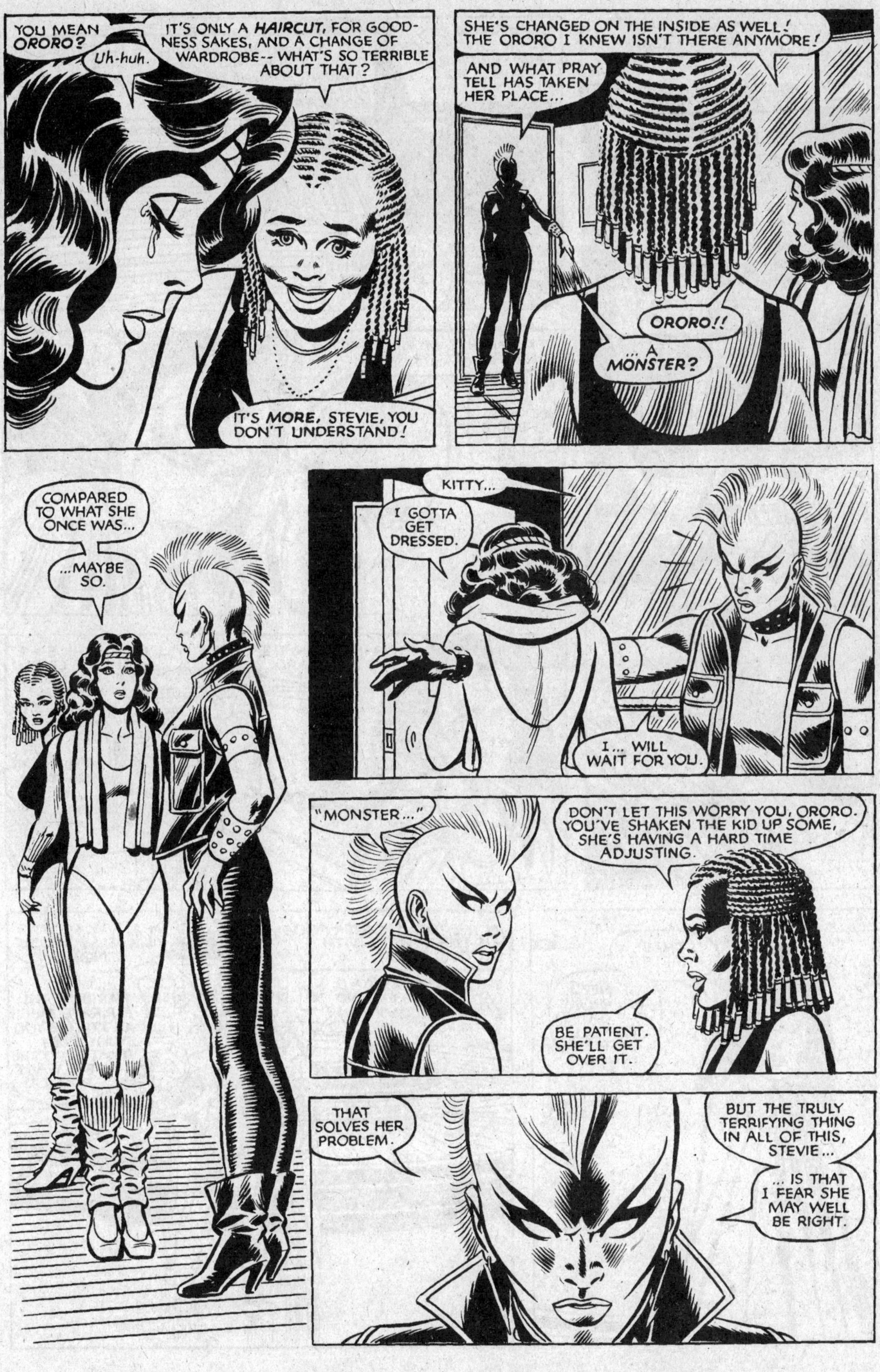
YOU MEAN ORORO?
Uh-huh.
IT'S ONLY A HAIRCUT, FOR GOODNESS SAKES, AND A CHANGE OF WARDROBE-- WHAT'S SO TERRIBLE ABOUT THAT?
IT'S MORE, STEVIE, YOU DON'T UNDERSTAND!
SHE'S CHANGED ON THE INSIDE AS WELL! THE ORORO I KNEW ISN'T THERE ANYMORE!
AND WHAT PRAY TELL HAS TAKEN HER PLACE...
...A MONSTER?
ORORO!!
COMPARED TO WHAT SHE ONCE WAS...
...MAYBE SO.
KITTY...
I GOTTA GET DRESSED.
I... WILL WAIT FOR YOU.
"MONSTER..."
DON'T LET THIS WORRY YOU, ORORO. YOU'VE SHAKEN THE KID UP SOME, SHE'S HAVING A HARD TIME ADJUSTING.
BE PATIENT. SHE'LL GET OVER IT.
THAT SOLVES HER PROBLEM.
BUT THE TRULY TERRIFYING THING IN ALL OF THIS, STEVIE...
... IS THAT I FEAR SHE MAY WELL BE RIGHT.

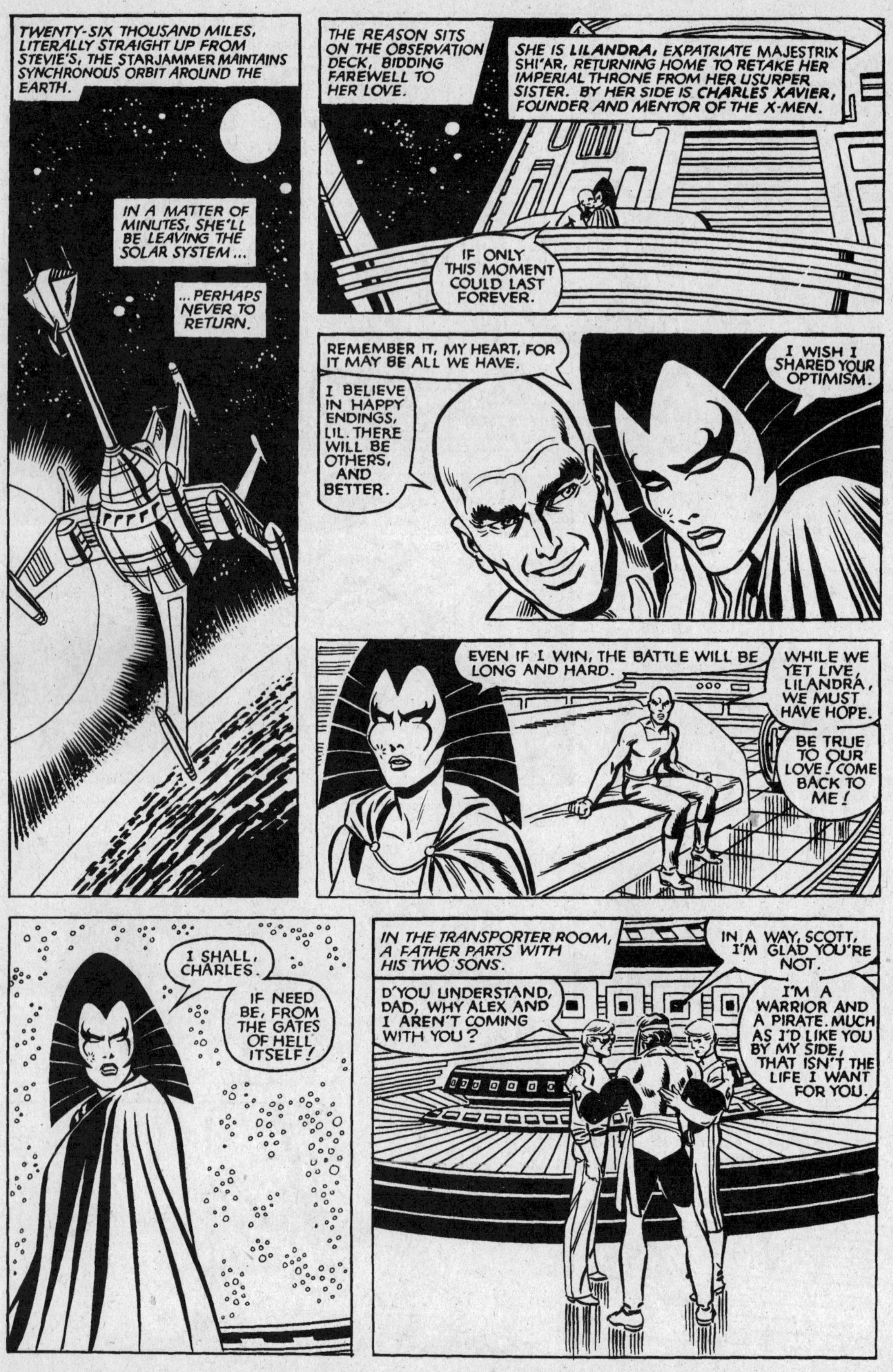
TWENTY-SIX THOUSAND MILES, LITERALLY STRAIGHT UP FROM STEVIE'S, THE STARJAMMER MAINTAINS SYNCHRONOUS ORBIT AROUND THE EARTH.
IN A MATTER OF MINUTES, SHE'LL BE LEAVING THE SOLAR SYSTEM...
...PERHAPS NEVER TO RETURN.
THE REASON SITS ON THE OBSERVATION DECK, BIDDING FAREWELL TO HER LOVE.
SHE IS LILANDRA, EXPATRIATE MAJESTRIX SHI'AR, RETURNING HOME TO RETAKE HER IMPERIAL THRONE FROM HER USURPER SISTER. BY HER SIDE IS CHARLES XAVIER, FOUNDER AND MENTOR OF THE X-MEN.
IF ONLY THIS MOMENT COULD LAST FOREVER.
REMEMBER IT, MY HEART, FOR IT MAY BE ALL WE HAVE.
I BELIEVE IN HAPPY ENDINGS, LIL. THERE WILL BE OTHERS, AND BETTER.
I WISH I SHARED YOUR OPTIMISM.
EVEN IF I WIN, THE BATTLE WILL BE LONG AND HARD.
WHILE WE YET LIVE, LILANDRA, WE MUST HAVE HOPE.
BE TRUE TO OUR LOVE! COME BACK TO ME!
I SHALL, CHARLES.
IF NEED BE, FROM THE GATES OF HELL ITSELF!
IN THE TRANSPORTER ROOM, A FATHER PARTS WITH HIS TWO SONS.
D'YOU UNDERSTAND, DAD, WHY ALEX AND I AREN'T COMING WITH YOU?
IN A WAY, SCOTT, I'M GLAD YOU'RE NOT.
I'M A WARRIOR AND A PIRATE. MUCH AS I'D LIKE YOU BY MY SIDE, THAT ISN'T THE LIFE I WANT FOR YOU.

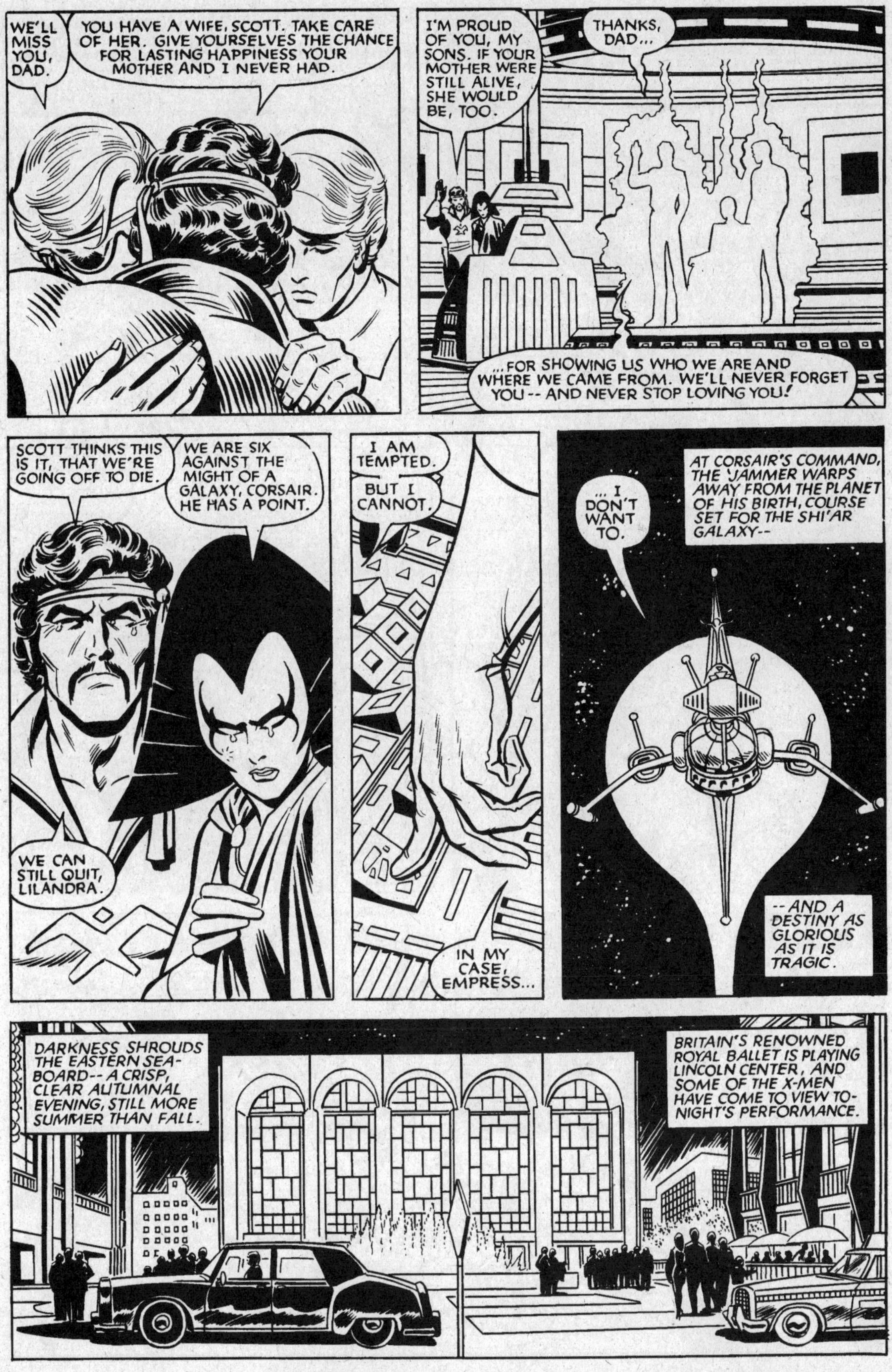
WE'LL MISS YOU, DAD.
YOU HAVE A WIFE, SCOTT. TAKE CARE OF HER. GIVE YOURSELVES THE CHANCE FOR LASTING HAPPINESS YOUR MOTHER AND I NEVER HAD.
I'M PROUD OF YOU, MY SONS. IF YOUR MOTHER WERE STILL ALIVE, SHE WOULD BE, TOO.
THANKS, DAD...
...FOR SHOWING US WHO WE ARE AND WHERE WE CAME FROM. WE'LL NEVER FORGET YOU -- AND NEVER STOP LOVING YOU!
SCOTT THINKS THIS IS IT, THAT WE'RE GOING OFF TO DIE.
WE ARE SIX AGAINST THE MIGHT OF A GALAXY, CORSAIR. HE HAS A POINT.
WE CAN STILL QUIT, LILANDRA.
I AM TEMPTED.
BUT I CANNOT.
IN MY CASE, EMPRESS...
... I DON'T WANT TO.
AT CORSAIR'S COMMAND, THE 'JAMMER WARPS AWAY FROM THE PLANET OF HIS BIRTH, COURSE SET FOR THE SHI'AR GALAXY--
-- AND A DESTINY AS GLORIOUS AS IT IS TRAGIC.
DARKNESS SHROUDS THE EASTERN SEA-BOARD-- A CRISP, CLEAR AUTUMNAL EVENING, STILL MORE SUMMER THAN FALL.
BRITAIN'S RENOWNED ROYAL BALLET IS PLAYING LINCOLN CENTER, AND SOME OF THE X-MEN HAVE COME TO VIEW TO-NIGHT'S PERFORMANCE.

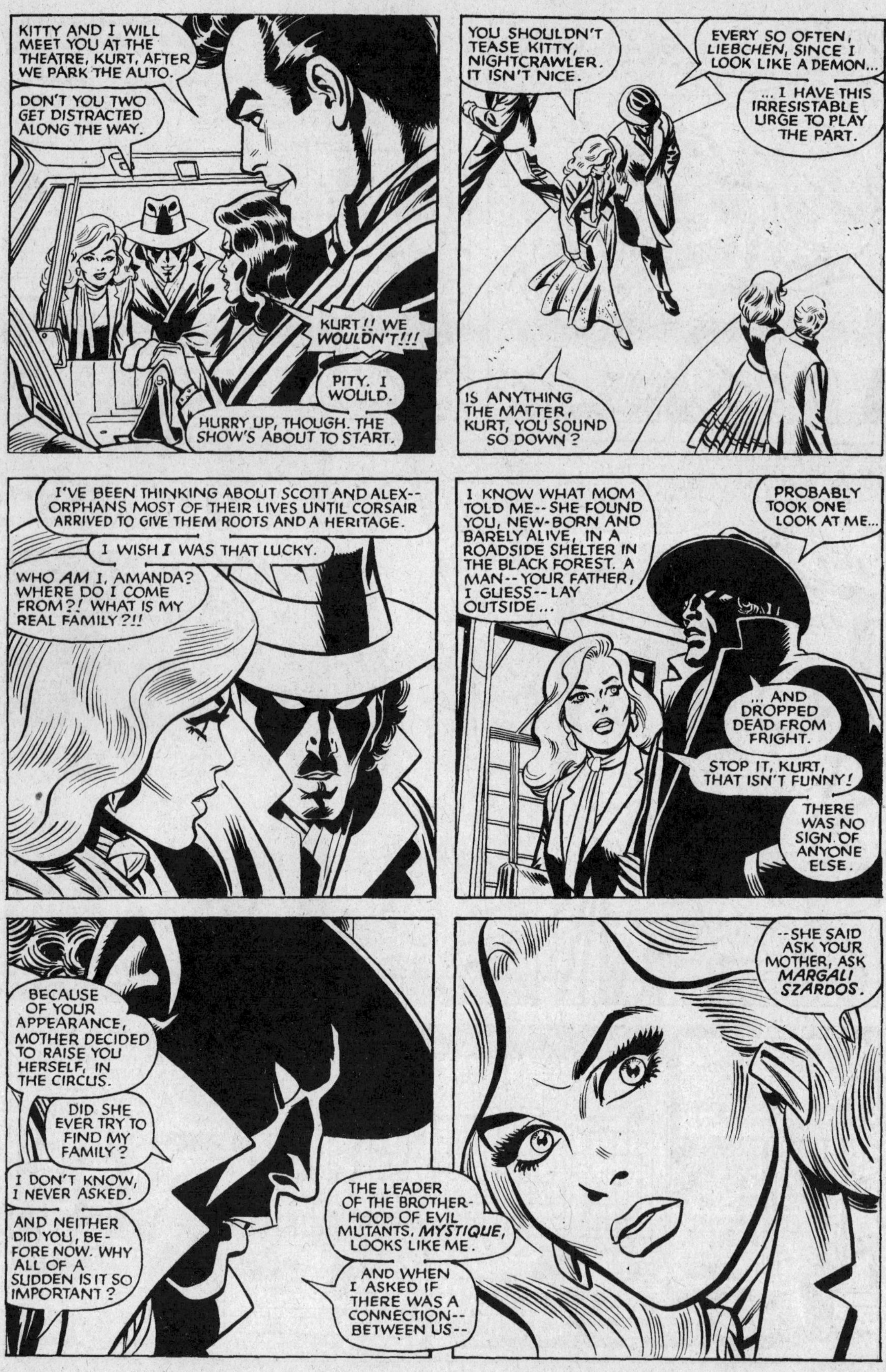
KITTY AND I WILL MEET YOU AT THE THEATRE, KURT, AFTER WE PARK THE AUTO.
DON'T YOU TWO GET DISTRACTED ALONG THE WAY.
KURT!! WE WOULDN'T!!!
PITY. I WOULD.
HURRY UP, THOUGH. THE SHOW'S ABOUT TO START.
YOU SHOULDN'T TEASE KITTY, NIGHTCRAWLER. IT ISN'T NICE.
EVERY SO OFTEN, LIEBCHEN, SINCE I LOOK LIKE A DEMON...
... I HAVE THIS IRRESISTABLE URGE TO PLAY THE PART.
IS ANYTHING THE MATTER, KURT, YOU SOUND SO DOWN?
I'VE BEEN THINKING ABOUT SCOTT AND ALEX-- ORPHANS MOST OF THEIR LIVES UNTIL CORSAIR ARRIVED TO GIVE THEM ROOTS AND A HERITAGE.
I WISH I WAS THAT LUCKY.
WHO AM I, AMANDA? WHERE DO I COME FROM?! WHAT IS MY REAL FAMILY?!!
I KNOW WHAT MOM TOLD ME-- SHE FOUND YOU, NEW-BORN AND BARELY ALIVE, IN A ROADSIDE SHELTER IN THE BLACK FOREST. A MAN-- YOUR FATHER, I GUESS-- LAY OUTSIDE...
PROBABLY TOOK ONE LOOK AT ME...
... AND DROPPED DEAD FROM FRIGHT.
STOP IT, KURT, THAT ISN'T FUNNY!
THERE WAS NO SIGN OF ANYONE ELSE.
BECAUSE OF YOUR APPEARANCE, MOTHER DECIDED TO RAISE YOU HERSELF, IN THE CIRCUS.
DID SHE EVER TRY TO FIND MY FAMILY?
I DON'T KNOW, I NEVER ASKED.
AND NEITHER DID YOU, BEFORE NOW. WHY ALL OF A SUDDEN IS IT SO IMPORTANT?
THE LEADER OF THE BROTHERHOOD OF EVIL MUTANTS, MYSTIQUE, LOOKS LIKE ME.
AND WHEN I ASKED IF THERE WAS A CONNECTION-- BETWEEN US--
--SHE SAID ASK YOUR MOTHER, ASK MARGALI SZARDOS.

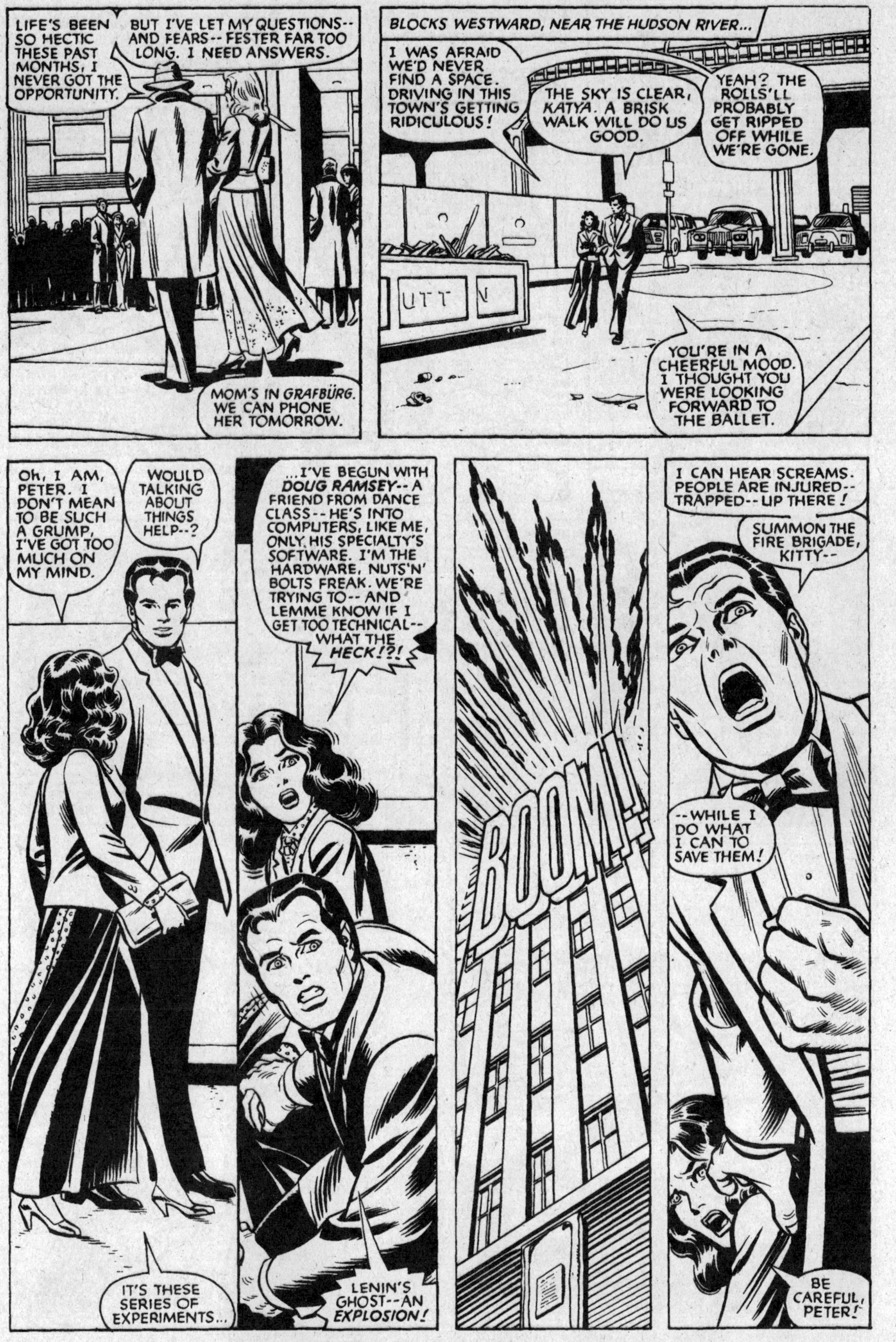
LIFE'S BEEN SO HECTIC THESE PAST MONTHS, I NEVER GOT THE OPPORTUNITY.
BUT I'VE LET MY QUESTIONS-- AND FEARS-- FESTER FAR TOO LONG. I NEED ANSWERS.
MOM'S IN GRAFBÜRG. WE CAN PHONE HER TOMORROW.
BLOCKS WESTWARD, NEAR THE HUDSON RIVER...
I WAS AFRAID WE'D NEVER FIND A SPACE. DRIVING IN THIS TOWN'S GETTING RIDICULOUS!
THE SKY IS CLEAR, KATYA. A BRISK WALK WILL DO US GOOD.
YEAH? THE ROLLS'LL PROBABLY GET RIPPED OFF WHILE WE'RE GONE.
YOU'RE IN A CHEERFUL MOOD. I THOUGHT YOU WERE LOOKING FORWARD TO THE BALLET.
Oh, I AM, PETER. I DON'T MEAN TO BE SUCH A GRUMP, I'VE GOT TOO MUCH ON MY MIND.
WOULD TALKING ABOUT THINGS HELP--?
IT'S THESE SERIES OF EXPERIMENTS...
...I'VE BEGUN WITH DOUG RAMSEY-- A FRIEND FROM DANCE CLASS-- HE'S INTO COMPUTERS, LIKE ME, ONLY HIS SPECIALTY'S SOFTWARE. I'M THE HARDWARE, NUTS'N' BOLTS FREAK. WE'RE TRYING TO-- AND LEMME KNOW IF I GET TOO TECHNICAL-- WHAT THE HECK!?!
LENIN'S GHOST--AN EXPLOSION!
BOOM!!
I CAN HEAR SCREAMS. PEOPLE ARE INJURED-- TRAPPED-- UP THERE!
SUMMON THE FIRE BRIGADE, KITTY--
--WHILE I DO WHAT I CAN TO SAVE THEM!
BE CAREFUL, PETER!

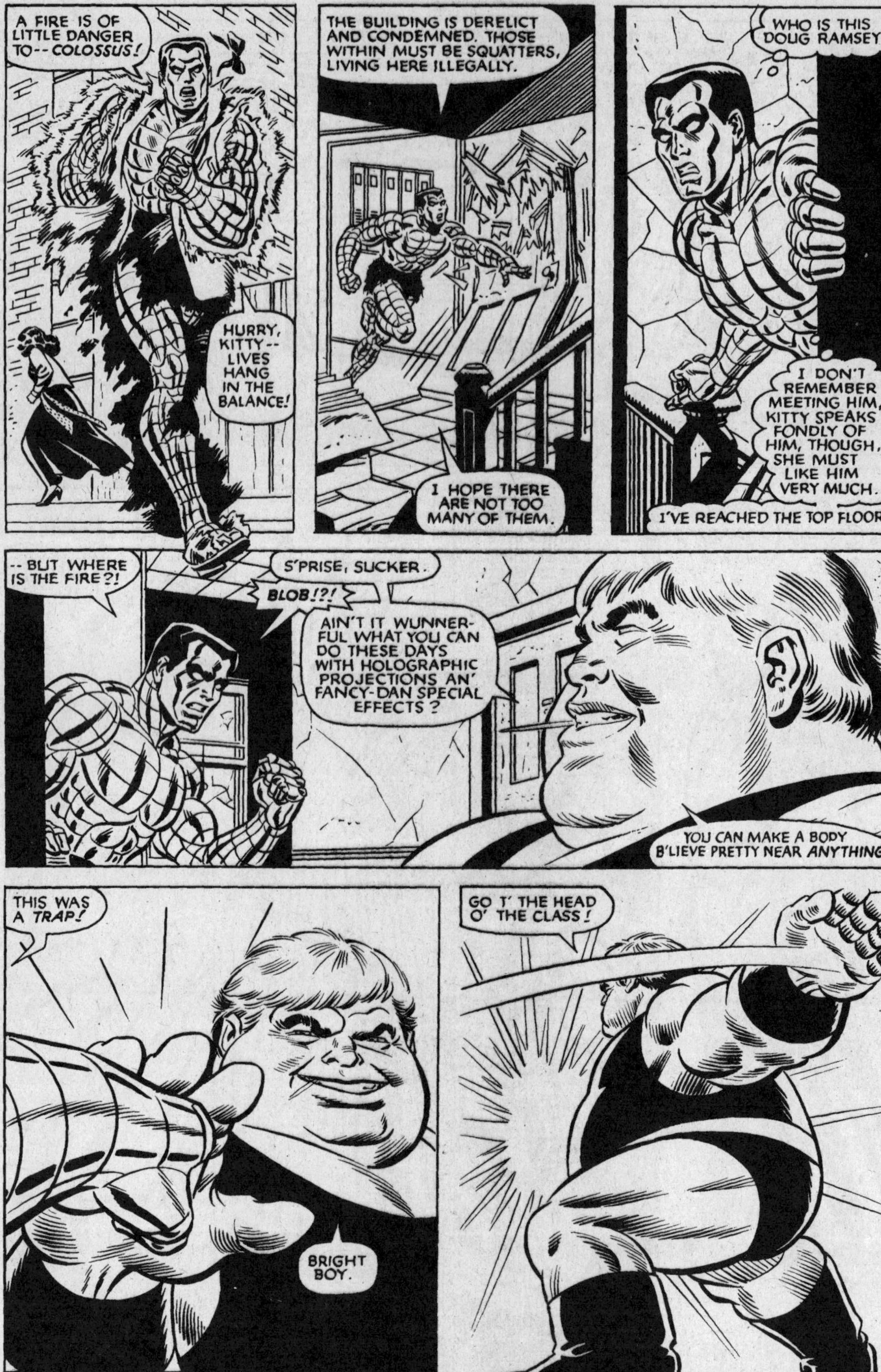
A FIRE IS OF LITTLE DANGER TO-- COLOSSUS!
HURRY, KITTY-- LIVES HANG IN THE BALANCE!
THE BUILDING IS DERELICT AND CONDEMNED. THOSE WITHIN MUST BE SQUATTERS, LIVING HERE ILLEGALLY.
I HOPE THERE ARE NOT TOO MANY OF THEM.
WHO IS THIS DOUG RAMSEY?
I DON'T REMEMBER MEETING HIM, KITTY SPEAKS FONDLY OF HIM, THOUGH. SHE MUST LIKE HIM VERY MUCH.
I'VE REACHED THE TOP FLOOR--
-- BUT WHERE IS THE FIRE?!
S'PRISE, SUCKER.
BLOB!?!
AIN'T IT WUNNERFUL WHAT YOU CAN DO THESE DAYS WITH HOLOGRAPHIC PROJECTIONS AN' FANCY-DAN SPECIAL EFFECTS?
YOU CAN MAKE A BODY B'LIEVE PRETTY NEAR ANYTHING.
THIS WAS A TRAP!
BRIGHT BOY.
GO T' THE HEAD O' THE CLASS!

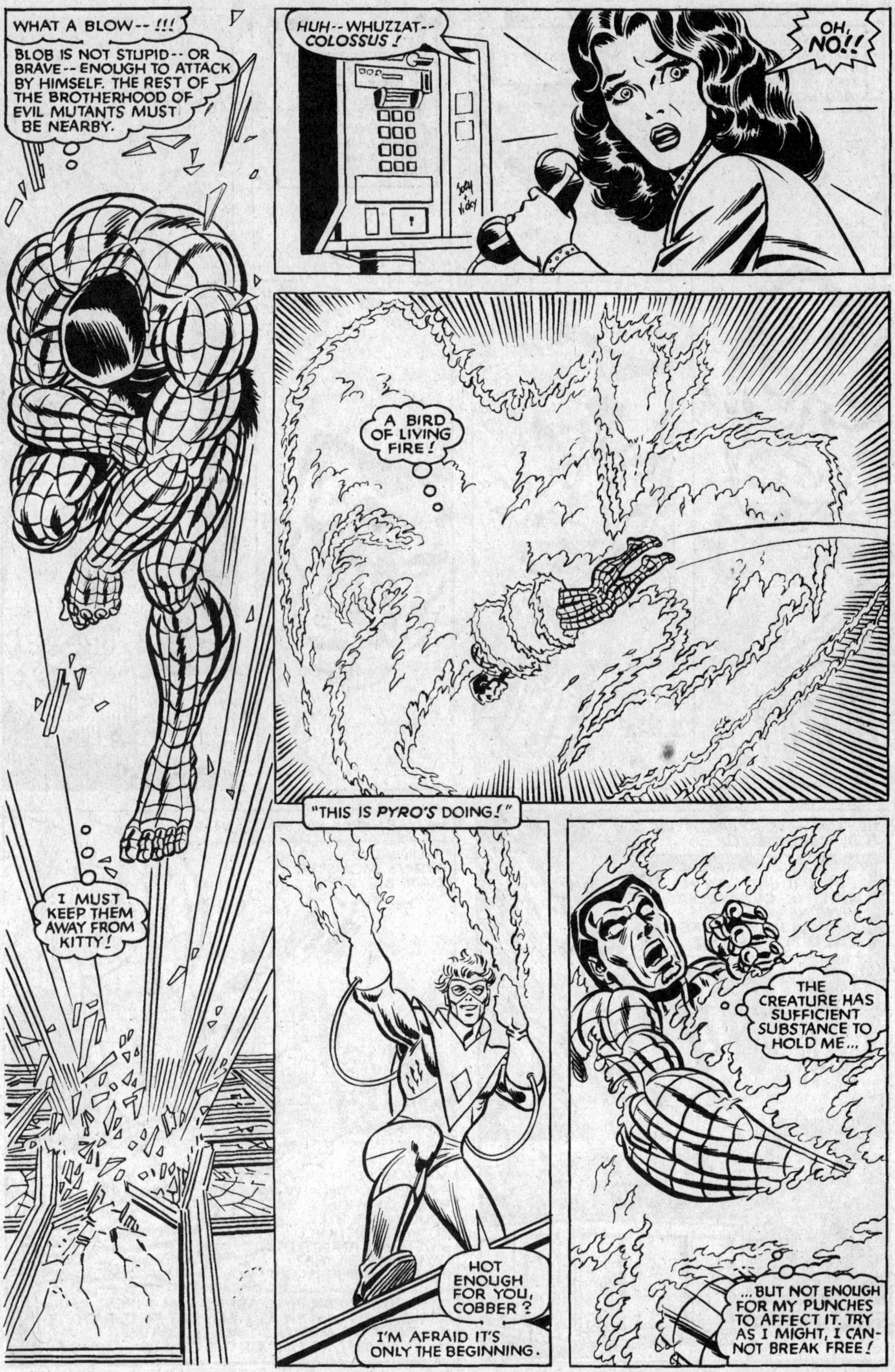
WHAT A BLOW-- !!!
BLOB IS NOT STUPID-- OR BRAVE-- ENOUGH TO ATTACK BY HIMSELF. THE REST OF THE BROTHERHOOD OF EVIL MUTANTS MUST BE NEARBY.
I MUST KEEP THEM AWAY FROM KITTY!
HUH--WHUZZAT-- COLOSSUS!
OH, NO!!
A BIRD OF LIVING FIRE!
"THIS IS PYRO'S DOING!"
HOT ENOUGH FOR YOU, COBBER?
I'M AFRAID IT'S ONLY THE BEGINNING.
THE CREATURE HAS SUFFICIENT SUBSTANCE TO HOLD ME...
...BUT NOT ENOUGH FOR MY PUNCHES TO AFFECT IT. TRY AS I MIGHT, I CANNOT BREAK FREE!

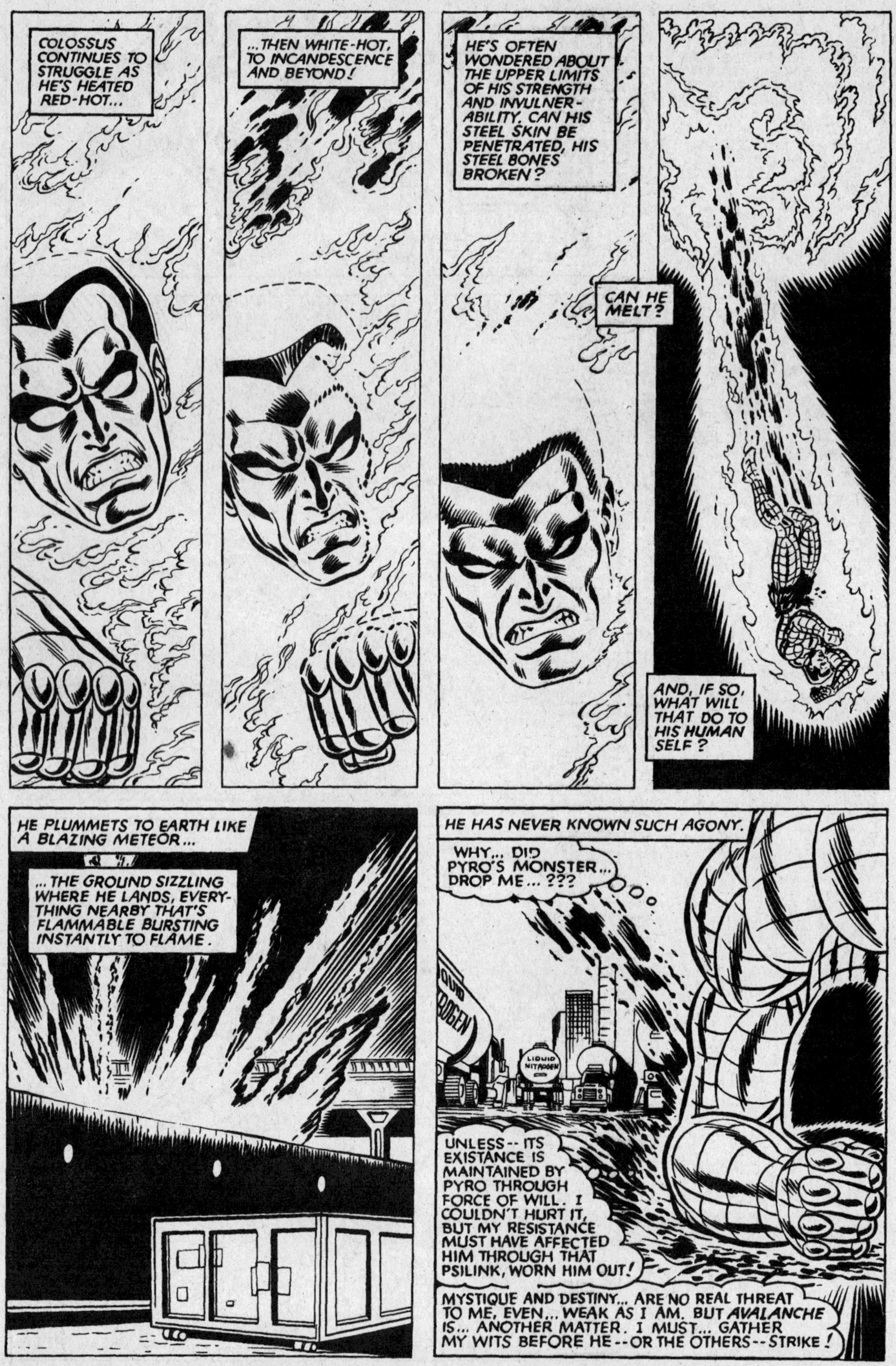

COLOSSUS CONTINUES TO STRUGGLE AS HE'S HEATED RED-HOT...
...THEN WHITE-HOT, TO INCANDESCENCE AND BEYOND!
HE'S OFTEN WONDERED ABOUT THE UPPER LIMITS OF HIS STRENGTH AND INVULNER-ABILITY. CAN HIS STEEL SKIN BE PENETRATED, HIS STEEL BONES BROKEN?
CAN HE MELT?
AND, IF SO, WHAT WILL THAT DO TO HIS HUMAN SELF?
HE PLUMMETS TO EARTH LIKE A BLAZING METEOR...
...THE GROUND SIZZLING WHERE HE LANDS, EVERY-THING NEARBY THAT'S FLAMMABLE BURSTING INSTANTLY TO FLAME.
HE HAS NEVER KNOWN SUCH AGONY.
WHY... DID PYRO'S MONSTER... DROP ME...???
LIQUID NITROGEN
UNLESS-- ITS EXISTANCE IS MAINTAINED BY PYRO THROUGH FORCE OF WILL. I COULDN'T HURT IT, BUT MY RESISTANCE MUST HAVE AFFECTED HIM THROUGH THAT PSILINK, WORN HIM OUT!
MYSTIQUE AND DESTINY... ARE NO REAL THREAT TO ME, EVEN... WEAK AS I AM. BUT AVALANCHE IS... ANOTHER MATTER. I MUST... GATHER MY WITS BEFORE HE--OR THE OTHERS--STRIKE!

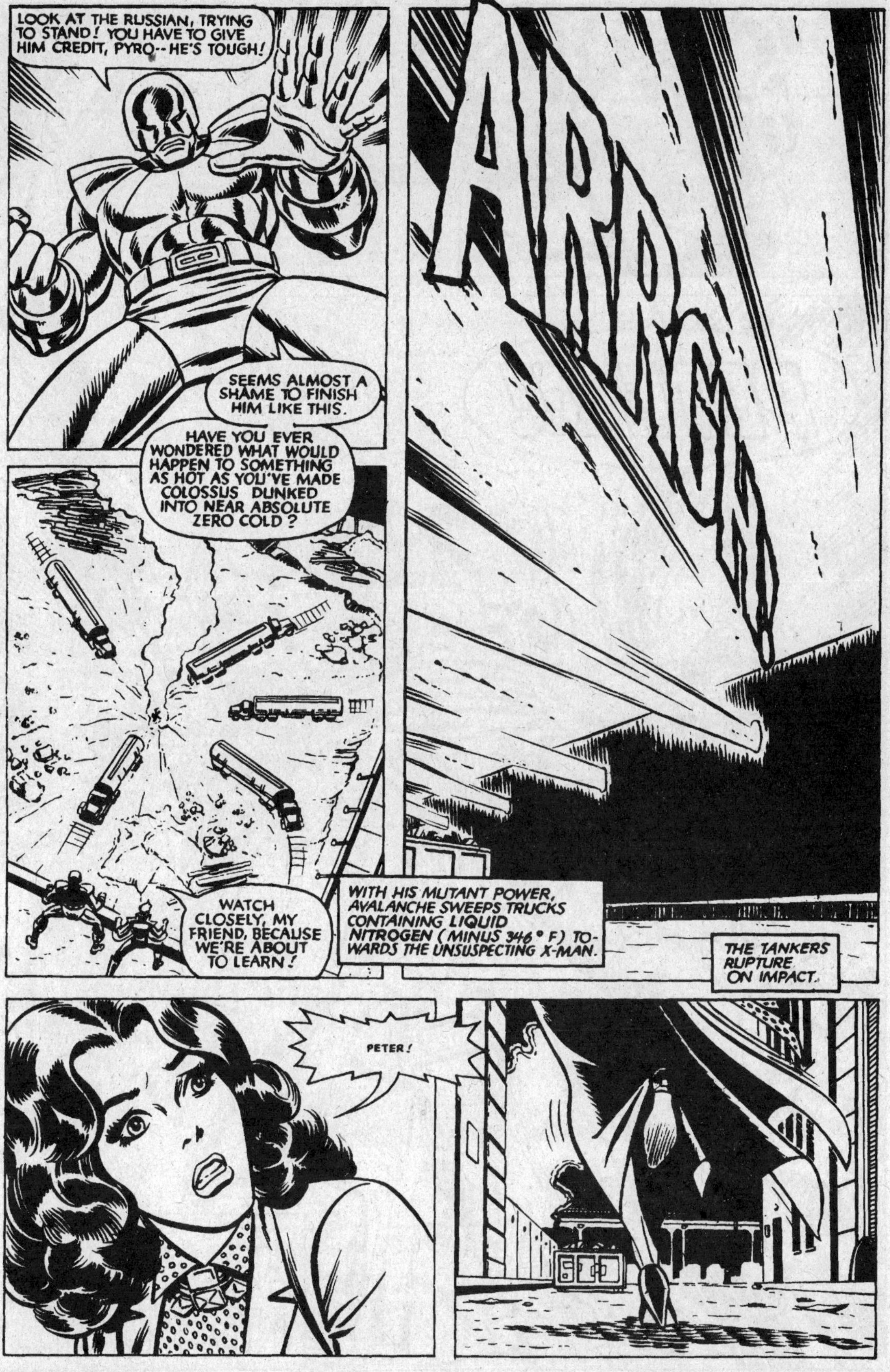

LOOK AT THE RUSSIAN, TRYING TO STAND! YOU HAVE TO GIVE HIM CREDIT, PYRO-- HE'S TOUGH!
SEEMS ALMOST A SHAME TO FINISH HIM LIKE THIS.
HAVE YOU EVER WONDERED WHAT WOULD HAPPEN TO SOMETHING AS HOT AS YOU'VE MADE COLOSSUS DUNKED INTO NEAR ABSOLUTE ZERO COLD?
WATCH CLOSELY, MY FRIEND, BECAUSE WE'RE ABOUT TO LEARN!
WITH HIS MUTANT POWER, AVALANCHE SWEEPS TRUCKS CONTAINING LIQUID NITROGEN (MINUS 346° F) TOWARDS THE UNSUSPECTING X-MAN.
ARRGH!
THE TANKERS RUPTURE ON IMPACT.
PETER!

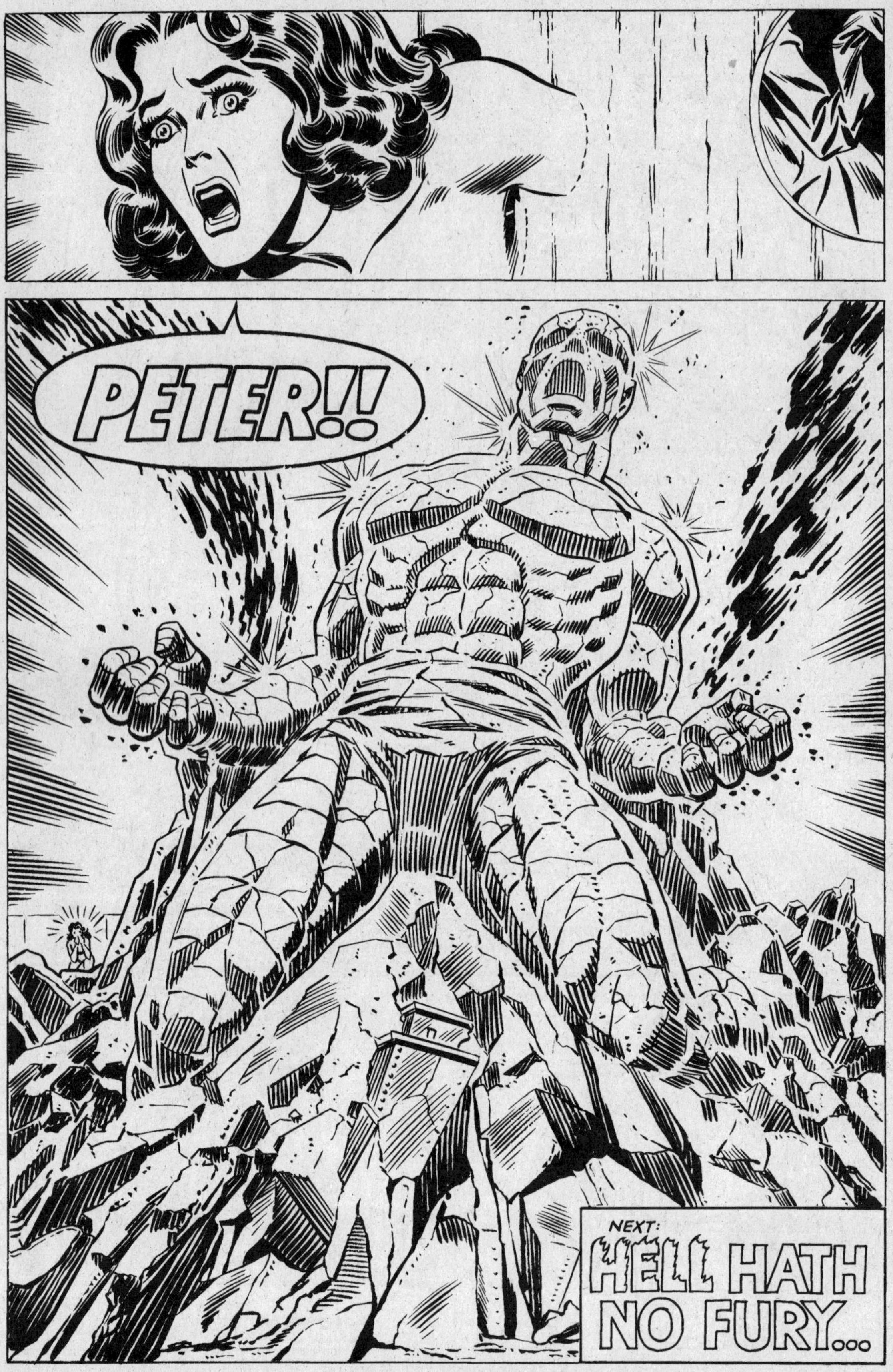
PETER!!
NEXT:
HELL HATH NO FURY...

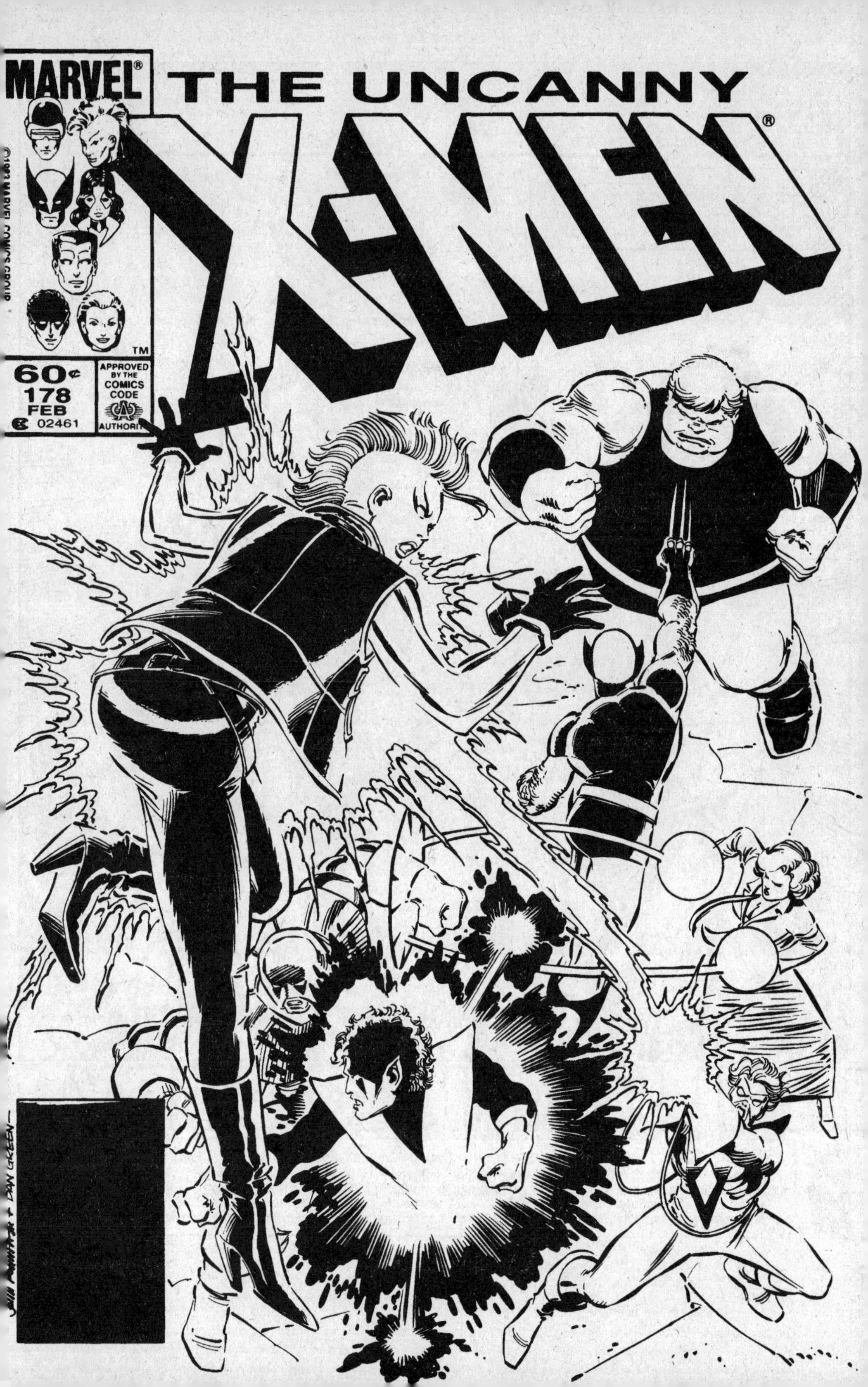
MARVEL®
THE UNCANNY
X-MEN®
TM
60¢
178
FEB
02461
APPROVED BY THE COMICS CODE AUTHORITY

HEAT METAL WHITE-HOT, THEN SUBJECT IT TO NEAR ABSOLUTE-ZERO COLD-- A TEMPERATURE SO LOW THAT MOLECULAR MOTION VIRTUALLY CEASES-- AND THAT METAL BLISTERS, CRACKS, ULTIMATELY SHATTERS.

THAT IS WHAT'S JUST HAPPENED TO COLOSSUS, IN THIS CONSTRUCTION SITE ON THE WEST SIDE OF MANHATTAN.

FOR A MAN COMPOSED, AS HE IS, OF ORGANIC STEEL, THE PROCESS WOULD SURELY SEEM TO MEAN CERTAIN DEATH.

HELL HATH NO FURY...

A **STAN LEE** PRESENTATION, STARRING THE UNCANNY **X-MEN** -- AS CHRONICLED BY

| CHRIS CLAREMONT writer | JOHN ROMITA, Jr. penciler | BOB WIACEK & BRETT BREEDING inkers | GLYNIS WEIN colorist | TOM ORZECHOWSKI letterer | LOUISE JONES editor | JIM SHOOTER chief |

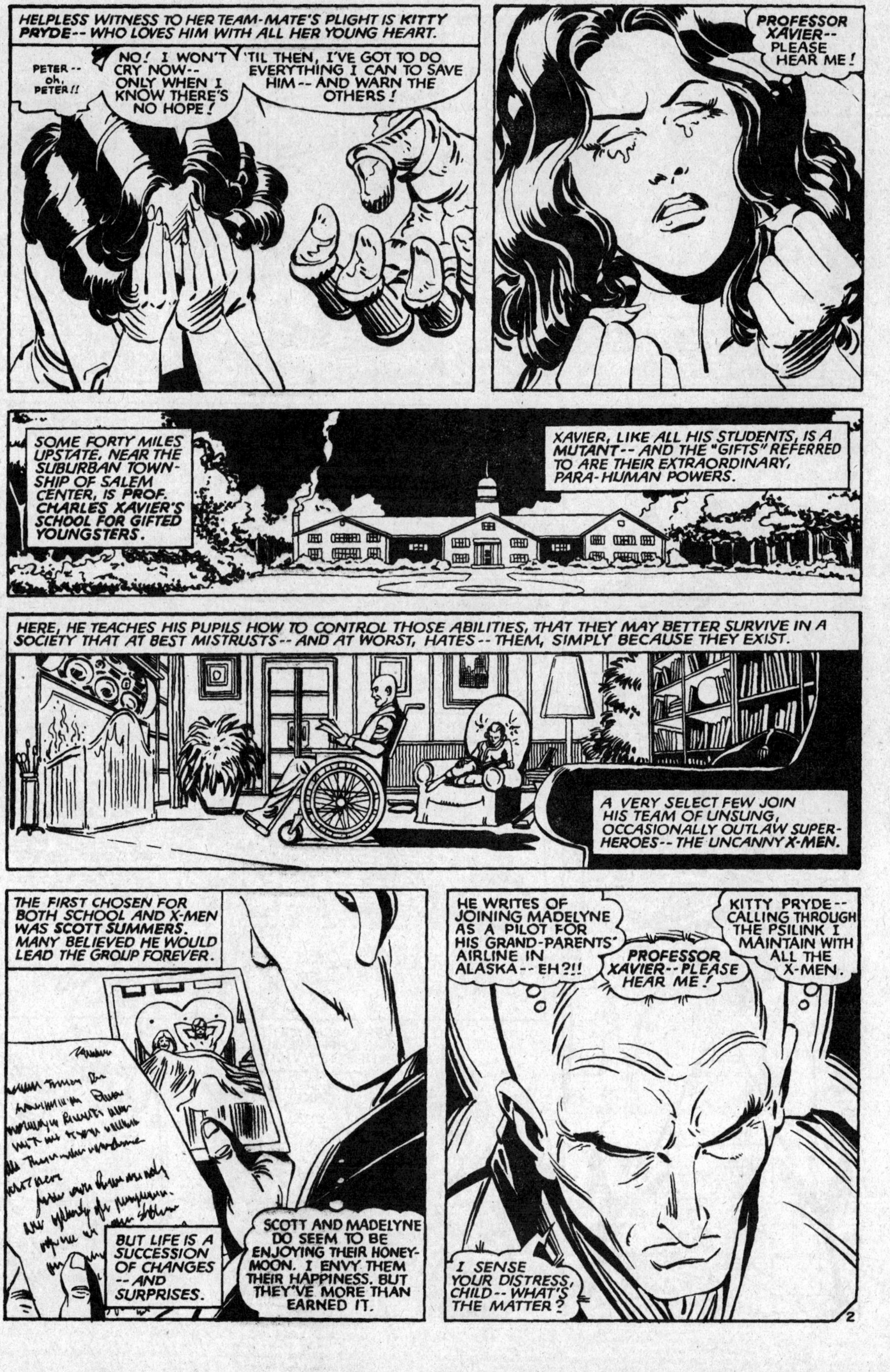

HELPLESS WITNESS TO HER TEAM-MATE'S PLIGHT IS KITTY PRYDE-- WHO LOVES HIM WITH ALL HER YOUNG HEART.
PETER -- oh, PETER!!
NO! I WON'T CRY NOW-- ONLY WHEN I KNOW THERE'S NO HOPE!
'TIL THEN, I'VE GOT TO DO EVERYTHING I CAN TO SAVE HIM -- AND WARN THE OTHERS!
PROFESSOR XAVIER-- PLEASE HEAR ME!
SOME FORTY MILES UPSTATE, NEAR THE SUBURBAN TOWNSHIP OF SALEM CENTER, IS PROF. CHARLES XAVIER'S SCHOOL FOR GIFTED YOUNGSTERS.
XAVIER, LIKE ALL HIS STUDENTS, IS A MUTANT-- AND THE "GIFTS" REFERRED TO ARE THEIR EXTRAORDINARY, PARA-HUMAN POWERS.
HERE, HE TEACHES HIS PUPILS HOW TO CONTROL THOSE ABILITIES, THAT THEY MAY BETTER SURVIVE IN A SOCIETY THAT AT BEST MISTRUSTS-- AND AT WORST, HATES -- THEM, SIMPLY BECAUSE THEY EXIST.
A VERY SELECT FEW JOIN HIS TEAM OF UNSUNG, OCCASIONALLY OUTLAW SUPER-HEROES-- THE UNCANNY X-MEN.
THE FIRST CHOSEN FOR BOTH SCHOOL AND X-MEN WAS SCOTT SUMMERS. MANY BELIEVED HE WOULD LEAD THE GROUP FOREVER.
BUT LIFE IS A SUCCESSION OF CHANGES --AND SURPRISES.
SCOTT AND MADELYNE DO SEEM TO BE ENJOYING THEIR HONEY-MOON. I ENVY THEM THEIR HAPPINESS. BUT THEY'VE MORE THAN EARNED IT.
HE WRITES OF JOINING MADELYNE AS A PILOT FOR HIS GRAND-PARENTS' AIRLINE IN ALASKA-- EH?!!
PROFESSOR XAVIER-- PLEASE HEAR ME!
KITTY PRYDE-- CALLING THROUGH THE PSILINK I MAINTAIN WITH ALL THE X-MEN.
I SENSE YOUR DISTRESS, CHILD-- WHAT'S THE MATTER?

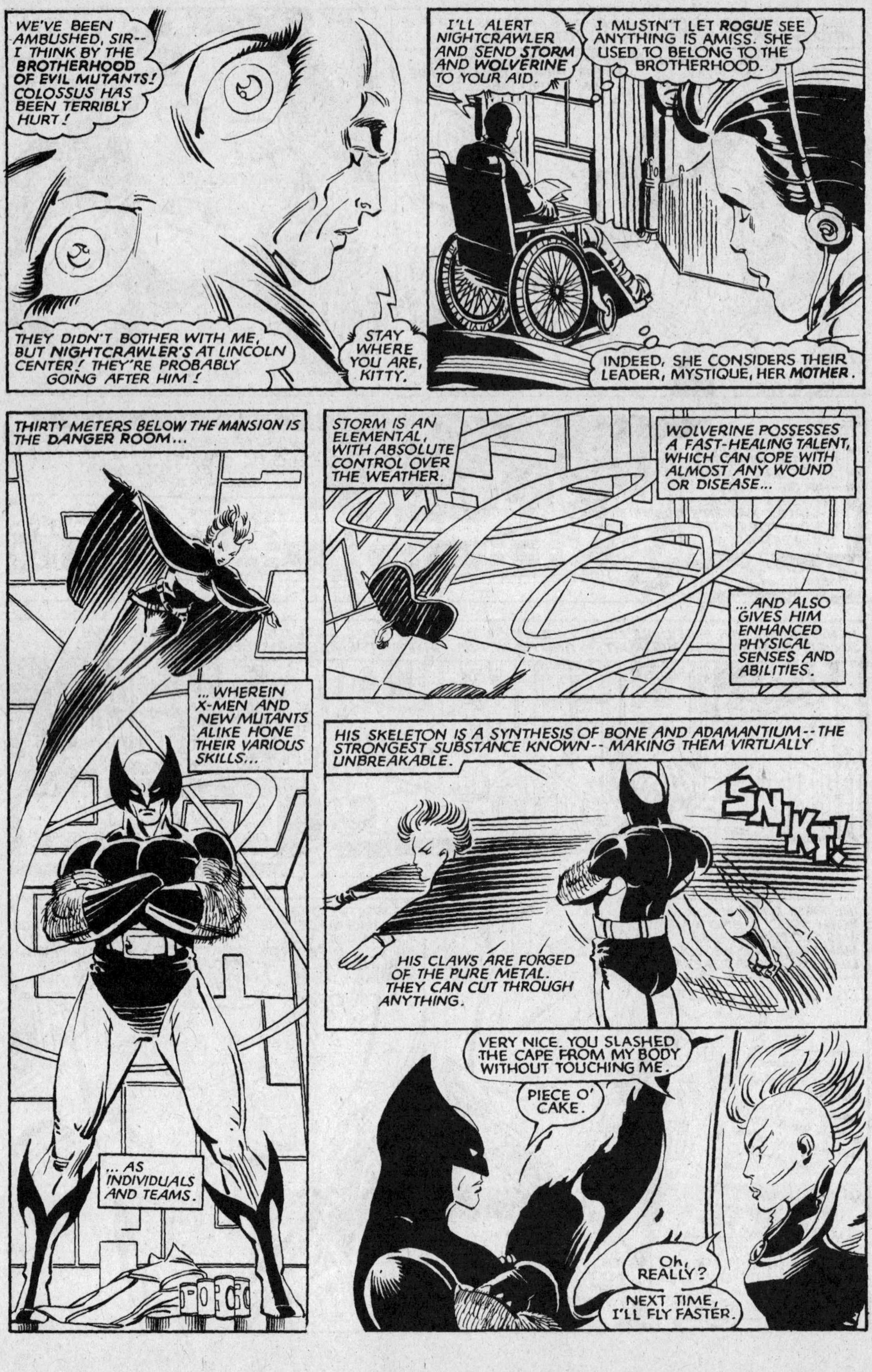

WE'VE BEEN AMBUSHED, SIR-- I THINK BY THE BROTHERHOOD OF EVIL MUTANTS! COLOSSUS HAS BEEN TERRIBLY HURT!
THEY DIDN'T BOTHER WITH ME, BUT NIGHTCRAWLER'S AT LINCOLN CENTER! THEY'RE PROBABLY GOING AFTER HIM!
STAY WHERE YOU ARE, KITTY.
I'LL ALERT NIGHTCRAWLER AND SEND STORM AND WOLVERINE TO YOUR AID.
I MUSTN'T LET ROGUE SEE ANYTHING IS AMISS. SHE USED TO BELONG TO THE BROTHERHOOD.
INDEED, SHE CONSIDERS THEIR LEADER, MYSTIQUE, HER MOTHER.
THIRTY METERS BELOW THE MANSION IS THE DANGER ROOM...
...WHEREIN X-MEN AND NEW MUTANTS ALIKE HONE THEIR VARIOUS SKILLS...
...AS INDIVIDUALS AND TEAMS.
STORM IS AN ELEMENTAL, WITH ABSOLUTE CONTROL OVER THE WEATHER.
WOLVERINE POSSESSES A FAST-HEALING TALENT, WHICH CAN COPE WITH ALMOST ANY WOUND OR DISEASE...
...AND ALSO GIVES HIM ENHANCED PHYSICAL SENSES AND ABILITIES.
HIS SKELETON IS A SYNTHESIS OF BONE AND ADAMANTIUM -- THE STRONGEST SUBSTANCE KNOWN -- MAKING THEM VIRTUALLY UNBREAKABLE.
SNIKT!
HIS CLAWS ARE FORGED OF THE PURE METAL. THEY CAN CUT THROUGH ANYTHING.
VERY NICE. YOU SLASHED THE CAPE FROM MY BODY WITHOUT TOUCHING ME.
PIECE O' CAKE.
Oh, REALLY?
NEXT TIME, I'LL FLY FASTER.

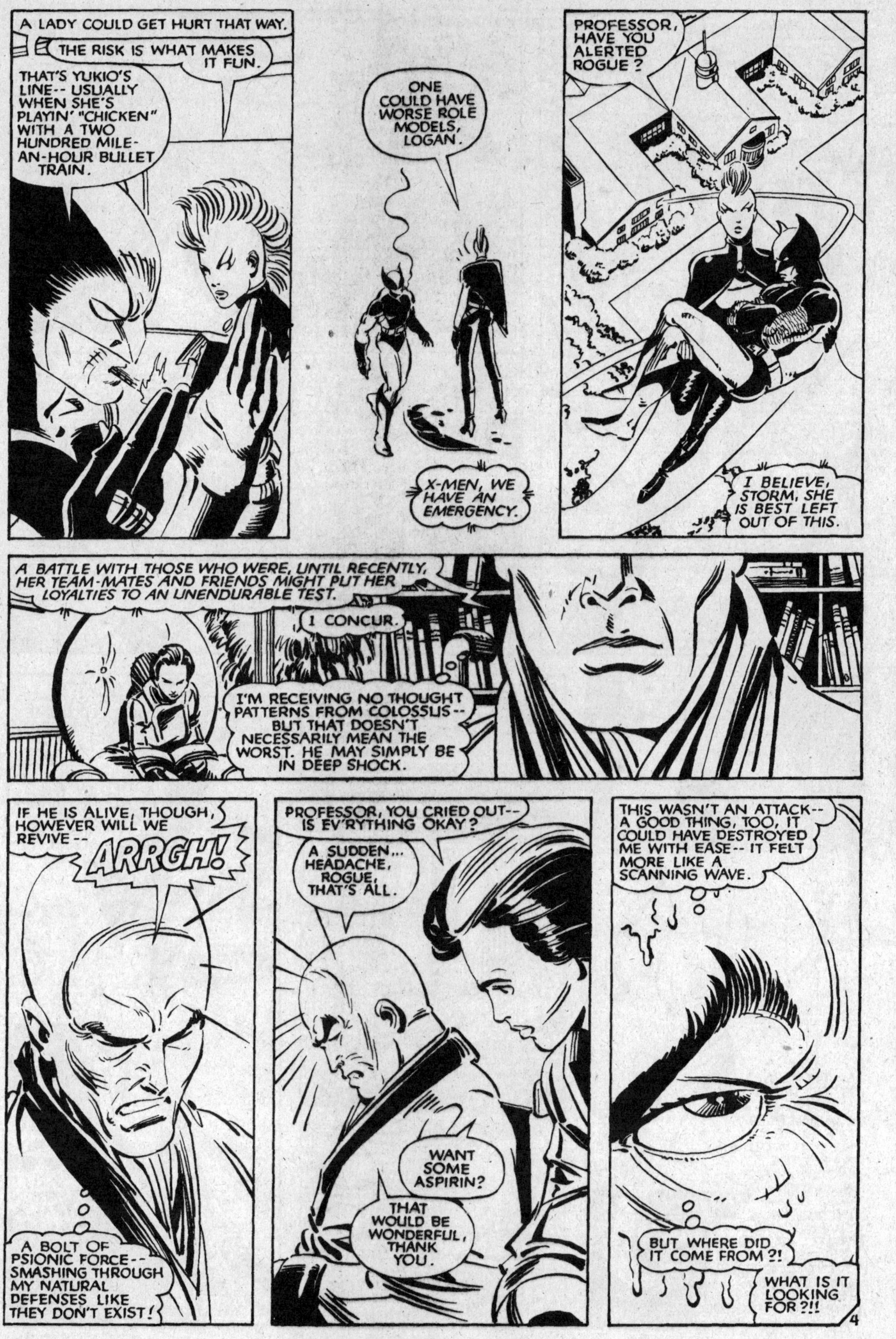

A LADY COULD GET HURT THAT WAY.
THE RISK IS WHAT MAKES IT FUN.
THAT'S YUKIO'S LINE-- USUALLY WHEN SHE'S PLAYIN' "CHICKEN" WITH A TWO HUNDRED MILE-AN-HOUR BULLET TRAIN.
ONE COULD HAVE WORSE ROLE MODELS, LOGAN.
X-MEN, WE HAVE AN EMERGENCY.
PROFESSOR, HAVE YOU ALERTED ROGUE?
I BELIEVE, STORM, SHE IS BEST LEFT OUT OF THIS.
A BATTLE WITH THOSE WHO WERE, UNTIL RECENTLY, HER TEAM-MATES AND FRIENDS MIGHT PUT HER LOYALTIES TO AN UNENDURABLE TEST.
I CONCUR.
I'M RECEIVING NO THOUGHT PATTERNS FROM COLOSSUS-- BUT THAT DOESN'T NECESSARILY MEAN THE WORST. HE MAY SIMPLY BE IN DEEP SHOCK.
IF HE IS ALIVE, THOUGH, HOWEVER WILL WE REVIVE--
ARRGH!
A BOLT OF PSIONIC FORCE-- SMASHING THROUGH MY NATURAL DEFENSES LIKE THEY DON'T EXIST!
PROFESSOR, YOU CRIED OUT-- IS EV'RYTHING OKAY?
A SUDDEN... HEADACHE, ROGUE, THAT'S ALL.
WANT SOME ASPIRIN?
THAT WOULD BE WONDERFUL, THANK YOU.
THIS WASN'T AN ATTACK-- A GOOD THING, TOO, IT COULD HAVE DESTROYED ME WITH EASE-- IT FELT MORE LIKE A SCANNING WAVE.
BUT WHERE DID IT COME FROM?!
WHAT IS IT LOOKING FOR?!!
4

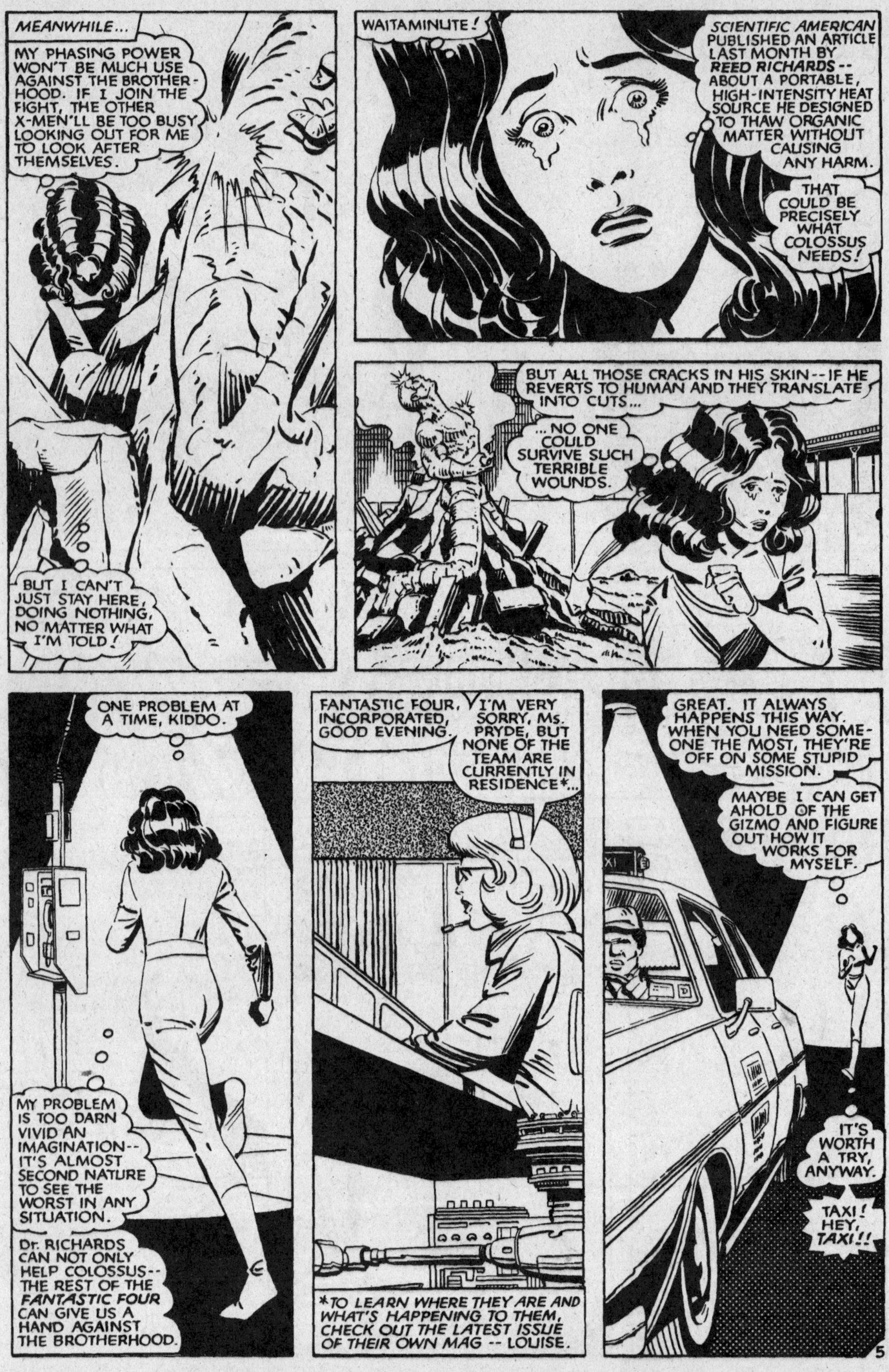
MEANWHILE...
MY PHASING POWER WON'T BE MUCH USE AGAINST THE BROTHERHOOD. IF I JOIN THE FIGHT, THE OTHER X-MEN'LL BE TOO BUSY LOOKING OUT FOR ME TO LOOK AFTER THEMSELVES.
BUT I CAN'T JUST STAY HERE, DOING NOTHING, NO MATTER WHAT I'M TOLD!
WAITAMINUTE!
SCIENTIFIC AMERICAN PUBLISHED AN ARTICLE LAST MONTH BY REED RICHARDS -- ABOUT A PORTABLE, HIGH-INTENSITY HEAT SOURCE HE DESIGNED TO THAW ORGANIC MATTER WITHOUT CAUSING ANY HARM.
THAT COULD BE PRECISELY WHAT COLOSSUS NEEDS!
BUT ALL THOSE CRACKS IN HIS SKIN -- IF HE REVERTS TO HUMAN AND THEY TRANSLATE INTO CUTS...
...NO ONE COULD SURVIVE SUCH TERRIBLE WOUNDS.
ONE PROBLEM AT A TIME, KIDDO.
MY PROBLEM IS TOO DARN VIVID AN IMAGINATION -- IT'S ALMOST SECOND NATURE TO SEE THE WORST IN ANY SITUATION.
Dr. RICHARDS CAN NOT ONLY HELP COLOSSUS -- THE REST OF THE FANTASTIC FOUR CAN GIVE US A HAND AGAINST THE BROTHERHOOD.
FANTASTIC FOUR, INCORPORATED, GOOD EVENING.
I'M VERY SORRY, Ms. PRYDE, BUT NONE OF THE TEAM ARE CURRENTLY IN RESIDENCE*...
*TO LEARN WHERE THEY ARE AND WHAT'S HAPPENING TO THEM, CHECK OUT THE LATEST ISSUE OF THEIR OWN MAG -- LOUISE.
GREAT. IT ALWAYS HAPPENS THIS WAY. WHEN YOU NEED SOMEONE THE MOST, THEY'RE OFF ON SOME STUPID MISSION.
MAYBE I CAN GET AHOLD OF THE GIZMO AND FIGURE OUT HOW IT WORKS FOR MYSELF.
IT'S WORTH A TRY, ANYWAY.
TAXI! HEY, TAXI!!
5

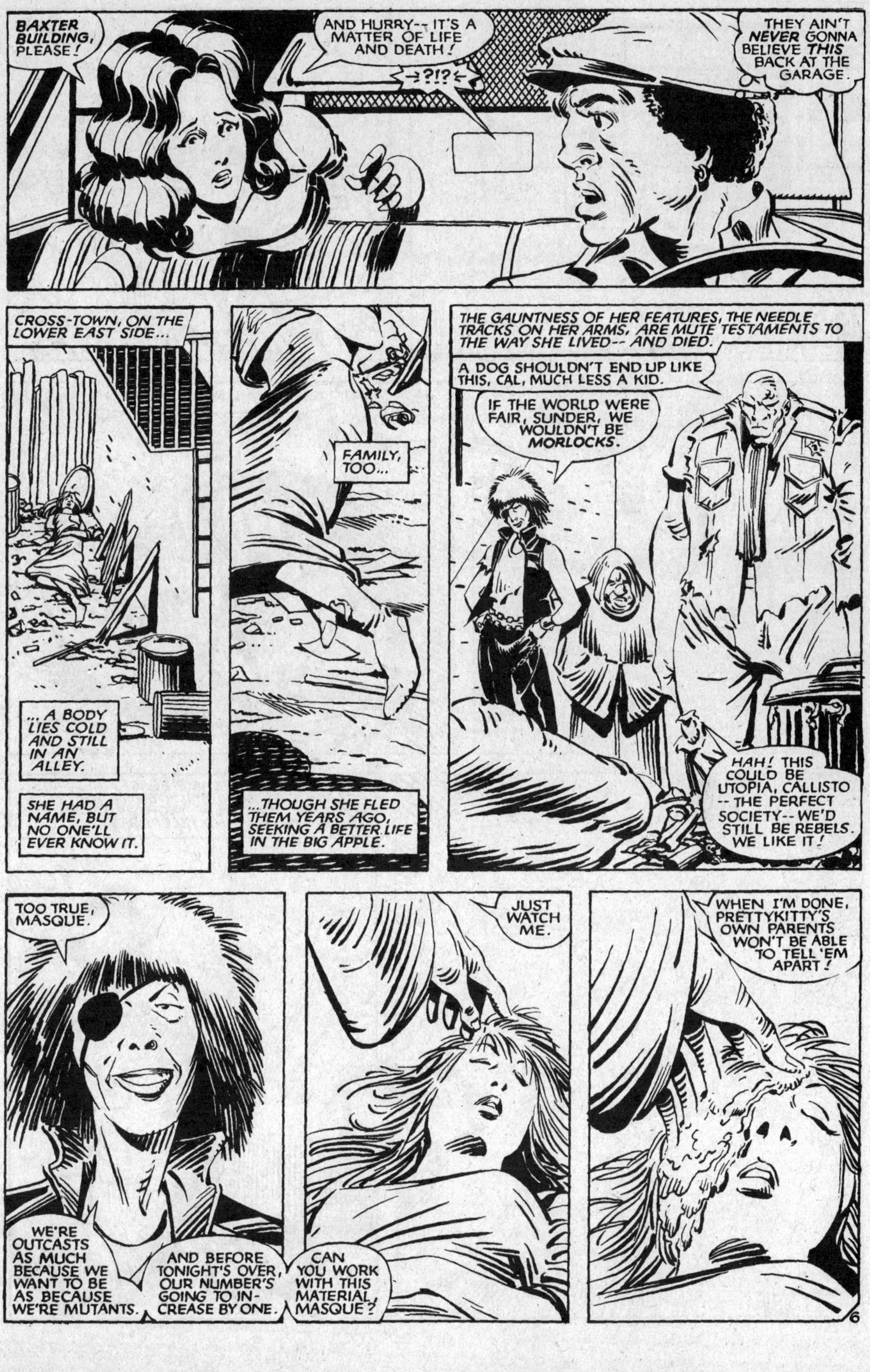
BAXTER BUILDING, PLEASE!
AND HURRY-- IT'S A MATTER OF LIFE AND DEATH!
?!?
THEY AIN'T NEVER GONNA BELIEVE THIS BACK AT THE GARAGE.
CROSS-TOWN, ON THE LOWER EAST SIDE...
...A BODY LIES COLD AND STILL IN AN ALLEY.
SHE HAD A NAME, BUT NO ONE'LL EVER KNOW IT.
FAMILY, TOO...
...THOUGH SHE FLED THEM YEARS AGO, SEEKING A BETTER LIFE IN THE BIG APPLE.
THE GAUNTNESS OF HER FEATURES, THE NEEDLE TRACKS ON HER ARMS, ARE MUTE TESTAMENTS TO THE WAY SHE LIVED-- AND DIED.
A DOG SHOULDN'T END UP LIKE THIS, CAL, MUCH LESS A KID.
IF THE WORLD WERE FAIR, SUNDER, WE WOULDN'T BE MORLOCKS.
HAH! THIS COULD BE UTOPIA, CALLISTO -- THE PERFECT SOCIETY-- WE'D STILL BE REBELS. WE LIKE IT!
TOO TRUE, MASQUE.
WE'RE OUTCASTS AS MUCH BECAUSE WE WANT TO BE AS BECAUSE WE'RE MUTANTS.
AND BEFORE TONIGHT'S OVER, OUR NUMBER'S GOING TO IN-CREASE BY ONE.
CAN YOU WORK WITH THIS MATERIAL, MASQUE?
JUST WATCH ME.
WHEN I'M DONE, PRETTYKITTY'S OWN PARENTS WON'T BE ABLE TO TELL 'EM APART!
6

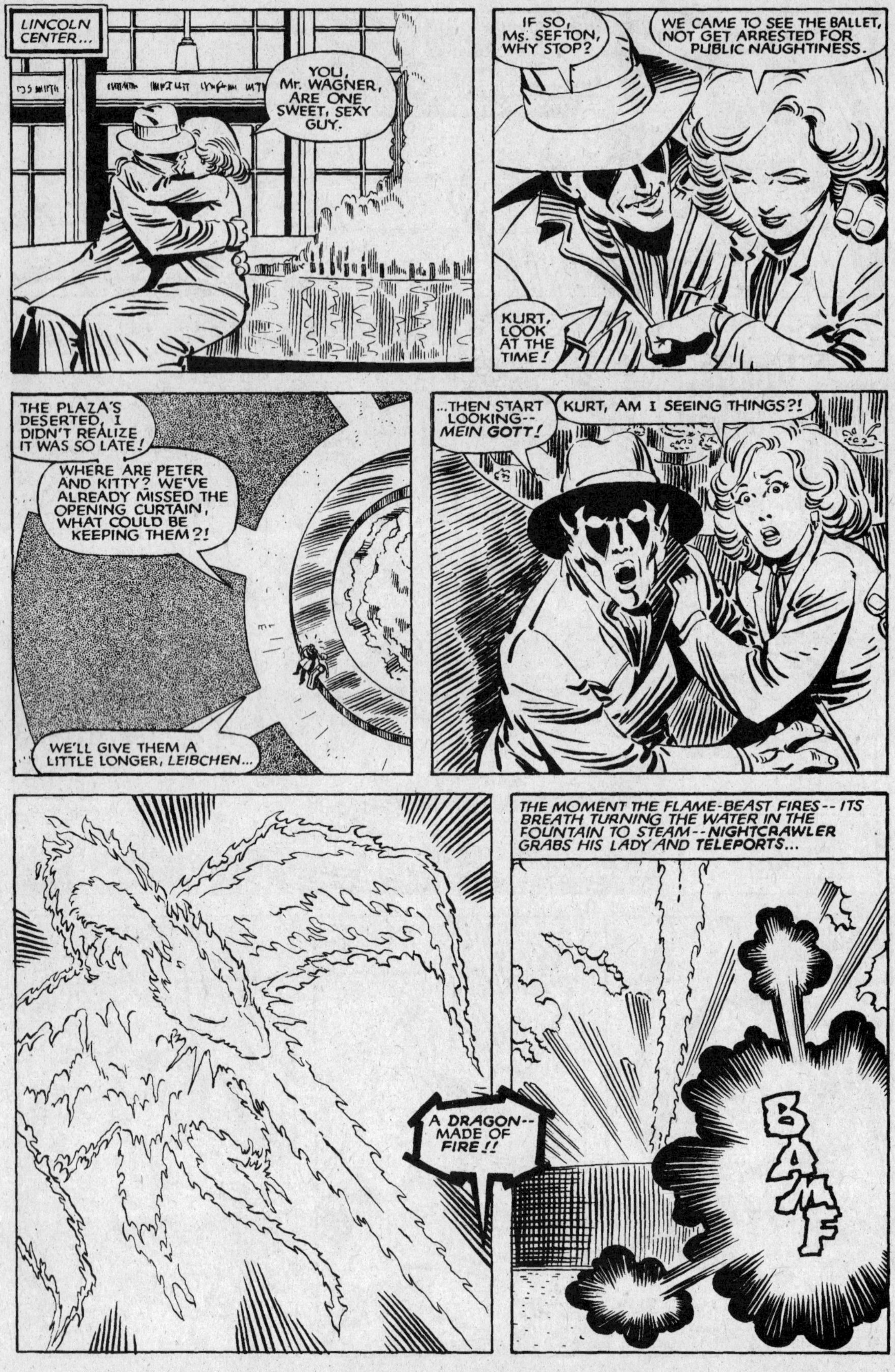
LINCOLN CENTER...
YOU, Mr. WAGNER, ARE ONE SWEET, SEXY GUY.
IF SO, Ms. SEFTON, WHY STOP?
WE CAME TO SEE THE BALLET, NOT GET ARRESTED FOR PUBLIC NAUGHTINESS.
KURT, LOOK AT THE TIME!
THE PLAZA'S DESERTED, I DIDN'T REALIZE IT WAS SO LATE!
WHERE ARE PETER AND KITTY? WE'VE ALREADY MISSED THE OPENING CURTAIN, WHAT COULD BE KEEPING THEM?!
WE'LL GIVE THEM A LITTLE LONGER, LEIBCHEN...
...THEN START LOOKING-- MEIN GOTT!
KURT, AM I SEEING THINGS?!
A DRAGON-- MADE OF FIRE!!
THE MOMENT THE FLAME-BEAST FIRES-- ITS BREATH TURNING THE WATER IN THE FOUNTAIN TO STEAM--NIGHTCRAWLER GRABS HIS LADY AND TELEPORTS...
BAMF

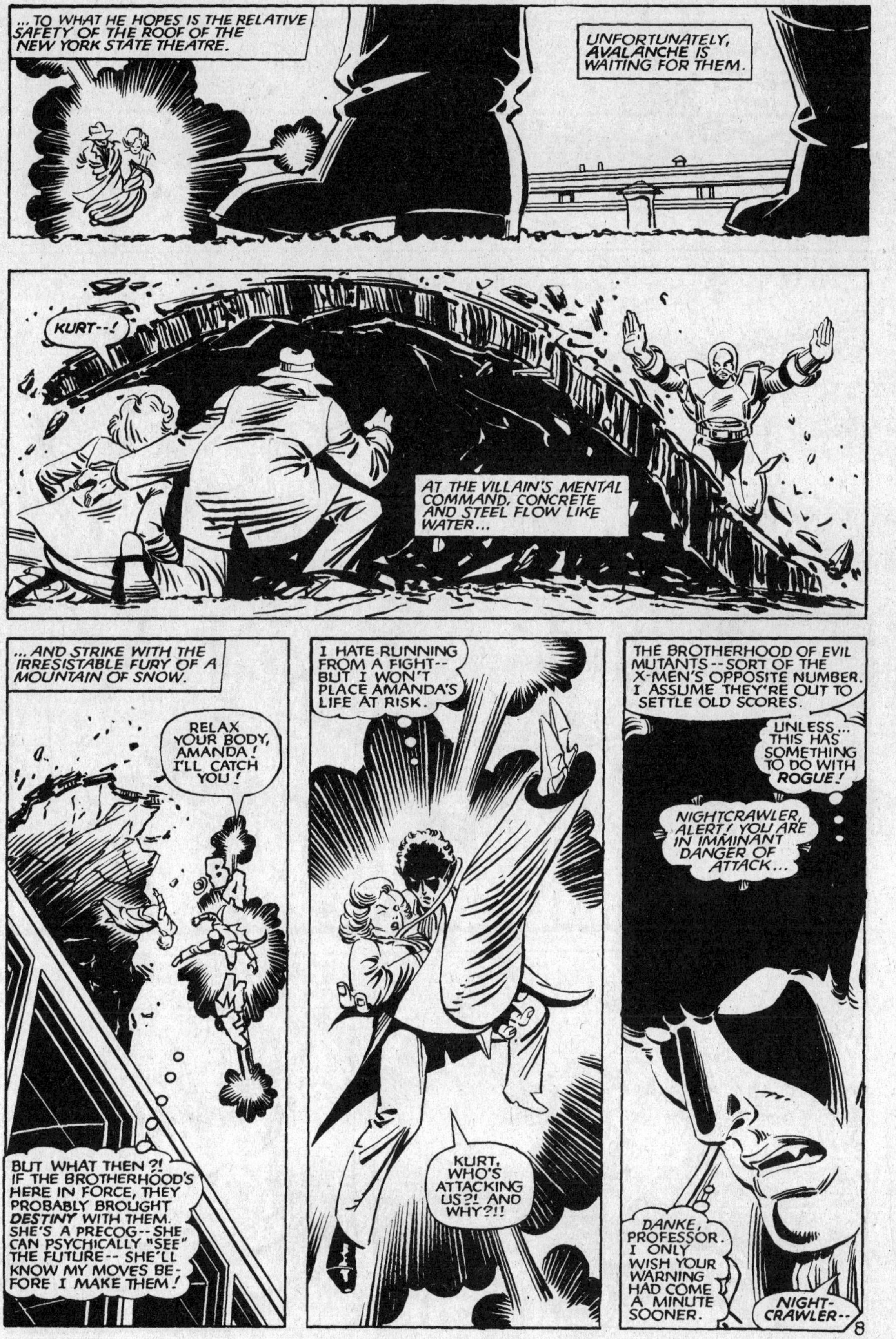

...TO WHAT HE HOPES IS THE RELATIVE SAFETY OF THE ROOF OF THE NEW YORK STATE THEATRE.
UNFORTUNATELY, AVALANCHE IS WAITING FOR THEM.
KURT--!
AT THE VILLAIN'S MENTAL COMMAND, CONCRETE AND STEEL FLOW LIKE WATER...
...AND STRIKE WITH THE IRRESISTABLE FURY OF A MOUNTAIN OF SNOW.
RELAX YOUR BODY, AMANDA! I'LL CATCH YOU!
BAMF
BUT WHAT THEN?! IF THE BROTHERHOOD'S HERE IN FORCE, THEY PROBABLY BROUGHT DESTINY WITH THEM. SHE'S A PRECOG--SHE CAN PSYCHICALLY "SEE" THE FUTURE--SHE'LL KNOW MY MOVES BEFORE I MAKE THEM!
I HATE RUNNING FROM A FIGHT--BUT I WON'T PLACE AMANDA'S LIFE AT RISK.
KURT, WHO'S ATTACKING US?! AND WHY?!!
THE BROTHERHOOD OF EVIL MUTANTS--SORT OF THE X-MEN'S OPPOSITE NUMBER. I ASSUME THEY'RE OUT TO SETTLE OLD SCORES.
UNLESS... THIS HAS SOMETHING TO DO WITH ROGUE!
NIGHTCRAWLER, ALERT! YOU ARE IN IMMINANT DANGER OF ATTACK...
DANKE, PROFESSOR. I ONLY WISH YOUR WARNING HAD COME A MINUTE SOONER.
NIGHT-CRAWLER--

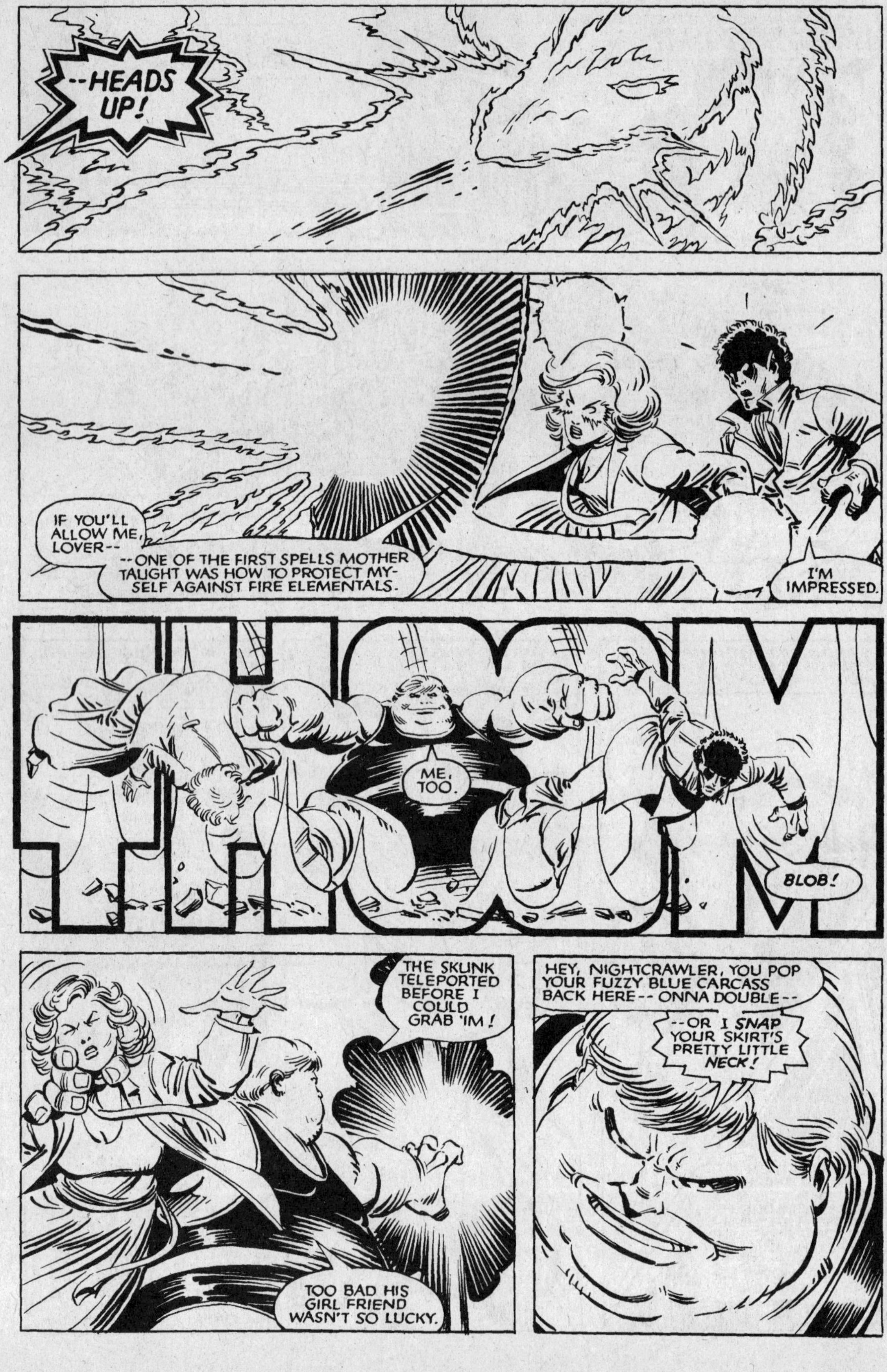
--HEADS UP!
IF YOU'LL ALLOW ME, LOVER--
--ONE OF THE FIRST SPELLS MOTHER TAUGHT WAS HOW TO PROTECT MY-SELF AGAINST FIRE ELEMENTALS.
I'M IMPRESSED.
THOOM
ME, TOO.
BLOB!
THE SKUNK TELEPORTED BEFORE I COULD GRAB 'IM!
TOO BAD HIS GIRL FRIEND WASN'T SO LUCKY.
HEY, NIGHTCRAWLER, YOU POP YOUR FUZZY BLUE CARCASS BACK HERE-- ONNA DOUBLE--
--OR I SNAP YOUR SKIRT'S PRETTY LITTLE NECK!

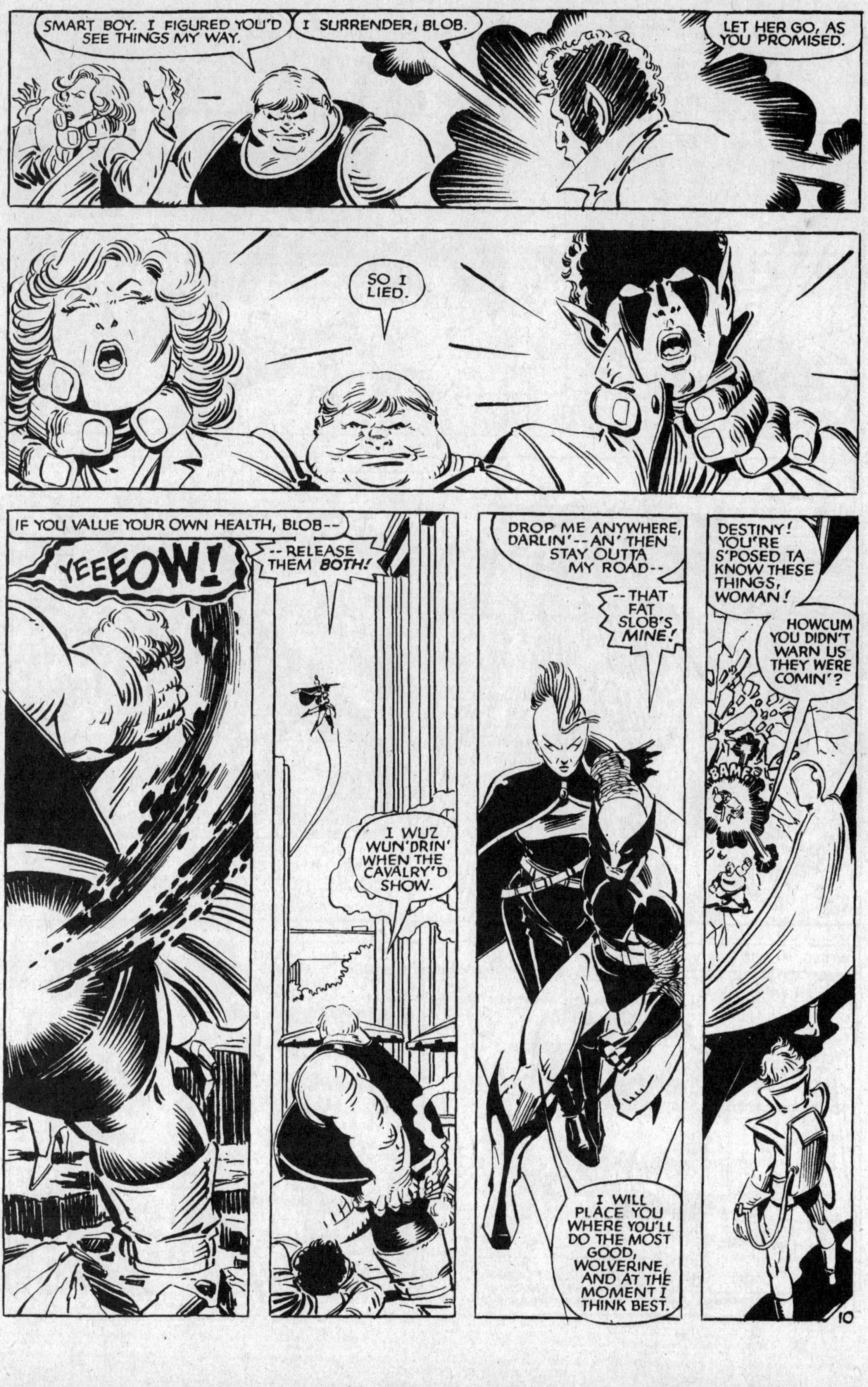

SMART BOY. I FIGURED YOU'D SEE THINGS MY WAY.
I SURRENDER, BLOB.
LET HER GO, AS YOU PROMISED.
SO I LIED.
IF YOU VALUE YOUR OWN HEALTH, BLOB--
YEEEOW!
--RELEASE THEM BOTH!
I WUZ WUN'DRIN' WHEN THE CAVALRY'D SHOW.
DROP ME ANYWHERE, DARLIN'--AN' THEN STAY OUTTA MY ROAD--
--THAT FAT SLOB'S MINE!
I WILL PLACE YOU WHERE YOU'LL DO THE MOST GOOD, WOLVERINE, AND AT THE MOMENT I THINK BEST.
DESTINY! YOU'RE S'POSED TA KNOW THESE THINGS, WOMAN!
HOWCUM YOU DIDN'T WARN US THEY WERE COMIN'?
BAMF
10

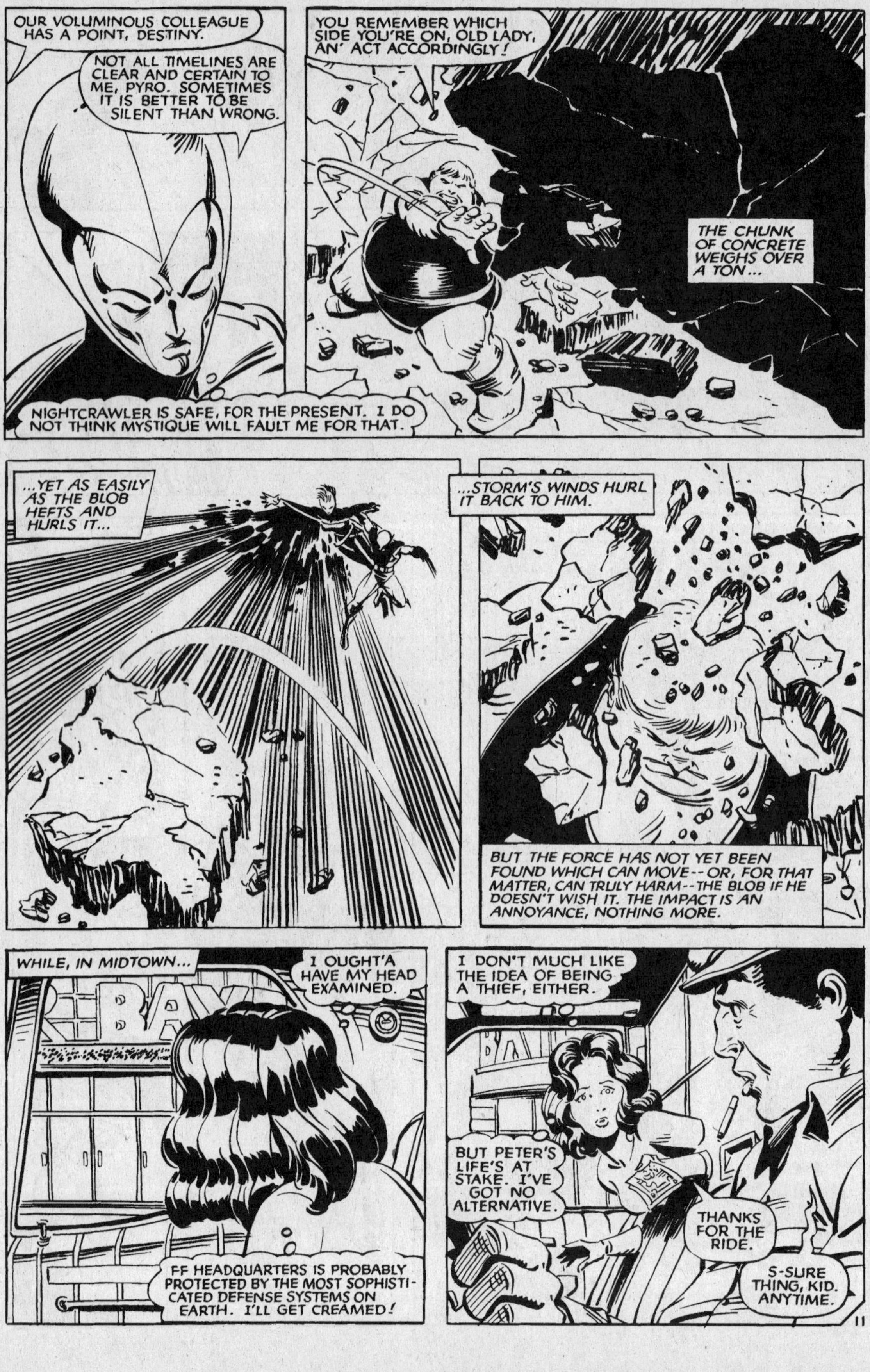
OUR VOLUMINOUS COLLEAGUE HAS A POINT, DESTINY.
NOT ALL TIMELINES ARE CLEAR AND CERTAIN TO ME, PYRO. SOMETIMES IT IS BETTER TO BE SILENT THAN WRONG.
YOU REMEMBER WHICH SIDE YOU'RE ON, OLD LADY, AN' ACT ACCORDINGLY!
THE CHUNK OF CONCRETE WEIGHS OVER A TON...
NIGHTCRAWLER IS SAFE, FOR THE PRESENT. I DO NOT THINK MYSTIQUE WILL FAULT ME FOR THAT.
...YET AS EASILY AS THE BLOB HEFTS AND HURLS IT...
...STORM'S WINDS HURL IT BACK TO HIM.
BUT THE FORCE HAS NOT YET BEEN FOUND WHICH CAN MOVE--OR, FOR THAT MATTER, CAN TRULY HARM--THE BLOB IF HE DOESN'T WISH IT. THE IMPACT IS AN ANNOYANCE, NOTHING MORE.
WHILE, IN MIDTOWN...
I OUGHT'A HAVE MY HEAD EXAMINED.
FF HEADQUARTERS IS PROBABLY PROTECTED BY THE MOST SOPHISTICATED DEFENSE SYSTEMS ON EARTH. I'LL GET CREAMED!
I DON'T MUCH LIKE THE IDEA OF BEING A THIEF, EITHER.
BUT PETER'S LIFE'S AT STAKE. I'VE GOT NO ALTERNATIVE.
THANKS FOR THE RIDE.
S-SURE THING, KID. ANYTIME.

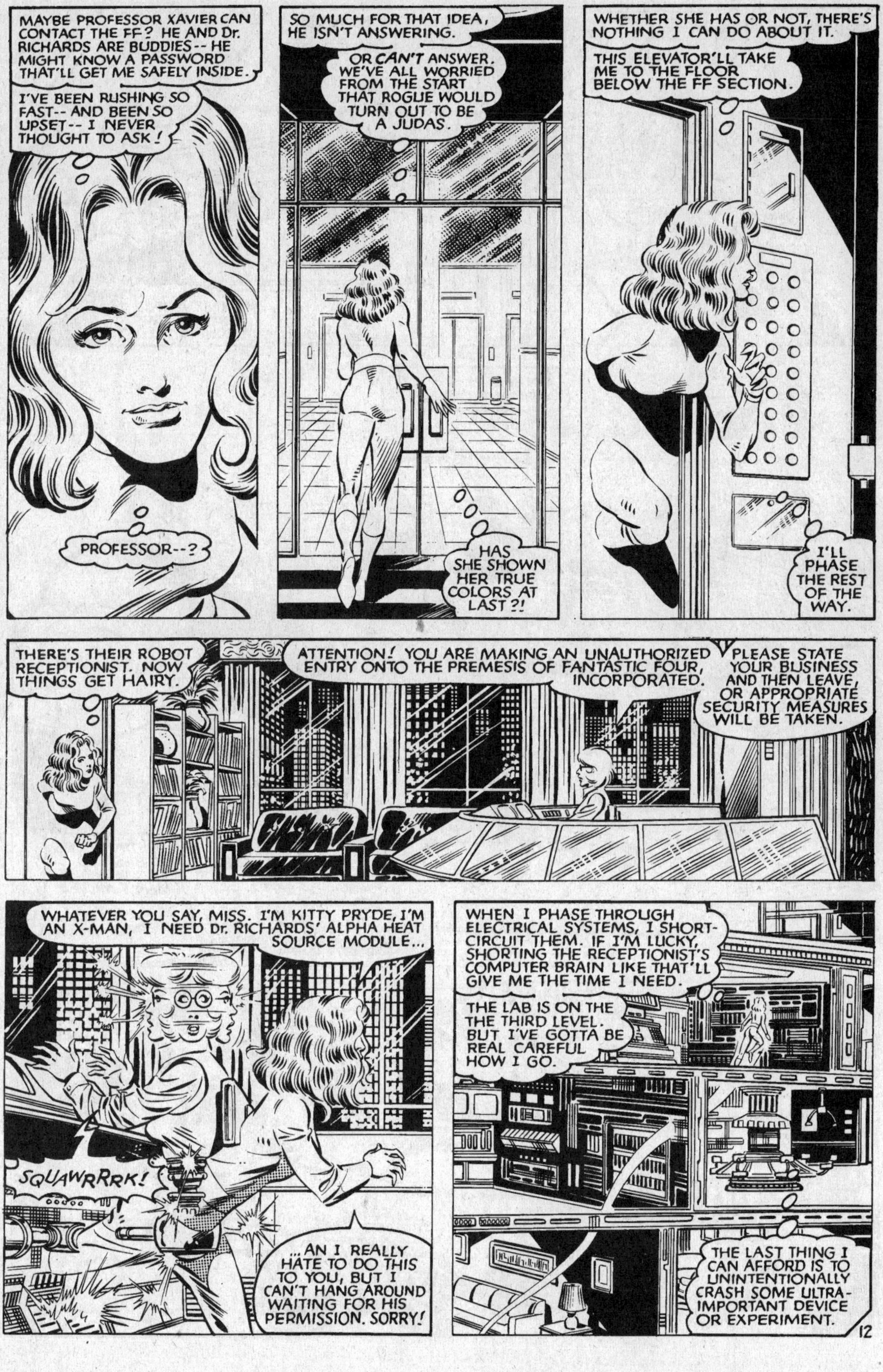
MAYBE PROFESSOR XAVIER CAN CONTACT THE FF? HE AND Dr. RICHARDS ARE BUDDIES-- HE MIGHT KNOW A PASSWORD THAT'LL GET ME SAFELY INSIDE.
I'VE BEEN RUSHING SO FAST-- AND BEEN SO UPSET-- I NEVER THOUGHT TO ASK!
PROFESSOR--?
SO MUCH FOR THAT IDEA, HE ISN'T ANSWERING.
OR CAN'T ANSWER. WE'VE ALL WORRIED FROM THE START THAT ROGUE WOULD TURN OUT TO BE A JUDAS.
HAS SHE SHOWN HER TRUE COLORS AT LAST?!
WHETHER SHE HAS OR NOT, THERE'S NOTHING I CAN DO ABOUT IT.
THIS ELEVATOR'LL TAKE ME TO THE FLOOR BELOW THE FF SECTION.
I'LL PHASE THE REST OF THE WAY.
THERE'S THEIR ROBOT RECEPTIONIST. NOW THINGS GET HAIRY.
ATTENTION! YOU ARE MAKING AN UNAUTHORIZED ENTRY ONTO THE PREMESIS OF FANTASTIC FOUR, INCORPORATED.
PLEASE STATE YOUR BUSINESS AND THEN LEAVE, OR APPROPRIATE SECURITY MEASURES WILL BE TAKEN.
WHATEVER YOU SAY, MISS. I'M KITTY PRYDE, I'M AN X-MAN, I NEED Dr. RICHARDS' ALPHA HEAT SOURCE MODULE...
SQUAWRRRK!
...AN I REALLY HATE TO DO THIS TO YOU, BUT I CAN'T HANG AROUND WAITING FOR HIS PERMISSION. SORRY!
WHEN I PHASE THROUGH ELECTRICAL SYSTEMS, I SHORT-CIRCUIT THEM. IF I'M LUCKY, SHORTING THE RECEPTIONIST'S COMPUTER BRAIN LIKE THAT'LL GIVE ME THE TIME I NEED.
THE LAB IS ON THE THE THIRD LEVEL. BUT I'VE GOTTA BE REAL CAREFUL HOW I GO.
THE LAST THING I CAN AFFORD IS TO UNINTENTIONALLY CRASH SOME ULTRA-IMPORTANT DEVICE OR EXPERIMENT.

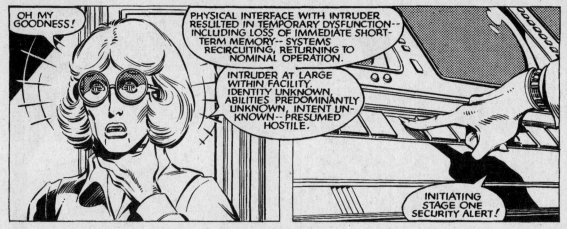

OH MY GOODNESS!

PHYSICAL INTERFACE WITH INTRUDER RESULTED IN TEMPORARY DYSFUNCTION-- INCLUDING LOSS OF IMMEDIATE SHORT-TERM MEMORY-- SYSTEMS RECIRCUITING, RETURNING TO NOMINAL OPERATION.

INTRUDER AT LARGE WITHIN FACILITY. IDENTITY UNKNOWN, ABILITIES PREDOMINANTLY UNKNOWN, INTENT UN-KNOWN-- PRESUMED HOSTILE.

INITIATING STAGE ONE SECURITY ALERT!

ON THE PLAZA AT LINCOLN CENTER...

...DESTINY DOES HER BEST TO ANTICIPATE THE X-MEN'S MOVES.

UNFORTUNATELY, IT'S ONE THING TO WARN A TEAM-MATE THAT NIGHTCRAWLER IS ABOUT TO TELEPORT AWAY FROM HIS PUNCH...

...AND SOMETHING ELSE AGAIN FOR HIM TO REACT FAST AND EFFECTIVELY ENOUGH TO DO ANYTHING ABOUT IT.

BAMF

KRAK!

13

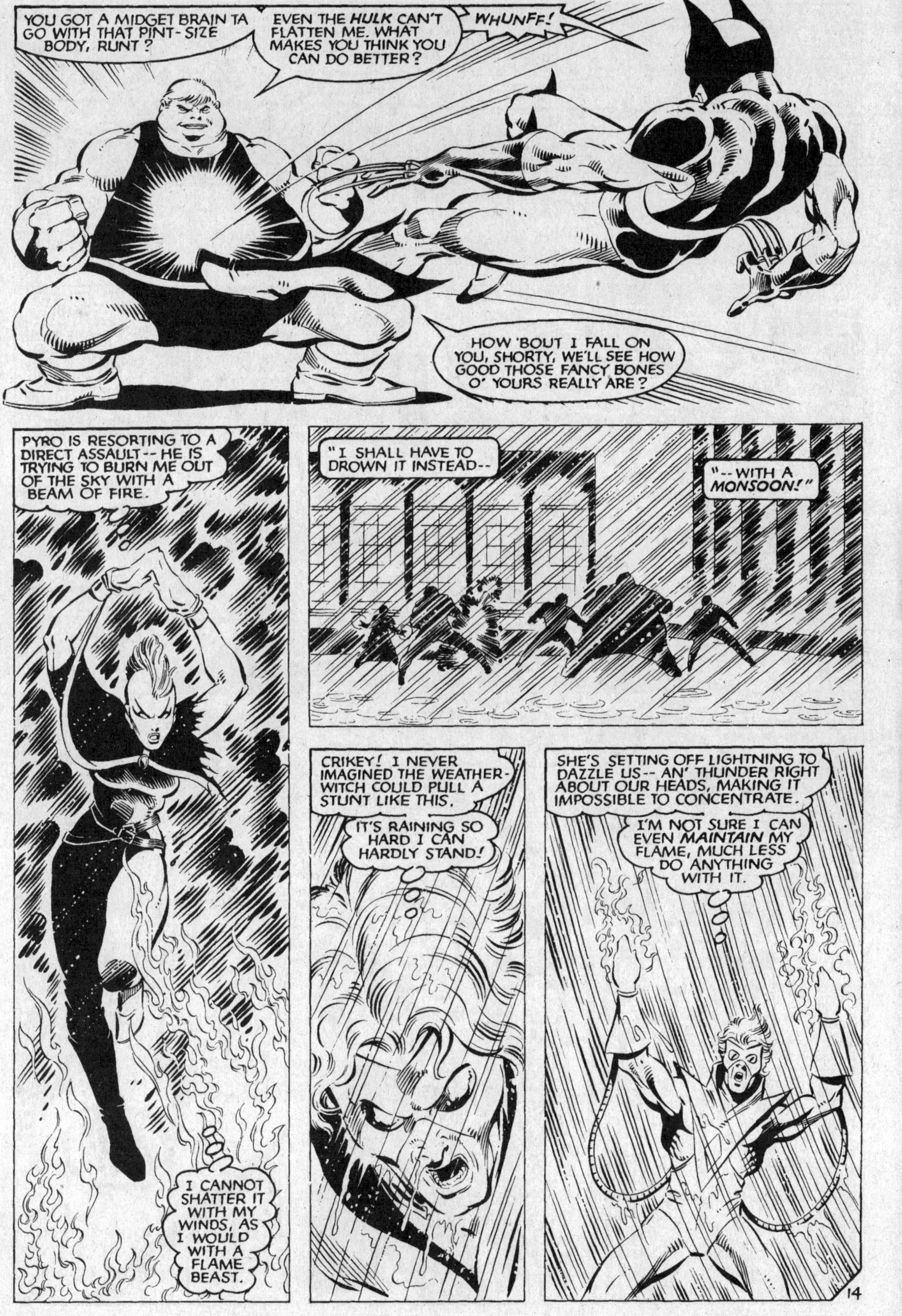
YOU GOT A MIDGET BRAIN TA GO WITH THAT PINT-SIZE BODY, RUNT?
EVEN THE HULK CAN'T FLATTEN ME. WHAT MAKES YOU THINK YOU CAN DO BETTER?
WHUNFF!
HOW 'BOUT I FALL ON YOU, SHORTY, WE'LL SEE HOW GOOD THOSE FANCY BONES O' YOURS REALLY ARE?
PYRO IS RESORTING TO A DIRECT ASSAULT-- HE IS TRYING TO BURN ME OUT OF THE SKY WITH A BEAM OF FIRE.
I CANNOT SHATTER IT WITH MY WINDS, AS I WOULD WITH A FLAME BEAST.
"I SHALL HAVE TO DROWN IT INSTEAD--
"--WITH A MONSOON!"
CRIKEY! I NEVER IMAGINED THE WEATHER-WITCH COULD PULL A STUNT LIKE THIS.
IT'S RAINING SO HARD I CAN HARDLY STAND!
SHE'S SETTING OFF LIGHTNING TO DAZZLE US-- AN' THUNDER RIGHT ABOUT OUR HEADS, MAKING IT IMPOSSIBLE TO CONCENTRATE.
I'M NOT SURE I CAN EVEN MAINTAIN MY FLAME, MUCH LESS DO ANYTHING WITH IT.

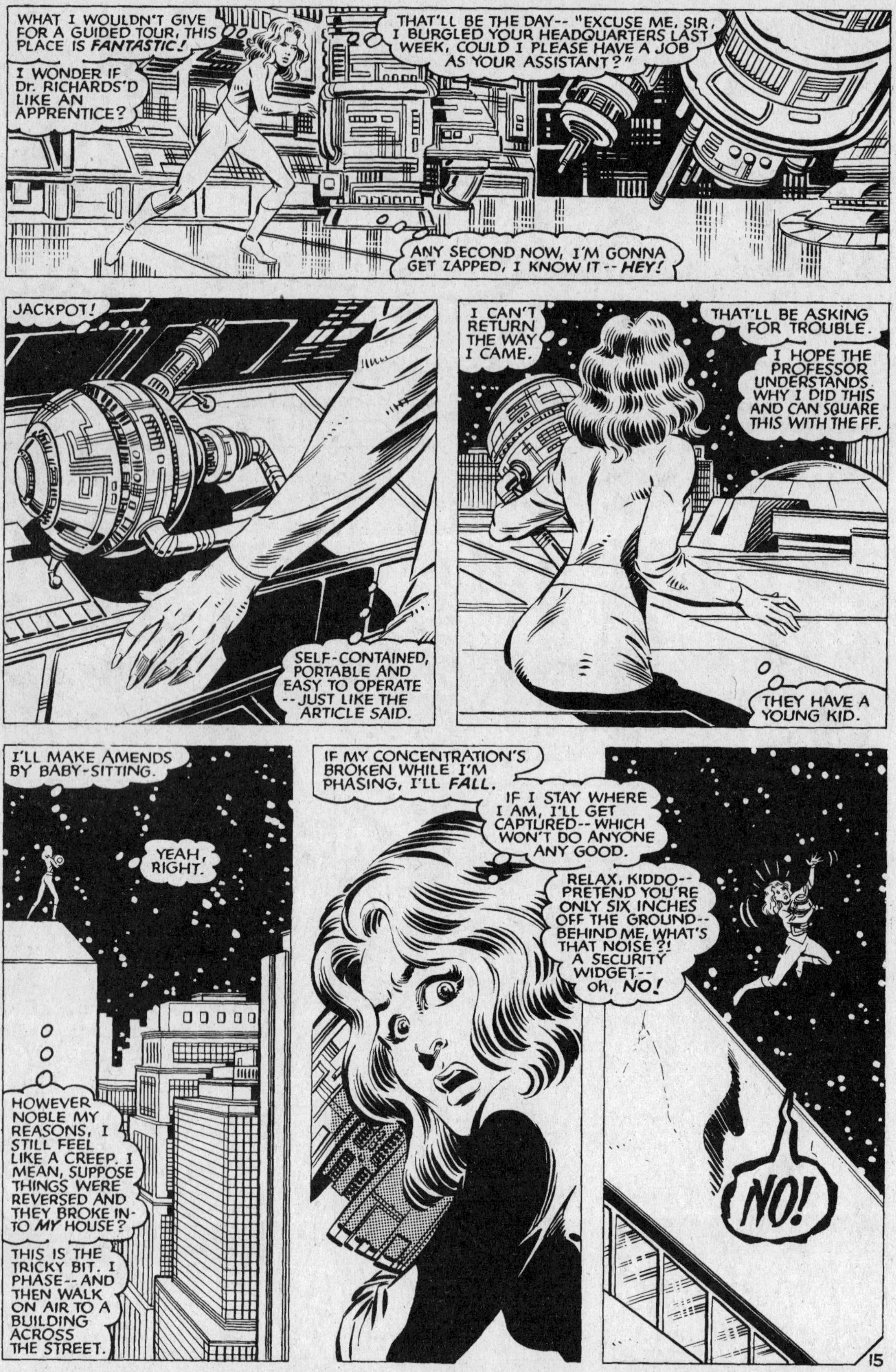

WHAT I WOULDN'T GIVE FOR A GUIDED TOUR, THIS PLACE IS FANTASTIC!
I WONDER IF Dr. RICHARDS'D LIKE AN APPRENTICE?
THAT'LL BE THE DAY-- "EXCUSE ME, SIR, I BURGLED YOUR HEADQUARTERS LAST WEEK, COULD I PLEASE HAVE A JOB AS YOUR ASSISTANT?"
ANY SECOND NOW, I'M GONNA GET ZAPPED, I KNOW IT -- HEY!
JACKPOT!
SELF-CONTAINED, PORTABLE AND EASY TO OPERATE -- JUST LIKE THE ARTICLE SAID.
I CAN'T RETURN THE WAY I CAME.
THAT'LL BE ASKING FOR TROUBLE.
I HOPE THE PROFESSOR UNDERSTANDS WHY I DID THIS AND CAN SQUARE THIS WITH THE FF.
THEY HAVE A YOUNG KID.
I'LL MAKE AMENDS BY BABY-SITTING.
YEAH, RIGHT.
HOWEVER NOBLE MY REASONS, I STILL FEEL LIKE A CREEP. I MEAN, SUPPOSE THINGS WERE REVERSED AND THEY BROKE INTO MY HOUSE?
THIS IS THE TRICKY BIT. I PHASE-- AND THEN WALK ON AIR TO A BUILDING ACROSS THE STREET.
IF MY CONCENTRATION'S BROKEN WHILE I'M PHASING, I'LL FALL.
IF I STAY WHERE I AM, I'LL GET CAPTURED-- WHICH WON'T DO ANYONE ANY GOOD.
RELAX, KIDDO-- PRETEND YOU'RE ONLY SIX INCHES OFF THE GROUND-- BEHIND ME, WHAT'S THAT NOISE?! A SECURITY WIDGET-- oh, NO!
NO!

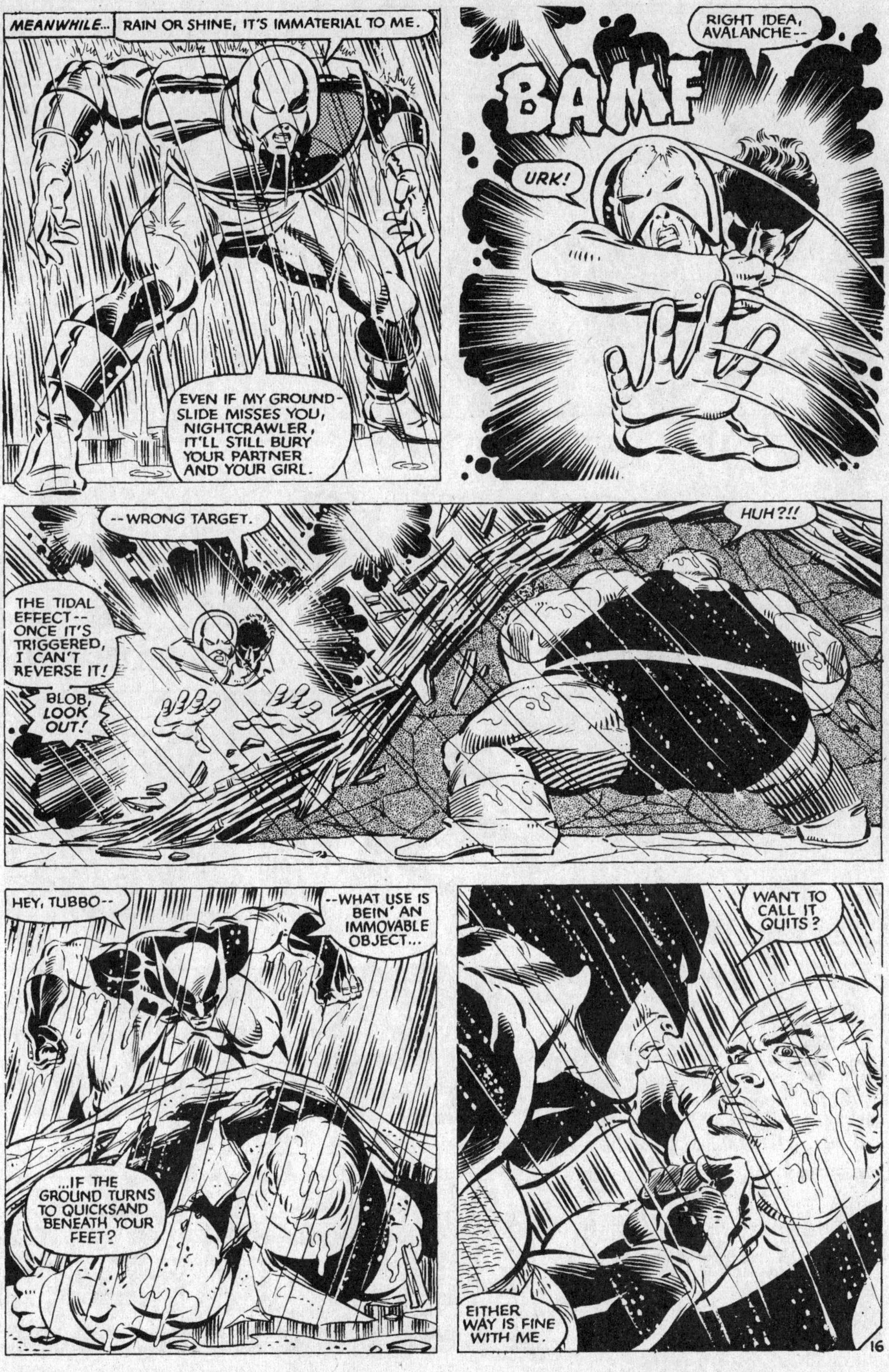
MEANWHILE...
RAIN OR SHINE, IT'S IMMATERIAL TO ME.
EVEN IF MY GROUND-SLIDE MISSES YOU, NIGHTCRAWLER, IT'LL STILL BURY YOUR PARTNER AND YOUR GIRL.
RIGHT IDEA, AVALANCHE--
BAMF
URK!
--WRONG TARGET.
THE TIDAL EFFECT-- ONCE IT'S TRIGGERED, I CAN'T REVERSE IT!
BLOB, LOOK OUT!
HUH?!!
HEY, TUBBO--
--WHAT USE IS BEIN' AN IMMOVABLE OBJECT...
...IF THE GROUND TURNS TO QUICKSAND BENEATH YOUR FEET?
WANT TO CALL IT QUITS?
EITHER WAY IS FINE WITH ME.

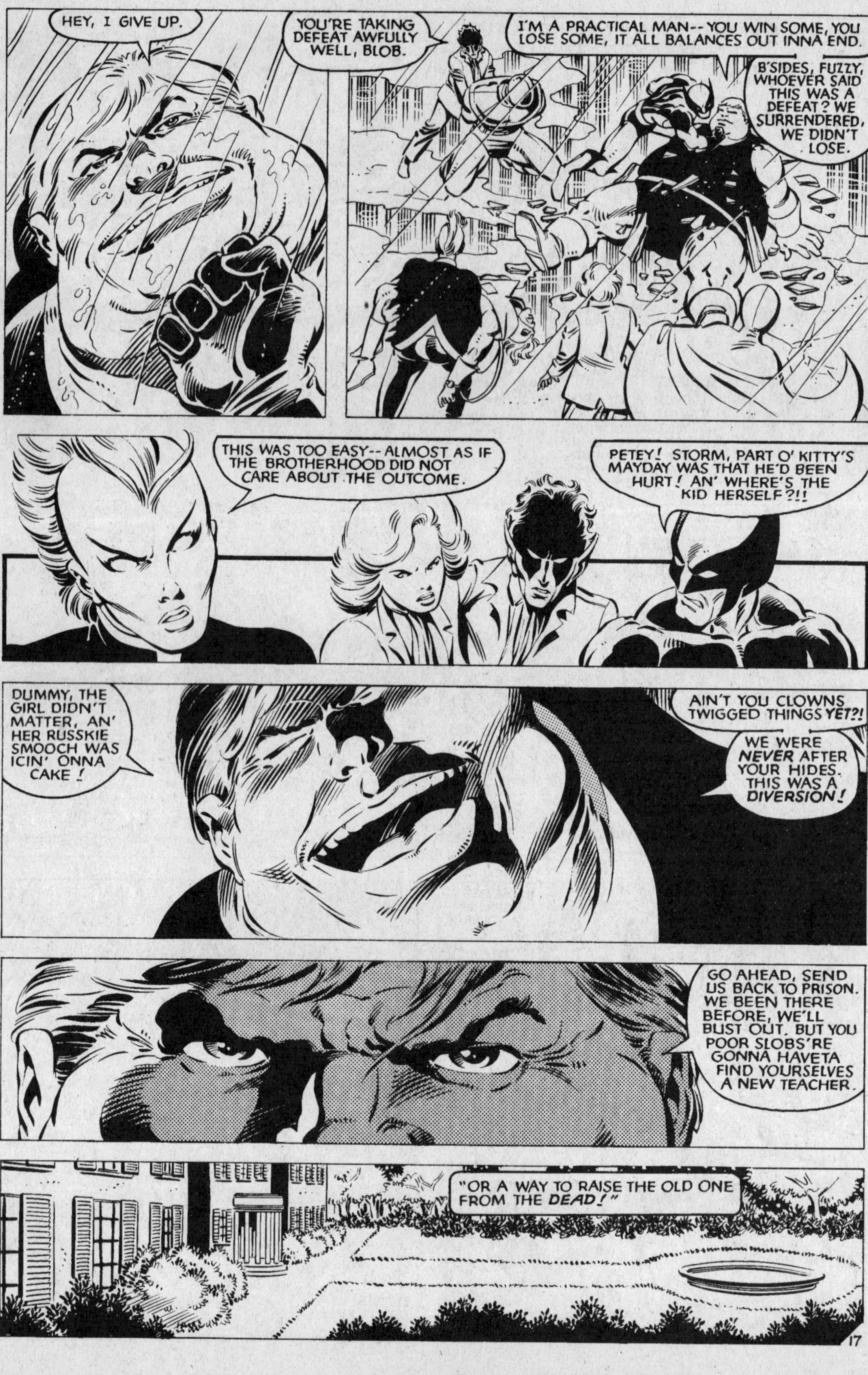
HEY, I GIVE UP.
YOU'RE TAKING DEFEAT AWFULLY WELL, BLOB.
I'M A PRACTICAL MAN-- YOU WIN SOME, YOU LOSE SOME, IT ALL BALANCES OUT INNA END.
B'SIDES, FUZZY, WHOEVER SAID THIS WAS A DEFEAT? WE SURRENDERED, WE DIDN'T LOSE.
THIS WAS TOO EASY-- ALMOST AS IF THE BROTHERHOOD DID NOT CARE ABOUT THE OUTCOME.
PETEY! STORM, PART O' KITTY'S MAYDAY WAS THAT HE'D BEEN HURT! AN' WHERE'S THE KID HERSELF?!!
DUMMY, THE GIRL DIDN'T MATTER, AN' HER RUSSKIE SMOOCH WAS ICIN' ONNA CAKE!
AIN'T YOU CLOWNS TWIGGED THINGS YET?!
WE WERE NEVER AFTER YOUR HIDES. THIS WAS A DIVERSION!
GO AHEAD, SEND US BACK TO PRISON. WE BEEN THERE BEFORE, WE'LL BUST OUT. BUT YOU POOR SLOBS'RE GONNA HAVETA FIND YOURSELVES A NEW TEACHER.
"OR A WAY TO RAISE THE OLD ONE FROM THE DEAD!"

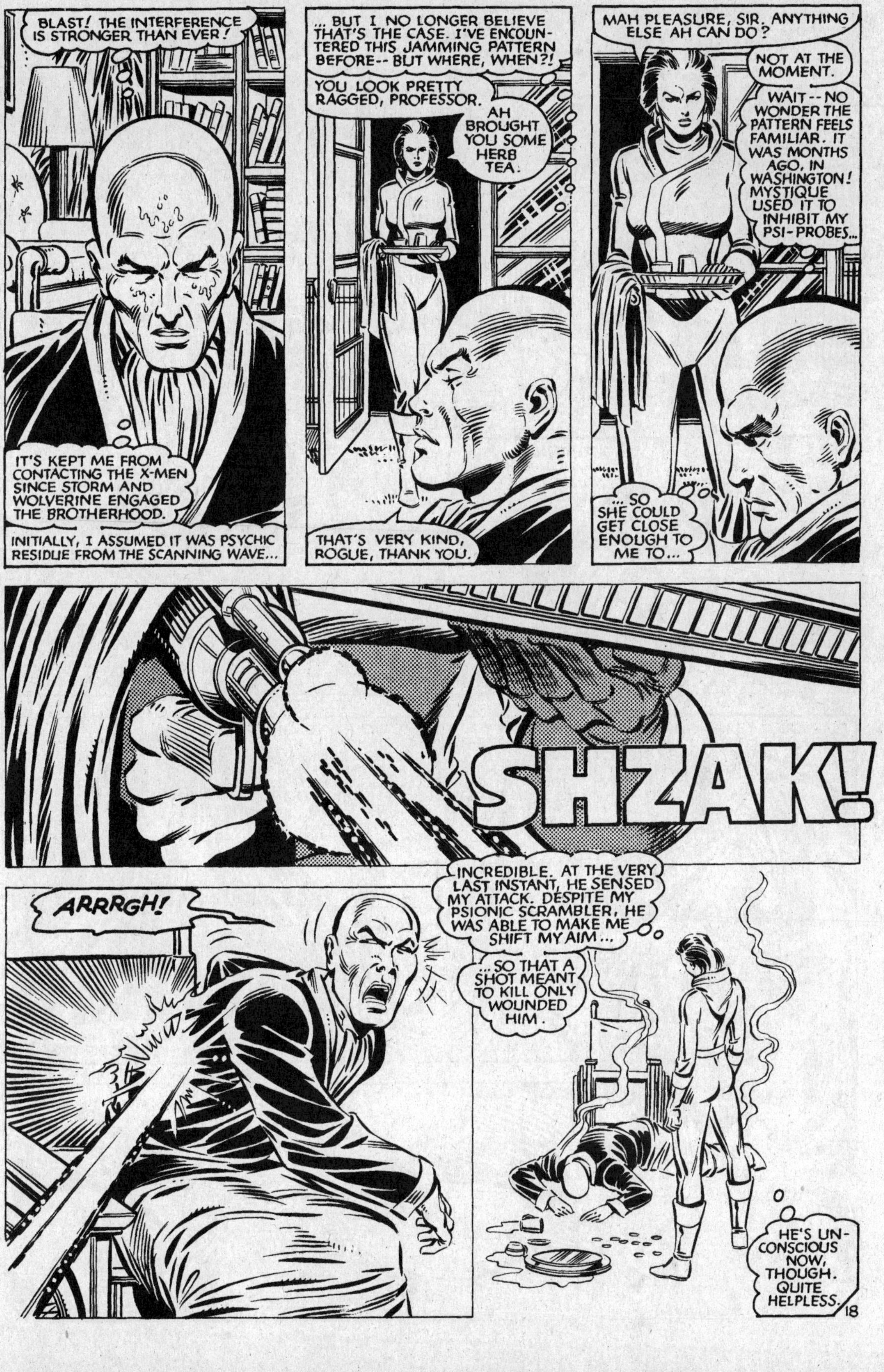
BLAST! THE INTERFERENCE IS STRONGER THAN EVER!
IT'S KEPT ME FROM CONTACTING THE X-MEN SINCE STORM AND WOLVERINE ENGAGED THE BROTHERHOOD.
INITIALLY, I ASSUMED IT WAS PSYCHIC RESIDUE FROM THE SCANNING WAVE...
... BUT I NO LONGER BELIEVE THAT'S THE CASE. I'VE ENCOUNTERED THIS JAMMING PATTERN BEFORE-- BUT WHERE, WHEN?!
YOU LOOK PRETTY RAGGED, PROFESSOR.
AH BROUGHT YOU SOME HERB TEA.
THAT'S VERY KIND, ROGUE, THANK YOU.
MAH PLEASURE, SIR. ANYTHING ELSE AH CAN DO?
NOT AT THE MOMENT.
WAIT--NO WONDER THE PATTERN FEELS FAMILIAR. IT WAS MONTHS AGO, IN WASHINGTON! MYSTIQUE USED IT TO INHIBIT MY PSI-PROBES...
... SO SHE COULD GET CLOSE ENOUGH TO ME TO...
SHZAK!
ARRRGH!
INCREDIBLE. AT THE VERY LAST INSTANT, HE SENSED MY ATTACK. DESPITE MY PSIONIC SCRAMBLER, HE WAS ABLE TO MAKE ME SHIFT MY AIM...
... SO THAT A SHOT MEANT TO KILL ONLY WOUNDED HIM.
HE'S UNCONSCIOUS NOW, THOUGH. QUITE HELPLESS.

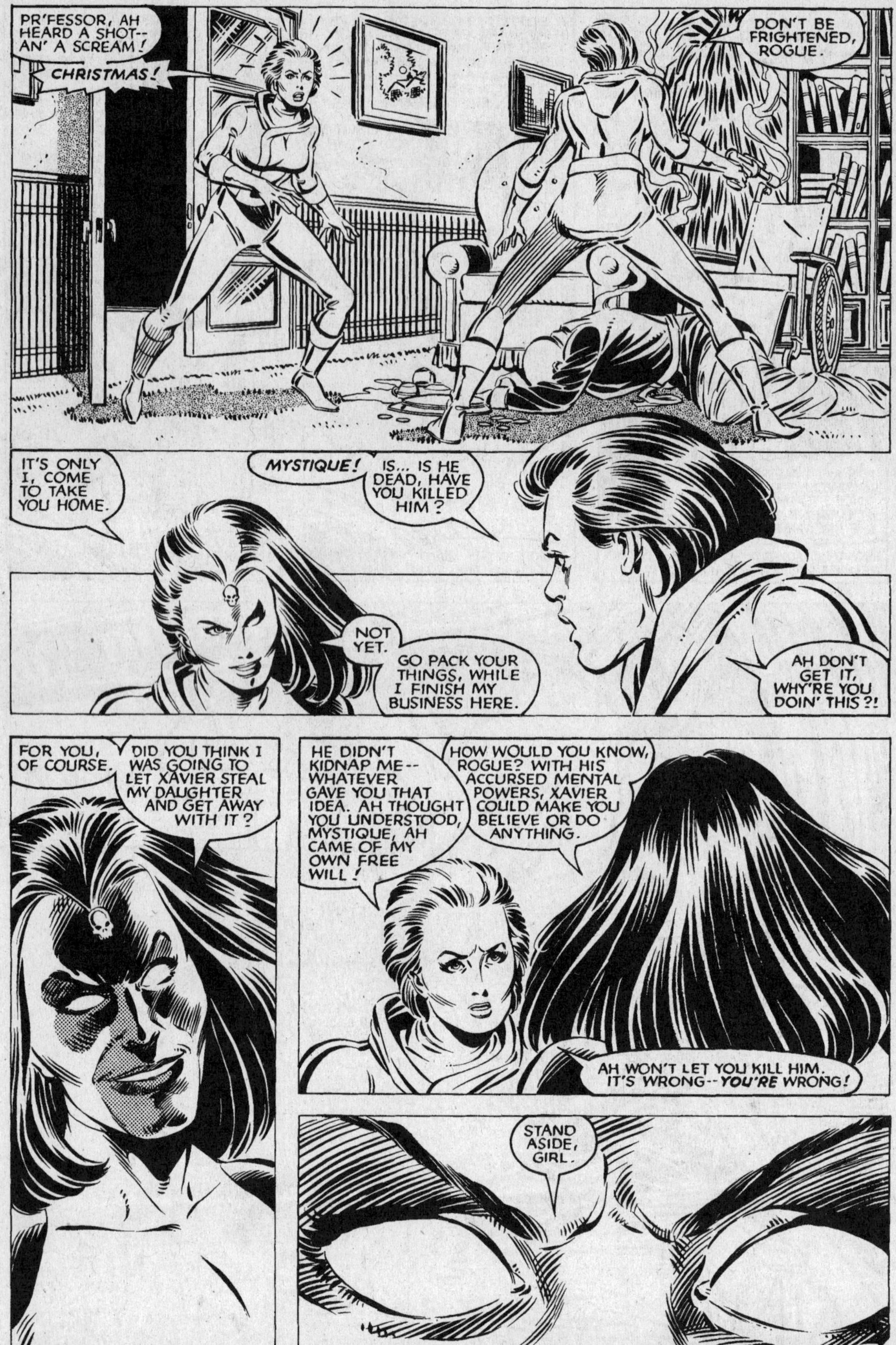
PR'FESSOR, AH HEARD A SHOT-- AN' A SCREAM!
CHRISTMAS!
DON'T BE FRIGHTENED, ROGUE.
IT'S ONLY I, COME TO TAKE YOU HOME.
MYSTIQUE!
IS... IS HE DEAD, HAVE YOU KILLED HIM?
NOT YET.
GO PACK YOUR THINGS, WHILE I FINISH MY BUSINESS HERE.
AH DON'T GET IT, WHY'RE YOU DOIN' THIS?!
FOR YOU, OF COURSE.
DID YOU THINK I WAS GOING TO LET XAVIER STEAL MY DAUGHTER AND GET AWAY WITH IT?
HE DIDN'T KIDNAP ME-- WHATEVER GAVE YOU THAT IDEA. AH THOUGHT YOU UNDERSTOOD, MYSTIQUE, AH CAME OF MY OWN FREE WILL!
HOW WOULD YOU KNOW, ROGUE? WITH HIS ACCURSED MENTAL POWERS, XAVIER COULD MAKE YOU BELIEVE OR DO ANYTHING.
AH WON'T LET YOU KILL HIM. IT'S WRONG--YOU'RE WRONG!
STAND ASIDE, GIRL.
19

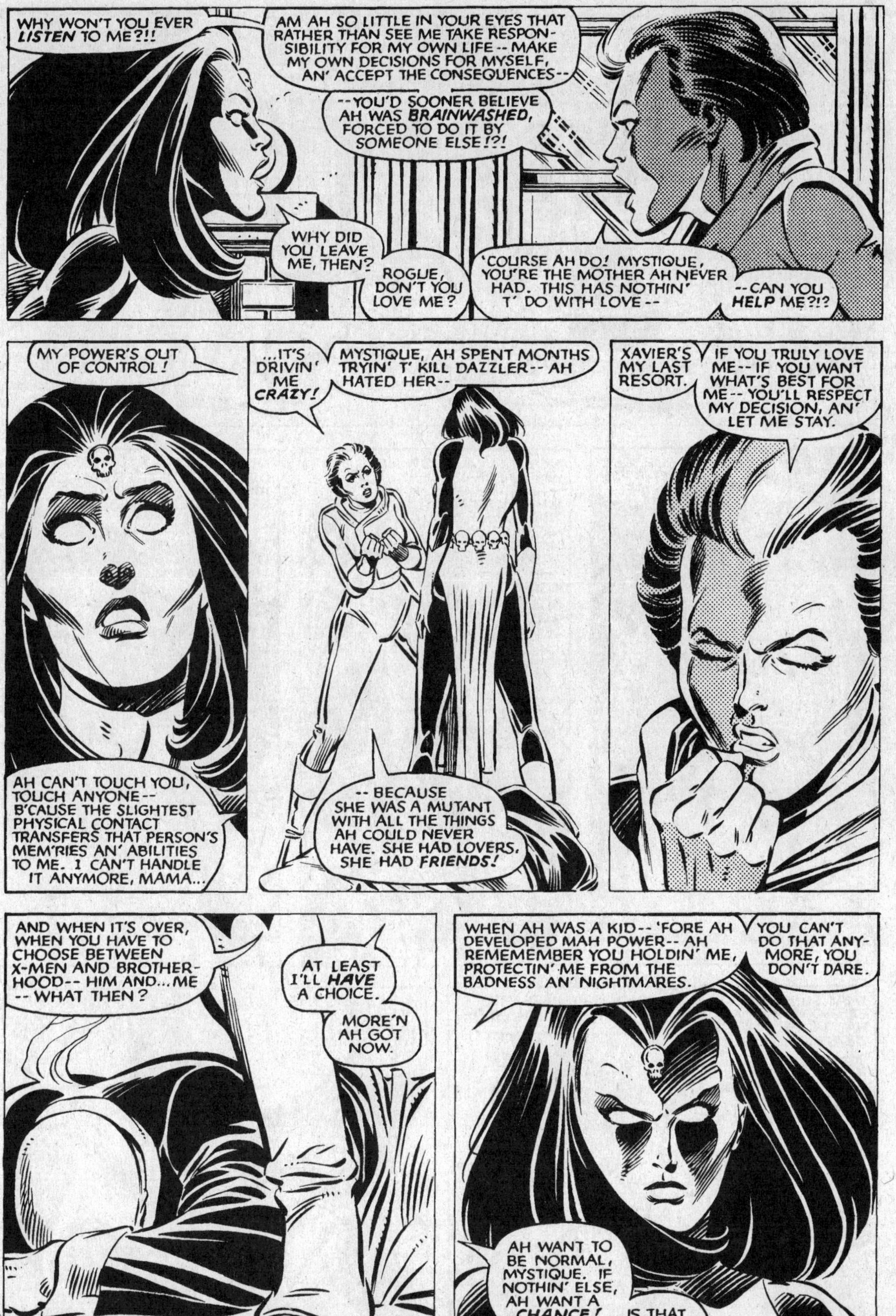

WHY WON'T YOU EVER LISTEN TO ME?!!
AM AH SO LITTLE IN YOUR EYES THAT RATHER THAN SEE ME TAKE RESPONSIBILITY FOR MY OWN LIFE -- MAKE MY OWN DECISIONS FOR MYSELF, AN' ACCEPT THE CONSEQUENCES --
-- YOU'D SOONER BELIEVE AH WAS BRAINWASHED, FORCED TO DO IT BY SOMEONE ELSE!?!
WHY DID YOU LEAVE ME, THEN?
ROGUE, DON'T YOU LOVE ME?
'COURSE AH DO! MYSTIQUE, YOU'RE THE MOTHER AH NEVER HAD. THIS HAS NOTHIN' T' DO WITH LOVE --
-- CAN YOU HELP ME?!?
MY POWER'S OUT OF CONTROL!
AH CAN'T TOUCH YOU, TOUCH ANYONE -- B'CAUSE THE SLIGHTEST PHYSICAL CONTACT TRANSFERS THAT PERSON'S MEM'RIES AN' ABILITIES TO ME. I CAN'T HANDLE IT ANYMORE, MAMA...
...IT'S DRIVIN' ME CRAZY!
MYSTIQUE, AH SPENT MONTHS TRYIN' T' KILL DAZZLER -- AH HATED HER --
-- BECAUSE SHE WAS A MUTANT WITH ALL THE THINGS AH COULD NEVER HAVE. SHE HAD LOVERS. SHE HAD FRIENDS!
XAVIER'S MY LAST RESORT.
IF YOU TRULY LOVE ME -- IF YOU WANT WHAT'S BEST FOR ME -- YOU'LL RESPECT MY DECISION, AN' LET ME STAY.
AND WHEN IT'S OVER, WHEN YOU HAVE TO CHOOSE BETWEEN X-MEN AND BROTHERHOOD -- HIM AND... ME -- WHAT THEN?
AT LEAST I'LL HAVE A CHOICE.
MORE'N AH GOT NOW.
WHEN AH WAS A KID -- 'FORE AH DEVELOPED MAH POWER -- AH REMEMEMBER YOU HOLDIN' ME, PROTECTIN' ME FROM THE BADNESS AN' NIGHTMARES.
YOU CAN'T DO THAT ANYMORE, YOU DON'T DARE.
AH WANT TO BE NORMAL, MYSTIQUE. IF NOTHIN' ELSE, AH WANT A CHANCE!
IS THAT SO MUCH TO ASK?

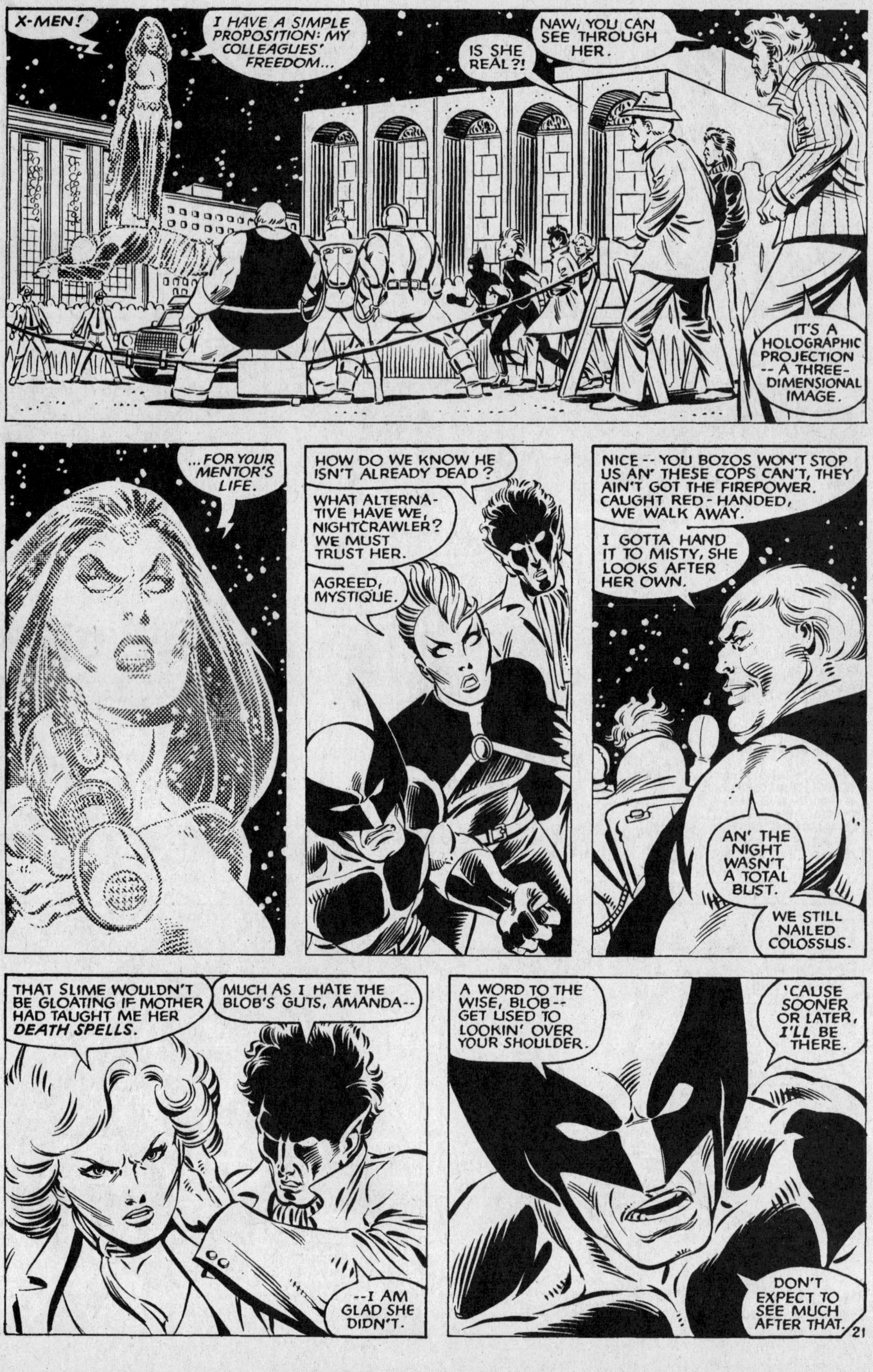
X-MEN!
I HAVE A SIMPLE PROPOSITION: MY COLLEAGUES' FREEDOM...
IS SHE REAL?!
NAW, YOU CAN SEE THROUGH HER.
IT'S A HOLOGRAPHIC PROJECTION -- A THREE-DIMENSIONAL IMAGE.
...FOR YOUR MENTOR'S LIFE.
HOW DO WE KNOW HE ISN'T ALREADY DEAD?
WHAT ALTERNATIVE HAVE WE, NIGHTCRAWLER? WE MUST TRUST HER.
AGREED, MYSTIQUE.
NICE -- YOU BOZOS WON'T STOP US AN' THESE COPS CAN'T, THEY AIN'T GOT THE FIREPOWER. CAUGHT RED-HANDED, WE WALK AWAY.
I GOTTA HAND IT TO MISTY, SHE LOOKS AFTER HER OWN.
AN' THE NIGHT WASN'T A TOTAL BUST.
WE STILL NAILED COLOSSUS.
THAT SLIME WOULDN'T BE GLOATING IF MOTHER HAD TAUGHT ME HER DEATH SPELLS.
MUCH AS I HATE THE BLOB'S GUTS, AMANDA--
--I AM GLAD SHE DIDN'T.
A WORD TO THE WISE, BLOB -- GET USED TO LOOKIN' OVER YOUR SHOULDER.
'CAUSE SOONER OR LATER, I'LL BE THERE.
DON'T EXPECT TO SEE MUCH AFTER THAT.

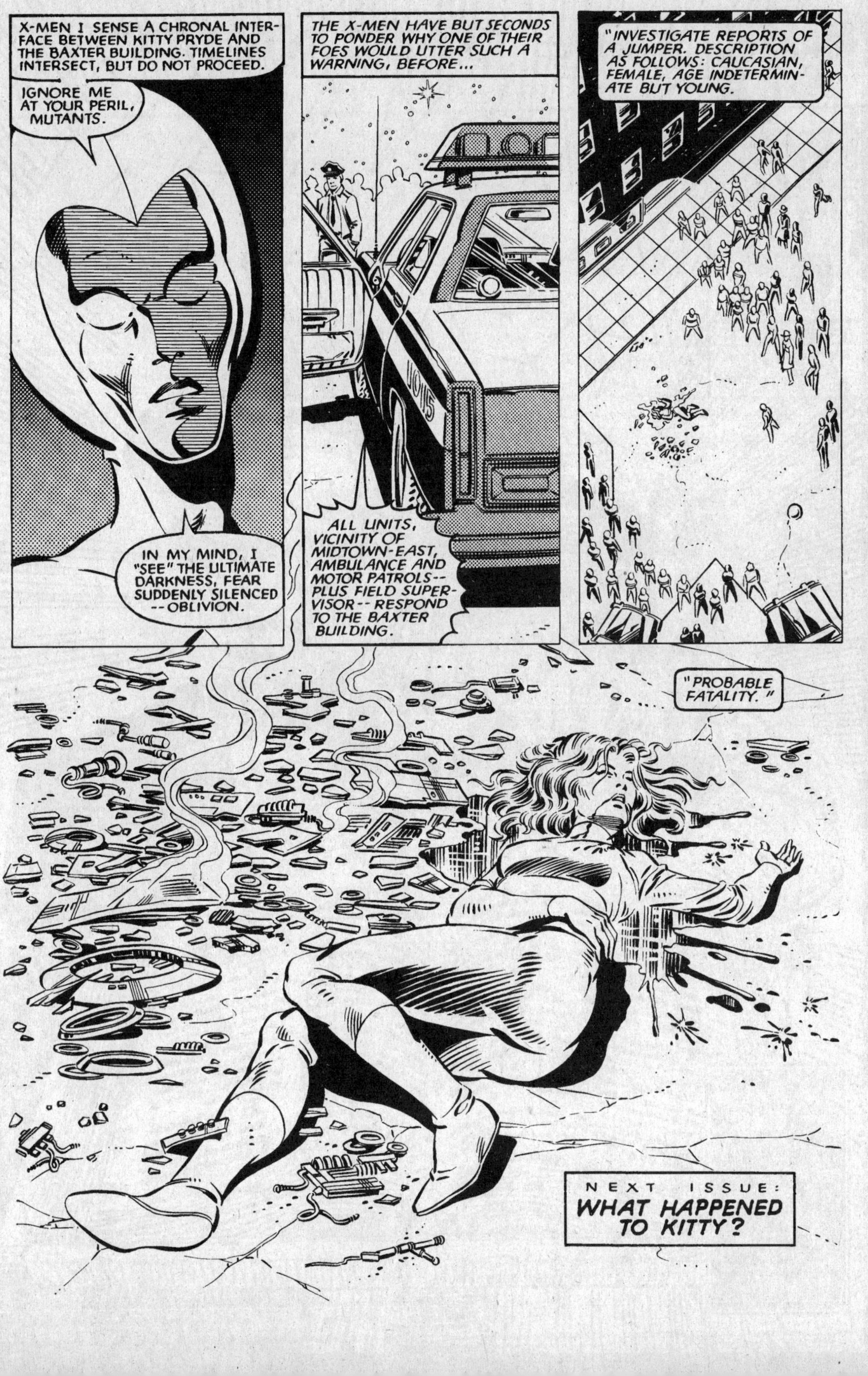
X-MEN I SENSE A CHRONAL INTERFACE BETWEEN KITTY PRYDE AND THE BAXTER BUILDING. TIMELINES INTERSECT, BUT DO NOT PROCEED.
IGNORE ME AT YOUR PERIL, MUTANTS.
IN MY MIND, I "SEE" THE ULTIMATE DARKNESS, FEAR SUDDENLY SILENCED --OBLIVION.
THE X-MEN HAVE BUT SECONDS TO PONDER WHY ONE OF THEIR FOES WOULD UTTER SUCH A WARNING, BEFORE...
ALL UNITS, VICINITY OF MIDTOWN-EAST, AMBULANCE AND MOTOR PATROLS-- PLUS FIELD SUPERVISOR-- RESPOND TO THE BAXTER BUILDING.
"INVESTIGATE REPORTS OF A JUMPER. DESCRIPTION AS FOLLOWS: CAUCASIAN, FEMALE, AGE INDETERMINATE BUT YOUNG.
"PROBABLE FATALITY."
NEXT ISSUE:
WHAT HAPPENED TO KITTY?

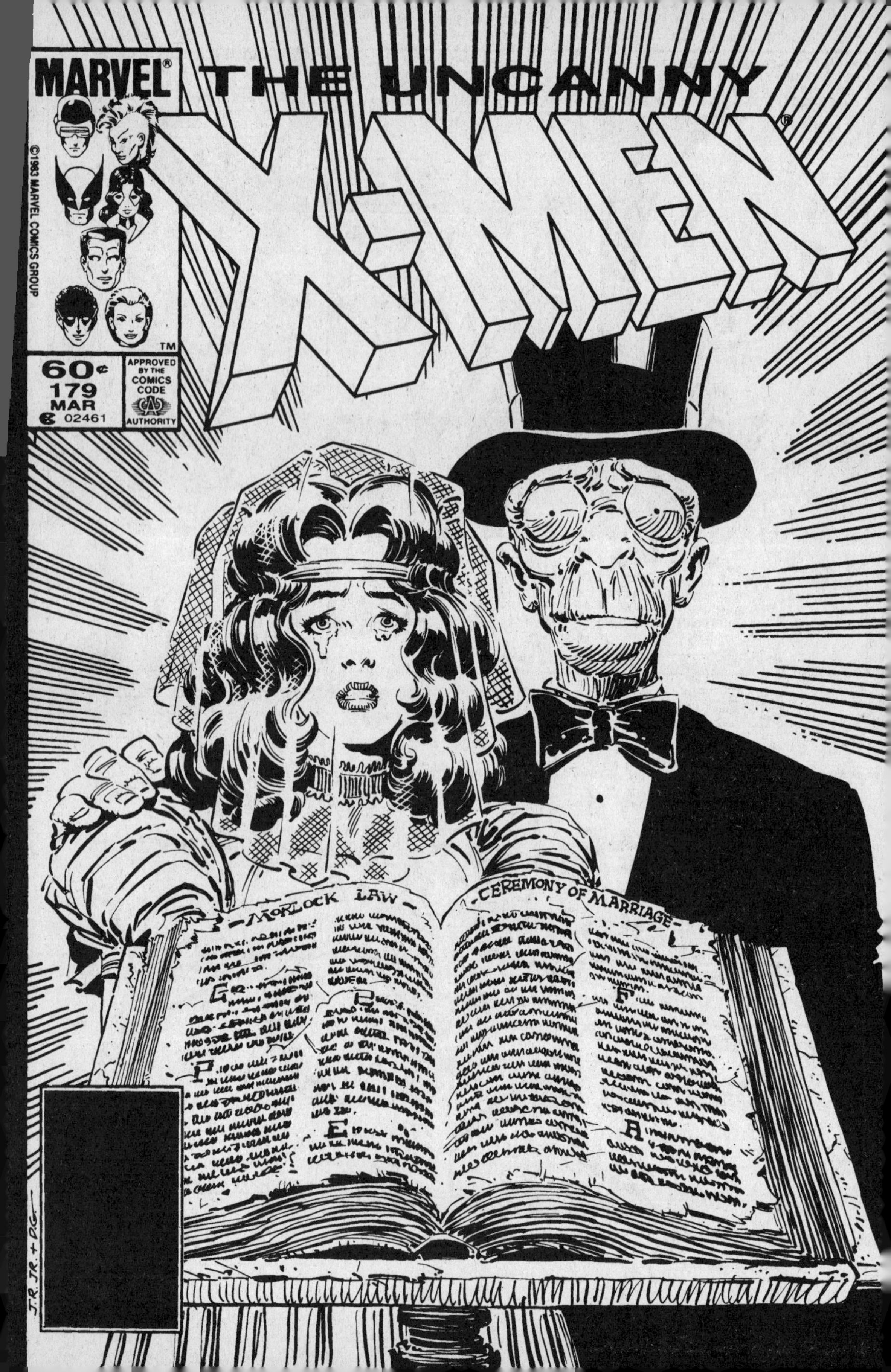

MARVEL®
THE UNCANNY
X-MEN®
©1963 MARVEL COMICS GROUP
TM
60¢
179
MAR
02461
APPROVED BY THE COMICS CODE AUTHORITY
MORLOCK LAW
CEREMONY OF MARRIAGE
J.R. JR. + D.G.

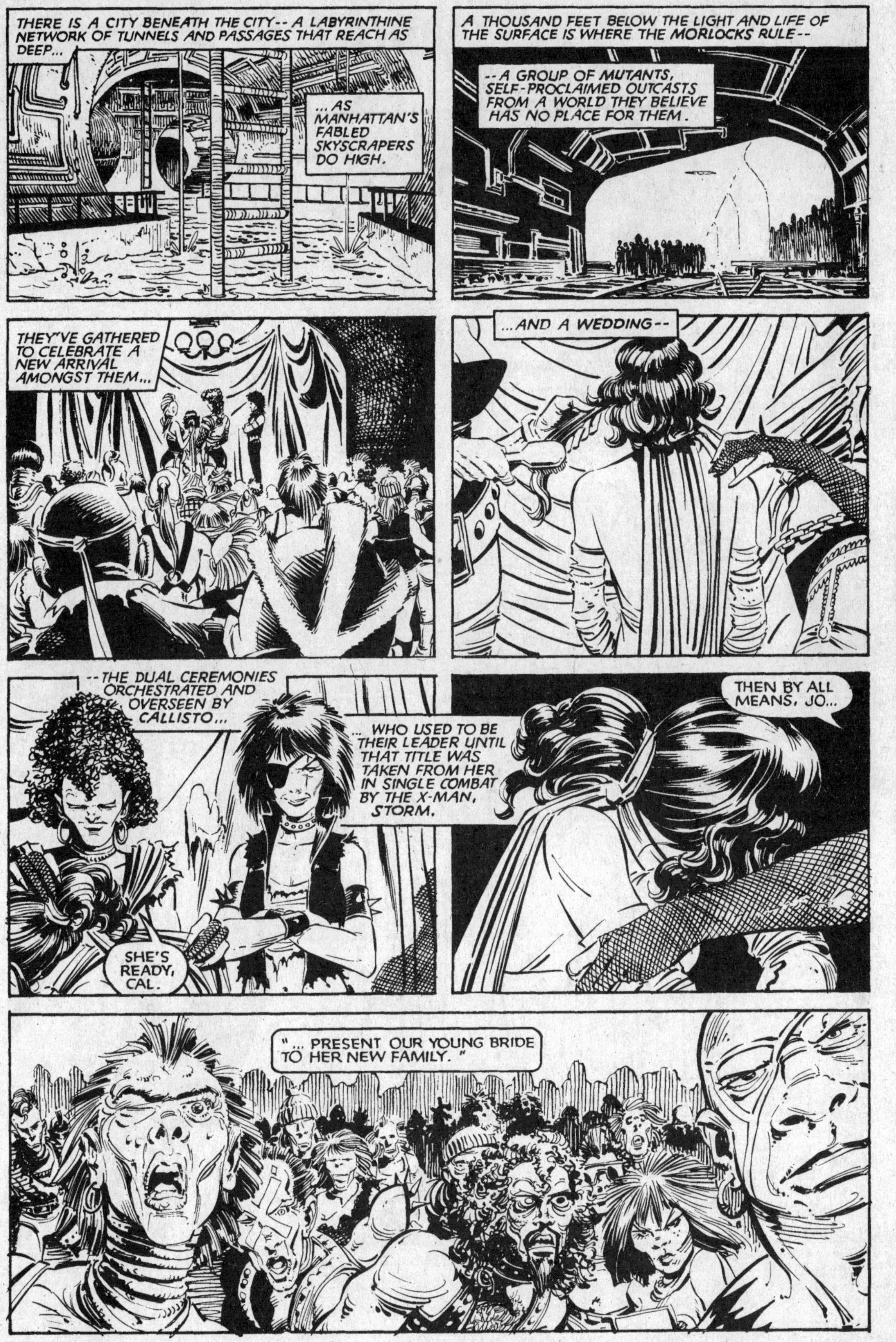
THERE IS A CITY BENEATH THE CITY-- A LABYRINTHINE NETWORK OF TUNNELS AND PASSAGES THAT REACH AS DEEP...
...AS MANHATTAN'S FABLED SKYSCRAPERS DO HIGH.
A THOUSAND FEET BELOW THE LIGHT AND LIFE OF THE SURFACE IS WHERE THE MORLOCKS RULE--
--A GROUP OF MUTANTS, SELF-PROCLAIMED OUTCASTS FROM A WORLD THEY BELIEVE HAS NO PLACE FOR THEM.
THEY'VE GATHERED TO CELEBRATE A NEW ARRIVAL AMONGST THEM...
...AND A WEDDING--
--THE DUAL CEREMONIES ORCHESTRATED AND OVERSEEN BY CALLISTO...
...WHO USED TO BE THEIR LEADER UNTIL THAT TITLE WAS TAKEN FROM HER IN SINGLE COMBAT BY THE X-MAN, STORM.
SHE'S READY, CAL.
THEN BY ALL MEANS, JO...
"...PRESENT OUR YOUNG BRIDE TO HER NEW FAMILY."

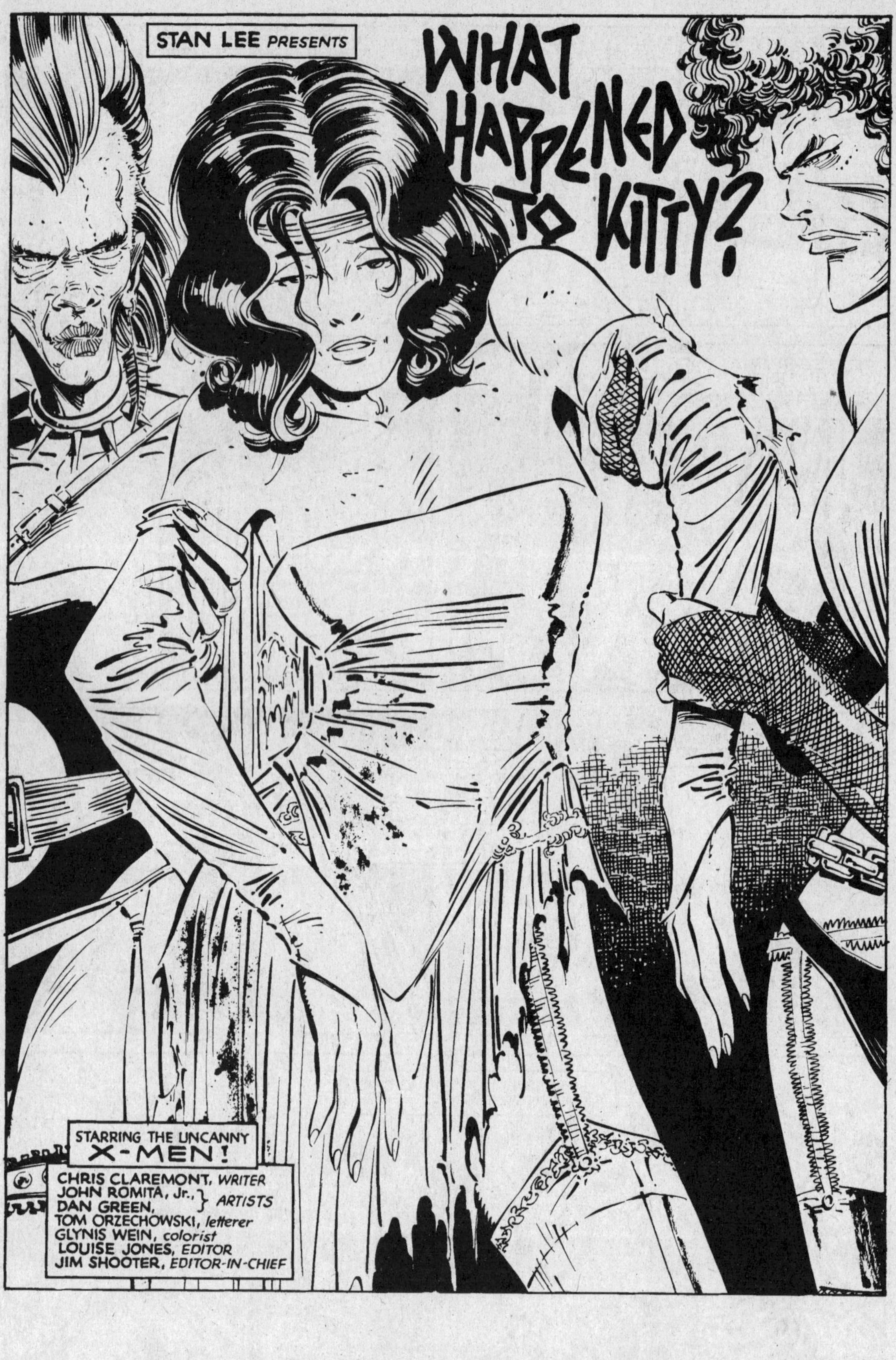
STAN LEE PRESENTS
WHAT HAPPENED TO KITTY?
STARRING THE UNCANNY X-MEN!
CHRIS CLAREMONT, WRITER
JOHN ROMITA, Jr., DAN GREEN, ARTISTS
TOM ORZECHOWSKI, letterer
GLYNIS WEIN, colorist
LOUISE JONES, EDITOR
JIM SHOOTER, EDITOR-IN-CHIEF

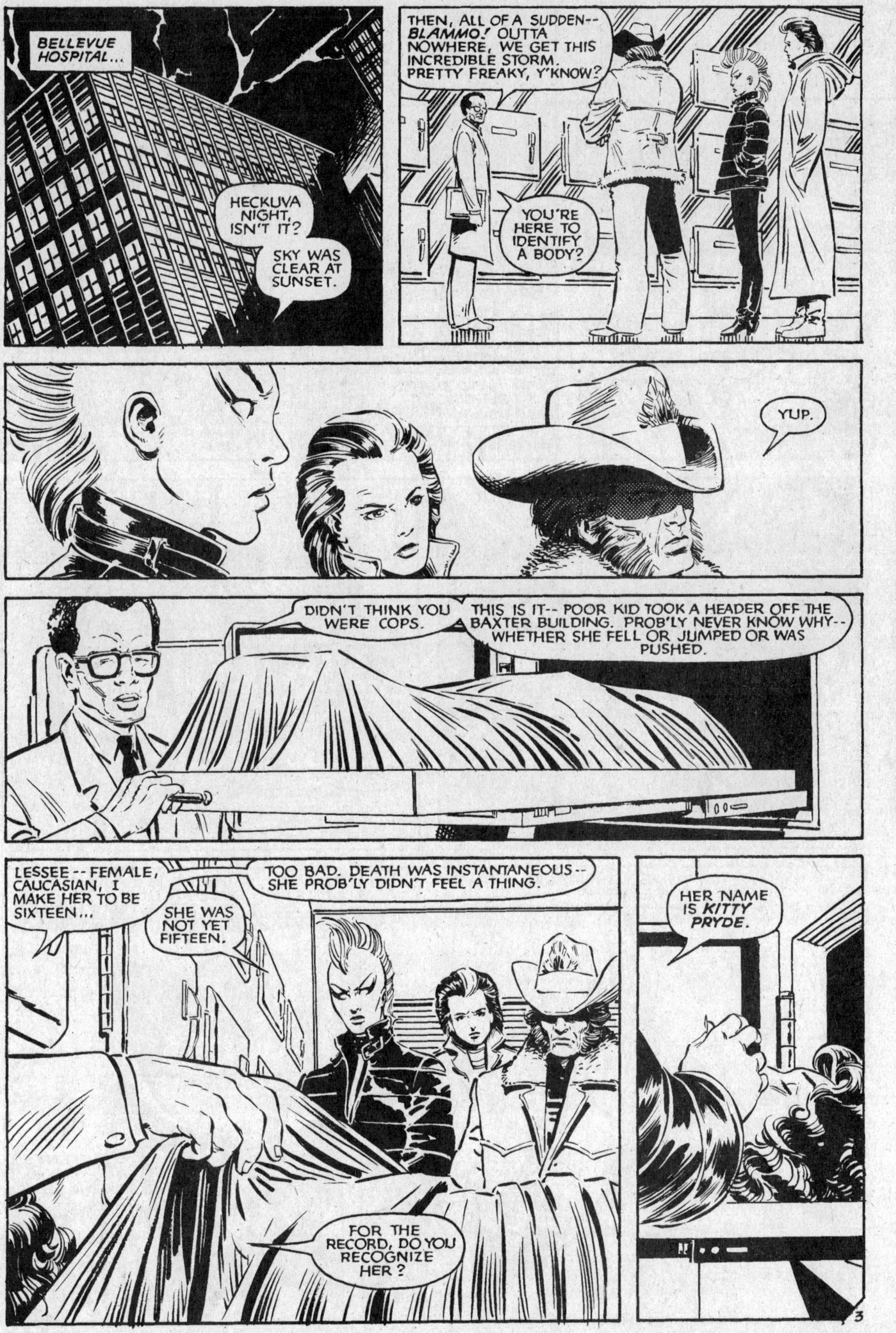
BELLEVUE HOSPITAL...
HECKUVA NIGHT, ISN'T IT?
SKY WAS CLEAR AT SUNSET.
THEN, ALL OF A SUDDEN-- BLAMMO! OUTTA NOWHERE, WE GET THIS INCREDIBLE STORM. PRETTY FREAKY, Y'KNOW?
YOU'RE HERE TO IDENTIFY A BODY?
YUP.
DIDN'T THINK YOU WERE COPS.
THIS IS IT-- POOR KID TOOK A HEADER OFF THE BAXTER BUILDING. PROB'LY NEVER KNOW WHY-- WHETHER SHE FELL OR JUMPED OR WAS PUSHED.
LESSEE-- FEMALE, CAUCASIAN, I MAKE HER TO BE SIXTEEN...
SHE WAS NOT YET FIFTEEN.
TOO BAD. DEATH WAS INSTANTANEOUS-- SHE PROB'LY DIDN'T FEEL A THING.
FOR THE RECORD, DO YOU RECOGNIZE HER?
HER NAME IS KITTY PRYDE.
3

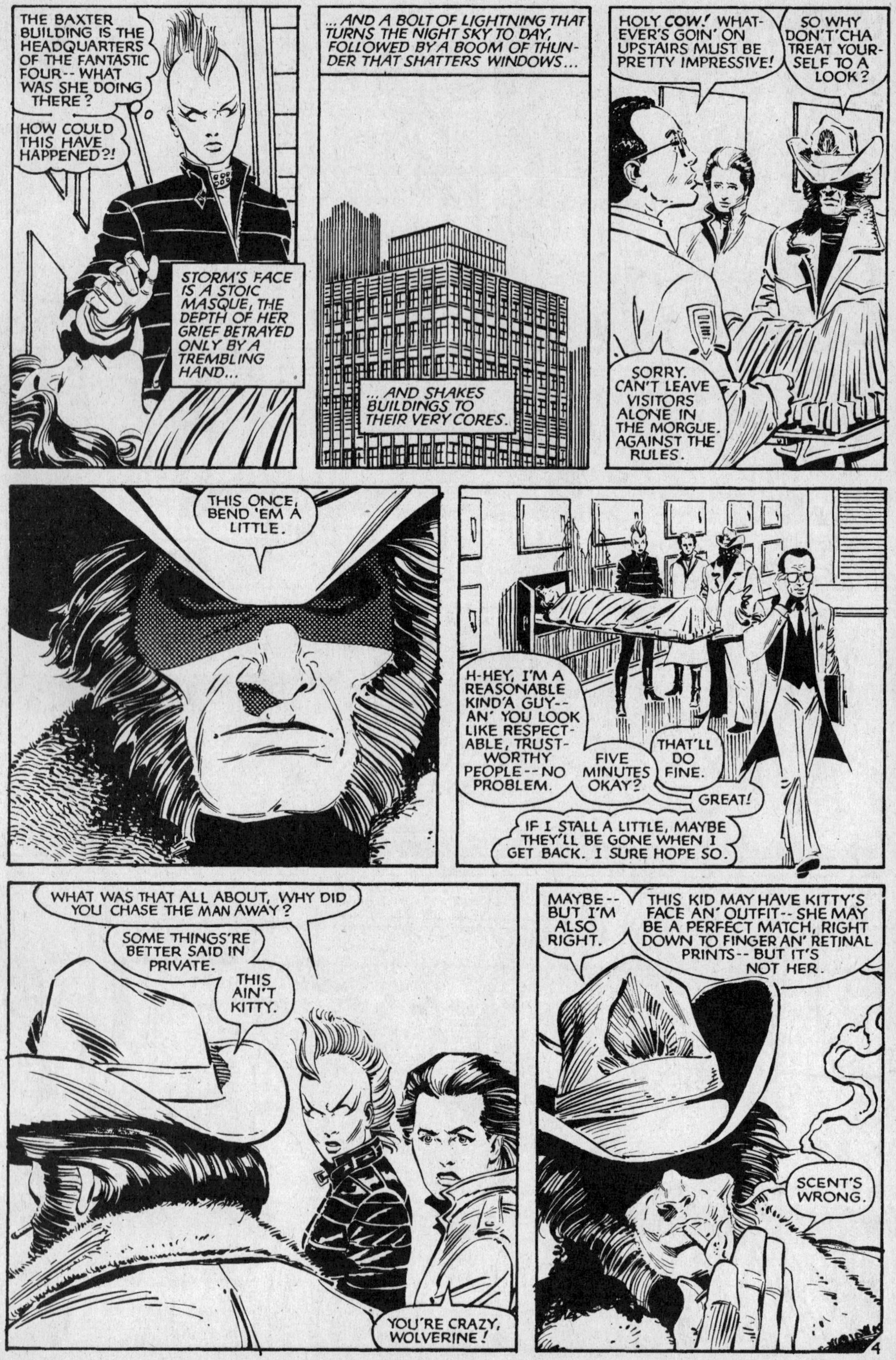
THE BAXTER BUILDING IS THE HEADQUARTERS OF THE FANTASTIC FOUR-- WHAT WAS SHE DOING THERE?
HOW COULD THIS HAVE HAPPENED?!
STORM'S FACE IS A STOIC MASQUE, THE DEPTH OF HER GRIEF BETRAYED ONLY BY A TREMBLING HAND...
...AND A BOLT OF LIGHTNING THAT TURNS THE NIGHT SKY TO DAY, FOLLOWED BY A BOOM OF THUNDER THAT SHATTERS WINDOWS...
...AND SHAKES BUILDINGS TO THEIR VERY CORES.
HOLY COW! WHAT-EVER'S GOIN' ON UPSTAIRS MUST BE PRETTY IMPRESSIVE!
SO WHY DON'T'CHA TREAT YOUR-SELF TO A LOOK?
SORRY. CAN'T LEAVE VISITORS ALONE IN THE MORGUE. AGAINST THE RULES.
THIS ONCE, BEND 'EM A LITTLE.
H-HEY, I'M A REASONABLE KIND'A GUY-- AN' YOU LOOK LIKE RESPECT-ABLE, TRUST-WORTHY PEOPLE--NO PROBLEM.
FIVE MINUTES OKAY?
THAT'LL DO FINE.
GREAT!
IF I STALL A LITTLE, MAYBE THEY'LL BE GONE WHEN I GET BACK. I SURE HOPE SO.
WHAT WAS THAT ALL ABOUT, WHY DID YOU CHASE THE MAN AWAY?
SOME THINGS'RE BETTER SAID IN PRIVATE.
THIS AIN'T KITTY.
YOU'RE CRAZY, WOLVERINE!
MAYBE-- BUT I'M ALSO RIGHT.
THIS KID MAY HAVE KITTY'S FACE AN' OUTFIT-- SHE MAY BE A PERFECT MATCH, RIGHT DOWN TO FINGER AN' RETINAL PRINTS-- BUT IT'S NOT HER.
SCENT'S WRONG.

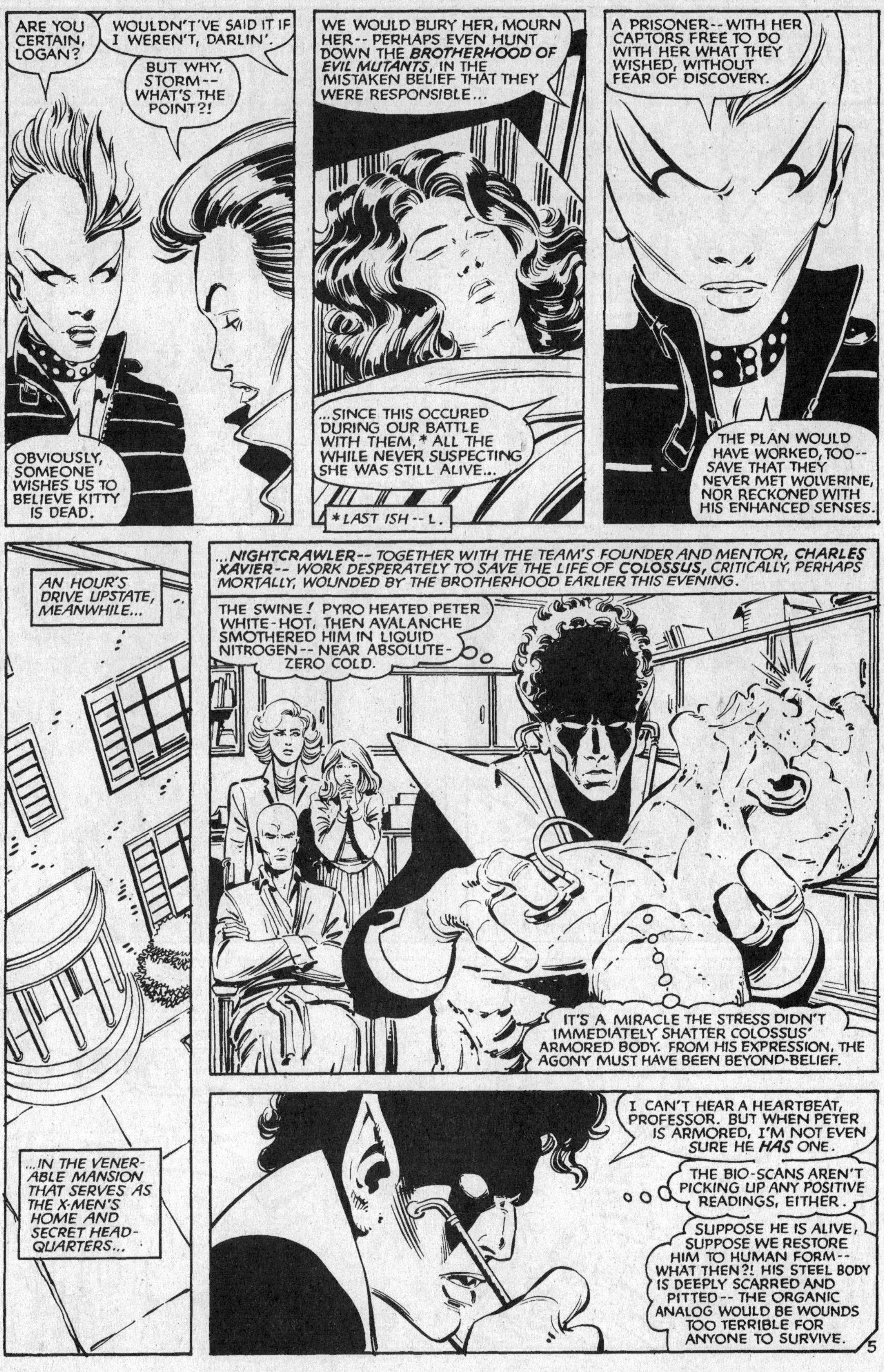
ARE YOU CERTAIN, LOGAN?
WOULDN'T'VE SAID IT IF I WEREN'T, DARLIN'.
BUT WHY, STORM-- WHAT'S THE POINT?!
OBVIOUSLY, SOMEONE WISHES US TO BELIEVE KITTY IS DEAD.
WE WOULD BURY HER, MOURN HER-- PERHAPS EVEN HUNT DOWN THE BROTHERHOOD OF EVIL MUTANTS, IN THE MISTAKEN BELIEF THAT THEY WERE RESPONSIBLE...
...SINCE THIS OCCURED DURING OUR BATTLE WITH THEM,* ALL THE WHILE NEVER SUSPECTING SHE WAS STILL ALIVE...
*LAST ISH -- L.
A PRISONER-- WITH HER CAPTORS FREE TO DO WITH HER WHAT THEY WISHED, WITHOUT FEAR OF DISCOVERY.
THE PLAN WOULD HAVE WORKED, TOO-- SAVE THAT THEY NEVER MET WOLVERINE, NOR RECKONED WITH HIS ENHANCED SENSES.
AN HOUR'S DRIVE UPSTATE, MEANWHILE...
...IN THE VENERABLE MANSION THAT SERVES AS THE X-MEN'S HOME AND SECRET HEADQUARTERS...
...NIGHTCRAWLER-- TOGETHER WITH THE TEAM'S FOUNDER AND MENTOR, CHARLES XAVIER-- WORK DESPERATELY TO SAVE THE LIFE OF COLOSSUS, CRITICALLY, PERHAPS MORTALLY, WOUNDED BY THE BROTHERHOOD EARLIER THIS EVENING.
THE SWINE! PYRO HEATED PETER WHITE-HOT, THEN AVALANCHE SMOTHERED HIM IN LIQUID NITROGEN-- NEAR ABSOLUTE-ZERO COLD.
IT'S A MIRACLE THE STRESS DIDN'T IMMEDIATELY SHATTER COLOSSUS' ARMORED BODY. FROM HIS EXPRESSION, THE AGONY MUST HAVE BEEN BEYOND-BELIEF.
I CAN'T HEAR A HEARTBEAT, PROFESSOR. BUT WHEN PETER IS ARMORED, I'M NOT EVEN SURE HE HAS ONE.
THE BIO-SCANS AREN'T PICKING UP ANY POSITIVE READINGS, EITHER.
SUPPOSE HE IS ALIVE, SUPPOSE WE RESTORE HIM TO HUMAN FORM-- WHAT THEN?! HIS STEEL BODY IS DEEPLY SCARRED AND PITTED-- THE ORGANIC ANALOG WOULD BE WOUNDS TOO TERRIBLE FOR ANYONE TO SURVIVE.

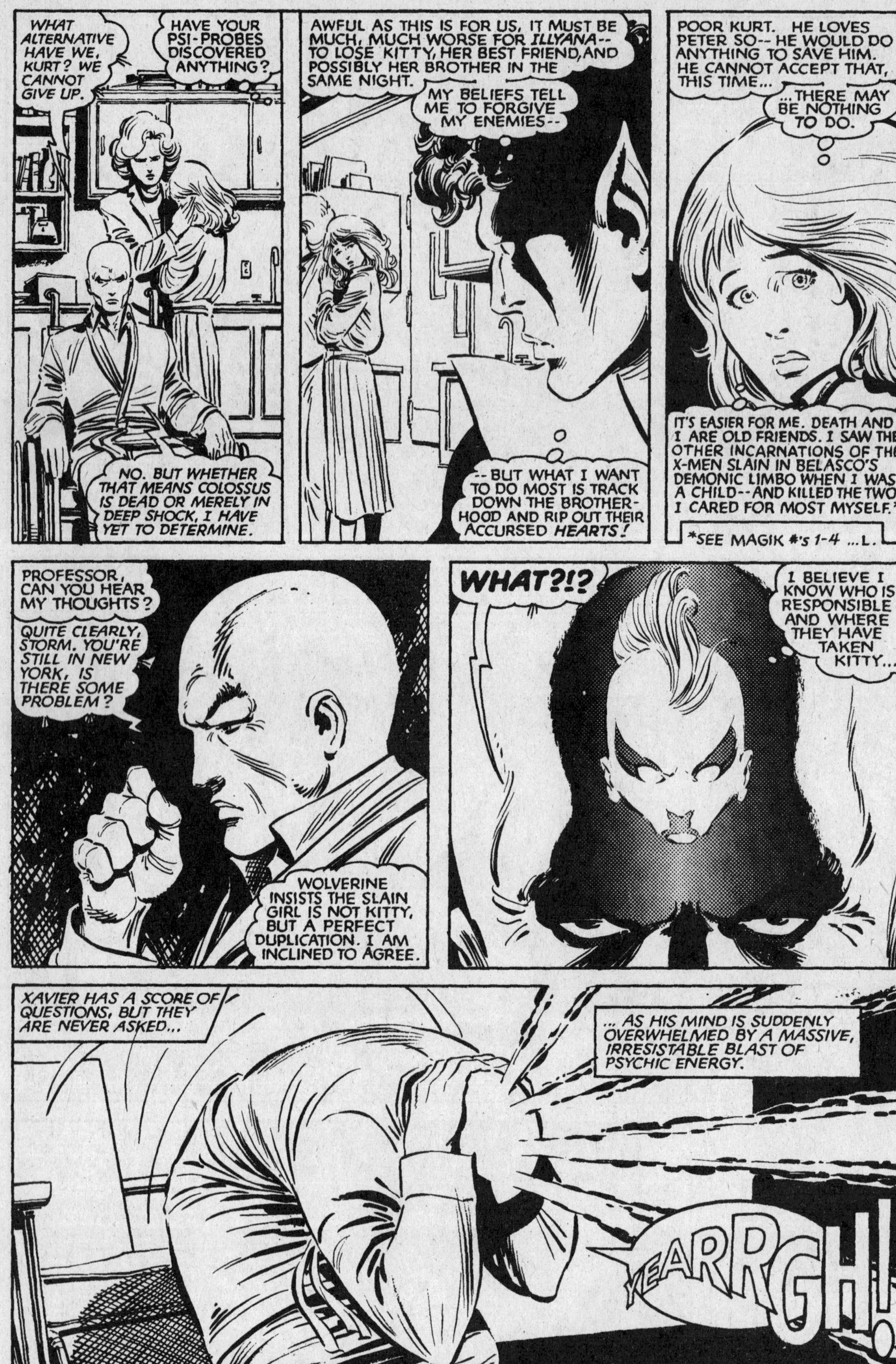
WHAT ALTERNATIVE HAVE WE, KURT? WE CANNOT GIVE UP.
HAVE YOUR PSI-PROBES DISCOVERED ANYTHING?
NO. BUT WHETHER THAT MEANS COLOSSUS IS DEAD OR MERELY IN DEEP SHOCK, I HAVE YET TO DETERMINE.
AWFUL AS THIS IS FOR US, IT MUST BE MUCH, MUCH WORSE FOR ILLYANA-- TO LOSE KITTY, HER BEST FRIEND, AND POSSIBLY HER BROTHER IN THE SAME NIGHT.
MY BELIEFS TELL ME TO FORGIVE MY ENEMIES--
--BUT WHAT I WANT TO DO MOST IS TRACK DOWN THE BROTHERHOOD AND RIP OUT THEIR ACCURSED HEARTS!
POOR KURT. HE LOVES PETER SO-- HE WOULD DO ANYTHING TO SAVE HIM. HE CANNOT ACCEPT THAT, THIS TIME...
...THERE MAY BE NOTHING TO DO.
IT'S EASIER FOR ME. DEATH AND I ARE OLD FRIENDS. I SAW THE OTHER INCARNATIONS OF THE X-MEN SLAIN IN BELASCO'S DEMONIC LIMBO WHEN I WAS A CHILD--AND KILLED THE TWO I CARED FOR MOST MYSELF.*
*SEE MAGIK #'s 1-4 ...L.
PROFESSOR, CAN YOU HEAR MY THOUGHTS?
QUITE CLEARLY, STORM. YOU'RE STILL IN NEW YORK, IS THERE SOME PROBLEM?
WOLVERINE INSISTS THE SLAIN GIRL IS NOT KITTY, BUT A PERFECT DUPLICATION. I AM INCLINED TO AGREE.
WHAT?!?
I BELIEVE I KNOW WHO IS RESPONSIBLE AND WHERE THEY HAVE TAKEN KITTY...
XAVIER HAS A SCORE OF QUESTIONS, BUT THEY ARE NEVER ASKED...
... AS HIS MIND IS SUDDENLY OVERWHELMED BY A MASSIVE, IRRESISTABLE BLAST OF PSYCHIC ENERGY.
YEARRRGH!
6

THE SHOCK IS SO GREAT, HE LOSES CONTROL OF HIS OWN TELEPATHIC POWERS, SPRAYING THE INFIRMARY WITH PSI-BOLTS CAPABLE OF INSTANTLY FRYING THE BRAIN OF WHOMEVER THEY STRIKE.

AS NIGHTCRAWLER'S LADY FRIEND, AMANDA SEFTON, PUSHES ILLYANA TO THE FLOOR...

...THE GERMAN-BORN MUTANT RESPONDS BY...

BAMF

...TELEPORTING TO HIS TEACHERS' SIDE.

HERR PROFESSOR, GET AHOLD OF YOURSELF, BEFORE YOU KILL US ALL!

PERHAPS I SHOULD SEDATE HIM-- OR WILL THAT ONLY MAKE MATTERS WORSE?

AAAHHHH-- MY HEAD... NEVER IMAGINED SUCH PAIN...

SCANNING WAVE... OF EXTRA-TERRESTRIAL ORIGIN-- ENCOUNTERED IT BEFORE. UNABLE TO PINPOINT ITS SOURCE-- FOCUS IS ON ME-- DON'T KNOW WHY. WON'T RESPOND TO... MY ATTEMPTS TO MAKE CONTACT.

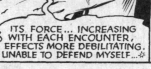

ITS FORCE... INCREASING WITH EACH ENCOUNTER, EFFECTS MORE DEBILITATING. UNABLE TO DEFEND MYSELF...✷

PROFESSOR? PROFESSOR?!!

AMANDA, HELP ME GET HIM INTO A LIFE SUPPORT CELL!

I'VE GOT TO WARN STORM, THROUGH OUR RADIO COMLINK-- BUT OF WHAT?! IS THIS ANOTHER ATTACK, BY SOME NEW FOE?!

WHAT IS HAPPENING, WHAT DOES THIS MEAN?!!

ELSEWHERE...

...THE BRIDE-TO-BE ENJOYS THE HAPPIEST EVENING OF HER LIFE...

...HER FELLOW MORLOCKS AS HAPPY TO WELCOME HER AS SHE IS TO BE WELCOMED.

7

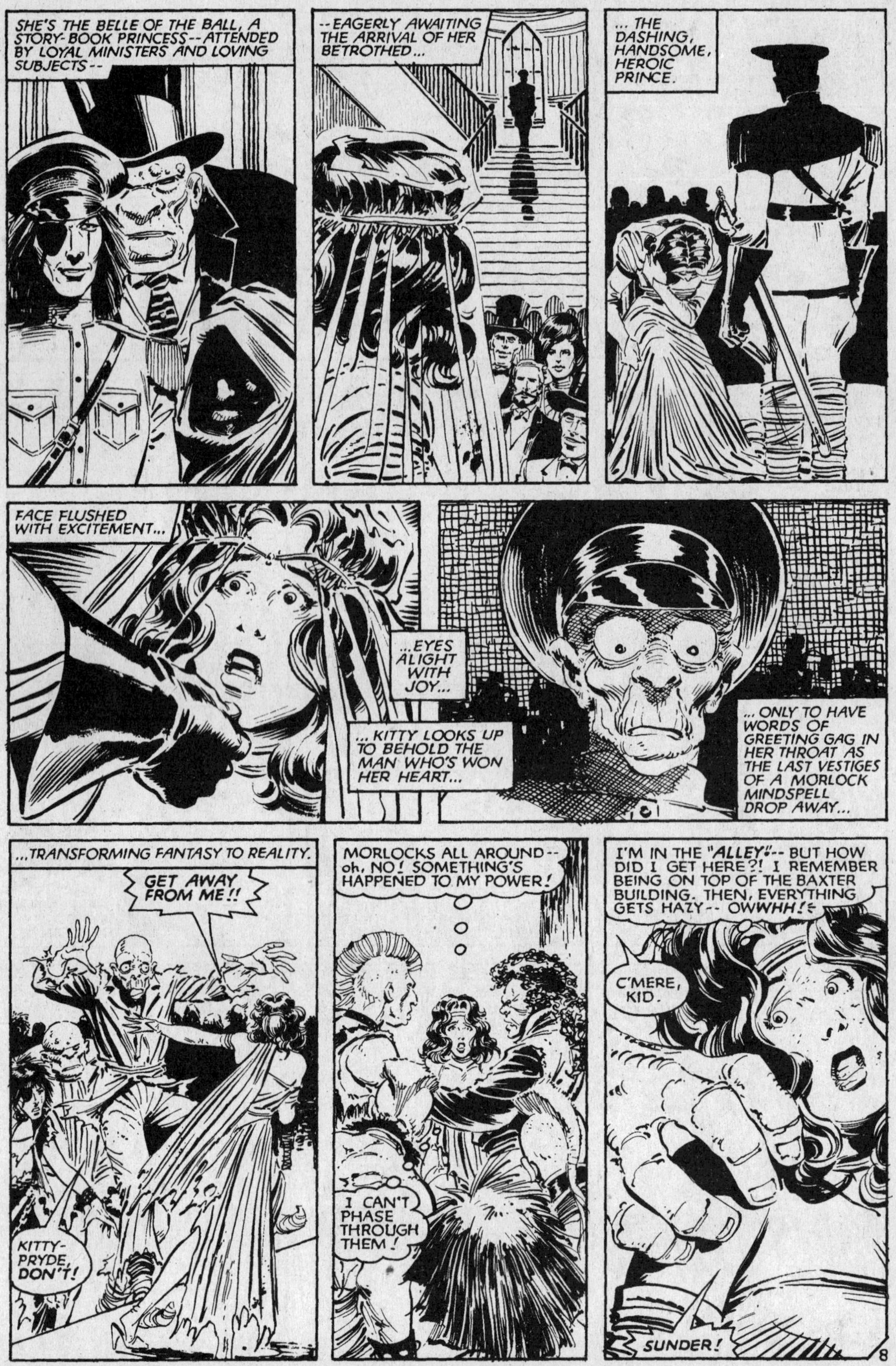

SHE'S THE BELLE OF THE BALL, A STORY-BOOK PRINCESS--ATTENDED BY LOYAL MINISTERS AND LOVING SUBJECTS--
--EAGERLY AWAITING THE ARRIVAL OF HER BETROTHED...
...THE DASHING, HANDSOME, HEROIC PRINCE.
FACE FLUSHED WITH EXCITEMENT...
...EYES ALIGHT WITH JOY...
...KITTY LOOKS UP TO BEHOLD THE MAN WHO'S WON HER HEART...
...ONLY TO HAVE WORDS OF GREETING GAG IN HER THROAT AS THE LAST VESTIGES OF A MORLOCK MINDSPELL DROP AWAY...
...TRANSFORMING FANTASY TO REALITY.
GET AWAY FROM ME!!
KITTY-PRYDE, DON'T!
MORLOCKS ALL AROUND-- oh, NO! SOMETHING'S HAPPENED TO MY POWER!
I CAN'T PHASE THROUGH THEM!
I'M IN THE "ALLEY"-- BUT HOW DID I GET HERE?! I REMEMBER BEING ON TOP OF THE BAXTER BUILDING. THEN, EVERYTHING GETS HAZY-- OWWHH!
C'MERE, KID.
SUNDER!

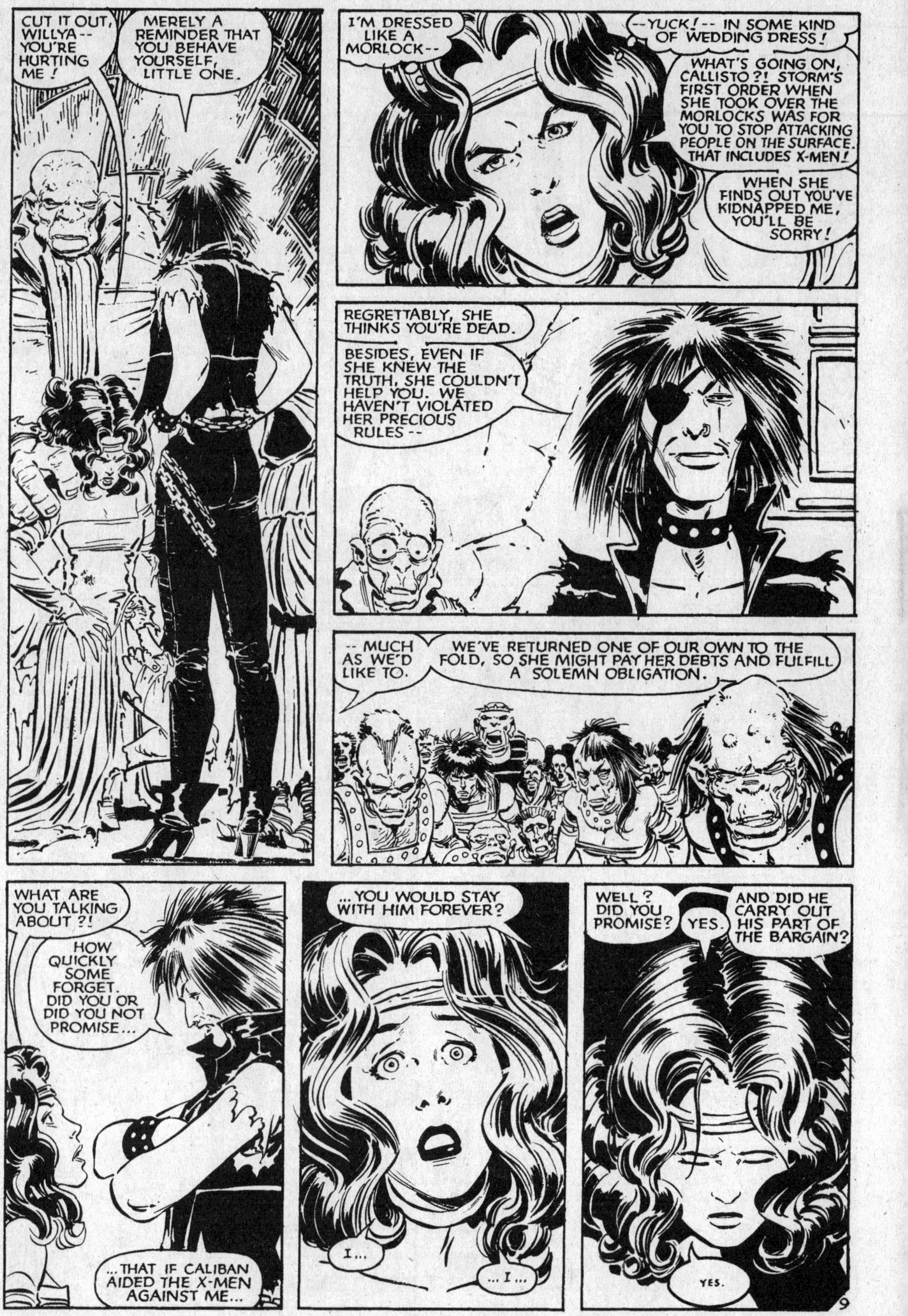
CUT IT OUT, WILLYA-- YOU'RE HURTING ME!
MERELY A REMINDER THAT YOU BEHAVE YOURSELF, LITTLE ONE.
I'M DRESSED LIKE A MORLOCK--
--YUCK!-- IN SOME KIND OF WEDDING DRESS!
WHAT'S GOING ON, CALLISTO?! STORM'S FIRST ORDER WHEN SHE TOOK OVER THE MORLOCKS WAS FOR YOU TO STOP ATTACKING PEOPLE ON THE SURFACE. THAT INCLUDES X-MEN!
WHEN SHE FINDS OUT YOU'VE KIDNAPPED ME, YOU'LL BE SORRY!
REGRETTABLY, SHE THINKS YOU'RE DEAD.
BESIDES, EVEN IF SHE KNEW THE TRUTH, SHE COULDN'T HELP YOU. WE HAVEN'T VIOLATED HER PRECIOUS RULES--
-- MUCH AS WE'D LIKE TO.
WE'VE RETURNED ONE OF OUR OWN TO THE FOLD, SO SHE MIGHT PAY HER DEBTS AND FULFILL A SOLEMN OBLIGATION.
WHAT ARE YOU TALKING ABOUT?!
HOW QUICKLY SOME FORGET. DID YOU OR DID YOU NOT PROMISE...
...THAT IF CALIBAN AIDED THE X-MEN AGAINST ME...
...YOU WOULD STAY WITH HIM FOREVER?
I...
...I...
WELL? DID YOU PROMISE?
YES.
AND DID HE CARRY OUT HIS PART OF THE BARGAIN?
YES.

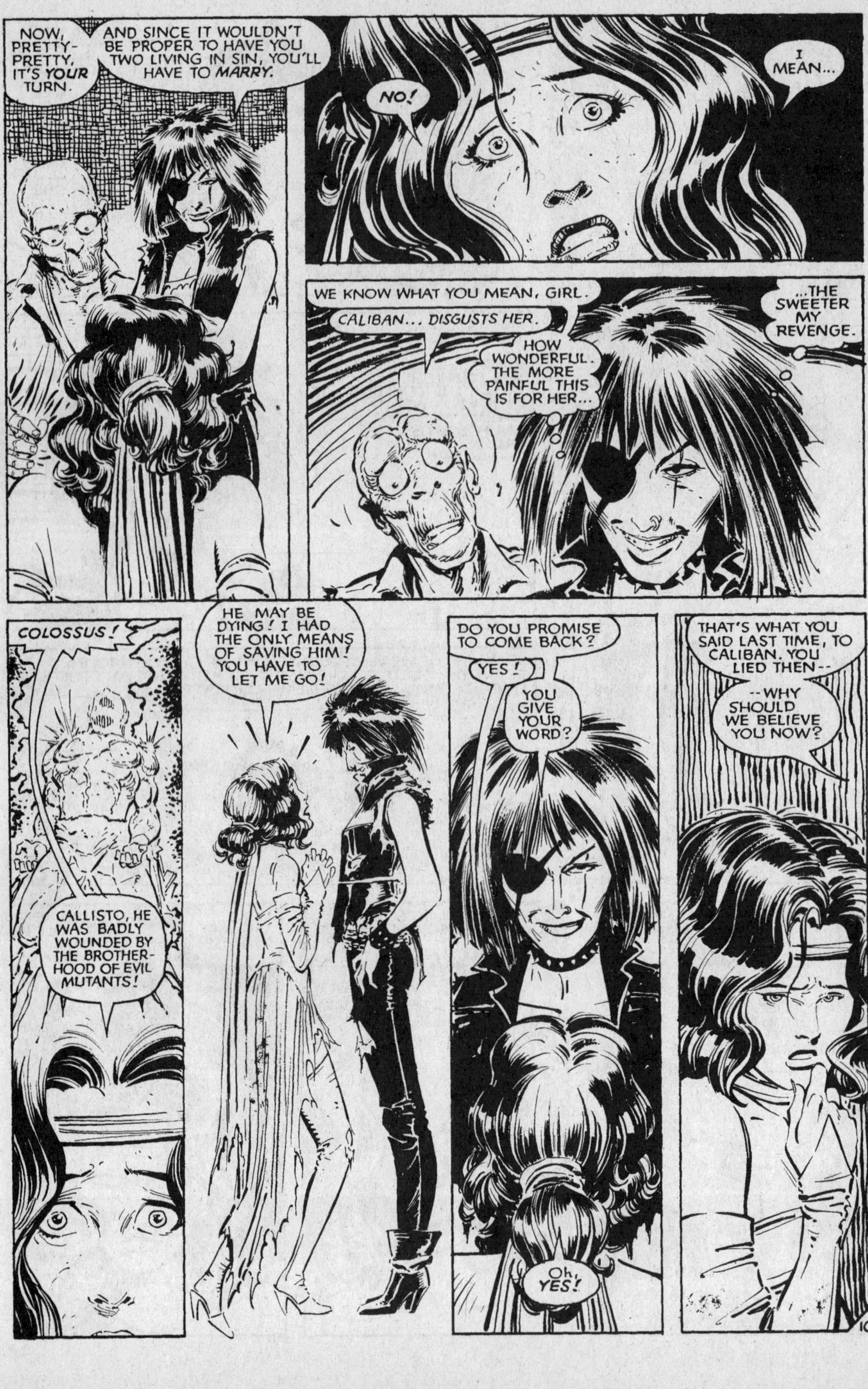
NOW, PRETTY-PRETTY, IT'S YOUR TURN.
AND SINCE IT WOULDN'T BE PROPER TO HAVE YOU TWO LIVING IN SIN, YOU'LL HAVE TO MARRY.
NO!
I MEAN...
WE KNOW WHAT YOU MEAN, GIRL.
CALIBAN... DISGUSTS HER.
HOW WONDERFUL. THE MORE PAINFUL THIS IS FOR HER...
...THE SWEETER MY REVENGE.
COLOSSUS!
CALLISTO, HE WAS BADLY WOUNDED BY THE BROTHER-HOOD OF EVIL MUTANTS!
HE MAY BE DYING! I HAD THE ONLY MEANS OF SAVING HIM! YOU HAVE TO LET ME GO!
DO YOU PROMISE TO COME BACK?
YES!
YOU GIVE YOUR WORD?
Oh, YES!
THAT'S WHAT YOU SAID LAST TIME, TO CALIBAN. YOU LIED THEN--
--WHY SHOULD WE BELIEVE YOU NOW?

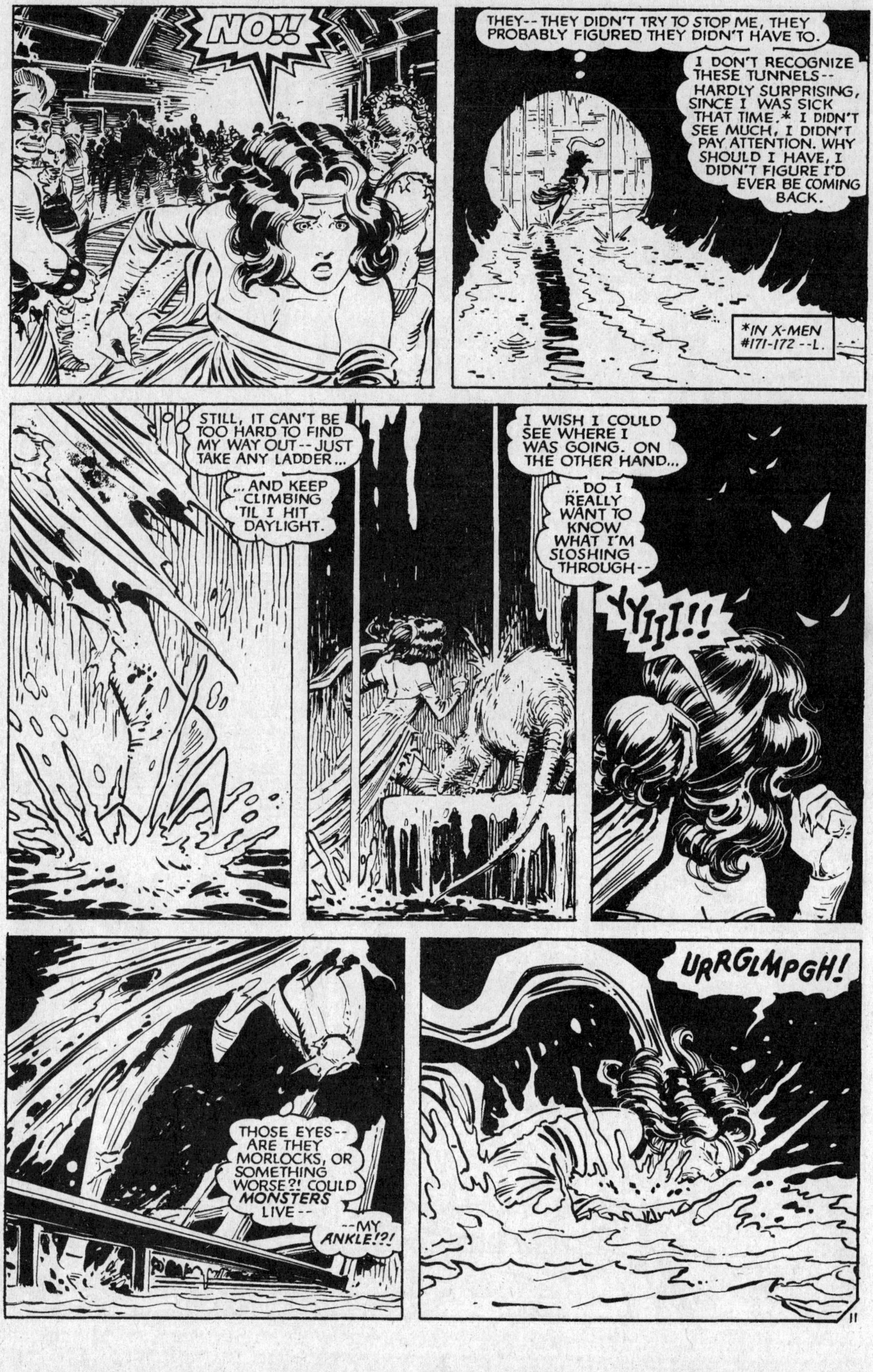
NO!!
THEY-- THEY DIDN'T TRY TO STOP ME, THEY PROBABLY FIGURED THEY DIDN'T HAVE TO.
I DON'T RECOGNIZE THESE TUNNELS-- HARDLY SURPRISING, SINCE I WAS SICK THAT TIME.* I DIDN'T SEE MUCH, I DIDN'T PAY ATTENTION. WHY SHOULD I HAVE, I DIDN'T FIGURE I'D EVER BE COMING BACK.
*IN X-MEN #171-172 --L.
STILL, IT CAN'T BE TOO HARD TO FIND MY WAY OUT-- JUST TAKE ANY LADDER...
...AND KEEP CLIMBING 'TIL I HIT DAYLIGHT.
I WISH I COULD SEE WHERE I WAS GOING. ON THE OTHER HAND...
...DO I REALLY WANT TO KNOW WHAT I'M SLOSHING THROUGH--
YYIII!!
THOSE EYES-- ARE THEY MORLOCKS, OR SOMETHING WORSE?! COULD MONSTERS LIVE--
--MY ANKLE!?!
URRGLMPGH!
11

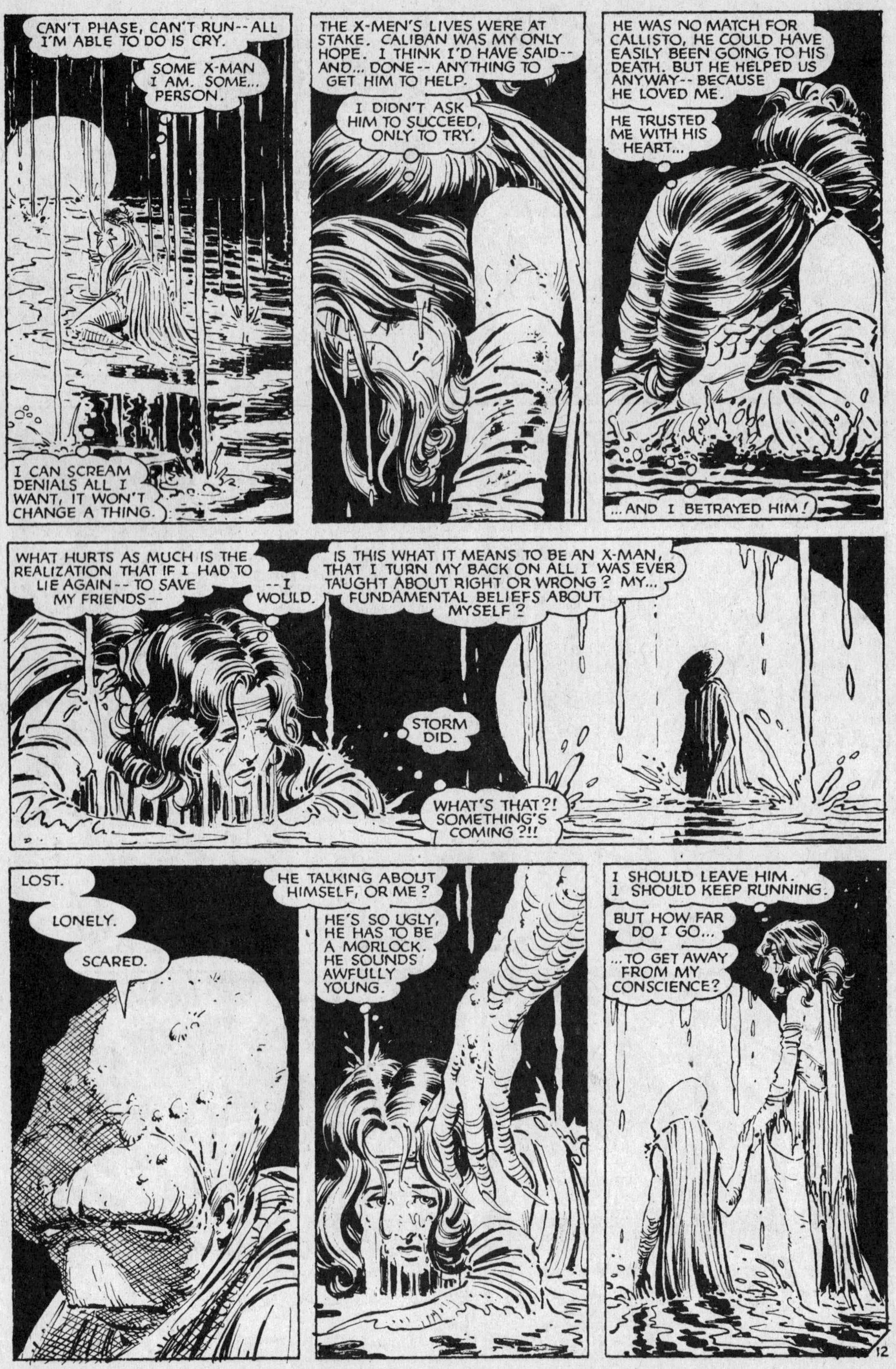

CAN'T PHASE, CAN'T RUN--ALL I'M ABLE TO DO IS CRY.
SOME X-MAN I AM. SOME... PERSON.
I CAN SCREAM DENIALS ALL I WANT, IT WON'T CHANGE A THING.
THE X-MEN'S LIVES WERE AT STAKE. CALIBAN WAS MY ONLY HOPE. I THINK I'D HAVE SAID--AND... DONE--ANYTHING TO GET HIM TO HELP.
I DIDN'T ASK HIM TO SUCCEED, ONLY TO TRY.
HE WAS NO MATCH FOR CALLISTO, HE COULD HAVE EASILY BEEN GOING TO HIS DEATH. BUT HE HELPED US ANYWAY--BECAUSE HE LOVED ME.
HE TRUSTED ME WITH HIS HEART...
...AND I BETRAYED HIM!
WHAT HURTS AS MUCH IS THE REALIZATION THAT IF I HAD TO LIE AGAIN--TO SAVE MY FRIENDS--
--I WOULD.
IS THIS WHAT IT MEANS TO BE AN X-MAN, THAT I TURN MY BACK ON ALL I WAS EVER TAUGHT ABOUT RIGHT OR WRONG? MY... FUNDAMENTAL BELIEFS ABOUT MYSELF?
STORM DID.
WHAT'S THAT?! SOMETHING'S COMING?!!
LOST.
LONELY.
SCARED.
HE TALKING ABOUT HIMSELF, OR ME?
HE'S SO UGLY, HE HAS TO BE A MORLOCK. HE SOUNDS AWFULLY YOUNG.
I SHOULD LEAVE HIM. I SHOULD KEEP RUNNING.
BUT HOW FAR DO I GO...
...TO GET AWAY FROM MY CONSCIENCE?
12

WELCOME... ...HOME. HOW NICE OF YOU TO BRING ONE OF OUR STRAYS WITH YOU.

I GAVE MY WORD, CALLISTO. I'LL KEEP IT.

I KNEW YOU WOULD.

BUT, PLEASE, IF IT'S WITHIN YOUR POWER TO SAVE COLOSSUS, DO SO. HE MEANS THE WORLD TO ME.

I BEG YOU, CALLISTO.

NO NEED FOR THAT, SWEET SISTER. YOU'RE ONE OF US...

...AND MORLOCKS LOOK AFTER THEIR OWN.

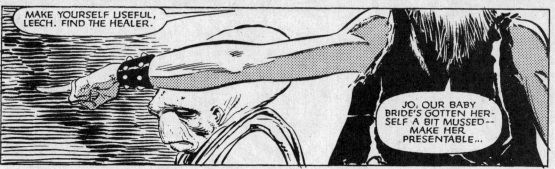

MAKE YOURSELF USEFUL, LEECH. FIND THE HEALER.

JO, OUR BABY BRIDE'S GOTTEN HER-SELF A BIT MUSSED-- MAKE HER PRESENTABLE...

"...THEN BRING HER TO MASQUE."

YOU BECOME MORLOCK, YOU GET NEW FACE-- IF YOU LIKE, WHOLE NEW BODY.

WHY?

WE OUTCASTS-- OUTLAWS! THIS SYMBOLIZES REJECTION BY YOU OF LIFE YOU LED, WORLD YOU KNEW...

...PEOPLE YOU LOVED.

WILL IT HURT?

DOES IT MATTER?

13

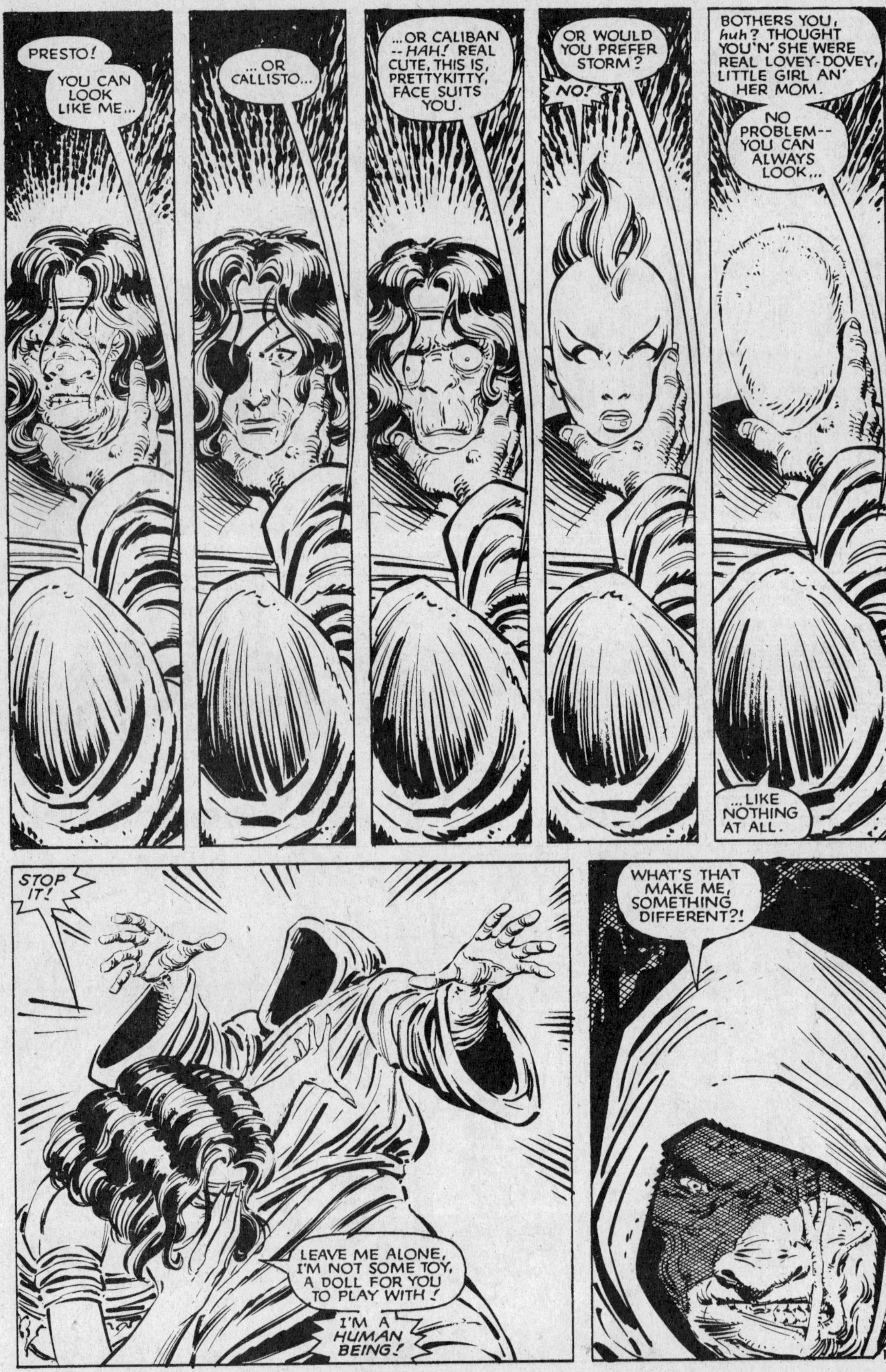
PRESTO!
YOU CAN LOOK LIKE ME...
...OR CALLISTO...
...OR CALIBAN --HAH! REAL CUTE, THIS IS, PRETTYKITTY, FACE SUITS YOU.
OR WOULD YOU PREFER STORM?
NO!
BOTHERS YOU, huh? THOUGHT YOU'N' SHE WERE REAL LOVEY-DOVEY, LITTLE GIRL AN' HER MOM.
NO PROBLEM-- YOU CAN ALWAYS LOOK...
...LIKE NOTHING AT ALL.
STOP IT!
LEAVE ME ALONE, I'M NOT SOME TOY, A DOLL FOR YOU TO PLAY WITH!
I'M A HUMAN BEING!
WHAT'S THAT MAKE ME, SOMETHING DIFFERENT?!

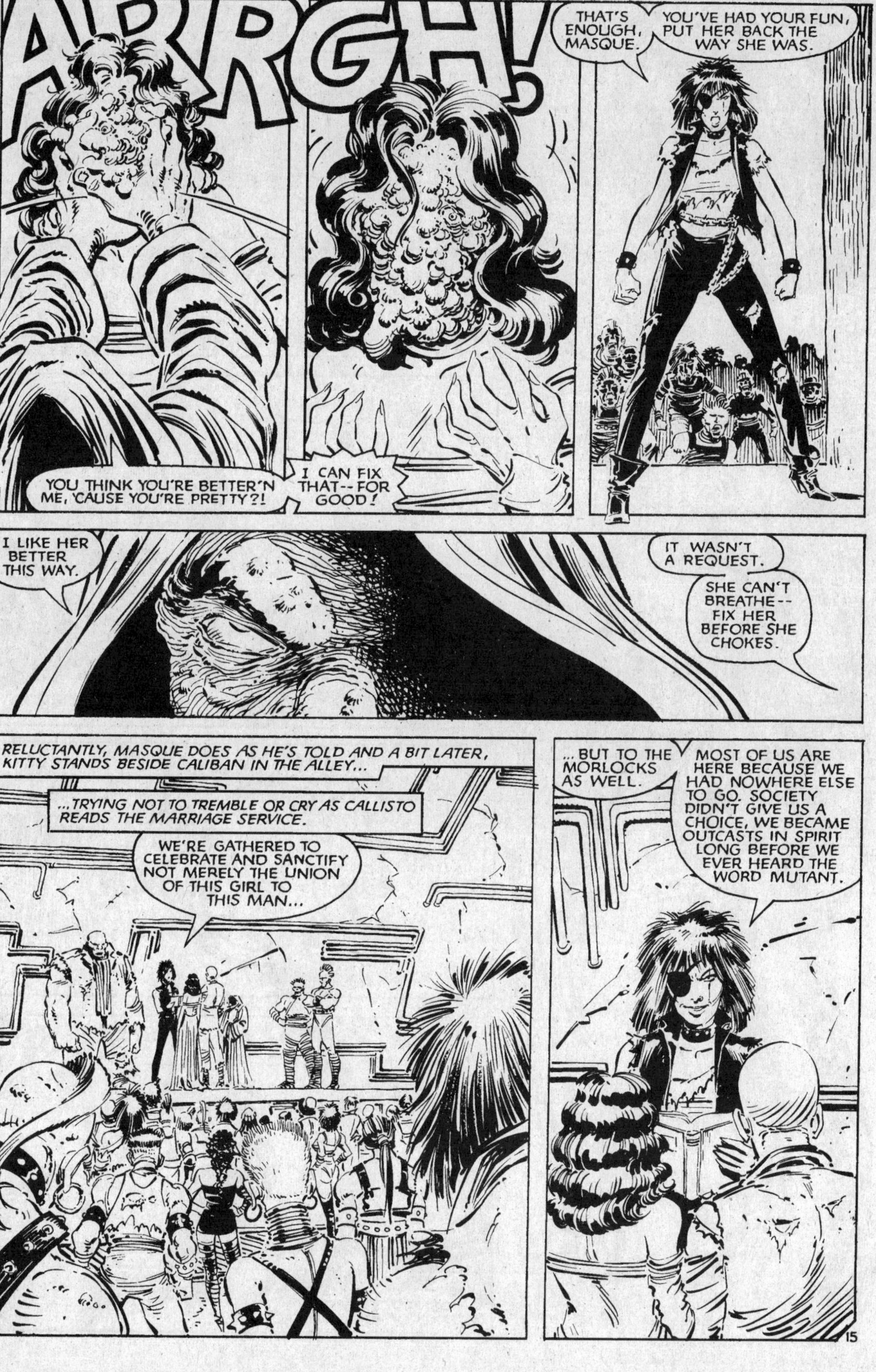
ARRGH!
YOU THINK YOU'RE BETTER'N ME, 'CAUSE YOU'RE PRETTY?!
I CAN FIX THAT-- FOR GOOD!
THAT'S ENOUGH, MASQUE.
YOU'VE HAD YOUR FUN, PUT HER BACK THE WAY SHE WAS.
I LIKE HER BETTER THIS WAY.
IT WASN'T A REQUEST.
SHE CAN'T BREATHE-- FIX HER BEFORE SHE CHOKES.
RELUCTANTLY, MASQUE DOES AS HE'S TOLD AND A BIT LATER, KITTY STANDS BESIDE CALIBAN IN THE ALLEY...
...TRYING NOT TO TREMBLE OR CRY AS CALLISTO READS THE MARRIAGE SERVICE.
WE'RE GATHERED TO CELEBRATE AND SANCTIFY NOT MERELY THE UNION OF THIS GIRL TO THIS MAN...
...BUT TO THE MORLOCKS AS WELL.
MOST OF US ARE HERE BECAUSE WE HAD NOWHERE ELSE TO GO. SOCIETY DIDN'T GIVE US A CHOICE, WE BECAME OUTCASTS IN SPIRIT LONG BEFORE WE EVER HEARD THE WORD MUTANT.

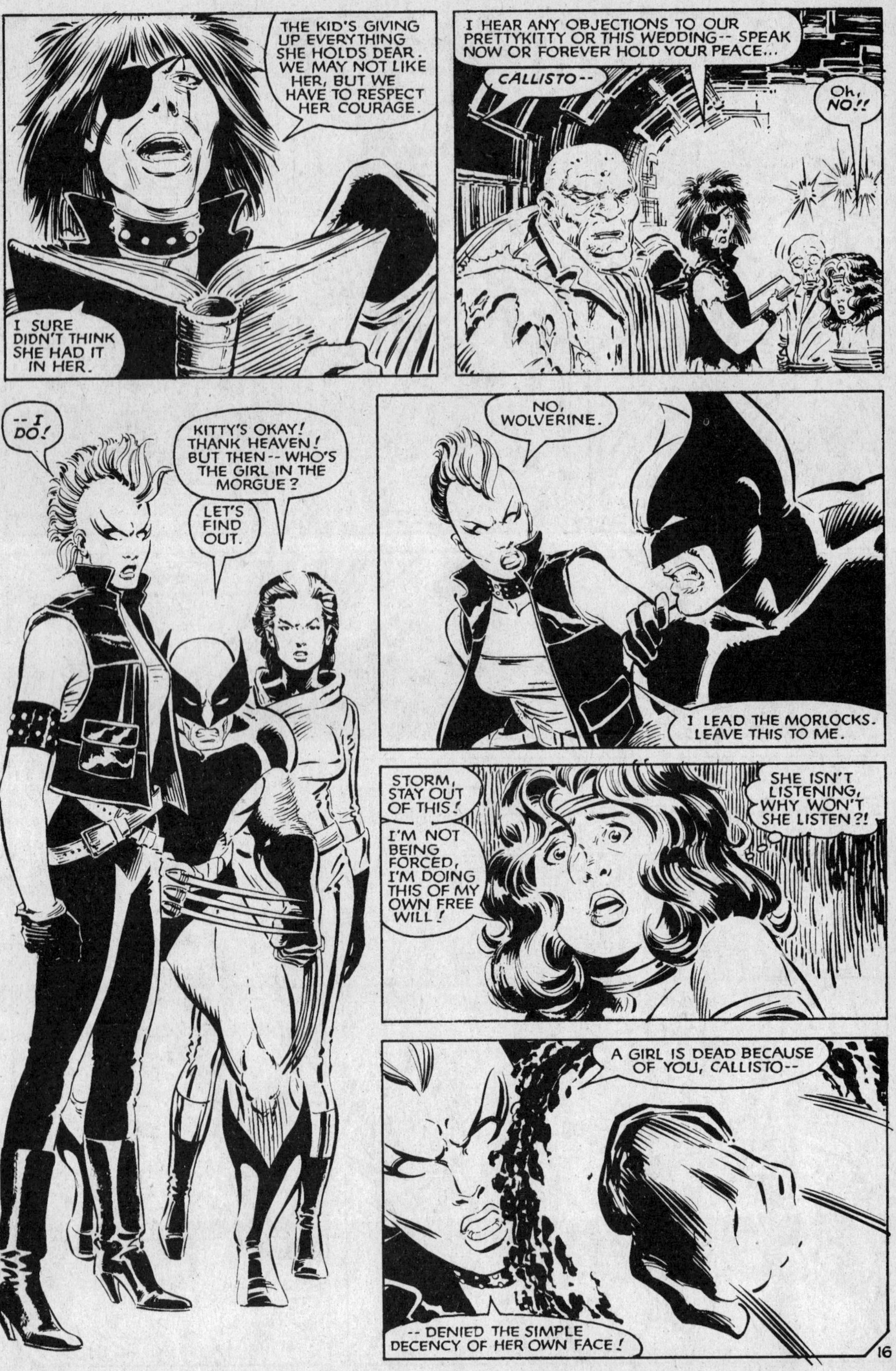

THE KID'S GIVING UP EVERYTHING SHE HOLDS DEAR. WE MAY NOT LIKE HER, BUT WE HAVE TO RESPECT HER COURAGE.
I SURE DIDN'T THINK SHE HAD IT IN HER.
I HEAR ANY OBJECTIONS TO OUR PRETTYKITTY OR THIS WEDDING-- SPEAK NOW OR FOREVER HOLD YOUR PEACE...
CALLISTO--
Oh, NO!!
--I DO!
KITTY'S OKAY! THANK HEAVEN! BUT THEN--WHO'S THE GIRL IN THE MORGUE?
LET'S FIND OUT.
NO, WOLVERINE.
I LEAD THE MORLOCKS. LEAVE THIS TO ME.
STORM, STAY OUT OF THIS!
I'M NOT BEING FORCED, I'M DOING THIS OF MY OWN FREE WILL!
SHE ISN'T LISTENING, WHY WON'T SHE LISTEN?!
A GIRL IS DEAD BECAUSE OF YOU, CALLISTO--
--DENIED THE SIMPLE DECENCY OF HER OWN FACE!

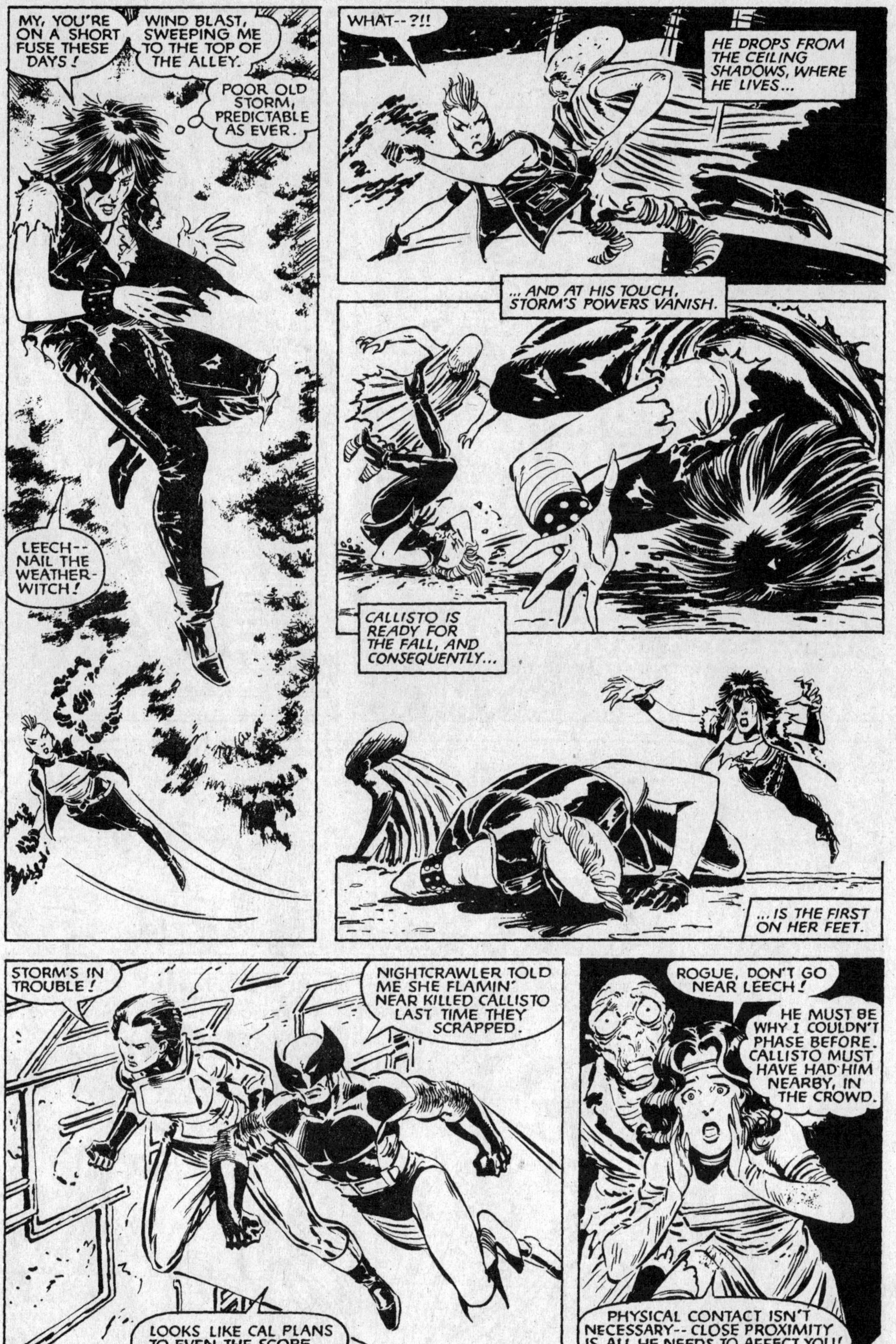
MY, YOU'RE ON A SHORT FUSE THESE DAYS!
WIND BLAST, SWEEPING ME TO THE TOP OF THE ALLEY.
POOR OLD STORM, PREDICTABLE AS EVER.
LEECH-- NAIL THE WEATHER-WITCH!
WHAT--?!!
HE DROPS FROM THE CEILING SHADOWS, WHERE HE LIVES...
...AND AT HIS TOUCH, STORM'S POWERS VANISH.
CALLISTO IS READY FOR THE FALL, AND CONSEQUENTLY...
...IS THE FIRST ON HER FEET.
STORM'S IN TROUBLE!
NIGHTCRAWLER TOLD ME SHE FLAMIN' NEAR KILLED CALLISTO LAST TIME THEY SCRAPPED.
LOOKS LIKE CAL PLANS TO EVEN THE SCORE.
ROGUE, DON'T GO NEAR LEECH!
HE MUST BE WHY I COULDN'T PHASE BEFORE. CALLISTO MUST HAVE HAD HIM NEARBY, IN THE CROWD.
PHYSICAL CONTACT ISN'T NECESSARY-- CLOSE PROXIMITY IS ALL HE NEEDS TO AFFECT YOU!

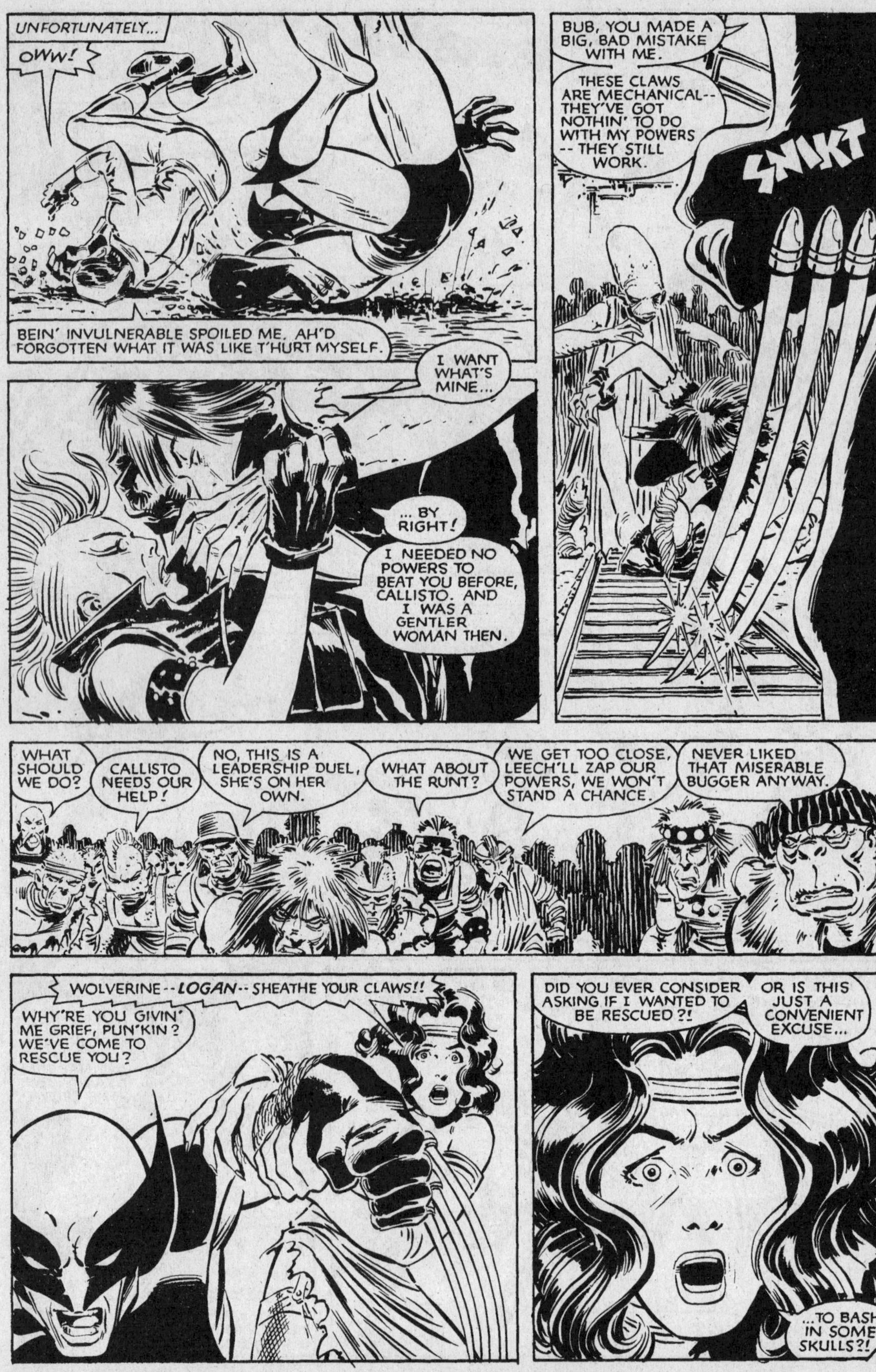
UNFORTUNATELY...
OWW!
BEIN' INVULNERABLE SPOILED ME. AH'D FORGOTTEN WHAT IT WAS LIKE T'HURT MYSELF.
BUB, YOU MADE A BIG, BAD MISTAKE WITH ME.
THESE CLAWS ARE MECHANICAL-- THEY'VE GOT NOTHIN' TO DO WITH MY POWERS -- THEY STILL WORK.
SNIKT
I WANT WHAT'S MINE...
... BY RIGHT!
I NEEDED NO POWERS TO BEAT YOU BEFORE, CALLISTO. AND I WAS A GENTLER WOMAN THEN.
WHAT SHOULD WE DO?
CALLISTO NEEDS OUR HELP!
NO, THIS IS A LEADERSHIP DUEL, SHE'S ON HER OWN.
WHAT ABOUT THE RUNT?
WE GET TOO CLOSE, LEECH'LL ZAP OUR POWERS, WE WON'T STAND A CHANCE.
NEVER LIKED THAT MISERABLE BUGGER ANYWAY.
WOLVERINE--LOGAN--SHEATHE YOUR CLAWS!!
WHY'RE YOU GIVIN' ME GRIEF, PUN'KIN? WE'VE COME TO RESCUE YOU?
DID YOU EVER CONSIDER ASKING IF I WANTED TO BE RESCUED?!
OR IS THIS JUST A CONVENIENT EXCUSE...
...TO BASH IN SOME SKULLS?!

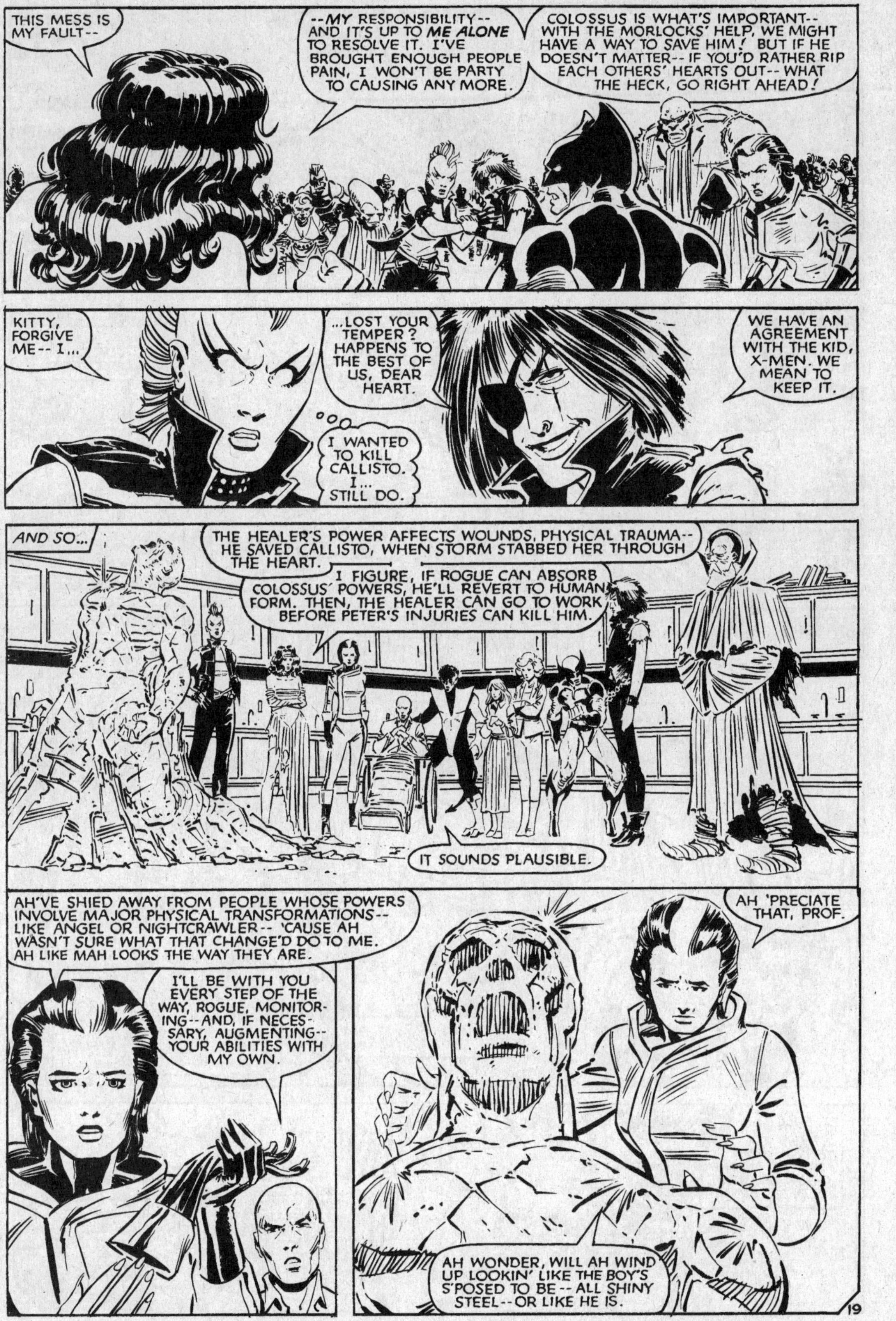
THIS MESS IS MY FAULT--
--MY RESPONSIBILITY-- AND IT'S UP TO ME ALONE TO RESOLVE IT. I'VE BROUGHT ENOUGH PEOPLE PAIN, I WON'T BE PARTY TO CAUSING ANY MORE.
COLOSSUS IS WHAT'S IMPORTANT-- WITH THE MORLOCKS' HELP, WE MIGHT HAVE A WAY TO SAVE HIM! BUT IF HE DOESN'T MATTER-- IF YOU'D RATHER RIP EACH OTHERS' HEARTS OUT-- WHAT THE HECK, GO RIGHT AHEAD!
KITTY, FORGIVE ME-- I...
...LOST YOUR TEMPER? HAPPENS TO THE BEST OF US, DEAR HEART.
I WANTED TO KILL CALLISTO. I... STILL DO.
WE HAVE AN AGREEMENT WITH THE KID, X-MEN. WE MEAN TO KEEP IT.
AND SO...
THE HEALER'S POWER AFFECTS WOUNDS, PHYSICAL TRAUMA-- HE SAVED CALLISTO, WHEN STORM STABBED HER THROUGH THE HEART.
I FIGURE, IF ROGUE CAN ABSORB COLOSSUS' POWERS, HE'LL REVERT TO HUMAN FORM. THEN, THE HEALER CAN GO TO WORK BEFORE PETER'S INJURIES CAN KILL HIM.
IT SOUNDS PLAUSIBLE.
AH'VE SHIED AWAY FROM PEOPLE WHOSE POWERS INVOLVE MAJOR PHYSICAL TRANSFORMATIONS-- LIKE ANGEL OR NIGHTCRAWLER-- 'CAUSE AH WASN'T SURE WHAT THAT CHANGE'D DO TO ME. AH LIKE MAH LOOKS THE WAY THEY ARE.
I'LL BE WITH YOU EVERY STEP OF THE WAY, ROGUE, MONITORING--AND, IF NECESSARY, AUGMENTING-- YOUR ABILITIES WITH MY OWN.
AH 'PRECIATE THAT, PROF.
AH WONDER, WILL AH WIND UP LOOKIN' LIKE THE BOY'S S'POSED TO BE -- ALL SHINY STEEL--OR LIKE HE IS.

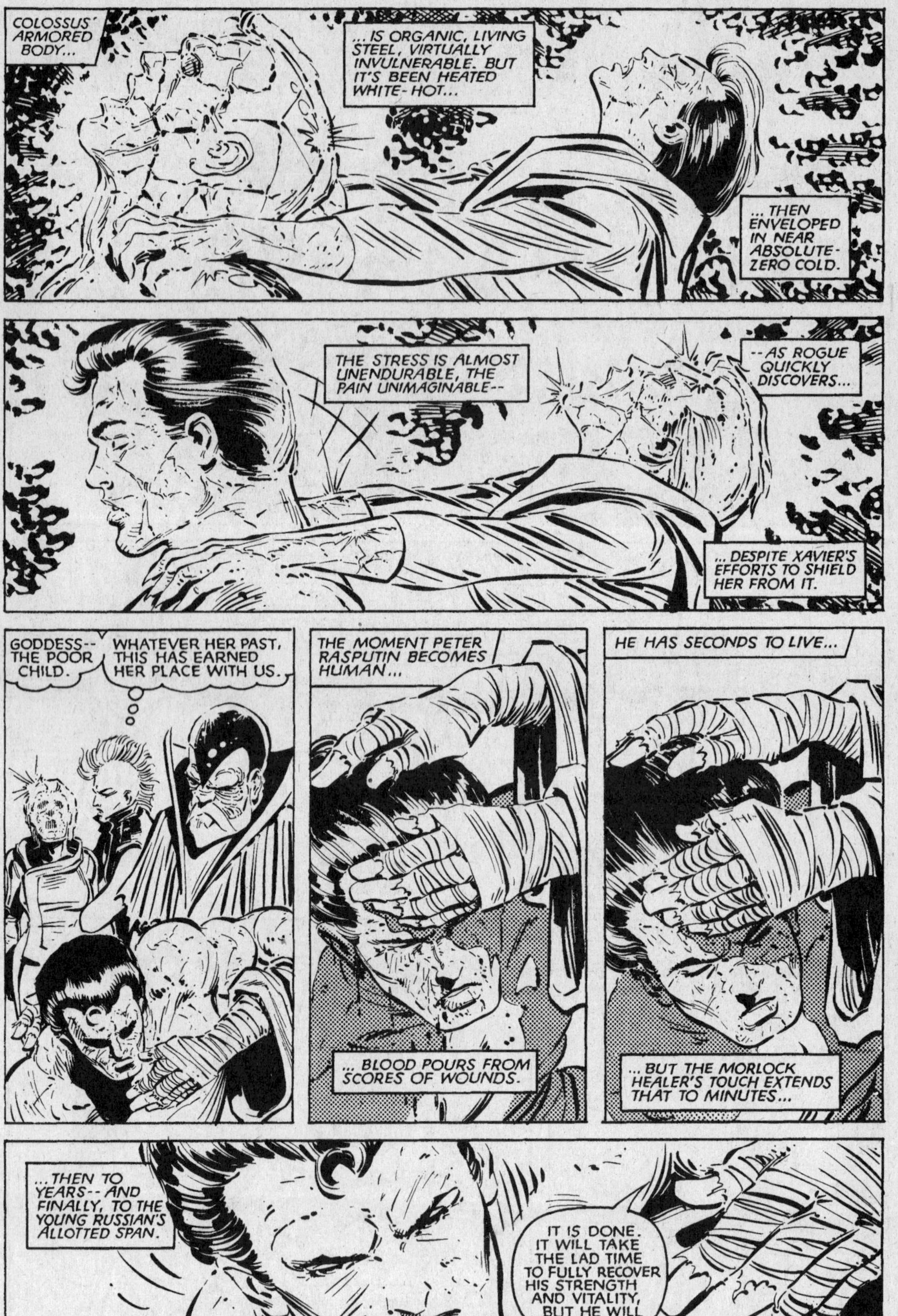
COLOSSUS' ARMORED BODY...
...IS ORGANIC, LIVING STEEL, VIRTUALLY INVULNERABLE. BUT IT'S BEEN HEATED WHITE-HOT...
...THEN ENVELOPED IN NEAR ABSOLUTE-ZERO COLD.
THE STRESS IS ALMOST UNENDURABLE, THE PAIN UNIMAGINABLE--
--AS ROGUE QUICKLY DISCOVERS...
...DESPITE XAVIER'S EFFORTS TO SHIELD HER FROM IT.
GODDESS-- THE POOR CHILD.
WHATEVER HER PAST, THIS HAS EARNED HER PLACE WITH US.
THE MOMENT PETER RASPUTIN BECOMES HUMAN...
...BLOOD POURS FROM SCORES OF WOUNDS.
HE HAS SECONDS TO LIVE...
...BUT THE MORLOCK HEALER'S TOUCH EXTENDS THAT TO MINUTES...
...THEN TO YEARS-- AND FINALLY, TO THE YOUNG RUSSIAN'S ALLOTTED SPAN.
IT IS DONE. IT WILL TAKE THE LAD TIME TO FULLY RECOVER HIS STRENGTH AND VITALITY, BUT HE WILL SURVIVE.

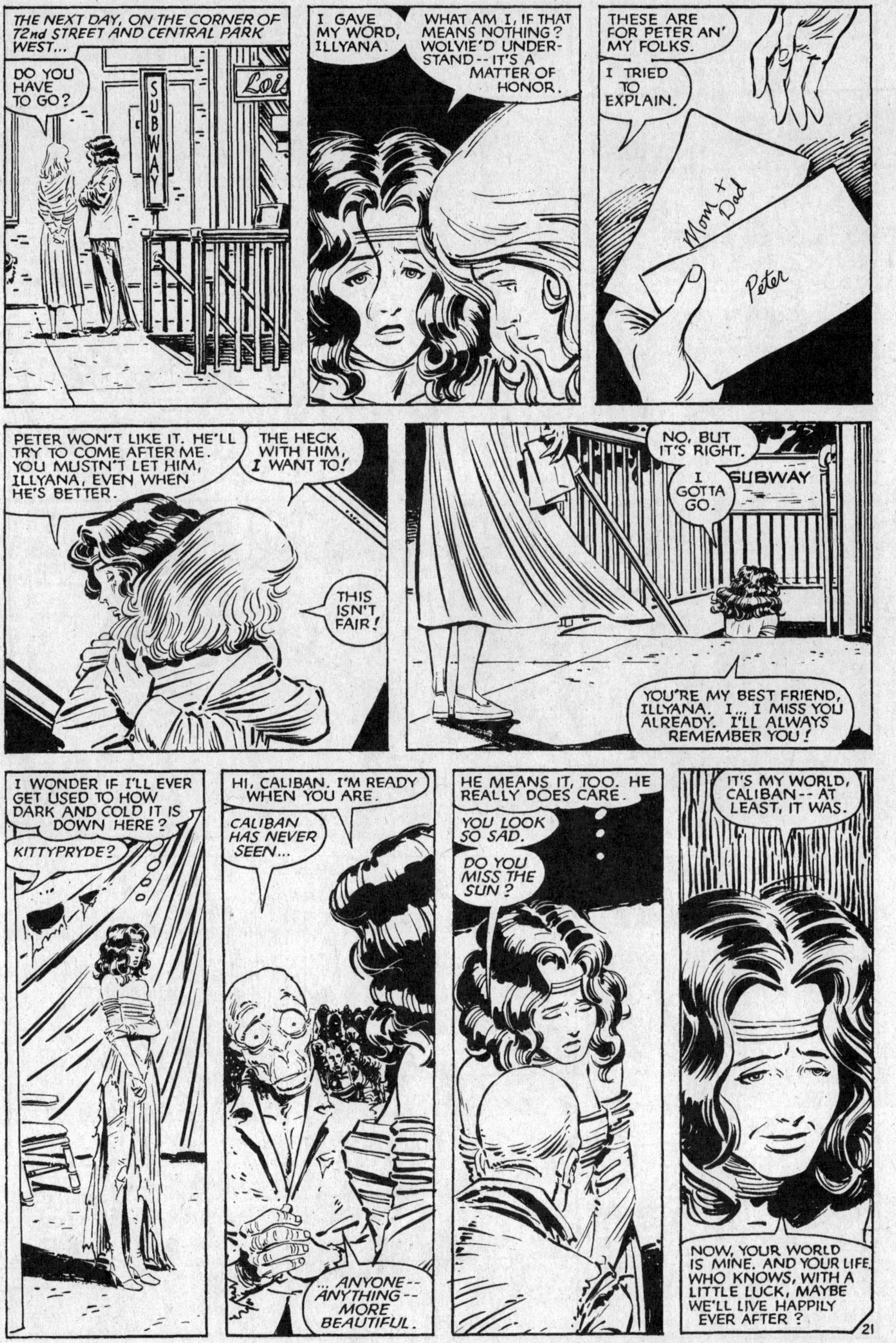
THE NEXT DAY, ON THE CORNER OF 72nd STREET AND CENTRAL PARK WEST...
DO YOU HAVE TO GO?
SUBWAY
Lois
I GAVE MY WORD, ILLYANA.
WHAT AM I, IF THAT MEANS NOTHING? WOLVIE'D UNDERSTAND-- IT'S A MATTER OF HONOR.
THESE ARE FOR PETER AN' MY FOLKS.
I TRIED TO EXPLAIN.
Mom + Dad
Peter
PETER WON'T LIKE IT. HE'LL TRY TO COME AFTER ME. YOU MUSTN'T LET HIM, ILLYANA, EVEN WHEN HE'S BETTER.
THE HECK WITH HIM, I WANT TO!
THIS ISN'T FAIR!
NO, BUT IT'S RIGHT.
I GOTTA GO.
SUBWAY
YOU'RE MY BEST FRIEND, ILLYANA. I... I MISS YOU ALREADY. I'LL ALWAYS REMEMBER YOU!
I WONDER IF I'LL EVER GET USED TO HOW DARK AND COLD IT IS DOWN HERE?
KITTYPRYDE?
HI, CALIBAN. I'M READY WHEN YOU ARE.
CALIBAN HAS NEVER SEEN...
...ANYONE-- ANYTHING-- MORE BEAUTIFUL.
HE MEANS IT, TOO. HE REALLY DOES CARE.
YOU LOOK SO SAD.
DO YOU MISS THE SUN?
IT'S MY WORLD, CALIBAN-- AT LEAST, IT WAS.
NOW, YOUR WORLD IS MINE. AND YOUR LIFE. WHO KNOWS, WITH A LITTLE LUCK, MAYBE WE'LL LIVE HAPPILY EVER AFTER?

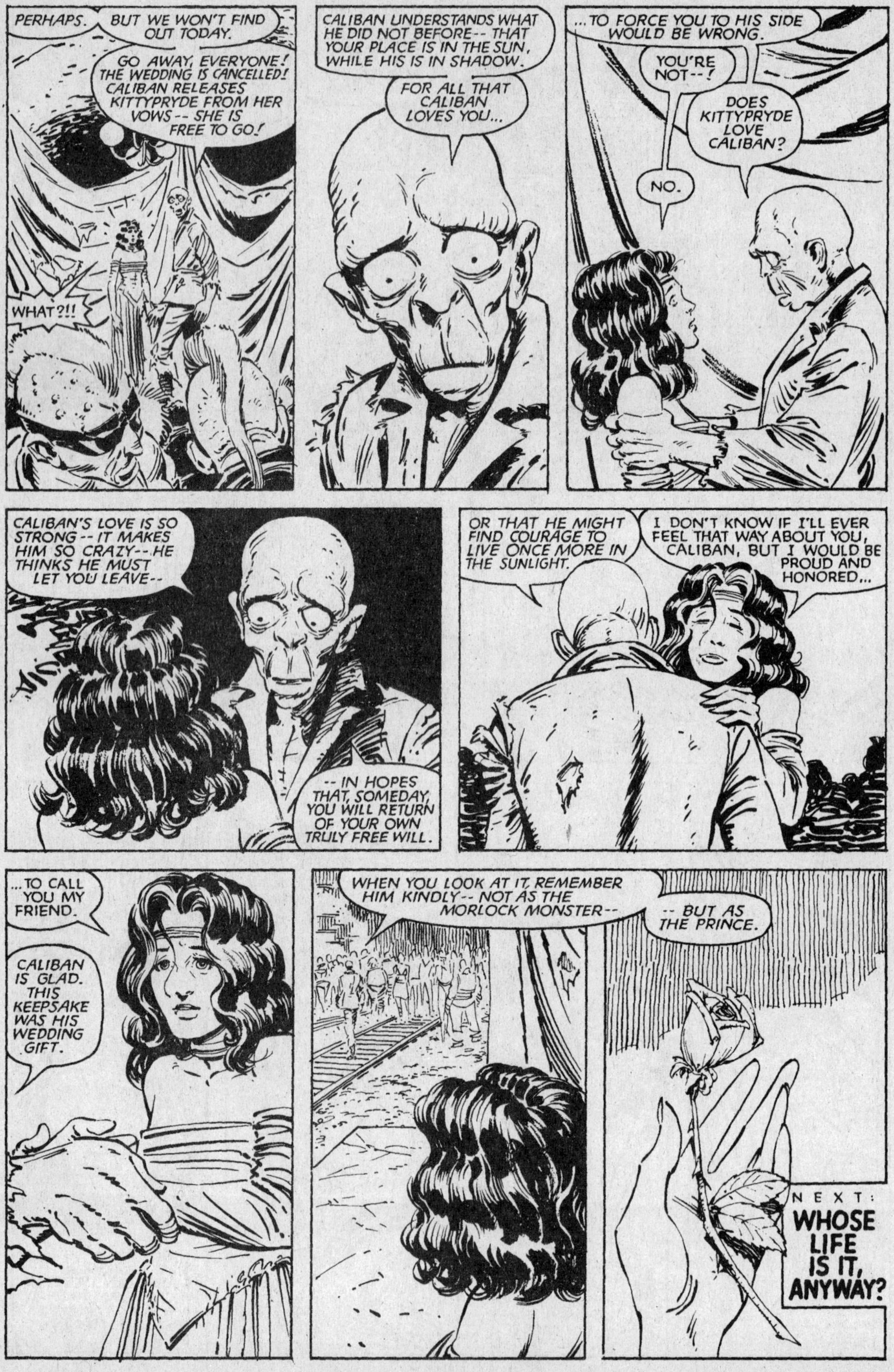
PERHAPS.
BUT WE WON'T FIND OUT TODAY.
GO AWAY, EVERYONE! THE WEDDING IS CANCELLED! CALIBAN RELEASES KITTYPRYDE FROM HER VOWS -- SHE IS FREE TO GO!
WHAT?!!
CALIBAN UNDERSTANDS WHAT HE DID NOT BEFORE -- THAT YOUR PLACE IS IN THE SUN, WHILE HIS IS IN SHADOW.
FOR ALL THAT CALIBAN LOVES YOU...
...TO FORCE YOU TO HIS SIDE WOULD BE WRONG.
YOU'RE NOT--!
DOES KITTYPRYDE LOVE CALIBAN?
NO.
CALIBAN'S LOVE IS SO STRONG -- IT MAKES HIM SO CRAZY -- HE THINKS HE MUST LET YOU LEAVE--
-- IN HOPES THAT, SOMEDAY, YOU WILL RETURN OF YOUR OWN TRULY FREE WILL.
OR THAT HE MIGHT FIND COURAGE TO LIVE ONCE MORE IN THE SUNLIGHT.
I DON'T KNOW IF I'LL EVER FEEL THAT WAY ABOUT YOU, CALIBAN, BUT I WOULD BE PROUD AND HONORED...
...TO CALL YOU MY FRIEND.
CALIBAN IS GLAD. THIS KEEPSAKE WAS HIS WEDDING GIFT.
WHEN YOU LOOK AT IT, REMEMBER HIM KINDLY -- NOT AS THE MORLOCK MONSTER--
-- BUT AS THE PRINCE.
NEXT:
WHOSE LIFE IS IT, ANYWAY?

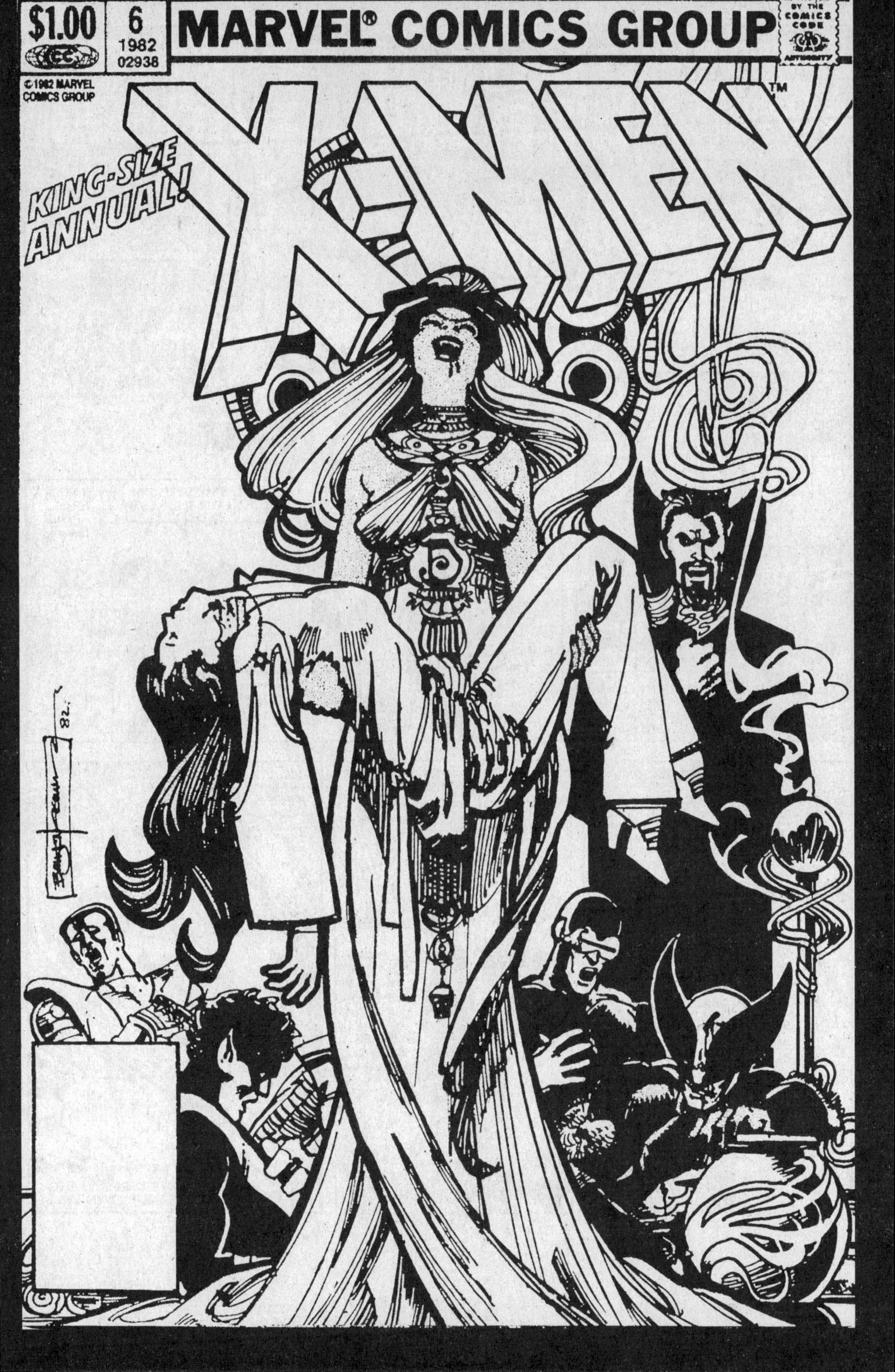

$1.00
6
1982
02938
MARVEL® COMICS GROUP
APPROVED BY THE COMICS CODE AUTHORITY
© 1982 MARVEL COMICS GROUP
X-MEN™
KING-SIZE ANNUAL!

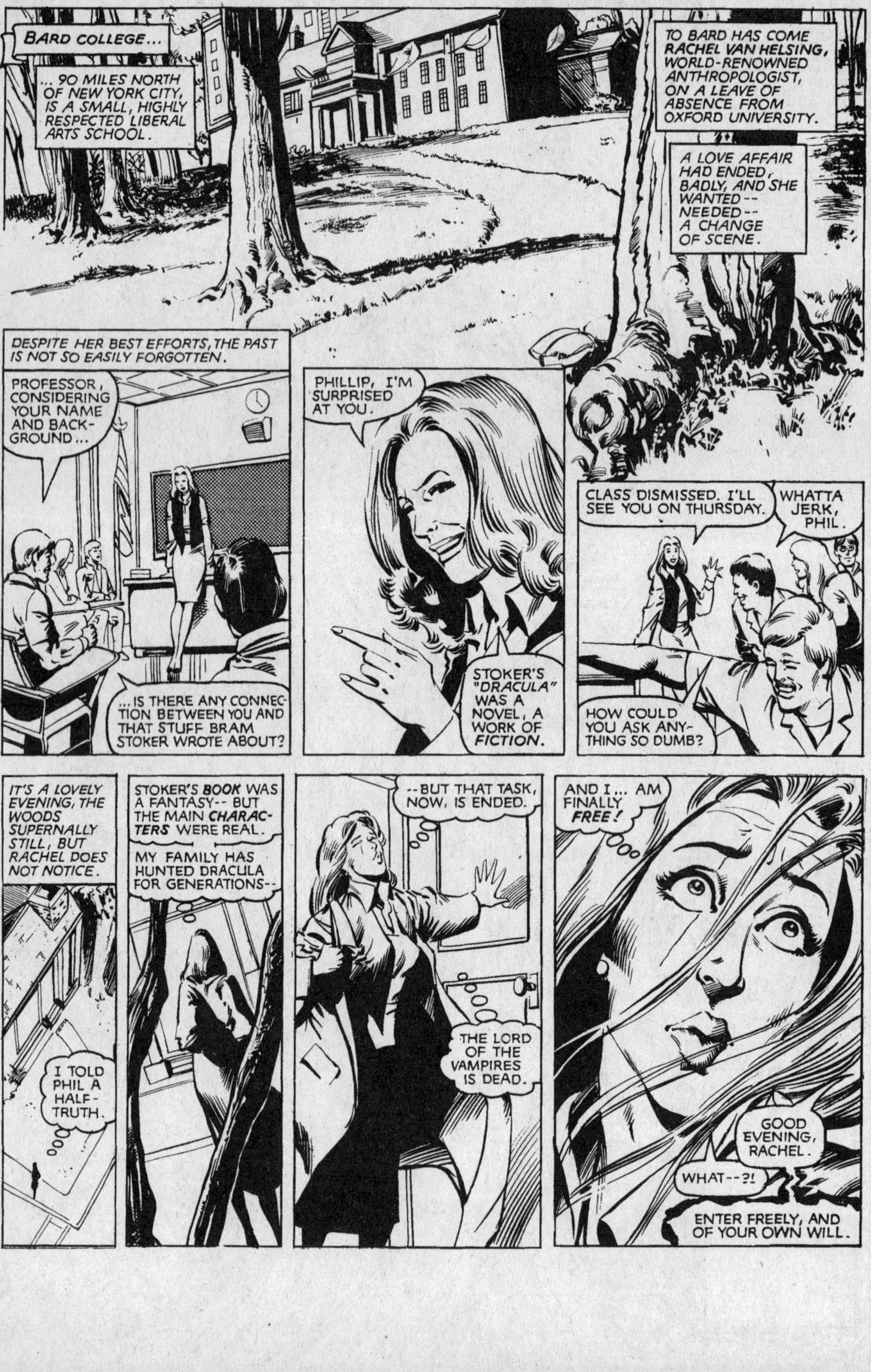
BARD COLLEGE...
... 90 MILES NORTH OF NEW YORK CITY, IS A SMALL, HIGHLY RESPECTED LIBERAL ARTS SCHOOL.
TO BARD HAS COME RACHEL VAN HELSING, WORLD-RENOWNED ANTHROPOLOGIST, ON A LEAVE OF ABSENCE FROM OXFORD UNIVERSITY.
A LOVE AFFAIR HAD ENDED, BADLY, AND SHE WANTED-- NEEDED-- A CHANGE OF SCENE.
DESPITE HER BEST EFFORTS, THE PAST IS NOT SO EASILY FORGOTTEN.
PROFESSOR, CONSIDERING YOUR NAME AND BACKGROUND...
...IS THERE ANY CONNECTION BETWEEN YOU AND THAT STUFF BRAM STOKER WROTE ABOUT?
PHILLIP, I'M SURPRISED AT YOU.
STOKER'S "DRACULA" WAS A NOVEL, A WORK OF FICTION.
CLASS DISMISSED. I'LL SEE YOU ON THURSDAY.
WHATTA JERK, PHIL.
HOW COULD YOU ASK ANYTHING SO DUMB?
IT'S A LOVELY EVENING, THE WOODS SUPERNALLY STILL, BUT RACHEL DOES NOT NOTICE.
I TOLD PHIL A HALF-TRUTH.
STOKER'S BOOK WAS A FANTASY-- BUT THE MAIN CHARACTERS WERE REAL.
MY FAMILY HAS HUNTED DRACULA FOR GENERATIONS--
--BUT THAT TASK, NOW, IS ENDED.
THE LORD OF THE VAMPIRES IS DEAD.
AND I... AM FINALLY FREE!
GOOD EVENING, RACHEL.
WHAT--?!
ENTER FREELY, AND OF YOUR OWN WILL.

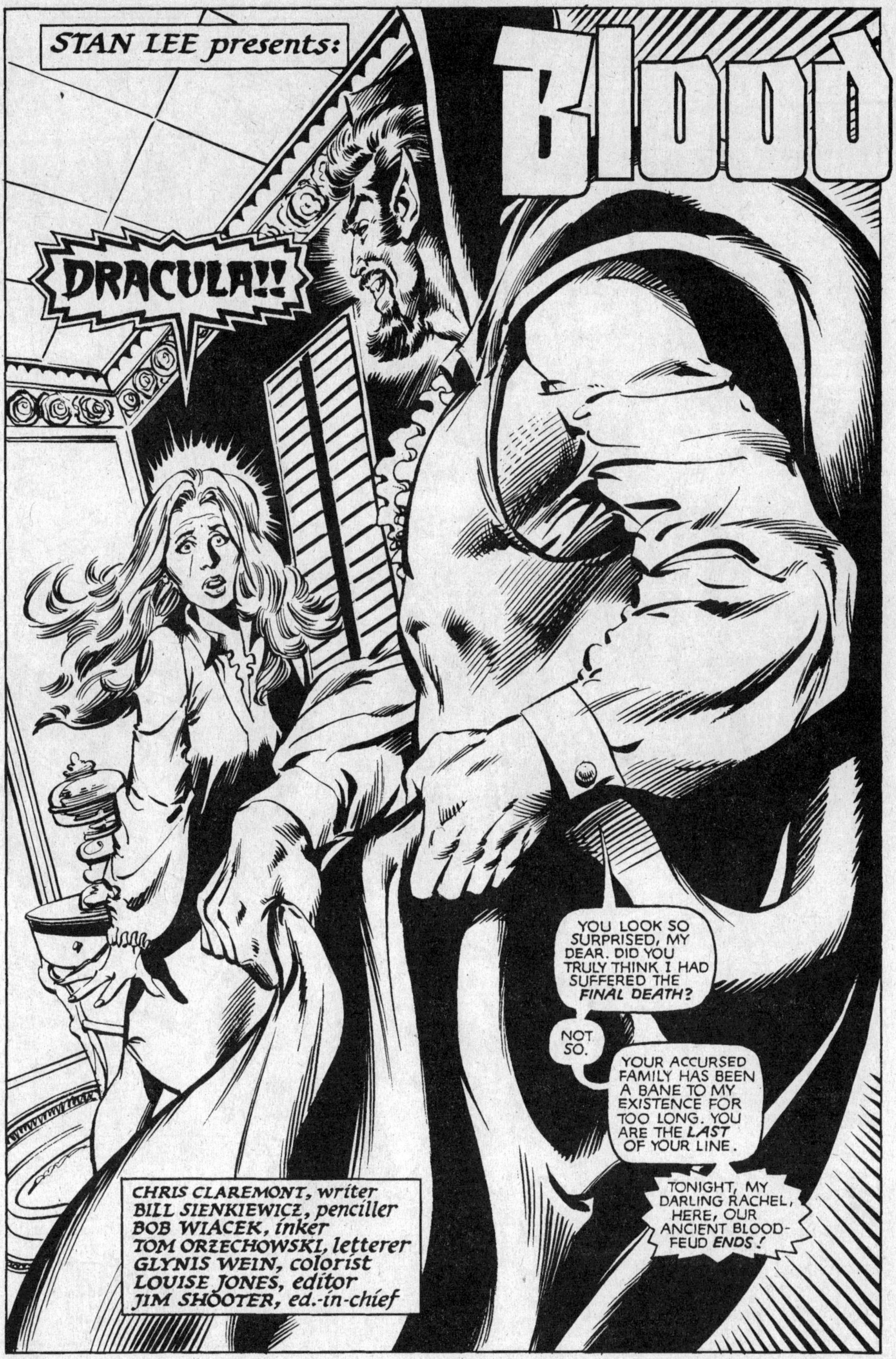
STAN LEE presents:
BLOOD
DRACULA!!
YOU LOOK SO SURPRISED, MY DEAR. DID YOU TRULY THINK I HAD SUFFERED THE FINAL DEATH?
NOT SO.
YOUR ACCURSED FAMILY HAS BEEN A BANE TO MY EXISTENCE FOR TOO LONG. YOU ARE THE LAST OF YOUR LINE.
TONIGHT, MY DARLING RACHEL, HERE, OUR ANCIENT BLOOD-FEUD ENDS!
CHRIS CLAREMONT, writer
BILL SIENKIEWICZ, penciller
BOB WIACEK, inker
TOM ORZECHOWSKI, letterer
GLYNIS WEIN, colorist
LOUISE JONES, editor
JIM SHOOTER, ed.-in-chief

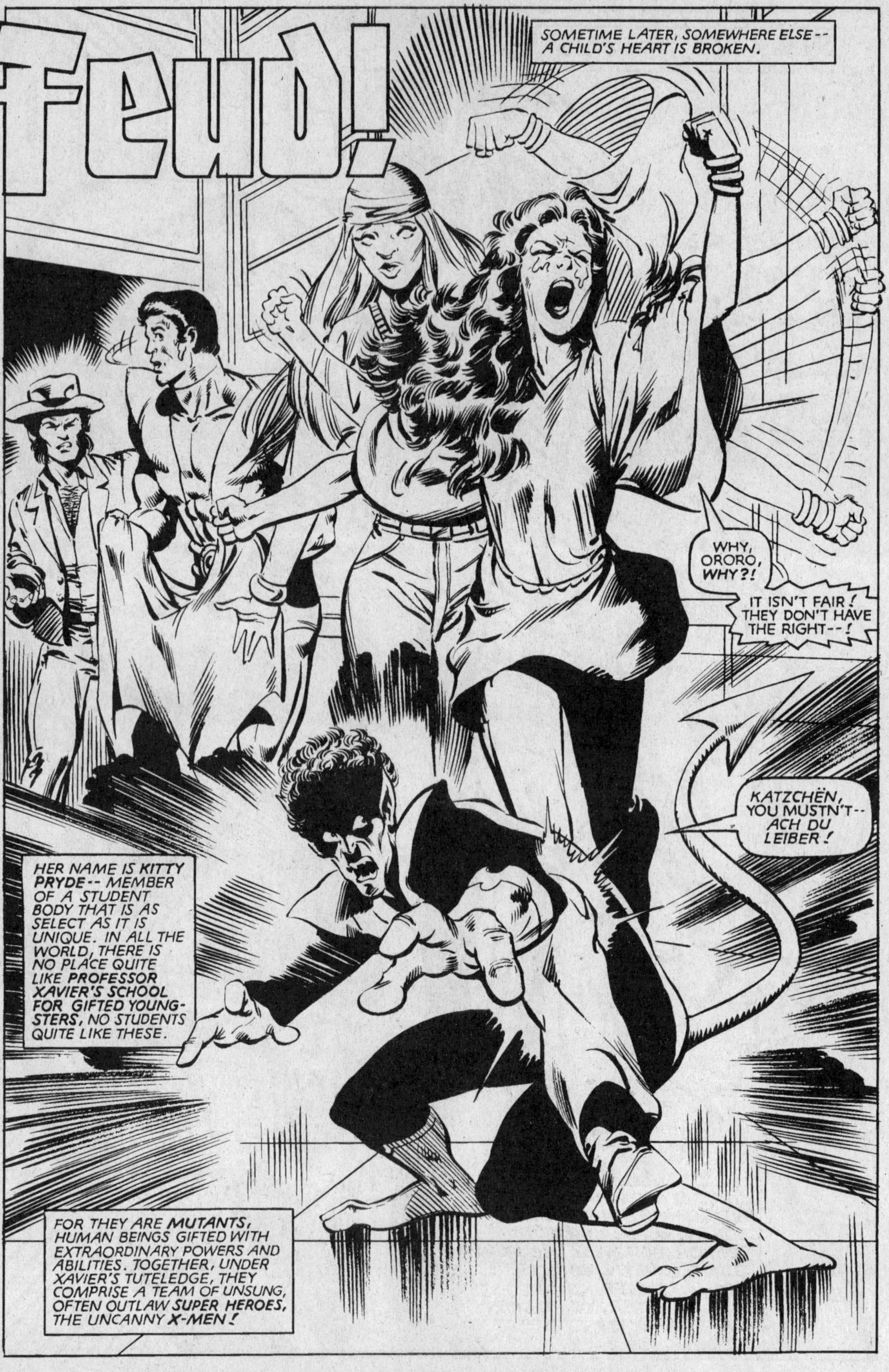

FEUD!
SOMETIME LATER, SOMEWHERE ELSE-- A CHILD'S HEART IS BROKEN.
WHY, ORORO, WHY?!
IT ISN'T FAIR! THEY DON'T HAVE THE RIGHT--!
KATZCHËN, YOU MUSTN'T-- ACH DU LEIBER!
HER NAME IS KITTY PRYDE-- MEMBER OF A STUDENT BODY THAT IS AS SELECT AS IT IS UNIQUE. IN ALL THE WORLD, THERE IS NO PLACE QUITE LIKE PROFESSOR XAVIER'S SCHOOL FOR GIFTED YOUNGSTERS, NO STUDENTS QUITE LIKE THESE.
FOR THEY ARE MUTANTS, HUMAN BEINGS GIFTED WITH EXTRAORDINARY POWERS AND ABILITIES. TOGETHER, UNDER XAVIER'S TUTELEDGE, THEY COMPRISE A TEAM OF UNSUNG, OFTEN OUTLAW SUPER HEROES, THE UNCANNY X-MEN!

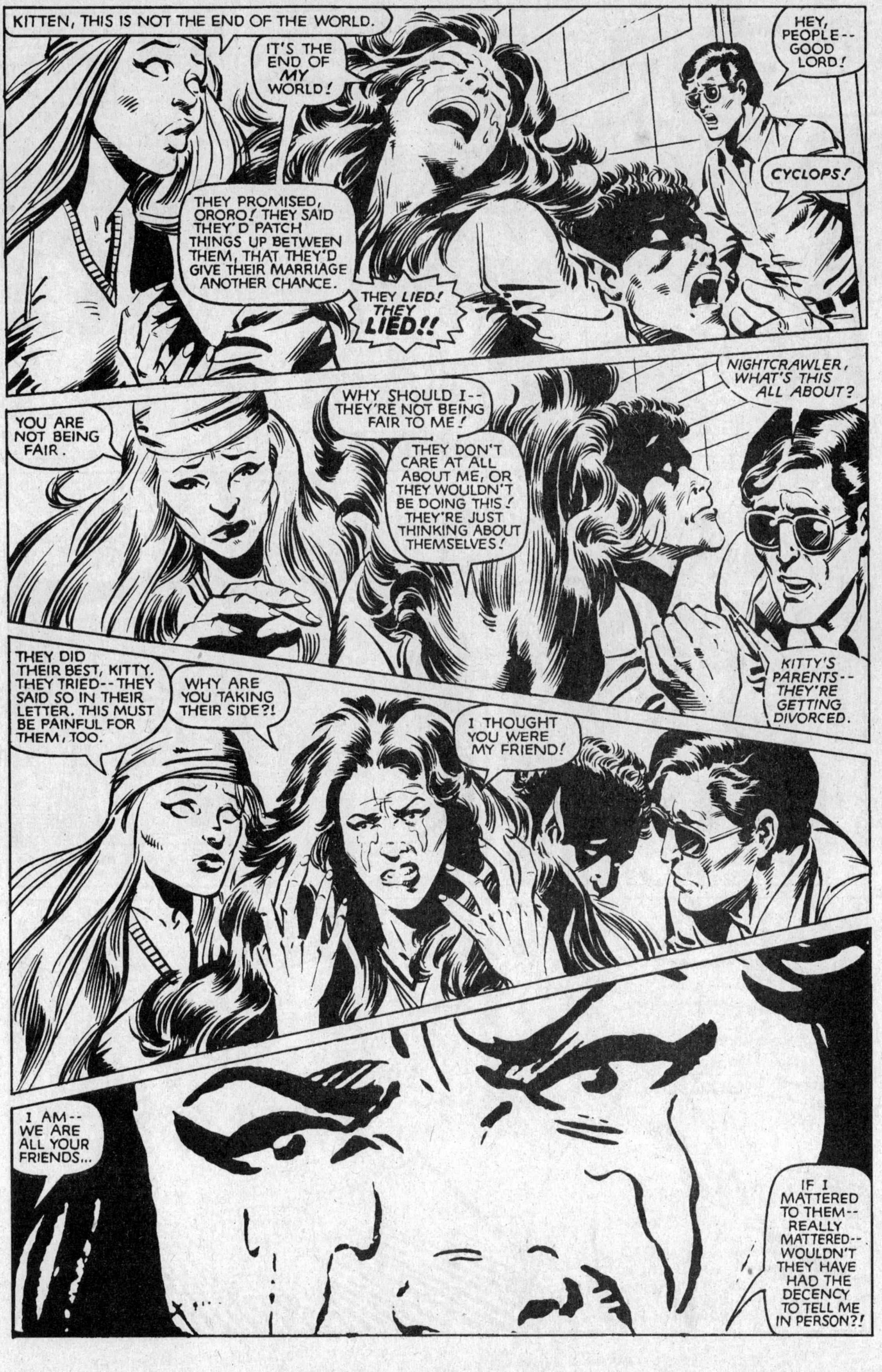
KITTEN, THIS IS NOT THE END OF THE WORLD.
IT'S THE END OF MY WORLD!
THEY PROMISED, ORORO! THEY SAID THEY'D PATCH THINGS UP BETWEEN THEM, THAT THEY'D GIVE THEIR MARRIAGE ANOTHER CHANCE.
THEY LIED! THEY LIED!!
HEY, PEOPLE-- GOOD LORD!
CYCLOPS!
YOU ARE NOT BEING FAIR.
WHY SHOULD I-- THEY'RE NOT BEING FAIR TO ME!
THEY DON'T CARE AT ALL ABOUT ME, OR THEY WOULDN'T BE DOING THIS! THEY'RE JUST THINKING ABOUT THEMSELVES!
NIGHTCRAWLER, WHAT'S THIS ALL ABOUT?
THEY DID THEIR BEST, KITTY. THEY TRIED--THEY SAID SO IN THEIR LETTER. THIS MUST BE PAINFUL FOR THEM, TOO.
WHY ARE YOU TAKING THEIR SIDE?!
I THOUGHT YOU WERE MY FRIEND!
KITTY'S PARENTS-- THEY'RE GETTING DIVORCED.
I AM-- WE ARE ALL YOUR FRIENDS...
IF I MATTERED TO THEM-- REALLY MATTERED-- WOULDN'T THEY HAVE HAD THE DECENCY TO TELL ME IN PERSON?!

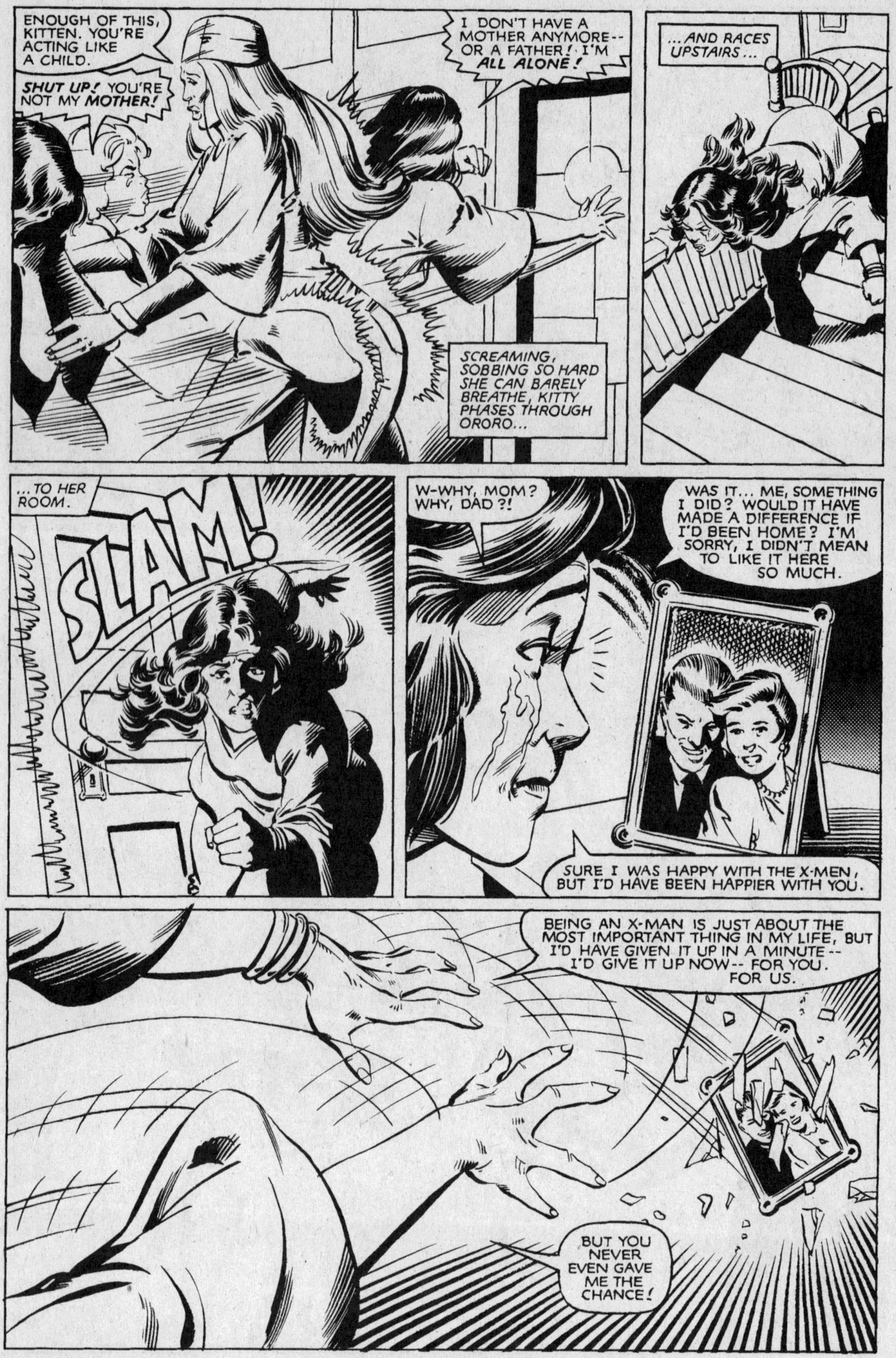

ENOUGH OF THIS, KITTEN. YOU'RE ACTING LIKE A CHILD.
SHUT UP! YOU'RE NOT MY MOTHER!
I DON'T HAVE A MOTHER ANYMORE-- OR A FATHER! I'M ALL ALONE!
SCREAMING, SOBBING SO HARD SHE CAN BARELY BREATHE, KITTY PHASES THROUGH ORORO...
...AND RACES UPSTAIRS...
...TO HER ROOM.
SLAM!
W-WHY, MOM? WHY, DAD?!
WAS IT... ME, SOMETHING I DID? WOULD IT HAVE MADE A DIFFERENCE IF I'D BEEN HOME? I'M SORRY, I DIDN'T MEAN TO LIKE IT HERE SO MUCH.
SURE I WAS HAPPY WITH THE X-MEN, BUT I'D HAVE BEEN HAPPIER WITH YOU.
BEING AN X-MAN IS JUST ABOUT THE MOST IMPORTANT THING IN MY LIFE, BUT I'D HAVE GIVEN IT UP IN A MINUTE -- I'D GIVE IT UP NOW-- FOR YOU. FOR US.
BUT YOU NEVER EVEN GAVE ME THE CHANCE!

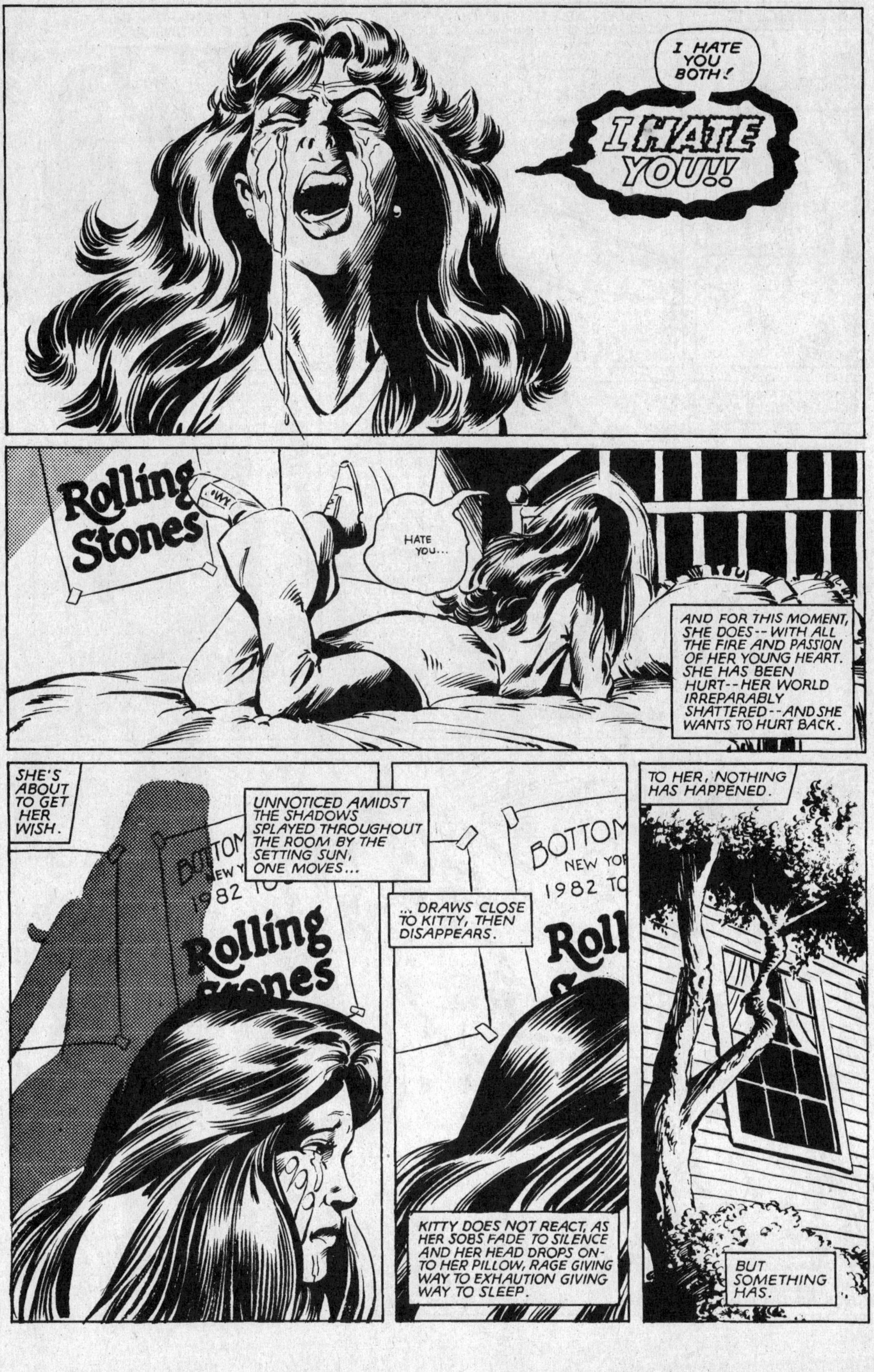
I HATE YOU BOTH!
I HATE YOU!!
Rolling Stones
HATE YOU...
AND FOR THIS MOMENT, SHE DOES--WITH ALL THE FIRE AND PASSION OF HER YOUNG HEART. SHE HAS BEEN HURT--HER WORLD IRREPARABLY SHATTERED--AND SHE WANTS TO HURT BACK.
SHE'S ABOUT TO GET HER WISH.
UNNOTICED AMIDST THE SHADOWS SPLAYED THROUGHOUT THE ROOM BY THE SETTING SUN, ONE MOVES...
Rolling
...DRAWS CLOSE TO KITTY, THEN DISAPPEARS.
BOTTOM
NEW YO
1982 TO
KITTY DOES NOT REACT, AS HER SOBS FADE TO SILENCE AND HER HEAD DROPS ONTO HER PILLOW, RAGE GIVING WAY TO EXHAUTION GIVING WAY TO SLEEP.
TO HER, NOTHING HAS HAPPENED.
BUT SOMETHING HAS.

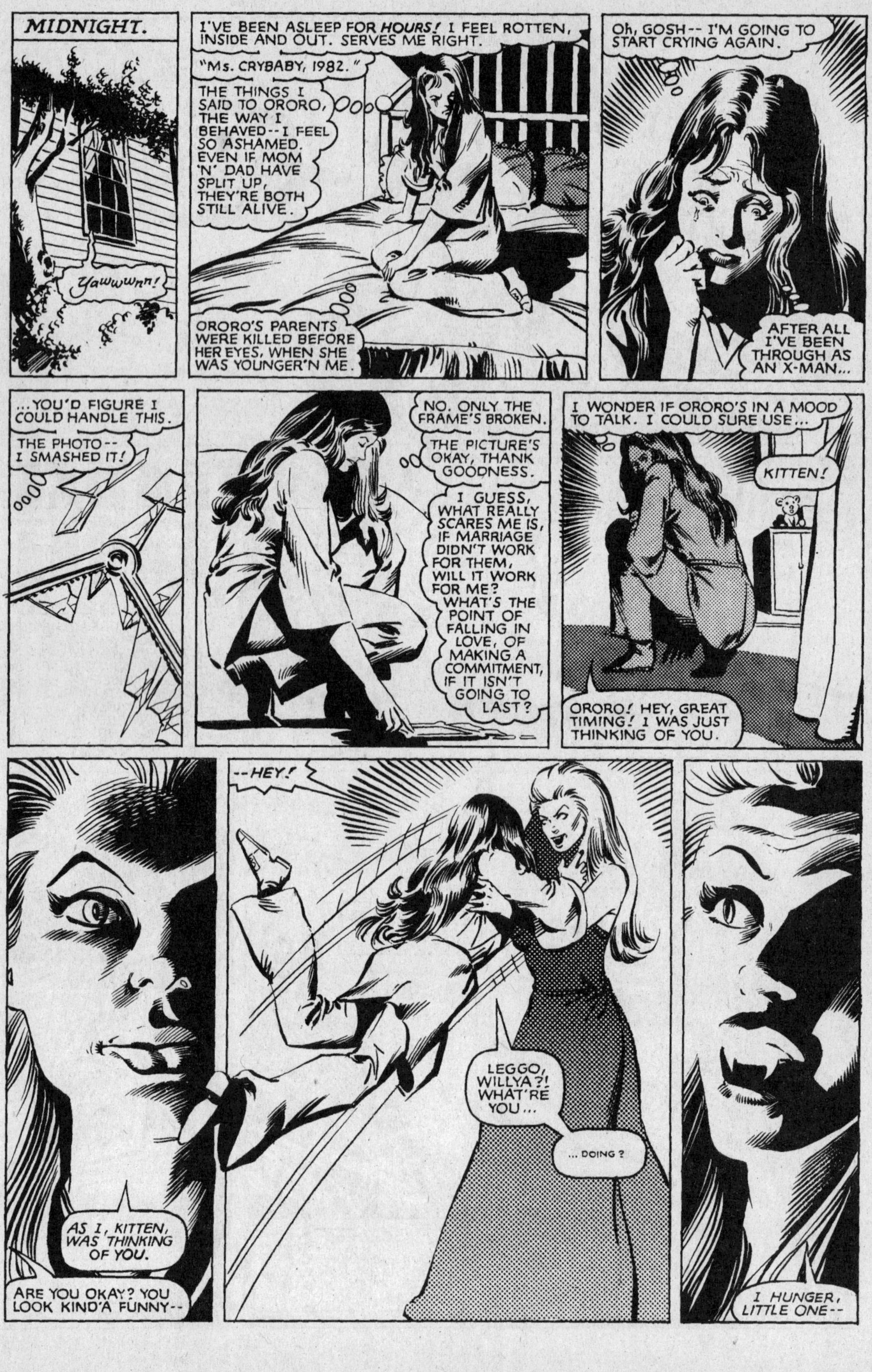
MIDNIGHT.
Yawwwnn!
I'VE BEEN ASLEEP FOR HOURS! I FEEL ROTTEN, INSIDE AND OUT. SERVES ME RIGHT.
"Ms. CRYBABY, 1982."
THE THINGS I SAID TO ORORO, THE WAY I BEHAVED-- I FEEL SO ASHAMED. EVEN IF MOM 'N' DAD HAVE SPLIT UP, THEY'RE BOTH STILL ALIVE.
ORORO'S PARENTS WERE KILLED BEFORE HER EYES, WHEN SHE WAS YOUNGER'N ME.
Oh, GOSH-- I'M GOING TO START CRYING AGAIN.
AFTER ALL I'VE BEEN THROUGH AS AN X-MAN...
...YOU'D FIGURE I COULD HANDLE THIS.
THE PHOTO-- I SMASHED IT!
NO. ONLY THE FRAME'S BROKEN.
THE PICTURE'S OKAY, THANK GOODNESS.
I GUESS, WHAT REALLY SCARES ME IS, IF MARRIAGE DIDN'T WORK FOR THEM, WILL IT WORK FOR ME? WHAT'S THE POINT OF FALLING IN LOVE, OF MAKING A COMMITMENT, IF IT ISN'T GOING TO LAST?
I WONDER IF ORORO'S IN A MOOD TO TALK. I COULD SURE USE...
KITTEN!
ORORO! HEY, GREAT TIMING! I WAS JUST THINKING OF YOU.
AS I, KITTEN, WAS THINKING OF YOU.
ARE YOU OKAY? YOU LOOK KIND'A FUNNY--
--HEY!
LEGGO, WILLYA?! WHAT'RE YOU...
...DOING?
I HUNGER, LITTLE ONE--

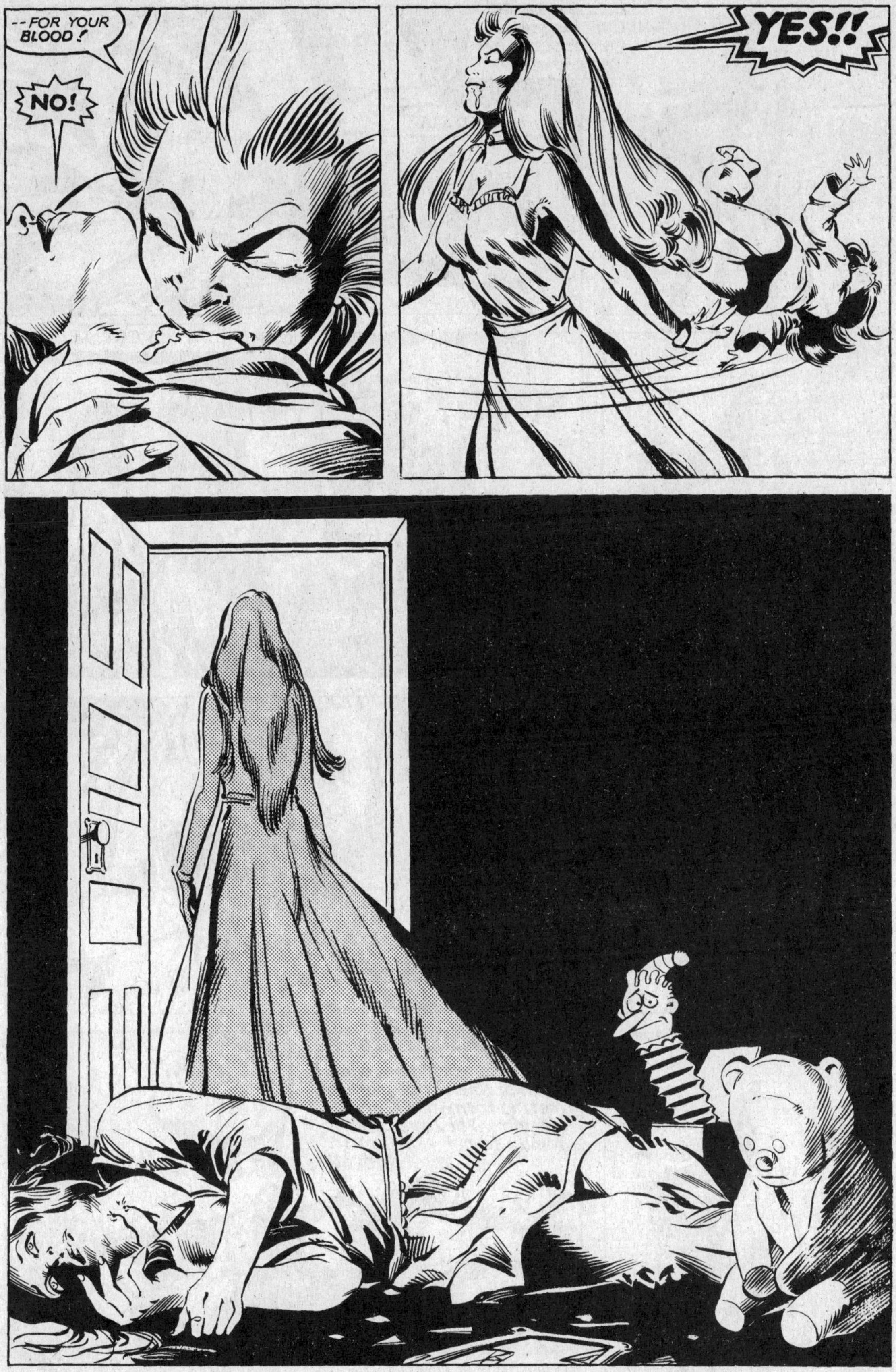
--FOR YOUR BLOOD!
NO!
YES!!

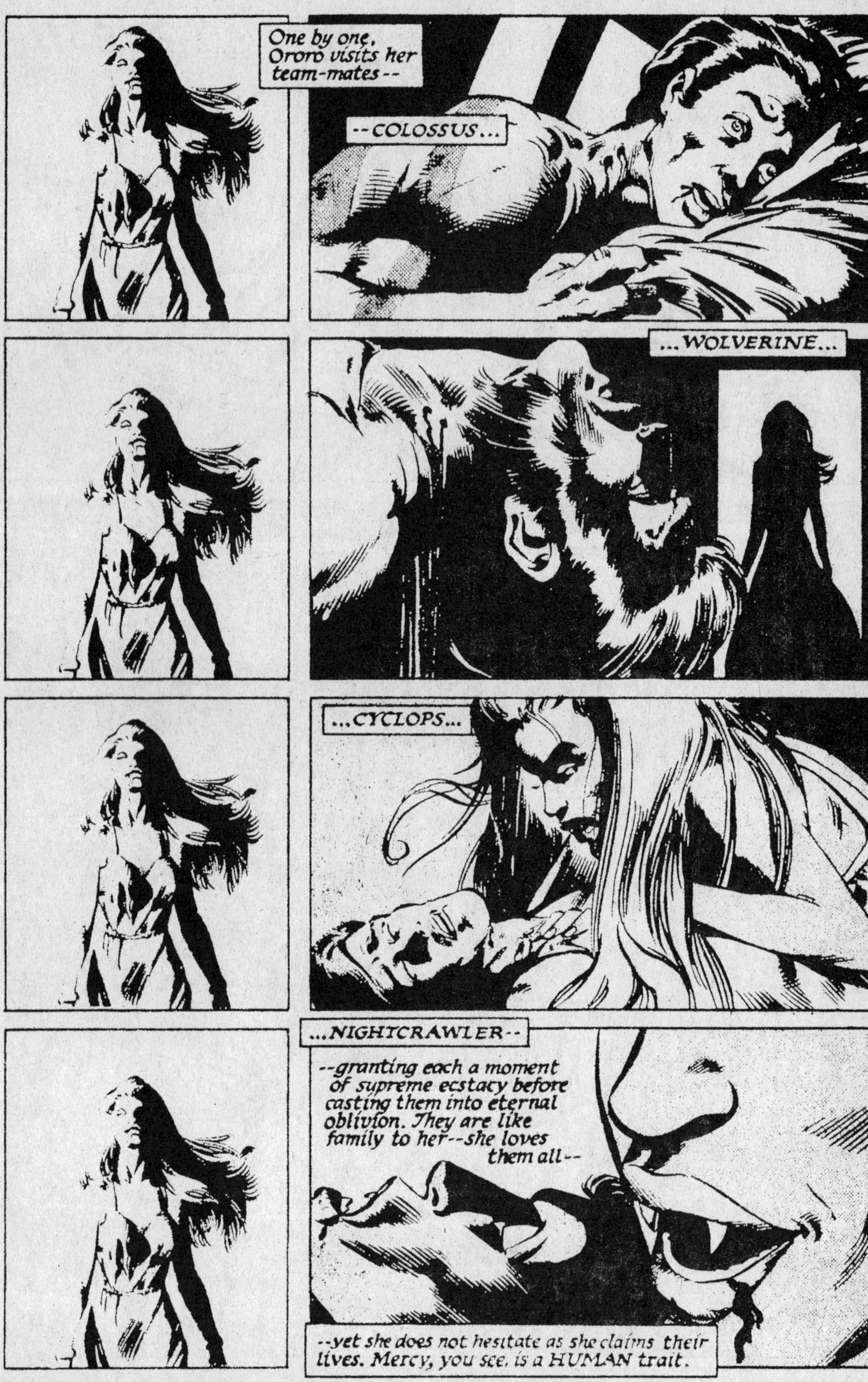
One by one, Ororo visits her team-mates--
--COLOSSUS...
...WOLVERINE...
...CYCLOPS...
...NIGHTCRAWLER--
--granting each a moment of supreme ecstacy before casting them into eternal oblivion. They are like family to her--she loves them all--
--yet she does not hesitate as she claims their lives. Mercy, you see, is a HUMAN trait.

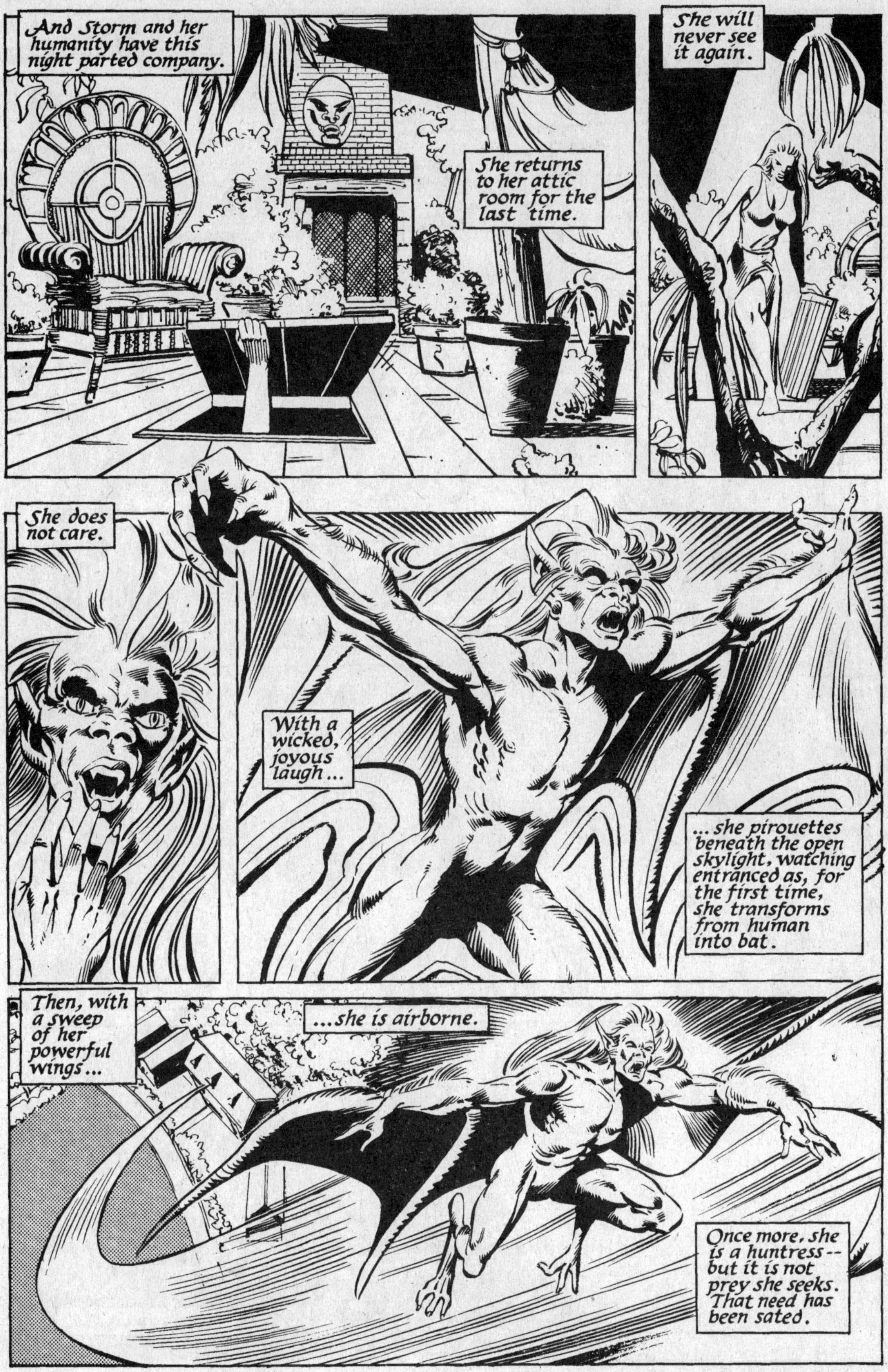
And Storm and her humanity have this night parted company.
She returns to her attic room for the last time.
She will never see it again.
She does not care.
With a wicked, joyous laugh...
... she pirouettes beneath the open skylight, watching entranced as, for the first time, she transforms from human into bat.
Then, with a sweep of her powerful wings...
...she is airborne.
Once more, she is a huntress -- but it is not prey she seeks. That need has been sated.

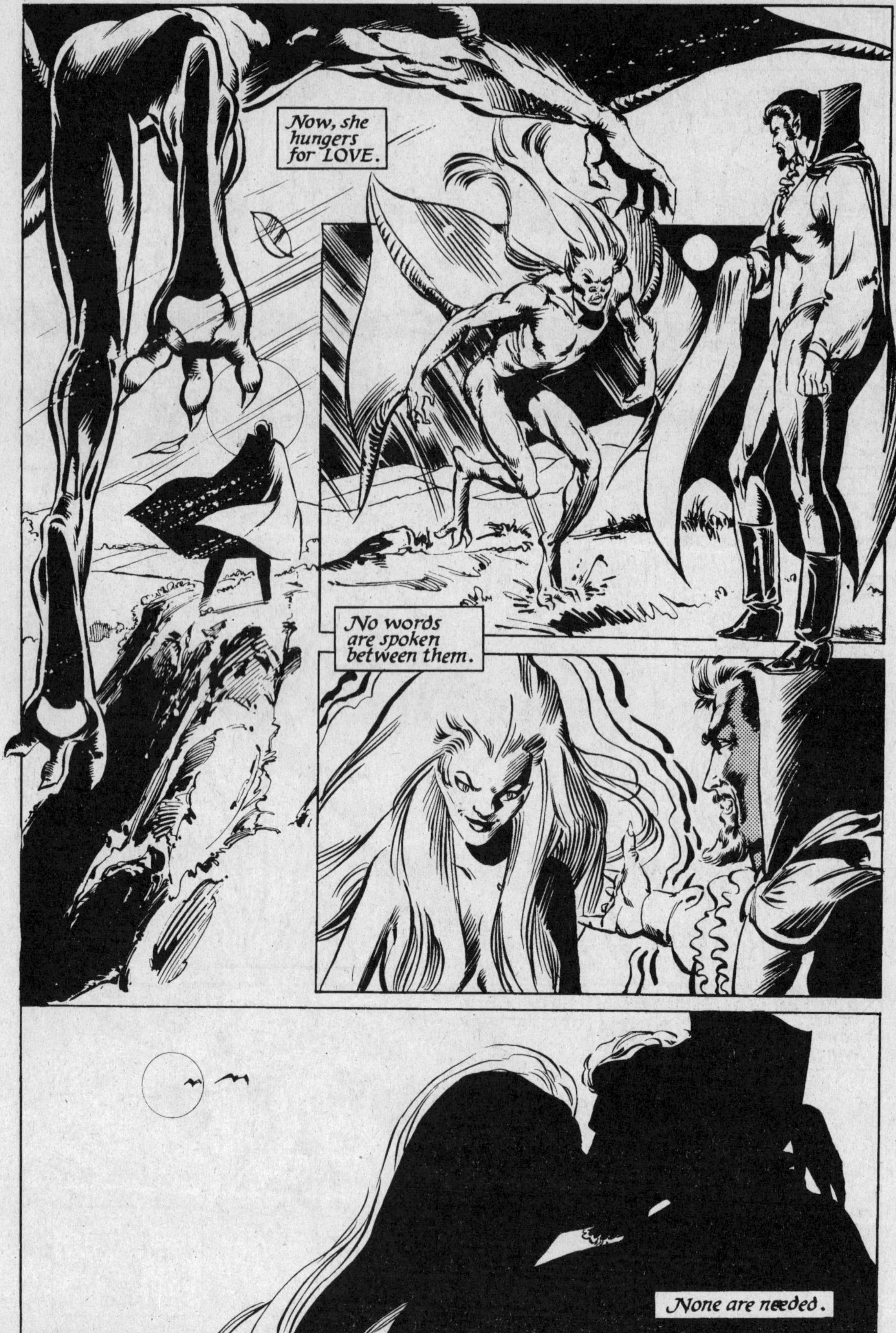
Now, she hungers for LOVE.
No words are spoken between them.
None are needed.

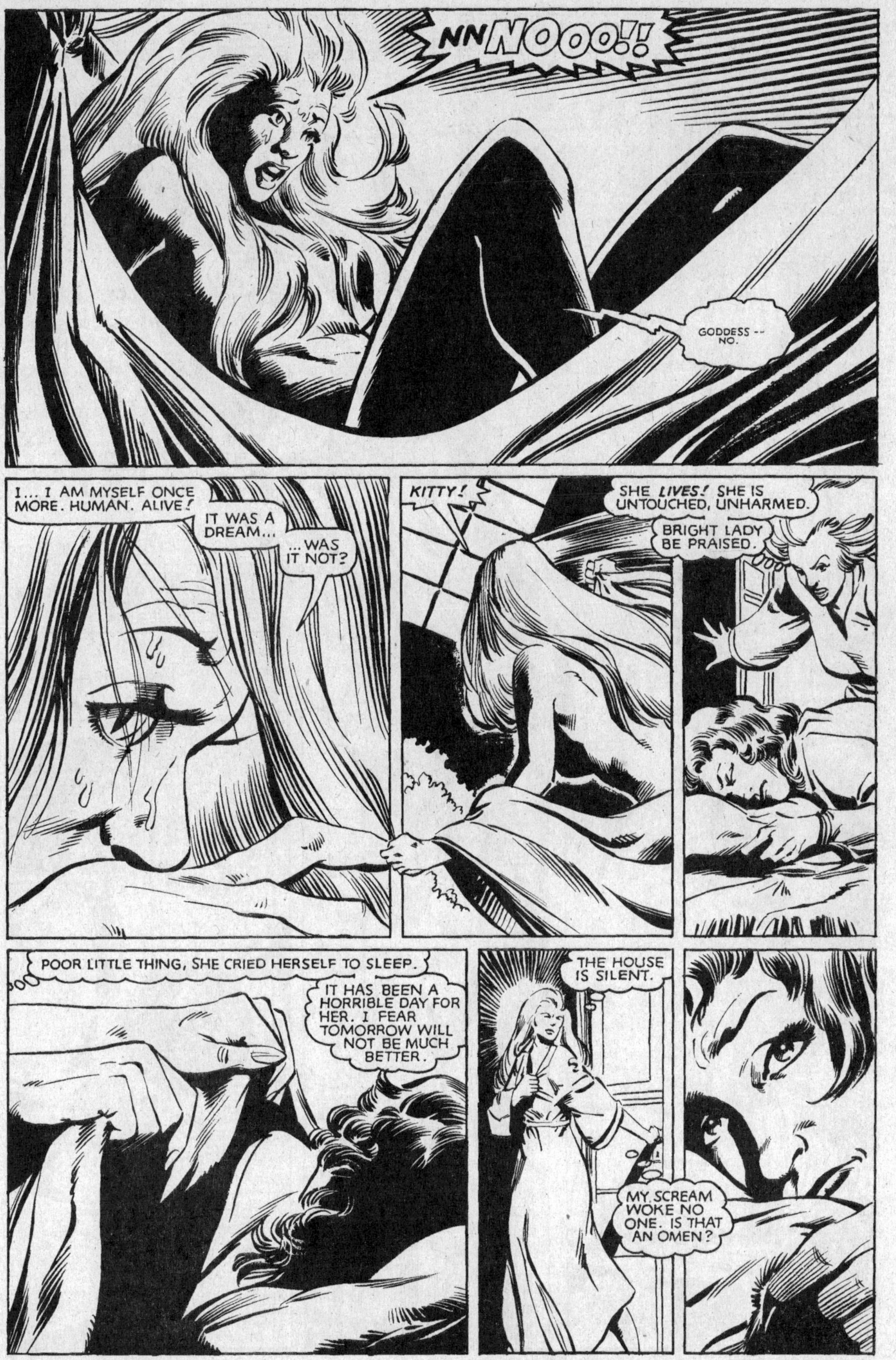
NNNOOOO!!
GODDESS -- NO.
I... I AM MYSELF ONCE MORE. HUMAN. ALIVE!
IT WAS A DREAM...
...WAS IT NOT?
KITTY!
SHE LIVES! SHE IS UNTOUCHED, UNHARMED.
BRIGHT LADY BE PRAISED.
POOR LITTLE THING, SHE CRIED HERSELF TO SLEEP.
IT HAS BEEN A HORRIBLE DAY FOR HER. I FEAR TOMORROW WILL NOT BE MUCH BETTER.
THE HOUSE IS SILENT.
MY SCREAM WOKE NO ONE. IS THAT AN OMEN?

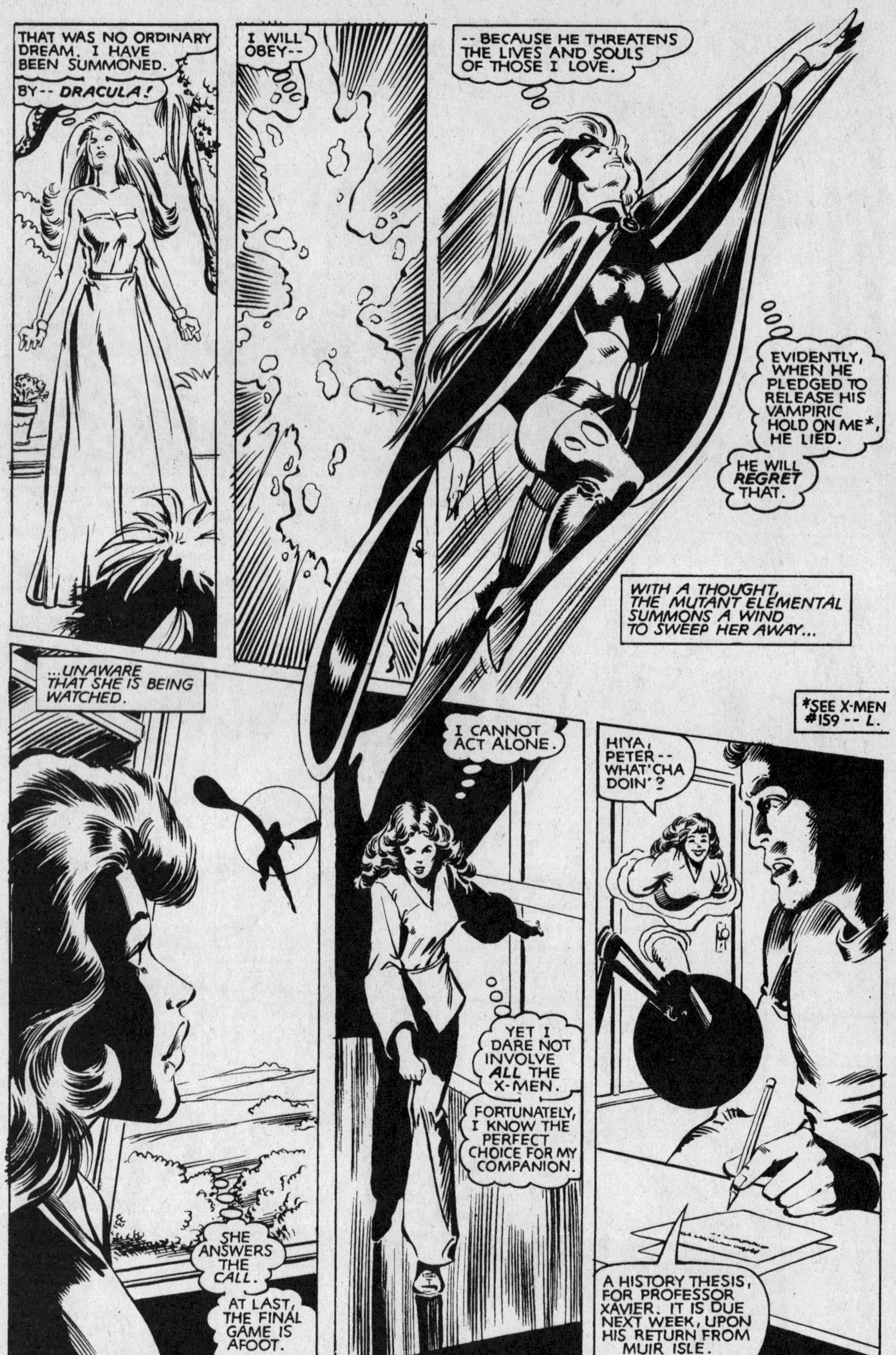

THAT WAS NO ORDINARY DREAM. I HAVE BEEN SUMMONED.
BY-- DRACULA!
I WILL OBEY--
-- BECAUSE HE THREATENS THE LIVES AND SOULS OF THOSE I LOVE.
EVIDENTLY, WHEN HE PLEDGED TO RELEASE HIS VAMPIRIC HOLD ON ME*, HE LIED.
HE WILL REGRET THAT.
WITH A THOUGHT, THE MUTANT ELEMENTAL SUMMONS A WIND TO SWEEP HER AWAY...
...UNAWARE THAT SHE IS BEING WATCHED.
SHE ANSWERS THE CALL.
AT LAST, THE FINAL GAME IS AFOOT.
I CANNOT ACT ALONE.
YET I DARE NOT INVOLVE ALL THE X-MEN.
FORTUNATELY, I KNOW THE PERFECT CHOICE FOR MY COMPANION.
*SEE X-MEN #159 -- L.
HIYA, PETER-- WHAT'CHA DOIN'?
A HISTORY THESIS, FOR PROFESSOR XAVIER. IT IS DUE NEXT WEEK, UPON HIS RETURN FROM MUIR ISLE.

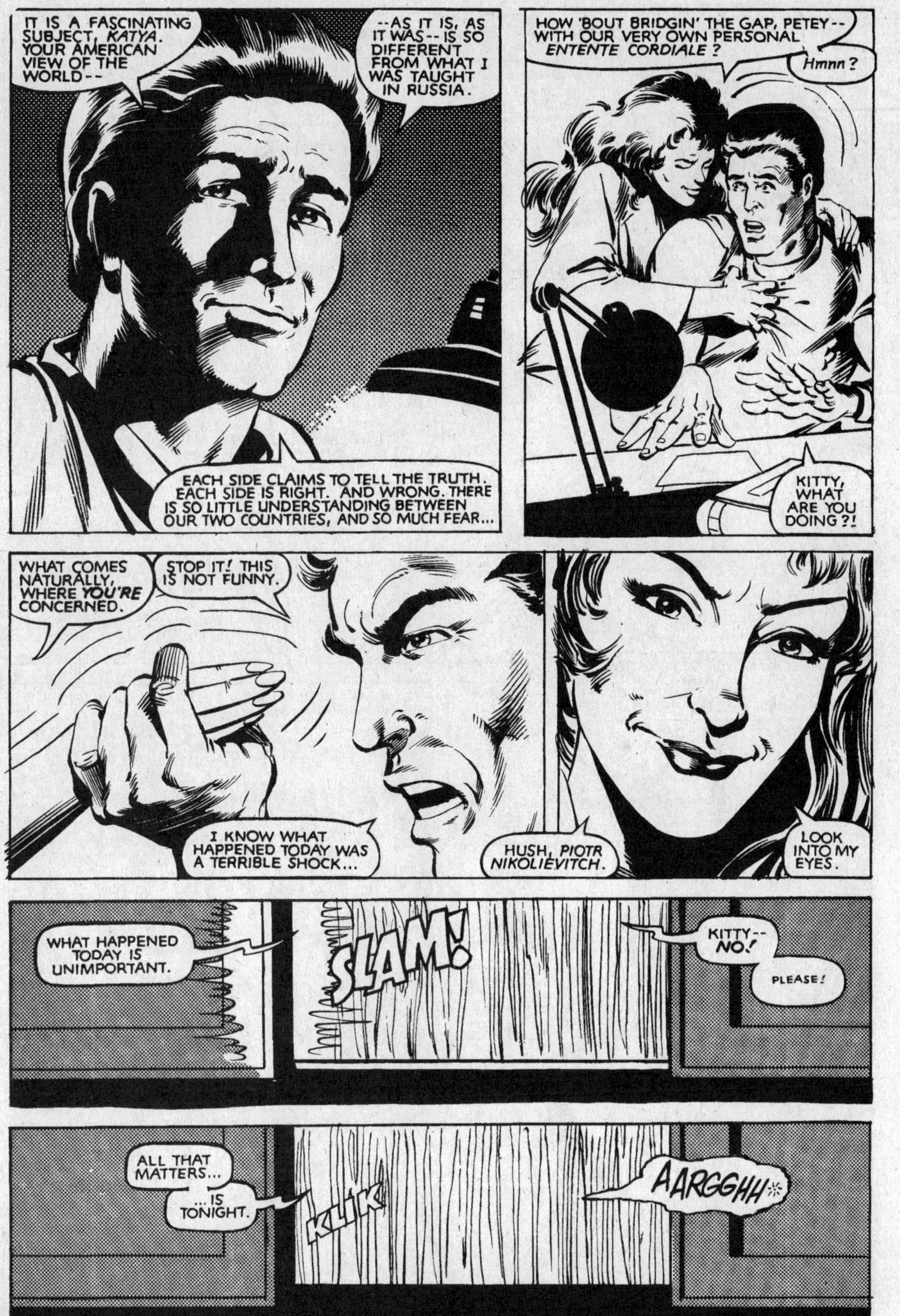
IT IS A FASCINATING SUBJECT, *KATYA*. YOUR AMERICAN VIEW OF THE WORLD--
--AS IT IS, AS IT WAS--IS SO DIFFERENT FROM WHAT I WAS TAUGHT IN RUSSIA.
EACH SIDE CLAIMS TO TELL THE TRUTH. EACH SIDE IS RIGHT. AND WRONG. THERE IS SO LITTLE UNDERSTANDING BETWEEN OUR TWO COUNTRIES, AND SO MUCH FEAR...
HOW 'BOUT BRIDGIN' THE GAP, PETEY--WITH OUR VERY OWN PERSONAL *ENTENTE CORDIALE*?
Hmnn?
KITTY, WHAT ARE YOU DOING?!
WHAT COMES NATURALLY, WHERE *YOU'RE* CONCERNED.
STOP IT! THIS IS NOT FUNNY.
I KNOW WHAT HAPPENED TODAY WAS A TERRIBLE SHOCK...
HUSH, *PIOTR NIKOLIEVITCH*.
LOOK INTO MY EYES.
WHAT HAPPENED TODAY IS UNIMPORTANT.
SLAM!
KITTY--*NO!*
PLEASE!
ALL THAT MATTERS...
...IS TONIGHT.
KLIK
AARGGHH

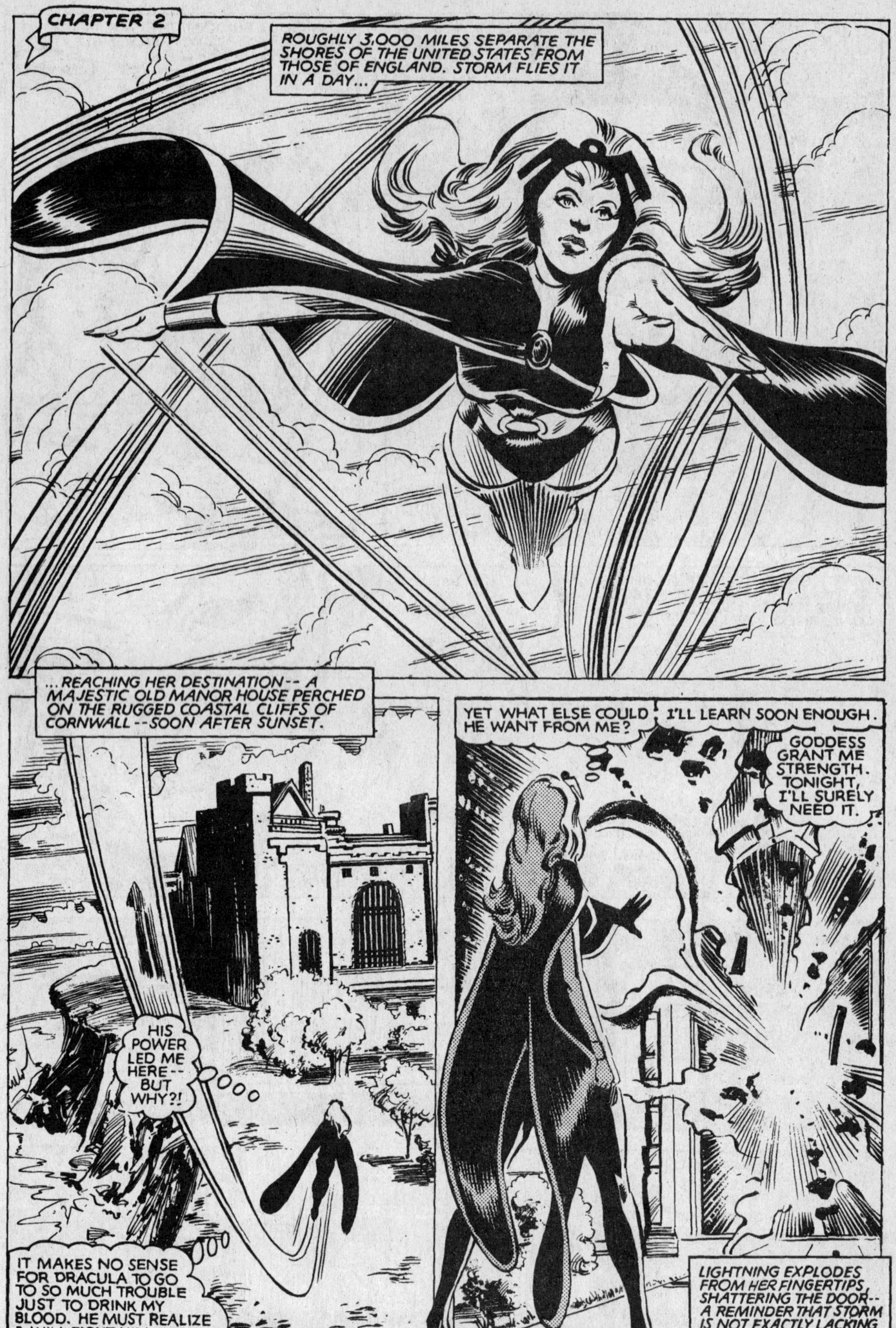
CHAPTER 2
ROUGHLY 3,000 MILES SEPARATE THE SHORES OF THE UNITED STATES FROM THOSE OF ENGLAND. STORM FLIES IT IN A DAY...
...REACHING HER DESTINATION-- A MAJESTIC OLD MANOR HOUSE PERCHED ON THE RUGGED COASTAL CLIFFS OF CORNWALL--SOON AFTER SUNSET.
HIS POWER LED ME HERE-- BUT WHY?!
IT MAKES NO SENSE FOR DRACULA TO GO TO SO MUCH TROUBLE JUST TO DRINK MY BLOOD. HE MUST REALIZE I WILL FIGHT HIM--TO MY DEATH, AND BEYOND.
YET WHAT ELSE COULD HE WANT FROM ME?
I'LL LEARN SOON ENOUGH.
GODDESS GRANT ME STRENGTH. TONIGHT, I'LL SURELY NEED IT.
LIGHTNING EXPLODES FROM HER FINGERTIPS, SHATTERING THE DOOR-- A REMINDER THAT STORM IS NOT EXACTLY LACKING IN POWER, EITHER.

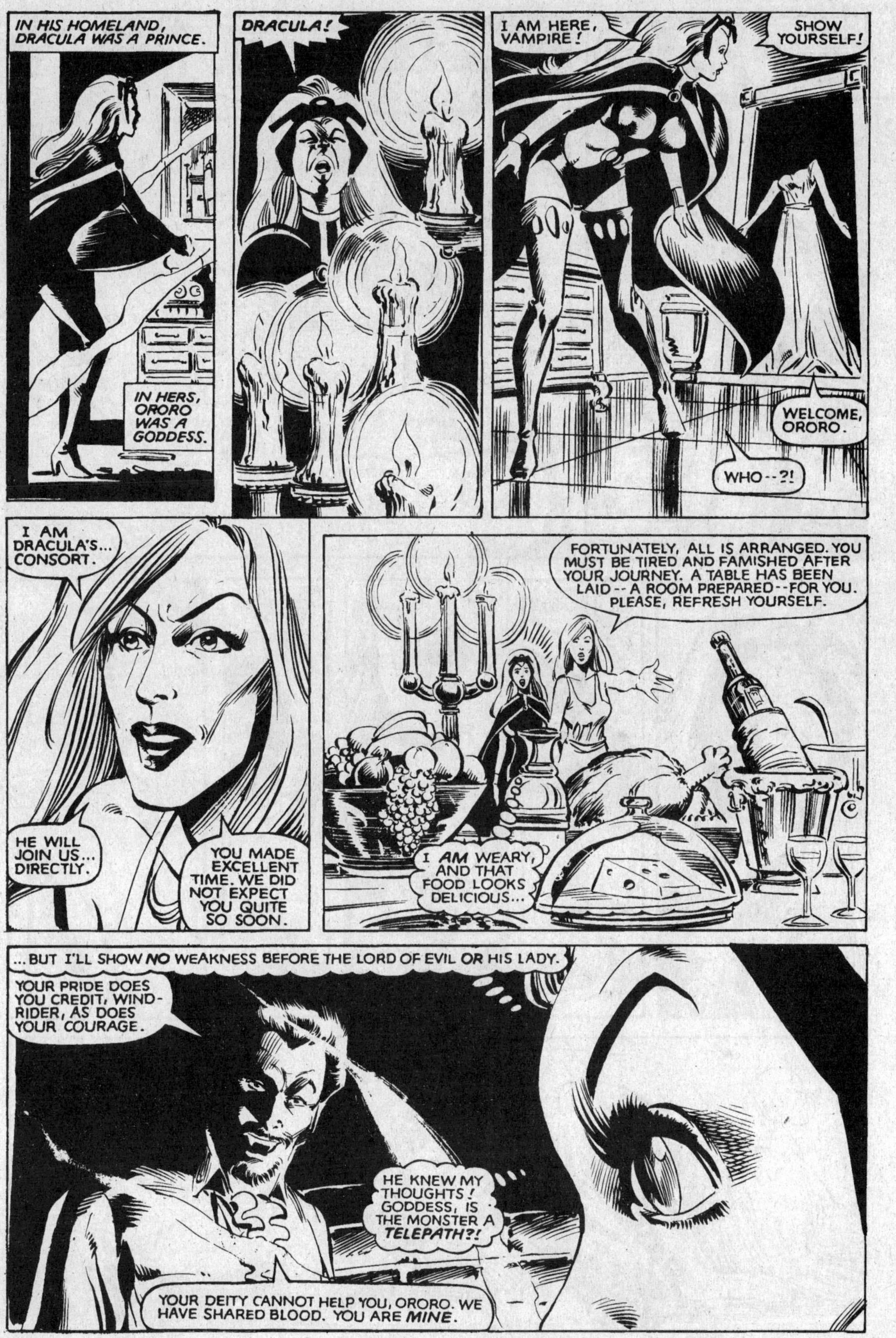
IN HIS HOMELAND, DRACULA WAS A PRINCE.
IN HERS, ORORO WAS A GODDESS.
DRACULA!
I AM HERE, VAMPIRE!
SHOW YOURSELF!
WELCOME, ORORO.
WHO--?!
I AM DRACULA'S... CONSORT.
HE WILL JOIN US... DIRECTLY.
YOU MADE EXCELLENT TIME. WE DID NOT EXPECT YOU QUITE SO SOON.
FORTUNATELY, ALL IS ARRANGED. YOU MUST BE TIRED AND FAMISHED AFTER YOUR JOURNEY. A TABLE HAS BEEN LAID--A ROOM PREPARED--FOR YOU. PLEASE, REFRESH YOURSELF.
I AM WEARY, AND THAT FOOD LOOKS DELICIOUS...
...BUT I'LL SHOW NO WEAKNESS BEFORE THE LORD OF EVIL OR HIS LADY.
YOUR PRIDE DOES YOU CREDIT, WIND-RIDER, AS DOES YOUR COURAGE.
HE KNEW MY THOUGHTS! GODDESS, IS THE MONSTER A TELEPATH?!
YOUR DEITY CANNOT HELP YOU, ORORO. WE HAVE SHARED BLOOD. YOU ARE MINE.

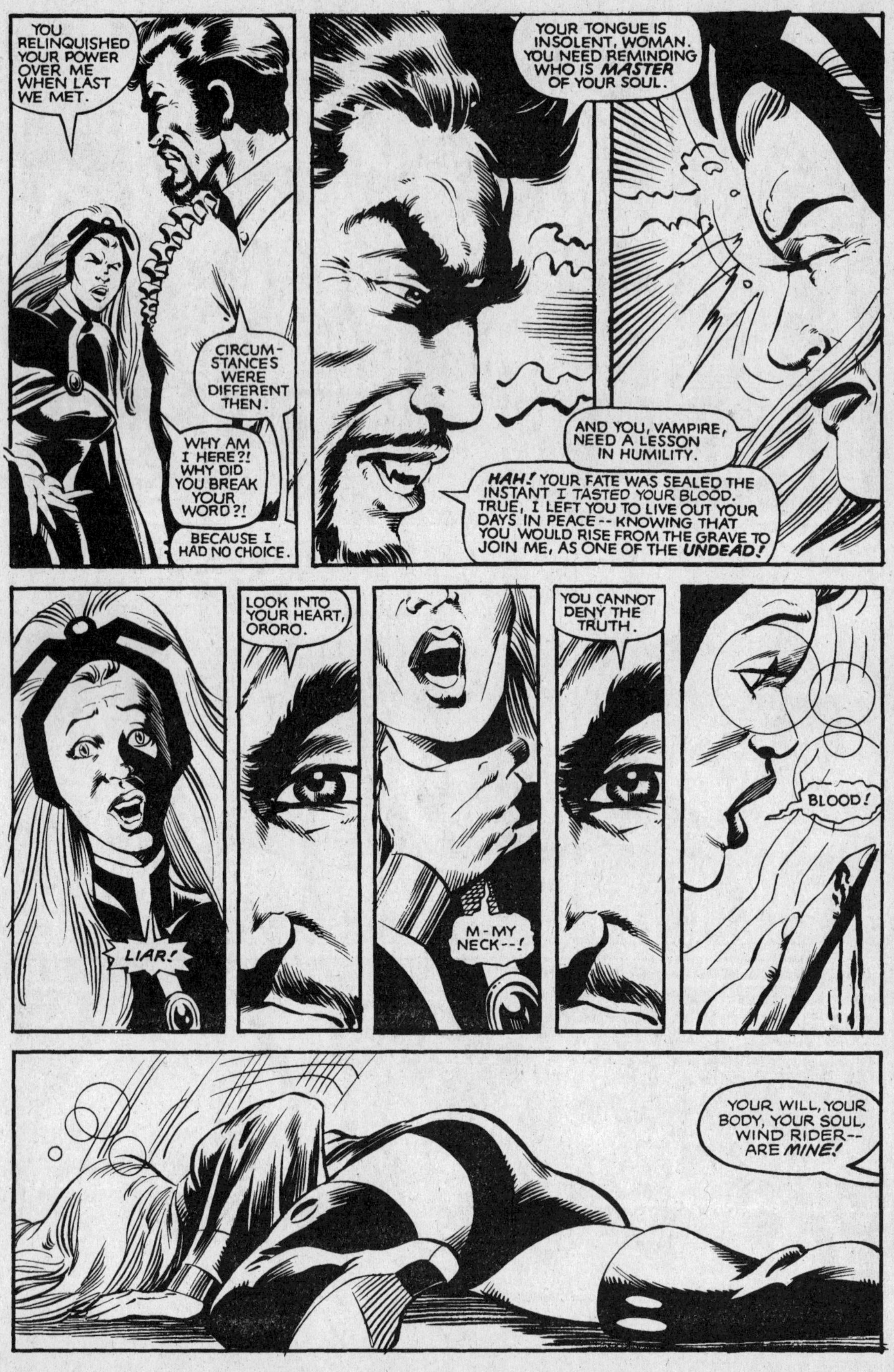

YOU RELINQUISHED YOUR POWER OVER ME WHEN LAST WE MET.
CIRCUM-STANCES WERE DIFFERENT THEN.
WHY AM I HERE?! WHY DID YOU BREAK YOUR WORD?!
BECAUSE I HAD NO CHOICE.
YOUR TONGUE IS INSOLENT, WOMAN. YOU NEED REMINDING WHO IS MASTER OF YOUR SOUL.
AND YOU, VAMPIRE, NEED A LESSON IN HUMILITY.
HAH! YOUR FATE WAS SEALED THE INSTANT I TASTED YOUR BLOOD. TRUE, I LEFT YOU TO LIVE OUT YOUR DAYS IN PEACE -- KNOWING THAT YOU WOULD RISE FROM THE GRAVE TO JOIN ME, AS ONE OF THE UNDEAD!
LIAR!
LOOK INTO YOUR HEART, ORORO.
M-MY NECK--!
YOU CANNOT DENY THE TRUTH.
BLOOD!
YOUR WILL, YOUR BODY, YOUR SOUL, WIND RIDER-- ARE MINE!

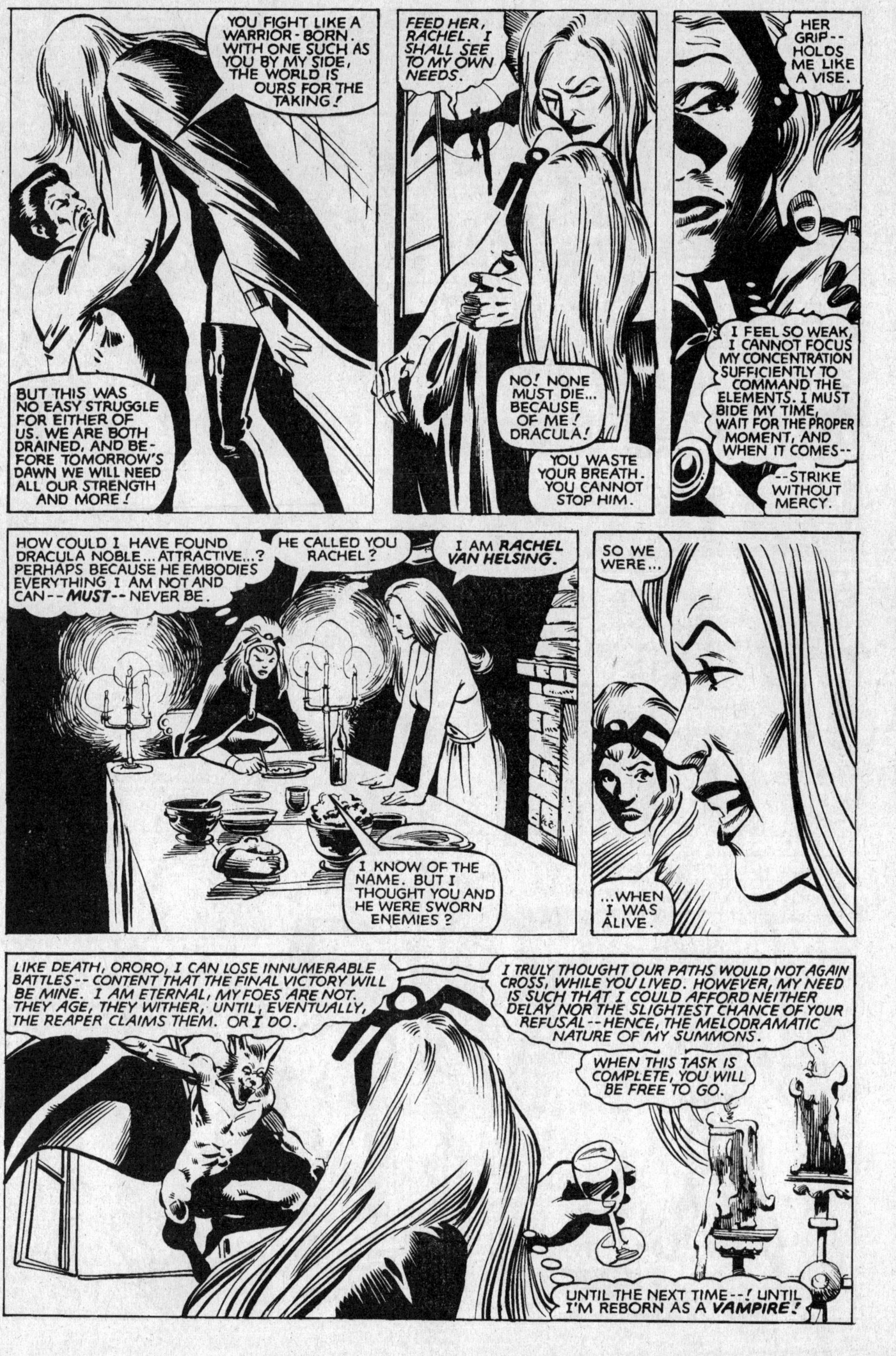

YOU FIGHT LIKE A WARRIOR-BORN. WITH ONE SUCH AS YOU BY MY SIDE, THE WORLD IS OURS FOR THE TAKING!
BUT THIS WAS NO EASY STRUGGLE FOR EITHER OF US. WE ARE BOTH DRAINED, AND BEFORE TOMORROW'S DAWN WE WILL NEED ALL OUR STRENGTH AND MORE!
FEED HER, RACHEL. I SHALL SEE TO MY OWN NEEDS.
NO! NONE MUST DIE... BECAUSE OF ME! DRACULA!
YOU WASTE YOUR BREATH. YOU CANNOT STOP HIM.
HER GRIP-- HOLDS ME LIKE A VISE.
I FEEL SO WEAK, I CANNOT FOCUS MY CONCENTRATION SUFFICIENTLY TO COMMAND THE ELEMENTS. I MUST BIDE MY TIME, WAIT FOR THE PROPER MOMENT, AND WHEN IT COMES--
--STRIKE WITHOUT MERCY.
HOW COULD I HAVE FOUND DRACULA NOBLE... ATTRACTIVE...? PERHAPS BECAUSE HE EMBODIES EVERYTHING I AM NOT AND CAN--MUST--NEVER BE.
HE CALLED YOU RACHEL?
I AM RACHEL VAN HELSING.
I KNOW OF THE NAME. BUT I THOUGHT YOU AND HE WERE SWORN ENEMIES?
SO WE WERE...
...WHEN I WAS ALIVE.
LIKE DEATH, ORORO, I CAN LOSE INNUMERABLE BATTLES--CONTENT THAT THE FINAL VICTORY WILL BE MINE. I AM ETERNAL, MY FOES ARE NOT. THEY AGE, THEY WITHER, UNTIL, EVENTUALLY, THE REAPER CLAIMS THEM. OR I DO.
I TRULY THOUGHT OUR PATHS WOULD NOT AGAIN CROSS, WHILE YOU LIVED. HOWEVER, MY NEED IS SUCH THAT I COULD AFFORD NEITHER DELAY NOR THE SLIGHTEST CHANCE OF YOUR REFUSAL--HENCE, THE MELODRAMATIC NATURE OF MY SUMMONS.
WHEN THIS TASK IS COMPLETE, YOU WILL BE FREE TO GO.
UNTIL THE NEXT TIME--! UNTIL I'M REBORN AS A VAMPIRE!

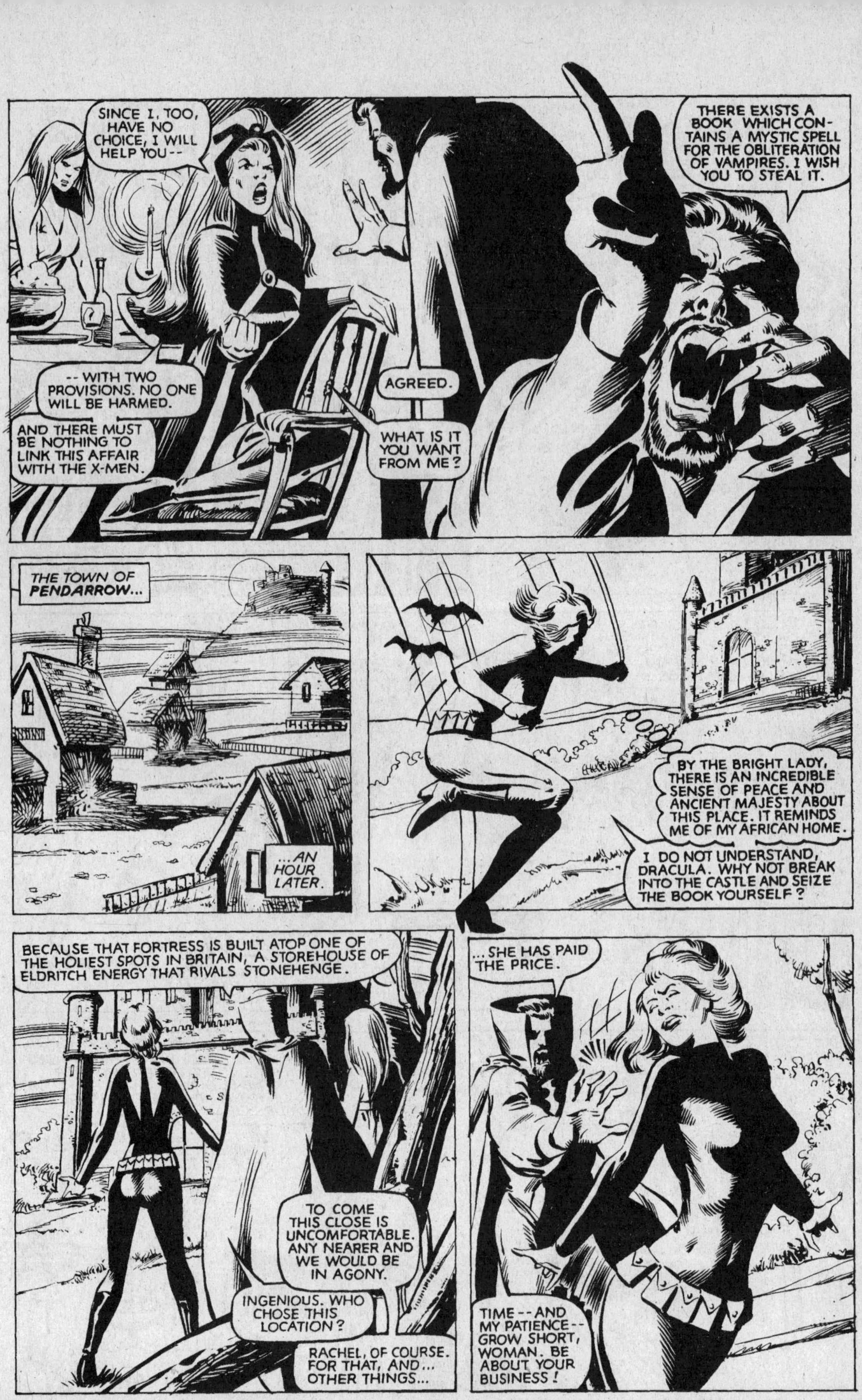
SINCE I, TOO, HAVE NO CHOICE, I WILL HELP YOU--
--WITH TWO PROVISIONS. NO ONE WILL BE HARMED.
AND THERE MUST BE NOTHING TO LINK THIS AFFAIR WITH THE X-MEN.
AGREED.
WHAT IS IT YOU WANT FROM ME?
THERE EXISTS A BOOK WHICH CONTAINS A MYSTIC SPELL FOR THE OBLITERATION OF VAMPIRES. I WISH YOU TO STEAL IT.
THE TOWN OF PENDARROW...
...AN HOUR LATER.
BY THE BRIGHT LADY, THERE IS AN INCREDIBLE SENSE OF PEACE AND ANCIENT MAJESTY ABOUT THIS PLACE. IT REMINDS ME OF MY AFRICAN HOME.
I DO NOT UNDERSTAND, DRACULA. WHY NOT BREAK INTO THE CASTLE AND SEIZE THE BOOK YOURSELF?
BECAUSE THAT FORTRESS IS BUILT ATOP ONE OF THE HOLIEST SPOTS IN BRITAIN, A STOREHOUSE OF ELDRITCH ENERGY THAT RIVALS STONEHENGE.
TO COME THIS CLOSE IS UNCOMFORTABLE. ANY NEARER AND WE WOULD BE IN AGONY.
INGENIOUS. WHO CHOSE THIS LOCATION?
RACHEL, OF COURSE. FOR THAT, AND... OTHER THINGS...
...SHE HAS PAID THE PRICE.
TIME--AND MY PATIENCE--GROW SHORT, WOMAN. BE ABOUT YOUR BUSINESS!

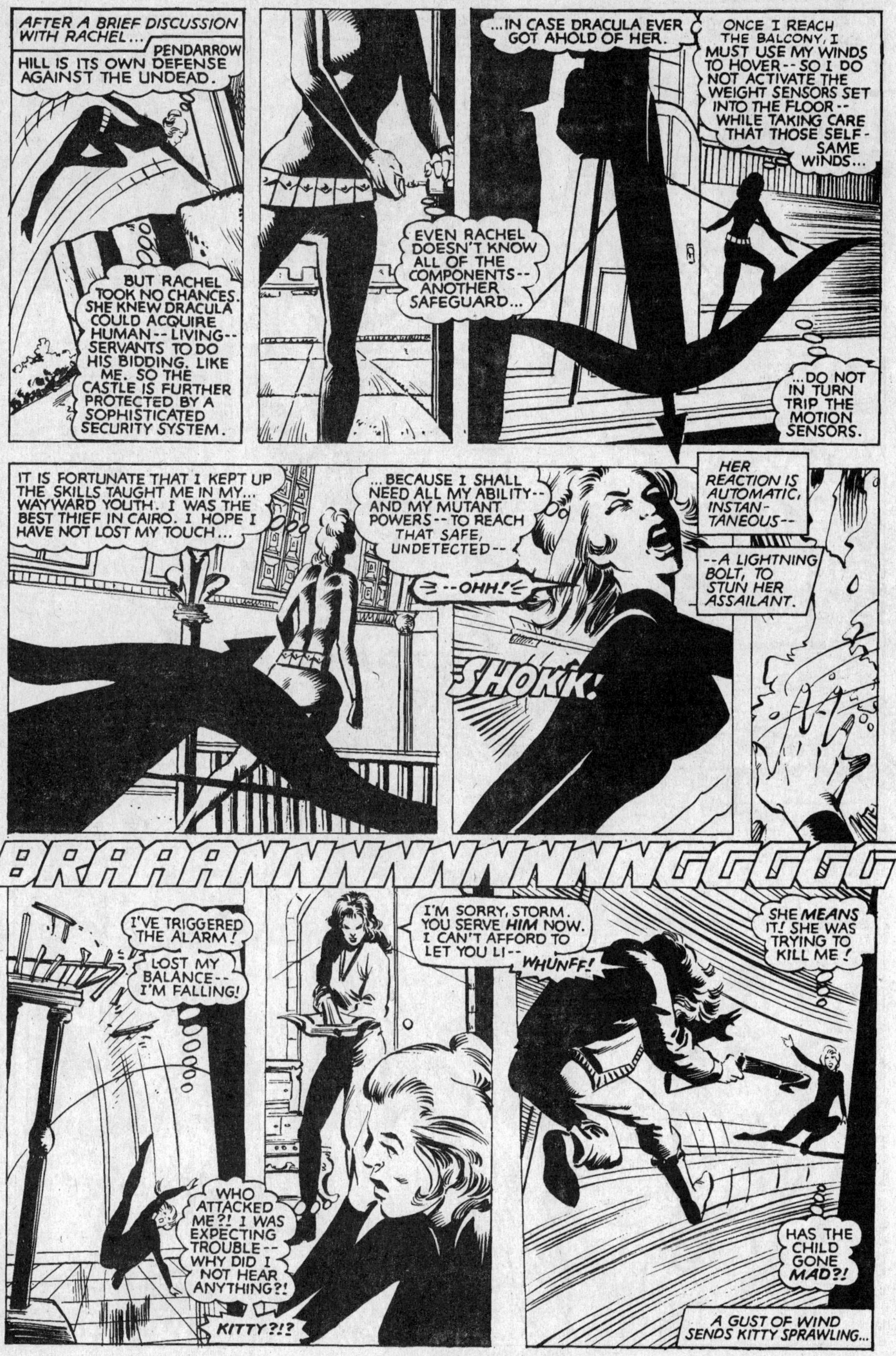
AFTER A BRIEF DISCUSSION WITH RACHEL...
PENDARROW HILL IS ITS OWN DEFENSE AGAINST THE UNDEAD.
BUT RACHEL TOOK NO CHANCES. SHE KNEW DRACULA COULD ACQUIRE HUMAN--LIVING--SERVANTS TO DO HIS BIDDING. LIKE ME. SO THE CASTLE IS FURTHER PROTECTED BY A SOPHISTICATED SECURITY SYSTEM.
EVEN RACHEL DOESN'T KNOW ALL OF THE COMPONENTS--ANOTHER SAFEGUARD...
...IN CASE DRACULA EVER GOT AHOLD OF HER.
ONCE I REACH THE BALCONY, I MUST USE MY WINDS TO HOVER--SO I DO NOT ACTIVATE THE WEIGHT SENSORS SET INTO THE FLOOR--WHILE TAKING CARE THAT THOSE SELF-SAME WINDS...
...DO NOT IN TURN TRIP THE MOTION SENSORS.
IT IS FORTUNATE THAT I KEPT UP THE SKILLS TAUGHT ME IN MY... WAYWARD YOUTH. I WAS THE BEST THIEF IN CAIRO. I HOPE I HAVE NOT LOST MY TOUCH...
...BECAUSE I SHALL NEED ALL MY ABILITY--AND MY MUTANT POWERS--TO REACH THAT SAFE, UNDETECTED--
--OHH!
SHOKK!
HER REACTION IS AUTOMATIC, INSTANTANEOUS--
--A LIGHTNING BOLT, TO STUN HER ASSAILANT.
BRAAANNNNNNNNNGGGGG
I'VE TRIGGERED THE ALARM!
LOST MY BALANCE--I'M FALLING!
WHO ATTACKED ME?! I WAS EXPECTING TROUBLE--WHY DID I NOT HEAR ANYTHING?!
KITTY?!?
I'M SORRY, STORM. YOU SERVE HIM NOW. I CAN'T AFFORD TO LET YOU LI--
WHUNFF!
SHE MEANS IT! SHE WAS TRYING TO KILL ME!
HAS THE CHILD GONE MAD?!
A GUST OF WIND SENDS KITTY SPRAWLING...

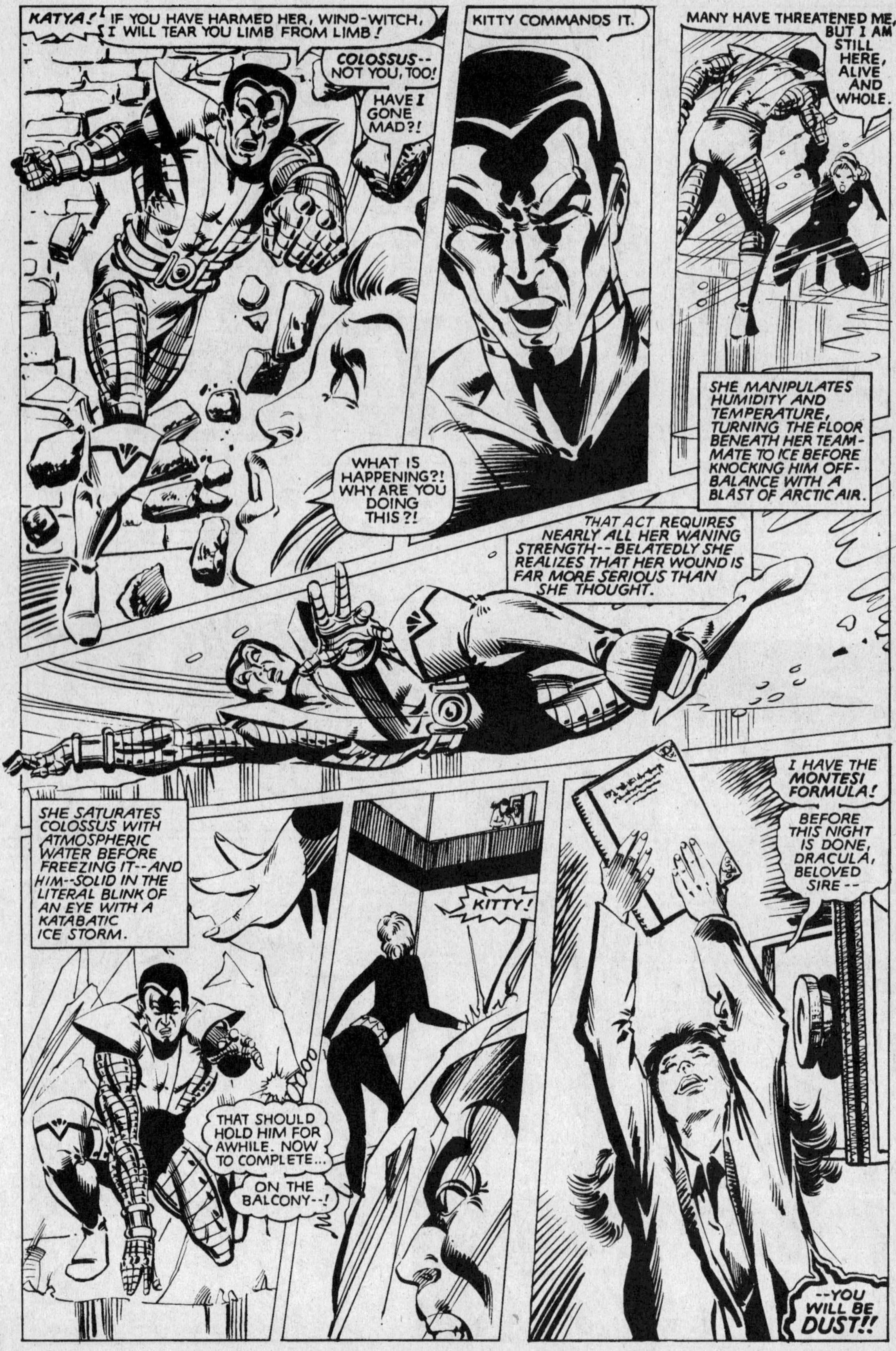
KATYA! IF YOU HAVE HARMED HER, WIND-WITCH, I WILL TEAR YOU LIMB FROM LIMB!
COLOSSUS-- NOT YOU, TOO!
HAVE I GONE MAD?!
WHAT IS HAPPENING?! WHY ARE YOU DOING THIS?!
KITTY COMMANDS IT.
MANY HAVE THREATENED ME, BUT I AM STILL HERE, ALIVE AND WHOLE.
SHE MANIPULATES HUMIDITY AND TEMPERATURE, TURNING THE FLOOR BENEATH HER TEAM-MATE TO ICE BEFORE KNOCKING HIM OFF-BALANCE WITH A BLAST OF ARCTIC AIR.
THAT ACT REQUIRES NEARLY ALL HER WANING STRENGTH-- BELATEDLY SHE REALIZES THAT HER WOUND IS FAR MORE SERIOUS THAN SHE THOUGHT.
SHE SATURATES COLOSSUS WITH ATMOSPHERIC WATER BEFORE FREEZING IT--AND HIM--SOLID IN THE LITERAL BLINK OF AN EYE WITH A KATABATIC ICE STORM.
THAT SHOULD HOLD HIM FOR AWHILE. NOW TO COMPLETE...
KITTY!
ON THE BALCONY--!
I HAVE THE MONTESI FORMULA!
BEFORE THIS NIGHT IS DONE, DRACULA, BELOVED SIRE --
--YOU WILL BE DUST!!

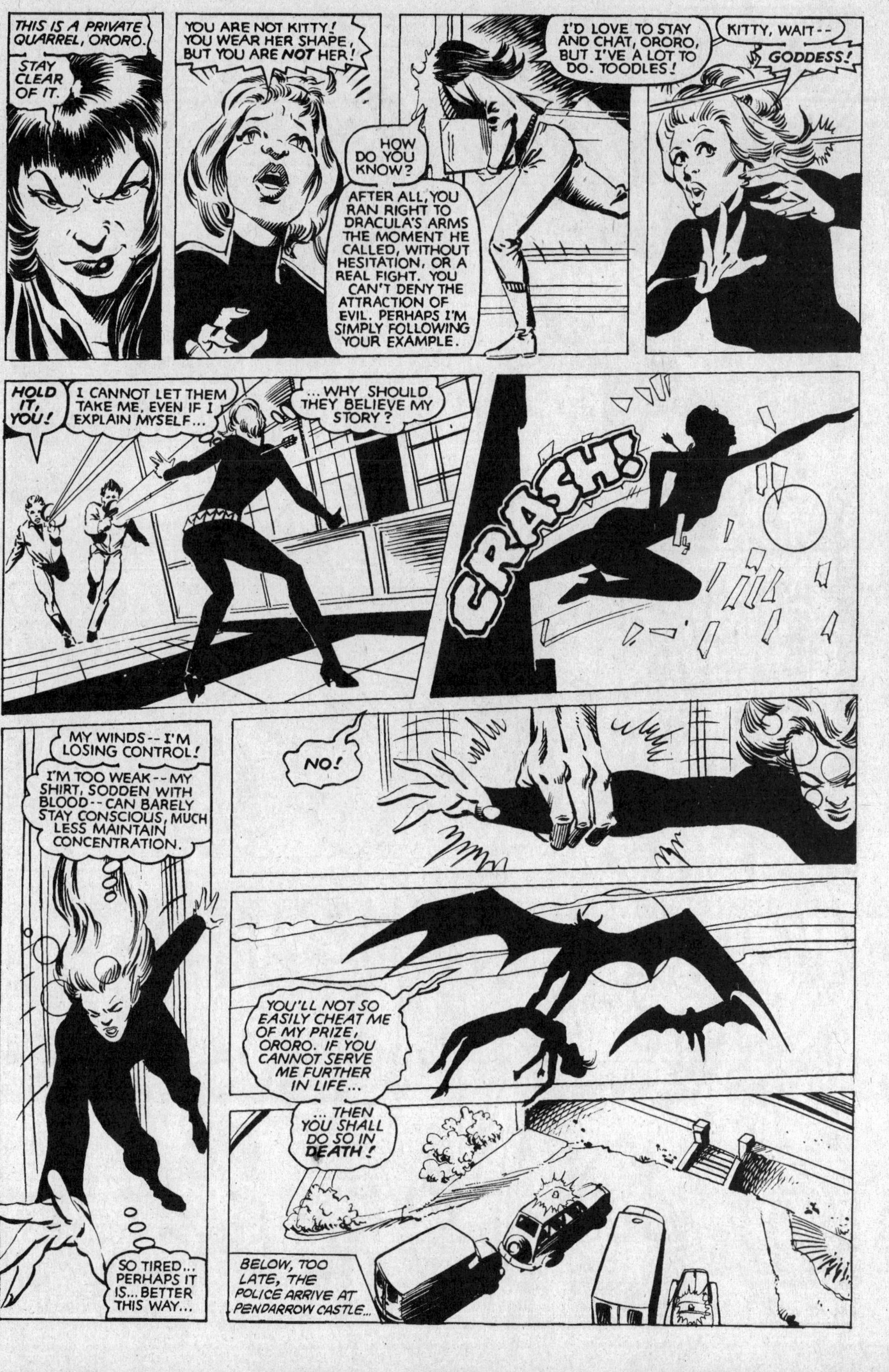
THIS IS A PRIVATE QUARREL, ORORO.
STAY CLEAR OF IT.
YOU ARE NOT KITTY! YOU WEAR HER SHAPE, BUT YOU ARE NOT HER!
HOW DO YOU KNOW?
AFTER ALL, YOU RAN RIGHT TO DRACULA'S ARMS THE MOMENT HE CALLED, WITHOUT HESITATION, OR A REAL FIGHT. YOU CAN'T DENY THE ATTRACTION OF EVIL. PERHAPS I'M SIMPLY FOLLOWING YOUR EXAMPLE.
I'D LOVE TO STAY AND CHAT, ORORO, BUT I'VE A LOT TO DO. TOODLES!
KITTY, WAIT--
GODDESS!
HOLD IT, YOU!
I CANNOT LET THEM TAKE ME, EVEN IF I EXPLAIN MYSELF...
...WHY SHOULD THEY BELIEVE MY STORY?
CRASH!
MY WINDS--I'M LOSING CONTROL!
I'M TOO WEAK--MY SHIRT, SODDEN WITH BLOOD--CAN BARELY STAY CONSCIOUS, MUCH LESS MAINTAIN CONCENTRATION.
SO TIRED... PERHAPS IT IS... BETTER THIS WAY...
NO!
YOU'LL NOT SO EASILY CHEAT ME OF MY PRIZE, ORORO. IF YOU CANNOT SERVE ME FURTHER IN LIFE...
...THEN YOU SHALL DO SO IN DEATH!
BELOW, TOO LATE, THE POLICE ARRIVE AT PENDARROW CASTLE...

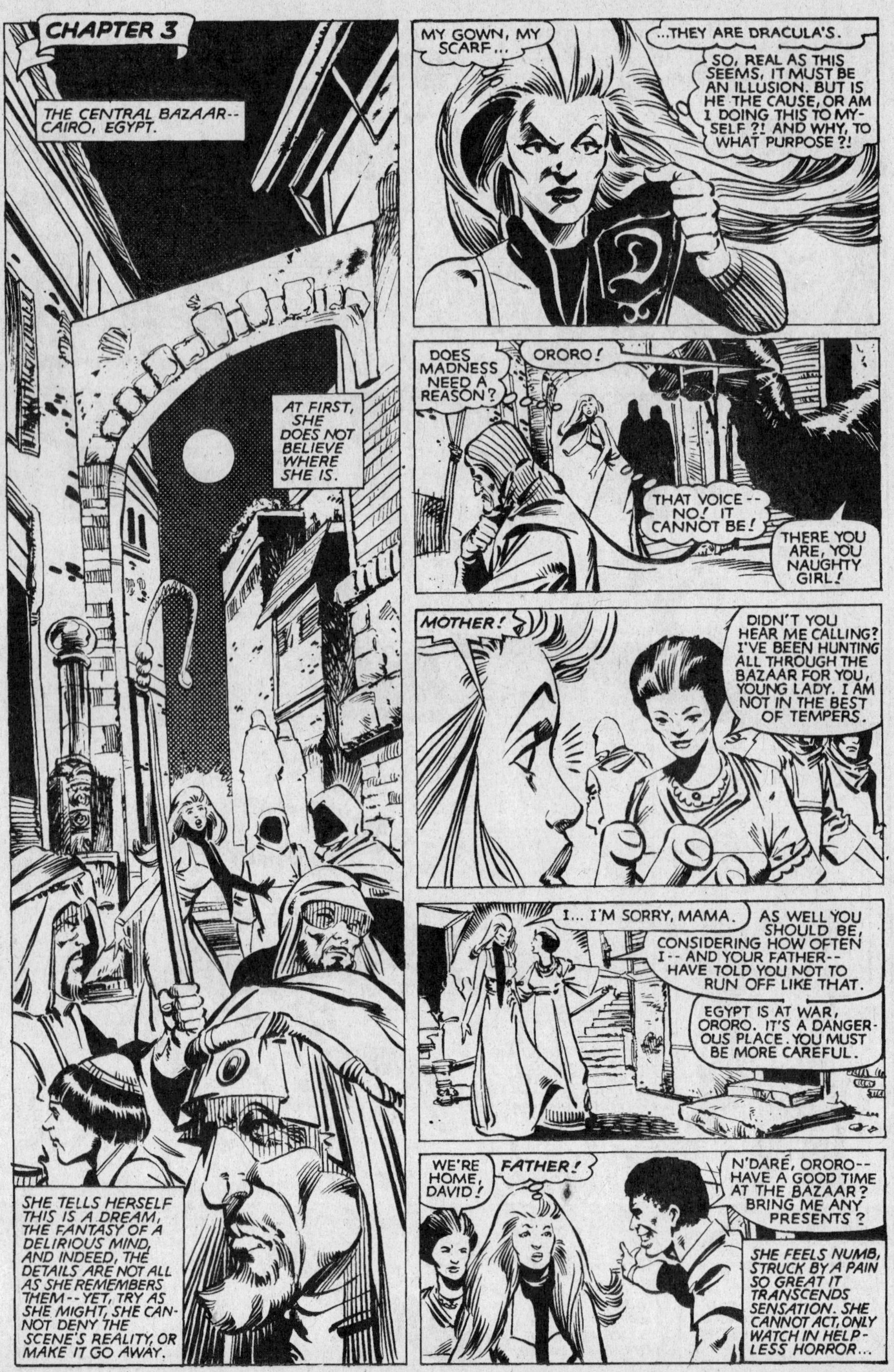
CHAPTER 3
THE CENTRAL BAZAAR-- CAIRO, EGYPT.
AT FIRST, SHE DOES NOT BELIEVE WHERE SHE IS.
SHE TELLS HERSELF THIS IS A DREAM, THE FANTASY OF A DELIRIOUS MIND, AND INDEED, THE DETAILS ARE NOT ALL AS SHE REMEMBERS THEM--YET, TRY AS SHE MIGHT, SHE CANNOT DENY THE SCENE'S REALITY, OR MAKE IT GO AWAY.
MY GOWN, MY SCARF...
...THEY ARE DRACULA'S.
SO, REAL AS THIS SEEMS, IT MUST BE AN ILLUSION. BUT IS HE THE CAUSE, OR AM I DOING THIS TO MYSELF ?! AND WHY, TO WHAT PURPOSE ?!
DOES MADNESS NEED A REASON?
ORORO!
THAT VOICE-- NO! IT CANNOT BE!
THERE YOU ARE, YOU NAUGHTY GIRL!
MOTHER!
DIDN'T YOU HEAR ME CALLING? I'VE BEEN HUNTING ALL THROUGH THE BAZAAR FOR YOU, YOUNG LADY. I AM NOT IN THE BEST OF TEMPERS.
I... I'M SORRY, MAMA.
AS WELL YOU SHOULD BE, CONSIDERING HOW OFTEN I-- AND YOUR FATHER-- HAVE TOLD YOU NOT TO RUN OFF LIKE THAT.
EGYPT IS AT WAR, ORORO. IT'S A DANGEROUS PLACE. YOU MUST BE MORE CAREFUL.
WE'RE HOME, DAVID!
FATHER!
N'DARÉ, ORORO-- HAVE A GOOD TIME AT THE BAZAAR? BRING ME ANY PRESENTS?
SHE FEELS NUMB, STRUCK BY A PAIN SO GREAT IT TRANSCENDS SENSATION. SHE CANNOT ACT, ONLY WATCH IN HELPLESS HORROR...

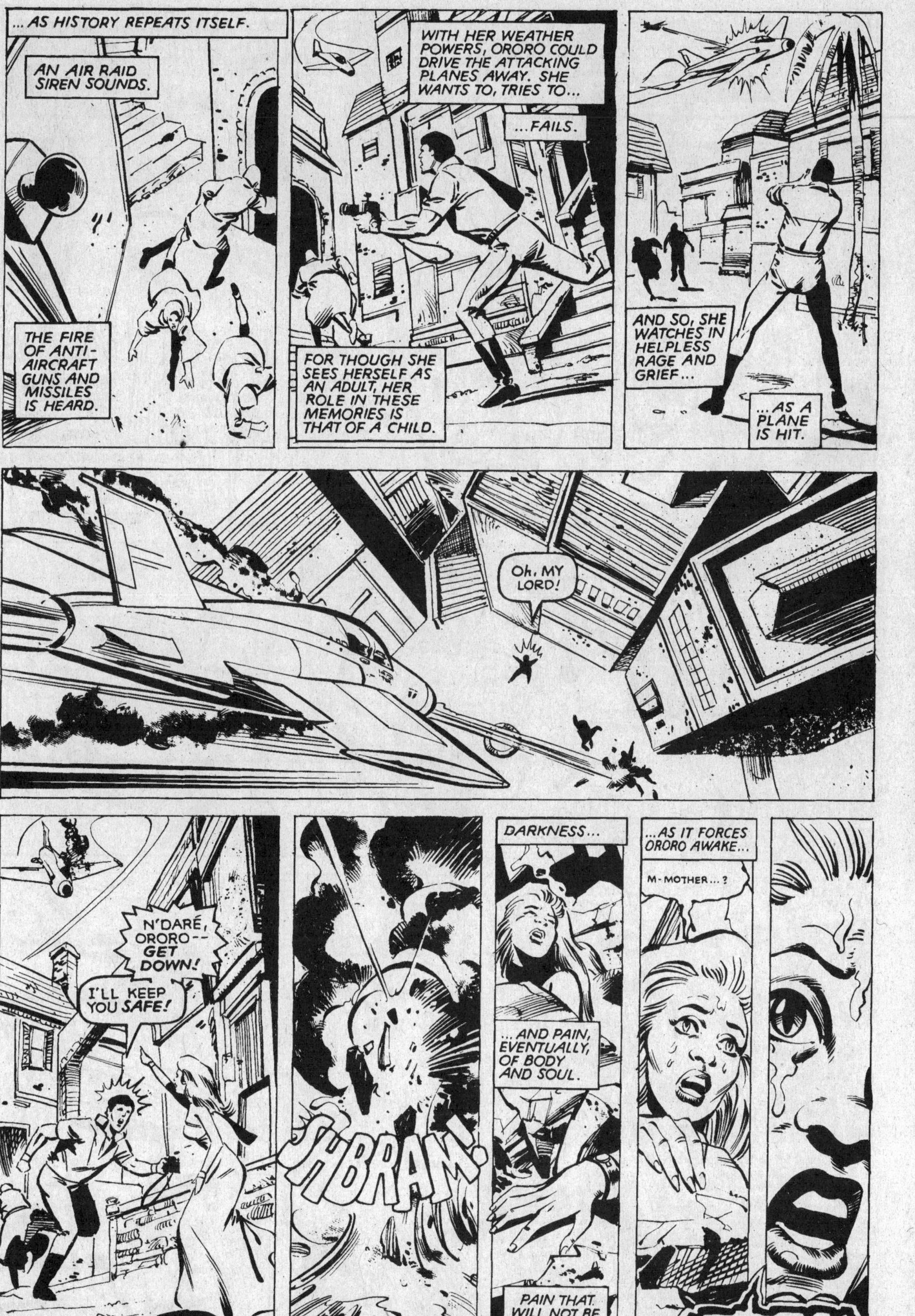
...AS HISTORY REPEATS ITSELF.
AN AIR RAID SIREN SOUNDS.
THE FIRE OF ANTI-AIRCRAFT GUNS AND MISSILES IS HEARD.
WITH HER WEATHER POWERS, ORORO COULD DRIVE THE ATTACKING PLANES AWAY. SHE WANTS TO, TRIES TO...
...FAILS.
FOR THOUGH SHE SEES HERSELF AS AN ADULT, HER ROLE IN THESE MEMORIES IS THAT OF A CHILD.
AND SO, SHE WATCHES IN HELPLESS RAGE AND GRIEF...
...AS A PLANE IS HIT.
OH, MY LORD!
N'DARÉ, ORORO-- GET DOWN!
I'LL KEEP YOU SAFE!
SHBRAM!
DARKNESS...
...AND PAIN, EVENTUALLY, OF BODY AND SOUL.
PAIN THAT WILL NOT BE IGNORED...
...AS IT FORCES ORORO AWAKE...
M-MOTHER...?
MOTHER!!

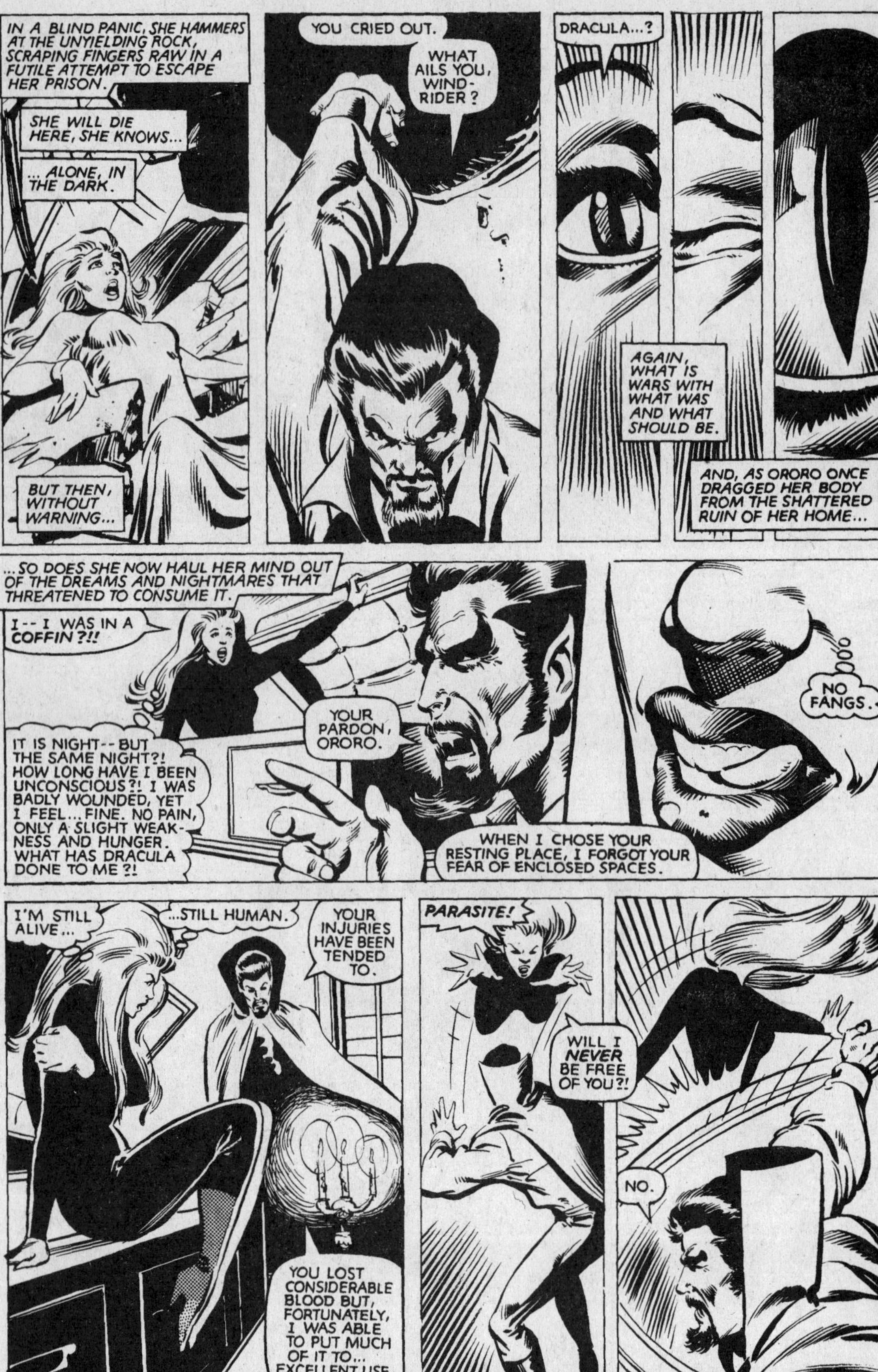

IN A BLIND PANIC, SHE HAMMERS AT THE UNYIELDING ROCK, SCRAPING FINGERS RAW IN A FUTILE ATTEMPT TO ESCAPE HER PRISON.
SHE WILL DIE HERE, SHE KNOWS...
... ALONE, IN THE DARK.
BUT THEN, WITHOUT WARNING...
YOU CRIED OUT.
WHAT AILS YOU, WIND-RIDER?
DRACULA...?
AGAIN, WHAT IS WARS WITH WHAT WAS AND WHAT SHOULD BE.
AND, AS ORORO ONCE DRAGGED HER BODY FROM THE SHATTERED RUIN OF HER HOME...
...SO DOES SHE NOW HAUL HER MIND OUT OF THE DREAMS AND NIGHTMARES THAT THREATENED TO CONSUME IT.
I -- I WAS IN A COFFIN?!!
YOUR PARDON, ORORO.
IT IS NIGHT-- BUT THE SAME NIGHT?! HOW LONG HAVE I BEEN UNCONSCIOUS?! I WAS BADLY WOUNDED, YET I FEEL... FINE. NO PAIN, ONLY A SLIGHT WEAKNESS AND HUNGER. WHAT HAS DRACULA DONE TO ME?!
WHEN I CHOSE YOUR RESTING PLACE, I FORGOT YOUR FEAR OF ENCLOSED SPACES.
NO FANGS.
I'M STILL ALIVE...
...STILL HUMAN.
YOUR INJURIES HAVE BEEN TENDED TO.
YOU LOST CONSIDERABLE BLOOD BUT, FORTUNATELY, I WAS ABLE TO PUT MUCH OF IT TO... EXCELLENT USE.
PARASITE!
WILL I NEVER BE FREE OF YOU?!
NO.

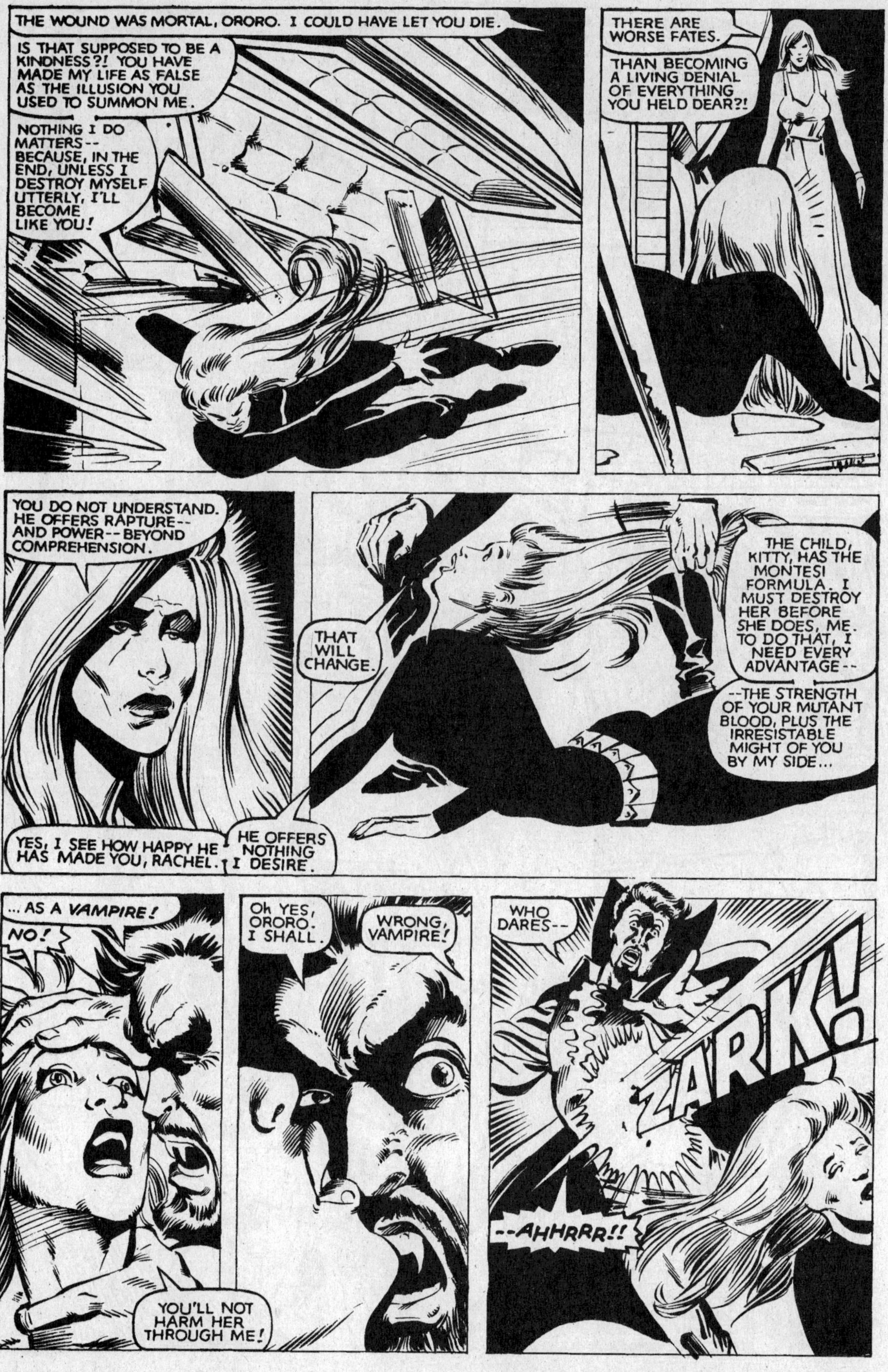

THE WOUND WAS MORTAL, ORORO. I COULD HAVE LET YOU DIE.
IS THAT SUPPOSED TO BE A KINDNESS?! YOU HAVE MADE MY LIFE AS FALSE AS THE ILLUSION YOU USED TO SUMMON ME.
NOTHING I DO MATTERS-- BECAUSE, IN THE END, UNLESS I DESTROY MYSELF UTTERLY, I'LL BECOME LIKE YOU!
THERE ARE WORSE FATES.
THAN BECOMING A LIVING DENIAL OF EVERYTHING YOU HELD DEAR?!
YOU DO NOT UNDERSTAND. HE OFFERS RAPTURE-- AND POWER-- BEYOND COMPREHENSION.
YES, I SEE HOW HAPPY HE HAS MADE YOU, RACHEL.
HE OFFERS NOTHING I DESIRE.
THAT WILL CHANGE.
THE CHILD, KITTY, HAS THE MONTESI FORMULA. I MUST DESTROY HER BEFORE SHE DOES, ME. TO DO THAT, I NEED EVERY ADVANTAGE--
--THE STRENGTH OF YOUR MUTANT BLOOD, PLUS THE IRRESISTABLE MIGHT OF YOU BY MY SIDE...
... AS A VAMPIRE!
NO!
YOU'LL NOT HARM HER THROUGH ME!
Oh YES, ORORO. I SHALL.
WRONG, VAMPIRE!
WHO DARES--
ZARK!
--AHHRRR!!

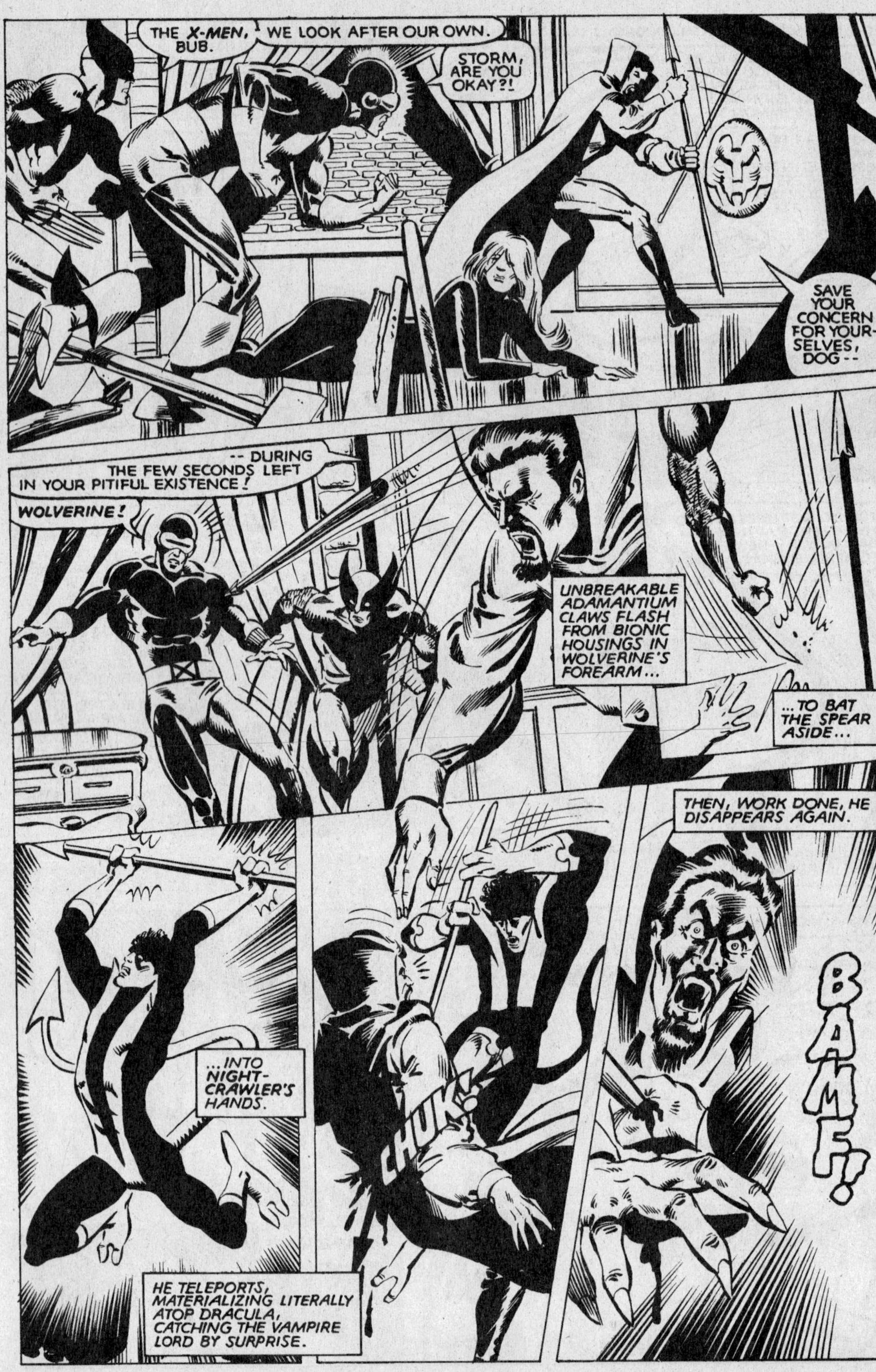
THE X-MEN, BUB.
WE LOOK AFTER OUR OWN.
STORM, ARE YOU OKAY?!
SAVE YOUR CONCERN FOR YOUR-SELVES, DOG --
-- DURING THE FEW SECONDS LEFT IN YOUR PITIFUL EXISTENCE!
WOLVERINE!
UNBREAKABLE ADAMANTIUM CLAWS FLASH FROM BIONIC HOUSINGS IN WOLVERINE'S FOREARM...
...TO BAT THE SPEAR ASIDE...
...INTO NIGHT-CRAWLER'S HANDS.
HE TELEPORTS, MATERIALIZING LITERALLY ATOP DRACULA, CATCHING THE VAMPIRE LORD BY SURPRISE.
CHUK!
THEN, WORK DONE, HE DISAPPEARS AGAIN.
BAMF!

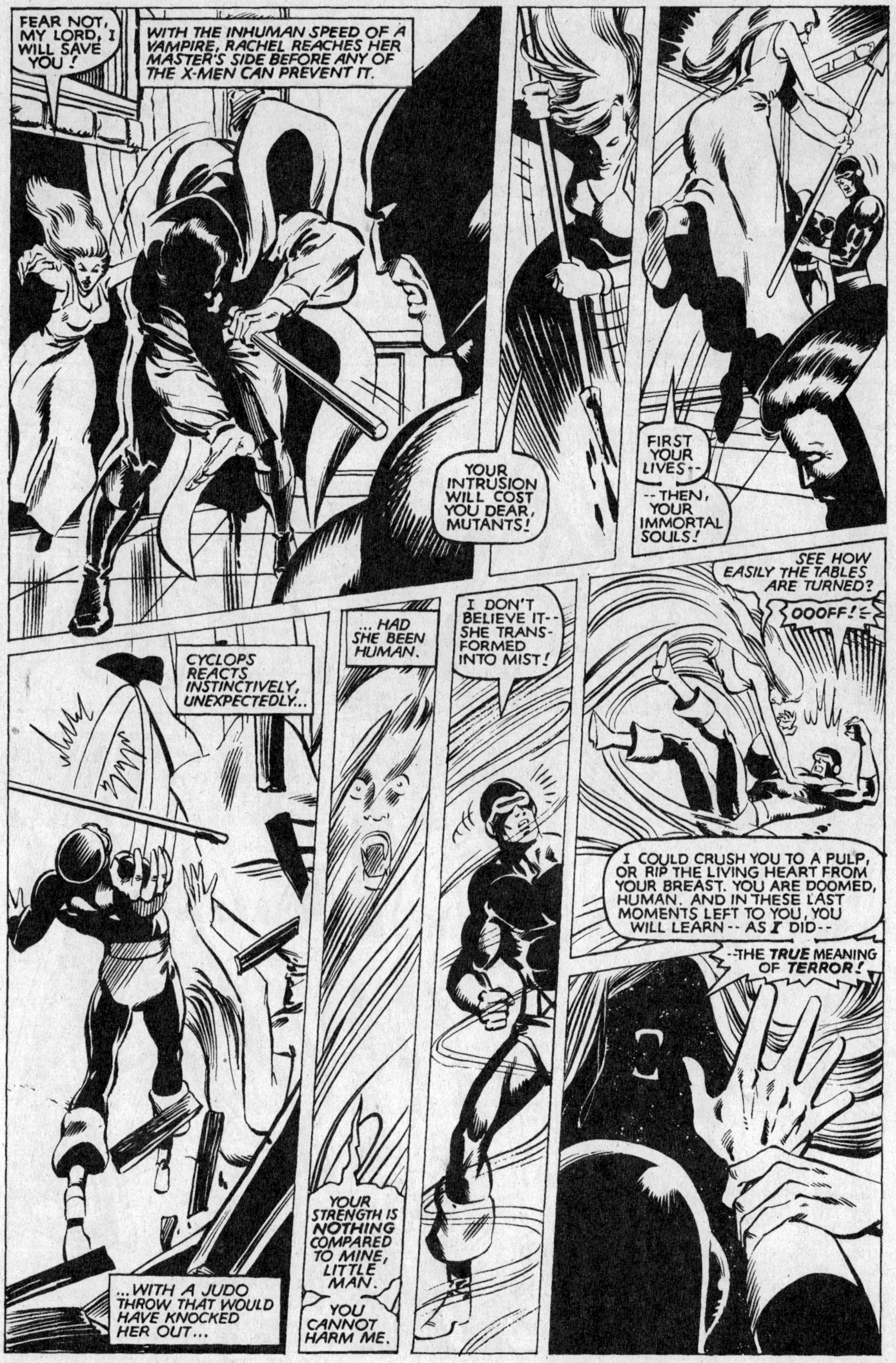
FEAR NOT, MY LORD, I WILL SAVE YOU!
WITH THE INHUMAN SPEED OF A VAMPIRE, RACHEL REACHES HER MASTER'S SIDE BEFORE ANY OF THE X-MEN CAN PREVENT IT.
YOUR INTRUSION WILL COST YOU DEAR, MUTANTS!
FIRST YOUR LIVES--
--THEN, YOUR IMMORTAL SOULS!
CYCLOPS REACTS INSTINCTIVELY, UNEXPECTEDLY...
...WITH A JUDO THROW THAT WOULD HAVE KNOCKED HER OUT...
...HAD SHE BEEN HUMAN.
YOUR STRENGTH IS NOTHING COMPARED TO MINE, LITTLE MAN.
YOU CANNOT HARM ME.
I DON'T BELIEVE IT-- SHE TRANSFORMED INTO MIST!
SEE HOW EASILY THE TABLES ARE TURNED?
OOOFF!
I COULD CRUSH YOU TO A PULP, OR RIP THE LIVING HEART FROM YOUR BREAST. YOU ARE DOOMED, HUMAN. AND IN THESE LAST MOMENTS LEFT TO YOU, YOU WILL LEARN -- AS I DID--
--THE TRUE MEANING OF TERROR!

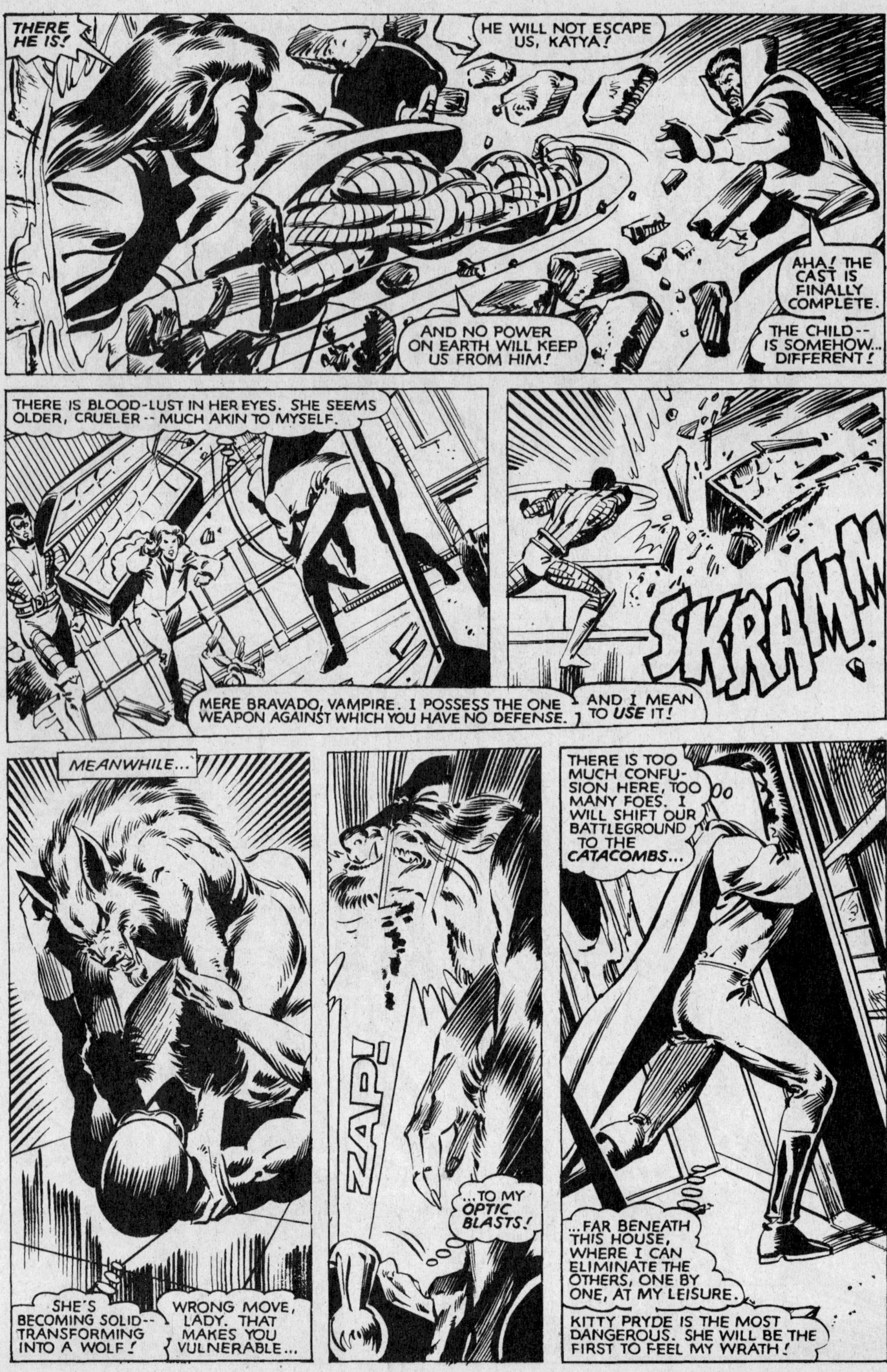
THERE HE IS!
HE WILL NOT ESCAPE US, KATYA!
AND NO POWER ON EARTH WILL KEEP US FROM HIM!
AHA! THE CAST IS FINALLY COMPLETE.
THE CHILD-- IS SOMEHOW... DIFFERENT!
THERE IS BLOOD-LUST IN HER EYES. SHE SEEMS OLDER, CRUELER -- MUCH AKIN TO MYSELF.
SKRAMM
MERE BRAVADO, VAMPIRE. I POSSESS THE ONE WEAPON AGAINST WHICH YOU HAVE NO DEFENSE.
AND I MEAN TO USE IT!
MEANWHILE...
SHE'S BECOMING SOLID-- TRANSFORMING INTO A WOLF!
WRONG MOVE, LADY. THAT MAKES YOU VULNERABLE...
ZAP!
...TO MY OPTIC BLASTS!
THERE IS TOO MUCH CONFUSION HERE, TOO MANY FOES. I WILL SHIFT OUR BATTLEGROUND TO THE CATACOMBS...
...FAR BENEATH THIS HOUSE, WHERE I CAN ELIMINATE THE OTHERS, ONE BY ONE, AT MY LEISURE.
KITTY PRYDE IS THE MOST DANGEROUS. SHE WILL BE THE FIRST TO FEEL MY WRATH!

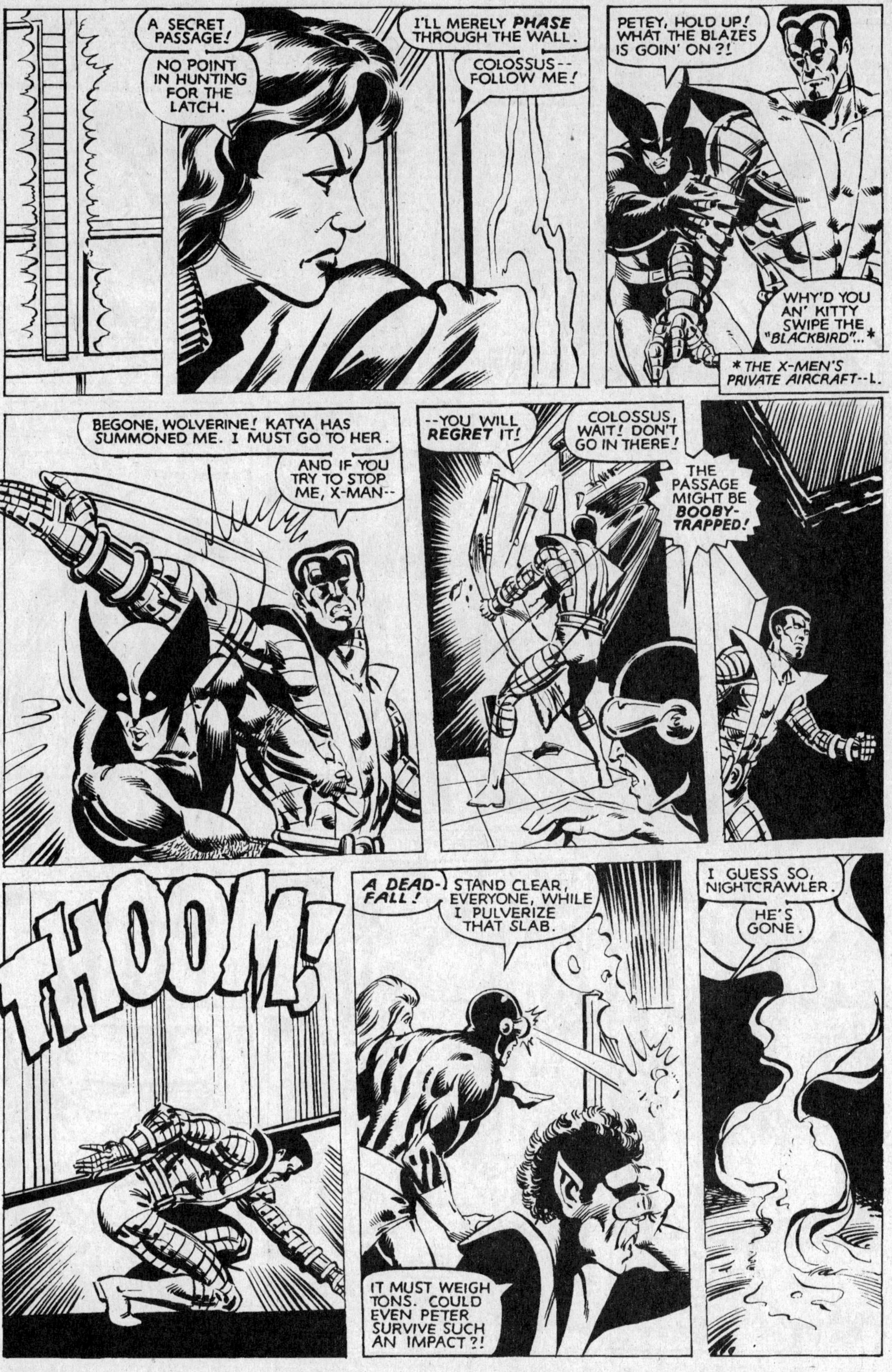
A SECRET PASSAGE!
NO POINT IN HUNTING FOR THE LATCH.
I'LL MERELY PHASE THROUGH THE WALL.
COLOSSUS-- FOLLOW ME!
PETEY, HOLD UP! WHAT THE BLAZES IS GOIN' ON?!
WHY'D YOU AN' KITTY SWIPE THE "BLACKBIRD"...*
*THE X-MEN'S PRIVATE AIRCRAFT--L.
BEGONE, WOLVERINE! KATYA HAS SUMMONED ME. I MUST GO TO HER.
AND IF YOU TRY TO STOP ME, X-MAN--
--YOU WILL REGRET IT!
COLOSSUS, WAIT! DON'T GO IN THERE!
THE PASSAGE MIGHT BE BOOBY-TRAPPED!
THOOM!
A DEAD-FALL!
STAND CLEAR, EVERYONE, WHILE I PULVERIZE THAT SLAB.
IT MUST WEIGH TONS. COULD EVEN PETER SURVIVE SUCH AN IMPACT?!
I GUESS SO, NIGHTCRAWLER.
HE'S GONE.

Panel 1:

HEARTFELT GREETINGS-- AND MUTUAL EXPLANATIONS-- ARE SPEEDILY EXCHANGED...

HOW DID YOU FIND ME?

WHEN KITTY SWIPED THE *BLACKBIRD*, SHE SET-OFF THE ALARMS. THE JET'S AUTOMATIC TRACER BEACON ALLOWED US TO FOLLOW IT TO ENGLAND.

ON ARRIVAL, WE HEARD ABOUT THE BREAK-IN AT PENDARROW CASTLE. THAT BECAME OUR NEXT STOP. WOLVERINE'S ENHANCED SENSES AND TRACKING ABILITIES DID THE REST.

KURT, GET ORORO TO SAFETY. WOLVIE AND I WILL...

Panel 2:

I AM TEAM LEADER, CYCLOPS. MY PLACE IS HERE.

DON'T BE RIDICULOUS. YOU'RE IN NO SHAPE FOR A FIGHT.

Panel 3:

SUPPOSE DRACULA REGAINS CONTROL OF YOU.

IN A BURST OF LIGHT, STORM CHANGES INTO HER COSTUME...

I KNOW THE RISK. BUT IF I AM TO BE TRUE TO MYSELF -- AS ORORO AND STORM-- I MUST STAY.

Panel 4:

WIN OR LOSE, I MUST AT LEAST TRY.

ALL RIGHT.

Panel 5:

SOMETHING ELSE, THOUGH-- I BELIEVE KITTY AND PETER ARE UNDER ANOTHER'S INFLUENCE.

Panel 6:

SOUNDS LOGICAL, THE WAY THEY'VE BEEN ACTING.

NASTY WEATHER OUTSIDE, ALL OF A SUDDEN. YOUR DOIN', DARLIN'?

IN PART, I FEAR SO, WOLVERINE.

A REFLECTION OF MY MOOD. SHALL I BANISH IT?

Panel 7:

SAVE YOUR STRENGTH, WE'LL NEED IT.

THE PASSAGE IS OPEN, CYCLOPS...

...BUT THERE MAY BE MORE BOOBY-TRAPS.

FORGET ABOUT THAT, NIGHT-CRAWLER.

Panel 8:

WE'LL MAKE OUR OWN WAY INTO THE CATACOMBS.

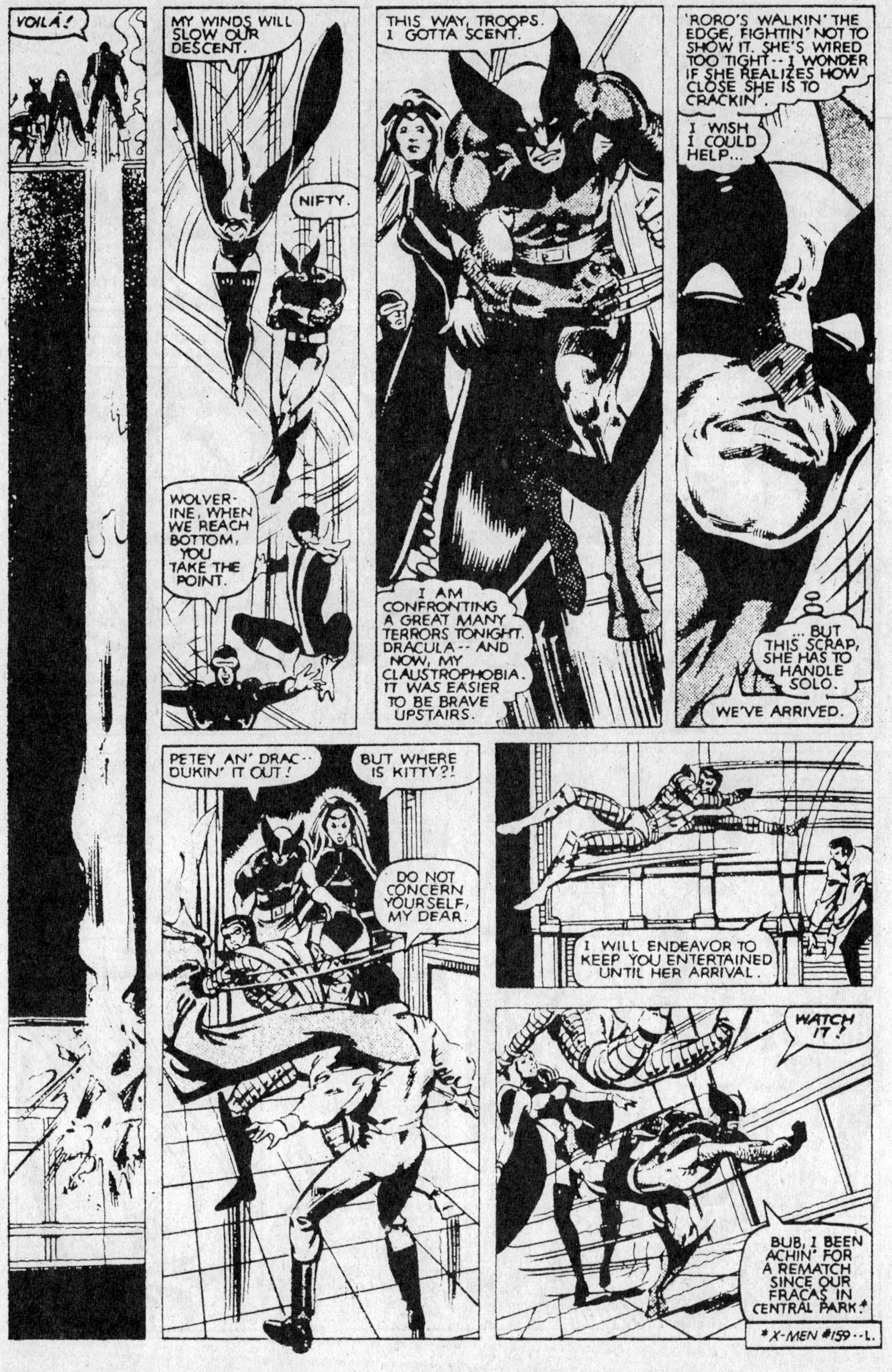
VOILÀ!
MY WINDS WILL SLOW OUR DESCENT.
NIFTY.
WOLVERINE, WHEN WE REACH BOTTOM, YOU TAKE THE POINT.
THIS WAY, TROOPS. I GOTTA SCENT.
I AM CONFRONTING A GREAT MANY TERRORS TONIGHT. DRACULA -- AND NOW, MY CLAUSTROPHOBIA. IT WAS EASIER TO BE BRAVE UPSTAIRS.
'RORO'S WALKIN' THE EDGE, FIGHTIN' NOT TO SHOW IT. SHE'S WIRED TOO TIGHT -- I WONDER IF SHE REALIZES HOW CLOSE SHE IS TO CRACKIN'.
I WISH I COULD HELP...
... BUT THIS SCRAP, SHE HAS TO HANDLE SOLO.
WE'VE ARRIVED.
PETEY AN' DRAC -- DUKIN' IT OUT!
BUT WHERE IS KITTY?!
DO NOT CONCERN YOURSELF, MY DEAR.
I WILL ENDEAVOR TO KEEP YOU ENTERTAINED UNTIL HER ARRIVAL.
WATCH IT!
BUB, I BEEN ACHIN' FOR A REMATCH SINCE OUR FRACAS IN CENTRAL PARK!*
*X-MEN #159 -- L.

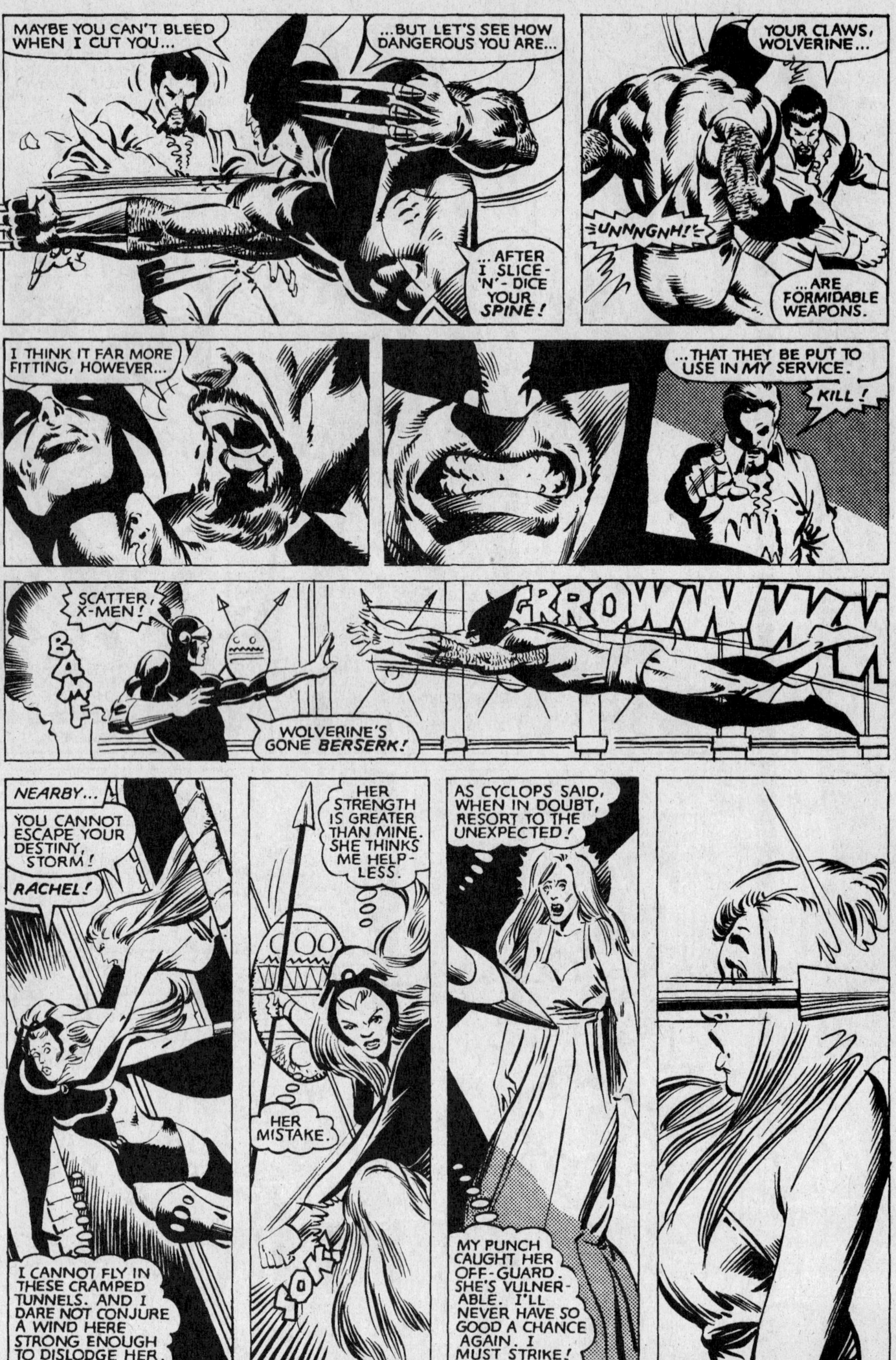
MAYBE YOU CAN'T BLEED WHEN I CUT YOU...
...BUT LET'S SEE HOW DANGEROUS YOU ARE...
...AFTER I SLICE-'N'-DICE YOUR SPINE!
YOUR CLAWS, WOLVERINE...
UNNNGNH!
...ARE FORMIDABLE WEAPONS.
I THINK IT FAR MORE FITTING, HOWEVER...
...THAT THEY BE PUT TO USE IN MY SERVICE.
KILL!
SCATTER, X-MEN!
BAMF
GRROWWWW
WOLVERINE'S GONE BERSERK!
NEARBY...
YOU CANNOT ESCAPE YOUR DESTINY, STORM!
RACHEL!
I CANNOT FLY IN THESE CRAMPED TUNNELS. AND I DARE NOT CONJURE A WIND HERE STRONG ENOUGH TO DISLODGE HER.
HER STRENGTH IS GREATER THAN MINE. SHE THINKS ME HELP-LESS.
HER MISTAKE.
SOK
AS CYCLOPS SAID, WHEN IN DOUBT, RESORT TO THE UNEXPECTED!
MY PUNCH CAUGHT HER OFF-GUARD. SHE'S VULNER-ABLE. I'LL NEVER HAVE SO GOOD A CHANCE AGAIN. I MUST STRIKE!

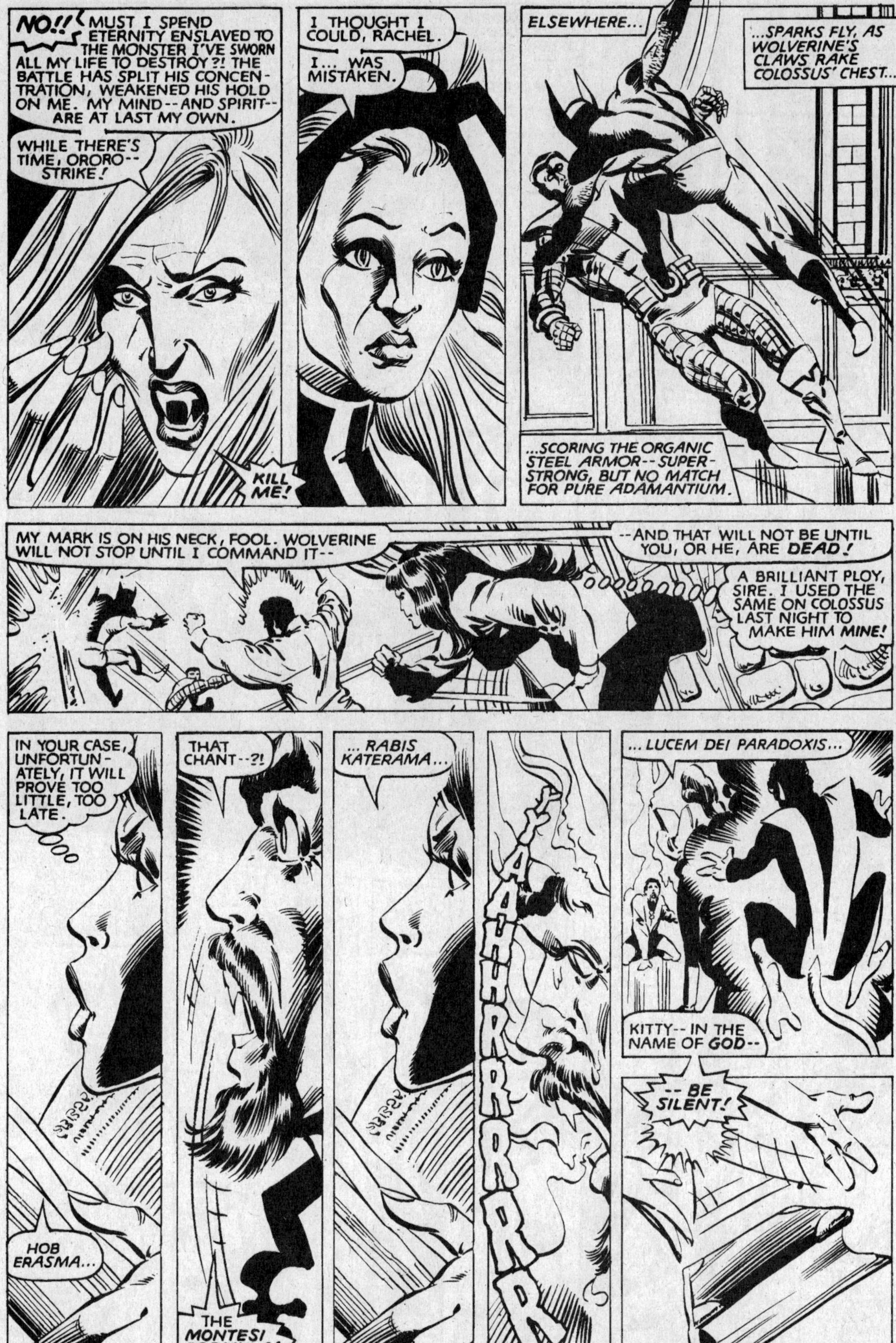
NO!! MUST I SPEND ETERNITY ENSLAVED TO THE MONSTER I'VE SWORN ALL MY LIFE TO DESTROY?! THE BATTLE HAS SPLIT HIS CONCENTRATION, WEAKENED HIS HOLD ON ME. MY MIND--AND SPIRIT--ARE AT LAST MY OWN.
WHILE THERE'S TIME, ORORO--STRIKE!
KILL ME!
I THOUGHT I COULD, RACHEL.
I... WAS MISTAKEN.
ELSEWHERE...
...SPARKS FLY, AS WOLVERINE'S CLAWS RAKE COLOSSUS' CHEST...
...SCORING THE ORGANIC STEEL ARMOR--SUPER-STRONG, BUT NO MATCH FOR PURE ADAMANTIUM.
MY MARK IS ON HIS NECK, FOOL. WOLVERINE WILL NOT STOP UNTIL I COMMAND IT--
--AND THAT WILL NOT BE UNTIL YOU, OR HE, ARE DEAD!
A BRILLIANT PLOY, SIRE. I USED THE SAME ON COLOSSUS LAST NIGHT TO MAKE HIM MINE!
IN YOUR CASE, UNFORTUNATELY, IT WILL PROVE TOO LITTLE, TOO LATE.
HOB ERASMA...
THAT CHANT--?!
THE MONTESI FORMULA!
... RABIS KATERAMA...
YAAHHRRRRRRR
... LUCEM DEI PARADOXIS...
KITTY-- IN THE NAME OF GOD--
-- BE SILENT!

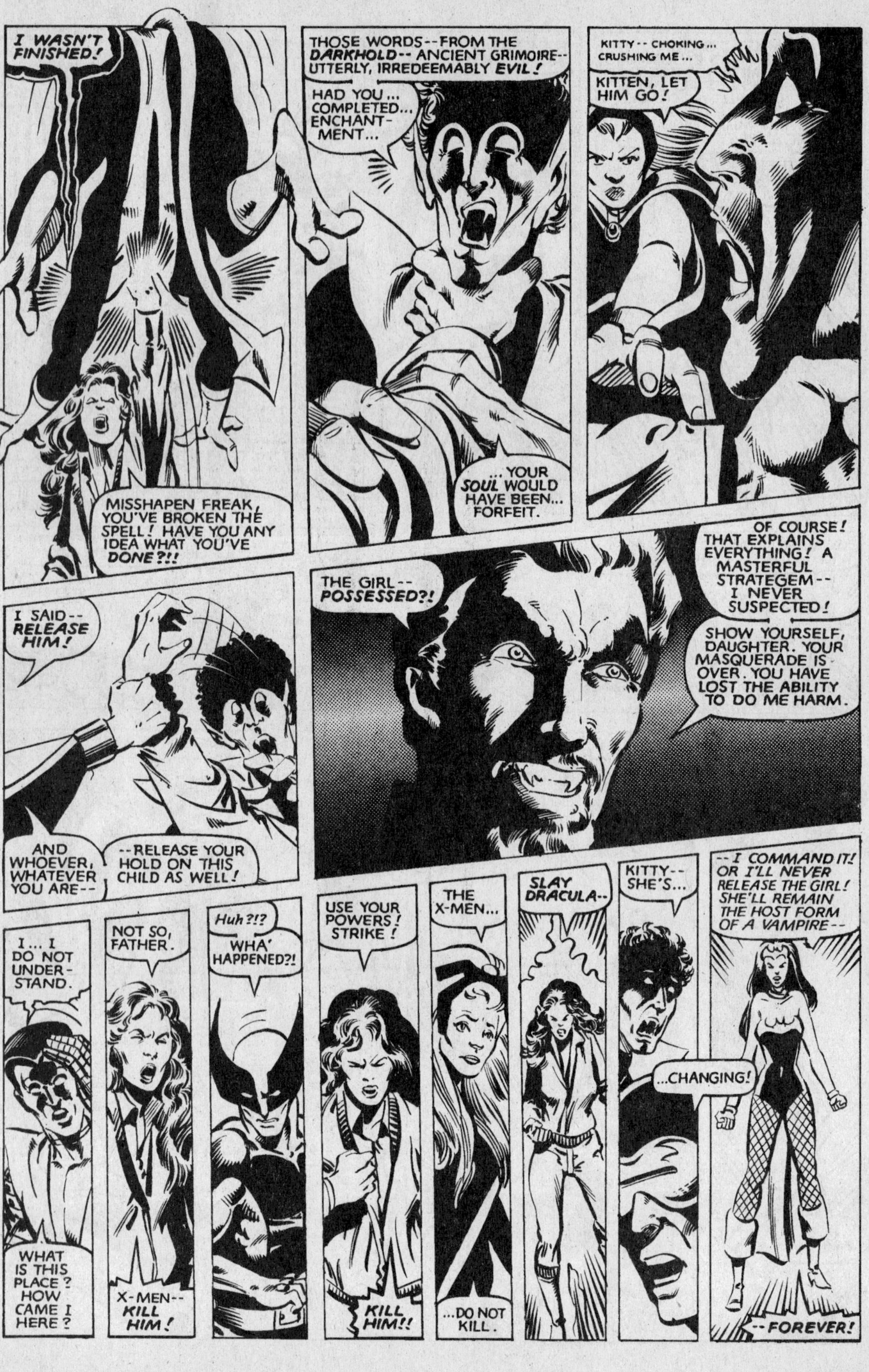
I WASN'T FINISHED!
MISSHAPEN FREAK, YOU'VE BROKEN THE SPELL! HAVE YOU ANY IDEA WHAT YOU'VE DONE?!!
THOSE WORDS--FROM THE DARKHOLD--ANCIENT GRIMOIRE--UTTERLY, IRREDEEMABLY EVIL!
HAD YOU... COMPLETED... ENCHANT-MENT...
...YOUR SOUL WOULD HAVE BEEN... FORFEIT.
KITTY--CHOKING... CRUSHING ME...
KITTEN, LET HIM GO!
I SAID--RELEASE HIM!
AND WHOEVER, WHATEVER YOU ARE--
--RELEASE YOUR HOLD ON THIS CHILD AS WELL!
THE GIRL--POSSESSED?!
OF COURSE! THAT EXPLAINS EVERYTHING! A MASTERFUL STRATEGEM--I NEVER SUSPECTED!
SHOW YOURSELF, DAUGHTER. YOUR MASQUERADE IS OVER. YOU HAVE LOST THE ABILITY TO DO ME HARM.
I... I DO NOT UNDER-STAND.
WHAT IS THIS PLACE? HOW CAME I HERE?
NOT SO, FATHER.
X-MEN--KILL HIM!
Huh?!? WHA' HAPPENED?!
USE YOUR POWERS! STRIKE!
KILL HIM!!
THE X-MEN...
...DO NOT KILL.
SLAY DRACULA--
KITTY--SHE'S...
...CHANGING!
--I COMMAND IT! OR I'LL NEVER RELEASE THE GIRL! SHE'LL REMAIN THE HOST FORM OF A VAMPIRE--
--FOREVER!

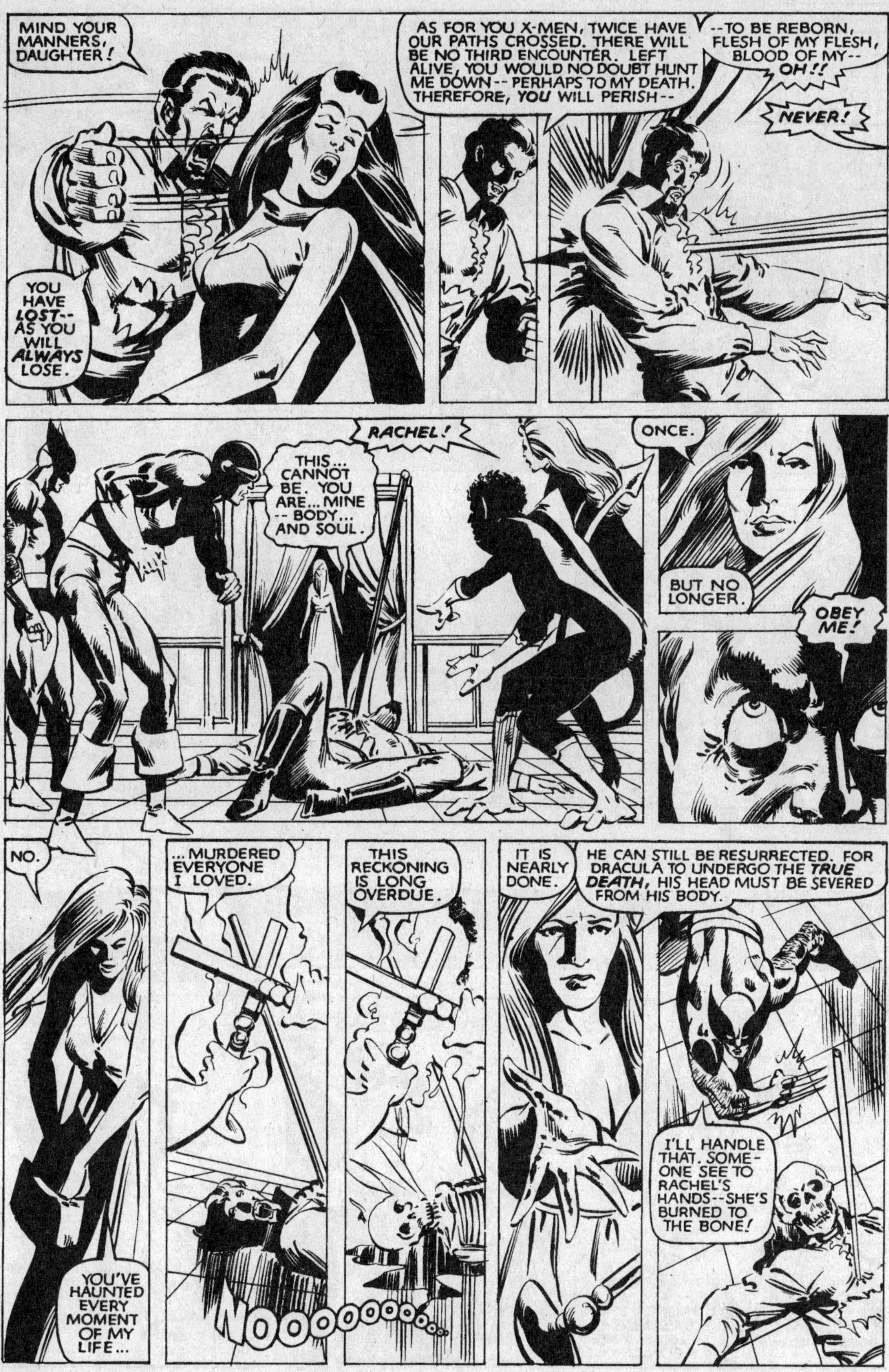
MIND YOUR MANNERS, DAUGHTER!
YOU HAVE LOST-- AS YOU WILL ALWAYS LOSE.
AS FOR YOU X-MEN, TWICE HAVE OUR PATHS CROSSED. THERE WILL BE NO THIRD ENCOUNTER. LEFT ALIVE, YOU WOULD NO DOUBT HUNT ME DOWN-- PERHAPS TO MY DEATH. THEREFORE, YOU WILL PERISH--
--TO BE REBORN, FLESH OF MY FLESH, BLOOD OF MY-- OH!!
NEVER!
RACHEL!
THIS... CANNOT BE. YOU ARE... MINE -- BODY... AND SOUL.
ONCE.
BUT NO LONGER.
OBEY ME!
NO.
YOU'VE HAUNTED EVERY MOMENT OF MY LIFE...
...MURDERED EVERYONE I LOVED.
THIS RECKONING IS LONG OVERDUE.
NOOOOOOOO...
IT IS NEARLY DONE.
HE CAN STILL BE RESURRECTED. FOR DRACULA TO UNDERGO THE TRUE DEATH, HIS HEAD MUST BE SEVERED FROM HIS BODY.
I'LL HANDLE THAT. SOME-ONE SEE TO RACHEL'S HANDS--SHE'S BURNED TO THE BONE!

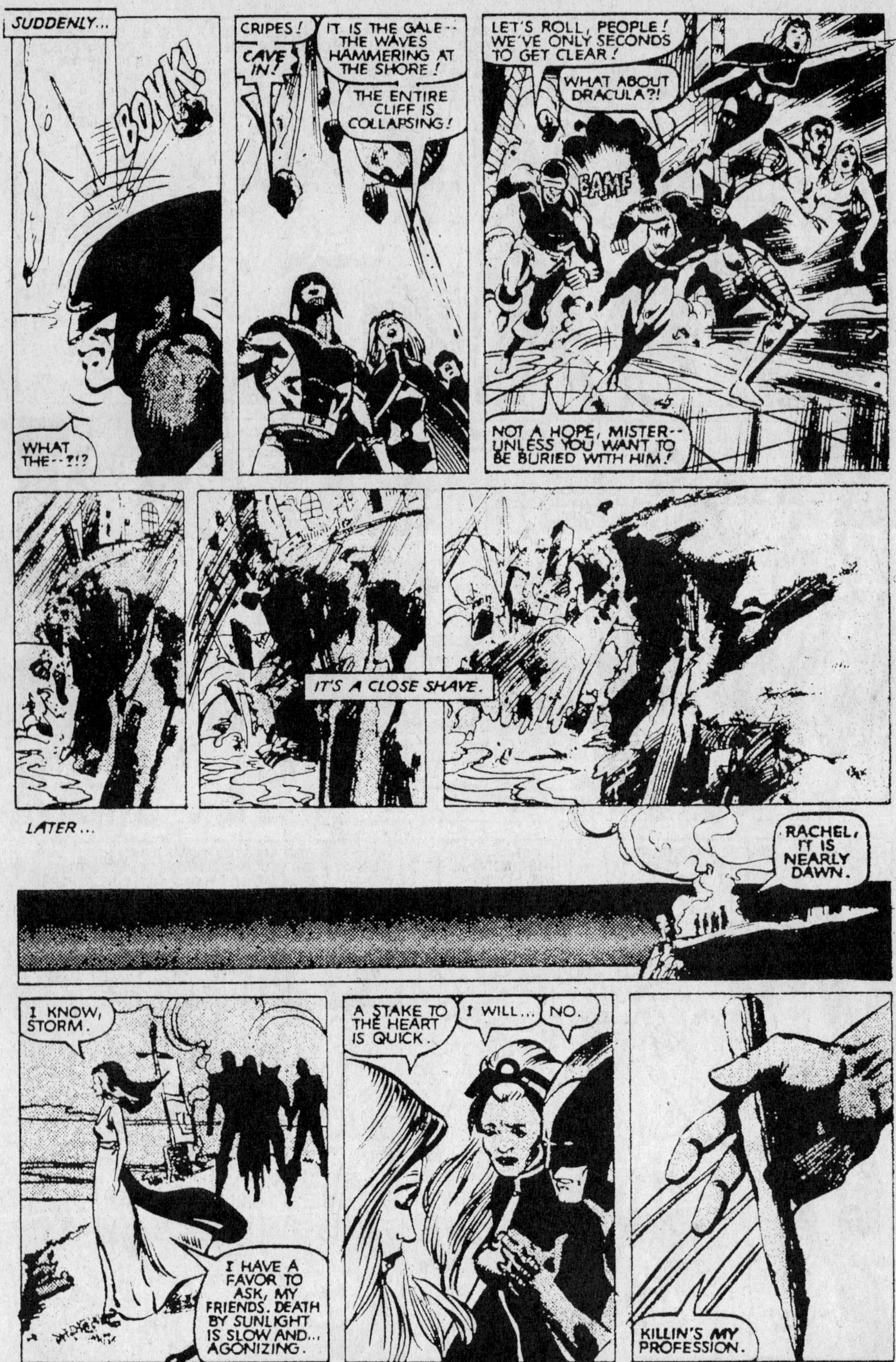
SUDDENLY...
BONK!
WHAT THE--?!?
CRIPES!
CAVE IN!
IT IS THE GALE-- THE WAVES HAMMERING AT THE SHORE!
THE ENTIRE CLIFF IS COLLAPSING!
LET'S ROLL, PEOPLE! WE'VE ONLY SECONDS TO GET CLEAR!
WHAT ABOUT DRACULA?!
BAMF
NOT A HOPE, MISTER-- UNLESS YOU WANT TO BE BURIED WITH HIM!
IT'S A CLOSE SHAVE.
LATER...
RACHEL, IT IS NEARLY DAWN.
I KNOW, STORM.
I HAVE A FAVOR TO ASK, MY FRIENDS. DEATH BY SUNLIGHT IS SLOW AND... AGONIZING.
A STAKE TO THE HEART IS QUICK.
I WILL...
NO.
KILLIN'S MY PROFESSION.

YOU'RE A VAMPIRE-- BUT THE SUN DOESN'T AFFECT YOU!

NOR DO CROSSES OR GARLIC OR ANY OF THE TRADITIONAL DEFENSES.

I AM UNIQUE.

I WAS CREATED AS A VAMPIRE TO BE MY FATHER'S ETERNAL NEMESIS. I COULD DO ANYTHING BUT DESTROY HIM, YET TO DESTROY HIM WAS MY SOLE DESIRE.

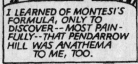

I LEARNED OF MONTESI'S FORMULA, ONLY TO DISCOVER-- MOST PAINFULLY-- THAT PENDARROW HILL WAS ANATHEMA TO ME, TOO.

I LEAKED WORD OF MY QUEST FOR THE FORMULA, KNOWING DRACULA WOULD SUMMON STORM TO STEAL IT. I POSSESSED KITTY BOTH TO GAIN THE ABILITY TO ENTER PENDARROW CASTLE AND TO DRAW THE X-MEN INTO THE FRAY.

AS KITTY, I APPROACHED PETER AND TOOK HIS BLOOD, MAKING HIM MY DEVOTED SLAVE. I THOUGHT OF FANGING YOU ALL...

...BUT YOUR WILLS ARE TOO STRONG-- I COULD NEVER MAINTAIN CONTROL OVER THE ENTIRE GROUP FOR LONG. THE REST, AS THE SAYING GOES, IS HISTORY.

YOUR CHILD IS RETURNED, X-MEN, UNHARMED IN MIND OR BODY OR-- THANKS TO NIGHTCRAWLER'S TIMELY INTERVENTION-- SOUL.

MY WORK IS DONE. WE SHALL NOT MEET AGAIN.

OH! STORM-- WITH DRACULA'S DEATH, HIS HOLD ON YOU AND WOLVERINE IS TRULY ENDED. YOU WILL NOT RISE AFTER DEATH AS A VAMPIRE. PITY.

COLOSSUS IS IN NO DANGER, EITHER. HE DIDN'T LOSE ENOUGH BLOOD. FAREWELL, X-MEN. IT'S BEEN... FUN.

WH-WHERE AM I...?

GUYS! WHAT'S GOING ON?! I WAS IN MY ROOM-- OH, ORORO, THE AWFUL THINGS I SAID TO YOU ALL... I'M SO SORRY...

IT'S ALL RIGHT, KITTEN. EVERYTHING'S ALL RIGHT, NOW.

LATER...

HOW'S THE KID?

CONFUSED. TIRED. SHE REMEMBERS NOTHING SINCE HER TANTRUM THE OTHER DAY.

GOOD. THAT'S IT, THEN, IT'S OVER.

IS IT?

THE END...?

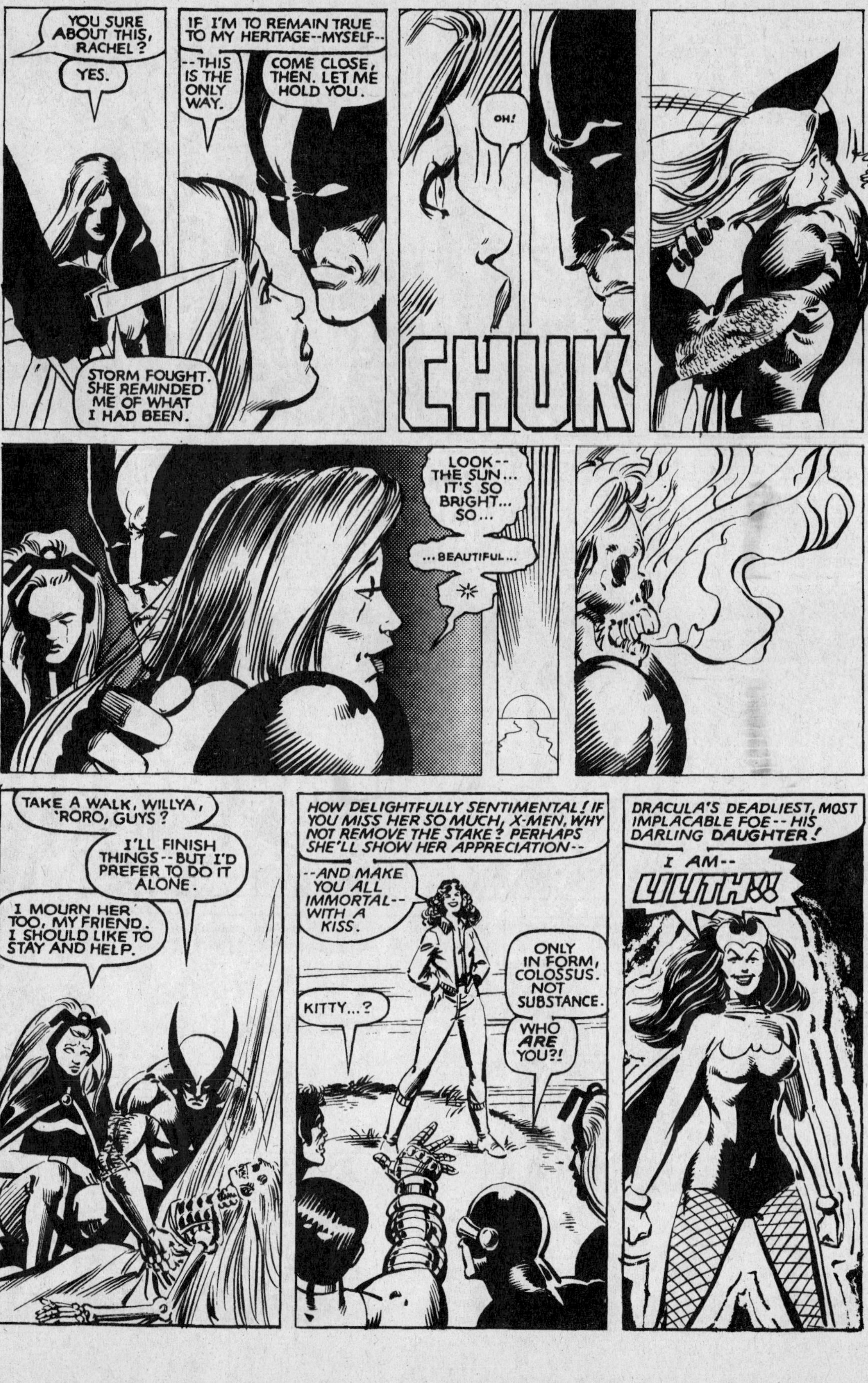
YOU SURE ABOUT THIS, RACHEL?
YES.
STORM FOUGHT. SHE REMINDED ME OF WHAT I HAD BEEN.
IF I'M TO REMAIN TRUE TO MY HERITAGE--MYSELF--
--THIS IS THE ONLY WAY.
COME CLOSE, THEN. LET ME HOLD YOU.
OH!
CHUK
LOOK-- THE SUN... IT'S SO BRIGHT... SO...
...BEAUTIFUL...
TAKE A WALK, WILLYA, 'RORO, GUYS?
I'LL FINISH THINGS--BUT I'D PREFER TO DO IT ALONE.
I MOURN HER TOO, MY FRIEND. I SHOULD LIKE TO STAY AND HELP.
HOW DELIGHTFULLY SENTIMENTAL! IF YOU MISS HER SO MUCH, X-MEN, WHY NOT REMOVE THE STAKE? PERHAPS SHE'LL SHOW HER APPRECIATION--
--AND MAKE YOU ALL IMMORTAL--WITH A KISS.
KITTY...?
ONLY IN FORM, COLOSSUS. NOT SUBSTANCE.
WHO ARE YOU?!
DRACULA'S DEADLIEST, MOST IMPLACABLE FOE--HIS DARLING DAUGHTER!
I AM-- LILITH!!

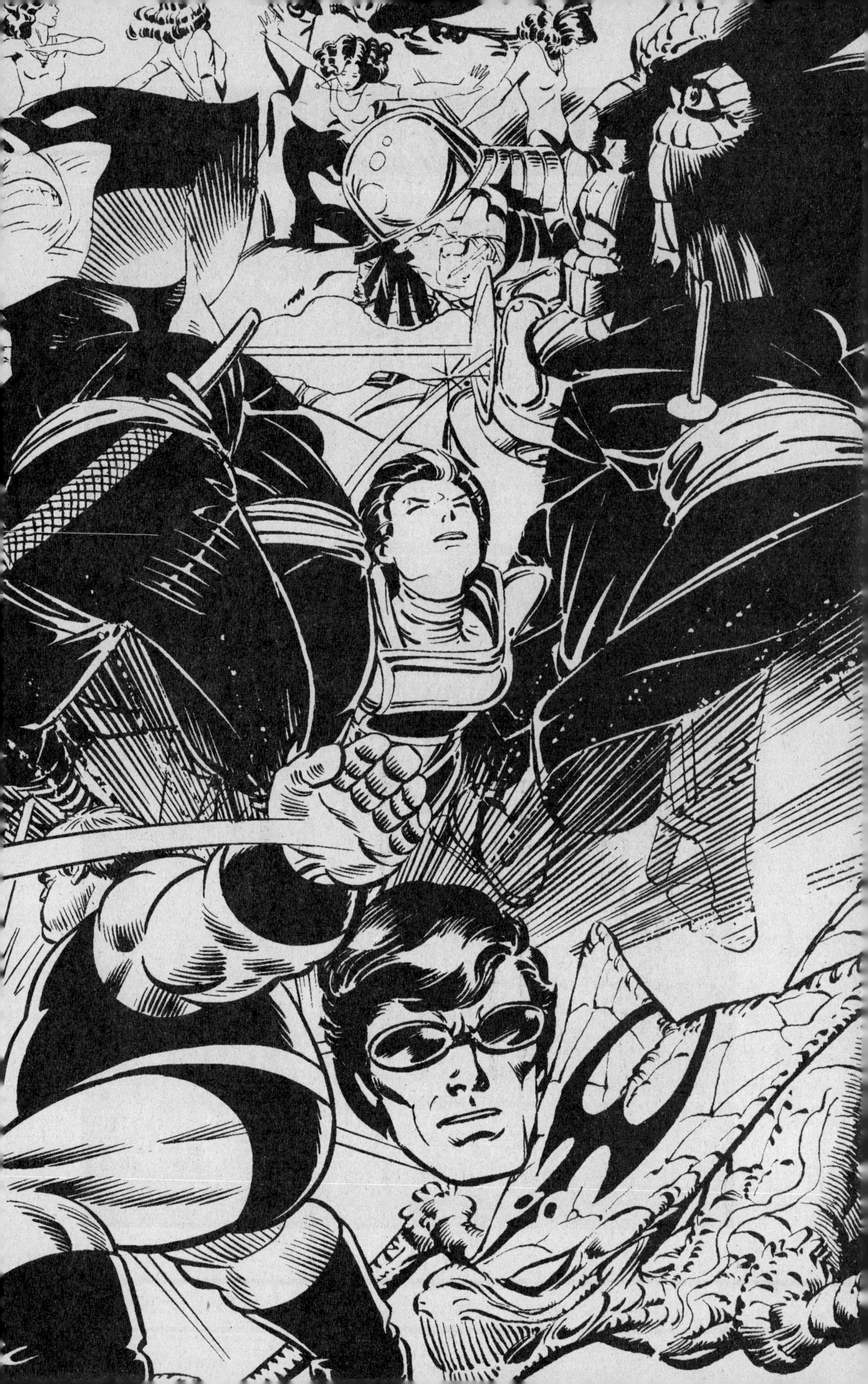

ALSO AVAILABLE: